AF796995

New Syllabus

2026-2015

Andhra Pradesh

EAPCET

CHAPTER-WISE & TOPIC-WISE

PREVIOUS YEAR QUESTIONS

Chemistry

DISHA™
Publication Inc

DISHA Publication Inc.

A-23 FIEE Complex, Okhla Phase II
New Delhi-110020
Tel: 49842349/ 49842350

Typeset By
DISHA DTP Team

Write To Us At

feedback_disha@aiets.co.in

www.dishapublication.com

DISHA™ Publication Inc

CONTENTS

CLASS XI

Hints & Solutions (Class XI)

CLASS XII B1 - B88

Hints & Solutions (Class XII) B89 - B140

CLASS–XI

1 Some Basic Concepts of Chemistry

CHAPTER SYNOPSIS

- 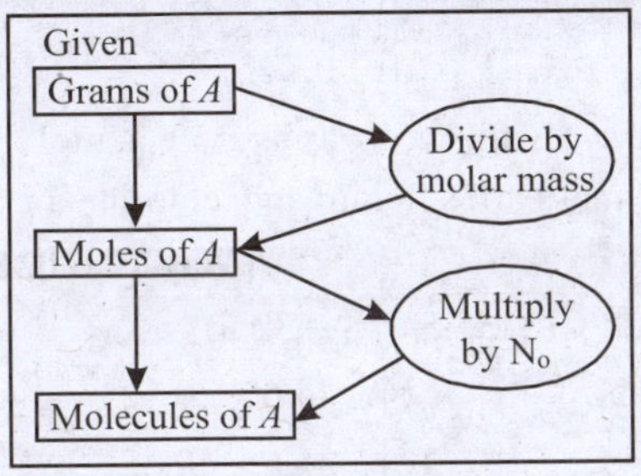

- One atomic mass unit (amu)

$$= \frac{1}{N_0} = \frac{1}{6.023 \times 10^{23}} \text{ g} = 1.66 \times 10^{-24} \text{ g} = 1.66 \times 10^{-27} \text{ kg}$$

- The volume of 1 mole of gas at NTP (normal temperature and pressure) or STP (Standard temperature and pressure) is 22.4 litre. NTP or STP refers for pressure = 1 atm and T = 0°C or 273K.

- Molarity of mixing :

$$M_1V_1 + M_2V_2 + M_3V_3 = M_R(V_1 + V_2 + V_3)$$

M_R = resultant molarity

- $$V = \frac{nRT}{P} = \frac{1 \times 0.0821 \times 273}{1} = 22.4 \text{ L}$$

1 mole of gas at S.T.P. = 22.4 L

To convert : g $\longrightarrow$ mol $\longrightarrow$ litre

- Molality (m) expressed in terms of mole fraction of solute (X_1) is given by relation :

$$m = \frac{1000X_1}{(1 - X_1)m_2}$$

where m_2 is the molar mass of the solvent.

- Molality (m) is related to molarity (M) by relation : $m = \dfrac{1000M}{1000d - Mm_1}$

where d is the density (g mL^{-1}) and m_1 is the molar mass of the solute.

Topic 1 Significant Figures, Laws of Chemical Combinations and Mole Concept

1. The number of significant figures present in 0.010200×10^3 is [May 14, 2026 (II)]
(a) 7 (b) 5 (c) 6 (d) 10

2. Chlorophyll contains 2.4% of magnesium. The number of magnesium atoms present in 2.0 g of chlorophyll is ($N = 6 \times 10^{23}$ mol^{-1}, At.wt of Mg = 24 u) [May 12, 2026 (II)]
(a) 1.8×10^{21} (b) 2.4×10^{21}
(c) 1.2×10^{21} (d) 3.6×10^{21}

3. Consider the following [May 22, 2025 (II)]
(A) 0.0025 (B) 500.0 (C) 2.0034
Number of significant figures in A, B and C respectively, are
(a) 5, 4, 4 (b) 2, 4, 2 (c) 4, 3, 2 (d) 2, 4, 5

4. Observe the following [May 21, 2025 (I)]
I. 0.0063 II. 132.00 III. 1004
The number of significant figures in I, II and III is respectively.
(a) 4, 3, 5 (b) 4, 5, 4 (c) 4, 3, 4 (d) 2, 5, 4

5. A flask contains 98 mg of H_2SO_4. If 3.01×10^{20} molecules of H_2SO_4 are removed from the flask, the number of moles of H_2SO_4 remained in flask is ($N = 6.02 \times 10^{23}$) [May 21, 2024 (II)]
(a) 1×10^{-4} (b) 5×10^{-4}
(c) 1.66×10^{-4} (d) 9.95×10^{-3}

6. 0.1 mole of potassium permanganate was heated at 300°C. What is the weight (in g) of the residue? (Mn = 55 u; K = 39 u: O = 16 u) [May 21, 2024 (I)]
(a) 14.2 (b) 1.6 (c) 15.8 (d) 7.1

7. The formula of nickel oxide is $Ni_{0.98}\,O_{1.00}$. What is the approximate percentage of Ni^{+2} in it? [May 17, 2023 (II)]
(a) 92 (b) 94 (c) 96 (d) 98

8. The statement related to law of definite proportions is [July 4, 2022 (I)]
(a) The ratio of oxygen in H_2O and H_2O_2 with respect to fixed mass of Hydrogen atom is a whole number
(b) % of oxygen in H_2O is constant irrespective of the source
(c) Equal volume of all gases at the same temperature and pressure should contain equal number of molecules
(d) Matter can neither be created nor destroyed.

9. If one atom of an element *X* weighs 6.643×10^{-23} g. Then, find the number of moles of atoms in 50 kg of element *X*. [Aug. 23, 2021 (I)]
(a) 500 moles (b) 125 moles
(c) 1250 moles (d) 50 moles

10. Vapour density of a metal chloride is 83. If equivalent weight of the metal is 6, its atomic weight will be .... [Sept. 21, 2020 (I)]
(a) 12 (b) 24 (c) 18 (d) 60

11. 3.011×10^{22} atoms of an element weighs 1.15 g. The atomic mass of the element is [2015]
(a) 23 (b) 10 (c) 16 (d) 35.5

Topic 2 Percentage Composition and Empirical Formula

12. A gas mixture contains 64% methane and 36% ethane by mass. The density of the mixture at 27°C and 750 mm pressure (in g L^{-1}) is [May 14, 2026 (II)]
(at. wt C = 12 u, H = 1 u, R = 0.082 L atm K^{-1} mol^{-1})
(a) 0.57 (b) 0.87
(c) 0.67 (d) 0.77

13. The molar mass of mustard gas is 159 g mol^{-1}. The percentage by mass of sulphur and chlorine in it are respectively [May 12, 2026 (II)]
(Atomic weight : Cl = 35.5 u, S = 32 u)
(a) 20.12, 44.65 (b) 44.65, 20.12
(c) 40, 24.65 (d) 24.65, 40

14. The mass of a mixture containing Na*Cl* and NaBr is 4.0 g. If Na is 30% of the total mixture, the composition of NaCl in the mixture is [May 26, 2025 (II)]
(Na = 23 u, *Cl* = 35.5 u. Br = 80 u)
(a) 48% (b) 55% (c) 45% (d) 52%

15. The composition of a sample of wustite is $Fe_{0.93}O_{100}$. Percentage of iron in the form of Fe^{3+} ion is nearly [May 23, 2025 (I)]
(a) 85 (b) 15 (c) 93 (d) 7

16. 1.84 g of a mixture of $CaCO_3$ and $MgCO_3$ is strongly heated to get a residue of 0.96 g. The percentage of $CaCO_3$ in the mixture is [May 22, 2025 (I)]
(a) 50.34 (b) 49.66
(c) 54.34 (d) 45.66

17. 200 g of 20% w/w urea solution is mixed with 400 g of 40% w/w urea solution. What is the weight percentage (w/w %) of resultant solution? [May 19, 2024 (II)]
(a) 30.33 (b) 33.33
(c) 36.33 (d) 28.33

18. An oxide of chlorine with water gives the strongest acid. The ratio of chlorine and oxygen in its formula is [May 19, 2023 (I)]
(a) 2:1 (b) 1:2 (c) 2:7 (d) 1:3

19. The weight percentage of C and H in a hydrocarbon is in the ratio of 4 : 1. What is its empirical formula? [May 16, 2023 (I)]
(a) CH (b) CH_2 (c) CH_3 (d) CH_4

20. 6 g of urea (molar mass = 60 g mol^{-1}) and 9 g of glucose (molar mass = 180 g mol^{-1}) were dissolved in 35 g of water. The mass percent of urea and glucose is respectively [May 15, 2023 (II)]
(a) 18, 12 (b) 6, 9 (c) 12, 18 (d) 9, 6

21. What is the atomic mass of Fe? [July 6, 2022 (I)]
Given abundance of $^{54}Fe = 10\%$, $^{56}Fe = 85\%$, $^{57}Fe = 5\%$
(a) 55.65 (b) 55.75 (c) 55.85 (d) 55.95

22. An alloy of metals X and Y weighs 12 g and contains atoms X and Y in the ratio of 2 : 5. The percentage of metal X in the alloy is 20 by mass. If the atomic mass of X is 40 amu what is the atomic mass of metal Y? **[Aug. 20, 2021 (I)]**
(a) 64 amu (b) 32 amu (c) 60 amu (d) 50 amu

23. 0.12 g of an organic compound 'X' containing phosphorus on reacting with magnesia mixture gave 0.22 g of magnesium pyrophosphate ($Mg_2P_2O_7$). The percentage of phosphorus in the compound 'X' is .... **[Sept. 18, 2020 (I)]**
(a) 45.30% (b) 28.70% (c) 64.25% (d) 51.20%

24. One mole of oxygen gas at STP is equal to **[Sept. 17, 2020 (II)]**
(a) 6.022×10^{23} molecules of oxygen
(b) 6.022×10^{23} atoms of oxygen
(c) 16 g of oxygen
(d) 3.2 g of oxygen

25. Two oxides of a X contain 50% and 40% of non-metal respectively. If the formula of the first oxide is XO_2. Then the formula of second oxide is **[2017]**
(a) X_2O_3 (b) X_2O_5 (c) XO_3 (d) X_2O

26. A carbon compound contains 12.8% of carbon, 2.1% of hydrogen and 85.1% of bromine. The molecular weight of the compound is 187.9. Calculate the molecular formula of the compound. **[2015]**
(Atomic weight: H = 1.008, C = 12.0, Br = 79.9)
(a) CH_3Br (b) CH_2Br_2I (c) $C_2H_4Br_2$ (d) $C_2H_3Br_3$

Topic 3 Stoichiometric Calculations

27. White phosphorus reacts with aqueous NaOH to form $PH_3(g)$ and sodium hypophosphite. When 6.2g of white phosphorus reacted with 500 mL of xM NaOH solution, the concentration of sodium hypophosphite in the resultant solution was 0.3 mol L^{-1}. What are x (in M) and weight (in g) of PH_3 formed respectively?
(P = 31 u ; H = 1 u; O = 16 u) **[May 15, 2026 (I)]**
(a) 0.6, 17 (b) 03, 3.4
(c) 0.3, 1.7 (d) 0.6, 3.4

28. 5.4 g of a metal (M) reacts with chlorine to form 26.7 g of metal chloride. What is the weight (in g) of M that reacts with 48 g of oxygen? **[May 14, 2026 (I)]**
(a) 67.5 (b) 40.5
(c) 54 (d) 27

29. Identify the correct statements about the following stoichiometric equation. **[May 27, 2025 (I)]**

$$aP_4 + bOH^- + cH_2O \longrightarrow dPH_3 + eH_2PO_2^-$$

I. $a + b + c = 5$
II. $b + c - e = 3$
III. The oxidation state of P in $H_2PO_2^-$ is +1.
(a) I, II, III (b) I, II only
(c) I, III only (d) II, III only

30. Two acids A and B are titrated separately, 25 mL of 0.5 M Na_2CO_3 solution requires 10 mL of A and 40 mL of B for complete neutralisation. The volume (in L) of A and B required to produce 1 L of 1 N acid solution respectively are **[May 24, 2025 (I)]**
(a) 0.2, 0.8 (b) 0.8, 0.2 (c) 0.3, 0.7 (d) 0.7, 0.3

31. Complete combustion of ethane gives only gaseous products. In a closed vessel, 15 g of ethane and 112 g of O_2 were allowed to completely react. What is the total number of moles of gaseous substances present in the vessel at the end of the reaction? **[May 23, 2025 (II)]**
(a) 4.25 (b) 2.5 (c) 1.75 (d) 8.50

32. 4 mL of 'X volume' H_2O_2 on heating gives 80 mL of oxygen at STP. The value of X is **[May 22, 2025 (II)]**
(a) 10 (b) 20 (c) 15 (d) 40

33. 209 g of an element reacts with chlorine to form 315.5 g of its chloride. What is the weight (in g) of oxygen that reacts with 418 g of same element? (Cl = 35.5 u; O = 16 u) **[May 21, 2025 (II)]**
(a) 24 (b) 48 (c) 96 (d) 36

34. 100 mL of 0.1 M Fe^{2+} solution was titrated with $\frac{1}{60}$ M $Cr_2O_7^{2-}$ solution in acid medium. What is the volume (in L) of $Cr_2O_7^{2-}$ solution consumed? **[May 22, 2024 (II)]**
(a) 100 (b) 10 (c) 1 (d) 0.1

35. 10 g of a metal (M) reacts with oxygen to form 11.6 g of oxide. What is the equivalent weight of M? **[May 22, 2024 (I)]**
(a) 50 g (b) 0.02 (c) 0.02 g (d) 50

36. At STP 'x' g of a metal hydrogen carbonate ($MHCO_3$) (molar mass 84 g mol^{-1}) on heating gives CO_2, which can completely react with 0.2 moles of MOH (molar mass 40 g mol^{-1}) to give $MHCO_3$. The value of 'x' is **[May 20, 2024 (II)]**
(a) 67.2 (b) 33.6 (c) 11.2 (d) 22.4

37. A hydrocarbon containing C and H has 92.3% C. When 39 g of hydrocarbon was completely burnt in O_2, x moles of water and y moles of CO_2 were formed. x moles of water is sufficient to liberate 0.75 moles of H_2 with Na metal. What is the weight (in g) of oxygen consumed?
(C = 12 u; H = 1 u) **[May 18, 2024 (I)]**
(a) 120 (b) 240 (c) 360 (d) 480

38. x g of methane was burnt completely in the presence of oxygen. The liberated gases were passed into a solution containing 370 g of $Ca(OH)_2$. The weight of white precipitate obtained was 500 . What is the value of x (in g)? **[May 18, 2023 (II)]**
(Given : C = 12; H = 1; Ca = 40; O = 16 u)
(a) 16 (b) 80 (c) 160 (d) 120

39. Observe the following reaction
$I_2 + 10\ HNO_3 \rightarrow 2\ HIO_3 + 10\ NO_2 + 4\ H_2O$
The equivalent wt. of HNO_3 is
(molar mass of HNO_3 = M) **[July 8, 2022 (I)]**
(a) M (b) $\frac{M}{4}$ (c) $\frac{M}{2}$ (d) $\frac{M}{5}$

40. If 50% of 1 M Na_2SO_4 is dissociated in aqueous solution of density 1.2 g mL^{-1}, what is the molality of Na^+ ion in the solution? **[July 6, 2022 (I)]**
(a) 0.95 (b) 1.89 (c) 1.00 (d) 2.00

41. How many grams of Mg is required to completely reduce 100 ml, 0.1 M NO_3^- solution using the following reaction

$NO_3^- + Mg \longrightarrow Mg^{2+} + NH_3$ **[July 4, 2022 (II)]**

(a) 0.96 (b) 0.62
(c) 0.24 (d) 0.75

42. What amount of conc. H_2SO_4 solution should be used to prepare 500 mL of 0.5 M H_2SO_4? (The concentration of H_2SO_4 solution being used is 90% and molecular mass of $H_2SO_4 = 98.079$ g mol^{-1}) **[Aug. 23, 2021 (II)]**

(a) 22.06 g (b) 24.52 g
(c) 11.03 g (d) 27.24 g

43. 100 mL of 0.2 M acetic acid is completely neutralised using a standard solution of NaOH. The volume of ethane obtained at STP after complete electrolysis of the resulting solution is **[Aug. 23, 2021 (II)]**

(a) 11.2 L (b) 2.24 L
(c) 0.224 L (d) 22.4 L

44. For formation of 3.40 g of ammonia gas, what volumes of hydrogen gas and nitrogen gas, respectively are required at NTP conditions? **[Aug. 23, 2021 (I)]**

(a) 2.24 L and 2.24 L (b) 2.24 L and 1.24 L
(c) 6.72 L and 2.24 L (d) 6.72 L and 1.12 L

45. When 20 g of $CaCO_3$ is treated with 20 g of HCl, the mass of CO_2 formed would be **[Aug. 19, 2021 (II)]**

(a) 10 g (b) 8.8 g
(c) 22.2 g (d) 20 g

46. Calculate the amount of CO_2 gas produced, when 32 g moles of CH_4 is burned with sufficient amount of oxygen. (Given, atomic weights of C = 12, O = 16, H = 1) **[Sept. 18, 2020 (I)]**

(a) 132 g (b) 44 g
(c) 88 g (d) 176 g

47. 20 mL of Fe^{2+} solution of certain concentration has completely reacted with 20 mL of 0.01 M $K_2Cr_2O_7$ in acidic medium. If 20 mL of same Fe^{2+} solution has reacted completely with 20 mL of $KMnO_4$ solution in acid medium, the molarity of $KMnO_4$ solution is **[Apr. 22, 2019 (I)]**

(a) 0.01 M (b) 0.12 M
(c) 0.10 M (d) 0.012 M

48. The volume of 0.02 M acidified permanganate solution required for complete reaction of 60 mL, of 0.01 M I^- ion solution to from I_2 in mL is **[Apr. 20, 2019 (I)]**

(a) 60 (b) 20
(c) 40 (d) 6

49. One litre of 0.15 M Na_2SO_3 aqueous solution is mixed with 500 mL of 0.2 M $K_2Cr_2O_7$ aqueous solution in acid medium. What is the number of moles of $K_2Cr_2O_7$ remaining in the solution after the reaction? **[2018]**

(a) 0.1 (b) 0.0125
(c) 0.025 (d) 0.05

50. 40 mL of xM $KMnO_4$ solution is required to react completely with 200 mL of 0.02 M oxalic acid solution in acidic medium. The value of x is **[2016]**

(a) 0.04 (b) 0.01 (c) 0.03 (d) 0.02

2 Structure of Atom

CHAPTER SYNOPSIS

- **Photoelectric effect**

$1/2\ mv^2 = h\nu - h\nu_0(w)$ (work function)

ν_0 = Threshold frequency

- **Radii of Orbits**

$$r = \frac{(4\pi \in_0)n^2h^2}{4\pi^2 mZe^2}$$

By putting value of constants

$$r = 0.529 \times \frac{n^2}{Z} \text{Å}$$

$$r = 0.529 \times \frac{n^2}{Z} \times 10^{-10} \text{m}$$

$$r = 0.529 \times 10^{-8} \times \frac{n^2}{Z} \text{cm}$$

For H-like atoms.

Thus $r_n = r_1 \times n^2$

- **The Energy of Electron**

$$E_n = -\frac{21.79 \times 10^{-19} Z^2}{n^2} \text{ J/atom} = -\frac{13.6}{n^2} Z^2 \text{ eV per atom}$$

$$= -\frac{313.6 \times Z^2}{n^2} \text{ kcal/mol}$$

- **Rydberg Equation**

The wavelength (λ), wave number ($\bar{\nu}$) for the electromagnetic radiation can be calculated by Rydberg equation.

$$\bar{\nu} = \frac{1}{\lambda} = R \times Z^2 \left[\frac{1}{n_1^2} - \frac{1}{n_2^2}\right]$$

Z = atomic number

R = 109743 cm^{-1} - Rydberg constant

n_2 = higher orbit

n_1 = lower orbit

λ = wavelength

- **Total number of spectral lines**

(i) $\frac{n(n-1)}{2} \rightarrow$ when electron jumps from n^{th} level to ground level

(ii) $\frac{(n_2 - n_1)(n_2 - n_1 + 1)}{2} \rightarrow$ when electron returns from n_2 to n_1.

- The wavelength of limiting line $= \frac{n_1^2}{R_H}$ for all series. So, for lyman series $= \frac{1}{R_H}$

-

	Spectral Series	n_1	n_2	Region
(i)	Lyman Series	1	2, 3, 4 ...	UV
(ii)	Balmer Series	2	3, 4 ...	Visible
(iii)	Paschen Series	3	4, 5, 6 ...	IR
(iv)	Brackett Series	4	5, 6, 7 ...	IR
(v)	Pfund Series	5	6, 7 ...	IR
(vi)	Humphrey	6	7, 8 ...	Far IR

- In terms of time and energy Heisenberg's uncertainty principle may be given as $\Delta E\ \Delta t \geq \frac{h}{4\pi}$ (for energy and time)

- **(n + *l*) rule**

This rule states that electrons are filled in orbitals according to their increasing values of $n + \ell$. When $(n + \ell)$ is same for sub energy levels, the electrons first occupy the sublevels with lowest "n" value. Thus, order of filling up of orbitals is as follows:

1s < 2s < 2p < 3s < 3p < 4s < 3d < 4p < 5s < 4d < 5p < 6s < 4f < 5d

- **Orbital & Spin Angular Momentum**

$$\frac{h}{2\pi}\sqrt{\ell(\ell+1)},\ \frac{h}{2\pi}\sqrt{s(s+1)}$$

Topic 1 Atomic Models and Dual Nature of Electromagnetic Radiation

1. Threshold frequencies of the metals A, B respectively are 4×10^{14} Hz and 6×10^{14} Hz. If both are irradiated with light of frequency 10^{15} Hz, what is the ratio of the kinetic energy of electrons emitted from A and B? **[May 18, 2026 (I)]**
(a) 2 : 3 (b) 3 : 2
(c) 4 : 9 (d) 9 : 4

2. The threshold frequency of a metal is 1.15×10^{15} Hz. If electrons with kinetic energy of 0.20 eV are ejected when this metal surface is irradiated with photons of frequency 'v', the value of v is **[May 15, 2026 (I)]**
($h = 6.60 \times 10^{-34}$ Js, 1 eV = 1.6×10^{-19} J)
(a) 1.20×10^{14} Hz (b) 1.20×10^{15} Hz
(c) 1.98×10^{14} Hz (d) 1.98×10^{15} Hz

3. Consider the following two statements
Statement - I: The order of energies of 2s - orbitals of H, Li and Na is $E_{2s}(H) < E_{2s}(Li) < E_{2s}(Na)$
Statement - II : The photoelectric effect explains the wave nature of light
The correct answer is **[May 14, 2026 (II)]**
(a) Both statements - I and II are correct
(b) Statement - I is correct but Statement - II is not correct
(c) Statement - I is not correct but Statement - II is correct
(d) Both statements - I and II are not correct

4. In a photoelectric effect, the kinetic energy of electrons is 1.3×10^{-19}J. If work function of the metal is 2.27 eV, then the frequency (in Hz) of the incident radiation is
($h = 6.6 \times 10^{-34}$ Js, 1 eV = 1.6×10^{-19} J) **[May 14, 2026 (II)]**
(a) 7.47×10^{15} (b) 7.47×10^{14}
(c) 6.47×10^{15} (d) 3.47×10^{14}

5. The work function of Mg, Cu, Ag, Li are 3.7, 4.8, 4.3, 2.5 eV respectively. A wavelength of 300 nm light is shined on them. The metals which undergo photoelectric effect are **[May 14, 2026 (I)]**
(a) Mg, Cu (b) Cu, Ag
(c) Ag, Li (d) Mg, Li

6. The work functions (in eV) of Mg, Cu, Ag, Na respectively are 3.7, 4.8, 4.3, 2.3. From how many metals, the electrons will be ejected if their surfaces are irradiated with an electromagnetic radiation of wavelength 300 nm?
($h = 6.6 \times 10^{-34}$ Js , 1 eV = 1.6×10^{-19} J) **[May 24, 2025 (I)]**
(a) 1 (b) 4 (c) 2 (d) 3

7. Identify the region of spectral lines of electromagnetic spectrum, when electron transition takes place from higher energy levels to n = 3, 4, 5 in atomic spectrum of hydrogen is **[May 17, 2023 (I)]**
(a) Ultraviolet (b) Visible
(c) Infrared (d) Microwave

8. Vijayawada FM radio station broadcasts at frequency of 103.4 MHz. The wavelength of the corresponding radio waves (in m) is **[May 15, 2023 (I)]**
(a) 2.90 (b) 29.0
(c) 9.20 (d) 92.0

9. With what velocity must an electron travel, so that its momentum is equal to that of a photon of wavelength 663 nm? **[Aug. 23, 2021 (I)]**
(a) 1098 m/s (b) 109.8 m/s
(c) 10.98 m/s (d) 1.098 m/s

10. The number of protons, neutrons and electrons in $^{13}_{6}C$ respectively are **[Aug. 20, 2021 (I)]**
(a) 6, 7, 6 (b) 13, 6, 6
(c) 6, 7, 13 (d) 6, 6, 13

11. The masses of an electron, a proton and a neutron respectively will be in the ratio **[Aug. 20, 2021 (I)]**
(a) 1 : 1836.15 : 1838.68 (b) 1 : 1856.15 : 1858.68
(c) 1 : 1834.15 : 1836.68 (d) 1 : 1846.15 : 1848.68

12. Match the following species with the correct number of electrons present in them. **[Aug. 20, 2021 (I)]**

	Species		Number of electrons
A.	Be^{2+}	(i)	0
B.	H^+	(ii)	10
C.	Na^+	(iii)	2
D.	Mg^+	(iv)	11
		(v)	4

Codes

	A	B	C	D		A	B	C	D
(a)	(iv)	(iii)	(ii)	(i)	(b)	(i)	(ii)	(iii)	(iv)
(c)	(v)	(iv)	(i)	(iii)	(d)	(iii)	(i)	(ii)	(iv)

13. If two particles *A* and *B* are moving with the same velocity, but wavelength of *A* is found to be double than that of *B*. Which of the following statement is correct? **[Aug. 19, 2021 (I)]**
(a) Both *A* and *B* have same mass.
(b) Mass of *A* is half that of *B*.
(c) Mass of *B* is half that of *A*.
(d) Mass of *B* is one-fourth that of *A*.

14. Calculate the wave number and frequency of orange radiation having wavelength 6300 Å. **[Sept. 17, 2020 (I)]**
(a) 1.587×10^{8} m^{-1}, 4.761×10^{16}s^{-1}
(b) 1.587×10^{4} m^{-1}, 4.761×10^{14}s^{-1}
(c) 1.587×10^{6} m^{-1}, 4.761×10^{14}s^{-1}
(d) 1.587×10^{6} m^{-1}, 4.761×10^{16}s^{-1}

15. Isochores are drawn at .... **[Sept. 17, 2020 (I)]**
(a) constant volume, pressure *vs* temperature
(b) constant pressure, volume *vs* temperature
(c) constant temperature, pressure *vs* volume
(d) constant temperature, volume *vs* temperature

16. The wavelength of a microscopic particle of mass 9.1×10^{-31} kg is 182 nm, its kinetic energy in J is ($h = 6.625 \times 10^{-34}$ J s) **[Apr. 20, 2019 (I)]**
(a) 7.28×10^{-23} (b) 7.28×10^{-24}
(c) 3.64×10^{-23} (d) 3.64×10^{-24}

Topic 2 Bohr's Model for Hydrogen Atom (Emission and Absorption Spectra)

17. Wavelength of a particular line in Balmer series of atomic spectrum of hydrogen is 656.4 nm. What is the wavelength (in nm) of corresponding line in the spectrum of He^+? **[May 18, 2026 (II)]**
(a) 328.2 (b) 164.1
(c) 492.3 (d) 246.1

18. The radius of first Bohr orbit of hydrogen is a_0 nm. What is the de Broglie wavelength (in nm) associated with electron present in fourth orbit of hydrogen? **[May 15, 2026 (II)]**
(a) $2\pi a_0$ (b) $\frac{2\pi a_0}{3}$
(c) $8\pi a_0$ (d) $4\pi a_0$

19. The wavelength of spectral line (X) of hydrogen spectrum is same as that of spectral line of He^+ spectrum corresponding to $n = 4 \rightarrow n = 2$ electron transition. The correct electron transition corresponding to X is **[May 15, 2026 (II)]**
(a) $n = 2 \rightarrow n = 1$ (b) $n = 3 \rightarrow n = 2$
(c) $n = 4 \rightarrow n = 2$ (d) $n = 3 \rightarrow n = 1$

20. If the energy required to remove an electron from the ground state of He^+ is x J, the energy (in J) required to remove an electron from the ground state of Li^{2+} is **[May 15, 2026 (I)]**
(a) $\frac{3}{2}x$ (b) $\frac{2}{3}x$
(c) $\frac{9}{4}x$ (d) $\frac{4}{9}x$

21. The energy of spectral line of lowest frequency in Lyman series of Li^{2+} spectrum is x J. The energy of second spectral line in Balmer series of He^+ spectrum is y J. The ratio of x and y is **[May 13, 2026 (I)]**
(a) 3 : 1 (b) 1 : 3
(c) 1 : 9 (d) 9 : 1

22. Wavelength of a photon emitted during electron transition from n = 4 state to n = 2 state in the hydrogen atom is $\underline{x}$ nm. Wavelength of a photon emitted during electron transition from n = 4 state to n = 1 state in the same atom is $\underline{y}$ nm. $\frac{y}{x}$ is equal to **[May 12, 2026 (II)]**
(a) 0.4 (b) 0.2
(c) 0.5 (d) 0.3

23. In an atomic spectrum of hydrogen, a series of lines with wavelengths at 656.46, 486.27, x and 410.29 nm was obtained. What is the value of x (in nm)? ($R_H = 1.097 \times 10^7$ m^{-1}) **[May 12, 2026 (I)]**
(a) 453.15 (b) 449.32
(c) 434.17 (d) 428.37

24. The energy of second Bohr orbit of hydrogen atom is –3.4 eV. The energy of the fourth Bohr orbit of the He^+ ion will be **[May 27, 2025 (I)]**
(a) –3.4 eV (b) –13.6 eV
(c) –6.8 eV (d) –0.85 eV

25. Which of the following represents the wavelength of spectral line of Balmer series of He^+ ion? (R = Rydberg constant, $n > 2$) **[May 24, 2025 (I)]**
(a) $\frac{n^2}{R(n-2)(n+2)}$ (b) $\frac{R(n-2)(n+2)}{n^2}$
(c) $\frac{n^2}{4R(n-2)(n+2)}$ (d) $\frac{4R(n-2)(n+2)}{n^2}$

26. The radius of fourth orbit in He^+ ion is 'R_1' pm and radius of third orbit in Li^{2+} ion is 'R_2' pm. The value of $(R_1 - R_2)$ in pm is **[May 23, 2025 (I)]**
(a) 132.25 (b) 529.00 (c) 264.50 (d) 793.50

27. The difference between the radii of 3rd and 2nd orbit of H-atom is x pm. The difference between the radii of 4th and 3rd orbit of Li^{2+} ion is y pm. $y : x$ is equal to **[May 22, 2025 (II)]**
(a) 15 : 7 (b) 7 : 15
(c) 3 : 1 (d) 1 : 3

28. The wavenumber of the first line ($n_2 = 3$) in the Balmer series of hydrogen is $\vec{v}_1$ cm^{-1}. What is the wavenumber (in cm^{-1}) of the second line ($n_2 = 4$) in the Balmer series of He^+? **[May 22, 2025 (I)]**
(a) $\frac{5\vec{v}_1}{27}$ (b) $\frac{27\vec{v}_1}{5}$ (c) $\frac{27\vec{v}_1}{20}$ (d) $\frac{20\vec{v}_1}{27}$

29. Which of the following statements are correct? **[May 21, 2025 (II)]**
(I) The energy of hydrogen atom in its ground state is –13.6 eV
(II) On the basis of Bohr's model, the radius of the 3rd orbit of hydrogen atom is 158.7 pm
(III) The order of radius of the first orbit of H, He^+, Li^{2+} and Be^{3+} is H > He^+ > Li^{2+} > Be^{3+}
(a) II and III only (b) I and III only
(c) I and II only (d) I, II, III

30. Identify the correct statements from the following : **[May 21, 2025 (I)]**

(I) Isotopes of an element show different chemical behaviour

(II) Lyman series of lines of hydrogen spectrum appear in UV region

(III) The oscillating electric and magnetic field components of electromagnetic radiation are perpendicular to each other and both are perpendicular to the direction of propagation of radiation

(a) II and III only (b) I and II only
(c) I and III only (d) I, II, III

31. The ratio of ground state energy of Li^{2+}, He^+, H is **[May 22, 2024 (II)]**

(a) 3 : 2 : 1 (b) 1 : 2 : 3
(c) 9 : 4 : 1 (d) 1 : 4 : 9

32. If the longest wavelength of spectral line of Paschen series of Li^{2+} ion spectrum is x Å, then the longest wavelength (in Å) of Lyman series of hydrogen spectrum is **[May 22, 2024 (I)]**

(a) $\frac{12}{7x}$ (b) $\frac{7x}{12}$ (c) $\frac{20x}{27}$ (d) $\frac{27x}{20}$

33. The difference in radii between fourth and third Bohr orbits of He^+ (in m) is **[May 21, 2024 (II)]**

(a) 2.64×10^{-10} (b) 1.85×10^{-12}
(c) 1.85×10^{-10} (d) 1.85×10^{-9}

34. The energy of third orbit of Li^{2-} ion (in J) is **[May 21, 2024 (I)]**

(a) -2.18×10^{-18} (b) -6.54×10^{-18}
(c) -7.3×10^{-19} (d) $+2.18 \times 10^{-18}$

35. The energy (in J) released when an excited electron of 5th orbit of hydrogen atom returns to its ground state is **[May 18, 2023 (II)]**

(a) 2.091×10^{-18} (b) 4.182×10^{-18}
(c) 6.273×10^{-18} (d) 8.364×10^{-18}

36. The radius of the first orbit of Li^{2+} is x Å. The radius of the third orbit of He^+ (in Å) is **[July 8, 2022 (I)]**

(a) $\frac{18}{2}x$ (b) $\frac{18}{3}x$ (c) $\frac{27}{4}x$ (d) $\frac{27}{2}x$

37. The wavelength of the electron in the ground state of hydrogen atom is y Å. What is the wavelength of the electron in the fourth orbit of He^+ ion (in Å) is **[July 6, 2022 (I)]**

(a) 2y (b) 3y (c) y (d) $\frac{3y}{2}$

38. The wavelength of electron in the first orbit of hydrogen atom is 3.3×10^{-10} m. The kinetic energy of electron (in J) is **[July 5, 2022 (II)]**

($h = 6.6 \times 10^{-34}$ Js, $m_e = 9.0 \times 10^{-31}$ kg)

(a) 3.33×10^{-17} (b) 1.11×10^{-18}
(c) 2.22×10^{-18} (d) 2.22×10^{-17}

39. The spectrum of helium is expected to be similar to that of **[Aug. 19, 2021 (I)]**

(a) Li^+ (b) H (c) Na (d) He^+

40. On the basis of Bohr's model, the radius of the 3rd orbit is **[Aug. 19, 2021 (I)]**

(a) equal to the radius of 1st orbit
(b) 3 times the radius of 1st orbit
(c) 5 times the radius of 1st orbit
(d) 9 times the radius of 1st orbit

41. Which of the following statements is correct about the cathode rays? **[Sept. 21, 2020 (I)]**

1. These rays start from anode and move towards cathode.
2. They are visible with human eye.
3. In presence of electric and magnetic fields, they behave like positively charged particles.
4. Their characteristic does not depend on the nature of material at electrode.

(a) 1 (b) 2 (c) 3 (d) 4

42. The energies of an electron in first orbit of He^+ and in third orbit of Li^{2+} in J are respectively **[Apr. 21, 2019 (I)]**

(a) $-8.72 \times 10^{-18}, -2.18 \times 10^{-18}$
(b) $-8.72 \times 10^{-18}, -1.96 \times 10^{-17}$
(c) $-1.96 \times 10^{-17}, -2.18 \times 10^{-18}$
(d) $-8.72 \times 10^{-17}, -1.96 \times 10^{-17}$

43. The energy of an electron in an orbit of hydrogen like ion with an orbit radius of 52.9 pm in J is
(ground state energy of electron in hydrogen atom is $= -2.18 \times 10^{-18}$ J) **[Apr. 20, 2019 (I)]**

(a) -4.36×10^{-18} (b) -1.09×10^{-17}
(c) -8.72×10^{-18} (d) -6.54×10^{-18}

44. If the radius of electron orbit in the excited state of hydrogen atom is 476.1 pm, the energy of electron in that excited state in J is
(Radius and energy of electron in the first orbit of hydrogen atom are 52.9 pm and -2.18×10^{-18}J respectively) **[2018]**

(a) -2.42×10^{-18} (b) -19.62×10^{-18}
(c) -2.42×10^{-19} (d) -6.05×10^{-19}

45. The energy and radius of electron present in second orbit of He^+ respectively are **[2017]**

(a) -1.09×10^{-18} J, 105.8 pm
(b) -8.72×10^{-18} J, 211.6 pm
(c) -4.36×10^{-18} J, 52.9 pm
(d) -2.18×10^{-18} J, 105.8 pm

Topic 3 Dual Behaviour of Matter and Heisenberg Uncertainty Principle

46. In an atom, electron is moving with a speed of x ms^{-1}. If its speed is measured within an accuracy of 0.001%, what is its uncertainty in position (in m)? **[May 18, 2026 (II)]**

($m_e = 9 \times 10^{-31}$ kg, h = 6.6×10^{-34} Js)

(a) $\frac{3\pi x}{55}$ (b) $\frac{55\pi}{3x}$

(c) $\frac{55}{3\pi x}$ (d) $\frac{55}{3\pi}$

47. A ball has a mass of 50g and a speed of 50 m/s. If the speed is measured within an accuracy of 2%, the uncertainty in its position (in m) is **[May 14, 2026 (I)]**
(h = 6.626×10^{-34} J s, π = 3.14)

(a) 2.12×10^{-34} (b) 1.06×10^{-33}
(c) 2.12×10^{-33} (d) 1.06×10^{-34}

48. If the radius of the first Bohr orbit of He^+ is 26.45 pm, then the de Broglie wavelength (in m) associated with the electron present in its fourth orbit is (π = 3.14) **[May 13, 2026 (II)]**

(a) 3.13×10^{-11} (b) 1.33×10^{-11}
(c) 2.33×10^{-10} (d) 3.32×10^{-10}

49. The de Broglie wavelength associated with a pebble of mass 6.63 g travelling with velocity x ms^{-1} is 10^{-24} nm. What is the value of x?
(h = 6.63×10^{-34} js) **[May 12, 2026 (II)]**

(a) 1.0×10^{-1} (b) 1.0×10^{2}
(c) 1.0×10^{3} (d) 1.0×10^{-2}

50. If two particles have same kinetic energy, then the ratio of their de Broglie wavelengths ($\lambda_A : \lambda_B$) is (Given : $m_A = 4m_B$) **[May 12, 2026 (I)]**

(a) 1 : 2 (b) 2 : 1
(c) 1 : 4 (d) 4 : 1

51. The wavelength of a particular electron transition for He^+ is 100 nm. The wavelength (in Å) of H atom for the same transition is **[May 27, 2025 (I)]**

(a) 1000 (b) 100 (c) 4000 (d) 2000

52. *a, b, c, d* are electromagnetic radiations. Frequencies of *a, b* are 3×10^{15} Hz, 2×10^{14} Hz, respectively, whereas wavelength of *c, d* are 400 nm, 750 nm, respectively. The increasing order of their energies is **[May 26, 2025 (II)]**

(a) *b, d, c, a* (b) *a, d, c, b*
(c) *a, b, c, d* (d) *b, c, d, a*

53. The work function of Cu is 7.68×10^{-19} J. If photons of wave length 221 nm are made to strike the surface of the metal, the kinetic energy (in J) of the ejected electrons will be ($h = 6.63 \times 10^{-34}$ Js) **[May 26, 2025 (I)]**

(a) 2.64×10^{-18} (b) 1.32×10^{-19}
(c) 2.64×10^{-19} (d) 6.60×10^{-19}

54. The uncertainty in the velocities of two particles A and B are 0.03 and 0.01 m s^{-1} respectively. The mass of B is four times to the mass of A. The ratio of uncertainties in their positions is **[May 23, 2025 (II)]**

(a) $\frac{4}{3}$ (b) $\frac{3}{4}$ (c) $\frac{16}{9}$ (d) $\frac{9}{16}$

55. The de Broglie wavelengths of two fast moving particles *X, Y* are 1 nm, 3 nm respectively. Mass of *X* is nine times the mass of *Y*. The ratio of kinetic energies of *X, Y* is **[May 23, 2025 (I)]**

(a) 1 : 3 (b) 1 : 1 (c) 9 : 1 (d) 1 : 9

56. The de Broglie wavelength of an electron in the third Bohr orbit of H-atom is **[May 22, 2025 (II)]**

(a) $3\pi \times 5.29$ pm (b) $4\pi \times 52.9$ pm
(c) $6\pi \times 52.9$ pm (d) $2\pi \times 5.29$ pm

57. Which of the following sets of quantum numbers is not possible for the electron? **[May 22, 2025 (I)]**

(a) $n = 3, l = 1, m = 0, s = +\frac{1}{2}$

(b) $n = 4, l = 0, m = 0, s = -\frac{1}{2}$

(c) $n = 3, l = 3, m = -3, s = +\frac{1}{2}$

(d) $n = 1, l = 0, m = 0, s = -\frac{1}{2}$

58. The uncertainty in the position of electron (Δx) is approximately 100 pm. The uncertainty in momentum (in kg ms^{-1}) of an electron is [$h = 6.626 \times 10^{-34}$ Js] **[May 21, 2025 (II)]**

(a) 1.104×10^{-22} (b) 0.527×10^{-27}
(c) 0.527×10^{-24} (d) 1.055×10^{-24}

59. When a metal surface is irradiated with light of frequency *x* Hz, the kinetic energy of emitted photoelectrons is *z* J. When the same metal is irradiated with light of frequency *y* Hz, the kinetic energy of emitted electrons is $\frac{z}{3}$ J. What is the threshold frequency (in Hz) of metal? **[May 21, 2025 (I)]**

(a) $\frac{3}{2}(y-x)$ (b) $\left(\frac{3y-x}{2}\right)$

(c) $\left(\frac{2y-x}{3}\right)$ (d) $\frac{2}{3}(y-x)$

60. If the position of the electron was measured with an accuracy of +0.002 nm. the uncertainty in the momentum of it would be (in kg ms^{-1}) (h = 6.626×10^{-34} J s) **[May 23, 2024 (I)]**

(a) 2.637×10^{-23} (b) 2.637×10^{-24}
(c) 8.283×10^{-23} (d) 8.283×10^{-24}

61. The de Broglie wavelength of an electron with kinetic energy of 2.5 eV is (in m) **[May 22, 2024 (II)]**
(1 eV = 1.6×10^{-19} J, $m_e = 9 \times 10^{-31}$ kg)

(a) $\frac{h \times 10^{-25}}{\sqrt{72}}$ (b) $\frac{h \times 10^{25}}{\sqrt{72}}$

(c) $\frac{\sqrt{72}}{h \times 10^{-25}}$ (d) $\frac{\sqrt{72}}{h \times 10^{25}}$

62. If v_0 is the threshold frequency of a metal X, the correct relation between de Broglie wavelength (λ) associated with photoelectron and frequency (v) of the incident radiation is **[May 22, 2024 (I)]**

(a) $\lambda \propto \frac{1}{\sqrt{v-v_0}}$ (b) $\lambda \propto \frac{1}{(v-v_0)^{\frac{1}{4}}}$

(c) $\lambda \propto \frac{1}{(v-v_0)^{\frac{3}{4}}}$ (d) $\lambda \propto \sqrt{v-v_0}$

63. If λ_0 and λ are respectively the threshold wavelength and wavelength of incident light, the velocity of photo electrons ejected from the metal surface is **[May 21, 2024 (II)]**

(a) $\sqrt{\frac{2h}{m}(\lambda_0-\lambda)}$ (b) $\sqrt{\frac{2hc}{m}\left(\frac{\lambda_0-\lambda}{\lambda\lambda_0}\right)}$

(c) $\sqrt{\frac{2hc}{m}(\lambda_0-\lambda)}$ (d) $\sqrt{\frac{2hc}{m}\left(\frac{1}{\lambda_0}-\frac{1}{\lambda}\right)}$

64. If uncertainty in position and momentum of an electron are equal, then uncertainty in its velocity is **[May 20, 2024 (II)]**

(a) $\frac{1}{2m}\sqrt{\frac{h}{\pi}}$ (b) $\frac{1}{m}\sqrt{\frac{h}{\pi}}$

(c) $\sqrt{\frac{h}{\pi}}$ (d) $m\sqrt{\frac{h}{\pi}}$

65. In the ground state of hydrogen atom. electron absorbs 1.5 times energy than the minimum energy (2.18×10^{-18} J) to escape from the atom. The wavelength of the emitted electron (in m) is ($me = 9 \times 10^{-31}$ kg) **[May 19, 2024 (II)]**

(a) $\frac{h\times10^{24}}{\sqrt{1.962}}$ (b) $\frac{h}{\sqrt{1.962}}\times10^{23}$

(c) $\frac{h}{\sqrt{1.962}}\times10^{25}$ (d) $\frac{h}{\sqrt{1.962}}\times10^{22}$

66. A golf ball of mass 'm' g has a speed of 50 ms^{-1}, If the speed can be measured within accuracy of 2%, the uncertainty in the position is **[May 19, 2024 (II)]**

(a) $\frac{h}{4\pi m}$ (b) $\frac{h}{16\pi m}$

(c) $\frac{h}{4\pi m}\times10^3$ (d) $\frac{h}{16\pi m}\times10^3$

67. The de Broglie wavelength of a particle of mass 1 mg moving with a velocity of
10 ms^{-1} is ($h = 6.63 \times 10^{-34}$ J s) **[May 18, 2024 (I)]**

(a) 6.63×10^{-29} m (b) 6.63×10^{-31} m
(c) 6.63×10^{-34} m (d) 6.63×10^{-22} m

68. The de Broglie wavelength of a particle is 1000 nm. What is its momentum?
($h = 6.6\times10^{-34}$ J s) **[May 18, 2023 (I)]**

(a) 6.6×10^{-25} J s m^{-1} (b) 6.6×10^{-25} J s m
(c) 6.6×10^{-28} J s m^{-1} (d) 6.6×10^{-26} J s m

69. A photon of wavelength 3000 Å strikes a metal surface. The work function of the metal is 2.13 eV. What is the kinetic energy of the emitted photoelectron?
($h = 6.626 \times 10^{-34}$ Js) **[May 17, 2023 (II)]**

(a) 4.0 eV (b) 3.0 eV (c) 2.0 eV (d) 1.0 eV

70. The de Broglie wavelength of an electron travelling with 20% of velocity of light is
($h = 6.626 \times 10^{-34}$ Js ; $m_e = 9.1 \times 10^{-31}$ kg)
[May 15, 2023 (II); Similar to May 18, 2023 (I)]

(a) 2.4×10^{-11} m (b) 1.2×10^{-11} m
(c) 3.6×10^{-11} m (d) 4.8×10^{-11} m

71. Work function (W_o) values of six metals (in eV) are given below:

Li	Mg	Cu	Ag	K	Na
2.42	3.7	4.8	4.3	2.25	2.3

How many of the above metals do not eject the electrons when they are made to strike with radiation of wavelength 400 nm? **[July 7, 2022 (II)]**
($h = 6.62 \times 10^{-34}$Js)

(a) 4 (b) 2 (c) 3 (d) 5

72. The work function of a metal M is 6.3 eV. The wave length of the incident radiation required to just eject the electrons from its surface (in nm) is **[July 7, 2022 (II)]**

(a) 102 (b) 330 (c) 197 (d) 310

73. The value of work function of a metal X is 3.1 eV. The threshold frequency of it (in Hz) ($h = 6.62 \times 10^{-34}$ Js) **[July 6, 2022 (I)]**

(a) 6.49×10^{13} (b) 5.49×10^{13}
(c) 6.49×10^{14} (d) 7.49×10^{14}

74. If Δx is the uncertainity in position and Δv is the uncertainity in velocity of a particle are equal, the correct expression for uncertainity in momentum for the same particle is **[July 4, 2022 (I)]**

(a) $\frac{1}{4}\sqrt{\frac{mh}{\pi}}$ (b) $\frac{1}{3}\sqrt{\frac{mh}{2\pi}}$ (c) $\frac{1}{2}\sqrt{\frac{mh}{\pi}}$ (d) $\frac{1}{2}\sqrt{\frac{h}{m\pi}}$

75. Two particles of masses m and $2m$ have equal kinetic energies. The de-Broglie wavelengths are in the ratio of **[Aug. 23, 2021 (I)]**

(a) 1 : 1 (b) 1 : 2 (c) $1:\sqrt{2}$ (d) $\sqrt{2}:1$

76. If, the binding energy of electrons in a metal is 250 kJ/mol, what should be the threshold frequency of the striking photons in order to free an electron from the metal surface? **[Sept. 21, 2020 (I)]**

(a) 6.26×10^{14} s^{-1} (b) 12.4×10^{14} s^{-1}
(c) 6.26×10^{12} s^{-1} (d) 12.4×10^{12} s^{-1}

77. Which of the following statements is correct about photoelectric effect? **[Sept. 18, 2020 (I)]**

1. The number of electrons ejected from metal surface is inversely proportional to intensity of light.

2. Below threshold frequency, photoelectric effect can be observed.
3. At higher frequency than threshold frequency, the ejected electrons have certain kinetic energy.
4. At higher frequency than threshold frequency, the electron is still on the metal surface.

(a) 1 (b) 2 (c) 3 (d) 4

78. If the kinetic energy of an electron of mass 9.0×10^{-31} kg is 2.0×10^{-25}J, the wavelength of the electron in nm is approximately **[Apr. 22, 2019 (I)]**

(a) 1004.3 (b) 1204.3 (c) 1104.3 (d) 994.3

79. If a suitable photon is employed to locate an electron (mass = 9.11×10^{-31} kg) in an atom within a distance of 10.98 nm, the uncertainty involved in the measurement of its velocity in ms^{-1} is **[Apr. 22, 2019 (I)]**

(a) $\frac{1.6565 \times 10^6}{\pi}$ (b) $\frac{1.6565 \times 10^4}{\pi}$

(c) $\frac{1.6565 \times 10^{-8}}{\pi}$ (d) $\frac{1.6565 \times 10^8}{\pi}$

80. A light of frequency 1.6×10^{16} Hz when falls on a metal plate emits electrons that have double the kinetic energy compared to the kinetic energy of emitted electrons when frequency of 1.0×10^{16} Hz falls on the same plate. The threshold frequency (v_0) of the metal in Hz is **[2018]**

(a) 1×10^{15} (b) 4×10^{15}

(c) 3×10^{15} (d) 4×10^{13}

81. The work functions of Ag, Mg, K and Na respectively in eV are 4.3, 3.7, 2.25, 2.30. When an electromagnetic radiation of wavelength of 300 nm is allowed to fall on these metal surface, the number of metals from which the electrons are ejected is
(1eV = 1.6022×10^{-19}J) **[2017]**

(a) 4 (b) 3 (c) 2 (d) 5

82. The product of uncertainty in velocity and uncertainty in position of a micro particle of mass '*m*' is not less than which of the following? **[2016]**

(a) $h \times \frac{3\pi}{m}$ (b) $\frac{h}{3\pi} \times m$ (c) $\frac{h}{4\pi} \times \frac{1}{m}$ (d) $\frac{h}{4\pi} \times m$

83. If the kinetic energy of a particle is reduced to half, de-Broglie wavelength becomes **[2015]**

(a) 2 times (b) $\frac{1}{\sqrt{2}}$ times

(c) 4 times (d) $\sqrt{2}$ times

Topic 4 Quantum Mechanical Model of Atom

84. The number of radial nodes possible for 3p orbital is x and number of angular nodes possible for 4d-orbital is y. What is x : y? **[May 18, 2026 (I)]**

(a) 3 : 2 (b) 2 : 1

(c) 1 : 2 (d) 1 :1

85. Quantum number sets of four electrons I, II, III, IV are given below. The correct order of the energy of these electrons is **[May 13, 2026 (I)]**

I. $n = 3, l = 1, m_l = -1, m_s = +\frac{1}{2}$

II. $n = 4, l = 1, m_l = 0, m_s = +\frac{1}{2}$

III. $n = 4, l = 2, m_l = -2, m_s = +\frac{1}{2}$

IV. $n = 3, l = 2, m_l = -1, m_s = -\frac{1}{2}$

The correct answer is

(a) I > IV > II > III (b) III > II > I > IV

(c) III > IV > II > I (d) III > II > IV > I

86. The number of electrons with magnetic quantum number, *ml* = 0 in the elements with atomic numbers Z = 24 and Z = 29 are respectively **[May 26, 2025 (II)]**

(a) 12, 13 (b) 12, 12 (c) 13, 12 (d) 14, 15

87. In an element with atomic number (Z) 25, the number of electrons with ($n + l$) value equal to 3 and 4 are x and y respectively. The value of ($x + y$) is **[May 26, 2025 (I)]**

(a) 21 (b) 12 (c) 14 (d) 16

88. The total maximum number of electrons possible in 3d, 6d, 5s and 4f orbitals with m*l* (magnetic quantum number) value –2 is **[May 23, 2025 (II)]**

(a) 6 (b) 8 (c) 10 (d) 12

89. The sum of number of angular nodes and radial nodes for 4d orbital is **[May 23, 2024 (I)]**

(a) 2 (b) 3 (c) 4 (d) 5

90. The graph between variation of probability density, $\psi^2(r)$ and distance of the electron from the nucleus, r is shown below. This represents **[May 20, 2024 (II)]**

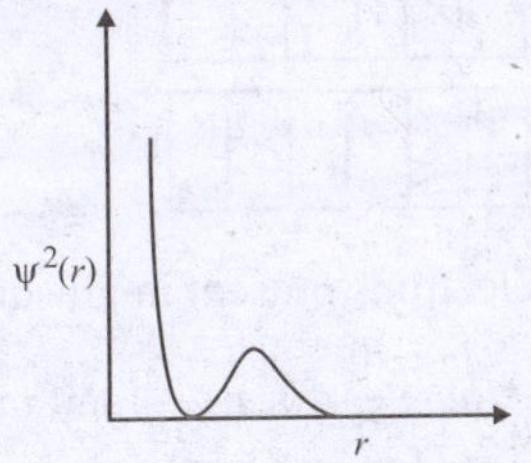

(a) 1*s* – orbital (b) 2*s* – orbital

(c) 3*s* – orbital (d) 2*p* – orbital

91. The angular momentum of an electron in a stationary state of Li^{2+} (Z = 3) is $\frac{3h}{\pi}$. The radius and energy of that stationary state are respectively **[May 20, 2024 (I)]**

(a) 3.174 Å, -5.45×10^{-19} J

(b) 6.348 Å, -5.45×10^{-19} J

(c) 6.348 Å, $+5.45 \times 10^{-18}$ J

(d) 2.116 Å, -5.45×10^{-19} J

92. Correct set of four quantum numbers for the valence electron of strontium (Z = 38) is **[May 18, 2024 (I)]**

(a) $5, 0, 0, +\frac{1}{2}$ (b) $5, 1, 0, +\frac{1}{2}$

(c) $5, 1, 1, +\frac{1}{2}$ (d) $6, 0, 0, +\frac{1}{2}$

93. Which of the following sets of quantum numbers is correct for an electron in 4f orbital?

[May 19, 2023 (I); Similar to May 15, 2023 (I)]

(a) $n = 3, \ell = 2, m_l = -2, m_s = +½$

(b) $n = 4, \ell = 3, m_l = +1, m_s = +½$

(c) $n = 4, \ell = 3, m_l = +4, m_s = +½$

(d) $n = 4, \ell = 4, m_l = +4, m_s = -½$

94. In which of the following, orbitals are correctly arranged in the increasing order of their energies?

[May 18, 2023 (II)]

(a) 4f < 5p < 5d < 6s (b) 5p < 4f < 6s < 5d

(c) 5p < 6s < 4f < 5d (d) 5p < 5d < 4f < 6s

95. Maximum number of electrons theoretically possible for an orbit with principal quantum number n = 6 in an atom is **[May 17, 2023 (I)]**

(a) 27 (b) 98 (c) 72 (d) 50

96. Which of the following electron arrangement does not obey Hund's rule? **[May 15, 2023 (II)]**

(a) 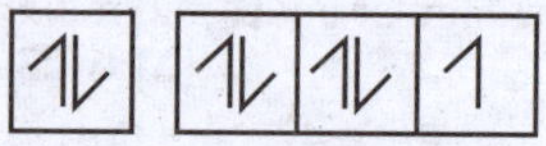

(b) 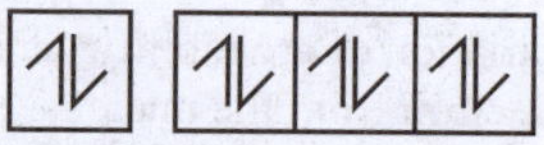

(c) 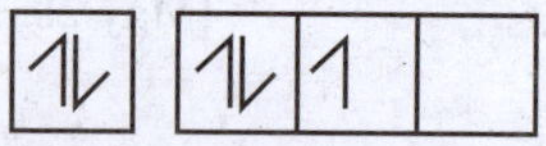

(d) 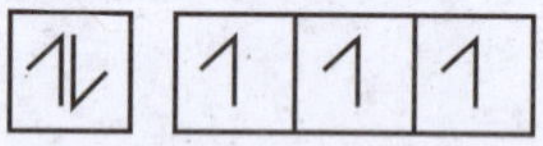

97. The sum of electrons present in all sub shells of an atom with m_s value of $+\frac{1}{2}$ for n = 4 and m_s value of $-\frac{1}{2}$ for n = 3 is **[July 8, 2022 (I)]**

(a) 25 (b) 16 (c) 09 (d) 32

98. Maximum number of electrons possible with spin quantum number $+\frac{1}{2}$ with principal quantum number n = 4 in an atom is **[July 5, 2022 (II)]**

(a) 16 (b) 9 (c) 4 (d) 25

99. The maximum number of electrons present in an orbital with n = 4, l = 3 is **[July 4, 2022 (II)]**

(a) 06 (b) 14 (c) 10 (d) 2

100. Which quantum number provides information about the shape of an orbital? **[July 4, 2022 (II)]**

(a) Spin quantum number

(b) Azimuthal quantum number

(c) Magnetic quantum number

(d) Principal quantum number

101. The number of radial nodes, angular nodes of a 4f-orbital are respectively **[July 4, 2022 (I)]**

(a) 0, 3 (b) 1, 2 (c) 2, 1 (d) 2, 0

102. Which orbital among the following has zero radial nodes and 2 angular nodes? **[Aug. 23, 2021 (I)]**

(a) 4*s* (b) 3*d* (c) 2*p* (d) 5*s*

103. Choose the correct option regarding:

Assertion: Energy of the orbital decreases with increase of '*n*'.

Reason: Energy is required in shifting away the negatively charged electron from positively charged nucleus. **[Sept. 21, 2020 (I)]**

(a) Assertion and Reason are correct statements and Reason is the correct explanation for Assertion

(b) Assertion and Reason are correct statements and Reason is not the explanation for Assertion

(c) Assertion is correct, Reason is wrong

(d) Assertion is wrong, Reason is correct

104. "No two electrons in an atom can have the same set of all four quantum numbers". This principle of called

[Sept. 18, 2020 (I)]

(a) Zeeman effect

(b) Pauli's exclusion principle

(c) Stark effect

(d) Heisenberg principle

105. The uncertainty in the position of an electron moving with velocity of 3×10^4 cm/s is (given mass of electron = 9.1×10^{-28} g, uncertainty in velocity = 0.02%)

[Sept. 18, 2020 (I)]

(a) 1.8×10^{-3} cm (b) 9×10^{-3} cm

(c) 3.8×10^{-2} cm (d) 1.8×10^{-4} cm

106. How many orbitals is/are possible with $n = 3, l = 1$ and $m_l = -1$ value? **[Apr. 21, 2019 (I)]**

(a) 2 (b) 3

(c) 5 (d) 1

107. Which of the following sets of quantum numbers is correct for an electron in 3*d*-orbital? **[2015]**

(a) $n = 3, l = 2, m = -3, s = +\frac{1}{2}$

(b) $n = 3, l = 3, m = +3, s = -\frac{1}{2}$

(c) $n = 3, l = 2, m = -2, s = +\frac{1}{2}$

(d) $n = 3, l = 2, m = -3, s = -\frac{1}{2}$

3 Classification of Elements and Periodicity in Properties

CHAPTER SYNOPSIS

- Isoelectronic ions have different size.
- Inert pair effect in *p*-block. Stability of higher state decreases and that of lower state increases going along a group $Ge^{2+} < Sn^{2+} < Pb^{2+}$.
- Reducing nature of hydride increases in a group and decreases in a period.
- Noble gases have largest atomic sizes (van der waal radii). However, their covalent radii are smaller e.g. Xe.
- Size of Ga and Al are same, [Z_{eff} increasing]
- Period no. is equal to the valence shell present in the configuration. Also for *s* and *p*-block elements.
- Period no. = valence shell, for d-block = shell + 1, for *f*-block = shell + 2 and so on.
- Lower atomic volume leads to higher density, increased hardness higher melting point, boiling point, less malleability and ductility.
- Lowest electronegativity : Cs
- Highest electronegativity : F
- Highest ionisation potential : He
- Lowest ionisation potential : Cs
- Highest electron affinity : Chlorine (Cl)
- Least electropositive element : Fluorine (F)
- *s*-block elements and *p*-block elements both are called main group or representative elements
- *d*-block elements are called transition elements and *f*-block elements are called inner transition elements
- Largest atomic size : Cs
- Most electropositive element : Cs (in stable element), Fr (In all element)
- Group containing maximum no. of gaseous elements in periodic table : Zero gp ; next to zero group is VII group or halogen group (F_2 and Cl_2)
- Total number of gaseous elements in periodic table : 11 (H_2, He, N_2, O_2, F_2 Ne, Cl_2, Ar, Kr, Xe, Rn)
- Total number of liquid elements in periodic table : 4 (Ga, Br, Cs, Hg) (Fr is also liquid)

Topic 1 Modern Periodic Table

1. Which of the following sets contain atomic numbers of only representative elements? **[May 14, 2026 (II)]**
I. 3, 33, 53, 87 II. 2, 10, 22, 36
III. 9, 35, 51, 88 IV. 17, 25, 37, 48
The correct answer is
(a) I & II only (b) II & III only
(c) I & III only (d) II & IV only

2. Consider the elements with atomic number (Z) from 11 to 18. The ratio of number of s-electrons to p-electrons in element X is 2 : 3 and in element Y is 3 : 5. What are X and Y? **[May 13, 2026 (II)]**
(a) Mg, Al (b) Si, P
(c) P, S (d) S, Cl

3. Match the following : **[May 21, 2025 (I)]**

List-I (Atomic number, Z)		List-II (Block)	
(A)	112	(I)	*s*
(B)	116	(II)	*p*
(C)	88	(III)	*d*
(D)	100	(IV)	*f*

The correct answer is
(a) A-III, B-I, C-II, D-IV
(b) A-III, B-II, C-I, D-IV
(c) A-IV, B-II, C-III, D-I
(d) A-II, B-III, C-IV, D-I

4. Match the following **[May 23, 2024 (I)]**

List -I Symbol of element		List-II Group number	
A	Mc	I	16
B	Lv	II	17
C	Fl	III	15
D	Ts	IV	14

The correct answer is
(a) A-III, B-IV, C-I, D-II (b) A-IV, B-III, C-I, D-II
(c) A-III, B-I, C-IV, D-II (d) A-II, B-IV, C-I, D-III

5. The number of *d* electrons in Fe is equal to which of the following? **[May 21, 2024 (I)]**
i. Total number of '*s*' electrons of Mg
ii. Total number of '*p*' electrons of Cl
iii. Total number of '*p*' electrons of Ne
The correct option is
(a) i, ii only (b) ii, iii only
(c) i, iii only (d) i, ii, iii

6. Match the following: **[May 20, 2024 (II)]**

List-I		List-II	
A.	Titanium	I.	Non-metal
B.	Fluorine	II.	Transition metal
C.	Tellurium	III.	Lanthanoid
D.	Dysprosium	IV.	Metalloid

(a) A-II, B-I, C-III, D-IV
(b) A-III, B-I, C-IV, D-II
(c) A-II, B-I, C-IV, D-III
(d) A-IV, B-I, C-II, D-III

7. Identify the pair of elements in which number of electrons in (*n*–1) shell is same
(a) Fe, Mn (b) Zn, Fe
(c) K, Sc (d) Mn, Cr

8. The number of metalloids in the following elements are **[May 19, 2023 (I)]**
Si, Mn, B,F,Cu, Ag, K, Sb, As, Na, Ge
(a) 4 (b) 5 (c) 6 (d) 7

9. Match the following **[May 16, 2023 (I)]**

List-I (Elements)	List-II (Valence shell Configuration)
A. Alkali metals	I. ns^2np^6
B. Alkaline earth metals	II. ns^2np^5
C. Halogens	III. ns^2
D. Noble gases	IV. ns^1

(a) A-I, B-II, C-III, D-IV
(b) A-IV, B-III, C-II, D-I
(c) A-II, B-I, C-III, D-IV
(d) A-IV, B-I, C-III, D-II

10. Which of the following element has two electrons in Q shell in its ground state? **[July 8, 2022 (I)]**
(a) Ba (b) Ra (c) La (d) Pb

11. The general formula of the compound formed when a metal (M) of group-1 reacts with non metal (x) of group-16 is **[July 7, 2022 (II)]**
(a) MX_6 (b) M_2X_3 (c) MX_2 (d) M_2X

12. The number of valence electrons present in an element with atomic number117 is **[July 5, 2022 (II)]**
(a) 7 (b) 8 (c) 6 (d) 5

13. In second period of the long form of the periodic table an element X has second lowest first ionization enthalpy and element Y has second highest first ionization enthalpy values. What are X and Y? **[July 4, 2022 (II)]**
(a) Be, F (b) Be, Ne (c) Be, O (d) C, O

14. To which group of the periodic table does an element having electronic configuration $[Ar]3d^54s^2$ belong? **[Aug. 19, 2021 (I)]**
(a) Second (b) Fourth
(c) Seventh (d) Third

15. "The properties of elements are periodic functions of their atomic weights." This periodic law was given by **[Sept. 17, 2020 (I)]**

(a) Dobereiner (b) Lothar Meyer
(c) Mendeleev (d) Alexander

16. An element has [Ar] $3d^1$ configuration in its +2 oxidation state. Its position in the periodic table is **[2016]**

(a) period-3, group-3 (b) period-3, group-7
(c) period-4, group-3 (d) period-3, group-9

17. Match the following. **[2015]**

List I	List II
A. Rubidium	(1) Germanium
B. Platinum	(2) Radioactive chalcogen
C. Eka-silicon	(3) s-block element
D. Polonium	(4) Atomic number 78

	A	B	C	D
(a)	4	3	2	1
(b)	3	4	1	2
(c)	2	1	4	3
(d)	4	3	1	2

Topic 2 Periodic Trends in Properties of Elements

18. In which of the following, elements are not in correct order with respect to the property mentioned in brackets? **[May 18, 2026 (II)]**

(a) $S < P < N < O$ (Electronegativity)
(b) $Br < Ge < Ga < Ca$ (Atomic radius)
(c) $Al < Mg < S < P$ (First ionization enthalpy)
(d) $Mg < Ca < K < Cs$ (Metallic nature)

19. Which of the following statements are correct?

I. In third period, two elements have higher ionization enthalpy than the element immediately following them in the same period.
II. Electro negativity of carbon is higher than that of phosphorus.
III. An element X belongs to group 14 and period 3. The number of electrons present in it is 14.

The correct answer is **[May 18, 2026 (I)]**

(a) I, II, III (b) I, II only
(c) II, III only (d) I, III only

20. The amount of energy released (in k cal mol^{-1}) when 7.1 g of gaseous chlorine atoms are completely converted to Cl^- (g) ions is **[May 15, 2026 (II)]**
(Given ; $\Delta_{eg}H(Cl) = -3.6$ eV, 1 eV = 23 k cal mol^{-1}, At, Wt; Cl = 35.5u)

(a) 15.66 (b) 16.56
(c) 31.32 (d) 33.12

21. Which of the following sets of molecules/ions represent isoelectronic species? **[May 15, 2026 (I)]**

I. NO^+, CN^-, CO, O_2^{2+}
II. NH_3, Al^{3+}, Ne, F^-
III. O_2^+, NO, N_2^-, H_2O

The correct answer is

(a) I, II only (b) I, II, III
(c) II, III only (d) I, III only

22. Which of the following is not the correct order of atomic radius of the elements given? **[May 15, 2026 (I)]**

(a) $Br < Ge < Ga < Ca$ (b) $Cr < V < Ti < Sc$
(c) $F < Cl < K < Cs$ (d) $O < P < K < Ge$

23. In which of the following, the number of valence electrons is maximum? **[May 14, 2026 (II)]**

(a) PO_4^{3-} (b) SO_3^{2-}
(c) CO_3^{2-} (d) CNO^-

24. Match the following **[May 14, 2026 (I)]**

List-I (Pair of elements having similar values of property mentioned in List-II)	List-II (Property)
A. Co, Ni	I. Electronegativity
B. K, Ba	II. Electron gain enthalpy
C. N, Cl	III. Metallic radius
D. Ar, Kr	IV. Standard reduction potential (–ve)

The correct answer is

(a) A-III, B-I, C-IV, D-II (b) A-IV, B-III, C-II, D-I
(c) A-IV, B-III, C-I, D-II (d) A-III, B-IV, C-I, D-II

25. Which of the following statements is not correct regarding third period elements? **[May 13, 2026 (II)]**

(a) Cl has the highest electron gain enthalpy
(b) Ar has the highest first ionization enthalpy
(c) Mg has higher ionization enthalpy than Al.
(d) P has a lower first ionization enthalpy than S

26. Identify the correct pair of species having same number of valency electrons **[May 13, 2026 (I)]**

(a) SF_4, ClO_3^- (b) PO_4^{3-}, SF_4
(c) ClF_3, SO_3^{2-} (d) CCl_4, PO_4^{3-}

27. Which of the following statement is not correct? **[May 13, 2026 (I)]**

(a) The increasing order of first ionization enthalpy of Be, B, C, is $B < Be < C$
(b) The IUPAC name of element Livermorium is unhunhexium
(c) The element Tennessene belongs to group 16 in periodic table
(d) Al_2O_3, As_2O_3 are amphoteric oxides

28. Which of the following sets are correctly matched?

Order	Property
I. K > Li > C > F	Atomic radius
II. F > C > Li > K	First ionization enthalpy
III. F > C > K > Li	Electronegativity

The correct answer is **[May 12, 2026 (II)]**
(a) I, II only (b) II, III only
(c) I, III only (d) I, II, III

29. Observe the following pairs of elements
I. P, H
II. C, S
III. N, Cl
Which pairs contain the elements having same electronegativity? **[May 12, 2026 (I)]**
(a) I, II only (b) II, III only
(c) I, III only (d) I, II, III

30. Observe the following data: **[May 27, 2025 (I)]**

Ion	Q^{a+}	X^{b+}	Y^{c+}	Z^{d+}
Radius (pm)	53	66	40	100

Q^{a+}, X^{b+}, Y^{c+}, Z^{d+} are respectively
(a) $Mg^{2+}, Al^{3+}, Na^+, Si^{4+}$ (b) $Al^{3+}, Si^{4+}, Mg^{2+}, Na^+$
(c) $Mg^{2+}, Si^{4+}, Al^{3+}, Na^+$ (d) $Al^{3+}, Mg^{2+}, Si^{4+}, Na^+$

31. Which of the following orders is not correct for the given property? **[May 26, 2025 (II)]**
(a) Li < Na < K - metallic radius
(b) Br < F < C*l* - electron gain enthalpy
(c) C < N < O - first ionization enthalpy
(d) $Mg^{2+} < Na^+ < F^-$ - ionic radius

32. Among the ions Mg^{2+}, O^{2-}, Al^{3+}, F^-, Na^+ and N^{3-}, the ion with largest size and ion with smallest size are respectively **[May 26, 2025 (I)]**
(a) N^{3-}, Mg^{2+} (b) O^{2-}, F^-
(c) Al^{3+}, N^{3-} (d) N^{3-}, Al^{3+}

33. The order of negative electron gain enthalpy of Li, Na, S, Cl is **[May 24, 2025 (I)]**
(a) Na > S > Cl > Li (b) Cl > S > Li > Na
(c) Cl > Li > S > Na (d) Li > Na > S > Cl

34. The period and group numbers of the element having maximum elctronegativity in the long form of periodic table, respectively, are **[May 23, 2025 (II)]**
(a) 2, 17 (b) 3,17 (c) 1, 18 (d) 2, 16

35. Electronic configurations of four elements *A, B, C, D* are given below is: **[May 23, 2025 (I)]**
(A) $1s^2 2s^2 2p^6 3s^1$ (B) $1s^2 2s^2 2p^6 3s^2 3p^1$
(C) $1s^2 2s^2 2p^6 3s^2$ (D) $1s^2 2s^2 2p^6 3s^2 3p^2$
The correct order of first ionization enthalpy of these elements is:
(a) D > B > C > A (b) C > D > B > A
(c) C > A > B > D (d) D > C > B > A

36. The correct order of the non-metallic character among the elements B, C, N, F and Si is **[May 22, 2025 (II)]**
(a) B > C > Si > N > F (b) Si > C > B > N > F
(c) F > N > C > B > Si (d) F > N > C > Si > B

37. The correct order of atomic radii of C, Al and S is **[May 22, 2025 (I)]**
(a) C < Al < S (b) S < Al < C
(c) Al < S < C (d) C < S < Al

38. Which of the following orders is not correct about the property shown against it? **[May 21, 2025 (II)]**
(a) N > O > P > S - First ionisation enthalphy
(b) F > Cl > O > S - Negative electron gain enthalpy
(c) $Fe^{3+} < Fe^{2+} <$ Fe - Size
(d) O > N > S > P - Non-metallic character

39. Two statements are given below:
Statement I: Nitrogen has more ionization enthalpy and electronegativity than beryllium.
Statement II: CrO_3, B_2O_3 are acidic oxides. **[May 22, 2024 (II)]**
(a) Both statements I and II are correct
(b) Both statements I and II are not correct
(c) Statement I is correct, but statement II is not correct
(d) Statement I is not correct, but statement II is correct

40. In which of the following sets, elements are not correctly arranged with the property shown in brackets? **[May 22, 2024 (I)]**
(a) S > Se > O (Electron gain enthalpy)
(b) F > O > Cl (Electronegativity)
(c) Na > Li > Al (Metallic radius)
(d) Na > K > Ba (Metallic nature)

41. The correct order of atomic radii of N, F, Al, Si is **[May 21, 2024 (II)]**
(a) F > N > Si > Al (b) F > N > Al > Si
(c) Al > Si > F > N (d) Al > Si > N > F

42. The correct order of atomic radii of given elements is **[May 21, 2024 (I)]**
(a) B < Be < Mg (b) Mg < Be < B
(c) Be < B < Mg (d) B < Mg < Be

43. The correct order of density of Be, Mg, Ca, Sr is **[May 20, 2024 (II)]**
(a) Sr > Be > Mg > Ca
(b) Be > Mg > Ca > Sr
(c) Mg > Ca > Sr > Be
(d) Ca > Sr > Be > Mg

44. Which of the following orders is not correct against the given property **[May 20, 2024 (II)]**
(a) Ga < In < Tl < Al < B - melting point
(b) Al < Ga < In< Tl < B - Electronegativity
(c) B < Al < Ga < In < Tl - density
(d) B < Al < Ga < In < Tl - atomic radius

45. Match the following: **[May 20, 2024 (I)]**

List-I		List-II	
(A)	Ionization enthalpy	(I)	P < Si < Mg < Na
(B)	Metallic character	(II)	I < N < O < F
(C)	Electron gain enthalpy	(III)	B < Be < C < O < N
(D)	Electro negativity	(IV)	I < Br < F < Cl

Then the correct match is

(a) (A) - (III), (B) - (IV), (C) - (I), (D) - (II)
(b) (A) - (III), (B) - (I), (C) - (IV), (D) - (II)
(c) (A) - (IV), (B) - (II), (C) - (I), (D) - (III)
(d) (A) - (IV), (B) - (III), (C) - (I), (D) - (II)

46. If the first ionisation enthalpy of Li, Be and C respectively are 520, 899, 1086 kJ mol^{-1}, the first ionisation enthalpy (in kJ mol^{-1}) of B will be **[May 19, 2024 (II)]**

(a) 487 (b) 950 (c) 801 (d) 1402

47. The correct order of decomposition temperature of $MgCO_3$ (X). $BaCO_3$ (Y), $CaCO_3$ (Z) is **[May 19, 2024 (II)]**

(a) Y > Z > X (b) X > Y > Z
(c) Y > X > Z (d) X > Z > Y

48. Match the following:

List-I (Element)		List-II (Electron gain enthalpy) (in kJ mol^{-1})	
(A)	F	(I)	– 141
(B)	Cl	(II)	– 328
(C)	O	(III)	– 200
(D)	S	(IV)	– 349

[May 18, 2024 (I)]

(a) (A) - (II), (B) - (IV), (C) - (I), (D) - (III)
(b) (A) - (IV), (B) - (II), (C) - (I), (D) - (III)
(c) (A) - (III), (B) - (II), (C) - (IV), (D) - (I)
(d) (A) - (II), (B) - (III), (C) - (IV), (D) - (I)

49. The correct order of the metallic nature of the following elements is

[May 18, 2023 (II); Similar to May 17, 2023 (II)]

(a) Si > Al > Na > Hg (b) Na > Mg > Al > Si
(c) Al > Mg > Na > Si (d) Mg > Na > Al > Si

50. The number of following pairs of elements which exhibit diagonal relationship is: **[May 18, 2023 (I)]**

1. B & Si 2. Be & Al
3. Li & Mg 4. Al & S

(a) 2 (b) 1 (c) 3 (d) 4

51. Which one of the following indicates correct order of atomic size of the given elements?

[May 17, 2023 (II); Similar to May 18, 2023 (II)]

(a) Li > B > F > N (b) N > F > Li > B
(c) F > N > B > Li (d) Li > B > N > F

52. The correct order of electron gain enthalpy of N, O, Cl, Al is **[May 17, 2023 (I)]**

(a) Cl < N < O < Al (b) Al < N < O < Cl
(c) O < N < Al < Cl (d) N < O < Cl < Al

53. Consider the elements Ne, Na, Mg. The element with highest first ionization enthalpy and element with lowest second ionization enthalpy respectively are

[May 16, 2023 (II)]

(a) Na, Ne (b) Ne, Mg
(c) Na, Na (d) Mg, Na

54. Which of the following oxides is highly basic?

[May 16, 2023 (I)]

(a) Cr_2O_3 (b) Al_2O_3
(c) MgO (d) Na_2O

55. The correct order of covalent radii of Si, Ge, Sn is:

[May 15, 2023 (II)]

(a) Ge < Si < Sn (b) Sn < Si < Ge
(c) Si < Ge < Sn (d) Sn < Ge < Si

56. Identify the pair of elements with the highest and lowest electronegativity respectively **[May 15, 2023 (I)]**

(a) K and Rb (b) I and F
(c) F and Fr (d) Fr and Li

57. Consider the following

(I) The order of first ionisation enthalpy of first three elements of 3rd period is Mg > Al > Na
(II) The element with electronegativity of 3.5 is chlorine
(III) The order of sizes of ions Mg^{2+}, Na^+, F^- and O^{2-} is $Mg^{2+} < Na^+ < F^- < O^{2-}$
(IV) The IUPAC name of the element with atomic number 106 is Bohrium. **[May 17, 2023 (I)]**

The correct statements are

(a) I & II only (b) II & III only
(c) I & III only (d) II & IV only

58. The electronic configuration which is associated with highest first ionisation enthalpy is: **[July 8, 2022 (I)]**

(a) [Ne] $3s^23p^2$ (b) [Ne] $3s^23p^3$
(c) [Ne] $3s^23p^4$ (d) [Ne] $3s^23p^1$

59. In which of the following, elements are correctly arranged in the decreasing order of their second ionization enthalpies.

[July 7, 2022 (II)]

(a) O > F > N > C (b) N > O > F > C
(c) F > O > N > C (d) C > N > O > F

60. Identify the element which has highest second ionization enthalpy **[July 7, 2022 (II)]**

(a) Carbon (b) Phosphorus
(c) Nitrogen (d) Oxygen

61. The set of amphoteric oxides among ZnO, Tl_2O_3, In_2O_3, B_2O_3, PbO, SnO_2 is **[July 6, 2022 (I)]**

(a) ZnO, Tl_2O_3, PbO (b) ZnO, PbO, SnO_2
(c) ZnO, In_2O_3, SnO_2 (d) ZnO, In_2O_3, PbO

62. In which of the following the elements are in correct order of their chemical reactivity in terms of oxidizing property? **[July 6, 2022 (I)]**

(a) F > O > Cl > N (b) O > F > Cl > N
(c) Cl > F > O > N (d) F > Cl > N > O

63. In which of the following, the elements Al, B, Mg and K are correctly arranged in the increasing order of their metallic character? **[July 5, 2022 (II)]**

(a) B < Al < Mg < K (b) B < Mg < Al < K
(c) Al < Mg < K < B (d) B < Mg < K < Al

64. In which of the following, elements are arranged in the correct order of their electron gain enthalpies. **[July 4, 2022 (II)]**

(a) F > S > O > N (b) F > O > S > N
(c) F > O > N > S (d) F > N > O > S

65. Lithium shows diagonal relationship with element 'X' and aluminum with Y . X and Y respectively are **[July 4, 2022 (I)]**

(a) Mg, Be (b) Be, Mg
(c) Na, Si (d) B, Be

66. The correct order of the metallic character of the elements Be, Al, Na, K is **[July 4, 2022 (I)]**

(a) K > Na > Al > Be (b) K > Al > Na > Be
(c) Al > K > Na > Be (d) Na > K > Be > Al

67. The ions S^{2-}, Cl^-, K^+, Ca^{2+} are isoelectronic. Their ionic radii show **[Aug. 23, 2021 (I)]**

(a) a decrease from S^{2-} to Cl^- and then increase from K^+ to Ca^{2+}.
(b) an increase from S^{2-} to Cl^- and then decrease from K^+ to Ca^{2+}.
(c) a significant decrease from S^{2-} to Ca^{2+}
(d) a significant increase from S^{2-} to Ca^{2+}

68. Which among the following isoelectronic species has the smallest size? **[Aug. 23, 2021 (I)]**

O^{2+}, F^-, Ne, Na^+, Mg^{2+}, Al^{3+}, Si^{4+}

(a) F^- (b) Ne (c) Si^{4+} (d) Na^+

69. **Assertion (A) :** The first ionisation energy of Be is greater than that of B. **[Aug. 23, 2021 (II)]**

Reason (R) : 2*p* orbital has lower energy than 2*s* orbital.

(a) Both A and R are true and R is a correct explanation for A.
(b) Both A and R are true but R is not a correct explanation for A.
(c) A is true but R is false.
(d) A is false but R is true.

70. The correct order of electronegativity of carbon in various hybridisation states is **[Aug. 20, 2021 (I)]**

(a) $sp < sp^2 < sp^3$ (b) $sp > sp^2 > sp^3$
(c) $sp^2 > sp < sp^3$ (d) $sp = sp^2 < sp^3$

71. Given that ionisation potential and electron gain enthalpy of chlorine are 13eV and 4eV respectively. The electronegativity of chlorine on Mulliken scale, approximately equals to **[Aug. 19, 2021 (I)]**

(a) 8.5 eV (b) 6.0 eV
(c) 3.0 eV (d) 1.5 eV

72. Which of the following represents the correct order of increasing electron gain enthalpy with negative sign for the elements? **[Aug. 19, 2021 (II)]**

1. Nitrogen (N) 2. Phosphorus (P)
3. Chlorine (Cl) 4. Fluorine (F)

(a) P < N < F < Cl (b) N < P < F < Cl
(c) Cl < F < P < N (d) F < Cl < N < P

73. The second ionisation energies of Li, Be, B and C are in the order .... **[Sept. 21, 2020 (I)]**

(a) Li > C > B > Be (b) Li > B > C > Be
(c) Be > C > B > Li (d) B > C > Be > Li

74. Choose the smallest ion from the following. **[Sept. 17, 2020 (I)]**

(a) Mg^{2+} (b) S^{2-} (c) Na^+ (d) Cl^-

75. **Assertion :** Boron has a smaller first ionisation enthalpy than beryllium. **[Sept. 17, 2020 (II)]**

Reason : The penetration of a 2*s*-electron to the nucleus is more than the 2*p*-electron hence, 2*p*-electron is more shielded by the inner core of electrons than 2s-electrons.

(a) Assertion and Reason both are correct statements but Reason is not correct explanation for Assertion.
(b) Assertion is correct statement but Reason is wrong statement.
(c) Assertion and Reason both are correct statements and Reason is correct explanation for Assertion
(d) Assertion and Reason both are wrong statements.

76. If four elements with atomic numbers $Z-2$, $Z-1$, Z and $Z+1$ are forming isoelectronic ions, the atomic number of the ion having largest size is **[Apr. 21, 2019 (I)]**

(a) $Z-2$ (b) $Z-1$ (c) Z (d) $Z+1$

77. Identify the set of acidic oxides. **[Apr. 20, 2019 (I); Similar to 2015]**

(a) Na_2O, CaO, BaO (b) ZnO, PbO, BeO
(c) CO, NO, N_2O (d) Mn_2O_7, CrO_3, V_2O_5

78. **Assertion (A) :** Na^+ and Mg^{2+} ions are isoelectronic but the ionic radius of Na^+ is greater than that of Mg^{2+}.

Reason (R) : The effective nuclear charge of Na^+ ion is less than that of Mg^{2+} ion. **[2017]**

(a) Both (A) and (R) are correct but (R) is not the correct explanation of (A).
(b) Both (A) and (R) are correct and (R) is correct explanation of (A).
(c) (A) is not correct but (R) is correct.
(d) (A) is correct but (R) is not correct.

79. Identify the correct statement. **[2015]**

(a) Lead forms compounds in +2 oxidation state due to inert pair effect
(b) All halogens show only negative oxidation state
(c) Catenation property increases from boron to oxygen
(d) Oxidation state of oxygen is –1 in ozonides

4 Chemical Bonding and Molecular Structure

CHAPTER SYNOPSIS

- Formation of an ionic compound is favoured by:-
  (a) Low ionization energy (IE) of the metal.
  (b) High electron affinity (EA) of the other element.
  (c) Higher lattice energy (U) of the resulting compound.
- Bond order (B.O.) = $\frac{\text{No. of electrons in BMO} - \text{No. of electrons in ABMO}}{2}$
- In order to determine the number of $p\pi - p\pi$ or $p\pi - d\pi$ bonds, the following formula can be used.
  (i) Calculate the number of σ bonds = number of surrounding atoms
  (ii) π bonds = number of oxygen atoms – number of negative charge
  (iii) Lone pair = 1/2 (Valence electron – number of covalent bond)
  (iv) Hybridization = σ bonds + number of lone pairs
  (v) Now, number of pπ – pπ bonds = number of unhybridized p orbitals left
  (vi) pπ – dπ bonds will be formed when π bonds are more than the number of unhybridized *p*–orbitals left.
- Types of Hybridization and orbital involved in it:

Hybridization	**Atomic orbital involve**
sp	s + any p-orbitals (p_x or p_y or p_z)
sp^2	s + any two p-orbitals (p_x or p_y or p_z)
sp^3	$s + p_x + p_y + p_z$
sp^3d	$s + p_x + p_y + p_z + d_z^2$ – trigonal bipyramidal
sp^3d	$s + p_x + p_y + p_z + d_{x^2-y^2}$ – Square pramidal
dsp^2	$(n-1)d_{x^2-y^2} + ns + np_x + np_y$ – Square planar
sp^3d^2	$ns + np_x + np_y + np_z + nd_{x^2-y^2} + nd_{z^2}$
d^2sp^3	$(n-1)d_{x^2-y^2} + (n-1)d_{z^2} + ns + np_x + np_y + np_z$
sp^3d^3	$n_x + np_x + np_y + nd_{x^2-y^2} + ndxy + np_z + nd_{z^2}$

- For General Formula of Hybridization:

Simple Molecule

$$H = \frac{1}{2}[V + M]$$

Polyatomic Anion

$$X = \frac{1}{2}[V + M + A]$$

Polyatomic Cation

$$X = \frac{1}{2}[V + M - C]$$

$$\text{Overall} = \frac{1}{2}(V + M - C + A)$$

In the above formulae,
V = Number of outer shell electrons in ground state of the central atom
M = Number of monovalent atoms or groups attached to the central atom
A = Magnitude of charge on anion
C = Magnitude of charge on cation

- **For the molecules having molecular mass more than N_2** the sequence in the order of increasing energy is

$$\sigma 1s < \sigma^* 1s < \sigma 2s < \sigma^* 2s < \sigma 2p_z < \pi 2p_x = \pi 2p_y < \pi^* 2p_x = \pi^* 2p_y < \sigma^* 2p_z$$

- **For the molecules having molecular mass up to N_2** like Li_2, Be_2, B_2, C_2, N_2 etc. $s2p_z$ the order of increasing energy is

$$\sigma 1s < \sigma^* 1s < \sigma 2s < \sigma^* 2s < \pi 2p_x = \pi 2p_y < \sigma 2p_z < \pi^* 2p_x = \pi^* 2p_y < \sigma^* 2p_z$$

Topic 1 Electrovalent, Covalent and Co-ordinate Bonding

1. Formal change on sulphur atom in the following three Lewis structure I, II, III respectively is

I. $S=C=N$ II. $S-C\equiv N$

III. $S\equiv C-N$ **[May 18, 2026 (I)]**

(a) 0, +1, –1 (b) +1, 0, –1

(c) 0, –1, + 1 (d) +1, –1, 0

2. Identify the set containing isoelectronic species. **[May 23, 2025 (II)]**

(a) N_2, O_2^{2-}, NO^+ (b) N_2, CO, NO^+

(c) F_2, O_2^{2-}, N_2 (d) N_2, O_2^{2+}, C_2

3. The correct order of covalent bond character of BCl_3, CCl_4, $BeCl_2$, LiCl is **[May 21, 2024 (II)]**

(a) $LiCl < BeCl_2 < BCl_3 < CCl_4$

(b) $CCl_4 < BeCl_2 < BCl_3 < LiCl$

(c) $CCl_4 < BCl_3 < BeCl_2 < LiCl$

(d) $LiCl < BCl_3 < BeCl_2 < CCl_4$

4. Which of the following orders are correct regarding their covalent character? **[May 21, 2024 (I)]**

i. KF < KI ii. LiF < KF

iii. $SnCl_2 < SnCl_4$ iv. NaCl < CuCl

The correct option is

(a) i, ii, iii only (b) ii, iii, iv only

(c) i, iii, iv only (d) i, ii, iv only

5. Given below are two statements

Assertion (A): Ionic compounds are formed by non-directional bonds

Reasoning (R): They are soluble in nonpolar solvents

The correct answer is **[May 17, 2023 (II)]**

(a) Both (A) and (R) are correct and (R) is the correct explanation of (A)

(b) Both (A) and (R) are correct and (R) is not the correct explanation of (A)

(c) (A) is correct but (R) is not correct

(d) (A) is not correct but (R) is correct

6. Which of the following is not the property of covalent substances? **[May 15, 2023 (II)]**

(a) have definite shape

(b) have low melting points

(c) good conductors of electricity

(d) soluble in non- polar solvents

7. How many lone pairs of electrons are present in a hydroxyl ion? **[Sept. 17, 2020 (I)]**

(a) Two pairs (b) Three pairs

(c) One pair (d) Four pairs

Topic 2 Octet Rule, Resonance and Hydrogen Bonding

8. Which of the following statements are correct about CO_3^{2-} ion? **[May 14, 2026 (II)]**

I. The hybridisation of central atom is sp^3

II. The average formal charge on each oxygen atom is 0.67

III. The resonance hybrid structure has one C–O single bond and two C=O double bonds

IV. All C–O bond lengths are equal

(only =)

(a) II & IV only (b) I & II only

(c) II & III only (d) I & III only

9. In which of the following intramolecular H-bonding is absent? **[May 21, 2025 (I)]**

(a) Salicylic acid (b) Salicylaldehyde

(c) Quinol (d) Catechol

10. Observe the following structure **[May 20, 2024 (I)]**

$O=N-O$
(1) (2) (3)

The formal charges on the atoms 1, 2, 3 respectively are

(a) +1, 0, –1 (b) 0, 0, –1

(c) –1, 0, +1 (d) 0, 0, 0

11. The correct formula used to determine the formal charge (Q_f) on an atom in the given Lewis structure of a molecule or ion is

(V = number of valence electrons in free atom, U = number of unshared electrons on the atom, B = number of bonds around the atom) **[May 18, 2024 (I)]**

(a) $Q_f = V - \left(\frac{U}{B}\right)$ (b) $Q_f = V + (U - B)$

(c) $Q_f = V - (U + B)$ (d) $Q_f = V - \left(\frac{B}{U}\right)$

12. The correct order of C – O bond length in CO, CO_3^{2-}, CO_2 is **[May 16, 2023 (II)]**

(a) $CO < CO_3^{2-} < CO_2$ (b) $CO_3^{2-} < CO_2 < CO$

(c) $CO < CO_2 < CO_3^{2-}$ (d) $CO_2 < CO_3^{2-} < CO$

13. Identify incorrectly matched set from the following **[May 15, 2023 (I); Similar to July 4, 2022 (II)]**
(a) Molecules with incomplete octet–BeH_2, BCl_3
(b) Polar molecules–BF_3, CCl_4
(c) Molecules with expanded octet–PCl_5, SF_6
(d) Odd electron molecules–NO, NO_2

Topic 3 Dipole Moment and Bond Polarity

14. In which of the following sets, molecules are correctly arranged in the decreasing order of covalent character?
I. $AlCl_3 > MgCl_2 > NaCl$
II. $BeCl_2 > MgCl_2 > CaCl_2$
III. $CaI_2 > CaBr_2 > CaCl_2$
Correct answer is **[May 18, 2026 (II)]**
(a) I, II only (b) I, II, III
(c) II, III only (d) I, III only

15. Which one of the following orders is not correctly matched with the property mentioned against it? **[May 13, 2026 (II)]**
(a) $HCl < O_2 < N_2$ – Bond dissociation energy
(b) $H_2O < O_3 < SO_2$ – Bond angle
(c) $CHCl_3 < NF_3 < NH_3$ – Dipole moment
(d) $KF < NaF < LiF$ – Covalent character

16. Observe the following sets of molecules and identify the set in which all molecules have dipole moment **[May 12, 2026 (I)]**
(a) H_2S, C_6H_6, CO_2 (b) H_2O, NH_3, HCl
(c) $BeCl_2$, CS_2, BBr_3 (d) $PbCl_2$, $SnCl_2$, $HgCl_2$

17. The order of dipole moment of H_2O (A), $CHCl_3$ (B) and NH_3 (C) is **[May 27, 2025 (I)]**
(a) B < A < C (b) B < C < A
(c) C < B < A (d) C < A < B

18. Match the following **[May 26, 2025 (II)]**

List-I (Molecule)	List-II (Dipole moment in D)
(A) HCl	(I) 1.85
(B) NH_3	(II) 1.07
(C) H_2O	(III) 0.23
(D) NF_3	(IV) 1.47

The correct answer is
(a) A-II, B-IV, C-I, D-III
(b) A-IV, B-III, C-I, D-II
(c) A-II, B-I, C-IV, D-III
(d) A-III, B-II, C-IV, D-I

19. The correct order of increasing bond lengths of C – H, O – H, C – C and H – H is **[May 26, 2025 (I)]**
(a) O – H < H – H < C – C < C – H
(b) C – C < C – H < H – H < O – H
(c) C – C < O – H < H – H < C – H
(d) H – H < O – H < C – H < C – C

20. Consider the following **[May 22, 2025 (I)]**
Assertion (A) : Dipole moment of NF_3 is lesser than NH_3.
Reason (R) : In NF_3, the orbital dipole due to lone pair of electrons is in the opposite direction to the resultant dipole moment of the three N-F bonds.
The correct answer is
(a) Both (A) and (R) are correct and (R) is the correct explanation of (A).
(b) Both (A) and (R) are correct but (R) is not the correct explanation of (A).
(c) (A) is correct, but (R) is not correct.
(d) (A) is not correct, but (R) is correct.

21. Identify the correct set of molecules with zero dipole moment. **[May 21, 2025 (I)]**
(a) CO_2, NH_3, H_2O (b) NH_3, NF_3, BF_3
(c) PF_3, NH_3, CH_4 (d) CH_4, BF_3, CO_2

22. In which of the following pairs, both molecules possess dipole moment? **[May 21, 2024 (II)]**
(a) CO_2, BCl_3 (b) BCl_3, NF_3
(c) CO_2, SO_2 (d) SO_2, NF_3

23. Observe the following sets. **[May 21, 2024 (I)]**

	Order	Property
i.	$NH_3 > H_2O > SO_2$	Bond angle
ii.	$H_2O > NH_3 > H_2S$	Dipole moment
iii.	$N_2 > O_2 > H_2$	Bond enthalpy
iv.	$NO^+ > O_2 > O_2^{2-}$	Bond order

Which of the above sets are correctly matched?
(a) i, ii, iv only (b) ii, iii only
(c) ii, iii, iv only (d) i, iii, iv only

24. What are the formal charges on terminal oxygens of ozone molecule? **[May 19, 2023 (I)]**
(a) +1, –1 (b) +1, +1
(c) –1, –1 (d) 0, –1

25. Match the following

List – I (Molecules)	List – II (Dipolemoment μ, D)
A. H_2O	I. 0
B. BF_3	II. 0.23
C. NH_3	III. 1.47
D. NF_3	IV. 1.85

The correct answer is [May 18, 2023 (I)]

(a) A – IV, B – I, C – II, D – III

(b) A – IV, B – I, C – III, D – II

(c) A – IV, B – III, C – I, D – II

(d) A – III, B –IV, C – II, D – I

26. The combination of which of the following gives an ionic compound with maximum covalent character. **[July 5, 2022 (II)]**

(a) Mg^{2+} and Cl^- (b) Mg^{2+} and O^{2-}

(c) Na^+ and Br (d) Na^+ and O^{2-}

27. Choose the correct option from the following **[July 4, 2022 (I)]**

(a) KF is more covalent than KI

(b) $SnCl_4$ is less covalent than $SnCl_2$

(c) LiF is more covalent than KF

(d) $ZnCl_2$ is less covalent than NaCl

28. The bond lengths of C_2, N_2 and B_2 molecules are X_1, X_2 and X_3 pm respectively. The correct order of their bond lengths is **[July 4, 2022 (I)]**

(a) $X_3 > X_1 > X_2$ (b) $X_2 > X_3 > X_1$

(c) $X_1 > X_2 > X_3$ (d) $X_1 > X_3 > X_2$

29. Which of the following molecule has the maximum dipole moment?

[Aug. 20, 2021 (I); Similar to Aug. 19, 2021 (I)]

(a) NH_3 (b) CS_2

(c) C_2H_6 (d) NCl_3

30. Which compound among the following will have a permanent dipole moment? **[Aug. 20, 2021 (I)]**

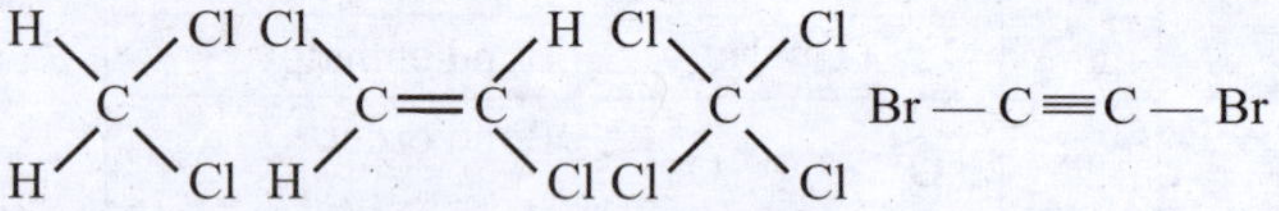

(i) (ii) (iii) (iv)

(a) Only (i) (b) Only (ii)

(c) Only (iii) (d) Only (iv)

31. For which molecules among the following, the resultant dipole moment (μ) ≠ 0? **[Aug. 19, 2021 (I)]**

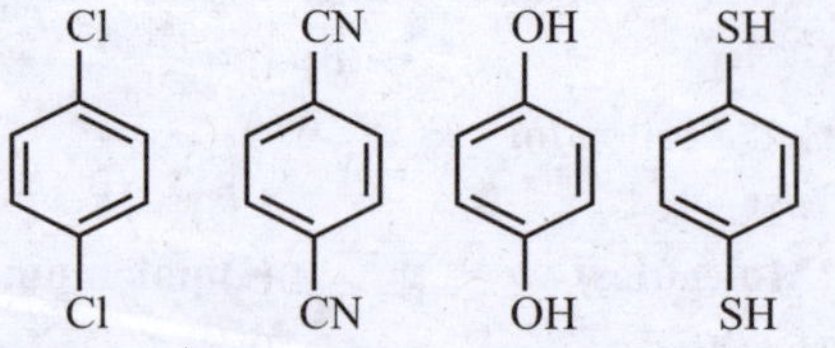

(i) (ii) (iii) (iv)

(a) (iii) and (iv) (b) (i) and (ii)

(c) (ii) and (iii) (d) Only (iv)

Topic 4 VSEPR Theory and Hybridisation

32. Which of the following sets contain isostructural molecules?

I. H_2O, OF_2, SCl_2 II. CO_2, $BeCl_2$, $HgCl_2$

III $SiCl_4$, SF_4, XeF_4

Correct answer is **[May 18, 2026 (I)]**

(a) I, II, III (b) I, III only

(c) II, III only (d) I, II only

33. Identify the correct set of molecules/ions in which hybridization of central atom is not same **[May 15, 2026 (II)]**

(a) H_2O, NH_3, CH_4 (b) H_3O^+, NH_4^+, ClO_4^-

(c) CH_3^+, BF_3, SO_2 (d) SF_4, XeF_4, SO_3

34. How many of the following molecules are linear with no lone pairs of electrons on the central atom?

$BeCl_2$, O_3, SCl_2, XeF_2, $SnCl_2$, $PbCl_2$, $HgCl_2$

[May 14, 2026 (I)]

(a) 2 (b) 3

(c) 4 (d) 1

35. The pair of molecules with same type of hybridisation is **[May 12, 2026 (II)]**

(a) H_3BO_3, H_3PO_3 (b) NO_2, SO_3

(c) XeO_3, BF_3 (d) PCl_3, ClF_3

36. Which of the following sets are correctly matched? **[May 27, 2025 (I)]**

	Molecule	Hybridization	Geometry
I.	BrF_5	sp^3d^2	square pyramidal
II.	XeF_6	sp^3d^3	Distorted octahedral
III.	SF_4	dsp^2	square planar
IV.	$PbCl_2$	sp	linear

(a) I & IV (b) II & III

(c) III & IV (d) I & II

37. Which of the following sets are correctly matched ? **[May 26, 2025 (II)]**

Molecule	Number of lone pairs of electrons on central atom	Hybridization
(I) PCl_3	1	sp^3
(II) SO_2	2	sp^3
(III) SF_4	2	$sp^3 d^2$
(IV) ClF_3	2	$sp^3 d$

(a) I & II (b) II & III

(c) II & IV (d) I & IV

38. The number of molecules having lone pair of electrons on central atom in the following is **[May 24, 2025 (I)]**
BF_3, SF_4, $SiCl_4$, XeF_4, NCl_3, XeF_6, PCl_5, $HgCl_2$, $SnCl_2$
(a) 6 (b) 3 (c) 4 (d) 5

39. Identify the pair of molecules which have same hybridisation as the hybridisation in Xenon (II) fluoride. **[May 23, 2025 (II)]**
(a) XeO_3, SF_4 (b) BrF_5, PF_5
(c) ClF_3, SF_4 (d) PCl_3, NH_3

40. A molecule has T-shape. The total number of electron pairs in the valence shell of central atom of it is **[May 23, 2025 (I)]**
(a) 4 (b) 5 (c) 6 (d) 3

41. How many of the following molecules have two lone pairs of electrons on central atom? **[May 22, 2025 (II)]**
SF_6, BF_3, ClF_3, PCl_5, BrF_5, XeF_4, H_2O, SF_4
(a) 5 (b) 4 (c) 3 (d) 2

42. How many of the following molecules / ions have trigonal planar structure? **[May 22, 2025 (I)]**
BO_3^{3-}, NH_3, PCl_3, BCl_3, ClF_3, XeO_3
(a) 5 (b) 2 (c) 4 (d) 3

43. The increasing order of number of lone pair of electrons on the central atom of the following molecules is **[May 21, 2025 (II)]**
(I) ClF_3 (II) XeF_2
(III) SF_4 (IV) SiH_4
(a) IV < III < II < I (b) I < II < III < IV
(c) II < I < III < IV (d) IV < III < I < II

44. Identify the set of molecules in which the central atom has only one lone pair of electrons in their valence shells **[May 23, 2024 (I)]**
(a) BrF_5, SF_4, $SnCl_2$ (b) BrF_5, XeF_4, $SnCl_2$
(c) XeF_4, NH_3, ClF_3 (d) XeF_6, ClF_3, SF_4

45. The number of lone pairs of electrons on the central atom of BrF_5, XeO_3, SO_2 respectively are **[May 22, 2024 (II)]**
(a) 1, 1, 2 (b) 1, 2, 2
(c) 2, 2, 1 (d) 1, 1, 1

46. In which of the following, there is no change in hybridisation of the central atom? **[May 22, 2024 (I)]**
(a) $NH_3 + H^+ \rightarrow NH_4^+$ (b) $BF_3 + F^- \rightarrow BF^-_4$
(c) $PCl_3 + Cl_2 \rightarrow PCl_5$ (d) $ClF_3 + F_2 \rightarrow ClF_5$

47. Observe the following reactions. Identify the reaction in which the hybridisation of underlined atom is changed **[May 20, 2024 (II)]**
(a) $\underline{N}H_3 + H^+ \rightarrow NH_4^+$
(b) $\underline{P}Cl_3 + 3\,H_2O \rightarrow H_3PO_3 + 3HCl$
(c) $NaNO_3 + H_2SO_4 \rightarrow NaH\underline{S}O_4 + HNO_3$
(d) $\underline{Xe}F_6 + H_2O \rightarrow \underline{Xe}OF_4 + 2\,HF$

48. Among the following species, correct set of isostructural pairs are **[May 20, 2024 (II)]**
XeO_3, CO_3^{2-}, SO_3, H_3O^+, ClF_3
(a) (XeO_3, CO_3^{2-}) and (SO_3, HO^+)
(b) (XeO_3, SO_3) and (CO_3^{2-}, H_3O^+)
(c) (XeO_3, H_3O^+) and (SO_3, CO_3^{2-})
(d) (SO_3, ClF_3) and (XeO_3, CO_3^{2-})

49. The correct order of bond angles of the molecules $SiCl_4$, SO_3, NH_3, $HgCl_2$ is **[May 20, 2024 (I)]**
(a) $SO_3 > SiCl_4 > NH_3 > HgCl_2$
(b) $SiCl_4 > NH_3 > HgCl_2 > SO_3$
(c) $HgCl_2 > SO_3 > NH_3 > SiCl_4$
(d) $HgCl_2 > SO_3 > SiCl_4 > NH_3$

50. In which of the following sets of molecules, the central atoms of molecules have same hybridisation? **[May 19, 2024 (II)]**
(a) NH_3, ClF_3 (b) H_2O, SO_3
(c) SF_4, CH_4 (d) XeF_6, IF_7

51. The correct increasing order of number of lone pair of electrons on the central atom of $SnCl_2$, XeF_2, ClF_3 and SO_3 is **[May 19, 2024 (II)]**
(a) $SO_3 < ClF_3 < SnCl_2 < XeF_2$
(b) $SO_3 < SnCl_2 < ClF_3 < XeF_2$
(c) $XeF_2 < SnCl_2 < ClF_3 < SO_3$
(d) $XeF_2 < ClF_3 < SnCl_2 < SO_3$

52. Which of the following pairs of molecules is isostructural? **[May 19, 2023 (I)]**
(a) $HgCl_2$, SO_2 (b) $SnCl_2$, $PbCl_2$
(c) SF_4, XeF_4 (d) NH_3, SO_3

53. Match the following

List-I (Hybridisation)	**List-II (Shape)**
A. dsp^2	I. Square planar
B. sp^3	II. Tetrahedral
C. d^2sp^3	III. Octahedral
D. Sp^3d	IV. Trigonal bipyramidal

[May 18, 2023 (II)]
(a) A-II, B-I, C-III, D-IV
(b) A-I, B-II, C-III, D-IV
(c) A-III, B-IV, C-II, D-I
(d) A-IV, B-III, C-II, D-I

54. Which of the following is the correct order of increasing number of lone pair of electrons on the central atom? **[May 18, 2023 (I)]**

(a) $IF_5 < XeF_2 < IF_7 < ClF_3$
(b) $IF_7 < ClF_3 < XeF_2 < IF_5$
(c) $IF_7 < XeF_2 < ClF_2 < IF_5$
(d) $IF_7 < IF_5 < ClF_3 < XeF_2$

55. Match the following **[May 17, 2023 (II)]**

List-I (Molecule/Ion)	**List-II (Shape)**
A. I_3^-	1. T-shaped
B. ClF_3	2. See-Saw
C. H_2O	3. Angular
D. SF_4	4. Linear

(a) A-4, B-1, C-3, D-2 (b) A-4, B-1, C-2, D-3
(c) A-2, B-3, C-4, D-1 (d) A-3, B-2, C-4, D-1

56. The number of bond pairs of electrons and total number of lone pairs of electrons in $XeOF_4$ are respectively **[May 17, 2023 (I)]**

(a) 6, 10 (b) 5, 15
(c) 5, 10 (d) 6, 15

57. The correct order of bond angles of the following is

H_2O (I) NH_3 (II) CH_4 (III) SO_2 (IV) **[May 16, 2023 (I)]**

(a) IV > III > II > I (b) IV > III > I > II
(c) I > II > III > IV (d) I > II > IV > III

58. Hybridization of positively charged and negatively charged carbons of the following respectively are

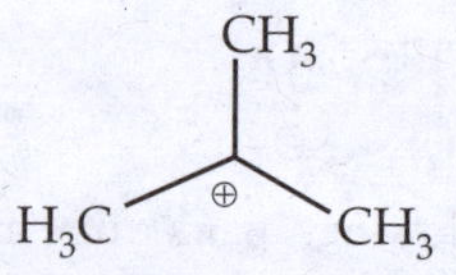

$CH_3C \equiv C^{\ominus}$

[May 16, 2023 (I)]

(a) sp^2, sp (b) sp^2, sp^2
(c) sp^3, sp^3 (d) sp^3, sp^2

59. Which of the following sets is correct?

	Molecule	**Hybridization**	**Geometry**	**Number of lone pairs of electrons on central atom**
I	SiH_4	sp^3	tetrahedral	0
II	$BeCl_2$	sp^2	linear	1
III	SF_4	dsp^3	square planar	1
IV	$SnCl_2$	sp	linear	0

[May 15, 2023 (II)]

(a) I (b) II (c) III (d) IV

60. In which of the following molecules, the number of line pairs of electrons on central atom and the number d-orbitals involved in the hybridisation of central atom, is same? **[May 13, 2023 (II)]**

(a) ClF_3 (b) PCl_5 (c) BrF_5 (d) SF_4

61. The hybridizations of the central atom in the molecules BF_3, BeF_2, BrF_3 are respectively **[Sept. 18, 2020 (I)]**

(a) sp^2, sp, sp^3d (b) sp, sp^2, sp^3
(c) sp^3, sp, sp^3d (d) sp^2, sp^3, dsp^2

62. Match the following **[July 6, 2022 (I)]**

List-I (Molecule/ion)	**List-II (Hybridisation)**
(A) ICl_4^-	(P) sp^3
(B) NO_3^-	(Q) sp^3d
(C) PCl_4^+	(R) sp^3d^2
(D) SiF_6^{2-}	(S) sp^2
	(T) sp

	A	**B**	**C**	**D**
(a)	P	S	Q	T
(b)	Q	T	P	S
(c)	R	S	P	T
(d)	S	Q	R	P

63. Identify the pair of species with same geometries **[July 6, 2022 (I)]**

(a) XeF_4, PCl_4^+ (b) NH_3, ClF_3
(c) SF_4, NH_4^+ (d) XeF_2, I_3^-

64. The tetra atomic molecules/ions with different shapes are **[July 5, 2022 (II)]**

(a) $TeCl_4$, SeF_4 (b) CH_4, PCl_4^+
(c) SF_4, NH_4^+ (d) SiH_4, CCl_4

65. In which of the following molecules/ions, the central atom is sp^2 hybridised? **[Aug. 19, 2021 (I)]**

BF_3, NO_2^-, NH_2^- and H_2O

(a) NH_2^- and H_2O (b) NO_2^- and H_2O
(c) BF_3 and NO_2^- (d) NO_2^- and NH_2^-

66. The linear shape of CO_2 is due to .... **[Sept. 21, 2020 (I)]**

(a) sp^3-hybridisation of carbon
(b) sp-hybridisation of carbon
(c) pπ-dπ bonding between carbon and oxygen
(d) sp^2-hybridisation of carbon

67. Which of the following molecules can be represented as AB_2E_2, where *A*-central atom, *B*-bond pairs of electrons, *E*-lone pairs of electrons? **[Sept. 18, 2020 (I)]**

(a) SO_2 (b) H_2O_2 (c) H_2O (d) XeF_2

68. The types of hybridisation on the five carbon atoms from left to right in pent-1-en-4-yne are

(a) sp^2, sp^2, sp^3, sp, sp **[Sept. 18, 2020 (I)]**

(b) sp, sp, sp^3, sp^2, sp^2

(c) sp^2, sp^3, sp, sp, sp^3

(d) sp^2, sp, sp^3, sp, sp^2

69. The geometry with respect to the central atom of the molecules $N(SiH_3)_3 \cdot Me_3N, (SiH_3)_3P$, respectively are

(a) planar, pyramidal, planar **[Sept. 17, 2020 (I)]**

(b) planar, pyramidal, pyramidal

(c) pyramidal, pyramidal, pyramidal

(d) pyramidal,planar, pyramidal

70. Match the following :

List-I	List-II
(a) BF_3	I. Tetrahedral
(b) ClF_3	II. Trigonal planar
(c) NH_3	III. T-shape
(d) NH_4^+	IV. Trigonal pyramidal

The correct answer is **[Apr. 22, 2019 (I)]**

	A	B	C	D
(a)	III	II	IV	I
(b)	III	II	I	IV
(c)	II	III	IV	I
(d)	II	III	I	IV

71. Identify the molecule in which the arrangement of electron pairs around the central atom is octahedral and shape is not octahedral. **[Apr. 21, 2019 (I)]**

(a) SF_6 (b) XeF_6

(c) BrF_5 (d) XeO_2F_4

72. Which set of the following molecules has only one lone pair of electrons on their respective central atoms? **[2018]**

(i) SO_2 (ii) XeF_4 (iii) $PbCl_2$ (iv) SF_4

(v) ClF_3

(a) (i), (iii), (iv) (b) (ii), (iii), (iv)

(c) (i), (ii), (v) (d) (i), (iii), (v)

73. In which of the following molecules, all bond lengths are not equal? **[2016]**

(a) SF_6 (b) PCl_5 (c) BCl_3 (d) CCl_4

74. In which of the following molecules, maximum number of lone pairs is present on the central atom? **[2016]**

(a) NH_3 (b) H_2O (c) ClF_3 (d) XeF_2

75. In which one of the following pairs the two species have identical shape, but differ in hybridisation? **[2015]**

(a) $I_3^-, BeCl_2$ (b) NH_3, BF_3

(c) XeF_2, I_3^- (d) NH_4^+, SF_4

Topic 5 Valence Bond and Molecular Orbital Theory

76. Observe the following statements

Statement-I: The correct order of O - O bond length in O_2, H_2O_2 and O_3 is $H_2O_2 > O_3 > O_2$

Statement-II: Hybridisation of carbon in graphite and pyridine is same

The correct answer is **[May 18, 2026 (II)]**

(a) Both statements I and II are correct

(b) Statement I is correct, but statement II is not correct

(c) Statement I is not correct, but statement II is correct

(d) Both statements I and II are not correct

77. Match the following **[May 15, 2026 (II)]**

List-I (molecule/Ion)		List-II (Bond order and magnetic property)
A O_2^-	I	1.5 - Paramagnetic
B O_2	II	2.0 - Paramagnetic
C C_2^{2-}	III	3.0 - Diamagnetic
D B_2	IV	1.0 - Paramagnetic

The correct answer is

(a) A-I, B-III, C-II, D-IV (b) A-I, B-II, C-III, D-IV

(c) A-IV, B-II, C-I, D-III (d) A-IV, B-I, C-II, D-III

78. Following is the structural representation of N_2O_3 molecule in which x, y, z are bond angles and p, q, r are bond lengths **[May 14, 2026 (I)]**

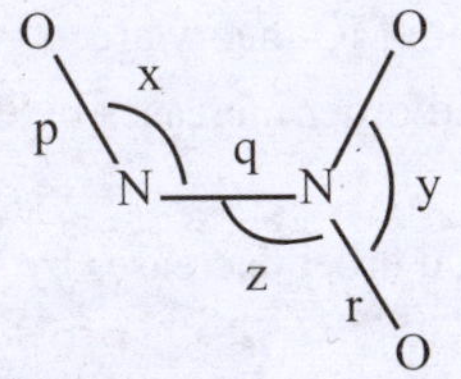

The correct orders of bond angles and bond lengths respectively are

(a) $x < z < y$ & $p < q < r$ (b) $x < y < z$ & $p < r < q$

(c) $x < z < y$ & $p < r < q$ (d) $x < y < z$ & $p < q < r$

79. Which of the following statements is not correct? **[May 13, 2026 (II)]**

(a) CO, N_2, O_2^{2+} have same bond order.

(b) The bond between third element of 1st group and second element of 17th group is ionic in nature.

(c) The total number of sp^2 hybrid orbitals in benzene is 12.

(d) *o*-Nitro phenol has intramolecular H-bonding

80. Which of the following orders is not correct for the property mentioned against them? [May 13, 2026 (I)]
(a) $H_2O > HF > NH_3 > H_2S$ boiling point
(b) $H_2O > NH_3 > NF_3 > CF_4$ dipole moment
(c) $C-C > N-O > C-O > C-H$ bond length
(d) $O_2^+ > O_2 > O_2^- > O_2^{2-}$ bond order.

81. The number of species having bond order ≥ 2 from the following is [May 12, 2026 (II)]
$N_2, O_2^{2-}, NO^-, O_2^+, NO^+, NO$
(a) 4 (b) 6
(c) 5 (d) 3

82. The sum of the bond orders of $O_2^{2+}, O_2^{2-}, O_2^+, O_2^-, O_2$ and sum of the unpaired electrons present in them respectively are [May 26, 2025 (I)]
(a) 10, 4 (b) 10, 6 (c) 8, 4 (d) 8, 6

83. The sum of bond order values of C_2 and O_2^{2+} is x, which is equal to sum of bond order values of *a, b* and *c*. What are *a, b* and *c*? [May 23, 2025 (I)]
(a) O_2^-, O_2^+, O_2 (b) B_2, N_2, F_2
(c) He_2^+, F_2, N_2 (d) O_2^{2-}, N_2, Be_2

84. The pair of molecules / ions with the same bond order value is [May 22, 2025 (II)]
(a) B_2, C_2 (b) O_2, C_2 (c) O_2^+, O_2^- (d) H_2^+, Li_2

85. Consider the following changes I and II
$$O_2^- \xleftarrow{II} O_2 \xrightarrow{I} O_2^+$$
The correct statements about these changes (I) and (II) in accordance with MO theory are [May 21, 2025 (II)]
(A) In (I) bond order increases by 0.5 from the existing value
(B) In (II) bond order decreases by 1.0 from the existing value
(C) In both (I) and (II) magnetic property is not changed
(D) In both (I) and (II) magnetic property is changed
(a) A, B and C only (b) A and C only
(c) A and D only (d) B and C only

86. The bond order of which of the following two species is same? [May 23, 2024 (I)]
(a) O_2, N_2 (b) C_2, O_2
(c) B_2, C_2 (d) F_2, C_2

87. In which of the following sets the sum of bond orders of three species is maximum? [May 22, 2024 (I)]
(a) B_2, CN^-, O_2^{2-} (b) O_2, F_2, O_2^{2+}
(c) O_2^-, N_2, O_2^+ (d) C_2, O_2, He_2^{2+}

88. The bond lengths of diatomic molecules of elements X, Y and Z respectively are 143, 110 and 121 pm. The atomic numbers of X. Y and Z respectively are: [May 18, 2024 (I)]
(a) 9, 7, 8 (b) 7, 8, 9 (c) 9, 8, 7 (d) 7, 9, 8

89. The hybridization of central atom of ClF_3, NH_3, SO_3 are respectively [May 18, 2023 (II)]
(a) sp^2, sp^2, sp^2 (b) sp^3d, sp^3, sp^2
(c) sp^2, sp^3, sp^3d (d) sp^3d, sp^3, sp^3

90. The correct order of bond enthalpy of given molecules is [May 17, 2023 (I)]
(a) $O_2 < N_2 < H_2$ (b) $N_2 < O_2 < H_2$
(c) $H_2 < N_2 < O_2$ (d) $H_2 < O_2 < N_2$

91. If the bond order in C_2 is 'x' then the bond order in B_2 and O_2, respectively are [May 15, 2023 (I)]
(a) $\frac{1}{2}x, 2x$ (b) x, x
(c) $\frac{1}{2}x, x$ (d) x, 2x

92. The bond order of Be_2^- is x. The bond orders of H_2^+, Li_2^{2-} only are respectively [July 8, 2022 (II)]
(a) $\frac{5}{3}x, \frac{5}{6}x$ (b) $\frac{3}{5}x, \frac{6}{5}x$
(c) $\frac{2}{5}x, \frac{3}{5}x$ (d) $\frac{5}{2}x, \frac{5}{3}x$

93. As per molecular orbital theory the pair of molecules which do not exist is [July 8, 2022 (I)]
(a) Li_2, B_2 (b) He_2, C_2
(c) Be_2, C_2 (d) Be_2, Ne_2

94. Arrange the following species in the decreasing order of their bond orders. [July 7, 2022 (II)]
NO (I) NO^+ (II) NO^- (III)
(a) (I) > (II) > (III) (b) (II) > (I) > (III)
(c) (II) > (III) > (I) (d) (III) > (II) > (I)

95. Bond order is an inverse measure of [Aug. 20, 2021 (I)]
(a) bond length
(b) bond angle
(c) bond dissociation energy
(d) stability

96. The bond stability of N_2, N_2^- and N_2^{2-} varies as [Sept. 21, 2020 (I)]
(a) $N_2 < N_2^- < N_2^{2-}$ (b) $N_2^- < N_2 < N_2^{2-}$
(c) $N_2^{2-} < N_2^- < N_2$ (d) $N_2^- < N_2^{2-} < N_2$

97. Which of the following sets of species have similar bond order? **[Sept. 17, 2020 (I)]**

(a) N_2, O_2^{2-}, NO^+ (b) N_2, F_2, O_2^{2-}

(c) N_2, N_2^{2-}, O_2^- (d) N_2, CO, NO^+

98. Observe the following molecules/ions H_2, N_2, O_2, N_2^+, O_2^+, O_2^-, F_2. Identify correct statement. **[Apr. 22, 2019 (I)]**

(a) H_2, N_2, O_2, F_2 show diamagnetic property

(b) O_2, O_2^+, O_2^-, N_2^+ show paramagnetic property

(c) N_2, F_2, O_2^+, O_2^- show diamagnetic property

(d) H_2, N_2^+, O_2^+, O_2^- show paramagnetic property

99. The wave functions of 1*s*- orbitals of two hydrogen atoms are ψ_A and ψ_B. ψ_A and ψ_B are linearly combined to form two molecular orbitals (σ and σ^*). Which of the following statements are correct?

I. σ^* is equal to $(\psi_A - \psi_B)$.

II. In σ-orbital, one nodal plane is present in between two nuclei.

III. The energy of σ-orbital is lower than the energy of σ^*–orbital. **[Apr. 21, 2019 (I)]**

(a) I, II, III (b) I, II only

(c) II, III only (d) I, III only

100. Which of the following orders are correct against the property given ? **[Apr. 20, 2019 (I)]**

(i) Dipole moment $NF_3 > NH_3 > BF_3$

(ii) Covalent bond length C—O > N—O > O—H

(iii) Bond order $C_2 > B_2 > He_2$

(a) i, ii only (b) ii, iii only

(c) i, iii only (d) i, ii, iii

101. The molecule on having diamagnetic nature and a bond order of 1.0 is **[Apr. 20, 2019 (I)]**

(a) He_2^+ (b) Li_2^+

(c) B_2 (d) C_2

102. How many of the following species are diamagnetic?

He_2^+, H_2, H_2^+, H_2^-, He **[2017]**

(a) 1 (b) 2

(c) 3 (d) 0

103. Which of the following does not have triple bond between the atoms? **[2015]**

(a) N_2 (b) CO

(c) NO (d) C_2^{2-}

5 Thermodynamics

CHAPTER SYNOPSIS

- Work done by a gas for expansion from volume V_1 to volume V_2 against a constant external pressure P is $w = -P(V_2 - V_1) = -P\Delta V$ (1 litre atm = 101.3 J)
- Sign conventions for ΔE, q and w

  If work is done on the system, w is positive

  If work is done by the system, w is negative

  If heat is absorbed by the system, q is positive

  If heat is given out by the system, q is negative

  If energy is absorbed by the system, i.e., internal energy increases, ΔE is positive.

  If energy is released, i.e., internal energy of the system decreases, ΔE is negative.
- $\Delta H_{Reaction} = \Sigma\, \Delta H^\circ_f\,(\text{products}) - \Sigma\, \Delta H^\circ_f\,(\text{Reactants})$
- $\Delta H_{Reaction} = \Sigma$ Bond energies (B.E.) of Reactants $- \Sigma$ Bond energies (B.E.) of Products
- Heat capacity, $C = \dfrac{q}{T_2 - T_1}$ where q is the heat absorbed to raise the temperature from T_1 to T_2.
- $C_v = \left(\dfrac{\partial E}{\partial T}\right)_v$ and $C_p = \left(\dfrac{\partial H}{\partial T}\right)_p$
- Work done in isothermal reversible expansion,

  $w = -2.303\, nRT \log\left(\dfrac{V_2}{V_1}\right) = -2.303\, nRT \log\left(\dfrac{P_1}{P_2}\right)$

  This is the maximum work obtained and is represented as w_{max}.
- For reversible adiabatic expansion, $PV^{\gamma} = \text{const.}$,

  $TV^{\gamma-1} = \text{const.}$ and $TP^{(1-\gamma)/\gamma} = \text{const.}$ where $\gamma = \dfrac{C_p}{C_v}$.
- Work done during adiabatic expansion of n moles of an ideal gas $= nC_v(T_2 - T_1)$.
- Work done in expansion/ from same initial state to same final volume:-

  $$W_{adiabatic} < W_{isothermal} < W_{isobaric}$$
- Entropy change, $\Delta S = \dfrac{q_{rev}}{T}$.
- $\Delta S_{system} + \Delta S_{surr} \geq 0$, where sign '=' refers to a reversible process (equilibrium) and sign '>' to an irreversible process (spontaneous process).
- $\Delta S_f = \dfrac{\Delta H_f}{T_f}$ and $\Delta S_{vap} = \dfrac{\Delta H_{vap}}{T_b}$
- $\Delta G^\circ = \Sigma G^\circ\,(\text{Products}) - \Sigma G^\circ\,(\text{Reactants})$
- $\Delta S^\circ = \Sigma S^\circ\,(\text{Products}) - \Sigma S^\circ\,(\text{Reactants})$
- If ΔG is negative, process is spontaneous.

  If ΔG is positive, process is non-spontaneous.

  If ΔG is zero, process is in equilibrium.

Topic 1 First Law and Basic Fundamentals of Thermodynamics

1. At constant temperature, one mole of an ideal gas of volume 2L was expanded to 100 L against an external pressure of 1 atm under reversible conditions. What is the change in internal energy? **[May 18, 2026 (II)]**
(1L atm = 101.3 J; log 5 = 0.7)
(a) Zero (b) 793.2 J
(c) 3266 J (d) 326.6 J

2. For the reaction, **[May 15, 2026 (II)]**
$2Al_2O_3(s) \rightarrow 4Al(s) + 3O_2(g), \Delta H = 3340$ kJ.
What is the enthalpy of formation of $Al_2O_3(s)$ (in kJ)?
(a) +1670 (b) – 3340
(c) +3340 (d) – 1670

3. At 27°C, 1.6 g of O_2 exerting a pressure of 5 atm is allowed to expand isothermally against a constant pressure of 1 atm. What is the work done (in J)?
(1L – atm = 100 J, R = 0.082 L atm K^{-1} mol^{-1})
[May 15, 2026 (II)]
(a) – 49.2 (b) – 98.4
(c) +98.4 (d) +49.2

4. At constant temperature, one mole of an ideal gas of volume 2L expanded to 100 L against an external pressure of 1 atm under reversible conditions. What is the work done (in J)? **[May 15, 2026 (I)]**
(1L atm = 101.3 J; log 5 = 0.7)
(a) – 163.3 (b) – 793.2
(c) +793.2 (d) +326.6

5. Match the following **[May 14, 2026 (II)]**

List-I (Δ_rH° Δ_rS° Δ_rG°)	List-II (Description about the reaction)
A. + – +	I. Non spontaneous at low temperature
B. – – –	II. Spontaneous at high temperature
C. + + +	III. Non spontaneous at all temperatures
D. + + –	IV. Spontaneous at low temperature

(a) A-III, B-IV, C-II, D-I
(b) A-III, B-IV, C-I, D-II
(c) A-IV, B-III, C-II, D-I
(d) A-II, B-IV, C-I, D-III

6. Identify the set with only extensive properties
[May 14, 2026 (II)]
(a) Temperature, Pressure, Number of moles
(b) Heat capacity, Enthalpy, Entropy
(c) Pressure, Specific heat, Molar heat capacity
(d) Density, Mole fraction, viscosity

7. At 27°C, 10 g of argon (at. wt = 40 u) is compressed isothermally and reversibly from 50 L to 5 L. What is q for this process? **[May 13, 2026 (II)]**
(Assume Ar as an ideal gas) (R = 8.3 JK^{-1} mol^{-1})
(a) +1.433 kJ (b) –1.433 kJ
(c) –2.866 kJ (d) +2.866 kJ

8. At 300 K, 1 mole of an ideal gas is allowed to expand isothermally and reversibly from a pressure of 20 atm to 2 atm. The work done (in kJ mol^{-1}) in the process is (R = 8.3 J K^{-1} mo^{-1}) **[May 13, 2026 (I)]**
(a) –57.34 (b) +5.734
(c) –5.734 (d) +57.34

9. Consider the following reaction **[May 12, 2026 (II)]**
$A_2B_4(g) \rightarrow 2AB_2(g)$
At 300 K, Δ_rH for this reaction is –x kJ mol^{-1}. What is its Δ_rU (in kJ mol^{-1}) at the same temperature? (R = 8.3 J mol^{-1} K^{-1})
(a) – (x + 2490) (b) (x + 2490)
(c) – (x + 2.49) (d) (x + 2.49)

10. 1 mole of an ideal gas is allowed to expand isothermally and reversibly from 1L to 5L at 300 K. The change in enthalpy (in kJ) is (R = 8.3 J K^{-1} mol^{-1}) **[May 27, 2025 (I)]**
(a) 1.74 (b) 2.48 (c) 0.0 (d) 4.22

11. 5 moles of a gas is allowed to pass through a series of changes as shown in the graph in a cyclic process. The processes C → A, B → C and A → B respectively are **[May 27, 2025 (I)]**

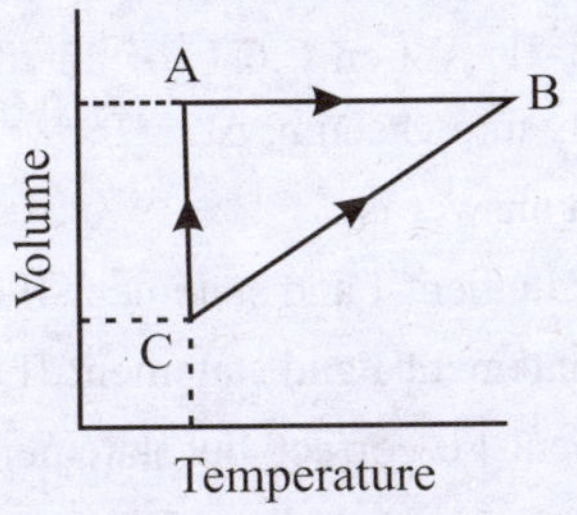

(a) Isothermal, Isochoric, Isobaric
(b) Isochoric, Isobaric, Isothermal
(c) Isobaric, Isochoric, Isothermal
(d) Isothermal, Isobaric, Isochoric

12. Consider the following. [May 26, 2025 (I)]

Statement-I: Both internal energy (U) and work (w) are state functions.

Statement-II: During the free expansion of an ideal gas into vacuum, the work done is zero.

The correct answer is

(a) Both statement-I and statement-II are correct.
(b) Both statement-I and statement-II are not correct.
(c) Statement-I is correct, but statement-II is not correct.
(d) Statement-I is not correct, but statem ent-II is correct.

13. The C_P of $H_2O(l)$ is 75.3 J mol^{-1} K^{-1}. What is the energy (in J) required to raise 180 g of liquid water from 10°C to 15°C? (H_2O = 18 u) [May 24, 2025 (I)]

(a) 3.765 (b) 3765 (c) 753 (d) 376.5

14. For which reaction $\Delta H \neq \Delta U$? [May 23, 2025 (I)]

(a) $H_2(g) + I_2(g) \longrightarrow 2HI(g)$
(b) $2NO(g) \longrightarrow N_2(g) + O_2(g)$
(c) $N_2(g) + 3H_2(g) \longrightarrow 2NH_3(g)$
(d) $C(s) + O_2(g) \longrightarrow CO_2(g)$

15. Identify the correct statements from the following:

(I) Work is a path function. [May 22, 2025 (I)]
(II) Enthalpy is an extensive property.
(III) Lattice enthalpy of ionic compounds can be obtained from Born-Haber cycle.

(a) I, II only (b) I, III only
(c) II, III only (d) I, II, III

16. The energy required to increase the temperature of 180 g of liquid water from 10°C to 15°C is 3765 J. What is C_p of water in J mol^{-1} K^{-1}? (H_2O = 18u) [May 21, 2025 (II)]

(a) 75.3 (b) 376.5 (c) 753 (d) 37.65

17. Consider the following. [May 21, 2025 (II)]

Statement-I: During isothermal expansion of an ideal gas its enthalpy decreases.

Statement-II: When 2.0 L of an ideal gas expands isothermally into vaccum, $\Delta U = 0$.

The correct answer is

(a) Both statement-I and statement-II are correct.
(b) Both statement-I and statement-II are not correct.
(c) Statement-I is correct, but statement-II is not correct.
(d) Statement-I is not correct, but statement-II is correct.

18. At 273 K the maximum work done when pressure on 10 g of hydrogen is reduced from 10 atm to 1 atm under isothermal, reversible conditions is (Assume the gas behaves ideally) (R = 8.3 JK^{-1} mol^{-1}) [May 21, 2025 (I)]

(a) – 52.18 kJ (b) + 26.09 kJ
(c) – 26.09 kJ (d) + 52.18 kJ

19. A vessel of volume V L contains an ideal gas at T (K). The vessel is partitioned into two equal parts. The volume (in L) and temperature (in K) in each part is respectively [May 22, 2024 (II)]

(a) $V, \frac{T}{2}$ (b) $\frac{V}{2}, T$ (c) V, T (d) $\frac{V}{2}, \frac{T}{2}$

20. The number of extensive properties in the following list is enthalpy, density, volume, internal energy, temperature. [May 21, 2024 (II)]

(a) 4 (b) 2 (c) 3 (d) 5

21. The volume of an ideal gas contracts from 1 0.0 L to 2.0 L under an applied pressure of 2.0 atm. During contraction the system also evolved 900 J of heat. The change in internal energy (in J) involved in the system is (1 L atm = 101.3 J) [May 20, 2024 (II)]

(a) 720.8 (b) 360.4 (c) 1620.8 (d) 810.4

22. Given below are two statements. [May 19, 2024 (II)]

Statement - I: For isothermal irreversible change of an ideal gas, $q = -w = P_{ext}(V_{final} - V_{initial})$

Statement - II: For adiabatic change, $\Delta U = W_{adiabatic}$

(a) Both Statement-I and statement-II are correct
(b) Both Statement-I and statement-II are not correct
(c) Statement-I is correct but statement-II is not correct
(d) Statement-I is not correct but statement-II is correct

23. A thermodynamic process (B → E) was completed as shown below. The work done is equal to area under the limits [May 19, 2024 (II)]

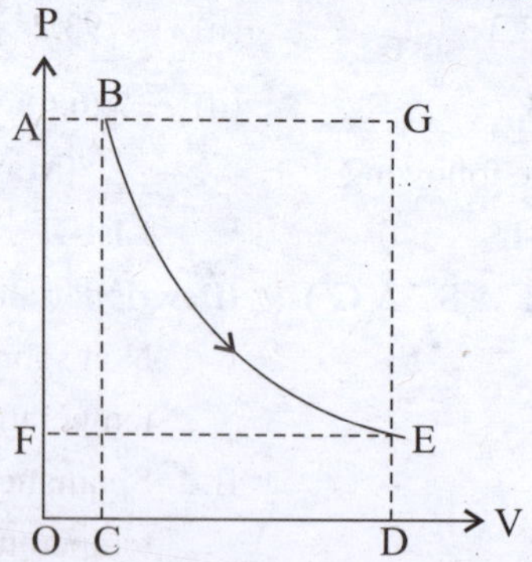

(a) 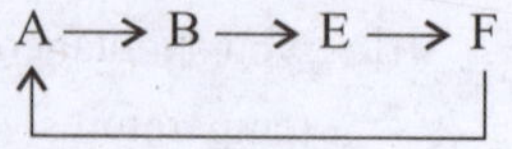

(b) 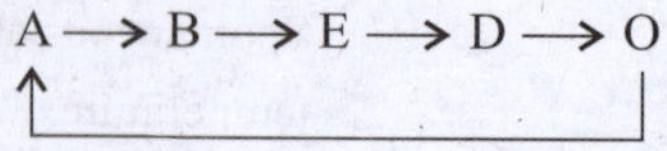

(c) 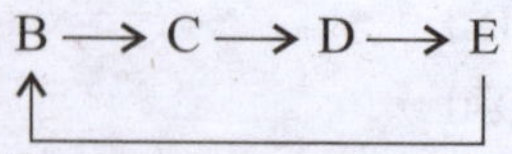

(d) 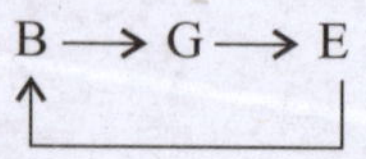

24. The number of extensive and intensive properties in the following list is respectively Mass, temperature, pressure, enthalpy, heat capacity, internal energy, density **[May 18, 2023 (II)]**

(a) 2, 5 (b) 3, 4 (c) 4. 3 (d) 5, 2

25. If one litre of an ideal gas at a pressure of 20 atm expands isothermally and reversibly to a final volume of 'X' L by absorbing 92.12 L. atm heat, 'X' (in L) is **[May 18, 2023 (II)]**

(a) 200 (b) 20 (c) 15 (d) 100

26. Identify the pair in which both are not extensive properties **[May 18, 2023 (I); Similar to July 4, 2022 (II)]**

(a) Internal energy, enthalpy
(b) Mass, volume
(c) Density, pressure
(d) Heat capacity Gibbs energy

27. 11.0 L of an ideal gas at a constant external pressure of 5 atm is compressed isothermally to a final volume of one liter. The heat absorbed and work done respectively, during this compression (in L atm) are **[May 17, 2023 (I); Similar to May 17, 2023 (II)]**

(a) –50, –50 (b) 50, –50
(c) –50, 50 (d) 50, 50

28. If the work done by 2 mol of an ideal gas during isothermal reversible expansion from 5L to 50L is –189.1 L atm at constant pressure, the temperature of the gas (in °C) is **[May 15, 2023 (II)]**

(a) 500 (b) 227 (c) 327 (d) 127

29. Which of the followings is not a state function? **[July 8, 2022 (I)]**

(a) Internal Energy (b) Work
(c) Enthalpy (d) Entropy

30. Identify the correct statements from the following. **[July 7, 2022 (II)]**

(i) For adiabatic process, $\Delta U = W_{adiabatic}$
(ii) Work is a path function.
(iii) Volume is an extensive property.
(a) i, ii, iii (b) i, iii only (c) ii, iii only (d) i, ii only

31. Which of the following equations are correct? **[July 5, 2022 (II)]**

(A) U = H – PV
(B) G = H – TS
(C) U = q + W
(a) A, B and C (b) A and B only
(c) A and C only (d) B and C only

32. State 1 $\rightleftarrows$ State 2 $\rightleftarrows$ State 3

State 1	State 2	State 3
T = 300K	T = 300K	T = 300K
P = 15bar	P = 10bar	P = 5bar
1mole	1mole	1mole

Above shows a cyclic process. Calculate the total work done during one complete cycle. **[July 4, 2022 (I)]**

(Assume a single step to reach the next state).

(a) 25/3 L bar (b) –25/3 L bar
(c) 50/3 L bar (d) –50/3 L bar

33. Which of the following is not an intensive property? **[Sept. 17, 2022 (I)]**

(a) Entropy (b) Melting point
(c) Specific gravity (d) Refractive index

34. Work done by an ideal gas at a constant volume is .... **[Sept. 21, 2020 (I)]**

(a) $-\frac{\Delta p}{p}$ (b) $-V\Delta p$ (c) 0 (d) $\frac{nR}{p}$

35. The heat required to rise the temperature of 54 g of aluminium from 40°C to 60°C in J is (molar heat capacity of aluminium in this temperature range is 24 J mol^{-1} K^{-1}; atomic weight of Al is 27) **[Apr. 21, 2019 (I)]**

(a) 480 (b) 800 (c) 960 (d) 1280

36. 6g of graphite is burnt in a bomb calorimeter at 25°C and 1 atm pressure. The temperature of water increased from 25°C to 31°C. If ΔH of this reaction is –248 kJ mol^{-1}, find out C_V (in kJ K^{-1}) of bomb calorimeter.

(a) 20.667 (b) 41.33 (c) 1488 (d) 0.145

37. Which one of the following is applicable for an adiabatic expansion of an ideal gas? **[2015]**

(a) $\Delta E = 0$ (b) $\Delta W = \Delta E$
(c) $\Delta W = -\Delta E$ (d) $\Delta W = 0$

Topic 2 Laws of Thermochemistry

38. What is the enthalpy change (in J mol^{-1}) for the conversion of 1 mole of H_2O (l) at 10°C to 1 mole of H_2O (s) at – 10°C?

(At 0°C, H_2O (s) + x kJ mol^{-1} $\rightarrow$ H_2O (l) ;
C_p (H_2O) (l)) = yJ mol^{-1} K^{-1}
C_p (H_2O (s)) = z J mol^{-1} K^{-1}) **[May 18, 2026 (II)]**

(a) – (1000x + 10y + 10z)
(b) – (x + y + z)
(c) – (1000x + y – z)
(d) –(1000x – y + z)

39. At 298 K, the value of ($\Delta H - \Delta U$) for the combustion of 1 mole C_4H_{10}(g) is x kJ and for the combustion of 1 mole glucose, the value of ($\Delta H - \Delta U$) is y kJ. The value of (x – y) (in kJ) is (R = 8.3 J K^{-1} mol^{-1}) **[May 18, 2026 (I)]**

(a) +8.657 (b) –8.657
(c) –9.659 (d) +4.329

40. At T(K), in a reaction $A(g) \rightarrow B(g) + C(g)$, x J of heat was absorbed and y J of work is done by the system. What is $\Delta_r H$ (in J) for the reaction?
(R = gas constant) **[May 15, 2026 (I)]**
(a) (x + y + RT) (b) (x – y + RT)
(c) (x + y + 2RT) (d) (x – y + 2RT)

41. Combustion of methane gives $CO_2(g)$ and $H_2O(l)$. What is enthalpy of combustion ($\Delta_c H^\ominus$ in kJ mol^{-1}) of $CH_4(g)$ at 298 K? **[May 14, 2026 (I)]**
($\Delta_f H^\ominus$ ($CH_4(g)$) = – x kJ mol^{-1} ; $\Delta_f H^\ominus$ ($CO_2(g)$) = – y kJ mol^{-1}; $\Delta_f H^\ominus$ ($H_2O(l)$) = – z kJ mol^{-1})
(a) – (y + 2z – x) (b) (2z – y + x)
(c) (2z + x – y) (d) – (2y + z + x)

42. At T (K), enthalpy of combustion of C(s), $H_2(g)$ and $CH_4(g)$ are –393.5, –286, –890 kJ mol^{-1} respectively. What is the enthalpy of formation of methane (in kJ mol^{-1})?
[May 13, 2026 (I)]
(a) 54.6 (b) –75.5
(c) 99.7 (d) 89.6

43. The $\Delta_f H^\ominus$ of AO (g), $AO_2(g)$, B_2O (g) and B_2O_4 (g) is respectively – 110, – 393, + 81 and + 9.7 kJ mol^{-1}. What is $\Delta_r H^\ominus$ (in kJ mol^{-1}) of the following reaction at 298 K?
$B_2O_4(g) + 3\,AO(g) \rightarrow B_2O\,(g) + 3\,AO_2\,(g)$
[May 12, 2026 (I)]
(a) – 777.7 (b) – 1179
(c) +777.7 (d) +1179

44. Enthalpy of formation of $CO_2(g)$, $H_2O(l)$ and $C_6H_{12}O_6(s)$ are –393, –286 and –1170 kJ mol^{-1} respectively. The quantity of heat liberated when 18g of $C_6H_{12}O_6(s)$ is burnt completely in oxygen is **[May 23, 2025 (II)]**
(a) 520 kJ (b) 145 kJ (c) 290 kJ (d) 420 kJ

45. One mole of C_2H_5OH (*l*) was completely burnt in oxygen to form CO_2 (g) and H_2O (*l*). The standard enthalpy of formation ($\Delta_f H^\ominus$) of C_2H_5OH (*l*), CO_2 (g) and H_2O (*l*) is *x*, *y*, *z* kJ mol^{-1} respectively. What is $\Delta_r H^\ominus$ (in kJ mol^{-1}) for this reaction? **[May 22, 2025 (II)]**
(a) $(2y + 3z + x)$ (b) $(2y - 3z + x)$
(c) $(x - 2y - 3z)$ (d) $(2y + 3z - x)$

46. A 10 L vessel contains 1 mole of an ideal gas with pressure of P(atm) and temperature of T(K). The vessel is divided into two equal parts. The pressure (in atm) and temperature (in K) in each part is respectively **[May 23, 2024 (I)]**
(a) $\frac{P}{2}, \frac{T}{2}$ (b) $\frac{P}{2}, T$ (c) P, T (d) $P, \frac{T}{2}$

47. Observe the following reaction
$$ABO_3(s) \xrightarrow{1000K} AO(s) + BO_2(g)$$
$\Delta_r H$ for this reaction is x kJ mol^{-1}. What is its $\Delta_r U$ (in kJ mol^{-1}) at the same temperature?
(R = 8.3 J mol^{-1} K^{-1}) **[May 22, 2024 (II)]**
(a) $x - 8300$ (b) $x + 8.3$
(c) $x + 8300$ (d) $x - 8.3$

48. What is the enthalpy change (in J) for converting 9 g of H_2O (l) at +10°C to H_2O (l) at +20°C? (C_P (H_2O (l)) = 75 J mol^{-1} K^{-1}) (density of H_2O (l) = 1 g mL^{-1})
[May 22, 2024 (I)]
(a) 750 (b) 75 (c) 37.5 (d) 375

49. A, B, C and D are some compounds. The enthalpy of formation of A (g), B (g), C (g) and D (g) is 9.7, –110, 81 and –393 kJ mol^{-1} respectively. What is $\Delta_r H$ (in kJ mol^{-1}) for the given reaction? **[May 22, 2024 (I)]**
$A\,(g) + 3B\,(g) \longrightarrow C\,(g) + 3D\,(g)$
(a) – 777.7 (b) + 777.7
(c) – 1418.3 (d) + 1418.3

50. Identify the correct equation relating ΔH, ΔU and ΔT for 1 mole of an ideal gas from the following (R = gas constant)
[May 21, 2024 (II)]
(a) $(\Delta H)^2 = \Delta U + R\Delta T$ (b) $\Delta H = (\Delta U)^2 + R\Delta T$
(c) $\Delta U = \Delta H - R\Delta T$ (d) $\Delta U = \Delta H + R\Delta T$

51. Observe the following reactions **[May 21, 2024 (I)]**
$AB(g) + 25\,H_2O(l) \rightarrow AB_{(50\,H_2O)}$; $\Delta H = x$ kJ mol^{-1}
$AB(g) + 50\,H_2O(l) \rightarrow AB_{(50\,H_2O)}$; $\Delta H = y$ kJ mol^{-1}
The enthalpy of dilution (ΔH_{dil}) in kJ mol^{-1} is
(a) $(y - x)$ (b) $(y + x)$ (c) $\frac{y}{x}$ (d) $\frac{x}{y}$

52. The molar heats of fusion and vapourisation of benzene are 10.9 and 31.0 kJ mol^{-1} respectively. The changes in entropy for the solid → liquid and liquid → vapour transitions for benzene are *x* and *y*. JK^{-1} mol^{-1}, respectively. The value of $(y - x)$ (in JK^{-1} mol^{-1}) is (At 1 atm, benzene melts at 5.5 °C and boils at 80 °C) **[May 20, 2024 (II)]**
(a) 87.8 (b) 48.7 (c) 39.1 (d) 28.7

53. Observe the following reaction **[May 20, 2024 (I)]**
$$2A_2(g) + B_2(g) \xrightarrow{T(K)} 2A_2B(g) + 600\text{ kJ}$$
The standard enthalpy of formation ($\Delta_f H^!$) of A_2B (g) is
(a) 600 kJ mol^{-1} (b) 300 kJ mol^{-1}
(c) –300 kJ mol^{-1} (d) –600 kJ mol^{-1}

54. Identify the molecule for which the enthalpy of atomization ($\Delta_a H^-$) and bond dissociation enthalpy ($\Delta_{BOND}H^-$) are not equal) **[May 20, 2024 (I)]**

(a) H_2 (b) Cl_2 (c) F_2 (d) CH_4

55. The standard enthalpy of atomization of ethane according to the equation $C_2H_6(g) \rightarrow 2C(g) + 6H(g)$ is 622 kJ mol^{-1}. If standard mean C-H bond dissociation enthalpy is 90 kJ mol^{-1}, the standard mean dissociation enthalpy of C-C bond (in kJ mol^{-1}) is **[May 19, 2023 (I)]**

(a) 540 (b) 90 (c) 85 (d) 82

56. If standard molar enthalpy change and standard molar internal energy change measured in bomb calorimeter are equal, which one of the following statements is correct? **[May 19, 2023 (I)]**

(a) $\Delta n > 0$, with increase in pressure
(b) $\Delta n > 0$, with decrease in pressure
(c) $\Delta n < 0$, with increase in pressure
(d) $\Delta n = 0$, at constant pressure

57. The standard enthalpy of formation of $CO_2(g)$, $CaO(s)$ and $CaCO_3(s)$ are –393, –634, –1210 kJ mol^{-1} respectively. If all the substances are in standard state, the standard enthalpy of decomposition of calcium carbonate to $CaO(s)$ and $CO_2(g)$ (in kJ mol^{-1}) is **[May 18, 2023 (I)]**

(a) 969 (b) 183
(c) –969 (d) –183

58. If for the reaction $CCl_4(g) \rightarrow C(g) + 4Cl(g)$ the following data is given

$\Delta_{vap}H^{\circ}_{CCl_4}(l) = 30$ kJ mol^{-1}, vap = vaporization

$\Delta_f H^{\circ}_{CCl_4} = -136.0$ kJ mol^{-1}, f = formation

$\Delta_a H_C = 714.0$ kJ mol^{-1}, a = atomization

$\Delta_a H^{\circ}_{Cl_2} = 242.0$ kJ mol^{-1}, a = atomization

the bond mean enthalpy of C-Cl in CCl_4 (l) is **[May 17, 2023 (II)]**

(a) –319 (b) 326
(c) –326 (d) 292

59. If the standard enthalpy of sublimation ($\Delta_{sub}H°$) of solid CO_2, naphthalene, Li and Na are 25.2, 73.0, 162, 108 kJ mol respectively, the order of sublimation of these substances with temperature is **[May 16, 2023 (I)]**

(a) Na > Li > Naphthalene > Solid CO_2
(b) Solid CO_2 > Na > Naphthalene > Li
(c) Solid CO_2 > Naphthalene > Na > Li
(d) Li > Na > Naphthalene > Solid CO_2

60. When 'X' g of graphite is completely burnt in a bomb calorimeter in excess of O_2 at 298 K and 1 atm pressure as given in the equation

$C(graphite) + O_2(g) \rightarrow CO_2(g)$.

The temperature of calorimeter raised from 298 K to 302 K. If the heat capacity of the calorimeter and molar enthalpy change for the reaction at 1 atm and 298 K are 20.7 kJ K^{-1} and –248.4 kJ mol^{-1}, 'X' in g is **[May 16, 2023 (I)]**

(a) 8 (b) 2 (c) 3 (d) 4

61. At 300 K the enthalpy change for the following reaction is –2800 kJ mol^{-1}

$C_6H_{12}O_6(S) + 6O_2(g) \rightarrow 6CO_2(g) + 6H_2O(l)$

What is the ΔU for the same reaction at 300K (kJ mol^{-1})? **[May 15, 2023 (II)]**

(a) –2802.49 (b) –2800.00
(c) –2814.94 (d) +2802.49

62. If the standard enthalpy change $(\Delta_r H^{\theta})$ for reaction $H_2(g) + Br_2(l) \rightarrow 2HBr(g)$ is –72.8 kJ, the standard enthalpy of formation $(\Delta_f H^{\theta})$ of HBr (g) (in kJ mol^{-1}) is **[May 15, 2023 (I)]**

(a) –36.4 (b) +36.4
(c) –18.2 (d) –18.2

63. Calculate $\Delta_r H$ (kJ mol^{-1}) of the following reaction **[July 8, 2022 (I)]**

$C_2H_5OH(l) + 7/2\ O_2(g) \rightarrow 2\ CO_2(g) + 3\ H_2O\ (l)$

Molecule	$\Delta_f H^0$ **(kJ mol^{-1})**
$C_2H_5OH(l)$	–280
$CO_2(g)$	–400
$H_2O(l)$	–290

(a) –1950 (b) –1100 (c) –1390 (d) –700

64. From the following data at 25°C, calculate the $\Delta_r H^0$ for $H_2O(g) \rightarrow 2H(g) + O(g)$. **[July 6, 2022 (I)]**

Reaction	$\Delta_r H^0$ **(kJ mol^{-1})**
$\frac{1}{2}H_2(g) + \frac{1}{2}O_2(g) \rightarrow OH(g)$	42.09
$H_2(g) + \frac{1}{2}O_2(g) \rightarrow H_2O(g)$	–242
$H_2(g) \rightarrow 2H(g)$	436
$O_2(g) \rightarrow 2O(g)$	496

(a) 1174 kJ mol^{-1} (b) 742 kJ mol^{-1}
(c) 926 kJ mol^{-1} (d) 690 kJ mol^{-1}

65. Calculate the energy required to convert all atoms in 4.8 g of Mg to Mg^{2+} in the vapour state. IE_1 and IE_2 of Mg are 740 kJ/mol and 1450 kJ/mol respectively. **[Sept. 21, 2020 (I)]**

(a) + 740 kJ/mol (b) – 740 kJ/mol
(c) – 1450 kJ/mol (d) + 438 kJ/mol

66. The enthalpy of formation (ΔH_f) of methanol, formaldehyde and water are –239, –116 and –286 kJ mol^{-1} respectively. The enthalpy change for the oxidation of methanol to formaldehyde and water in kJ is **[2017]**

(a) – 136 (b) – 173 (c) 163 (d) – 163

67. Given that,

$C(s) + O_2(g) \longrightarrow CO_2(g); \Delta H° = -x$ kJ mol^{-1}

$2CO(g) + O_2(g) \longrightarrow 2CO_2(g); \Delta H° = -y$ kJ mol^{-1}

The enthalpy of formation of CO will be **[2016]**

(a) $\frac{y-2x}{3}$ (b) $\frac{y-2x}{2}$

(c) $\frac{2x-y}{2}$ (d) $\frac{x-y}{2}$

Topic 3 Entropy and Second Law of Thermodynamics

68. At 298 K for the reaction **[May 18, 2026 (I)]**

$N_2(g) + 3H_2(g) \rightleftharpoons 2NH_3(g)$, $\Delta H = -92.4$ kJ, log K_C value is 5.75. What is the entropy charge (in JK^{-1}) for this reaction at the same temperature?

($R = 8.3$ J K^{-1} mol^{-1})

(a) –300 (b) –400
(c) –200 (d) –100

69. Identify the correct statements from the following

I. Bomb calorimeter is used to determine the heat absorbed by water in a chemical reaction at constant volume

II. Heat capacity is an extensive property

III. The units of entropy are J K

The correct answer is **[May 14, 2026 (I)]**

(a) I, II, III (b) I, II only
(c) I, III only (d) II, III only

70. Consider the unbalanced equation given below

$a\,Cr(OH)_3 + b\,IO_3^- + c\,OH^- \rightarrow d\,CrO_4^{2-} + eI^- + fH_2O$

Identify the correct statements/equations given below.

I. $Cr(OH)_3$ is reduced to CrO_4^{2-}

II. $a + b + c = 7$

III. $a + c = d + f$

IV. IO_3^- acts as an oxidizing agent in this reaction.

The correct answer is **[May 13, 2026 (II)]**

(a) I, II, IV only (b) II, IV only
(c) I, III only (d) I, II, III, IV

71. Identify the incorrect statements from the following.

(I) For adiabatic process, $\Delta U = W_{ad}$

(II) Enthalpy is an intensive property

(III) For the process, $H_2O\,(l) \rightarrow H_2O\,(s)$, the entropy increases

The correct answer is **[May 23, 2025 (II)]**

(a) I, II only (b) I, II, III
(c) I, III only (d) II, III only

72. For which of the following processes entropy change (ΔS) is negative? **[May 22, 2025 (I)]**

(I) Sublimation of dry ice

(II) Freezing of water

(III) Crystallisation of the dissolved substance

(IV) Burning of rocket fuel

(a) I and II only (b) II and III only
(c) III and IV only (d) I and IV only

73. Observe the following reactions **[May 23, 2024 (I)]**

I. $CaCO_3(s) \rightarrow CaO(s) + CO_2(g)$

II. $Cl_2(g) \rightarrow 2Cl(g)$

III. $H_2O(1) \rightarrow H_2O(s)$

Identify the reactions in which entropy increases

(a) I, II, III (b) I, II Only
(c) I, III Only (d) II, III Only

74. At 300 K, for the reaction A → P, the ΔS_{sys} is 5 JK^{-1} mol^{-1}. What is the heat absorbed (in kJ mol^{-1}) by the system? **[May 18, 2024 (I)]**

(a) 1.5 (b) 15 (c) 1500 (d) 0.6

75. Identify the incorrect statements from the following

I. $\Delta S_{system} = (\Delta S_{total} + \Delta S_{sum})$

II. $A(l) \rightarrow A(s)$: for this process entropy change decreases

III. Entropy units are $JK\,mol^{-1}$ **[May 18, 2024 (I)]**

(a) I, III only (b) I, II only
(c) I, II, III (d) II, III only

76. Identify the reaction/process in which the entropy decreases **[July 6, 2022 (I)]**

(a) $H_2O(l) \longrightarrow H_2O\,(s)$
(b) $H_2O(l) \longrightarrow H_2O\,(g)$
(c) $H_2O(g) \longrightarrow 2H\,(g)$
(d) Crystal (100 K) $\longrightarrow$ Crystal (200 K)

77. Identify the reaction/process in which the entropy increases. **[July 4, 2022 (I)]**

(a) $H(g) + H(g) \rightarrow H_2(g)$ (b) $H_2O (g) \rightarrow H_2O (s)$
(c) $H_2O (1) \rightarrow H_2O (g)$ (d) $A(g)+B(g)+C(s) \rightarrow 2D(s)$

78. For the reaction, $H_2O(l) \longrightarrow H_2O(g)$ at $T = 100°C$ and $p = 1$ atm, choose the correct option. **[Aug. 20, 2021 (I)]**

(a) $\Delta S_{system} > 0$ and $\Delta S_{surrounding} > 0$
(b) $\Delta S_{system} > 0$ and $\Delta S_{surrounding} < 0$
(c) $\Delta S_{system} < 0$ and $\Delta S_{surrounding} > 0$
(d) $\Delta S_{system} < 0$ and $\Delta S_{surrounding} < 0$

79. If, $\Delta H > 0$ and $\Delta S > 0$, the reaction can proceed spontaneously at .... **[Sept. 21, 2020 (I)]**

(a) low temperature (b) high temperature
(c) all temperature (d) will never be spontaneous

Topic 4 Spontaneity and Gibb's Free Energy

80. At 17°C, the enthalpy change and entropy change of the reaction given below are respectively – 12.55 kJ mol^{-1} and 5.0 JK^{-1} **[May 12, 2026 (II)]**

$Zn(s) + 2HCl(aq) \rightarrow ZnCl_2(aq) + H_2(g)$

What is ΔG (in kJ mol^{-1}) for this reaction?

(a) – 14 (b) + 14
(c) – 28 (d) +56

81. What is $\Delta_r G^\ominus$ for the following reaction at 298 K?

$2X(g) + Y(g) \rightarrow 2Z(g)$

($\Delta U^\ominus = -10.5$ kJ; $\Delta S^\ominus = -44$ JK^{-1}; R = 8.3 J K^{-1} mol^{-1}) **[May 12, 2026 (I)]**

(a) 12973 J (b) 13112 J
(c) 139.0 J (d) 0.1390 J

82. The signs of $\Delta_r H°$ and $\Delta_r S°$ for a reaction to be spontaneous at all temperatures respectively are **[May 26, 2025 (I)]**

(a) positive, positive (b) positive, negative
(c) negative, negative (d) negative, positive

83. If $\Delta_r H^\ominus$ and $\Delta_r S^\ominus$ are standard enthalpy change and standard entropy change respectively for a reaction, the incorrect option is **[May 24, 2025 (I)]**

(a) $\Delta_r H^\ominus$ = negative; $\Delta_r S^\ominus$ = positive; spontaneous at all temperatures
(b) $\Delta_r H^\ominus$ = negative; $\Delta_r S^\ominus$ = negative; non–spontaneous at low temperatures
(c) $\Delta_r H^\ominus$ = positive; $\Delta_r S^\ominus$ = positive; non–spontaneous at low temperatures
(d) $\Delta_r H^\ominus$ = negative; $\Delta_r S^\ominus$ = negative; spontaneous at low temperatures

84. At 298 K, $\Delta_r U^\ominus$ and $\Delta_r S^\ominus$ for the following reaction are –10.5 kJ and +44.1 JK^{-1}; $2X(g) + Y(g) \longrightarrow 2Z(g)$

What is $\Delta_r G^\ominus$ (in kJ) for this reaction?

($R = 8.314$ $JK^{-1}mol^{-1}$) **[May 23, 2025 (I)]**

(a) +0.164 (b) –26.119 (c) –2.6119 (d) –0.082

85. Consider the following reaction **[May 22, 2025 (II)]**

$A(g) + 3B(g) \longrightarrow 2C(g)$; $\Delta H^\ominus = -24$ kJ.

At 25°C if $\Delta G^\ominus$ of the reaction is –9 kJ, the standard entropy change (in JK^{-1}) of the same reaction at same temperature is

(a) –5.33 (b) –50.33 (c) –500.33 (d) –0.533

86. At 298 K, $\Delta_r G^\ominus$ for the following reaction is 165.469 kJ mol^{-1}. What is the equilibrium constant for this reaction? ($R = 8.3$ J mol^{-1} K^{-1}) **[May 21, 2025 (I)]**

$\frac{3}{2}O_2(g) \longrightarrow O_3(g)$

(a) 10^{29} (b) 10^{-29}
(c) 5×10^{-27} (d) $5 \times 10^{+27}$

87. Two statements are given below.

Statement I: The reaction $Cr_2O_3 + 2Al \rightarrow Al_2O_3 + 2Cr$ ($\Delta G^Q = -421$ kJ) is thermodynamically feasible.

Statement II: The above reaction occurs at room temperature. **[May 22, 2024 (II)]**

(a) Both the statements I & II are correct
(b) Both the statements I & II are not correct
(c) Statement I is correct, but statement II is not correct
(d) Statement I is not correct, but statement II is correct

88. Identify the correct statements from the following

I. $\Delta_r G$ is zero for $A \rightleftharpoons B$ reaction
II. The entropy of pure crystalline solids approaches zero as the temperature approaches absolute zero
III. ΔU of a reaction can be determined using bomb calorimeter **[May 21, 2024 (I)]**

(a) I, II only (b) I, III only
(c) II, III only (d) I, II, III

89. If the enthalpy and entropy change for a reaction at 298 K are –145 kJ mol^{-1} and –650 J K^{-1} mol^{-1} respectively, which one of the following statements is correct? **[May 17, 2023 (I)]**

(a) $\Delta G = -50$ kJ mol^{-1}, the reaction is spontaneous
(b) $\Delta G = -48.7$ kJ mol^{-1}, the reaction is non–spontaneous
(c) $\Delta G = +50$ kJ mol^{-1}, the reaction is spontaneous
(d) $\Delta G = 48.7$ kJ mol^{-1}, the reaction is non–spontaneous

90. If ΔG and ΔS for the reaction $A(g) \rightarrow B(g) + 2C(g)$ at 2000 K are -40 kJ mol^{-1} and 0.22 kJ K^{-1} mol^{-1} respectively, the change in internal energy for the same reaction approximately (in kJ mol^{-1}) is **[May 16, 2023 (II)]**

(a) 366.7 (b) –366.7 (c) 433.3 (d) –433.3

91. If the standard enthalpy change $\left(\Delta_r H^\circ\right)$ for a certain reaction at 298 K and constant pressure is –1860 kJ mol^{-1}, the standard entropy change $\left(\Delta_{sys} S^\circ\right)$ of the same reaction is –550 J K^{-1} mol^{-1}, which one of the following statements is correct? **[May 15, 2023 (I)]**

(a) $\left(\Delta_{sys} S^\circ\right) + \Delta_{surr} S^\circ = -7692$ J mol^{-1} K^{-1}, the reaction is spontaneous

(b) $\left(\Delta_{sys} S^\circ\right) + \Delta_{surr} S^\circ = -5692$ J mol^{-1} K^{-1}, the reaction is non–spontaneous

(c) $\left(\Delta_{sys} S^\circ\right) + \Delta_{surr} S^\circ = +5692$ J mol^{-1} K^{-1}, the reaction is spontaneous

(d) $\left(\Delta_{sys} S^\circ\right) + \Delta_{surr} S^\circ = +7692$ J mol^{-1} K^{-1}, the reaction is non–spontaneous

92. For a reaction $2CO(g) + O_2(g) \rightleftharpoons 2CO_2(g)$, $\Delta_r G^0 = -128$ kJ at 300 K. If $\Delta_r S^o$ of the reaction is –40 J K^{-1}, calculate $\Delta_r U$ of the reaction. **[July 5, 2022 (II)]**

(a) –137.5 kJ (b) –128 kJ

(c) –140 kJ (d) 126.2 kJ

93. At 60°C, dinitrogen tetroxide is 50% dissociated. Find it's standard free energy change at this temperature and one atmosphere. [Given log1.33 = 0.1239] **[Aug. 20, 2021 (I)]**

(a) – 650 J mol^{-1} (b) – 830 J mol^{-1}

(c) – 790 J mol^{-1} (d) – 875 J mol^{-1}

94. If a chemical reaction is known to be non-spontaneous at 298 K but spontaneous at 350 K, then which among the following conditions is true for the reaction? **[Aug. 19, 2021 (I)]**

(a) $\Delta G = -ve, \Delta H = -ve, \Delta S = +ve$

(b) $\Delta G = +ve, \Delta H = +ve, \Delta S = +ve$

(c) $\Delta G = -ve, \Delta H = +ve, \Delta S = +ve$

(d) $\Delta G = +ve, \Delta H = +ve, \Delta S = -ve$

6 Equilibrium

CHAPTER SYNOPSIS

- Equilibrium constant for gaseous homogenous equilibrium can be expressed in two ways K_P and K_C. This means value of equilibrium constant depends upon choice of standard state in which concentrations of reactants and products are expressed.
- The equilibrium constant for a reaction decreases with increase in temperature, if the reaction is exothermic and if the reaction is endothermic the equilibrium constant increases with increase in temperature
- **Effect of pressure (or volume) at equilibrium**

Reaction Type	**Effect of P or V**
n = 0	Equilibrium is not affected
n = +ve	Increase in P or decrease in V shift the equilibrium to left
n = -ve	Increase in P or decrease in volume shift the equilibrium to right

- **Effect of addition of inert gas at equilibrium**

Reaction Type	**Effect**
$\Delta n = 0$	Equilibrium is not affected at constant P or V
$\Delta n = +ve$	At constant V : Equilibrium is not affected At constant P : Equilibrium shifts to right
$\Delta n = -ve$	At constant V : Equilibrium is not affected At constant P : Equilibrium shifts to left

- Variation of equilibrium constant with variation of the reaction equation (K = equilibrium constant for original reaction) is given as below:

When the equation	**the change in equilibrium constant**
Reversed	$1/K$
Divided by 2	$\sqrt{K}$
Multiplied by 2	K^2
Divided into two steps	$K = K_1 \times K_2$

- The value of the equilibrium constant is not affected by the addition of a catalyst to the reaction. This is because the catalyst increases the speed of the forward reaction and the backward reaction to the same extent.
- K_P is related to K_C as $\mathbf{K_P = K_C (RT)^{\Delta n}}$
- Relation between $\Delta G°$ and K

$\Delta G°$	lnK	R	Reaction
–ve	+ve	>1	Spontaneous
+ve	–ve	<1	Non-spontaneous
0	0	=1	Equilibrium

- Prediction of the direction of the reaction using following relation
  - If $Q_c < K_c$, net reaction goes from left to right
  - If $Q_c > K_c$, net reaction goes from right to left
  - If $Q_c = K_c$, no net reaction.
- $\Delta G°$ is related to K by the relation $\mathbf{\Delta G° = -RT \ln K}$
- Ionic product of water is the product of concentration of H^+ ions and OH^- ions in pure water. It is constant at constant temperature.
- The ionic product of water increases with increase in temperature.
- Salt hydrolysis is reverse of neutralisation.
- The aqueous solution of salts of weak acid and strong base is alkaline in nature (pH > 7).
- The aqueous solution of strong acid and weak base is acidic in nature (pH < 7).
- The nature of salts of weak acid and weak base on hydrolysis depends upon the relative hydrolysis of the cation or anion of the salt.
- The aqueous solution of salts of strong acid and strong base is neutral.
- Solubility product is defined as the product of ionic concentration of sparingly soluble electrolyte in a saturated solution and is constant at constant temperature.

Topic 1 Law of Mass Action, Equilibrium Constant (K_c and K_p) and its Application

1. At T(K), in a 10 L flask, the following equilibrium is established $2SO_2(g) + O_2(g) \rightleftharpoons 2SO_3(g)$
The value of K_c for this reaction is 100. At equilibrium, the number of moles of $SO_3(g)$ is equal to twice the number of moles of $SO_2(g)$. What is the number of moles of $O_2(g)$ equilibrium? **[May 18, 2026 (II)]**
(a) 0.04 (b) 0.4
(c) 0.02 (d) 0.2

2. At T(K) in a 10.0 L flask, 2 moles of $N_2O_4(g)$ was heated. At equilibrium 20% of $N_2O_4(g)$ was dissociated into $NO_2(g)$. What is the K_C for this reaction? **[May 15, 2026 (II)]**
(a) 2×10^{-2} (b) 4×10^{-2}
(c) 3×10^{-2} (d) 6×10^{-2}

3. Observe the following reaction **[May 15, 2026 (I)]**
$$A(g) + B(g) \xrightleftharpoons{T(K)} C(g)$$
In a 1L closed flask, 2 moles of A(g) and 1 mole of B(g) were taken and heated to T(K). At equilibrium, the concentration of B(g) is equal to twice the equilibrium concentration of C(g). What is the value of K_c?
(a) 0.3 (b) 0.6
(c) 1.2 (d) 1.5

4. At T(K), 15 moles of H_2 reacts with 5.2 moles of I_2 and forms of HI. The equilibrium constant for the reaction $2HI(g) \rightleftharpoons H_2(g) + I_2(g)$ is **[May 14, 2026 (II)]**
(a) 50 (b) 100
(c) 2×10^{-2} (d) 1×10^{-2}

5. Observe the following reaction **[May 14, 2026 (I)]**
$$A(g) + B(g) \xrightleftharpoons{T(K)} C(g) + D(g)$$
In a 1L closed flask, 2 moles of A(g) and 1 mole of B(g) were taken and heated to T(K). At equilibrium, the concentration of C(g) is thrice the concentration of B(g). What is the value of K_C?
(a) 7.2 (b) 3.6
(c) 0.9 (d) 1.8

6. At T(K) in a closed 2.0 L vessel, 1 mole of H_2 and 2 moles of I_2 are taken initially and allowed to react till equilibrium is established. At equilibrium, the number of moles of H_2 is found to be 0.2. The equilibrium constant for the dissociation of HI is **[May 13, 2026 (II)]**
(a) 1.066×10^1 (b) 93.75×10^{-2}
(c) 2.132×10^2 (d) 9.375×10^{-2}

7. For the reaction $2HI(g) \rightleftharpoons H_2(g) + I_2(g)$, the correct expression relating the degree of dissociation (α) of HI and equilibrium constant K_p is **[May 13, 2026 (I)]**
(a) $\alpha = \dfrac{1+2\sqrt{K_p}}{2}$ (b) $\alpha = \sqrt{1+\dfrac{2K_p}{2}}$
(c) $\alpha = \dfrac{2\sqrt{K_p}}{1+2\sqrt{K_p}}$ (d) $\alpha = \sqrt{\dfrac{2K_p}{1+2K_p}}$

8. At 540 K, 0.1 mol of PCl_5 is heated in a 8.0 L flask. The total pressure of the equilibrium mixture is 1 atm. The K_p (in atm) for the reaction is ($R = 0.082 L\ atm\ K^{-1}\ mol^{-1}$) **[May 12, 2026 (II)]**
(a) 1.77 (b) 0.77
(c) 2.77 (d) 3.77

9. The equilibrium constants $\sqrt{\dfrac{10gh}{7}}$ and $\sqrt{\dfrac{6gh}{5}}$ for the gaseous reactions, $X \rightleftharpoons 2Y$ and $Z \rightleftharpoons P + Q$ respectively are in the ratio of 1:9. If the degree of dissociation of X and Z are equal, then the ratio of their total pressures at these equilibria is **[May 12, 2026 (I)]**
(a) 1 : 36 (b) 1 : 3
(c) 9 : 1 (d) 4 : 1

10. Consider the following equilibrium reaction in gaseous state at T(K). **[May 27, 2025 (I)]**
$$A + 2B \rightleftharpoons 2C + D$$
The initial concentration of B is 1.5 times that of A. At equilibrium, the concentrations of A and B are equal. The equilibrium constant for the reaction is
(a) 6 (b) 16 (c) 12 (d) 4

11. A and B are ideal gases. At T(K). 2 L of 'A' with a pressure of 1 bar is mixed with 4 L of 'B' with a pressure P_B bar in a 100 L flask. The pressure exerted by gaseous mixture is 0.1 bar. What is the value of P_B in bar ? **[May 26, 2025 (II)]**
(a) 2 (b) 0.04 (c) 0.02 (d) 1

12. At T(K), K_c value of $AO_2(g) + BO_2(g) \rightleftharpoons AO_3(g) + BO(g)$ is 16. In a closed 1 L flask, one mole each of AO_2, BO_2, AO_3 and BO are taken and heated to T(K). Identify the correct statements about this equilibrium.
I. Total number of moles at equilibrium is 4
II. At equilibrium, the ratio of moles of AO_2 and AO_3 is 1 : 4
III. Total number of moles of AO_2 and BO_2 at equilibrium is 0.8 **[May 26, 2025 (I)]**
(a) I, II only (b) I, III only
(c) II, III only (d) I, II, III

13. At T(K), consider the following gaseous reaction, which is in equilibrium **[May 24, 2025 (I)]**
$$N_2O_5 \rightleftharpoons 2NO_2 + \frac{1}{2}O_2$$
What is the fraction of N_2O_5 decomposed at constant volume and temperature, if the initial pressure is 300 mm Hg and pressure at equilibrium is 480 mm Hg? (Assume all gases as ideal)
(a) 0.2 (b) 0.6 (c) 0.4 (d) 0.8

14. At 298 K, the value of K_p for $N_2O_4(g) \rightleftharpoons 2NO_2(g)$ is 0.113 atm. The partial pressure of N_2O_4 at equilibrium is 0.2 atm. What is the partial pressure (in atm) of NO_2 at equilibrium? **[May 23, 2025 (II)]**

(a) 0.05 (b) 0.075 (c) 0.30 (d) 0.15

15. Consider the following gaseous equilibrium reactions (I), (II) and (III) with equilibrium constants K_1, K_2 and K_3 respectively. **[May 23, 2025 (I)]**

(I) $\frac{1}{2}N_2 + \frac{3}{2}H_2 \rightleftharpoons NH_3$

(II) $2NO \rightleftharpoons N_2 + O_2$

(III) $H_2 + \frac{1}{2}O_2 \rightleftharpoons H_2O$

The correct expression for the equilibrium constant for the gaseous equilibrium reaction

$2NH_3 + \frac{5}{2}O_2 \rightleftharpoons 2NO + 3H_2O$ is

(a) $\frac{K_3^2}{K_1 \times K_2}$ (b) $\frac{K_3^3}{K_1^2 \times K_2}$

(c) $\frac{K_3^2}{K_1^2 \times K_2}$ (d) $\frac{K_3}{K_1^{1/2} \times K_2^2}$

16. At T(K), the following gaseous equilibrium is established.

$W + X \rightleftharpoons Y + Z$

The initial concentration of W is two times to the initial concentration of X. The system is heated to T(K) to establish the equilibrium. At equilibrium the concentration of Y is four times to the concentration of X. What is the value of K_c? **[May 22, 2025 (II)]**

(a) 0.375 (b) 1.333 (c) 2.666 (d) 5.333

17. At T(K), K_c value for **[May 22, 2025 (I)]**

$AO_2(g) + BO_2(g) \rightleftharpoons AO_3(g) + BO(g)$ is 16. In a closed 1 L flask, one mole each of AO_2, BO_2, AO_3 and BO are taken and heated to T(K). What is the concentration (in mol L^{-1}) of AO_3 at equilibrium?

(a) 0.4 (b) 0.6 (c) 1.6 (d) 1.4

18. At 298 K, the value of K_c for the following reaction is x mol L^{-1}. What is the approximate K_p value for this reaction? (R = 0.082 L atm mol^{-1} K^{-1})

$A_2O_4(g) \rightleftharpoons 2AO_2(g)$ **[May 21, 2025 (II)]**

(a) $24.4x$ (b) $12.2x$ (c) $\frac{x}{24.4}$ (d) $\frac{24.4}{x}$

19. The following equilibrium is established at STP.

$B_2(g) \rightleftharpoons 2B(g)$

Atoms of B occupy 20% of total volume at STP. The total pressure of the system is 1 bar. What is its K_p? (STP volume = 22.7 L) **[May 21, 2025 (I)]**

(a) 0.05 (b) 0.1 (c) 0.5 (d) 0.025

20. At 300 K, K_C for the reaction.

$A_2B_2(g) \rightleftharpoons A_2(g) + B_2(g)$ is 100 mol L^{-1}. What is its K_p (in atm) at the same temperature?

(R = 0.082 L atm mol^{-1} K^{-1}) **[May 23, 2024 (I)]**

(a) 100 (b) 2460 (c) 4.06 (d) 246

21. At equilibrium for the reaction **[May 22, 2024 (I)]**

$A_2(g) + B_2(g) \rightleftharpoons 2AB(g)$

the concentrations of A_2, B_2 and AB respectively are 1.5×10^{-3} M, 2.1×10^{-3} M and 1.4×10^{-3} M in a sealed vessel at 800 K. What will be K_p for the decomposition of AB at same temperature?

(a) 0.62 (b) 1.6 (c) 0.44 (d) 2.27

22. 15 moles of H_2 and 5.2 moles of I_2 are mixed and allowed to attain equilibrium at 773 K. At equilibrium, the number of moles of HI is found to be 10. The equilibrium constant for the dissociation of HI is **[May 21, 2024 (II)]**

(a) 2×10^{-2} (b) 50

(c) 2×10^{-1} (d) 5.0

23. K_c for the reaction

$A_2(g) \xrightleftharpoons{T(K)} B_2(g)$

is 39.0. In a closed one litre flask, one mole of $A_2(g)$ was heated to T(K). What are the concentrations of $A_2(g)$ and $B_2(g)$ (in mol L^{-1}) respectively at equilibrium? **[May 21, 2024 (I)]**

(a) 0.025, 0.975 (b) 0.975, 0.025

(c) 0.05, 0.95 (d) 0.02, 0.98

24. At T(K), the equilibrium constant for the reaction $H_2(g) + Br_2(g) \rightleftharpoons 2HBr(g)$ is 1.6×10^5. If 10 bar of HBr is introduced into a sealed vessel at T(K), the equilibrium pressure of HBr (in bar) is approximately **[May 20, 2024 (II)]**

(a) 10.20 (b) 10.95 (c) 9.95 (d) 11.95

25. K_c for the reaction, $A_2(g) \xrightleftharpoons{T(K)} B_2(g)$ is 99.0. In a 1 L closed flask two moles of $B_2(g)$ is heated to T (K). What is the concentration of $B_2(g)$ (in mol L^{-1}) at equilibrium? **[May 20, 2024 (I)]**

(a) 0.02 (b) 1.98 (c) 0.198 (d) 1.5

26. K_c for the following reaction is 99.0

$A_2(g) \xrightleftharpoons{T(K)} B_2(g)$

In a one litre flask, 2 moles of A_2 was heated to T(K) and the above equilibrium is reached. The concentrations at equilibrium of A_2 and B_2 are $C_1(A_2)$ and $C_2(B_2)$ respectively. Now, one mole of A_2 was added to flask and heated to T(K) to establish the equilibrium again. The concentrations of A_2 and B_2 are $C_3(A_2)$ and $C_4(B_2)$ respectively. What is the value of $C_3(A_2)$ in mol L^{-1}? **[May 19, 2024 (II)]**

(a) 1.98 (b) 0.01 (c) 0.03 (d) 2.97

27. At T (K), K_c for the reaction. $A_2(g) \rightleftharpoons B_2(g)$ is 99.0. Two moles of A_2 (g) was heated to T (K) in a 1L closed flask to reach the above equilibrium. What are the concentrations (in mol L^{-1}) of A_2 (g) and B_2(g) respectively at equilibrium? **[May 18, 2024 (I)]**
(a) 1.86,0.0187 (b) 1.98,0.02
(c) 0.0187,1.86 (d) 0.02,1.98

28. At T(K), the K_p for the reaction $A_2B_6(g) \rightarrow A_2B_4(g) + B_2(g)$ is 0.04 atm. The equilibrium pressure (in atm) of A_2B_6)g) when it is placed in a flask at 4 atm pressure and allowed to come to above equilibrium is **[May 19, 2023 (I)]**
(a) 0.362 (b) 0.380 (c) 3.62 (d) 2.62

29. At 1000 K, the value of K_c for the below reaction is 10 mol L^{-1}. Value of K_p (in atm) is **[May 18, 2023 (I)]**
$A(g) \rightleftharpoons B(g)+C(g)$
(given R = 0.082 atm L mol^{-1} K^{-1})
(a) 82 (b) 0.82 (c) 8.2 (d) 820

30. One mole of A(g) is heated to T(K) till the following equilibrium is obtained
$A(g) \xrightleftharpoons{T(K)} B(g)$
The equilibrium constant of this reaction is 10^{-1}. After reaching the equilibrium, 0.5 moles of A(g) is added and heated. The equilibrium is again established. The value of $\frac{[A]}{[B]}$ is **[May 17, 2023 (II)]**
(a) 10^{-1} (b) 10 (c) 10^{-2} (d) 100

31. One mole H_2O(g) and one mole CO(g) are taken in 1L flask and heated to 725K. At equilibrium, 40% (by mass) of water reacted with CO(g) as follows.
$H_2O(g)+CO(g) \rightleftharpoons H_2(g)+CO_2(g)$. Its K_p value is **[May 17, 2023 (I); Similar to May 15, 2023 (I)]**
(a) 2.220 (b) 0.444 (c) 4.440 (d) 0.222

32. One mole of PCl_5(g) was heated in a 1L closed flask at 500 K. At equilibrium, 0.1 mole of Cl_2 (g) was formed. What is its K_p (in atm)?
(Given R = 0.082 L atm mol^{-1} K^{-1}) **[May 16, 2023 (I)]**
(a) 2.7×10^{-4} (b) 0.455
(c) 0.0111 (d) 90.0

33. At T(K), the equilibrium constant for the reaction a A(g) ż b B (g) is K_c. If the reaction takes place in the following form 2aA(g) → 2b B(g) its equilibrium constant is K'_c. The correct relationship between K_c and K_c is **[May 15, 2023 (II)]**
(a) $K'_c = (K_c)^2$ (b) $K'_c = (K_c)^{\frac{1}{2}}$
(c) $K'_c = (K_c)^{-1}$ (d) $K'_c = K_c$

34. K_p/K_C for the reaction at T(K) is **[July 8, 2022 (I)]**
$CO(g)+\frac{1}{2}O_2(g) \rightleftharpoons CO_2(g)$
(a) $\sqrt{RT}$ (b) 2RT (c) RT (d) $1/\sqrt{RT}$

35. For ammonia formation from constituent elements, the expression for K_C is **[July 6, 2022 (I)]**
(a) $K_C = \frac{[NH_3]^3}{[N_2]^3[H_2]^3}$ (b) $K_C = \frac{[NH_3]^2}{[N_2][H_2]^3}$
(c) $K_C = \frac{[NH_3]}{[N_2][H_2]}$ (d) $K_C = [NH_3]^2$

36. Identify the correct expression for the equilibrium constant of the following reaction. **[Aug. 23, 2021 (I)]**
$2X(g)+Y(g) \rightleftharpoons 3Z(g)$
(a) $k = \frac{[X]^2[Y]}{[Z]^3}$ (b) $k = \frac{[Z]^3}{[X]^2[Y]}$
(c) $k = \frac{3[Z]}{2[X][Y]}$ (d) $k = [Z]^3[X]^2[Y]$

37. Which among the following denotes the correct relationship between K_p and K_c for the reaction,
$2A(g) \rightleftharpoons B(g)+C(g)$ **[Aug. 19, 2021 (II)]**
(a) $K_p > K_c$ (b) $K_c > K_p$
(c) $K_c = (K_p)^2$ (d) $K_p = K_c$

38. For a reversible reaction, if the concentration of the reactants is reduced to half, the equilibrium constant will be .... **[Sept. 18, 2020 (I)]**
(a) doubled (b) halved
(c) reduced to one-fourth (d) remains same

39. What is the equilibrium constant (K_c) for the given reaction?
$N_2 + O_2 \rightleftharpoons 2NO$
Where the equilibrium concentration of N_2, O_2 and NO are found to be 4×10^{-3}, 3×10^{-3} and 3×10^{-3} M respectively. **[Apr. 21, 2019 (II)]**
(a) 0.750 (b) 0.622
(c) 9×10^{-3} (d) 12.8×10^{-6}

40. At 1000 K, the equilibrium constant. K_C for the reaction $2NOCl(g) \rightleftharpoons 2NO(g)+Cl_2(g)$ is 4.0×10^{-6} mol L^{-1}. The K_P (in bar) at the same temperature is **[2018]**
(R = 0.083 L bar $K^{-1}mol^{-1}$)
(a) 3.32×10^{-6} (b) 3.32×10^{4}
(c) 3.32×10^{-4} (d) 3.32×10^{-3}

41. The equilibrium constant (K_C) for the following equilibrium **[2017]**
$2SO_2(g)+O_2(g) \rightleftharpoons 2SO_3(g)$
at 563 K is 100. At equilibrium, the number of moles of SO_3 in the 10 litre flask is twice the number of moles of SO_2, then the number of moles of oxygen is
(a) 0.4 (b) 0.3 (c) 0.2 (d) 0.1

42. (i) $H_3PO_4(aq) \rightleftharpoons H^+(aq) + H_2PO_4^-(aq)$

(ii) $H_2PO_4^-(aq) \rightleftharpoons H^+(aq) + HPO_4^{2-}(aq)$

(iii) $HPO_4^{2-}(aq) \rightleftharpoons H^+(aq) + PO_4^{3-}(aq)$

The equilibrium constants for the above reactions at a certain temperature are K_1, K_2 and K_3 respectively. The equilibrium constant for the reaction $H_3PO_4(aq) \rightleftharpoons 3H^+(aq) + PO_4^{3-}(aq)$ in terms of K_1, K_2 and K_3 is **[2017]**

(a) $K_1 + K_2 + K_3$ (b) $\frac{K_1}{K_2 + K_3}$

(c) $\frac{K_3}{K_1 K_2}$ (d) $K_1 K_2 K_3$

43. At 400 K, in a 1.0 L vessel, N_2O_4 is allowed to attain equilibrium, $N_2O_4(g) \rightleftharpoons 2NO_2(g)$ At equilibrium, the total pressure is 600 mm Hg, when 20% of N_2O_4 is dissociated. The value of K_p for the reaction is **[2016]**

(a) 50 (b) 100 (c) 150 (d) 200

Topic 2 Relation between K, Q and G and Factors Effecting Equilibrium

44. At 450 K, for the reaction $2SO_2(g) + O_2(g) \rightleftharpoons 2SO_3(g)$, the value of K_p is 2.0×10^{10}. What is the value of K_C for the decomposition of sulphur trioxide at the same temperature? **[May 18, 2026 (I)]**
[$R = 0.083$ L bar mol^{-1} K^{-1}]

(a) 7.47×10^{11} (b) 1.34×10^{-12}

(c) 7.47×10^{-12} (d) 1.34×10^{12}

45. At 298 K for the reaction,
$N_2(g) + 3H_2(g) \rightleftharpoons 2NH_3(g)$, enthalpy and entropy changes are –92.4 kJ and –200 J K^{-1} respectively. The value of log K_c for the reaction is
($R = 8.3$ J K^{-1} mol^{-1}) **[May 13, 2026 (II)]**

(a) 5.75 (b) 6.75

(c) 7.65 (d) 5.67

46. At 300 K, $\Delta_r G^\circ$ for the reaction $A_2(g) \rightleftharpoons B_2(g)$ is –11.5 kJ mol^{-1}. The equilibrium constant at 300 K is approximately ($R = 8.314$ J mol^{-1} K^{-1}) **[May 22, 2024 (II)]**

(a) 10 (b) 100 (c) 1000 (d) 25

47. Observe the following equilibrium
$Fe^{3+}(aq) + SCN^-(aq) \rightleftharpoons [Fe(SCN)]^{2+}(aq)$
yellow colourless deep red
Addition of aqueous oxalic acid solution to the above equilibrium **[May 18, 2023 (II)]**

(a) Shifts the equilibrium towards the formation of $[Fe(SCN)]^{2+}$
(b) Deep red color increases
(c) Intensity of deep red color decreases
(d) No change in equilibrium

48. Observe the following equilibrium at T (K)
$H_2(g) + I_2(g) \rightleftharpoons 2HI(g)$
Which one of the following does not disturb the above equilibrium? **[May 16, 2023 (II)]**

(a) Addition of H_2 (g) (b) Removal of HI(g)

(c) Addition of I_2(g) (d) Addition of He(g)

49. For a reaction

$$A(g) + \frac{1}{2}B(g) \rightleftharpoons C(g) + \text{heat}$$

favorable conditions for the reaction to occur in the forward direction are **[July 5, 2022 (II)]**

(a) Low T and Low P (b) Low T and high P

(c) High T and Low P (d) High T and high P

50. Which of the following expression is correct **[July 4, 2022 (II)]**

(a) $\Delta G = -RT \ln K$ (b) $\Delta G = \frac{1}{RT^2 \ln K}$

(c) $\Delta G^0 = -RT \ln K$ (d) $\Delta G^0 = -\frac{1}{RT^2 \ln K}$

51. The formation of ammonia from its constituent elements is an exothermic reaction. The effect of increase temperature on the reaction equilibrium is **[July 4, 2022 (I)]**

(a) The rate of the forward reaction becomes zero
(b) No effect of temperature.
(c) Forward reaction is favored
(d) Backward reaction is favored

52. When reaction is carried out at standard states then, at the equilibrium **[Aug. 23, 2021 (II)]**

(a) $\Delta H^\circ = 0$
(b) $\Delta S^\circ = 0$
(c) equilibrium constant (K) = 0
(d) equilibrium constant (K) = 1

53. Le-Chateliers' principle is not applicable to **[Aug. 20, 2021 (I)]**

(a) $H_2(g) + I_2(g) \rightleftharpoons 2HI(g)$

(b) $Fe(s) + S(s) \rightleftharpoons FeS(s)$

(c) $N_2(g) + 3H_2(g) \rightleftharpoons 2NH_3(g)$

(d) $N_2(g) + O_2(g) \rightleftharpoons 2NO(g)$

54. Standard entropies of X_2, Y_2 and XY_3 are 60, 40 and 50 JK^{-1} mol^{-1} respectively. At what temperature, the following reaction will be at equilibrium?
[given : $\Delta H^\circ = -30$ kJ] **[Aug. 19, 2021 (II)]**

$$\frac{1}{2}X_2 + \frac{3}{2}Y_2 \rightleftharpoons XY_3$$

(a) 500 K (b) 750 K (c) 1000 K (d) 1250 K

55. For the reaction $SO_2(g) + \frac{1}{2}O_2(g) \rightleftharpoons SO_3(g)$, the percentage yield of product at different pressure is shown in the figure. Then, which among the following is true? **[Aug. 19, 2021 (II)]**

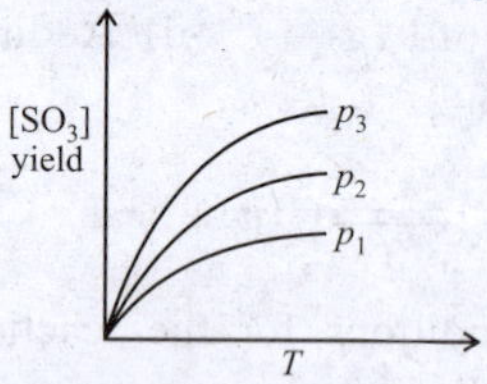

(a) Pressure has no effect (b) $p_1 < p_2 < p_3$
(c) $p_1 > p_2 > p_3$ (d) $p_1 = p_2 = p_3 \neq 0$

56. K_P for the conversion of oxygen to ozone at 400 K is 1.0×10^{-30}, its standard Gibbs energy change in kJ mol^{-1} is approximately **[Apr. 22, 2019 (I)]**
(a) 229.8 (b) 114.9 (c) –229.8 (d) –114.9

57. On increasing temperature, the equilibrium constant of exothermic and endothermic reactions, respectively **[2015]**
(a) increases and decreases
(b) decreases and increases
(c) increases and increases
(d) decreases and decreases

Topic 3 Theories of Acids and Bases, Ionic Product of Water and pH Scale

58. What is the conjugate acid of $H_3P_2O_6^-$? **[May 18, 2026 (II)]**
(a) Orthophosphorus acid (b) Hypophosphorus acid
(c) Pyrophosphoric acid (d) Hypophosphoric acid

59. Identify the correct statements from the following
I. Conjugate base of nitrous acid is NO_2^-
II. The concentration of OH^- ions in 0.1 M aqueous pyridine solution is $\sqrt{2} \times 10^{-5}$ M. (K_b of pyridine = 2×10^{-9})
III. The acid strength of aqueous hydrogen halides follow the order
HF > HCl > HBr > HI
The correct answer is **[May 18, 2026 (I)]**
(a) I, II, III (b) I, II only
(c) I, III only (d) II, II only

60. In the reaction given below, water behaves as
$NH_3 + H_2O \rightleftharpoons NH_4^+ + OH^-$
(a) A Lewis base **[May 15, 2026 (I)]**
(b) A Bronsted- Lowry acid
(c) A Bronsted-Lowry base
(d) A Lewis acid

61. The conjugate base of hydrogen carbonate ion is X. The hybridization of central atom in X is **[May 13, 2026 (II)]**
(a) sp (b) sp^2
(c) sp^3 (d) sp^3d

62. The conjugate base of phosphorus acid is x. The conjugate base of oleum is y. What are x and y, respectively? **[May 26, 2025 (I)]**
(a) $H_2PO_4^-, HS_2O_7^-$ (b) $H_2PO_4^-, HSO_5^-$
(c) $H_2PO_3^-, HS_2O_7^-$ (d) $H_2PO_3^-, HSO_4^-$

63. Observe the following molecules/ions. **[May 24, 2025 (I)]**
$NH_4^+, NH_3, BF_3, OH^-, CH_3^+, H^+, CO, C_2H_4$
The number of Lewis bases in the above list is
(a) 2 (b) 3 (c) 4 (d) 5

64. The percentage of ionization of 1 L of x M acetic acid is 4.242 and is called solution "A". The percentage of ionization of 1 L of y M acetic acid is 3 and is called solution "B". Solution "A" is mixed with solution "B". What is the concentration of acetic acid in the resultant solution? **[May 23, 2025 (II)]**
(K_a of acetic acid = 1.8×10^{-5})
(a) 0.05 M (b) 0.015 M (c) 0.02 M (d) 0.15 M

65. 100 mL of 0.1 M HA (weak acid) and 100 mL of 0.2 M NaA are mixed. What is the pH of resultant solution? (K_a of HA is 10^{-5}; log 2 = 0.3) **[May 22, 2024 (II)]**.
(a) 4.7 (b) 5.0 (c) 5.3 (d) 4.0

66. Which of the following when added to 20 mL of a 0.01 M solution of HCl would decrease its pH? **[May 22, 2024 (I)]**
(a) 20 mL of 0.02 M HCl (b) 20 mL of 0.005 M HCl
(c) 20 mL of 0.01 M HCl (d) 40 mL of 0.005 M HCl

67. At 27°C. 100 mL of 0.4 M HCl is mixed with 100 mL of 0.5 M NaOH solution. To the resultant solution. 800 mL of distilled water is added. What is the pH of final solution? **[May 20, 2024 (I)]**
(a) 12 (b) 2 (c) 1.3 (d) 1.0

68. Observe the following stoichiometric equation
$P_4 + 3\,OH^- + 3H_2O \rightarrow PH_3 + 3x^-$ **[May 19, 2024 (II)]**
What is the conjugate acid of x^- ?
(a) Phosphorous acid
(b) Hypophosphorous acid
(c) Phosphoric acid
(d) Pyrophosphoric acid

69. What is the conjugate base of chloric acid? **[May 19, 2024 (II)]**
(a) ClO_4^- (b) ClO^- (c) ClO_2^- (d) ClO_3^-

70. Observe the following species
$AlCl_3, NH_3, H^+, Co^{3+}, {}^-OH, Mg^{2+}, BF_3, Cl^-$
How many Lewis acids are present in the above list?
[May 18, 2023 (II); Similar to May 17, 2023 (II)]
(a) 5 (b) 4 (c) 2 (d) 3

71. Given below are two statements
Statement I: The changes in pH with temperature are so small that we often ignore it
Statement II: When the hydrogen ion concentration changes by a factor of 100, the pH changes by one unit
In the light of above statements, identify the correct answer from the options given below
[May 17, 2023 (I)]
(a) Both statements I and II are correct.
(b) Both statements I and II are not correct.
(c) Statement I is correct but statement II is not correct.
(d) Statement I is not correct but statement II is correct.

72. Observe the following solutions
I. Black coffee II. 0.2M NaOH
III. Lemon juice IV. Lime water
V. Human Saliva VI. Tomato juice
The number of solutions with pH less than 7 is
[May 16, 2023 (II); Similar to May 15, 2023 (II)]
(a) 2 (b) 5 (c) 4 (d) 3

73. Conjugate acid and conjugate base of HCO_3^- are respectively **[May 16, 2023 (I)]**
(a) $H_2CO_3, H_3CO_3^+$ (b) H_2CO_3, CO_3^{2-}
(c) CO_3^{2-}, H_2CO_3 (d) CO_3^{2-}, CO_2

74. The conjugate base of H_3O^+ is **[July 6, 2022 (I)]**
(a) H_2O (b) OH^- (c) H^+ (d) H^-

75. The pH of 0.01 N lime water is **[July 4, 2022 (II)]**
(a) 13.09 (b) 10 (c) 12 (d) 9.8

76. Which of the following gas has the highest pH at 25°C?
[Aug. 23, 2021 (I)]
(a) Distilled H_2O (b) 1 M *aq* NH_3
(c) 1 M NaOH (d) 1 M HCl

77. Strongest conjugate base among the following is
[Sept. 18, 2020 (I)]
(a) Cl^- (b) F^- (c) Br^- (d) I^-

78. At *T* (*K*), if the ionisation constant of ammonia in solution is 2.5×10^{-5}, the pH of 0.01 M ammonia solution and the ionisation constant of its conjugate acid respectively at that temperature are (log 2 = 0.30)
[Apr. 22, 2019 (II)]
(a) 10.7, 4.0×10^{-8} (b) 10.7, 4.0×10^{-10}
(c) 3.3, 4.0×10^{-8} (d) 3.3, 4.0×10^{-10}

79. The number of species of the following that can act both as Bronsted acids and bases is **[Apr. 20, 2019 (I)]**
HCl, ClO_4^-, ^-OH, H^+, H_2O, HSO_4^-, SO_4^-, H_2SO_4, Cl^-
(a) 4 (b) 3 (c) 1 (d) 2

80. What is the pH of the NaOH solution when 0.04 g of it dissolved in water and made to 100 mL solution? **[2015]**
(a) 2 (b) 1 (c) 13 (d) 12

Topic 4 Ionisation of Weak Acids and Bases and Relation between K_a and K_b

81. The dissociation constants of H_2A are $K_{a1} = 6 \times 10^{-2}$ and $K_{a2} = 6 \times 10^{-5}$ respectively. At equilibrium, $[A^{2-}] = [H_2A]$. What is the approximate concentration of H^+ at equilibrium? **[May 14, 2026 (I)]**
(a) 1.9×10^{-3} (b) 2×10^{-4}
(c) 1.9×10^{-5} (d) 1.9×10^{-2}

82. For the following given equilibrium reaction $\frac{K_c}{K_p}$ is equal to 1076 at T(K). What is the value of T (in K) ? (R = 0.082 L-atm K^{-1} mol^{-1}) **[May 26, 2025 (II)]**
$N_2(g) + 3H_2(g) \rightleftharpoons 2NH_3(g)$
(a) 500 (b) 600 (c) 400 (d) 450

83. 100 mL of aqueous solution of 0.05 M Cu^{2+} is added to 1 L of 0.1 M KI solution. The resultant solution was titrated with 0.01 M $Na_2S_2O_3$ solution using starch indicator till blue color disappeared. What is the volume (in mL) of $Na_2S_2O_3$ used? **[May 26, 2025 (I)]**
(a) 2000 (b) 1000 (c) 500 (d) 250

84. At 25°C, K_a of formic acid is 1.8×10^{-4}. What is the K_b of $HCOO^-$? **[May 22, 2025 (II)]**
(a) 1.8×10^{-10} (b) 5.55×10^{-4}
(c) 5.55×10^{-11} (d) 5.55×10^{-12}

85. At 25°C, the percentage of ionization of '*x*' M acetic acid is 4.242. What is the value of *x*? ($K_a = 1.8 \times 10^{-5}$)
[May 22, 2025 (I)]
(a) 0.05 (b) 0.04 (c) 0.02 (d) 0.01

86. At 25°C, the percentage of ionization of *x* M acetic acid is 4.242. What is the pH of the acetic acid solution? (log 4.242 = 0.6275); (log 0.04242 = –1.372)
($K_a = 1.8 \times 10^{-5}$) **[May 21, 2025 (II)]**
(a) 3.37 (b) 1.70 (c) 1.37 (d) 2.37

87. At 27°C. the degree of dissociation of HA (weak acid) in 0.5 M of its solution is 1%. The concentrations of H_3O^+, A^- and HA at equilibrium (in mol L^{-1}) are respectively
[May 23, 2024 (I)]
(a) 0.005, 0.005, 0.495 (b) 0.05, 0.05, 0.45
(c) 0.01, 0.01, 0.49 (d) 0.005, 0.495, 0.005

88. At 27°C, the degree of dissociation of weak acid (HA) in its 0.5M aqueous solution is 1%. Its K_a value is approximately
[May 18, 2024 (I)]
(a) 5×10^{-4} (b) 5×10^{-5}
(c) 5×10^{-6} (d) 5×10^{-8}

89. The pH of 0.01M BOH solution is 10. What is its degree of dissociation? **[May 19, 2023 (I)]**
(Given K_b of BOH is 1×10^{-6})
(a) 10% (b) 5%
(c) 2% (d) 1%

90. The K_a values of A, B and C are 1.8×10^{-4}, 5×10^{-10} and 3×10^{-8} respectively. The correct order of their acidic strength is **[July 5, 2022 (II)]**
(a) B > A > C (b) B > C > A
(c) A > B > C (d) A > C > B

91. Equal volumes of 0.5 N acetic acid and 0.5 N sodium acetate are mixed. What is the pH of resultant solution? (pK_a of acetic acid = 4.75) **[July 4, 2022 (I)]**
(a) 4.85 (b) 4.65 (c) 4.75 (d) 7.0

92. The pH of 10^{-8} M HCl solution is **[Sept. 21, 2020 (II)]**
(a) 8 (b) – 8
(c) Between 7-8 (d) Between 6-7

93. Which acid among the following has the highest pK_a value? **[Sept. 21, 2020 (I)]**
(a) HCl (b) HF (c) HI (d) HBr

94. The ionic product of water .... with increase in temperature. **[Sept. 21, 2020 (I)]**
(a) remains constant (b) increases
(c) decreases (d) may increase or decrease

95. 30.0 mL of the given HCl solution requires 20.0 mL of 0.1 M sodium carbonate solution for complete neutralisation. What is the volume of this HCl solution required to neutralise 30.0 mL of 0.2 M NaOH solution? **[Apr. 21, 2019 (II)]**
(a) 25 mL (b) 50 mL (c) 90 mL (d) 45 mL

96. If the pK_a of acetic acid and pK_b of dimethylamine are 4.76 and 3.26 respectively, the pH of dimethyl ammonium acetate solution is **[2018]**
(a) 7.75 (b) 6.75 (c) 7.0 (d) 8.5

Topic 5 Common Ion Effect, Salt Hydrolysis, Buffer Solutions and Solubility Product

97. The minimum volume of water (in L) needed to dissolve 1.5 g of $CaSO_4$ **[May 15, 2026 (II)]**
(molar mass = 136 g mol^{-1}) at 298 K is
(K_{S_p} ($CaSO_4$) at 298 K = 9×10^{-6})
(a) 6.37 (b) 7.37
(c) 3.67 (d) 3.73

98. A solution is prepared by adding 0.5 L of 0.5 M NaOH to 0.5 L of 0.55 M formic acid. What is the pH of resultant solution? **[May 15, 2026 (I)]**
(K_a of formic acid = 1.8×10^{-4} ; log (1.8) = 0.26)
(a) 3.74 (b) 4.74
(c) 2.74 (d) 3.26

99. Solution of HCN and NaCN forms a buffer solution x moles of HCN is required to prepare 1.0 L of a buffer solution of pH 9 using 0.01 moles of NaCN. What is the value of x ? **[May 14, 2026 (II)]**
(Given K_a (HCN) = 10^{-10})
(a) 9×10^{-1} (b) 9×10^{-2}
(c) 9×10^{-3} (d) 9×10^{-4}

100. Observe the following data given below. Whice set of buffer solution has highest pH? **[May 13, 2026 (I)]**

Buffer solution	Volume (in mL) of 1M solution of weak acid	Volume (in mL) of 0.1 M sodium salt of weak acid
I	4.0	4.0
II	4.0	40.0
III	40.0	4.0
IV	0.1	10.0

(a) I (b) II
(c) III (d) IV

101. The mass of CaC_2O_4 (in g) to be dissolved in distilled water to make 1.0 L of saturated solution is
(K_{SP} of $CaC_2O_4 = 2.5 \times 10^{-9}$ mol^2 L^{-2})
molar mass of CaC_2O_4 = 128 g mol^{-1})
[May 12, 2026 (II)]
(a) 0.0064 (b) 0.0032
(c) 0.0128 (d) 0.0640

102. The pH of a solution obtained by mixing 250 mL of 0.5 M NaOH, 100 mL of 0.5 M HCl and 400 mL of water is **[May 12, 2026 (I)]**
(a) 12 (b) 2
(c) 1 (d) 13

103. At T(K) K_{sp} of two ionic salts MX_2 and MX is 5×10^{-13} and 1.6×10^{-11} respectively. The ratio of molar solubility of MX_2 and MX is **[May 27, 2025 (I)]**
(a) 12.5 (b) 1.25 (c) 6.25 (d) 7.50

104. The molar solubility of PbI_2 in 0.2 M $Pb(NO_3)_2$ solution in terms of K_{sp} (solubility product) is **[May 26, 2025 (II)]**
(a) $\left(\frac{K_{sp}}{0.2}\right)^{1/2}$ (b) $\left(\frac{K_{sp}}{0.4}\right)^{1/4}$
(c) $\left(\frac{K_{sp}}{0.8}\right)^{1/2}$ (d) $\left(\frac{K_{sp}}{0.8}\right)^{1/3}$

105. What is the indicator used in Argentometric titrations ? **[May 24, 2025 (I)]**
(a) Starch solution (b) Eosin dye
(c) $KMnO_4$ solution (d) Phenolphthalein

106. When 30 mL of 0.2 M NH_4OH is added to 30 mL of 2 M NH_4Cl solution. If the pH of the buffer formed is 8.2, what is the pK_b of NH_4OH? **[May 23, 2025 (I)]**
(a) 7.2 (b) 5.8 (c) 6.8 (d) 4.8

107. At T(K), the solubility product of AgBr is 4×10^{-13}. What is its solubility in 0.1 M KBr solution? **[May 21, 2025 (I)]**
(a) 2×10^{-6} M (b) 4×10^{-10} M
(c) 4×10^{-12} M (d) 4×10^{-14} M

108. The solubility of barium phosphate of molar mass 'M' g mol^{-1} in water is x g per 100 mL at 298 K. Its solubility product is $1.08 \times \left(\frac{x}{M}\right)^a \times (10)^b$. The values of a and b respectively are **[May 21, 2024 (II)]**

(a) 7, 5 (b) 5, 7 (c) 5, 5 (d) 7, 7

109. At T(K), the solubility product of AX is 10^{-10}. What is the molar solubility of AX in 0.1 M HX solution? **[May 21, 2024 (I)]**

(a) 10^{-5} (b) 10^{-10} (c) 10^{-9} (d) 10^{-8}

110. Which of the following will make a basic buffer solution. **[May 20, 2024 (II)]**

(a) 100 mL of 0.1 M CH_3COOH + 100 mL of 0.1 M NaOH
(b) 100 mL of 0.1 M HCl + 100 mL of 0.1 M NaOH
(c) 50 mL of 0.1 M KOH + 25 mL of 0.1 M CH_3COOH
(d) 100 mL of 0.1 M HCl + 200 mL of 0.1 M NH_4OH

111. Observe the following solutions
(i) 1L of 10^{-6} M Ag NO_3
(ii) 1L of 10^{-7} M $AgNO_3$
(iii) 1L of 10^{-9} M Ag NO_3
(iv) 1L of 10^{-3} M $AgNO_3$
(v) 1L of 10^{-5} M NaCl

Which of the above two solutions when mixed will give a white precipitate, AgCl? **[May 18, 2023 (I)]**
(Given K_{sp} of AgCl = 1×10^{-10})

(a) (i), (v) (b) (ii), (v)
(c) (iv), (v) (d) (iii), (v)

112. **Statement A :** pH of buffer increases with increasing temperature.
Statement B : The value of K_W of water decreases with decreasing temperature. **[July 8, 2022 (I)]**

(a) A is correct, but B is wrong.
(b) Both A and B are correct
(c) Both A and B are wrong
(d) A is wrong but B is correct

113. At 25°C, the solubility product of MCl is 1×10^{-10}. What is its molar solubility in 0.1 M NaCl solution at same temperature? **[July 7, 2022 (II)]**

(a) 0.1 M (b) 0.05 M
(c) 10^{-9} M (d) 10^{-5} M

114. The solubility products of NiS, ZnS, CdS and HgS are 4.7×10^{-5}, 1.6×10^{-24}, 8×10^{-27} and 4×10^{-53} respectively. An aqueous solution contains Ni^{2+}, Zn^{2+}, Cd^{2+}, and Hg^{2+} of equal concentration. H_2S gas was passed into this solution very slowly. The first and the last ions that precipitate as sulphides are respectively **[July 7, 2022 (II)]**

(a) Ni^{2+}, Hg^{2+} (b) Hg^{2+}, Cd^{2+}
(c) Zn^{2+}, Hg^{2+} (d) Hg^{2+}, Ni^{2+}

115. The solubility of AgBr(s), having solubility product 5×10^{-10} in 0.2 M NaBr solution equals **[Aug. 20, 2021 (I); Similar to Sep. 21, 2020 (I)]**

(a) 5×10^{-10} M (b) 25×10^{-10} M
(c) 0.5 M (d) 0.002 M

116. The solubility product of $Ni(OH)_2$ at 298 K is 2×10^{-15} mol^3 dm^{-9}. The pH value if, its aqueous and saturated solution is **[Sept. 17, 2020 (I)]**

(a) 5 (b) 7.5
(c) 9 (d) 13

117. The solubility product of a sparingly soluble salt A_2B is 3.2×10^{-11}. Its solubility in mol L^{-1} is **[Apr. 21, 2019 (II)]**

(a) 4×10^{-4} (b) 2×10^{-4}
(c) 6×10^{-4} (d) 3×10^{-4}

118. In which of the following salts, only cationic hydrolysis is involved? **[2016]**

(a) CH_3COONH_4 (b) CH_3COONa
(c) NH_4Cl (d) Na_2SO_4

7 Redox Reactions

CHAPTER SYNOPSIS

- The reducing agent is the substance that is oxidized.

  The oxidizing agent is the substance that is reduced.

- A redox reaction is a chemical reaction in which change in oxidation numbers occurs.

- Oxidation is an increase in oxidation number. Reduction is a decrease in oxidation number.

- Ion-electron method-Acidic solution

  Step 1 : Divide the equation into two half-reactions.

  Step 2 : Balance atoms other than H and O.

  Step 3 : Balance O by adding H_2O.

  Step 4 : Balance H by adding H^+.

  Step 5 : Balance net charge by adding e^-.

  Step 6 : Make e^- gain equal e^- loss, then add half-reactions.

  Step 7 : Cancel anything that's the same on both sides.

  Additional steps in the ion-electron method for basic solutions :

  Step 8 : Add to both sides of the equation the same number of OH^- as there are H^+.

  Step 9 : Combine H^+ and OH^- to form H_2O.

  Step 10 : Cancel any H_2O that you can.

- The oxidation number of N in NO_2 is + 4. In NO, the oxidation number is +2.

Topic 1 Oxidation and Reduction Reactions

1. Observe the following reactions **[May 23, 2024 (I)]**

(i) $2KClO_3(s) \xrightarrow{\Delta} 2KCl(s)+3O_2\ (g)$

(ii) $2H_2O_2\ (aq) \xrightarrow{\Delta} 2H_2O(l) + O_2(g)$

(iii) $AgNO_3(aq)+KCl(aq) \longrightarrow AgCl(s)+KNO_3(aq)$

(iv) $2Na(s) + \frac{1}{2}O_2\ (g) \longrightarrow Na_2O(s)$

The number of redox reactions in this list is

(a) 3 (b) 4
(c) 2 (d) 1

2. In the reaction of sulphur with concentrated sulphuric acid, the oxidised product is X and reduced product is Y. X and Y are respectively **[May 21, 2024 (I)]**

(a) SO_3, SO_2 (b) SO_2, SO_2
(c) SO_2, H_2S (d) SO_2, H_2O

3. Which among the following species acts as a self-indicator? **[Aug. 19, 2021 (I)]**

(a) H_2O_2 (b) I^- (c) $Cr_2O_7^{2-}$ (d) MnO_4^-

4. The number of elements among O, Cl, F, N, P, Sn, Ti, K, Sc, which show more than one non-zero oxidation state is **[Sept. 21, 2020 (II)]**

(a) 2 (b) 3 (c) 6 (d) 8

Topic 2 Oxidation Number

5. If the molar masses of $Na_2S_2O_3$ and I_2 are M_1 and M_2 respectively, then the equivalent weights of $Na_2S_2O_3$ and I_2 in the following reaction are respectively

$2Na_2S_2O_3 + I_2 \rightarrow 2\ NaI + Na_2S_4O_6$

[May 15, 2026 (II)]

(a) M_1, M_2 (b) $M_1, \frac{M_2}{2}$

(c) $2M_1, M_2$ (d) $\frac{M_1}{2}, M_2$

6. The volume (in mL) of 10 volume H_2O_2 solution required to completely react with 200 mL of 0.4 M $KMnO_4$ solution in acidic medium is **[May 21, 2025 (I)]**

(a) 112 (b) 336 (c) 224 (d) 448

7. What is the oxidation state of S in the sulphur containing product of the following reaction?

$SO_3^{2-}(aq) + Br_2(l) + H_2O \rightarrow$ **[July 4, 2022 (II)]**

(a) +6 (b) +4 (c) +2.5 (d) +2

8. What are the oxidation states of three Br atoms in Br_3O_8 molecule **[July 4, 2022 (I)]**

(a) +5, +6, +5 (b) +6, +4, +6
(c) +7, +2, +7 (d) +6, +3, +7

9. The oxidation number of an element in a compound is evaluated on the basis of certain rules. Which of the following rules is not correct? **[Sept. 18, 2020 (I)]**

1. The oxidation number of hydrogen is always +1.
2. The algebraic sum of all the oxidation numbers of all elements in a compound is zero.
3. An element in the free or the uncombined state bears oxidation number zero.
4. In all its compounds, the oxidation number of fluorine is – 1.

(a) 1 (b) 2 (c) 3 (d) 4

Topic 3 Disproportionation and Balancing of Redox Reactions

10. Observe the following unbalanced equation

$aS_8 + b\ OH^-\ (aq) \rightarrow cS^{2-}\ (aq) + dS_2O_3^{2-}\ (aq) + eH_2O\ (l)$

In the balanced equation, the ratio of c and d is **[May 18, 2026 (II)]**

(a) 1 : 2 (b) 2 : 1 (c) 1 : 3 (d) 3 : 1

11. Observe the following unbalanced reactions

$KO_2 \xrightarrow{HOH} X + Y\uparrow + KOH$

$KMnO_4 \xrightarrow[\text{basic medium}]{X} Y + Z + KOH + H_2O$

Y and Z are respectively **[May 18, 2026 (I)]**

(a) O_2, MnO (b) O_2, MnO_2
(c) O_3, MnO_2 (d) O_3, MnO

12. Consider the following **[May 13, 2026 (I)]**

$H_3PO_2, Se_2Cl_2, HNO_2, HNO_3, H_2SO_4, H_2O_2$

How many of the above compounds under goes disproportionation reaction ?

(a) 2 (b) 3 (c) 4 (d) 5

13. Hydrolysis of chlorine nitrate gives oxoacid of chlorine $\underline{X}$ and oxoacid of nitrogen $\underline{Y}$. The oxidation states of Cl in $\underline{X}$, N in _ are respectively **[May 12, 2026 (II)]**

(a) +1, +3 (b) –1, +3
(c) +1, +5 (d) +3, +5

14. Observe the following unbalanced equation

$a\ S_8(s) + b\ OH^-\ (aq) \rightarrow$
$c\ S^{2-}\ (aq) + d\ S_2O_3^{-2}\ (aq) + e\ H_2O\ (l)$

From the balanced equation, identify the correct relations from the following sets **[May 12, 2026 (I)]**

I. $a + b = c + d + e + 1$

II. $b = 2e + d$

III. $b - a = c + e + 1$

IV. $b + d = 2c + e - 1$

The correct answer is

(a) I, II, III only (b) II, IV only

(c) I, III only (d) I, IV only

15. H_2O_2 reduces $KMnO_4$ in acidic medium to '*x*' and in basic medium to '*y*'. What are *x* and *y* ? **[May 23, 2025 (II)]**

(a) $x = MnO_2, y = Mn^{2+}$ (b) $x = Mn^{2+}, y = MnO_2$

(c) $x = MnO_4^{2-}, y = Mn^{2+}$ (d) $x = MnO_2, y = MnO_4^{2-}$

16. H_2O_2 with $KMnO_4$ in acidic medium gives a manganese compound 'X' and in basic medium gives another manganese compound 'Y'. The oxidation state of manganese in X and Y, respectively are **[May 21, 2025 (II)]**

(a) +2, +4 (b) +4, +2 (c) +3, +4 (d) +4, +3

17. The standard reduction potentials of $2H^+/H_2$, Cu^{2+}/Cu. Zn^{2+}/Zn and NO_3^-, H^+/NO are 0.0, –0.34, – 0.76 and 0.97 V respectively. Observe the following reactions

I. $Zn + HCl \rightarrow$ **[May 20, 2024 (II)]**

II. $Cu + HCl \rightarrow$

III. $Cu + HNO_3 \rightarrow$

Which reactions does not liberate H_2 (g)?

(a) II, III only (b) I, II only

(c) I, III only (d) I. II, III

18. Given below are two statements.

Statement I: In the decomposition of potassium chlorate. Cl is reduced.

Statement II: Reaction of Na with O_2 to form Na_2O is a redox reaction. **[May 20, 2024 (I)]**

(a) Both statements-I and II are correct

(b) Both statements-I and II are not correct

(c) Statement-I is correct but statement-II is not correct

(d) Statement-I is not correct but statement-II is correct

19. The disproportionation products of ortho phosphorous acid are **[May 19, 2024 (II)]**

(a) H_3PO_4, PH_3 (b) H_3PO_2, H_3PO_3

(c) H_3PO_4, HPO_3 (d) H_3PO_2, P_2H_4

20. In neutral or faintly alkaline medium, MnO_4^- oxidizes I^- to iodate. What is the volume (in L) of 0.02M $KMnO_4$ required to completely convert 1 L of 0.5 M KI solution to iodate in neutral or faintly alkaline medium?

[May 19, 2023 (I)]

(a) 5 (b) 50 (c) 20 (d) 30

21. In neutral or faintly alkaline medium, MnO_4^- oxidizes I^- to iodate. What is the number of moles of $KMnO_4$ required to completely convert 1 L of 0.5 M KI to iodate?

[May 18, 2023 (I)]

(a) 0.5 (b) 4.0 (c) 2.0 (d) 1.0

22. Observe the following reaction

$$a\,P_4\,(s) + b\,OH^-(aq) + H_2O\,(l) \rightarrow c PH_3\,(g) + d\,H_2PO_2^-\,(aq)$$

a, b, c and d are respectively **[May 17, 2023 (II)]**

(a) 1, 3, 3, 1 (b) 1, 3, 2, 3

(c) 3, 1, 3, 1 (d) 1,3, 1,3

23. What are x, y and z respectively in the following reaction?

$$xFe^{2+}(aq) + yH^+(aq) + zCr_2O_7^{2-}(aq) \rightarrow \frac{y}{2}H_2O(l) + xFe^{3+}(aq) + 2zCr^{3+}(aq)$$

[May 17, 2023 (I)]

(a) 14, 1, 6 (b) 14, 6, 1

(c) 6, 1, 14 (d) 6, 14, 1

24. Observe the following reaction

$$x\,S_8(s) + y\,OH^-(aq) \rightarrow zS^{2-}(aq) + 2S_2O_3^{2-}(aq) + 6H_2O(l)$$

x, y and z are respectively.

[May 16, 2023 (II)]

(a) 1, 12, 4 (b) 1, 12, 2

(c) 1, 4, 12 (d) 2, 12, 2

25. Observe the following reaction

$$Cl_2\,(g) + 2OH^-\,(aq) \rightarrow ClO^-\,(aq) + Cl^-\,(aq) + H_2O(l)$$

Identify the correct statements about this reaction

I. Cl_2 (g) is oxidized to ClO^- (aq)

II. Cl_2 (g) is oxidized to Cl^- (aq)

III. Cl_2 (g) is reduced to ClO^- (aq)

IV. Cl_2 (g) is reduced to Cl^- (aq)

The correct answer is **[May 15, 2023 (I)]**

(a) I, IV only (b) I, III only

(c) I, II, IV only (d) II, III only

26. Match the following **[July 7, 2022 (II)]**

List-I (Type of reaction)	**List-II (Unbalanced equation)**
(A) Combination reaction	(i) $AgNO_3 + CaCl_2 \rightarrow AgCl + Ca(NO_3)_2$
(B) Decomposition reaction	(ii) $Cl_2 \rightarrow Cl^- + ClO_3^-$
(C) Disproportionation reaction	(iii) $Mg + N_2 \rightarrow Mg_3N_2$
(D) Displacement reaction	(iv) $KClO_3 \xrightarrow{\Delta} KCl + O_2$

	A	B	C	D
(a)	(iii);	(ii);	(iv);	(i)
(b)	(i);	(iv);	(ii);	(iii)
(c)	(i);	(ii);	(iii);	(iv)
(d)	(iii);	(iv);	(ii);	(i)

27. Which of the following reactions is not a disproportionation reaction? **[July 5, 2022 (II); Similar to July 5, 2022 (II)]**

(a) $CaCO_3 \longrightarrow CaO + CO_2$
(b) $P_4 + 3NaOH + 3H_2O \longrightarrow 3NaH_2PO_2 + PH_3$
(c) $2H_2O_2 \longrightarrow 2H_2O + O_2$
(d) $2Cu^+ \longrightarrow Cu^{2+} + Cu$

28. Among P_4, S_8 and N_2, the elements which undergo disproportionation when heated with NaOH solution **[July 4, 2022 (II)]**

(a) P_4, S_8 only (b) N_2, S_8 only
(c) N_2, P_4 only (d) P_4, N_2, S_8

29. Which among the following species does not shown disproportionation reaction? **[Aug. 20, 2021 (II)]**

(a) ClO^- (b) ClO_2^- (c) ClO_3^- (d) ClO_4^-

30. Which of the following represents disproportionation of potassium chlorate? **[Sept. 21, 2020 (II)]**

(a) $2KClO_3 \longrightarrow 2KCl + 3O_2$
(b) $3KClO_3 \longrightarrow 2KClO_2 + KClO_3$
(c) $4KClO_3 \longrightarrow 3KClO_4 + KCl$
(d) None of the above

31. Which species among the following doesn't show disproportionation reactions? **[Sept. 21, 2020 (I)]**

(a) ClO_2^- (b) ClO_3^- (c) ClO^- (d) ClO_4^-

Topic 4 Electrode Potential and Oxidising, Reducing Agents

32. X, Y and Z represent three electrodes Al^{3+}/Al. $Cu^{2+}Cu$ and Ag^+/Ag^1 with E° values –1.66. 0.34 and 0.80 V respectively. The correct order of oxidising power of these three electrodes is **[May 13, 2026 (I)]**

(a) X > Y > Z (b) Z > Y > X
(c) X = Y = Z (d) Y > Z > X

33. Which one of the following reactions is not feasible? **[May 23, 2025 (I)]**

(a) $Cl_2(g) + 2KBr(aq) \longrightarrow 2KCl(g) + Br_2(l)$
(b) $Cl_2(g) + 2KI(aq) \longrightarrow 2KCl(aq) + I_2(s)$
(c) $Br_2(l) + 2KI(aq) \longrightarrow 2KBr(aq) + I_2(s)$
(d) $I_2(s) + 2KBr(aq) \longrightarrow 2KI(aq) + Br_2(l)$

34. Which one of the following alkali metals is the weakest reducing agent as per their E° values? **[May 22, 2024 (II)]**

(a) K (b) Cs (c) Li (d) Na

35. The standard reduction potentials of $2H^+/H_2$, Cu^{2+}/Cu, Zn^{2+}/Zn and NO_3^-, H^+/NO are 0.0, 0.34, – 0.76 and 0.97 V respectively. Identify the correct statements from the following **[May 21, 2024 (II)]**

I. H^+ does not oxidize Cu to Cu^{2+}
II. Zn reduces Cn^{2+} to Cu
III. NO_3^- oxidizes Cu to Cu^{2+}

(a) I, II only (b) I, II, III
(c) I, III only (d) II, III only

36. As per standard reduction potential values, which is the strongest reducing agent among the given elements? **[May 21, 2024 (I)]**

(a) Rb (b) Sr (c) Na (d) Mg

37. Which of the following statement is incorrect? **[Aug. 20, 2021 (I)]**

(a) Tl^{3+} salts are oxidising agents.
(b) Ga^+ salts are reducing agents.
(c) Pb^{4+} salts are better oxidising agents.
(d) As^{+5} salts are better oxidising agents.

8 Organic Chemistry – Some Basic Principles & Techniques

CHAPTER SYNOPSIS

- In the common system of nomenclature, prefixes iso and neo are used for the groups $Me_2CH–$ (isopropyl) and $Me_3C–$ (*tert*-butyl) groups respectively.
- Isocyanides or isonitriles or carbylamines have no IUPAC name.
- The aldehyde group (a terminal group) can be represented by two types of prefixes, i.e., *oxo* (when –CHO is at the end of the carbon chain, here its carbon is counted in the chain) and formyl when –CHO is present as a substituent, its carbon is not counted in the chain). For example,

$$\overset{3}{O=CH}-\overset{2}{CH_2}-\overset{1}{C}OOH$$

3–Oxo propanoic acid

$$HOO\overset{1}{C}-\overset{2}{CH}(CHO)-\overset{3}{C}OOH$$

2 – Formylpropan -1, 3 – dioic acid

- In IUPAC system, while using prefixes like carboxy, formyl and oxo, the carbon of the substituent group is not counted in the principal chain.
- Due to different systems of nomenclature, a given organic compound can have two or more IUPAC names but one IUPAC name can't represent two compounds.

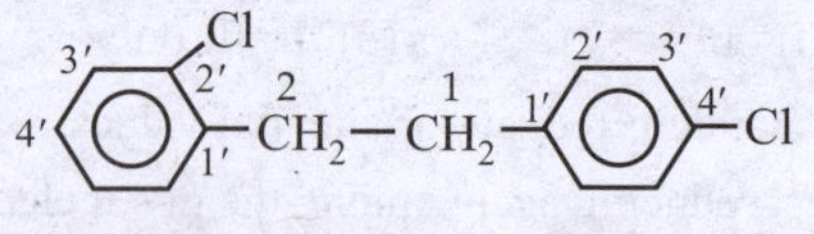

1–(4′–Chlorophenyl)–2–(2′-chlorophenyl)ethane

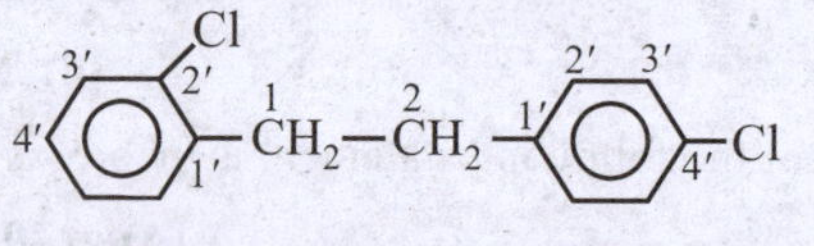

1–(2′–Chlorophenyl)–2–(4′-chlorophenyl)ethane

- When two or more prefixes consist of identical words, (e.g. chlorophenyl in the given example) the priority for citation is given to that group which contains the lowest locant at the first point of difference.
- Hydrocarbons containing double as well as triple bond is always named as **alkenyne** and not alkynene. However, in such cases numbering should be done in a way that it follows the lowest locant rule (sum of locants should be minimum). However, if there is a choice, the double bond should be given preference over the triple bond. For example,

correct numbering (←)

$$\overset{5}{CH}\equiv\overset{4}{C}-\overset{3}{CH_2}-\overset{2}{CH}=\overset{1}{CH_2}$$

wrong numbering (→)

Pent–1–en–4–yne

$$\overset{1}{CH_2}=\overset{2}{CH}-\overset{3}{CH}=\overset{4}{CH}-\overset{5}{C}\equiv\overset{6}{CH}$$

Hexa - 1, 3 - dien - 5 - yne **(correct)**

Hexa - 3, 5 - dien - 1 - yne **(wrong)**

- The order of decreasing electronegativity of hybrid orbitals is $sp > sp^2 > sp^3$.
- Conformational isomers are those isomers which arise due to rotation around a single bond.
- A meso compound is optically inactive, (due to internal compensation of rotation of plane polarised light) even though it has asymmetric centres.

- An equimolar mixture of enantiomers is called racemic mixture, which is optically inactive due to external compensation.
- Tautomerism is the type of isomerism arising by the migration of hydrogen.
- Reaction intermediates and reagents :
- Homolytic fission → Free radicals
- Heterolytic fission → Ions (Carbocations and Carbanions)
- Nucleophiles – electron rich

  Two types : (i) Anions (ii) Neutral molecules with lone pair of electrons (Lewis bases)

  Electrophiles – electron deficient.

  Two types : (i) Cations (ii) Neutral molecules with vacant orbitals (Lewis acids).
- Inductive effect is due to σ electron displacement along a chain and is permanent effect.
- +I (inductive effect) increases basicity, – I effect increases acidity of compounds.
- Characteristic reactions :

Homologous series	**Type of reactions**
(a) Alkanes	Substitution (Mostly free radical)
(b) Alkenes and alkynes	Electrophilic addition
(c) Arenes	Electrophilic substitution
(d) Alkyl halides	Nucleophilic substitution
(e) Aldehydes and ketones	Nucleophilic addition

- **Comparison of substitution and elimination reaction under different conditions.**

Type of alkyl halide	Poor nucleophile (e.g.H_2O, ROH)	Weak basic nucleophile (e.g. I^-, RS^-)	Strongly basic unhindered nucleophile (e.g. RO^-)	Strongly basic hindered nucleophile (e.g. Me_3CO^-)
Methyl halide	No reaction	S_N2	S_N2	S_N2
1°unhindered RX	No reaction	S_N2	S_N2	E2
1° hindered RX	No reaction	S_N2	E2	E2
2° alkyl halide	S_N1, E1(slow)	S_N2	E2	E2
3° alkyl halide	E1 or S_N1	S_N1, E1	E2	E2
$CH_3C(=O)CH_2CH(X)CH_3$	E1cB	E1cB	E1cB	E1cB

Topic 1 Classification and Nomenclature of Organic Compounds

1. The IUPAC name of the given compound is

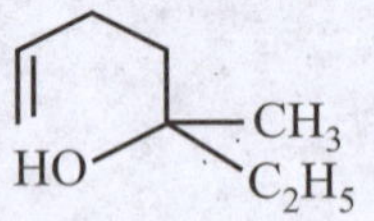

[May 15, 2026 (II)]

(a) 5-Ethylhex-1-en-5-ol
(b) 2-Ethylhex-5-en-2-ol
(c) 5-Methylhept-1-en-5-ol
(d) 3-Methylhept-6-en-3-ol

2. The IUPAC name of the following hydrocarbon is

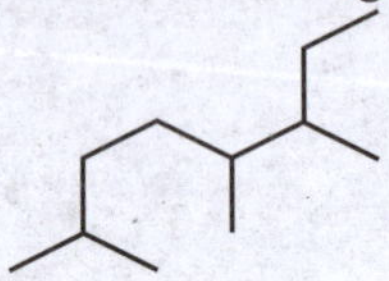

[May 15, 2026 (I)]

(a) 2, 5, 6 - Trimethyloctane
(b) 2-Ethyl - 3, 6 - dimethylheptane
(c) 3, 4, 7-Trimethyloctane
(d) 2-Ethyl - 2, 6- dimethylheptane

3. The correct IUPAC names of the compounds X and Y given below are respectively [May 14, 2026 (I)]

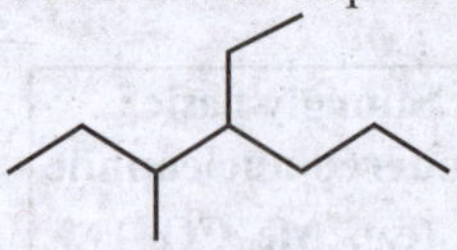
X

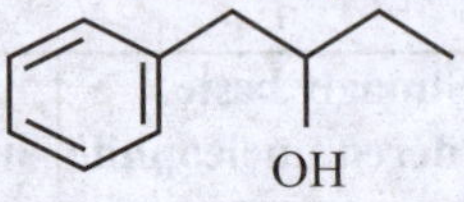

Y

(a) 3-Methyl-4-ethylheptane ; 1-Phenylbutan-2-ol
(b) 4-Ethyl-3-Methylheptane ; 1-Phenylbutan-2-ol
(c) 3-(sec-butyl)-hexane ; 2-Hydroxy-1-phenylbutane
(d) 3-Methyl-4-Ethylheptane ; 2-Hydroxybutylbenzene

4. The IUPAC name of the following structure is

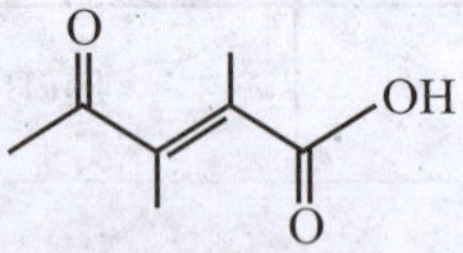

(a) 2-Carboxy-3-methylpent-2-en-3-one
(b) 4-Carboxy-3-methylpent-3-en-2-one
(c) 4-oxo-2, 3-dimethylpent-2-enoic acid
(d) 2, 3-Dimethyl-4-oxopent-2-enoic acid

5. IUPAC names of the given compounds (I) and (II) are respectively [May 26, 2025 (II)]

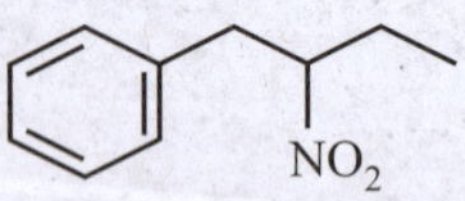

(I)

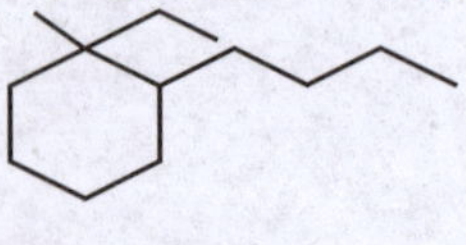
(II)

(a) 5-Phenyl-3-nitrobutane; 2-ethyl-2-methy l-l-propylcyclohexane
(b) 2-Nitro-1-phenylbutane; 2-ethyl-2-methy l-l -propylcyclohexane
(c) 2-Nitro-1-phenylbutane; l-ethyl-l-methy l-2-propylcyclohexane
(d) 3-Nitro-5-phenylbutane; 1-ethyl-1-methy l-2-propylcyclohexane

6. IUPAC name of the following compound is [May 23, 2025 (II)]

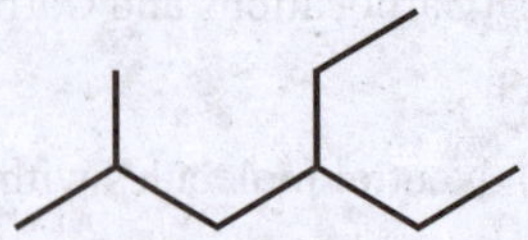

(a) 2 – Methyl – 4 – ethylhexane
(b) 4 – Ethyl – 2 – methylhexane
(c) 5 – Methyl – 3 – ethylhexane
(d) 3 – Ethyl – 5 – methylhexane

7. IUPAC names of mesityl oxide and oxalic acid are respectively [May 23, 2025 (I)]

(a) 4-Methylpent-3-en-2-one; Ethanedioic acid
(b) 4-Methylpent-3-en-2-one; Propanedioic acid
(c) 3-Methylpent-3-en-2-one; Propanedioic acid
(d) 3-Methylpent-3-en-2-one; Ethanedioic acid

8. The correct decreasing order of priority for the functional group of organic compounds in the IUPAC method of nomenclature is [May 22, 2025 (I)]

(a) –CHO > –OH > $-CONH_2$ > COCl
(b) $-CONH_2$ > –CHO > –COCl > –OH
(c) –COCl > $-CONH_2$ > –CHO > –OH
(d) –CHO > $-CONH_2$ > –COCl > –OH

9. The IUPAC name of the following compound is [May 21, 2025 (I)]

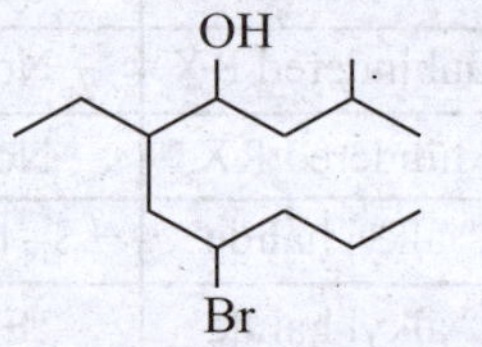

(a) 6-Ethyl-9-methyl-4-bromodec-5-en-7-ol
(b) 7-Bromo-2-methyl-5-ethyldec-5-en-4-ol
(c) 7-Bromo-5-ethyl-2-methyldec-5-en-4-ol
(d) 4-Bromo-6-ethyl-9-methyldec-5-en-7-ol

10. IUPAC names of the following compounds A and B are [May 21, 2024 (II)]

A. 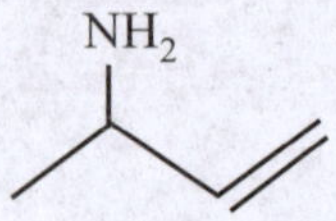

B. 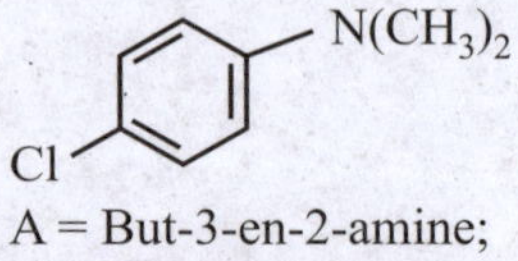

(a) A = But-3-en-2-amine;
B = 4-N. N-dimethylaminochlorobenzene
(b) A = But-l -en-3-amine;
B = 4-N, N-dimethylaminochlorobenzene
(c) A = But-l -en-3-amine;
B = 4-Chloro-N. N-dimethylbenzenamine
(d) A = But-3-en-2-amine;
B = 4-Chloro-N. N-dimethylbenzenamine

11. The number of nucleophiles in the following list is
CH_3NH_2, CH_3CHO, C_2H_4, CH_3SH **[May 20, 2024 (I)]**
(a) 3 (b) 2 (c) 4 (d) 1

12. Tropolone is an example for which of the following class of compounds? **[May 19, 2024 (II)]**
(a) Benzenoid aromatic compound
(b) Non-benzenoid aromatic compound
(c) Alicyclic compound
(d) Heterocyclic aromatic compound

13. The IUPAC name of the following molecule is

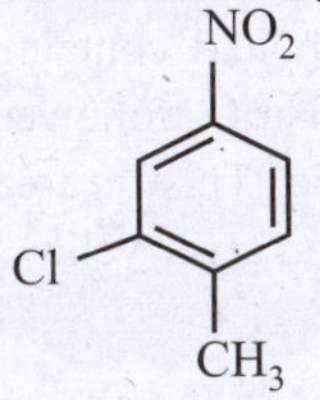

[May 19, 2023 (I)]
(a) 2-Methyl-5 nitro-1-chlorobenzene
(b) 3-Chloro-4 methyl-1-nitrobenzene
(c) 2-Chloro-1 methyl-4-nitorbenzene
(d) 2-Chloro-4 nitro-1-methylbenzene

14. The decreasing order of priority for the following functional groups in the IUPAC nomenclature is
$-SO_3H$, –CN, –COOH, –OH, CHO **[May 17, 2023 (I)]**
(a) $-COOH > -SO_3H > -CN > -CHO > -OH$
(b) $-SO_3H > -COOH > -CN > -CHO > -OH$
(c) $-COOH > -SO_3H > -CHO > -CN > -OH$
(d) $-SO_3H > COOH > -CHO > -CN > -OH$

15. IUPAC name of the following molecule is

$$CH_3-CH=\underset{\underset{Cl}{|}}{\overset{\overset{C_2H_5}{|}}{C}}-CH-\overset{\overset{O}{||}}{C}-\underset{\underset{Br^-}{|}}{CH}-\overset{\overset{C_2H_5}{|}}{CH}-C\equiv CH$$

[May 16, 2023 (I)]
(a) 6-Bromo-4-chloro-3,7-diethyl-5-oxo-8-yne-2-nonene
(b) 6-Chloro-4-bromo-3,7-diethyl-5-keto-7-ene-1-nonene
(c) 4-Chloro-6-bromo-3,7-diethyl-5-keto-8-yn-2-nonene
(d) 4-Bromo-6-chloro-3,7-diethylnon-7-en-1-yn-5-one

16. The IUPAC name of the following compound is **[July 6, 2022 (I)]**

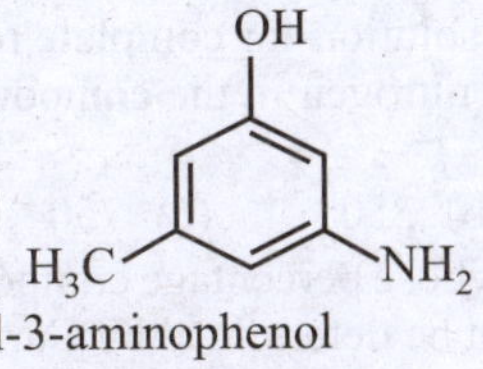

(a) 5-Methyl-3-aminophenol
(b) 3-Amino-5-methylphenol
(c) 3-Amino-5-hydroxy toluene
(d) 3-Hydroxy-5-methylaniline

17. IUPAC name of 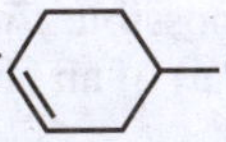 $-OCH_3$ is **[Apr. 22, 2019 (II)]**
(a) 5-methoxycyclohexene (b) methoxycyclohex-3-ene
(c) methoxycyclohex-4-ene (d) 4-methoxycycohexene

18. The IUPAC name of the following compound is **[2018]**

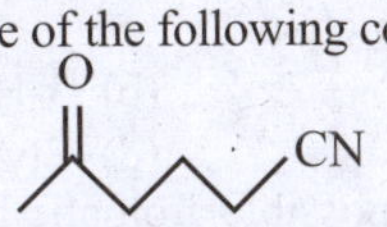

(a) 5-cyanopentan-2-one (b) 5-oxohexanenitrile
(c) 4-oxopentanenitrile (d) 2-oxopentanenitrile

19. Which of the following belongs to the homologous series of $C_5H_8O_2N$? **[2016]**
(a) $C_6H_{10}O_3N$ (b) $C_6H_8O_2N_2$
(c) $C_6H_{10}O_2N_2$ (d) $C_6H_{10}O_2N$

20. The IUPAC name of **[2016]**

$$(CH_3)_2CH-CH=CH-CH=CH-\underset{\underset{C_2H_5}{|}}{CH}-CH_3 \text{ is}$$

(a) 2, 7-dimethyl-3, 5-nonadiene
(b) 2, 7-dimethyl-2-ethylheptadiene
(c) 2-methyl-7-ethyl-3, 5-octadiene
(d) 1, 1-dimethyl-6-ethyl-2, 4-heptadiene

Topic 2 Isomerism in Organic Compounds

21. Which of the following exhibit cis-trans isomerism?
(I) 2-Methylpent-2 ene (II) Styrene
(III) 2-Chlorobut-2 ene (IV) 1-Phenylprop-1-ene
The correct answer is **[May 15, 2026 (II)]**
(a) I & II only (b) III & IV only
(c) I & III only (d) II & IV only

22. Which of the following compounds will show geometrical isomerism? **[May 13, 2026 (I)]**
I. $(CH_3)_2C=CH\,C_2H_5$ II. $C_6H_5\,CH=CH\,C_2H_5$
III. $C_6H_5\,CH=CH_2$ IV. $CH_3CH=C(Cl)CH_3$
The correct answer is
(a) I & II only (b) II & III only
(c) I & III only (d) II & IV only

23. Identify the most stable carbocation from the following **[May 26, 2025 (II)]**

(a) 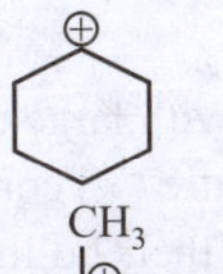

(b) 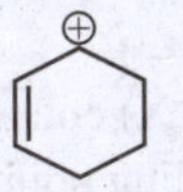

(c) 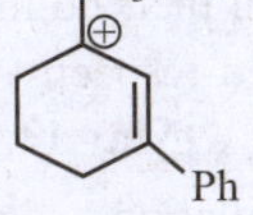

(d) 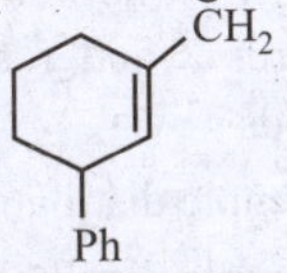

24. The number of primary (1°), secondary (2°) and tertiary (3°) alcohols possible for the formula $C_5H_{12}O$ respectively are **[May 21, 2025 (II)]**
(a) 3, 3, 2 (b) 4, 2, 2 (c) 4, 3, 1 (d) 3, 4, 1

25. The number of isomers possible for a dibromo derivate (Molecular weight = 186 u) of an alkene is (Br = 80 u) **[May 22, 2024 (I)]**
(a) 2 (b) 3 (c) 4 (d) 6

26. Which of the following compound does not exhibit geometrical isomerism? **[May 17, 2023 (II)]**
(a) 2- Butene (b) 3-Hexene
(c) But-2-enal (d) Styrene

27. The number of possible aromatic benzenoid isomers for $C_6H_4Cl_2$ are **[July 8, 2022 (I)]**
(a) 2 (b) 3 (c) 4 (d) 5

Topic 3 Concept of Reaction Mechanism in Organic Compounds and Purification

28. Consider the following carbocations

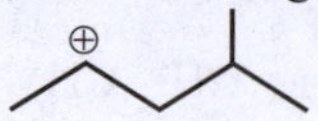
(A)

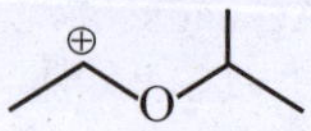
(B)

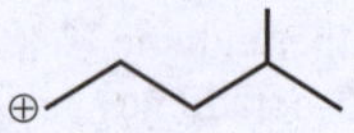
(C)

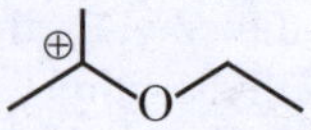
(D)

The correct stability order for the above carbocations is **[May 18, 2026 (II)]**
(a) (B) > (A) > (D) > (C) (b) (B) > (D) > (C) > (A)
(c) (D) > (B) > (C) > (A) (d) (D) > (B) > (A) > (C)

29. In the estimation of sulphur by Carius method, x g of an organic compound gave 0.233 g of $BaSO_4$. If the percentage of sulphur in it is 8.89%, the value of x is (At. wt; Ba = 137 u, S = 32 u, O = 16 u) **[May 18, 2026 (II)]**
(a) 0.12 (b) 0.24
(c) 0.36 (d) 0.48

30. 1.5 g of an organic compound was analysed by Kjeldahl's method for estimation of nitrogen. The ammonia liberated was passed into 30 mL of 1N HCl solution. The remaining HCl was further neutralised by 120 mL of N/10 NaOH solution. The percentage of nitrogen in the compound is **[May 15, 2026 (I)]**
(a) 18.6 (b) 16.8
(c) 36.3 (d) 28.4

31. A mixture (X) contains two liquids with large difference in their boiling points. Another mixture (Y) contains two liquids with not much difference in their boiling points. Mixtures X and Y can be separated respectively by the methods **[May 14, 2026 (I)]**
(a) Simple distillation, Steam distillation
(b) Simple distillation, Fractional distillation
(c) Fractional distillation, Simple distillation
(d) Steam distillation, Fractional distillation

32. In the four species (I, II, III and IV) given below, σ and π-electrons are delocalized in two species (X). Only π-electrons are delocalized in other two species (Y). What are X and Y respectively? **[May 13, 2026 (II)]**

But-2-ene	Tropylium cation
I	II
Nitrobenzene	Toluene
III	IV

(a) X = II, IV; Y = I, III (b) X = II, III; Y = I, IV
(c) X = I, III; Y = II, IV (d) X = I, IV; Y = II, III

33. An organic compound containing an extra element E on reaction with Na_2O_2 followed by boiling with HNO_3 gives a compound. This on treatment with ammonium molybdate solution gives yellow precipitate. What is E? **[May 13, 2026 (I)]**
(a) S (b) N
(c) P (d) I

34. Which of the following will be suitable for estimation of nitrogen by Kjeldahl's method? **[May 12, 2026 (II)]**
(a) Benzene diazonium chloride
(b) Nitrobenzene
(c) Amino benzene
(d) Pyridine

35. 0.248 g of an organic compound was strongly heated in a Carius tube with fuming HNO_3. Phosphoric acid so produced was precipitated as $MgNH_4PO_4$. This on ignition gave 0.444 g of $Mg_2P_2O_7$. The percentage of phosphorus in the compound is **[May 12, 2026 (I)]**
(Atomic weight : Mg = 24 u, P = 31 u, O = 16 u)
(a) 25 (b) 34
(c) 50 (d) 68

36. In compound (X), hyperconjugation is present and in (Y), resonance effect is present. What are X and Y, respectively?
(a) Toluene, prop–2–en–1–ol **[May 24, 2025 (I)]**
(b) Aniline, 2–propenal
(c) Toluene, nitrobenzene
(d) 1–Bromopropane, phenol

37. 'x' mg of an organic compound was analysed by Kjeldahl method. The ammonia evolved was absorbed in 50 mL of 0.5 M H_2SO_4. The unused acid required 60 mL of 0.5 M NaOH solution for complete neutralisation. If the percentage of nitrogen in the compound is 56, the value of x is **[May 23, 2025 (I)]**
(a) 500 (b) 250 (c) 750 (d) 375

38. The element whose percentage composition in an organic compound can be determined by Carius method is **[May 23, 2025 (I)]**
(a) Nitrogen (b) Sulphur
(c) Carbon (d) Oxygen

39. Which method is used to purify liquids having very high boiling points and liquids which decompose at or below their boiling point? **[May 22, 2025 (II)]**
(a) Distillation
(b) Fractional distillation
(c) Distillation under reduced pressure
(d) Steam distillation

40. Species A, B, C, D formed in the following bond cleavages respectively are **[May 22, 2024 (II)]**

$CH_3CH_2 - I \longrightarrow A + B$

$CH_3CH_2 - Cu \longrightarrow C + D$

(a) $CH_3CH_2^+$, I^-, $CH_3CH_2^-$, Cu^+
(b) $CH_3CH_2^+$, I^-, $CH_3CH_2^+$, Cu^-
(c) $CH_3CH_2^-$, I^+, $CH_3CH_2^+$, Cu^-
(d) $CH_3CH_2^-$, I^+, $CH_3CH_2^-$, Cu^+

41. Assertion (A): Carboxylic acids are more acidic than phenols.
Reason (R): Resonance structures of carboxylate ion are equivalent, while resonance structures of phenoxide ion are not equivalent. **[May 22, 2024 (II)]**
(a) Both (A) and (R) are correct and (R) is the correct explanation of (A)
(b) Both (A) and (R) are correct But (R) is not the correct explanation of (A)
(c) (A) is correct but (R) is incorrect
(d) (A) is incorrect but (R) is correct

42. Arrange the following in the correct order of their acidic strength **[May 22, 2024 (I)]**

I. 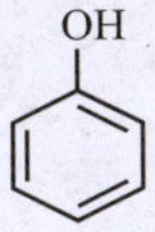

II. 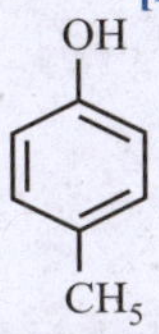

III. 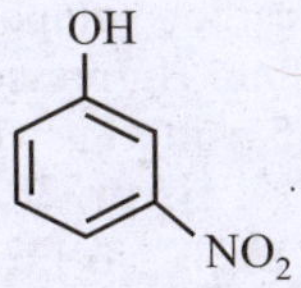

IV. 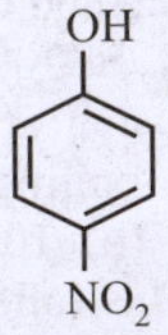

(a) III > IV > I > II (b) IV > III > I > II
(c) II > I > III > IV (d) I > IV > III > II

43. Number of deactivating groups of the following is
$-Cl$, $-SO_3H$, $-OH$, $-NHC_2H_5$, $-COOCH_3$, $-CH_3$ **[May 21, 2024 (II)]**
(a) 4 (b) 3 (c) 2 (d) 1

44. Arrange the following in decreasing order of their basicity **[May 21, 2024 (I)]**

A. 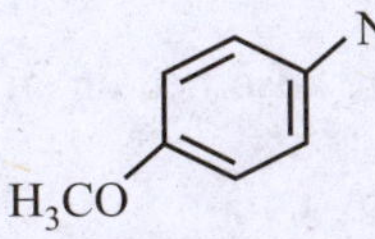

B. 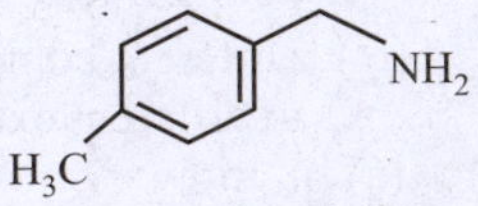

C. 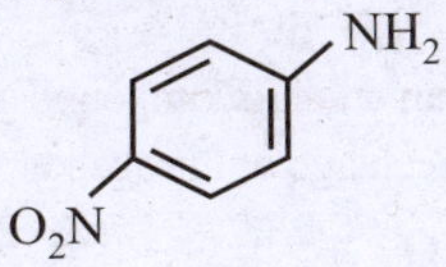

(a) B > C > A (b) B > A > C
(c) A > B > C (d) A > C > B

45. A mixture of substances A, B, C, D is subjected to column chromatography. The degree of adsorption is in the order of D > B > C > A. The column is eluted with suitable solvent. Identify the correct statement with respect to separation of mixture **[May 20, 2024 (II)]**
(a) D comes out first from the column
(b) A comes out first from the column
(c) C comes out after B from the column
(d) B comes out after D from the column

46. From the following identify the groups that exhibit negative resonance (–R) effect when attached to conjugated system **[May 18, 2024 (I)]**

formyl	amino	alkoxy	cyano	nitro
A	B	C	D	E

(a) A, C, E only (b) B, C, D only
(c) A, D, E only (d) B, D, E only

47. Arrange the following in decreasing order of their acidity **[May 18, 2024 (I)]**

(A) 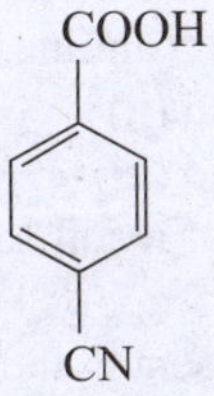

(B) 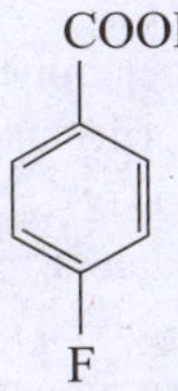

(C) 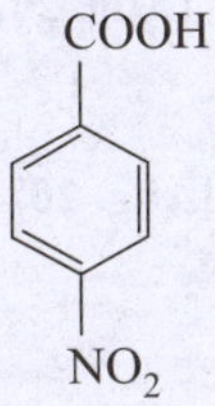

(a) C > B > A (b) C > A > B
(c) B > C > A (d) B > A > C

48. Arrange the following free radicals in the correct order of their stability

(i) $CH_2 = \dot{C}H$ (ii) $\dot{C}H_3$

(iii) $CH_3 - \dot{C}H - CH_3$ (iv) $(CH_3)_3\dot{C}$

[May 17, 2023 (I)]

(a) i > ii > iii > iv (b) iv > iii > ii > i
(c) i < ii < iii < iv (d) iv > iii > i > ii

49. Identify the molecules which have sp-hybridized carbon(s) from the list given under. **[July 7, 2022 (II)]**
I. Ethane nitrile, II. Buta-1, 3 - diene,
III. Propa-1, 2-diene, IV. Ethyne V. Benzene
(a) I, II, III only (b) II, III, IV only
(c) III, IV, V only (d) I, III, IV only

50. The correct order of acidity of the following is **[July 4, 2022 (I)]**

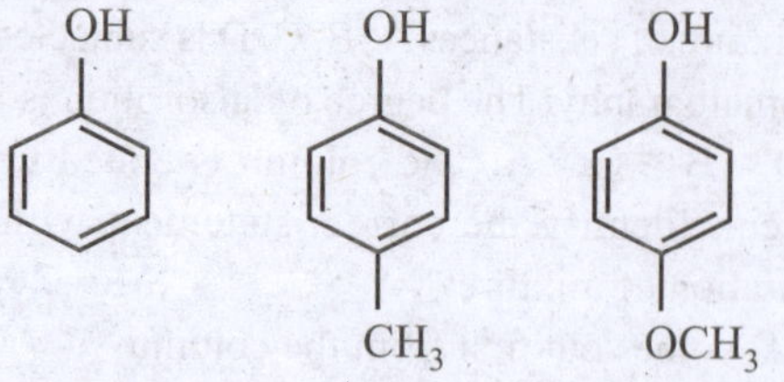

I II III

(a) III > II > I (b) II > III > I
(c) I > II > III (d) III > I > II

51. In Lassaigne sodium fusion test, N and S of an organic compounds are converted into **[Aug. 23, 2021 (I)]**
(a) NaCN (b) Na_2S (c) NaCNS (d) NaNS

52. Which of the following statements are correct? **[Aug. 23, 2021 (I)]**
(i) Inductive effect and resonance effect is possible in chlorobenzene.
(ii) Resonance effect dominates over inductive effect in anisole.
(iii) *p*-Nitrobenzoic acid is less acidic than *m*-Nitrobenzoic acid.
(iv) Diphenylamine is more basic than aniline.
(a) (i), (ii), (iii) and (iv) (b) (i) and (ii)
(c) (iii) and (iv) (d) (i) and (iii)

53. Using Kjeldahl's method over 1 g of a soil sample, the ammonia evolved could neutralise 25 mL of 1 MH_2SO_4. Then, the percentage of nitrogen present in the sample is **[Aug. 20, 2021 (I)]**
(a) 100% (b) 60% (c) 70% (d) 25%

54. Which of the following is not explained by hyperconjugation? **[Aug. 20, 2021 (II)]**
(a) Stability order of carbanions
(b) Stability order of free radicals
(c) Stability order of carbocations
(d) Stability of alkenes

55. When difference in boiling points of two liquids is too small, then the separation is carried out by **[Aug. 19, 2021 (I)]**
(a) steam distillation (b) simple distillation
(c) fractional distillation (d) vacuum distillation

56. In Lassaigne's test for halogens, it is necessary to remove *X* and *Y* from the sodium fusion extract, if nitrogen and sulphur are present. This is done by boiling the extract with *Z*. Identify *X, Y* and *Z*. **[Aug. 19, 2021 (II)]**
(a) $X = NaNO_3$, $Y = Na_2SO_4$, $Z =$ conc. HNO_3
(b) $X = NaNH_2$, $Y = NaSH$, $Z =$ conc. HCl
(c) $X = Na_2NO_2$, $Y = NaSO_3H$, $Z =$ conc. H_2SO_4
(d) $X = NaCN$, $Y = Na_2S$, $Z =$ conc. HNO_3

57. Which of the products indicates the presence of sulphur atom in an organic compound, in qualitative elemental analysis? **[Sept. 18, 2020 (I)]**
(a) Fe_2SO_4 (b) ZnS (c) MgS (d) PbS

58. Which of the following is most stable form for the given structure, after rearrangement? **[Sept. 17, 2020 (I)]**

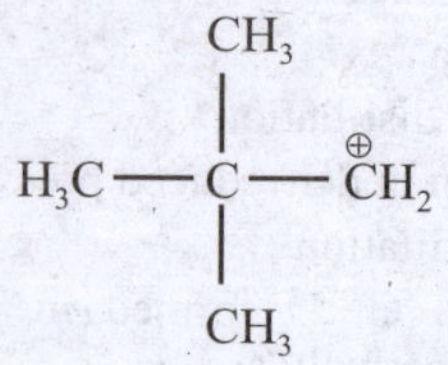

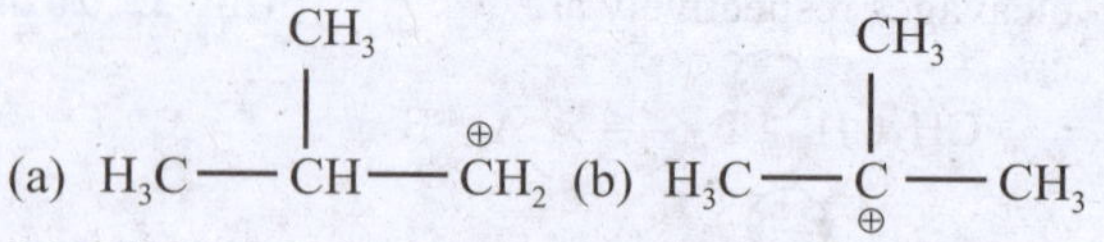

(c) $CH_3-\overset{\oplus}{C}H-CH_2-CH_3$

(d) $CH_3-CH_2-CH_2-\overset{\oplus}{C}H_2$

59. For which of the following, Kjeldahl's method is not used for the estimation of nitrogen? **[Apr. 21, 2019 (I)]**
I. Aniline II. Azobenzene
III. Nitrobenzene IV. Pyridine
(a) II, III, IV (b) II, III only
(c) III, IV only (d) I, III, IV

60. Identify the compound, which has maximum number of no bond resonance structures. **[Apr. 21, 2019 (I)]**

(a) 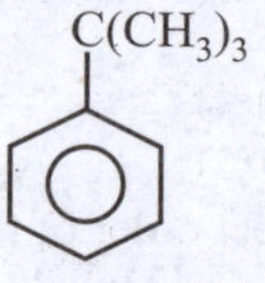
(b) 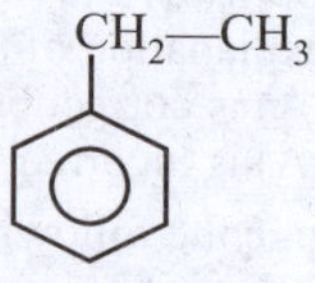
(c) 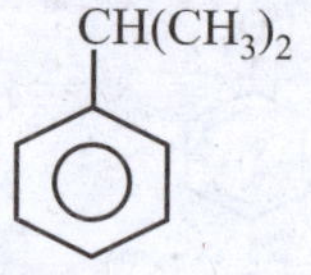
(d) 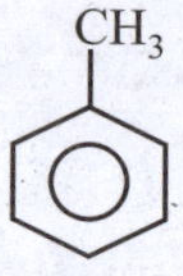

61. In Dumas method one gram of carbon compound gives 50 mL of N_2 at 300 K and 740 mm Hg pressure. If the aqueous tension at 300 K is 15 mm Hg, what is the percentage of nitrogen in it? **[Apr. 20, 2019 (I)]**
(a) 5.42 (b) 10.84 (c) 21.68 (d) 2.71

62. Which of the following is used in the estimation of carbon monoxide? **[2017]**
(a) I_2O_4 (b) BrO_3 (c) Cl_2O_7 (d) I_2O_5

63. Identify the correct statements from the following **[2017]**
(i) Electromeric effect is a permanent effect.
(ii) Hyperconjugation is a temporary effect.
(iii) Fractional distillation is used to separate two liquids from a mixture if the difference in their boiling points is less.
(iv) Different compounds are adsorbed on an adsorbent to different extents.
(a) ii, iii, iv (b) i, ii, iii
(c) ii, iv (d) iii, iv

64. In Dumas method, 0.3 g of an organic compound gave 45 mL of nitrogen at STP. The percentage of nitrogen is **[2016]**
(a) 16.9 (b) 18.7 (c) 23.2 (d) 29.6

9 Hydrocarbons

CHAPTER SYNOPSIS

- Pyrolytic cracking is a process in which higher alkanes decompose to a mixture of smaller hydrocarbons, when it is heated strongly, in absence of oxygen.
- Combustion is a process in which hydrocarbons decompose to CO_2 and H_2O (ℓ) when they are completely burnt in air/O_2.
- In dehydration and dehydrohalogenation the preferential order for removal of hydrogen is 3° > 2° > 1° (Saytzeff's rule).
- Alkenes undergo *anti*-Markownikov addition only with HBr in presence of peroxides.
- All *o*- and *p*-directing groups (except – X) are ring activating groups.

  They are : – OH, – NH_2, – R, – OR, etc.
- All *m*-directing groups are ring deactivating groups. They are : – CHO, – COOH, – NO_2, – CN, – $\overset{+}{N}R_3$, etc.

Group	Electronic effects and their net result	Rate controlling effect	Oreinting effect
— $\ddot{O}$:$^-$ (Phenoxide ion)	+ E, + M, + I (Electron release)	Strongly activating	*o, p*
— $\ddot{N}R_2$, — $\ddot{N}HR$, — $\ddot{N}H_2$, — $\ddot{O}H$, — $\ddot{O}R$	+ E, + M, – I (Electron release)	Strongly activating	*o, p*
—$\ddot{N}HCOR$, — $\ddot{O}COR$	+ E, + M, – I (Electron release)	Moderately activating	*o, p*
—C_6H_5	+ M, – I (Electron release)	Weakly activating	*o, p*
—R	+ I, hyperconjugation	Weakly activating	*o, p*
—CH = CH_2	+M (Electron release)		*o, p*
— $\ddot{Cl}$:, — $\ddot{Br}$:, $\ddot{I}$:	+ E, + M, – I (Electron release)	Weakly deactivating	*o, p*
—NO_2, —CN, —SO_3H, —COOH, —COOR, —CHO, —COR	– E, – M, – I (Electron withdrawl)	Strongly deactivating	*m*
— $\overset{+}{N}H_3$, — $\overset{+}{N}R_3$	– I (Electron withdrawl)	Strongly deactivating	*m*
—CCl_3	—I, hyperconjugation (Electron withdrawl)	Strongly deactivating	*m*

Topic 1 Alkanes

1. The number of monochloro derivatives possible for (i) Isopentane (ii) neopentane and (iii) 2, 3- dimethylbutane are x, y and z respectively. The sum of x, y and z is **[May 15, 2026 (II)]**

(a) 6 (b) 7

(c) 8 (d) 5

2. Consider the sets I, II and III. Identify the set(s) which is (are) correctly matched. **[May 27, 2025 (I)]**

I. Staggered ethane > eclipsed ethane ...... torsional strain.

II. 2, 2-Dimethyl butane > 2-methylpentane ......boiling point

III. cis-But-2-ene > trans-But-2-ene ....dipole moment

(a) I, II only (b) II, III only

(c) III only (d) I, II, III

3. The empirical formula weight of 'Z' in the given reaction sequence is n-propyl bromide **[May 23, 2025 (II)]**

$$\xrightarrow[\text{Dry ether}]{\text{Na}} X \xrightarrow[\substack{773K \\ 20atm}]{V_2O_5} Y \xrightarrow[\substack{UV \\ 500K}]{Cl_2} Z$$

(a) 47.5 (b) 54.5

(c) 84.5 (d) 48.5

4. Consider the following : **[May 22, 2025 (I)]**

Statement-I : Kolbe's electrolysis of sodium propionate gives n-hexane as product.

Statement-II : In Kolbe's process CO_2 is liberated at anode and H_2 is liberated at cathode.

Correct answer is

(a) Both statement-I and statement-II are correct.

(b) Both statement-I and statement-II are not correct.

(c) Statement-I is correct, but statement-II is not correct.

(d) Statement-I is not correct, but statement-II is correct.

5. The catalyst used for the isomerisation of *n*-alkanes to branched chain alkanes is **[May 21, 2025 (II)]**

(a) Anhy.$AlCl_3$ / HCl (b) Mo_2O_3

(c) $FeCl_3$ (d) $TiCl_4 + R_3Al$

6. What are X and Y respectively in the following reaction sequence? **[May 22, 2024 (II), May 15, 2023]**

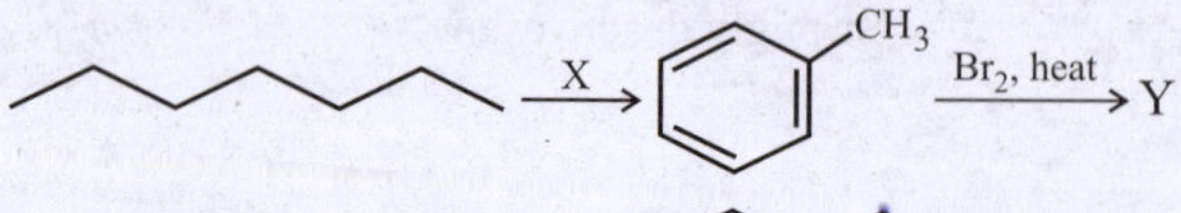

(a) $FeCl_3$, 773 K, 10-20 atm; 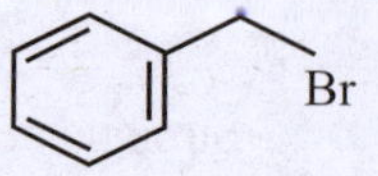

(b) Mo_2O_3, 770 K; 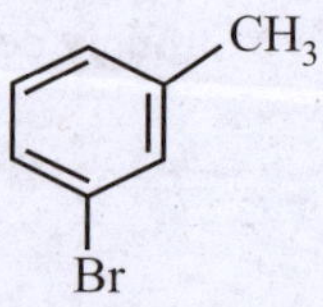

(c) $AlCl_3$, Δ, 10-20 atm; 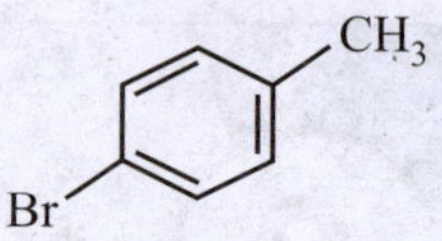

(d) Cr_2O_3, 773 K, 10-20 atm; 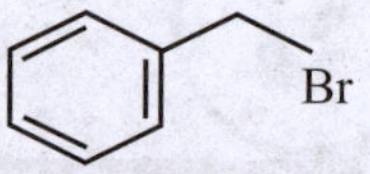

7. In Kolbe's electrolysis of sodium propanoate, products formed at anode and cathode are respectively **[May 22, 2024 (I); Similar to May 15, 2023 (I)]**

(a) C_2H_6, H_2 (b) C_3H_8, H_2

(c) C_4H_{10}, H_2 (d) H_2, C_4H_{10}

8. A mixture of ethyl iodide and n-propyl iodide is subjected to Wurtz reaction. The hydrocarbon which will not be formed is **[May 21, 2024 (I)]**

(a) Butane (b) Propane (c) Pentane (d) Hexane

9. A dibromide X ($C_4H_8Br_2$) on dehydrohalogenation gave Y which on reduction with Z gave non polar isomer of C_4H_8. What are X and Z respectively? **[May 18, 2024 (I)]**

(a) 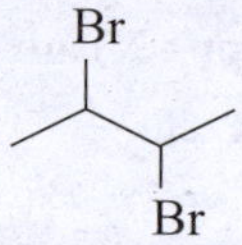 Na/NH_3 (*l*)

(b) 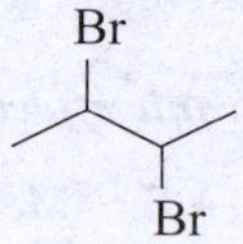 Pd / C

(c) 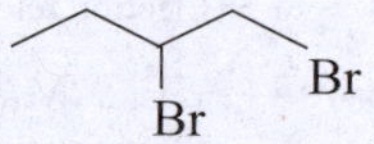 Na / NH_3(*l*)

(d) 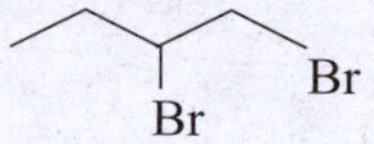 Pd/C

10. An alkyl halide C_3H_7Cl, on reaction with a reagent X gave the major product Y (C_4H_7N). Y on hydrolysis released gas which turns red litmus to blue. What are X and Y? **[May 18, 2024 (I)]**

(a) KCN/C_2H_5OH, 

(b) KCN/C_2H_5OH, 

(c) $AgCN/C_2H_5OH$, 

(d) $AgCN/C_2H_5OH$, 

11. Ethane on heating with a regulated supply of air at high pressure in presence of manganese acetate forms 'Q', 'Q' is **[May 19, 2023 (I)]**

(a) CH_3CH_2OH (b) CH_3CHO

(c) HCOOH (d) CH_3COOH

12. The correct order of boiling points of following molecules is

(i) n-Hexane (ii) 2-methylpentane

(iii) 2,3- dimethylbutane **[May 18, 2023 (II)]**

(a) i > ii > iii (b) iii > ii > i

(c) iii > i > ii (d) i > iii > ii

13. The major product of the following reaction is

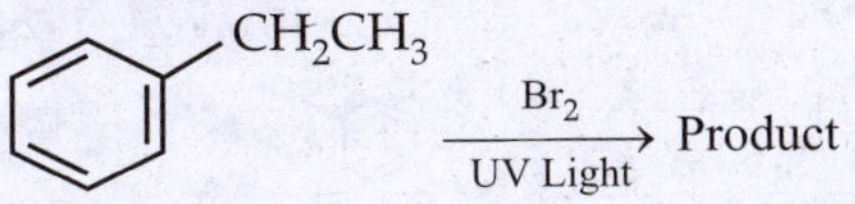

[May 16, 2023 (II)]

(a) 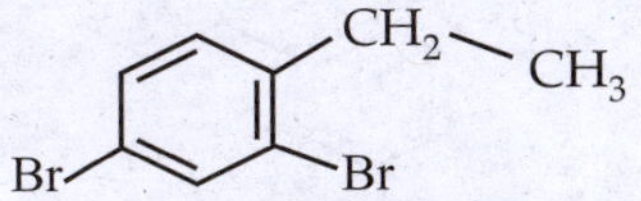

(b) 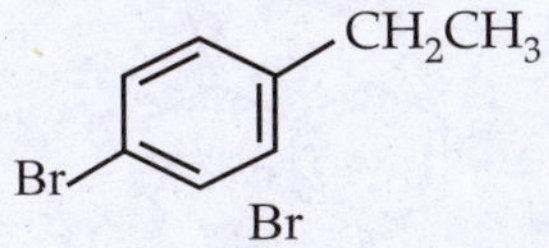

(c) 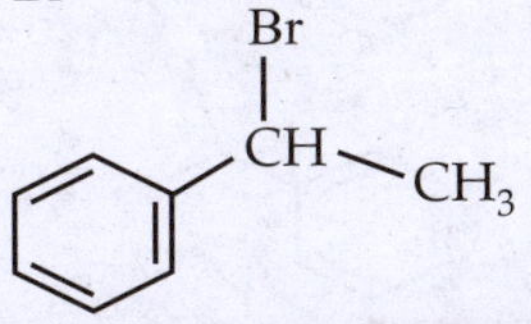

(d) 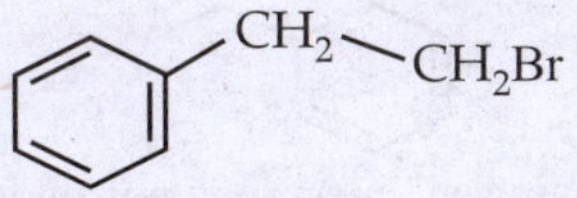

14. Identify the starting compound 'P' in the following reaction. [July 8, 2022 (I)]

$$P \xrightarrow{\text{Na / dry ether}} (CH_3)_2CHCH_2CH_2CH(CH_3)_2$$

(a) 1-Bromo-2-methylpropane
(b) 1-Bromobutane
(c) 2-Bromopropene
(d) 2-Bromobutane

15. The suitable reagents for the conversion of methane into methyl iodide are [Aug. 23, 2021 (II)]

(a) I_2, HNO_2 (b) I_2, H_2O_2
(c) I_2, H_2O (d) I_2, HNO_3

16. **Assertion (A):** Sodium acetate on Kolbe's electrolysis gives ethane.
Reason (R): Methyl free radical is formed at cathode. [Aug. 19, 2021 (I)]

(a) Both A and R are true and R is a correct explanation of A.
(b) Both A and R are true but R is not a correct explanation of A.
(c) A is true but R is false.
(d) A is false but R is true.

17. Wurtz reaction of bromoethane gives *n*-butane. Sodium salt of *X* on heating with sodalime also results in *n*-butane. Compound *X* is [Apr. 22, 2019 (I)]

(a) $CH_3CH_2CH_2COOH$ (b) $CH_3(CH_2)_3COOH$
(c) $CH_3(CH_2)_4COOH$ (d) CH_3CH_2COOH

18. Sodium acetate was electrolysed by Kolbe's method to form two gases *A* and *B* at anode. *C* and *D* are formed, when *B* is heated with regulated supply of O_2 or air in the presence of $(CH_3COO)_2Mn$. *C* reacts with NaOH to form a salt. *A* and *D* are respectively, [Apr. 20, 2019 (II)]

(a) CO_2, CH_3COOH (b) CO_2, H_2O
(c) C_2H_6, H_2O (d) CO_2, H_2O_2

19. Identify the correct statements from the following
(i) Petrol and CNG operated automobiles cause less pollution
(ii) Alkanes having tertiary hydrogen can be oxidised to alcohols by $KMnO_4$
(iii) Methane can be prepared by Kolbe's electrolytic method.
(iv) Alkyl chloride on reduction with zinc and dilute hydrochloric acid gives alkane [2018]

(a) (i), (iii), (iv) (b) (i), (ii)
(c) (i), (ii), (iv) (d) (iii), (iv)

Topic 2 Alkenes

20. Identify the end product Z in the given sequence of reactions. [May 18, 2026 (I)]

$$C_3H_6 \xrightarrow[(C_6H_5CO)_2O_2]{HBr} X \xrightarrow[\text{Anhy. } AlCl_3]{C_6H_6} Y \xrightarrow[\text{(ii) } H_3O^+ \text{ (iii) NaOH/CaO, } \Delta]{\text{(i) } KMnO_4/OH^-} Z$$

(a) Toluene (b) Cumene
(c) Benzene (d) Xylene

21. An alkene (X) with formula C_5H_{10} on ozonolysis gives butanone and methanal. X with HBr in the presence of organic peroxide gives Y as major product. When Y is subjected to Wurtz reaction gives Z. The number of 1°, 2° and 3° carbons in Z respectively are [May 15, 2026 (I)]

(a) 4, 4, 2 (b) 4, 2, 4
(c) 3, 3, 4 (d) 5, 3, 2

22. Observe the following reaction sequence

$$\underset{X}{CH_3CH_2CH=CH_2} \xrightarrow{HBr} \underset{\text{major}}{Y} \xrightarrow{\text{alc. KOH}} \underset{\text{major}}{Z}$$

Correct statement regarding Z is [May 14, 2026 (II)]

(a) Number of π bonds in it is two
(b) Number of hyper conjugative resonance structures possible for it is 6
(c) It does not exhibit cis-trans isomerism
(d) It is the chain isomer of X

23. An isomer of C_4H_8 is X, which exhibits cis-trans isomerism. Y is the chain isomer of X. Products obtained from ozonolysis of Y are [May 14, 2026 (II)]

(a) $CH_3CHO + CH_3CHO$
(b) $CH_3\,CH_2\,CHO + HCOOH$
(c) $CH_3\,CO\,CH_3 + HCHO$
(d) $CH_3\,CH_2\,COOH + CO_2$

24. What are X and Y in the following set of reactions respectively? **[May 14, 2026 (I)]**

I. 2-Methylpropene $\xrightarrow[H^+]{H_2O}$ X

II. 2-Methylpropane $\xrightarrow{KMnO_4}$ Y

(a) 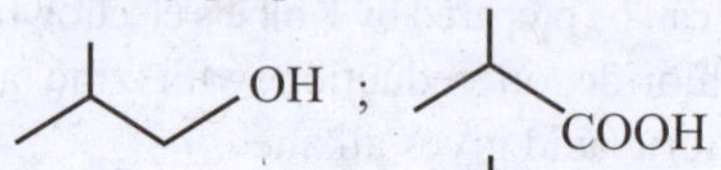

(b) 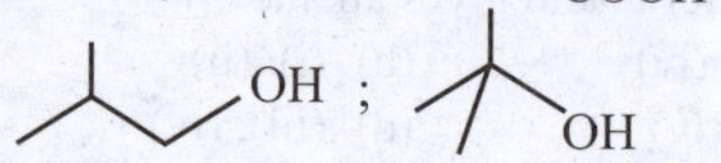

(c) 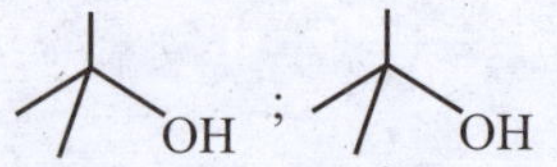

(d) 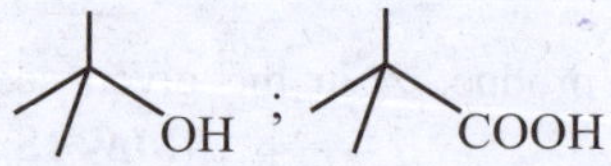

25. The number of hyperconjugative hydrogens present in the product Y is **[May 13, 2026 (I)]**

$CH_2 = CH_2 \xrightarrow{HBr} X \xrightarrow[\text{Anhy. } AlCl_3]{C_6H_6} Y$

(a) 2 (b) 3
(c) 5 (d) 1

26. Consider the following reactions in which 'P' is the major product **[May 12, 2026 (I)]**

$CH_3 - CH = CH_2 \xrightarrow[\text{Benzoyl peroxide}]{HBr} P \xrightarrow{\text{Finkelstein reaction}} Q$

$P \xrightarrow{\text{Swarts reaction}} R$

The correct order of reactivity of P, Q and R towards S_N2 reaction is

(a) P > Q > R (b) R > Q > P
(c) Q > P > R (d) Q > R > P

27. The IUPAC name of the end product Z in the given reaction sequence is **[May 12, 2026 (I)]**

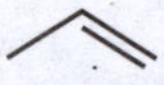

$\xrightarrow[\text{ii) alc. KOH } \Delta]{\text{i) } Br_2/CCl_4} X \xrightarrow[\Delta]{NaNH_2} Y \xrightarrow{\text{Excess HBr}} Z$

(a) 1, 1-Dibromopropane (b) 1,2-Dibromopropane
(c) 1, 3-Dibromopropane (d) 2, 2-Dibromopropane

28. What are X, Y, Z in the following reaction sequence? **[May 22, 2025 (II)]**

But-2-ene $\xrightarrow{X}$ Ethanoic acid $\xrightarrow{Y}$ Ethanoyl chloride $\xrightarrow[\text{Anhy. } AlCl_3]{\text{Benzene}}$ Z

(a) $KMnO_4 / H^+$; $SOCl_2$; Acetophenone
(b) $KMnO_4 / H^+$; Cl_2; Propiophenone
(c) Cold $KMnO_4$; $SOCl_2$; Propiophenone
(d) Cold $KMnO_4$; Cl_2; Acetophenone

29. Which of the following sequence of reagents convert 3-hexene to propane ? **[May 23, 2024 (I)]**

(a) $KMnO_4 | H^+$: NaOH, CaO
(b) (i) O_3 (ii) Zn H_2O: $NaBH_4$
(c) (i) O_3, (ii) Zn, H_2O ; Zn-Hg, HCl
(d) $KMnO_4 | H^+$; $LiAlH_4$, H_2O

30. What are X and Y respectively in the following reaction sequence? **[May 21, 2024 (II)]**

$C_3H_6 \xrightarrow[(C_6H_5CO)_2 O_2]{HBr} X \xrightarrow[\text{Na/ dry ether}]{} Y$ 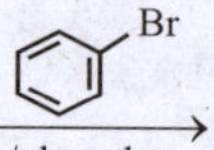

(a) 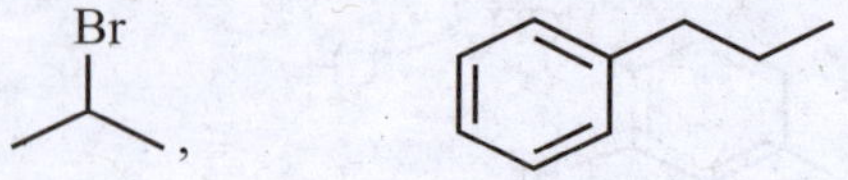

(b) 

(c) 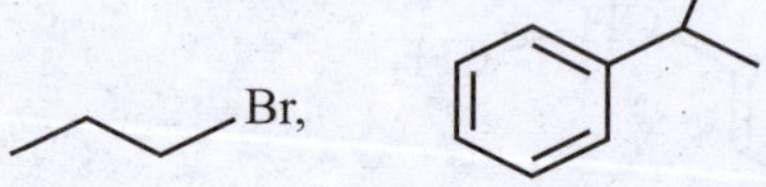

(d) 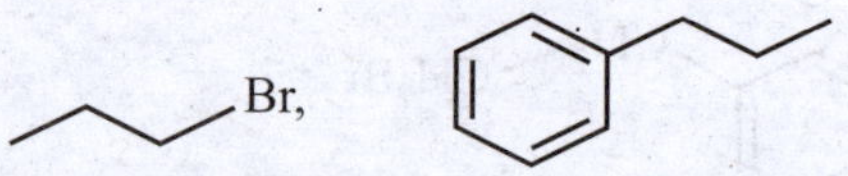

31. Which of the following alkenes does not undergo anti-Markovnikov addition of HBr? **[May 21, 2024 (I)]**

(a) Propene (b) 1 -Butene
(c) 2-Butene (d) 3-Methyl-2-pentene

32. What is X in the following reaction? **[May 20, 2024 (II)]**

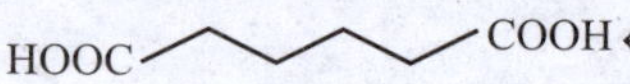

$\xleftarrow[\Delta]{KMnO_4-H_2SO_4} C_6H_{10} \xrightarrow[\text{UV light}]{Br_2} X$

(a) $H_3C-CH_2-C \equiv C-CH_2-CH_2Br$

(b) $H_3C-CH_2-C \equiv C-\underset{\displaystyle Br}{\underset{|}{CH}}-CH_3$

(c) 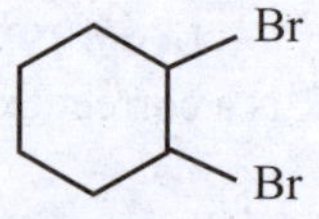

(d) 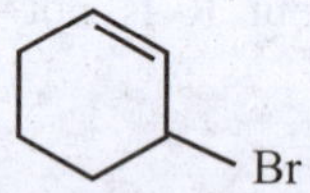

33. An alkene X (C_4H_8) on reaction with HBr gave Y (C_4H_9Br). Reaction of Y with benzene in the presence of anhydrous $AlCl_3$ gave Z which is resistant to oxidation with $KMnO_4$ - KOH. What are X, Y, Z respectively? **[May 20, 2024 (I)]**

(a) 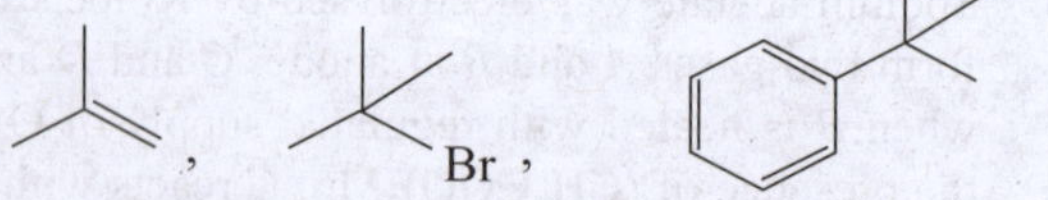

(b) 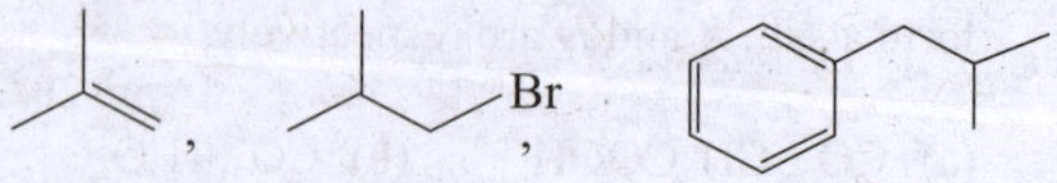

(c) 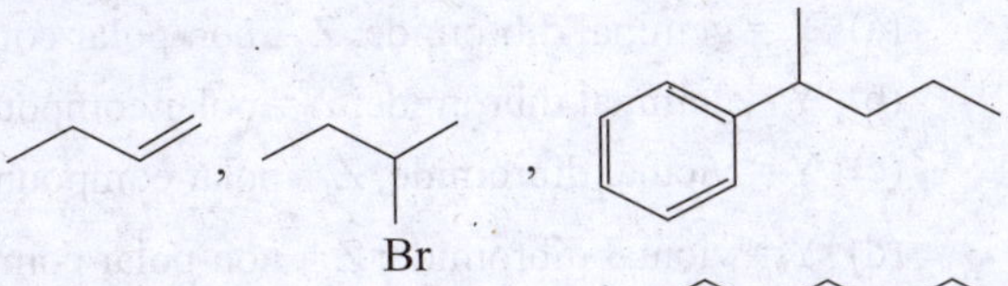

(d) 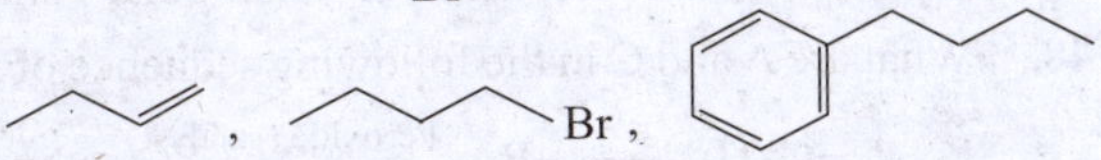

34. An alkene X (C_4H_8) does not exhibit cis trans isomerism. Reaction of X with Br_2 in the presence of UV light gave Y. What is Y? **[May 20, 2024 (I)]**

(a) 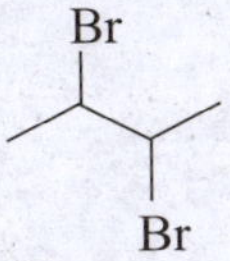
(b) 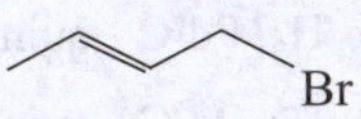

(c) 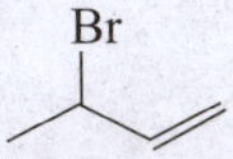
(d) 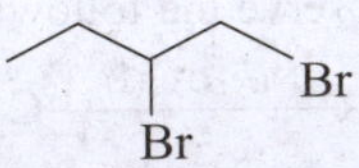

35. Consider the reactions **[May 20, 2024 (I)]**

$$(H_3C)_2C=CH_2 \xrightarrow[(2)\,Zn/H_2O]{(1)\,O_3} X + Y$$

$$X + Y \xrightarrow[(2)\,\Delta]{(1)\,\text{dil. NaOH}} Z$$

The IUPAC name of 'Z' is

(a) But-1-en-3-one (b) 4-Hydroxybutan-2-one
(c) But-3-en-2-one (d) 1-Hydroxybutan-3-one

36. What are X and Y respectively in the following reaction sequence? **[May 19, 2024 (II)]**

$$\text{Isopentane} \xrightarrow{KMnO_4} X \xrightarrow{\text{dehydration}} \underset{\text{Major}}{Y}$$

(a) 

(b) 

(c) 

(d) 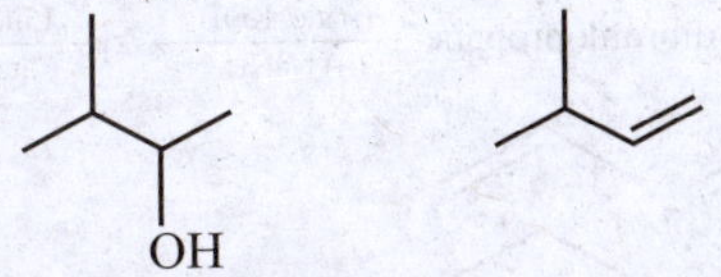

37. Identify the correct statements with respect to cis/trans-2-butene from the following

I. cis-2- Butene is more polar than trans-2-butene

II. Melting point of cis-2-butene is greater than that of trans- 2- butene

III. Boiling point of cis-2-butene is greater than that of trans- 2-butene

Correct answer is **[May 17, 2023 (II)]**

(a) I, II only (b) II, III only
(c) I, III only (d) I, II, III

38. Which of the following reaction is not feasible? **[May 15, 2023 (II)]**

(a) $CH_3-CH_2-OH \xrightarrow[443K]{95\%\ H_2SO_4} CH_2=CH_2$

(b) $H_3C-CH_2-CH_2-CH_2-OH \xrightarrow[300K]{75\%\ H_2SO_4} CH_3-CH_2-CH=CH_2$

(c) $H_3C-CH_2-\underset{}{\overset{OH}{\overset{|}{C}H}}-CH_3 \xrightarrow[440K]{85\%\ H_3PO_4} CH_3-CH=CH-CH_3$

(d) $CH_3-\overset{CH_3}{\overset{|}{\underset{CH_3}{\underset{|}{C}}}}-OH \xrightarrow[358K]{20\% H_3PO_4} CH_3-\overset{CH_3}{\overset{|}{C}}=CH_2$

39. An unsaturated organic compound, X on reaction with hot, acidified $KMnO_4$ gives succinic acid. What is X? **[July 6, 2022 (I)]**

(a) Cyclopentene (b) Cyclopropene
(c) Cyclobutene (d) 2-Butene

40. The major product of the following reaction is **[July 4, 2022 (II)]**

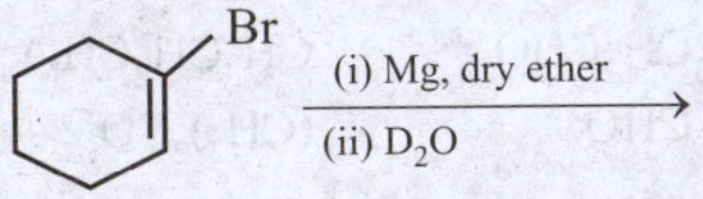

(a) 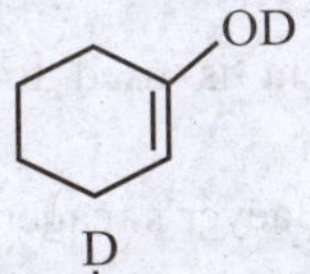
(b) 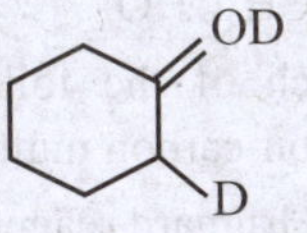

(c) 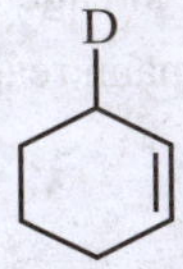
(d) 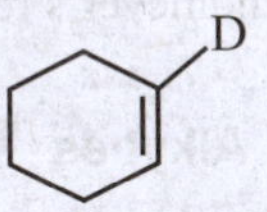

41. The following effect is known as **[Aug. 19, 2021 (I)]**

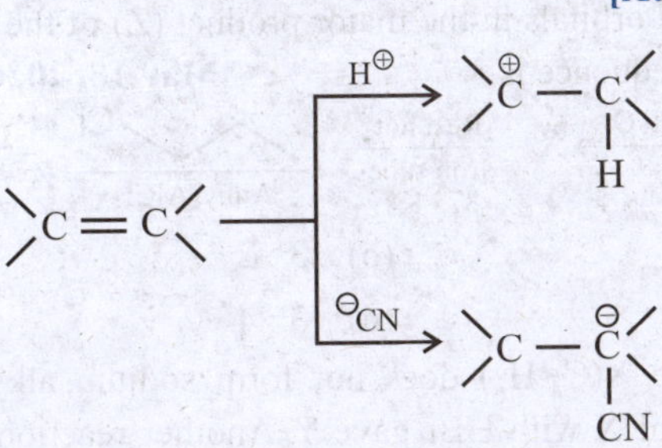

(a) inductive effect (b) electromeric effect
(c) resonance effect (d) hyperconjugation

42. Geometrical isomerism can be found in which of the following? **[Sept. 17, 2020 (I)]**
(a) Butyric acid (b) Aspartic acid
(c) Palmitic acid (d) Cinnamic acid

43. What are *Y* and *Z* in the following reaction sequence ? **[Apr. 20, 2019 (I)]**

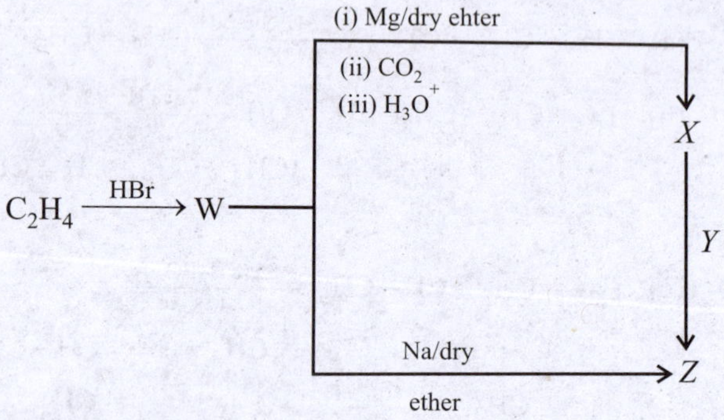

	Y	**Z**
(a)	NaOH/CaO	$CH_3(CH_2)_2CH_3$
(b)	NaOH/electrolysis	$H_3C—CH_3$
(c)	NaOH/CaO	$H_3C—CH_3$
(d)	NaOH/electrolysis	$CH_3(CH_2)_2CH_3$

44. What are *X* and *Y* in the following reaction? **[2018]**

$$\text{Pent}-2-\text{ene} \xrightarrow[\text{(ii) Zn / H}_2\text{O}]{\text{(i) O}_3} X + Y$$

	X	**Y**
(a)	CH_3CHO	CH_3CH_2CHO
(b)	CH_3CH_2CHO	CH_3CH_2CHO
(c)	CH_3CHO	$(CH_3)_2CO$
(d)	CH_3CHO	CH_3CHO

45. Which of the following reagent is used to find out carbon-carbon multiple bonds? **[2015]**
(a) Grignard reagent (b) Baeyer's reagent
(c) Sandmeyer's reagent (d) Gattermann reagent

Topic 3 Alkynes

46. The ratio of number of sp^3 hybrid orbitals to number of sp^2 hybrid orbitals in the major product (Z) of the given reaction sequence is **[May 18, 2026 (II)]**

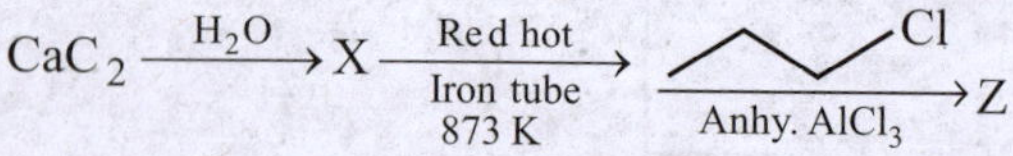

(a) 3 : 5 (b) 3 : 2
(c) 2 : 3 (d) 3 : 4

47. An alkyne $X(C_4H_6)$ does not form sodium alkynide. Reaction of X with HBr gave Y. Another reaction of X with Na/liq, NH_3 gave Z. Identify Y and Z **[May 18, 2026 (I)]**
(a) Y = geminal dibromide; Z = non-polar compound
(b) Y = geminal dibromide; Z = polar compound
(c) Y = vicinal dibromide; Z = polar compound
(d) Y = vicinal dibromide; Z = non-polar compound

48. What are A and C in the following sequence of reactions?

$$C_2H_2 \xrightarrow{A} B \xrightarrow[\substack{350-370\text{ K}\\ 1000-2000\text{ atm}}]{\text{Peroxide (catalyst)}}$$

[May 15, 2026 (I)]
(a) Pd/H_2 ; LDP
(b) Pd/H_2 ; HDP
(c) H_2, Pd/C - quinoline ; LDP
(d) H_2, Pd/C - quinoline ; HDP

49. Observe the following set of reactions

$$Y \xleftarrow{Na/NH_3(l)} C_2H_2 \xrightarrow{H_2/Pt} X$$

Hybridization of carbon in X and Y respectively is **[May 14, 2026 (II)]**
(a) sp^2, sp^2 (b) sp^3, sp^3
(c) sp^2, sp^3 (d) sp^3, sp^2

50. What are A and B respectively in the following set of reactions? **[May 13, 2026 (II)]**

$$\text{But}-2-\text{yne} \xrightarrow{A} \underset{\text{(polar)}}{X}$$

$$\text{But}-2-\text{ene} \xrightarrow{B} \underset{\text{(acid)}}{Y}$$

(a) Na/liq NH_3; $KMnO_4/H^+$
(b) Na/liq NH_3; dil. $KMnO_4$, 273K
(c) H_2/Pd-quinoline; dil. $KMnO_4$, 273K
(d) H_2/Pd-quinoline; $KMnO_4/H^+$

51. Consider the given sequence of reactions

$$CH_3-C\equiv CH \xrightarrow{HBr} X \xrightarrow{HBr} Y$$

Total number of isomers possible for the product Y is **[May 12, 2026 (II)]**
(a) 1 (b) 2
(c) 4 (d) 3

52. What are B and C respectively in the following set of reactions? **[May 27, 2025 (I)]**

$$C \xleftarrow[\Delta]{Zn} 1,2-\text{dibromopropane} \xrightarrow[\text{(ii) NaNH}_2]{\text{(i) alc. KOH}} A \xrightarrow[\text{Catalyst}]{\text{Lindlar}} B$$

(a) 
(b) 
(c) 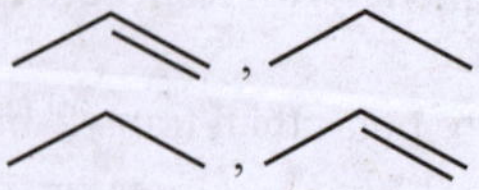
(d) 

53. What is 'Z' in the following reaction sequence ? **[May 26, 2025 (I)]**

$$C_3H_6 \xrightarrow[CCl_4]{Br_2} \underset{\text{(colourless)}}{X} \xrightarrow[\text{(ii) } NaNH_2,\Delta]{\text{(i)KOH/alcohol}}$$

$$Y \xrightarrow[\substack{Hg^{2+},H^+\\333K}]{H_2O} Z$$

(a) Acetone (b) Propanal
(c) Propanol-2 (d) Methoxy ethane

54. An alcohol $X(C_4H_{10}O)$ on dehydration gave alkene (C_4H_8) as major product, which on bromination followed by treatment with Y gave alkyne C_4H_6. Alkyne C_4H_6 does not react with sodium metal. What are X and Y? **[May 24, 2025 (I)]**

(a) 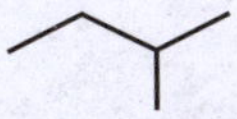 OH; aq. KOH

(b) 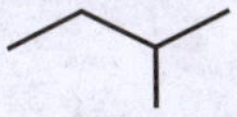 OH; (i) alc. KOH (ii) $NaNH_2$

(c)  OH; alc. KOH

(d)  OH; (i) alc. KOH (ii) $NaNH_2$

55. Aluminum carbide on reaction with D_2O gives $Al(OD)_3$ and 'X'. What is 'X'? **[May 18, 2024 (I)]**

(a) C_2D_2 (b) C_3D_4
(c) C_2D_4 (d) CD_4

56. Which of the following reactions is not correct? **[May 18, 2023 (II)]**

(a) $CH_2Br-CH_2Br \xrightarrow{Zn} CH_2=CH_2$

(b) $CH_3-C\equiv C-CH_3 \xrightarrow[Na]{\text{Liq. }NH_3}$ 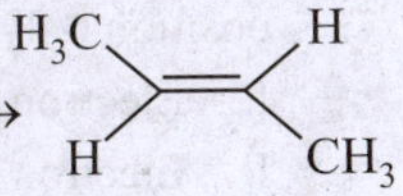

(c) $CH_3-C\equiv C-H \xrightarrow[Hg^{+2},H^+]{H_2O} CH_3-CH_2-CHO$

(d) $Ph-CH_2-Br \xrightarrow[\text{Dry ether}]{Na} Ph-(CH_2)_2-Ph$

57. Which of the following reactions are not feasible?

I. $CH_3CH=CH_2 \xrightarrow[(C_6H_5CO)_2O_2]{HCl} CH_3CH_2CH_2Cl$

II. $C_6H_6+CH_3CH_2CH_2Cl \xrightarrow{AlCl} C_6H_5CH(CH_3)_2$

III. $CH_3CHClCH_2Cl \xrightarrow[\Delta]{KOH} CH_3C\equiv CH$

IV. $CH_3CH=CHCH_3 \xrightarrow{KMnO_4/H^+} CH_3COOH$

[May 18, 2023 (I)]

(a) I & IV only (b) II & III only
(c) II & IV only (d) I & III only

58. Match the following

List -I	List -II
A. $HC\equiv CH \xrightarrow[H_2O]{Hg^+,H^+}$	I. $H_3C-COOH$
B. $CH_4 \xrightarrow[Mo_2O_3,\Delta]{O_2}$	II. $CH_3-\overset{O}{\overset{\Vert}{C}}-CH_3$
C. 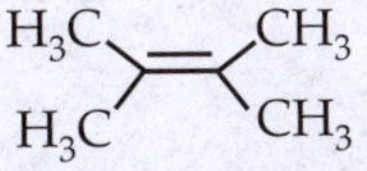 $\xrightarrow[Zn,H_2O]{O_3}$	III. H_3C-CHO
D. $CH_3-CH=CH-CH_3 \xrightarrow[H^+]{KMnO_4}$	IV. HCHO

[May 15, 2023 (II)]

(a) A-I, B-II, C-III, D-IV (b) A-III, B-IV, C-II, D-I
(c) A-I, B-IV, C-III, D-II (d) A-III, B-II, C-IV, D-I

59. The decreasing order of acidic nature of the following compounds is **[July 7, 2022 (II)]**

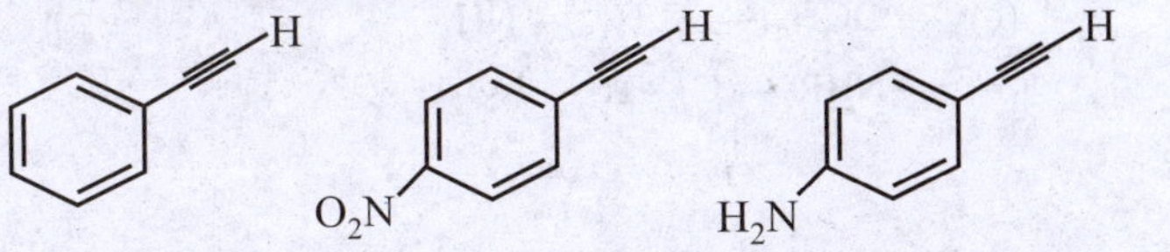

I II III

(a) III > II > I (b) II > III > I
(c) II > I > III (d) I > III > II

60. The correct order of acidic nature of the following alkynes is **[July 5, 2022 (II)]**

I. C_2H_2 II. $(CH_3)_2C_2$ III. $(CH_3)\,C_2H$

(a) I < III < II (b) II < III < I
(c) III < II < I (d) II < I < III

61. Decreasing order of acidity of the following terminal acetylenes is **[Sept. 17, 2020 (I)]**

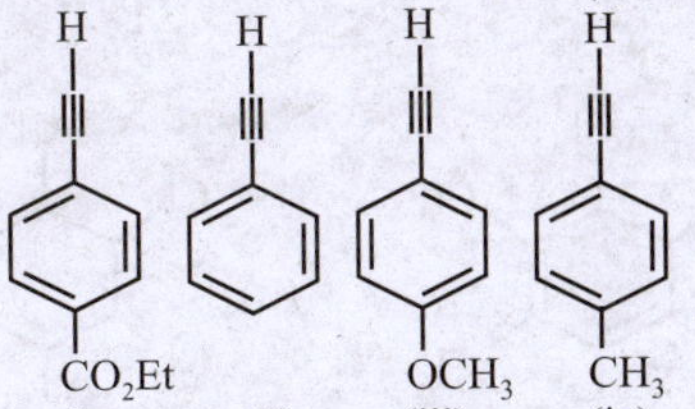

(i) (ii) (iii) (iv)

(a) (i) > (iii) > (ii) > (iv) (b) (i) > (ii) > (iv) > (iii)
(c) (i) > (iv) > (ii) > (iii) (d) (i) > (iii) > (iv) > (ii)

Topic 4 Aromatic Hydrocarbons

62. From the following list, identify the number of substituents which exert +R effect when present on benzene ring

$-Cl$, $-COCH_3$, $-NHC_2H_5$, $-OCH_3$, $-NHCOCH_3$, $-COOCH_3$ **[May 18, 2026 (I)]**

(a) 5 (b) 6
(c) 3 (d) 4

63. What are X and Y in the following set of reactions? **[May 13, 2026 (II)]**

$$\underset{\text{(major product)}}{\text{Cumene}} \xleftarrow[\text{anhy. AlCl}_3]{Y} C_6H_6 \xrightarrow{X} C_6H_6Cl_6$$

(a) Cl_2/anhy $AlCl_3$, dark; 

(b) Cl_2/ dark; 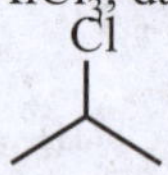

(c) Cl_2/ UV light; 

(d) Cl_2/ anhy $AlCl_3$; 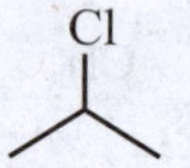

64. Identify the set with only meta directing groups **[May 12, 2026 (II)]**

(a) $-CH_3$, $-\underset{\underset{O}{\|}}{C}-R$, $-NH-\underset{\underset{O}{\|}}{C}-CH_3$

(b) $-CN$, $-CO-R$, $-COOH$

(c) $-OCH_3$, $-C_2H_5$, $-NH_2$

(d) $-NHR$, $-\underset{\underset{O}{\|}}{C}-H$, $-NO_2$

65. The structure of the product 'Z' in the reaction sequence is **[May 23, 2025 (I)]**

$$\begin{array}{l}CHO\\ |\\ (CHOH)_4\\ |\\ CH_2OH\end{array} \xrightarrow{HI,\ \Delta} X \xrightarrow[10-20\ \text{atm}]{Cr_2O_3,\ 773K} Y \xrightarrow[UV]{Cl_2} Z$$

(a) 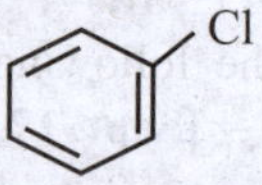

(b) 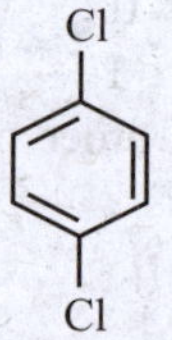

(c) 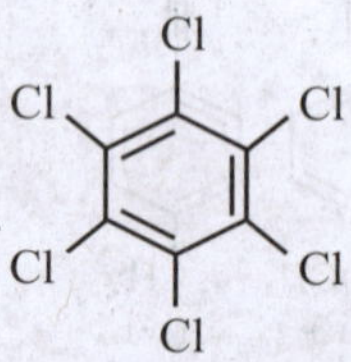

(d) 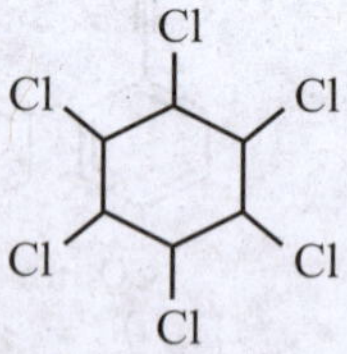

66. Consider the following reaction sequence

$$\text{Vinylbenzene} \xrightarrow[\Delta]{KMnO_4+KOH} X \xrightarrow[\Delta]{NaOH+CaO} Y$$

'Y' can also be formed from **[May 21, 2025 (I)]**

(a) Polymerisation of ethylene

(b) Polymerisation of propyne

(c) Aromatisation of *n*-hexane

(d) Aromatisation of *n*-heptane

67. The number of alicyclic compounds from the following is Cyclohexene. Anisole. Pyridine. Tetrahydrofuran Biphenyl **[May 23, 2024 (I)]**

(a) 2 (b) 3

(c) 1 (d) 4

68. What are X, Y in the following reaction sequence?

$$CH_3(CH_2)_5CH_3 \xrightarrow{X} C_7H_8 \xrightarrow[\Delta]{Br_2} Y$$

[May 18, 2023 (I)]

(a) X = Cr_2O_3, 773 K, 10–20 atm

Y = 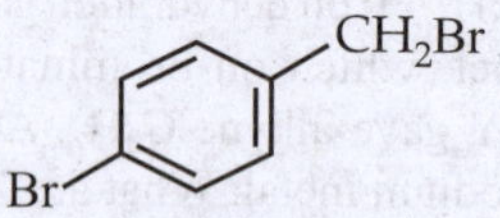

(b) X = V_2O_5, 773 K, 10–20 atm

Y = 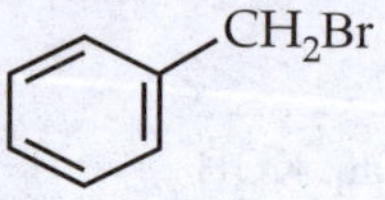

(c) X = $KMnO_4$

Y = 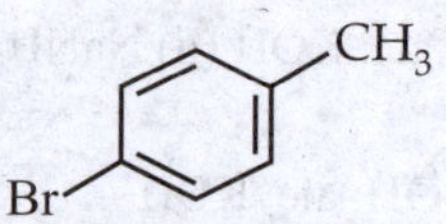

(d) X = Anhydrous $AlCl_3$

Y = 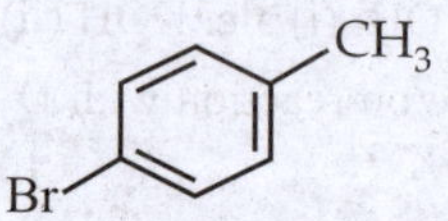

69. 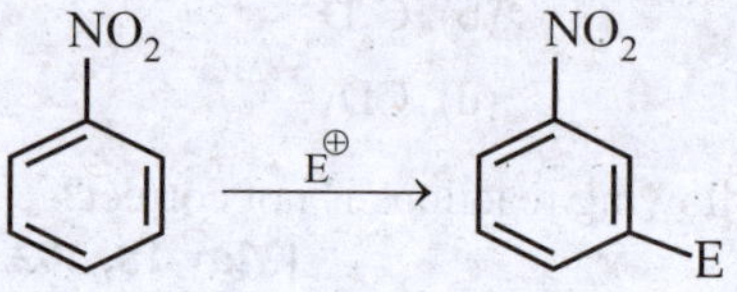

In the above reaction electrophile is substituted at meta position only, due to

I. Electron density is more at ortho & para position

II. Electron density is relatively less at ortho & para position

III. Electron density is less at meta position

IV. Electron density is relatively more at meta position

Correct answer is **[May 16, 2023 (I)]**

(a) I, III only (b) II, IV only

(c) I only (d) III only

70. Which of the following molecule is not aromatic? **[May 15, 2023 (I)]**

(a) 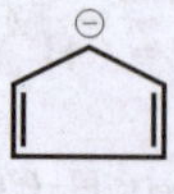 (b) 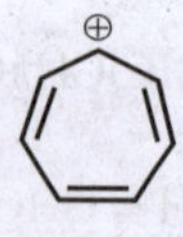

(c)  (d) 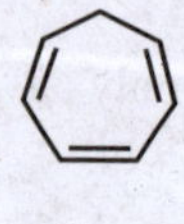

71. The product(s) formed when toluene is reacted with Cl_2 in presence of Fe in dark is/are **[July 8, 2022 (I)]**

(a) 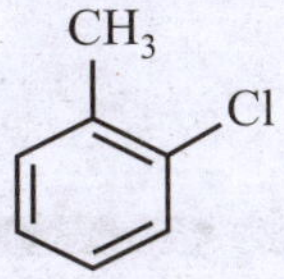 , 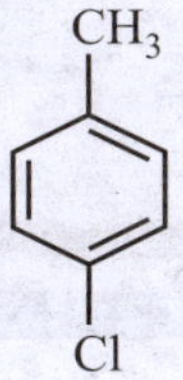

(b) 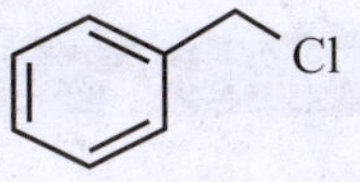

(c) 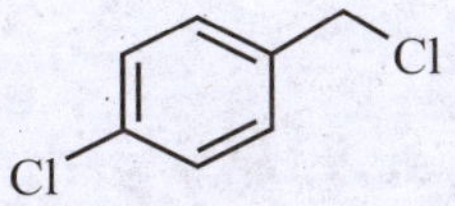 , 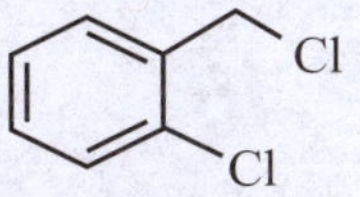

(d) 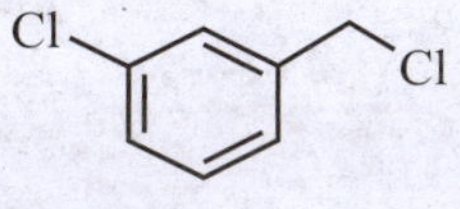 , 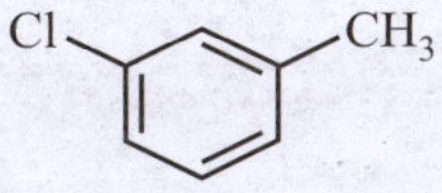

72. Identify the ortho and para directing groups towards aromatic electrophilic substitution reactions from the following list **[July 4, 2022 (II)]**

–OH	–CN	$–CO_2H$	$–OCH_3$	$–NHCOCH_3$	–CHO
I	II	III	IV	V	VI

(a) I, IV, V (b) II, III, VI
(c) I, II, IV (d) IV, V, VI

73. The compound or ion which is not aromatic in the following is **[July 4, 2022 (I)]**

(a) 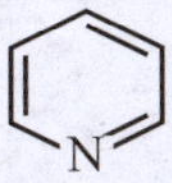 (b) 

(c) 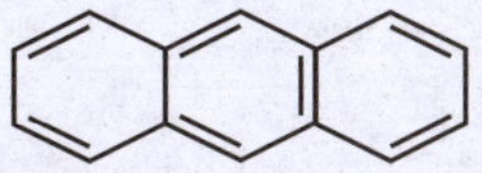 (d) 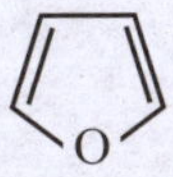

74. An organic compound of molecular formula $C_6H_6Br_2$ has six carbon atoms in a ring system, two non-conjugate double bonds and two bromo groups at 1, 4-positions. Then the compound is **[Aug. 20, 2021 (I)]**

(a) aromatic but non-homo-cyclic
(b) aromatic and hetero-cyclic
(c) homo-cyclic but not aromatic
(d) neither homo-cyclic nor hetero-cyclic

75. Which compound among the following is most reactive towards electrophilic reagents? **[Aug. 20, 2021 (I)]**

(a) 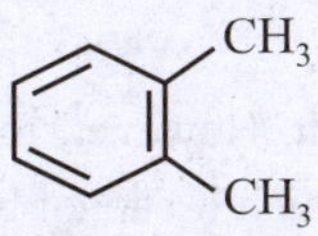 (b) 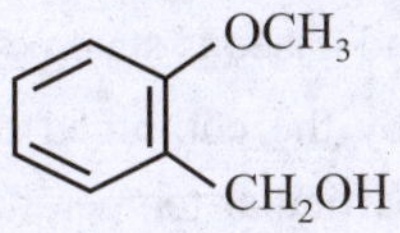

(c) 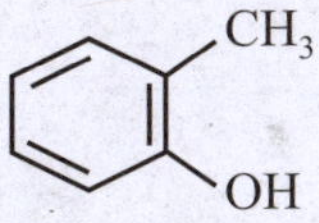 (d) 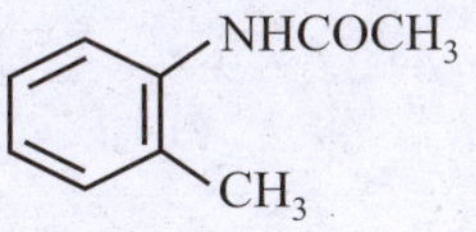

76. The non-aromatic compound among the following is **[Sept. 18, 2020 (I)]**

(a) 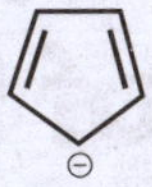 (b) 

(c)  (d) 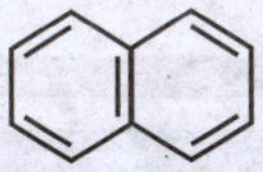

77. What will be the product A in the reaction given below? **[Sept. 18, 2020 (I)]**

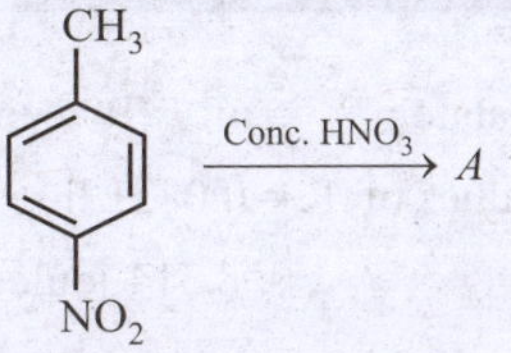

(a) 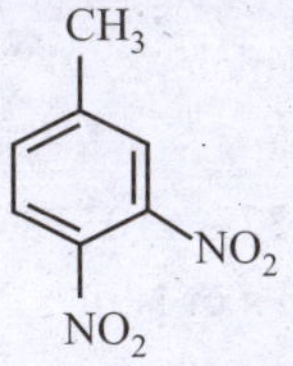 (b) 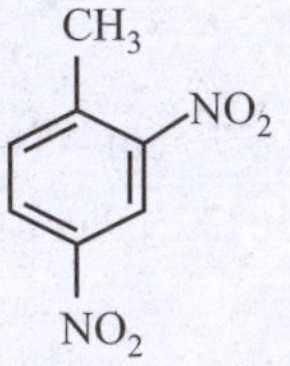

(c) 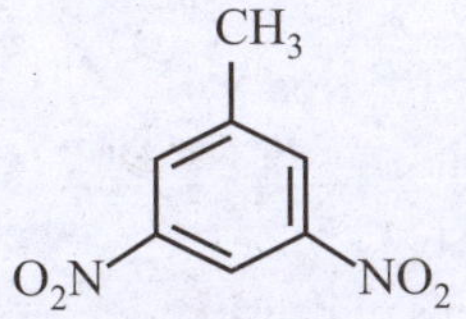 (d) 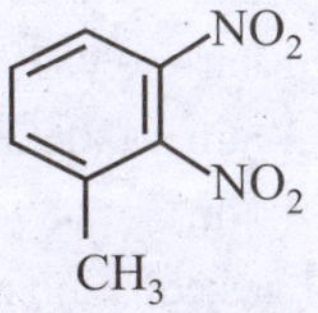

78. Identify *ortho* and *para* directing groups from the following : **[Apr. 22, 2019 (I)]**

—CHO,	$—NHCOCH_3$,	$—OCH_3$,	$—SO_3H$
I	II	III	IV

(a) III, IV (b) II, III
(c) II, IV (d) I, IV

79. Which of the following statements are correct? **[Apr. 21, 2019 (I)]**

I. In nitrating mixture, nitric acid participates as an acid.
II. σ-Complex is the intermediate substance in electrophilic substitution of benzene.
III. Benzene on Friedel-Crafts alkylation with *n*-propyl chloride gives isopropyl benzene.

(a) II, III only (b) I, II only
(c) I, III only (d) I, II, III

80. Which one of the following functional groups is not *meta* directing? **[Apr. 21, 2019 (I)]**

(a) —COOH (b) $—NO_2$
(c) —CHO (d) $—OCH_3$

81. Identify the correct statements for a ring system to exhibit aromaticity **[2017]**

(I) It must not be planar.
(II) It must possess $(4n + 2)$ π-electrons.
(III) It must be planar.
(III) It must possess $4n$ π-electrons.

The correct answer is

(a) II, IV (b) I, II
(c) I, IV (d) II, III

Appendix-I

States of Matter

CHAPTER SYNOPSIS

- Equation of state : $PV = nRT$ (R = universal gas constant)

  Units and values of R = 0.0821 litre atm/ mole–K

  = 8.314 joule/mole – K(N–m/mole–K)

  = 8.314×10^7 ergs/mole–K

  = 1.99 cal/mole–K

- 1 atm = 76 cm = 760 mm = 760 torr

  = 101325 Pa or N m^{-2} = 1.01325×10^5 Pa or N m^{-2}

  = 10^5 Pa or N m^{-2}

  1 atm = 1.013 bar

  1 bar = 0.987 atm = 10^2 Kpa

  1 atm = 0.06805 psi

  1 Nm^{-2} = 6894.8 psi

- Ideal gas equation in terms of density :

  $$PV = \frac{m}{M}RT \Rightarrow P = d\frac{RT}{M} \Rightarrow d = \frac{PM}{RT}$$

  (i) $\frac{d_1 T_1}{P_1} = \frac{d_2 T_2}{P_2}$ (for same gas at different temperatures and pressures)

  (ii) $\frac{d_1}{d_2} = \frac{M_1}{M_2}$ (for different gases at same temperature and pressure) (Where d = density of gas)

- On removal of nozzel the gas from higher pressure will travel towards heat of lower pressure so as to have equal pressure at both the containers. From idea of total moles and final temperature each parameter can be calculated.
- **Collision frequency :** The total number of collisions occurring in a unit volume of a gas per second under given set of conditions.

  $z \propto T^{1/2}$ (at constant P)

  $z \propto P^2$ (at constant T)

- Greater the value of 'a' more easily the gas is liquifiable $a = \frac{PV^2}{n^2}$
- Normal boiling point of liquid $\approx \frac{2}{3}$ of its T_C. At T_C both liquid and gaseous state co-exist.
- A gas can be liquefied by cooling or by applying pressure or by the combined effect of both. However, the effect of temperature is more important because for every gas there is a particular temperature above which it cannot be liquefied howsoever high pressure is applied.

Topic 1 Intermolecular Forces, Gas Laws and Ideal Gas Equation

1. At 300 K, one mole of a gas present in a 10 L flask exerted a pressure of 2.71 atm. What is its compressibility factor? ($R = 0.082$ L atm mol^{-1} K^{-1}) **[May 18, 2026 (II)]**
(a) 1.15 (b) 0.95
(c) 1.10 (d) 0.91

2. At 27°C, a real gas of molar mass 44 g mol^{-1} occupies a volume of 0.4 L at 40 atm pressure. If the compressibility factor of it is 0.65, what is its weight (in g)? ($R = 0.082$ L-atm K^{-1} mol^{-1}) **[May 18, 2026 (I)]**
(a) 42 (b) 44
(c) 46 (d) 28

3. Given below are two statements **[May 15, 2026 (I)]**
Statement-I: London forces between two particles are proportional to r^{-6}, where 'r' is the distance between two particles
Statement-II: The dipole-dipole interaction energy in a solid is proportional to r^{-3}, where r is the distance between two polar molecules
Correct answer is
(a) Both statement-I and statement-II are correct
(b) Both statement-I and statement-II are not correct
(c) Statement-I is correct, but statement-II is not correct
(d) Statement-I is not correct, but statement-II is correct

4. At 300 K, air is present in an open round bottom flask of volume 10 L. The flask is heated to 750 K. Some air is expelled from the flask. What is the fraction of air expelled from the flask? (Assume air as an ideal gas) **[May 13, 2026 (I)]**
(a) $\frac{2}{5}$ (b) $\frac{3}{5}$
(c) $\frac{1}{5}$ (d) $\frac{4}{5}$

5. The number of extensive and intensive properties in the list given below is respectively **[May 26, 2025 (II)]**
density, enthalpy, mass, temperature, volume, pressure
(a) 4, 2 (b) 1, 5 (c) 2, 4 (d) 3, 3

6. At 27°C, 1 L of H_2 with a pressure of 1 bar is mixed with 2 L of O_2 with a pressure of 2 bar in a 10 L flask. What is the pressure exerted by gaseous mixture in bar ? (Assume H_2 and O_2 as ideal gases) **[May 24, 2025 (I)]**
(a) 4 (b) 0.05 (c) 1 (d) 0.5

7. Consider the following: **[May 24, 2025 (I)]**
Statement-I: If thermal energy is stronger than intermolecular forces, the substance prefers to be in gaseous state.
Statement-II: At constant temperature, the density of an ideal gas is proportional to its pressure.
(a) Statement-I is correct, but Statement-II is not correct.
(b) Statement-I is not correct, but Statement-II is correct.
(c) Both Statement-I and Statement-II are correct.
(d) Both Statement-I and Statement-II are not correct.

8. Observe the following substances. **[May 24, 2025 (I)]**
Ethanol, acetic acid, ethylamine, trimethylamine, salicylic acid, ethanal. In the above list, the number of substances with H-bonding is
(a) 4 (b) 3 (c) 5 (d) 2

9. An ideal gas mixture of C_2H_6 and C_2H_4 occupies a volume of 28 L at 1 atm and 273 K. This mixture reacts completely with 128 g of O_2, to produce CO_2 and $H_2O(l)$. What is the mole fraction of C_2H_4 in the mixture? **[May 23, 2025 (II)]**
(a) 0.4 (b) 0.8 (c) 0.5 (d) 0.6

10. At T(K), hydrogen and oxygen gases are mixed in the ratio of 1 : 2 by mass in a closed vessel of volume 'V' litres. If the total pressure of gaseous mixture is 'p' atm, the partial pressure of oxygen (in atm) is **[May 23, 2025 (I)]**
(a) $\frac{p}{9}$ (b) $9p$ (c) $\frac{8p}{9}$ (d) $\frac{p}{6}$

11. For one mole of an ideal gas an isochore is obtained. The slope of the isochore is 0.082 atm K^{-1}. What will be its pressure (in atm) when the temperature is 12.2 K? ($R = 0.082$ L atm $mol^{-1}K^{-1}$). **[May 22, 2025 (II)]**
(a) 10.0 (b) 0.1 (c) 1.0 (d) 0.5

12. At T(K), a gaseous mixture contains H_2 and O_2. The total pressure of the mixture is 2 bar. The partial pressure of H_2 is 1.778 bar. What is the weight (w/w) percentage of H_2 in the mixture? **[May 22, 2025 (I)]**
(a) 66.67 (b) 33.33
(c) 80.00 (d) 20.00

13. Which of the following is correct for an ideal gas? **[May 21, 2025 (II)]**

(a) 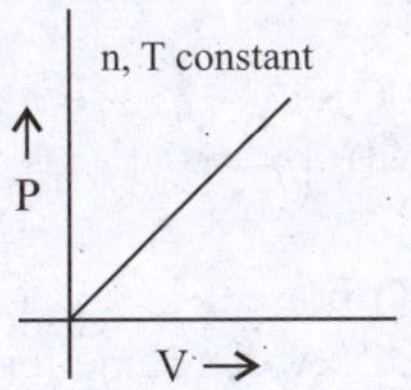

(b) 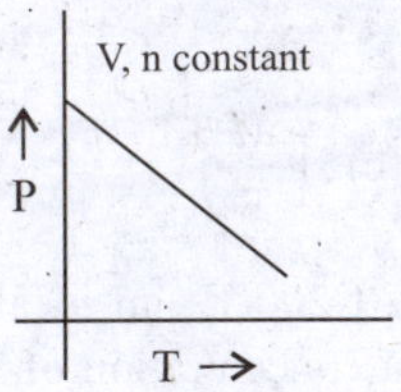

(c) 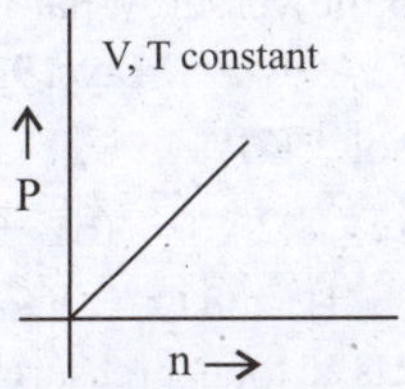

(d) 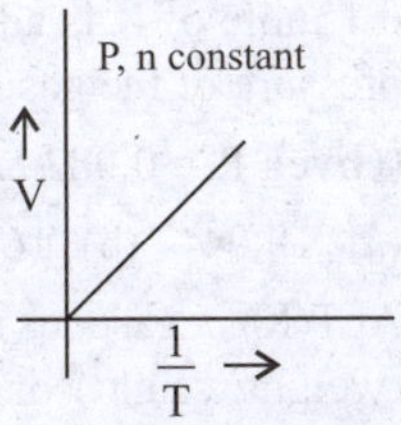

14. Consider the following : **[May 21, 2025 (I)]**
Statement-I: If the intermolecular forces are stronger than thermal energy, the substance prefers to be in gaseous state.
Statement-II: Among all elements, the total number of elements available as gases at room temperature is 10.

The correct answer is

(a) Both statement-I and statement-II are correct.

(b) Both statement-I and statement-II are not correct.

(c) Statement-I is correct, but statement-II is not correct.

(d) Statement-I is not correct, but statement-II is correct.

15. At T (K) for one mole of an ideal gas, the graph of P (on *y*-axis) and V^{-1} (on *x*-axis) gave a straight line with slope of 32.8 L atm mol^{-1}. What is the temperature (in K)? ($R = 0.082$ L atm mol^{-1} K^{-1}) **[May 22, 2024 (II)]**

(a) 600 (b) 200 (c) 800 (d) 400

16. At STP, a closed vessel contains 1 mole each of He and CH_4. Through a small hole, 2L of He and 1L of CH_4 was escaped from vessel in '*t*' minutes. What are the mole fractions of He and CH_4 respectively remaining in the vessel? (Assume He and CH_4 as ideal gases. At STP one mole of an ideal gas occupies 22.4 L of volume) **[May 22, 2024 (I)]**

(a) 0.512, 0.488 (b) 0.5, 0.5

(c) 0.329, 0.671 (d) 0.488, 0.512

17. At T(K), the P, V and u_{rms} of 1 mole of an ideal gas were measured. The following graph is obtained. What is its slope (m)? (*x*-axis=PV; *y*-axis u_{rms}^2, M = Molar mass) **[May 21, 2024 (II)]**

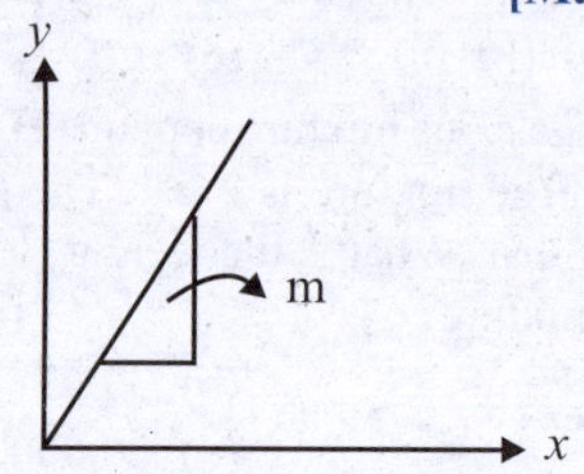

(a) $\frac{3}{M}$ (b) $\frac{M}{3}$

(c) $\left(\frac{M}{3}\right)^{1/2}$ (d) $\left(\frac{3}{M}\right)^{1/2}$

18. At 200 K, an ideal gas (X) present in a 1 L flask has a concentration of 1 mol L^{-1}. At the same temperature, 0.1 mole of X is added into the vessel. What is the final pressure of the gas in atm? **[May 19, 2023 (I)]**
(Given $R = 0.082$ L atom mol^{-1} K^{-1})

(a) 18.04 (b) 16.4 (c) 8.2 (d) 9.02

19. At T(K), a gaseous mixture of H_2 and O_2 containing 20% (weight/weight) of H_2 exerts a total pressure of 2 bar. What is the partial pressure of O_2 (in bar)?
[May 18, 2023 (II); Similar to May 17, 2023 (II)]

(a) 0.2 (b) 0.1 (c) 0.4 (d) 0.6

20. The following data is obtained for one mole of a gas
The gas behaves as an ideal gas in the pressure range (in bar)

P(bar)	$\frac{PV}{RT}$
1	1
2	1
3	1
4	1.5
5	2.0

[May 18, 2023 (II); Similar to May 17, 2023 (II)]

(a) 1 to 3 (b) 1 to 5

(c) 4 to 5 (d) Above 5

21. The vapors of 1 g of an element occupy 2.5625 L exerting a pressure of 0.5 atm at 1000 K. What is the molar mass (in g mol^{-1}) of the element?
(Assume vapors follow ideal gas equation.
Given $R = 0.082$ L atm mol^{-1} K^{-1})
[May 18, 2023 (I); Similar to May 15, 2023 (I)]

(a) 64 (b) 16 (c) 32 (d) 128

22. A gas obeys Charles law in the temperature range 0–500 K at a given pressure. Its volume changes to zero at temperature of **[May 18, 2023 (I)]**

(a) 273.15°C (b) 0 °C

(c) –273.15°C (d) 500 K

23. At T (K), an ideal gas (Z) present in V L flask exerted a pressure of 16.4 atm. Its concentration is 1 mol L^{-1}. What is the value of T in K? **[May 17, 2023 (I)]**

(a) 100 (b) 400 (c) 300 (d) 200

24. At 300 K, the following graph is obtained for one mole of an ideal gas. If its pressure is 10 atm, then its volume (in L) will be

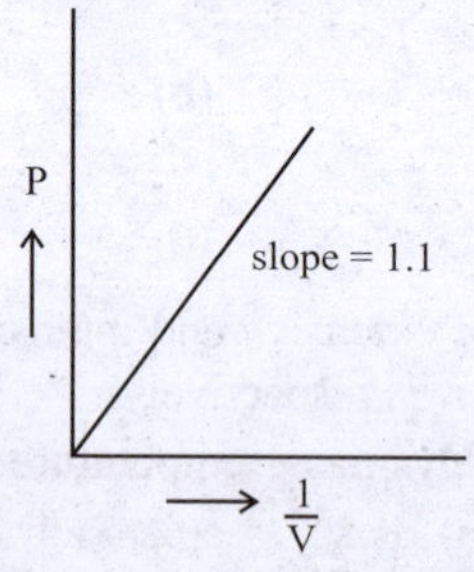

[May 17, 2023 (I)]

(a) 0.11 (b) 1.1 (c) 2.0 (d) 4.0

25. At a given temperature , the density of an ideal gas is proportional to
(P = pressure of ideal gas)
[May 16, 2023 (I); Similar to Aug. 19, 2023 (I)]

(a) $\frac{1}{P}$ (b) P (c) P^2 (d) $\sqrt{P}$

26. At T(K), equal weights of H_2, D_2, and T_2 are present in closed vessel. The pressure exerted by this gaseous mixture is P atm. The ratio of partial pressures of T_2, D_2 and H_2 is approximately
(H, D and T are isotopes of hydrogen). **[May 15, 2023 (II)]**

(a) 0.33 : 0.33 : 0.33 (b) 0.18 : 0.27: 0.54
(c) 0.25 : 0.50 : 0.25 (d) 0.54 : 0.27 : 0.18

27. A 100 L cylinder containing H_2 exerted a pressure of 4 atm at 300 K. It was accidentally opened and some H_2 was escaped. When it was closed, it exerted a pressure of 3 atm at 300 K. The number of moles of H_2 remaining in the cylinder is equal to **[May 15, 2023 (I)]**
(Assume H_2 as an ideal gas; R = gas constant)

(a) $\frac{1}{2R}$ (b) R (c) $\frac{1}{R}$ (d) 2R

28. What is the density of one mole of He (molar mass = 4 g mol^{-1}) at 300 K and a pressure of 0.82 atm? (R = 0.082 L atm mol^{-1} K^{-1}) **[July 8, 2022 (I)]**

(a) 1.33×10^{-2} g mL^{-1} (b) 1.33×10^{-2} g L^{-1}
(c) 1.33×10^{-1} g L^{-1} (d) 1.33×10^{-1} g mL^{-1}

29. The standard molar enthalpy of vaporisation ($\Delta_{vap}H°$) of A, B and C liquids is 23.3, 41 and 29 kJ mol^{-1} respectively. The correct order of dipole-dipole attractive forces in these liquids is: **[July 7, 2022 (II)]**

(a) B > C > A (b) B > A > C
(c) A > C > B (d) A > B > C

30. From the following plots, find the correct option. **[July 4, 2022 (II)]**

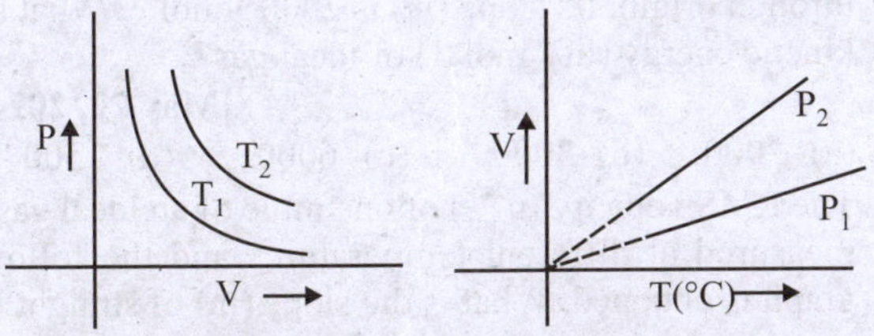

(a) $T_1 > T_2 : P_1 > P_2$ (b) $T_1 > T_2 : P_2 > P_1$
(c) $T_2 > T_1 : P_2 > P_1$ (d) $T_2 > T_1 : P_1 > P_2$

31. A person living in Shimla observed that, cooking food without using pressure cooker takes more time. The reason is that at high altitude **[Aug. 23, 2021 (I)]**

(a) temperature decrease (b) pressure increases
(c) pressure decreases (d) temperature increases

32. Which of the following graphs correctly represents Boyle's Law? **[Aug. 19, 2021 (I)]**

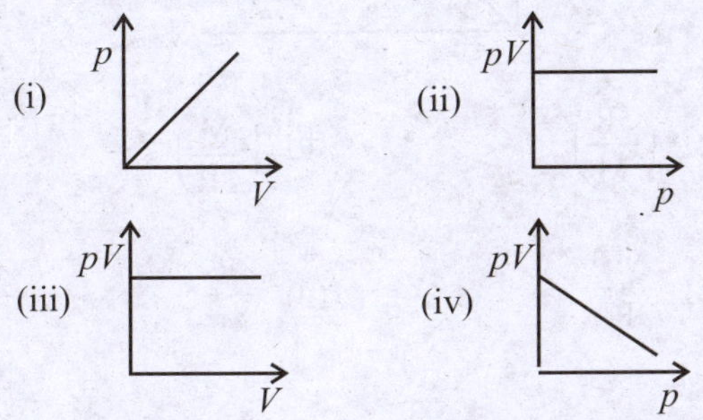

(a) (i), (ii) and (iii) (b) (ii) and (iii)
(c) (iii) and (iv) (d) (ii) and (iv)

33. The temperature at which 4 moles of a gas occupy 5 dm^3 volume at 3.32 bar pressure is **[Sept. 18, 2020 (I)]**

(a) 50 K (b) 50°C
(c) 27°C (d) 100 K

34. A gaseous mixture of 3 gases *A, B* and *C* has a pressure 10 atm. The total number of moles are 10. If partial pressure of gases *A* and *B* are 3 atm and 1 atm respectively and if molar mass of gas *C* is 2. Calculate the weight of *C* in the mixture. **[Sept. 17, 2020 (I)]**

(a) 12 g (b) 24 g (c) 8 g (d) 2 g

35. Which among the following statements is correct? **[Sept. 17, 2020 (I)]**

A. There is a complete order of molecules in gases.
B. There is a complete disorder of molecules in gases.
C. Molecules are not always in random motion in gases.
D. Molecules are fixed at respective position in gases.

(a) A (b) B (c) C (d) D

36. The variation of vapour pressure (*b*) as a function of temperature (*a*) is studied for $C_2H_5OC_2H_5$, CCl_4 and H_2O at 760 mm Hg and is shown in the figure below. The boiling temperatures of $C_2H_5OC_2H_5$, CCl_4 and H_2O are 308, 350 and 373 K respectively. Curves *A, B, C* respectively correspond to **[Apr. 21, 2019 (I)]**

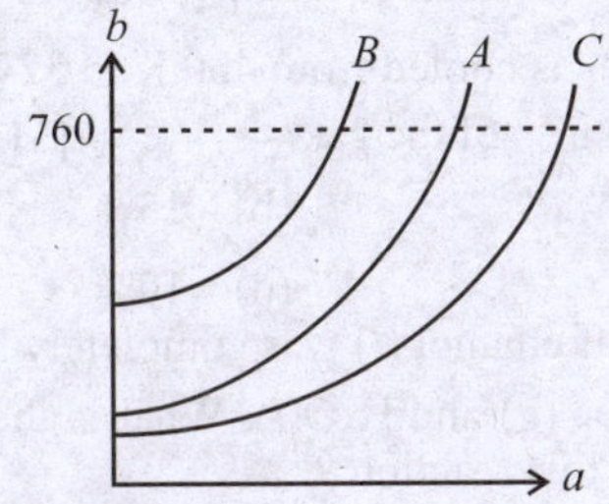

(a) $H_2O, C_2H_5OC_2H_5, CCl_4$
(b) $C_2H_5OC_2H_5, CCl_4, H_2O$
(c) $CCl_4, C_2H_5OC_2H_5, H_2O$
(d) $CCl_4, H_2O, C_2H_5OC_2H_5$

37. 16 g each of H_2, He and O_2 are present in a container exerting 10 atm. pressure at *T*(K). The pressure in atm exerted by 16 g each of He and O_2 in the second container of same volume and temperature is **[2018]**

(a) 1.8 (b) 6.4 (c) 3.6 (d) 5.4

38. At 27°C in a 10 L flask 4.0 g of an ideal gaseous mixture containing. He (molar mass 4.0 g mol^{-1}) and Ne (molar mass 20g mol^{-1}) has a pressure of 1.23 atm. What is the mass % of neon ? (*R* = 0.082 L atm $K^{-1}mol^{-1}$) **[2017]**

(a) 25.2 (b) 62.5
(c) 84.2 (d) 74.2

39. On the top of a mountain, water boils at **[2015]**

(a) high temperature (b) same temperature
(c) high pressure (d) low temperature

Topic 2 Kinetic Theory of Gases and Molecular Speeds

40. An ideal gas with density 3.0 g L^{-1} has a pressure of 684 mm Hg at 25°C. The rms speed (in m s^{-1}) of it is (1 atm = 10^5 Pa) **[May 15, 2026 (II)]**
(a) 3×10^2 (b) 3×10^3
(c) 4×10^2 (d) 4×10^3

41. At T(K), the rms velocity of an ideal gas is x m s^{-1}. At what temperature (in K), the rms velocity of gas becomes 3x ms^{-1}? **[May 14, 2026 (I)]**
(a) 3T (b) 4T (c) 9T (d) 18T

42. At T(K), the kinetic energy of one mole of an ideal gas (molar mass = M g mol^{-1}) is Y kJ mol^{-1}. What is its most probable velocity (U_{mp}) in s^{-1}? **[May 13, 2026 (II)]**
(a) $10^3\sqrt{\frac{3M}{Y}}$ (b) $10^3\sqrt{\frac{Y}{3M}}$
(c) $2\times10^3\sqrt{\frac{3M}{Y}}$ (d) $2\times10^3\sqrt{\frac{Y}{3M}}$

43. The rms velocity of SO_2 molecules at 400 K is same as the most probable velocity of O_2 molecules at T(K). What is the kinetic energy (in kJ) of 5 moles of O_2 at T(K)? (At. wt: S = 32 u, O = 16u), (R = 8.3 J K^{-1} mol^{-1}) **[May 12, 2026 (II)]**
(a) 16.875 (b) 18.675 (c) 17.685 (d) 15.768

44. An ideal gas is cooled from 400 K to 324 K. What is the decrease in u_{rms} of the gas? **[May 12, 2026 (I)]**
(a) 5% (b) 15%
(c) 20% (d) 10%

45. One mole of ethanol (*l*) was completely burnt in oxygen to form CO_2 (g) and H_2O(*l*). What is the $\Delta_r H^\ominus$ (in kJ mol^{-1}) for this reaction ?
(The standard enthalpy of formation ($\Delta_f H^\ominus$) of C_2H_5OH(*l*), CO_2(g) and H_2O (*l*) is respectively – 277, – 393 and – 286 kJ mol^{-1}.) **[May 26, 2025 (II)]**
(a) +1921 (b) – 1921 (c) +1367 (d) – 1367

46. At T(K), the u_{rms} of CO_2 is 412 ms^{-1}. What is its kinetic energy (in kJ mol^{-1}) at the same temperature ? (CO_2 = 44 u). **[May 26, 2025 (I)]**
(a) 3.7343 (b) 7.4687 (c) 14.9374 (d) 3734.3

47. 2.0 g of H_2 diffuses through a porous container in 10 minutes. How many grams of O_2 would diffuse from the same container in the same time under similar conditions ? **[May 26, 2025 (I)]**
(a) 2.0 (b) 4.0 (c) 16.0 (d) 8.0

48. At 27°C kinetic energy of 4 g of H_2 is *x* J. What is the kinetic energy (in J) of 6.4 g of oxygen at 127°C? **[May 23, 2025 (I)]**
(a) $\frac{x}{15}$ (b) $\frac{4x}{15}$ (c) $\frac{8x}{15}$ (d) $\frac{2x}{15}$

49. At what temperature (in K) the rms velocity of SO_2 molecules is equal to rms velocity of O_2 molecules at 27°C. **[May 22, 2025 (II)]**
(a) 300 (b) 1200 (c) 600 (d) 900

50. The most probable speed (u_{mp}) of 8 g of H_2 is 2×10^2 ms^{-1}. The kinetic energy (in J) of same amount of H_2 gas is **[May 22, 2025 (I)]**
(a) 480 (b) 240 (c) 720 (d) 120

51. At 256 K, rms speed of SO_2 gas molecules is 3.16×10^2 ms^{-1}. What is the most probable velocity (in ms^{-1}) of same gas at same temperature? **[May 21, 2025 (II)]**
(a) 2.911×10^2 (b) 2.58×10^2
(c) 5.16×10^2 (d) 1.29×10^2

52. The rms velocity (u_{rms}), mean velocity (u_{av}) and most probability (u_{mp}) of a gas differ from each other at a given temperature. Which of the following ratios regarding them is correct? **[May 23, 2024 (I)]**
(a) $\frac{u_{rms}}{u_{av}} = 1.20$ (b) $\frac{u_{av}}{u_{mp}} = 1.12$
(c) $\frac{u_{rms}}{u_{mp}} = 1.15$ (d) $\frac{u_{av}}{u_{rms}} = 0.98$

53. 60 cm^3 of SO_2 gas diffused through a porous membrane in '*x*' min. Under similar conditions 360 cm^3 of another gas (molar mass 4 g mol^{-1}) diffused 'y' min. The ratio of *x* and *y* is **[May 23, 2024 (I)]**
(a) 3 : 2 (b) 2 : 3 (c) 1 : 3 (d) 3 : 1

54. At 240.55 K, for one mole of an ideal gas, a graph of P (on *y*-axis) and V^{-1} (on *x*-axis) gave a straight line passing through origin. Its slope (*m*) is 2000 J mol^{-1}. What is the kinetic energy (in J mol^{-1}) of ideal gas? **[May 22, 2024 (I)]**
(a) 2000 (b) 3000 (c) 6000 (d) 1500

55. The RMS velocity (u_{rms}) of one mole of an ideal gas was measured at different temperatures and the following graph is obtained. What is the slope (m) of straight line? (*x*-axis = T(K); *y*-axis = $(u_{rms})^2$; M = molar mass; R = gas constant)

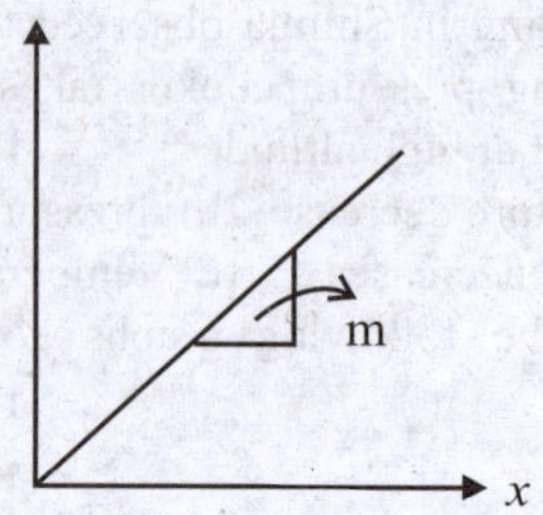

(a) $\left(\frac{3R}{M}\right)^{1/2}$ (b) $\left(\frac{M}{3R}\right)^{1/2}$
(c) $\frac{M}{3R}$ (d) $\frac{3R}{M}$

56. What is the ratio of kinetic energies of 3 g of hydrogen and 4 g of oxygen at a certain temperature? **[May 20, 2024 (II)]**

(a) 3 : 4 (b) 6 : 1 (c) 12 : 1 (d) 1 : 12

57. What is the kinetic energy (in J mol^{-1}) of one mole of an ideal gas (molar mass = 0.1 kg mol^{-1}) if its rms velocity is 4×10^2 ms^{-1} at T (K)? **[May 20, 2024 (II)]**

(a) 2×10^5 (b) 8×10^4
(c) 8×10^2 (d) 8×10^3

58. At 133.33 K. the RMS velocity of an ideal gas is (M = 0.083 kg mol^{-1}: R= 8.3 J mol^{-1} K^{-1}) **[May 20, 2024 (I)]**

(a) 200 ms^{-1} (b) 150 ms^{-1}
(c) 2000 ms^{-1} (d) 400 ms^{-1}

59. Identify the correct statements from the following. **[May 19, 2024 (II)]**

I. For an ideal gas, the compressibility factor is 1.0
II. The kinetic energy of NO (g) (molar mass = 30 g mol^{-1}) at T(K) is x J mol^{-1}. The kinetic energy of N_2O_4 (g) (molar mass = 92 g mol^{-1}) at T (K) is $2x$ J mol^{-1}
III. The rate of diffusion of a gas is inversely proportional to square root of its density

(a) I, II, III (b) II, III only
(c) I, III only (d) I, II only

60. The following graph is obtained for a gas at different temperatures (T_1, T_2, T_3). What is the correct order of temperature? (x-axis = velocity; y-axis = number of molecules) **[May 19, 2024 (II)]**

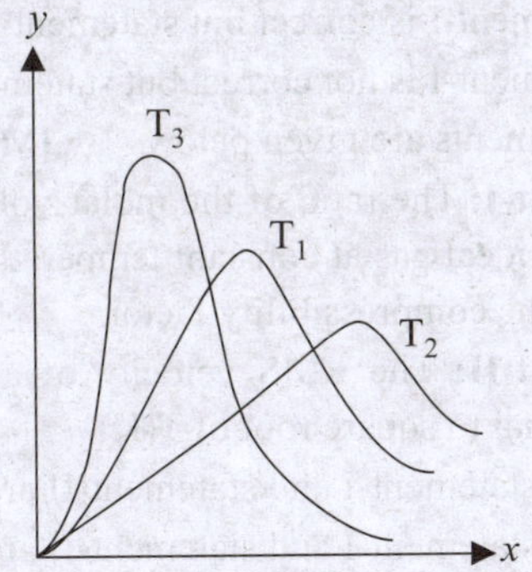

(a) $T_2 > T_1 > T_3$ (b) $T_2 > T_3 > T_1$
(c) $T_3 > T_1 > T_2$ (d) $T_3 > T_2 > T_1$

61. RMS velocity of one mole of an ideal gas was measured at different temperatures. A graph of $(v_{rms})^2$ (on y-axis) and T(K) (on x-axis) gave straight line passing through the origin and its slope is 249 $m^2s^{-2}K^{-1}$. What is the molar mass (in kg mol^{-1}) of ideal gas? (R = 8.3 J $mol^{-1}K^{-1}$) **[May 18, 2024 (I)]**

(a) 10 (b) 1.0 (c) 24.9 (d) 1×10^{-1}

62. At T (K) and pressure P, the diffusion rate of an ideal gas is 120 mL min^{-1}. What is the time taken (in sec.) for 3000 mL of this gas for diffusion at same temperature and pressure? **[May 16, 2023 (II)]**

(a) 25 (b) 1500 (c) 250 (d) 150

63. 20 mL of gas A and 10 mL of gas B diffuses through a porous membrane separately in 1 minute. If the vapor density of B is X, what is the vapor density of A? **[July 7, 2022 (II)]**

(a) 2x (b) 4x (c) $\frac{x}{4}$ (d) $\frac{x}{2}$

64. If two gases CH_4 and SO_2, are allowed to enter from the two ends of a 1 km long vacuum tube at the same time, where will the gases meet from the CH_4 end? **[July 6, 2022 (I)]**

(a) 500 m (b) 620 m (c) 667 m (d) 720 m

65. Find the false statement for ideal gases. **[July 5, 2022 (II)]**

(a) Kinetic energy of 1 mol of gas depends on mass of the gas molecule.
(b) Kinetic energy increases with increase in temperature.
(c) Kinetic energy of 1g of H_2 is higher than that 8g of O_2 at the same temperature.
(d) At a given temperature, kinetic energy does not depend on the pressure of the gas.

66. If the most probable speed of CO_2 at 27°C is 400 ms^{-1}. The root mean square velocity of CO_2 at the same temperature in ms^{-1} is approximately **[Apr. 22, 2019 (I)]**

(a) 600 (b) 490 (c) 267 (d) 245

67. If the kinetic energy of O_2 gas is 4.0 kJ mol^{-1}, its RMS speed in cm s^{-1} is **[Apr. 20, 2019 (I)]**

(a) 5.0×10^2 (b) 5.0×10^3
(c) 5.0×10^4 (d) 5.0×10^{-4}

68. Which one of the following is the kinetic energy of a gaseous mixture containing 3 g of hydrogen and 80 g of oxygen at temperature $T(K)$? **[2016]**

(a) $3RT$ (b) $6RT$ (c) $4RT$ (d) $8RT$

69. The given figure shows the Maxwell distribution of molecular speeds of a gas at three different temperatures T_1, T_2 and T_3. The correct order of temperature is **[2016]**

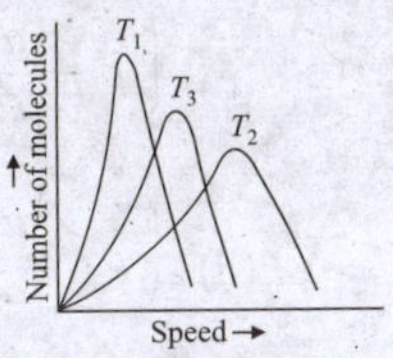

(a) $T_1 > T_2 > T_3$
(b) $T_1 > T_3 > T_2$
(c) $T_3 > T_2 > T_1$
(d) $T_2 > T_3 > T_1$

Topic 3 van der Waals Equation and Liquefaction of Gases

70. Identify the correct statements from the following.

I. Glass is an extremely viscous liquid.
II. Increase in temperature decreases the surface tension of liquids. **[May 27, 2025 (I)]**
III. Compressibility factor for an ideal gas is zero.

(a) I, II, III (b) I, II only
(c) I, III only (d) II, III only

71. Identify the correct graph for an ideal gas **[May 27, 2025 (I)]**

(y-axis = compressibility factor, Z: x-axis = pressure, p)

(a) 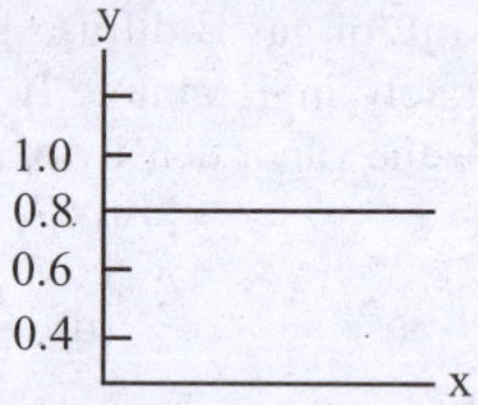

(b) 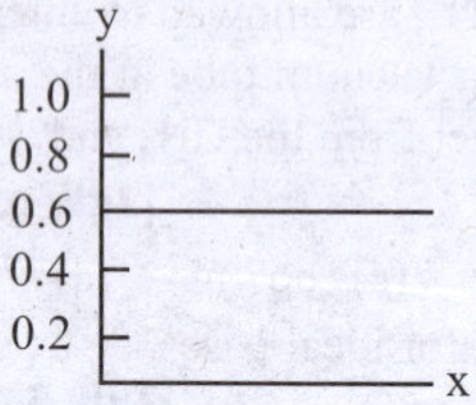

(c) 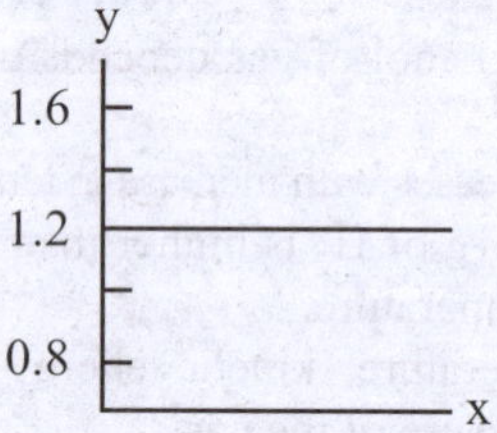

(d) 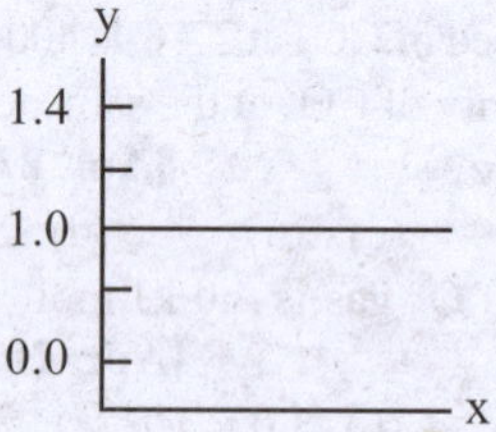

72. The correct equation for one mole of a real gas is (a, b are constants) **[May 26, 2025 (II)]**

(a) $\left(p+\frac{a}{V^2}\right)(V-b)=RT$

(b) $\left(p-\frac{a}{V^2}\right)(V-b)=RT$

(c) $\left(p+\frac{a}{V^2}\right)(V+b)=RT$

(d) $\left(p+\frac{a}{V^2}\right)(V-b)=RT$

73. Choose the incorrect statement from the following: **[May 23, 2025 (II)]**

(a) At Boyle temperature a real gas obeys ideal gas law over an appreciable range of pressure

(b) Critical temperature of CO_2 is 27.5° C

(c) Above critical temperature, a real gas behaves like an ideal gas

(d) At room temperature and 1 atm pressure the compressibility factor (Z) for H_2 gas is greater than 1

74. Identify the conditions at which van der Waals equation of state changes to ideal gas equation. **[May 21, 2025 (I)]**

(a) high temperature and high pressure

(b) low temperature and high pressure

(c) high temperature and low pressure

(d) low temperature and low pressure

75. Three layers of liquid are flowing over fixed solid surface as shown below. The correct order of velocity of liquid in these layers is **[May 21, 2024 (II)]**

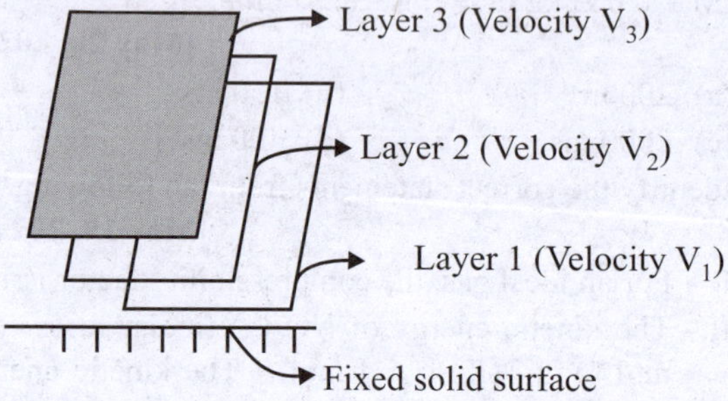

(a) $V_1 > V_2 > V_3$ (b) $V_1 = V_2 = V_3$

(c) $V_3 > V_2 > V_1$ (d) $V_3 > V_1 > V_2$

76. Two statements are given below.

Statement-I: Viscosity of liquid decreases with increase in temperature.

Statement-II: The units of viscosity coefficient are Pascal sec. **[May 21, 2024 (I)]**

(a) Both statement-I and statement-II are correct.

(b) Both statement-I and statement-II are not correct.

(c) Statement-I is correct but statement-II is not correct.

(d) Statement-I is not correct but statement-II is correct.

77. Two statements are given below. **[May 20, 2024 (I)]**

Statement-I: The ratio of the molar volume of a gas to that of an ideal gas at constant temperature and pressure is called the compressibility factor.

Statement-II: The RMS velocity of a gas is directly proportional to square root of T(K)

(a) Both statement-I and statement-II are correct

(b) Both statement-I and statement-II are not correct

(c) Statement-I is correct but statement-II not correct

(d) Statement-I is not correct but statement-II is correct

78. Given below are two statements.

Statement-I: Viscosity of liquid decreases with increase in temperature.

Statement-II: The units of viscosity are kg $m^{-1}s^{-2}$. **[May 18, 2024 (I)]**

(a) Both statement-I and statement-II are correct

(b) Both statement-I and statement-II are not correct

(c) Statement-I is correct but statement-II is not correct

(d) Statement-I is not correct but statement-II is correct

79. At 300 K, the compressibility factor of 1 mole of a gas is 1.1. Its pressure is 2.706 atm. What is its volume in L? (Given R = 0.082 L atm mol^{-1} K^{-1}).

[May 16, 2023 (II); Similar to May 15, 2023 (II)]

(a) 1 (b) 10
(c) 100 (d) 0.1

80. Identify the correct statements from the following

(A) The compressibility factor (Z) for an ideal gas is 1
(B) Urananium isotopes (^{235}U and ^{238}U) are separated by converting them into UF_6 vapours
(C) Decrease in temperature increases the kinetic energy of gas molecules **[May 16, 2023 (I)]**

(a) A, B, C (b) A, C only
(c) B, C only (d) A, B only

81. Among the gases a, b, c, d, e and f, the gases that show only positive deviation from ideal behavior at all pressures in the graph are **[July 4, 2022 (I)]**

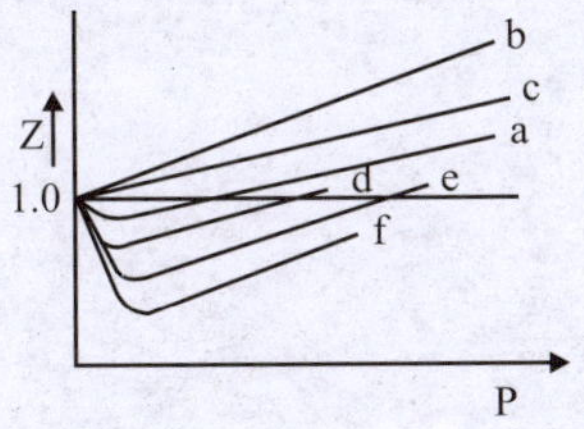

(a) b, c only (b) b, c, a only
(c) d, e only (d) d, e, f only

82. Which among the following statements is/are incorrect regarding real gases? **[Aug. 20, 2021 (I)]**

(i) Their compressibility factor is never equal to unity ($Z \neq 1$).
(ii) The deviations from ideal behaviour are less at low pressure and high temperatures.
(iii) Intermolecular forces among gas molecules are equal to zero.
(iv) They obey van der Waal's equation, $pV = nRT$

(a) (i), (ii) and (iv) (b) (ii) and (iv)
(c) Only (ii) (d) (iii) and (iv)

83. Which of the following statements is incorrect? **[Sept. 18, 2020 (I)]**

1. The property of liquid drops to have minimum surface area is called surface tension.
2. Surface tension of liquids decreases with rise in temperature.
3. The SI unit of surface tension in Nm^{-1}.
4. Magnitude of surface tension is less, when there is strong attractive force between the molecules.

(a) 1 (b) 2 (c) 3 (d) 4

84. *A, B, C* and *D* are four different gases with critical temperatures 304.1, 154.3, 405.5 and 126.0 K respectively. While cooling the gas, which gets liquefied first? **[2016]**

(a) *B* (b) *A* (c) *D* (d) *C*

85. Which one of the following is the wrong statement about the liquid? **[2015]**

(a) It has intermolecular force of attraction
(b) Evaporation of liquids increase with the decrease of surface area
(c) It resembles a gas near the critical temperature
(d) It is an intermediate state between gaseous and solid state

Appendix-II

The s-Block Elements

CHAPTER SYNOPSIS

- Atomic radii : Li < Na < K < Rb < Cs
- Ionic radii : $Li^+ < Na^+ < K^+ < Rb^+ < Cs^+$
- Electronegativity : Li > Na > K > Rb > Cs
- First ionization potential : Li > Na > K > Rb > Cs
- Melting point Li > Na > K > Rb > Cs
- Density : Li > Na < K > Rb > Cs
- Colour of the flame : Li - Red, Na - Golden, K - Violet, Rb - Red, Cs - Blue, Ca - Brick red, Sr - Blood red, Ba-Apple green
- Rb and Cs show photoelectric effect.
- Stability of hydrides : LiH > NaH > KH > RbH > CsH
- Basic nature of hydroxides : LiOH < NaOH < KOH < RbOH < CsOH
- Washing soda, $Na_2CO_3 . 10H_2O$; Efflorescent soda, $Na_2CO_3 .10H_2O$

Topic 1 General Characteristics of Alkali Metals

1. Which of the given statements are not correct for Li and Mg? **[May 18, 2026 (II)]**
   I. Both Li and Mg mainly give monoxides only
   II. Both Li and Mg react slowly with water
   III. Both Li and Mg give flame test
   IV. On combustion in air Mg forms Mg_3N_2 but Li does not form Li_3N
   (a) I & II (b) I & III
   (c) I & IV (d) III & IV

2. In group 13 elements, element Y has the lowest boiling point and element Z has lowest melting point. The nature of oxides of Y and Z is respectively **[May 15, 2026 (I)]**
   (a) Acidic, amphoteric (b) Amphoteric, Basic
   (c) Basic, amphoteric (d) Amphoteric, amphoteric

3. Identify the incorrect statement regarding alkali metal halides (M = alkali metal) **[May 13, 2026 (II)]**
   (a) The order of melting points is MF > MCl > MBr > MI.
   (b) The order of boiling points is MI > MBr > MCl > MF.
   (c) Low solubility of LiF in water is due to its high lattice energy.
   (d) Low solubility of CsI is due to smaller hydration enthalpy of its two ions.

4. Identify the correct statements from the following: **[May 26, 2025 (II)]**
   (A) Among alkali metal ions, Li^+ has highest hydration enthalpy
   (B) Boiling point of alkali metals increases from Li to Cs
   (C) Density of K is less than that of Na and Rb
   (D) Li has strong tendency to form superoxide
   The correct answer is
   (a) A & B (b) B & C
   (c) A & C (d) A & D

5. Which of the following statements are correct regarding lithium and magnesium?
   (I) They react slowly with water.
   (II) Their bicarbonates are solids.
   (III) Their chlorides are not soluble in ethanol.
   (IV) Their nitrates decompose easily on heating.
   The correct option is **[May 22, 2025 (I)]**
   (a) II and III only (b) I and III only
   (c) I and IV only (d) III and IV only

6. Two of the products formed by the reaction of 'X' with HCl are gases. What is 'X'? **[May 22, 2024 (I)]**
   (a) $NaNO_2$ (b) Na_2S
   (c) Ca_3P_2 (d) Na_2SO_3

7. Lithium forms an alloy with 'X'. This alloy is used to make armour plates. What is 'X'? **[May 18, 2024 (I)]**
   (a) Mg (b) Pb (c) Al (d) Cr

8. Among the following, the incorrect statement is **[May 18, 2023 (II)]**
   (a) Cesium forms superoxide
   (b) Sodium peroxide is paramagnetic
   (c) Lithium chloride is deliquescent
   (d) White metal is an alloy of lithium and lead

9. Which of the following statement(s) is (are) correct?
   (i) LiF is less soluble in water
   (ii) NaCl is less ionic than CsCl
   (iii) Formation of alkali metal halide is an endothermic reaction **[May 18, 2023 (I)]**
   (a) i & ii only (b) i, ii & iii
   (c) ii & iii only (d) i only

10. Two alkali halide salts, ACl and BCl gave crimson red and violet in their flame test respectively. A and B are respectively **[May 16, 2023 (II)]**
    (a) K, Li (b) Li, K (c) Li, Na (d) Na, K

11. The nitrate of which of the following metals does not liberate NO_2 gas on heating? **[July 8, 2022 (I)]**
    (a) Pb (b) Ba
    (c) Li (d) K

12. Identify the correct statements from the following: **[July 7, 2022 (II)]**
    A. Alkali metals are strong reducing agents.
    B. KO_2 is a diamagnetic oxide.
    C. Lithium chloride exists as $LiCl.\ 2H_2O$
    (a) A, B only (b) A, C only
    (c) B, C only (d) A, B, C

13. Metal 'M' in the following reaction is
    $$2MNO_3 \rightarrow M_2O + 2NO_2 + \frac{1}{2}O_2$$ **[July 5, 2022 (II)]**
    (a) Cs (b) K (c) Na (d) Li

14. Which among the following compound shows the highest lattice energy? **[Aug. 23, 2021 (I)]**
    (a) LiF (b) CsF
    (c) NaF (d) KF

15. Alkali metals are powerful reducing agents because **[Aug. 23, 2021 (I)]**
    (a) they are metals
    (b) they are monovalent
    (c) their ionic radii are large
    (d) their ionisation energies are low

16. Which of the following does not form double salts? **[Aug. 20, 2021 (I)]**
    (a) Li_2SO_4 (b) Na_2SO_4
    (c) K_2SO_4 (d) Rb_2SO_4

17. **Assertion (A) :** K, Rb and Cs form superoxides.
Reason (R) : The stability of superoxides increases from K to Cs due to decrease in lattice energy. **[Aug. 19, 2021 (I)]**
(a) Both A and R are true and R is a correct explanation of A.
(b) Both A and R are true but R is not a correct explanation of A.
(c) A is true but R is false.
(d) A is false but R is true.

18. Which factor makes Li the strongest reducing agent in aqueous solution ? **[Sept. 21, 2020 (I)]**
(a) Sublimation enthalpy (b) Ionization enthalpy
(c) Hydration enthalpy (d) Electron gain enthalpy

19. KO_2, reacts with water to form *A, B* and *C*. *B* forms *C* when it reacts with iodine in basic medium. What are *B* and *C* respectively? **[Apr. 21, 2019 (I)]**
(a) KOH, H_2O_2 (b) K_2O_2, H_2O_2
(c) KOH, O_2 (d) H_2O_2, O_2

20. Identify the correct statements from the following : **[Apr. 20, 2019 (I)]**
I. Tendency to form halide hydrates gradually increases from Be to Ba down the group.
II. Tendency to form stable super oxides increases from Li to Cs down the group.
III. Low solubility of LiF is due to its high lattice energy.
IV. Solubility of carbonates of group-2 elements increases down the group.
(a) I, II (b) III, IV (c) II, III (d) I, III

21. Which one of the following statements is not correct? **[2017]**
(a) The hydration enthalpies of alkali metal ions decrease down the group.
(b) Lithium halides are some what covalent in nature.
(c) Alkali metals react with water liberating oxygen gas.
(d) KO_2 is paramagnetic.

22. Calgon is **[2016]**
(a) Na_2HPO_4 (b) Na_3PO_4
(c) $Na_2P_6O_{18}$ (d) NaH_2PO_4

23. Consider the following statements. **[2016]**
I. Cs^+ ion is more highly hydrated than other alkali metal ions.
II. Among the alkali metals, only lithium forms a stable nitride by direct combination with nitrogen.
III. Among the alkali metals Li, Na, K, Rb, the metal, Rb has the highest melting point.
IV. Among the alkali metals Li, Na, K, Rb, only Li forms peroxide when heated with oxygen.
Select the correct statement is
(a) I (b) II (c) III (d) IV

24. **Assertion (A) :** Alkali metals are soft and have low melting and boiling points.
Reason (R) : This is because interatomic bonds are weak. **[2015]**
(a) Both (A) and (R) are not true
(b) (A) is true but (R) is not the correct explanation of (A)
(c) (A) is true but (R) is false
(d) Both (A) and (R) are true and (R) is the correct explanation of (A)

Topic 2 Some Important Compounds of Alkali Metals

25. X, Y, Z are calcium compounds. X is a primary raw material for manufacturing cement. Y is used to recover ammonia in Solvay process and Z is employed for making casts of statues. Identify the incorrect statement from the following **[May 15, 2026 (II)]**
(a) Y is prepared by adding water to X
(b) Y is also used as a starting material to manufacture bleaching powder
(c) Z is formed by heating gypsum at 373 K
(d) X with P_4O_{10} forms calcium phosphate

26. Consider the following statements
Statement-I: In three dimensional network of SiO_2, if few Si atoms are replaced by Al atoms, the resulting structure acquires a positive charge
Statement-II: Silicones are organo - silicon polymers which have $\left(R_2SiO\right)$ as a repeating unit
The correct answer is **[May 15, 2026 (I)]**
(a) Both statements-I and II are correct
(b) Statement-I is correct but Statement-II is not correct
(c) Statement-I is not correct but Statement-II is correct
(d) Both statements-I and II are not correct

27. Which of the following is not the raw material in Solvay process? **[May 14, 2026 (II)]**
(a) NH_3 (b) NaCl
(c) $CaCl_2$ (d) $Ca(OH)_2$

28. When lithium nitrate and calcium nitrate are heated in separate test tubes, which of the following observations would be identical for both? **[May 14, 2026 (I)]**
(a) Evolution of colorless, non-flammable gas
(b) Evolution of brown fumes and gas that supports combustion
(c) The formation of a metal that reacts vigorously with water
(d) Gases are not liberated

29. In Solvay process, NH_3 is recovered when the solution containing NH_4Cl is treated with compound 'X'. What is 'X' ? **[May 26, 2025 (I)]**
(a) $Ca(OH)_2$ (b) $CaCl_2$
(c) NaOH (d) NaCl

30. White metal is an alloy of **[May 16, 2023 (I)]**
(a) Li & Mg (b) Li & Pb
(c) Pb & Sn (d) Pb & Al

31. A few grams of sodium carbonate is added to 1 L of water. What is the pH or pH range of resultant solution? **[July 6, 2022 (I)]**
(a) 7 – 14 (b) 7.0 (c) 1.0 (d) 1 – 4

32. Identify A and B from the following reaction
$NaNO_3 \xrightarrow{\Delta} xA + yB$ **[July 4, 2022 (I)]**
(a) $NaNO_2, O_2$ (b) Na_2O, NO_2
(c) Na_2O, NO (d) Na, NO_2

33. Which of the following nitrates on heating does not give its oxide? **[2018]**
(a) $LiNO_3$ (b) $NaNO_3$ (c) $Ba(NO_3)_2$ (d) $Be(NO_3)_2$

Topic 3 General Characteristics of Alkaline Earth Metals and their Compounds

34. The oxide and hydroxide of which metal are amphoteric in nature? **[May 12, 2026 (II)]**
(a) Li (b) Na
(c) Mg (d) Be

35. Identify the correct statements from the following
I. All alkaline earth metals give hydrides on heating with hydrogen. **[May 27, 2025 (I)]**
II. Calcium hydroxide is used to purify sugar.
III. $BeCl_2$ is a dimer in gaseous phase.
(a) I & III only (b) II & III only
(c) I, II, III (d) I & II only

36. Consider the following. **[May 24, 2025 (I)]**
Statement-I: Both $BeSO_4$ and $MgSO_4$ are readily soluble in water.
Statement-II: Among the nitrates of alkaline earth metals, only $Be(NO_3)_2$ on strong heating gives its oxide, NO_2 and O_2.
(a) Both Statement-I and statement-II are correct.
(b) Statement-I is correct, but statement-II is not correct.
(c) Statement-I is not correct, but statement-II is correct.
(d) Both statement-I and statement-II are not correct.

37. Which chloride does not exist as hydrate ? **[May 23, 2025 (II)]**
(a) $MgCl_2$ (b) $CaCl_2$ (c) LiCl (d) KCl

38. The correct order of density of Be, Mg, Ca, Sr is **[May 23, 2025 (I)]**
(a) Sr > Be > Mg > Ca (b) Sr > Ca > Mg > Be
(c) Be > Mg > Ca > Sr (d) Be > Mg > Sr > Ca

39. Which of the following orders are correct against the stated property? **[May 21, 2025 (II)]**
(I) $NaO_2 < KO_2 < RbO_2 < CsO_2$ - stability
(II) $Mg(OH)_2 < Ca(OH)_2 < Sr(OH)_2$ - basic strength
(III) $MgCO_3 < CaCO_3 < SrCO_3$ - thermal stability
(a) I and III only (b) II and III only
(c) I and II only (d) I, II and III

40. Which of the following statements is incorrect with reference to alkaline earth metals? **[May 21, 2025 (I)]**
(a) Solubility of carbonates in water decreases down the group
(b) All the sulphates are thermally stable
(c) All the nitrates decompose on heating
(d) All halides are ionic in nature

41. Well of the following, on thermal decomposition, form both acidic and basic oxides along with O_2?
(i) $NaNO_3$ (ii) $Ca(NO_3)_2$ (iii) $Be(NO_3)_2$ (iv) $LiNO_3$
The correct option is **[May 23, 2024 (I)]**
(a) ii, iii only (b) iii, iv only
(c) ii, iv only (d) i, ii, iii

42. Which one of the following alkaline earth metals does not form hydride when it is heated with hydrogen directly? **[May 22, 2024 (I)]**
(a) Be (b) Mg (c) Ca (d) Sr

43. Which one of the following statements is NOT correct about the compounds of alkaline earth metals? **[May 21, 2024 (II)]**
(a) Basic nature increases from $Mg(OH)_2$ to $Ba(OH)_2$
(b) Thermal stability decreases from $BeCO_3$ to $BaCO_3$
(c) Solubility of sulphates in water decreases from $BeSO_4$ to $BaSO_4$
(d) Nitrates of these on heating give oxides

44. Ba, Ca, Sr form halide hydrates. Their formulae are $BaCl_2, xH_2O$, $CaCl_2, yH_2O$, $SrCl_2, zH_2O$. The values of x, y, z respectively are **[May 20, 2024 (I)]**
(a) 2, 6, 6 (b) 8, 6, 2 (c) 8, 6, 6 (d) 6, 4, 2

45. The alkaline earth metal with lowest density is **[May 19, 2023 (I)]**
(a) Be (b) Mg (c) Ca (d) Sr

46. Which of the following statement(s) is/are correct?
(i) Li NO_3, Ba $(NO_3)_2$ both will give NO_2 on heatiing
(ii) $BaSO_4$ is less soluble in water than $CaSO_4$
(iii) Alkaline earth metals do not dissolve in liquid ammonia **[May 17, 2023 (I)]**
(a) i only (b) i, ii only
(c) i, ii & iii (d) i, iii only

47. Match the following

List I (alkaline earth metal)	List II (density/ g cm^{-3})
A. Be	I. 1.74
B. Mg	II. 1.84
C. Ca	III. 2.63
D. Sr	IV. 1.55

[May 15, 2023 (II)]
(a) A-III, B-II, C-I, D-IV (b) A-IV, B-I, C-II, D-III
(c) A-II, B-I, C-III, D-IV (d) A-II, B-I, C-IV, D-III

48. Observe the following reactions

$$\text{Dimer} \xleftarrow{\text{Vapour phase}} MCl_2 \xrightarrow{1200\,K} \text{linear monomer}.$$

What is M? **[July 8, 2022 (I)]**

(a) Ca (b) Sr (c) Mg (d) Be

49. Hydration enthalpy of which of the following ions is highest? **[July 7, 2022 (II)]**

(a) Mg^{2+} (b) Na^+ (c) Ca^{2+} (d) K^+

50. The pair of elements that form both oxides and nitrides, when burnt in air are **[July 4, 2022 (II)]**

(a) Na, Mg (b) Na, Be (c) Mg, Ca (d) Be, Mn

51. **Assertion (A) :** $MgSO_4$ is readily soluble in water

Reason (R) : The greater hydration enthalpy of Mg^{2+} ions overcome its lattice enthalpy. **[July 4, 2022 (I)]**

(a) A and R both are correct and R is the correct explanation of A.

(b) A and R both are correct but R is not the correct explanation of A.

(c) A is correct but R is not correct.

(d) A is incorrect but R is correct.

52. Two metals *A* and *B* having similar ionic radii, react with oxygen to give only monoxides and react with nitrogen to give nitrides. Then, *A* and *B* respectively are **[Sept. 17, 2020 (I)]**

(a) Li and Na (b) Na and Ca

(c) Li and Mg (d) Na and Be

Topic 4 Some Important Compounds of Alkaline Earth Metals

53. Identify the sets in which both the metals react with water? **[May 18, 2026 (I)]**

I. Be, Mg II. Li, Mg

III. Na, K IV. K, Ca

Correct answer is

(a) II, IV only (b) II, III, IV only

(c) III, IV only (d) I, II only

54. An element X reacts with air to form monoxide and nitride. This oxide is amphoteric. It can be converted to its chloride by heating with carbon and chlorine. Which of the following is correct for X? **[May 15, 2026 (I)]**

(a) The oxide of X has rock-salt structure

(b) X belongs to group I of the periodic table

(c) X shows diagonal relationship with aluminium

(d) Carbonate of X is thermally very stable

55. Which one of the carbonates is unstable in air and is kept in CO_2 atmosphere to avoid decomposition? **[May 13, 2026 (I)]**

(a) $MgCO_3$ (b) $CaCO_3$

(c) $BaCO_3$ (d) $BeCO_3$

56. Identify the incorrect statement from the following **[May 12, 2026 (I)]**

(a) Among the oxides of alkaline earth metals, oxide of Be is only amphoteric in nature

(b) Reducing power of alkaline earth metals is less than those of their corresponding alkali metals

(c) All alkaline earth metals combine with hydrogen upon heating and form MH_2 type of hydrides

(d) All alkaline earth metals liberate H_2 on reaction with acids

57. The enamel present on teeth becomes much harder due to the conversion of $[3\,Ca_3(PO_4)_2, X]$ into $[3\,Ca_3(PO_4)_2, Y]$. What are X and Y? **[May 21, 2024 (II)]**

(a) $X = Ca(OH)_2$, $Y = CaF_2$

(b) $X = Ca(OH)_2$, $Y = CaCl_2$

(c) $X = Ca(OH)_2$, $Y = NaCl$

(d) $X = CaO$, $Y = CaCl_2$

58. Which of the following alloys are correctly matched with their uses? **[May 15, 2023 (I)]**

(i) Li/Mg armour plates

(ii) Cu/Be high strength springs

(iii) Mg/Al aircraft construction

(a) i, ii only (b) ii, iii only

(c) i, iii only (d) i, ii, iii

59. $CaCO_3$ was reacted with dil HCl to form three products. One of the products formed, when passed into slaked lime gave X. What is X? **[July 6, 2022 (I)]**

(a) $CaCl_2$ (b) $CaCO_3$

(c) $Ca(OH)_2$ (d) $Ca(HCO_3)_2$

60. The colour of $Mg(OH)_2$ precipitate formed when it is precipitated in the presence of magneson reagent is **[July 6, 2022 (I)]**

(a) Green (b) Yellow (c) Brown (d) Blue

61. The compound that is used in smoke screens is **[July 5, 2022 (II)]**

(a) Mg_3N_2 (b) MgO (c) NaN_3 (d) Ca_3P_2

Appendix-III

The *p*-Block Elements (Group-13)

CHAPTER SYNOPSIS

General electronic configuration: ns^2np^1

- Anomalous Behaviour of Boron
  - Characteristics shown by boron and not by other elements of the group are followings:
  - B is a non-metal and forms covalent compounds
  - B is a bad conductor of electricity
  - Trihalides of B exist as monomer.
  - Hydroxides and oxides of B are acidic in nature
  - B exhibits maximum covalency of four.
- Atomic radii
- B < Ga < Al < In < Tl (Poor screening effect of d-electrons in Ga)
- Ionic radii (+3 o.s)
- B < Al < Ga < In < Tl (regular trend)
- All elements of group 13 form trihalides of the formula MX_3.
- Boric acid (H_3BO_3) has a hydrogen bonded structure.
- Zeolites are alumino silicates of the general formula,

  $$M_{x/n}[(AlO_2)_x.(SiO_2)_y].mH_2O$$

  where, M may be a simple cation like Na^+, K^+, or Ca^{2+}

  n is the charge on the simple cation, m is the number of molecules of water of hydration.
- Properties of Al are different from Ga, In and Tl.
- First ionization energy is in the order

  B > Tl > Ga > Al > In
- Inert pair effect increases after *n* (principal quantum no.) > 4 and increases with increasing value of *n*.
- Al and Ga are amphoteric. In is more basic than Ga.
- Lewis acid character of boron halides is in the order

  $$BI_3 > BBr_3 > BCl_3 > BF_3$$
- (+ 1) B < Al < Ga < In < Tl (inert pair effect)
- (+ 3) B > Al > Ga > In > Tl
- The nature of oxides varies down the group
- B_2O_3 (Acidic) Al_2O_3, Ga_2O_3 (Amphoteric) In_2O_3, Tl_2O_3, TlO_2 (Basic)
- Reaction with acids: $2M + 6H^+ \longrightarrow 2M^{3+} + 3H_2$
- Reaction with alkalies:
- $2M + 2NaOH + 6H_2O \longrightarrow 2Na^+ [M(OH)_4]^- + 3H_2$
- Boron does not react with acid or base even at moderate temperature however 'Al' shows amphoteric character.
- Reaction with halogens: $2M + 3X_2 \longrightarrow 2MX_3$
- (except TlI_3)
- Lewis acid strength trends:
- $BF_3 < BCl_3 < BBr_3 < BI_3$ (due to back bonding BF_3 is less acidic)

1. The structure of Al_2Cl_6 is given below

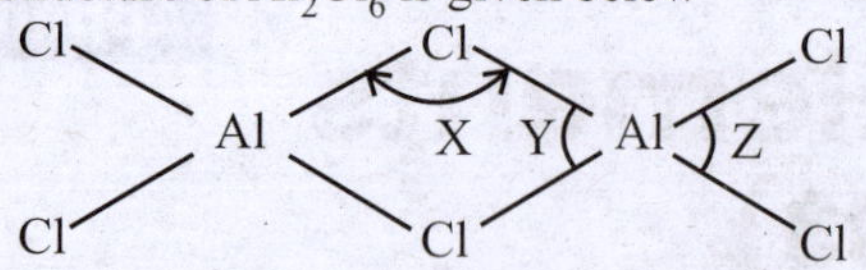

The correct order of bond angles X, Y and Z is **[May 18, 2026 (II)]**

(a) X > Y > Z (b) Z > X > Y
(c) Y > X > Z (d) Z > Y > X

2. The reaction between X and Y produces a solid substance and a mixture of two gases, one of which is a colorless toxic gas. X and Y respectively are. **[May 18, 2026 (I)]**

(a) $LiAlH_4$, BF_3 (b) $NaBH_4$, I_2
(c) NaH, BF_3 (d) $LiBH_4$, BCl_3

3. $NaBH_4$ reacts with I_2 and gives a salt and two gases Y, Z. The gas Y is toxic in nature. Z is a combustible gas. The correct statements regarding Y, Z are

I. Y with NaH forms a compound which acts as a good reducing agent
II. Y on hydrolysis gives a monobasic acid
III. Z is used in Haber's process

The correct answer is **[May 15, 2026 (II)]**

(a) I, II only (b) I, III only
(c) I, II, III (d) II, III only

4. Observe the following reaction **[May 15, 2026 (I)]**

$Na_2B_4O_7 \xrightarrow{H_2O}$ Acid + alkali

The hybridisation of central atom of acid is

(a) sp^3 (b) sp^2
(c) dsp^2 (d) sp^3d^2

5. In which of the following boron and boron related substances are not correctly matched with the application shown against it? **[May 14, 2026 (I)]**

(a) Boron fibres - manufacture of glass wool
(b) Metal borides - protective shields in nuclear industry
(c) Borax - flux for soldering metals
(d) Boric acid - mild antiseptic

6. Observe the following sequence of reactions

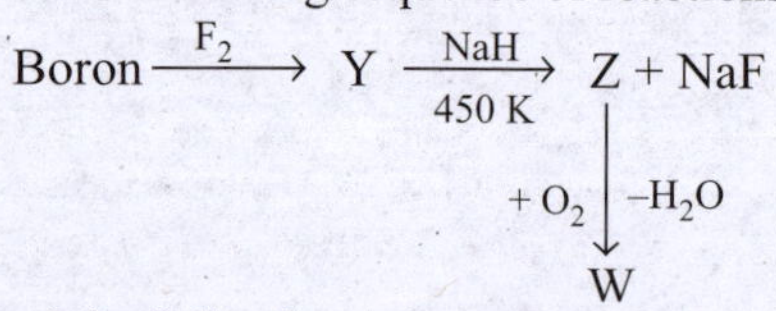

Which of the following is not correct?

[May 13, 2026 (II)]

(a) Z forms adducts with Lewis bases.
(b) Y & Z both are electron deficient molecules.
(c) W is an acidic oxide.
(d) Y on hydrolysis gives a weak monobasic acid in which hybridisation of central atom is sp^3.

7. Total number of electrons involved in the formation of bridge bonds in the structure of diborane is **[May 13, 2026 (I)]**

(a) 6 (b) 2
(c) 4 (d) 3

8. A boron compound X̲ is obtained when aqueous solution of borax is treated with HCl. The incorrect statement about X̲ is **[May 12, 2026 (II)]**

(a) It has layer structure
(b) Its basicity is 3
(c) On heating it gives an acidic oxide
(d) It is highly soluble in hot water

9. BCl_3 on hydrolysis gives a complex ion $\sqrt{\frac{4gh}{3}}$. $AlCl_3$ in acidified aqueous solution forms a complex ion $2\sin\left(\frac{2\pi}{3}\right)t$. The hybridization of central atoms in X and Y are respectively. **[May 12, 2026 (I)]**

(a) sp^3, sp^3 (b) sp^3, sp^3d
(c) sp^2, sp^3d^2 (d) sp^3, sp^3d^2

10. Select the correct statements from the following.

(A) Aluminium liberates H_2 gas with dil. HCl but not with aqueous NaOH. **[May 27, 2025 (I)]**
(B) Formula of sodium metaborate is Na_3BO_3
(C) Boric acid is a weak monobasic acid
(D) For thallium, +1 state is more stable than +3 state.

(a) A & B (b) B & C (c) C & D (d) A & D

11. The correct order of electronegativity of group 13 elements is **[May 26, 2025 (II)]**

(a) B > Ga > Al > Tl > In (b) B > Al > Tl > Ga > In
(c) B > Al > Ga > In > Tl (d) B > Tl > In > Ga > Al

12. Which of the following reactions give H_2 as one of the products ? **[May 26, 2025 (I)]**
(Reactions are not balanced)

I. $NaBH_4 + I_2 \rightarrow$
II. $B_2H_6 + N(CH_3)_3 \rightarrow$
III. $Al + NaOH + H_2O \rightarrow$
IV. $BF_3 + NaH \rightarrow$

(a) I, II & III only (b) II & IV only
(c) I & III only (d) II, III & IV only

13. Which of the following is not associated with water molecules? **[May 24, 2025 (I)]**

(a) cryolite (b) bauxite (c) kernite (d) borax

14. Identify the incorrect statement about the group 13 elements **[May 23, 2025 (II)]**

(a) Nature of aqueous solution of borax is alkaline.
(b) Orthoboric acid is a weak tribasic acid.
(c) Metaboric acid on heating gives an acidic oxide.
(d) $LiBH_4$ acts as a reducing agent.

15. Identify the reaction in which diborane is produced on industrial scale? **[May 23, 2025 (I)]**
(a) Reaction of BF_3 with $LiAlH_4$ in diethyl ether
(b) Oxidation of $NaBH_4$ with I_2
(c) Reaction of BF_3 with NaH at 450 K
(d) By heating H_3BO_3 to above 370 K temperature

16. Consider the following **[May 22, 2025 (II)]**
Statement-I : Al_2O_3 is amphoteric in nature.
Statement-II : Tl_2O_3 is more basic than Ga_2O_3
The correct answer is
(a) Both statement-I and statement-II are correct.
(b) Both statement-I and statement-II are not correct.
(c) Statement-I is correct, but statement-II is not correct.
(d) Statement-I is not correct, but statement-II is correct.

17. The incorrect statement from the following is **[May 22, 2025 (I)]**
(a) Aluminium dissolves in conc. HNO_3 and liberates H_2 gas
(b) Borazole contains 12σ and 3π bonds
(c) Gallium oxide is amphoteric in nature
(d) BF_3 is a Lewis acid

18. In the structure of diborane, the number of 2-centre-2-electron bonds is X and 3-centre-2-electron bonds is Y. The value of (X + Y) is **[May 21, 2025 (II)]**
(a) 5 (b) 6 (c) 4 (d) 8

19. Consider the following. **[May 21, 2025 (I)]**
Statement-I : The order of electronegativity of B, Al, In, Tl is B > Tl > Al > In
Statement-II : Boric acid is a weak protonic acid.
The correct answer is
(a) Both statement-I and statement-II are correct.
(b) Both statement-I and statement-II are not correct.
(c) Statement-I is correct, but statement-II is not correct.
(d) Statement-I is not correct, but statement-II is correct.

20. Identify the correct sets **[May 23, 2024 (I)]**
i. Boron fibres - bullet proof vest
ii. Metal borides - protective shields
iii. Borax - glass wool
Correct option is
(a) i, ii only (b) i, ii, iii
(c) i, iii only (d) ii, iii only

21. In the given structure of Diborane θ_1, θ_2 are respectively **[May 22, 2024 (I)]**

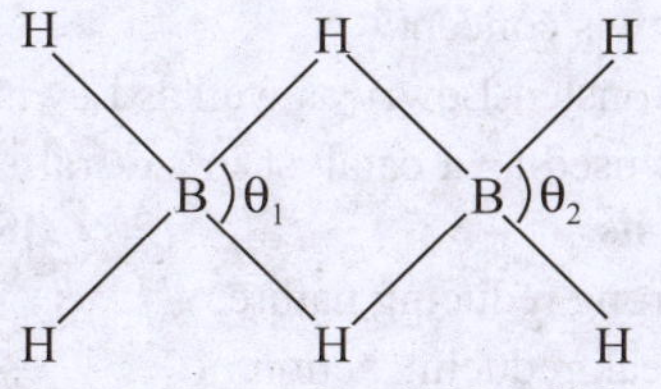

(a) 101°, 118° (b) 118°, 101°
(c) 97°, 120° (d) 120°, 97°

22. A Lewis acid ‘X’ reacts with $LiAlH_4$ in ether medium to give a highly toxic gas, ‘Y’. ‘Y’ when heated with NH_3 gives a compound known as inorganic benzene. ‘Y’ bums in oxygen and gives H_2O and ‘Z’. ‘Z’ is **[May 21, 2024 (I)]**
(a) Basic oxide (b) Acidic oxide
(c) Amphoteric acid (d) Neutral oxide

23.

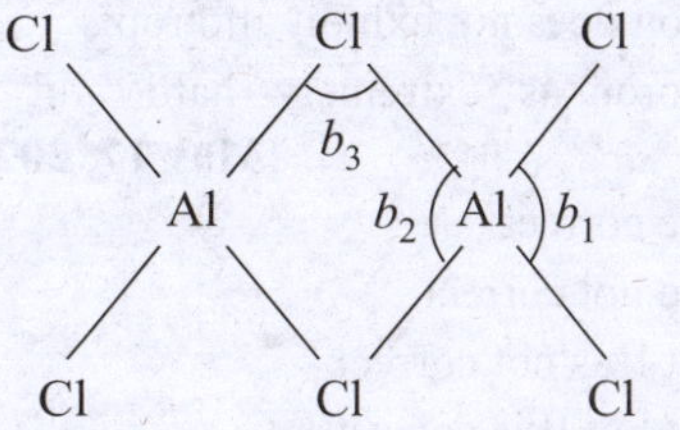

The bond angles b_1, b_2, b_3 in the above structure are respectively (in °) **[May 20, 2024 (I)]**
(a) 79, 101, 118 (b) 118, 101, 79
(c) 79, 118, 101 (d) 118, 79, 101

24. Identify the correct statements. **[May 19, 2024 (II)]**
i. Oxidation of $NaBH_4$ with I_2 gives B_2H_6
ii. B_2H_6 burns in oxygen and releases an enormous amount of energy
iii. B_2H_6 on hydrolysis gives a tribasic acid
(a) i, ii, iii (b) i, iii only
(c) i, ii only (d) ii, iii only

25. Which one of the following is used as piezoelectric material? **[May 19, 2024 (II)]**
(a) tridymite (b) quartz
(c) zelolite (d) mica

26. In which of the following reaction, dihydrogen is not evolved? **[May 18, 2024 (I)]**
(a) Oxidation of sodium borohydride with iodine
(b) Hydrolysis of boranes
(c) Heating the adduct formed by reaction of ammonia with diborane
(d) Burning of diborane in oxygen

27. Relative stability orders of +1, +3 oxidation states of Ga, In, T1 are respectively **[May 19, 2023 (I)]**
(a) $Tl^+ > In^+ > Ga^+$, $Ga^{3+} > In^{3+} > Tl^{3+}$
(b) $Ga^+ > In^+ > Tl^+$, $Tl^{3+} > In^{3+} > Ga^{3+}$
(c) $Ga^+ > In^+ > Tl^+$, $Ga^{3+} > In^{3+} > Tl^{3+}$
(d) $Tl^+ > In^+ > Ga^+$, $Tl^{3+} > In^{3+} > Ga^{3+}$

28. The standard electrode potential (in V) values for Al^{3+}/Al, Tl^{3+}/T1 are respectively **[May 18, 2023 (II)]**
(a) –1.66, –1.26 (b) +1.66, +1.26
(c) –1.66, +1.26 (d) +1.66, –1.26

29. Which one of the following is correct? **[May 18, 2023 (I)]**
(a) Thallium is more electropositive than aluminium
(b) Boron has high electrical conductivity
(c) An aqueous solution of ortho boric acid is generally used as a mild antiseptic
(d) Boron – 11 (^{11}B) isotope has high ability to absorb neutrons

30. In the below reaction, geometry of BCl_3, X respectively are
$BCl_3 + NH_3 \rightarrow X$ **[May 17, 2023 (II)]**
(a) Pyramidal, tetrahedral
(b) Pyramidal, octahedral
(c) Trigonal planar, tetrahedral
(d) Trigonal planar, octahedral

31. Statement-I: Boron does not exhibit allotropy
Statement-II: Boron is extremely hard and black coloured solid **[May 17, 2023 (I)]**
(a) Both I & II are correct
(b) Both I & II are not correct
(c) I is correct but II is not correct
(d) I is not correct but II is correct

32. Which of the following statements are not correct?
i. Atomic radius of Ga is less than that of Al
ii. The order of ionization enthalpy of group 13 elements is B > Al > Ga > In > T1
iii. Boron trioxide is amphoteric in nature
[May 16, 2023 (I)]
(a) ii, iii only (b) i, iii only
(c) i, ii only (d) i, ii, iii

33. The correct order of melting points of Al, Ga, In is
[May 15, 2023 (II)]
(a) Ga < In < Al (b) In < Ga < Al
(c) Al < Ga < In (d) Ga < Al < In

34. Match the following

List-I (Group 13 element)	**List-II (Metallic radius, pm)**
A. Al	I. 135
B. Ga	II. 143
C. In	III. 170
D. Tl	IV. 167

The correct answer is **[May 15, 2023 (I)]**
(a) A–I, B–II, C–IV, D–III (b) A–II, B–I, C–IV, D–III
(c) A–III, B–IV, C–II, D–I (d) A–II, B–I, C–III, D–IV

35. The structures of BCl_3 and $BCl_3.NH_3$, respectively are
[July 8, 2022 (I)]
(a) Planar trigonal and Tetrahedral
(b) Planar trigonal and Pyramidal
(c) Pyramidal and Tetrahedral
(d) Pyramidal and Pyramidal

36. Aluminium chloride in acidified aqueons solution gives a complex ion 'X'. The hybridization of central atom in X is **[July 7, 2022 (II)]**
(a) sp^3 (b) sp^2d (c) d^2sp^3 (d) sp^3d^2

37. Borax dissolves in water and forms a product of boron (X). Identify the compound X. **[July 6, 2022 (I)]**
(a) HBO_2 (b) B_2O_3 (c) $NaBO_2$ (d) H_3BO_3

38. The reaction of diborane in diethylether with X gives metalborohydride. X is a **[July 5, 2022 (II)]**
(a) Metal (b) Metal halide
(c) Metal hydride (d) Metal oxide

39. Identify the correct statements about the anomalous behavior of Boron **[July 4, 2022 (II)]**
I. Boron trihalides can form dimeric structures.
II. Boron shows + 1 as stable oxidation state
III. Maximum covalency of boron is four.
IV. Boron does not form BF_6^{6-} ion.
(a) I, II only (b) II, III only
(c) III, IV only (d) I, IV only

40. Identify the correct statements about Boron.
I. It has high melting point. **[July 4, 2022 (I)]**
II. It has high density.
III. It has high electrical conductivity
IV. B-10 isotope of it has high ability to absorb neutrons
(a) I, II only (b) II, III only
(c) III, IV only (d) I, IV only

41. Consider the following reaction **[Aug. 23, 2021 (I)]**
$BCl_3 + NH_3 \longrightarrow BCl_3 \cdot NH_3$
The geometries of BCl_3 and $BCl_3 \cdot NH_3$ respectively are
(a) trigonal planar and tetrahedral
(b) tetrahedral and square planar
(c) tetrahedral and trigonal bipyramidal
(d) square planar and trigonal pyramidal

42. AlF_3 is soluble in HF only in the presence of KF due to formation of **[Aug. 20, 2021 (I)]**
(a) AlH_3 (b) $[AlH_6]^{3-}$
(c) $[AlF_6]^{3-}$ (d) $K[AlF_3H]$

43. When borax is dissolved in water, it gives an alkaline solution. The alkaline solution consists the following products **[Aug. 19, 2021 (I)]**
(a) NaOH and BH_3 (b) NaOH and H_3BO_3
(c) $NaHCO_3$ and H_3BO_3 (d) Na_2CO_3 and H_3BO_3

44. Which of the following compounds are formed, when boron trichloride is treated with water?
[Sept. 18, 2020 (II)]
(a) $H_3BO_3 + HCl$ (b) $B_2H_6 + HCl$
(c) $B_2O_3 + HCl$ (d) $HBO_3 + HCl$

45. Acidity of BF_3 can be explained on the basis of which of the following concepts? **[Sept. 17, 2020 (I)]**
(a) Arrhenius concept
(b) Bronsted-Lowry concept
(c) Lewis concept
(d) Bronsted-Lowry as well as Lewis concept

46. BF_3 is used as a catalyst in several industrial processes due to its **[Sept. 17, 2020 (II)]**
(a) strong reducing nature.
(b) weak reducing action
(c) strong Lewis acid nature
(d) weak Lewis acid character

47. What is X in the following reaction? **[Apr. 22, 2019 (I)]**

$$NaH + B_2H_6 \xrightarrow{\text{Diethyl ether}} X$$

(a) $Na[BH_4]$ (b) $NaBO_2$

(c) H_3BO_3 (d) $(C_2H_5OC_2H_4)^+(BH_4)^-$

48. Identify the correct statements from the following : **[Apr. 21, 2019 (I)]**

I. Ga_2O_3 is an amphoteric oxide.

II. The dimer of aluminium chloride has three Al—Cl—Al bridge bonds.

III. Boron is very hard refractory solid of high melting temperature.

(a) I, II only (b) I, III only

(c) II, III only (d) I, II, III

49. BF_3 reacts with NaH at 450 K to form NaF and X. When X reacts with LiH in diethyl ether, Y is formed. What is Y? **[2018]**

(a) $LiBO_2$ (b) $Li_2B_4O_7$

(c) $LiBH_4$ (d) B_2H_6 .LiH

50. In which of the following reactions, hydrogen is liberated? **[2017]**

(i) $Al(s) + HCl(aq) \longrightarrow$

(ii) $Al(s) + NaOH(aq) \longrightarrow$

(iii) $NaBH_4 + I_2 \longrightarrow$

(a) i, ii (b) ii, iii

(c) i, iii (d) i, ii, iii

51. **Assertion (A) :** $AlCl_3$ exists as a dimer through halogen bridged bonds.

Reason (R) : $AlCl_3$ gets stability by accepting electrons from the bridged halogen. **[2016]**

(a) Both (A) and (R) are true and (R) is the correct explanation of (A)

(b) Both (A) and (R) are true but (R) is not the correct explanation of (A)

(c) (A) is true, but (R) is false

(d) (A) is false, but (R) is true

Appendix-IV

The *p*-Block Elements (Group-14)

CHAPTER SYNOPSIS

- **General electronic configuration: ns^2np^2**

Physical Properties

- On moving down in a group from C to Pb
- atomic and ionic radius increases
- m. p and b. p decreases
- I.E decreases up to Sn
- The trend is : C > Si > Ge > Sn < Pb
- electronegativity decreases up to Si and from Si to Pb are almost same
- Density: Si < C < Ge < Sn < Pb

Chemical Properties

- Carbon form three types of carbides.
  - (a) Ionic (salt-like) carbides – CaC_2, Al_4C_3, Mg_2C_3.
  - (b) Covalent carbides – B_4C, SiC
  - (c) Interstitial carbides – WC, carbides of Cr, Mn, and iron group metals
- Silicates are the metal derivatives of silicic acid (H_4SiO_4). The basic building unit of silicates is the SiO_4^{4-} anion.
- Silicones are water-repellent.
- **Anomalous Behaviour of Carbon**
  - Characteristics shown by carbon and not by other elements of the group are followings:
  - exhibit covalence upto four only
  - ability to form pπ-pπ multiple bonds.
  - maximum tendency for catenation.
- **Oxidation state**

C, Si,	Ge	Sn	Pb
+4	+ 4 >	+ 4 >	+ 4
	+ 2 <	+ 2 <	+ 2

- Reaction with air : $2M + O_2 \longrightarrow 2MO$; $M + O_2 \longrightarrow MO_2$
- (CO_2, SiO_2, GeO_2), (SnO_2, PbO_2), CO
  acidic — amphoteric — neutral
- GeO, SnO, PbO
  acidic — amphoteric
- Reaction with water : $Sn + 2H_2O \xrightarrow{\Delta} SnO_2 + 2H_2$
- C, Si and Ge are not affected by water while pb also not affected by H2O due to protective oxide film formation.
- Reaction with halogens :Except carbon all other elements react directly with halogens.
- Order of catenation : C >> Si > Ge ≈ Sn

1. Which of the following reaction is not correct? [May 18, 2026 (II)]
(a) $SiF_4 + 2F^- \rightarrow [SiF_6]^{2-}$
(b) $GeCl_4 + 2Cl^- \rightarrow [GeCl_6]^{2-}$
(c) $Sn(OH)_4 + 2OH^- \rightarrow [Sn(OH)_6]^{2-}$
(d) $SiCl_4 + 2Cl^- \rightarrow [SiCl_6]^{2-}$

2. X, Y and Z are three allotropes of carbon. They are used in black ink, in water filters and as reducing agent in metallurgy respectively. The correct statement about their production is [May 18, 2026 (I)]
(a) X is produced by heating wood at high temperatures in absence of air
(b) Y is produced by burning hydrocarbons in limited air
(c) Z is produced by heating coal at high temperatures in absence of air
(d) All three are produced by same chemical process

3. Which of the following compounds is not correctly matched with the property given? [May 15, 2026 (II)]
(a) Silica - Has high melting point
(b) Silicones - water-repellent and heat-resistant
(c) Zeolites - ion-exchangers
(d) Stannous chloride - good oxidizing agent

4. Which of the following carbon allotropes is not correctly matched with its use? [May 14, 2026 (II)]
(a) Graphite - as electrode in batteries
(b) Diamond - as abrasive for cutting hard tools
(c) Coke - as reducing agent in extraction of metals
(d) Carbon black - in adsorbing poisonous gases

5. Which of the following statements regarding the similarities between boron and silicon is not correct? [May 14, 2026 (II)]
(a) Both form halides that undergo hydrolysis
(b) Both form electron precise hydrides
(c) Both form acidic oxides
(d) Density of both is almost same

6. The number of amphoteric oxides in the following is
CO_2, GeO_2, SnO_2, PbO_2, CO, GeO, SnO, PbO
The correct answer is [May 14, 2026 (I)]
(a) 5 (b) 3
(c) 2 (d) 4

7. Which pair of oxides is acidic in nature? [May 13, 2026 (II)]
(a) GeO, GeO_2 (b) CO, CO_2
(c) SnO, SnO_2 (d) PbO, PbO_2

8. Consider the following statements [May 13, 2026 (I)]
Statement-I: Silica in its normal form is almost non-reactive because of very high Si-O bond enthalpy.
Statement-II: Silica has no reaction with HF
The correct answer is
(a) Both the statements-I & II are correct.
(b) Statement-I is correct but statement-II is NOT correct
(c) Statement-I is NOT correct but statement-II is correct
(d) Both the statements-I & II are NOT correct

9. Observe the following statements about the oxides of group 14 elements [May 12, 2026 (II)]
I. CO_2 is an acidic oxide but CO is a neutral oxide
II. Cristobalite is the crystalline form of silica
III. Liquid CO is called dry ice
IV. Both CO and CO_2 act as Lewis acids
The correct statements are
(a) I & II only (b) I & III only
(c) I & IV only (d) III & IV only

10. Galena is the sulphide ore of element $\frac{1}{r}$ and cassiterite is the oxide ore of $\frac{1}{r^2}$. What are X and Y respectively? [May 12, 2026 (I)]
(a) Pb, Sn (b) Sn, Pb
(c) Ge, Sn (d) Pb, Si

11. The number of amphoteric oxides from the following is
CO_2, GeO_2, SnO_2, PbO_2, CO, GeO, SnO, PbO [May 27, 2025 (I)]
(a) 3 (b) 4 (c) 6 (d) 5

12. Identify the correct statements. [May 26, 2025 (II)]
(I) CO reduces the oxygen carrying ability of blood
(II) Producer gas contains CO & N_2
(III) C-O bond length in CO_2 is 115 pm
(a) I & III only (b) I, II & III
(c) I & II only (d) II & III only

13. Which one of the following gases is the major contributor to global warming ? [May 26, 2025 (I)]
(a) CO (b) CO_2 (c) CH_4 (d) N_2O

14. Consider the following. [May 26, 2025 (I)]
Statement-I: CCl_4 does not undergo hydrolysis. But $SiCl_4$ undergoes hydrolysis.
Statement-II: Thermal and chemical stability of GeX_4 is more than GeX_2
The correct answer is
(a) Both statement-I and statement-II are correct.
(b) Both statement-I and statement-II are not correct.
(c) Statement-I is correct, but statement-II is not correct.
(d) Statement-I is not correct, but statement-II is correct.

15. Identify the incorrect statement about silica. [May 24, 2025 (I)]
(a) It is acidic in nature.
(b) It has no reaction with most of acids except HF.
(c) With NaOH it forms sodium silicate.
(d) Like graphite, it has two dimensional structure.

16. Which of the following statements are correct? [May 23, 2025 (II)]
(I) SnF_4, is ionic in nature.
(II) Stability of dihalides of group 14 elements increases down the group.
(III) $GeCl_2$ is more stable than $GeCl_4$.

(a) I, II & III (b) I & III only
(c) II & III only (d) I & II only

17. Which of the following properties is not correct for silicones? **[May 23, 2025 (I)]**
(a) bio compatible
(b) high thermal stability
(c) low dielectric strength
(d) water repelling in nature

18. Identify the incorrect order against the stated property. **[May 22, 2025 (II)]**
(a) Ge > Sn > Pb - Ionization enthalpy
(b) Ge > Pb > Sn - Melting point
(c) Pb > Sn > Ge - Density
(d) Ge > Pb > Sn - Electrical resistivity

19. In Buckminster fullerene, the number of six membered carbon rings is '*x*' and five membered carbon rings is '*y*', $(x + y)$ value is **[May 22, 2025 (I)]**
(a) 30 (b) 31 (c) 32 (d) 33

20. Match the following : **[May 21, 2025 (II)]**

List-I (Compound)		List-II (Use)	
(A)	Kieselghur	(I)	Chromotographic material
(B)	Silica gel	(II)	Softening of hard Water
(C)	ZSM-5	(III)	Filtration plants
(D)	Hydrated zeolites	(IV)	To convert alcohol directly into gasoline

The correct answer is
(a) A-IV, B-III, C-II, D-I
(b) A-IV, B-I, C-II, D-III
(c) A-III, B-IV, C-I, D-II
(d) A-III, B-I, C-IV, D-II

21. Consider the following. **[May 21, 2025 (I)]**
Assertion (A): CO is poisonous to living beings.
Reason (R): CO binds to haemoglobin forming carboxyhaemoglobin, which is less stable than oxygen-haemoglobin complex.
Correct answer is
(a) (A) and (R) both are correct and (R) is the correct explanation for (A).
(b) (A) and (R) both are correct and (R) is not the correct explanation for (A).
(c) (A) is correct, but (R) is not correct.
(d) (A) is not correct, but (R) is correct.

22. Which of the following does not exist? **[May 21, 2025 (I)]**
(a) $[SiCl_6]^{2-}$ (b) $[GeCl_6]^{2-}$
(c) $[SiF_6]^{2-}$ (d) $[Sn(OH)_6]^{2-}$

23. Which of the following is / are ionic in nature?
(i) GeF_4 (ii) SnF_4 (iii) PbF_4 **[May 23, 2024 (I)]**
(a) iii only (b) ii, iii only
(c) i only (d) i, ii only

24. Two statements are given below. **[May 22, 2024 (II)]**
Statement-I: SnF_4, PbF_4 are ionic in nature.
Statement-II: $GeCl_2$ is more stable than $GeCl_4$.
The correct answer is
(a) Both statements-I & II are correct
(b) Both statements-I & II are not correct
(c) Statement-I is correct, but statement-II is not correct
(d) Statement-I is not correct, but statement II is correct

25. In which of the following sets allotropes of carbon are correctly matched with their uses?
i. graphite - crucibles **[May 22, 2024 (I)]**
ii. activated charcoal - water filters
iii. carbon black - fuel
The correct answer is
(a) i, iii only (b) ii, iii only
(c) i, ii, iii (d) i, ii only

26. Hydrated sodium aluminium silicate is called **[May 21, 2024 (II)]**
(a) Calgon (b) Zeolite
(c) Dead burnt plaster (d) Kaolinite

27. Which of the allotropic forms of carbon is aromatic in nature? **[May 21, 2024 (II)]**
(a) Diamond (b) Graphite
(c) Buckminster fullerene (d) coke

28. Which of the following are correct?
i. Basic structural unit of silicates is $-R_2SiO-$
ii. Silicones are biocompatible
iii. Producer gas contains CO and N_2
The correct option is **[May 20, 2024 (II)]**
(a) i, ii, iii (b) ii, iii only
(c) i, iii only (d) i, ii only

29. Which of the following oxides is acidic in nature? **[May 20, 2024 (I)]**
(a) GeO_2 (b) CO (c) PbO_2 (d) SnO

30. Match the following **[May 18, 2024 (I)]**

List-I (Bond)		List-II (Bond enthalpy (in kJ mol^{-1}))	
(A)	Si - Si	(I)	240
(B)	C - C	(II)	297
(C)	Sn - Sn	(III)	348
(D)	Ge - Ge	(IV)	260

The correct answer is
(a) (A) - (II), (B) - (III), (C) - (I), (D) - (IV)
(b) (A) - (II), (B) - (IV), (C) - (III), (D) - (I)
(c) (A) - (III), (B) - (II), (C) - (I), (D) - (IV)
(d) (A) - (III), (B) - (I), (C) - (IV), (D) - (II)

31. Which element of group 14 decomposes steam to form dioxide and dihydrogen gas? **[May 19, 2023 (I)]**
(a) C (b) Pb
(c) Ge (d) Sn

32. Match the following

List-I		List-II
A.	Carbon black	I. Electrodes in batteries
B.	Graphite	II. Extraction of metals
C.	Diamond	III. Abrasive
D.	Activated charcoal	IV. Filler in automobile tyres
		V. Air conditioning system

[May 18, 2023 (II)]

(a) A-IV B-III C-II D-V (b) A-III B-I C-II D-IV
(c) A-V B-I C-III D-II (d) A-IV B-I C-III D-V

33. Thermodynamically most stable allotrope of carbon is **[May 18, 2023 (I)]**

(a) Graphite (b) Diamond
(c) Fullerene (d) Coke

34. In which one of the following pairs, both oxides are acidic? **[May 17, 2023 (II)]**

(a) CO, CO_2 (b) SnO, PbO_2
(c) GeO, SiO_2 (d) SnO, PbO

35. Which of the following is not correct? **[May 17, 2023 (I)]**

(a) Lead does not show catenation
(b) Buckminster fullerene contains 20 six–membered rings and 12 five–membered rings
(c) Stability order of GeX_2, SnX_2 and PbX_2 is $GeX_2 < SnX_2 < PbX_2$
(d) The number of metalloids in group 14 elements is 2

36. For a good quality cement the ratio of silica to alumina should be in the range of **[May 17, 2023 (II)]**

(a) 2.5 – 4.0 (b) 0.1 – 1.0
(c) 1.0 – 1.5 (d) 5.0 – 8.0

37. Given below are two statements

Assertion (A): The enthalpy of formation of graphite is taken as zero.

Reason (R): Graphite is thermodynamically most stable allotrope of carbon

The correct answer is **[May 16, 2023 (II)]**

(a) Both (A) and (R) are correct and (R) is the correct explanation of (A)
(b) Both (A) and (R) are correct but (R) is not the correct explanation of (A)
(c) (A) is correct but (R) is incorrect
(d) (A) is incorrect but (R) is correct

38. Identify the correct statements from the following.

i. Melting points and boiling points of group 13 elements are much higher than those of corresponding group 14 elements
ii. SiO only exists at high temperatures
iii. PbI_4 does not exist
iv. Buckminster fullerene contain twelve 6-membered carbon rings and twenty 5- membered carbon rings.

[May 16, 2023 (I)]

(a) i, iii only (b) ii, iii, iv only
(c) ii, iii only (d) i, iv only

39. Among the following the correct statements are

I. Germanium exists only in traces
II. PbF_4 molecule is tetrahedral in shape
III. GeX_2 is more stable than GeX_4 **[May 15, 2023 (II)]**

(a) II, III only (b) I, II only
(c) I, II, III (d) I, III only

40. Choose the acidic oxide from the following **[May 15, 2023 (I)]**

(a) CO (b) GeO (c) SnO (d) PbO

41. Among the given group 14 elements, the one with highest density is **[July 8, 2022 (I)]**

(a) Carbon (b) Silicon
(c) Tin (d) Lead

42. Bond enthalpy of Ge-Ge bond is 260 kJ mol^{-1}. The bond enthalpies of Si-Si and Sn-Sn bonds in kJ mol^{-1} are respectively. **[July 7, 2022 (II)]**

(a) 240, 270 (b) 297, 297
(c) 297, 240 (d) 200, 348

43. The number of six membered carbon rings and five membered carbon rings present in Buckminster fullerene are x and y respectively. The sum of x and y is: **[July 6, 2022 (I)]**

(a) 32 (b) 23 (c) 30 (d) 42

44. The correct statements with respect to halides of group 14 elements are **[July 5, 2022 (II)]**

I. Both CCl_4 and $SiCl_4$ undergo hydrolysis
II. GeX_4 is more stable than GeX_2
III. PbX_4 is less stable than PbX_2
IV. Stability of dihalides decreases down the group.

(a) I, IV only (b) II, IV only
(c) II, III only (d) III, IV only

45. The hybridizations of carbon in graphite, diamond and C_{60} are respectively **[July 4, 2022 (II)]**

(a) sp^2, sp^3, sp (b) sp^2, sp^3, sp^2
(c) sp, sp^2, sp^3 (d) sp, sp^3, sp

46. Which of the following tetrahalides does not exist? **[July 4, 2022 (I)]**

(a) CCl_4 (b) $SiCl_4$
(c) $PbCl_4$ (d) PbI_4

47. Carbon and germanium belong to the 14th group. The maximum coordination number of carbon is less than germanium, because of **[Aug. 23, 2021 (I)]**

(a) larger size of germanium
(b) electronegativity difference
(c) availability of low-lying *d*-orbitals in germanium
(d) electrical conductivity

48. What would be the product of following reaction?

$SiCl_4 \xrightarrow{\text{Excess of } H_2O} ?\text{(Major product)}$

[Aug. 20, 2021 (I)]

(a) $SiCl_3(OH)$ (b) $Si(OH)_4$
(c) $SiCl_2(OH)_2$ (d) $SiCl_4$ (no reaction)

49. Identify (*P*) and (*Q*) in the following reaction.

$CH_3Cl + Si \xrightarrow[570\text{ K}]{\text{Cu-powder}} (P) \xrightarrow{H_2O} (Q)$

$\longrightarrow$ Straight chain polymer

[Aug. 19, 2021 (II)]

(a) $P : (CH_3)_3SiCl$, $Q : (CH_3)_3SiOH$
(b) $P : (CH_3)_2SiCl_2$, $Q : (CH_3)_2Si(OH)_2$
(c) $P : (CH_3)_2SiCl_2$, $Q : (CH_3)_2Si(OH)Cl$
(d) $P : (CH_3)_2SiCl_2$, $Q : (CH_3)_2SiO$

50. The 'dry ice' is .... **[Sept. 18, 2020 (I)]**

(a) dry CO_2 gas (b) solid CO_2
(c) dry SO_2 gas (d) solid NH_3

51. Among the following oxides, which one is weakly basic and yet a powerful oxidant? **[Sept. 17, 2020 (I)]**

(a) CO_2 (b) SnO_2 (c) SiO_2 (d) PbO_2

52. Which one of the following is used as refrigerant for ice-cream and frozen foods? **[Apr. 22, 2019 (I)]**

(a) Dry CO (b) Liquid CH_4
(c) Dry ice (d) Liquid H_2

53. Which one of the following methods is used to prepare carbon monoxide on commercial scale?

[Apr. 21, 2019 (II)]

(a) Dehydration of formic a d with conc. H_2SO_4
(b) Direct oxidation of C in limited supply of oxygen
(c) Passing steam over hot coke
(d) Heating lime stone

54. Formic acid is heated with conc. H_2SO_4 at 100°C to form *A* and *B*. When Fe_2O_3 is heated strongly with *B*, the products formed are *C* and *D*. *C* can also be obtained by reacting $CaCO_3$ with dil.HCl. What is *D*?

[Apr. 21, 2019 (I)]

(a) Fe (b) CO
(c) CO_2 (d) Fe_3O_4

55. **Assertion (A) :** $[SiF_6]^{2-}$ is formed but $[SiCl_6]^{2-}$ is not

Reason (R) : Electronegativity (EN) of F is higher than EN of Cl **[2018]**

(a) Both (A) and (R) are correct and (R) is the correct explanation of (A)
(b) Both (A) and (R) are correct but (R) is not the correct explanation of (A)
(c) (A) is correct but (R) is not correct
(d) (A) is not correct but (R) is correct

Hints & Solutions

1 Some Basic Concepts of Chemistry

1. **(b)** Zeros before decimal point are non-significant, while zeros after decimal point are significant after a non-zero digit.

The significant digit in 0.010200×10^3 are 1, 0, 2, 0, 0

Multiplying by power of ten doesn't count as significant figure.

2. **(c)** Mass of Mg in 2g of chlorophyll:

$$\text{Mass} = 2.4\% \text{ of } 2g = \frac{2.4}{100} \times 2 \Rightarrow 0.048g$$

$$\text{Moles of Mg} = \frac{0.048}{24} = 0.002 \text{ mol}$$

No. of atoms of Mg $\Rightarrow 0.002 \times 6 \times 10^{23}$

$\Rightarrow 1.2 \times 10^{21}$ atoms.

3. **(d)** For 0.0025 = 2 because zeroes preceding to first non zero digit are not significant. Such zero indicates the position of decimal point.

For 500.0 = 4 because zeros at the end or right of a number are significant, provided they are on the right side of the decimal point.

For 2.0034 = 5 because zeroes between two non zero digits are significant.

4. **(d)**

Number	**Significant figure**
0.0063	2
132.00	5
1004	4

5. **(b)**

Weight of H_2SO_4 (W) = 98 mg = 98×10^{-3}g

$$\text{No. of moles in flask } (n_1) = \frac{98 \times 10^{-3}}{98} = 10^{-3} \text{ mol}$$

No. of moles removed from the flask (n_2) =

$$\frac{3.01 \times 10^{20}}{6.023 \times 10^{23}} = \frac{1}{2} \times 10^{-3}$$

$\therefore$ Remaining no. of moles in the flask = $(n_1 - n_2)$

$$= 1 \times 10^{-3} - \frac{1}{2} \times 10^{-3} = 0.5 \times 10^{-3} = 5 \times 10^{-4} \text{ mol}$$

6. **(a)**

$$2KMnO_4 \xrightarrow{300°C} \underbrace{K_2MnO_4 + MnO_2}_{\text{Solid residue}} + O_2$$

Molecular weight of $KMnO_4$ = 158u; Mole = 0.1

Weight = Molecular weight × mole = 0.1 × 158

Weight of Total $KMnO_4$ = 15.8 g

After heat O_2 will evolved

$\therefore$ Weight of O_2 = mole × molecular weight = 0.1 × 16 = 1.6 g

$\therefore$ Weight of Residue = 15.8 – 1.6 = 14.2g

7. **(c)** Let there be 100 formula units of $Ni_{0.98}O_{1.00}$. Thus, for 100 O^{2-} ions, there are 98 nickel ions (Ni^{2+} or Ni^{3+}).

Let x = number of Ni^{2+} ions.

$\Rightarrow$ Number of Ni^{3+} ions = 98 – x.

For an electrically neutral compound:-

$2x + 3(98 - x) + 100(-2) = 0 \Rightarrow x = 94$

$$\text{So, \% of } Ni^{2+} = \frac{94}{98} \times 100 = 96\%$$

8. **(b)** Irrespective of source, a given compound is made up of same element with fixed composition.

9. **(c)** Mass of one atom = $\dfrac{50 \times 1000}{6.643 \times 10^{-23}}$

Mass of 6.022×10^{23} Atoms

$= 6.643 \times 10^{-23} \times 6.022 \times 10^{23}$

Number of moles

$$= \frac{\text{Given Mass}}{\text{Molar Mass}} = \frac{50000}{6.643 \times 10^{-23} \times 6.02 \times 10^{23}}$$

= 1250.3 moles = 1250 moles

10. **(b)** Valency of metal,

$$(n) = \frac{2 \times \text{vapour density}}{\text{Equiv. weight of metal} + 35.5}$$

$$= \frac{2 \times 83}{6 + 35.5} = 4$$

Atomic weight of metal = n × equivalent weight = 4 × 6 = 24

11. **(a)** From Avogadro's law,

Avogadro's number = Atomic mass of the element

3.011×10^{22} atoms of an element weigh = 1.15 g

$\therefore$ 6.023×10^{23} atoms weigh

$$= \frac{1.15 \times 6.023 \times 10^{23}}{3.011 \times 10^{22}} = 23$$

12. **(d)** Let us assume total mass of gas mixture = 100 g

100g of gas mixture contains = 64g methane

$$\text{No. of moles of } CH_4 = \frac{64}{16} = 4 \text{ moles}$$

100g of gas mixture contains = 36g ethane

$$\text{No. of moles of } C_2H_6 = \frac{36}{30} = 1.2 \text{ moles}$$

Total moles = (4 + 1.2) = 5.2 moles

$$\text{Average molar mass} = \frac{100}{5.2} = 19.2 \text{ g/mol}$$

Using, $d = \dfrac{PM}{RT}$

Pressure = 750 mm (1 atm = 760 mm)

$$= \frac{750}{760} \text{ atm}$$

= 0.9868 atm

$$d = \frac{0.9868 \times 19.2}{0.082 \times 300}$$

= 0.77 g/l

13. **(a)** Mustard gas is : $(ClCH_2CH_2)_2S$

Molar Mass = 159 g/mol

$$\text{\% of S} = \frac{32}{159} \times 100 = 20.12\%$$

$$\text{\% of Cl} = \frac{71}{159} \times 100 = 44.65\%$$

14. **(c)** mass of Na (m) = 4 × 30% = 1.2g

mass of (Br + Cl) = 2.8g

mass of Cl = x

mass of Br = 2.8 – x

$$n_{Cl} = \frac{x}{35.5}, \; n_{Br} = \frac{2.8 - x}{80}$$

$$n_{Cl+Br} = \frac{x}{35.5} + \frac{2.8 - x}{80}$$

$$= \frac{80x + 35.5(2.8 - x)}{3.5 \times 80}$$

$\Rightarrow n_{Cl+Br} = 0.0156x + 0.035$

$$\Rightarrow n_{Cl+Br} = n_{Na} = \frac{12}{23} = 0.0521$$

$$\therefore x = \frac{0.0171}{0.0156} = 1.09$$

Mass of Cl = x = 1.09 g

$$\text{Moles of Cl} = \frac{1.09}{35.5} = 0.0307 \text{ mol}$$

n(Na) = 0.0307 mol

Mass of NaCl = 0.0307 × 23 + (0.0307 × 35.5) = 1.795g

$$\text{\% of NaCl} = \frac{1.795}{4} \times 100$$

= 44.875 ≈ 45%

15. **(b)** $Fe_{0.93}O_{1.00}$

Let $Fe^{3+} = x$

$3(0.93x) + 2(1 - x)0.93 = 2$

$2.79x + 1.86 - 1.86x = 2$

$2.79x - 1.86x = 2 - 1.86$

$0.93x = 0.14$

$$x = \frac{0.14}{0.93}$$

$$\text{\% of } Fe^{3+} = \frac{0.14}{0.93} \times 100 = 15.05 \approx 15$$

16. **(c)** $CaCO_3(s) \rightarrow CaO + CO_2(g)$

$MgCO_3(s) \rightarrow MgO + CO_2$

Let mass of $CaCO_3$ is x and mass of $MgCO_3$ is y

$x + y = 1.84$ or $y = 1.86 - x$

Mass of CaO_3 from $CaCO_3$

$$= \frac{56}{100} \times x$$

$$\text{Mass of MgO from } MgCO_3 = \frac{40}{84} y$$

$$\frac{56}{100} x + \frac{40}{84} y = 0.96$$

$$\frac{56}{100} x + \frac{40}{84}(1.84 - x) = 0.96$$

$0.56x + 0.877 - 0.476x = 0.96$
$0.084x = 0.96 - 0.877 = 0.083$
$x = 1$

% of $CaCO_3 = \frac{1}{1.84} \times 100 = 54.34\%$

17. (b) 200g of 20% urea contain 40g urea in 200g solution
400g of 40% urea contain 160g urea in 400g solution.
Total amount of solution = 600g
Total amount of urea in solution = 200g
$\Rightarrow$ Weight % of urea in solution $= \frac{200}{600} \times 100 = 33.33\%$

18. (c) Chlorine heptoxide Cl_2O_7 reacts with water to give perchloric acid $HClO_4$ which is the strongest acid.
Thus, the ratio of Cl to O is 2 : 7.

19. (c) M(C) = 12.01, M(H) = 1.0
m(C) = 4 × m(H) (Given)
If n(C) = 1 and n (H) = 3
$\Rightarrow$ m(C) = 12.01 and m(H) = 3
and C : H mass ratio = 4 : 1 $\Rightarrow$ Empirical formula $= CH_3$.

20. (c)

m % of urea $= \frac{6g}{(6+9+35)g} \times 100 = 12\%$

m % of glucose $= \frac{9\ g}{50\ g} \times 100 = 18\%$

21. (c) Average atomic mass of Fe = 54 × 0.1 + 56 × 0.85 + 57 × 0.05 = 55.85

22. (a) Mass of sample of alloy = 12 g
% of metal X in sample = 20
$\therefore$ If x is the mass of metal X in sample

$\frac{x}{12} \times 100 = 20 \Rightarrow x = 2.4$ g

If y is the mass of metal Y in sample, then
$y = 12 - 2.4 = 9.6$ g

Number of atoms of X $= \frac{6.022 \times 10^{23} \times 24}{40}$
$= 3.61 \times 10^{22}$

Atoms of X and atom of $y = \frac{2}{5}$

Number of atoms of $y = \frac{3.61 \times 10^{22} \times 5}{2}$
$= 9.025 \times 10^{22}$ atoms.
9.025×10^{22} atoms of Y are present in 9.6 g.
6.022×10^{23} atoms of Y are present in

$\frac{9.6}{9.025 \times 10^{22}} \times 6.022 \times 10^{23} = 64$ g

Hence, atomic mass of Y = 64 amu.

23. (d)

$P\% = \frac{62}{222} \times \frac{m_1}{m} \times 100 = \frac{62}{222} \times \frac{0.22}{0.12} \times 100 = 51.20\%$

24. (a) 1 mole of O_2 gas $= 6.022 \times 10^{23}$ molecules of O_2
= 32 g of O_2 = 22.4 L of O_2 at STP.

25. (c) In XO_2, X : O : : 50 : 50
Mass of oxygen = 2 × 16 = 32 g
Hence, mass of X = 32 g
In XO_n, X : O : : 40 : 60
Mass of X, in this case also remains = 32 g
40% ≡ 32 g

60% ≡ $\frac{32}{40} \times 60 = 48$ g

Mass of oxygen = 48 g $\Rightarrow n = \frac{48}{16} = 3$

Formula of oxide $= XO_3$

26. (c)

Element	% of element	Atomic weight	Relative number	Mole Ratio
Carbon	12.8	12	$\frac{12.8}{12} = 1.06$	$\frac{1.06}{1.06} = 1$
Hydrogen	2.1	1	$\frac{2.1}{1} = 2.1$	$\frac{2.1}{1.06} = 2$
Bromine	85.1	80	$\frac{85.1}{80} = 1.06$	$\frac{1.06}{1.06} = 1$

Empirical formula $= CH_2Br$
Empirical formula mass = 12 + 2 + 80 = 94

Factor, $n = \frac{\text{Molecular mass}}{\text{Empirical formula mass}}$

$= \frac{187.9}{94} = 2$

Molecular formula $= (CH_2Br)_2 = C_2H_4Br_2$

27. (c) $P_4 + 3NaOH + 3H_2O \longrightarrow PH_3 + 3NaH_2PO_2$

Given mass of P_4 = 6.2 g

Moles of $P_4 = \frac{6.2}{124} = 0.05$ mol
From stoichiometry, 1 mol of P_4 reacts with 3 mol of NaOH to produce 1 mol of PH_3 and 3 mol of NaH_2PO_2
So, 0.05 mol of P_4 produces 0.05 mol of PH_3
Mass of PH_3 = 0.05 × 34 = 1.7g
According to stoichiometry, 1 mol of P_4 3 mol of NaOH
So 0.05 mol of P_4 reacts with = 3 × 0.05 mol NaOH = 0.15 mol NaOH

Conc. of NaOH $= \frac{0.15\ \text{mol}}{0.5\ \text{L}} = 0.3$ mol L^{-1}
So, x = 0.3

28. (c) Given, Mass of Metal chloride = 26.7g
Mass of Metal = 5.4g
So, Mass of chlorine = 26.7 – 5.4 = 21.3g
Thus Mass of 5.4 g metal reacts with 21.3g of chlorine
According to law of reciprocal proportions.
The mass of chlorine and oxygen that combine with the same mass of metal are proportional to their equivalent masses.
Equivalent Mass of Cl = 35.5g, O = 8g
So, 21.3 of Cl is equivalent to:

21.3g of Cl $\rightarrow 21.3 \times \frac{8}{35.5} = 4.8$g of O

So, 5.4 g of metal react with 4.8 g of oxygen.
Mass of metal react with 48 g of oxygen.

Mass of metal $\frac{5.4 \times 48}{4.8} = 54$g

29. (d) Balanced chemical equation is
$P_4 + 3OH^- + 3H_2O \rightarrow PH_3 + 3H_2PO_2^-$
On comparing with equation with stoichiometry.
a = 1
b = 3
c = 3
d = 1
e = 3
Thus II. 3 + 3 – 3 = 3 (correct)

III. $H_2PO_2^-$
$(+1)2 + x + (-2)2 = -1$
$x = +4 - 2 - 1 = +1$

30. (a) For Na_2CO_3
Normality $= n_{factor} \times$ molarity
Here $n_{factor} = 2$
$\therefore$ Normality (N) for Na_2CO_3 = 2 × 0.5 = 1N
For acid (A)
Using dilution factor
$N_AV_A = NV$
Where, N_A = Normality of acid (A)
V_A = Volume of Acid (A) = 10 mL
N = Normality of Base = 1 N
V = volume of Base = 25 mL

$N_A = \frac{25 \times 1}{10}$

$N_A = 2.5$
For Acid (B)
Using dilution method again
$N_BV_B = NV$
Where, N_B = Normality of Acid (B)
V_B = Volume of Acid (B) = 40 mL

$N_B = \frac{25 \times 1}{40}$

$N_B = 0.625$
For mixture of acids A & B to produce 1 L of 1 N acid
$N_AV_1 + N_BV_2 = N_{mix}V_{mix}$
Where,
V_1 = Volume of acid A
V_2 = Volume of acid B
N_{mix} = 1 N
V_{mix} = 1 L = 1000 mL
So, $2.5\ V_1 + 0.625\ V_2 = 1 \times 1000$ ...(i)
As $V_1 + V_2 = 1000$
Hence, $V_2 = 1000 - V_1$
Substituting the V_2 in equation (i) we get :
$2.5V_1 + 0.625(1000 - V_1) = 1000$
$2.5V_1 + 0.625 \times 1000 - 0.625V_1 = 1000$
$2.5V_1 - 0.625V_1 = 1000 - 625$
$V_1 = 200$ mL
$\therefore$ $V_2 = 800$ mL
So, the volumes of acids A & B to mix are :
Volume of acid (V_1) = 0.2 L
Volume of acid (V_2) = 0.8 L

31. (a) $\underset{15\ g}{C_2H_6(g)} + \underset{112\ g}{\frac{7}{2}O_2(g)} \rightarrow 2CO_2(g) + 3H_2O(g)$

$n(C_2H_6) = \frac{15\ g}{30\ g\ mol^{-1}} = 0.5$ mol (Limiting reagent)

$n(O_2) = \frac{112\ g}{32\ g\ mol^{-1}} = 3.5$ mol

Thus, 0.5. mol of C_2H_6 reacts completely with $\frac{7}{2} \times 0.5 = 1.75$ mol of O_2
Thus, 3.5 – 1.75 = 1.75 moles of O_2 are left.
0.5 mol C_2H_6 gives 0.5 × 2 = 1 mol CO_2 and 0.5 × 3 = 1.5 mol H_2O.
Thus, final total number of gaseous moles = 1.75 + 1 + 1.5 = 4.25 mol.

32. **(b)** $\underset{4\,mL}{2H_2O_2} \rightarrow 2H_2O + \underset{80\,mL}{O_2}$

$X = \frac{80\,mL \times 1000\,mL}{4\,mL} = 20\,L$

33. **(b)** $\underset{209\,g}{xE} + \underset{xg}{yd^2} \rightarrow \underset{315.5\,g}{E_x d_y}$; $y = 3$

$209\,g + x = 315.5$

$x = 106.5\,g$

$\therefore \frac{106.5}{209} = 0.509$ g of Cl_2 per g of E

$= 0.007169$ mol per g of E

$\therefore$ moles of oxygen $= 418 \times 0.007169 = 3$ mol

$\therefore$ mass of oxygen $= 16 \times 3 = 48$ g

34. **(d)** $Cr_2O_7^{2-} + 14H^+ + 6\,Fe^{2+} \longrightarrow 2Cr^{3+} + 6Fe^{3+} + 7H_2O$

no. of equivalents $K_2Cr_2O_7$ = no. of equivalents $FeSO_4$

$\frac{1}{60} \times V_{ml} \times 6 = 1 \times 0.1 \times 100$

$\Rightarrow V_{ml} = 10 \times 0.1 \times 100$

$V_{ml} = 100$ ml $= 0.1$L

35. **(d)** Equivalent weight of metal

$= \left(\frac{10}{11.6 - 10}\right) \times 8 = 50$

36. **(b)** Given, 0.2 moles of MOH reacts completely with CO_2

$CO_2 + MOH \rightarrow MHCO_3$

0.2 moles   0.2 moles

Now, $2\,MHCO_3 \xrightarrow{\Delta} M_2CO_3 + CO_2 + H_2O$

1 mole of CO_2 is obtained from 2 moles of $MHCO_3$

0.2 mole of CO_2 will be obtain from

$= 2 \times 0.2 = 0.4$ mole of $MHCO_3$

Hence, amount 'x' $= 0.4 \times 84 = 33.6$ g

37. **(a)**

C = 92.3%	$\frac{92.3}{12} = 7.69$	1
H = 7.7%	$\frac{7.7}{1} = 7.7$	1

Empirical Ratio 1 : 1

CH possible hydrocarbon C_2H_2

$C_2H_2 + \frac{5}{2}O_2 \rightarrow 2CO_2 + H_2O$

$2H_2O + 2Na \longrightarrow 2NaOH + H_2$

2 mole of H_2O gives one mol H_2

0.7 H_2 Produced thus 1.5 mol H_2O used

mass of 1.5 mol $H_2O = 1.5 \times 18 = 17$

On balancing and multiplying with 1.5

mass of O_2 required $= 3.75 \times 32 = 120$ g

38. **(b)** $CH_4 + 2O_2 \rightarrow CO_2 + 2H_2O$

Thus, 1 mole of CH_4 gives 1 mole of CO_2 gas.

CO_2 gas combines with Ca $(OH)_2$ as :-

$Ca(OH)_2 + CO_2 \rightarrow CaCO_3 \downarrow + H_2O$

Thus, 1 mole of $Ca(OH)_2$ gives 1 mole of $CaCO_3$ precipitate or 74 g $Ca(OH)_2$ gives 100 g of $CaCO_3$ precipitate.

Therefore, 500 g of precipitate would be obtained by :

$74 \times 5 = 370$ g or 5 moles of Ca $(OH)_2$.

Since products are formed as per the stoichiometric coefficients, there would be 5 moles of CO_2 released in the first reaction. 5 moles of CO_2 would be released by 5 moles or $5 \times 16 = 80$ g of CH_4.

Thus, x = 80.

39. **(d)** $I_2 + 10HNO_3 \longrightarrow 2HIO_3 + 10NO_2 + 4H_2O$

For calculation of equivalent weight of HNO_3 in a redox reaction we must consider changes in both HNO_3 and I_2.

$\therefore$ Change in oxidation state of N per molecule is:

$(+5 \text{ to } +4) = \frac{1}{10 \times 1} = \frac{1}{10}$

$\therefore$ Change in oxidation state of I per molecule is:

$(0 \text{ to } +5) = \frac{1}{2 \times 5} = \frac{1}{10}$

Thus, equivalent weight of

$HNO_3 = \left(\frac{1}{10} + \frac{1}{10}\right)M = \frac{M}{5}$

40. **(a)** Density (d) of solution = 1.2 g/mL

$\underset{1\,mol}{Na_2SO_4} \longrightarrow \underset{2\,mol}{2Na^+} + SO_4^{2-}$;

MW of $Na_2SO_4 = 142$ g/mol

$\therefore$ 50% dissociation of Na_2SO_4 produces 1 mol of Na^+

$\therefore$ 1M Na_2SO_4 solution has 1M Na^+ ions in 1000 ml solution = 1200 g solution.

$\therefore$ Weight of solvent = (1200 – 142) = 1058g

$\therefore$ The molality of Na^+ ion $= \frac{1 \times 1000}{1058} = 0.95$m

41. **(a)**

$Mg \longrightarrow Mg^{2+} + 2e^{-1}$; $\overset{+5}{NO_3^-} + 8e^{-1} \longrightarrow \overset{-3}{NH_3}$

$\therefore$ After balancing the no. of e^{-1} involved in the reaction,

$4Mg + NO_3^- \longrightarrow 4Mg(NO_3)_2 + NH_3$

Now, balancing the NO_3^- ion, H atom and O atom,

$\underset{4\,mol\,Mg}{4\,Mg} + \underset{1\,mol}{9HNO_3} \rightarrow 4Mg(NO_3)_2 + NH_3 + 3H_2O$

4 mol Mg = 96 g of Mg

$\therefore$ 1 mol of NO is completely reduced by 96 g of Mg 100 ml 0.1(M) = 0.01 mol of NO_3^- is completely reduced by 0.96 g of Mg.

42. **(d)** Given, Molarity of H_2SO_4(m)

Molar mass = 98 ; V = 500 mL = 0.5 L

$M = \frac{\text{mass}(m)}{\text{molar mass} \times \text{volume}(L)}$

$0.5 = \frac{m}{98 \times 0.5} \Rightarrow m = 24.52$ g

$\Rightarrow$ Concentration of $H_2SO_4 = 90\%$

$\Rightarrow$ Mass of solution required = 27.24 g

43. **(c)** Moles of acetic acid = MV

$= 0.2 \times 100 = 20$ mili moles = 0.02 moles

$2CH_3COOH \rightarrow C_2H_6 + 2CO_2 + H_2$

2 moles CH_3COOH gives 1 moles of ethane *i.e.*, 22.4 L

0.02 moles of CH_3COOH will give ethane

$= \frac{22.4 \times 0.02}{2} = 0.224$ L

44. **(c)** Moles of Ammonia

$= \frac{\text{Mass}}{\text{Molar mass}} = \frac{3.4}{17} = 0.2$

$N_2(g) + 3H_2(g) \rightarrow 2NH_3(g)$

Since 1 mol   3 mol   2 mol

Hence, 0.1 mol   0.3 mol   0.2 mol

$\Rightarrow$ 1 mol of a gas = 22.4 L at STPor NTP

$\Rightarrow$ 0.3 mol $H_2 = 22.4 \times 0.3 = 6.72$ L at NTP

Similarly 0.1 mol $N_2 = 22.4 \times 0.1 = 2.24$ L at NTP

45. **(b)**

$\underset{\substack{\text{Calcium}\\\text{carbonate}\\(100g)}}{CaCO_3(s)} + \underset{\substack{\text{Hydrochloric}\\\text{acid}\\(73g)}}{2HCl} \rightarrow \underset{\substack{\text{Calcium}\\\text{chloride}}}{CaCl_2(aq)} + H_2O(l) + \underset{(44g)}{CO_2(g)}$

As amount of $CaCO_3$ and HCl are same, $CaCO_3$ will be the limiting reagent.

$\therefore$ 100g of $CaCO_3$ gives = 44g of CO_2 gas

$\therefore$ 20g of $CaCO_3$ will give

$= \frac{44}{100} \times 20$g of $CO_3 = 8.8$g of CO_2

46. **(c)** $\underset{\substack{16g\\32g}}{CH_4} + 2O_2 \longrightarrow \underset{\substack{44g\\88g}}{CO_2} + 2H_2O$

47. **(d)**

$Cr_2O_7^{2-} + 14H^+ + 6Fe^{2+} \rightarrow 2Cr^{3+} + 7H_2O + 6Fe^{3+}$

$MnO_4^- + 8H^+ + 5Fe^{2+} \rightarrow Mn^{2+} + 4H_2O + 5Fe^{3+}$

$Cr_2O_7^{2-}$ react with 6 moles of Fe^{2+} and 1 mole of MnO_4^- react with 5 moles of Fe^{2+} in a balanced equation.

Gram equivalent of Fe^{2+}

= gram equivalent of $K_2Cr_2O_7$

= gram equivalent of $KMnO_4$

Thus, $M_1 \times V_1 \times n_1 = M_2 \times V_2 \times n_2$

$\Rightarrow 0.01 \times 20 \times 6 = M_2 \times 20 \times 5$

$\Rightarrow M_2 = \frac{0.01 \times 6}{5} = 0.012$M

48. **(d)** $2\overset{+7}{KMnO_4} + 10I^- \longrightarrow \overset{0}{5I_2} + 2Mn^{+2}$

n-factor of $KMnO_4 = 7 - 2 = 5$

I^- convert into I_2 then, *n*-factor = 1 – 0 = 1

Number of equivalents of $KMnO_4$

= Number of equivalents of I^-

n-factor × moles of $KMnO_4$ = *n*-factor × moles of I^-

$\Rightarrow V \times 0.02 \times 5 = 60 \times 0.01 \times 1 \Rightarrow V = 6$ mL.

49. **(d)** When 0.15 M Na_2CO_3 (1L) mixed with 0.2 M $K_2Cr_2O_7$ (0.5 L) than total molarity (*M*).

M_1V_1 (Na_2SO_3) + M_2V_2 $(K_2Cr_2O_7)$ = M_3V_3 (total)

$M_3 = \frac{(0.15 \times 1) + (0.2 \times 0.5)}{1.5}$

$= 0.167 \approx 0.15$ mol/L

Remaining mole of $K_2Cr_2O_7 = 0.2 - 0.15 = 0.05$ mol/L

50. **(a)** $2\,KMnO_4 + 3\,H_2SO_4 + 5(COOH)_2 \rightarrow K_2SO_4 + 2\,MnSO_4 + 8\,H_2O + 10\,CO_2$

$\frac{M_1V_1}{n_2} = \frac{M_2V_2}{n_1} \Rightarrow \frac{x \times 40\,mL}{2} = \frac{0.02 \times 200\,mL}{5}$

(where $\frac{n_1}{n_2}$ = n-factor) $\Rightarrow x = 0.04$ M

2 Structure of Atom

1. **(b)** Threshold frequencies of the metal A $(v_o)_A = 4 \times 10^{14}$

Threshold frequencies of the metal B $(v_o)_B = 6 \times 10^{14}$

For 'A' and 'B' frequency of light $(v) = 10^{15}$

∴ The kinetic energy of electron emitted $= hv - hv_o$.

∴ Ratio of kinetic energy (KE)

$$\frac{(KE)_A}{(KE)_B} = \frac{(hv - hv_o)_A}{(hv - hv_o)_B} = \frac{10^{15} - 4\times10^{14}}{10^{15} - 6\times10^{14}}$$

$$= \frac{6}{4} = \frac{3}{2}$$

$\therefore KE_A : KE_B = 3:2$

2. **(b)** Given, $v_0 = 1.15 \times 10^{15}$ Hz

K.E = 0.20 eV

$= 0.20 \times 1.6 \times 10^{-19}$

$= 3.2 \times 10^{-20}$ J

According to photoelectric equation:

$hv = hv_0 + K.E$

$$v = v_0 + \frac{K.E}{h}$$

$$v = 1.15 \times 10^{15} + \frac{3.2\times10^{-20}}{6.6\times10^{-34}}$$

$v = 1.15 \times 10^{15} + 0.48 \times 10^{+14}$

$v = 1.15 \times 10^{15} + 0.048 \times 10^{15}$

$v = 1.198 \times 10^{15}$ Hz $\simeq 1.2 \times 10^{15}$ Hz

3. **(d)** I: As nuclear charge increases from (H to Na), the 2s electron helds more tightly to the nucleus, so orbital energy (2s) becomes more and more negative to a lower value not higher.

The correct order is:

E_{2s} (Na) < E_{2s} (Li) < E_{2s}(H)

Hence, statement I is incorrect.

II: The photoelectric effect explains the particle nature of the light not wave nature. Hence, statement II is also incorrect.

4. **(b)** According to photoelectric effect equation:

$hv = hv_0 + K.E$

v = Frequency of incident radiation,

hv_0 = Work function of metal

K.E = Kinetic energy of electrons

Given, work function = 2.27 eV

$= 2.27 \times 1.6 \times 10^{-19}$J

K.E $= 1.3 \times 10^{-19}$ J

$hv = 2.27 \times 1.6 \times 10^{-19} + 1.3 \times 10^{-19}$

$hv = 4.932 \times 10^{-19}$

$$v = \frac{4.932\times10^{-19}}{6.6\times10^{-34}}$$

$v = 7.47 \times 10^{+14}$ Hz

5. **(d)** Given, wavelength of incident radiation = 300 nm.

Energy of incident radiation:

$$E = \frac{hc}{\lambda}$$

$$E = \frac{6.6\times10^{-34}\times3\times10^{8}}{300\times10^{-9}}$$

$= 6.6 \times 10^{-19}$ J

$$= \frac{6.6\times10^{-19}}{1.6\times10^{-19}} = 4.125 \text{ eV}$$

Photoelectric effect occurs only if work function is < 4.125 eV

Out of given metals Mg having work function (3.7 eV) and Li having work function (2.5 eV) shown photoelectric effect. Cu and Ag does not shows photoelectric effect because their work function is greater than 4.125 eV.

6. **(c)** To eject the electron from the metallic surface the energy of incident electromagnetic radiation must be comparable with the work function of the metal.

So, the energy of electromagnetic radiation $= \dfrac{hc}{\lambda}$

Where, h = planck's constant $= 6.6 \times 10^{-34}$ Js

c = speed of light $= 3 \times 10^8$ m/s

λ = wavelength of electromagnetic radiation $= 300 \times 10^{-9}$ m

∴ The energy of electromagnetic radiation

$$= \frac{6.6\times10^{-34}\times3\times10^{8}}{300\times10^{-9}} \text{J}$$

$$= \frac{6.6\times10^{-19}}{1.6\times10^{-19}} \text{eV} = 4.1 \text{ eV}$$

So, the metals having work function < 4.1 eV do eject the electron but > 4.1 eV do not eject the electron. Hence, only 2 metals Mg and Na from which the electrons can be ejected.

7. **(c)** $n_2 = 1$ from $n_1 = 2, 3, 4$ ... ⇒ Lyman series (UV)

$n_2 = 2$ from $n_1 = 3, 4, 5$ ... ⇒ Balmer series (Visible)

$n_2 = 3$ from $n_1 = 4, 5, 6$ ... ⇒ Paschen Series (IR)

$n_2 = 4$ from $n_1 = 5, 6, 7$ ... ⇒ Brackett Series (IR)

$n_2 = 5$ from $n_1 = 6, 7, 8$ ... ⇒ P fund Series (IR)

8. **(a)** $$\lambda = \frac{c}{v} = \frac{3\times10^{8}\text{ ms}^{-1}}{1.034\times10^{8}\text{ s}^{-1}} \cong 2.90 \text{ m}$$

9. **(a)** Given, $\lambda = 663$ nm $= 663 \times 10^{-9}$ m

$$\lambda = \frac{h}{mv} \Rightarrow v = \frac{h}{m\lambda}$$

$$v = \frac{6.6\times10^{-34}}{9.1\times10^{-31}\times663\times10^{-9}}$$

$= 0.0010979 \times 10^6 \simeq 1098$ m/s.

10. **(a)** Atomic number of carbon = 6

Atomic mass of carbon = 13

Atomic number = no. of protons = no. of electrons = 6

Atomic mass = no. of protons + no. of neutrons

$13 = 6 + n \Rightarrow n = 7$

11. **(a)** Mass of proton $(p) = 1.6726 \times 10^{-27}$ kg

Mass of neutron $(n) = 1.6749 \times 10^{-27}$ kg

Mass of electron $(e) = 9.1 \times 10^{-31}$ kg

Mass of proton is 1836.16 times heavier than electron.

Mass of neutron is 1838.68 times heavier than electron.

Ratio of mass of electron, proton and neutron will be

1 : 1836.15 : 1838.68.

12. **(d)** A – (iii), B – (i), C – (ii), D – (iv)

Number of electron = Atomic no. – no. of +ve charge + no. of –ve charge

(i) Be^{2+} ⇒ Atomic number = 4, Number of electrons = 2

(ii) H^+ ⇒ Atomic number = 1, Number of electrons = 0

(iii) Na^+ ⇒ Atomic number = 11, Number of electrons = 10

(iv) Mg^+ ⇒ Atomic number = 12, Number of electrons = 11

13. **(b)** $$\lambda_A = 2\times\lambda_B;\ 2\times\frac{h}{m_B v_B} = \frac{h}{m_A v_A}$$

Given, $$v_A = v_B;\ \frac{2}{m_B} = \frac{1}{m_A} \Rightarrow m_A = \frac{m_B}{2}$$

14. **(c)** For orange radiation of $\lambda = 6300$ Å $= 63 \times 10^{-8}$ m

Wave number,

$$\bar{v} = \frac{1}{\lambda} = \frac{1}{63\times10^{-8}\text{ m}} = 1.587 \times 10^6 \text{ m}^{-1}$$

Frequency, $\nu = \frac{c}{\lambda} = \frac{3\times10^{8}\ \text{m s}^{-1}}{63\times10^{-8}\ \text{m}}$

$= 4.761 \times 10^{14}\ \text{s}^{-1}$.

15. (a) Isochores are drawn at constant volume between pressure vs temperature (T, in K) as;

For 1 mole of an ideal gas, $pV = RT$

At isochoric condition, $p \propto T$.

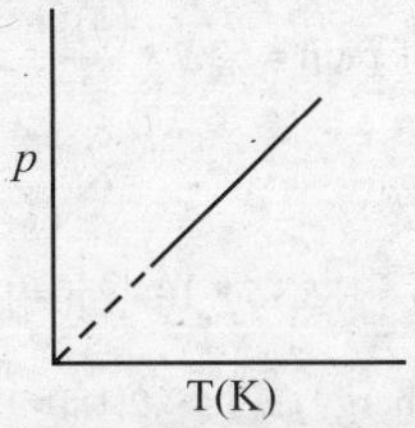

16. (b) $\lambda = \frac{h}{mv} \Rightarrow v = \frac{h}{m\times\lambda}$

$\Rightarrow \quad v = \frac{6.626\times10^{-34}\ \text{Js}}{9.1\times10^{-31}\ \text{kg}\times182\times10^{-9}\ \text{m}}$

$= 4 \times 10^{3}$ m/s

$KE = \frac{1}{2}mv^{2} = \frac{1}{2}\times9.1\times10^{-31}\times(4\times10^{3})^{2}$

$= 7.28 \times 10^{-24}$ J.

17. (b) According to Rydberg formula

$\lambda \propto \frac{1}{Z^{2}}$

$\frac{\lambda_{He}}{\lambda_{H}} = \frac{Z_{H}^{2}}{Z_{He}^{2}}$

$\lambda_{He} = \frac{1^{2}}{2^{2}}\times656.4$ nm

$\lambda_{He} = 164.1$ nm

18. (c) $2\pi r_n = n\lambda \quad n = 4$

$r_n = a_0 \cdot n^{2}$

$= a_0 \cdot 16$

$2\pi(16a_0) = 4\lambda$

$\lambda = 8\pi a_0$

19. (a) $\frac{1}{\lambda} = R_H \cdot Z^{2}\left(\frac{1}{n_1^{2}} - \frac{1}{n_2^{2}}\right)$

$\frac{1}{\lambda_{He^{+}}} = R_H \cdot 2^{2}\left(\frac{1}{2^{2}} - \frac{1}{4^{2}}\right)$

$= R_H \cdot \frac{3}{4}$

For hydrogen atom (α)

$\frac{1}{\lambda_H} = R_H \cdot 1^{2}\left(\frac{1}{n_1^{2}} - \frac{1}{n_2^{2}}\right) = R_H \cdot \frac{3}{4}$

Finding the transition $n_1 = 1$ and $n_2 = 2$

$\left(\frac{1}{1^{2}} - \frac{1}{2^{2}}\right) = 1 - \frac{1}{4} = \frac{3}{4}$

20. (c) $E_n = -13.6\frac{Z^{2}}{n^{2}}$

So $E_n \propto Z^{2}$

Energy required to remove electron from ground state $\propto Z^{2}$

He^{+} (Z = 2) : E = – 13.6 × $(2)^{2}$ = xJ ... (1)

For Li^{2+} (Z = 3) E = – 13.6 × $(3)^{2}$ ... (2)

Comparing (1) and (2)

$\frac{E_{Li^{2+}}}{E_{He^{+}}} = \frac{Z^{2}_{Li}}{Z^{2}_{He}} = \frac{9}{4}$

$E_{Li^{2+}} = \frac{9}{4}x$ J

21. (d) For H-like atoms

$\Delta E = 13.6z^{2}\left(\frac{1}{n_f^{2}} - \frac{1}{n_i^{2}}\right)$ eV

For Li^{2+}, lowest frequency will be from $n_i = 2$ to $n_f = 1$ and Z = 3

$\Delta E = x = 13.6 \times (3)^{2}\left(\frac{1}{1^{2}} - \frac{1}{2^{2}}\right)$ eV

x = 91.8 eV

For He^{+}, second line in Balmer series: $n_i = 4 \rightarrow n_f = 2$ and z = 2

$\Delta E = y = 13.6 \times (2)^{2}\left(\frac{1}{2^{2}} - \frac{1}{4^{2}}\right)$ eV

y = 10.2 eV

Ratio of x and y:

$\frac{x}{y} = \frac{91.8}{10.2} = \frac{9}{1} \Rightarrow 9:1$

22. (b) Using Rydberg formula:

$\frac{1}{\lambda} = R\left(\frac{1}{n_1^{2}} - \frac{1}{n_2^{2}}\right)$

For transition $4 \rightarrow 2$; $n_1 = 2$, $n_2 = 4$

$\frac{1}{x} = R\left(\frac{1}{(2)^{2}} - \frac{1}{(4)^{2}}\right) \quad (\because \lambda = x)$

$\frac{1}{x} = R\left(\frac{1}{4} - \frac{1}{16}\right)$

$\frac{1}{x} = R\left(\frac{4-1}{16}\right)$

$\frac{1}{x} = \frac{3R}{16}$ ... (1)

For transition : $4 \rightarrow 1$; $n_1 = 1$, $n_2 = 4$

$\frac{1}{y} = R\left(\frac{1}{(1)^{2}} - \frac{1}{(4)^{2}}\right)$

$\frac{1}{y} = R\left(\frac{15}{16}\right) \Rightarrow \frac{1}{y} = \frac{15R}{16}$ ... (2)

Dividing (1) ÷ (2)

$\frac{y}{x} = \frac{3}{15} = 0.2$

23. (c) As, the given wavelengths are of visible region and we know that in hydrogen spectrum wavelengths of visible region corresponds to Balmer Series.

According to Rydberg formula:

$\frac{1}{\lambda} = R_H\left(\frac{1}{n_1^{2}} - \frac{1}{n_2^{2}}\right)$

For Balmer Series $n_1 = 2$

So given wavelengths are:

(a) 656.46 nm : ($n_2 = 3$, $n_1 = 2$)

(b) 486.27 nm : ($n_2 = 4$, $n_1 = 2$)

(c) x nm : ($n_2 = 5$, $n_1 = 2$)

(d) 410.29 nm : ($n_2 = 6$, $n_1 = 2$)

For $n_1 = 2$, $n_2 = 5$:

$\frac{1}{\lambda} = 1.097\times10^{7}\left(\frac{1}{2^{2}} - \frac{1}{5^{2}}\right)$

$\frac{1}{\lambda} = 1.097\times10^{7}\times\frac{21}{100}$

$\frac{1}{\lambda} = 0.23037 \times 10^{7}$

$\lambda = 4.34 \times 10^{-7}$ Or 434 nm.

24. (a) Energy for Bohr orbit of hydrogen

$E_n = -\frac{R_H}{n^{2}} \Rightarrow \frac{E_2}{E_4} = \frac{n_4^{2}}{n_2^{2}}$

$E_4 = \frac{-3.4\times4^{2}}{2^{2}}$

$= -3.4 \times 4 = -13.6$ eV

25. (a) $\frac{1}{\lambda} = RZ^{2}\left[\frac{1}{n_1^{2}} - \frac{1}{n_2^{2}}\right]$

Where, λ = wavelength

R = Rydberg constant

z = atomic number

n_1 = lower energy level

n_1 = 2 (for Balmer series)

n_2 = higher energy level; $n_2 = n$

Z = atomic number = 2 for He^{+} ion

$\frac{1}{\lambda} = R(2)^{2}\left[\frac{1}{2^{2}} - \frac{1}{n^{2}}\right]$

$\frac{1}{\lambda} = R4\left[\frac{n^{2}-4}{4n^{2}}\right]$

$\frac{1}{\lambda} = 4R\left[\frac{n^{2}-4}{4n^{2}}\right]$

$\frac{1}{\lambda} = R\left[\frac{n^{2}-(2)^{2}}{n^{2}}\right]$

$\frac{1}{\lambda} = R\left[\frac{(n+2)(n-2)}{n^{2}}\right]$

$\therefore \lambda = \frac{n^{2}}{R(n+2)(n-2)}$

26. (c) Radius of hydrogen like species

$R_n = \frac{0.529n^{2}}{z}$

For 4th orbit of He^+ radius $= \frac{0.529(4)^2}{2}$

For 3rd orbit of Li^{+2} radius $= \frac{0.529(3)^2}{3}$

$R_1 - R_2 = 0.529\,(8-3)$

$= 0.529 \times 5 = 2.645$ Å $= 264.5$ pm (1Å = 100 pm)

27. (b) The radii expression is given by :

$$r_n = 52.9\left(\frac{n^2}{Z}\right) \text{pm}$$

Where, n is the orbit

Z is the atomic number

For H atom

$$r_2 = 52.9\left(\frac{2^2}{1}\right) \text{pm}$$

$r_2 = 52.9\,(2)^2$ pm

$$r_3 = 52.9\left(\frac{3^2}{1}\right) \text{pm}$$

$r_3 = 52.9\,(3)^2$ pm

The difference between the radii of 3rd & 2nd orbit is :

$r_3 - r_2 = 52.9(3)^2 - 52.9(2)^2 \text{pm} = x$

For Li^{+2} ion

$$r_4 = 52.9\frac{(4)^2}{3} \text{pm}$$

$$r_3 = 52.9\frac{(3)^2}{3} \text{pm}$$

The difference between the radii of 4th & 3rd orbit is :

$$r_4 - r_3 = 52.9\frac{(4)^2}{3} - 52.9\frac{(3)^2}{3} \text{pm} = y$$

The ratio of $y : x$ is :

$$\frac{r_4 - r_3}{r_3 - r_2} = \frac{\frac{52.9}{3}[(4)^2-(3)^2]}{52.9[(3)^2-(2)^2]} = \frac{16-9}{3(9-4)} = \frac{7}{15}$$

28. (b) The number for first line ($n_2 = 3$) in the Balmer series of hydrogen is given by $\overline{v_1}$ cm^{-1}. The wave number of second line ($n_2 = 4$) in the Balmer series of He^+ is also to be determined.

The Rydberg formula

$$\overline{v} = RZ^2\left(\frac{1}{n_1^2} - \frac{1}{n_2^2}\right)$$

Where $\overline{v}$ is the wave number, R is Rydberg constant, Z is atomic number, n_1 and n_2 are the principal Quantum numbers of lower and upper energy levels respectively.

For the Balmer series $n_1 = 2$

Step-1:

$$\overline{v_1} = R(1)^2\left(\frac{1}{2^2} - \frac{1}{3^2}\right)$$

$$\overline{v_1} = R\left(\frac{1}{4} - \frac{1}{9}\right) = R\left(\frac{5}{36}\right)$$

Step-2:

$$\overline{v_2} = R(2)^2\left(\frac{1}{2^2} - \frac{1}{4^2}\right)$$

$$\overline{v_2} = R\,2^2\left(\frac{1}{4} - \frac{1}{16}\right) = 4R\left(\frac{3}{16}\right)$$

$$\frac{\overline{v_2}}{\overline{v_1}} = \frac{\frac{3R}{4}}{\frac{5R}{36}} = \frac{3R}{4} \times \frac{36}{5R} = \frac{3\times 9}{5} = \frac{27}{5}$$

$$\overline{v_2} = \frac{27}{5}\overline{v_1}$$

29. (b) I. The energy of hydrogen in its ground state is –13 eV.

II. On the basis of Bohr's model, the radius of 3rd orbital of hydrogen atom is

$$r_n = 52.9 \times \frac{n^2}{Z} \text{ pm} = 52.9 \times \frac{3^2}{1} \text{ pm} = 476.1 \text{ pm}$$

III. $r_n \propto \frac{1}{Z}$

Be^{3+} has highest atomic mass so radius is smallest.

Order of radius will be $H > He^+ > Li^{2+} > Be^{3+}$

So only I and III are correct.

30. (a) Since isotope have same number of electron thus their chemical properties are same.

31. (c) Ground state energy of hydrogen like atom is

$$E = -13.6 \times \frac{Z^2}{n^2}$$

All are in ground state i.e n = 1

∴ $E \propto Z^2$

∴ The ratio of ground state energy of

$$E_{Li^{2+}} : E_{He^+} : E_H = (3)^2 : (2)^2 : (1)^2 = 9 : 4 : 1$$

32. (b) $\upsilon = R_H \times Z^2 \times \left(\frac{1}{n_1^2} - \frac{1}{n_2^2}\right)$

For paschen series longest wavelength

$n_1 = 3;\ n_2 = 4$

$$\upsilon = R_H \times (3)^2 \times \left(\frac{1}{(3)^2} - \frac{1}{(4)^2}\right) = R_H \times \frac{9\times 7}{9\times 16}$$

$$\upsilon = R_H \times \frac{7}{16} \Rightarrow \frac{1}{\lambda} = R_H \times \frac{7}{16}$$

or, $\lambda = \frac{16}{7\times R_H} = x$ ...(i)

for Lyman series of hydrogen spectrum.

$$\upsilon = R_H \times Z^2 \times \left[\frac{1}{N_1^2} - \frac{1}{N_2^2}\right]$$

$$\upsilon = R_H \times (1)^2 \times \left[\frac{1}{1^2} - \frac{1}{2^2}\right] \Rightarrow \upsilon = R_H \times \frac{3}{4}$$

$\lambda = \frac{4}{3R_H}$ ...(ii)

By equation (i) and (ii) we get

$$\lambda = \frac{7x}{12}$$

33. (c) Bohr radii (r_n) $= 52.9 \times \frac{n^2}{Z}$ pm

radii of fourth orbit of $He^+ = 52.9 \times \frac{(4)^2}{2}$

radii of third orbit of $He^+ = 52.9 \times \frac{(3)^2}{2}$

difference of radii $= 52.9 \times \frac{(4)^2}{2} - 52.9 \times \frac{(3)^2}{2}$

$= \frac{52.9}{2} \times 7$ pm

$= 185.15$ pm $= 185.15 \times 10^{-12}$m $= 1.85 \times 10^{-10}$m

34. (a) Energy (E_n) $= -2.18 \times 10^{-18}\left(\frac{Z^2}{n^2}\right)$ J

Z = 3; n = 3 (third orbit)

$$E_3 = -2.18 \times 10^{-18} \times \frac{(3)^2}{(3)^2} \text{J}$$

$E_3 = -2.18 \times 10^{-18}$ J

35. (a) $E = 2.18 \times 10^{-18}\left(\frac{1}{n_1^2} - \frac{1}{n_2^2}\right)$

$= 2.18 \times 10^{-18}\left(\frac{1}{5^2} - \frac{1}{1^2}\right) = 2.18 \times 10^{-18}(-0.96)$

$= -2.091 \times 10^{-18}$ J.

36. (d)

Radius of 1st Bohr orbit, $r = \frac{0.529n^2}{z}$ Å

$$\therefore r_{He^+} : r_{Li^{2+}} = \frac{0.529\times 3^2}{2} : \frac{0.529 \times 1^2}{3} = \frac{9}{2} : \frac{1}{3}$$

$$\therefore r_{He^+} = \frac{27}{2}x$$

37. (a) From Bohr's theory, $r_n = \frac{0.529n^2}{z}$ Å for hydrogen like systems.

For H, $r_1 = 0.529$Å

∴ For He^+, n = 4, $r_4 = \frac{0.529 \times 4^2}{2}$

$\Rightarrow r_1 : r_4 = 1 : 8$

We know, $n\lambda = 2\pi r$

$r_1 = \frac{\lambda_1}{2\pi}$ and $r_4 = \frac{4\lambda_4}{2\pi}$

∴ $r_1 : r_4 = 1 : 8$

or, $\frac{\lambda_1}{2\pi} : \frac{4\lambda_4}{2\pi} = 1:8$ or, $\frac{\lambda_1}{4\lambda_4} = \frac{1}{8}$ or, $\lambda_4 = \frac{8\lambda_1}{4}$

or, $\lambda_4 = 2y$ ($\because \lambda_1 = y$Å)

38. (c) From de-Broglie's equation

$p = \frac{h}{\lambda}$ or, $v = \frac{h}{m\lambda}$

$$\text{K.E.} = \frac{1}{2}mv^2 = \frac{1}{2}m.\frac{h^2}{m^2\left(3.3\times 10^{-10}\right)^2}$$

$= \frac{1}{2\times9\times10^{-31}}\times\left(\frac{6.6\times10^{-34}}{3.3\times10^{-10}}\right)^2$

$= \frac{2}{9}\times10^{-17}\,J = 0.222\times10^{-17}\,J = 2.22\times10^{-18}J$

39. (a) Number of electrons in Li^+ = Number of electrons in helium = 2.

40. (d) For first orbit (n = 1), r_1

$= \left(\frac{1}{z}\right)\times0.529Å$

For third orbit (n = 3), $r_3 = \left(\frac{9}{z}\right)\times0.529Å$

Hence, $r_3 = 9r_1$

41. (d)

42. (a) Energy of electron in nth orbitals is given by

$E_n = -2.18\times10^{-18}.\frac{Z^2}{n^2}J$

For helium ion (He^+) $Z = 2, n = 1$

$\therefore\ E_n = -2.18\times10^{-18}\times\frac{2^2}{1^2} = -8.72\times10^{-18}\,J$

For lithium ion (Li^{2+}) $Z = 3, n = 3$

$\therefore\ E_n = -2.18\times10^{-18}\times\frac{3^2}{3^2} = -2.18\times10^{-18}\,J$

43. (c) Ground state energy of electron in H atom= -2.18×10^{-18} J

$r_n = r_0\times\frac{n^2}{Z}$ 52.9pm= 52.9 pm $\times\frac{n^2}{Z}\Rightarrow Z = n^2$

Now $E_n = E_0\frac{Z^2}{n^2}\Rightarrow E_n = -2.18\times10^{-18}\times\frac{n^4}{n^2}$

$E_n = -2.18\times10^{-18}\times n^2$

When $n = 1$, $E_1 = 2.18\times10^{-18}$ J

$n = 2$, $E_2 = 4\times(-2.18\times10^{-18}) = -8.72\times10^{-18}$ J

44. (c) Given, r_n = 476.1 pm

r_1 = 52.9 pm

$r_n = \frac{n^2\times r_1}{Z}$; $476.1 = \frac{n^2\times52.9}{Z}$; $n = 3$ [Z = 1]

Now, $E_n = -2.18\times10^{-18}\cdot\frac{Z^2}{n^2}$

and $E_n = E_3 = -\frac{2.18\,Z^2\times10^{-18}\,J}{9}$

$= -2.42\times10^{-19}$ J

45. (d) For He^+ : $Z = 2, n = 2$

$E_n = -2.18\times10^{-18}.\frac{Z^2}{n^2}\cdot J$

$\therefore\ E_n = -2.18\times10^{-18}\times\frac{4}{4} = -2.18\times10^{-19}$ J

$r_n = 52.9\times\frac{n^2}{Z}$ pm $= 52.9\times\frac{4}{2} = 105.8$ pm

46. (c) v = x m/s

Speed is measured with accuracy of 0.001%

v = x × 0.001

$v = x\times\frac{0.001}{100}$

$v = x\times10^{-5}$ m/s

Using Heisenberg Uncertainty Principle

$\Delta x.\Delta p = \frac{h}{4\pi}$

$\Delta x.m\Delta v = \frac{h}{4\pi}$ [$1J = kg\ m^2/s^2$]

$\Delta x = \frac{6.6\times10^{-34}\,J\,s}{4\times3.14\times9\times10^{-31}\,kg\times x\times10^{-5}\,m/s}$

$\Delta x = \frac{6.6\times10^{-34}}{4\times3.14\times9\times10^{-31}\times x\times10^{-5}}$

$\Delta x = \frac{6.6\times100}{4\pi\times9\times x} = \frac{55}{3\pi x}$

47. (b) Given, mass of ball 50g = 0.05 kg

v = 50 m/s

accuracy in speed = 2%

so, $\Delta v = \frac{2}{100}\times50 = 1$ m/s

$\Delta p = m\Delta v$

$\Delta p = 0.05\times1$

= 0.05 kg m/s

According to Heisenberg uncertainty principle:

$\Delta x\cdot\Delta p = \frac{h}{4\pi}$

$\Delta x = \frac{h}{4\pi\cdot\Delta p}$

$\Delta x = \frac{6.6\times10^{-34}}{4\times3.14\times0.05} = 1.06\times10^{-33}$ m.

48. (N) $r_n = r_1\times n^2$, n = 4

$r_4 = 26.45\ pm\times4^2 = 423.2$ pm

$v = \frac{nh}{2\pi m_r}$ ...(i)

$\lambda = \frac{h}{mv}$ ...(ii)

Putting (i) in (ii), we get $\lambda = \frac{2\pi r_n}{n}$

$2\pi r_n = n\lambda$

$2\pi r_n = 4\lambda$

$\lambda = \frac{3.14\times423.2\ pm}{2} = 6.64\times10^{-10}$m

49. (b) Mass = 6.63g ⇒ 6.63×10^{-3} kg

Wavelength (λ) = 10^{-24} nm ⇒ 10^{-33}m

h = 6.63×10^{-34} J.S

$\lambda = \frac{h}{mv}\Rightarrow v = \frac{h}{m\lambda}$

$v = \frac{6.6\times10^{-34}}{6.63\times10^{-3}\times10^{-33}}$

= 1×10^2 m/s Or 100 m/s

50. (a) According to de-Broglie equation:

For a given kinetic energy 'K' : $\lambda = \frac{h}{\sqrt{2mK}}$

$\lambda\propto\frac{1}{\sqrt{m}}$

From the above relation:

$\frac{\lambda_A}{\lambda_B} = \sqrt{\frac{m_B}{m_A}} = \sqrt{\frac{m_B}{4m_B}}$ $(\because m_A = 4m_B)$

$\frac{y}{x} = \frac{3}{15} = 0.2$

$\lambda_A : \lambda_B = 1:2$

51. (c) According to Rydberg equation

For hydrogen atom

$\frac{1}{\lambda_H} = R(1)^2\left(\frac{1}{n_1^2}-\frac{1}{n_2^2}\right)$

For He^+

$\frac{1}{\lambda_{He^+}} = R(2)^2\left(\frac{1}{n_1^2}-\frac{1}{n_2^2}\right)$

$\lambda_H = 4\lambda_{He^+} = 4\times100$ nm = 400 nm = 4000 Å

52. (a) Energy (E) = $h\nu = \frac{hc}{\lambda}$ [ν = frequency

c = speed of light = (3×10^8 m/s) [λ = wavelength]

$a = 3\times10^{15}$ Hz

$b = 0.2\times10^{15}$ Hz

c = 400 nm

$h\nu = h\times\frac{3\times10^8}{4\times10^{-7}} = h\times0.75\times10^{15}$

$\nu = 0.75\times10^{15}$ Hz

For d = 750 nm

$h\nu = \frac{h\times3\times10^8}{750\times10^{-9}}$

$\nu = 0.4\times10^{15}$ HZ

$E\propto\nu$

So, order will be

$b\ (0.2\times10^{15}) < d\ (0.4\times10^{15}) < c\ (0.75\times10^{15}) <$ a (3×10^{15})

53. (b) The minimum energy required to eject the electron is $h\nu_0$ also called work function = 7.68×10^{-19} J

The striking photon has energy equal to $h\nu$

$\therefore\ E = h\nu = \frac{hc}{\lambda}$

$= \frac{6.63\times10^{-34}\,J.S\times3\times10^8\,m/s}{221\times10^{-9}\,m}$

$h\nu = 9\times10^{-19}$ J

The kinetic energy (in J) of the ejected electrons is

$= (9\times10^{-19} - 7.68\times10^{-19})$ J

$= 1.32\times10^{-19}$ J

54. (a) $\Delta V_A = 0.03\ ms^{-1}$, $\Delta V_B = 0.01\ ms^{-1}$

$m(B) = 4\,m(A),\ \frac{\Delta x_A}{\Delta x_B} = ?$

$\Delta x\,.\,\Delta p = \Delta x\,.\,m\Delta V = \frac{h}{4\pi}$

$\Rightarrow \Delta x = \frac{h}{4\pi m\Delta V}$

Thus, $\frac{\Delta x_A}{\Delta x_B} = \frac{h}{4\pi m(A)\Delta V_A} \times \frac{4\pi m(B)\Delta V_B}{h}$

$= \frac{m(B)\Delta V_B}{m(A)\Delta V_A} = \frac{4m(A)\Delta V_B}{m(A)\Delta V_A}$

$= \frac{4\Delta V_B}{\Delta V_A} = \frac{4\times 0.01}{0.03} = \frac{0.04}{0.03} = \frac{4}{3}$

55. (b)

	λ	m
X	1	9
Y	3	1

$\lambda = \frac{h}{\sqrt{2m\,KE}}$

$\frac{\lambda_x}{\lambda_y} = \sqrt{\frac{2M_y KE_y}{2m_x\ KE_x}}$

$\frac{1}{3} = \frac{1}{3}.\sqrt{\frac{KE_y}{KE_x}}$

$\frac{3}{3} = \sqrt{\frac{KE_y}{KE_x}} = \frac{1}{1}$

$\sqrt{\frac{KE_x}{KE_y}} = \frac{1}{1}$ ratio is 1 : 1

56. (c) As, $mvr = \frac{nh}{2\pi}$

Where, m is the mass v is the velocity r is the radius of orbit n is the orbit h is planck's constant λ is wavelength r_n is Bohr radius

So, $mv = \frac{nh}{2\pi r}$ ...(i)

and $\lambda = \frac{h}{mv}$

So, $mv = \frac{h}{\lambda}$ ...(ii)

From (i) & (ii)

$\frac{nh}{2\pi r} = \frac{h}{\lambda}$

$\therefore\ \lambda = \frac{2\pi r}{n}$ ...(iii)

as $r_n = 52.9\left(\frac{n^2}{Z}\right)$ pm ...(iv)

$\therefore$ Substituting the value of r_n of (iv) in (iii)

$\lambda = \frac{2\pi}{n} \times 52.9 \times \left(\frac{n}{Z}\right)^2$ pm

$\therefore\ \lambda = 2\pi \times 52.9 \times \frac{n}{Z}$ pm

as $n = 3, Z = 1$

$\therefore\ \lambda = 2\pi \times 52.9 \times \frac{3}{1}$ pm

$\therefore\ \lambda = 6\pi \times 52.9$ pm

57. (c) The value of l in O to $(n-1)$ thus for $n = 3$ value of l not more than 2.

58. (c) Heisenberg's uncertainty principle's Mathematical expression is

$\Delta x.\Delta p_x \geq \frac{h}{4\pi}$

$\Delta x = 100$ pm

$\therefore\ \Delta p_x = \frac{6.626\times10^{-34}\,J.S}{4\times3.14\times10^2\times10^{-12}\,m}$

$\Delta p_x = 0.527 \times 10^{-24}$ Kg ms^{-1}

59. (b) Given energy use for work done and kinetic energy as

$E = hv = W_0 + K$

$W_0 = hv_0$

$v_0 \Rightarrow$ Threshold frequency

When x H_z frequency of light fall on the metal surface the kinetic energy of electron is J the equation will be

$hx = hv_0 + J$ ...(1)

When metal irradiated with light of frequency Y H_z kinetic energy of emitted electron $\frac{J}{3}$ the equation is.

$hy = hv_0 + \frac{J}{3}$ ...(2)

from equation (1)

$J = hx - hv_0$

Putting the value of J in equation (2)

$h_y = hv_0 + \frac{x - hv_0}{3}$

$3hy = 3hv_0 + hx - hv_0$

$3hy - hx = 2hv_0$

$v_0 = \frac{3y - x}{2}$

60. (a) Heisenberg uncertainty principle,

$\Delta x\,.\,\Delta p = \frac{h}{4\pi}$

$\Delta x = 2 \times 10^{-3}$nm

$\Delta x = 2 \times 10^{-3} \times 10^{-9}$ m [1nm = 10^{-9}m]

$\therefore\ \Delta x = 2 \times 10^{-12}$m

h = 6.626×10^{-34} Js [1J = 1kg m^2 s^{-2}]

$\therefore\ \Delta x.\Delta p = \frac{h}{4\pi}$

$\Delta p = \frac{h}{4\pi.\Delta x} = \frac{6.626\times10^{-34}\,Js}{4\times3.14\times2\times10^{-12}\,m}$

$= 0.2637 \times 10^{-22}$ kg ms^{-1}

$= 2.637 \times 10^{-23}$ kg ms^{-1}

61. (b) $KE = \frac{1}{2}mv^2 \Rightarrow v = \sqrt{\frac{2.KE}{m}}$

de broglie wavelength $(\lambda) = \frac{h}{mv}$

$\therefore\ \lambda = \frac{h}{\sqrt{m\times 2.KE}}$

$\lambda = \frac{h}{\sqrt{9\times10^{-31}\times2\times2.5\times1.6\times10^{-19}}}$

$= \frac{h}{\sqrt{72}\times\sqrt{10^{-50}}}$

$\lambda = \frac{h}{\sqrt{72}}\times10^{25}$

62. (a) According to de Broglie wavelength,

$\lambda = \frac{h}{m\upsilon}$

$KE = \frac{1}{2}m\upsilon^2 \Rightarrow \upsilon = \sqrt{\frac{2\times K.E}{m}}$

$\therefore \lambda = \frac{h}{\sqrt{2m\times K.E}}$

From photoelectric effect,

$KE = h\upsilon - h\upsilon_0 \Rightarrow KE = h(\upsilon - \upsilon_0)$

$\therefore\ \lambda = \frac{h}{\sqrt{2mh(\upsilon-\upsilon_0)}} \Rightarrow \lambda = \sqrt{\frac{h}{2m(\upsilon-\upsilon_0)}}$

$\lambda \propto \left(\frac{1}{\upsilon-\upsilon_0}\right)^{1/2}$

63. (b) According to Einstein's equation of photoelectric effect.

$h\upsilon = h\upsilon_0 + K.E$

$\therefore\ \frac{1}{2}mv^2 = h(\upsilon-\upsilon_0) = \frac{hc}{\lambda} - \frac{hc}{\lambda_0}$

or, $v^2 = \frac{2hc}{m}\left(\frac{1}{\lambda} - \frac{1}{\lambda_0}\right)$

$v = \sqrt{\frac{2hc}{m}\left(\frac{\lambda_0-\lambda}{\lambda\lambda_0}\right)}$

64. (a) $\Delta x \times \Delta p = \frac{h}{4\pi}$

Given, $\Delta x = \Delta p$

$(\Delta p)^2 = \frac{h}{4\pi} \Rightarrow \Delta p = \sqrt{\frac{h}{4\pi}}$

$\Rightarrow m\Delta v = \frac{1}{2}\sqrt{\frac{h}{\pi}} \Rightarrow \Delta v = \frac{1}{2m}\sqrt{\frac{h}{\pi}}$

65. (a) Energy absorbed by the element

$= 1.5 \times 2.18 \times 10^{-18}$J

$= 1.5 \times 2.18 \times 10^{-18}$ kg m^2 s^{-2}

$= 3.27 \times 10^{-18}$ kg m^2 s^{-2}

Energy required = 2.18×10^{-18} J

Kinetic energy of the emitted electron

= Energy absorbed – energy required

= $(3.27 \times 10^{-18} - 2.18 \times 10^{-18})$ kg m^2 s^{-2}

KE = 1.09×10^{-18} kg m^2 s^{-2}

$m_e = 9 \times 10^{-31}$ kg

According to de. Broglie equation

$\lambda = \frac{h}{mv}$

$KE = \frac{1}{2}mv^2 \Rightarrow v = \left(\frac{2\times KE}{m}\right)^{1/2}$

$\therefore \lambda = \frac{h}{\sqrt{2m\,K.E}}$

or, $\lambda = \frac{h}{\sqrt{2\times 9\times 10^{-31}kg\times 1.09\times 10^{-18}kg\,m^2s^{-2}}}$

or, $\lambda = \frac{h}{\sqrt{19.62\times 10^{-49}}}$

$\lambda = \frac{h}{\sqrt{1.962\times 10^{-48}}} \Rightarrow \lambda = \frac{h\times 10^{24}}{\sqrt{1.962}}$

66. (c) The uncertainty in the speed is 2% i.e.

$50\times\frac{2}{100} = 1ms^{-1}$

According to Heisenberg uncertainty principle,

$\Delta x = \frac{h}{4\pi m\Delta v}$

$\Delta x = \frac{h}{4\pi m\times 1ms^{-1}g}$ $\left[1\,g = 10^{-3}\,kg\right]$

$\Delta x = \frac{h}{4\pi m\times 10^{-3}}$

$\Delta x = \frac{h}{4\pi m}\times 10^3$ $\left[1\,J = 1kgm^2s^{-2}\right]$

67. (a) According to de Broglie wavelength

$(\lambda) = \frac{h}{p}$ or, $\lambda = \frac{h}{mv}$

[$1\,J = Kg\,m^2\,s^{-2}$ $1\,mg = 10^{-3}g$ $1\,Kg = 10^3g$]

$\lambda = \frac{6.63\times 10^{-34}Js}{1\,mg\times 10\,ms^{-1}}$

$\Rightarrow \lambda = \frac{6.63\times 10^{-34}Kg\,m^2s^{-2}s}{10^{-3}\,mg\times 10\,ms^{-1}}$

$\lambda = \frac{6.63\times 10^{-34}\times 10^3\,gm^2s^{-1}}{10^{-2}gm\,s^{-1}}$

$\lambda = 6.63\times 10^{-34}\times 10^3\times 10^2$ m

$\Rightarrow \lambda = 6.63\times 10^{-29}$ m

68. (c) $\lambda = 1000$ nm

$= \mathbf{1000}\times 10^{-9}$ m $= 1.0\times 10^{-6}$ m

$\Rightarrow p = \frac{h}{\lambda} = \frac{6.626\times 10^{-34}}{1.0\times 10^{-6}} = 6.626\times 10^{-28}$ J s m^{-1}

69. (c) $\lambda = 3000Å = 3\times 10^{-7}$m, $\phi = 2.13$ eV

$K.E. = hv - hv_0 = hv - \phi = \frac{hc}{\lambda} - \phi$

$= \frac{(6.626\times 10^{-34}\times 3\times 10^8)}{3\times 10^{-7}} - (2.13\times 1.6\times 10^{-19})$

$= \frac{1.98\times 10^{-25}}{3\times 10^{-7}} - (3.408\times 10^{-19})$

$= (6.60\times 10^{-19}) - (3.408\times 10^{-19})$

$= 3.192\times 10^{-19}$ J $= 2.0$ eV

70. (b) $C = 3\times 10^8$ ms^{-1}

$\Rightarrow$ Velocity (V) $= \frac{20\times 3\times 10^8}{100} = 6\times 10^7$ ms^{-1}.

Thus, $\lambda = \frac{h}{m_eV} = \frac{6.626\times 10^{-34}}{(9.1\times 10^{-31})(6\times 10^7)}$

$= 1.2\times 10^{-11}$ m.

71. (c) The energy of photon

$= \frac{hc}{\lambda} = \frac{6.62\times 10^{-34}\times 3\times 10^8}{400\times 10^{-9}}$ J

$= \frac{0.0497\times 10^{-77}}{1.6\times 10^{-19}}$ eV $= 3.1$ eV

The metals having work function < 3.1 eV do eject the electron but > 3.1 eV do not eject

$\therefore$ Li, Na, K will eject the electron but Mg, Cu, Ag will not able to eject.

72. (c) To eject the electron from the metallic surface the energy of incident photon must be comparable with the work function of the metal.

$\therefore$ The energy of incident radiation = 6.3 eV

$\therefore$ $hv = 6.3\times 1.6\times 10^{-19}$J

$\frac{hc}{\lambda} = 6.3\times 1.6\times 10^{-19}$ J

or, $\lambda = \frac{6.62\times 10^{-34}\times 3\times 10^8}{6.3\times 1.6\times 10^{-19}} = 1.97\times 10^{-7}$ m

$= 197\times 10^{-9}$m $= 197$ nm.

73. (d) Work function $(\phi) = 3.1$ eV

$= 3.1\times 1.6\times 10^{-19}$J

Threshold frequency

$(v_0) = \frac{E}{h} = \frac{3.1\times 1.6\times 10^{-19}}{6.626\times 10^{-34}}$ s^{-1}

$= 0.748\times 10^{15}$ s^{-1} $= 7.48\times 10^{14}$ Hz

74. (c) Given condition, $\Delta x = \Delta v$

$\Delta p.\,\Delta x = \frac{h}{4\pi}$

or, $m\,\Delta v.\,\Delta v = \frac{h}{4\pi}$ or $\Delta v = \sqrt{\frac{h}{4\pi m}} = \frac{1}{2}\sqrt{\frac{h}{\pi m}}$

$\therefore$ Uncertainty in momentum,

$\Delta p = m\,\Delta v = \frac{m}{2}\sqrt{\frac{h}{\pi m}} = \frac{1}{2}\sqrt{\frac{hm}{\pi}}$

75. (d) As we know

$\lambda = \frac{h}{mv}$ $\left[\because E = \frac{1}{2}mv^2\right]$ $\lambda = \frac{h}{\sqrt{2mKE}}$

Since, h is a constant and kinetic energy is same for both particles, so,

Wavelength for particle one $(\lambda_1) = \frac{h}{\sqrt{2mKE}}$

Wavelength for particle two $(\lambda_2) = \frac{h}{\sqrt{4mKE}}$

The ratio will be $\frac{\lambda_1}{\lambda_2} = \frac{\sqrt{4m}}{\sqrt{2m}} = \frac{\sqrt{2}}{1}$

The ratio of de-Broglie wavelength is $\sqrt{2} : 1$.

76. (a) Binding energy of 1 mole (6.022×10^{23}) of electrons = 250 kJ

Binding energy of 1 electron

$= (250)/(6.022\times 10^{23})$ kJ $= 4.15\times 10^{-19}$ J

Threshold energy (hv_0) = Binding energy

$\therefore$ $hv_0 = 4.15\times 10^{-19}$ J

or $v_0 = (4.15\times 10^{-19}\,J)h$

$= (4.15\times 10^{-19}J)(6.626\times 10^{-34}J.s) = 6.25\times 10^{14}s^{-1}$

77. (c) Kinetic energy of photoelectrons

$KE = h(v - v_0)$ symbol

When $v > v_0$ (threshold frequency) $KE > 0$

78. (c) $\lambda = \frac{h}{\sqrt{2m(KE)}}$

$\lambda = \frac{6.626\times 10^{-34}\,Js}{\sqrt{2\times 9.0\times 10^{-31}kg\times 2\times 10^{-25}J}}$

$\lambda = 11043\times 10^{-6}$m $= 1104.3$nm

79. (b) According to Heisenberg uncertainty

$\Delta x.\Delta v = \frac{h}{4\pi\,m}$

$\Delta v = \frac{6.626\times 10^{-34}\,Js}{4\times\pi\times 911\times 10^{-31}.kg\times 10.98\times 10^{-9}\,m}$

$\Delta v = \frac{1.6565\times 10^4}{\pi}$

80. (b) $\frac{hv_1 - hv_0}{hv_2 - hv_0} = \frac{K.E_1}{K.E_2}$

$\frac{h(1.6\times 10^{16} - v_0)}{h(1.0\times 10^{16} - v_0)} = \frac{2K.E.}{K.E.}$

$1.6\times 10^{16} - v_0 = 2\times 1.0\times 10^{16} - 2v_0$

$v_0 = 1.6\times 10^{16} - 2(1.0\times 10^{16}) = v_0 = 4\times 10^{15}$ Hz

81. (b)

82. (c) According to uncertainty principle,

$\Delta p.\Delta x \geq \frac{h}{4\pi} \Rightarrow m.\Delta v\times\Delta x \geq \frac{h}{4\pi}$

$\Rightarrow \Delta v\times\Delta x \geq \frac{h}{4\pi\times m}$

83. (d) $\lambda \propto \frac{1}{\sqrt{K.E.}} \Rightarrow \frac{\lambda_1}{\lambda_2} = \sqrt{\frac{(KE)_2}{(KE)_1}}$

$KE_2 = \frac{(KE)_1}{2}$

Thus, $\frac{\lambda_1}{\lambda_2} = \sqrt{\frac{1}{2}} \Rightarrow \lambda_2 = \sqrt{2}\lambda_1$

84. (c)

The number of radial node for 3p = n – l – 1

(x) $\Rightarrow$ 3 – 1 – 1 = 1

The number of angular node for 3d = 1.

(y) = 2

$\therefore$ Ratio of x and y

$= \frac{x}{y} = \frac{1}{2}$

$\Rightarrow$ x : y = 1 : 2

85. (d) For energy comparison, (n + l) rule is followed. If (n + l) value is same, then lower n value has lower energy.

I. $(n + l) = (3 + 1) = 4$

II. $(n + l) = 5$ (n = 4)

III. $(n + l) = 6$

IV. $(n + l) = 5$ (n = 3)

Energy order : III > II > IV > I

86. (a) $z = 24 = 1s^2\, 2s^2\, 2p^6\, 3s^2\, 3p^2\, 3d^5\, 4s^1$

$z = 29 = 1s^2\, 2s^2\, 2p^6\, 3s^2\, 3p^6\, 3d^{10}\, 4s^1$

For $z = 24$, $m_l = 0$ orbital contain electrons are

$(1s + 2s + 2p + 3s + 3p + 3d + 4s)$

$2 + 2 + 2 + 2 + 2 + 1 + 1 = 12$

$z = 29$, $m_l = 0$ orbital contain electrons are

$(1s + 2s + 2p + 3s + 3p + 3d + 4s)$

$(2 + 2 + 2 + 2 + 2 + 2 + 1) = 13$

87. (d) $Z = 25$ means the element is Mn

$Mn = 1s^2\, 2s^2\, 2p^6\, 3s^2\, 3p^6\, 3d^5\, 4s^2$

For $(n + l) = 3$, we have $2p$ and $3s$ so number of such electrons $(x) = 6 + 2 = 8$

For $(n + l) = 4$, we have $3p$ and $4s$ so number of such electrons $(y) = 6 + 2 = 8$

$\therefore \quad (x + y) = 8 + 8 = 16$

88. (a) Number of subshells having $m_l = -2$ will be 3.

(3*d*, 6*d*, 4*f* = 3 orbitals)

Thus, number of electrons possible = 2 × 3 = 6

89. (b) Radial node = n – 1 – 1; Angular node = 1

$\therefore$ for 4d; n = 4, l = 2

Angular node = 2; Radial node = 4 – 2 – 1 = 1

$\therefore$ Sum of angular + radial node = 3

90. (b) The region where probability density function, $\psi^2_{(r)}$ reduces to zero is called model surfaces or simply nodes ns orbital has (n – 1) nodes.

Givengraphhasonenode.Soitshouldbe2s-orbital.

General formula for calculating radial nodes in $(n - \ell - 1)$.

91. (b) Angular momentum $= \dfrac{3h}{\pi}$

$m_e Vr = n\dfrac{h}{2\pi}$

$\dfrac{3h}{\pi} = n.\dfrac{h}{2\pi}$

n = 6

For the Radius$(r_n) = a_0 \times \dfrac{n^2}{Z}$

$\Rightarrow 52.9 \text{ pm} \times \dfrac{(6)^2}{3}$

$\Rightarrow \quad 634.8 \times 10^{-12}$ m. $\Rightarrow$ $\boxed{r_n = 6.348 A°}$

Energy of stationary state $(E_n) = -R_H \times \left(\dfrac{1}{n^2}\right)$

For Li^{+2} = (n = 2)

$F_2 = -2.18 \times 10^{-18}\text{ J} \times \dfrac{1}{2^2}$

$= -0.545 \times 10^{-18}\text{J} = -5.45 \times 10^{-19}$ J

92. (a) Electronic configuration of strontium (Sr) = [Kr] $5s^2$

(n) = 5; (l) = 0; $(m_\ell) = 0$; $(m_s) = \dfrac{1}{2}$

n	l	m_ℓ	m_s
5	0	0	$+\frac{1}{2}$

93. (b) For a 4f- orbital, n = 4 and l = 3

For a given value of *l*, there can be (2*l* + 1) values of m_l ranging from $-l$ to $+l$.

Thus, $m_l = +1$ is possible.

m_s can be $+\dfrac{1}{2}$ or $-\dfrac{1}{2}$

94. (c) For multielectron atoms, the energy of the orbitals increases with an increase in their (n + *l*) value.

Thus, the order will be :

5p < 6s < 4f < 5d

95. (c) Number of electrons = $2n^2 = 2\,(6)^2 = 72$

96. (c) According to Hund's rule, pairing of electrons does not take place in a subshell untill each orbital in that subshell has got one electron each.

Thus, configuration in option (c) violates Hund's rule.

97. (a) No. of electrons in 'n' shell = $2n^2$

$\therefore \quad n = 4;\ 2n^2 = 32e^-$ and $n = 3;\ 2n^2 = 18e^-$

Half of the electrons in one shell has $\left(+\dfrac{1}{2}\right)$ spin and half of them has $\left(-\dfrac{1}{2}\right)$ spin.

$\therefore \quad$ Total no. of electrons $= \dfrac{32}{2} + \dfrac{18}{2} = 25e^-$

98. (a) Maximum no. of electrons = $2n^2$ = 2 × 4 × 4 = 32 (when n = 4) in n = 4, $2n^2 = 32$

Half of the electrons have $\left(+\dfrac{1}{2}\right)$ spin, i.e, 16.

99. (d) According to Pauli's Exclusion Principle, maximum 2 electrons may exist in one orbital with opposite spin.

100. (b) Azimuthal quantum number (l).

101. (a) Radial nodes = n – *l* – 1

Angular nodes = the value of '*l*'

4f orbital, n= 4, *l* = 3

$\therefore$ Radial nodes = 4 – 3 – 1 = 0 and angular nodes = *l* = 3

102. (b) Two angular nodes are found in *d*-orbital.

Number of radial nodes = $(n - l - 1)$

for 3d : $n = 3$, $l = 2$

$\therefore$ Number of angular nodes = $l = 2$

Number of radial nodes = $n - l - 1 = 3 - 2 - 1 = 0$

103. (d) Assertion is wrong, reason is correct as we move away from the nucleus, in atom the potential energy of electron increase, as the value of *n* increase the distance from nucleus increase, consequently the kinetic energy of the electron decreases, but total energy as whole increases.

104. (b)

105. (b) $\Delta x \times m\Delta v \geq \dfrac{h}{4\pi} \Rightarrow \Delta x \geq \dfrac{h}{4\pi \times m \times \Delta v}$

$\geq \dfrac{6.626 \times 10^{-27}}{4 \times 3.14 \times 9.1 \times 10^{-28} \times 3 \times 10^4 \times 0.02 \times 10^{-2}}$

$\geq 9.66 \times 10^{-3}\text{ cm} \approx 9 \times 10^{-3}\text{ cm}$

106. (d) Given, $n = 3$, l = 1 and $m_l = -1$

Means an orbital is present in p-subshell of 3rd shell having orientation value = –1. (i.e. p_x or p_y).

Thus, only one orbital is possible for the given set of values of *n*, *l* and m_l.

107. (c) For 3*d*-orbitals; $n = 3$, $\ell = 2$. m_l can take values from $-\ell$ to $+\ell$, i.e., –2 to +2. m_s can take values $+\dfrac{1}{2}$ or $-\dfrac{1}{2}$

3 Classification of Elements and Periodicity in Properties

1. **(c)** Representative elements are elements from s and p block only.

I - 3(Li, s-block), 33(As, p-block), 53(I-p-block), 87 (Fr, s-block)

II- 2(He, p-block), 10(Ne, p-block), 22 (Ti, d-block), 36(Kr, p-block)

III-9(F, p-block) 35(Br, p-block), 51(Sb, p-block), 88(Ra, S-block)

IV- 17 (Cl, p-block), 25(Mn, d-block), 37(Rb, s-block), 48(Cd, d-block)

Hence, I, III contains s and p-block elements only.

2. **(c)** Phosphorus (Z = 15) electronic configuration-

$1s^2\ 2s^2\ 2p^6\ 3s^2\ 3p^3$

Total s-electrons = 2 + 2 + 2 = 6

Total p-electrons = 6 + 3 = 9 Ratio (s:p) = 6:9 = 2:3

Sulfur (Z = 16) electronic configuration

$1s^2\ 2s^2\ 2p^6\ 3s^2\ 3p^4$

Total s-electrons = 6, Total p-electrons = 10

Ratio (s:p) = 6:10 = 3:5

3. **(b)** A - 112 $[_{86}Rn]\ 5s^{14}\ 6d^{10}\ 7s^2$

B - 116 $[_{86}Rn]\ 5s^{14}\ 6d^{10}\ 7s^2\ 7p^4$

C - 88 $[_{86}Rn]\ 7s^2$

D - 100 $[_{86}Rn]\ 5f^{12}\ 7s^2$

4. **(c)** Mc (Moscovium) group 15.

Lv (Livermorium) group 16.

Fl (Flerovium) group 14.

Ts (Tennessine) Group 17

5. **(c)** Electronic configuration of Fe = [Ar] $3d^6\ 4s^2$

$\therefore$ iron have 6 electron in d orbital

Atom Electronic configuration

Mg $1s^2\ 2s^2\ 2p^6\ 3s^2$

Cl [Ne] $3s^2\ 3p^5$

Ne $1s^2\ 2s^2\ 2p^6$

$\therefore$ Ne have 6 electrons in p orbital which is same as Fe electrons in d orbital and Mg also have 6 electrons in all 's' orbital.

Hence (i) and (iii) are correct.

6. **(c)** A-II, B-I, C-IV, D-III

7. **(d)** (Mn, Cr)

(a) Fe electronic configuration
$= [Fe = 1s^2\ 2s^2\ 2p^6\ 3s^2\ 3p^6\ 4s^2\ 3d^6]$
Here (n – 1) shell is 3d which have 6 electron.

(b) Mn electronic configuration
$[Mn = 1s^2\ 2s^2\ 2p^6\ 3s^2\ 3p^6\ 4s^2\ 3d^5]$
(n – 1) shell have 5 electrons

(c) Zn electronic configuration
$[Zn = 1s^2\ 2s^2\ 2p^6\ 3s^2\ 3p^6\ 4s^2\ 3d^{10}]$
(n – 1) shell have 10 electron

(d) Sc electronic configuration
$[Sc = 1s^2\ 2s^2\ 2p^6\ 3s^2\ 3p^6\ 4s^2\ 3d^1]$
(n – 1) shell have 1 electron.
K electronic configuration is
$[K = 1s^2\ 2s^2\ 2p^6\ 3s^2\ 3p^6\ 4s^1]$
(n – 1) shell have 6 electron.
Cr electronic configuration is
$[Cr = 1s^2\ 2s^2\ 2p^6\ 3s^2\ 3p^6\ 4s^1\ 3d^5]$
Here (n – 1) shell have 5 electron.
So Mn, Cr have same Number of electron in (n – 1) shell.

8. **(a)** Metalloids : B, Sb, As, Ge
Metals = Mn, Cu, Ag, K, Na
Non-Metals = Si, F

9. **(b)** Alkali metals (group 1) = ns^1
Alkaline earth metals (group 2) = ns^2
Halogens (group 17) = $ns^2\ np^5$
Noble gases (group 18) = $ns^2\ np^6$

10. **(b)** Q shell $\Rightarrow$ n = 7 indicates the position of the element in period 7 in the periodic table.
Ra : outer electronic configuration = $4s^2$ (valence shell)

11. **(d)** The valency of gp. 1 metal is 1 and that of gp. 16 elements is 2.

12. **(a)** The element with atomic number 117 is Ts, Tennessive. Valence shell electronic configuration is $7s^2\ 7p^5$.

13. **(a)** IE increases along a period as the nuclear charge increases and the added electron comes in the same valence shell. But exception occurs when the element has completely filled and half-filled subshells.

The valence shell electronic configurations are:

$Be(4) \rightarrow 2s^2$; $B(5) \rightarrow 2s^2 2p^1$; $C(6) \rightarrow 2s^2 2p^2$;
$(I.E.)_1$ $(I.E.)_2$ $(I.E.)_3$

$O(8) \rightarrow 2s^2 2p^4$; $F(9) \rightarrow 2s^2 2p^5$; $Ne(10) \rightarrow 2s^2 2p^6$
$(I.E.)_4$ $(I.E.)_5$ $(I.E.)_6$

Order :

$(I.E.)_6 > (I.E.)_5 > (I.E.)_4 > (I.E.)_3 > (I.E.)_1 > (I.E.)_2$

The correct answer should be Be, F.

14. **(c)** For electronic configuration = [Ar] $3d^5 4s^2$

Group = number of valence electrons = 5 + 2 = 7

15. **(c)** According Mendeleev's periodic law "The properties of elements are periodic functions of their atomic weights."

16. **(c)** Electronic configuration of the element in +2 oxidation state is [Ar] $3d^1$. Its electronic configuration in neutral state:

[Ar] $3d^1 4s^2$

Period = Max. principal quantum no. $n = 4$

Group = Total number of valence shell electrons = 3

17. **(b)**

18. **(a)** Electronegativity increases across the period from left to right. So correct order will be P < S < N < O.

19. **(a)**

I. In third period, Mg and P have higher ionization enthalpy than the element immediately following them in the same period due to half field electronic configuration of Mg (s^2) and P(p^3)

II. Electronegativity of carbon is 2.5 and phosphorous is 2.1 so carbon electronegativity is higher than that of phosphorous.

III. In period 3 and group 14 element present is Si and it has 14 electrons.

So all three statements are correct.

20. **(b)** Energy per mole

$= 3.6 \times 23$ k cal mol^{-1} = 82.8 k cal mol^{-1}

Number of moles (n) = $\dfrac{7.1\,g}{35.5\,g\,mol^{-1}}$ = 0.2 moles

Total energy released = n × (Energy per mole)

= 0.2 moles × 82.8 k cal mol^{-1}

= 16.56

21. **(a)**

I : $NO^+ = 7 + 8 - 1 = 14$
$CN^- = 6 + 7 + 1 = 14$
$CO = 6 + 8 = 14$
$O_2^{2+} = 8 + 8 - 2 = 14$
all isoelectronic

II : $NH_3 = 7 + 3 = 10$
$Al^{3+} = 13 - 3 = 10$
$Ne = 10$
$F^- = 9 + 1 = 10$
all isoelectronic

III : $O_2^+ = 8 + 8 - 1 = 15$
$NO = 7 + 8 = 15$
$N_2^- = 7 + 7 + 1 = 15$
$H_2O = 8 + 2 = 10$
not isoelectronic

22. **(d)** Down the group atomic radii increases while along the period left to right atomic radii decreases.

The correct order of atomic radii is O<P<Ge<K not O < P < K < Ge because along the period moving from left to right atomic radii decreases.

23. **(a)** PO_4^{3-} : 5 + 4(6) + 3 = 32

SO_3^{2-} : 6 + 3(6) + 2 = 26

$CO_3^{2-}: 4 + 3(6) + 2 = 24$

$CNO^-: 4 + 5 + 6 + 1 = 16$

PO_4^{3-} has maximum valence electrons

24. (d)
- Co, Ni → have similar metallic radius (III)
- K, Ba → have similar standard reduction potential (IV)
- N, Cl → have similar electronegativity (I)
- Ar, Kr → have similar electron gain enthalpy (II)

So, A-III, B-IV, C-I, D-II

25. (d) Phosphorus (Z = 15) electronic configuration = [Ne] $3s^2\ 3p^3$ half-filled 3p subshell that is exceptionally stable.

Sulfur (Z = 16) electronic configuration = [Ne] $3s^2$, $3p^4$ removing an electron from s-orbital relieves inter electronic pairing repulsion in the 3p orbital, making it easier to ionize than phosphorus.

$IE_1(P) > IE_1(S)$

26. (d) $CCl_4: 4 + 4(7) = 32$

$PO_4^{3-}: 5 + 4(6) + 3 = 32$

They both have same number of valence electrons.

27. (c) Tennessine, Z = 117. It belongs to group 17, halogen.

28. (a)

I. K > Li > C > F - Down the group atomic radii increases, while going left to right along a period radii decreases.

II. F > C > Li > K - Down the group ionisation enthalpy decreases, while going left to right along a period ionisation enthalpy increases.

III. F > C > K > Li - Down the group electronegativity decreases, while going left to right along a period electronegativity increases, so correct order is F > C > Li > K

Hence, I, II are correct.

29. (d) All three pairs have equal electronegativities.

(a) $P \approx 2.1, H \approx 2.1$
(b) $C \approx 2.5, S \approx 2.5$
(c) $N \approx 3.0, Cl \approx 3.0$

All three have approx equal electronegativity on Pauling Scale.

So, option (d) is correct.

30. (d)

	Na^+	Mg^{2+}	Al^{3+}	Si^{4+}
$\frac{e}{p}$	$\frac{10}{11}$	$\frac{10}{12}$	$\frac{10}{13}$	$\frac{10}{14}$

Largest radius $\frac{10}{11} \Rightarrow Na^+ = 100$ pm

Smallest radius $\frac{10}{14} \Rightarrow Si^{4+} = 40$ pm

Thus from given data Mg^{2+} smaller than Na^+ and Al^{3+} larger than Si and sequence are

$Al^{3+}, Mg^{2+}, Si^{4+}, Na^+$

31. (c) First ionisation enthalpy of nitrogen is more than oxygen and carbon. In nitrogen three 2*p*-electrons reside in different atomic orbitals whereas in the oxygen atom, two of the four 2*p*-electrons must occupy the same 2*p*-orbital resulting in an increased electron-electron repulsion. So, its easy to remove fourth 2*p* electron from oxygen. So, order will be

N > O > C

32. (d) For isoelectric set of ions greater the charge on anion larger will be its size and ions of greater the charge on cation smaller will be its size. Hence N^{3-} is largest in size and Al^{3+} is smallest in size.

33. (b) Chlorine, a halogen has very high electron gain enthalpy because it can readily gain an electron to achieve a stable noble gas configuration.

Sulphur, also readily gains electrons, it's electron gain enthalpy is less negative than chlorine due to its larger size and greater shielding.

Lithium has a smaller atomic size compared to sodium. This smaller size allows lithium to hold onto its electrons more tightly.

Sodium is larger than lithium which means it has a lower effective nuclear charge and hence it is less effective at attracting an additional electron.

34. (a) Fluorine (F):- Period = 2, Groups = 17

35. (d) After removal of one electron the species having higher stability will have lesser ionisation potential

Thus order is

D > C > B > A

36. (c) Generally, non metallic character increases across the period and decreases down the group.

37. (d) C (2, 4) Al (2, 8, 3) S (2, 8, 6)

Carbon is smallest because only two shell present, Al and S have three shell but due to high effective nuclear charge atomic size of S is less than Al. Thus order is.

C < S < Al

38. (b) The order of negative electrone gain enthalpy is Cl > F > S > O.

39. (a) Ionization enthalpy depends on the

(i) Size of the atom

(ii) $Z_{effective}$ nuclear charge

(iii) electronic configuration.

In periodic table left to right ionisation enthalpy increases and nitrogen have half-filled electronic configuration so its ionisation enthalpy is more.

B_2O_3 (Borontrioxide) is acidic and reacts with basic (methalic) oxides forming metal borates.

CrO_3 is acidic oxide.

So both statements are correct.

40. (d) Electron gain enthalpy:- In a group there is decrease of electron gain enthalpy in general but for p-block elements only the EA_1 of second period element is less than EA_1 of third period element. The third period have larger size and vacant 3d orbitals, which can accommodate incoming electron easily.

So order will be S > Se > O

Electronegative along a period left to right increases and in a group it is decreases.

F > O > Cl

Metallic radius in a periodic table from left to right it is decrease and top to bottom it is increases so,

Na > Li > Al

Metallic character increases down the group

Ba > K > Na

41. (d) In periodic table, left to right atomic radii decreases and from top to bottom atomic radii increases.

∴ Al > Si > N > F

42. (a) In periodic table atomic radii decrease from left to right and increase from top to bottom.

Mg is placed in 3rd period and Be, B are in second period so, Mg have more atomic radii than Be and B.

$\xleftarrow[\text{Atomic radii}]{Mg>Be>B}$

43. (a)

Element	Density/g cm^{-3}
Be	1.84
Mg	1.74
Ca	1.55
Sr	2.63

Density of Be is higher than Mg and Ca due to small size.

44. (d) Atomic radius of gallium is less than aluminium.

Correct order : B < Al > Ga < In < Tl

45. (b) A → III, B → I, C → IV, D → II

46. (c) First ionisation enthalpy of Li, Be and C respectively are 520, 899, 1086 kJ mol^{-1}.

The ionisation energy depend on the

(i) Size of the atom

(ii) effective nuclear charge

(iii) Screening effect

(iv) Penetration effect

(v) Electronic configuration

Li - $1s^2\ 2s^1$

Be - $1s^2\ 2s^2$

B - $1s^2\ 2s^2\ 2p^1$

C - $1s^2\ 2s^2\ 2p^2$

(i) Left to right in the periodic table ionisation enthalpy increase.

(ii) Beryllium have full filled orbital so its ionisation energy is more than boron.

So, order will be

C > Be > B > Li

∴ Correct option will be (c).

47. (a) Thermal stability increases with increasing cationic size. So, correct order is $BaCO_3 > CaCO_3 > MgCO_3$

48. (a) Electron gain enthalpy generally becomes more negative across a period as we move from left to right. Within a group, electron gain enthalpy becomes less negative down a group.

When we are adding an electron to 'F' atom, 2p orbital leads to greater repulsion than adding an electron larger 3p orbital like chlorine, due to larger size of chlorine electron can accommodate easily so its value will be more negative as compare to fluorine. Same reason follow for oxygen and sulphur.

49. (b) Metallic nature decreases in a period from left to right due to an increase in the effective nuclear charge.

50. (c) Diagonal relationship is exhibited by an element and the element lying diagonally right to the next group in the next period.

$Li \rightarrow Mg$, $Be \rightarrow Al$, $B \rightarrow Si$.

51. (d) The atomic size/radius decreases in a period from left to right.

Thus, ${}_3Li > {}_5B > {}_7N > {}_9F$

52. (b) Correct order of electron gain enthalpy:-

$Al < N < O < Cl$

It is higher for non-metallic elements that have higher electronegativities (higher in magnitude)

53. (b) ${}_{10}Ne = 1s^2\ 2s^2\ 2p^6$, ${}_{11}Na = 1s^2\ 2s^2\ 2p^6\ 3s^1$, ${}_{12}Mg = 1s^2\ 2s^2\ 2p^6\ 3s^2$

$\Rightarrow$ Highest first ionization enthalpy: Ne, due to stable fully-filled configuration.

$\Rightarrow$ Lowest second ionization enthalpy: Mg, due to stable noble gas configuration obtained after losing two electrons.

54. (d) Strongly electropositive metals form strongly basic oxides that dissolve in water to give alkalis.

Na_2O has strongly electropositive Na-metal that forms NaOH in water which is a strong base.

55. (c) As we move down the group, the addition of shells causes an increase in the covalent radii of the group 14 elements.

Thus, $Si < Ge < Sn$.

56. (c) Fluorine (F) is the element with highest electronegativity, lying at the extreme right in the second period.

Francium (Fr) is the most electropositive or least electronegative element, lying at the bottom left of the periodic table.

57. (c) Statement (II) is **incorrect** as oxygen is the element with an electronegativity of 3.5 and not chlorine.

Statement (IV) is **incorrect** as the element with the atomic number 106 is seaborgium (Sg) and not Bohrium (Bh)

58. (b) Half-filled or completely filled orbitals attain extra stability due to symmetrical distribution of electrons and high exchange energy.

59. (a)

$$C \rightarrow 1s^2 2s^2 2p^2 \xrightarrow[\text{Ionization}]{\text{After Ist}} 1s^2 2s^2 2p^1$$

$$N \rightarrow 1s^2 2s^2 2p^3 \longrightarrow 1s^2 2s^2 2p^2$$

$$O \rightarrow 1s^2 2s^2 2p^4 \longrightarrow 1s^2 2s^2 2p^3 \text{ (Half – filled)}$$

$$F \rightarrow 1s^2 2s^2 2p^5 \longrightarrow 1s^2 2s^2 2p^4$$

All elements are in 1st Period. As the atomic number increases ionization energy increases. Oxygen gets extra stability due to half-filled p-orbital after first ionization.

60. (d) $O \rightarrow 1s^2\ 2s^2\ 2p^4$

After 1st ionization enthalpy becomes:

$O = 1s^2 2s^2 2p^3$

61. (b) Higher oxidation states of metals are acidic. Lower oxidation are basic as they produce bases reacting with water. Amphoteric oxides produce both acids and bases with water or reacts with both acid or bases.

Tl_2O_3, In_2O_3 $\rightarrow$ basic oxides; $B_2O_3 \rightarrow$ acidic oxide

ZnO, PbO, SnO_2 $\rightarrow$ amphoteric oxides

62. (a) Oxidizing property depends on the enthalpy of sublimation, ionization enthalpy of the element as well as solvation energy of the resulting anion of oxidizing agent.

63. (a) Metallic character decreases along a period from left to right and increases along a group from top to bottom.

64. (a) $X\ (g) + e \rightarrow X^-\ (g)$ at absolute zero temperature.

The electron gain enthalpy ($\Delta_{eg}H$) could be positive endothermic or negative exothermic. If $\Delta_{eg}H$ has high negative values, more is the stability of $X^-(g)$.

In case of F, O, $\Delta_{eg}H$ value is less negative compared to other elements present in their corresponding groups. However, $\Delta_{eg}H\ (S^-, g)$ greater negative value than $\Delta_{eg}H\ (O^-, g)$ due to the larger size of S, less interelectronic repulsion than O. So, $S^-(g) > O^-(g)$ in terms of stability.

$\therefore$ The correct order : $F > S > O > N$.

65. (a) $\begin{matrix} Li \\ Na \end{matrix} \searrow \begin{matrix} Be \\ Mg \end{matrix} \searrow \begin{matrix} B \\ Al \end{matrix}$ Diagonal relationship

66. (a) The metallic character increases down the group and decreases from left to right of a period.

67. (c) For isoelectronic species, the ionic radii decrease with increase in nuclear charge.

So, the cation with greater positive charge i.e. Ca^{2+} will have smaller radius and the anion with greater negative charge i.e. S^{2-} will have a larger radius.

Ionic radii : $S^{2-} > I^- > K^+ > Ca^{2+}$

68. (c) In isoelectronic species

Greater the charge on cation smaller is the size of cation.

Hence, Si^{4+} has the smaller size.

69. (c) The first IE of Be is greater than that of B because Be has stable complete electronic configuration ($1s^2\ 2s^2$), whereas, B has electronic configuration $1s^2\ 2s^2\ 3s^1$ which require lesser energy than that of Be to remove an electron. In atoms with more than one electron, 2*s*-orbital is lower in energy than 2*p*-orbital.

70. (b) $sp > sp^2 > sp^3$

$50\% > 33\% > 25\%$

71. (a) $EN = \dfrac{IE + EA}{2}$ ...(i)

$EN = \dfrac{13+4}{2} = \dfrac{17}{2} = 8.5$ eV

72. (b) Due to small size of F atom, it has lower EGE than that of Cl atom

Order of increasing electron gain enthalpy

$N < P < F < Cl$

73. (b) The second ionisation energy is the energy required to remove an electron from a 1+ cation in the gaseous state.

$X^+(g) \rightarrow X^{2+}(g) + e^-$

Second ionisation energy is also affected by size, effective nuclear charge, and electronic configuration.

Li has highest IE_2 than B because the second electron remove from stable noble gas configuration has higher IE_2 than C due to the extra stability of the $2s^2$ subshell in the B^+ ion. Therefore, the correct order $I.E_2$ will be : $Li > B > C > Be$.

74. (a) For isoelectronic set of ions greater the charge on cation smaller will be its size and greater the size on anion larger will be its size. Hence, the order of ionic radii will be

$Mg^{2+} < Na^+ < Cl^- < S^{2-}$.

75. (c) Electronic configuration of boron ($Z = 5$); [He] $2s^2 2p^1$. First ionisation will take place from unpaired p^1-electron. $2p^1$-electron of *B* experience lesser nuclear attractive force for ionisation.

Electronic configuration of Be ($Z = 4$) : [He]$2s^2$. Removal of electron takes place from paired $2s^2$-electrons which requires more energy.

76. (a) For an isoelectronic species, the species with more electrons with respect protons in nucleus has larger size.

If 'Z' represents number of protons in a nucleus. then, $Z - 2$ has least number of protons, whereas $Z + 1$ has maximum number of protons.

Hence, order of size for isoelectronic species will e

$Z - 2 > Z - 1 > Z > Z + 1$

Element with atomic number $Z - 2$ is of largest size and option (a) is the correct answer.

77. (d) Mn_2O_7, CrO_3, V_2O_5 are acidic.

Due to higher oxidation state of central metal oxides.

78. (b) Na^+ and Mg^{2+} are isoelectric species having $10e^-$ each. But Mg^{2+} has 12 protons while Na^+ has 11 protons. Hence effective nuclear charge is greater in case of Mg^{2+}.

$$\text{ionic radius} \propto \frac{1}{\text{effective nuclear charge}}$$

79. (a) Due to inert pair effect, +2 O.S. is more stable than +4 O.S. for lead.

4 Chemical Bonding and Molecular Structure

1. **(c)** Formal charge (F.C) on an atom in a Lewis structure
= [Total number of valence electrons in the free atom] – [Total number of non bonding (lone pair) electrons] – 1/2 [Total number of bonding (shared) electrons]
For Lewis structure I, II, III F.C of sulphur is

$(F.C)_I = 16 - 4 - \frac{1}{2} \times 4 = 0$

$(F.C)_{II} = 6 - 6 - \frac{1}{2} \times 2 = -1$

$(F.C)_{III} = 6 - 2 - \frac{1}{2} \times 6 = +1$

2. **(b)** $N_2 = CO = NO^+ = 14$ electrons.

3. **(a)** According to Fajan rule, for greater

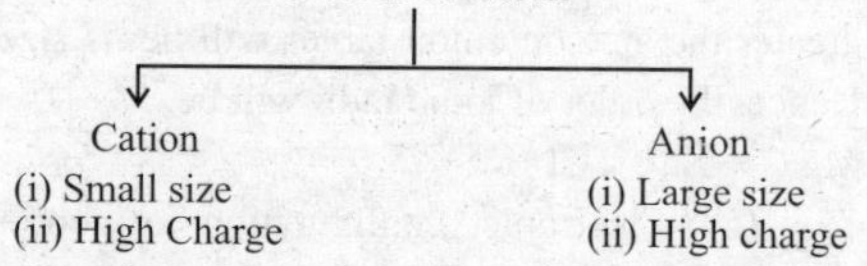

Covalent character :- $CCl_4 > BCl_3 > BeCl_2 > LiCl$

4. **(c)** According to Fajan's rule, for covalent character, cation should be small in size and contain high positive charge and anion should be large in size and contain high negative charge.
(i) Iodine have more size than anion fluorine so, KI > KF
(ii) K^+ have more size than Li^+ so, LiF > KF
(iii) Sn^{2+} and Sn^{4+}
in Sn^{4+} carry more charge than Sn^{2+}
so, $SnCl_4 > SnCl_2$
(iv) Cu^+ have pseudo configuration so it has more covalent character than NaCl.
CuCl > NaCl
∴ (i), (iii) and (iv) are correct

5. **(c)** Ionic bonds are electrostatic forces of attraction that are non-directional in nature. Thus, (A) is correct.
Ionic compounds are soluble in polar solvents that solvate them via ion-dipole interactions. Thus, (R) is incorrect.

6. **(c)** Covalent solids are bad conductors of electricity due to the absence of free electrons like in metallic solids.

7. **(b)** In hydroxyl ion, 3 lone pairs of electrons are present on oxygen atom of hydroxyl ion.

8. **(a)** I: CO_3^{2-} is sp^2 hybridised not sp^3

II: Average formal charge on each O = $-\frac{2}{3}$ = – 0.67

III: The resonance hybrid structure is a blend where all three C-O bonds are identical.

IV: Because of resonance delocalisation, all C–O bond lengths are equal.

Hence, statement II and IV are correct.

9. **(c)**

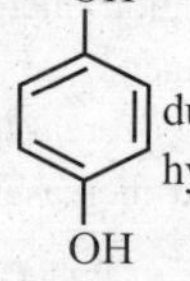

due to distant terminals of hydrogen no intramolecular hydrogen bond is formed.

10. **(b)** (0, 0, –1)
The formal charge can be calculated by this formula

$$\text{Formal charge} = \begin{bmatrix}\text{Total number of} \\ \text{Valence electron} \\ \text{in the free state}\end{bmatrix} - \begin{bmatrix}\text{total number of} \\ \text{non – Bonding (lone} \\ \text{pair) electron}\end{bmatrix} - \frac{1}{2}\begin{bmatrix}\text{total number of Bonding} \\ \text{(shared electrons)}\end{bmatrix}$$

For atom 1 ⇒ 6 – 4 – 1/2 [4] = 0
Atom 2 ⇒ 5 – 2 – 1/2 [6] = 0
Atom 3 ⇒ 6 – 6 = 1/2 [2] = – 1

11. **(c)** Formal charge (Q_f) on an atom = [Total number of valence electron in the free atom (v)] – [total number of non bonding/ unshared electron] – [number of bond around the atom]
$\therefore Q_f = V - (U) - (B)$
$Q_f = V - (U + B)$

12. **(a)**

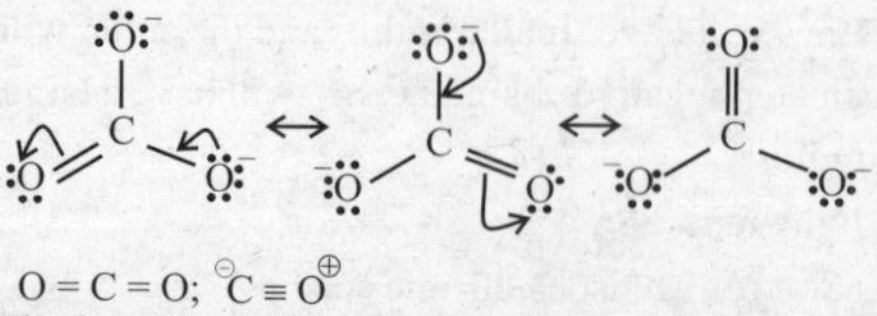

$O = C = O; \overset{\ominus}{C} \equiv \overset{\oplus}{O}$
The bond length is smallest for the C ≡ O bond due to strong triple bond.
Among CO_3^{2-} and CO_2, CO_3^{2-} has the smaller C – O bond length due to resonance stabilization that makes the bond stronger.

13. **(b)** BF_3 and CCl_4 are non-polar molecules due to symmetrical arrangement of the bond pairs that result in the cancellation of the individual bond dipoles(μ=0).

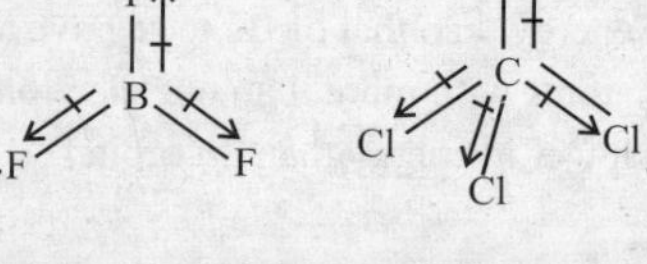

14. **(b)** According to Fajan's rule, small and highly charged cation and big size anion are most covalent.

15. **(c)** In NH_3 net dipole moment (≈ 1.47D)
In NF_3 the net dipole moment (≈ 0.23D)
In $CHCl_3$ the net dipole moment (≈ 1.01D)
The correct increasing order should be-
$NF_3 < CHCl_3 < NH_3$

16. **(b)** H_2O (Bent Shape, Polar)

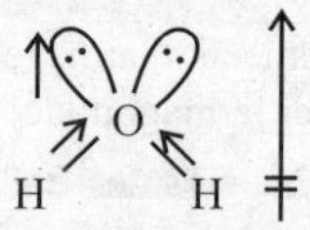

NH_3 (Pyramidal shape, Polar)

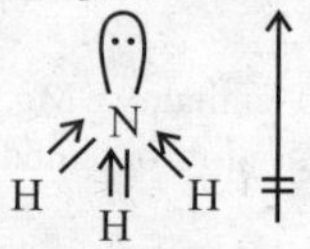

HCl (linear Shape, Polar)

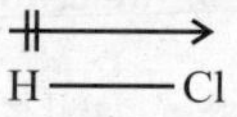

Only polar and non-symmetric molecules shows dipole moment.

17. **(b)**

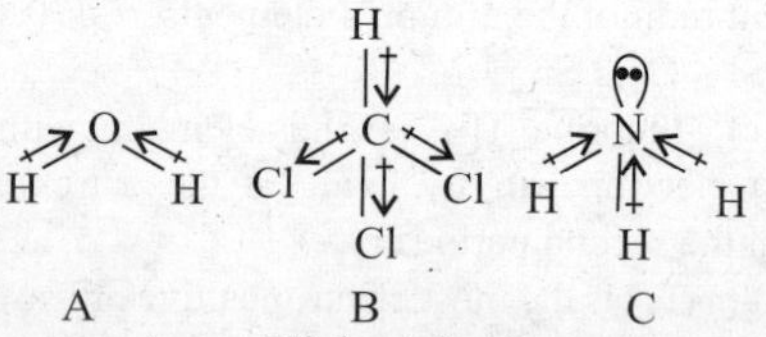

Lowest — Highest due to vector sum is high

18. **(a)**

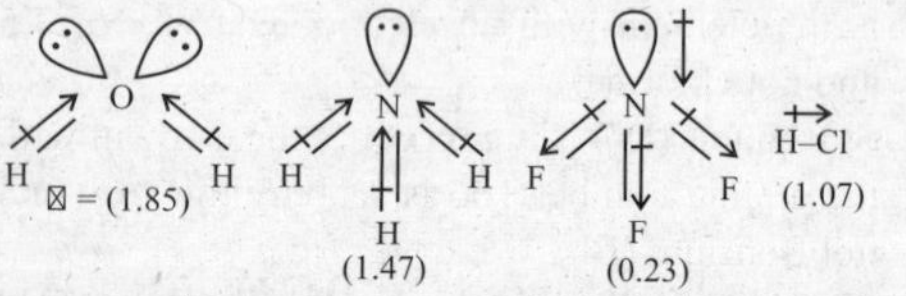

Water have more dipole moment due to oxygen electronegativity and in NH_3 and NF_3, the orbital dipole due to lone pair is in the same direction as the resultant dipole moment of the N-H bond but in NF_3 it is in the opposite direction which result in the low dipole moment as compare to NH_3.

19. **(d)** Bond length is affected by atomic size and electronegativity H – H = shortest length due to smallest atomic radii (0.74 Å)
In O – H and C – H; O – H have less bond length (0.96 Å) as compare to C – H (1.09 Å) due to electronega-tivity difference.

C–C has more bond length due to large atomic radii (1.54 Å)

So the order will be

H – H < O – H < C – H < C – C

20. (a) Dipole of NF_3 cancelled to other thus dipole moments of NH_3 is less than NH_3. NF_3 orbital dipole opposite direction which result decrease in dipole moment.

21. (d) CH_4,

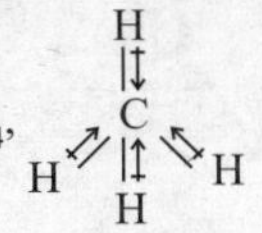

Dipole moment cancelled to each other thus CH_4, BF_3 and CO_2 have zero dipole moment.

BF_3,

CO_2, O⇄C⇄O

22. (d)

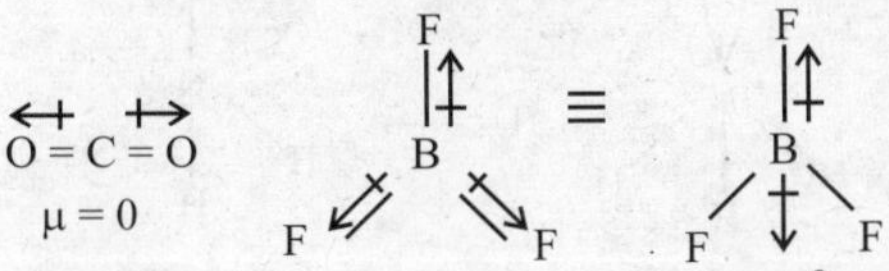

$\mu = 0$ $\mu = 0$

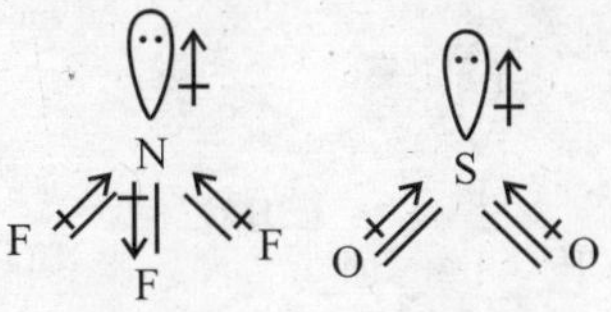

$\mu \neq 0$ $\mu \neq 0$

$\mu = 0.23$ $\mu = 1.60$

∴ SO_2 and NF_3 both pair have dipole moment.

23. (c) (i)

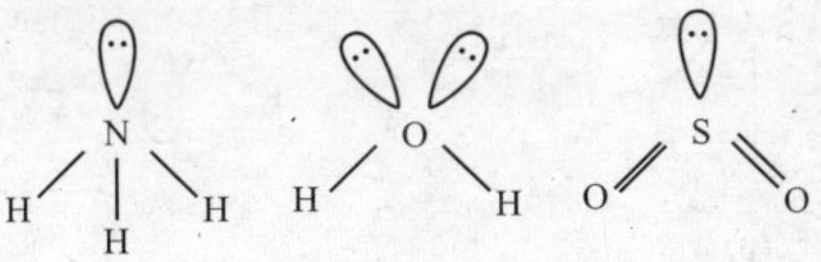

sp^3 sp^3 sp^2

107.3° 104.5° 119°

In NH_3 and H_2O bond angle should be 109.28° but in ammonia there is one lone pair-bone pair repulsion and in H_2O two lone pair and bone pair repulsion so which decrease the bond angle and SO_2 is planar structure and its bond angle should be 120° but also to lone-pair-bond pair it decreases.

$SO_2 > NH_3 > H_2O$

(ii)

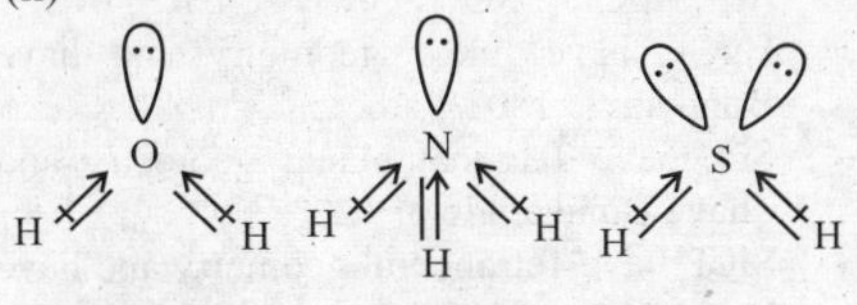

X = 1.85 1.47 0.95

Dipole moment ∝ Electronegativity

Oxygen is more electronegative then nitrogen so its dipole moment in H_2O is more as compare to NH_3 and H_2S

$H_2O > NH_3 > H_2S$

(iii) More the bond order more will be the bond enthalpy

Molecule	Bond order
N_2	3
O_2	2
H_2	1

∴ Bond enthalpy $N_2 > O_2 > H_2$

(iv)

Molecule	Bond order
NO^+	2.5
O_2	2
O_2^{2-}	1

Bond order $NO^+ > O_2 > O_2^{2-}$

∴ (ii), (iii) and (iv) are correct.

24. (d)

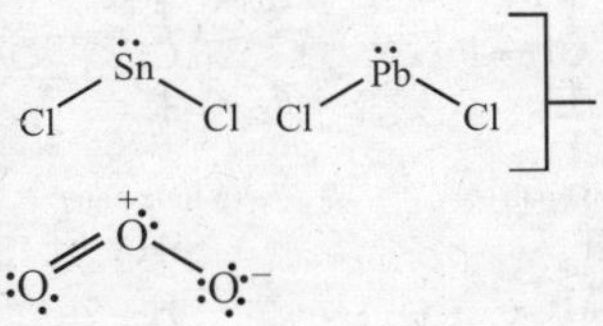

Formal charges on terminal oxygens = 0 and –1.

25. (b)

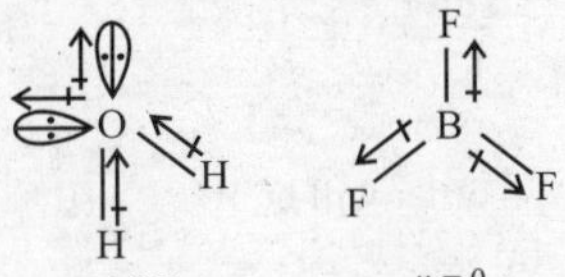

$\mu = 1.85$ $\mu = 0$ (Symmetrical)

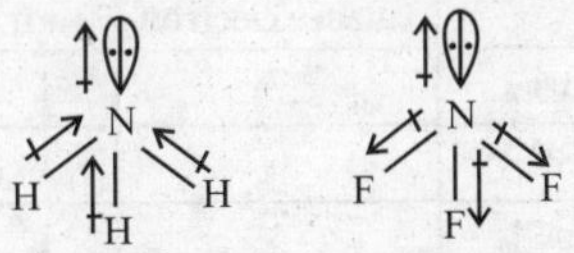

$\mu = 1.47$ (bond dipoles added) $\mu = 0.23$ (bond dipoles cancel out)

26. (b) According to the Fajan's rule, smaller the size of cation and larger size anion have greater covalent character.

27. (c) Small size and high positive charge of a cation highly polarizes the large sized, high negative charged anion. Therefore, enhances the posibility of covalency.

28. (a) M.O. : $B_2(10)$ = KK*

$\sigma 2s^2 (\sigma 2s^*)^2 \left(\pi^1 2p_x = \pi^1 2p_y\right);$

$$B.O. = \frac{1}{2}(4-2) = 1$$

$C_2(12) = KK^* \sigma 2s^2 \ (\sigma 2s^*)^2 \left(\pi^2 2p_x = \pi^2 2p_y\right);$

$$B.O. = \frac{1}{2}(6-2) = 2$$

$N_2(14) = KK^* \sigma 2s^2 \ (\sigma 2s^*)^2 \left(\pi^2 2p_x = \pi^2 2p_y\right) \sigma^2 2p_z;$

$$B.O. = \frac{1}{2}(8-2) = 3$$

Greater the bond order shorter is the bond length.

∴ $X_3 > X_1 > X_2$.

29. (a)

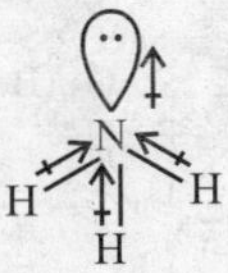

$\mu \neq 0$

(Resultant dipole moment and dipole due to lone pair are in same direction)

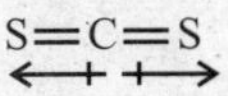

$\mu = 0$ (Symmetric)

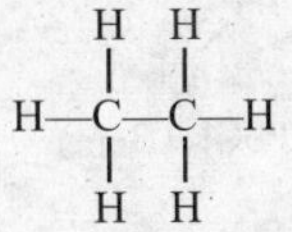

$\mu = 0$ (Symmetric)

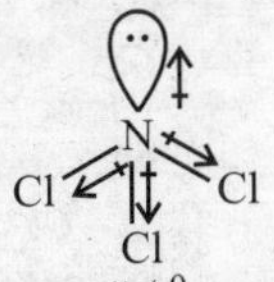

$\mu \neq 0$ (lone pair decreases the resultant N–Cl bond moments)

30. (a) (i)

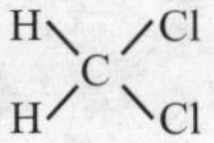

$\mu \neq 0$

(ii)

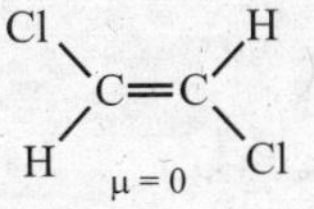

$\mu = 0$

(iii)

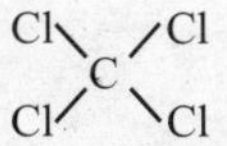

$\mu = 0$

(iv) Br — C ≡ C — Br $\mu = 0$

As dipole moment is vector quantity. Due to electron density in opposite direction, net dipole moment cancel out each other.

31. (a) The O–H and S–H bond dipoles in (iii) and (iv) molecules do not cancel each other as they exist in different conformations.

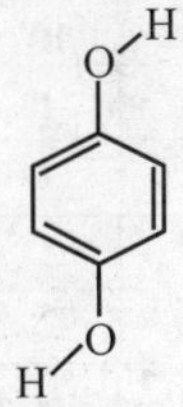

32. (d)

I. H_2O, OF_2 and SCl_2 all have bent structure.

II. CO_2, $BeCl_2$ and $HgCl_2$ all have Linear structure.

III. $SiCl_4$ is Tetrahedral, SF_4 have see saw and XeF_4 have square planer structure.

So only I and II are isostructural.

33. (d) $U = \frac{1}{2}$ [V + M – C + A]

U = Steric number

V = Valence electrons of central atom

M = Monovalent atoms bonded

C = Cationic charge

A = Anionic charge

SF_4, $U = \frac{1}{2}$ [6 + 4] = 5 ⟶ sp^3d

XeF_4, U = – [8 + 4] = 6 ⟶ sp^3d^2

SO_3, $U = \frac{1}{2}$[6 + 0] = 3 ⟶ sp^2

34. (a) Cl – Be – Cl

$BeCl_2$ (linear)

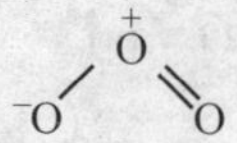

O_3 (Bent)

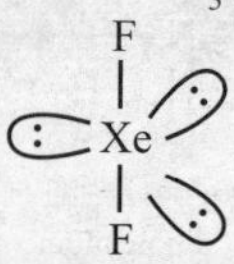

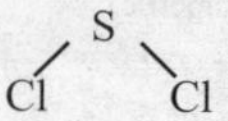

SCl_2 (Bent) XeF_2 (linear, but 3 L.P)

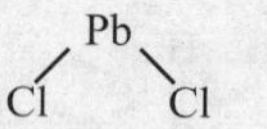

$PbCl_2$ (Bent)

$SnCl_2$ (Bent)

Cl – Mg – Cl

$HgCl_2$ (linear)

35. (b) NO_2 :

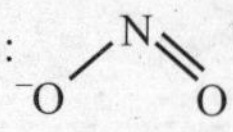

(sp^2)

SO_3 :

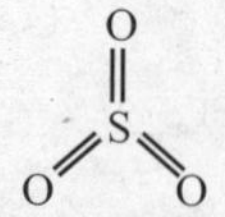

(sp^2)

- $H_3BO_3 – sp^2$, $H_3PO_3 – sp^3$
- $XeO_3 – sp^3$, $BF_3 – sp^2$
- $PCl_3 – sp^3$, $ClF_3 – sp^3d$

36. (d) SF_4 have sp^3d hybridisation and due to presence of lone pair on sulphur atom shape of molecule is distorted to see-saw shape. $PbCl_2$ is ionic compound thus exist in lattice form.

37. (d)

Molecule	Bond pair	Lone pair	Steric number	Hybridisation
I. PCl_3	3	1	4	sp^3
II. SO_2	2	1	3	sp^2
III. SF_4	4	1	5	sp^3d
IV. ClF_3	3	2	5	sp^3d

So only 'I' and IV are correctly matched.

38. (d)

Molecule	Lone pair of electrons in central atom
BF_3	0
SF_4	1
$SiCl_4$	0
XeF_4	2
NCl_3	1
XeF_6	1
PCl_5	0
$HgCl_2$	0 (*d* electrons are not taken)
$SnCl_2$	1

Hence, total number of molecules = 5

39. (c) $ClF_3 = sp^3d$ (3 b.p + 2 l.p.)

$SF_4 = sp^3d$ (4 b.p. + 3 l.p.)

$XeF_2 = sp^3d$ (2 b.p. + 3 l.p.)

40. (b) ClF_3 the trigonal bipyramidal deform into T-Shape due to two lone pair electron present on chlorine atom pushing the three bonded atoms ClF_3 contain 10 electron is 5 pair.

41. (c)

Molecules	Number of lone pairs
SF_6	0
BF_3	0
ClF_3	2
PCl_5	0
BrF_5	1
XeF_4	2
H_2O	2
SF_4	1

So, ClF_3, XeF_4, H_2O has 2 lone pair of electrons.

42. (b)

BO_3^{3-}	Trigonal planar
NH_3	Trigonal pyramidal
PCl_3	Trigonal pyramidal
BCl_3	Trigonal planar
ClF_3	T-shaped
XeO_3	Pyramidal

Only BO_3^{3-} and BCl_3 have Trigonal planar geometry.

43. (d) ClF_3 XeF_2

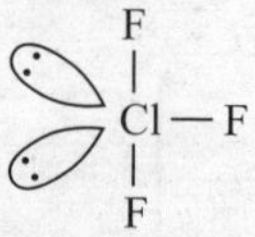

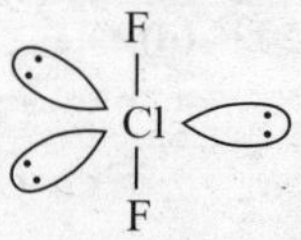

(2 lone pair) (3 lone pair)

SF_4 SiH_4

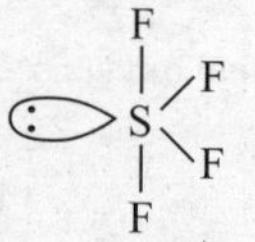

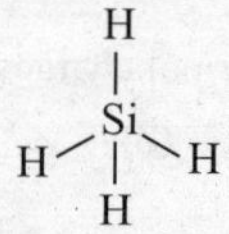

(One lone pair) ('0' lone pair)

So order will be II > I > III > IV

44. (a)

Molecule	central metal valence electron	Lone pair	Bond pair
BrF_5	7	1	5
SF_4	6	1	4
$SnCl_2$	4	1	2
XeF_4	8	2	4
NH_3	5	1	3
ClF_3	7	2	3

'So' BrF_5, SF_4 and $SnCl_2$ all have 1 lone pair of electrons.

45. (d)

Molecule	Valence electron of CM	Bond pair	Lone pair
BrF_5	7	5	1
XeO_3	8	3	1
SO_2	6	2	1

46. (a)

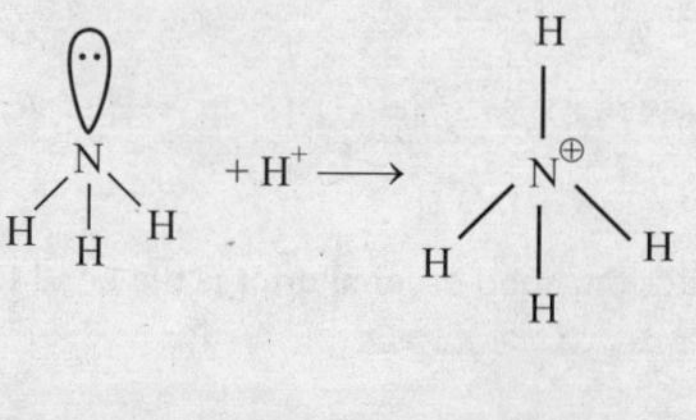

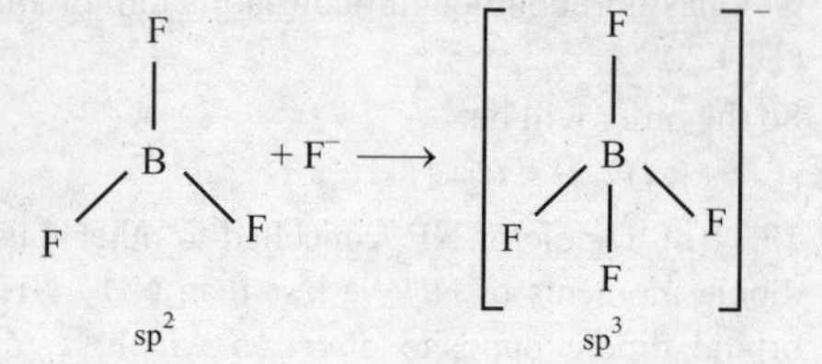

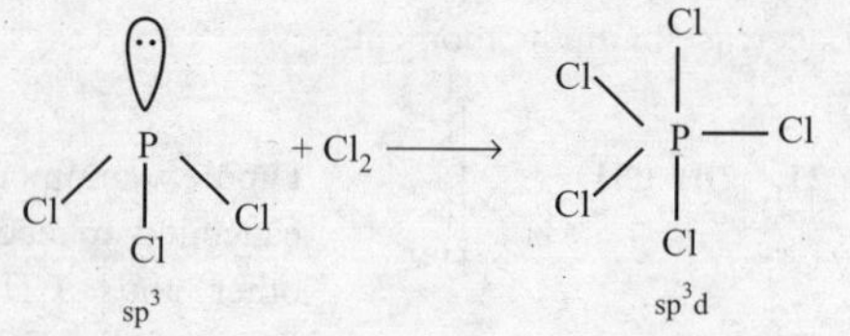

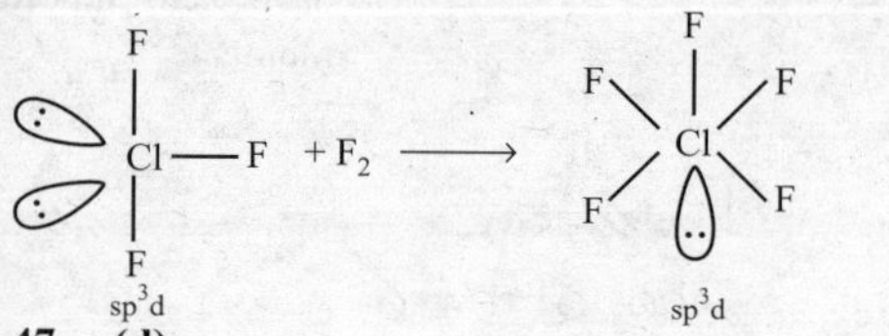

47. (d)

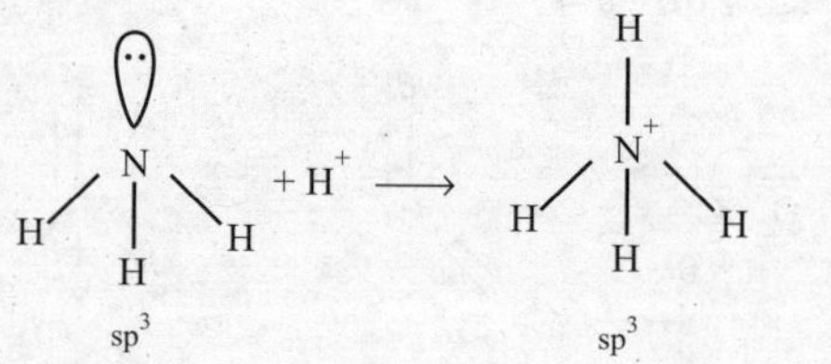

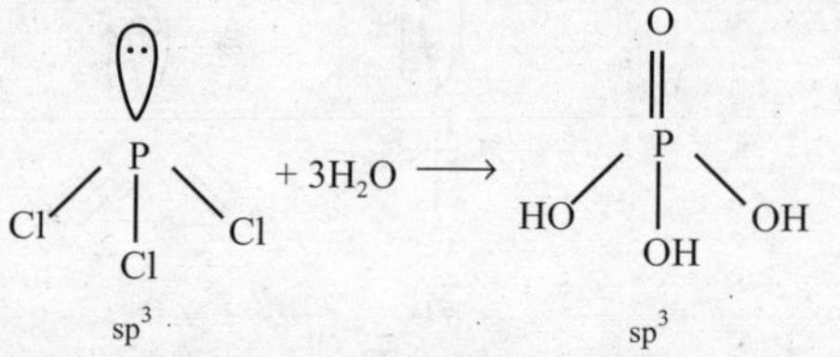

$NaNO_3 + H_2SO_4 \longrightarrow NaHSO_4 + HNO_3$

sp^3 sp^3

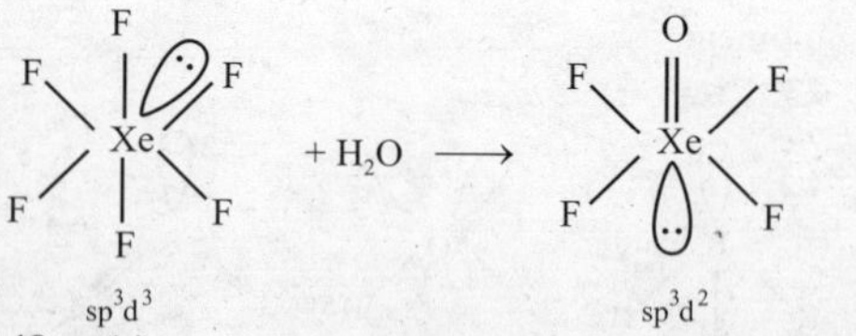

48. (c)

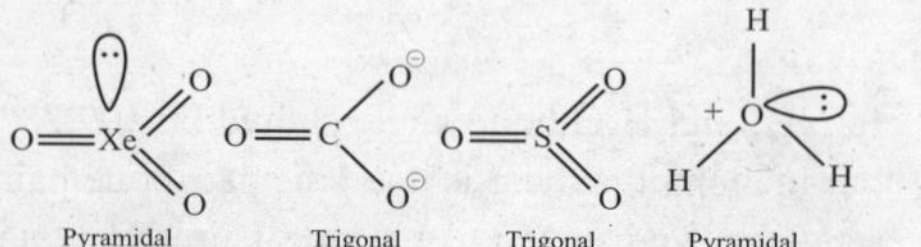

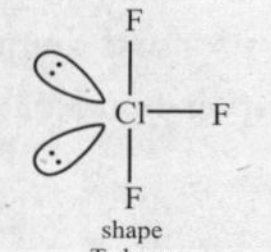

49. (d) $HgCl_2 > SO_3 > SiCl_4 > NH_3$

1. $HgCl_2$ have linear geometry and have Bond angle 180°.
2. SO_3 have Trigonal planar geometry and have Bond angle of 120°.
3. $SiCl_4$ have Tetrahedral geometry and have Bond angle of 109.5°.
4. NH_3 have Trigonal pyramidal geometry and have Bond angle of 107°.

50. (d)

Molecule	Bond pair	Lone pair	Steric No.	Molecular type	Hybridisation	Shape
1. NH_3	3	1	4	AB_3E	sp^3	Trigonal pyramidal
2. ClF_3	3	2	5	AB_3E_2	sp^3d	T-shape
3. H_2O	2	2	4	AB_2E_2	sp^3	Bent
4. SO_3	3	0	3	AB_3	sp^2	Trigonal planar
5. SF_4	4	1	5	AB_4E	sp^3d	See-Saw
6. CH_4	4	0	4	AB_4	sp^3	Tetrahedral
7. XeF_6	6	1	7	AB_6E	sp^3d^3	Square bipyramidal
8. IF_7	7	0	7	AB_7	sp^3d^3	Pentagonal Bipyramidal

$\therefore$ XeF_6 and IF_7 have same hybridisation.

51. (b)

Molecule	Valence electron of Central atom	Lone pair	Bond pair
$SnCl_2$	4	1	2
ClF_3	7	2	3
SO_3	6	0	3
XeF_2	8	3	2

52. (b) Sn and Pb both belong to group 14 of periodic table. Using two of their four valence electrons, they form $SnCl_2$ and $PbCl_2$ and both have bent/angular shape.

53. (b) sp^3 – tetrahedral
sp^3d^2 – trigonal bipyramidal
dsp^3 – square planar
sp^3d^2/d^2sp^3 – octahedral

54. (d)

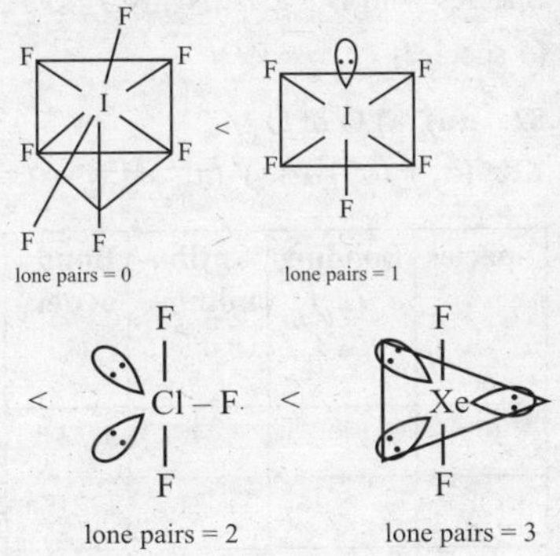

55. (a)

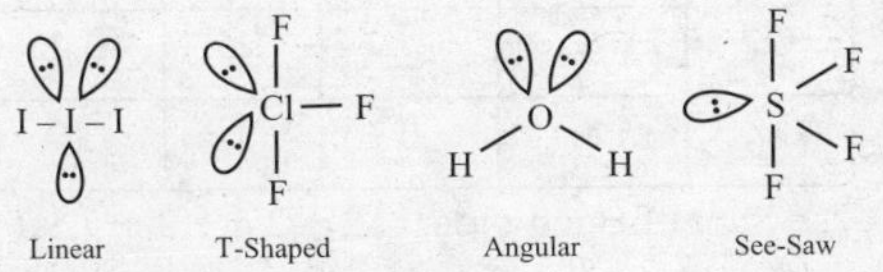

56. (d)

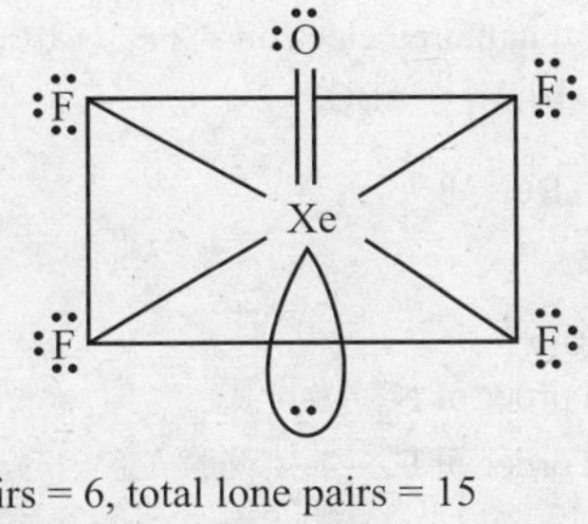

Bond pairs = 6, total lone pairs = 15

57. (a)

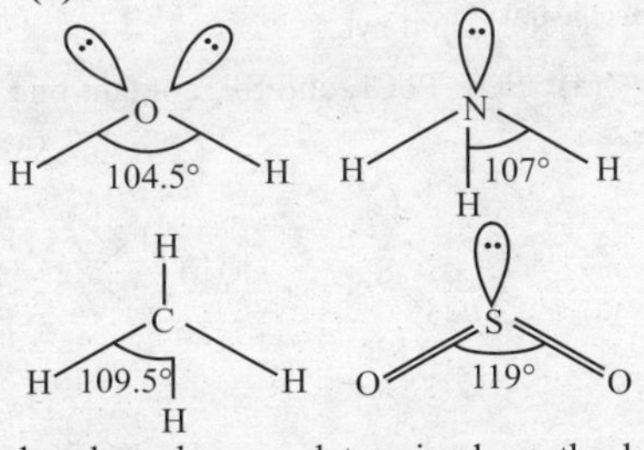

The bond angles are determined on the basis of hybridization of the central atom and the number of lone pairs and bond pairs that cause the repulsion and affect the bond angle.
Thus, bond angle varies as IV > III > II > I.

58. (a) Positively- charged carbon in carbocation
= sp^2- hybridized due to three bond pairs and zero lone pairs.
Negatively - charged carbon in carbanion = sp-hybridized due to one lone pair and one bond pair of electrons.

59. (a) SiH_4:
Si belongs to group 14, has 4 valence electrons, undergoes sp^3- hybridization to form a tetrahedral geometry.
Be in $BeCl_2$ is in sp-hybridization and forms linear shape.
S in SF_4 is in dsp^3 - hybridization and forms a square-pyramidal geometry with one lone pair.
$SnCl_2$ has Sn in sp^2 - hybridization and forms an angular geometry with one lone pair.
Thus, only I is correct.

60. (d) SF_4

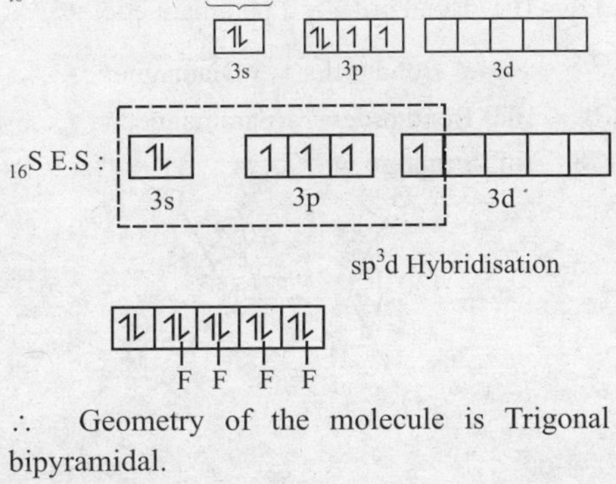

$\therefore$ Geometry of the molecule is Trigonal bipyramidal.

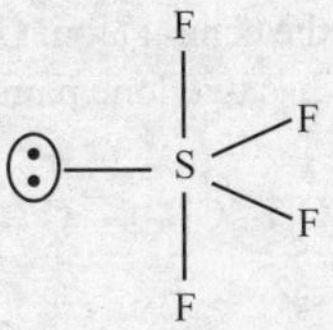

Here only one 'd' orbital takes part in bonding and the geometry also shows only one lone pair of electron.

61. (a) For BF_3:-
No. of bond pairs around B = 3
No. of lone pairs around B = 0
$\Rightarrow$ Hybridization state = sp^2
For BeF_2 :-
No. of bond pairs around Be = 2
No. of lone pairs around Be = 0
$\Rightarrow$ Hybridization state = sp
For BrF_3:-
No. of bond pairs around Br = 3
No. of lone pairs around Br = 2
$\Rightarrow$ Hybridization state = sp^3d.

62. (N)

(A) ICl_4^- : Steric Number

$$= \frac{1}{8}(7+(4\times7)+1) = \frac{36}{8}$$

$$= 4+4 \text{ ; b.p.} = 4, \text{ l.p.} = \frac{4}{2} = 2$$

$\therefore$ $ICl_4^- \rightarrow sp^3d^2$ hybridization

(B) $NO_3^- : \frac{1}{8}(5+(3\times6)+1)$

$$= \frac{1}{8}\times24 = 3 \text{ b.p., } sp^2 \text{ hybridization}$$

(C) $PCl_4^+ : \frac{1}{8}(5+(4\times7)-1)$

$$= \frac{1}{8}\times32 = 4 \text{ b.p., } sp^3 \text{ hybridization}$$

(D) $SiF_6^{2-} : \frac{1}{8}(4+(6\times7)+2)$

$$= \frac{1}{8}\times48 = 6 \text{ b.p., } sp^3d^2 \text{ hybridization}$$

Correct option is not given.

63. (d)

XeF_4 : square planar; PCl_4^+ : tetrahedral
NH_3 : pyramidal; ClF_3; T-shaped
SF_4 : see-saw; NH_4^+ : tetrahedral
XeF_2 : Linear; I_3^- : Linear

64. (c) $TeCl_4$, SeF_4 — square planar;
CH_4, PCl_4^+ — Tetrahedral
SF_4 — square planar, $\overset{+}{NH_4}$ —Tetrahedral
SiH_4, CCl_4 — Tetrahedral.

65. (c) The central atoms in BF_3 and NO_2^- are sp^2 hybridised.

66. (b) 180°
O = C = O
sp hybridised

67. (c) In H_2O, the central atom O forms two sigma bonds and it has two lone pairs of e^-

68. (a)

$$\overset{1}{CH_2} = \overset{2}{CH} - \overset{3}{CH_2} - \overset{4}{C} \equiv \overset{5}{CH_2}$$

$\uparrow sp^2$ $\uparrow sp^2$ $\uparrow sp^3$ $\uparrow sp$ $\uparrow sp$

69. (b)

$N(SiH_3)_3$

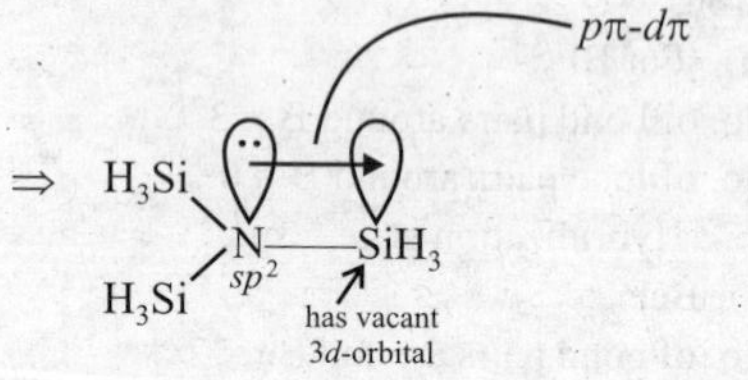

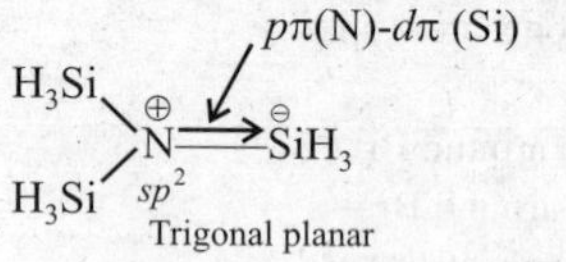

$Me_3N \Rightarrow$

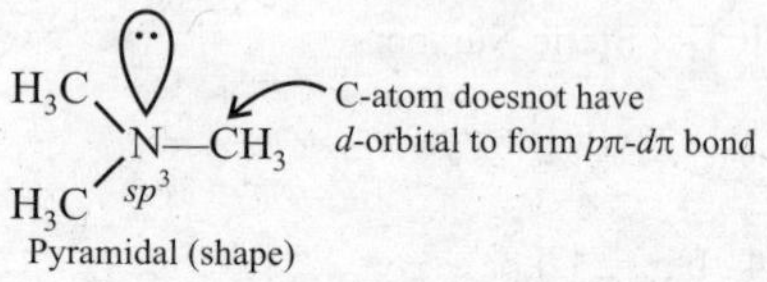

$(SiH)_3P \Rightarrow$

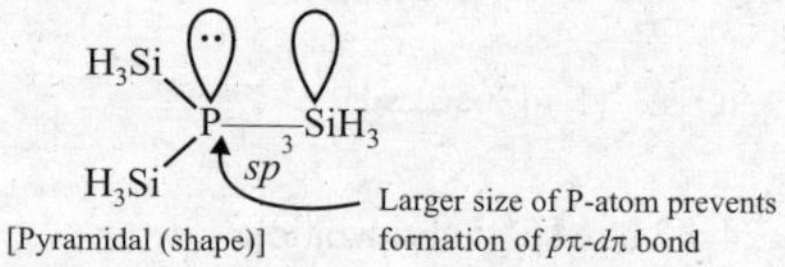

70. (c)

A-(II) B - (III) C - (IV) D - (I)

BF_3	sp^2	Trigonal planar
ClF_3	sp^3d	T-shape
NH_3	sp^3	Trigonal pyramidal
NH_4^+	sp^3	Tetrahedral

71. (c) The structure of given species are :

(a) SF_6

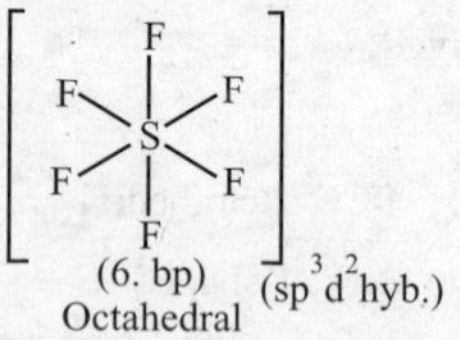

(b) XeF_6

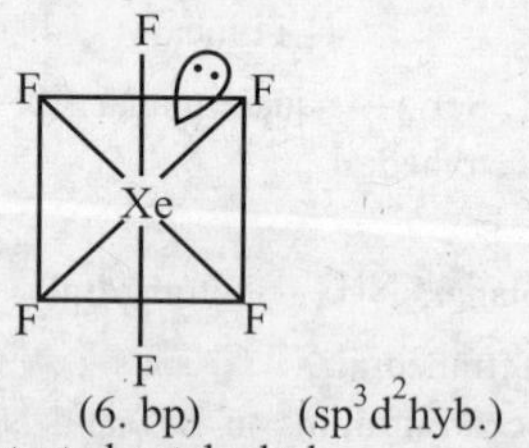

Distorted octahedral

(c) BrF_5

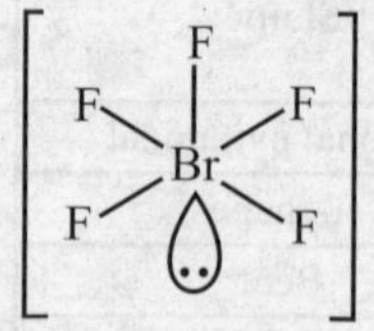

(5 bp, 1l.p.)(sp^3d^2hyb.)

Square pyramidal

(d) XeO_2F_4

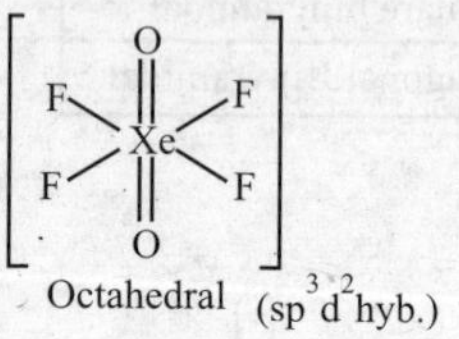

Octahedral (sp^3d^2 hyb.)

72. (a) SO_2, $PbCl_2$ and SF_4 contain one lone pair.

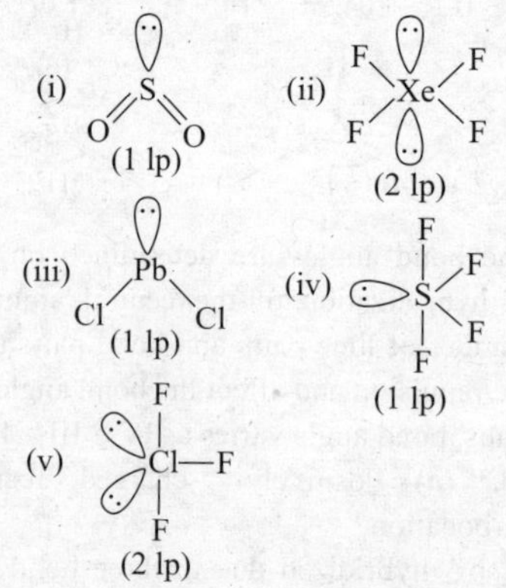

73. (b) In PCl_5 bond length of axial bond is greater than the length of equatorial bond.

74. (d) XeF_2 has 3 lone pairs and 2 bond pairs.

75. (a) Central I in I_3^- undergoes sp^3d hybridisation giving a linear shape with three lone pairs at equatorial positions. Beryllium chloride $BeCl_2$ has linear structure with *sp* hybridisation of Be atom.

76. (a) Both statement are correct.

77. (b) Bond order = $\frac{N_b - N_a}{2}$

Total electrons	10	11	12	13	14	15	16	17	18
Bond order	1	1.5	2	2.5	3	2.5	2	1.5	1

= $17e^-$ Bond order = 1.5 paramagnetic

$O_2 = 16e^-$ Bond order = 2 paramagnetic

$C_2^{2-} = 14e^-$ Bond order = 3 Diamagnetic

$B_2 = 10e^-$ Bond order = 1 paramagnetic

78. (c) Structure of N_2O_3:

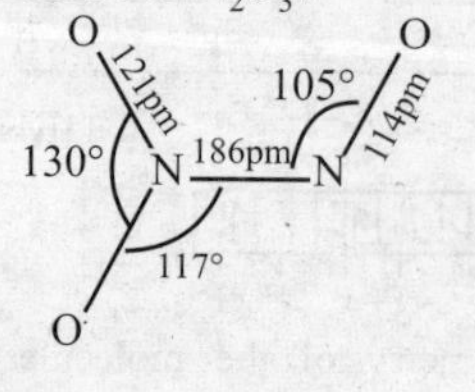

Order of bond angle - y > z > x

Order of bond length - q > r > p

79. (c)

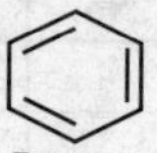

Benzene

Consist of 6 carbon atoms, and each individual carbon is sp^2 hybridized.

A single sp^2 hybridized atom produces 3 hybrid orbitals. Therefore, the total number of sp^2 hybrid orbitals across the entire benzene molecule is -18

80. (c) Bond length depends on 2 main factors:

(1) Size of atoms involved

(2) Bond order/electronegativity difference

Since C > N (size), So N – O bond length will be shorter than C–O bond length.

81. (c)

Species	Bond Order
N_2	3
O_2^{2-}	1
NO^-	2
O_2^+	2.5
NO^+	3
NO	2.5

Species with BO ≥ 2 : N_2, NO^-, O_2^+, NO^+, NO (5 species)

82. (a) M.O of O_2:

$KK^* (\sigma_{2s})^2 (\sigma^*_{2s})^2 (\sigma_{2p})^2 (\pi_{2p_x})^2 (\pi_{2p_y})^2 (\pi^*_{2p_x})^1 (\pi^*_{2p_y})^1$

Species	Bonding e^- (n_b)	Antibonding (n_a)	Bond order $\left[\frac{1}{2}(n_b - n_a)\right]$	Unpaired electron
O_2	8	4	2	2
O_2^+	8	3	2.5	1
O_2^{2+}	8	2	3	0
O_2^-	8	5	1.5	1
O_2^{2-}	8	6	1	0

∴ Sum of Bond order = 2 + 2.5 + 3 + 1.5 + 1 = 10

Sum of unpaired electron = 2 + 1 + 0 + 1 + 0 = 4

83. (b) C_2 BO = 2

O_2^{2+} BO = 3

2 + 3 = 5

BO B_2 = 1

Bond order of N_2 = 3

Bond order of F_2 = 1

84. **(b)** For O_2

$\sigma 1s^2\ \sigma^*1s^2\ \sigma 2s^2\ \sigma^*2s^2\ \sigma 2pz^2\ \pi 2px^2$

$= \pi 2py^2\ \pi^*2px^1 = \pi^*2py^1$

Bond order $= \frac{1}{2}(N_b - N_a)$

Where, N_b = number of electrons in bonding molecular orbitals

N_a = number of electrons in antibonding molecular orbitals

$\therefore$ Bond order $= \frac{1}{2}(10-6)$

Bond order $= \frac{4}{2} = 2$

For C_2

$\sigma 1s^2\ \sigma^*1s^2\ \sigma 2s^2\ \sigma^*2s^2\ \pi 2px^2 = \pi 2py^2$

$\therefore$ Bond order $= \frac{1}{2}(8-4) = 2$

85. **(b)** M.O. of O_2

$KK^*(\sigma_{2s})^2(\sigma^*_{2s})^2(\sigma_{2p})^2(\pi_{2p_x})^2(\pi_{2p_y})^2(\pi^*_{2p_x})^1(\pi^*_{2p_y})^1$

Species	Bond order	Magnetic property
O_2	2	Paramagnetic
O_2^+	1.5	Paramagnetic
O_2^-	2.5	Paramagnetic

So only A and C are correct.

86. **(b)**

Molecule	Total no. of electron	Bond order
O_2	16	2
N_2	14	3
C_2	12	2
B_2	10	1
F_2	18	1

O_2 and C_2 have same bond order.

87. **(c)**

Molecule	Total electron	Bond order
B_2	10	1
CN^-	14	3
O_2^{2-}	18	1
O_2	16	2
F_2	18	1
O_2^{2+}	14	3
O_2^-	17	1.5
N_2	14	3
O_2^+	15	2.5
C_2	12	2
O_2	16	2
He_2^{2+}	2	1

So, O_2^-, N_2 and O_2^+ the sum of order is 7 it has maximum bond order among the given options.

88. **(a)** We know that

Bond order $\propto \frac{1}{\text{Bond Length}}$

Bond order of a diatomic increases its bond length will decreases.

Diatomic	Bond Length	Atomic number	Total electron	Bond order
X	143	9	18	1
Y	110	7	14	3
Z	121	8	16	2

89. **(b)**

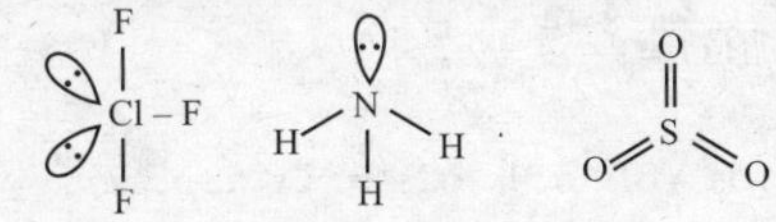

sp^3 d-hybridization (2lp + 3bp) sp^3-hybridization (3bp + 1lp) sp^2-hybridization (3bp)

90. **(d)** The correct order of bond enthalpy = $H_2 < O_2 < N_2$. This is due to increasing bond strength due to single, double and triple bonds respectively (H – H, O = O, N ≡ N).

91. **(c)** B.O. $= \frac{N_b - N_a}{2}$

$C_2 : \sigma 1s^2\ \sigma^*\ 1s^2\ \sigma 2s^2\ \sigma^*\ 2s^2\ \pi 2p_x{}^2\ \pi 2p_y{}^2$

$\Rightarrow$ B.O. $= \frac{8-4}{2} = 2$, so x = 2

$B_2 : \sigma 1s^2\ \sigma^*\ 1s^2\ \sigma 2s^2\ \sigma*\ 2s^2\ \pi 2p_x{}^1\ \pi 2p_y{}^1$

$\Rightarrow$ B .O. $= \frac{6-4}{2} = 1$, so B.O. $= \frac{1}{2}$x

$O_2 : \sigma 1s^2\ \sigma^*1s^2\ \sigma 2s^2\ \sigma^*2s^2\ \sigma 2p_z{}^2\ \pi 2p_x{}^2\ \pi 2p_y{}^2$

$\pi^*2p^1x\ \pi^*2p_y{}^1$

$\Rightarrow$ B.O. $= \frac{10-6}{2} = 2$, so B.O. = x.

92. **(b)** B.O $= \frac{N_b - Na}{2}$

For $O_2^+ = \sigma 1s^2\ \sigma^*\ 1s^2\ \sigma 2s^2\ \sigma^*\ 2s^2\ \sigma 2p_z^2\ \pi 2p_x^2\ \pi 2p_y^2\ \pi^*\ 2p_x^2\ \pi^*2p_y^0$

$\Rightarrow$ B.O. $= \frac{10-5}{2} = \frac{5}{2} = x$

For $O_2^- = \sigma 1s^2\ \sigma^*\ 1s^2\ \sigma 2s^2\ \sigma^*\ 2s^2\ \sigma 2p_z^2\ \pi 2p_x^2\ \pi 2p_y^2\ \pi^*\ 2p_x^2\ \pi^*2p_y^1$

$\Rightarrow$ B.O. $= \frac{10-7}{2} = \frac{3}{2}$

For $O_2^{2+} = \sigma 1s^2\ \sigma^*1s^2\ \sigma 2s^2\ \sigma^*2s^2\ \sigma 2p_z^2\ \pi 2p_x^2\ \pi 2p_y^2$

$\Rightarrow$ B.O. $= \frac{10-4}{2} = \frac{6}{2} = 3$

Therefore,

B.O. of $O_2^- = \frac{3}{5}$x and B.O. of $O_2^{2+} = \frac{6}{5}$x

93. **(d)**

Molecules	Total no. of e^-	e^- in bonding orbitals	e^- in anti-bonding orbital	Bond order
(a) He_2	4	2	2	0
(b) Be_2	8	4	4	0
(c) Li_2	6	4	2	1
(d) B_2	10	6	4	1
(e) C_2	12	8	4	2
(f) Ne_2	20	10	10	0

94. **(b)** M.O. of NO:

$kk^*\ \sigma_{2s}^2\ \sigma_{2s}^{*2}\left(\pi_{2p_x}^2 = \pi^2{}_{2p_y}\right)\sigma_{2p_z}^2\left(\pi_{2p_x}^{*1} = \pi_{2p_y}^0\right)$

B.O. of <u>NO</u> ; <u>NO^+</u> ; <u>NO^-</u>

$\frac{1}{2}(8-3)$; $\frac{1}{2}(8-2)$; $\frac{1}{2}(8-4)$

= 2.5 ; = 3 ; = 2

95. **(a)** Bond order $\propto \frac{1}{\text{Bond length}}$

96. **(c)** Stability of a molecule is related with bond order as:

Stability α Bond order

B.O of $N_2 = \frac{1}{2}[N_b - N_a] = \frac{1}{2}[10-4] = 3$

B.O of $N_2^- = \frac{1}{2}[10-5] = 2.5$

B.O of $N_2^{2-} = \frac{1}{2}[10-6] = 2$

Therefore, the bond stability order is

$N_2 > N_2^- > N_2^{2-}$

97. **(d)** Bond order, $\frac{N_b - N_a}{2}$

Bond order of N_2 ($14e^-$): B.O. $= \frac{10-4}{2} = 3$

Bond order of O_2^{2-} ($18e^-$): B.O. $= \frac{10-8}{2} = 1$

Bond order of NO^+ ($14e^-$): B.O. $= \frac{10-4}{2} = 3$

Bond order of F_2($18e^-$): B.O. $= \frac{10-8}{2} = 1$

Bond order of N_2^{2-} ($16e^-$): B.O. $= \frac{10-6}{2} = 2$

Bond order of O_2^- ($17e^-$): B.O. $= \frac{10-7}{2} = 1.5$

Bond oder of CO ($14e^-$): B.O. $= \frac{10-4}{2} = 3$

Hence, (N_2, CO, NO^+) have similar bond order, 3.

98. (b) N_2 does not have any unpaired electron hence diamagnetic in nature

$O_2 \rightarrow KK^1\ (\sigma 2s)^2(\sigma^* 2s)^2(\sigma 2p_z)^2(\pi 2p_x)^2(\pi 2p_y)^2 (\pi^* 2p_x)^1(\pi^* p_y)^1$

O_2 has two unpaired electrons, hence, paramagnetic in nature.

$O_2^+ \rightarrow KK'(\sigma 2s)^2(\sigma{*}2s)^2(\sigma 2p_z)^2(\pi 2p_x)^2$
$(\pi 2p_y)^2\ (\pi^{2*} p_x)^1\ (\pi^* 2p_y)^0$

$O_2^- \rightarrow KK'(\sigma 2s)^2(\sigma^* 2s)^2(\sigma 2p_z)^2(\pi 2p_x)^2$
$(\pi 2p_y)^2\ (\pi^{2*} p_x)^1\ (\pi^* 2p_y)^0$

$N_2 \rightarrow KK'\ (\sigma 2s)^2(\sigma^* 2s)^2\ (\pi 2p_x)^2\ (\pi 2p_y)^2(\sigma 2p_z)^2$
$\rightarrow KK^1(\sigma 2s)^2(\sigma^* 2s)^2\ (\pi 2p_x)^2 (\pi 2p_y)^2(\sigma 2p_z)^1$

N_2^+ have one unpaired electron, so it paramagnetic in nature.

99. (d) According to molecular orbital theory:

I. σ^*-orbital are formed by the substraction of two wave functions say ψ_A and ψ_B and therefore
$\sigma^* = \psi_A - \psi_B$.

II. σ-orbital are formed when two orbitals are in same phase Hence, they do not have nodal plane in between two nuclei.

III. Combination of two atomic orbitals give two types of molecular orbitals one is bonding molecular orbital σ and another one is antibonding molecular orbital (σ*). Energy of bonding molecular orbital is lower than that of antibonding molecular orbital.

100. (b)

(I) In BF_3, electronegativity of F-atom is greater than B.

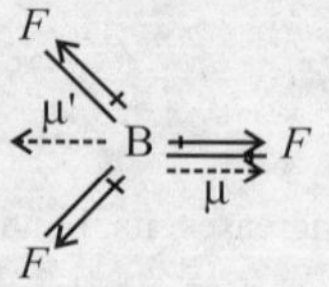

(II) Covalent bond length increases as
C—O > N—O > O—H

Due to increase in size of atom.

(III) Bond order $= \dfrac{N_b - N_a}{2}$

$C_2 = \sigma 1s^2 \sigma^* 1s^2 \sigma 2s^2 \sigma^* 2s^2 \pi 2p_x^2 \pi 2p_y^2$

$B.O. = \dfrac{8-4}{2} = 2$

$B_2 = \sigma 1s^2 \sigma^* 1s^2 \sigma 2s^2 \sigma^* 2s^2 \pi 2p_x^1 \pi 2p_y^1$

$B.O. = \dfrac{6-4}{2} = 1$

$He_2 = \sigma 1s^2\ \sigma^* 1s^2$

$B.O. = \dfrac{2-2}{2} = 0$

Hence, Bond order :
$C_2 > B_2 > He_2$.

101. (N) $He_2^+ : \sigma 1s^2 < \sigma^* 1s^1$

$BO = \dfrac{2-1}{2} = 0.5$

$Li_2^+ : \sigma 1s^2 < \sigma^* 1s^2 < \sigma 2s^1$

$BO = \dfrac{3-2}{2} = 0.5$

$B_2 : \sigma 1s^2 < \sigma^* 1s^2 < \sigma 2s^2 < \sigma^* 2s^2 < \pi 2p_x^1 = \pi 2p_y^1$

$BO = \dfrac{6-4}{2} = 1$

Due to 2 unpaired e^-, it is paramagnetic.

$C_2 : \sigma 1s^2 < {*}\sigma 1s^2 < \sigma 2s^2 < {*}\sigma 2s^2 < \pi 2p_x^2 = \pi 2p_y^2$

$BO = \dfrac{8-4}{2} = 2$

102. (b) According to molecular orbital theory, species with all paired electrons in their electronic configuration are diamagnetic in nature.

$He_2^+ : \sigma 1s^2\ \sigma^* 1s^1$

$H_2 : \sigma 1s^2\ \sigma^* 1s^0$

$H_2^+ : \sigma 1s^1$

$H_2^- : \sigma 1s^2\ \sigma^* 1s^1$

$He : \sigma 1s^2\ \sigma^* 1s^0$

Hence, among the given species, only H_2 and He which are diamagnetic and thus, option (b) is the correct answer.88. (c) Nitric oxide (NO) has 15 electrons in its valence shells and its bond order is 2.5. Hence, it does not contain triple bond between the atoms.

103. (c) Nitric oxide (NO) has 15 electrons in its valence shells and its bond order is 2.5. Hence, it does not contain triple bond between the atoms.

5 Thermodynamics

1. **(a)** At constant temperature, change in internal energy is zero.

2. **(d)** $2Al(s) + \frac{3}{2}O_2(g) \longrightarrow Al_2O_3(s)$

$2Al_2O_3(s) \longrightarrow 4Al(s) + 3O_2(g); \Delta H = 3340$ kJ

$4Al(s) + 3O_2(g) \longrightarrow 2Al_2O_3(s); \Delta H_{reversed} = -3340$ kJ

$\Delta H_f^\circ(Al_2O_3) = -\frac{3340\,kJ}{2} = -1670\,kJ$

3. **(b)** $W = -P_{ext}(V_2 - V_1)$

No. of moles of $O_2 = \frac{1.6\,g}{32\,g\,mol^{-1}} = 0.05$ moles

PV = nRT

Initial state $P_1 = 5$atm

$V_1 = \frac{nRT}{P_1} = \frac{0.05 \times 0.082 \times 300}{5} = 0.246L$

Final state $P_2 = 1$ atm

$V_2 = \frac{nRT}{P_2} = \frac{0.05 \times 0.082 \times 300}{1} = 1.23\,L$

$W = -1$ atm × (1.23 L – 0.246 L)

= – 0.984L -atm = –98.4 J

4. **(b)** Given, n = 1 mol

$V_1 = 2L, V_2 = 100$ L

$P_{ext} = 1$ atm

Work done in reversible isothermal expansion:

$W = -nRT \ln \frac{V_2}{V_1}$

$= -2.303\,nRT \log \frac{V_2}{V_1}$

For ideal gas, PV = nRT

$nRT = P_1V_1$

nRT = 1 × 2

nRT = 2L atm

$W = -2.303 \times 2 \times \log \frac{100}{2}$

$= -2.303 \times 2 \times \log 50$

$= -2.303 \times 2 \times 1.70$

= – 7.83 L atm

= – 7.83 × 101.3 J = 793.2 J

5. **(b)** According to the thermodynamic relation

$\Delta G = \Delta H - T\Delta S$

Σ A reaction is spontaneous (ΔG = – ve) at all T when ΔH is –ve and ΔS is +ve

Σ A reaction is non spontaneous (ΔG = +ve) at all temperature when ΔH is +ve and ΔS is –ve

Σ A reaction is spontaneous (ΔG = – ve) only at high temperature when ΔH is +ve and ΔS is +ve

Σ A reaction is spontaneous (ΔG = –ve) only at low temperature when ΔH is –ve and ΔS is –ve

Σ A reaction is non-spontaneous (ΔG = +ve) only at low temperature when ΔH is +ve and ΔS is +ve

So correct option is: A-III, B-IV, C-I, D-II

6. **(b)** An extensive property depends on the amount of substance (mass/moles) while intensive property does not.

Heat capacity, enthalpy, entropy depends on amount of substance so they are intensive.

7. **(b)** $w = -2.303\,nRT \log_{10}\left(\frac{V_2}{V_1}\right)$

n = 0.25 mol

$w = -2.303 \times 0.25 \times 8.3 \times 300 \log_{10}\left(\frac{5}{50}\right)$

= + 1433.6 J

q = – w = – 1.4336 kJ

8. **(c)** For reversible isothermal expansion,

$W = -nRT \ln\left(\frac{V_2}{V_1}\right) = -nRT \ln\left(\frac{P_1}{P_2}\right)$ ...(i)

From question

n = 1, T = 300K, $P_1 = 20$ atm, $P_2 = 2$ atm,

$R = 8.3\,J\,K^{-1}\,mol^{-1}$

Putting all the values in (i)

$W = -1 \times 8.3 \times 300 \times \ln\left(\frac{20}{2}\right)$

W = – 2490 ln 10.

W = – 2490 × 2.303 = – 5734.47 J/mol

$\boxed{W = -5.734\,kJ\,mol^{-1}}$

9. **(c)** For the reaction,

$A_2B_4(g) \longrightarrow 2AB_2(g)$

$\Delta n_g = 2 - 1 = 1$

$\Delta_rH = -x$ kJ/mol

T = 300 K

R = 8.3 J/mol. K

$\Delta_rU = \Delta_rH - \Delta n_gRT$

$\Delta_rU = -x - \frac{1 \times 8.3 \times 300}{1000}$

$\Delta_rU = (-x - 2.49)$ kJ/mol

$\Delta_rU = -(x + 2.49)$ kJ/mol

10. **(c)** For reversible isothermic process

$\Delta H = n\,C_V\Delta T$

∴ Process is isothermal.

Thus $\Delta T = 0 \Rightarrow \Delta H = 0$

11. **(d)** C → A Temperature remains same thus isothermal

B → C No change in pressure in the graph thus isobaric

A → B Volume remain same thus isochoric

12. **(d)** Internal energy (U) is a state function but work (W) is a path function. So statement-I is incorrect but statement II is correct.

13. **(b)** $C_p = 75.3\,JK^{-1}\,mol^{-1}$

$T_1 = 10°C = 283$ K

$T_2 = 15°C = 288$ K

Where, C_p = heat capacity at constant pressure

$T_1 = T_2$ = Temperature in kelvin

n = number of moles

ΔH = change in enthalpy

q_p = heat at constant pressure

Given mass(m) = 180 g

Molar mass (M) = 18 g/ mole

As per formula,

$q_p = \Delta H = nC_p\Delta T$

$q_p = \Delta H = \frac{m}{M}C_P(T_2 - T_1)$

$\therefore \quad q_p = \Delta H = \frac{180}{18} \times 75.3(288 - 283)$ J

$\therefore \quad q_p = 3765$ J

14. **(c)** $\Delta H = \Delta U + \Delta PV$

$\Delta PV = \Delta n_{(g)}RT$

In $N_{2(g)} + 3H_{2(g)} \rightarrow 2NH_{3(g)}$ number of moles of reactant not equal to product, thus $\Delta H \neq \Delta U$

15. **(d)** Work is path variable enthalpy depends on mass therefor extensive property Lattice enthalpy of ionic compound obtain by different steps used in Born-Haber Cycle.

16. **(a)** Mass = 180 g

Moles = $\frac{180}{18}$ = 10 moles

$T_1 = 10°C = 283$ K

$T_2 = 15°C = 288$ K

$\Delta T = T_2 - T_1 = 288 - 283 = 5K$

$q = 3765$ J

$C_p = \frac{q}{n\Delta T} = \frac{3765\,J}{10 \times 5}$ mol K $= 75.3\,J\,mol^{-1}\,K^{-1}$

17. **(d)** During isothermal expension enthalpy is zero so statement I is not correct.

For an isothermal system, $\Delta U = 0$

So statement II is correct.

18. (c) For isothermal and reversible process

$W = -nRT \ln\left(\frac{P_2}{P_1}\right)$

Where n = No. of mole

R is the gas constant (8.3 JK)

T = 273 K

P_1 initial pressure = 10 atm

P_2 final pressure = 1 atm

number of mole of hydrogen = $\frac{10}{2}$ = 5 mol

$W = -5 \text{ mol} \times 8.3 \text{ JK}^{-1} \text{ mol}^{-1} \times 273 \times \ln\left(\frac{1}{10}\right)$

$= -5 \times 8.3 \times 273 \ln(0.1)$

$W = -5 \times 8.3 \times 273 \times 2.303$

$W = -26091.83 \text{ J} = -26.091 \text{ kJ}$

19. (b) Volume is extensive property it depend on the quantity of matter but temperature is intensive properties it is independent of quantity of matter so. Volume will be halved but temperature will be constant.

20. (c) Extensive properties are depend on the quantity of matter.

Extensive property	**Intensive property**
enthalpy	density
Volume	temperature
Internal energy	

21. (a) Given,

Heat released = – 900 J

$\Delta u = q + w$

$= -900 \text{ J} + (-2 \text{ atm } (2 - 10)\text{L})$

$= -900 \text{ J} + 16 \text{ L atm}$

$= -900 \text{ J} + 16 \times 101.35 \text{ J}$

$= 721.6 \text{ J}$

22. (a) For isothermal process, $\Delta U = 0$

$\Rightarrow \quad q = -w = -\left(-P_{ext}\Delta V\right) = P_{ext}(V_{final} - V_{initial})$

for adiabatic process, q = 0

$\Rightarrow \quad \Delta U = W_{adibatic}$

23. (c) The process given in graph is isothermal reversible expansion. Work done is given by area under the curve (BE)

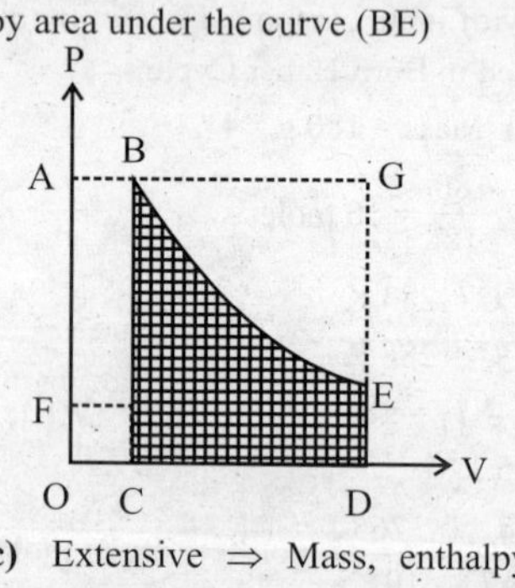

24. (c) Extensive ⇒ Mass, enthalpy, heat capacity, internal energy.

Intensive ⇒ Temperature, pressure, density

25. (d) $W_{rev} = -2.303 \text{ RT} \log\frac{V_2}{V_1}$

$= -2.303 \text{ } P_1 V_1 \log\frac{V_2}{V_1}$

$= -2.303 \text{ } (20)(1.0) \log\frac{V_2}{V_1} = -46.06 \log\frac{V_2}{1}$

$= -46.06 \log V_2 = -92.12 \text{ L atm}$

$\Rightarrow \log V_2 = 2 \Rightarrow V_2 = 100 \text{ L}$

26. (c) Extensive properties = Internal energy, enthalpy,

Mass, volume, Heat capacity, Gibbs energy

Intensive properties = Density, pressure

27. (c) Work done $= w = -p_{ext}\Delta V = -5(1 - 11) = +50$ L atm

Now, at constant pressure and temperature:-

$\Delta U = q + w = q + p\Delta V = 0$

$\Rightarrow q = -w = -50$ L atm.

28. (b) $W_{rev} = -2.303 \text{nRT} \log\left(\frac{P_1}{P_2}\right)$

$= -2.303 \text{ nRT} \log\left(\frac{V_2}{V_1}\right)$

We have, n = 2 mol, V_1 = 5L, V_2 = 50L,

W = – 189.1 L atm

$\Rightarrow \quad T = \frac{W_{rev}}{-2.303 \text{nR} \log\left(\frac{V_2}{V_1}\right)}$

$= \frac{-189.1}{-2.303(2)(0.082)\log\left(\frac{50}{5}\right)}$

$\cong 500 \text{ K} = 227°\text{C}$.

29. (b) State functions are thermodynamic properties whose values are not dependent on the path of the process rather on the states of matter.

30. (a) There is no exchange of energy (heat) between system and surrounding in adiabatic process.

Extensive property = The property depends on mass.

31. (b) (A) and (B) are correct.

32. (N) $W = -2.303 \text{ nRT} \log\frac{P_1}{P_2}$

From 1 → 2

$W_1 = -2.303 \text{ nRT} \log\frac{15}{10}$

$W_1 = -1009.7$ ... (1)

From 2 → 3

$W_2 = -2.303 \text{ nRT} \log\frac{10}{5}$

$W_2 = -1726.247$

From 3 → 2

$W_3 = -2.303 \text{ nRT} \log\frac{5}{10} = 1726.247$

From 2 → 1

$W_4 = -2.303 \text{ nRT} \log\frac{10}{15}$

= 1009.7

$W_{Total} = W_1 + W_2 + W_3 + W_4$

$= -1009.7 + (-1726.2) + 1726.2 + 1009.7 = 0$

33. (a) Entropy, $S = Q/T$ and $Q = mCT$

Thus, we can see that entropy (S) depends on mass (m) and hence, is an extensive property.

34. (c) The work done is given as $p\Delta V$.

The volume is held constant ($\Delta V = 0$)

Hence, work done = 0

35. (c) Moles of (Al), $(n) = \frac{w}{M} = \frac{54}{27} = 2$ mol

Heat required (Q) = $nC\Delta T$

$= 2 \times 24 \times 20 = 960$ J

Hence, option (c) is the correct answer.

36. (a) In bomb calorimeter,

$\Delta H = \Delta U = q$

Given, $\Delta H = -248$ kJ/mol

For, 12 g of graphite energy released = 248 kJ/mol.

For, 6 g of graphite energy released $= \frac{248 \times 6}{12}$

From, $q = C_V\Delta T$

$\Rightarrow \quad \frac{248 \times 6}{12} = C_v \times (31 - 25)$

$\Rightarrow \quad C_v = \frac{248}{2 \times 6} = 20.6 \text{ kJ/K}$

37. (b) $\Delta E = q + W$

For an adiabatic reaction, $q = 0$. So, $\Delta E = W$

38. (a)

At 0°C, H_2O (s) ⟶ H_2O(l) ΔH = –x kJ/mol

= – 1000x kJ/mol

$\therefore \quad \underset{283 \text{ K}}{H_2O(l)} \rightleftharpoons \underset{273 \text{ K}}{H_2O(l)}$ ... (i)

$\underset{273 \text{ K}}{H_2O(l)} \rightleftharpoons \underset{273 \text{ K}}{H_2O(s)}$ ... (ii)

$\underset{273 \text{ K}}{H_2O(s)} \rightleftharpoons \underset{263 \text{ K}}{H_2O(s)}$ ... (iii)

Given, for change in phase ΔH = – 1000 J/mol

$\therefore [\Delta H_2(273K) - \Delta H_2(283K)] + [\Delta H_2(263) - \Delta H_2(273K)] + [\Delta H] = C_p^l(273 - 283)K + C_p^s(263 - 273)K$

$\therefore \Delta H_2(263)K - \Delta H_2(283K)$

$= -10C_p^l - 10C_p^s - \Delta H$

$= -10y - 10z - 1000x$

$= -(1000x + 10y + 10z)$ J/mol

39. (b) $C_4H_{10} + \frac{13}{2}O_2 \rightarrow 4CO_2 + 5H_2O$

$\Delta n = 4 - \frac{13}{2} - 1 = -\frac{7}{2}$

$\therefore \Delta H - \Delta U = \Delta n_g RT = x$

$\Rightarrow x = \frac{-7}{2}RT$

$C_6H_{12}O_6 + 6O_2 \rightarrow 6CO_2 + 6H_2O$

$\Delta n_g = 6 - 6 = 0$

$\therefore \quad \Delta H - \Delta U = \Delta n_g RT = y$

$\Rightarrow \quad y = 0$

$\therefore x - y = -\frac{7}{2}RT - 0 = -\frac{7}{2}RT$

$= -\frac{7}{2} \times 8.3 \times 298\,J$

$= -8.657\ kJ$

40. (b) For the given reaction,

$A(g) \longrightarrow B(g) + C(g)$

heat absorbed = x J

Work done by system = y J

By first law of thermodynamics

$\Delta U = q - w = x - y$

$\Delta n_g = n_P - n_R = 2 - 1 = 1$

$\Delta H = \Delta U + \Delta n_g RT$

$\Delta H = (x - y) + 1 \times RT$

$\Delta H = x - y + RT$

41. (a) Combustion of methane:

$CH_4[g] + 2O_2(g) \rightarrow CO_2(g) + 2H_2O(l)$

$\Delta_C H° = [\Delta_f H(CO_2) + 2\Delta_f H(H_2O)] - [\Delta_f H(CH_4)]$

$= -y + 2(-z) - (-x) = -(y + 2z - x)$

42. (b) $C(s) + O_2 \longrightarrow CO_2(g)\ \Delta H = -393.5\ kJ\ mol^{-1}$

$H_2 + \frac{1}{2}O_2 \longrightarrow H_2O(l)\ \Delta H = -286\ kJ/mol$

$CH_4 + 2O_2 \longrightarrow CO_2 + 2H_2O(l)\ \ \Delta H = -890\ kJ/mol$

For combustion of CH_4

$\Delta_r H = \Delta H_f(CO_2) + \Delta H_f(H_2O) - \Delta H_f(CH_4)$

$-890 = -393.5 + 2(-286) - \Delta H_f(CH_4)$

$\Delta H_f(CH_4) = -75.5\ kJ/mol$

43. (a) According to the given reaction:

$B_2O_4(g) + 3AO(g) \longrightarrow B_2O(g) + 3AO_2(g)$

$\Delta_r H^{\ominus} = [\Delta_f H(B_2O) + 3\Delta_f H(AO_2)] - [\Delta_f H(B_2O_4)] + 3\Delta_f H(AO)]$

$= [81 + 3(-393)] - [9.7 + 3(-110)]$

$= [81 - 1179] - [9.7 - 330]$

$= -1098 + 320.3 = -777.7\ kJ/mol$

44. (c) $C_6H_{12}O_6(s) + 6O_2(g) \rightarrow 6CO_2(g) + 6H_2O(l)$

$\Delta H_r = [\Delta_f H(CO_2) + \Delta_f H(H_2O)] - [\Delta_f H(C_6H_{12}O_6) + \Delta_f H(O_2)]$

$= [(6 \times (-393)) - (6 \times (-286))] - [(-1170) + (0.01)]$

$= -2904\ kJ\ mol^{-1}$

Thus, for $\frac{18\ g}{180\ g\ mol^{-1}} = 0.1$ mol, the energy released will be :

$E = 0.1 \times 2904 = 290.4\ kJ$

45. (d) $C_2H_5OH + 3O_2 \rightarrow 2CO_2 + 3H_2O$

as, $\Delta_r H° = \Sigma_i a_i \Delta_f H°(P) - \Sigma_i b_i \Delta_f H°(R)$

Where, P = Products

R = reactants

$a_i = b_i$ = stoihiometric coefficients

$\because\ \Delta H_f°$ for $O_2 = 0$

because by convention standard enthalpy for formation of an element in its most stable state of aggregation is taken as zero.

and $\Delta_f H°$ of $C_2H_5OH = x$

$\Delta_f H°$ of $CO_2 = 2y$

$\Delta_f H°$ of $H_2O = 3z$

$\therefore\ \Delta_r H° = (2y + 3z - x)$

46. (c) Pressure and temperature both are extensive property, it does not depend on the quantity of matter. So pressure and temperature does not change.

47. (d) $\Delta_r H = \Delta_r U + \Delta n_g RT$

$\Delta_r H = x\ kJ\ mol^{-1}$

$R = 8.3\ J\ mol^{-1}\ k^{-1}$

$\Delta n_g = 1$

$T = 10^3 k$

$x\ kJ\ mol^{-1}\ \Delta_r U + \frac{1 \times 8.3 J\ mol^{-1}\ K^{-1} \times 10^3\ K}{10^3}$

$x = \Delta_r U + 8.3$ [1 kJ = 10^3 J]

$\Delta_r U = x - 8.3$

48. (d) We know that,

$\Delta H = nC_p \Delta T$

Given

$C_p = 75\ J\ mol^{-1}\ k^{-1}$

$T_1 = 283K$

$T_2 = 293K$

$\text{mole}(n) = \frac{\text{Weight of } H_2O}{\text{Molecular weight of } H_2O}$

$\Rightarrow \frac{9}{18} = \frac{1}{2}$ mol

$\therefore\ \Delta H = 75\ J\ mol^{-1}\ k^{-1}(293 - 283)k \times \frac{1}{2}$ mol

$\Delta H = \frac{750}{2} J$

$\Delta H = 375\ J$

49. (a) Given,

$\Delta H_A(g) = 9.7\ kJ\ mol^{-1}$

$\Delta H_B(g) = -110.81\ kJ\ mol^{-1}$

$\Delta H_C(g) = 81\ kJ\ mol^{-1}$

$\Delta H_D(g) = -393\ kJ\ mol^{-1}$

$A(g) + 3B(g) \rightarrow C(g) + 3D(g)$

$\Delta_r H = \sum_i a_i \Delta_f H(\text{Products}) - \sum_i b_i \Delta_f H(\text{Reactants})$

$= [3 \times (-393) + 81] - [9.7 + 3(-110)]$

$= -1098 + 320.3$

$\boxed{\Delta_r H = -777.7\ kJ\ mol^{-1}}$

50. (c) Relation between ΔH and ΔU is

$\Delta H = \Delta U + \Delta n_g RT$

or, $\Delta U = \Delta H - \Delta n_g RT$

for 1 mole,

$\Delta U = \Delta H - R\Delta T$

51. (a) Enthalpy of Dilution: Dilution of a solution from one concentration to another is accompanied by enthalpy change called enthalpy of dilution.

$AB(g) + 50\ H_2O(\ell) \rightarrow AB_{(50H_2O)}$

$\Delta H = y\ kJ\ mol^{-1}$

$AB_{(25H_2O)} \rightarrow AB(g) + 25\ H_2O(\ell)$

$\Delta H = -x\ kJ\ mol^{-1}$

$AB_{(25H_2O)} + 25H_2O(\ell) \rightarrow AB_{(50H_2O)};$

$\Delta H = (y - x)\ kJ\ mol^{-1}$

52. (b) $\Delta H_{fus}(C_6H_6) = 10.9\ kJ\ mol^{-1}$

$\Delta H_{vap}(C_6H_6) = 31.0\ kJ\ mol^{-1}$

Melting point of benzene = 5.5°C

= (5.5 + 273.15) K

= 278.65 K

Boiling point of benzene = 80°C

= (80 + 273.15) K

= 353.15 K

$y - x = \frac{\Delta H_{vap}}{T_{b.p}} - \frac{\Delta H_{fus}}{T_{m.p}}$

$= \frac{31 \times 1000}{353.15} - \frac{10.9 \times 1000}{278.65}$

$= 48.66\ JK^{-1}\ mol^{-1}$.

53. (c) $-300\ kJ\ mol^{-1}$

Given reaction - $2A_2 + B_2 \rightarrow 2A_2B + 600\ kJ$

By this equation indicates that the formation of 2 moles of A_2B releases 600 kJ energy.

$\Delta H_f^0(A_2B) = \frac{\text{Total enthalpy change}}{\text{Number of moles of } A_2B}$

$\Delta H_f^0(A_2B) = \frac{600kJ}{2} = 300\ kJ/mol$

Since reaction releases energy (Exothermic). The enthaipy of formation is negative.

$\Delta H_f^0 = -300\ kJ/mol$

54. (d) CH_4

1. For H_2
- Atomization $H_2 \rightarrow 2H$
- Bond dissociation $H_2 \rightarrow 2H$

so ΔH atomization = ΔH dissociation

2. For Cl_2
- Atomization $Cl_2 \rightarrow 2Cl$
- Bond dissociation $Cl_2 \rightarrow 2Cl$

so $\Delta H_{atom} = \Delta H_{dissociation}$

3. For F_2
- Atomization $F_2 \rightarrow 2F$
- Bond dissociation $F_2 \rightarrow 2F$

so $\Delta H_{atomization} = \Delta H_{dissociation}$

4. CH_4

Atomization $CH_4 \rightarrow C + 4H$

Bond dissociation – Each C – H bond in CH_4 has its own dissociation enthalpy and these are not necessarily the same as enthalpy of atomization.

ΔH atomization ≠ ΔH dissociation.

55. (d) $\Delta_a H° = \Delta_{C-H}H° + \Delta_{C-C}H°$

$622 = [6 \times 90] + [\Delta_{C-C}H°] = 540 + \Delta_{C-C}H°$

$\Rightarrow \Delta_{C-C}H° = 622 - 540 = 82\ kJ\ mol^{-1}$.

56. (d) $\Delta H° = \Delta U°$ (given)

$\Delta H° = \Delta U° + P\Delta V = \Delta U° + \Delta nRT = \Delta U°$

$\Rightarrow \Delta nRT = 0$ which means $\Delta n = 0$ with constant pressure.

57. (b) $CaCO_3(s) \xrightarrow{\Delta} CaO(s) + CO_2(g)$
$\Delta H^\circ_r = [\Delta_f H^\circ(CaO) + \Delta_f H^\circ(CO_2)] - [\Delta_f H^\circ(CaCO_3)]$
$= [(-634) + (-393)] - [-1210] = +183\ kJ\ mol^{-1}$

58. (b) $CCl_4(g) \rightarrow C(g) + 4Cl(g)$
or $CCl_4(g) \longrightarrow C(g) + 2Cl_2(g)$
$\Delta H^\circ_r = \Delta_a H^\circ(C) + 2\Delta_a H^\circ(Cl_2) - \Delta_{vap} H^\circ - \Delta_f H^\circ(CCl_4)$
$= (714) + [2 \times 242.0] - (30.0) - (-136.0) = 1304\ kJ\ mol^{-1}$
$\Rightarrow$ Average bond enthalpy of C–Cl bond
$= \frac{1304}{4} = 326\ kJ\ mol^{-1}$

59. (c) The lower the sublimation enthalpy, the lower is the heat required to sublime it and easier for that substance to get sublimed.
Thus, the order of ease of sublimation will be:-
solid CO_2 > Naphthalene > Na > Li

60. (d) Heat released in the reaction with 'X' g carbon
$Q = C_P\,\Delta T = (20.7)(4) = 82.8\ kJ$
1 mole or 12 g of carbon (graphite) gives 248.4 kJ heat
'X' g carbon gives 82.8 kJ heat
$\Rightarrow X = \frac{12 \times 82.8}{248.4} = 4\,g$

61. (b) $\Delta H = \Delta U + P\Delta V = \Delta U + \Delta n_g RT$
$\Rightarrow \Delta U = \Delta H - \Delta n_g RT = (-2800) - (0 \times 0.082 \times 300)$
$= -2800\ kJ\ mol^{-1}$

62. (a) ΔH_f° (H_2 gas) = 0.0 kJ mol^{-1}, ΔH_f° (Br_2 liquid) = 0.0 kJ mol^{-1}
$\Delta H_r^\circ = -72.8$ kJ for 2 moles of HBr.
$\Rightarrow \Delta H_r^\circ = [2\Delta H_f^\circ(HBr\ gas) - (\Delta H_f^\circ(H_2\ gas)) + (\Delta H_f^\circ(Br_2\ liq.))]$
$-72.8 = 2\,\Delta H_f^\circ(HBr\ gas) - (0.0 + 0.0)$
$= 2\,\Delta H_f^\circ(HBr\ gas)$
$\Rightarrow \Delta H_f^\circ(HBr\ gas) = \frac{-72.8}{2} = -36.4\ kJ\ mol^{-1}$.

63. (c)
$\Delta_r H^\circ = 2\Delta_f H^\circ_{CO_2} + 3\Delta_f H^\circ_{H_2O} - \Delta_f H^\circ_{C_2H_5OH}$
$= 2(-400) + 3(-290) - (-280)kJ$
$= -800 - 870 + 280 = -1390\ kJ$

64. (c) $H_2O(g) \longrightarrow H_2(g) + \frac{1}{2}O_2(g)$;
$\Delta H = +242\ kJ/mol$
$H_2(g) \longrightarrow 2H$; $\Delta H = +436\ kJ/mol$
$\frac{1}{2}O_2(g) \longrightarrow O$;
$\Delta H = +\frac{496}{2}\ kJ/mol = 248\ kJ/mol$
By adding up above three equations:
$\Delta_r H = 242 + 436 + 248 = 926\ kJ/mol$

65. (d) Number of moles in 4.8g of Mg = 4.8/24 = 0.2 mol
For 1 mole of ($Mg \rightarrow Mg^{2+}$)
$IE = IE_1 + IE_2 = (740 + 1450) = 2190\ kJ/mol.$
For 1 mole energy reqired = 2190 kJ/mol.
For 0.2 mole energy required = 2190 × 0.2 = 438 kJ

66. (d)
Given ΔH_f for $CH_3OH = -239\ kJ\ mol^{-1}$
ΔH_f of H.CHO = – 116 kJ mol^{-1}
ΔH_f of H_2O = – 286 kJ mol^{-1}
Required relation:
$2CH_3OH + O_2 \longrightarrow 2HCHO + 2H_2O$
$\Delta_r H = \Sigma(\Delta_f H_{Product}) - \Sigma(\Delta_f H_{Reactant})$
$= (-116 + (-286)) - (293 + 0) = -163\ kJ\ mol^{-1}$

67. (b) $C(s) + O_2(g) \rightarrow CO_2(g)$,
$\Delta H^0 = -x\ kJ\ mol^{-1}$ .... (i)
$2CO(g) + O_2(g) \rightarrow 2CO_2 g$,
$\Delta H^0 = -y\ kJ\ mol^{-1}$ .... (ii)
by applying eq. (i) – $\frac{1}{2}$ × Eq. (ii)
$C(s) + \frac{1}{2}O_2(g) \rightarrow CO(g)$
$\therefore\ \Delta_f H(CO) = -x - \left(-\frac{y}{2}\right) = -x + \frac{y}{2} = \frac{y-2x}{2}$

68. (c) Given,
$\Delta H = -92.4\ kJ$
$10g\ K_c = 5.75$
$\therefore \Delta G = -RT \ln K_c$
$= -2.303 \times 8.3 \times 298 \times 5.75$
$= -32.75\ kJ\ mol^{-1}$
$\therefore$ for 1 mol ΔG is –32.75 k J
We know that
$\Delta G = \Delta H - T\Delta S$
$\Rightarrow \Delta S = -\frac{\Delta G - \Delta H}{T} = \frac{32.75 - 92.4}{298}$
$= -0.200\ kJ$
$\therefore \Delta S = -200J$

69. (b) Statement I: A bomb calorimeter measure the heat released or absorbed by the reaction (not by water) at constant volume. Hence, statement I is incorrect.
Statement II: Heat capacity is an entensive property, it depends on the amount of substance. Hence, statement II is correct.
Statement III: The unit of entropy is JK^{-1} not JK. Hence, statement III is incorrect.

70. (b) $aCr(OH)_3 + bIO_3^- + cOH^- \longrightarrow dCrO_4^{2-} + eI^- + fH_2O$
Oxidation half reaction- $Cr(OH)_3 \longrightarrow CrO_4^{2-}$
$Cr(OH)_3 + 5OH^\ominus \longrightarrow CrO_4^{2-} + 4H_2O + 3e^-$ ... (1)
Reduction half reaction $IO_3^- \longrightarrow I^\ominus$
$IO_3^- + 3H_2O + 6e^- \longrightarrow I^\ominus + 6OH^\ominus$ ... (2)
$2Cr(OH)_3 + IO_3^- + 4OH^+ \longrightarrow 2CrO_4^{2-} + I^\ominus + 5H_2O$
a = 2, b = 1, c = 4, d = 2, e = 1, f = 5

71. (d) ΔH or enthalpy change in an extensive property as its value depends on the amount of substance in the system.
Thus, II is incorrect.
For going from liquid to solid the water molecules become ordered due to H-bonding.
Thus, entropy decreases.
Thus, III is incorrect.

72. (b) During crystallization entropy decrease and molecule closes to each other.

73. (b) When the number of gaseous atom increases entropy is increases. So in reaction I and II gaseous molecule produced so entropy increase.

74. (a) $\Delta S_{sys} = \frac{q_{sys}}{T}$
$q_{sys} = \Delta S_{sys} \times T$
$= 5\ JK^{-1}\ mol^{-1} \times 300\ K$
$= 1500\ J\ mol^{-1}$
$= \frac{1500}{1000}\ kJ\ mol^{-1}$
[1 KJ = 1000 J]
$\boxed{q_{sys} = 1.5\ kJ\ mol^{-1}}$

75. (a) (I) The total entropy change (ΔS_{total}) for the system and surrounding of a spontaneous process is given by
$\Delta S_{total} = \Delta S_{sys} + \Delta S_{surr}$
(II) $A(l) \rightarrow A(S)$:
for this process liquid to solid randomness or disorder in the system decreases. So entropy change decreases.
Entropy will increases in following cases.
(i) $A(S) \longrightarrow A(l)$
(ii) $A(l) \longrightarrow A(g)$
(iii) $A(s) \longrightarrow A(g)$
(iv) On increasing temperature S will increase
(v) On decreasing pressure, S will increases.
(III) Unit of entropy (S) is JK^{-1} mol^{-1} or cal k^{-1} mole

76. (a) Solid to liquid phase transition decreases the entropy

77. (c) Entropy increases from liquid phase to gaseous phase.

78. (b) $H_2O(l) \rightarrow H_2O(g)$ at T = 100°C
$\Rightarrow p = 1$ atm
The system containing water is an open system (P = 1 atm) and it gains heat from the surroundings. Therefore, the entropy of system increases and that of the surroundings decreases. (For reversible process ΔS total = 0)
$\therefore$ If $\Delta S_{system} > 0$ then $\Delta S_{surrounding} < 0$.

79. (b) When both ΔH and ΔS are Positive for a system then the process will be an endothermic which involves an increase in the entropy of system. In this case, ΔG will be negative, if the magnitude of the $T\Delta S$ term is greater than ΔH. Hence, such a process spontaneous at high temperatures and non-spontaneous at low temperatures.

80. **(a)** For the reaction:

$Zn(S) + 2HCl(aq.) \longrightarrow ZnCl_2(aq.) + H_2(g)$

$T = 17°C \Rightarrow 290K$

$\Delta H = -12.55$ kJ/mol

$\Delta S = 5.0 J/k/mol \Rightarrow 0.005$ kJ/K/mol

$\Delta G = \Delta H - T\Delta S$

$= -12.55 - 290 \times 0.005$

$= -12.55 - 1.45$

$= -14$ kJ/mol

81. **(c)** For the given reaction:

$2X(g) + Y(g) \longrightarrow 2Z(g)$

$\Delta n_g = n_P - n_R = 2 - 3 = -1$

$\Delta H^\ominus = \Delta U^\ominus + \Delta n_g RT$

$= -10500 + (-1) \times 8.3 \times 298$

$= -10500 - 2473.4$

$= -12973.4$ J

As we know, $\Delta G = \Delta H - T\Delta S$

$\Delta G = -12973.4 - 298(-44)$

$= -12973.4 + 13112$

$= 138.6 \simeq 139$ J

82. **(d)** For a spontaneous process $\Delta_r G°$ should be negative and $\Delta_r S°$ should be positive.

$\Delta_r G° = \Delta_r H° - T\Delta_r S°$

for all temperature $\Delta_r H°$ will be negative.

83. **(b)** For a spontaneous reaction, $\Delta_r G^\ominus$ should be negative.

As per the formula, $\Delta_r G^\ominus = \Delta_r H^\ominus - T\Delta_r S^\ominus$

If $\Delta_r H^\ominus = -ve$

$\Delta_r S^\ominus = -ve$

Thus, $\Delta_r G^\ominus$ is also –ve at lower temperature hence, will become spontaneous.

84. **(b)** The change in internal energy $\Delta U = -10.5$ kJ

The change in entropy $\Delta S = +44.1$ J/K

The Temperature T = 298 k

The gas constant $R = 8.314$ JK^{-1} mol^{-1}

The reaction is $2X_{(g)} + Y_{(g)} \rightarrow 2Z_{(g)}$

$\Delta G = \Delta H - T\Delta S$ ...(i)

Since ΔH not given directly is can be appoximated by ΔU because change is volume in negligible

$\Delta G \approx \Delta U - \Delta T \Delta S$

$$\Delta S = +44.1 \frac{J}{K} = +44.1 \times 10^{-3} \frac{kJ}{K}$$

Substituting the value in eq (1).

$$\Delta G = -10.5 - 298 K \times 0.441 \frac{kJ}{K}$$

$= -10.5 - 13.1418$ kJ

$= -23.6418$ kJ ≈ -23.642

Gibbs free energy for the reaction in approximately – 23.642 kJ the closest option to this value is – 26.119 kJ. This is due to ΔH and ΔU not considered.

85. **(b)** At 25°C or 298 K

$\Delta G° = -9$ kJ

$\Delta H° = -24$ kJ

$\Delta S° = ?$

as $\Delta G° = \Delta H° - T\Delta S°$

Where, $\Delta G°$ = change in standard Gibb's free energy

$\Delta H°$ = change in standard enthalpy

$\Delta S°$ = change in standard entropy

So, $T\Delta S° = \Delta H° - \Delta G°$

$$\therefore \quad \Delta S° = \frac{\Delta H° - \Delta G°}{T}$$

$$\text{so, } \Delta S° = \frac{-24+9}{298} \text{ kJ/K}$$

$\Delta S° = -0.05033$ kJ/K

OR

$\Delta S° = -50.33$ J/K as, 1 kJ = 1000 J

86. **(b)** $\Delta G° = -RT \ln K$

$$\ln K = -\frac{\Delta G°}{RT} = \frac{165.469 \times 10^3}{8.3 \times 298}$$

$\ln K = -66.86$

$$\log K = -\frac{66.86}{2.303}$$

$\log K = -29$

$K = 10^{-29}$

87. **(c)** Certain amount of activation energy is essential ever for such reactions which are thermodynamically feasible therefore heating is required.

So statement I is correct but II is incorrect.

88. **(d)** (I) For equilibrium reaction Gibb's free energy i.e $\Delta_r G = 0$

(II) According to third law of thermodynamics the entropy of pure crystalline solid approaches zero as the temperature approaches absolute zero. This is because there is perfect order in a crystal at absolute zero.

(III) For a chemical reactions, heat absorbed at constant volume i.e ΔU is measured in a bomb calorimeter.

89. **(d)** $\Delta G = \Delta H - T\Delta S$

We have, $\Delta H = -145$ kJ mol^{-1} and $\Delta S = -650$ J K^{-1} mol^{-1}

$\Rightarrow \quad \Delta G = (-145 \text{ kJ mol}^{-1}) - 298(-650 \times 10^{-3} \text{ kJ mol}^{-1} \text{ k}^{-1}) = +48.7 \text{ kJ mol}^{-1}$ and the reaction is non- Spontaneous.

90. **(a)** $\Delta G = \Delta H - T\Delta S$

$\therefore \quad \Delta G + T\Delta S = \Delta H$

$-40 + 2000 \times 0.22 = 400$

$\Delta H = \Delta U + P\Delta V$

$\Delta H - P\Delta V = \Delta U$

$\Delta H - \Delta n_g RT = \Delta U$

$$400 - 2 \times 8.3 \times \frac{2000}{1000} \Delta U$$

$\therefore \quad \Delta U = 366.8$ kJ mol^{-1}

91. **(c)** $\Delta G° = \Delta H° - T\Delta s°$

$= (-1860 \times 10^3) - 298(-550)$

$= -1696.1$ kJ Mol^{-1}

Thus, the reaction is Spontaneous as $\Delta G°$ is negative.

Now, Since the system loses the heat, the surrounding must gain it and therefore,

$\Delta H°_{Surrounding} = +1860 \times 10^3$ J mol^{-1}.

$$\Rightarrow \Delta S°_{surrounding} = \frac{\Delta H°_{surrounding}}{T}$$

$$= \frac{+1860 \times 10^3}{298}$$

$= 6241.6$ J

$\Rightarrow \Delta S°_{total} = \Delta S°_{system} + \Delta S°_{surrounding}$

$= (-550) + (6241.6)$

$= +5692$ J mol^{-1} K^{-1}.

92. **(a)** $\Delta_r G° = \Delta_r H° - T\Delta_r S°$

or $\quad -128 = \Delta_r H° + (300 \times 40 \times 10^{-3})$

or $\quad \Delta_r H° = -140$ kJ or $\Delta_r U° + \Delta nRT = -140$

or $\quad \Delta_r U° = -140 + (8.314 \times 10^{-3} \times 300)$

$[\because \Delta n = -1]$

or $\quad \Delta_r U° = -140 + 2.5 = -137.5$ kJ

93. **(c)**

	$N_2O_4(g)$ $\rightleftharpoons$	$2NO_2(g)$
Initial moles	1 mol	0 mol
At equilibrium	(1 – 0.5) mol	2 × 0.5 mol

Total number of m oles = 0.5 + 1 = 1.5 mol

According to law of chemical equilibrium

$$K_p = \frac{}{N_2O_4} = \frac{\left(\frac{}{1.5} \times\right)}{\left(\frac{0.5}{1.5} \times\right)} = 1.33 \text{ atr}$$

We know,

$\Delta G° = -2.303RT \log K_p$

$\Delta G° = -2.303 \times 0.082$ JK^{-1} mol^{-1} $\times 333$ K $\times \log 1.33$

$= -7.79$ atm L

atm L = 101.32500 joules = – 789.2 J mol^{-1}

$= -790$ J mol^{-1}

94. **(c)** $\Delta G = \Delta H - T\Delta S$

If ΔH and ΔS are +ve then, ΔG will be positive till $\Delta H > T\Delta S$.

When the temperature is increased further, then $\Delta H < T\Delta S$ and ΔG becomes –ve. Which is the essential condition for spontaneous reaction.

6 Equilibrium

1. **(b)** $2SO_2 + O_2 \rightleftharpoons 2SO_3$

$$K_c = \frac{[SO_3]^2}{[SO_2]^2[O_2]}$$

$$K_c = \frac{\left(\frac{n_{SO_3}}{10}\right)^2}{\left(\frac{n_{SO_2}}{10}\right)^2\left(\frac{n_{O_2}}{10}\right)} = 100$$

$$\left(\frac{n_{SO_3}}{n_{SO_2}}\right)^2 \times \frac{10}{n_{O_2}} = 100$$

ATQ

$$n_{SO_3} = 2n_{SO_2}$$

$$\left(\frac{2n_{SO_2}}{n_{SO_2}}\right)^2 \times \frac{10}{n_{O_2}} = 100$$

$$n_{O_2} = \frac{4}{10}$$

$$n_{O_2} = 0.4$$

2. **(b)** $N_2O_4(g) \rightleftharpoons 2NO_2(g)$

Moles of $N_2O_4 = 2 \times (1 - 0.2) = 1.6$ moles

Moles of $NO_2 = 4 \times 0.2 = 0.8$ moles

$$N_2O_4 = \frac{1.6 \text{ moles}}{10.0L} = 0.16 \text{ M}$$

$$NO_2 = \frac{0.8 \text{ moles}}{10.0L} = 0.08 \text{ M}$$

$$K = \frac{[NO\ \ ]}{[N_2O_4]} = \frac{(0.08)}{(0.16)} = 4 \times 10$$

3. **(a)** For the reaction,

$A(g) + B(g) \rightleftharpoons C(g)$

	A	B	C
at t = 0	2	1	0
at eq^m	2 – x	1 – x	x

at equilibrium : [B] = 2[C]

$1 - x = 2x$

$$x = \frac{1}{3}$$

So, $[A] = 2 - x = 2 - \frac{1}{3} = \frac{5}{3}$

$[B] = 1 - x = 1 - \frac{1}{3} = \frac{2}{3}$

$$K_c = \frac{[C]}{[A][B]} = \frac{\frac{1}{3}}{\left(\frac{5}{3}\right)\left(\frac{2}{3}\right)} = \frac{3}{10} = 0.3$$

4. **(c)** As per Question

	H_2	+ I_2	⇌ 2HI
t = 0	15	5.2	0
Change at	–x	–x	+2x
equilibrium	15–5 = 10	5.2 – 5 = 0.2	10

Let volume of container V

$$K_c = \frac{\left(\frac{10}{V}\right)^2}{\left(\frac{10}{V}\right)\times\left(\frac{0.2}{V}\right)}$$

For $2HI \rightleftharpoons H_2 + I_2$

$$K_c = \frac{\left(\frac{10}{V}\right)\times\left(\frac{0.2}{V}\right)}{\left(\frac{10}{V}\right)^2}$$

$$= \frac{10\times0.2}{(10)^2} = \frac{2}{100} = 0.02$$

$= 2\times10^{-2}$

5. **(d)** $A(g) + B(g) \rightleftharpoons C(g) + D(g)$

	A	B	C	D
Initially no. of modes	2	1	0	0
At. equilibrium	2 – x	1 – x	x	x

At equilibrium, [C] = 3[B]

$x = 3(1 - x)$

$x = 3 - 3x$

$$x = \frac{3}{4} = 0.75$$

so, $[A] = 2 - x = 2 - 0.75 = 1.25$

$[B] = 1 - x = 1 - 0.75 = 0.25$

$[C] = x = 0.75$

$[D] = x = 0.75$

$$K_C = \frac{[C][D]}{[A][B]}$$

$$= \frac{0.75\times0.75}{1.25\times0.25}$$

$$= \frac{0.5625}{0.3125} = 1.8$$

6. **(d)** $K_f = \frac{[HI]^2}{[H_2][I_2]} = \frac{(1.6)^2}{0.2\times1.2} = \frac{32}{3}$

$2HI(g) \rightleftharpoons H_2(g) + I_2(g)$

$$K_d = \frac{1}{K_f} = \frac{3}{32} = 9.375 \times 10^{-2}$$

7. **(c)**

	2HI	⇌ H_2	+ I_2
Initial	1	0	0
At eq^m	$1 - \alpha$	$\frac{\alpha}{2}$	$\frac{\alpha}{2}$

Total moles at eq^m $\quad 1 - \alpha + \frac{\alpha}{2} + \frac{\alpha}{2}$

Since there is no change in moles

$\Delta n = 0$

$\therefore \quad K_P = K_C$

$$K_P = \frac{P_{H_2}\cdot P_{I_2}}{(P_{HI})^2} \quad \text{... (1)}$$

$$P_{H_2} = \frac{\alpha}{2}P$$

$$P_{I_2} = \frac{\alpha}{2}P$$

$P_{HI} = (1 - \alpha)P$

Putting these values in (1)

$$K_P = \frac{\frac{\alpha}{2}P.\frac{\alpha}{2}P}{((1-\alpha)P)^2}$$

$$K_P = \frac{\alpha^2P^2}{4(1-\alpha)^2P^2}$$

$$\sqrt{K_P} = \frac{\alpha}{2(1-\alpha)}$$

$$\alpha = 2\sqrt{K_P} - 2\alpha\sqrt{K_P}$$

$$2\sqrt{K_P} = \alpha\left(1 + 2\sqrt{K_P}\right)$$

$$\boxed{\alpha = \frac{2\sqrt{K_P}}{1+2\sqrt{K_P}}}$$

8. **(a)** $PCl_5(g) \rightleftharpoons PCl_3(g) + Cl_2(g)$

	PCl_5	PCl_3	Cl_2
at t = 0	0.1	0	0
at eq^m	0.1 – x	x	x

$n_T = 0.1 - x + x + x = 0.1 + x$

$\Delta n_g = n_p - n_R = 2 - 1 = 1$

Using ideal gas equation:

PV = nRT

$1 \times 8 = (0.1 + x) \times 0.0821 \times 540$

$x = 0.08$

$$K_c = \frac{[PCl_3][Cl_2]}{[PCl_5]}$$

$$K_c = \frac{\left(\frac{x}{8}\right)\left(\frac{x}{8}\right)}{\left(\frac{0.1-x}{8}\right)}$$

$$K_c = \frac{x^2}{(0.1-x)8}$$

$$K_c = \frac{(0.08)^2}{8(0.1-0.08)}$$

$K_c = 0.04 \text{ mol L}^{-1}$

As we know,

$K_p = K_c (RT)^{\Delta n_g}$

$K_p = 0.04 \times (0.0821 \times 540)^1$

$K_p = 1.77$ atm

9. (a) For the reaction:

$X \rightleftharpoons 2Y$

at t = 0   1   0

at eq^m $1-\alpha$ 2α

$$K_{P_1} = \frac{(P_Y)^2}{P_X} = \frac{4\alpha^2}{1-\alpha^2}P_1 \quad \dots (1)$$

For the reaction :

$Z \rightleftharpoons P + Q$

at t = 0   1   0   0

at eq^m $1-\alpha$ α α

$$K_{P_2} = \frac{(P_P)(P_Q)}{P_Z} = \frac{\alpha^2}{1-\alpha^2}P_2 \quad \dots (2)$$

According to question : $K_{P_1} : K_{P_2} = 1:9$

Dividing (1) ÷ (2)

$$\frac{K_{P_1}}{K_{P_2}} = \frac{4P_1}{P_2}$$

$$\frac{4P_1}{P_2} = \frac{1}{9} \;;\; \frac{P_1}{P_2} = \frac{1}{36}$$

So, $P_1 : P_2 = 1 : 36$

10. (d) $A + 2B \rightleftharpoons 2C + D$

$t = 0$ a $1.5a$

at eq. $(a-x)$ $(1.5a-2x)$ $2x$ x

$$K_C = \frac{(2x)^2 \cdot x}{(a-x)(1.5a-2x)^2}$$

Given at equilibrium

$(a-x) = (1.5a-2x)$

$a - 1.5a = x - 2x$

$-0.5a = -x$

$a = 2x$

Putting the value

$$K_C = \frac{(2x)^2 \cdot x}{(2x-x)(1.5 \times 2x - 2x)^2}$$

$$= \frac{4x^3}{x^3} = 4$$

11. (a) $P_A = 1$ bar, $P_B = ?$

$V_A = 2L$, $V_B = 4L$

$P = 0.1$

$V = 100$ L

$PV = P_A V_A + P_B V_B$

$0.1 \times 100 = 1 \times 2 + P_B \times 4$

$10 = 2 + 4P_B$

$P_B = \frac{8}{4} = 2$ bar.

12. (d) $AO_2(g) + BO_2(g) \rightleftharpoons AO_3(g) + BO(g)$

initial moles   1   1   1   1

At equilibrium $1-x$ $1-x$ $1+x$ $1+x$

Volume is 1L

so $[AO_2] = 1-x$, $[BO_2] = 1-x$

$[AO_3] = 1+x$, $[BO] = 1+x$

$$Kc = \frac{[AO_2][BO]}{[AO_2][BO_2]} = \frac{(1+x)^2}{(1-x)^2}$$

$$16 = \left(\frac{1+x}{1-x}\right)^2$$

$4 - 4x = 1 + x$

$x = \frac{3}{5} = 0.6$

Concentration of equilibrium will be

$[AO_2] = 0.4$, $[BO_2] = 0.4$

$[AO_3] = 1.6$, $[BO] = 1.6$

I. Total number of moles at equilibrium $= 0.4 + 0.4 + 1.6 + 1.6 = 4$

II. $AO_2 : AO_3 = 0.4 : 1.6 = 1 : 4$

III. $AO_2 + BO_2 = 0.4 + 0.4 = 0.8$

13. (c) For the reaction:

$$N_2O_5 \rightarrow 2NO_2 + \frac{1}{2}O_2$$

Initial p_i 0   0

At Equilibrium $(p_i - x)$ $2x$ $\frac{x}{2}$

Where, p_i = initial pressure = 300 mm Hg

x = decrease in pressure of N_2O_5

Further, we can write at equilibrium

$$(p_i - x) + 2x + \frac{x}{2} = 480$$

Substituting the value of p_i and finding out the value of x:

$$(300 - x) + \frac{5x}{2} = 480$$

$$\frac{5x - 2x}{2} = 180$$

$$\frac{3x}{2} = 180$$

$$x = \frac{2}{3} \times 180 = 120$$

∴ Fraction of N_2O_5 decomposed

$$= \frac{x}{p_i} = \frac{120}{300} = \frac{2}{5} = 0.4$$

14. (d) $N_2O_4(g)\ 2NO_2(g)$

$$K_p = \frac{(P_{NO_2})^2}{P_{N_2O_4}} = \frac{(P_{NO_2})^2}{0.2} = 0.113$$

$\Rightarrow P_{NO_2} = \sqrt{0.2 \times 0.113} = 0.150$ atm.

15. (b) $\frac{1}{2}N_2 + \frac{3}{2}H_2 \rightleftharpoons NH_3;\ k_1$

$2NH_3 \rightleftharpoons N_2 + 3H_2;\ \frac{1}{k^2}$ ...(i)

$2NO \rightleftharpoons N_2 + O_2;\ k_2$

$O_2 + N_2 \rightleftharpoons 2NO;\ \frac{1'}{k_2}$ ...(ii)

$H_2 + \frac{1}{2}O_2 \rightleftharpoons H_2;\ k_3$

$3H_2 + \frac{3}{2}O_2 \rightleftharpoons 3H_2O;\ k_3^3$ ...(iii)

On adding eq.(i), (ii) & (iii)

$$2NH_3 + \frac{5}{2}O_2 \rightleftharpoons 2NO + 3H_2O;\ \frac{K_3^3}{K_1^2 \cdot K_2}$$

Correct option is $\frac{K_3^3}{K_1^2 \cdot K_2}$.

16. (c) $W + X \rightleftharpoons Y + Z$

$t = 0$ $2x$ x 0   0

t = at equilibrium $(2x-a)$ $(x-a)$ a a

Given : $a = 4(x-a)$

∴ $a = 4x - 4a$

$5a = 4x$

∴ $a = \frac{4}{5}x$

$$\text{Now, } K_c = \frac{[Y][Z]}{[W][X]} = \frac{a^2}{(2x-a)(x-a)}$$

$$= \frac{\left(\frac{4}{5}\right)^2 x^2}{\left(2x - \frac{4x}{5}\right)\left(x - \frac{4x}{5}\right)}$$

$$K_c = \frac{\frac{16}{25}x^2}{\left(\frac{6x}{5}\right)\left(\frac{x}{5}\right)} = \frac{16}{6} = \frac{8}{3} = 2.66$$

17. (c) As per question

$AO_2(g) + BO_2(g) \rightleftharpoons AO_3(g) + BO(g)$

t = 0   1 M   1 M   1 M   1 M

at equilibrium $(1-x)$ M $(1-x)$ M $(1+x)$ M $(1+x)$ M

$$K = \frac{(1+x)\,(1+x)}{(1-x)\,(1-x)} = \left(\frac{1+x}{1-x}\right)^2 = 16$$

$$4 = \frac{1+x}{1-x}$$

$4(1-x) = 1 + x$

$4 - 4x = 1 + x$

$-4x - x = 1 - 4$

$-5x = -3$

$x = \frac{3}{5} = 0.6$

AO_3 concentration at equilibrium = 1 + 0.6 = 1.6

18. (a) $A_2O_4(g) \rightleftharpoons 2AO_2(g)$

$\Delta n_g = 2 - 1 = 1$

$K_p = K_c \times (RT)^{\Delta n} \Rightarrow K_p = K_c \times RT$

$\Rightarrow K_p = x \times 0.082 \times 298 \Rightarrow K_p = 24.4x$

19. (a) For the reaction $B_2 \rightleftharpoons 2B$

at equilibrium $\frac{80}{100}$ $\frac{20}{100}$

$$K_p = \frac{(0.2)^2}{(0.8)^2} = \frac{0.04}{0.8} = 0.05$$

$K_p = 0.05$

20. (b) $K_p = K_c \times (RT)^{\Delta n}$

Given,

$K_c = 100 \text{ mol } L^{-1}$

$R = 0.082 \text{ L atm mol}^{-1} K^{-1}$

$T = 300 \text{ K}$

Δn = (No. of gaseous product) – (no. of gaseous reactant)

$= 2 - 1 = 1$

$\therefore K_p = 100 \text{ mol } L^{-1} \times (0.082 \text{ L atm mol}^{-1} k^{-1} \times 300K)^1$

$K_p = 2460$ atm

21. (b) $A_2(g) + B_2(g) \rightleftharpoons 2AB(g)$

At equilibrium $1.5 \times 10^{-3}M$ $\quad 2.1 \times 10^{-3}M$ $\quad 1.4 \times 10^{-3}M$

$$K_c = \frac{[AB]^2}{[A_2][B_2]}$$

$$K_c = \frac{1.4\times10^{-3}\times1.4\times10^{-3}}{1.5\times10^{-3}\times2.1\times10^{-3}}$$

$K_c = 0.622$

$K_p = K_c X(RT)^{\Delta n}$

$\Delta n = 0$

$K_p = K_c = 0.622$

For the decomposition of AB(K′) $= \frac{1}{K_p}$

$= \frac{1}{0.622}$

$\Rightarrow K' = 1.60$

22. (a) $H_2 + I_2 \rightleftharpoons 2HI$

Initial $\quad 15 \quad 5.2 \quad 0$

At equilibrium $\quad 15 - x \quad 5.2 - x \quad 2x$

Let 'V' is volume in litre

Given, $2x = 10$

$x = 5$

Concentration of H_2 at equilibrium = 15 – 5

$[H_2] = 10/V$; $[I_2] = \frac{0.2}{V}$; $[HI] = \left[\frac{10}{V}\right]$

$$K_c = \frac{\left[\frac{10}{V}\right]^2}{\left[\frac{10}{V}\right]\times\left[\frac{0.2}{V}\right]}$$

$$K_c = \frac{10\times10}{10\times0.2} = 50$$

$\therefore$ K_c' for the dissociation of HI is $= \frac{I}{K_c}$

$= \frac{1}{50} = 0.2\times10^{-1} = 2\times10^{-2}$

23. (a) $A_2(g) \xrightleftharpoons{T(K)} B_2(g)$

Initial $\quad 1 \quad 0$

Equilibrium $\quad 1 - x \quad x$

$$K_c = \frac{[B_2]}{[A_2]}$$

$$39 = \frac{\left[\frac{x}{1}\right]}{\left[\frac{1-x}{1}\right]}$$

or, $39 - 39x = x$

$\Rightarrow 40x = 39$

$\Rightarrow x = \frac{39}{40}$

$x = 0.975$

Concentration of $B_2 = 0.975$

Concentration of $A_2 = 1 - 0.975 = 0.025$

24. (c) Given

$H_2(g) + Br_2(g) \rightleftharpoons 2HBr(g)$. $K_p = 1.6 \times 10^5$

Reverse reaction,

$2HBr(g) \rightleftharpoons H_2(g) + Br_2(g)$, $K_p' = \frac{1}{K_p}$

$$HBr(g) \rightleftharpoons \frac{1}{2}H_2(g) + \frac{1}{2}Br_2(g),\ K_p'' = \left(\frac{1}{K_p}\right)^{1/2}$$

At t = 0 $\quad$ 10 bar $\quad 0 \quad 0$

At equilibrium $\quad 10 - x \quad \frac{x}{2} \quad \frac{x}{2}$

$$\left(\frac{1}{K_p}\right)^{\frac{1}{2}} = \frac{p_{H_2}^{1/2} \times p_{Br_2}^{1/2}}{P_{HBr}}$$

$$\left(\frac{1}{1.6\times10^5}\right)^{1/2} = \frac{\left(\frac{x}{2}\right)^{1/2}\left(\frac{x}{2}\right)^{1/2}}{(10-x)}$$

$\therefore 10 >> x$

$$2.5\times10^{-3} = \frac{x}{20}$$

$\Rightarrow x = 0.05 \Rightarrow p_{HBr} = 10 - 0.05 = 9.95$ bar.

25. (b) 1.98

$A_2(g) \xrightleftharpoons{T(K)} B_2(g)$, $K_c = 99.0$

moles of $B_2 = 2$

$$K_c = \frac{[B_2]^2}{[A_2]} \quad ...(1)$$

$$99 = \frac{[B_2]^2}{[A_2]}$$

Initial concentration of $A_2 = 0$

Initial concentration of $B_2 = 2$

Let x be the concentration of A_2 so the change in B_2 would be – 2x

Equilibrium concentration are

$[A_2] = x$, $[B_2] = 2 - 2x$

Putting the value in eq. (1)

$$99 = \frac{(2-2x)^2}{x}$$

$$99 = 4\frac{(1-x)^2}{x}$$

Let's simplify the equation – $[(a - b)^2 = a^2 - 2ab + b^2]$

$$99 = \frac{4(1-2x+x^2)}{x}$$

$99x = 4 - 8x + 4x^2$

$4x^2 - 107x + 4 = 0$

Solving the quadratic equation we use the Quadratic formula:-

$$x = \frac{-b\pm\sqrt{b^2-4ac}}{2a} \qquad a = 4, b = -107, c = 4$$

$$x = \frac{-(-107)\pm\sqrt{(-107)^2-4(4)(4)}}{2\times4}$$

$$x = \frac{107\pm\sqrt{11449-64}}{8}$$

$$x = \frac{107\pm\sqrt{11385}}{8}$$

$$x = \frac{107\pm106.70}{8}$$

$$x = \frac{213.65}{8} \approx 26.71,$$

$$x = \frac{0.30}{x} \approx 0.030$$

Putting the value of x to finding the concentration of B_2

$B_2 = 2 - 2x$

$B_2 = 2 - 2 \times 0.03$

$B_2 = 2 = 0.06 = 1.94$

26. (c) I. $A_2(g) \rightleftharpoons B_2(g)$

t = 0 $\quad$ 2 moles $\quad 0$

t = Equilibrium, $\quad C_1 \quad C_2$

$\quad (2 - x) \quad (x)$

II. $A_2(g) \rightleftharpoons B_2(g)$

t = 0 $\quad (2 - x) + 1 \quad x$

t = Equilibrium $\quad C_3 \quad C_4$

$\quad (3 - x) - x \quad x + x$

$\quad (3 - 2x) \quad 2x$

$$\therefore K_c = \frac{[B_2]}{[A_2]} = \frac{2x}{(3-2x)}$$

As, $K_c = 99$

$$\therefore 99 = \frac{2x}{3-2x}$$

$99(3 - 2x) = 2x$

$99 \times 3 = 2x + 99 \times 2x$

$297 = 2x + 198x$

$x = 1.485$

$\therefore$ for $C_3 (A_2) = 3 - 2x$

$= 3 - 2 \times 1.485 = 0.03$

27. (d) given $K_c = 99.0$

n = 2 moles of A_2

V = 1L

$A_2 \rightleftharpoons B_2$

Initial $\quad 2 \quad 0$

At equilibrium, $\quad 2 - x \quad x$

$$K_c = \frac{[\text{Product}]}{[\text{Reactant}]}$$

$$K_c = \frac{[x/1]}{\left[\frac{2-x}{1}\right]}$$

$$99 = \frac{x}{2-x}$$

$19 - 99x = x$

$\therefore x = \frac{198}{100} = 1.98$

concentration of B_2 at equilibrium is 1.98 mol L^{-1}

concentration of A_2 at equilibrium is (2 – 198)

= 0.02 mol L^{-1}

= 0.02 mo1 L^{-1}

28. (c) $A_2B_6(g) \rightleftharpoons A_2B_4(g) + B_2(g)$

Initial	p = 4 atm	0.0	0.0
Equilibrium	4 – 4α = 4 (1 – α)	pα = 4α	pα = 4α

$$K_p = \frac{P(A_2B_4) \times P(B_2)}{P(A_2B_6)} = 0.04 \text{ atm}$$

$$= \frac{(4\alpha)(4\alpha)}{4(1-\alpha)} = \frac{4\alpha^2}{1-\alpha} \approx 4\alpha^2$$

$\Rightarrow \quad \alpha = 0.1$

Therefore, $P(A_2B_6)$ at equilibrium = 4 (1 – α) = 4(1 – 0.1) = 3.62

29. (d) $K_p = K_c (RT)^{\Delta n_g}$

$K_c = 10 \text{ mol L}^{-1}$, T = 1000 K,

$R = 0.082 \text{ L atm mol}^{-1} \text{ K}^{-1}$

$\Delta n_g = (1 + 1) - 1 = 1$

$\Rightarrow K_p = (10)(0.082 \times 1000)^1 = 820$

30. (b) $K_C = \frac{[B]}{[A]} = 10^{-1}$ or $\frac{1}{10}$

Since K_C remains constant at a given temperature, the value of $\frac{[B]}{[A]}$ will still be the same.

$$\Rightarrow \frac{[B]}{[A]} = \frac{1}{10} \Rightarrow \frac{[A]}{[B]} = 10$$

31. (b) $K_p = K_c (RT)^{\Delta n_g}$

$H_2O(g) + CO(g) \rightleftharpoons H_2(g) + CO_2(g)$

$\Rightarrow \quad \Delta n_g = (1 + 1) - (1 + 1) = 0$

$\Rightarrow \quad K_p = K_c.$

Now, 40% of mass of water reacted with CO.

$\Rightarrow \quad \alpha = 0.4$

	H_2O	CO	H_2	CO_2
Initial moles	1.0	1.0	0.0	0.0
At equilibrium	1 – 0.4 = 0.6	1 – 0.4 = 0.6	0.4	0.4

Thus, $[H_2O] = \frac{0.6}{1.0} = 0.6$ M, [CO] = 0.6 M,

$[H_2] = 0.4$ M, $[CO_2] = 0.4$ M

$$\Rightarrow K_C = \frac{[H_2][CO_2]}{[H_2O][CO]} = \frac{(0.4)(0.4)}{(0.6)(0.6)} = 0.444$$

Thus, $K_p = 0.444$.

32. (b) $K_p = K_c (RT)^{\Delta n_g}$

$PCl_5(g) \xrightarrow{\Delta} PCl_3(g) + Cl_2(g)$

Initial	1	0	0
Equilibrium	1 – x	x	x

x = 0.1 (given) so 1 – x = 0.9

$$\Rightarrow K_c = \frac{x^2}{1-x} = \frac{(0.1)^2}{0.9} = 0.011$$

Thus, $K_p = (0.011)(0.082 \times 500)^{(2-1)}$ = 0.451.

33. (a) $K_c = \frac{[B]^b}{[A]^a}$ and $K'_c = \frac{[B]^{2b}}{[A]^{2a}}$

$\Rightarrow \quad K'_c = (K_c)^2$

34. (d) $K_p = K_c(RT)^{\Delta n}$

[Δn = Change in the no. gaseous molecules from reactant to product.]

In this equation,

$$\Delta n = \left(1 - 1 - \frac{1}{2}\right) = -\frac{1}{2}$$

$$\therefore \frac{K_p}{K_c} = (RT)^{-1/2} = \frac{1}{\sqrt{RT}}$$

35. (b)

$$N_2 + 3H_2 \rightarrow 2NH_3;\ K_c = \frac{[NH_3]^2}{[N_2][H_2]^3}$$

36. (b) Given reaction is

$2X + Y \rightleftharpoons 3Z$

Equilibrium constant $k = \frac{[Z]^3}{[X]^2[Y]}$

37. (d) $2(A)g \rightleftharpoons B(g) + C(g)$

$\Delta n = 2 - 2 = 0$

$K_p = K_C (RT)^0 \Rightarrow K_p = K_C$

38. (d) The value of equilibrium constant does not depend on initial concentrations of reactants and products.

39. (a) $N_2 + O_2 \rightleftharpoons 2NO$

K_C for the above reaction can be given as,

$$K_C = \frac{[NO]^2}{[N_2][O_2]}$$

$$K_C = \frac{[3\times10^{-3}]^2}{[4\times10^{-3}][3\times10^{-3}]} \Rightarrow K_C = \frac{3\times10^{-3}}{4\times10^{-3}} = 0.75$$

40. (c) Given, $K_C = 4 \times 10^{-6}$ mol/L

$(\Delta n = n_P - n_R \Rightarrow 3 - 2 = 1)$

$K_p = K_C \times (RT)^{\Delta n_g}$

$= 4 \times 10^{-6} \text{ mol L}^{-1} \times (0.083 \text{ L bar k}^{-1} \text{ mol}^{-1} \times 1000 \text{ K})^1$

$K_p = 3.32 \times 10^{-4}$ bar

41. (a) Let, number of moles of $SO_2 = x$

moles of $SO_3 = 2x$

$2SO_2(g) + O_2(g) \rightleftharpoons 2SO_3(g)$

At equilibrium,

$$K_c = \frac{[SO_3]^2}{[SO_2]^2[O_2]}$$

$$100 = \frac{\left[\frac{2x}{10}\right]^2}{\left[\frac{x}{10}\right]^2\left[\frac{n_{O_2}}{10}\right]}$$

$$100 = \frac{40}{n_{O_2}}$$

$$n_{O_2} = \frac{40}{100} = 0.4$$

Hence, number of moles of oxygen = 0.4

42. (d) Required relation

$H_3PO_4(aq.) \rightleftharpoons 3H^+(aq.) + PO_4^{3-}(aq.)$

For reaction (i)

$$K_1 = \frac{[H^+]_{(aq)}[H_2PO_4^-]_{(aq)}}{H_3PO_{4(aq.)}} \quad \text{...(i)}$$

For reaction (ii)

$$K_2 = \frac{[H^+]_{(aq.)}[HPO_4^{2-}]_{(aq.)}}{[H_2PO_4^-]_{(aq.)}} \quad \text{...(ii)}$$

For reaction (iii)

$$K_3 = \frac{[H^+]_{(aq.)}[PO_4^{3-}]_{(aq.)}}{[HPO_4^{2-}]_{(aq.)}} \quad \text{...(iii)}$$

On multiplying (i), (ii), (iii)

$K = K_1 \times K_2 \times K_3$

43. (b) $N_2O_4 \rightleftharpoons 2NO_2$

Initial moles	1	0
At equilibrium	(1 – 0.2)	2 × 0.2 = 0.4

Total moles = 0.4 + 0.8 = 1.2

$$K_p = \frac{(P_{NO_2})^2}{(P_{N_2O_4})} \Rightarrow K_p = \frac{\left(\frac{0.4}{1.2}\times600\right)^2}{\left(\frac{0.8}{1.2}\times600\right)} = 100$$

44. (b) For decomposition of SO_3 reaction will be reversible

$$\therefore 2SO_3(g) \rightleftharpoons 2SO_2(g) + O_2(g)\ K_p^1 = \frac{1}{K_p}$$

$$\therefore K_p^1 = \frac{1}{2\times10^{10}} = 0.5\times10^{-10}$$

$= 5 \times 10^{-11}$

$\Delta n_g = 3 - 2 = 1$

$\Rightarrow K_p^1 = K_c \times (RT)^{\Delta n_g}$

$$\Rightarrow K_c = \frac{K_p^1}{RT} = \frac{5\times10^{-11}}{0.083\times450}$$

$K_c = 1.34 \times 10^{-12}$

45. (a) $N_2(g) + 3H_2(g) \rightleftharpoons 2NH_3(g)$

$\Delta G° = \Delta H° - T\Delta S°$

$\Delta G° = -92400 + 298 \times 200$

$\Delta G° = -32800$ J

$\Delta G° = -2.303 RT \log K_c$

$$\log K_c = \frac{-32800}{-2.303\times8.3\times298} \approx 5.758$$

46. (b) We know that,

$\Delta_r G° = -RT\ln K_{eq}$

given,

$\Delta_r G° = -11.5 \text{ kJ mol}^{-1}$

T = 300 K

$R = 8.314 \text{ J mol}^{-1} \text{ K}^{-1}$

$\therefore \quad -11.5 \times 10^3 \text{ J mol}^{-1}$

$= -8.314 \text{J mol}^{-1} \text{ K}^{-1} \times 300 \text{ K} \times \ln K_{eq}$

or, $\quad 4.6106 = 2.303 \log_{10} K_{eq}$

$\therefore \quad \log_{10} K_{eq} = 2$

$\Rightarrow \quad K_{eq} = (10)^2$

$\boxed{K_{eq} = 100}$

47. (c) Addition of oxalic acid $H_2C_2O_4$ causes the oxalate ions $C_2O_4^{2-}$ to react with Fe^{3+} ions and form a complex that decreases the concentration of Fe^{3+} ions.

Thus, the equilibrium would shift towards the direction where the concentration of Fe^{3+} ions would increase which is towards left and this decreases the intensity of deep red colour.

48. (d) Addition of He gas (inert gas) at constant pressure or volume will not have any effect on the equilibrium of the given reaction as a change of pressure will not affect the number of gaseous moles that are equal on reactant and product side.

49. (b) $A(g)+\frac{1}{2}B(g) \rightleftharpoons C(g)+\text{heat};$

exothermic reaction

∴ Low temperature is favourable.

$$\Delta n = +1-\left(1+\frac{1}{2}\right)=1-\frac{3}{2}=-\frac{1}{2}$$

no. of gas molecules decreases in the forward reaction. So, high pressure is favourable for forward reaction.

50. (c) At equilibrium, the equilibrium constant = K and Gibb's Free Energy = $\Delta G = 0$

Non-equilibrium condition,

$\Delta G = \Delta G° + RT \ln K$

or, $0 = \Delta G° + RT \ln K$

or, $\Delta G° = - RT \ln K$

51. (d) $N_2(g) + 3H_2(g) \rightleftharpoons 2NH_3(g) + \Delta H$, Exothermic reaction.

According to Le Chatelier's principle, the reaction will proceed in backward reaction as the temperature increases.

52. (d) As equilibrium $\Delta G = 0$

$\Delta G° = - RT \ln K_c$

At equilibrium [Product] = [Reactant]

Hence, equilibrium constant

$K_c = 1$.

53. (b) Le-Chatelier principle is not applicable to pure solids and liquids because they experience negligible change in concentration during chemical equilibrium.

54. (b) $\frac{1}{2}X_2+\frac{3}{2}Y_2 \rightleftharpoons XY_3; \Delta H=-30kJ$

$X_2+3Y_2 \rightleftharpoons 2XY_3; \Delta H=-60kJ$

$\Delta S_r = 2 \times 50 - 3 \times 40 - 1 \times 60 = -80\ JK^{-1}\ mol^{-1}$

$\Delta G = \Delta H - T\Delta S$

When, $\Delta G = 0$

$0 = \Delta H - T\Delta S \Rightarrow \Delta H = T\Delta S$

$1000 \times (-60) = T \times (-80) \Rightarrow T = 750$ K.

55. (b) $SO_2+\frac{1}{2}O_2(g) \rightleftharpoons SO_3(g)$

When pressure is increased forward reaction is favoured because product side has lower no. of moles.

From p_1 to p_3, yield of SO_3 is increasing because higher pressure favours forward reaction.

56. (a) $\Delta G° = - RT\, lnK_p$

$= - 8.314 \times 400 \times 2.303 \times \log 10^{-30}$

$= 22976570\ J\ mol^{-1} = 229.8\ J\ mol^{-1}$

57. (b) For exothermic reaction, k_f decreases and k_b increases with increase of temperature so that K_{eq} decreases. For endothermic reaction, k_f increases and k_b decreases with increase of temperature so that K_{eq} increases.

58. (d) Conjugate acid of $H_3P_2O_6^-$ is $H_4P_2O_6$ (hypophosphoric acid)

59. (b) I. Nitrous acid = HNO_2

conjugate base of Nitrous acid = NO_2^-

II.

$$[^-OH]=\sqrt{K_b \times C}=\sqrt{2\times10^{-9}\times10^{-1}}=\sqrt{2}\times10^{-5}$$

III. Acid strength of Hydride of Halogen increases down the group due to size of halogen increases so easy to remove $[H^+]$ ion so correct acidity order will be HI > HBr > HCl > HF.

So only I and II are correct.

60. (b) In the reaction,

$NH_3 + H_2O \rightleftharpoons NH_4^+ + OH^-$

Water donates H^+ to NH_3 forming NH_4^+ and itself becomes OH^-

Since, water donates H^+, water acts as Bronsted – Lowry acid.

61. (b)

$$HCO_3^- \xrightarrow{-H^{\oplus}} \underset{(X)}{CO_3^{2-}} \rightarrow sp^2 \text{hybridization}$$

62. (c)

$$\underset{\text{(phosphorus acid)}}{H_3PO_3} \xrightarrow{-H^+} \underset{\text{conjugate base } (x)}{H_2PO_3^-}$$

$$\underset{\text{(oleum)}}{H_2S_2O_7} \xrightarrow{-H^+} \underset{\text{conjugate base } (y)}{HS_2O_7^-}$$

63. (c) NH_3, $\overset{\ominus}{O}H$, CO are acting as Lewis bases because they have lone pair of electrons in them.

Whereas, C_2H_4 has one double bond that means it has pielectrons which are electron rich.

64. (b) $\alpha_A = 4.242\% = 0.04242$, $[A] = x$M, $V_A = 1$ L

$\alpha_B = 3\% = 0.030$, $[B] = y$M, $V_B = 1$ L

$K_a = C\alpha^2 \Rightarrow C = \frac{K_a}{\alpha^2}$

$$\Rightarrow [A]=x=\frac{K_a}{\alpha_A^2}=\frac{1.8\times10^{-5}}{(0.04242)^2}=0.01\text{ M}$$

$$[B]=y=\frac{K_a}{\alpha_B^2}=\frac{1.8\times10^{-5}}{(0.030)^2}=0.02\text{ M}$$

$\Rightarrow n_A = 0.01$ mol, $n_B = 0.02$ mol

$$\Rightarrow C_{final}=\frac{n_A+n_B}{V_{final}}=\frac{0.01+0.02}{2}=0.015\text{ M}$$

65. (c) $pH = pK_a + \log\frac{[Salt]}{[Acid]}$

$pH = 5 + \log\frac{0.2}{0.1}$ $[pK_a = -\log K_a = -\log 10^{-5} = 5]$

$pH = 5 + \log 2$

$pH = 5 + 0.3$

$pH = 5.3$

66. (a) For an acid,

pH of an acid solution will be lower as the solution is more concentrated.

$pH = -\log[H^+]$

$$M_a=\frac{M_1V_1+M_2V_2}{V_1+V_2}$$

$$=\frac{2\times10^{-2}\times10^{-2}+2\times10^{-2}\times2\times10^{-2}}{4\times10^{-2}}=1.5\times10^{-2}$$

$$M_b=\frac{2\times10^{-2}\times10^{-2}+2\times10^{-2}\times5\times10^{-3}}{4\times10^{-2}}=0.75\times10^{-2}$$

$$M_c=\frac{2\times10^{-2}\times10^{-2}+2\times10^{-2}\times1\times10^{-2}}{4\times10^{-2}}$$

$M_c = 1 \times 10^{-2}$

$$M_d=\frac{2\times10^{-2}\times10^{-2}+4\times10^{-2}\times5\times10^{-3}}{6\times10^{-2}}$$

$$=\frac{4\times10^{-4}}{6\times10^{-2}}$$

$M_d = 0.66 \times 10^{-2}$

Order of concentration : $M_a > M_c > M_b > M_d$

Order of pH :- $M_d > M_b > M_c > M_a$

∴ Ma have the lowest pH.

67. (a) 12

Moles of HCl = 0.4m × 0.1L = 0.04 moles

For NaOH:-

Moles of NaOH = 0.5 M × 0.1 L = 0.05 moles

HCl and NaOH react in 1 : 1 Ratio

$HCl + NaOH \rightarrow NaCl + H_2O$

NaOH is in excess since 0.05 moles of NaOH react with 0.04 moles of HCl

0.05 moles – 0.04 moles = 0.01 moles of NaOH remaining

The total volume after mixing – 100ml of HCl + 100 ml

of NaOH + 800 ml of

distilled water

⇒ 1000 ml or 1 L

so the concentration of NaOH

$$=\frac{0.01\text{ moles}}{1L}=0.01\text{ m}$$

$pOH = -\log[OH^-]$

$pOH = -\log[0.01] = 2$

As we know pH + pOH = 14

pH = 14 – pOH = 14 – 2 = 12

68. (b) Balanced stoichiometric equation is:

$P_4 + 3OH^- + 3H_2O \rightarrow PH_3 + 3H_2PO_2^-$

conjugate of $H_2PO_2^-$ is H_3PO_2.

H_3PO_2 is hypophosphorous acid.

69. (d) $\underset{\text{chloric acid}}{HClO_3} \rightleftharpoons \underset{\text{Conjugate base}}{ClO_3^- + H^+}$

70. (a) Lewis acids = $AlCl_3$, H^+, Co^{3+}, Mg^{2+}, BF_3.

71. (c) A small change in temperature has little impact on the pH of a solution as the concentration of the H^+ ions does not change much.

Thus, statement I is correct.

$pH_1 = -\log [H^+]_1$ so if $[H^+]_2 = 100 [H^+]_1$

$\Rightarrow \quad pH_2 = -\log [H^+]_2 = -\log (100[H^+]_1)$

$= -\log (100) + [-\log [H^+]_1]$

$= -2 + pH_1 = pH_1 - 2$

Thus, pH changes by two units.

Therefore, statement II is incorrect.

72. (c) Acidic solutions (pH < 7) are Black coffee, Lemon juice, Human Saliva, Tomato juice.

73. (b) Conjugate acid of $HCO_3^- = H_2CO_3$ (has an extra H^+)

Conjugate base of $HCO_3^- = CO_3^{2-}$ (has an less H^+)

74. (a) $H_3O^+ \longrightarrow H^+ + \underset{\text{conjugate base}}{H_2O}$

75. (c) $\underset{0.01\ (N)}{Ca(OH)_2} \rightarrow Ca^{2+} + 2OH^-$

At 298K, pH = 14 – pOH = 14 – [– log (0.01)]

$= 14 + \log 10^{-2} = 14 - 2 = 12$

76. (c) Base have pH value more than seven. Distilled H_2O is neutral, HCl is acidic, NaOH and NH_3 both are base but, NaOH is a strong base among the given options. Therefore, it has highest pH.

77. (b) HF is weakest acid, thus, F^- is the strongest conjugate base.

78. (b) $K_a \times K_b = K_w = 10^{-14}$ (at 25°C)

$\Rightarrow \quad K_a(NH_4^+).K_b(NH_3) = 10^{-14}$

$K_a(NH_4^+) \times 2.5 \times 10^{-5} = 10^{-14}$

$K_a(NH_4^+) = \dfrac{10^{-14}}{2.5 \times 10^{-5}} = 4 \times 10^{-10}$

For pH of 0.01 M ammonia (NH_3)

$\therefore$ NH_4OH dissociate as :

At equilibrium $\underset{0.01(1-\alpha)}{NH_4OH} \rightleftharpoons \underset{0.01\alpha}{NH_4^+} + \underset{0.01\alpha}{OH^-}$

Also, $\alpha = \sqrt{\dfrac{K_b}{C}} = \sqrt{\dfrac{2.5 \times 10^{-5}}{0.01}} = 0.05$

and $[OH^-] = C\alpha = 0.01 \times 0.05 = 5.0 \times 10^{-4}$

$pOH = -\log[OH^-] = -\log(5.0 \times 10^{-4})$

or, $pH = 14 - pOH = 14 - 3.3 \Rightarrow pH = 10.7$

79. (d)

$H_2O + H_2O \longrightarrow H_3O^+ + OH^-$ (Bronsted acid as well as base)

(Acid: $H_2O \to H_3O^+$; Base: $H_2O \to OH^-$)

$HSO_4^- \xrightarrow{H^+} H_2SO_4$ (acting as acid)

$HSO_4^- \xrightarrow{-H^+} SO_4^{2-}$ (acting as base)

80. (d)

Molecular mass of NaOH = 23 + 16 + 1 = 40

$\text{Molarity} = \dfrac{\text{Mass of solute (in g)}}{\text{Molecular mass of the solute} \times \text{Volume of solution (in L)}}$

$= \dfrac{0.04 \times 1000}{40 \times 100} = 10^{-2}$

$OH^- = 10^{-2}$ mol/L

So, $pOH = -\log[OH^-]$

$pOH + pH = 14$ or $pH = 14 - 2 = 12$

81. (a) Given, $K_{a_1} = 6 \times 10^{-2}$

At Equilibrium : $[A^{2-}] = [H_2A]$

First dissociation: $H_2A \rightleftharpoons H^+ + HA^-$

$K_{a_1} = \dfrac{[H^+][HA^-]}{[H_2A]}$ ..... (1)

Second dissociation: $HA^- \rightleftharpoons H^+ + A^{2-}$

$K_{a_2} = \dfrac{[H^+][A^{2-}]}{[H_2A]}$ ..... (2)

Multiply (1) and (2)

$K_{a_1} \times K_{a_2} = \dfrac{[H^+][HA^-]}{[H_2A]} \times \dfrac{[H^+][A^{2-}]}{[HA^-]}$

$K_{a_1} \times K_{a_2} = \dfrac{[H^+]^2[A^{2-}]}{[H_2A]}$

$K_{a_1} \times K_{a_2} = [H^+]^2$. $\quad (\because [A^{2-}] = [H_2A])$

$[H^+] = \sqrt{K_{a_1} \times K_{a_2}}$

$[H^+] = \sqrt{6 \times 10^{-2} \times 6 \times 10^{-5}}$

$= 1.89 \times 10^{-3}$ M or 1.9×10^{-3}M

82. (c) $\dfrac{K_C}{K_P} = 1076$

$N_2(g) + 3H_2(g) \rightleftharpoons 2NH_3(g)$

$\Delta n_g = 2 - 4 = -2$

$K_P = K_C \times (RT)^{\Delta n_g}$

$K_P = K_C \times (RT)^{-2}$

$(RT)^2 = \dfrac{K_C}{K_P} = 1076$

$RT = \sqrt{1076} = 32.80$

$T = \dfrac{32.80}{0.082} = 400K$

83. (c) $2Cu^{2+} + 4KI \rightarrow 2CuI(s) + I^2 + 2K^+$

moles of $Cu^{2+} = 0.05 \times \dfrac{100}{1000} = 0.005$ moles

$\therefore$ Cu^{2+} produce half mole of I_2.

moles of $I_2 = \dfrac{0.005}{2} = 0.0025$ moles

$I_2 + 2Na_2S_2O_3 \rightarrow 2NaI + Na_2S_4O_6$

One mole of I_2 reacts with 2 mole of $Na_2S_2O_3$

$\therefore$ Required moles of $Na_2S_2O_3$

$= 0.0025 \times 2 = 0.005$ moles

Volume of 0.01 M $Na_2S_2O_3$ required

$V = \dfrac{0.005 \text{ moles}}{0.01 \text{ M}} = 0.5 \text{ L} = 500 \text{ mL}$

84. (a) $\underset{C(1-\alpha)}{CH_3COOH} \rightleftharpoons \underset{C\alpha}{CH_3COO^-} + \underset{C\alpha}{H^+}$

$K_a = \dfrac{C\alpha^2}{(1-\alpha)}$ if $\alpha <<< 1$

$K_a = C\alpha^2$

$C = \dfrac{K_a}{\alpha^2} = \dfrac{1.8 \times 10^{-5}}{(0.04242)^2} \quad \left[\alpha = \dfrac{\%\text{ dissociation}}{100}\right]$

$C = 1000.32 \times 10^{-5} = 0.01$ M

85. (d) $\underset{C(1-\alpha)}{CH_3COOH} \rightleftharpoons \underset{C\alpha}{CH_3COO^-} + \underset{C\alpha}{H^+}$

$K_a = \dfrac{C\alpha^2}{(1-\alpha)}$ if $\alpha <<< 1$

$K_a = C\alpha^2$

$C = \dfrac{K_a}{\alpha^2} = \dfrac{1.8 \times 10^{-5}}{(0.04242)^2} \quad \left[\alpha = \dfrac{\%\text{ dissociation}}{100}\right]$

$C = 1000.32 \times 10^{-5} = 0.01$ M

86. (a) $\alpha = 0.04242$

$K_a = 1.8 \times 10^{-5}$

$K_a = C\alpha^2$

$\therefore \quad C = \dfrac{1.8 \times 10^{-5}}{(0.04242)^2} = \dfrac{1.8 \times 10^{-5}}{0.0018} = 0.01$

$[H^+] = C\alpha = 10^{-2} \times 0.04242$

$pH = -\log[H^+] = -\log 10^{-2} \times 0.04242$

$= 2 + 1.37 = 3.37$

87. (a) $HA \rightleftharpoons H_3O^+ + A^-$

	HA	H_3O^+	A^-
	0.5	0	0
	0.5 – x	x	x

$[H^+] = c\alpha$

$= 0.5 \times (10^{-2})$

$= 0.005$

$\therefore \quad [H_3O]^+ = 0.005$

$[A^-] = 0.005$

$[HA] = 0.5 - x$

$= 0.5 - 0.005$

$= 0.495$

88. (b) degree of dissociation of weak acid (HA) = 1%

$\alpha = 1\%$

$\Rightarrow \dfrac{1}{100} = 0.01$

Dissociation constant $(K_a) = C\alpha^2$

where,

C(concentration) = 0.5 M

α (degree of dissociation) = 0.01

$\therefore K_a = 0.5 \times (0.01)^2$

$= 5 \times 10^{-1} \times (10^{-2})^2$

$= 5 \times 10^{-1} \times 10^{-4}$

$\boxed{K_a = 5 \times 10^{-5}}$

89. (a) $BOH \rightleftharpoons B^+ + OH^-$

$K_b = \dfrac{[B^+][OH^-]}{[BOH]} = 1 \times 10^{-6}$

$pH = 10 \Rightarrow pOH = 14 - 10 = 4$

$\Rightarrow [OH^-] = 10^{-4}$ M.

Now, $K_b = \dfrac{C\alpha^2}{1-\alpha} = \dfrac{[OH^-]\alpha^2}{1-\alpha}$

$\Rightarrow \dfrac{K_b}{[OH^-]} = \dfrac{\alpha^2}{1-\alpha} \cong \alpha^2 = \dfrac{10^{-6}}{10^{-4}} = 10^{-2}$

$\Rightarrow \quad \alpha = 10^{-1}$ or 0.1 or 10%

90. (d) Larger the K_a values, higher is the acidic strength.

91. (c) According to Henderson's equation-

$$pH = pK_a + \log\frac{[salt]}{[acid]} = 4.75 + \log\frac{0.5}{0.5} = 4.75$$

92. (d) Given, $[HCl] = 10^{-8}$ M

$[H^+] = 10^{-8} + 10^{-7} = 10^{-8}(1 + 10)$

$10^{-8}(11) = 4 \times 10^{-8}$

$pH = -\log(H^+) = -\log(11 \times 10^{-8}) = 6.96$

10^{-8} M is a very low concentration and hence the protons from water are also considered.

93. (b) HF $\{pK_a = 3.1\}$

HCl $\{pK_a = -6.0\}$

HBr $\{pK_a = -9.0\}$

HI $\{pK_a = -9.5\}$

Acidic nature of hydrogen halides incerease down the group –17.

Hence k_a = HF < HCl < HBr < HI

pK_a = HF > HCl > HBr > HI

94. (b) With an increase in temperature, there is an increase in dissociation of H_2O which gives rise to an increase ion the concentration of H^+ and OH^- ions. Hence, the ionic product of water increases with an increase in temperature.

95. (d) Applying, Volume of HCl solution $(V_1) = 30$ mL

Volume of sodium carbonate solution (Na_2CO_3) $(V_2) = 20$ mL

Concentration of Na_2CO_3 solution $(M_2) = 0.1$ M

Volume of NaOH solution $(V_3) = 30.0$ mL

Concentration of NaOH solution $(M_3) = 0.2$ M

$N_1V_1 (Na_2CO_3) \Rightarrow M_1 \times n_f \times v_1 (HCl) = M_2 \times n_f \times v_2 (Na_2CO_3)$

$N = M \times nf_i$ n_f of HCl = 1 n_f of $Na_2CO_3 = 2$

$M_1 \times 30 = 20 \times 2 \times 0.1 \Rightarrow M_1 = 0.133$

Now, volume of HCl solution required to neutralise 30 mL of 0.2 M NaOH can be calculated by

Applying $M_1V_1 = M_3V_3$

$0.133 \times V_1 = 0.2 \times 30 \Rightarrow V_1 = 45.1$ mL

96. (a) pH of the solution of salts of weak acid e.g. acetic acid and weak base e.g. dimethylamine can be calculated as

$$pH = 7 + \frac{1}{2}[pK_a - pK_b]$$

Here, $pK_a = 4.76$, $pK_b = 3.26$

$$= 7 + \frac{1}{2}[4.76 - 3.26] \Rightarrow 7 + \frac{1}{2}[1.50]$$

$\Rightarrow 7 + 0.75 = 7.75$

97. (c) $CaSO_4(s) \rightleftharpoons Ca^{2+}(aq) + SO_4^{2-}(aq)$

$[Ca^{+2}] = S$ and $[SO_4^{2-}] = S$

$K_{sp} = [Ca^{+2}][SO_4^{2-}] = S \times S = S^2$

$S = \sqrt{K_{SP}} = \sqrt{9 \times 10^{-6}} = 3 \times 10^{-3}$ mol L^{-1}

$$n = \frac{mass}{molar\ mass} = \frac{1.5\,g}{136\,g\ mol^{-1}} \approx 0.01103 \text{ moles}$$

$$s = \frac{n}{V} = \frac{\left(\frac{1.5}{136}\right)}{3 \times 10^{-3}} \approx 3.676\,L$$

98. (b) No. of moles of NaOH = Molarity × volume = 0.5 × 0.5 = 0.25

No. of Moles of HCOOH = 0.55 × 0.5 = 0.275

Reaction involved : $HCOOH + NaOH \longrightarrow HCOONa + H_2O$

NaOH is limiting reagent

Remaining HCOOH = 0.275 – 0.25 = 0.025 mol

HCOONa formed = 0.25 mol

Using Henderson – Hasselbalch equation:

$$pH = pK_a + \log\frac{[Salt]}{[acid]}$$

$pK_a = -\log(K_a) \Rightarrow -\log(1.8 \times 10^{-4}) = 3.74$

$$pH = 3.74 + \log\frac{(0.25)}{(0.025)}$$

$pH = 3.74 + \log 10 = 3.74 + 1$

$pH = 4.74$

99. (c) According to Henderson - Hasselbalch equation:

$$pH = pK_a + \log\frac{[salt]}{[acid]} \quad ...(1)$$

Given, $K_a(HCN) = 10^{-10}$

so $pK_a = -\log(K_a)$

$= -\log(10^{-10}) = 10$

Putting in equation (1)

⇒ If x moles of HCN is required than, no. of moles of NaCN is left = 0.01 – x.

$$9 = 10 + \log\left(\frac{0.01 - x}{x}\right) \quad -1 = \log\left(\frac{0.01 - x}{x}\right)$$

Taking antilog on both sides

$$0.1 = \frac{0.01 - x}{x} \Rightarrow 0.1x = 0.01 - x$$

$1.1x = 10^{-2}$

$$x = \frac{10^{-2}}{1.1}$$

$x = 0.9 \times 10^{-2}$

∴ 9×10^{-3} moles of HCN is required.

100. (d) For acidic buffer

$$pH = pKa + \log\left(\frac{(Salt)}{(Acid)}\right)$$

Since acid is same, pK_a becomes constant

$$\therefore \quad pH \propto \left(\frac{\text{moles of salt}}{\text{moles of acid}}\right)$$

Buffer solution	n_{acid} (1.0 m × v)	n_{salt} (0.1m×v)	Ratio $\left(\frac{n_{salt}}{n_{acid}}\right)$
I	1.0 × 4.0 = 40	0.1 × 4.0 = 0.4	0.4/4.0 = 0.1
II	1.0 × 4.0 = 4.0	0.1 × 40 = 4	$\frac{4}{4} = 1$
III	1 × 40 = 40	0.1 × 4 = 0.4	$\frac{0.4}{40} = 0.01$
IV	1.0 × 0.1 = 0.1	0.1 × 10 = 1	$\frac{1}{0.1} = 10$

Since IV buffer has highest $\left(\frac{n_{salt}}{n_{acid}}\right)$ value,

∴ pH of IV solution is highest.

101. (a) $CaC_2O_4(s) \rightleftharpoons Ca^{2+} + C_2O_4^{2-}$
S S

$K_{sp} = S^2$

$S = \sqrt{K_{sp}}$

$S = \sqrt{2.5 \times 10^{-9}}$

$S = 5 \times 10^{-5}$ mol/L

Mass of CaC_2O_4 required = S × Molar mass of CaC_2O_4

$= 5 \times 10^{-5} \times 128$

= 0.0064g

102. (d) As we know,

$$\text{Molarity} = \frac{\text{No. of moles of solute}}{\text{Volume of solution in litres}}$$

So, No. of moles of NaOH = 0.5M × 0.250 L = 0.125 mol

No. of moles of HCl = 0.5M × 0.100L = 0.050

After neutralisation, Excess OH^- present in the solution:

Excess OH^- = 0.125 – 0.05 = 0.075 mol

Total volume = 250 + 100 + 400 = 750 ml or 0.75 L

$$\text{So, } [OH^-] = \frac{0.075}{0.75} = 0.1\text{ M}$$

So pOH = 1 and pH = 14 – pOH

pH = 14 – 1 = 13

103. (a) K_{sp} $MX_2 = 5 \times 10^{-13}$

$\Rightarrow K_{sp} = s \times (2s)^2 = 4s^3$

$MX = 1.6 \times 10^{-11} \Rightarrow K_{sp} = s \times s = s^2$

$$\text{Solubility } MX_2 = \sqrt[3]{\frac{K_{sp}}{4}}$$

$$\text{Solubility } MX = \sqrt{K_{sp}}$$

$$\text{Ratio of solubility} = \frac{\sqrt[3]{\frac{5 \times 10^{-13}}{4}}}{\sqrt{1.6 \times 10^{-11}}}$$

$$= \frac{\sqrt[3]{1.25 \times 10^{-13}}}{4 \times 10^{-6}} = \frac{\sqrt[3]{125 \times 10^{-15}}}{4 \times 10^{-6}}$$

$$= \frac{5 \times 10^{-5}}{4 \times 10^{-6}} = 1.25 \times 10 = 12.5$$

104. (c) $Pb(NO_3)_2 \rightleftharpoons Pb^{2+} + NO_3^-$
0.2 0.2

$PbI_2 \rightleftharpoons Pb^{2+} + 2I^-$
S + 0.2 2S

Solubility of Pb^{2+} = S + 0.2

$K_{SP} = (S + 0.2) \times (2S)^2$

$K_{SP} = 4S^3 + 0.8S^2$

$4S^3 << 0.8S^2$

$\therefore 0.8S^2 = K_{SP}$

$$S = \sqrt{\frac{K_{sp}}{0.8}} = \left(\frac{K_{sp}}{0.8}\right)^{\frac{1}{2}}$$

105. (b) Eosin, a red dye is an adsorption indicator used in argentometric titrations to detect the endpoint of the titration.

106. (d) $pOH = pK_b + \log \frac{[salt]}{[base]}$

Mole of $NH_4OH = 30 \times 0.2 = 6$m mol = 0.006 mol

Mole of $NH_4Cl = 30 \times 2 = 60$ m mol = 0.06 mol

$pH + pOH = 14$

$pOH = 14 - pH = 14 - 8.2 = 5.8$

$pOH = pK_b + \log \frac{0.06}{0.006}$

$5.8 = pK_b + \log 10$

$5.8 = pK_b + 1 \Rightarrow pK_b = 5.8 - 1 = 4.8$

107. (c) $\underset{}{AgBr} \rightleftharpoons \underset{s}{Ag^+} + \underset{s}{Br^-}$

$K_{sp} = 4 \times 10^{-13}$

In presence of strong electrolyte 0.1 M K Br

Br^- ion increases and dissociation of AgBr as

$[Ag^+] = 5$

$[Br^-] = 0.1 + 5$

$K_{sp} = 5 \times (0.1 + 5)$

$= 0.15 + s^2$

for very diluted $s^2 <<< 1$ thus s^2 ignored

$K_{sp} = 0.15$

$S = \frac{4 \times 10^{-13}}{0.1}$

$= 4 \times 10^{-12}$ M

108. (b) $Ba_3(PO_4)_2 \longrightarrow 3Ba^{2+} + 2PO_4^{3-}$

Solubility of Barium $= \left(\frac{\frac{x}{M}}{10^{-1}}\right)$

$= \left(\frac{x}{M} \times 10\right)$ mol / L

$Ba_3(PO_4)_2 \longrightarrow 3Ba^{2+} + 2PO_4^{3-}$

$\left(3\frac{x}{M} \times 10\right)\left(2\frac{x}{M} \times 10\right)$

$K_{sp} = \left(\frac{3x}{M} \times 10\right)^3 \times \left(\frac{2x}{M} \times 10\right)^2$

$= 27 \times \left(\frac{x}{M}\right)^3 \times 10^3 \times 4 \times \left(\frac{x}{M}\right)^2 \times 10^2$

$= 108 \times \left(\frac{x}{M}\right)^5 \times 10^5$

$K_{sp} = 1.08 \times \left(\frac{x}{M}\right)^5 \times 10^7$

$\therefore$ a = 5

b = 7

109. (c) Solubility product (K_{sp}) of Ax = 10^{-10}

$[H^+] = [X^-] = 10^{-1}$ M

$[K_{sp}] = [H^+] [X^-]$

$10^{-10} = [10^{-1}] \times [S]$

$\therefore \quad S = \frac{10^{-10}}{10^{-1}} = 10^{-9}$

110. (d) Basic buffer solution is made by mixing a weak base with strong acid.

111. (c) A solution that has the concentration of Ag^+ or Cl^- greater than or equal to the solubility of Ag^+ or Cl^- from the value of K_{sp}, will precipitate out.

$K_{sp} = [Ag^+] [Cl^-] = (s) (s) = s^2 = 1 \times 10^{-10}$ M^2

$\Rightarrow \quad s = 10^{-5}$ M

Thus, (iv) 1L of 10^{-3} M $AgNO_3$ and (v) 1L of 10^{-5} M NaCl will precipitate

112. (b) Dissociation of electrolytes increases with increase in temperature: So, $K_w = [H^+] [OH^-]$ also increases.

$\therefore$ pH of the buffer solution increases.

113. (c) $K_{sp} = 1 \times 10^{-10}$

$MCl \rightarrow M^+ + Cl^-$

In NaCl soln., total $[Cl^-] = (0.1 + s)$M

$\therefore \quad s(s + 0.1) = 10^{-10}$

or, $\quad 0.1s = 10^{-10}$

[$\because$ s + 0.1 $\because$ 0.1 as s <<< 0.1]

or, $\quad s = \frac{10^{-10}}{0.1} = 10^{-9}$ M

114. (d) Smaller the value of K_{sp} of the salt, quicker is the formation of precipitate.

Sequence of precipitation : HgS, CdS, ZnS, NiS.

115. (b) Given, $[K_{sp}]$ of AgBr = 5×10^{-10}

[NaBr] = 0.2 M; $[Na^+] = [Br^-] = 0.2$ M

Now, $[K_{sp}] = [Ag^+] [Br^-]$

$s(0.2) = 5 \times 10^{-10} \quad (s << 0.2)$

$s = \frac{5 \times 10^{-10}}{0.2} = 25 \times 10^{-10}$ M

116. (c) $Ni(OH)_2 \rightleftharpoons \underset{s\text{ mol/L}}{Ni^{2+}} + \underset{2s\text{ mol/L}}{2OH^-}$

$\Rightarrow K_{sp} = [Ni^{2+}] [OH^-]^2 = s \times (2s)^2 = 4s^3$

2×10^{-15} (mol/L)$^3 = 4s^3$

$\Rightarrow s = \left(\frac{2}{4} \times 10^{-15}\right)^{1/3}$

$= 7.9 \times 10^{-6} = 8 \times 10^{-6}$ mol/L

$[OH^-] = 2s = 2 \times 8 \times 10^{-6}$ mol/L

pOH = 6 – log 16 = 4.983 $\simeq$ 5

$\therefore$ pH = 14 – pOH = 14 – 5 = 9 at 25°C.

117. (b) $\underset{}{A_2B} \rightarrow \underset{2s}{2A^+} + \underset{s}{B^{2-}}$

$K_{sp} = [A^+] [B^{2-}] = (2s)^2 (s) = 4s^3$

Given, K_{sp} for $A_2B = 3.2 \times 10^{-11}$

$\therefore \quad 3.2 \times 10^{-11} = 4s^3$

$s = \left(\frac{3.2}{4} \times 10^{-11}\right)^{1/3} = \left(8 \times 10^{-12}\right)^{1/3} = 2 \times 10^{-4}$

Thus $s = 2 \times 10^{-4}$

118. (c) Dissolution $NH_4Cl \rightarrow NH_4^+ + Cl^-$

Cl^- will Cl^- (aq) and will not undergo hydrolysis.

Hydrolysis $NH_4^+ + H_2O \rightleftharpoons NH_3 + H_3O^+$

7 Redox Reactions

1. (a)

$\overset{+1+5}{K}Cl\overset{-2}{O_3}(s) \xrightarrow{\Delta} 2\overset{+1}{K}\overset{-1}{Cl} + 3\overset{0}{O_2}(g)$

Redox Reaction

$2\overset{+1}{H_2}\overset{-1}{O_2}(aq) \xrightarrow{\Delta} 2\overset{+1}{H_2}\overset{-2}{O}(l) + \overset{0}{O_2}(g)$ Redox Reaction

$2\overset{0}{Na}(s) + \frac{1}{2}\overset{0}{O_2} \rightarrow \overset{+2}{Na_2}\overset{-2}{O}(s)$ Redox Reaction

$\overset{+1}{Ag}\overset{-1}{NO_3}(aq) + \overset{+1}{K}\overset{-1}{Cl}(aq) \rightarrow \overset{+1}{Ag}\overset{-1}{Cl}(S) + \overset{+1}{K}\overset{-1}{NO_3}(aq)$

No change in oxidation state so it is not a redox reaction.

'So' '3' reactions are redox.

2. (b)

$\overset{0}{S} + H_2\overset{+6}{SO_4} \longrightarrow \overset{+4}{SO_2} + H_2O$

(oxidation: S → SO_2; Reduction: H_2SO_4 → SO_2)

$\therefore$ Oxidised product = SO_2

Reduced product = SO_2

3. (d) Pink colour of MnO_4^- converts to colourless MnO_2 after reduction.

4. (c) The oxidation states of oxygen –1, –2, +2.

The oxidation states of chlorine –1 to +7.

The oxidation state of fluorine: – 1

The oxidation states of tin (Sn) range from +2 to +4.

The oxidation states of scandium +3.

Scandium (Z = 21) does not exhibit variable oxidation states.

The oxidation states of titanium + 2, + 3, + 4 respectively.

The oxidation states of Potassium: +1.

5. (b) $2Na_2S_2O_3 + I_2 \longrightarrow 2NaI + Na_2S_4O_6$

Equivalent weight = $\frac{\text{molar mass}}{\text{n – factor}}$

n-factor for $Na_2S_2O_3 = 2 \times 0.5 = 1$

Equivalent weight of $Na_2S_2O_3 = \frac{M}{1}$

n-factor for $I_2 = 2 \times 1 = 2$

Therefore equivalent weight of $I_2 = \frac{M_2}{2}$

6. (c) Molarity of H_2O_2

$= \frac{\text{V strength of } H_2O_2 \times 2}{22.4}$

$= \frac{10 \times 2}{22.4} = 0.89$ M

$KMnO_4 + 5H_2O_2 + 6H^+ \rightarrow Mn^{2+} + 5O_2 + 8H_2O$

$M_1V_1 = M_2V_2 \times \frac{2}{5}$

$0.4 \times 200 = 0.89 \times V_2 \times \frac{2}{5}$

$V_2 = \frac{0.4 \times 200 \times 5}{0.89 \times 2}$

$= 224.7 \approx 224$ ml H_2O_2 required

7. (a)

$\overset{0}{Br_2}(l) + \overset{+4}{SO_3^{2-}}(aq) + H_2O \longrightarrow Br^- + \overset{+6}{SO_4^{2-}} + H^+$

8. (b)

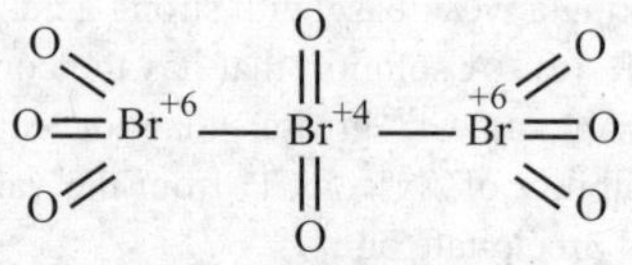

Br_3O_8.

9. (a) In alkali and alkaline earth metal hydride oxidation state of hydrogen atom is –1.

10. (b) On balancing, we get

$S_8 + 12OH^- \longrightarrow 4S^{2-} + 2S_2O_3^{2-} + 6H_2O$

Ratio of c and d = 2:1

11. (b) $2KO_2 + 2H_2O \rightarrow$

$2K^+ + 2\,OH + H_2O_2 + O_2\uparrow$

$2KMnO_4 \xrightarrow[\text{basic medium}]{3H_2O_2}$

$2MnO_2 + 3O_2 + 2KOH + 2H_2O$

$\therefore$ X = O_2; Y = MnO_2.

12. (b) H_3PO_2, HNO_2, H_2O_2 can undergo disproportionation reaction.

13. (c) Chlorine nitrate is ($ClONO_2$)

$ClONO_2 + H_2O \longrightarrow \underset{(X)}{HOCl} + \underset{(Y)}{HNO_3}$

Oxidation state of Cl in HOCl ⇒ x – 1 ⇒ x = + 1

Oxidation state of N in HNO_3 ⇒ x + 1 – 6

⇒ x = + 5. So, answer is +1, +5

14. (c) Balancing the disproportionation of S_8 in basic medium. The balanced equation is:

$S_8 + 12OH^- \longrightarrow 4S^{2-} + 2S_2O_3^{2-} + 6H_2O$

So, a = 1, b = 12, c = 4, d = 2, e = 6

(I) a + b = 1 + 12 = 13 ; c + d + e + 1 = 4 + 2 + 6 + 1 = 13 (Correct)

(II) b = 12 ; 2e + d = 2 (6) + 2 = 14 (Incorrect)

(III) b – a = 12 – 1 = 11;

c + e + 1 = 4 + 6 + 1 = 11 (Correct)

(IV) b + d = 12 + 2 = 14;

2c + e – 1 = 2(4) + 6 – 1 = 13 (Incorrect)

So, option (c) I, III is correct relation.

15. (b) Acidic medium :

$2MnO_4^- + 6H^+ + 5H_2O_2 \rightarrow 2Mn^{2+} + 8H_2O + 5O_2$ (x)

Basic medium :

$2MnO_4^- + 3H_2O_2 \rightarrow$

$2MnO_2 + 3O_2 + 2H_2O + 2OH^-$ (y).

16. (a) In acidic medium

$2MnO_4^- + 6H^+ + 5H_2O_2 \rightarrow 2Mn^{2+} + 8H_2O + 5O_2$ (x)

In basic medium,

$2MnO_4^- + 3H_2O_2 \rightarrow 2MnO_2 + 3O_2 + 2H_2O + OH^-$ (y)

Oxidation state *x* is = +2

Oxidation state *y* is = +4

17. (a) Higher the reduction potential less in the tendency to liberate H_2 gas.

18. (a) Both statement I and II are correct.

19. (a) Orthophosphorous acid on heating disproportionate to give orthophosphoric acid and phosphine.

$4H_3PO_3 \xrightarrow{\Delta} 3H_3PO_4 + PH_3$

20. (b) $2KMnO_4 + H_2O + KI \rightarrow$

$2MnO_2 + 2KOH + KIO_3$

⇒ 1 mole of I^- requires 2 moles of MnO_4^-.

Now, number of moles of 1L × 0.5 M = 0.5 mol.

⇒ Number of moles of MnO_4^- required = 2 × 0.5 = 1.0 mol.

⇒ Volume = $\frac{n}{M} = \frac{1.0}{0.02} = 50$ L

21. (d) $2KMnO_4 + H_2O + KI \rightarrow$

$2MnO_2 + 2KOH + KIO_3$.

Thus, according to the balanced equation, 1 mole of KI or I^- requires 2 moles of $KMnO_4$ or MnO_4^-. Therefore, 1 × 0.5 = 0.5 moles of I^- would require 2 × 0.5 = 1.0 moles of $KMnO_4$.

22. (d) The balanced equation is :-

$P_4(s) + 3OH^-(aq) + H_2O(l) \rightarrow$

$PH_3(g) + 3H_2PO_2^-(aq.)$

Thus, a = 1, b = 3, c = 1 and d = 3

23. **(d)** The balanced chemical equation is :-

$6\,Fe^{2+}(aq.) + 14\,H^+(aq.) + Cr_2O_7^{2-}(aq.) \rightarrow$

$7\,H_2O\,(l) + 6\,Fe^{3+}(aq.) + 2\,Cr^{3+}(aq.)$

Thus, x = 6, y = 14 and z = 1

24. **(a)** The balanced equation is:-

$S_8(s) + 12\,OH^-(aq.) \rightarrow$

$4S^{2-}(aq) + 2S_2O_3^{2-}(aq) + 6\,H_2O\,(l)$

Thus, x = 1, y = 12 and z = 4

25. **(a)** In the given reaction, Cl_2 is getting disproportionated into +1 state in ClO^- and –1 state in Cl^-.

Cl_2 to ClO^- is oxidation while Cl_2 to Cl^- is reduction.

26. **(d)** $\overset{0}{Cl_2} \longrightarrow \overset{-1}{Cl^-} + Cl\,O_3$ (Reduction: $Cl_2 \rightarrow Cl^-$; Oxidation: $Cl_2 \rightarrow ClO_3$)

(i) Displacement reaction,
(ii) Disproportionation reaction
(iii) Combination reaction
(iv) Decomposition reaction

27. **(a)**

$CaCO_3 \xrightarrow{\Delta} CaO + CO_2$ (Decomposition reaction).

28. **(a)**

$\overset{0}{P_4} + 3NaOH + 3H_2O \longrightarrow \overset{-3}{PH_3} + 3Na\overset{+1}{H_2PO_2}$

$\overset{0}{S_8} + 12NaOH \longrightarrow 4Na_2\overset{-2}{S} + 2Na_2S_2O_3 + 6H_2O$

Structure of $S_2O_3^{2-}$: 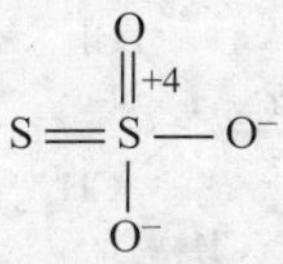

29. **(d)** In disproportionation reaction a species simultaneously undergo reduction and oxidation to form two different products.

In ClO_4^-, chlorine is present in its highest oxidation state +7 and cannot further undergo oxidation.

30. **(c)** Potassium chlorate disproportionate into potassium perchlorate and potassium chloride at higher temperature.

$4K\overset{(+5)}{ClO_3} \rightarrow 3K\overset{(-7)}{ClO_4} + K\overset{(-1)}{Cl}$

31. **(d)** Disproportionation is a type of redox reaction on which a species simultaneously undergoes reduction and oxidation to form two different products.

In ClO_4^- chlorine cannot undergo oxidation

32. **(b)** Highest E° values → stronger oxidising agent and vice-versa.

∴ Oxidising Power : Z > Y > X

33. **(d)** $I_2(s) + 2KBr(aq) \rightarrow$ No reaction because halogen having lower atomic number cannot oxidise a halide of higher atomic number.

34. **(d)** Standard electrode potential

E° (in volts)

Li^+/Li – 3.05

Na^+/Na – 2.71

K^+/K – 2.93

Rb^+/Rb – 2.92

Cs^+/Cs – 2.92

Lithium has the most negative standard potential while sodium has the lowest negative standard potential.

35. **(b)** The greater the negative value of the reduction potential value in the electrochemical series, the greater will be the tendency to act as a reducing agent that means it can reduce other element whose value is high.

Zn^{2+}/Zn – 0.76 V

$2H^+/H_2$ 0 V

Cu^{2+}/Cu 0.34 V

$NO_3^-, H^+/NO$ 0.97 V

Zinc acts as a good reducing agent than copper. This implies that zinc can reduce copper.

$2H^+/H_2$ cannot oxides Cu/Cu^{2+} because it have lower reduction potential than copper.

NO_3^- have high reduction potential it can oxides copper.

36. **(a)** The tendency of an element to lose an electron is measured by its oxidation potential more the value of E° of an element stronger will be its reducing character.

The alkali metals have a low value of ionization energy which decreases down the group and so can easily lose their valence electrons and thus act as good reducing agent.

So, Rb is the strongest reducing agent.

37. **(d)**

(a) Tl in +1 oxidation state is more stable than +3 oxidation state because of inert pair effect therefore Tl^{3+} salts are oxidising agents.

(b) Ga^+ is a reducing agent because it is more stable in +3 O.S.

(c) Pb^{2+} is more stable than Pb^{4+} hence Pb^{4+} is an oxidising agent.

(d) $As^{5+} + 2e^- \rightarrow As^{3+}$ (Less stable)

Thus, As cannot be reduced easily hence, it is not a good oxidising agent.

An oxidising agent is defined as substance whose oxidation number decreases while reducing agent defined as substance whose oxidation number increases.

8 Organic Chemistry—Some Basic Principles & Techniques

1. (d) 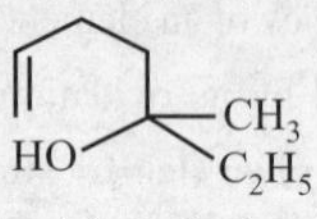

3-methylhept 6-en-3-ol

2. (a) 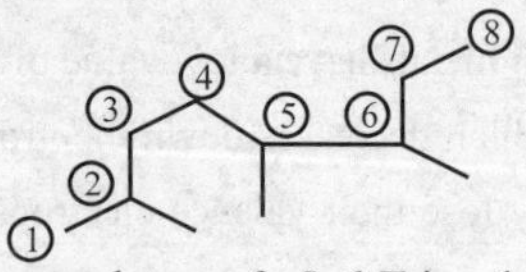

IUPAC nomenclature : 2, 5, 6-Trimethyloctane.

3. (b) 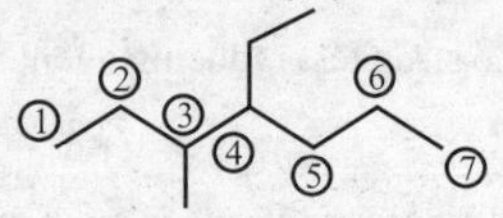 (X)

3-Methyl-4-ethyl heptane

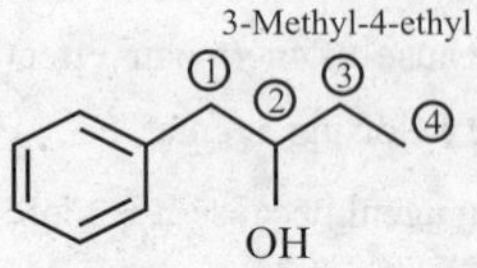

1-phenyl butan-2-ol

4. (d) 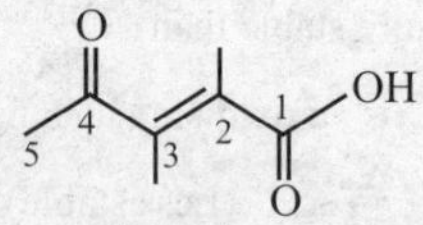

The IUPAC name of the following compound is: 2, 3-Dimethyl-4-oxopent-2-enoic acid.

Main functional group in carboxylic acid not ketone according to preference order.

5. (c)

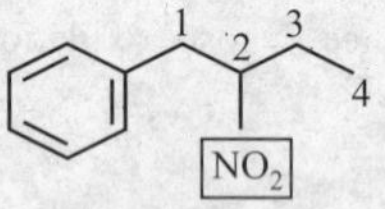

2-Nitro-1-phenylbutane

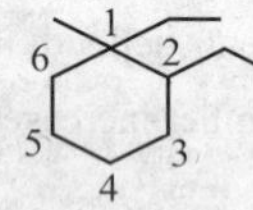

1-ethyl-1-methyl-2-Propylcyclohexane

6. (b) 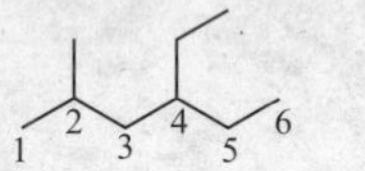

4-Ethyl-2-methylhexane.

7. (a) **Mesityl oxide**

$$H_3C-C=CH-\overset{\overset{O}{\|}}{C}-CH_3$$
$$\quad\;\; |$$
$$\quad\;\; CH_3$$

Oxalic acid

COOH
|
COOH

Ethanedioic acid

4-methylpent-3-en-2-one

8. (c) Priority order of functional group of organic compounds in the IUPAC nomenclature is

$-COCl > -CONH_2 > -CHO > -OH$

9. (c) 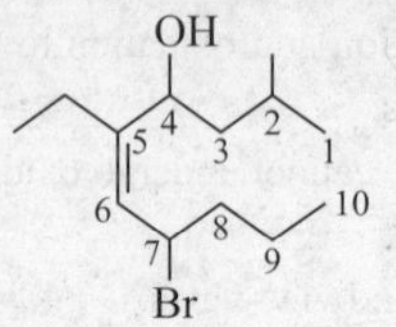

7-Bromo-5-ethyl-2-methyldec-5-ene-4-ol

10. (d) 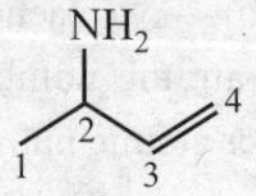

But-3-en-2-amine

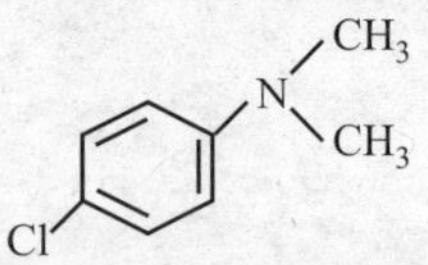

4-Chloro-N.N-dimethyl benzenamine

11. (b) (2)

$CH_3\ddot{N}H_2$ having lone pair on the nitrogen that can be donated. So it is a good nucleophile.

$CH_3\ddot{S}H$ has sulfur. Sulfur is much larger atom than nitrogen and has more electron pairs. So it can act as nucleophile.

12. (b) Tropolone is a non-benzenoid aromatic compound, its structure is:

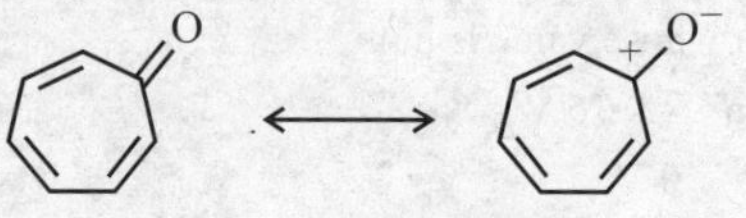

Aromatic compound ($6\pi e^-$)

13. (c) $-NO_2$ and $-Cl$ are written as prefixes with $-CH_3$ being given the highest preference for numbering (C – 1).

Thus, the name of the compound will be 2-chloro-1-methyl-4-nitrobenzene.

14. (a) The correct priority order is:

$-COOH > -SO_3H > -CN > -CHO > -OH$

15. (d)

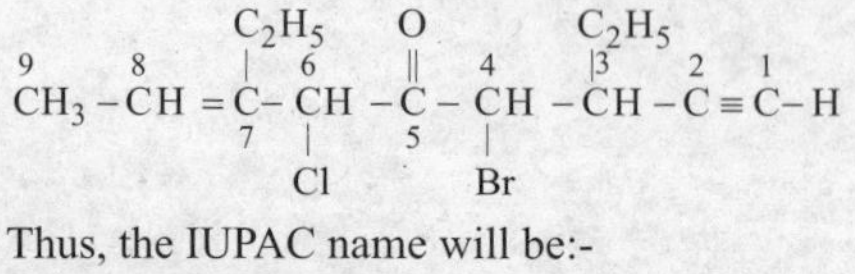

Thus, the IUPAC name will be:-

4-Bromo-6- chloro-3, 7- diethylnon-7-. en-l-yn-5- one

16. (b)

Priority order : $-OH > -NH_2 > -CH_3$

IUPAC name : 3-Amino-5-methylphenol

17. (d) 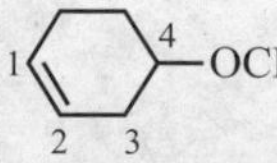

4-Methoxycyclohexene

18. (b) 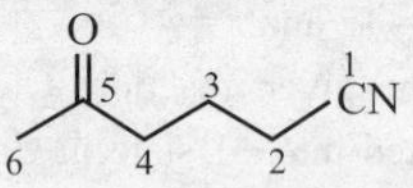

5-Oxohexanenitrile

19. (d) The general formula for this series is C_nH_{2n-2}. Hence, $C_6H_{10}O_2N$ belongs to the given homologous series.

20. (a) 2, 7-dimethyl-3, 5 - nonadiene

21. (b) 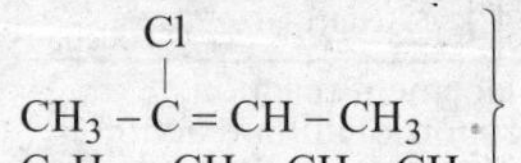

Both exhibits cis trans isomerism

22. (d) Compound showing geometrical isomerism must have double bond and carbon atom of double bond must be attached with different groups.

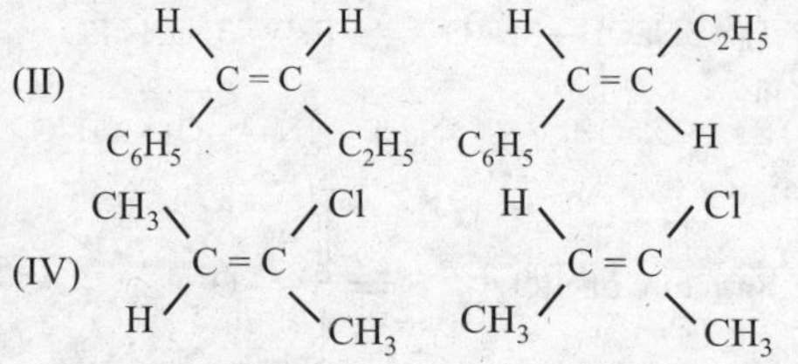

23. (c) 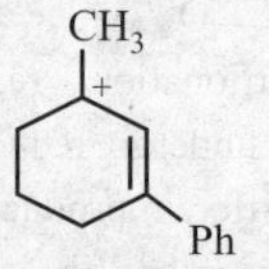

This compound is more stable as compared to other due to resonance and hyper conjugation.

24. (c) For $C_5H_{12}O$

Primary alcohols

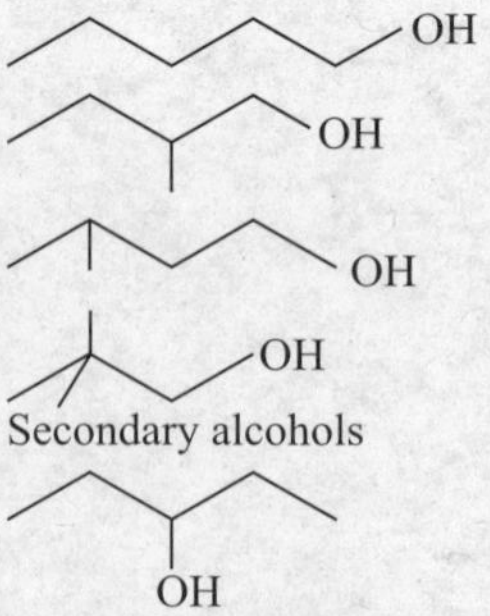

Secondary alcohols

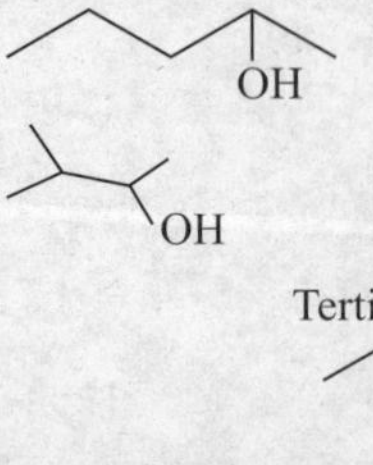

Tertiary alcohols

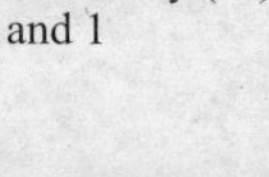

So primary (1°), secondary (2°) and tertiary (3°) alcohols are 4, 3 and 1

25. (b) Molecular weight of dibromo derivative = 186u

2 Br = 160

alkene = 26, i.e., C_2H_2 (24 + 2)

Possible structures will be

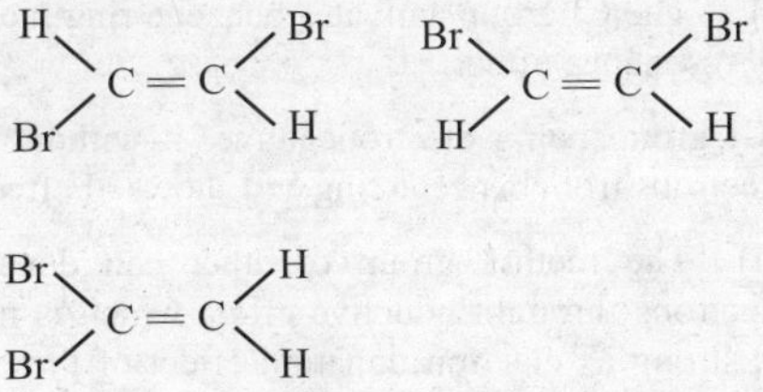

26. (d)

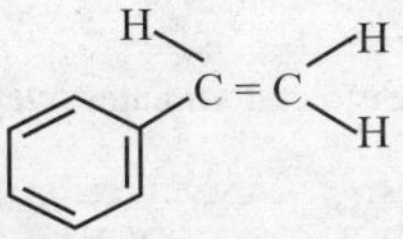

Styrene does not exhibit geometrical isomerism as it has three identical groups (H-atoms) on the doubly-bonded carbon atoms.

27. (b)

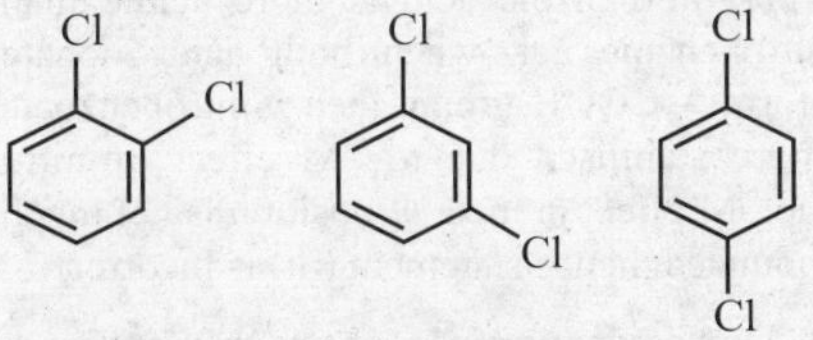

28. (d) D > B > A > C

Stability order for carbocations = 3° > 2° > 1° > methyl – o being EDG, donates its e^- density to C^+ making it stable.

29. (c) $BaSO_4 = 137 + 32 + 64 = 233$ g/mol

233g of $BaSO_4$ contains 32g of S

So in 0.233 g of $BaSO_4 = \frac{32}{233} \times 0.233 = 0.032$ g

$$\% S = \frac{\text{mass of sulphur}}{\text{mass of organic compound}} \times 100$$

$$8.89 = \frac{0.032}{x} \times 100$$

$$x = \frac{3.2}{8.89} \approx 0.36\text{g}$$

30. (b) Milliequivalents of HCl = Normality × Vol. in ml = 1 × 30 = 30 meq.

Milliequivalents of unreacted HCl which is neutralized by NaOH.

Meq. of NaOH = 0.1 × 120 = 12 Meq.

Milliequivalents of HCl neutralized by NH_3

= Total Meq. of HCl - Meq. of unreacted HCl

= 30 – 12 = 18

$$\% \text{ of N} = \frac{1.4 \times (\text{Meq of acid neutralized by } NH_3)}{\text{Mass of org. compound (g)}}$$

$$\% \text{ of N} = \frac{1.4 \times 18}{1.5}$$

= 16.8%

31. (b) Two liquids with large difference in their boiling points can be separated by simple distillation while two liquids with less difference in their boiling points can be separated by fractional distillation.

32. (d) (I) $CH_3–CH = CH–CH_3$(But-2-ene)

The σ electrons of the alpha carbon-hydrogen bonds overlap with π* orbital of the double bond. This is called hyperconjugation ⟶ Belongs to X.

(II) 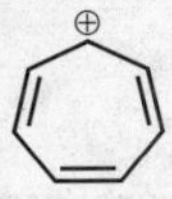

Tropylium Cation

highly stable aromatic ring belongs to Y.

(III) 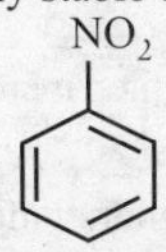

NO_2 group conjugates directly with the benzene ring, delocalizing π-electrons out of the ring through resonance belongs to Y.

(IV) 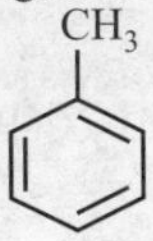

Show hyperconjugation, belongs to X

33. (c) This is ammonium phosphomolybdate test used for the identification of phosphorus.

34. (c) Kjeldhal's method converts organic nitrogen to NH_3/ $(NH_4)_2$ SO_4. It fails for compound with N = N, aromatic ring N directly bonded to the ring, and nitro groups since that nitrogen is not converted efficiently to ammonium sulphate.

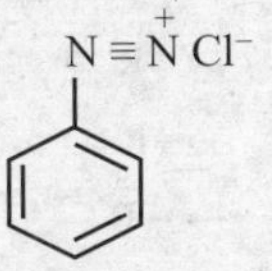

Benzene dizonium chloride (Not suitable)

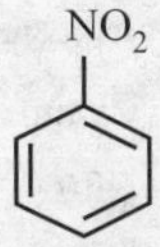

Nitrobenzene (Not suitable)

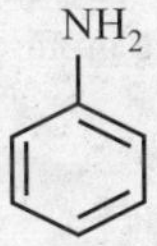

Amino benzne (Suitable)

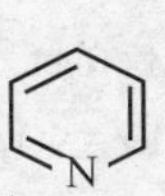

Pyridine (Not suitable)

35. (c) % of phosphorus by Carius method:

Molar mass of Mg_2 P_2 O_7 : 2 (24) + 2 (31) + 7 (16) = 222 g/mol

No. of moles of Mg_2 P_2 $O_7 = \frac{0.444}{222} = 0.002$ mol

Each mole of Mg_2 P_2O_7 contains 2 mole of P. So, no. of moles of P is 0.002 × 2 = 0.004 mol

Mass of P = 0.004 × 31 = 0.124 g

$$\% \text{ of P} = \frac{\text{Mass of P}}{\text{Mass of organic compound}} \times 100$$

$$\% \text{ of P} = \frac{0.124}{0.248} \times 100 = 50\%$$

36. (c) Hyperconjugative effect in Toluene:

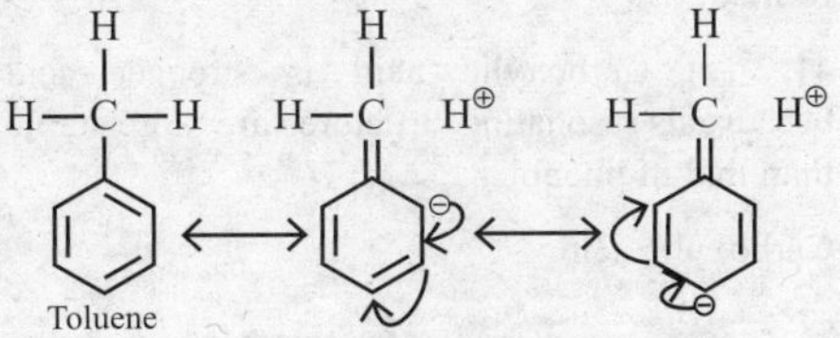

Toluene

Resonance effect in nitro benzene:

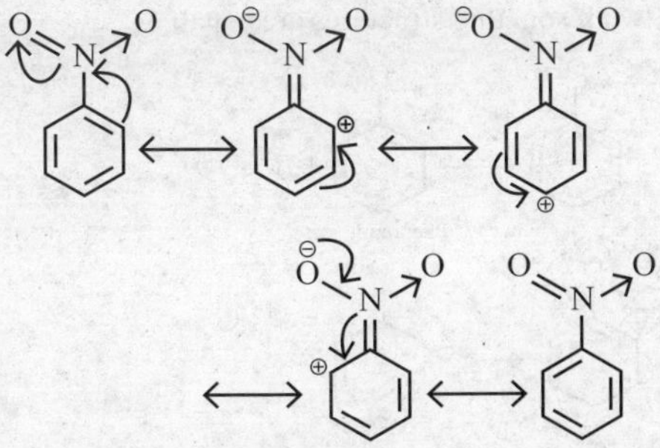

37. (a) % of nitrogen = 56.

Let volume of NaOH V_1 and volume of H_2SO_4V

$$\% \text{ of Nitrogen} = \frac{1.4 \times M \times 2\left(V - \frac{V_1}{2}\right)}{X}$$

$$= \frac{1.4 \times 0.5 \times 2\left(50 - \frac{60}{2}\right)}{x}$$

$$x = \frac{1.4 \times 0.5 \times 2(20)}{56}$$

= 0.5 g = 500 mg

Thus $x = 500$

38. (b) Carius method us for halogen, sulphur phosphorous.

39. (c) Distillation under reduced pressure also known as vacuum distillation is a process used to separate liquids with high boiling points or those that decompose at or below their boiling points. Under the conditions of reduced pressure, the liquid will boil at a temperature lower than its boiling point and as a result the liquids will not degrade as they would otherwise.

40. (a)

$$CH_3 - CH_2 - I \longrightarrow CH_3 - \overset{+}{C}H_2 + I^-$$

Iodine is good living group so it generate the carbocation.

$$CH_3 - CH_2 - Cu \longrightarrow CH_3 - \overset{\ominus}{C}H_2 + Cu^+$$

Here, Cu is giving electron to the carbon atom so it acts as a reducing agent. So a carbanion is formed.

41. (a) Carboxylic acid is stronger acid because its resonating structures are more stable than that of phenol.

Carboxylic acid

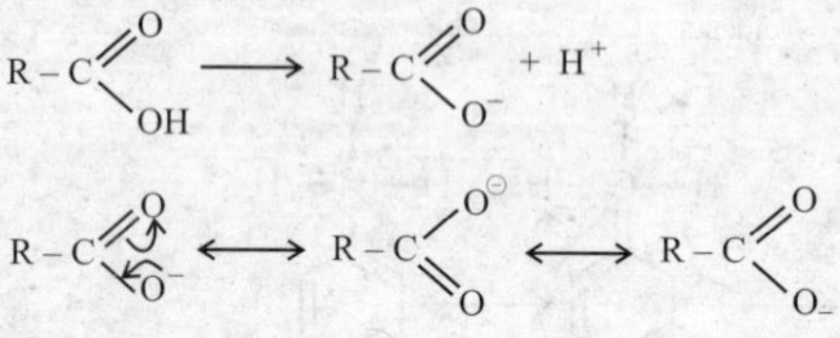

Carboxylate ions are stable. The negative charge is on more electronegative oxygen atom and its two resonating structures are equal.

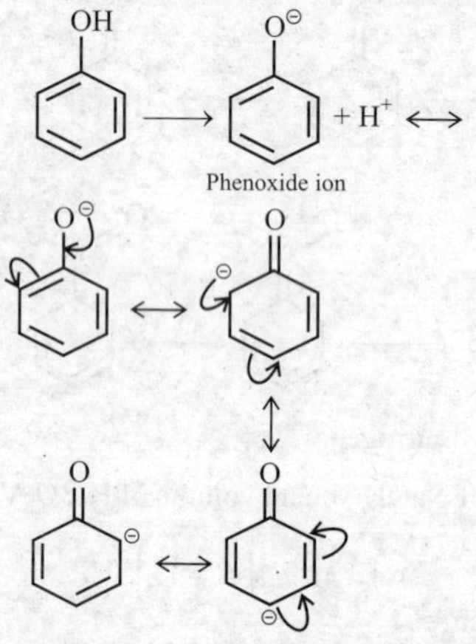

Negative charge is on carbon which leads to less stability of phenoxide than carboxylate ion.

Moreover, its resonating structures are not equivalent.

42. (b) Acidity $\propto$ Electron withdrawing group.

(IV) Nitro group in *p*-position exhibits negative mesomeric effect (–M) which attracts electrons and thus it makes phenoxide

ion 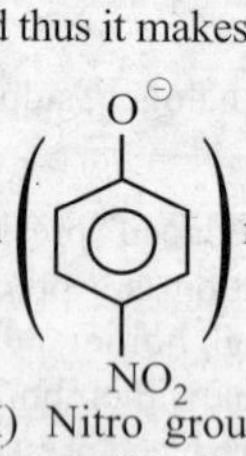 more stable.

(III) Nitro group in meta position withdraws electron density by negative inductive effect which makes phenoxide ion less stable than (IV)

(II) Methyl group is in para position it donates electrons which destabilizes the phenoxide ion, so it is less acidic.

Acidic order :- (IV) > (III) > (I) > (II).

43. (b) Those groups which withdraw electron density from the benzene ring and makes the benzene ring less reactive towards electrophilic substitution reactions. Such groups are called deactivating groups.

Thus the three deactivating groups are

$-Cl$, $-\overset{O}{\overset{\|}{\underset{\underset{O}{\|}}{S}}}-OH$, $-\overset{O}{\overset{\|}{C}}-OCH_3$

Due to (–I effect) (–M effect) (–M effect)

44. (b) Basicity $\propto$ + I effect

$\propto$ + M effect

(B) In B, nitrogen lone pair is not part of conjugation, it is more easily available for donation so it is more basic.

(A) $-OCH_3$ group is +M group which increases the basicity of nitrogen.

(C) $-NO_2$ group is electron withdrawing (–I effect) and also shows –M effect.

Thus the decreasing order of basicity is

$$B > A > C$$

45. (b) The degree of adsorption of A is smallest, so it will come out first followed by C, B and then D.

46. (c) Negative resonance (–R): A group which withdraws electron density from a conjugated system.

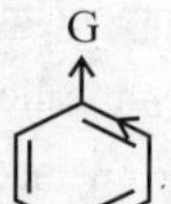

(A) Formyl $\rightarrow -\overset{O}{\overset{\|}{C}}-H \rightarrow -R$

(B) Amino $\rightarrow NH_2 \rightarrow +R$

(C) Alkoxy $\rightarrow -OR \rightarrow +R$

(D) Cyano $\rightarrow -CN \rightarrow -R$

(E) Nitro $\rightarrow -NO_2 \rightarrow -R$

$\therefore$ A, D, E group Show – R effect.

47. (b)

Acidity $\propto$ Electron withdrawing group

$\propto$ –M effect

–M effect order $-NO_2 > -CN > -F$

So, order of acidity: C > A > B

48. (b) The stability of free radicals follows the order:-

$CH_2=\dot{C}H < \dot{C}H_3 < 1° < 2° < 3°$

Thus, stability order will be :-

iv > iii > ii > i.

49. (d)

$H_3C-C_{sp}\equiv N$, $H_2C=CH-CH=CH_2$, $H_2C=C_{sp}=CH_2$

$HC_{sp}\equiv C_{sp}H$, 

50. (c) Order of stability of conjugate base: I > II > II Greater the stability of conjugate base higher is the acidity.

+I and +R effects of $-CH_3$, $-OCH_3$, respectively destabilize the conjugate base.

51. (c) If a compound contains both nitrogen and sulphur, then they are converted to sodium thiocyanate (NaCNS).

52. (b)

(i) The Cl group activates benzene ring more by resonance effect.

–Cl group being electronegative, it withdraws electrons from benzene ring and shows –I effect.

(ii) The methyl group of ether can donate electrons through inductive effect which is not as strong as electron donation effect of the pi-system.

Thus, resonance effect dominates over inductive effect in anisole.

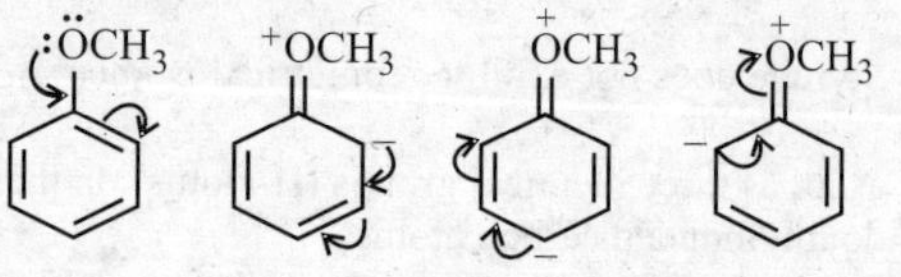

(iii) *p*-Nitorbenzoic acid is more acidic than m-nitrobenzoic aci. when both acids donate H^+ form —COOH group, then *p*-nitrobenzoate is more stabilised due to –M effect of nitro group –M effect in meta *m*-position is not much pronounced, hence statement (iii) is incorrect.

(iv) Diphenylamine is less basic than aniline.

The lone pair of electron on the N-atom in diphenylamine is delocalised on two benzene rings due to which it is less available to donate resulting into decrease in basicity. In aniline, it is delocalised on one benzene ring, so lone pair is more available for donation. Hence, it is more basic.

53. (c) 25 mL of 1M H_2SO_4 corresponds to 25 mili mol.

It will neutralise 50 mili mol of NH_3.

Weight of N in $NH_3 = 14 \times 50 \times 10^{-3}$ g = 0.70 g

Thus 1 g of sample of organic compound contains 0.70 g of nitrogen.

% of nitrogen in organic sample is $\frac{0.70}{1} \times 100 = 70\%$.

54. (a) Hyperconjugation is the delocalisation of σ electron with adjacent *p*-orbital.

It helps in explaining stability order of free radicals, carbocations and alkenes but cannot explain stability of carbanion due to absence of vacant π or *p*-orbitals.

55. (c) Fractional distillation is used for the separation of a mixture of miscible liquids for which the difference in boiling points is very small (less than 25°C).

56. (d) Conc. HNO_3 is used to remove NaCN(X) and Na_2S (Y) so that they do not interfere with the test for halogen.

$NaCN + HNO_3 \xrightarrow{boil} NaNO_3 + HCN\uparrow$

$Na_2S + 2HNO_3 \longrightarrow 2NaNO_3 + H_2S\uparrow$

57. (d) Lassaigne test

$$Na_2S \xrightarrow{(CH_3COO)_2Pb} \underset{\text{Black}}{PbS\downarrow} + 2CH_3COONa$$

58. (N)

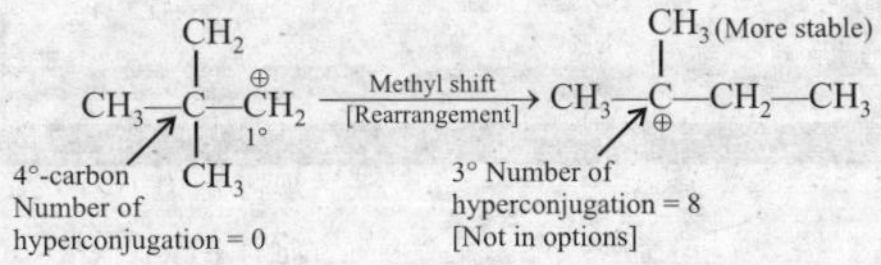

59. (a) The groups in which nitrogen contain double bond or present in heterocyclic ring can not be estimated by Kjeldahl's method, viz. $C_6H_5-\underset{\underset{O}{\|}}{N}\rightarrow O$, $C_6H_5-N=N-C_6H_5$ and pyridine.

Nitrogen in aniline does not contain double bond, it so estimated by Kjeldahl's method.

60. (d) No bond resonance is a special case of resonance in which delocalization of sigma electron or orbital containg lone pair of electron with adjacent p-orbital. It is also called hyperconjugation.

More the H-atoms associated (bonded) with C-atom, which is bonded with the benzene ring, more will be the number of **'no bond resonance' hyperconjugation.**

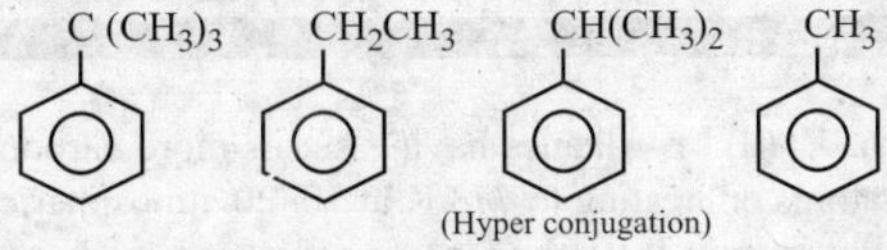

(Hyper conjugation)

Number of hyperconjugative –H

61. (a) $\frac{p_1V_1}{T_1} = \frac{p_2V_2}{T_2}$

$$\Rightarrow \frac{725\times 50}{300} = \frac{760\times V_2}{273}$$

$$\Rightarrow V_2 = \frac{725\times 50\times 273}{300\times 760} = 43.4 \text{ mL}$$

$$\Rightarrow 22400 \text{ mL of } N_2 \equiv 28 \text{ g of } N_2 \text{ at STP}$$

$$\Rightarrow 43.4\text{mL of}N_2 \equiv \frac{28\times 43.4}{22400} = 0.054 \text{ g of } N_2$$

$$\% \text{ mass of } N_2 = \frac{0.054 \text{ g}}{1 \text{ g}}\times 100 = 5.4\%.$$

62. (d) Carbon monoxide is estimated using I_2O_5 as per the following reaction:

$$I_2O_5 + 5CO \longrightarrow \underset{\text{Violet}}{I_2} + 5CO_2$$

63. (d)

(i) Electromeric effect is a temporary effect, it takes place only in the prescence of reagent.

(ii) Hyperconjugation is a permanent effect which allows delocalisation of sigma electrons to adjacent carbon.

64. (b) % of nitrogen at STP = $\frac{28V\times 100}{22400\times W}$

V = 45 ml, W = 0.3

$$\% \text{ of Nitrogen} = \frac{28\times 45\times 100}{22400\times 0.3} = 18.75\%$$

9 Hydrocarbons

1. **(b)** $CH_3-CH-CH_2-CH_3$ with CH_3 on the CH

Total structurally distinct monochloro derivatives (x) = 4

$CH_3-C(CH_3)_2-CH_3$

Total structurally distinct monochloro derivatives (y) = 1

$(CH_3)_2CH-CH(CH_3)_2$ Total structurally distinct monochloro derivatives (z) = 2

Calculate the sum = x + y + z = 4 + 1 + 2 = 7

2. **(c)** I. Staggered conformation have less torsional strain than eclipsed

II. $H_3C-CH_2-C(CH_3)_2-CH_3$

$H_3C-CH_2-CH_2-CH(CH_3)-CH_3$

High branching have less boiling point.

3. **(d)**

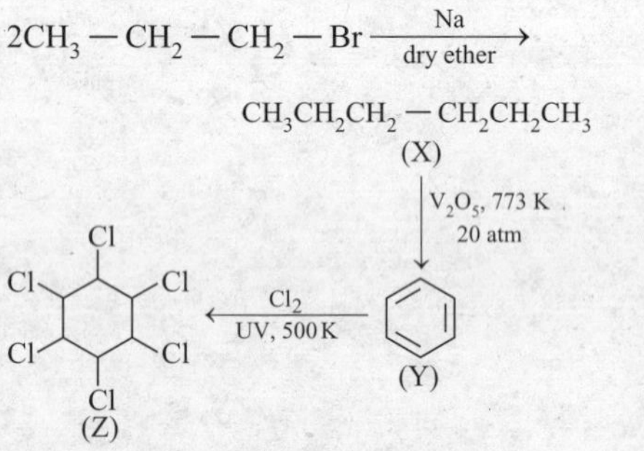

Z = Benzene Hexachloride = $C_6H_6Cl_6$

⇒ Empirical Formula = CHCl

⇒ Empirical Formula mass = 12 + 1 + 35.5 = 48.54

4. **(d)** Kolbe's electrolysis of sodium propionate gives *n*-butane as a product

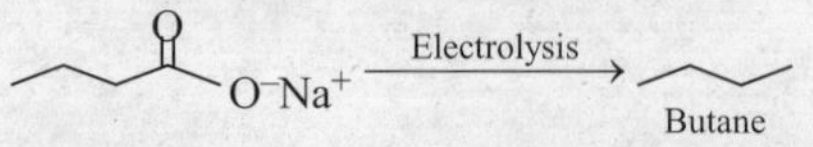

So statement-I is incorrect but statement-II is correct.

5. **(a)** Anhy. $AlCl_3/HCl$ is used for the isomerisation of *n*-alkanes to branched chain alkane.

6. **(d)** n-Alkanes having six or more carbon atoms on heating to 773 K at 10–20 atmospheric pressure in the presence of oxides of vanadium, molybdenum or chromium supported over alumina get dehydrogenated and cyclised to benzene and its homologues. The reaction is known as aromatization or reforming.

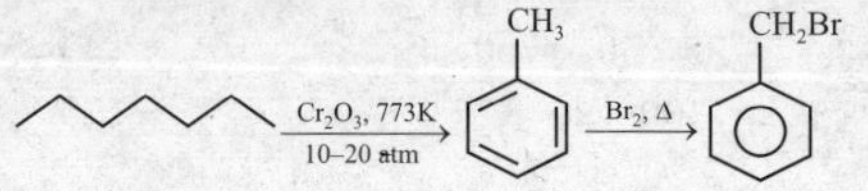

7. **(c)** $2CH_3CH_2COO\bar{O}\overset{+}{Na}\xrightarrow[2H_2O]{\text{electrolysis}}$

$CH_3CH_2-CH_2CH_3+2CO_2+H_2+2NaOH$

At anode (oxidation):

$2CH_3CH_2-\overset{O}{\overset{\|}{C}}-O^-\xrightarrow{2e^-}2CH_3\dot{C}H_2+2CO_2$

$CH_3\dot{C}H_2+CH_3\dot{C}H_2\rightarrow CH_3CH_2CH_2CH_3$

Butane (X)

At cathode (reduction):

$2H_2O\rightarrow 2OH^-+2H^+$

$2H^++2e^-\rightarrow 2H^\bullet\rightarrow H_2\ (Y)$

$2Na^++2OH^-\rightarrow 2NaOH$

8. **(b)**

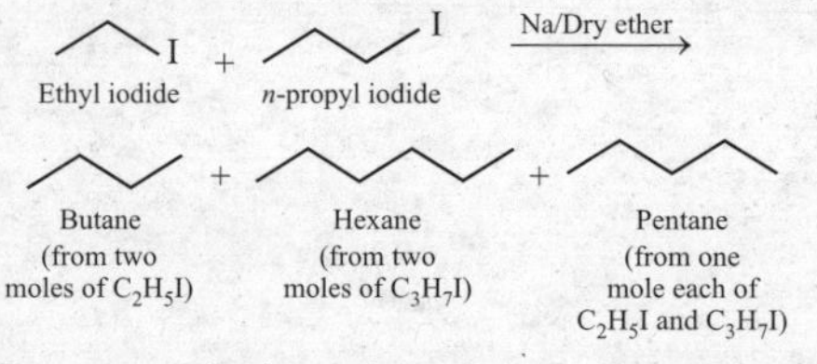

9. **(a)** Final product C_4H_8 (alkene) is an isomer of non-polar alkene which indicates it to be *trans*-2-butene. Further *trans*-2-butene is formed by the redcution of *Y* with *Z*, so *Y* is butyne-2 and *Z* is Na/liquid NH_3. So the complete set of reactions can be represented as

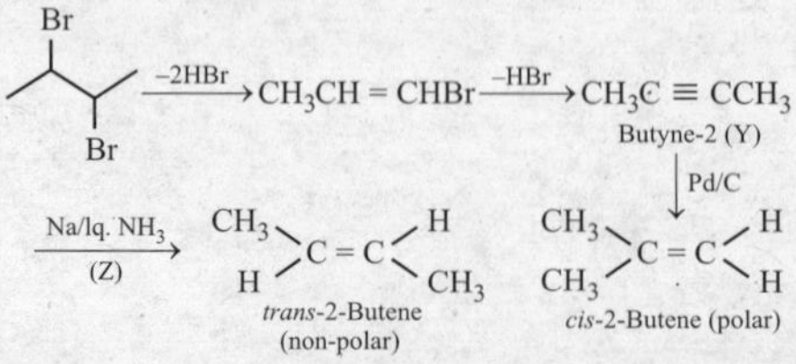

Note that reduction of butyne-2 (Y) with Pd/C will give *cis*-2-butene (polar isomer of trans-2-butene).

10. **(b)**

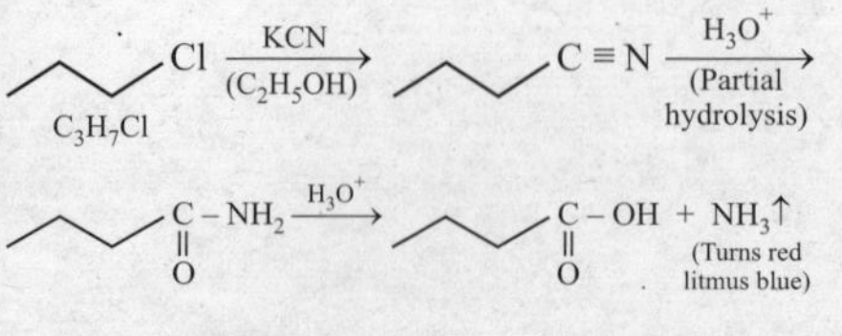

11. **(d)** $2CH_3-CH_3+3O_2\xrightarrow[\Delta]{(CH_3COO)_2Mn}2CH_3COOH+2H_2O$ (Q)

12. **(a)** Boiling point of isomeric alkanes decreases with increasing branching due to a decrease in the exposed surface area that leads to weaker van der Waal forces.

Thus, the order will be :-

$CH_3-(CH_2)_4-CH_3>CH_3-CH(CH_3)-CH_2-CH_2-CH_3>CH_3-CH(CH_3)-CH(CH_3)-CH_3$
(i) (ii) (iii)

13. **(c)**

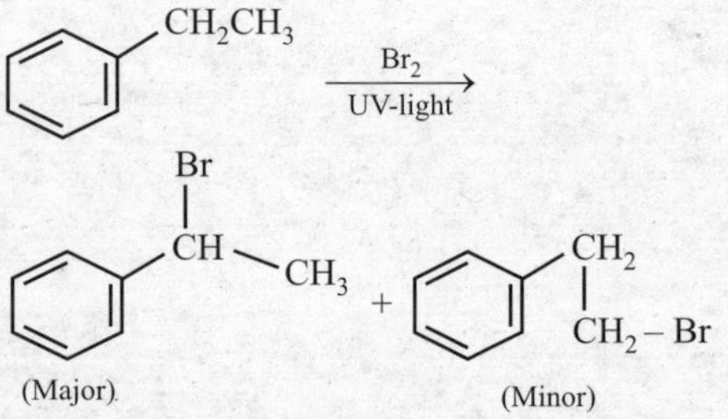

14. **(a)** It is an example of Wurtz reaction which is used for synthesizing alkanes of even no. of carbon atoms.

$\overset{3}{CH_3}-\overset{2}{CH}(CH_3)-\overset{1}{CH_2}-Br+Br-CH_2-CH(CH_3)-CH_3$

1-Bromo-2 methylpropane

↓ Na/Dry ether

$CH_3-CH(CH_3)CH_2CH_2CH(CH_3)-CH_3$

15. **(d)** $CH_4+I_2\rightleftharpoons CH_3I+HI$

Reaction between methane and iodine is reversible, because HI is a reducing agent and it reduces methyl iode back to methane, therefore HNO_3 (a strong oxidising agent) is used to decompose HI into I_2.

$2HNO_3+2HI\rightarrow 2NO_2+2H_2O+I_2$

16. **(c)** Kolbe's electrolysis

$2CH_3COONa+2H_2O\rightarrow CH_3-CH_3+2CO_2+2NaOH+H_2$

Reaction at anode :

$2CH_3CO\dot{O}\longrightarrow 2\dot{C}H_3+2CO_2$

$2\dot{C}H_3\longrightarrow C_2H_6$

$\dot{C}H_3$ radical is produced at anode, not cathode. (consult Q. 2)

17. (b) $CH_3 — CH_2 — Br + 2Na + Br — CH_2 — CH_3 \rightarrow$

$$CH_3 — CH_2 — CH_2 — CH_3 + 2NaBr$$

n- Butane can also be obtained when sodium salt of pentanoic acid (*X*) is heated with sodalime.

$$\underset{(x)}{CH_3(CH_2)_3COOH} \xrightarrow{NaOH} \underset{\text{Sodium salt of pentanoic acid}}{CH_3CH_2CH_2CH_2COONa} \xrightarrow{NaOH + CaO(\text{Sada lime})} \underset{n\text{-Butane}}{CH_3CH_2CH_2CH_3} + Na_2CO_3$$

18. (b) Kolbe electrolysis of $CH_3COO^-Na^+$.

At anode,

$$CH_3 — \overset{O}{\overset{||}{C}} — O^- \longrightarrow CH_3 — \overset{O}{\overset{||}{C}} — O^\bullet + e^-$$

$$CH_3 — \overset{O}{\overset{||}{C}} — O^\bullet \longrightarrow CO_2\uparrow + \underset{(A)}{\dot{C}H_3}$$

$$^\bullet CH_3 + {}^\bullet CH_3 \longrightarrow \underset{(B)}{H_3C - CH_3}\uparrow$$

$$\underset{(B)}{CH_3 - CH_3} + 5O_2 \xrightarrow{(CH_3COO)_2Mn} \underset{(C)}{2CO} + \underset{(D)}{3H_2O}$$

$$\underset{(C)}{CO} + NaOH \rightleftharpoons \underset{(\text{Salt})}{HCOONa}$$

Hence, *A* is CO_2 and *D* is H_2O.

19. (c)

(i) Petrol and CNG operated automobiles cause less pollution.

(ii)
$$R - \overset{R}{\underset{R}{C}} - H \xrightarrow{KMnO_4} R - \overset{R}{\underset{R}{C}} - OH \text{ (Not acid)}$$

(iii) Kolbe's electrolysis gives hydrocarbons containing at least two carbon atoms ($\dot{R} + '\dot{R} \longrightarrow R - R'$)

(iv) Alkyl halide on reduction with zinc and dilute HCl gives alkane.

$$\underset{\text{Alkyl chloride}}{R - Cl} \xrightarrow{Zn + HCl} \underset{\text{Alkane}}{R - H}$$

20. (c)

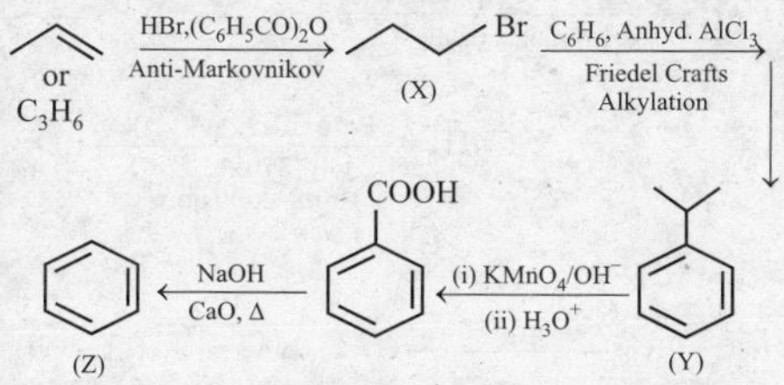

21. (a) (X) on ozonolysis give butanone $\left(CH_3\overset{O}{\overset{||}{C}}CH_2CH_3\right)$ and methanal (HCHO)

$$\underset{(X)}{CH_2 = \overset{CH_3}{\overset{|}{C}} - CH_2 - CH_3} \xrightarrow{O_3/Zn} \underset{(\text{Butanone})}{CH_3 - \overset{O}{\overset{||}{C}} - CH_2 - CH_3} + \underset{(\text{Methanal})}{HCHO}$$

$$\underset{(X)}{CH_2 = \overset{CH_3}{\overset{|}{C}} - CH_2 - CH_3} \xrightarrow{HBr/Peroxide} \underset{\underset{(Y)}{\text{1-Bromo-2-methyl Butane}}}{Br - CH_2 - \overset{CH_3}{\overset{|}{C}H} - CH_2 - CH_3}$$

$$2CH_3 - CH_2 - \overset{CH_3}{\overset{|}{CH}} - CH_2Br \xrightarrow{Na/\text{dry ether}} \underset{\underset{(Z)}{\text{3,6 dimethyl Octane}}}{CH_3 - CH_2\overset{CH_3}{\overset{|}{CH}} - CH_2 - CH_2 - \overset{CH_3}{\overset{|}{CH}} - CH_2 - CH_3}$$

No. of 1° carbons in (Z) = 4

No. of 2° carbons in (Z) = 4

No. of 3° carbons in (Z) = 2

22. (b)

$$\underset{(X)}{CH_3CH_2CH_2 = CH_2} \xrightarrow[\text{Markovnikov addition}]{HBr} \underset{\text{2-Bromo butane (Y)}}{CH_3CH_2\underset{Br}{\underset{|}{Cr_2}} - CH_3}$$

$$\downarrow \text{alc. KOH (Dehydro halogenation)}$$

$$\underset{\text{But-2-ene (Z)}}{CH_3–CH = CH–CH_3}$$

In But-2-ene each terminal CH_3 groups has 3 C–H bonds available for hyperconjugation giving 6 hyperconjugative structures.

23. (c) Isomers of C_4H_8 are:

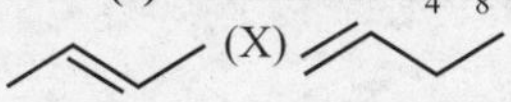

2-Butene 1-Butene

Out of 1-Butene and 2-Butene, 2-Butene shows cis trans isomerism.

Chain isomer of 2-Butene is

$$H_3C - \underset{CH_3}{\underset{|}{C}} = CH_2 \quad (Y)$$

(Having same formula, but different carbon skeleton)

Oronolysis is Y gives.

$$H_3C - \underset{CH_3}{\underset{|}{C}} = CH_2 \xrightarrow{O_3/Zn} \begin{matrix} H_3C \\ H_3C \end{matrix}\!\!> C = O + HCHO$$

24. (c)

I:
$$\underset{\text{2-Methylpropene}}{H_3C - \overset{CH_3}{\overset{|}{C}} = CH_2} \xrightarrow[\text{Markovnikov addition}]{H_2O/H^+} \underset{\underset{\text{2 - Methyl propane - 2 - ol}}{(x)}}{H_3C - \overset{CH_3}{\overset{|}{\underset{OH}{\underset{|}{C}}}} - CH_3}$$

II:
$$\underset{\text{2-Methyl propane}}{H_3C - \overset{CH_3}{\overset{|}{C}} = CH_3} \xrightarrow{KMnO_4} \underset{\underset{\text{2 - Methyl propan - 2 - ol.}}{(Y)}}{H_3C - \overset{CH_3}{\overset{|}{\underset{OH}{\underset{|}{C}}}} - CH_3}$$

Since, $KMnO_4$ is strong oxidising agent it oxides the 3° C – H to 3° alcohol.

25. (a)

$$CH_2 = CH_2 \xrightarrow{HBr} CH_3CH_2 - B_2$$

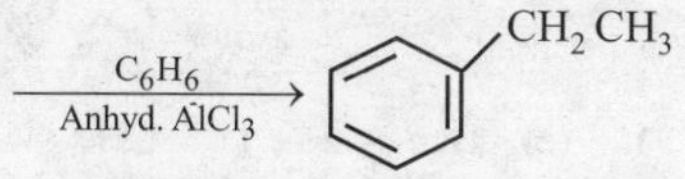

No. of hyper-conjugative H = no. of H on carbon adjacent to unsaturated ring.

No. of hyper-conjugative H = 2

26. (c)

$$CH_3 - CH = CH_2 \xrightarrow[\text{(Anti–Markovnikov Addition)}]{\underset{\text{Benzoyl peroxide}}{HBr}} CH_3 - CH_2 - CH_2Br \text{ (P)}$$

Swarts Reaction AgF → $CH_3–CH_2–CH_2–F$ (R)

Finkelstein Reaction NaI/Acetone Δ → $CH_3–CH_2–CH_2–I$ (Q)

S_N2 reactivity depends on how good the leaving group is : $I^- > Br^- > F^-$

So reactivity order is : Q > P > R

27. (d)

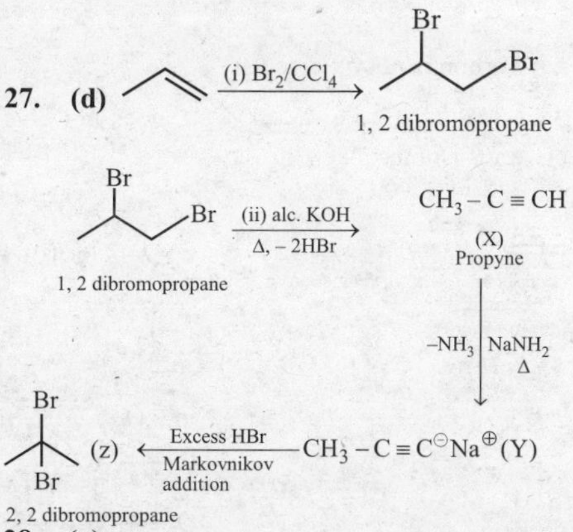

28. (a)

$$\underset{\text{But-2-ene}}{CH_3 - CH = CH - CH_3} \xrightarrow[H^+]{KMnO_4} \underset{\text{Ethanoic acid}}{CH_3COOH}$$

$$\xrightarrow{SOCl_2} \underset{\text{Ethanoyl chloride}}{CH_3COCl} \xrightarrow[\text{Anhyd. } AlCl_3]{\text{Benzene}}$$

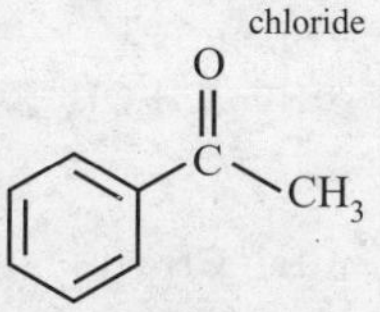

Acetophenone

29. (c)

$$\underset{\text{3-Hexene}}{CH_3CH_2CH = CHCH_2CH_3} \xrightarrow[\text{(ii) Zn, } H_2O]{\text{(i) } O_3} 2CH_3CH_2CHO \xrightarrow{Zn - Hg / HCl} \underset{\text{Propane}}{2CH_3CH_2CH_3}$$

Step-I reaction is reductive ozonolysis and Step-II reaction is reduction.

30. (d) First step is anti-Markovnikov and second step is Wurtz-Fittig reaction.

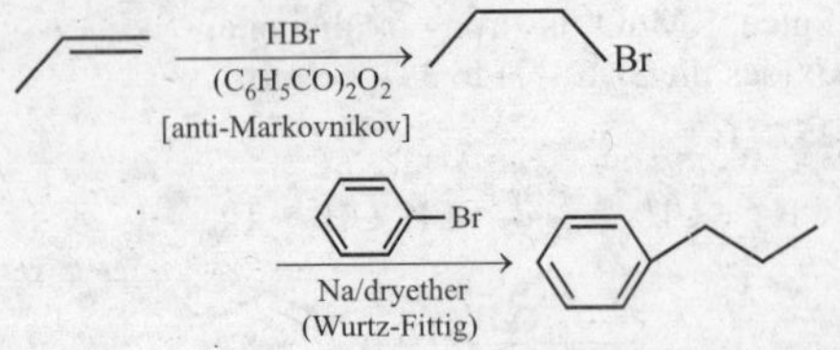

31. (c) But-2-ene i.e $CH_3–HC=CH–CH_3$ is the symmetrical alkene among the given alkenes. Hence anti-Markovnikov addition is not observed in but-2-ene.

32. (d)

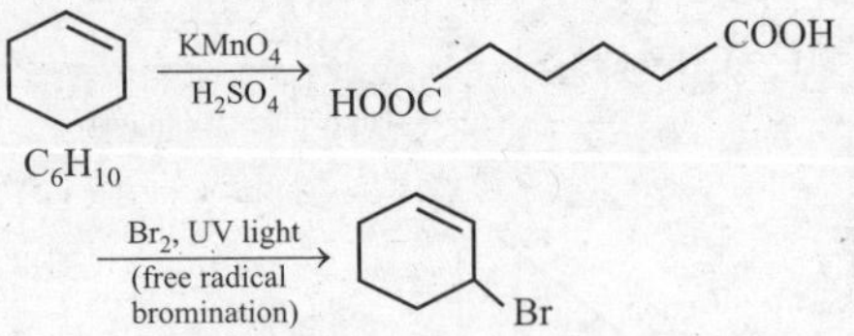

33. (a)

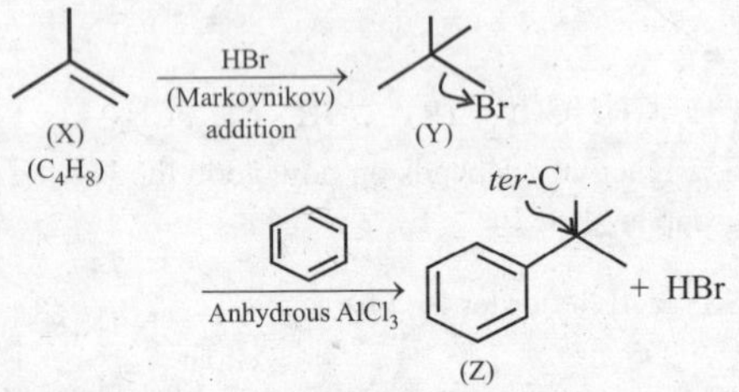

ter-Carbon is not oxidised.

34. (c) C_4H_8 i.e. 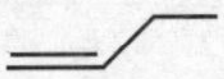 does not give cis-trans isomer

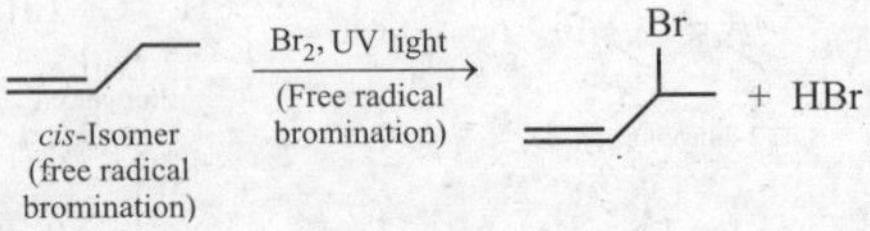

35. (c)

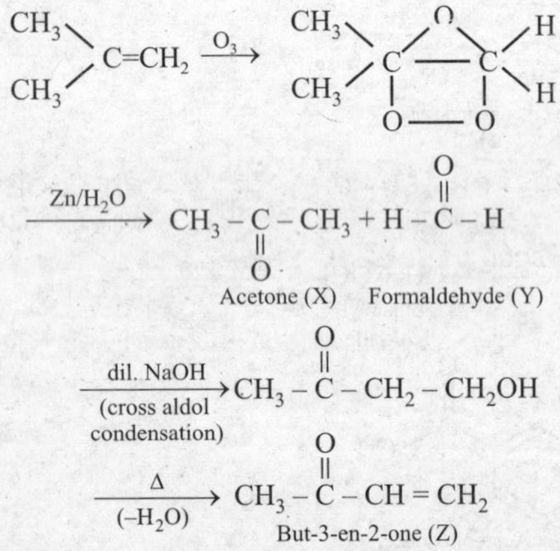

36. (a) Reactions takes place as:

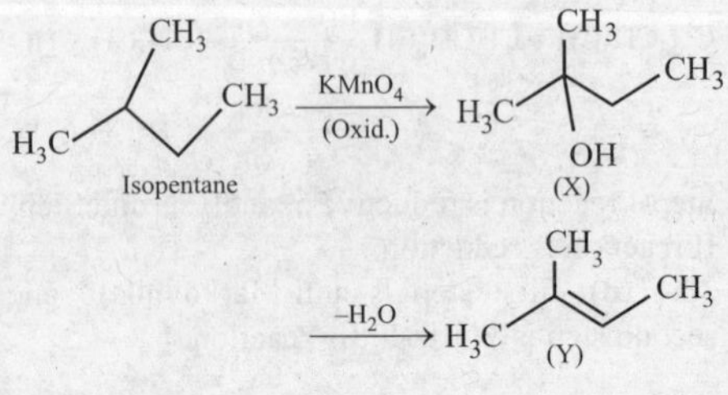

37. (c) cis-2-Butene is more polar than trans-2-butene as the bond dipole moment gets cancelled out in trans-2- butene.

Thus, statement I is correct.

Due to polar nature, cis-2-butene boils at a higher temperature.

Thus, III is correct.

Due to symmetric structure, the melting point of trans-2-butene is higher than that of cis-2-butene.

Thus, II is incorrect.

38. (b)

$$CH_3CH_2CH_2CH_2OH \xrightarrow[(-H_2O)]{H^+} CH_3CH_2CH_2\overset{+}{C}H_2 \text{ (1° Carbocation)}$$

$$\longrightarrow CH_3CH_2\overset{+}{C}HCH_3 \text{ (2° Carbocation)} \xrightarrow{-H^+} CH_3CH=CHCH_3 \text{ (More stable)}$$

39. (c)

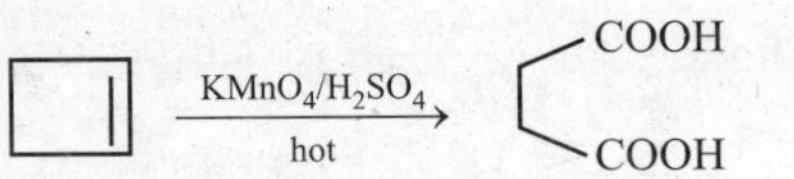

40. (d)

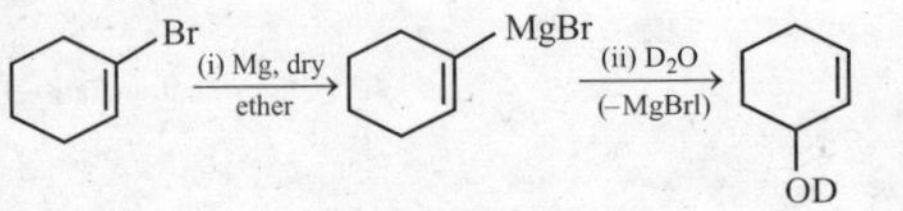

41. (b) Positive electromeric effect (+E)

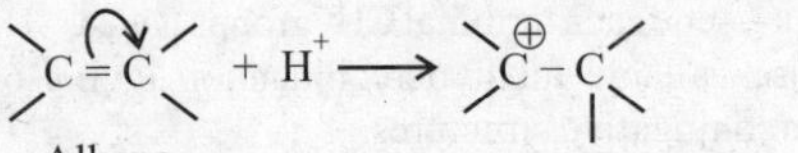

Negative electromeric effect (–E)

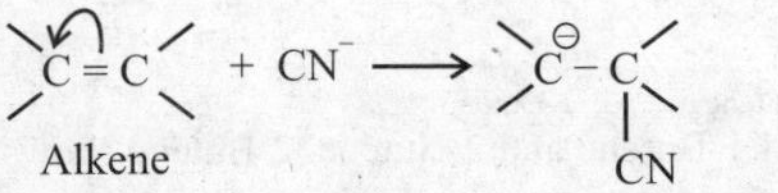

42. (d) Cinnamic acid is able to show geometrical isometrism.

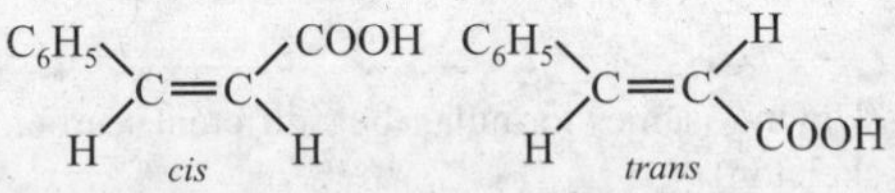

No olefinic C=C is present in butyric acid, aspartic acid and palmitic acid.

43. (d)

$$H_2C=CH_2 + HBr \longrightarrow H_3C-CH_2-Br \text{ (W)}$$

$$\xrightarrow{\text{(i) Mg/dry ether}} H_3C-CH_2-MgBr$$

$$\xrightarrow{\text{(ii) } O=C=O} H_3C-CH_2-\underset{\underset{O}{\|}}{C}-OMgBr$$

$$\xrightarrow{\text{(iii) } H_3O^+} CH_3-CH_2-COOH \text{ (X)} + Mg\begin{smallmatrix}OH\\Br\end{smallmatrix}$$

$$CH_3-CH_2-COOH \xrightarrow[\text{electrolysis (Y)}]{NaOH} CH_3-CH_2-CH_2-CH_3 \text{ (Z)}$$

$$H_3C-CH_2-Br \text{ (W)} \xrightarrow[\text{dry/ether}]{Na} CH_3-CH_2-CH_2-CH_3 \text{ (Z)}$$

44. (a)

$$CH_3-CH_2-CH_2=CH-CH_3 \xrightarrow[Zn/H_2O]{O_3} CH_3CH_2CHO + CH_3CHO$$

Pent-2-ene

(X) Ethanal (Y) Propanal

45. (b) With cold dilute alkaline $KMnO_4$ (Baeyer's reagent), alkenes give addition products and the purple colour of $KMnO_4$ disappears.

46. (c)

$$CaC_2 \xrightarrow{H_2O} CH\equiv CH \xrightarrow[\text{Fe tube}]{\text{Red hot}}$$

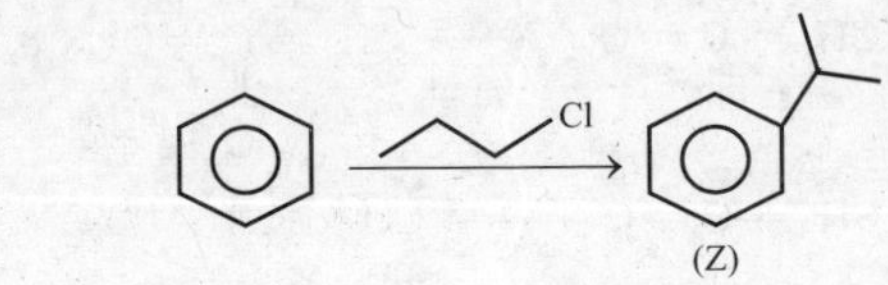

sp^3 hybrid orbital: $3 \times 4 = 12$ (each C of isopropyl group has 4 sp^3 hybrid orbital)

sp^2 hybrid orbital: $6 \times 3 = 18$

Ratio = 12:18 = 2:3

47. (a)

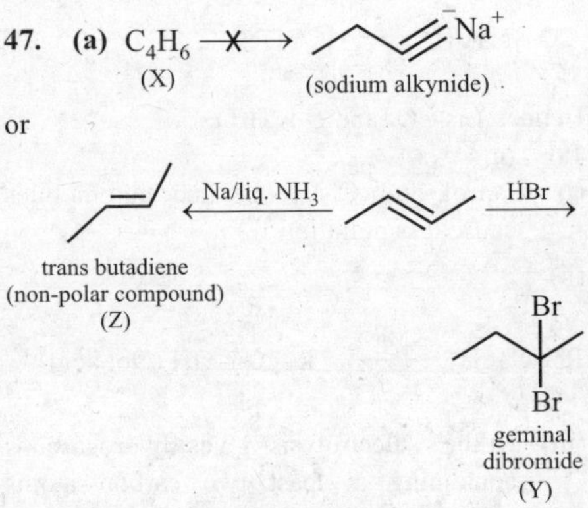

48. (c) According to question,

B under gels high pressure peroxide catalyzed free radical polymerization to form LDP (low density polyethylene)

So B is ethene

$$C_2H_2 \xrightarrow[\text{Lindlar's catalyst}]{H_2,\ Pd/c\text{–quinoline}}$$

$$C_2H_4 \xrightarrow[\substack{350\text{–}370k \\ 1000\text{–}2000 \text{ atms}}]{\text{Peroxide (catalyst)}} LDP$$

49. (d)

$$\underset{\substack{\text{Ethene}\\(Y)}}{H_2C=CH_2} \xleftarrow{Na(NH_3(l))} \underset{\text{Ethyne}}{H-C\equiv C-H} \xrightarrow{H_2/Pt} \underset{\substack{\text{Ethane}\\(X)}}{H_3C-CH_3}$$

Carbon in ethene (X) is sp^3 hybridised

Carbon in ethene (Y) is sp^2 hybridised

50. (d)

$$CH_3-C\equiv C-CH_3 \xrightarrow[\text{Lindlar's catalyst}]{H_2/Pd/CaCO_3}$$

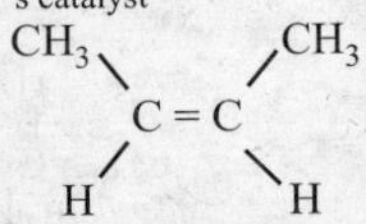

$$CH_3-CH=CH-CH_3 \xrightarrow{KMnO_4/H^+} 2CH_3-\overset{\overset{O}{\|}}{C}-OH$$

51. (c) $CH_3-C\equiv CH + HBr \longrightarrow CH_3-\underset{\underset{Br}{|}}{C}=CH_2 \xrightarrow{HBr} CH_3-\underset{\underset{Br}{|}}{\overset{\overset{Br}{|}}{C}}-CH_3$

2, 2–Dibromopropane

Only one isomer is possible

But given answer is (d)

52. (a)

$$CH_2=CH-CH_3 \xleftarrow[\Delta]{Zn} \underset{\underset{Br}{|}}{H_2C}-\underset{\underset{Br}{|}}{CH}-CH_3$$

1, 2-dibromopropane

$$\xrightarrow[(ii)\ NaNH_2]{(i)\ alc.\ KOH} CH_3-C\equiv CNH_2 \xrightarrow[Catalyst]{Lindlar} CH_3-CH=CH_2$$

53. (a)

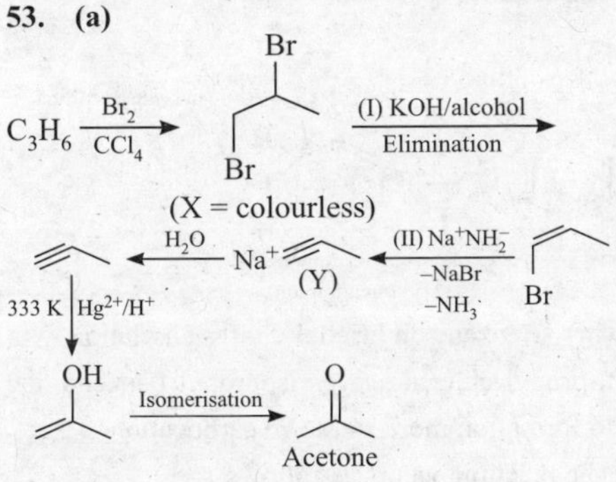

54. (b) Alcohol $X = C_4H_{10}O =$

$$CH_3-CH_2-\underset{\underset{CH_3}{|}}{CH}-OH$$

$$CH_3-CH_2-\underset{\underset{CH_3}{|}}{CH}-OH \xrightarrow[\Delta\ (Dehydration)]{conc.\ H_2SO_4}$$

(X)

$$\underset{(Major)}{CH_3-CH=CH-CH_3} + \underset{(Minor)}{CH_3-CH_2-CH=CH_2}$$

$$\underset{(C_4H_8)\ (Major)}{CH_3-CH=CH-CH_3} \xrightarrow[(Bromination)]{Br_2} CH_3-\underset{\underset{Br}{|}}{CH}-\underset{\underset{Br}{|}}{CH}-CH_3$$

$$CH_3-\underset{\underset{Br}{|}}{CH}-\underset{\underset{Br}{|}}{CH}-CH_3 \xrightarrow{alc.\ KOH}$$

(Y) = alc. KOH and $NaNH_2$

$$CH_3-\overset{\overset{H}{|}}{C}=\underset{\underset{Br}{|}}{C}-CH_3 \xrightarrow{NaNH_2} \underset{(C_4H_6)}{CH_3-C\equiv C-CH_3}$$

Internal alkyne doesn't react with Na metal

55. (d) Aluminium carbide = Al_4C_3

$Al_4C_3 = Al^{3+}$ or C^{4-}

Now, satisfy the value of C^{4-}

$Al_4C_3 + 12D_2O \rightarrow 4Al(OD)_3 + 3CD_4$.

56. (c)

$$CH_3-C\equiv C-H \xrightarrow[Hg^{2+},\ H^+]{H_2O} \left[CH_3-\overset{\overset{OH}{|}}{C}=CH_2\right]_{enol} \xrightleftharpoons{H^+} CH_3-\overset{\overset{O}{||}}{C}-CH_3$$

57. (d) $CH_3CH = CH_2$ to $CH_3CH_2CH_2Cl$ in the presence of HCl in presence of peroxide is not feasible as peroxide/Kharash effect is not observed for HCl and HI.

$CH_3\underset{\underset{Cl}{|}}{CH}-\underset{\underset{Cl}{|}}{CH_2}$ to $CH_3C\equiv CH$ using KOH/Δ is not feasible as this reaction would give an alkene which when treated with sodamide gives alkyne. Thus, I and III are not feasible.

58. (b)

$$\underset{(A)}{CH\equiv CH} \xrightarrow[H_2O]{Hg^+,\ H^+} \overset{H}{\underset{|}{C}}H=\overset{OH}{\underset{|}{C}}H \rightleftharpoons \underset{III}{CH_3-\overset{\overset{O}{||}}{C}-H}$$

$$\underset{(B)}{CH_4} \xrightarrow[Mo_2O_3,\Delta]{O_2} \underset{(IV)}{H-\overset{\overset{O}{||}}{C}-H}$$

$$\underset{(C)}{(H_3C)_2C=C(CH_3)_2} \xrightarrow[Zn,H_2O]{O_3} \underset{(II)}{2\ CH_3-\overset{\overset{O}{||}}{C}-CH_3}$$

$$\underset{(D)}{CH_3-CH=CH-CH_3} \xrightarrow[H^+]{KMnO_4} \underset{I}{2CH_3COOH}$$

59. (c) (–I) effect of p-NO_2 group stabilizes the conjugate base of the acid. (+R) effect of p-NH_2 group destabilizes the conjugate base.

60. (b)

$\underset{(I)}{HX\equiv XH}$ $\quad \underset{(II)}{H_3C-C\equiv C-CH_3}$ $\quad \underset{(III)}{CH_3-C\equiv C-H}$

Due to the (+I) effect of methyl group the stability of conjugate bases decreases from (III) to (II):

∴ Correct order of acidity : (II) < (III) < (I)

61. (b) Acidic strength of an acid can be predicted by determining the stability of its conjugated base.

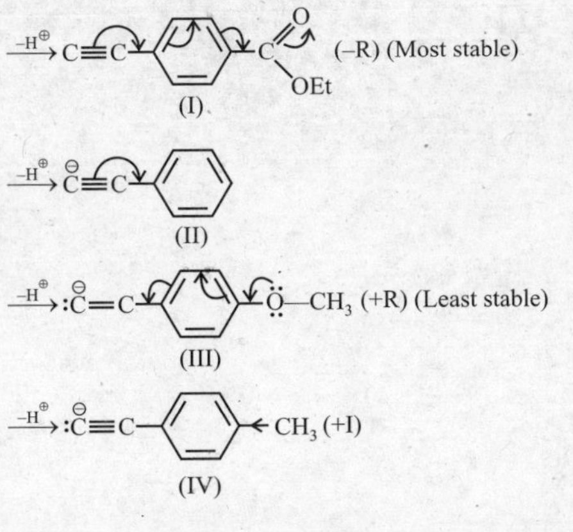

Electron withdrawing groups (– R) stabilise carbanions but electron donating groups (+R > + I) destabillise carbanions.

A stronger acid produces stable conjugate base. So, the order of acidity will be

(i) > (ii) > (iv) > (iii).

62. (d) –Cl, – NHC_2H_5, –OCH_3, –$NHCOCH_3$ substitutes show +R effect when present at benzene ring.

Note: Halogen atoms are ortho-para directors by resonance, but they deactivate the ring by their electronegativity. Their unshared electron pairs stabilize the areniun ion by resonance, but the stabilization is limited by the atomic size and orbital overlap between carbon and halogen. So –I effect is dominant over +R effects.

63. (c)

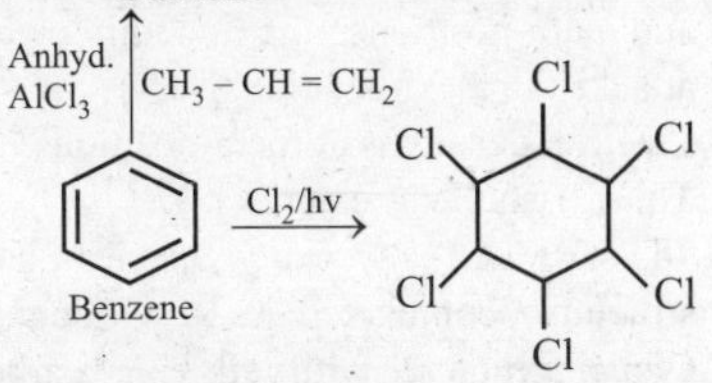

64. (b) Electron withdrawing groups are meta directing groups while electron donating groups are ortho and para directing.

$-CN$, $-\overset{\overset{O}{||}}{C}-R$, $-\overset{\overset{O}{||}}{C}-OH$ are meta directing groups.

65. (d)

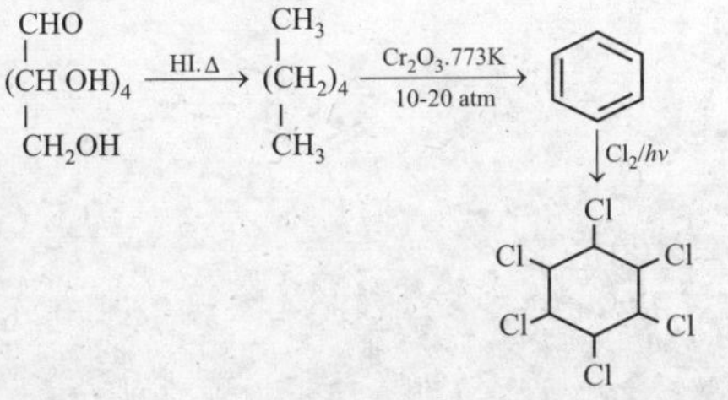

66. (c)

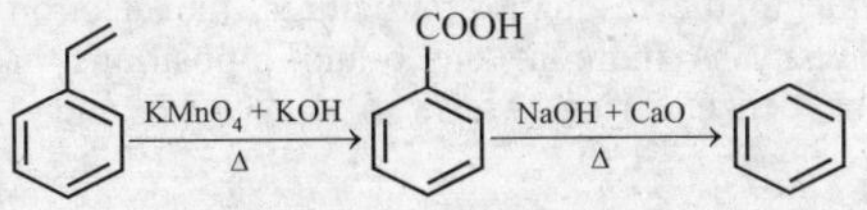

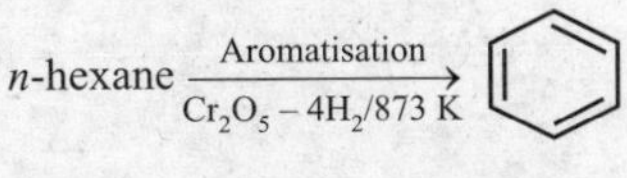

67. (a)

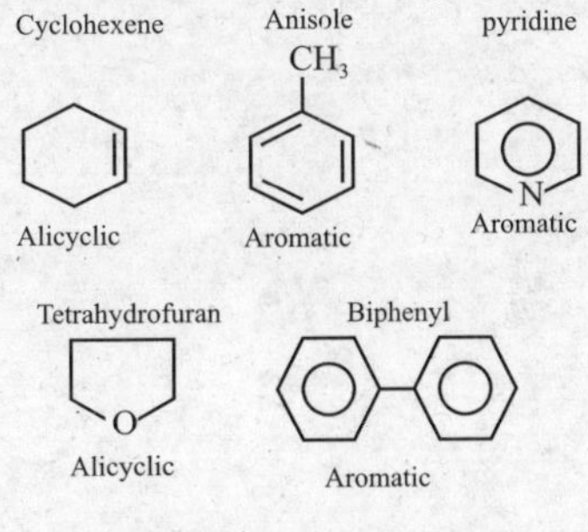

68. (b)

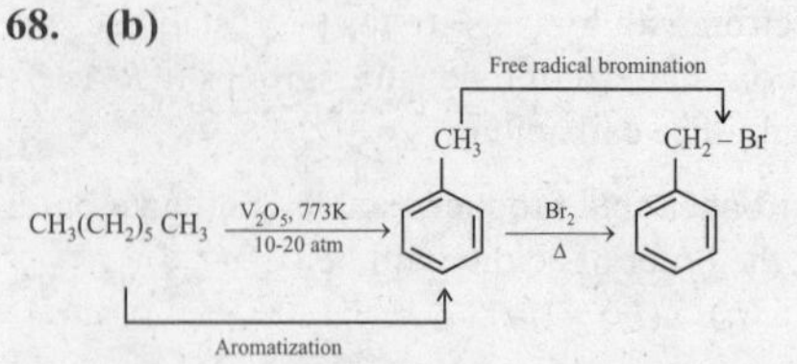

69. (b)

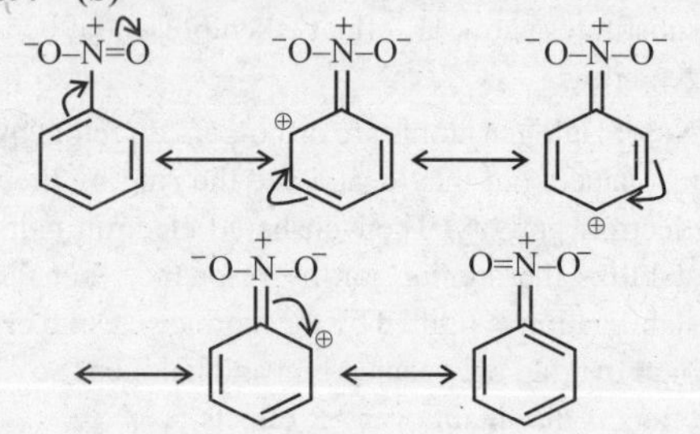

Since the positive charge resides only at the ortho and para-positions, the incoming electrophile attacks the meta-positions.

Electron density is at meta-positions.

Thus, II and IV are correct.

70. (d) An aromatic species has planar structure, conjugated C = C double bonds, cyclic structure with all ring carbon atoms with sp^2-hybridization and having a total of (4n + 2) π electrons. **Cycloheptatriene (d)** has a total of six π- electrons but one ring carbon is sp^3 - hybridized that restricts the conjugated movement of π-electrons.

Thus, it is not aromatic.

71. (a)

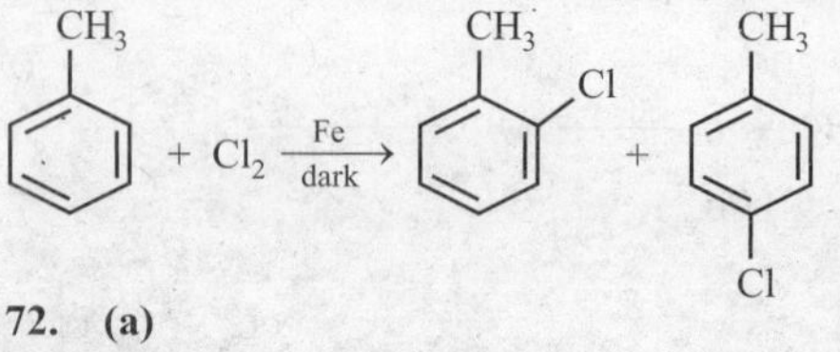

72. (a)

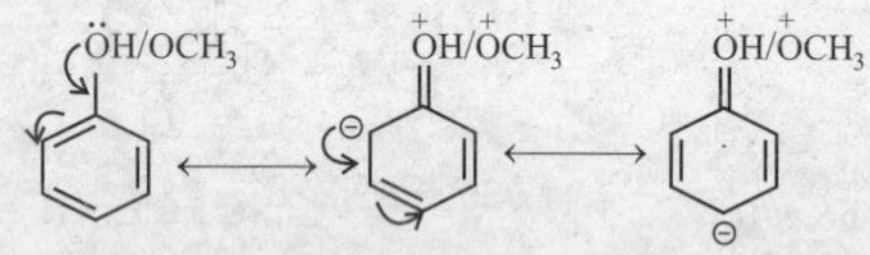

Due to the resonating structures, the electron density is more at the o-and p-positions of the benzene ring. Thus, –OH, $-OCH_3$ and $-NHCOCH_3$ groups direct the electrophile to *o*- and *p*-positions in electrophilic aromatic substitution.

73. (b) Condition for aromaticity: (4n + 2) no. of π electrons should be present in the planar moleculae, where n is any positive integer.

Anti-aromatic compound: 4n π electrons.

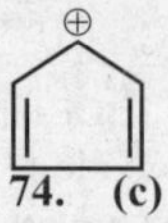 ⟶ 4n = 4 (when n = 1) π electrons

74. (c) The compound contains ring system, with two non-conjugate double bonds and two bromo groups at 1, 4-positions.

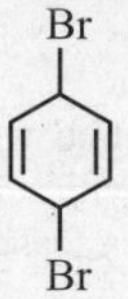

Two double bonds mean 4π-electrons are present in the compound. Therefore, it is anti-aromatic as aromatic compound must have (4*n* + 2) π-electrons.

75. (c) The decreasing order of activating influence of substituents towards electrophilic reagent is

NR_2 > —NHR > $—NH_2$ > —OH > —OR > —NHCOR > —Ph > —R.

Thus the most reactive towards electrophilic reagent is *o*-cresol.

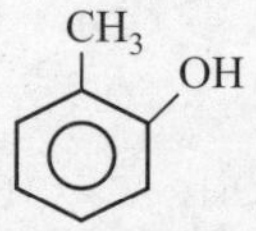

76. (b) Due to 4n e^-, cyclopentadiene is non-aromatic.

77. (b)

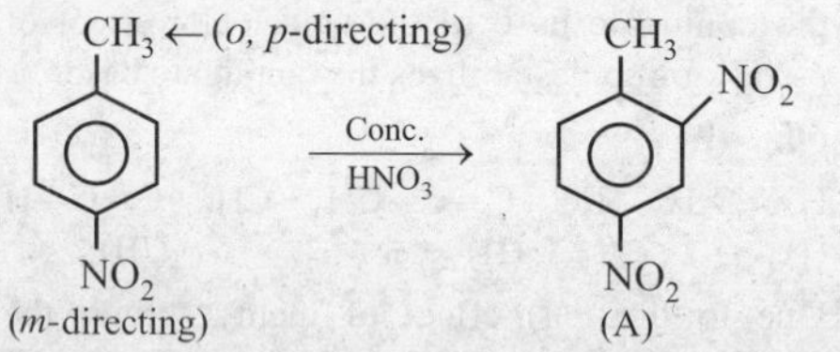

Thus both groups ($-CH_3$ and $-NO_2$) direct the new entering $-NO_2$ group to same position giving (b) as the final product.

78. (b) (i) Groups in which key atom (the atom attached to benzene ring) has lone pair of electrons are *o, p*-directing like $-\ddot{N}H_2$, $-\ddot{N}HCOCH_3$, $-\ddot{O}H$, $-\ddot{O}CH_3$, etc. (except halogens)

(ii) All alkyl groups like $-CH_3$, $-CH_2CH_3$, $-CH(CH_3)_2$, etc. are also *o, p*-directing due to +I effect.

(iii) On the other hand, key atom of *m*-directing (electron withdrawing) groups have at least one double bond like $-\overset{O}{\overset{\|}{C}}H$, $-\overset{O}{\overset{\|}{C}}-CH_3$, $-\overset{O}{\overset{\|}{N}}\rightarrow O$, etc.

They decrease the electron density in benzene ring especialy in *o, p*-positions due to –R effect. Hence all are *m*-directing.

79. (a)

(i) In nitrating mixture ($HNO_3 + H_2SO_4$), nitric acid behaves as a base.

(ii)

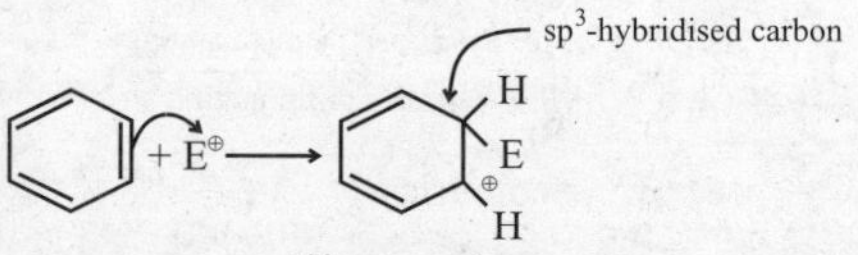

Sigma complex
(arenium ion)

(iii) Benzene on Friedel-Craft's alkylation with n-propyl chloride gives isopropyl benzene due to formation more stable 2° carbocation.

The reaction occurs as follows

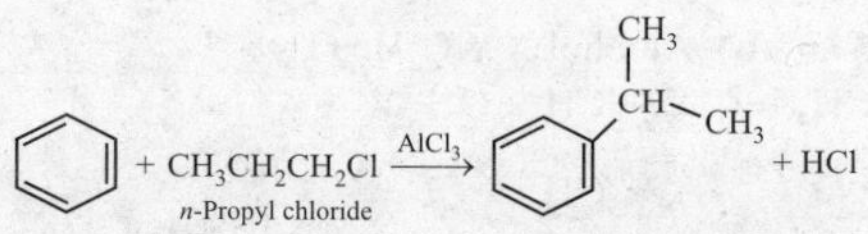

80. (d) $-OCH_3$ due to +R effect increases electron density at *o* and *p* positions. Hence, it is *o, p*-directing.

81. (d) (*i*) For a compound to be aromatic

(*ii*) The ring system must contain (4n + 2)π electrons.

(*iii*) The ring system must be planar.

States of Matter

1. **(c)** Compressibility factor, $Z = \frac{PV}{nRT}$

$Z = \frac{2.71 \times 10}{1 \times 0.082 \times 300}$

$Z = 1.1016$

$Z \approx 1.10$

2. **(b)** Compressibility factor

$(Z) = \frac{PV}{nRT}$

Given, P – 40 atm

$R = 0.082\ L - atm\ K^{-1}\ mol^{-1}$

T = 27°C = 300K

V = 0.4L

$n = \frac{\text{weight (w)}}{\text{Molecular weight}} = \frac{(w)}{44g\ mol^{-1}}$

$\Rightarrow Z = 0.65 = \frac{40 \times 0.4 \times 44}{w \times 0.082 \times 300}$

$\Rightarrow w = \frac{16 \times 44}{0.65 \times 0.082 \times 300} = 44g$

3. **(a) Statement I:** London dispersion forces $\propto \frac{1}{r^6}$

Hence, statement I is correct.

Statement II: Dipole - Dipole interaction energy in

Solid $\propto \frac{1}{r^3}$

Hence, statement II is also correct.

4. **(b)** Since its an open system, pressure remains constant V = 10L (fixed)

Using ideal gas eq^n

PV = nRT

$n \propto \frac{1}{T}$

$\therefore \frac{n_1}{n_2} = \frac{T_2}{T_1}$

Let n_1 = moles at 300K

n_2 = moles at 750K

$\frac{n_1}{n_2} = \frac{750}{300} = \frac{5}{2}$

$n_1 = \frac{5}{2}n_2$ or $n_2 = \frac{2}{5}n_1$

moles expelled = $n_1 - n_2$

$= n_1 - \frac{2}{5}n_1 = \frac{3}{5}n_1$

Fraction expelled = $\frac{\text{moles expelled}}{n_1} = \frac{3}{5}$

5. **(d)** Extensive properties : enthalpy, mass, volume

Intensive properties: density, temperature, pressure

6. **(d)** For H_2

$P_{H_2} = 1$ bar

$V_{H_2} = 1$ L

$P_T = ?$ $\because P_T$ = total pressure

$V_T = 10$ L $\because V_T$ = total volume

As, temperature & number of moles are constant

$\therefore \quad P_{H_2} V_{H_2} = P_T V_T$

$1 \times 1 = P_T \times 10$

$\therefore \quad P_T = 0.1$ bar

For O_2

$P_{O_2} = 2$ bar

$V_{O_2} = 2$ L

$P_T = ?$

$V_T = 10$ L

As temperature and number of moles are constant

$\therefore \quad P_{O_2} V_{O_2} = P_T V_T$

$\therefore \quad 2 \times 2 = P_T \times 10$

$\frac{4}{10} = P_T = 0.4$ bar

Hence, total pressure for the mixture is 0.1 bar + 0.4 bar = 0.5 bar.

7. **(c)** Both the statement I & statement II are correct because in statement I that is in gaseous state, thermal energy significantly dominates over intermolecular forces causing the gas molecules to move freely & independently. This is because high thermal energy provides gas particles with sufficient kinetic energy to overcome the relatively weak intermolecular attractions and in statement II where at constant temperature, the density of an ideal gas is proportional to its pressure, this can also be proved by the formula given below:

$PM = dRT$

Where, P is pressure

M is molar mass

d is density

T is temperature and R is universal gas constant

$P = \frac{dRT}{M}$

At constant temperature

$\boxed{\therefore P \propto d}$

8. **(a)** Here 4 molecules *i.e.*, ethanol, acetic-acid, ethylamine, salicylicacid show H-bonding due to the presence of a H atom bonded to a highly electronegative atom that is with oxygen or nitrogen.

9. **(d)** $C_2H_6 + 3.5O_2 \rightarrow 2CO_2 + 3H_2O$

$C_2H_4 + 3O_2 \rightarrow 2CO_2 + 2H_2O$

$\left[\text{from } C_xH_y + \left(x + \frac{y}{4}\right)O_2 \rightarrow xCO_2 + \frac{y}{2}H_2O\right]$

Total volume = 28 L

$\Rightarrow \quad V_{C_2H_6} = x$ L, $V_{C_2H_4} = (28 - x)$ L

Number of moles of O_2 :

$n_{O_2} = \frac{128\ g}{32\ g\ mol^{-1}} = 4$ mol

Thus, $V_{O_2} = 22.4\ L\ mol^{-1} \times 4$ mol (at STP) = 89.6 L

Volume of O_2 would be equal to sum of volume reacting with C_2H_6 and the volume reacting with C_2H_4.

$\Rightarrow \quad V_{O_2} = 89.6 = 3.5x + 3\,(28 - x)$

$= 3.5x + 84 - 3x = 0.5x + 84$

$\Rightarrow \quad x = 11.2$ L, so $V_{C_2H_6} = 11.2$ L

$\Rightarrow \quad V_{C_2H_4} = 28 - 11.2 = 16.8$ L

For constant T, P and V $\propto n$.

Thus, mole fraction = Volume fraction

$\Rightarrow \quad x_{C_2H_4} = \frac{n_{C_2H_4}}{n_{total}} = \frac{V_{C_2H_4}}{V_{total}} = \frac{16.8\ L}{28\ L} = 0.6$

10. **(a)** Mole of $H_2 = \frac{1}{2}$

Mole of $O_2 = \frac{2}{32} = \frac{1}{16}$

Ratio of mol of H_2 and O_2

$\frac{H_2}{O_2} = \frac{1/2}{1/16} = \frac{1 \times 16}{2 \times 1} = \frac{8}{1}$

$H_2 : O_2 = 8 : 1$

Mole fraction of oxygen $= \frac{\frac{1}{16}}{\frac{1}{2} + \frac{1}{16}} = \frac{1}{9}$

Partial pressure of oxygen = Mole fraction × P

$= \frac{1}{9} \times P = \frac{P}{9}$

11. **(c)** For an ideal gas equation :

$PV = nRT$

$P = \left(\frac{nR}{V}\right)T$

Where, R is universal gas constant

T is temperature in Kelvin

For, $n = 1$ mole

V = constant (isochore means volume constant)

$\therefore \quad P = \left(\frac{1 \times R}{V}\right) T$

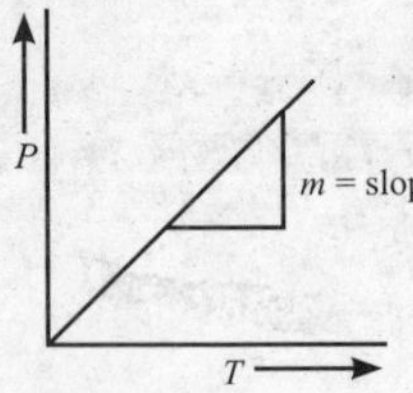

where, m = is slope

$y = P = 0.082$ atm K^{-1}

$x = T = 12.2$ K

$y = mx$

$\therefore \quad P = 0.082 \frac{atm}{K} \times 12.2 K$

$\therefore \quad P = 0.082 \times 12.2$ atm

$\therefore \quad P = 1.0004 \approx 1$ atm

12. (b) $p_{total} = p_{O_2} + p_{H_2}$

$p_{O_2} = P_{total} - p_{H_2}$

$= 2 - 1.778 = 0.222$

$x_{H_2} = \frac{1.778}{2} = 0.889$

$x_{O_2} = \frac{0.222}{2} = 0.111$

mass of gas can be calculated by assuming total one mole of mixture thus mole fraction equal to mol

mass of $O_2 = 0.111 \times 32 = 3.552$ g

mass of $H_2 = 0.889 \times 2 = 1.778$ g

Total mass $= 1.778 + 3.552 = 5.33$ g

mass percentage of $H_2 = \frac{1.778}{5.33} \times 100 = 33.33\%$

13. (c) For an ideal gas

$PV = nRT$

$P = n \times \frac{RT}{V}$

At constant, T and V,

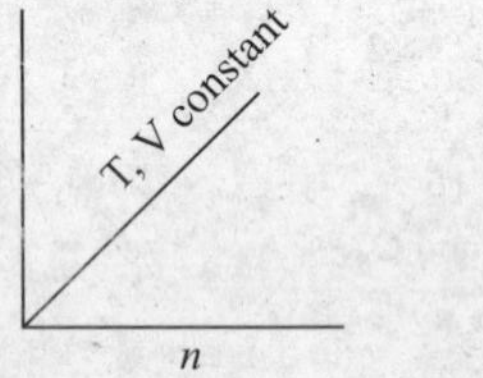

14. (b) Intermolecular forces are much weaker than thermal energy to if intermolecular force stronger than thermal energy substance preferred to condensed state not in gaseous state. Actual number of element exist in gas at room temperature is 11 i.e., H_2, N_2, O_2, F_2, Cl_2 and Noble gases.

15. (d) Ideal gas equation is

$PV = nRT$

for 1 mole, $PV = RT$

$P = V^{-1} RT$

$y = x\,m + C$

m (slope) = RT; C (intercept) = 0

Slope (m) = 32.8 L atm mol^{-1}

$\therefore \quad RT = 32.8$ L atm mol^{-1}

or, $\quad T = \frac{32.8 \text{ Latmmol}^{-1}}{0.082 \text{ atm L mol}^{-1} \text{K}^{-1}}$

$\boxed{T = 400K}$

16. (d) Initial mole of He $(n_1) = 1$

Initial mole of CH_4 $(n_2) = 1$

No. of mole of He escaped $(n'_1) = \frac{2}{22.4} = 0.089$

No. of mole of CH_4 escaped $(n'_2) = \frac{2}{22.4} = 0.044$

Remaining no. of mole $(n''_1) = n_1 - n'_1$

$= 1 - 0.089$

$= 0.90$

Remaining no. of mole $(n''_2) = 1 - 0.044$

$= 0.95$

Mole fraction of He $(\chi_{He}) = \frac{0.90}{1.85} = 0.488$

Mole fraction of CH_4 $(\chi_{CH_4}) = \frac{0.95}{1.85} = 0.512$

17. (a) Root mean square velocity

$(u_{rms}) = \sqrt{\frac{3RT}{M}}$ for 1 mole ideal gas equation

$PV = RT$

$u_{rms} = \sqrt{\frac{3PV}{M}} \Rightarrow u^2_{rms} = \frac{3PV}{M}$

$y = mx + C$

$M(\text{slope}) = \frac{3}{M}$; Intercept (C) = 0

18. (a) At a constant temperature, and volume,

$\frac{P_1}{n_1} = \frac{P_2}{n_2} \Rightarrow P_2 = \frac{P_1}{n_1} \times n_2$

Now, $P_1 = \frac{n_1 RT}{V} = \frac{(1)(0.082)(200)}{1} = 16.4$ atm

Thus, $P_2 = \frac{P_1}{n_1} \times n_2 = \frac{16.4}{1} \times 1.1 = 18.04$ atm

19. (c) $P_{total} = 2$ bar, $P_{O_2} = x_{O_2} P_{total}$

For 100 g of this gaseous mixture, W (H_2) = 20g, W(O_2) = 80g.

$\Rightarrow n_{H_2} = \frac{20}{2} = 10$ mol, $n_{O_2} = \frac{80}{32} = 2.5$ mol

$\Rightarrow x_{O_2} = \frac{2.5}{2.5 + 10} = 0.2$

$\Rightarrow P_{O_2} = 0.2 \times 2 = 0.4$ bar

20. (a) For an ideal gas, $Z = \frac{PV}{RT} = 1$

Thus, the given gas behaves ideally from P = 1 to 3.

21. (a) $PV = nRT = \frac{m}{M} RT \Rightarrow M = \frac{mRT}{PV}$

$= \frac{(1)(0.082)(1000)}{(0.5)(2.5625)} = 64$ g mol^{-1}.

22. (c) The volume approaches zero at absolute zero which is

0.0 K or –273. 15 °C

23. (d) $pV = nRT \Rightarrow p = \frac{n}{V} RT = CRT$

$\Rightarrow T = \frac{P}{CR} = \frac{16.4 \text{ atm}}{(1 \text{ mol L}^{-1})(0.082 \text{ L atm mol}^{-1}\text{K}^{-1})}$

= 200 K.

24. (a) $PV = nRT$ or $P = \frac{1}{V} nRT$ $(y = mx + 0)$

$\Rightarrow$ Slope = nRT = 1.1 (given)

$\Rightarrow V = \frac{nRT}{P} = \frac{1.1}{10} = 0.11$ L

25. (b) $d = \frac{m}{V} = \frac{(n \times M)}{\frac{nRT}{P}} = \frac{PM}{RT} = \left(\frac{M}{RT}\right) P$

Thus, $d \propto P$

26. (b) Let's take the equal weights of the three isotopes as 2g.

$\Rightarrow \quad n_1 = 1$ mol, $n_2 = \frac{1}{2}$ mol, $n_3 = \frac{1}{3}$ mol

$n_{total} = 1 + \frac{1}{2} + \frac{1}{3} = \frac{11}{6}$

$\Rightarrow x_1 = \frac{1}{\frac{11}{6}} = 0.54, \; x_2 = \frac{\frac{1}{2}}{\frac{11}{6}} = 0.27, \; x_3 = \frac{\frac{1}{3}}{\frac{11}{6}} = 0.18$

From Dalton's law of partial pressures:-

$P_i = x_i P_{total}$

$\Rightarrow \frac{P_3}{P_2} = \frac{x_3 P}{x_2 P} = \frac{0.18}{0.27}$ and $\frac{P_2}{P_1} = \frac{x_2}{x_1} = \frac{0.27}{0.54}$

$\Rightarrow \quad P_3 : P_2 : P_1 = 0.18 : 0.27 : 0.54.$

27. (c) $n_1 = \frac{P_1 V}{RT} = \frac{4V}{RT}$ and $n_2 = \frac{P_2 V}{RT} = \frac{3V}{RT}$

$\Rightarrow$ Number of moles remaining $= \frac{4V}{RT} - \frac{3V}{RT} = \frac{1}{R}$

28. (c) From ideal gas equation,

PV = nRT or, PM = dRT

[d = density of gas and M = molecular/atomic weight of the gas]

$\therefore \quad d = \frac{PM}{RT}$

$= \frac{0.82 \times 4}{0.082 \times 300} = \frac{4}{30} = 1.33 \times 10^{-1}$ gL^{-1}

29. (a) More the dipole-dipole attractive forces more is the standard molar enthalpy of vapourization.

30. (d) In plot (I): Higher the curvature higher is the temperature.

$PV = nRT; P_1 = \frac{nRT_1}{V_1}$ and $P_2 = \frac{nRT_2}{V_2}; T_2 > T_1$

In plot (II) : $V = \frac{nRT}{P}; P_1 > P_2$

Higher pressure lower is the slope.

31. (c) At higher altitudes atmospheric pressure decreases pressure. Decrease in atmospheric pressure decreases boiling point of water. Thus, food requies longer time to cook. So, cooking without pressure cooker at higher altitudes take more time.

32. (b) pV = constant at cons. T and n.

33. (a) $pV = nRT$

$\Rightarrow T = \frac{pV}{nR} = \frac{3.32 \times 5}{4 \times 0.082}$

$= 50.60$ K $\approx$ 50 K

34. **(a)** $p_{total} = p_A + p_B + p_C$
(According to Dalton's law)
$\Rightarrow p_C = p_{total} - (p_A + p_B) = 10 - (3+1) = 6$ atm
$\Rightarrow p_C = X_C \cdot p_{total}$

$$\Rightarrow p_C = \frac{n_C}{n_A + n_B + n_C} \times p_{total}$$

$$\Rightarrow \frac{6}{10} \times 10 = n_C \quad \Rightarrow n_C = 6.$$

Weight of C is the mixture = n_C × molar mass of $C = 6 \times 2 = 12$ g.

35. **(b)** Molecules in gases are in constant random motion with high velocity. Hence, there is a complete disorder of molecules in gases.

36. **(c)** Boiling point of a liquid is that temperature at which its vapour pressure becomes equal to the atmospheric pressure. Now, weaker is the attractive force between the molecues of given species, more is its volatile nature and smaller is its boiling point.

Volatile nature ∝ vapour pressure of $\frac{1}{\text{B.Pt}}$

Force of attraction; $C_2H_5OC_2H_5 < CCl_4 < H_2O$
order of B.Pt ; $C_2H_5OC_2H_5 < CCl_4 < H_2O$
308 k 350k 373k

Now, drawing perpendicular on x-axis, i.e. on (a) from points B, A and C, we have

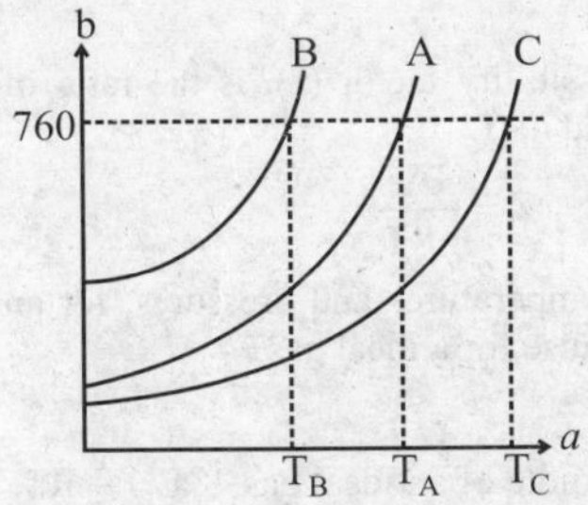

Hence, (A) = CCl_4, (B) = $C_2H_5OC_2H_5$, (C) = H_2O

37. **(c)** Moles of $H_2 = 16/2 = 8$
Moles of He = 16/4 = 4
Moles of $O_2 = 16/32 = 0.5$
Total moles at pressure 10 atm.
$(P_1) = 8 + 4 + 0.5 = 12.5$
Total moles at $(P_2) = 4.5$ (only He and O_2)

$$\frac{P_1V_1}{P_2V_2} = \frac{n_1RT}{n_2RT} \Rightarrow \frac{10}{P_2} = \frac{12.5}{4.5}$$

$P_2 = 3.6$

38. **(b)** Given
$T = 27 + 273 = 300K$
$V = 10L$
$W = W_1(He) + W_2(Ne) = g$ ...(i)
Molar mass (He) = 4
Molar mass (Ne) = 20
$P = 123$ atm
$R = 0.082$ L atm K^{-1} mol^{-1}

(i) $\because \quad PV = (n_1 + n_2)RT = \left[\frac{W_1}{4} + \frac{W_2}{20}\right]RT$

$$\therefore \quad \left[\frac{W_1}{4} + \frac{W_2}{20}\right] = \frac{1.23 \times 10}{0.082 \times 300} = 0.5$$

$25W_1 + 5W_2 = 50 \quad 5W_1 + W_2 = 10$ ...(ii)
On solving equation (ii) with the help of eq. (i)
$5W_1 + 4 - W_1 = 10 \quad \Rightarrow \quad W_1 = 1.5$
$W_2 = 2.5$

$$\text{Mass \% of neon} = \frac{2.5 \times 100}{4} = 62.5\%$$

39. **(d)** As we go higher in altitude, the atmospheric pressure decreases. We know that, P ∝ T. This results in decreasing the boiling point at higher altitude.

40. **(a)** d = 30 kg m^{-3}, P = 684 mmHg

$$PV = \frac{m}{M}RT$$

$$P = \left(\frac{m}{V}\right)\frac{RT}{M}$$

$$P = \frac{dRT}{M}, \quad \frac{RT}{M} = \frac{P}{d}$$

$$\frac{RT}{M} = 30{,}397.5 \text{ J kg}^{-1}$$

$$\mu_{rms} = \sqrt{\frac{3RT}{M}}$$

$$U_{rms} = \sqrt{3 \times 30{,}397.5} = 301.98 \text{ ms}^{-1} = 3 \times 10^2$$

41. **(c)** $v_{rms} = \sqrt{\frac{3RT}{M}}, \; V_{rms} \propto \sqrt{T}$
at temperature T, rms velocity = x
at temperature T^1, velocity = 3x
Using the proportionality,

$$\frac{v_2}{v_1} = \sqrt{\frac{T^1}{T}}$$

$$\frac{3x}{x} = \sqrt{\frac{T^1}{T}}$$

$$3 = \sqrt{\frac{T^1}{T}}$$

$$\Rightarrow \frac{T^1}{T} = 9$$

$T^1 = 9T$

42. **(d)** KE = $\frac{3}{2}$RT
Given KE = Y kJ mol^{-1} ⇒ KE = Y × 10^3 J mol^{-1}

$$Y \times 10^3 \text{ J mol}^{-1} = \frac{3}{2}RT, \quad RT = \frac{2}{3} \times Y \times 10^3$$

$$U_{mp} = \sqrt{\frac{2RT}{M}}$$

$$mp = \frac{M}{10^3} \text{ Kg mol}^{-1}$$

$$U_{mp} = \sqrt{\frac{2 \times \left(\frac{2}{3} \times Y \times 10^3\right)}{\frac{M}{10^3}}}$$

$$= 2 \times 10^3 \sqrt{\frac{Y}{3M}}$$

43. **(b)** According to question:
V_{rms} (SO_2, 400K) = V_{mp} (O_2, T)

$$\sqrt{\frac{3RT}{M_{SO_2}}} = \sqrt{\frac{2MT}{M_{O_2}}}$$

$$\frac{3 \times 400}{64} = \frac{2T}{32}$$

T = 300K
Translational K.E of 5 mol of O_2:

$$K.E = \frac{3}{2}nRT = \frac{3}{2} \times 5 \times 8.3 \times 300$$

= 18675 J Or 18.675 kJ

44. **(d)** u_{rms} is the root mean square speed of gas molecules:

$$u_{rms} = \sqrt{\frac{3RT}{M}}$$

$u_{rms} \propto \sqrt{T}$
$u_1 \propto \sqrt{400} = 20$ $(\therefore T_1 = 400K)$
$u_2 \propto \sqrt{324} = 18$ $(\therefore T_2 = 324K)$

$$\% \text{ decrease} = \frac{20 - 18}{20} \times 100 = 10\%$$

45. **(d)** $C_2H_5OH + 3O_2 \rightarrow 2CO_2 + 3H_2O$
$\Delta_rH^\ominus = (2\Delta_fH^\ominus_{CO_2} + 3\Delta_fH^\ominus_{H_2O)}) - (\Delta_fH^\ominus C_2H_5OH + 3\Delta_fHO_2^\ominus)$
$= [2 \times (-393) + 3 \times (-286) - (-277) + (3 \times 0)]$
$= (-786 - 858) - (-277)$
$= -1644 + 277$
$\Delta_rH^\ominus = -1367$

46. **(a)** Kinetic Energy $(KE) = -RT$ ...(i)

$$\therefore \quad \mu_{rms} = \sqrt{\frac{RT}{}} \quad \text{...(ii)}$$

From eq. (i) and eq. (ii) we get

$$\mu_{rms} = \sqrt{\frac{2KE}{M}} \quad [M = \text{molecular weight}]$$

$$\therefore KE = 412 \times 412 \, m^2s^{-2} \times \frac{44}{2} \text{ kg mol}^{-1} \times 10^{-3}$$

$= 3734.3$ kg m^2s^{-2} mol^{-1}
$= 3734.3 \times 10^{-3}$ kJ mol^{-1}
$= 3.7343$ kJ mol^{-1}

47. **(d)** Rate of diffusion (r) = $\frac{V}{t} \propto \frac{l}{\sqrt{M}}$

$$\Rightarrow \quad \frac{r_{H_2}}{r_{O_2}} = \frac{V_{H_2}}{V_{O_2}} = \frac{n_{H_2}}{n_{O_2}} = \sqrt{\frac{M_{O_2}}{M_{H_2}}}$$

$$\Rightarrow \quad \frac{\frac{2}{2}}{w/32} = \sqrt{\frac{32}{2}}$$

n = number of mole
w = weight of O_2
M = Molecular weight
v = Volume

$\Rightarrow \quad w = 8g$

48. **(d)** Kinetic energy of gas molecule directly proportional to absolute temperature. This relationship given by equation

$$KE = \frac{3}{2} KT$$

Where K is Boltzmann constant and T is absolute temperature
Total kinetic energy of gas sample is proportional to number of mole of gas as

$$KE = \frac{3}{2} n KT$$

Where n = number of moles of gas
R = gas constant
T = absolute temperature
$T_1 = 27\ ^\circ C = 300$ K
$T_2 = 127\ ^\circ C = 400$ K

Number of mole of hydrogen $= \frac{4g}{2g/mol} = 2$ mol

No. of mole of oxygen $= \frac{6.4g}{32g/mol^{-1}} = 0.2$ mol

$$\frac{KE_2}{KE_1} = \frac{\frac{3}{2}n_2RT_2}{\frac{3}{2}n_1RT_1}$$

$$\frac{x_2}{x_1} = \frac{n_2T_2}{n_1T_1} = \frac{0.2\times 400}{2\times 300} = \frac{80}{600} = \frac{2}{15}\quad x_2 = \frac{2}{15}x_1$$

Thus kinetic energy of 6.4 g oxygen at 127 ºC is $\frac{2}{15}\times$ J

49. (c) For *rms* velocity

$$V_{rms} = \sqrt{\frac{3RT}{M}}$$

Where, *R* is universal gas constant
T is temperature in Kelvin
M is molar mass
For SO_2 molecules

$$V_{SO_2} = \sqrt{\frac{3RT}{64}} \quad ...(i)$$

For O_2 molecules

$$V_{O_2} = \sqrt{\frac{3R(300)}{32}} \quad ...(ii)$$

Equating (i) & (ii) we get

$$\sqrt{\frac{3RT}{64}} = \sqrt{\frac{3R(300)}{32}}$$

Squaring both the sides we get

$$\frac{3RT}{64} = \frac{3R(300)}{32}$$

$$\frac{T}{2} = 300$$

$\therefore\quad T = 600$ K

50. (b) mass of $H_2 = 8$ g = 0.008 kg
Most probable velocity $(u_{mp}) = 2\times 10^2\ ms^{-1}$

Most probable velocity $u_{mp} = \sqrt{\frac{2RT}{M}}$

Molar mass of H_2 in kg = 0.002 kg mol^{-1}

$$u_{mp}^2 = \frac{2RT}{M} \Rightarrow RT = \frac{M\,u_{mp}^2}{2}$$

$$RT = \frac{0.002\times(2\times 10^2)^2}{2} = 40\ J\ mol^{-1}$$

number of mole $= \frac{8\ g}{2\ g/mol} = 4$ mol

$$KE = \frac{3}{2}nRT = \frac{3}{2}\times 4\times 40 = \frac{480}{2} = 240\ g$$

51. (b) $\mu_{rms} = \sqrt{\frac{3RT}{M}} = 3.16\times 10^2\ ms^{-1}$ ...(I)

μ (most probable velocity) $= \sqrt{\frac{2RT}{M}}$ ...(II)

$$\sqrt{\frac{3RT}{M}} = 3.16\times 10^2$$

$$\Rightarrow \frac{3RT}{M} = (3.16\times 10^2)^2$$

$$\Rightarrow \frac{RT}{M} = \frac{(3.16\times 10^2)^2}{3}$$

$$\mu_{\text{most probable velocity}} = \sqrt{\frac{2RT}{M}}$$

$$= \sqrt{\frac{2\times(3.16)^2\times 10^4}{3}} = \sqrt{\frac{2}{3}}\times 3.16\times 10^2$$

$= 2.58\times 10^2\ ms^{-1}$

52. (b) rms velocity $(\mu_{rms}) = \sqrt{\frac{3RT}{M}}$

Mean velocity $(\mu_{av}) = \sqrt{\frac{8RT}{\pi M}}$

Most probability $(\mu_{mp}) = \sqrt{\frac{2RT}{M}}$

Ratio	Value
$\frac{\mu_{rms}}{\mu_{av}} = \frac{\sqrt{3RT/M}}{\sqrt{8RT/\pi M}}$	= 1.08
$\frac{\mu_{av}}{\mu_{mp}} = \frac{\sqrt{8RT/\pi M}}{\sqrt{2RT/M}}$	= 1.12
$\frac{\mu_{rms}}{\mu_{mp}} = \sqrt{\frac{3RT/M}{2RT/M}}$	= 1.22
$\frac{\mu_{av}}{\mu_{rms}} = \sqrt{\frac{8RT/\pi M}{3RT/M}}$	= 0.91

53. (b) $V_1 = 60cm^3$, $M_1 = 64$, $t_1 = x$
$V_2 = 360\ cm^3$, $M_2 = 4$, $t_2 = y$
rate of diffusion,

$$r = \frac{V}{t} = \frac{\text{volume of gas diffused}}{\text{Time taken for diffusion}}$$

$$\frac{r_1}{r_2} = \sqrt{\frac{M_2}{M_1}} = \frac{v_1t_2}{v_2t_1} \quad \therefore \sqrt{\frac{4}{64}} = \frac{60}{360}\times\frac{y}{x}$$

$$\text{or, } \frac{1}{4}\times 6 = \frac{y}{x} \qquad \therefore \frac{y}{x} = \frac{3}{2}\ \therefore\ \frac{x}{y} = \frac{2}{3}$$

54. (b) Kinetic energy (K.E) $= \frac{3}{2}PV$

$$\therefore\quad P = \frac{2KE}{3}\times\frac{1}{V}$$

$$\frac{2}{3}KE\ V^{-1} = P$$

mx = y

where, $m = \frac{2}{3}KE$

$$\therefore\quad 2000 = \frac{2}{3}KE$$

$$\therefore\quad \frac{2000\times 3}{2} = 3000\ J\ mol^{-1}$$

55. (d) RMS velocity $(v_{rms}) = \sqrt{\frac{3RT}{M}}$

$$(v_{rms})^2 = \frac{3RT}{M}$$

$$\therefore\quad (v_{rms})^2 = \frac{3R}{M}.T + 0$$

y = mx + C
y-axis $= (v_{rms})^2$; x axis = T

$\Rightarrow$ Slope $= \frac{3R}{M}$; intercept (C) = 0

56. (c) At same temperature,

$$\frac{KE_1}{KE_2} = \frac{n_H}{n_{O_2}}$$

$$\eta_H = \frac{3}{2} = 1.5 \text{ moles};\ \eta_{O_2} = \frac{4}{32} = 0.125 \text{ moles}$$

$$\frac{KE_1}{KE_2} = \frac{1.5}{0.125} = \frac{12}{1} \Rightarrow 12:1$$

57. (d) $K.E = \frac{1}{2}mv^2 = \frac{1}{2}\ (0.1)\ (4\ \times 10^2)^2$
$= 8\times 10^3\ J\ mol^{-1}$

58. (a) To Find the RMS velocity of an ideal gas the formula is-

$$v_{rms} = \sqrt{\frac{3RT}{M}}$$

putting the value in the formula.

$$v_{rms} = \sqrt{\frac{3\times 8.3J\ mol^{-1}K^{-1}\times 133.33k}{0.083\ kg/mol}}$$

$$v_{rms} = \sqrt{\frac{3323.99}{0.083}} \Rightarrow v_{rms} = \sqrt{40048.14\ J\ kg^{-1}}$$

$v_{rms} = 200.12$ m/s

59. (c)
(I) Compressibility factor (z), is the ratio of product PV and nRT.

Mathematically, $Z = \frac{PV}{nRT}$

Z = 1 at all temperatures and pressures, for an ideal gas, because for a ideal gas.
PV = nRT.

(II) For one mole of an ideal gas, $K.E = \frac{3}{2}RT$
$\Rightarrow$ Kinetic energy is directly proportional to the absolute temperature, it is independent of the mass of the gas.
Hence, Statement (II) is incorrect.
(III) According to Graham's law of diffusion rate of diffusion (r) is inversely proportional to the square root of density. Hence, Statement (III) is correct.

60. (a) According to Maxwell - Boltzmann distribution of molecular speeds, $T_2 > T_1 > T_3$.

61. (d) RMS velocity $(v_{rms}) = \sqrt{\frac{3RT}{M}}$

$$\Rightarrow v_{rms}^2 = \frac{3RT}{M}$$

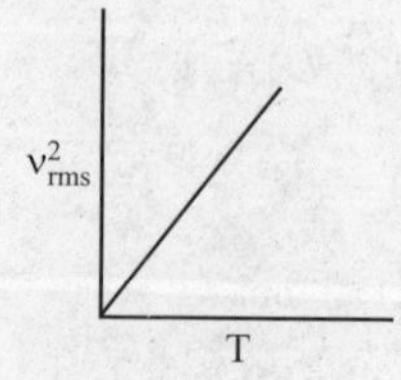

Slope (m) $= \frac{3R}{M}$ $[R = 83\ J\ mol^{-1}\ K^{-1}]$

$$\frac{3R}{M} = 249 m^2s^{-2}K^{-1}$$

$$M = \frac{3 \times 8.3 \text{ J mol}^{-1}\text{K}^{-1}}{249\text{m}^2\text{s}^{-2}\text{K}^{-1}} \quad [1\text{J} = 1 \text{ kg}]$$

$$M = \frac{3 \times 8.3 \text{ kg m}^2\text{s}^{-2}\text{mol}^{-1}\text{k}^{-1}}{249 \text{ m}^2\text{s}^2\text{k}^{-1}} [1\text{J} = 1 \text{ kg m}^2\text{s}^{-2}]$$

$$M = \frac{24.9 \text{ Kg mol}^{-1}}{249} \Rightarrow M = 0.1 \text{ Kg mol}^{-1}$$

$\therefore$ M (molar mass) = 1×10^{-1} Kg mol^{-1}

62. (b) Diffusion rate = 120 mL in one minute.

$\Rightarrow$ Time required for the diffusion of 3000 mL will be :-

$$t = \frac{3000}{120} = 25 \text{ minutes} = 25 \times 60 = 1500 \text{ seconds.}$$

63. (c) Molecular weight (M) = 2 × Vapour Density (VD)

Rate of diffusion (r)

$$= \frac{\text{Vol. of the gas}}{\text{Time}} = \frac{1}{\sqrt{M}} = \frac{1}{\sqrt{2(VD)}}$$

$$r_A = \frac{V_1}{t_1}; r_B = \frac{V_2}{t_2}$$

$$\text{or, } r_A = \frac{20\text{ml}}{60\text{s}} = \frac{1}{3}; r_B = \frac{10\text{ml}}{60\text{s}} = \frac{1}{6}$$

$$\therefore \frac{r_A}{r_B} = \sqrt{\frac{(VD)_B}{(VD)_A}} = \frac{1/3}{1/6}$$

$$\text{or, } \sqrt{\frac{x}{(VD)_A}} = 2 \ (VD)_A = \frac{x}{4}$$

64. (c)

$$M_{CH_4} = 16; (C_{CH_4})_{rms} = \sqrt{\frac{3RT}{16}} = \frac{\sqrt{3RT}}{4} \text{m/s}$$

$$M_{SO_2} = 64; (C_{SO_2})_{rms} = \sqrt{\frac{3RT}{64}} = \frac{\sqrt{3RT}}{8} \text{m/s}$$

$$\therefore (C_{CH_4})_{rms} > (C_{SO_2})_{rms}$$

Suppose, at time 't', both the gas will meet.

At time t, CH_4 molecules travel $\frac{\sqrt{3RT}}{4}$ t m and

At time SO_2 molecules travel $\frac{\sqrt{3RT}}{8}$ t m.

$$\therefore \frac{\sqrt{3RTt}}{4} + \frac{\sqrt{3RTt}}{8} = 1000$$

$$\text{or } \frac{\sqrt{3RTt}}{4}\left(1+\frac{1}{2}\right) = 1000$$

$$\text{or } \frac{\sqrt{3RTt}}{4} \times \frac{3}{2} = 1000 \text{ or } t = \frac{8000}{3\sqrt{3RT}}$$

$\therefore$ Distance travelled by time 't'

$$= \frac{\sqrt{3RT}}{4} \times \frac{8000}{3\sqrt{3RT}} = 667\text{m}$$

65. (a, d)

$$KE = \frac{1}{2}mv_{rms}^2 = \frac{1}{2} m \frac{3RT}{M} = \frac{1}{2} n \ 3RT$$

$\therefore$ KE $\propto$ n and KE $\propto$ T

$\therefore$ KE depends on no. of moles of gas

$$KE = \frac{3p}{2}V \quad ...(i)$$

KE depends on pressure of the gas from (i)

$\therefore$ wrong statement are (a, d).

For a given moles of a gas KE is independent of the mass of the gas molecule.

66. (b) Given,

Temperature (T) is same for most probable velocity (vmp) and for root mean square velocity [vrms]

Aslo, u(mp) = 400 ms–1

$$u_{(mp)} = \sqrt{\frac{2RT}{M}}$$

$$u_{(mp)}^2 = \frac{2RT}{M} \quad ...(i)$$

$$u_{rms} = \sqrt{\frac{3RT}{M}}$$

$$\Rightarrow u_{rms}^2 = \frac{3RT}{M} \quad ...(ii)$$

Dividing Eqs. (ii) by (i):

$$\frac{u_{rms}^2}{u_{mp}^2} = \frac{3}{2} \Rightarrow u_{rms}^2 = \frac{3}{2} \times (400)^2$$

$= 490\text{ms}^{-1}$

67. (c) $KE = \frac{3RT}{2}$ and $v_{rms} = \sqrt{\frac{3RT}{M}}$

$$v_{rms} = \sqrt{\frac{2KE}{M}} = \sqrt{\frac{2 \times 4 \times 10^3 \text{ J}}{32 \times 10^{-3} \text{ kg mol}^{-1}}}$$

$= 5 \times 10^2$ m/s $= 5 \times 10^4$ cm/s.

68. (b) Number of moles of hydrogen

$$= \frac{3\text{g}}{2\text{g mol}^{-1}} = 1.5$$

Number of moles of oxygen

$$= \frac{80\text{g}}{32\text{g mol}^{-1}} = 2.5$$

Total number of moles in gaseous mixture of hydrogen and oxygen,

$n = 1.5 + 2.5 = 4$

$$KE = \frac{3}{2}nRT = \frac{3}{2} \times 4 \times RT = 6RT$$

69. (d) At higher temperatures, the molecules have more energy. Hence, the molecular speeds are higher. Thus, as the temperature increases, distribution range narrows.

70. (b) I & II only correct.

I. Glass is super cooled liquid and highly viscous.

II. As the temperature incorrect kinetic energy increase, thus surface tension decrease.

III. Compressibility factor for ideal gas is unity (one)

71. (d) Compressibility factor $Z = 1 + \frac{Pb}{RT}$

For ideal gas compressibility factor remains unchange i.e. unity.

Thus option (d) is correct.

72. (a) $\left(P + \frac{an^2}{V^2}\right)(v - nb) = nRT$

This equation is known as Van der Waals equation for real gases.

For $n = 1$ mole.

$$\left(P + \frac{a^2}{V^2}\right)(v - b) = RT$$

73. (b) The critical temperature of CO_2 is 30.98 °C

74. (c) Under high temperature and Low pressure gas have highest kinetic energy and follow ideal gas equation.

75. (c) Layer 1 is near to the solid surface so its interaction will be more with the surface which tends to decrease it velocity. While the velocity of other layer increases with distance from the fixed layer.

$\therefore$ Order will be $V_3 > V_2 > V_1$

76. (a) Viscosity depends strongly on temperature in liquids it usually decreases with increasing temperature because temperature increases the kinetic energy of the molecule as a result the molecule overcomes the intermolecular attractive force between them units of viscosity are pascal-second and kg m^{-1} s^{-1}.

77. (a) Both statement I and II are correct.

$v_{rms} = \sqrt{\frac{3kbT}{m}}$ For this equation $v_{rms} \propto \sqrt{T}$

78. (c) Viscosity depends strongly on temperature in liquids it usually decrease with increasing temperature because temperature increase the kinetic energy of the molecule as a result the molecule overcomes the intermolecular attractive force between them.

Units of viscosity are pascal-second and Kg m^{-1} s^{-1}.

79. (b)

$$Z = \frac{PV}{RT} \Rightarrow V = \frac{ZRT}{P} = \frac{(1.1)(0.082)(300)}{2.706}$$

= 10 L

80. (d) PV = RT for an ideal gas so

$$Z = \frac{PV}{RT} = 1$$

Both, $^{235}UF_6$ and $^{238}UF_6$ are separated on the basis of their molecular velocities which are different for them. Kinetic energy is directly proportional to the temperature so a decrease in temperature would decrease the kinetic energy.

Thus, (A) and (B) are correct.

81. (a) Z > 1 for a gas in all pressure is not compressible easily.

82. (d)

(i) For real gases compressibility factor (Z) cannot be unity, while compressibility factor for an ideal gas is one.

(ii) A gas can behave like an ideal gas at very high temperature and low pressure. Hence, show very less deviation.

(iii) Intermolecular forces among gas molecules are weak as compare to liquid and solid but, these forces cannot be zero.

(iv) Ideal gas follows van der Waal's equation $pV = nRT$

Gases which do not follow this equation are real gases.

83. (d) Stronger intermolecular attractive force between molecules will give higher magnitude of surface tension.

84. (d) C has highest critical temperature, i.e., 405.5K. Hence, it gets liquified first.

85. (b) When surface area decreases, less liquid will be exposed to air and therefore, less amount of water can evaporate in a given time period.

The s-Block Elements

1. **(d)** Lithium gives crimson-red colour flame while Mg does not impart a characteristic colour.

Li form Li_3N and Mg form Mg_3N_2 on combustion.

2. **(c)** Down the group basicity of oxides increases.

- $B_2O_3 \rightarrow$ acidic
- $Al_2O_3 \rightarrow$ amphoteric
- $Ga_2O_3 \rightarrow$ amphoteric
- $In_2O_3 \rightarrow$ Basic
- $Tl_2O_3 \rightarrow$ Basic

Z (Ga) has lowest melting point because of weak metallic bonding.

Y(Tl) has lowest boiling point because down the group boiling point decreases.

So Y (Tl) oxide - Tl_2O_3 - Basic

Z(Ga) oxide - Ga_2O_3 - amphoteric.

3. **(b)** The boiling points of alkali metal halides actually follow the same trend as their melting points.

MF > MCl > MBr > MI. This is because inter-ionic electrostatic forces in the smaller fluorides require much more thermal energy to break apart in the vapour phase compared to the iodides.

4. **(c)** Among alkali metals ions, Li^+ to Cs^+ Hydration enthalpy decreases.

Boiling points of alkali metals decreases from Li to Cs. Li has strong tendency to form oxide.

5. **(c)** Lithium and magnesium react slowly with water. Their oxides and hydroxides are much less soluble and their hydroxides decompose on heating Lithium and magnesium both form a nitride Li_3N and Mg_3N_2 and decompose easily on heating.

6. **(a)** $NaNO_2 + HCl \longrightarrow HNO_2 + NaCl$

7. **(a)** Alloy of Lithium and Magnesium is used to make armour plates Lithium-magnesium alloy is an extremely light and strong alloy with one of the lowest densities of metallic materials.

8. **(b)** Sodium peroxide has peroxide ion O_2^{2-} that has a total of 18 electrons and is diamagnetic.

The superoxide ion O_2^- is paramagnetic.

9. **(a)** LiF being predominantly covalent, has a high lattice enthalpy due to which it is less soluble in water. Thus, (i) is correct.

$Na^+ < Cs^+$ so the polarizing power of Na^+ is higher than that of Cs^+ which results in NaCl being more covalent or less ionic than CsCl.

Thus, (ii) is also correct.

Formation of alkali metal halides like NaCl, CsCl, KF, etc. is an exothermic reaction which gives rise to a stable crystal lattice.

Thus, (iii) is incorrect.

10. **(b)** Li = crimson red, Na = yellow, K = violet

11. **(d)** $2KNO_3 \xrightarrow{\Delta} 2KNO_2 + O_2$

12. **(b)** Alkali metals are highly intended to lose the valence electron.

O_2^- has one unpaired electron in π^*_{2p} orbital.

13. **(d)** $2LiNO_3 \longrightarrow Li_2O + 2NO_2 + \frac{1}{2}O_2$

14. **(a)** The lattice energy of LiF is greater due to the small sizc of F^- and Li^+ ions.

15. **(d)** Alkali metals have only one valence electron in their outermost shell. Due to low ionisation enthalpy get oxidised to reduces other compounds.

16. **(a)** Li_2SO_4 is the only alkali metal sulphate that does not form double salt due to small size.

17. **(c)** K, Rb and Cs form superoxides when they are burned in the air. As we move down the group, the size of an atom from K to Cs increases.

Bigger cation can stabilize bigger O_2^- more easily

Hence, stability of superoxide increases.

18. **(c)** Lithium has due to its highest hydration enthalpy, Lithium acts as strongest reducing agent in aqieor solution.

19. **(d)**

$$\underset{(B)}{2KO_2} + 2H_2O \longrightarrow \underset{(A)}{2KOH} + \underset{(B)}{H_2O_2} + \underset{(C)}{O_2}$$

$$\underset{(B)}{H_2O_2} + I_2 + 2KOH \xrightarrow{\text{Basic medium}} 2KI + 2H_2O + \underset{(C)}{O_2}$$

KOH can not reduce I_2,

20. **(c)**

(II) On moving down in the group the size of the atom increases. The bigger atom can stabilise more the bigger superoxide ion effectively.

(III) Lattice energy of LiF is more than the hydration energy. Hence, LiF has very low solubility.

21. **(c)**

$$2M(s) + 2H_2O \longrightarrow 2MOH + H_2(g)$$

(Where M = Alkali Metals)

22. **(c)**

23. **(b)** Li is the only alkali metal which reacts directly with N_2 to give nitride (Li_3N)

$6Li + N_2 \rightarrow 2Li_3N$

24. **(d)** Melting and boiling points of alkali metals are very low due to weak metallic bond.

25. **(c)** X = CaO $\Rightarrow$ Used in cement manufacturing $+2Na^+$

Y = $Ca(OH)_2$ (slaked lime) $\Rightarrow$ used to recover NH_3 in the solve ammonia process and to make bleaching powder ($CaOCl_2$).

Z = $CaSO_4 \cdot Y_2H_2O$ (Plaster of Paris) $\Rightarrow$ used for casts.

26. **(c) Statement I:** In 3D network of SiO_2, if Si atoms are replaced by Al atoms, the resulting structure acquires negative charge not positive charge since Al has less electrons than Si. So, statement I is incorrect.

Statement II: Silicones exists as organo-silicon polymers with repeating unit $-(R_2SiO)$. Hence, statement II is correct.

27. **(c)** The Solvay process used in manufacturing of Na_2CO_3 uses NaCl, NH_3 and $CaCO_3$ as raw material. $CaCl_2$ is generated as by-product of the process.

28. **(b)** Both $LiNO_3$ and $Ca(NO_3)_2$ decompose on heating as:

$$4LiNO_3 \xrightarrow{\Delta} 2\,Li_2O + 4NO_2 + O_2$$

$$2Ca(NO_3)_2 \xrightarrow{\Delta} 2\,CaO + 4NO_2 + O_2$$

Evolution of brown gas (NO_2) and gas that supports combustion (O_2) observed during decomposition of $LiNO_3$ and $Ca(NO_3)_2$.

29. (a) $2NH_4Cl + Ca(OH)_2 \rightarrow 2NH_3 + 2H_2O + CaCl_2$

In solvay process NH_4Cl can be recoverd as a by product.

30. (b) White metal = Pb + Li

31. (a)

$$Na_2CO_3 + H_2O \longrightarrow 2NaOH + H_2O$$
$$\downarrow$$
$$Na^+ + OH^-$$

32. (a) Chlorine can be manufactured by electrolysis of a sodium chloride solution (brine). The reaction takes place as follows:

At cathode: $2H^+(aq) + 2e^- \rightarrow H_2(g)$

At anode: $Cl^-(aq) \rightarrow \frac{1}{2}Cl_2(aq) + e^-$

or $2Cl^-(aq) \rightarrow Cl_2(g) + 2e^-$

33. (b)

(a) $4LiNO_3 \xrightarrow{\Delta} 2Li_2O + 4NO_2 + O_2$

(b) $2NaNO_3 \xrightarrow{\Delta} 2NaNO_2 + O_2$

(Thermal stable)

(c) $2Ba(NO_3)_2 \xrightarrow{\Delta} 2BaO + 4NO_2 + O_2$

(d) $2Be(NO_3)_2 \xrightarrow{\Delta} 2BeO + 4NO_2 + O_2$

$NaNO_3$ is thermally stable and does not gives its oxide.

34. (d) BeO and $Be(OH)_2$ are both amphoteric in nature, while metal oxides and hydroxides are basic in nature.

35. (b) Alkaline earth metal except beryllium and magnesium react with hydrogen to form corresponding hydride.

36. (b) Statement-I is correct because the greater hydration enthalpies of Be^{+2} & Mg^{+2} ions overcome the lattice enthalpy factor & therefore their sulphate are soluble in water.

But, statement-II is not correct because not only Be even Mg, Ca, Sr, Ba all of these in the nitrate form decompose on heating to give the oxide, NO_2 & O_2.

$2M(NO_3)_2 \rightarrow 2MO + 4NO_2 + O_2$

(M = Be, Mg, Ca, Sr, Ba)

37. (d) KCl does not form hydrate due to hydration energy.

Others form hydrates due to higher hydration energy because of smaller cationic size.

38. (a) density = $\frac{\text{mass}}{\text{volume}}$ $\longrightarrow$

As down the group atomic mass increase thus density increase but volume of m_g is less thus density greater than the calcium.

39. (d)

I. The increasing stability of the peroxide or superoxide, as the size of the metal ion increases is due to the stabilisation of large anions by larger cations through lattice energy effect.

II. Down the group the ionic character of the hydroxides of the alkaline earth metals increases which increases the basic strength.

III. Down the group the thermal stability of alkaline earth metal carbonates increases due to increase in the lattice enthalpy due to increase in the ionic character of the carbonates.

40. (d) Due to high difference in electronegativity.

All halogen form compound with alkaline earth metals.

41. (c) $2NaNO_3 \longrightarrow 2NaNO_2 + O_2$
(basic)

$4LiNO_3 \longrightarrow 2Li_2O + 4NO_2 + O_2$
(basic) (acidic)

$Be(NO_3)_2 \longrightarrow [Be_4O(NO_3)_6]$
basic

$2Ca(NO_3)_2 \longrightarrow 2CaO(s) + 4NO_2(g) + O_2$
basic acidic

So, $Ca(NO_3)_2$ and $LiNO_3$ give both acidic and basic oxide along with O_2.

42. (a) Beryllium does not directly react with hydrogen.

43. (b) $Be(OH)_2$ is amphoteric, but the hydroxides of Mg, Ca, Sr and Ba are basic. The strength increases from Mg to Ba.

Carbonates of group 2 elements become more thermally stable down the group. The larger compounds require more heat than the lighter compounds in order to decompose.

$BeCO_3$	$MgCO_3$	$CaCO_3$	$SrCO_3$	$BaCO_3$
< 100°C	540°C	900°C	1290°C	1360°C

The solubility of the sulphates in water decreases down the group. Be > Mg >> Ca > Sr > Ba. The higher solubilities of $BeSO_4$ and $MgSO_4$ have high enthalpy of solvation of the smaller Be^{2+} and Mg^{2+} ions.

On heading, the alkaline earth metal nitrates decompose 10 give metal oxide, nitrogen dioxide and oxygen

$$2M(NO_3)_2 \xrightarrow{\Delta} 2MO + 4NO_2 + O_2$$

(M = Be, Mg, Ca)

Only 2nd option is incorrect.

44. (a) (2, 6, 6)

$BaCl_2.2H_2O$, $CaCl_2.6H_2O$, $SrCl_2.6H_2O$

so x, y, z are 2, 6, 6.

45. (c) The density of alkaline earth metals varies in the following order:-

Ca < Mg < Be < Sr < Ba < Ra

This is due to low mass and high volume of Ca compared to other members.

46. (b) $4LiNO_3 \xrightarrow{\Delta} 2Li_2O + 4NO_2 + O_2$ (anomalous behaviour)

$2Ba(NO_3)_2 \xrightarrow{\Delta} 2BaO + 4NO_2 + O_2$

Thus, (i) is correct.

The solubility of alkaline earth metals decreases down the group due to a decrease in hydration enthalpy compared to the lattice enthalpy.

Thus, $BaSO_4$ will be less soluble in water than $CaSO_4$.

Thus, (ii) is also correct.

Alkaline earth metals dissolve in liquid ammonia to form a coloured solution.

$M + (x + y) NH_3 \rightarrow [M(NH_3)_x]^{2+} + 2[e(NH_3)_y]^-$

Thus, (iii) is incorrect.

47. (d) The density of the alkaline earth metals first decreases down the group and then increases.

The variation in the densities is a result of the cumulative effect of the atomic size and various inter molecular forces acting in the metal atoms.

The correct order of the density is:-

Ca (1.55) < Mg (1.74) < Be (1.84) < Sr (2.63)

48. (d)

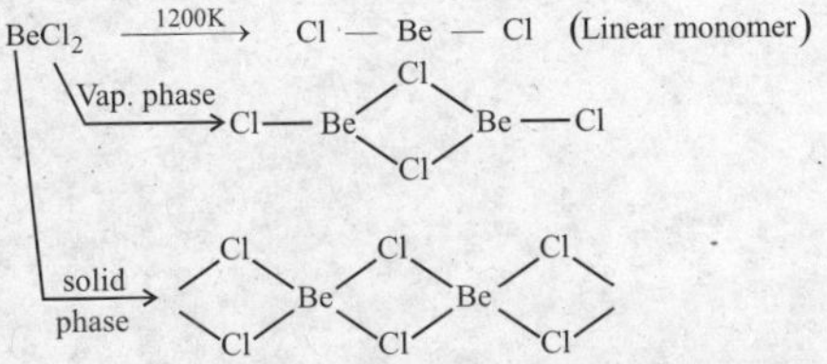

49. (a) Charge density over Mg^{2+} is highest as Mg^{2+} has the smallest ionic radius and highest cationic charge.

50. (c) (Mg, Ca) + Air(O_2, N_2) $\rightarrow$

(MgO, CaO) + (Mg_3N_2, Ca_3N_2)

51. (a) Smaller the size of the cation, greater is the hydration enthalpy.

52. (c) Li^+ among group-1 metals and Mg^{2+} of group-2 metals have similar ionic radii Li and Mg react with oxgen to give monoxide Li_2O and MgO respectively with nitrogen they give Li_3N and Mg_3N_2 respectively.

53. (c) Be and Mg are kinetically inert to oxygen and water because of the formation of an oxide film on their surface. So only III and IV pair are reacts with water.

54. (c) According to question, the monoxide (XO) is amphoteric. Among group 2 alkaline earth metals, Beryllium (Be) forms an amphoteric oxide (BeO) whereas oxides of other members of group 2 are basic in nature.

BeO can be converted to $BeCl_2$ by heating with carbon and chlorine.

$$BeO + C + Cl_2 \xrightarrow{\Delta} BeCl_2 + CO$$

Be shows diagonal relationship with Al due to their similar charge to size ratio. Both form amphoteric oxides and covalent chlorides.

55. (d) $BeCO_3$ is highly unstable due to small size and high polarising power of Be^{2+} ion (Fazan's Rule). It has a strong tendency to polarise CO_3^{2-} ion causing its decomposition even at room temperature.

56. (c) All alkaline earth metals combine with H_2 upon heating and form MH_2 type of hydrides is incorrect since, Be does not react directly with hydrogen to form BeH_2. BeH_2 is synthesized using organometallic precursors in an inert atmosphere.

57. (a) Calcium phosphate hydroxy apatite.

$$3Ca_3(PO_4)_2 . Ca(OH)_2 + 2F^- \longrightarrow 3[Ca_3(PO_4)_2 . CaF_2]$$

$X = Ca(OH)_2$

$Y = CaF_2$

58. (d) Li and Mg being hard metals are used as an alloy in armour plates.

Cu - Be alloy is used in high-strength springs due to ductility of Cu.

Mg - Al alloy is used in aircraft construction as Al is a versatile metal.

59. (b)

$$CaCO_3(s) + 2HCl(l) \longrightarrow CaCl_2(s) + CO_2(g) + H_2O(l)$$

$$CO_2 \xrightarrow{\text{slaked lime } Ca(OH)_2} \underset{\text{milky}}{CaCO_3 + H_2O}$$

60. (d)

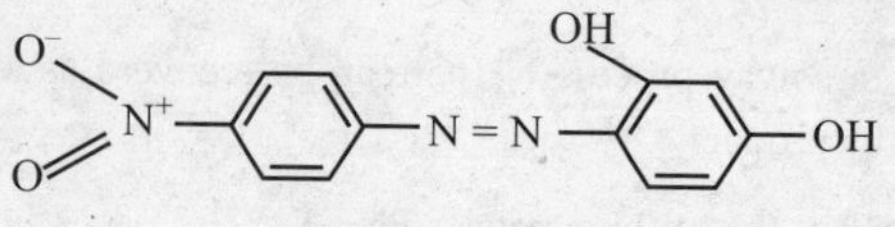

Magneson

It is a violet dye and experimentally as a pH indicator, appearing yellow below pH-11 and violet above pH-13.

In alkaline medium, it forms a complex with Mg^{2+}, which is deep blue in colour.

61. (d) A smoke screen is a dense cloud of fake smoke used to hide military areas.

$$Ca_3P_2 + 6H_2O \rightarrow 3Ca(OH)_2 + 2PH_3$$

PH_3 spontaneously catches fire to produce P_2O_5:

$$2PH_3 + 4O_2 \rightarrow P_2O_5 + 3H_2O$$

P_2O_5 forms a white dense smoke screen.

Appendix-III

The p-Block Elements (Group-13)

1. **(b)**

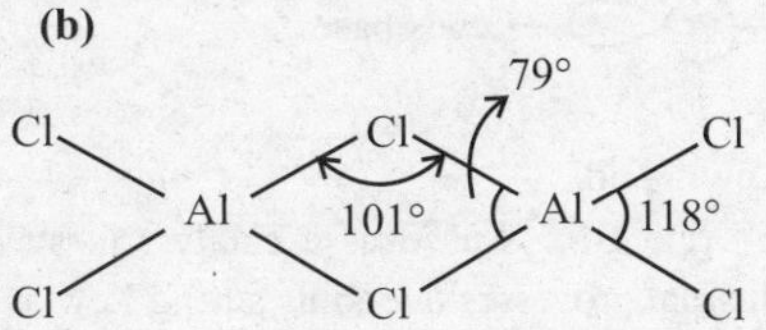

2. **(b)**

$2NaBH_4 + I_2 \rightarrow B_2H_6 \uparrow + 2NaI + H_2 \uparrow$

(X) (Y) (colourless toxic gas)

3. **(b)**

$2NaBH_4 + I_2 \longrightarrow 2NaI + B_2H_6(g) + H_2$

$2NaH + B_2H_6 \longrightarrow 2NaBH_4$

$B_2H_6 + 6H_2O \longrightarrow 2H_3BO_3 + 6H_2$

$B(OH)_3 + H_2O \rightleftharpoons [B(OH)_4]^- + H_3O^+$

Haber's process-

$N_2(g) + 3H_2(g) \rightleftharpoons 3NH_3(g)$

4. **(b)** $Na_2B_4O_7 + 7H_2O \longrightarrow 4H_3BO_3 + 2NaOH$

Acid formed = H_3BO_3 (Boric acid)

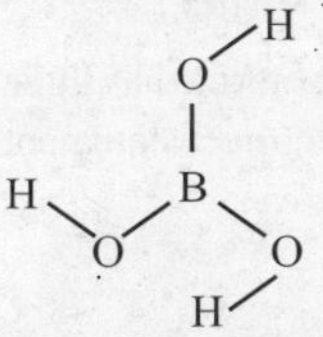

Central B atom hybridisation = sp^2

5. **(a)** Boron fibres are used in aerospace/ composite materials not for manufacturing of glass wool because boron fibres are high strength, light weight reinforcing materials, while glass wool is made up of silica (SiO_2) along with soda ash and limestone.

6. **(d)** $2B + 3F_2 \longrightarrow 2BF_3$ (Y)

$2BF_3 + 6NaH \xrightarrow{450K} B_2H_6 + 6NaF$ (Z)

$B_2H_6 + 3O_2 \longrightarrow B_2O_3 + 3H_2O$ (W)

7. **(c)** Diborane (B_2H_6) has two bridge bonds (banana bond) and each bond is 3-centre-2-etectron bond. So total number of e^- involved

$= 2 \times 2e^-/\text{bond} = 4$ electrons.

8. **(b)** $Na_2B_4O_7 + HCl \rightarrow H_3BO_3 + NaCl$

(Borax) (Boric acid)

H_3BO_3 is monobasic acid, it acts as a weak Lewis acid, it accepts OH^- from water rather than donating $3H^+$

$B(OH)_3 + H_2O \rightleftharpoons [B(OH)_4]^- + H^+$

9. **(d)** BCl_3 upon hydrolysis gives a complex ion (x) $[B(OH)_4]^-$ which is sp^3 hybridized (Tetrahedral).

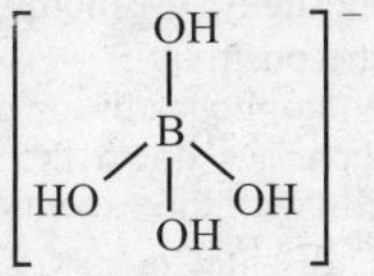

While, $AlCl_3$ in acidified aqueous solution forms the octahedral aqua complex $[Al(H_2O)_6]^{3+}$ (Y), where Al is sp^3d^2 hybridized.

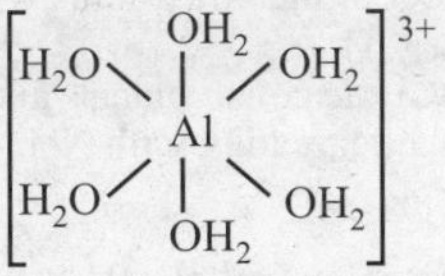

10. **(c)** Boric acid H_3BO_3 is a tribaric acid. Thalium more stable in +3 oxidation state.

$Th^{+3} \Rightarrow [Xe]\ 4f^{14}\ 5d^{10}\ 6s^0\ 6p^0$

11. **(d)** Due to weaker sheilding of electrons, Ga, In, and Tl have greater effective nuclear charge that results in higher electronegativity. Among these three elements, the order of electronegativity is Tl > In > Ga due to weaker sheilding 5d, 4f, 4d and 3d orbitals respectively. Therefore the complete order is

B > Tl > In > Ga > Al

12. **(c)** I. $2Na[BH_4] + I_2 \rightarrow B_2H_6 + H_2 + 2NaI$

II. $B_2H_6 + 2(Me)_3N \rightarrow 2[Me_3N.BH_3]$

III. $2Al + 2NaOH + 6H_2O \rightarrow 2Na^+[Al(OH)_4]^- + 3H_2$

IV. $2BF_3 + 6NaH \rightarrow B_2H_6 + 6NaF$

So I and III reactions produce H_2 gas.

13. **(a)** Cryolite is not associated with water molecules because its chemical formula is Na_3AlF_6 whereas in others like Bauxite, $Al_2O_3 \cdot 2H_2O$, Borax, $Na_2B_4O_7 \cdot 10H_2O$ and Kernite, $Na_2B_4O_7 \cdot 4H_2O$ these are associated with water molecules in their formula.

14. **(b)** Orthoboric acid (H_3BO_3) is a weak Lewis acid and not a Bronsted-Lowry tribasic acid.

15. **(c)** $2BF_3 + 6\,LiAl\,H_4 \xrightarrow{\text{Diethyl ether}} B_2H_6 + 6LiF + 6AlF_3$

On large scale (Industrial preparation)

$2BF_3 + 6\,NaH \xrightarrow{450\,K} B_2H_6 + 6NaF$

16. **(a)** Al_2O_3 is amphoteric in nature because it reacts with both acid as well as base.

$Al_2O_3 + 6HCl\ \ 2AlCl_3 + 3H_2O$

$Al_2O_3 + 2NaOH\ \ 2NaAlO_2 + H_2O$

Tl_2O_3 is more basic than Ga_2O_3 because down the group metallic character increases and metallic oxides are basic in nature.

17. **(a)** Aluminium does not react with concentrated nitric acid due to formation of protective oxide layer on the surface.

18. **(b)**

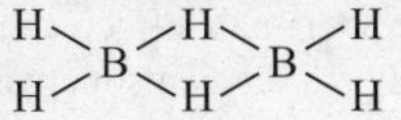

(x) 2c – 2e = 4

(y) 3c – 2e = 2

∴ $x + y = 6$

19. **(b)** Order of electronegativity of boron family

B > Al > In > Tl

Boric acid is monobasic acid but not protonic acid it is Lewis acid.

Thus both statement is incorrect.

20. **(b)** Boron fibres are used for making bullet-proof vests metal borides used as protective shield because it has the capacity to absorb neutrons. Borates are used in a range of glass and glass product where they increase the meachanical strength of glass.

21. **(c)**

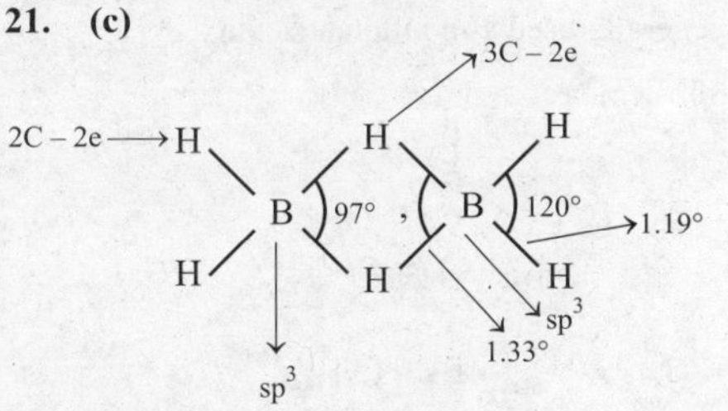

22. **(b)** $4BF_3 + 3LiAlH_4 \longrightarrow 2B_2H_6 + 3LiF + 3AlF_3$

Lewis acid [toxic gas]

$\downarrow O_2$ $\downarrow NH_3$

$B_2O_3 + H_2O$ (Acidic oxide) $B_3N_3H_6$ (Inorganic Benzene)

23. **(d)** 118, 79, 101

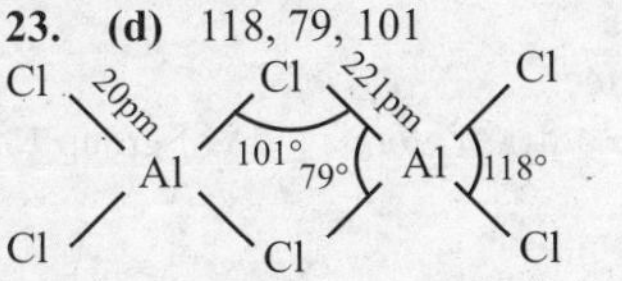

b_1, b_2, b_3 is 118, 79, 101.

24. **(c)**

(i) $2NaBH_4 + I_2 \rightarrow B_2H_6 + 2NaI + H_2$

(ii) $B_2H_6 + 3O_2 \rightarrow B_2O_3 + 3H_2O + \text{Energy}$

(iii) $B_2H_6\,(g) + 6H_2O \rightarrow 2B\,(OH)_3 + 6H_2$

$B(OH)_3 + H_2O \rightleftharpoons B(OH)_4^- + H^+$

$B(OH)_3$ is a monobasic acid.

25. **(b)** Quartz is a piezoelectric material. Piezoelectric material involves development of electric charge due to movement of electron upon application of stress.

26. (d) 1. $2\,NaBH_4 + I_2 \rightarrow B_2H_6 + 2NaI + H_2\uparrow$

2. $B_2H_6 + 6H_2O \rightarrow 2B(OH)_3 + 6H_2\uparrow$

3. $3B_2H_6 + 6NH_3 \rightarrow 3[BH_2(NH_3)_2]^+[BH_4]^-$

$$\xrightarrow{heat} 2B_3NH_3H_6 + 12H_2\uparrow$$

4. $B_2H_6 + 3O_2 \rightarrow B_2O_3 + 3H_2O$

27. (a) Due to inert pair effect, the stability of +1 state in group 13 elements increases down the group.
Opposite trend is observed for +3 state stability.

28. (c) Al^{3+} is much more stable than Al and due to electropositive nature, the standard reduction potential of Al^{3+}/Al is negative.
Tl is not as electropositive as Al and therefore Tl^{3+} can easily be reduced to Tl because of which its SEP value is positive.

29. (c) Thallium electronegativity = 1.62 (Pauling scale)
Aluminium electronegativity = 1.61
Boron is a bad conductor of electricity at low temperatures.
B-11 isotope is a stable and non-radioactive isotope.
An aqueous solution of orthoboric acid is generally used as a mild antiseptic.

30. (c)

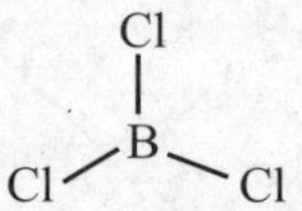

Trigonal planar

$BCl_3 + \ddot{N}H_3 \rightarrow BCl_3(NH_3)$;

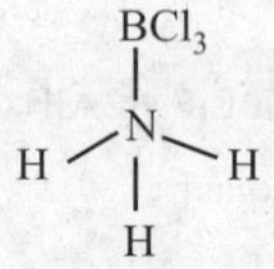

Tetrahedral

31. (d) Boron exists in crystalline and amorphous allotropes like α- and β-rhombohedral and β-tetragonal allotrope.
Thus, I is not correct.
Boron is extremely hard and black-coloured solid and high-melting due to high crystal lattice enthalpy.
Thus, II is correct.

32. (a). The order of atomic radii of group 13 elements varies as:-
B < Ga < Al < In < Tl
This is due to weak shielding of outermost electrons by 3d-subshell that causes Ga to become smaller than Al.
Thus, (i) is correct.
The correct order of ionization enthalpy of group 13 elements is :-
B > Tl > Ga > Al > In
This is due to poor shielding by d-subshells and f-subshells that result in ionization enthalpy being higher for Tl and Ga.
Thus, statement (ii) is incorrect.
Boron trioxide B_2O_3 is acidic in nature as it is a non-metal oxide and dissolves in water to form H_3BO_3.
Thus, statement (iii) is incorrect.

33. (a) The melting points of group 13 elements follow the order:-
B > Al > Tl > In > Ga
This is due to strong crystalline structure of B and soft metallic nature of the rest of the metals.
Gallium has unusually low melting point due to very high electro positivity.

34. (b) The atomic radii or metallic radii of elements increases down the group due to increasing shells with the exception of Gallium (Ga) in the 13th group.
This is due to the presence of d-subshell that offers poorer shielding of the outermost p-electrons.
Thus, the order of metallic radius will be:-
Ga < Al < In < Tl

35. (a) BCl_3 trigonal planar and it acts as Lewis acid while treating with NH_3.

36. (d)

$$2AlCl_3 + 6HCl \longrightarrow 2\left[Al(H_2O)_6\right]^{3+} + 6Cl^- + 3H_2$$

6-coordinated Al, sp^3d^2

37. (d) Borax = $Na_2B_4O_7 \cdot 10H_2O$
= $Na_2[B_4O_5(OH)_4] \cdot 8H_2O$
$Na_2B_4O_7 \cdot 10H_2O + H_2O \rightarrow NaOH + H_3BO_3$

38. (c) $B_2H_6 + LiH \longrightarrow LiBH_4$
∴ X should be metal hydride.

39. (c) Maximum covalency of B is 4 as it has only 2p orbital at the outermost shell.

40. (d) Boron is highly crystalline black coloured solid. ^{10}B isotopic has high ability to absorb neutrons. That's why metal borides are used in nuclear chemistry as protective shields and control rods.
Boron has high melting point, low density and very low conductivity of electricity.

41. (a) The molecular geometry of BCl_3 is trigonal planar.
In BCl_3, NH_3, the central atom B has 6 valence electrons that makes it an electron deficient molecule. BCl_3 acts as a Lewis acid as it requires 2 electrons to complete its octet. NH_3 can donate its lone pair to boron. The resulting structure is tetrahedral.

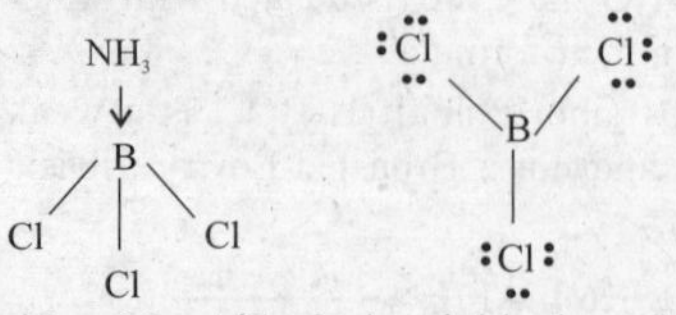

42. (c) AlF_3 is insoluble in anhydrous HF because F^- ion is not available for H-bonding but it is soluble in HF only in presence of KF due to formation of $K_3[AlF_6]$.

$$\underset{\text{Aluminium trifluoride}}{AlF_3(s)} \xrightarrow{HF} AlF_3 + 3KF \xrightarrow[KF]{HF} \underset{\substack{\text{(Soluble)}\\ \text{Potassium hexafluorido aluminate (III)}}}{K_3[AlF_6]}$$

43. (b)

$$\underset{\text{Borax}}{Na_2B_4O_7} + 7H_2O \longrightarrow \underset{\text{Sodium hydroxide}}{2\,NaOH} + \underset{\text{Boric acid}}{4H_3BO_3}$$

44. (a)

$$\underset{\text{Boron trichloride}}{BCl_3} + 3H_2O \longrightarrow \underset{\text{Boric acid}}{H_3BO_3} + 3HCl$$

45. (c) B in BF_3 has incomplete octet and thus it is electron deficiency due to which it can accept lone-pair of electrons and acts as Lewis acid.

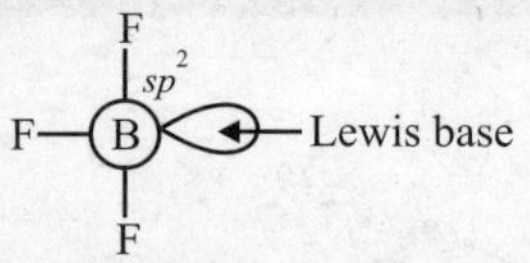

Lewis acid

46. (c) BF_3 is used as a catalyst in several industrial processes due to its strong Lewis acid nature.
BF_3 has sp^2 hybridisation and is electron deficient. Thus, acts as Lewis acid.

47. (a)

$$2NaH + B_2H_6 \xrightarrow{\text{Diethlether}} \underset{\text{'X'}}{2\,Na\left[BH_4\right]}$$

Hence, X is $Na[BH_4]$.

48. (b) Ga_2O_3 is an amphoteric oxide
Reaction with an acid
$Ga_2O_3 + 6HCl \rightarrow 2GaCl_3 + 3H_2O$
Reaction with a base :
$Ga_2O_3 + 2NaOH \rightarrow 2\,NaGaO_2 + H_2O$
(II) The dimer of aluminium chloride has three Al-Cl-Al bridge bond is not the correct statement as structure of Al_2Cl_6 is as follows:

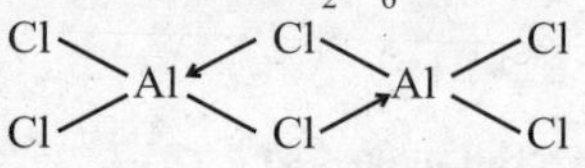

(i.e. has only two Al—Cl—Al bridge bonds)
(III) Boron is very hard refractory solid of high melting temperature as its melting point is 2349 K.

49. (c)

$$2BF_3 + 6NaH \xrightarrow{450\,K} 6NaF + \underset{(X)}{B_2H_6}$$

$$\underset{\text{Diborane}}{B_2H_6} + 2LiH \xrightarrow{\text{Diethyl ether}} \underset{\substack{(Y)\\ \text{Lithiumborohydride}}}{2LiBH_4}$$

50. (d) (i)

$$2Al(s) + 6HCl(aq) \longrightarrow 2AlCl_3(aq) + 3H_2$$

(ii)

$$2Al(s) + 2NaOH(aq) \longrightarrow \underset{\text{Sodium tetrahydroxi aluminate (III)}}{2Na\left[Al(OH)_4\right]} + 3H_2$$

(iii) $NaBH_4 + I_2 \longrightarrow B_2H_6 + 2NaI + H_2$

51. (a) $AlCl_3$ exists as a dimer through halogen bridged bonds. In dimer $AlCl_3$ aluminium completes its loctet through coordinates bond by chloine atom.

The p-Block Elements (Group-14)

1. **(d)** $[SiCl_6]^{2-}$ is not possible due to excessive steric hindrance. Si being a smaller element cannot bond with 6 Cl atoms.

2. **(c)**

Allotrope of carbon		Production		Uses	
(i)	Carbon Black (X)	(i)	Burning hydrocarbon in a limited supply of air	(i)	Black pigment in black ink
(ii)	Activated Charcoal (Y)	(ii) & (iii)	Charcoal and coke are obtained by heating wood or coal at high temperature in the absence of air	(ii)	Water to remove filters organic contamination, air-conditioning system
(iii)	Coke (Z)			(iii)	Fuel and reducing agent in metallurgy

3. **(d)** Silanes (SiH_4) are silicons hydrides. Silicons has 4 valence electrons and forms 4 covalent bond with hydrogen because it has no lone pair of electrons left to donate it cannot act as a Lewis base.

4. **(d)** Carbon black is used in tyres, inks and pigments not for adsorbing poisonous gase, to adsorb poisonous gase, activated charcoal is used.

5. **(b)** Boron and silicon having diagonal relationship they both form hydrides, acidic oxides and covalent halides that can go undergo hydrolysis but boron hydrides are electron deficient (e.g.: B_2H_6) while silicon hydrides (silones) are electron precise.

6. **(d)** Among the given oxides the amphoteric oxides are GeO_2, SnO_2, PbO_2 and PbO.

7. **(a)** Germanium is metalloid its lower oxides, GeO, is amphoteric. However, its higher oxide, GeO_2 is purely acidic in nature.

8. **(b)** SiO_2 react with HF.

$$SiO_2 + 4HF \longrightarrow SiF_4 + 2H_2O$$

With excess HF

$$SiO_2 + 6HF \longrightarrow H_2SiF_6 + 2H_2O$$

9. **(a)** (I) CO_2 is acidic, CO is neutral- Correct

(II) Cristobalite is a crystalline form of silica- Correct

(III) Solid CO_2 is called as dry ice (not liquid CO)

(IV) CO acts as Lewis Base because of lone pair on 'C'

Hence, only statement I, II are correct.

10. **(a)**

- Galena (PbS) is a sulphide ore of Pb so X is Pb
- Cassiterite (SnO_2) is an oxide ore of Sn, so Y is Sn

11. **(b)** The oxide which acts acid as well as base are called amphoteric oxide

CO_2 - Acidic oxide

GeO_2-Acidic oxide

SnO_2 - Acidic oxide

PbO_2 - Can act as an amphoteric oxide

CO - Neutral oxide

GeO - can act as an amphoteric

SnO- can act as an amphoteric oxide

PbO - This is a amphoteric oxide

12. **(b)**

$$\underbrace{2C(s) + O_2(g) + 4N_2(g)}_{\text{producer gas}} \xrightarrow{1273K} 2CO(g) + 4N_2(g)$$

In producer gas H_2 is present in small amount and is used for combustion.

13. **(b)** CO_2 gas is a green house gas and a major contributor of global warming.

14. **(a)** CCl_4 does not hydrolysed by water due to unavailable of vacant orbital but $SiCl_4$ have vacent *d* orbital and central atom Si can accommodate the lone pair of electrons.

Ge(+IV) is more stable than Ge(+II). So both statements are correct.

15. **(d)** Silica also known as Silicon dioxide is a covalent, 3D network solid in which each Si atom is covalently bonded in a tetrahedral manner to four oxygen atoms.

16. **(d)** $GeCl_2$ is less stable than $GeCl_4$ as +4 state is more stable than the +2 state for Ge.

+2 state becomes more stable for heavier elements like Sn and Pb due to inert pair effect. Thus, III is incorrect.

17. **(c)** Silicones are stable at high temperature biocompatible, so used in medical devices and water repelling in nature.

18. **(a)** Ge > Sn > Pb for Ionisation enthalpy small decrease in $\Delta_i H$ from Si to Ge to Sn and slight increase in $\Delta_i H$ from Sn to Pb is the consequence of poor shielding effect of intervening *d* & *f* orbitals and increase in size of the atom.

19. **(c)** In Buckminster Fullerene C_{60} has 12 five member and 20 six member rings are present and their sum is (20 + 12) 32.

20. **(d)**

Compound	Use
Kieselghur	Filtration plant
Silica gel	Chromotographic material
ZSM - 5	To convert alcohol directly into gasoline
Hydrated zeolies	Softening of hand water

21. **(c)** CO is poisonous to living beings it bind with hemoglobin more effectively than oxygen causing oxygen defficiency.

22. **(a)** $[SiCl_6]^{2-}$ does not exist because six large chloride ion cannot be effectively accomodated around Si^{4+} silicon atom due to relatively small size limited ability to expend its coordination sphere.

23. **(b)** Most of the MX_4 (X = F, Cl, Br, I) are covalent in nature in group 14 element but exception are SnF_4 and PbF_4 which are ionic in nature.

24. **(c)** In group 14, most of the MX_4 are covalent in nature exceptions one SnF_4 and PbF_4 because there is more electro-negativity difference make the bond ionic. So statement I is correct.

Ge electronic configuration : $[Ar]3d^{10}\,4s^2\,4p^2$ the Ge^{+4} oxidation is more stable because its allows germanium to achieve a full valence shell, which is energetically more favorable than having an incomplete valence shell in the Ge^{+2} oxidation state.

'So' only statement I is correct.

25. **(d)** A graphite crucible is a container used for melting and casting non-ferrous, non-iron metals shape as gold, silver, aluminium.

Activated charcoal is the ideal water filter because it remove toxins from water without stripping the water of salt S and important minerals.

Black carbon is used as a colorant and reinforcing filler in tires and other rubber products.

So, only (i) and (ii) are true.

26. **(b)** Hydrated sodium aluminium silicate is zeolite.

It is $Na_2\,Al_2\,Si_2O_8.x\,H_2O$

27. (c) Allotropic forms of carbon is aromatic is buck minister fullerene (C_{60}).
(i) The number of five membered ring in all fullerenes is 12.
(ii) The number of six membered ring in C_{60} is 20.

28. (b) Basic unit of silicates is SiO_4^{4-}.

29. (a) GeO_2
1. GeO is acidic in nature.
2. CO is a neutral
3. PbO_2 is Amphoteric in nature
4. SnO is Amphoteric in nature

30. (a) Bond enthalpy is the measure of strength of a chemical bond. Higher the bond energy more will be the energy require to break the bond. Among the element carbon show maximum catenation so its bond enthalpy is high as compare to other as we go down the group size of atom increase and their bond will become easy to break. So bond energy decrease.

31. (d) $Sn(s) + 2H_2O(g) \rightarrow SnO_2(s) + 2H_2(g)$

32. (d) Carbon black is used as a filler in automobile tyres due to its amorphous nature.
Graphite is used as electrodes in batteries due to being an electrical conductor.
Diamond is used as an abrasive due to its hard nature. Activated charcoal is used in air conditioning systems due to absorbing nature.

33. (a) Thermodynamic stability order :-
Graphite > Diamond > Fullerene > Coke
$\Delta H°$ (allotropic transformation) graphite to diamond $= +1.9$ kJ mol^{-1}.

34. (c) Acidic oxides = CO_2, SiO_2, GeO
Amphoteric oxides = SnO, PbO, PbO_2
Neutral oxides = CO

35. (d) Metalloids in group 14 = Ge
Non – metals = C, Si
Metals = Sn, Pb
Thus, Statement in option (d) is incorrect.

36. (a) For a good quality cement :-
Silica (SiO_2) : Alumina (Al_2O_3) = 2.5 – 4.0
Lime (CaO) : $SiO_2 + Al_2O_3 + Fe_2O_3 = 2$

37. (a) The enthalpy of formation of a substance is the amount of energy required to prepare it from its onstituents in their most stable states.
Since graphite is the most stable allotrope of carbon, its enthalpy of formation is zero.
Thus, both Assertion (A) and Reason (R) are correct statements and Reason (R) explains Assertion (A).

38. (c) The melting and boiling points of group 13 elements are lower than those of corresponding group 14 elements due to higher atomic masses and greater number of bonds between the atoms of group 14 elements.
Thus, (i) is incorrect.
SiO is less stable than SiO_2 so it exists only at higher temperatures.
Thus, (ii) is correct.
PbI_4 does not exist as Pb prefers +2 state rather than +4 state due to inert pair effect.
Thus, (iii) is correct
Buckminster fullerene contains 20 six-membered and 12 five-membered rings.
Thus, (iv) is incorrect.

39. (b) Statement-I is correct as Ge and Sn exist on earth's crust in trace amounts (1 – 2 ppm).
Statement-II is correct as Pb belongs to group 14 and thus has four valence electrons out of which all four are used to make the four Pb - F bonds. The resultant geometry is tetrahedral.
Statement-III is incorrect as the stability of the +2 oxidation state increases down the group due to inert pair effect and is predominant for heavier elements.
Ge prefers +4 state over +2 so Ge X_4 is more stable than Ge X_2.

40. (b) GeO = Acidic oxide (Metalloid)
CO = Neutral oxide
SnO, PbO = Amphoteric oxides

41. (d) Higher the atomic weight higher is the density.

42. (c) As the radii of atoms increase the bond lengths increase and thus, the bond enthalpy decrease.
Order of Atomic Radii: Si < Ge < Sn
Order of Bond length: Si – Si < Ge – Ge < Sn – Sn
∴ Order o f Bond enthalpy: Si – Si > Ge – Ge > Sn – Sn

43. (a) 20 six membered and 12 five membered rings are in Buckminster fullerene.

44. (c) CCl_4 does not undergo hydrolysis since C does not have 'd' orbital to accept the electrons from donor.
∴ (I) is incorrect.
GP. 14 elements have 4 electrons in their valence shells. So, (+4) and (+2) are the common oxidate states (O.S.) from C to Pb. However, the stability of (+4) O.S. decreases from Ge to Pb (Ge < Sn < Pb) due to inert pair effect. Therefore, Ge forms stable compound in (+4) O.S. and Pb in (+2) O.S. ∴ (II) & (III) are correct.
Stability of dihalides increases down the group.
∴ (IV) is incorrect.

45. (b) Graphite has benzene like planar structure.
Diamond has tetrahedrally bonded C atoms.
Fullerence, C_{60} has 20 six membered and 12 five membered rings. Spherical fullness are also called bucky balls.

46. (d) PbI_4 does not exist because Pb-I bond initially formed during the reaction does not release enough energy to unpair $6s^2$ electrons and excite them to higher orbital in order to get 4 unpaired electrons around Pb atom.

47. (c) Carbon is placed in 2nd period and electronic configuration of C_6 is $1s^2\ 2s^2\ 2p^2$. Hence it does not have vacant *d*-orbital, and its maximum covalency is 4.
While germanium belongs to 3rd period of the periodic table. Electronic configuration of Ge is [Ar] $3d^{10}\ 4s^2\ 4p^2$. Hence, It has vacant *d*-orbital.

48. (b)
$$\underset{\text{Silicon tetrachloride}}{SiCl_4} + 4H_2O \longrightarrow \underset{\textit{ortho}\text{-silicic acid}}{Si(HO)_4} + 4HCl$$

49. (b)
$$\underset{\text{methyl chloride}}{2CH_3Cl} + Si \xrightarrow[570\,K]{Cu-powder} \underset{\text{Dimethyl silanes}}{(CH_3)_2} - \underset{\text{dichloro (P)}}{SiCl_2}$$
$$\xrightarrow[-2HCl]{2H_2O} \underset{(Q)}{(CH_3)_2\,Si(OH)_2} \longrightarrow$$

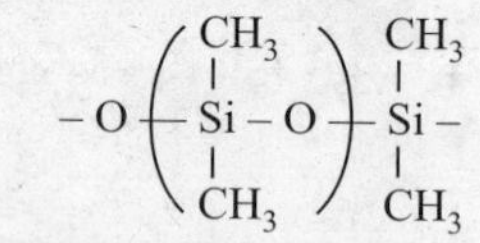

50. (b) Dry ice is solid CO_2.

51. (d) PbO_2 is weakly basic in nature. In PbO_2, Pb is in + 4 which is less stable than its + 2 oxidation state because of inert pair effect.
Hence, Pb^{4+} of PbO_2 has a tendency to be reduced into more stable Pb^{2+} (PbO) showing strong oxidising nature of PbO_2.

52. (c) The most common use of dry ice is to preserve food, using non-cyclic refrigeration. It is frequently used to pack items that must remain cold or frozen such as ice-cream or biological samples, without use of mechanical cooling.

53. (c)
(a) $HCOOH + H_2SO_4(conc.) \rightarrow CO + H_2O + H_2SO_4$
But this process is not used on commercial scale.
(b) Direct oxidation of carbon in limited supply of oxygen can give CO but the process is not used on commericial scale.
$$2C + O_2 \text{(limited supply)} \rightarrow 2CO$$
(c) When stream (H_2O) is passed over coke (C), it gives $CO + H_2$, as :
$$Coke(C) + \underset{\text{(stream)}}{H_2O} \xrightarrow[Ni]{\Delta} CO(g) + H_2(g)$$
The above process is used to produce (CO) on commercial scale.
(d) Lime stone is $CaCO_3$, on heating it gives oxygen (O_2) and CaO as :
$$CaCO_3 \xrightarrow{\Delta} CaO + O_2$$

54. (a)
$$HCOOH \xrightarrow{Conc.\ H_2SO_4} \underset{(B)}{CO} + \underset{(A)}{H_2O}$$
$$\underset{(B)}{3CO} + Fe_2O_3 \longrightarrow \underset{(D)}{2Fe} + \underset{(C)}{3CO_2}$$
$$CaCO_3 + 2HCl\,(dil.) \longrightarrow \underset{(C)}{CO_2} + H_2O + CaCl_2$$

55. (b) Assertion and Reason both are correct but Reason (R) is not the correct explanation of (A).
SiF_6^{2-} is formed but $SiCl_6^{2-}$ is not because Si can accomodate six F^- due to its smaller size but it can not accomodate six Cl^- due to its larger size and steric hindrance.
Electronegativity of F is higher than Cl

CLASS-XII

1 Solutions

CHAPTER SYNOPSIS

- Raoult's law

$$P_S = p_A + p_B = p^o_A x_A + p^o_B x_B$$

$$= (1 - x_B) p^o_A + p^o_B x_B = (p^o_B - p^o_A) x_B + p^o_A$$

$$\frac{P^o - P_S}{P^o} = \frac{n_A}{n_B} = \frac{w_A \times M_B}{M_A \times w_B}$$

Here, P_S = Total pressure

p^o_A or p^o_B = vapour pressure in pure state of component A or B, x_A or x_B =mole fraction of component A or B n_A and n_B = no. of moles of solute and solvent w_A and w_B are the masses and M_A and M_B are the molar masses of the solute and solvent respectively.

- Colligative properties $\propto$ Number of particles
  - $\propto$ Number of molecules (in case of non-electrolytes)
  - $\propto$ Number of ions (in case of electrolytes)
  - $\propto$ Number of moles of solute
  - $\propto$ Mole fraction of solute
- Elevation in boiling point $\Delta T_b = K_b m$, where,
  m = Molality
  K_b = Boiling point elevation constant or Ebullioscopic constant
- Depression of freezing point, $\Delta T_f = K_f m$

$$\left(m = \text{Molality} = \frac{w_A \text{ (g)}}{M_A \text{ (g/mol)} \times w_B \text{ (g)}} \times 1000 \right)$$

- Osmotic pressure (P or π) with depression in freezing point $\pi = \frac{\Delta T_f}{K_f m} CRT$
- $$i = \frac{\text{Normal molar mass}}{\text{Observed molar mass}} = \frac{\text{Observed colligative property}}{\text{Normal colligative property}}$$

$$i = \frac{\text{Observed osmotic pressure}}{\text{Normal osmotic pressure}} = \frac{\text{Total number of particles after association/dissociation}}{\text{No. of particles before association/dissociation}}$$

degree of association $\alpha = (i - 1) \dfrac{n}{1-n}$ and degree of dissociation $(\alpha) = \dfrac{i-1}{n-1}$

- The phenomenon of osmosis, first observed by **Abbe Nollet**, may be defined as a process in which pure solvent molecules pass through a semipermeable membrane from a solution of low concentration (or from solvent) to a solultion of higher concentration (or to a solution).
  - (a) **Exosmosis** is the outward flow of water into a cell containing an aqueous solution through a semipermeable membrane, e.g., grape in NaCl solution.
  - (b) **Endosmosis** is the inward flow of water into a cell containing an aqueous solution through a semipermeable membrane, e.g., grape in water.

Topic 1 Solubility and Concentration of Solutions

1. The mole fraction of NaOH in aqueous NaOH solution is 0.02. What is the volume (in mL) of this solution that reacts completely with 1L of 0.5 M HCl solution? (density of water = 1 g mL^{-1}) **[May 13, 2026 (II)]**
(a) 220.5 (b) 661.5
(c) 441.3 (d) 882.6

2. The mole fraction of CH_3OH in an aqueous solution is 0.02. What is the molality of this solution? **[May 12, 2026 (I)]**
(a) 4.52 m (b) 3.39 m
(c) 2.26 m (d) 1.13 m

3. What is the approximate molality of 10% (w/w) aqueous glucose solution ? **[May 26, 2025 (II)]**
(Molar mass of glucose = 180 g mol^{-1})
(a) 0.31 m (b) 0.62 m (c) 0.93 m (d) 1.24 m

4. In aqueous glucose solution, the mole fraction of water is 40 times to mole fraction of glucose. What is the weight percentage (w/w) of glucose in the solution? **[May 23, 2025 (II)]**
(a) 40 (b) 30 (c) 20 (d) 10

5. The mole fractions of glucose and water in aqueous glucose solution are 0.0244 and 0.9756 respectively. What is the weight percentage (w/w) of glucose in this solution? **[May 22, 2025 (I)]**
(a) 40 (b) 25 (c) 20 (d) 10

6. 248 g of ethylene glycol ($C_2H_6O_2$) is added to 200 g of water to prepare antifreeze. What is the molality of resultant solution? **[May 21, 2025 (I)]**
(C = 12 u; H = 1 u; O = 16 u)
(a) 5 m (b) 10 m (c) 20 m (d) 40 m

7. In water, which of the following gases has the highest Henry's law constant at 293 K? **[May 22, 2024 (II)]**
(a) N_2 (b) O_2 (c) He (d) H_2

8. 100 mL of $\frac{M}{10}$ Ca $(NO_3)_2$ and 200 mL of $\frac{M}{10}$ KNO_3 solutions are mixed. What is the normality of resulted solution with respect to NO_3^- ? **[May 21, 2024 (I)]**
(a) 0.1 N (b) 0.2 N (c) 0.13 N (d) 0.066 N

9. The mass % of urea solution is 6. The total weight of the solution is 1000 g. What is its concentration in mol L^{-1}? (density of water = 1.0 g mL^{-1}) **[May 20, 2024 (II)]**
(C = l2u, N =14u, O =16u, H = lu)
(a) 1.5 (b) 1.064 (c) 1.12 (d) 0.80

10. The density of nitric acid solution is 1.5 g mL^{-1}. Its weight percentage is 68. What is the approximate concentration (in mol L^{-1}) of nitric acid? (N =14*u*; O =16*u*; H = 1*u*) **[May 20, 2024 (I)]**
(a) 14.2 (b) 11.6 (c) 18.2 (d) 16.2

11. The concentration of 1L of $CaCO_3$ solution is 1000 ppm. What is its concentration in mol L^{-1}?
(Ca = 40u, O = 16u, C = 12 u) **[May 18, 2024 (I)]**
(a) 10^{-3} (b) 10^{-1} (c) 10^{-4} (d) 10^{-2}

12. At 293 K, methane gas was passed into 1 L of water. The partial pressure of methane is 1 bar. The number of moles of methane dissolved in 1 L water is (K_H of methane = 0.4 kbar) **[May 18, 2024 (I)]**
(a) 1.38 (b) 1.38×10^{-2}
(c) 1.38×10^{-3} (d) 1.38×10^{-1}

13. At 293 K, the Henry law constant in water for N_2 and O_2 are 76.48 k bar and 34.86 k bar respectively. What is the ratio of mole fractions of N_2 and O_2 in water?
(Assume partial pressures of N_2 and O_2 same at 293 K) **[May 18, 2023 (II)]**
(a) 2.19 (b) 0.95 (c) 0.60 (d) 0.45

14. The molarity of the solution when 4.9 g of H_2SO_4 dissolved in 250 mL of solution is **[May 18, 2023 (I); Similar to May 17, 2023 (I)]**
(a) 0.1 (b) 0.2 (c) 0.3 (d) 0.4

15. 20 mL of 0.1 M HCl is added to the 30 mL of 0.1 M NaOH. To this solution extra 50 mL of water was added. What is the molarity of the final solution formed? **[May 15, 2023 (I)]**
(a) 0.1 M (b) 0.01 M (c) 0.5 M (d) 0.05 M

16. The molarity of one molal glucose solution having density of 1.2 g/mL is **[May 15, 2023 (I)]**
(a) 0.101 M(b) 1.01 M (c) 2.01 M (d) 0.001 M

17. At T (K), the partial pressure of dissolved oxygen in 1 L water is 1 bar. The concentration of oxygen is ppm is (K_H of O_2 at T(K) is 50 kbar) **[July 8, 2022 (I)]**
(a) 71.0 (b) 35.50 (c) 17.75 (d) 81.10

18. **Assertion (A) :** For an endothermic dissolution process, increase in temperature increases the solubility in a nearly saturated solution. **[July 8, 2022 (I)]**
Reason (R) : In saturated solution dynamic equilibrium exists between dissolved solute and undissolved solute.
(a) Both (A) and (R) are correct and R is the correct explanation of A
(b) Both (A) and (R) are correct, but R is not the correct explanation of A
(c) (A) is correct but (R) is not correct
(d) (A) is incorrect but (R) is correct

19. If 2 g of NaOH is dissolved to make 200 mL solution at 25°C, the molarity (M) at 90°C is **[Sept. 17, 2020 (I)]**
(a) M < 0.25 (b) 0.5 > M > 0.25
(c) M = 0.25 (d) 0.5 < M < 1.0

20. If the K_H values for Ar(*g*), CO_2(*g*), HCHO(*g*) and CH_4(*g*) respectively are 40.39,1.67, 1.83×10^{-5} and 0.413, then identify the correct increasing order of their solubilities. **[Aug. 20, 2021 (II)]**

(a) $HCHO < CH_4 < CO_2 < Ar$
(b) $HCHO < CO_2 < CH_4 < Ar$
(c) $Ar < CO_2 < HCHO < CH_4$
(d) $Ar < CO_2 < CH_4 < HCHO$

21. If 500 mL of $CaCl_2$ solution contains 3.01×10^{22} chloride ions, molarity of the solution will be **[Aug. 20, 2021 (I)]**
(a) 0.05 M (b) 0.01 M
(c) 0.1 M (d) 0.02 M

22. The molarity of 0.2 N Na_2CO_3 solution will be **[Sept. 21, 2020 (I)]**
(a) 0.05 M (b) 0.2 M (c) 0.1 M (d) 0.4 M

23. A 40% HCl solution has density 1.2 g mL^{-1}. The molarity of the solution is nearly .... **[Sept. 17, 2020 (II)]**
(a) 11 M (b) 12 M
(c) 13 M (d) 14 M

24. The number of moles of solute present in the solutions of I, II and III is respectively **[Apr. 20, 2019 (I)]**
I. 500 mL of 0.2 M NaOH
II. 200 mL of 0.1 N H_2SO_4
III. 6 g of urea in 1 kg of water
(a) 0.1, 0.01, 0.1 (b) 0.1, 0.02, 0.1
(c) 0.2, 0.01, 0.1 (d) 0.1, 0.01, 0.2

25. Dissolving 120 g of a compound (mol. wt = 60) in 1000 g of water gave a solution of density 1.12 g mL^{-1}. The molarity of solution is **[2018]**
(a) 1.0 M (b) 2.0 M
(c) 2.5 M (d) 4.0 M

26. A gas '*X*' is dissolved in water at 2 bar pressure. Its mole fraction is 0.02 in solution. The mole fraction of water when the pressure of gas is doubled at the same temperature is **[2015]**
(a) 0.04 (b) 0.98 (c) 0.96 (d) 0.02

Topic 2 Vapour Pressure, Laws of Solutions and Ideal, Non-ideal Solutions

27. The following graph is obtained for an ideal solution containing a non-volatile solute. *x*- and *y*-axis represent, respectively **[May 27, 2025 (I)]**

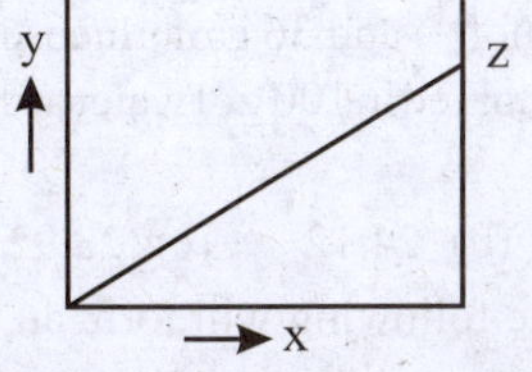

(a) mole fraction of solute, vapour pressure of solute.
(b) mole fraction of solvent, vapour pressure of solution.
(c) mole fraction of solute, vapour pressure of solution.
(d) concentration of solution, vapour pressure of solution.

28. At T(K), the vapour pressure of pure benzene and toluene are 75 and 22 mm Hg respectively. 23.4 g of benzene and 64.4 g of toluene are mixed to form an ideal solution. If the vapours are in equilibrium with the liquid mixture, the mole fraction of toluene in vapour phase is (At. wt of C = 12; H = 1) **[May 23, 2025 (I)]**
(a) 0.406 (b) 0.594 (c) 0.539 (d) 0.461

29. At 298 K, 0.714 moles of liquid A is dissolved in 5.555 moles of liquid B. The vapour pressure of the resultant solution is 475 torr. The vapour pressure of pure liquid A at the same temperature is 280.7 torr. What is the vapour pressure of pure liquid B in torr? **[May 22, 2025 (II)]**
(a) 486 (b) 550 (c) 514 (d) 500

30. At T(K), the vapour pressure of an aqueous solution of a non-volatile solute, whose mole fraction is 0.02 is found to be 34.65 mm Hg. What is the vapour pressure (in mm Hg) of pure water at the same temperature? **[May 22, 2025 (I)]**
(a) 35.70 (b) 35.36 (c) 35.00 (d) 34.30

31. At 300 K vapour pressure of a pure liquid. 'A' is 70 mm Hg. It forms an ideal solution with another liquid 'B'. The mole fraction of B in the solution is 0.2 and total vapour pressure of solution is 84 mm Hg at same temperature. What is the vapour pressure (in mm) of pure liquid B at 300 K? **[May 21, 2025 (II)]**
(a) 140 (b) 70 (c) 280 (d) 560

32. A solution containing 7.5 g of urea (molar mass = 60 g mol^{-1}) in 1 kg of water freezes at the same temperature as another solution containing 15 g of solute X, in the same amount of water. The molar mass of X (g mol^{-1}) is **[May 21, 2025 (I)]**
(a) 60 (b) 180 (c) 120 (d) 240

33. Two statements are given below.
Statement - I: Liquids A and B form a non-ideal solution with positive deviation. The interactions between A and B are weaker than A-A and B-B interactions
Statement - II: For an ideal solution. $\Delta_{mix}H = 0 : \Delta_{min}V = 0$
The correct answer is **[May 23, 2024 (I)]**
(a) Both Statements -I and Statement -II are correct
(b) Both Statements -I and Statement -II are not correct
(c) Statement-I is correct but Statement -II is not correct
(d) Statement-I is not correct but Statement-II is correct

34. At 300 K, the vapour pressures of A and B liquids are 500 and 400 mm Hg respectively. Equal moles of A and B are mixed to form an ideal solution, The mole fraction of A and B in vapour state is respectively **[May 23, 2024 (I)]**
(a) 0.5, 0.5 (b) 0.666, 0.333
(c) 0.444, 0.555 (d) 0.555, 0.444

35. At 290 K, a vessel (I) contains equal moles of three liquids (A, B, C). The boiling points of A, B and C are 350, 373 and 308 K respectively. Vessel (I) is heated to 300 K and vapours were collected into vessel (II). Identify the correct statements. (Assume vessel (I) contains liquids and vapours and vessel (II) contains only vapours)

I. Vessel – I is rich in liquid B **[May 22, 2024 (II)]**

II. Vessel – II is rich in vapour of C

III. The vapour pressures of A, B, C in Vessel (I) at 290K follows the order C > A > B.

(a) I, II, III (b) I, II only

(c) I, III only (d) II, III only

36. At T (K) two liquids A and B form an ideal solution. The vapour pressures of pure liquids A and B at that temperature are 400 and 600 mm Hg respectively. If the mole fraction of liquid B is 0.3 in the mixture, the mole fractions of A and B in vapour phase respectively are **[May 22, 2024 (I)]**

(a) 0.391, 0.609 (b) 0.509, 0.491

(c) 0.609, 0.391 (d) 0.491, 0.509

37. The following graph is obtained for vapour pressure (in atm) (on *y*-axis) and T (in K) (on *x*-axis) for aqueous urea solution and water. What is the boiling point (in K) of urea solution? (Atmospheric pressure = 1 attn) **[May 21, 2024 (II)]**

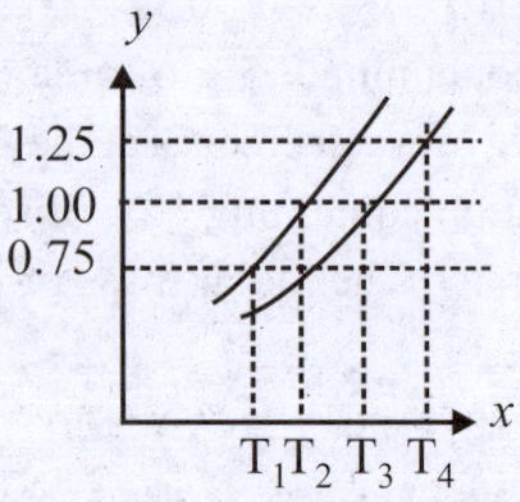

(a) T_1 (b) T_2 (c) T_3 (d) T_4

38. A solution was prepared by dissolving 0.1 mole of a non-volatile solute in 0.9 moles of water. What is the relative lowering of vapour pressure of solution? **[May 21, 2024 (I)]**

(a) 0.9 (b) 0.5 (c) 0.1 (d) 0.05

39. Which of the following is not correct? **[May 19, 2023 (I)]**

(a) n-hexane + n-heptane-Ideal solution

(b) $C_2H_5OH + H_2O$ – Positive deviation from Raoult's Law

(c) $CHC\ell_3 + CH_3-\overset{\overset{O}{\|}}{C}-CH_3$ – Negative deviation from Raoult's Law

(d) $C_2H_5OH + CH_3-\overset{\overset{O}{\|}}{C}-CH_3$ – Ideal solution

40. At 298 K, if the vapour pressure of pure liquids toluene, benzene, chloroform and dichloromethane are 60, 160, 200 and 415 torr respectively. Then which liquid is having high boiling point? **[May 18, 2023 (II)]**

(a) Toluene (b) Benzene

(c) Chloroform (d) Dichloromethane

41. A solution is formed by the combination of two liquids such as dichloromethane and chloroform. The partial pressures of dichloromethane and chloroform in solution are 285.5 and 62.4 mm Hg respectively. What is the total pressure of the solution? **[May 17, 2023 (II)]**

(a) 223.1 mm Hg (b) 347.9 mm Hg

(c) 357.9 mm Hg (d) 337.9 mm Hg

42. Which of the following does not belong to an ideal solution? **[May 15, 2023 (II)]**

(a) $\Delta H_{mix} = 0$

(b) $\Delta V_{mix} = 0$

(c) Obeys Raoult's law over the entire range of concentration

(d) Does not obey Raoult's law

43. 3.1 g of a compound, 'X' (molar mass = 62 g mol^{-1}) is dissolved in 19.5 g of other compound, Y (molar mass = 78 g mol^{-1}). The ratio of mole fractions of X and Y in the solution is **[July 7, 2022 (II)]**

(a) 1:5 (b) 5:1 (c) 4:1 (d) 1:4

44. For which of the following liquid mixtures $\Delta_{mix}H = 0$ and $\Delta_{mix}V = 0$? **[July 7, 2022 (II)]**

(a) ethyl chloride, ethyl bromide

(b) ethanol, acetone

(c) phenol, aniline

(d) chloroform, acetone

45. Which of the following condition is correct for reverse osmosis? **[July 5, 2022 (II)]**

[C = Concentration of solution in mol L^{-1}; T = Temperature in Kelvin scale; n = no of moles of solute]

(a) $P_{ext} = CRT$ (b) $P_{ext} > CRT$

(c) $P_{ext} < CRT$ (d) $P_{ext} > nRT$

46. At 298 K, the vapour pressure of pure water is 25 torr. The vapour pressure of water, when 12 g of urea (molar mass, 60 g mol^{-1}) and 36 g of glucose (molar mass, 180 g mol^{-1}) is dissolved in 100 g of water at the same temperature (in torr) is **[July 6, 2022 (I)]**

(a) 25.02 (b) 24.12 (c) 23.92 (d) 23.32

47. Which of the following will form an ideal solution? **[Aug. 19, 2021 (I)]**

(a) C_2H_5OH and H_2O

(b) HNO_3 and H_2O

(c) $CHCl_3$ and CH_3COCH_3

(d) C_6H_6 and $C_6H_5CH_3$

48. Which of the following units is useful in relating concentration of solution with its vapour pressure? **[Sept. 21, 2020 (II)]**
(a) Mole fraction (b) Parts per million
(c) Mass percentage (d) Molality

49. 160 g of non-volatile solute '*A*' is dissolved in 54 mL of water at 373 K. What is the vapour pressure of aqueous solution of *A*. **[Sept. 17, 2020 (I)]**
(Given, molecular weight of *A* = 160 g mol^{-1})
(a) 760 Torr (b) 720 Torr
(c) 570 Torr (d) 450 Torr

50. At 300 K an ideal solution is formed by mixing 460 g of toluene with 390 g benzene. If the vapour pressure of pure toluene and benzene at 300 K are 32 and 40 mm respectively, the mole fraction of toluene in vapour phase is **[Apr. 22, 2019 (I)]**
(a) 0.196 (b) 0.588 (c) 0.294 (d) 0.444

51. A solution is prepared by dissolving 10 g of a non-volatile solute (molar mass, '*M*' g mol^{-1}) in 360 g of water. What is the molar mass in g mol^{-1} of solute if the relative lowering of vapour pressure of solution is 5×10^{-3}? **[Apr. 21, 2019 (II)]**
(a) 199 (b) 99.5 (c) 299 (d) 149.5

52. The vapour pressure of pure benzene and toluene are 160 and 60 mm Hg respectively. The mole fraction of benzene in vapour phase in contact with equimolar solution of benzene and toluene is **[2016]**
(a) 0.073 (b) 0.027 (c) 0.27 (d) 0.73

Topic 3 Colligative Properties and Abnormal Molecular Masses

53. What mass (in g) of glycerol is required to produce the same anti-freezing effect in 0.1 L of water as that of 20 g of NaCl in 1.0 L of water?
(molar mass of glycerol = 92 g mol^{-1}, assume NaCl is 97% dissociated) **[May 18, 2026 (II)]**
(a) 52.96 (b) 61.96
(c) 41.91 (d) 72.96

54. At 300 K, x moles of $CaCl_2$ (i = 2.5; molar mass = 111 g mol^{-1}) is dissolved in 2.5 L of water. The osmotic pressure of resultant solution is 0.75 atm. What is ΔT_b of solution? **[May 18, 2026 (I)]**
(density of water – 1g mL^{-1}; K_b = 0.52 kg mol^{-1}; R = 0.08 L atm / $mol^{-1}K^{-1}$)
(a) 0.016 K (b) 0.032 K
(c) 0.048 K (d) 0.064 K

55. The boiling point of 1M aqueous solution of KCl (85% dissociation) having density 1.04 g mL^{-1} is
(Given : $K_b(H_2O)$ = 0.52 K kg mol^{-1}, molar mass of KCl = 74.5 g mol^{-1}) **[May 15, 2026 (II)]**
(a) 100.096°C (b) 100.996°C
(c) 100.896°C (d) 100.796°C

56. At 27°C, x g of $C_6H_{12}O_6$ (molar mass = 180 g mol^{-1}) and y g of a non-volatile, non-electrolyte (molar mass = 92 g mol^{-1}) were present separately in 1.0 L solutions. The osmotic pressure of two solutions is equal. What is x/y? **[May 15, 2026 (I)]**
(a) 45/23 (b) 23/45
(c) 32/54 (d) 54/32

57. At 300 K, a decimolar solution of potassium ferrocyanide is 50% dissociated. The osmotic pressure (in atm) of the solution is **[May 14, 2026 (II)]**
(R = 0.082 L atm K^{-1} mol^{-1})
(a) 6.83 (b) 3.87
(c) 7.38 (d) 7.83

58. 1.0 g of a non-electrolytic and non-volatile solute (X) was dissolved in 20.4 g of water. At 760 mm Hg the freezing point of solution was found to be –1.05°C. The molar mass (in g mol^{-1}) of the solute is
(K_f (H_2O) = 1.86 K kg mol^{-1}) **[May 14, 2026 (I)]**
(a) 96.8 (b) 43.4
(c) 86.8 (d) 48.4

59. An aqueous solution of a non-volatile and non-electrolytic solute boils at 100.5°C. What will be the freezing point of the same solution? **[May 13, 2026 (I)]**
(Given K_b = 0.512 K kg mol^{-1} and K_f = 1.86 K kg mol^{-1})
(a) –2.816 °C (b) –1.816 °C
(c) –0.908 °C (d) –3.632 °C

60. The value of K_f (in K kg mol^{-1}) of a solvent (X) is four times the value of its K_b. 2g of a non-volatile, non-electrolytic solute A is dissolved in 200 g of solvent X. The ΔT_b of resultant solution in YK. 4g of A is dissolved in 200 g of X and ΔT_f of resultant solution is Z K. What is the ratio of Y and Z? **[May 12, 2026 (II)]**
(Molar mass of A = 100 g mol^{-1})
(a) 1 : 2 (b) 1 : 4
(c) 1 : 8 (d) 1 : 16

61. A solution is prepared by adding 124 g of ethylene glycol (molar mass = 62 g mol^{-1}) to *x* g of water to get 10 m solution. What is the value of *x* (in g) ? **[May 27, 2025 (I)]**
(a) 100 (b) 400 (c) 800 (d) 200

62. The van't Hoff factor for 0.5 m aqueous CH_2FCOOH solution is 1.075. What is the experimentally observed ΔT_f (in K) for this solution ? **[May 26, 2025 (II)]**
(K_f = 1.86 K kg mol^{-1})
(a) 1.156 (b) 1.075 (c) 1.0 (d) 0.95

63. Elements X and Y form two non-volatile compounds (XY and XY_3). When 10 g of XY is dissolved in 50 g of ethanol, the depression in freezing point (ΔT_f) was 5.333 K. When 10 g of XY_3 is dissolved in 50 g of ethanol, the was (ΔT_f) 2.2857 K. What are the atomic weights of X and Y respectively? ($K_f = 2$ K kg mol^{-1}) **[May 26, 2025 (I)]**

(a) 50 u, 50 u (b) 25 u, 25 u
(c) 75 u, 100 u (d) 25 u, 50 u

64. At T(K), the vapour pressure of water is x kPa. What is the vapour pressure (in kPa) of 1 molal solution containing non-volatile solute? **[May 26, 2025 (I)]**

(a) 1.018 x (b) 0.8 x (c) 0.972 x (d) 0.982 x

65. At T(K), the vapour pressure of x molal aqueous solution containing a non-volatile solute is 12.078 kPa. The vapour pressure of pure water at T(K) is 12.3 kPa. What is the value of x? **[May 24, 2025 (I)]**

(a) 10 (b) 1.018 (c) 0.1018 (d) 0.018

66. An aqueous solution containing 0.2 g of a non volatile solute 'A' in 21.5 g of water freezes at 272.814 K. If the freezing point of water is 273.16 K, the molar mass (in g mol^{-1}) of solute A is [$K_f(H_2O) = 1.86$ K kg mol^{-1}] **[May 24, 2025 (I)]**

(a) 80 (b) 75 (c) 100 (d) 50

67. Benzoic acid molecules undergo dimerisation in benzene. 2.44 g of benzoic acid when dissolved in 30 g of benzene caused depression in freezing point of 2 K. What is the percentage of association of it?
(Given $K_f(C_6H_6) = 5$ K kg mol^{-1}; molar mass of benzoic acid = 122 g mol^{-1}) **[May 23, 2025 (II)]**

(a) 80 (b) 70 (c) 60 (d) 90

68. A solution of urea in water has a boiling point of 100.18°C. What is the freezing point of the same solution, if K_f and K_b of water are 1.86 and 0.52 K kg mol^{-1}, respectively? (Boiling point of water = 100°C) **[May 23, 2025 (I)]**

(a) –0.34°C (b) –0.22°C
(c) –0.64°C (d) –0.32°C

69. 1.95 g of non-volatile and non-electrolyte solute dissolved in 100 g of benzene lowered the freezing point of it by 0.64 K. The molar mass of the solute (in g mol^{-1}) ($K_f(C_6H_6)$ = 5.12 K kg mol^{-1}) **[May 22, 2025 (II)]**

(a) 240 (b) 156 (c) 165 (d) 265

70. A centi molar solution of acetic acid is 50% dissociated at 27°C. The osmotic pressure of the solution (in atm) is (R = 0.083 L atm K^{-1} mol^{-1}) **[May 21, 2025 (II)]**

(a) 0.37 (b) 3.7 (c) 0.037 (d) 0.73

71. At 300 K, 6 g of urea was dissolved in 500 mL of water. What is the osmotic pressure (in atm) of resultant solution? (R = 0.082 L atm K^{-1} mol^{-1}) **[May 22, 2024 (II)]**
(C = 12; N = 14; O = 16; H = 1)

(a) 0.492 (b) 2.46 (c) 4.92 (d) 49.2

72. Benzoic acid undergoes dimerization in benzene. x g of benzoic acid (molar mass 122 g mol^{-1}) is dissolved in 49 g of benzene. The depression in freezing point is 1.12K. If degree of association of acid is 88%, what is the value of x? (K_f for benzene = 4.9 K kg mol^{-1}) **[May 22, 2024 (I)]**

(a) 2.44 (b) 1.22 (c) 3.66 (d) 4.88

73. Given below are two statements.

Statement I: Liquids A and B form a non-ideal solution with negative deviation. The interactions between A and B are weaker than A-A and B-B interactions

Statement II: In reverse osmosis, the applied pressure must be higher than the osmotic pressure of solution

The correct answer is **[May 21, 2024 (II)]**

(a) Both Statement-I and Statement-II are correct
(b) Both Statement-I and Statement-II are not correct
(c) Statement-I is correct but Statement-II is not correct
(d) Statement-I is not correct but Statement-II is correct

74. A non-volatile solute is dissolved in water. The ΔT_b of resultant solution is 0.052 K. What is the freezing point of the solution (in K)? **[May 20, 2024 (II)]**
(K_b of water = 0.52 K kg mol^{-1}; K_f of water = 1.86 K kg mol^{-1}, Freezing point of water = 273 K)

(a) 272.628 (b) 273.186
(c) 273.000 (d) 272.814

75. The osmotic pressure of sea water is 1.05 atm. Four experiments were carried as shown in table. In which of the following experiments, pure water can be obtained in part-II of vessel. **[May 20, 2024 (I)]**

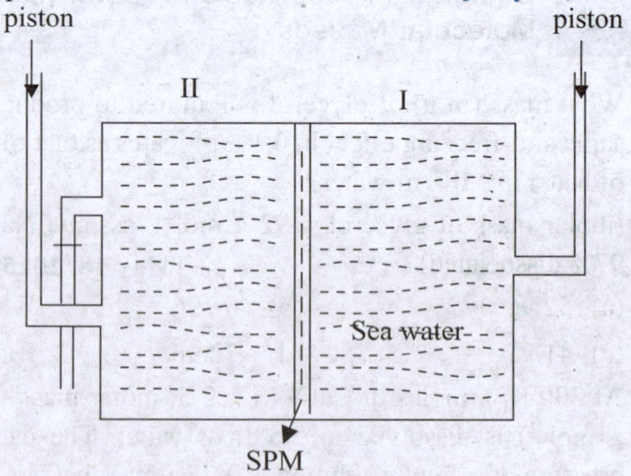

Tables

Expt. No.	Pressure applied in part-I of Vessel	Pressure applied in part-II of vessel
I	10 atm	-
II	-	10 atm
III	15 atm	-
IV	-	15 atm

(a) I, III only (b) II, IV only
(c) I, II, III, IV (d) IV only

76. The ΔT_b value for 0.01 m KCI solution is 0.01 K. What is the van't Hoff factor? **[May 19, 2024 (II)]**
(K_b for water = 0.52 K kg mol^{-1})
(a) 1.92 (b) 1.72 (c) 0.96 (d) 0.86

77. Distilled water boils at 373.15 K and freezes at 273.15 K. A solution of glucose in distilled water boils at 373.202 K. What is the freezing point (in K) of the same solution? (For water, K_b = 0.52 K kg mol^{-1}, K_f = 1.86 K kg mol^{-1}) **[May 18, 2024 (I)]**
(a) 273.15 (b) 273.0
(c) 272.964 (d) 273.336

78. What is the depression of freezing point, when mole fraction of non-electrolyte solute in aqueous solution is 0.01? (K_f of H_2O = 1.86 K kg mol^{-1}) **[May 19, 2023 (I)]**
(a) 1.246 K (b) 1.380 K
(c) 1.528 K (d) 1.043 K

79. What is the boiling point of solution of 0.1m KCl? K_b of water is 0.52 K kg mol^{-1}. (α = 100%) (water boil at 373 K) **[May 18, 2023 (I)]**
(a) 100.104 K (b) 373.104 K
(c) 273.104 K (d) 373.052 K

80. If the osmotic pressure of cane sugar solution is 2.46 atm at 27 °C, then what is the concentration (in mol L^{-1}) of the solution (R = 0.0821 L atm mol^{-1} K^{-1}) **[May 17, 2023 (II)]**
(a) 0.1 (b) 0.2 (c) 0.01 (d) 0.02

81. 6 g of a non–volatile solute (x) is dissolved in 100 g of water. The relative lowering of vapour pressure of resultant solution is 0.006. What is the molar mass (in g mol^{-1}) of x? **[May 17, 2023 (I)]**
(a) 60 (b) 360 (c) 100 (d) 180

82. When 10^{-3} M solution of glucose in water, freezes at –0.0186 °C, then at what temperature 10^{-3} M solution of NaCl will freeze? **[May 16, 2023 (II)]**
(a) 0 °C (b) 0.186 °C
(c) –0.186 °C (d) –0.0372 °C

83. Molal depression constant (K_f) is dependent on **[May 16, 2023 (II)]**
(a) Nature of solvent
(b) Nature of solute
(c) Number of moles of solvent
(d) Number of moles of solute

84. What is the osmotic pressure (in atm) of 0.02M aqueous glucose solution at 300 K?
(R = 0.082 L atm $mol^{-1}K^{-1}$) **[May 16, 2023 (I)]**
(a) $\frac{1}{0.492}$ (b) 0.492
(c) 0.988 (d) $\frac{1}{0.988}$

85. The elevation in the boiling point of aqueous urea solution is 0.104 K. What is its ΔT_f (in K) value? (for Water K_b = 0.52 K kg mol^{-1}, K_f = 1.86 K kg mol^{-1}) **[May 16, 2023 (I)]**
(a) 0.0186 (b) 0.186
(c) 0.372 (d) 0.0372

86. What is the van't Hoff factor of Ferric Sulphate (Assume 100% ionization) **[May 15, 2023 (II)]**
(a) 2 (b) 4 (c) 5 (d) 3

87. Which of the following solution has the highest freezing point? **[July 6, 2022 (I)]**
(a) 0.1 mol KCl in 1 kg water
(b) 0.1 mol K_2SO_4 in 1 kg water
(c) 0.1 mol Urea in 1 kg water
(d) 30 g of glucose in 1 kg water

88. A solution containing 6.0 g of urea is isotonic with a solution containing 10g of a non-electrolytic solute X. The molar mass of X (in g mol^{-1}) is **[July 4, 2022 (II)]**
(a) 50.0 (b) 100 (c) 75.0 (d) 68.0

89. x% (w/v) solution of urea is isotonic with 4% (w/v) solution of a non-volatile solute of molar mass 120 g mol^{-1}. The value of x is **[July 4, 2022 (II)]**
(a) 2 (b) 4 (c) 3 (d) 5

90. At T(K) x g of a non-volatile solid (molar mass 78 g mol^{-1}) when added to 0.5 kg water, lowered its freezing point by 1.0°C. What is x (in g)? (K_f of water at T(K) = 1.86 K Kg mol^{-1}) **[July 4, 2022 (I)]**
(a) 10.48 (b) 20.96 (c) 41.92 (d) 5.24

91. **Assertion (A) :** Blood cells collapse when suspended in saline water **[July 4, 2022 (I)]**
Reason (R) : Cell membrane dissolves in saline water
(a) Both (A) and (R) are correct and R is the correct explanation of A
(b) Both (A) and (R) are correct, but R is not the correct explanation of A
(c) (A) is correct but (R) is not correct
(d) (A) is incorrect but (R) is correct

92. Which of the following pair of solutions is isotonic? **[July 5, 2022 (II)]**
A. 18 g/L of glucose of solution and 6 g/L of Urea solution
B. 10 g/L of glucose solution and 10 g/L of Urea solution
C. 0.01 M NaOH solution and 0.02 M glucose solution
D. 0.01 M NaCl solution and 0.01 M glucose solution
(Assume that NaCl undergoes complete dissociation)
(a) A and B (b) A and C
(c) B and D (d) B and C

93. The molal elevation constant is the ratio of elevation in boiling point to **[Aug. 19, 2021 (I)]**
(a) molarity
(b) molality
(c) mole fraction of solute
(d) mole fraction of solvent

94. **Assertion:** Standard boiling point of a liquid is slightly higher than the normal boiling point.

Reason: 1 bar pressure is slightly less than 1 atm pressure. **[Sept. 18, 2020 (I)]**

(a) Assertion and Reason are correct statements and Reason is the correct explanation for Assertion.

(b) Assertion and Reason are correct statement and Reason is not the explanation for Assertion.

(c) Assertion is correct, Reason is incorrect.

(d) Assertion is incorrect, Reason is correct.

95. If aqueous solution contains 9% and 1% (*w/w*) of two non-volatile non-electrolytes *X* (molecular weight 180) and *Y* (molecular weight 50) respectively, the boiling point of solution in °C approximately is

(K_b = 0.52 K kg mol^{-1}) **[Apr. 22, 2019 (I)]**

(a) 101.4 (b) 100.4
(c) 102.4 (d) 100.8

96. *x* g of $MgSO_4$(i = 1.8) is in 2.5 L of solution has an osmotic pressure of 2.463 atm at 27°C. What is the value of *x* in g? **[Apr. 21, 2019 (I)]**

(a) 33.2 (b) 6.6 (c) 3.3 (d) 16.6

97. 6 g of a mixture of naphthalene ($C_{10}H_8$) and anthracene ($C_{14}H_{10}$) is dissolved in 300 gram of benzene. If the depression in freezing point is 0.70 K, the composition of naphthalene and anthracene in the mixture respectively in g are (molal depression constant of benzene is 5.1 K kg mol^{-1}) **[Apr. 20, 2019 (II)]**

(a) 2.60, 3.40 (b) 3.40, 2.60
(c) 2.90, 3.10 (d) 3.10, 2.90

98. The measured osmotic pressure of a solution prepared by dissolving 17.4 mg of K_2SO_4 in 2L of water at 27°C is 3.735×10^{-3} bar. The van't Hoff factor is

(R = 0.083 L bar K^{-1}mol^{-1}; atomic weights K = 39, S = 32; O = 16) **[2018]**

(a) 2.84 (b) 3.0
(c) 2.0 (d) 2.32

99. 31g of ethylene glycol ($C_2H_6O_2$) is dissolved in 600 g of water. The freezing point depression of the solution is (K_f for water is 1.86 K kg mol^{-1}) **[2017]**

(a) 0.77 K (b) 1.55 K
(c) 4.65 K (d) 3.10 K

100. Which one of the following solutions of compounds show highest osmotic pressure? (*AB*, AB_2 and A_2B_3 are ionic compounds) **[2017]**

(a) 5.0 M urea i = 1.0 and temperature is 67°C

(b) 1.5 M A_2B_3 type i = 4.1 and temperature is 27°C

(c) 3.0 M *AB* type i = 1.6 and temperature is 27°C

(d) 2.5 M AB_2 type i = 2.5 and temperature is 57°C

101. 6 g of a non-volatile, non-electrolyte *X* dissolved in 100 g of water freezes at –0.93°C. The molar mass of *X* in g mol^{-1} is (K_f of H_2O = 1.86 K kg mol^{-1}) **[2016]**

(a) 60 (b) 140 (c) 180 (d) 120

102. 18 g of glucose is dissolved in 90 g of water. The relative lowering of vapour pressure of the solution is equal to **[2015]**

(a) 6 (b) 0.2
(c) 5.1 (d) 0.02

2 Electrochemistry

CHAPTER SYNOPSIS

- E°_{cell} : In electrochemical cell, anode is the electrode with higher oxidation potential or lower reduction potential and cathode is vice-versa

  $E^{\circ}_{cell} = (E^{\circ}_{red})_{Cathode} - (E^{\circ}_{red})_{Anode}$ or $(E^{\circ}_{oxid})_{Anode} - (E^{\circ}_{oxid})_{Cathode}$

$$E^{\circ}_{cell} = E^{\circ}_{oxi} + E^{\circ}_{red}$$

  Nernst equation:- $E_{cell} = E^{\circ}_{cell} - \frac{0.0591}{n}\log\frac{[P]}{[R]}$

- Conductance of electrolytic solution.

Name	Formula	SI Unit
Resistance (R)	$R = \frac{\text{Potential difference (E)}}{\text{Current (I)}}$	ohm (Volts/Amperes)
Conductance (G)	$\frac{1}{R}$	ohm^{-1}(Ω^{-1}) or siemens (S)
Specific resistance (ρ)	$\rho = R \times \frac{a}{l}$	ohm metre (Ω m)
Specific conductance (κ)	$\kappa = \rho^{-1}$	ohm^{-1} metre^{-1}($\Omega^{-1}m^{-1}$) or S/m
Equivalent conductivity (Λ_{eq})	$\Lambda_{eq} = \frac{\kappa \times 1000}{N}$	$Sm^2\ eq^{-1}$
Molar conductivity (Λ_m)	$\Lambda_m = \frac{\kappa \times 1000}{M}$	$Sm^2\ mol^{-1}$

- Conductance (G), molar conductance (Λ_m) and equivalent conductance (Λ_{eq}) increase with dilution where as specific conductance (k) decrease with dilution
- . Huckel-Onsager equation for strong electrolytic at concentration 'c'

$$\left.\begin{aligned}\Lambda^{c}_{m} &= \Lambda^{\circ}_{m} - A\sqrt{c}\\ \Lambda^{c}_{eq} &= \Lambda^{\circ}_{eq} - A\sqrt{c}\end{aligned}\right\}$$ where A = constant (depends upon the nature of solvent and term)

Topic 1 Conductance and Conductivity

1. The Λ_m (on y - axis) of NaCl and CsCl was plotted against $\sqrt{c}$ (c = concentration on x - axis). Identify the correct figure for these electrolytes **[May 18, 2026 (I)]**
(λ^0 of Na^+ and Cs^+ is 50 and 77 S cm^2 mol^{-1} respectively)

(a) 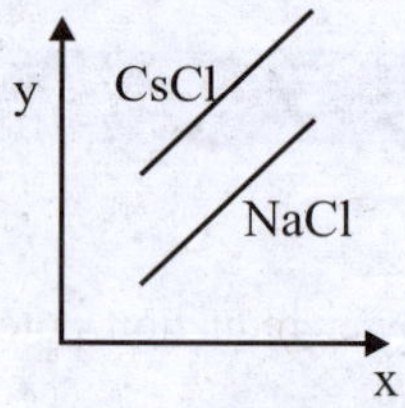

(b) 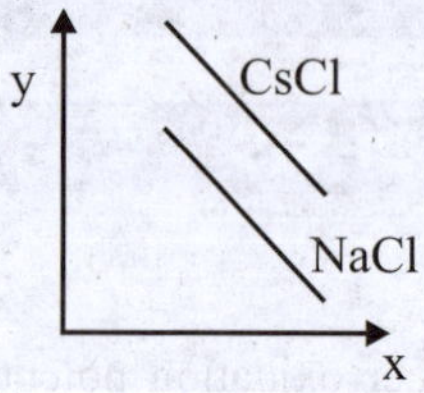

(c) 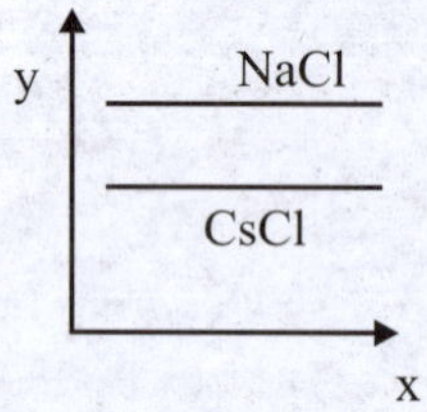

(d) 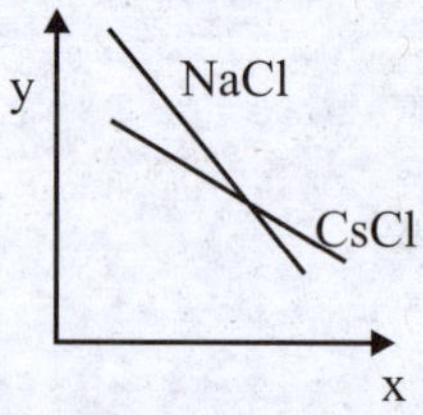

2. The resistance of a conductivity cell filled with 0.02M KCl solution is 85 Ω at 25°C. Conductivity of this solution is 0.3 S m^{-1}. Resistance of 0.0025 M K_2SO_4 solution taken in the same cell is 300 Ω. The molar conductivity of 0.0025 M K_2SO_4 solution (in S m^2 mol^{-1}) is **[May 15, 2026 (I)]**

(a) 6.8×10^{-3} (b) 2.4×10^{-2}
(c) 3.4×10^{-2} (d) 3.4×10^{-3}

3. The conductivity of 0.001 M acetic acid is 5×10^{-5} S cm^{-1}. If the molar conductivity of acetic acid solution at infinite dilution is 390 S cm^2 mol^{-1}. What is its degree of dissociation? **[May 14, 2026 (II)]**

(a) 0.218 (b) 0.128
(c) 0.138 (d) 0.238

4. The molar conductivity of three electrolytes, NaCl, KCl and CsCl, was plotted against $\sqrt{c}$ (c = concentration) and the obtained figure is shown below.
The λ^0 of Na^+, K^+ and Cs^+ is 50, 73 and 77 S cm^2 mol^{-1} respectively. Identify the electrolytes **[May 13, 2026 (II)]**

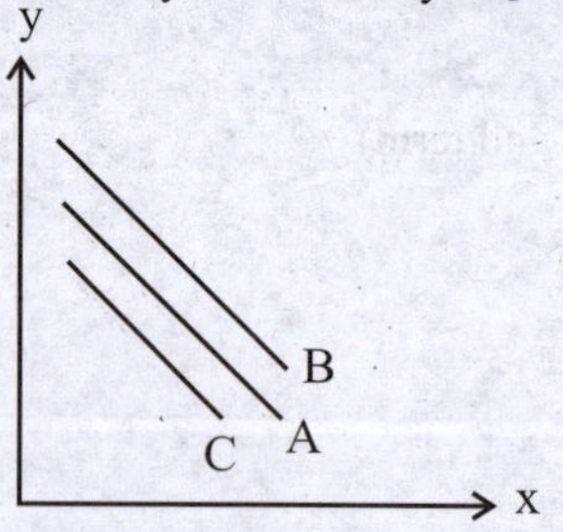

y = axis = Λ_m(in S^2 cm^2 mol^{-1})
x = axis = $\sqrt{c}$

(a) A = KCl; B = CsCl; C = NaCl
(b) A = KCl; B = NaCl; C = CsCl
(c) A = CsCl; B = NaCl; C = KCl
(d) A = NaCl; B = KCl, C = CsCl

5. The conductivity of 0.01 M KCl solution is 'p' ohm^{-1} cm^{-1}. When conductivity cell is filled with the above solution, the observed conductance is 'q' ohm^{-1}. When the same cell is filled with 0.01 M H_2SO_4, the observed conductance is 'r' ohm^{-1}. The conductivity of 0.01 M H_2SO_4 in ohm^{-1} cm^{-1} is **[May 12, 2026 (I)]**

(a) pq (b) qr
(c) $\frac{r}{pq}$ (d) $\frac{pr}{q}$

6. Match the following:

List-I (symbol of electrical property)	List-II (units)
(A) Λ_m	(I) S cm^{-1}
(B) G	(II) m^{-1}
(C) k	(III) S cm^2 mol^{-1}
(D) G*	(IV) S

The correct answer is **[May 26, 2025 (II)]**

(a) A-IV, B-III, C-I, D-II (b) A-III. B-IV, C-I, D-II
(c) A-III , B-IV, C-II, D-I (d) A-II, B-I , C-IV, D-III

7. The resistance of a conductivity cell filled with 0.1 M KCl solution is 100Ω. If the resistance of the same cell when filled with 0.2 M KCl solution is 520Ω, the molar conductivity of 0.02 M solution (in S cm^2 mol^{-1}) is (Given: conductivity of 0.1 M KCl solution = 1.29 Sm^{-1}) **[May 22, 2025 (II)]**

(a) 124 (b) 186 (c) 248 (d) 104

8. The specific conductance of 0.05 M NaOH solution is 0.0115 S cm^{-1}. What is its molar conductance ($\wedge_m$) in S cm^2 mol^{-1}? **[May 21, 2025 (II)]**

(a) 23 (b) 5.75×10^{-7}
(c) 2300 (d) 230

9. At 98K, the conductivity of KCl solutions of molarity 0.1, 0.01 and 1.0 M are recorded as X, Y and Z, Scm^{-1} respectively. The correct relation between X, Y and Z is **[May 19, 2023 (I)]**

(a) X > Y > Z (b) Z > X >Y
(c) Y > X > Z (d) X > Z > Y

10. The molar conductivity of 0.027 M methanoic acid is 40.42 Scm^2 mol^{-1}. The value of dissociation constant of this acid is
(Given $\overset{\circ}{\lambda}_{H^+}$ = 349.6 S cm^2 mol^{-1} and $\overset{\circ}{\lambda}_{HCOO^-}$ = 54.6 S cm^2 mol^{-1}) **[May 17, 2023 (I)]**

(a) 1.5×10^{-5} (b) 6.0×10^{-5}
(c) 4.5×10^{-4} (d) 3.0×10^{-4}

11. Given below are two statements
Assertion (A): Conductivity of an electrolyte decreases on dilution
Reason (R): On dilution number of ions per unit volume increases
The correct answer is **[May 16, 2023 (II)]**
(a) Both (A) and (R) are correct and (R) is the correct explanation of (A)
(b) Both (A) and (R) are correct and (R) is not the correct explanation of (A)
(c) (A) is correct but (R) is not correct
(d) (A) is not correct but (R) is correct

12. The conductivity of a solution containing 2.08 g of anhydrous barium chloride in 200 mL solution is 6×10^{-3} ohm^{-1} cm^{-1}. The molar conductivity of the solution (in ohm^{-1} cm^2 mol^{-1}) is $\underline{x} \times 10^2$. The value of $\underline{x}$ is
(Atomic mass of Ba = 137, Cl = 35.5) **[May 15, 2023 (I)]**
(a) 1.2 (b) 2.4 (c) 3.6 (d) 3.0

13. What is the molar conductivity of CH_3CO_2H at infinite dilution? **[July 6, 2022 (I)]**
Given that,
$\wedge_m^o(CH_3CO_2)_2Ba = x_1 S\,cm^2\,mol^{-1}$
$\wedge_m^o(BaCl_2) = x_2 S\,cm^2\,mol^{-1}$
$\wedge_m^o(HCl) = x_3\,S\,cm^2\,mol^{-1}$
(a) $\frac{x_1 - x_2}{2} + x_3$ (b) $\frac{x_1 - x_3}{2} + x_2$
(c) $\frac{x_2 - x_3}{2} + x_1$ (d) $x_1 + x_3 - x_2$

14. Resistance of a conductivity cell filled with 0.1 mol L^{-1} NaCl is 100 ohm. If the resistance of the same cell when filled with 0.02 mol L^{-1} NaCl solution is 258 ohm, the conductivity of 0.02 mol L^{-1} NaCl solution is (Conductivity of 0.1 mol L^{-1} NaCl is 1.29 S m^{-1}) **[July 5, 2022 (II)]**
(a) 1.0 S m^{-1} (b) 0.2 S m^{-1}
(c) 2.0 S m^{-1} (d) 0.5 S m^{-1}

15. If the resistance of 0.1 M KCl solution in a conductance cell is 300 Ω and conductivity is 0.013 Scm^{-1}, then the value of cell constant is **[Aug. 23, 2021 (II)]**
(a) 3.9 cm^{-1} (b) 39 m^{-1}
(c) 3.9 m^{-1} (d) 0.39 cm^{-1}

16. Molar conductivities at infinite dilution $\wedge^\circ_m$ for $Ba(OH)_2$, $BaCl_2$ and NH_4Cl are 457.0, 240.6 and 2130 Scm^2 mol^{-1} respectively. The $\wedge^\circ_m$ for ammonium hydroxide (in Scm^2 mol^{-1}) is
[May 16, 2023 (I); Similar to Aug. 19, 2021 (I)]
(a) 1683.2 (b) 1080.2
(c) 2130.0 (d) 2238.2

Topic 2 Electrolysis and Types of Electrolysis

17. The number of moles of H_2 gas liberated at cathode, when 10 milli-ampere current is passed through dilute aqueous solution of NaCl for about 19.3×10^4 seconds is (F = 96500 C mol^{-1}) **[May 18, 2026 (II)]**
(a) 0.50 (b) 0.02
(c) 0.01 (d) 0.15

18. Aqueous $CuSO_4$ solution was electrolysed by passing 2 amp of current for 10 min. What is the weight (in g) of copper deposited at cathode? **[May 20, 2024 (I)]**
(Cu = 63 u; F = 96500 C mol^{-1})
(a) 0.195 (b) 0.39
(c) 0.78 (d) 1.56

19. 2.644 g of metal (M) was deposited when 8040 coulombs of electricity was passed through molten MF_2 salt. What is the atomic mass of M (F = 96500 C mol^{-1})
[May 19, 2024 (II)]
(a) 63.47 *u* (b) 65.54 *u* (c) 31.74 *u* (d) 61.48 *u*

20. The minimum voltage (in V) required to bring about the electrolysis of 1M copper (II) sulphate solution at 298 K is **[May 18, 2023 (II)]**
$\left(\text{Given } E^\circ_{Cu^{2+}/Cu} = 0.34V \text{ and } E^\circ_{H_2O/H^+} = -1.23V\right)$
(a) +1.57 (b) +0.89
(c) –0.89 (d) –1.57

21. The time required (in hours) to reduce 3 mol of Fe^{3+} ions to Fe^{2+} ions with 2.0 amperes of current is (1F = 96500 C mol^{-1}) **[May 16, 2023 (I)]**
(a) 30.2 (b) 40.2 (c) 10.2 (d) 15.2

22. The number of Faradays required to completely deposit magnesium from 1 L of 0.1 M $MgCl_2$ aq. solution is
[May 15, 2023 (II)]
(a) 0.2 (b) 2 (c) 0.1 (d) 0.4

23. If 5 ampers of current is passed for 193 seconds through a solution containing Copper salt, 0.32 g of copper is deposited. What is the oxidation state of the Cu in the salt? **[July 8, 2022 (I)]**
(a) +2 (b) +1 (c) +3 (d) $+\frac{3}{2}$

24. On passing a current of 1.2 A through a solution of salt of 40 min, 0.96 g of copper was deposited. The equivalent weight of copper in g is **[July 7, 2022 (II)]**
(a) 21.2 (b) 31.75 (c) 63.5 (d) 15.9

25. 38.6 amperes of current is passed for 100 seconds through an aqueous $CuSO_4$ solution using platinum electrodes. The mass of copper consumed from the solution and volume of gas liberated at STP are respectively (molar mass of Cu = 63.54 g mol^{-1}). **[July 4, 2022 (II)]**
(a) 6.37 g, 0.448 L (b) 0.63 g, 0.224 L
(c) 1.27 g, 0.224 L (d) 4 g, 0.448 L

26. When a current of 10 A is passes through molten $AlCl_3$ for 1.608 minutes. The mass of Al deposited will be [Atomic mass of Al = 27 g] **[Aug. 19, 2021 (I)]**

(a) 0.09 g (b) 0.81 g
(c) 1.35 g (d) 0.27 g

27. A 200 W, 100 V bulb is connected in series with an electrolytic cell. If an aqueous solution of an Sn-salt is electrolysed for 5 hrs, 11.1 g of Sn gets deposited. The chemical formula of the compound is .... (Given atomics weight of Sn is 118.7 g mol^{-1}). **[Sept. 18, 2020 (I)]**

(a) SnO (b) $SnCl_2$ (c) $SnCl_4$ (d) SnO_2

28. When an aqueous solution of $CuCl_2$ is electrolysed using Pt inert electrodes, the reaction at cathode and anode respectively are **[2018]**

(a) $4H_2O(l) \xrightarrow{+4e^-} 2H_2(g) + 4\bar{O}H_2(aq);$

$2H_2O(l) \xrightarrow{-4e^-} O_2(g) + 4H^+(aq)$

(b) $2Cu^{2+}(aq) \xrightarrow{+4e^-} 2Cu(s);$

$2H_2O(l) \xrightarrow{-4e^-} O_2(g) + 4H^+(aq)$

(c) $Cu^{2+}(aq) \xrightarrow{+2e^-} Cu(s);$

$2Cl^-(aq) \xrightarrow{-2e^-} Cl_2(g)$

(d) $2H_2O(l) \xrightarrow{+2e^-} H_2(g) + 2\bar{O}H(aq);$

$2Cl^-(aq) \xrightarrow{-2e^-} Cl_2(g)$

29. Same amount of electricity is passed through aqueous solutions of $AgNO_3$ and $CuSO_4$. The number of Ag and Cu atoms deposited are x and y respectively. The correct relationship between x and y is **[2017]**

(a) $x < y$ (b) $x = 2y$
(c) $x = y$ (d) $y = 2x$

30. The gaseous products formed at cathode (X) and anode (Y), when an aqueous solution of sodium acetate is electrolysed are **[2017]**

	X	Y
(a)	CO_2	C_2H_6, H_2
(b)	H_2, CO_2	C_2H_6
(c)	H_2	C_2H_6, CO_2
(d)	C_2H_6, H_2	CO_2

31. The products obtained at the cathode and anode respectively during the electrolysis of aqueous K_2SO_4 solution using platinum electrodes are **[2016]**

(a) O_2, H_2 (b) H_2, O_2
(c) H_2, SO_2 (d) K, SO_2

Topic 3 Cells and Electrode Potential, Nernst Equation

32. The value of log K_c for the given cell reaction at 298 K is

$Cu(s) + 2Ag^+(aq) \rightarrow Cu^{2+}(aq) + 2Ag(s)$

(Given : $E^\circ_{Cu^{2+}/Cu} = 0.34V, E^\circ_{Ag^+/Ag} = 0.80V; \frac{2.303RT}{F} = 0.06$) **[May 18, 2026 (II)]**

(a) 45.33 (b) 20.33
(c) 15.33 (d) 30.66

33. Observe the following cell **[May 18, 2026 (I)]**

$M(s) | M^{2+}(xm) || H^+(0.02\,m) | 1\,bar\ H_2(g), Pt(s)$

What is the value of x?

Given: $\frac{2.303\,RT}{F} = 0.06V; E_{Cell} = 0.077V;$

$E^o_{M^{2+}|M} = -0.14V; E^o_{H^+|H_2} = 0.0V; \log 4 = 0.602;$

$(\text{antilog}(\bar{2}.7) = 0.05; \text{antilog}(\bar{2}.60) = 0.04)$

(a) 0.05 (b) 0.04
(c) 0.002 (d) 0.001

34. E_1, E_2 and E_3 are the emf values of three galvanic cells I, II, III respectively. The correct order of E_1, E_2 and E_3 is **[May 15, 2026 (II)]**

(I) $Zn | Zn^{2+}(1M) || Cu^{2+}(0.1\,M) | Cu$
(II) $Zn | Zn^{2+}(1M) || Cu^{2+}(1M) | Cu$
(III) $Zn | Zn^{2+}(0.1M) || Cu^{2+}(1M) | Cu$

(a) $E_3 > E_2 > E_1$ (b) $E_1 > E_2 > E_3$
(c) $E_2 > E_3 > E_1$ (d) $E_1 > E_3 > E_2$

35. E_{cell}, for the cell given below is 0.82 V. What is its E° value? **[May 15, 2026 (I)]**

$Fe|Fe^{2+}(0.001\,M) ||Cu^{2+}(0.1\,M)| Cu$

(Given : $\frac{2.303RT}{F} = 0.06$ V)

(a) 0.63 V (b) 0.69 V
(c) 0.76 V (d) 0.87 V

36. Molten Al_2O_3 was electrolyzed between carbon electrodes. The mass (in g) of aluminium produced at cathode when 965 amperes current is passed through it for 1000 seconds is (F = 96500 C mol^{-1}) **[May 14, 2026 (I)]**

(a) 30 (b) 90 (c) 60 (d) 45

37. ΔG° (in kJ mol^{-1}) for the cell reaction given below is

$2\,Al(s) + 3\,Cu^{2+}(aq) \rightarrow 2Al^{3+}(aq) + 3\,Cu(s)$

(Given : $E^\circ_{Al^{3+}|Al} = -1.66V$; $E^\circ_{Cu^{2+}|Cu} = +0.34$ V ; F = 96500 C mol^{-1}) **[May 14, 2026 (I)]**

(a) – 1158 (b) – 579
(c) – 386 (d) – 772

38. At 298 K, the following reaction takes place in a cell $2\,M^{3+}(aq) + 2I^-(aq) \rightarrow 2M^{2+}(aq) + I_2(s)$. The value of log K_c for this reaction is 7.98. What is E°_{cell} (in V)?
($F = 96500\ C\ mol^{-1}$, $R = 8.3\ J\ mol^{-1}\ K^{-1}$) **[May 13, 2026 (II)]**
(a) 0.455 (b) 0.135
(c) 0.235 (d) 0.938

39. Given below are two statements **[May 12, 2026 (II)]**
Statement I: The correct relationship between $\Delta_r G^\ominus$ and K_c is, $\Delta_r G^\ominus = -RT \ln K_c$
Statement II: At 298 K, the correct relationship between $E^\ominus_{cell}$ and K_c is, $E^\ominus_{cell} = \frac{0.059}{n} \ln K_c$
The correct answer is
(a) Both statement I and statement II are correct
(b) Both statement I and statement II are not correct
(c) Statement I is correct but statement II is not correct
(d) Statement I is not correct but statement II is correct

40. Consider the following cell containing two hydrogen electrodes at 298 K Pt, $H_2(g) \mid H^+ (10^{-8}M) \parallel H^+ (0.01\ M) \mid H_2(g)$, Pt
What is its cell potential (in V)? **[May 12, 2026 (I)]**
$\left(\text{Given}: \frac{2.303RT}{F} = 0.06\right)$
(a) +0.36 (b) –0.30
(c) –0.60 (d) +0.60

41. In a cell a copper electrode was used as a cathode. What is the elecrode potential (in V) of the copper electrode dipped in 0.1 M Cu^{2+} solution at 298 K? **[May 26, 2025 (I)]**
$(E^\ominus_{Cu^{2+}/Cu} = 0.34V; \frac{2.303RT}{F} = 0.06V)$
(a) 0.34 (b) 0.31 (c) 0.37 (d) 0.40

42. Consider the following cell reaction **[May 24, 2025 (I)]**
$$2Fe^{3+}(aq) + 2I^+(aq) \rightleftharpoons 2Fe^{2+}(aq) + I_2(s)$$
At 298 K, the cell emf is 0.237 V. The equilibrium constant for the reaction is 10*x*. The value of *x* is
($F = 96500\ C\ mol^{-1}$; $R = 8.3\ J\ K^{-1}\ mol^{-1}$).
(a) 8 (b) 7 (c) 6 (d) 9

43. At 298 K, the following reaction takes place for a cell at the hydrogen electrode **[May 23, 2025 (I)]**
$$H^+(aq) + e^- \longrightarrow \frac{1}{2}H_2\ (1\ bar)$$
The solution pH is 10.0. What is the hydrogen electrode potential in volts? $\left(\frac{2.303\ RT}{F} = 0.06\ V\right)$
(a) –0.6 (b) –0.06
(c) +0.6 (d) +0.06

44. If $E^0_{Fe^{2+}/Fe} = -0.441V$ and $E^0_{Fe^{3+}/Fe^{2+}} = 0.771V$, the standard emf of the cell reaction **[May 22, 2025 (I)]**
$Fe(s) + 2Fe^{3+}(aq) \longrightarrow 3Fe^{2+}(aq)$ is
(a) –1.212 V (b) +1.212 V
(c) –2.424 V (d) +2.424 V

45. What is E_{cell} (in V) of the following cell at 298 K? **[May 21, 2025 (I)]**
$(E^\ominus_{Zn^{2+}/Zn} = -0.76\ V;\ E^\ominus_{Ni^{2+}/Ni} = -0.25\ V;\ \frac{2.303\ RT}{F} = 0.06\ V)$
$Zn(s) \mid Zn^{2+}(0.01\ M) \parallel Ni^{2+}(0.1\ M) \mid Ni(s)$
(a) 0.51 (b) 0.48 (c) 0.57 (d) 0.54

46. At 300 K. the E°_{cell} of
$$A(s) + B^{2+}(aq) \rightleftharpoons A^{2+}(aq) + B(s)$$
is 1.0 V. If $\Delta_r S^\circ$ of this reaction is 100 JK^{-1}, what is $\Delta_r H^\circ$ (in $kJ\ mol^{-1}$) of this reaction?($F=96500\ Cmol^{-1}$) **[May 23, 2024 (I)]**
(a) – 163 (b) –223 (c) – 193 (d) –163000

47. Consider the cell reaction, at 300 K
$A(s) + B^{2+}(aq) \rightleftharpoons A^{2+}(aq) + B(s)$
Its E° is 1.0 V. The $\Delta_r H^\circ$ of the reaction is $-163\ kJ\ mol^{-1}$. What is $\Delta_r S^\circ$ (in JK^{-1}) of the reaction?
($F = 96500\ C\ mol^{-1}$) **[May 22, 2024 (II)]**
(a) 10 (b) 100 (c) 1000 (d) 10000

48. In which of the following Galvanic cells emf is maximum?
(Given: $E^0_{Mg^{2+}|Mg} = -2.36V$ and $E^0_{Cl_2|2Cl^-} = +1.36V$) **[May 22, 2024 (I)]**
(a) $Mg \mid Mg^{2+}(1M) \parallel 2Cl^-(1M) \mid Cl_2$ (1 atm), Pt
(b) $Mg \mid Mg^{2+}(0.01M) \parallel 2Cl^-(1M) \mid Cl_2$ (1 atm), Pt
(c) $Mg \mid Mg^{2+}(1M) \parallel 2Cl^-(0.01M) \mid Cl_2$ (1 atm), Pt
(d) $Mg \mid Mg^{2+}(0.01M) \parallel 2Cl^-(0.01M) \mid Cl_2$ (1 atm), Pt

49. Consider the following standard electrode potentials (E^0 in volts) in aqueous solution **[May 21, 2024 (II)]**

Element	M^{3+}/M	M^+/M
Al	– 1.66	+0.55
Tl	+1.26	–0.34

Based on this data, which of the following statements is correct?

(a) Tl^{3+} is more stable than Al^{3+}
(b) Tl^{+} is more stable than Al^{3+}
(c) Al^{+} is more stable than Al^{3+}
(d) Tl^{+} is more stable than Al^{+}

50. The standard free energy change (ΔG^o)for the following reaction (in kJ) at 25°C is $3Ca(s) + 2Au^{3+}(aq.\ 1M) \rightarrow 3Ca^{2+}(aq, 1M) + 2Au(s)$ **[May 21, 2024 (I)]**
(given : $E^o_{Au^{3+}/Au} = +1.50V, E^o_{Ca^{2+}/Ca} = -2.87\ V$, $1\ F = 96500\ C\ mol^{-1}$)
(a) -2.53×10^3 (b) $+2.53 \times 10^3$
(c) -2.53×10^4 (d) $+2.53 \times 10^4$

51. The E°of $M|M^{2+}||Cu^{2+}/Cu$ is 0.3 V, at what concentration of Cu^{2+} (in mol L^{-1}), the E_{cell} value becomes zero? $\left(\frac{2.303RT}{F} = 0.06\right)$ (Conc. of $M^{2+} = 0.1$ M) **[May 18, 2024 (I)]**
(a) 10^{-9} (b) 10^{-8} (c) 10^{-11} (d) 10^{-10}

52. The cell potential for the following cell notation is approximately **[July 8, 2022 (I)]**
$M(s)|M^{3+}(aq, 0.01M)||N^{2+}(aq, 0.1M)|N(s)$
$E^0_{M^{3+}/M} = 0.6\ V$ and $E^0_{N^{2+}/N} = 0.1\ V$
(a) 0.51 V (b) 1.5 V (c) 2.0 V (d) 2.5 V

53. The standard Gibbs energy (ΔG^0) for the following reaction is **[July 7, 2022 (II)]**
$A(s) + B^{2+}(aq) \rightarrow A^{2+}(aq) + B(s)$, $K_c = 10^{12}$ at 25°C (K_c = equilibrium constant)
(a) –150 kJ (b) –96.80 kJ
(c) –68.47 kJ (d) –100 kJ

54. The reduction potential of hydrogen electrode at 25°C in a neutral solution is $(p_{H_2} = 1\ bar)$ **[July 4, 2022 (I)]**
(a) 0.059V (b) –0.059V (c) –0.413V (d) 0.0V

55. If hydrogen electrodes dipped in two solutions of pH = 3 and pH = 6 are connected by a salt bridge, the emf of the resulting cell is **[Aug. 20, 2021 (I)]**
(a) 0.177 V (b) 0.3 V (c) 0.052 V (d) 0.104 V

56. In the Daniell cell, $Zn|Zn^{2+}||Cu^{2+}|Cu$, when an external voltage is applied such that $E_{external} > E_{cell}$, current flows from .... **[Sept. 21, 2020 (I)]**
(a) Zn to Cu (b) Cu to Zn
(c) no current flows (d) data insufficient

57. Find the observed EMF of the cell $Cd | Cd^{2+}(0.01\ M) || Cu^{2+}(0.01M) | Cu$ under conditions, internal resistance of 4 Ω and producing a current of 0.15 A. **[Sept. 17, 2020 (II)]**
(Given, $E^\circ_{Cu^{2+}/Cu} = 0.35$ V and $E^\circ_{Cd^{2+}/Cd} = -0.4$ V)
(a) 0.75 V (b) 0.15 V
(c) 0.6 V (d) 0.9 V

58. If the E°_{cell} of an equilibrium reaction
$$A(s) + 2B^{2+}(aq) \longrightarrow A^{2+}(aq) + 2B(s)$$
at 298 K is 0.59 V, the equilibrium constant K_c is **[Apr. 22, 2019 (I)]**
(a) 1.0×10^{10} (b) 1.0×10^{2}
(c) 1.0×10^{-20} (d) 1.0×10^{20}

59. The electrode potential for
$M^{2+}(aq) + e^- \longrightarrow M^+(aq)$
$M^+(aq) + e^- \longrightarrow M(s)$
are + 0.15 V and +0.50 V respectively. The value of $E^\circ_{M^{2+}/M}$ will be **[Apr. 21, 2019 (II)]**
(a) 0.150 V (b) 0.300 V
(c) 0.325 V (d) 0.650 V

60. Under which of the following conditions *E* value of the cell, for the cell reaction given is maximum ? **[Apr. 20, 2019 (I)]**
$$Zn(s) + Cu^{2+}(aq, c_1) \longrightarrow Cu(s) + Zn^{2+}(aq, c_2)$$
$$\left(\frac{2.303\ RT}{F} \text{ at } 298\ K = 0.059\ V,\ E^\circ_{Zn^{2+}/Zn} = -0.76V,\ E^\circ_{Cu^{2+}/Cu} = +0.34\ V\right)$$
(a) $C_1 = 0.1\ M, C_2 = 0.01\ M$
(b) $C_1 = 0.01\ M, C_2 = 0.1\ M$
(c) $C_1 = 0.1\ M, C_2 = 0.2\ M$
(d) $C_1 = 0.2\ M, C_2 = 0.1\ M$

61. Calculate ΔG° for the following cell reaction. **[2015]**
$$Zn(s) + Ag_2O(s) + H_2O(l) \longrightarrow Zn^{2+}(aq) + 2Ag(s) + 2^-OH(aq)$$
$E^\circ_{Ag^+/Ag} = +0.80V$ and $E^\circ_{Zn^{2+}/Zn} = -0.76$ V
(a) –305 kJ/mol (b) –301 kJ/mol
(c) 305 kJ/mol (d) 301 kJ/mol

Topic 4 Commercial Cells and Corrosion

62. Which of the following statements are correct about a dry cell? **[May 15, 2026 (II)]**
(I) It is also known as leclanche cell
(II) Electrolyte is a moist paste of NH_4Cl and $ZnCl_2$
(III) Reaction of cathode is $MnO_2 + NH_4^+ + e^- \rightarrow MnO(OH) + NH_3$
(IV) It can be charged
The correct answer is
(a) I, II, III only (b) II, III, IV only
(c) I, III, IV only (d) I, II, IV only

63. Which of the following are the correct statements about lead storage battery? **[May 14, 2026 (II)]**

I. It is a secondary battery

II. In this lead is cathode and a grid of lead packed with PbO_2 is anode

III. In this 98% H_2SO_4 acts as electrolyte

IV. During use of battery, concentration of H_2SO_4 decreases

The correct answer is

(a) I & II only (b) I & IV only

(c) II & III only (d) II & IV only

64. Given below are two statements **[May 13, 2026 (I)]**

Statement I: The electrical conductivity of a solution decreases with dilution.

Statement II: The overall reaction in $H_2 - O_2$ fuel cell is, $2H_2O(l) \rightarrow 2H_2(g) + O_2(g)$

The correct answer is

(a) Both statements I and statement II are correct.

(b) Both statements I and statement II are not correct.

(c) Statement I is correct but statement II is not correct.

(d) Statement I is not correct but statement II is correct.

65. Observe the following statements about dry cell

I. It is a primary battery.

II. Zinc vessel acts as cathode.

III. A paste of moist NH_4Cl, MnO_2 and $ZnCl_2$ is present between two electrodes.

IV. The potential of this cell is 1.5 V.

The correct statements are **[May 27, 2025 (I)]**

(a) I, II, III, IV (b) I, II, III only

(c) I, III, IV only (d) II, III, IV only

66. When the lead storage battery is in use (during discharge) the reaction that occurs at the anode is **[May 23, 2025 (II)]**

(a) $PbSO_4(s) + 2H_2O(l) \rightarrow PbO_2(s) + SO_4^{2-}(aq) + 4H^+(aq) + 2e^-$

(b) $Pb(s) + PbO_2(s) + 2H_2SO_4(aq) \rightarrow 2PbSO_4(s) + 2H_2O(l)$

(c) $Pb(s) + SO_4^{2-}(aq) \rightarrow PbSO_4(s) + 2e^-$

(d) $PbO_2(s) + SO_4^{2-}(aq) + 4H^+(aq) + 2e^- \rightarrow PbSO_4(s) + 2H_2O(l)$

67. Some statements about Lechlanche cell are

(I) Anode is zinc metal

(II) Cathode is graphite rod surrounded by powdered MnO_2 and carbon

(III) Electrolyte is a moist paste of ZnO and KOH

(IV) Oxidation product is ZnO

The correct statements are **[May 18, 2023 (I)]**

(a) I & II only (b) II & III only

(c) I & IV only (d) I, II & III only

68. The electrolyte used in mercury cell is **[May 17, 2023 (II)]**

(a) Moist paste of NH_4Cl and $ZnCl_2$

(b) 38% solution of H_2SO_4

(c) Paste of KOH and ZnO

(d) Paste of $MgCl_2$ and HgO

3 Chemical Kinetics

CHAPTER SYNOPSIS

- Plot of concentration vs. time.

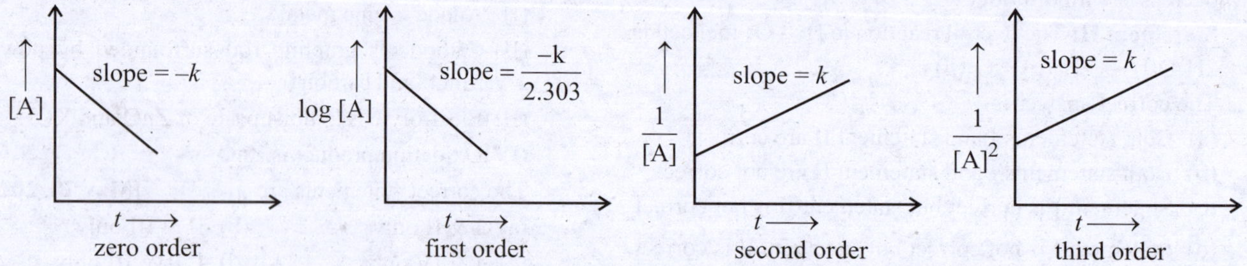

- Plot of rate vs. concentration : [rate $\propto$ (conc.)^n]

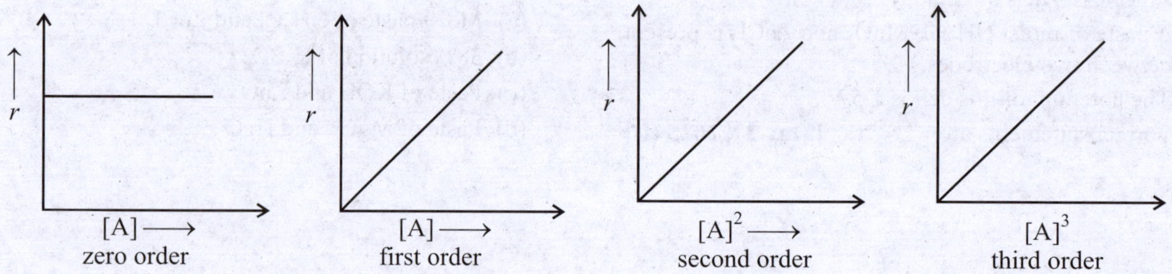

- Plot of half-life vs. concentration : [$t_{1/2} \propto (\text{conc.})^{1-n}$]

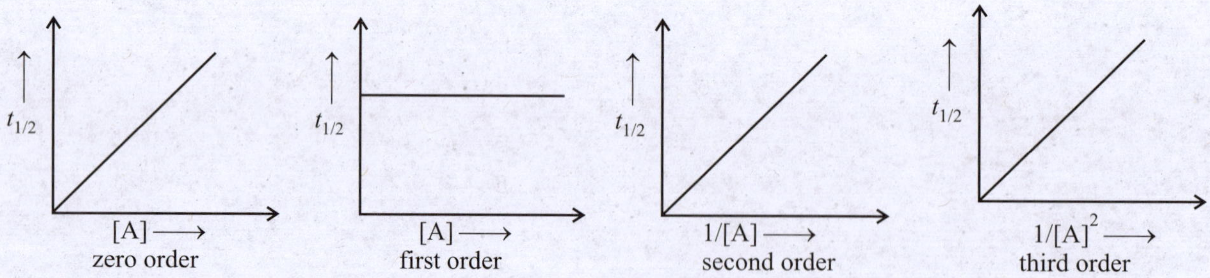

Topic 1 Rate of Reaction, Rate Laws and Rate Constant

1. N_2O_5 decomposes as shown below

$$N_2O_5 \rightarrow N_2O_4 + \frac{1}{2}O_2$$

When 50 mL of 2M solution of N_2O_5 was heated, 0.28 L of O_2 was formed at STP after 30 minutes. The concentration of unreacted N_2O_5 is $\underline{X}$ M and average rate of reaction (in mol L^{-1} min^{-1}) is $\underline{Y}$. What are X and Y respectively? **[May 18, 2026 (II)]**

(molar volume = 22.4 L, molar mass of N_2O_5 = 108 g mol^{-1})

(a) 0.5, 1.66×10^{-2} (b) 1.0, 3.33×10^{-2}
(c) 1.5, 1.66×10^{-2} (d) 0.75, 2.50×10^{-2}

2. $R \rightarrow P$ is a first order reaction. The concentration of R changed from 0.04 to 0.03 mol L^{-1} in 40 min. What is the average velocity of the reaction in mol L^{-1} s^{-1}? **[May 26, 2025 (I)]**

(a) 2.5×10^{-4} (b) 4.167×10^{-6}
(c) 4.167×10^{6} (d) 2.5×10^{-5}

3. $A \rightarrow B$ is a first order reaction. The concentration of A is decreased from x mol L^{-1} to y mol L^{-1} in 100 min. What is the average velocity of the reaction in mol L^{-1} min^{-1}? **[May 23, 2025 (I)]**

(a) $\frac{|x-y|}{100}$ (b) $\frac{|y-x|^2}{100}$
(c) $\frac{100}{|x-y|}$ (d) $\frac{100}{|x+y|}$

4. Consider the reaction given below.

$A + 2B \longrightarrow 3C + 2D$ **[May 21, 2025 (II)]**

If rate of disappearance of B is $x \times 10^{-2}$ mol L^{-1} s^{-1}, the ratio of rate of reaction and rate of appearance of C is

(a) 1 : 3 (b) 3 : 1 (c) 1 : 2 (d) 2 : 1

5. A→P is a first order reaction. The following graph is obtained for this reaction, (x-axis = time: y-axis = conc, of A). The instantaneous rate of the reaction at point C is **[May 23, 2024 (I)]**

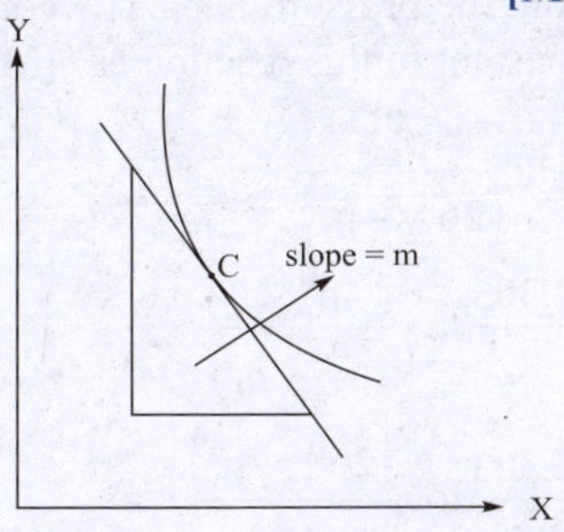

(a) $\frac{1}{m}$ (b) m
(c) 2.303 m (d) $\frac{1}{2.303m}$

6. Isomerisation of gaseous cyclobutene to butadiene is a first order reaction. At T (K), the rate constant of the reaction is 3.3×10^{-4} s^{-1}. What is the time required (in min) to complete 90% of this reaction at the same temperature? (log 2 = 0.3) **[May 22, 2024 (I)]**

(a) 116.67 (b) 233.34 (c) 58.34 (d) 350.0

7. $A \rightarrow P$ is a zero order reaction. At 298 K the rate constant of the reaction is 1×10^{-3} mol^{-1} s^{-1}. Initial concentration of 'A' is 0.1 mol L^{-1}. What is the concentration of 'A' after 10 sec? **[May 21, 2024 (II)]**

(a) 0.09 mol L^{-1} (b) 0.099 mol L^{-1}
(c) 0.087 mol L^{-1} (d) 0.011 mol L^{-1}

8. At 298 K the value of $-\frac{\Delta[Br^-]}{\Delta t}$ for the reaction $5Br^-(aq) + BrO_3^-(aq) + 6H^+(aq) \rightarrow 3Br_2(aq) + 3H_2O(l)$ is x mol $L^{-1}min^{-1}$. What is the rate (in mol L^{-1} min^{-1}) of this reaction? **[May 20, 2024 (II)]**

(a) $5x$ (b) x
(c) $\frac{x}{5}$ (d) $-\frac{x}{5}$

9. For a first order reaction, the concentration of reactant was reduced from 0.03 mol L^{-1} to 0.02 mol L^{-1} in 25 min. What is its rate (in mol L^{-1} s^{-1})? **[May 20, 2024 (I)]**

(a) 6.667×10^{-6} (b) 4×10^{-4}
(c) 6.667×10^{-4} (d) 4×10^{-6}

10. At 298 K, for a first order reaction (A→ P) the following graph is obtained. The rate constant (in s^{-1}) and initial concentration (in mol L^{-1}) of 'A' are respectively (y-axis = ln (a-x); x-axis = time in sec) **[May 18, 2024 (I)]**

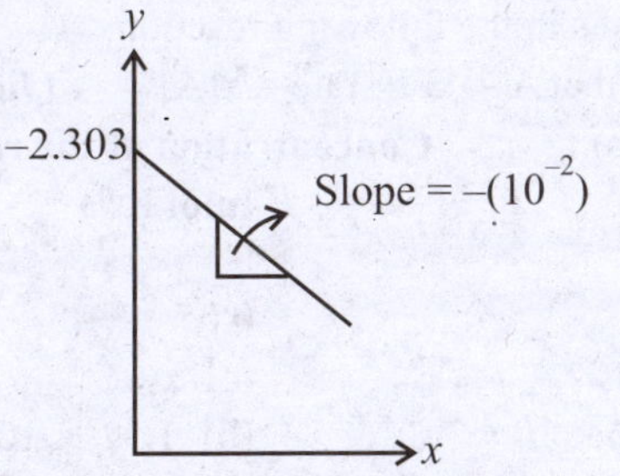

(a) 2.303; 10^{-1} (b) 10^{-2}; 2.303
(c) 10^{-1}; 10^{-2} (d) 10^{-2}; 10^{-1}

11. A reaction, $3X(g) \rightarrow 2Y(g) + Z(g)$ takes place in a closed vessel. What is the rate of formation of Y (in mol L^{-1}) if the rate of disappearance of X is 7.2×10^{-3} mol L^{-1} s^{-1}? **[May 18, 2023 (II); Similar to May 15, 2023 (I)]**

(a) 3.6×10^{-3} (b) 4.8×10^{-3}
(c) 2.4×10^{-3} (d) 1.2×10^{-3}

12. Consider a gas phase reaction which occurs in a closed vessel

$2A \rightarrow 4B + C$

The concentration of B is found to be increased by 5×10^{-3} mol L^{-1} in 10 seconds. **[May 17, 2023 (II)]**

The rate of disappearance of A (in mol L^{-1} s^{-1}) is

(a) 4.75×10^{-4} (b) 7.5×10^{-4}
(c) 1.25×10^{-4} (d) 2.5×10^{-4}

13. Consider the reaction carried out at T(K)
$A(g) + B(g) \rightarrow C(g)$
The rate law for this reaction is $r = k[A]^1 [B]^2$. The concentration of A in experiment 2 and rate in experiment 3 shown as x and z in the table, x and z are respectively

Experiment	[A] mol L^{-1}	[B] mol L^{-1}	Initial rate (mol L^{-1} s^{-1})
1	0.05	0.05	R
2	x	0.05	2R
3	0.20	0.10	z

[May 17, 2023 (I)]
(a) x = 0.10 z = 8R (b) x = 0.05 z = 4R
(c) x = 0.10 z = 16R (d) x = 0.20 z = 16R

14. A first order reaction has the rate constant of 1.15×10^{-3} s^{-1}. The time required to reduce 10 g of reactant to 6 g is $x \times 10^2$ sec. What is the approximate value of x? (log 5 = 0.7, log 3 = 0.48) **[May 16, 2023 (II)]**
(a) 2.2 (b) 3.3 (c) 4.4 (d) 1.1

15. The rate constant, k of a zero order reaction $2NH_3\,(g) \xrightarrow[1130K]{Pt} N_2\,(g) + 3H_2\,(g)$ is $y \times 10^{-4}$ mol L^{-1} s^{-1}. The rate of formation of hydrogen (in mol L^{-1} s^{-1}) is **[May 15, 2023 (II)]**
(a) $y \times 10^{-4}$ (b) $2y \times 10^{-4}$
(c) $3y \times 10^{-4}$ (d) $\frac{y}{3} \times 10^{-4}$

16. What is the concentration (in mol L^{-1}) of the product after 20 s in the following reaction.
Given that $A \rightarrow 3\,B$, rate = $k[A]^{\circ}$ **[July 7, 2022 (II)]**

Time(s)	**Concentration of the reactant (mol L^{-1})**
0	0.1
15	0.05
20	0.1-x

(a) 6.6×10^{-2} (b) 1.32×10^{-1}
(c) 1.98×10^{-1} (d) 2.2×10^{-2}

17. The rate constant for a zero order reaction A → products is 0.0030 mol L^{-1} s^{-1}. How long it will take for the initial concentration of A to fall from 0.10 M to 0.075M? **[July 4, 2022 (I)]**
(a) 10s (b) 20s (c) 8.33s (d) 1.33s

18. Which statement among the following is incorrect? **[Aug. 20, 2021 (I)]**
(a) Unit of rate of disappearance is M s^{-1}.
(b) Unit of rate of reaction is M s^{-1}.
(c) Unit of rate constant *k* depends upon order of reaction.
(d) Unit of rate constant *k* for a first order reaction is M s^{-1}.

19. In the first order thermal decomposition of $C_2H_5I(g) \rightarrow C_2H_4(g) + HI(g)$, the reactant in the beginning exerts a pressure of 2 bar in a closed vessel at 600 K. If the partial perssure of the reactant is 0.1 bar after 1000 minutes at the same temperature the rate constant in min^{-1} is (log 2 = 0.3010) **[Apr. 20, 2019 (I)]**
(a) 6.0×10^{-4} (b) 6.0×10^{-3}
(c) 3.0×10^{-3} (d) 3.0×10^{-4}

Topic 2 Order of Reaction and Half Life Period

20. At 1130 K, the decomposition of ammonia on Pt catalyst follows zero order kinetics. The rate of this reaction at t = 10 min is x mol L^{-1} min^{-1}. What will be its rate (in mol L^{-1} min^{-1}) at t = 20 min, at the same temperature? **[May 18, 2026 (I)]**
(a) $\frac{x}{2}$ (b) x
(c) 2x (d) $\sqrt{x}$

21. Hydrolysis of benzene diazonium chloride follows first order kinetics. The time taken for its decomposition to $1/8$ and $1/10$ of its original concentration are $\left[t_{1/8}\right]$ and $\left[t_{1/10}\right]$ respectively. What is the ratio of $\left[t_{1/8}\right]$ to $\left[t_{1/10}\right]$? **[May 15, 2026 (I)]**
[log 2 = 0.30, log 3 = 0.48, log 4 = 0.60]
(a) 9 : 10 (b) 10 : 9
(c) 3 : 5 (d) 5 : 3

22. Half-life of a first order reaction is 10 minutes. What is the rate of reaction after 20 minutes, if the initial concentration of the reactant is 10 M? **[May 14, 2026 (II)]**
(a) 1.73×10^{-1} M min^{-1} (b) 1.73×10^{-2} M min^{-1}
(c) 3.46×10^{-1} M min^{-1} (d) 4.19×10^{-2} M min^{-1}

23. At T(K), the following first order reaction takes place
$$A(g) \rightarrow B(g) + C(g)$$
Initial pressure (t = 0 min) of A(g) is p_A^0. After 10 min of the reaction, the pressure is p_t. The correct equation for the rate constant of this reaction is **[May 12, 2026 (II)]**

(a) $k = \frac{1}{t} \ln \frac{p_A^0}{(2p_A^0 - p_t)}$

(b) $k = \frac{2.303}{t} \ln \frac{p_A^0}{(2p_A^0 - p_t)}$

(c) $k = \frac{2.303}{t} \log \frac{(2p_A^0 - p_t)}{p_A^0}$

(d) $k = \frac{1}{t} \ln \frac{p_A^0}{(3p_A^0 - p_t)}$

24. At T(K), the rate constant of a reaction (A $\rightarrow$ products) is 0.02 mol L^{-1} min^{-1}. The initial concentration of A is 1.0 mol L^{-1}. What will be the concentration of A (in mol L^{-1}) after 20 min? (antilog (0.8264) = 6.705)

[May 12, 2026 (II)]

(a) 0.6705 (b) 0.6
(c) 0.5705 (d) 0.4

25. A(g) $\rightarrow$ products, follows first order kinetics. Initial concentration of A is 8×10^{-3} mol L^{-1}. For 80% decomposition of A, the time taken was 80 minutes. What is the rate constant for that reaction?
(log 2 = 0.3, log 3 = 0.48, log 4 = 0.60, log 5 = 0.70)

[May 12, 2026 (I)]

(a) 0.05 min^{-1} (b) 0.04 min^{-1}
(c) 0.02 min^{-1} (d) 0.06 min^{-1}

26. For a first order reaction, the ratio between the time taken to complete $\frac{3}{4}$th of the reaction and time taken to complete half of the reaction is **[May 24, 2025 (I)]**

(a) 2 (b) 3 (c) 1.5 (d) 2.5

27. In a first order reaction, the concentration of the reactant is reduced to 1/8 of the initial concentration in 75 minutes. The $t_{1/2}$ of the reaction (in minutes) is **[May 22, 2025 (II)]**
(log 2 = 0.30, log 3 = 0.47, log 4 = 0.60)

(a) 60.2 (b) 50.2
(c) 25.1 (d) 75.1

28. A $\rightarrow$ products, is a first order reaction. The following data is obtained for this reaction at T(K). The value of $x : y$ is

[May 21, 2025 (I)]

Rate (mol L^{-1} min^{-1})	[A]
0.2	0.02 M
0.4	x M
1.0	y M

(a) 1 : 5 (b) 2 : 3 (c) 5 : 2 (d) 2 : 5

29. The first order reaction A(g) $\rightarrow$ B(g) + 2C(g) occurs at 25°C. After 24 minutes the ratio of the concentration of products to the concentration of the reactant is 1:3. What is the half life of the reaction (in min)? (log 1.11 = 0.046)

[May 19, 2024 (II)]

(a) 150.5 (b) 142.2
(c) 157.8 (d) 15.78

30. Which of the following is correct with respect to the graph given?
[R] = Concentration at time 't'
$[R]_o$ = Initial concentration

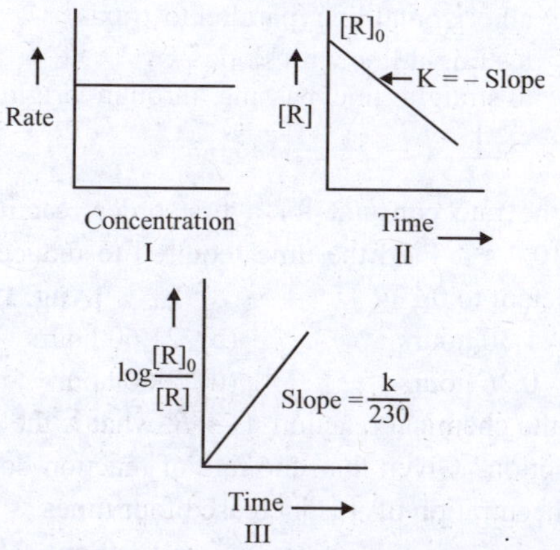

[May 18, 2023 (I)]

(a) I, III represent first order and II represents zero order reaction
(b) I, II represent zero order and III represents first order reaction
(c) I, II, III all represent zero order reactions
(d) I, II, III all represent first order reaction

31. For the reaction A + B $\rightarrow$ C, the following data were obtained

Exp	Initial concentration [A] M	[B] M	Initial rate (M min^{-1})
1.	0.1	0.1	1.0×10^{-4}
2.	0.1	0.3	9.0×10^{-4}
3.	0.3	0.3	2.7×10^{-3}

The order of reaction with respect to A and B are respectively **[May 15, 2023 (I)]**

(a) 1, 2 (b) 2, 1 (c) 1.5, 1.5 (d) 0, 3

32. In the reaction, A $\rightarrow$ products, If the concentration of the reactant is doubled rate of the reaction remains unchanged. The order of the reaction with respect to A is

[July 8, 2022 (I)]

(a) 1 (b) 2 (c) 0.5 (d) 0

33. A $\rightarrow$ products, is a first order reaction. The time required to decompose A to half its initial amount is 60 minutes. The rate constant of the reaction (in s^{-1}) is

[July 6, 2022 (I)]

(a) 1.05×10^{-2} (b) 1.15×10^{-2}
(c) 1.25×10^{-4} (d) 1.92×10^{-4}

34. The time required for completion of 93.75% of a first order reaction is x minutes. The half life of it (in minutes) is **[July 4, 2022 (II)]**

(a) x/8 (b) x/2 (c) x/4 (d) x/3

35. A reaction has rate constant $k = 2.4 \times 10^{-4}$ s^{-1}. Then, find the ratio of $t_{99.9}$ to t_{50}.

[Aug. 23, 2021 (II); Similar to 2015]

(a) 1 (b) 5 (c) 10 (d) 15

36. For zero order reaction, a plot of $t_{1/2}$ *versus* $[A]_0$ will be

[Aug. 20, 2021 (I)]

(a) a straight line passing through the origin and slope = k

(b) a horizontal line (parallel to x-axis)

(c) a straight line with slope $-k$

(d) a straight line passing through origin and slope $= \frac{1}{2k}$

37. If the rate constant for a first order reaction is $2.303 \times 10^{-3}\ s^{-1}$. Find the time required to reduce 4 g of the reactant to 0.2 g. **[Aug. 19, 2021 (I)]**

(a) 1.30 hours (b) 21.60 hours
(c) 0.36 hours (d) 2.60 hours

38. In the chemical reaction $A \rightarrow B$, what is the order of the reaction? Given that, the rate of reaction doubles if the concentration of A is increased four times. **[Sept. 21, 2020 (II)]**

(a) 2 (b) 1.5 (c) 0.5 (d) 1

39. Thermal decomposition of HCOOH is a first order reaction and the rate constant at T(K) is $4.606 \times 10^{-3}\ s^{-1}$. The time required to decompose 90% of initial quantity of HCOOH at T(K) in second is **[2018]**

(a) 100 (b) 500 (c) 1000 (d) 50

40. 20% of a first order reaction was found to be completed at 10:00 a.m at 11.30 a.m. on the same day, 20% of the reaction was found to be remaining. The half life period in minutes of the reaction is **[2017]**

(a) 90 (b) 45 (c) 60 (d) 30

Topic 3 Theories of Rate of Reaction

41. The k value of the reaction A → products is $5 \times 10^{3}\ s^{-1}$ at 300 K. Its activation energy is 50 kJ mol^{-1}. At T(K), its value becomes $1.0 \times 10^{4}\ s^{-1}$. What is the value of T (in K)? **[May 15, 2026 (II)]**

(R = 8.3 J mol^{-1} K^{-1}), (log 2 = 0.3)

(a) 397 (b) 311
(c) 286 (d) 345

42. At 300°C, decomposition of azomethane follows first order kinetics. Rate constant of this reaction at this temperature is $2.5 \times 10^{-4}\ S^{-1}$. If the activation energy of the reaction is 42 kcal mol^{-1}, what is the temperature (in K) at which the half-life of the reaction is 138.6 seconds? (R = 2 cal K^{-1} mol^{-1}, log 20 = 1.30) **[May 14, 2026 (I)]**

(a) 725 (b) 425
(c) 525 (d) 625

43. The rate constant of a first order reaction at 600 K is $1.6 \times 10^{-5}\ s^{-1}$. If its activation energy is 198.87 kJ mol^{-1}, what is the rate constant (in s^{-1}) at 700 K? **[May 13, 2026 (II)]**

(R = 8.3 J mol^{-1} K^{-1}) (antilog (0.4771) = 3.0)

(a) 4.8×10^{-4} (b) 4.8×10^{-3}
(c) 4.8×10^{-2} (d) 3.2×10^{-4}

44. In the Arrhenius equation, $\exp\left(\frac{\quad}{RT}\right)$ is equal to **[May 13, 2026 (I)]**

(a) Frequency factor

(b) Fraction of molecules that have energy higher than E_a

(c) Rate of the reaction

(d) Rate constant of the reaction.

45. For a reaction, the graph of ln k (on y-axis) and 1/T (on x-axis) is a straight line with a slope -2×10^{4} K. The activation energy of the reaction (in kJ mol^{-1}) is (R = 8.3 JK^{-1} mol^{-1}) **[May 27, 2025 (I)]**

(a) 332 (b) 432 (c) 166 (d) 216

46. The following graph is obtained for a first order reaction (A→P). The activation energy (E_a in kJ mol^{-1}) and heat of reaction (|ΔH| in kJ mol^{-1}) for this reaction are respectively **[May 26, 2025 (II)]**

(x = reaction coordinate; y = E in kJ mol^{-1})

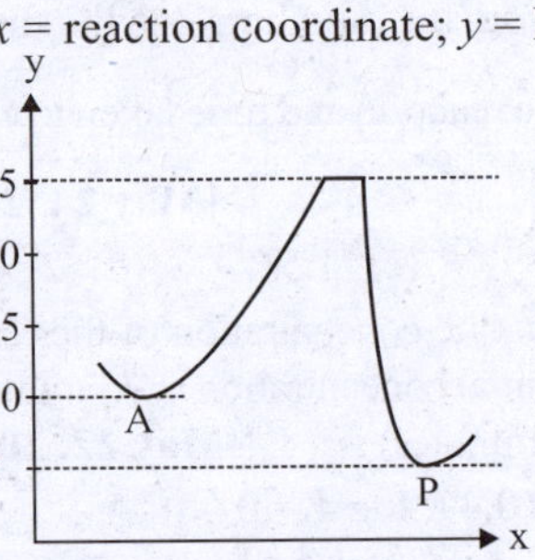

(a) 5, 15 (b) 15, 5 (c) 25, 5 (d) 10, 25

47. The following equation is obtained for a first order reaction at 300 K. **[May 23, 2025 (II)]**

$$\log_{10}\frac{K}{A} = 0.00174$$

What is the activation energy (in J mol^{-1}) of the reaction? (R = 8.314 J mol^{-1} K^{-1})

(a) 10.0 (b) 100.0 (c) 0.1 (d) 1.0

48. At T(K), the following equation is obtained for a first order reaction. **[May 22, 2025 (I)]**

$$\log\frac{k}{A} = -\frac{x}{T}$$

The activation energy for this reaction is equal to (R = gas constant)

(a) $2.303\,xR$ (b) $\frac{2.303R}{x}$
(c) $\frac{x}{2.303R}$ (d) $\frac{1}{2.303\,xR}$

49. Activation energy for the hydrolysis of sucrose by acid is X kJ mol^{-1} whereas activation energy for the hydrolysis of sucrose by sucrase is Y kJ mol^{-1}. X and Y respectively are **[May 21, 2025 (II)]**

(a) 6.22, 2.15 (b) 2.15, 6.22
(c) 6.22, 6.22 (d) 2.15, 2.15

50. The rate constant of a first order reaction was doubled when the temperature was increased from 300 to 310 K.

What is its approximate activation energy (in kJ mol^{-1})? (R = 8.3 J mol^{-1} K^{-1}; log 2 = 0.3)

[May 22, 2024 (II)]

(a) 5.33 (b) 533.3 (c) 53333 (d) 53.33

51. The rate constant of a first order reaction is 3.46×10^{-2} s^{-1} at 298K. What is the rate constant of the reaction at 350 K if its activation energy is 50.1 kJ mol^{-1}? (R= 8.314 $JK^{-1}mol^{-1}$)
(log 2 = 0.3010) **[May 21, 2024 (I)]**

(a) 0.592 s^{-1} (b) 0.692 s^{-1}
(c) 0.792 s^{-1} (d) 0.892 s^{-1}

52. The rate constant, k for a first order reaction, $C_2H_5I(g) \rightarrow C_2H_4(g) + HI(g)$ is x s^{-1} at 600 K and 4x s^{-1} at 700 K. **[May 19, 2023 (I)]**
The energy of activation of the reaction (in kJ mol^{-1}) is

(a) 48.16 (b) 58.16 (c) 38.16 (d) 28.16

53. The rate of a reaction doubles, when the temperature is changed from 300 K to 310 K. Activation energy of the change is .... **[Sept. 18, 2020 (I)]**
($R = 8.314$ JK^{-1} mol^{-1}, log 2 = 0.301)

(a) 53.6 kJ mol^{-1} (b) 48.6 kJ mol^{-1}
(c) 58.5 kJ mol^{-1} (d) 60.5 kJ mol^{-1}

54. Find the correct equation among the following.

[Sept. 17, 2020 (II)]

(a) $\ln k - \ln A = \frac{E_a}{RT}$ (b) $k = \frac{AE_a}{RT}$

(c) $\ln k + \ln A = \frac{E_a}{RT}$ (d) $\frac{E_a}{RT} = \ln A - \ln k$

55. Which one of the following statements is correct?

[Apr. 22, 2019 (I)]

(a) In collision theory, $e^{-E_a/RT}$ corresponds to the fraction of molecules that have energy equal or greater than E_a.
(b) The number of collisions of reacting molecules per second per unit volume of the reaction mixture is activated complex.
(c) Molecularity is the number of molecules involved in a complex reaction.
(d) A catalyst catalyses the non-spontaneous reaction.

56. The half-life period of a first order reaction at 300 K and 400 K are 50 s and 10 s respectively. The activation energy of the reaction in kJ mol^{-1} is (log 5 = 0.70)

[Apr. 21, 2019 (I)]

(a) 4.0 (b) 8.0
(c) 16.10 (d) 20.10

57. The slope of the graph drawn between ln k and $\frac{1}{T}$ as per Arrhenius equation gives the value (R = gas constant, E_α = Activation energy) **[2016]**

(a) $\frac{R}{E_a}$ (b) $\frac{E_a}{R}$ (c) $\frac{-E_a}{R}$ (d) $\frac{-R}{E_a}$

4 The *d*-and *f*-Block Elements

CHAPTER SYNOPSIS

- The highest oxidation states are found in fluorides and oxides because fluorine and oxygen are the most electronegative elements. The highest oxidation state shown by any transition metal is eight. The oxidation state of eight is shown by Ru and Os.
- Most of the transition elements and their compounds show paramagnetism due to the presence of one or more unpaired electrons in them. Paramagnetism in any transition series first increases, reaches a maximum value of d^5 cases and then decreases thereafter.
- The elements of first row transition metals (3*d*-series) form oxides of the type, MO, M_2O_3, M_3O_4, MO_2, M_2O_5 and MO_3.
- The oxides of metals in the intermediate oxidation states, are generally amphoteric. For example, CuO, Cr_2O_3, MnO_2 etc. are amphoteric.
- Halides of transition metals in the higher oxidation states exhibit a greater tendency towards hydrolysis.
- Potassium permanganate ($KMnO_4$) is the salt of an unstable acid $HMnO_4$ (permanganic acid).
- When a solid chloride salt is heated with potassium dichromate and conc. H_2SO_4, orange coloured vapours of chromyl chloride is obtained.
- Lanthanoids in aqueous solution and in the solid state exhibit oxidation states of +2, +3 and +4. The trivalent state (+3) being more stable.
- Trivalent ions of lanthanoids (except La^{3+} and Lu^{3+}) are paramagnetic.
- Direct consequences of the lanthanoid contraction are (a) almost equal size of Hf^{4+} and Zr^{4+}. (b) decrease in the basic character of lanthanoid hydroxides with increase in the atomic number. $La(OH)_3$ is the most basic, while $Lu(OH)_3$ is least basic.
- Actinoids show variable oxidation states. The oxidation state of +3 is the most common.

Topic 1 Characteristics of d-Block Elements

1. In which of the following sets, the alloy is correctly matched with its components? **[May 18, 2026 (I)]**

I. Brass : Cu, Zn
II. Bronze: Cu, Sn
III. German silver: Cu, Zn, Cr

Correct answer is

(a) I, III only (b) II, III only
(c) I, II, III (d) I, II only

2. A transition metal ion X^{3+} has a magnetic moment of $\sqrt{15}$ BM. The atomic number of the metal X is **[May 15, 2026 (II)]**

(a) 24 (b) 25
(c) 26 (d) 27

3. The spin only magnetic moment of the element having highest third ionization enthalpy among Ti, V, Cr, Mn, Fe in its +3 state (in BM) is **[May 14, 2026 (I)]**

(a) 3.87 (b) 4.90
(c) 5.92 (d) 2.84

4. In which of the following, elements are correctly arranged in the increasing order of unpaired electrons? **[May 13, 2026 (I)]**

(a) Fe < Co < Ni < Mn (b) Ni < Co < Mn < Fe
(c) Mn < Fe < Co < Ni (d) Ni < Co < Fe < Mn

5. Consider the following **[May 12, 2026 (I)]**

Ti, V, Cr, Mn, Fe

The spin only magnetic moment (in BM) of the metal with lowest melting point in its +3 oxidation state is

(a) $\sqrt{15}$ (b) $\sqrt{24}$
(c) $\sqrt{35}$ (d) $\sqrt{3}$

6. Identify the ion (hydrated in solution) which is not correctly matched with its spin only magnetic moment (in BM) given in brackets **[May 26, 2025 (II)]**

(a) Cr^{3+} (4.90) (b) Cu^{2+} (1.73)
(c) Co^{3+} (4.90) (d) Fe^{2+} (4.90)

7. Identify the incorrect statetment regarding the interstitial compounds **[May 26, 2025 (I)]**

(a) They have high melting points.
(b) They lose electrical conductivity during the formation from metal.
(c) They are chemically inert.
(d) They are very hard.

8. Match the following **[May 23, 2025 (II)]**

List-I (Transition metal, M)	List-II ($E^\circ M^{2+}/M$)
(A) Ni	(I) – 1.18
(B) Mn	(II) – 0.91
(C) Fe	(III) – 0.25
(D) Cr	(IV) – 0.44

The correct answer is

(a) A-III, B-II, C-IV, D-I (b) A-III, B-IV, C-I, D-II
(c) A-III, B-I, C-IV, D-II (d) A-I, B-IV, C-II, D-III

9. For which of the following the $E^\ominus(M^{3+}/M^{2+})$ is negative? **[May 22, 2025 (II)]**

(a) Mn (b) Co (c) Fe (d) Cr

10. Match the following. **[May 21, 2025 (II)]**

List-I (aquated ion)		List-II (colour)	
(A)	Ni^{2+}	(I)	Violet
(B)	Fe^{3+}	(II)	Blue
(C)	Mn^{3+}	(III)	Yellow
(D)	V^{4+}	(IV)	Red
		(V)	Green

Correct answer is

(a) A-V, B-III, C-IV, D-II (b) A-IV, B-V, C-I, D-III
(c) A-I, B-III, C-IV, D-V (d) A-V, B-III, C-I, D-II

11. The transition metal with highest melting point is **[May 20, 2024 (II)]**

(a) Re (b) Cr (c) Mo (d) W

12. Match the following

List I (Complex)	List II (Color)
A. $[Ni(en)_3]^{2+}$	I. Green
B. $[Ni(H_2O)_4(en)]^{2+}$	II. Blue
C. $[Ni(H_2O)_6]^{2+}$	III. Pale blue
D. $[Ni(H_2O)_6(en)_2]^{2+}$	IV. Violet

[May 19, 2023 (I)]

(a) A-IV, B-I, C-III, D-II (b) A-I, B-II, C-III, D-IV
(c) A-IV, B-III, C-I, D-II (d) A-I, B-III, C-II, D-IV

13. Which of the following are correct?

(i) V^{2+} liberates hydrogen from a dilute acid
(ii) The earlier members of lanthanide series behave more like aluminium
(iii) The 'silver' UK coins are made of Cu/Ni alloy
(iv) The maximum oxidation state exhibited by Neptunium is +7 **[May 18, 2023 (I)]**

(a) (i) (iii) only (b) (ii) (iv) only
(c) (i) (iii) (iv) only (d) (i) (ii) (iii) only

14. Arrange the oxides CrO, CrO_3 and Cr_2O_3 in the decreasing order of acidic strength **[May 17, 2023 (II)]**

(a) $CrO_3 > Cr_2O_3 > CrO$ (b) $CrO_3 > CrO > Cr_2O_3$
(c) $CrO > Cr_2O_3 > CrO_3$ (d) $CrO > CrO_3 > Cr_2O_3$

15. Among V, Cr, Zn, Fe, the metal having lowest enthalpy of atomization is **[May 17, 2023 (I)]**

(a) V (b) Cr (c) Zn (d) Fe

16. Arrange the following in order of increasing number of unpaired electrons in them

i. $[Fe(CN)_6]^{3-}$ ii. $[MnCl_6]^{3-}$
iii. $[FeF_6]^{3-}$ iv. $[Co(NH_3)_6]^{3+}$

[May 15, 2023 (II)]

(a) i, iv, ii, iii (b) iv, i, iii, ii
(c) iv, i, ii, iii (d) i, iv, iii, ii

17. Given below are two statements

Assertion (A): All Cu (II) halides are known except the iodide

Reason (R): Cu^{2+} oxidizes I^- to I_2

The correct answer is **[May 15, 2023 (I)]**

(a) Both (A) and (R) are correct and (R) is the correct explanation of (A)

(b) Both (A) and (R) are correct and (R) is the correct but (R) is not the correct explanation of (A)

(c) (A) is correct but (R) is not correct

(d) (A) is not correct but (R) is correct

18. **Assertion (A) :** Transition elements have higher enthalpies of atomization. **[July 8, 2022 (I)]**

Reason (R) : Large number of unpaired electrons present in transition elements facilitate strong interatomic interaction and strong bonding between atoms.

(a) Both (A) and (R) are correct and (R) is the correct explanation of (A)

(b) Both (A) and (R) are correct and (R) is not the correct explanation of (A).

(c) (A) Is correct and (R) is incorrect.

(d) (A) Is incorrect and (R) is correct.

19. Which of the following elements are not regarded as transition elements? **[July 7, 2022 (II)]**

(a) Zn, Cd, Hg (b) Cu, Zn, Hg

(c) Ag, Zn, Hg (d) Ag, Cd, Hg

20. Which of the following ions can reduce dilute acid to give hydrogen gas? **[July 6, 2022 (I)]**

(a) Ti^{2+}, Cr^{2+} (b) Mn^{3+}, Ti^{2+}

(c) Mn^{3+}, Cr^{2+} (d) Co^{3+}, Cr^{2+}

21. **Assertion (A) :** Transition metals and their complexes show catalytic activity. **[July 4, 2022 (II)]**

Reason (R) : The activation energy of a reaction is lowered by the catalyst.

(a) Both (A) and (R) are correct and (R) is the correct explanation of (A).

(b) Both (A) and (R) are correct but (R) is not the correct explanation of (A).

(c) (A) is correct but (R) is incorrect.

(d) (A) is incorrect but (R) is correct.

22. The catalyst used in the manufacture of polyethylene is a mixture of **[July 4, 2022 (I)]**

(a) Ti, $Al(CH_3)_3$ (b) Ti, CH_3MgBr

(c) $TiCl_3$, $Si(CH_3)_4$ (d) $TiCl_4$, $Al(CH_3)_3$

23. Which of the following is not arranged in the correct sequence? **[Aug. 20, 2021 (I)]**

(a) MO, M_2O_3, MO_2, M_2O_5 (Decreasing basic nature)

(b) Sc, V, Cr, Mn (Increasing number of oxidation states)

(c) d^5, d^3, d^1, d^4 (Increasing magnetic moment)

(d) Mn^{2+}, Fe^{2+}, Cr^{2+}, Co^{2+} (Decreasing stability)

24. What among the following is coloured? **[Aug. 20, 2021 (I)]**

(a) CuCl (b) $ScCl_3$

(c) $CuCl_2$ (d) $TiCl_4$

25. Which of the following is the common oxidation state for 'transition' elements? **[Sept. 21, 2020 (I)]**

(a) + 3 (b) + 1 (c) + 2 (d) + 4

26. Which transition metal oxide among the following has electrical conductivity similar to that of copper? **[Sept. 18, 2020 (I)]**

(a) MnO (b) FeO

(c) RgO_3 (d) TiO_2

27. The correct statement about Cr^{2+} and Mn^{3+} among the following is **[Sept. 17, 2020 (I)]**

(Given, atomic number of Cr = 24 and Mn = 25)

(a) Cr^{2+} is a reducing agent.

(b) Mn^{3+} is a reducing agent.

(c) Both Cr^{2+} and Mn^{3+} exhibit d^5 outer electronic configuration.

(d) When Cr^{2+} is used as reducing agent, it attains d^5 configuration.

28. Which of the following characteristics of the transition metals is associated with their catalytic activity? **[2016]**

(a) Colour of hydrated ions

(b) Diamagnetic behaviour

(c) Paramagnetic behaviour

(d) Variable oxidation states

Topic 2 Compounds of Transition Metals

29. The nature of chromium oxide formed by the thermal decomposition of ammonium dichromate is **[May 18, 2026 (II)]**

(a) acidic (b) basic

(c) neutral (d) amphoteric

30. x mL of 0.05 M $KMnO_4$ solution is required to oxidise completely 1.52 g of $FeSO_4$ in acidic medium. The value of x is **[May 18, 2026 (I)]**

(At. wt: Fe = 56 u, S = 32 u, O = 16 u)

(a) 40 (b) 20

(c) 30 (d) 50

31. The fusion of chromite ore with Na_2CO_3 in free access of air leads to the formation of yellow coloured solution of compound A and residue B along with the evolution of CO_2 gas. Identify the correct statements regarding A and B.

I. A contains Cr – O – Cr linkage **[May 15, 2026 (I)]**

II. B is Fe_2O_3

III. Oxidation state of chromium in A is +6

The correct answer is

(a) I, II only (b) II, III only

(c) I, III only (d) I, II, III

32. During the preparation of $K_2Cr_2O_7$ from chromite ore, in one of the steps, the yellow solution of sodium chromate is converted into orange sodium dichromate crystals. This is achieved by, **[May 14, 2026 (II)]**
(a) Increasing the pH
(b) Decreasing the pH
(c) Maintaining neutral pH
(d) Adding NaCl

33. Which of the following is not correct regarding $K_2Cr_2O_7$? **[May 12, 2026 (II)]**
(a) The angle Cr – O – Cr in it is 118°
(b) It oxidises Sn^{2+} to Sn^{4+} in acidic medium
(c) It is used as a primary standard in volumetric analysis
(d) It is an orange colored solid

34. In acidic medium, potassium permanganate oxidizes H_2O_2 to O_2 as per the equation given below **[May 12, 2026 (II)]**
$2MnO_4^- + 6H^+ + 5H_2O_2 \rightarrow 2Mn^{2+} + 8H_2O + 5O_2$
100 mL of 0.02 M $KMnO_4$ oxidises 10 mL of X vol H_2O_2 completely. The value of X approximately is
(a) 2.8 (b) 5.6
(c) 7.2 (d) 10.0

35. $KMnO_4$ oxidises hydrogen sulphide in acidic medium. The number of moles of $KMnO_4$ which react with one mole of hydrogen sulphide is **[May 27, 2025 (I)]**
(a) 2 (b) 4 (c) 0.4 (d) 2.5

36. Which one of the following statements is not correct? **[May 24, 2025 (I)]**
(a) CrO is basic but Cr_2O_3 is amphoteric
(b) Nitrite is oxidised to nitrate in acidic medium by $KMnO_4$
(c) $PdCl_2$ is the catalyst in Wacker process
(d) The reactivity of the earlier members of lanthanide series is similar to that of aluminium.

37. The amphoteric oxide of Vanadium (V) reacts with alkali and forms an oxoion 'X' and with acid forms an oxoion Y. The oxidation states of 'V' in X and Y are respectively
(a) +2, +5 (b) +3, +3 (c) +5, +5 (d) +5, +2

38. Which of the following is not correct? **[May 22, 2025 (I)]**
(a) Potassium permanganate on heating gives potassium manganate and manganese dioxide only
(b) Phosphine is used in smoke screens
(c) Bleaching action of chlorine is due to oxidation
(d) Noble gases have very low boiling points

39. Acidification of chromate gives 'Z'. The oxidation state of chromium in 'Z' is **[May 23, 2024 (I)]**
(a) +3 (b) +6 (c) +7 (d) +2

40. Which of the following reactions of $KMnO_4$ occurs in acidic medium? **[May 22, 2024 (II)]**
(a) Oxidation of thiosulphate to sulphate
(b) Precipitation of sulphur from H_2S
(c) Oxidation of iodide to iodate
(d) Oxidation of manganous salt to MnO_2

41. The correct order of oxidizing power of the given ions is **[May 22, 2024 (I)]**
(a) $VO_2^+ < Cr_2O_7^{2-} < MnO_4^-$
(b) $VO_2^+ < MnO_4^- < Cr_2O_7^{2-}$
(c) $MnO_4^- < Cr_2O_7^{2-} < VO_2^+$
(d) $Cr_2O_7^{2-} < VO_2^+ < MnO_4^-$

42. Which of the following occurs with $KMnO_4$ in neutral medium? **[May 21, 2024 (II)]**
(a) Oxidation of oxalate ion
(b) Precipitation of sulphur from hydrogen sulphide
(c) Oxidation of Fe^{2+} to Fe^{3+}
(d) Oxidation of iodide to iodate

43. Which transition metal does not form 'MO' type oxide? (M= transition metal) **[May 20, 2024 (I)]**
(a) V (b) Cr (c) Mn (d) Sc

44. In neutral medium potassium permanganate oxidises I^- to X. Identify the X **[May 19, 2024 (II)]**
(a) Iodine (b) Iodate
(c) Per iodate (d) Hypo iodite

45. Identify the basic oxide from the following **[May 18, 2024 (I)]**
(a) Cr_2O_3 (b) CrO_3 (c) V_2O_5 (d) V_2O_3

46. Identify the correctly matched pairs
i. TiO - pigment industry
ii. MnO_2 - dry battery cells
iii. Cu/Ni alloy - UK 'copper' coins **[May 15, 2023 (II)]**
(a) i, ii, iii (b) ii, iii only
(c) i, ii only (d) i, iii only

47. A compound *A* is used in paints instead of salts of lead. Compound *A* is obtained when a white compound *B* is strongly heated. Compound *B* is insoluble in water but dissolves in NaOH solution forming a solution of compound *C*. The compound *A* on heating with coke gives a volatile metal *D* and a gas *E* which burns with a blue flame. Identify the possible species *D* and *C* can be respectively? **[Aug. 19, 2021 (I)]**
(a) $D = Hg, C = Hg(OH)_2$ (b) $D = Cd, C = Na_2(CdO_2)$
(c) $D = Zn, C = Na_2ZnO_2$ (d) $D = Zn, C = Zn(OH)_2$

48. The yellow colour of chromate ion and orange colour of dichromate ion is due to **[Sept. 18, 2020 (I)]**
(a) *d-d* transition only
(b) charge transfer only
(c) both *d-d* transition and charge transfer
(d) *s-d* transitions only

49. Aqueous sulphite reacts with dilute sulphuric acid to form $X(g)$. The liberated $X(g)$ is passed into acidified $KMnO_4$ solution. What is the oxidation state of Mn in the product formed? **[Apr. 22, 2019 (I)]**

(a) +6 (b) +4 (c) +2 (d) +3

50. $KMnO_4$ oxidises $S_2O_3^{2-}$ to SO_4^{2-} in medium x and NO_2^- to NO_3^- in medium y, x and y are respectively **[Apr. 20, 2019 (I)]**

(a) acidic, basic (b) acidic, acidic
(c) acidic, neutral (d) neutral, acidic

51. What are X and Y in the following reactions? **[2017]**

(i) $MnO_4^- + I^- \xrightarrow{H^+} X$

(ii) $MnO_4^- + I^- \xrightarrow{H_2O} Y$

(a) I_2, IO_4^- (b) I_2, IO_3^-
(c) IO_3^-, IO_3^- (d) IO_3^-, I_2

Topic 3 Lanthanoids and Actinoids

52. Identify the pair of ions which act as good reducing agents **[May 18, 2026 (I)]**

(a) Ce^{4+}, Yb^{2+} (b) Ce^{4+}, Tb^{4+}
(c) Ce^{3+}, Tb^{2+} (d) Eu^{2+}, Yb^{2+}

53. How many of the following lanthanide elements exhibit +4 oxidation state? **[May 22, 2025 (I)]**
Ce, Pr, Nd, Pm, Sm, Eu, Gd, Tb, Dy

(a) 5 (b) 4 (c) 3 (d) 6

54. The ion with $4f^7$ configuration is **[May 21, 2025 (II)]**

(a) Pr^{3+} (b) Lu^{3+} (c) Eu^{2+} (d) Ce^{4+}

55. Which of the following lanthanoids have $[Xe]\, 4f^x\, 5d^1\, 6s^2$ configuration in their ground state? (x = 1–14) **[May 21, 2024 (I)]**

(a) Pr, Tb, Yb (b) Ce, Yb, Lu
(c) Ce, Gd, Lu (d) Gd, Tb, Lu

56. Identify the correct statement **[May 19, 2023 (I)]**

(a) Yb^{2+} is an oxidant
(b) Lu^{3+} is paramagnetic
(c) CrO is basic
(d) Brass is an alloy of Cu, Sn

57. Select the correct order of radii of the given ions **[May 17, 2023 (I)]**

(a) $Yb^{3+} < Sm^{3+} < Dy^{3+} < Pr^{3+}$
(b) $Yb^{3+} < Dy^{3+} < Sm^{3+} < Pr^{3+}$
(c) $Pr^{3+} < Sm^{3+} < Dy^{3+} < Yb^{3+}$
(d) $Pr^{3+} < Sm^{3+} < Yb^{3+} < Dy^{3+}$

58. Correct order of basic strength of metallic hydroxides **[May 16, 2023 (I)]**

(a) $Ce(OH)_3 < Lu(OH)_3 < Eu(OH)_3$
(b) $Ce(OH)_3 < Eu(OH)_3 < Lu(OH)_3$
(c) $Lu(OH)_3 < Eu(OH)_3 < Ce(OH)_3$
(d) $Lu(OH)_3 < Ce(OH)_3 < Eu(OH)_3$

59. From the list given below, the number of lanthanides which exhibit +4 state in their oxides is
Pr, Nd, Pm, Sm, Eu, Gd, Tb, Dy **[May 15, 2023 (I)]**

(a) 5 (b) 4 (c) 6 (d) 2

60. Which of the following statements is correct about "shielding effect"? **[Sept. 18, 2020 (I)]**

1. It is effective, when the orbitals in the inner shells are completely filled.'
2. Inner shells do not show any effect.
3. With increase of shielding down the group, ionisation energy increases.
4. With increasing nuclear charge, the shielding effect increases.

(a) 1 (b) 2 (c) 3 (d) 4

61. Identify the correct statements from the following : **[Apr. 22, 2019 (I)]**

I. The ionic radius of Pr^{3+}, Dy^{3+} and Sm^{3+} follow the order, $Sm^{3+} > Pr^{3+} > Dy^{3+}$.
II. Eu^{2+} acts as strong reducing reagent.
III. Pu exhibits +7 oxidation state.

(a) I, II only (b) I, III only
(c) I, II, III (d) II, III only

62. Which of the following set of elements do not possess f-electrons? **[Apr. 21, 2019 (I)]**

(a) La, U, Lr (b) La, Th, Lr
(c) La, Ac, Th (d) Ce, Ac, Th

63. In lanthanide series, the element well known to exhibit +4 oxidation state is **[2018]**

(a) Lu (b) Ce (c) Pm (d) Nd

64. The percentage of lanthanides and iron, respectively, in misch metal are **[2015]**

(a) 50, 50 (b) 75, 25
(c) 90, 10 (d) 95, 5

5 Co-ordination Compounds

CHAPTER SYNOPSIS

- Linkage isomerism is shown by the coordination compounds which contain ligands that are able to attach themselves to the central ion through more than one donor atoms, (ambidentate ligands).
- Square planar complexes
- $(Ma_4)^{n\pm}$, $(Ma_3\, b)^{n\pm}$, $[M(AA)_2]^{n\pm}$,
- $[M(AA)ab]^{n\pm}$, $[M(AA)a_2]^{n\pm}$
- Complex $[(Ma_6)^{n\pm}, (Ma_5b)^{n\pm}, (M(AA)_3)^{n\pm}]$ do not exhibit geometrical isomerism because all the possible arrangement of the ligands round the metal cation is the same.
- The most well-known cases of optical isomerism occur among octahedral complexes of the type $[M(aa)_3]$, where 'aa' is a bidentate ligand, e.g., trioxalatochromate (III) ion, and tris (ethylenediamine) cobalt (III) ion show optical isomerism.
- The ligands which cause only a small crystal field splitting are called weak field ligands. The ligands which cause a large crystal splitting are called strong field ligands.
- $I^- < Br^- < S^{2-} < SCN^- < Cl^- < N_3^- < F^- <$ urea
- $< OH^- < C_2H_5-OH < C_2O\bar{4} < O^{2-} < H_2O$
- $< NCS^- <$ gly $< NH_3, Py <$ en, $SO_3^{2-} < NH_2OH <$ bpy,
- phen $< NO_2^- < CH_3^- < C_6H_5^- < R_3P < CN^- < CO$
- High spin complex with electronic configuration t_{2g}^p, e_g^q CFSE = $[-0.4p + 0.6\, q]\,\Delta_0 + mp$
- Where p and q are the number of electrons in t_{2g} and e_g orbitals respectively.
- m = Number of pairs of electrons caused by the ligand
- p = pairing energy
- For a d^n tetrahedral complex with (Ma configuration.
- CFSE $= [-0.6p + 0.4q]\,\Delta_t$
- $= [-0.6p + 0.4q] \times \frac{4}{9}\,\Delta_0 \qquad (\because \Delta_t = \frac{4}{9}\Delta_0)$
- $= [-0.27p + 0.18q]\,\Delta_0$
- Since tetrahedral complexes are high spin and no pairing of d-electrons occurs ($\Delta_t < P$). Therefore no pair energy is included in the above equation.
- The organometallic compounds in which carbon monoxide (CO) acts as a ligand are called metal carbonyls.
- The ability of CO molecule to accept electron-density back into its empty orbitals is called π-acidity (or back donation).
- The stability of a complex depends upon the following factors.
- (a) Nature of the central ion – High charge, small size favours the stability of the complex.
- (b) Nature of the ligand – More basic ligand forms more stable complex.

Topic 1 Coordination Number, Nomenclature and Isomerism of Coordination Compounds

1. Which of the following exhibit only geometrical isomerism? [May 15, 2026 (I)]
(a) Diaquadioxalatochromate (III) ion
(b) Dichloridobis(ethane-1, 2-diamine) platinum (IV) ion
(c) Triamminetrinitrito - N cobalt (III)
(d) Tris(ethane-1, 2 - diamine) cobalt (III) ion

2. Which of the following complexes do not exhibit geometrical isomerism? [May 14, 2026 (II)]
I. $K[Cr(H_2O)_2(C_2O_4)_2]$
II. $[Co(en)_3]Cl_3$
III. $[Co(NH_3)_5(NO_2)] (NO_3)_2$
The correct answer is
(a) I, III only (b) II, III only
(c) I, II only (d) I, II, III

3. Identify the correct set containing only ambidentate ligands [May 14, 2026 (I)]
(a) NO_2^-, CN^-, SCN^-
(b) NH_3, CN^-, $C_2O_4^{2-}$
(c) SO_4^{2-}, SCN^-, CO
(d) $C_2O_4^{2-}$, $(CH_3)_3P$, CO

4. Choose the correct formula for tris (ethane-1, 2-diamine) cobalt (III) hexacyanido ferrate (II) [May 13, 2026 (II)]
(a) $[Co(en)_3] [Fe(CN)_6]$
(b) $[Co(en)_3]_2 [Fe(CN)_6]_3$
(c) $[Co(en)_3]_3 [Fe(CN)_6]_2$
(d) $[Co(en)_3]_4 [Fe(CN)_6]_3$

5. Aqueous solutions of which of the following compounds do not form AgCl precipitate with excess $AgNO_3$ solution? [May 12, 2026 (II)]
I. $PCl_4.2HCl$ II. $PtCl_2.2NH_3$
III. $CoCl_3.4NH_3$ IV. $PdCl_2.4NH_3$
The correct answer is
(a) I, II only (b) III, IV only
(c) I, II, III only (d) I, II, IV only

6. Identify the set which does not have ambidentate ligand(s) [May 27, 2025 (I)]
(a) NO_2^-, CN^-, $C_2O_4^{2-}$
(b) $C_2O_4^{2-}$, H_2O, SO_4^{2-}
(c) SCN^-, NH_3, CH_3COO^-
(d) CN^-, SCN^-, CH_3NH_2

7. The IUPAC name of the complex shown below is
$K_3[Co(ox)_3]$ [May 26, 2025 (II)]
(a) Tripotassium trioxalatocobaltate (III)
(b) Potassium trioxalatecobaltate (III)
(c) Potassium trioxalatecobalt (III)
(d) Potassium trioxalatocobaltate (III)

8. Which of the following exhibit ionization isomerism ?
I. $[Cr(NH_3)_4Cl_2]Cl$ [May 26, 2025 (I)]
II. $[Ti(H_2O)_5Cl](NO_3)_2$
III. $[Pt(en)(NH_3)Cl]NO_3$
IV. $[Co(NH_3)_4(NO_3)_2]NO_3$
(a) II & III only (b) I & II only
(c) II & IV only (d) III & IV only

9. The co-ordination number of chromium in
$K[Cr(H_2O)_2(C_2O_4)_2]$ is [May 24, 2025 (I)]
(a) 5 (b) 4 (c) 6 (d) 3

10. In $Fe_x[Fe_y(CN)_6]_3$, x, y respectively, are [May 22, 2025 (II)]
(a) 3, 2 (b) 4, 1 (c) 2, 3 (d) 1, 4

11. Cobalt (III) chloride forms a green coloured complex 'X' with NH_3. Number of moles of AgCl formed when excess of $AgNO_3$ solution is added to 100 mL of 1 M solution of 'X' is [May 21, 2024 (II)]
(a) 0.3 (b) 0.2 (c) 0.1 (d) 1

12. Impure silver ore $+CN^- + H_2O \xrightarrow{O_2} [X]^- + OH^-$
$[X]^- + Zn \longrightarrow [Y]^{2-} + Ag$ (pure)
The co-ordination numbers of the metals in [X]. (Y] are respectively [May 21, 2024 (I)]
(a) 3, 4 (b) 1, 4 (c) 4, 2 (d) 2, 4

13. How many of the following ligands are stronger than H_2O?
S^{2-}, Br^-, $C_2O_4^{2-}$, CN^-, en, NH_3, CO, OH^- [May 21, 2024 (I)]
(a) 5 (b) 3 (c) 4 (d) 6

14. Which of the following does not show optical isomerism?
(a) Cis – $[CrCl_2 (C_2O_4)_2]^{3-}$ [May 18, 2024 (I)]
(b) $[PtCl_2 (en)_2]^{2+}$
(c) $[Co(NH_3)_3 (NO_2)_3]$
(d) $[Co (en)_3]^{3+}$

15. Which of the following types of isomerism is exhibited by [May 18, 2023 (II)]
$[Co(NH_3)_5 (NO_2)] (NO_3)_2$
i. Optical ii. Linkage iii. Ionization iv. Coordination
(a) ii, iii only (b) i, ii, iii only
(c) i, iii only (d) ii, iv only

16. IUPAC name of $[Pt(NH_3)_2Cl(NH_2CH_3)]Cl$ is **[May 17, 2023 (II)]**
(a) (Amino methane) chloro (diammine) platinum (II) chloride.
(b) Chlorodiammine (methanamine) platinum (II) chloride.
(c) Diamminechloro (methanamine) platinum (II) chloride.
(d) Diamminechloro (methylamine) platinum (IV) chloride.

17. Which one of the following has the highest molar conductivity? **[May 16, 2023 (II)]**
(a) Diammine dichloroplatinum (II)
(b) Tetraamminedichlorocobalt (III) chloride
(c) Potassium hexacyano ferrate (II)
(d) Hexa aquo chromium (III) chloride

18. The formula of tris (ethane - 1, 2- diamine) cobalt (III) sulphate is: **[May 16, 2023 (I)]**
(a) $[Co(H_2NCH_2CH_2NH_2)_3]SO_4$
(b) $[Co(H_2NCH_2CH_2NH_2)_3]_3(SO_3)_2$
(c) $[Co(CH_3CH_2NHNH_2)_3]_2(SO_4)_3$
(d) $[Co(H_2NCH_2CH_2NH_2)_3]_2(SO_4)_3$

19. The set with only ambidentate ligands in the following is **[July 6, 2022 (I)]**
(a) $NO_3^{\ominus}, Br^{\ominus}, C_2O_4^{2\ominus}$ (b) $NO_2^{\ominus}, CN^{\ominus}, SCN^{\ominus}$
(c) $NO_2^{\ominus}, C_2O_4^{2\ominus}, NH_3$ (d) $SCN^{\ominus}, CO, NH_3$

20. What is coordination number of the metal in $[Co(en)_2Cl_2]^{2+}$? **[Aug. 19, 2021 (I)]**
(a) 3 (b) 4 (c) 5 (d) 6

21. Oxidation number of Cr in $[Cr(CO)_6]$ is **[Sept. 18, 2020 (I)]**
(a) +6 (b) – 6 (c) + 3 (d) 0

22. Select the correct IUPAC name of $[Co(NH_3)_5(CO_3)]Cl$. **[2016]**
(a) Penta ammoniacarbonate cobalt (III) chloride
(b) Pentaamminecarbonatecobalt chloride
(c) Pentaamminecarbonatocobalt (III) chloride
(d) Cobalt (III) pentaamminecarbonate chloride

23. When $AgNO_3$ solution is added in excess to 1M solution of $CoCl_3 \cdot X NH_3$, one mole of AgCl is formed. What is the value of 'X'? **[2015]**
(a) 1 (b) 4 (c) 3 (d) 2

Topic 2 Magnetic Moment, Valence Bond Theory and Crystal Field Theory

24. In which of the following given sets, complexes are correctly arranged in the increasing order of their spin only magnetic movement values?
I. $[Fe(CN)_6]^{4-} < [Fe(CN)_6]^{3-} < [Fe(H_2O)_6]^{3+}$
II. $[Co(NH_3)_6]^{3+} < [Ni(H_2O)_6]^{2+} < [Cr(H_2O)_6]^{3+}$
III. $[V(H_2O)_6]^{3+} < [Cr(CN)_6]^{3-} < [Fe(H_2O)_6]^{2+}$
The correct answer is **[May 18, 2026 (II)]**
(a) I, II only (b) I, II, III
(c) II, III only (d) I, III only

25. Which of the following has maximum number of electrons in t_{2g} orbitals? **[May 18, 2026 (I)]**
(a) $[Fe(CN)_6]^{3-}$ (b) $[FeCl_6]^{3-}$
(c) $[CoCl_6]^{3-}$ (d) $[Co(NH_3)_6]^{3+}$

26. How many of the following complex ions contain 4 unpaired electrons?
$[Cr(H_2O)_6]^{2+}$, $[Mn(H_2O)_6]^{2+}$, $[Fe(H_2O)_6]^{2+}$, $[Co(H_2O)_6]^{3+}$, $[Cu(H_2O)_6]^{2+}$, $[CoF_6]^{3-}$, $[Cr(CH)_6]^{4-}$, $[MnCl_4]^{2-}$
The correct answer is **[May 15, 2026 (II)]**
(a) 3 (b) 4
(c) 2 (d) 5

27. In which of the following, ratio of t_{2g} and e_g electrons is 3:2 ? **[May 12, 2026 (I)]**
(a) $FeF_6]^{3-}$ (b) $[CoF_6]^{3-}$
(c) $[Fe(CN)_6]^{3-}$ (d) $[Co(NH_3)_6]^{3+}$

28. Identify the complex ion with spin only magnetic moment of 4.90 BM. **[May 23, 2025 (II)]**
(a) $[Co(NH_3)_6]^{3+}$ (b) $[Cr(NH_3)_6]^{3+}$
(c) $[Mn(CN)_6]^{3-}$ (d) $[MnCl_6]^{3-}$

29. In which one of the following complexes the metal ion has $t_{2g}^3 e_g^2$ configuration? **[May 23, 2025 (I)]**
(a) $[Mn(H_2O)_6]^{2+}$ (b) $[Fe(H_2O)_6]^{2+}$
(c) $[Co(NH_3)_6]^{3+}$ (d) $[Ni(H_2O)_6]^{2+}$

30. In which of the following, complex ions are not in correct order with respect to their magnitude of crystal field splitting? **[May 22, 2025 (I)]**
(a) $[Fe(H_2O)_6]^{3+} > [FeF_6]^{3-}$
(b) $[Fe(en)_3]^{3+} > [Fe(NCS)_6]^{3-}$
(c) $[Fe(CN)_6]^{4-} > [Fe(H_2O)_6]^{2+}$
(d) $[Fe(H_2O)_6]^{2+} > [Fe(NH_3)_6]^{2+}$

31. Which of the following complexes exhibit geometrical isomerism? **[May 21, 2025 (I)]**
(I) $[Co(en)(NH_3)_2Cl_2]Cl$ (II) $[Co(NH_3)_4Cl_2]Cl$
(III) $[Co(en)_3]Cl_3$ (IV) $[Co(en)_2Cl_2]Br$
(a) I, II and III only
(b) II, III and IV only
(c) I, II and IV only
(d) II and III only

32. Arrange the following in the increasing order of their magnetic moments **[May 23, 2024 (I)]**

I. $[Mn(CN)_6]^{3-}$ II. $[Mn Cl_6]^{3-}$
III. $[Fe(CN)_6]^{3-}$ IV. $[FeF_6]^{3-}$

(a) III < I < IV < II (b) III < IV < II < I
(c) IV < II < I < III (d) III < I < II < IV

33. Which complex among the following is most paramagnetic? **[May 22, 2024 (II)]**

(a) $[Co(NH_3)_6]^{2+}$ (b) $[Co(NH_3)_6]^{3+}$
(c) $[Co(H_2O)_6]^{2+}$ (d) $[Co(H_2O)_6]^{3+}$

34. Match the complexes in List-I with their hybridization in List-II. **[May 22, 2024 (I)]**

List-I (Complex)		List-II (Hybridization)	
A.	$Ni(CO)_4$	I	sp^3d^2
B.	$[Ni(CN)_4]^{2-}$	II	d^2sp^3
C.	$[Co(NH_3)_6]^{3+}$	III	dsp^2
D.	$[CoF_6]^{3-}$	IV	sp^3

(a) I-C, II-D, III-A, IV-B (b) I-D, II-C, III-A, IV-B
(c) I-D, II-C, III-B, IV-A (d) I-C, II-D, III-B, IV-A

35. Arrange the following in the increasing order of number of unpaired electrons present in the central metal ion **[May 20, 2024 (II)]**

I. $[Mn Cl_6]^{3-}$ II. $[Fe F_6]^{3-}$
III. $[Mn (CN)_6]^{3-}$ IV. $[Fe (CN)_6]^{3-}$

(a) IV < I < III < II (b) I < III < II < IV
(c) IV < III < I < II (d) I < II < III < IV

36. The paramagnetic complex ion which has no unpaired electrons in t_{2g} orbitals is **[May 20, 2024 (I)]**

(a) $[Fe (CN)_6]^{4-}$ (b) $[Fe (CN)_6]^{3-}$
(c) $[Zn (NH_3)_6]^{2+}$ (d) $[Ni (NH_3)_6]^{2+}$

37. The spin only magnetic moments of the complexes $[Mn(CN)_6]^{3-}$ and $[Co(C_2O_4)_3]^{3-}$ are respectively **[May 19, 2024 (II)]**

(a) 2.84 BM, 0 BM (b) 0 BM, 2.84 BM
(c) 0 BM, 3.87 BM (d) 5.92 BM, 2.84 BM

38. The configurations of the complexes of manganese A, B respectively are $t_{2g}^3\ e_g^1$, $t_{2g}^4\ e_g^0$. Then A, B are **[May 18, 2023 (II)]**

(a) $[Mn(H_2O)_6]^{2+}$, $[Mn(CN)_6]^{3-}$
(b) $[Mn(H_2O)_6]^{2+}$, $[Mn(CN)_6]^{4-}$
(c) $[Mn(H_2O)_6]^{3+}$, $[Mn(CN)_6]^{4-}$
(d) $[Mn(H_2O)_6]^{3+}$, $[Mn(CN)_6]^{3-}$

39. The spin only magnetic moment of $[MnBr_4]^{x-}$ is 5.9 BM. The geometry of the complex and x respectively are **[May 18, 2023 (I)]**

(a) tetrahedral, 1 (b) square planar, 1
(c) square planar, 2 (d) tetrahedral, 2

40. Observe the following complexes
$[Mn(CN)_6]^{3-}$, $[Fe(CN)_6]^{-3}$, $[Co(C_2O_4)_3]^{3-}$, $[MnCl_6]^{3-}$, $[Fe(CN)_6]^{4-}$, $[CoF_6]^{3-}$
From the above, the number of inner orbital complexes with paramagnetic nature is **[May 16, 2023 (II)]**

(a) 2 (b) 1 (c) 3 (d) 4

41. Which of the following statements are correct?

i. $[Mn(CN)_6]^{3-}$, $[MnCl_6]^{3-}$ both are paramagnetic
ii. Both $[NiCl_4]^{2-}$, $[Ni(CO)_4]$ are tetrahedral and diamagnetic
iii. $[Co(NH_3)_6]^{3+}$ is inner orbital complex, but $[Ni(NH_3)_6]^{2+}$ is outer orbital complex

[May 16, 2023 (II)]

(a) i, ii only (b) i, iii only
(c) ii, iii only (d) i, ii, iii

42. According to valence bond theory the metal atom or ion can make use of which of the following orbitals to yield hybrid orbitals, that can form bonds with ligands. **[July 8, 2022 (I)]**

(a) (n – 1)d, (n – 1)s, np
(b) (n – 1)d, ns, np
(c) (n – 1)d, ns, (n – 1)p
(d) nd, (n – 1)s, (n – 1)p

43. The hybridization of metals involved in the following complexes, respectively are **[July 7, 2022 (II)]**
$[Mn(CN)_6]^{3-}$, $[CoF_6]^{3-}$

(a) sp^3d^2, sp^3d^2 (b) sp^3d^2, d^2sp^3
(c) d^2sp^3, d^2sp^3 (d) d^2sp^3, sp^3d^2

44. Calculated magnetic moment value for Fe^{2+} ion in BM is **[July 5, 2022 (II)]**

(a) 3.87 (b) 4.90
(c) 2.84 (d) 1.73

45. The crystal filed theory is successful in explaining which of the following? **[July 4, 2022 (II)]**

I. Ligands as point charges
II. Formation and structures of complexes
III. Colour
IV. Magnetic properties
V. Covalent character of metal-ligand bonding.

(a) I, II, III only (b) II, III, IV only
(c) III, IV, V only (d) II, IV, V only

46. Which of the following is correct related to the colours of $TiCl_3$ (X) $[Ti(H_2O)_6]Cl_3$(Y). **[July 4, 2022 (I)]**
(a) X = Colourless Y = Coloured
(b) X = Coloured Y = Coloured
(c) X = Colourless Y = Colourless
(d) X = Coloured Y = Colourless

47. Atomic number of Cr, Fe and Co are 24, 26 and 27 respectively. Which of the following inner orbital octahedral complexes are paramagnetic? **[Aug. 23, 2021 (I)]**
(a) $[Co(NH_3)_6]^{3+}$ (b) $[Co(CN)_3]^{3+}$
(c) $[Fe(CN)_6]^{4-}$ (d) $[Cr(CN)_6]^{3-}$

48. Which of the following complexes formed by nickel is tetrahedral and paramagnetic? **[Aug. 20, 2021 (I)]**
(a) $[Ni(CN)_4]^{2-}$ (b) $[Ni(CO)_4]$
(c) $[Ni(Cl)_4]^{2-}$ (d) $[Ni(NH_3)_6]^{2+}$

49. Which complex among the following has the highest value of spin only magnetic moment? **[Sept. 21, 2020 (I)]**
$[Fe(CN)_6]^{3-}$, $[Fe(CN)_6]^{4-}$, $[Ni(CN)_4]^{2-}$, $[NiCl_4]^{2-}$
(a) $[Fe(CN)_6]^{3-}$ (b) $[Fe(CN)_6]^{4-}$
(c) $[Ni(CN)_4]^{2-}$ (d) $[NiCl_4]^{2-}$

50. The correct order for wavelengths of absorption in the visible region for the following complexes will be **[Sept. 17, 2020 (I)]**
(a) $[Ni(NH_3)_6]^{2+} < [Ni(H_2O)_6]^{2+} < [Ni(NO_2)_6]^{4-}$
(b) $[Ni(NO_2)_6]^{4-} < [Ni(NH_3)_6]^{2+} < [Ni(H_2O)_6]^{2+}$
(c) $[Ni(NH_3)_6]^{2+} < [Ni(NO_2)_6]^{4-} < [Ni(H_2O)_6]^{2+}$
(d) $[Ni(NO_2)_6]^{4-} < [Ni(H_2O)_6]^{2+} < [Ni(NH_3)_6]^{2+}$

51. If the crystal field splitting energy of a tetrahedral complex (Δ_t) of the type $[ML_4]^{n+}$ is x eV, what is the crystal field splitting energy with respect to an octahedral complex, $[ML_6]^{n+}$? **[Apr. 22, 2019 (I)]**
(a) $\frac{9x}{4}$eV (b) $\frac{9x}{8}$eV (c) $\frac{4x}{9}$eV (d) $\frac{4x}{5}$eV

52. The Δ_0 of a coordination complex of a metal ion ($3d^1$) is 1000 kJ mol^{-1}. If the energy of t_{2g} orbitals is – 400 kJ mol^{-1}, the energy (in kJ mol^{-1}) of e_g orbitals is **[Apr. 21, 2019 (I)]**
(a) – 600 (b) 600 (c) 1000 (d) 400

53. The wavelengths of light absorbed by the complexes $[Ni(H_2O)_6]^{2+}$, $[Ni(en)_3]^{2+}$, $[Ni(H_2O)_4 en]^{2+}$ are λ_1, λ_2, λ_3 respectively. The correct order of wavelengths is **[Apr. 20, 2019 (I)]**
(a) $\lambda_1 > \lambda_2 > \lambda_3$ (b) $\lambda_3 > \lambda_2 > \lambda_1$
(c) $\lambda_1 > \lambda_3 > \lambda_2$ (d) $\lambda_2 > \lambda_3 > \lambda_1$

54. Crystal field splitting energies for octahedral (Δ_0) and tetrahedral (Δ_t) geometries caused by the same ligands are related through the expression **[2018]**
(a) $\Delta_0 = \Delta_t$ (b) $4\Delta_0 = 9\Delta_t$
(c) $9\Delta_0 = \Delta_t$ (d) $\Delta_0 = 2\Delta_t$

55. Identify, from the following, the diamagnetic, tetrahedral complex **[2017]**
(a) $[Ni(Cl)_4]^{2-}$ (b) $[Co(C_2O_4)_3]^{3-}$
(c) $[Ni(CN)_4]^{2-}$ (d) $[Ni(CO)_4]$

56. In which of the following coordination compounds, the central metal ion is in zero oxidation state? **[2015]**
(a) $[Fe(H_2O)_6]Cl_3$ (b) $K_4[Fe(CN)_6]$
(c) $[Fe(CO)_5]$ (d) $[Fe(H_2O)_6]Cl_2$

Topic 3 Organometallic Compounds

57. The metal ion, ligands present in Wilkinson catalyst are respectively. **[May 13, 2026 (I)]**
(a) Rh^{3+}, Cl^-, PPh_3 (b) Rh^+, Cl^-, PPh_3
(c) Rh^{2+}, Br^-, PH_3 (d) Re^+, I^-, $P(CH_3)_3$

58. In ruby and emerald, the metal ion(s) present is/are **[July 5, 2022 (II)]**
(a) Cr^{6+}, Mn^{3+} (b) Cr^{3+}
(c) Mn^{3+}, Co^{3+} (d) Co^{3+}h

59. Gadolinium (atomic number = 64) is a member of 4 f series. It's electronic configuration in + 3 oxidation state is [Xe] $4f^7$. What is the ground state electronic configuration of gadolinium? **[Aug. 23, 2021 (I)]**
(a) [Xe] $4f^{10}$ (b) [Xe] $4f^8 6s^2$
(c) [Xe] $4f^7 5d^3$ (d) [Xe] $4f^7 5d^1 6s^2$

6 Haloalkanes and Haloarenes

CHAPTER SYNOPSIS

- **Trends in nucleophilicity :**

  (i) A species with a negative charge is a stronger nucleophile than a similar neutral species. In particular, a base is a stronger nucleophile than its conjugate acid.

  $\ddot{\text{:}}\ddot{O}H^{-} > H_2\ddot{O}:$; $\quad \ddot{\text{:}}\ddot{S}H^{-} > H_2\ddot{S}:$; $\quad \ddot{\text{:}}NH_2^{-} > \ddot{N}H_3$

  (ii) With increase in electronegativity, nucleophilicity decreases from left to right in the periodic table.

  $\ddot{\text{:}}\ddot{O}H^{-} > \ddot{F}:^{-}$; $\quad :NH_3 > H_2\ddot{O}:$; $\quad R_3P: > R_2\ddot{S}:$

  (iii) Nucleophilicity increases down the periodic table, following the increase in size and polarizability.

  $I^- > Br^- > Cl^- > F^-$; $\quad {}^{-}SeH > {}^{-}SH > {}^{-}OH$; $\quad R_3P: > R_3N:$

  The rate of S_N1 is independent of the nature of the nucleophile (stronger or weaker) because here the nucleophile attacks on the carbocation (a fast step). The net result is that, other things being equal, *a strong nucleophile favours the* S_N2 *reaction, and a weak nucleophile favours the* S_N1 *reaction.*

- **Elimination Reactions :** They are classified into two categories :

  (a) α-Elimination reactions, (b) β-Elimination reactions.

  (i) α-Elimination reactions are those in which the two groups are eliminated from the same carbon. For ex:

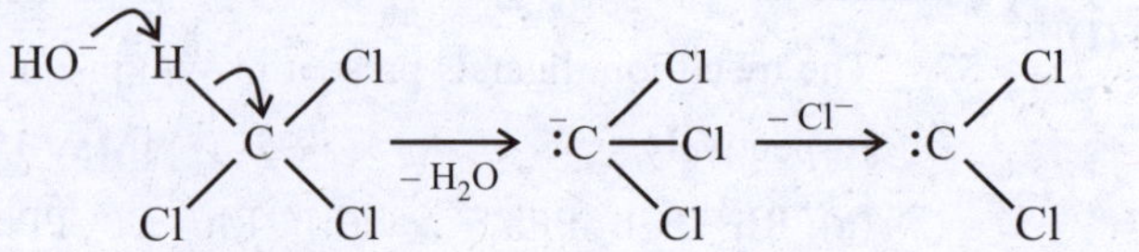

Chloroform $\quad$ Dichlorocarbene

  (ii) β-Elimination reactions are those reactions in which the two groups are eliminated from the adjacent carbon atoms: H from β- and the X from the α-carbon. For ex :

$$\overset{\beta}{CH_3}-\overset{\alpha}{CH_2}-Br \xrightarrow{NaOC_2H_5} CH_2 = CH_2 + C_2H_5OH + NaBr$$

The reactivity of halogen atom is increased by the presence of electron withdrawing group at ortho and or para positions wrt the halogen atom.Thus, the reactivity order of halogens is :

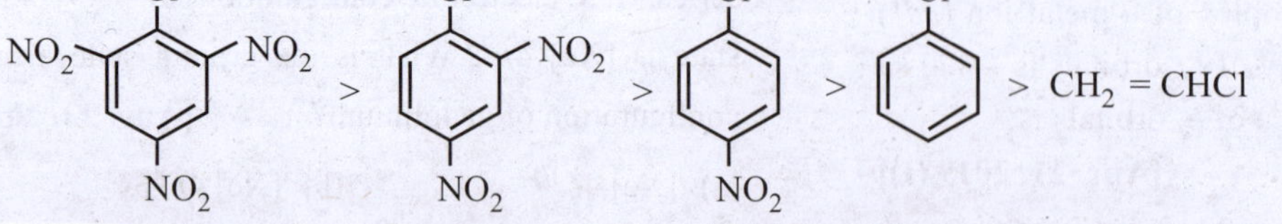

Picryl chloride $\quad$ 2, 4-dinitro chlorobenzene $\quad$ *p*-Nitrochloro benzene $\quad$ Chloro benzene $\quad$ Vinyl chloride

Topic 1 Preparation and Properties of Haloalkanes

1. In which of the following, the given four compounds (I to IV) are correctly arranged in the decreasing order of reactivity towards S_N2 reaction? **[May 18, 2026 (II)]**

1-Bromobutane (I) 1-Bromo-2,2-dimethylpropane (II)

1-Bromo-2-methylbutane (III) 1-Bromo-3-methylbutane (IV)

(a) I > IV > III > II (b) I > II > III > IV
(c) I > III > IV > II (d) IV > III > II > I

2. Consider the two chlorides given below
(I) (R)-2-Choloropentane (II) (R)-3-Chloroheptane
Chloride (I) undergoes nucleophilic substitution reaction (X) in single step
Chloride (II) undergoes nucleophilic substitution reaction (Y) in two steps
Stereochemistry involved in reactions X and Y respectively is **[May 15, 2026 (II)]**
(a) Retention ; racemisation
(b) Inversion ; retention
(c) Inversion ; racemisation
(d) Racemisation ; inversion

3. The number of α - hydrogens present in the major product (X) in the given reaction is **[May 15, 2026 (I)]**

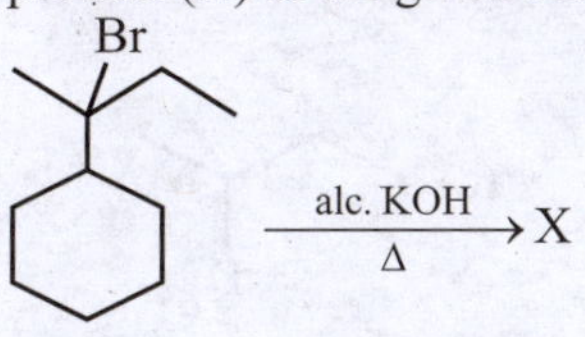

(a) 3 (b) 5 (c) 7 (d) 9

4. Consider the following **[May 14, 2026 (II)]**
(I) 1-Bromo - 1 - phenylpropane
(II) 1-Bromo - 3- n - butyl - 2- methyl benzene
Bromides I, II are classified respectively as
(a) Benzyl ; Aryl (b) Aryl ; Aryl
(c) Primary ; Benzyl (d) Aryl ; Primary

5. An isomer of C_4H_8 (A) exhibits cis-trans isomerism. Reaction of A with Br_2/CCl_4 gave B. Another organic compound C_4H_6 (C) forms sodium derivative with $NaNH_2$. Reaction of C with HBr gave D. what are B and D respectively? **[May 14, 2026 (I)]**

(a) 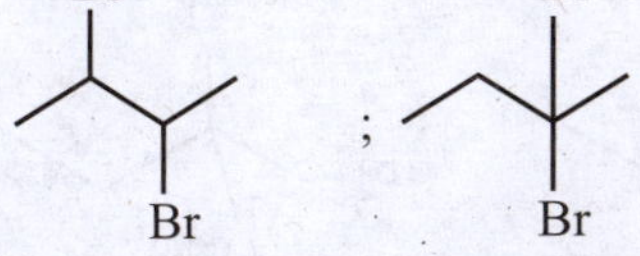

(b) 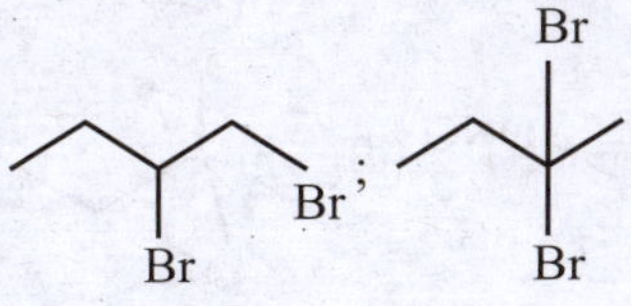

(c) 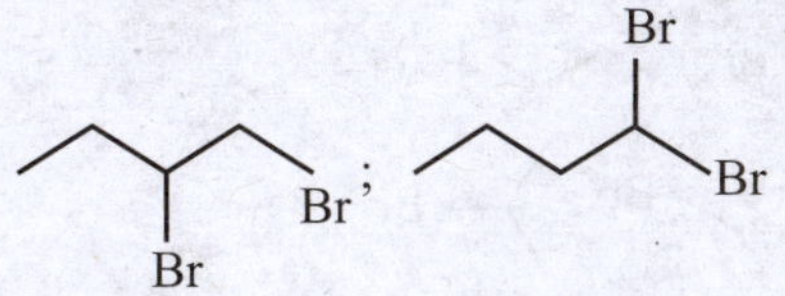

(d) 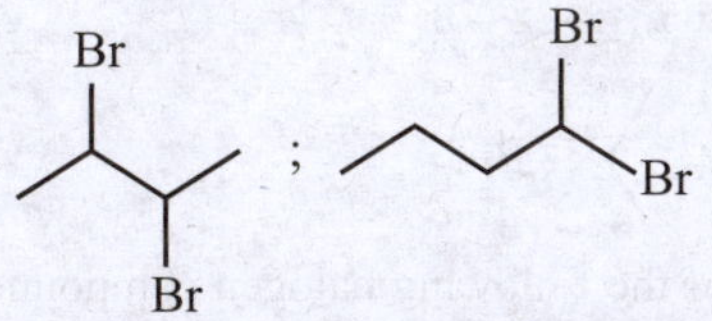

6. An organic compound C_4H_9Br(A) on reaction with Na/dry ether gave B. Photochemical chlorination of B gave two monochlorides. Correct statement regarding A is
(a) It is a chiral molecule **[May 14, 2026 (I)]**
(b) It undergoes nucleophilic substitution by S_N1 mechanism
(c) Reaction of it with $NaOC_2H_5$ gave predominantly substitution product
(d) It can be obtained by the addition of HBr to but-2-ene

7. Consider the following reactions I, II and III. The correct order of reactivity of X, Y and Z towards S_N1 reaction is **[May 13, 2026 (I)]**

I. 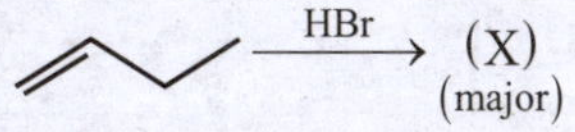

II. 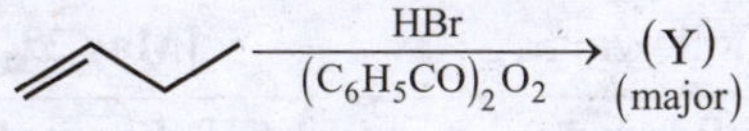

III. 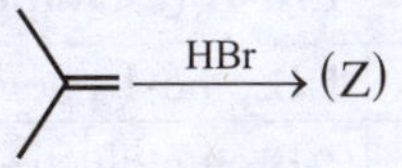

(a) Z > Y > X (b) X > Z > Y
(c) X > Y > Z (d) Z > X > Y

8. What are A and B in the following reaction sequence? **[May 12, 2026 (II)]**

$$C_4H_9Br \xrightarrow[S_N2]{A} \underset{\text{major Product}}{C_4H_9NO_2} \xrightarrow[HCl]{Sn} B$$

(a) $AgNO_2$; 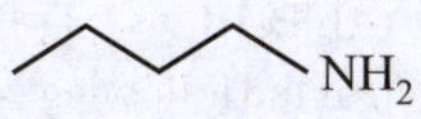

(b) $AgNO_2$; 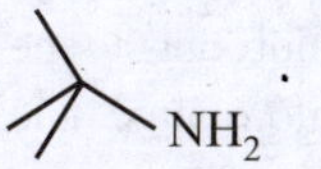

(c) KNO_2; 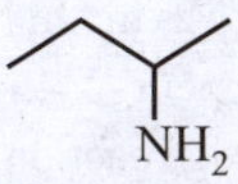

(d) KNO_2; 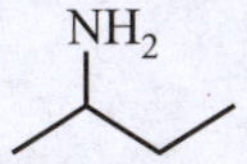

9. What are X and Y respectively in the following sets of reactions? **[May 27, 2025 (I)]**

I. 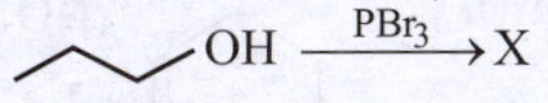

II. 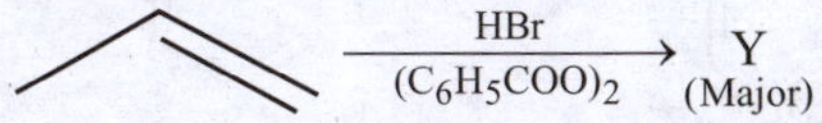

(a) 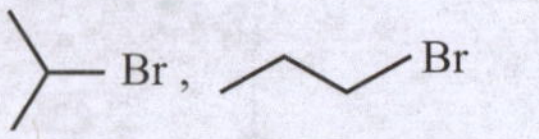

(b) 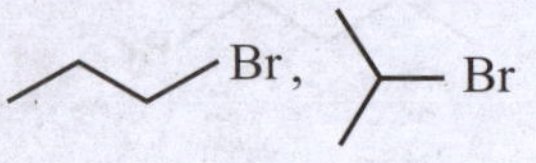

(c) 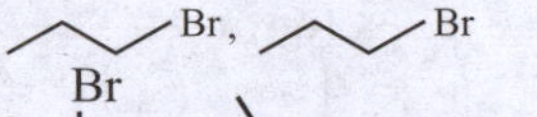

(d) 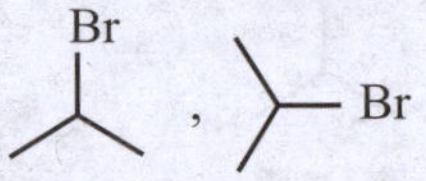

10. Which one of the following halogen compounds is least reactive towards hydrolysis by S_N1 mechanism? **[May 24, 2025 (I)]**

(a) Tertiary butyl chloride (b) Isopropyl chloride
(c) Allyl chloride (d) Ethyl chloride

11. An alkyl bromide $X(C_5H_{11}Br)$ undergoes hydrolysis in a two step mechanism. X is converted to Grignard reagent and then reacted with CO_2 in dry ether followed by acidification gave Y. What is Y ? **[May 23, 2025 (II)]**

(a) 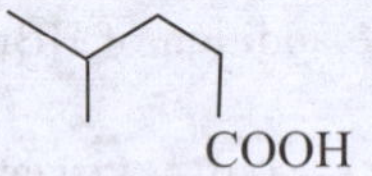

(b) 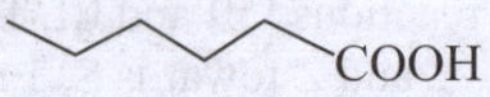

(c) 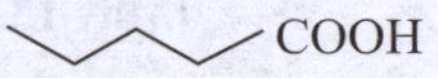

(d) 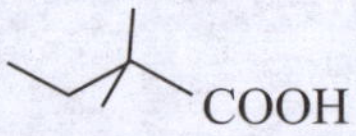

12. Match the following. **[May 22, 2025 (I)]**

List-I (Halide type)		List-II (Example)	
(A)	Vinyl	(I)	1-Bromo-1-phenylethane
(B)	Allyl	(II)	3-Bromotoluene
(C)	Benzyl	(III)	1-Bromo-3-methylcyclohexene
(D)	Aryl	(IV)	3-Bromo-4-methylcyclohexene

Correct answer is

(a) A-III, B-IV, C-II, D-I (b) A-III, B-IV, C-I, D-II
(c) A-II, B-III, C-I, D-IV (d) A-I, B-II, C-IV, D-III

13. Which of the following is not an example of allylic halide? **[May 22, 2024 (II)]**

(a) 4–chlorobut–1–ene
(b) 1–chlorobut–2–ene
(c) 3–chloro–2–methyl but–1–ene
(d) 4–chloropent–2–ene

14. In Wurtz-Fittig reaction a compound X reacts with alkyl halide. What is X? **[May 22, 2024 (I)]**

(a) 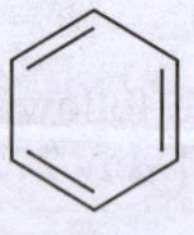 (b) 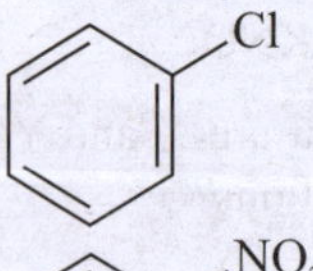

(c) 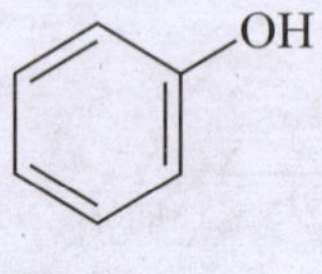 (d) 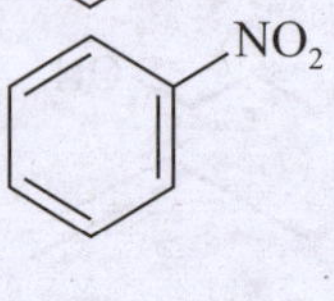

15. What are Y and Z respectively in the following reaction sequence? **[May 21, 2024 (II)]**

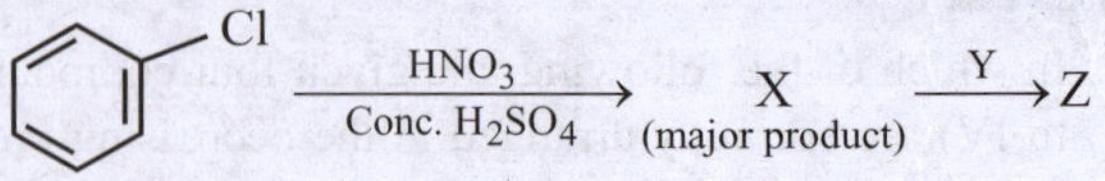

(a) (i) NaOH, 443 K, (ii) H^+; 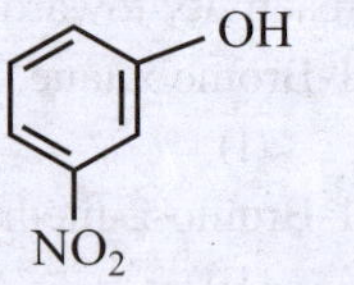

(b) (i) NaOH, 443 K, (ii) H^+, 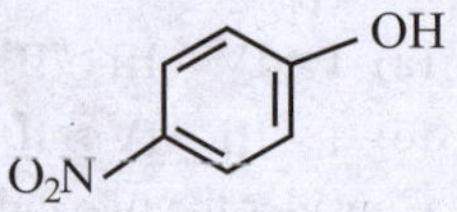

(c) H_2O, Δ; 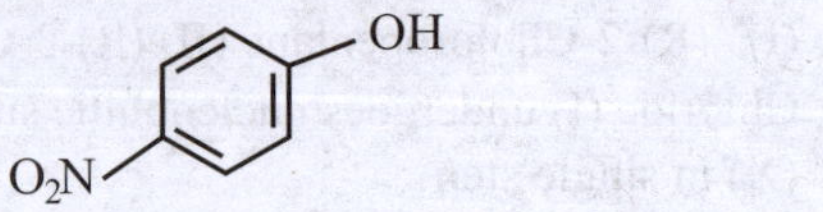

(d) H_2O, Δ; 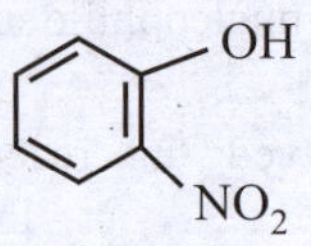

16. Hydrolysis of an alkyl bromide X $(C_5H_{11}Br)$ follows first order kinetics. Reaction of X with Mg in dry ether followed by treatment of D_2O gave Y. What is Y? **[May 21, 2024 (II)]**

(a) 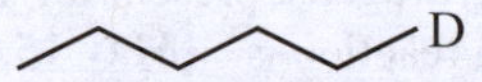 (b) 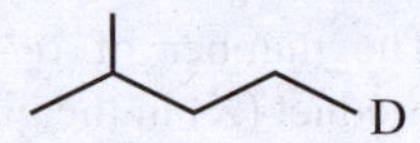

(c) 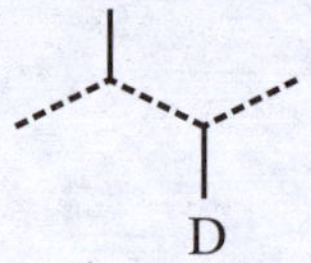 (d) 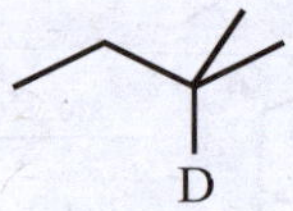

17. The major products X and Y respectively from the following reactions are **[May 21, 2024 (I)]**

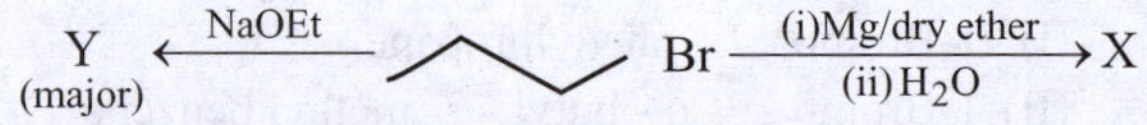

(a) 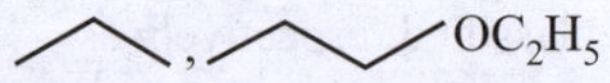

(b) 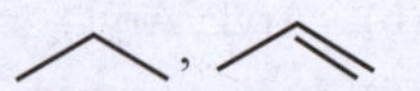

(c) 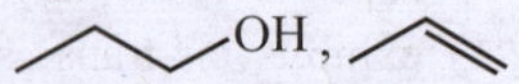

(d) 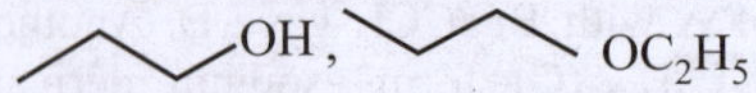

18. An isomer of C_5H_{12} on reaction with Br_2/ light gave only one isomer $C_5H_{11}Br$ (X). Reaction of X with $AgNO_2$ gave Y as major product. What is Y? **[May 21, 2024 (I)]**

(a) 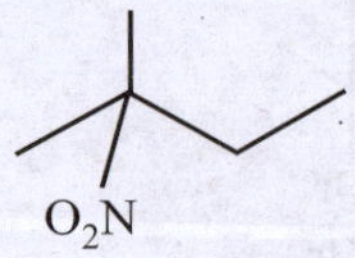 (b) 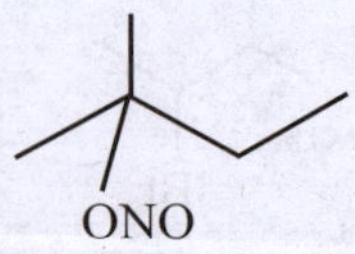

(c) 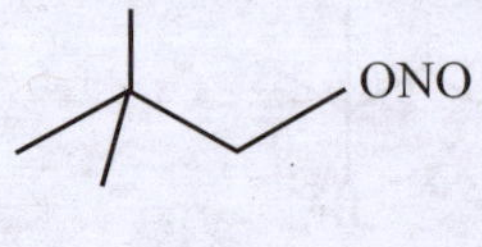 (d) 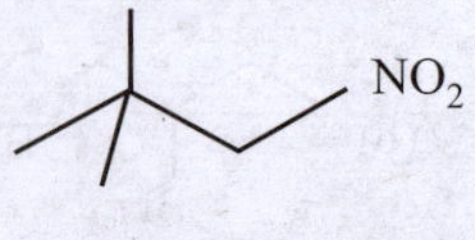

19. The major product (X) formed in the given reaction is an example of **[May 19, 2024 (II)]**

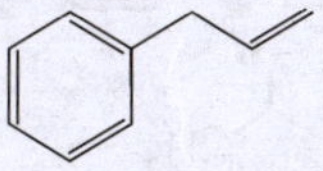 $\xrightarrow[(C_6H_5CO)_2O_2]{HBr}$ X

(a) Secondary alkyl halide (b) Primary alkyl halide
(c) Tertiary alkyl halide (d) Benzylic halide

20. Identify the Swarts reaction from the following: **[May 19, 2024 (II)]**

(a) $R-CH_2-Br + NaI \xrightarrow[\text{acetone}]{\text{dry}} R-CH_2-I + NaBr$

(b) $2R-CH_2-Br + 2Na \xrightarrow[\text{ether}]{\text{dry}} R-(CH_2)_2-R + 2\ NaBr$

(c) $2C_6H_5Cl + 2\ Na \xrightarrow[\text{ether}]{\text{dry}} C_6H_5-C_6H_5 + 2\ NaCl$

(d) $2R-CH_2-Br + CoF_2 \longrightarrow 2R-CH_2-F + CoBr_2$

21. Match the following reactions with the product obtained from them. **[May 18, 2024 (II)]**

List-I		List-II	
(A)	Sandmeyer reaction	(I)	R-I
(B)	Finkelstein reaction	(II)	R-F
(C)	Swarts reaction	(III)	Ar-Br
		(IV)	R-Br

The correct answer is
(a) (A) - (III), (B) - (I), (C) - (IV)
(b) (A) - (IV), (B) - (II), (C) - (I)
(c) (A) - (III), (B) - (IV), (C) - (II)
(d) (A) - (III), (B) - (I), (C) - (II)

22. How many distinct alkenes are obtained from 3-bromo-3-methylhexane upon treatment with alc. KOH? **[May 19, 2023 (I)]**

(a) 2 (b) 3 (c) 4 (d) 5

23. Below shown molecules are **[May 19, 2023 (I)]**

X

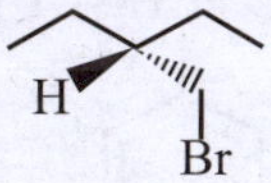

Y

(a) X = Y = Achiral (b) X = Y = Chiral
(c) X = Chiral, Y = Achiral (d) X = Achiral, Y = Chiral

24. How many asymmetric carbons are present in the following molecule? **[May 18, 2023 (II)]**

$HOH_2CCH(Br)CH(Br)CH_2OH$

(a) 3 (b) 1 (c) 4 (d) 2

25. Identify the correct products, when ethanol reacts with PCl_5 **[May 18, 2023 (II)]**

(a) Chloroethane, Hydrochloric acid and Phosphorus acid
(b) Chloroethane, Hydrochloric acid and Phosphoric acid
(c) Chloroethane, Sulfuric acid and Phosphorous oxy chloride
(d) Chloroethane, Hydrochloric acid and Phosphorous oxy chloride

26. Arrange the following in correct order towards S_N2 reaction. **[May 18, 2023 (I)]**

1 – Chloropropane (I) 2 – Chloropropane (II)
1 – Iodopropane (III) 2 – Iodopropane (IV)

(a) III > I > IV > II (b) III > IV > I > II
(c) I > II > III > IV (d) I > III > II > IV

27. Which of the following is an ambident nucleophile? **[May 18, 2023 (I)]**

(a) Ammonia (b) Chloride ion
(c) Water (d) Cyanide ion

28. Identify X and Y in the following reaction

$CH_2 = CH_2 \xrightarrow[\text{(ii)Y}]{\text{(i)X}} CH_3CH_2I$

[May 17, 2023 (II)]

(a) HBr, NaI/dry CH_3COCH_3
(b) HBr, I_2/dry CH_3COCH_3
(c) Br_2, NaI/dry CH_3COCH_3
(d) Br_2, I_2/dry CH_3COCH_3

29. Chlorocyclohexane is **[May 17, 2023 (II)]**

(a) Primary alkyl halide (b) Tertiary alkyl halide
(c) Allylic halide (d) Secondary alkyl halide

30. Which is the correct order of the following alkyl halides for an S_N2 reaction? **[May 17, 2023 (I)]**

(i) 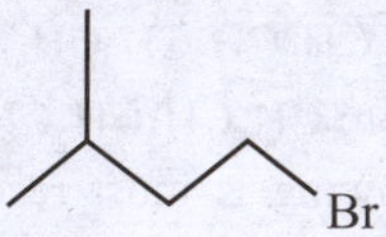

(ii) 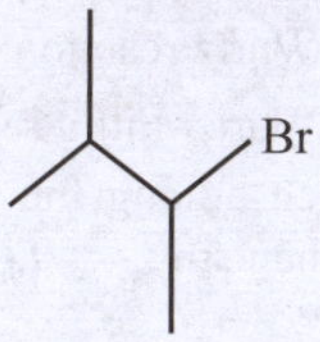

(iii) 

(a) (ii) > (i) > (iii) (b) (iii) > (i) > (ii)
(c) (iii) > (ii) > (i) (d) (ii) > (iii) > (i)

31. Arrange the following organic halides in the increasing order of their dehydrohalogenation reactions in the presence of alcoholic KOH **[May 16, 2023 (II)]**

CH_3CH_2Br (A) $CH_3CH_2CH_2Br$ (B)
$CH_3CH(Br)CH_3$ (C) $(CH_3)_3CBr$ (D)

(a) A < B < C < D (b) D < B < C < A
(c) A < C < B < D (d) B < A < C < D

32. Least reactive alkyl chloride in a S_N2 reaction is **[May 16, 2023 (II)]**

(a) 1–Chloro butane
(b) 1–Chloro 2–methyl propane
(c) 2–Chloro 2–methyl propane
(d) 2–Chloro butane

33. Which of the following alkyl halide is most reactive towards substitution by S_N1 mechanism? **[May 16, 2023 (II)]**

(a) $(CH_3)_3C–Br$ (b) $(CH_3)_3C–I$
(c) $(CH_3)_3C–F$ (d) $(CH_3)_3C–Cl$

34. Which of the following is the geminal dichloride? **[May 16, 2023 (I)]**
(a) 1, 1-Dichloropropane
(b) 1, 2-Dichloropropane
(c) 1, 3-Dichloropropane
(d) 2, 3-Dichloropropane

35. Which of the following is not correct about Grignard reagent? **[May 16, 2023 (I)]**
(a) It is a nucleophile
(b) Forms new carbon-carbon bond
(c) Reacts with carbonyl compounds
(d) It is an organomanganese compound

36. In S_N2 reaction, the carbon in the transition state is **[May 15, 2023 (II)]**
(a) Tri coordinated (b) Penta coordinated
(c) Tetra coordinated (d) Hexa coordinated

37. The optically inactive compound from the following is **[May 15, 2023 (I)]**
(a) 2–Bromopropanal
(b) 3–Bromopropanal
(c) 3–Bromo 2–iodopropanal
(d) 2–Bromo 3–iodopropanal

38. Which is correct option for the following reaction?
$$2\,CH_3CH_2Br \xrightarrow{2\,Na\,/\,Dry\,ether} ?$$
[May 15, 2023 (I)]
(a) Wurtz reaction; $CH_3CH_2CH_2CH_3$
(b) Wurtz–Fittig reaction; $CH_3CH_2CH_2CH_3$
(c) Wurtz reaction; $CH_3CH_2CH_2CH_2CH_3$
(d) Wurtz–Fittig reaction; $CH_3CH_2CH_2CH_2CH_3$

39. Which among the following is most reactive via S_N2 mechanism **[July 8, 2022 (I); Similar to April 20, 2019 (I), 2017]**

(a) 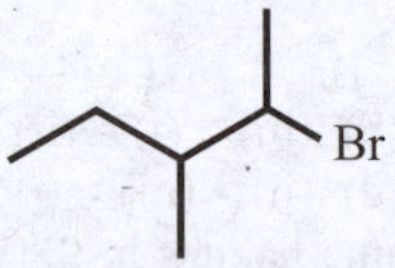
(b) 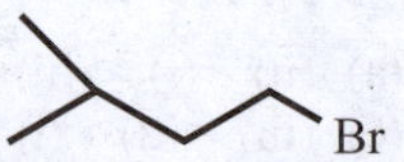
(c) 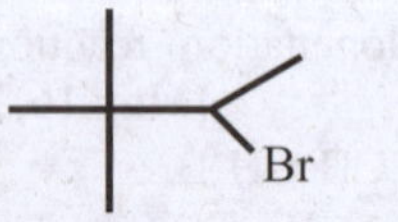
(d) 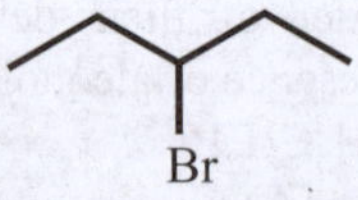

40. The rate of reaction of t-butyl bromide and NaOH in water depends on the concentration of **[July 7, 2022 (II)]**
(a) Both t-butyl bromide & NaOH
(b) NaOH
(c) Independent of concentration
(d) t-Butyl bromide

41. The reaction of 1-bromohexane with aqueous NaOH solution follows the order **[July 6, 2022 (I)]**
(a) zero order kinetics (b) first order kinetics
(c) second order kinetics (d) third order kinetics

42. The rate S_N1 reaction will be faster for which of the following bromides? **[July 5, 2022 (II)]**

(a) 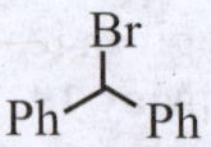
(b) 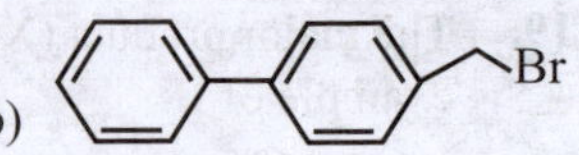
(c) 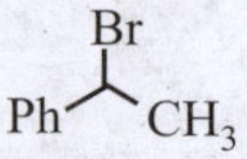
(d) 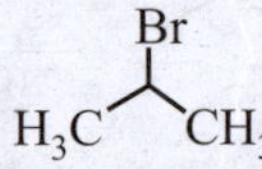

43. **Assertion (A) :** I- Bromopentane reacts with AgCN to give pentylisocyanide **[July 5, 2022 (II)]**
Reason (R) : AgCN is mainly ionic in nature
(a) A is true, R is true and R is correct explanation of A
(b) A is true, R is true but R is not correct explanation of A
(c) A is true, R is false
(d) A is false, R is true

44. Finkelstein reaction is used for the synthesis of **[July 4, 2022 (II)]**
(a) RF (b) RI (c) RCl (d) RBr

45. Which among the following will have highest density? **[July 4, 2022 (II)]**
(a) CCl_4 (b) $n\text{-}C_3H_7I$
(c) $n\text{-}C_3H_7Br$ (d) $n\text{-}C_3H_7Cl$

46. When 1-chloro butane is treated with aqueous KOH, it gives P. However, when it is treated with alcoholic KOH, it gives Q. Identify the products P and Q respectively **[July 4, 2022 (I)]**
(a) P = 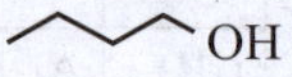 Q = 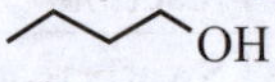
(b) P = 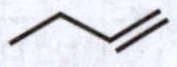 Q = 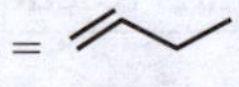
(c) P = 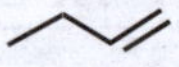 Q = 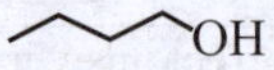
(d) P = 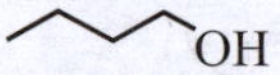 Q = 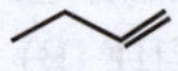

47. A compound *A* contains C and H only and has molecular mass 72. It's photochlorination gives a mixture containing only one monochloro and two dichloro hydrocarbons. The IUPAC name of *A* is **[Aug. 23, 2021 (I)]**
(a) 2, 2-dimethylpropane (b) *n*-pentane
(c) 2-methyl butane (d) cyclopentane

48. Identify the product of the following reaction. **[Aug. 20, 2021 (I)]**

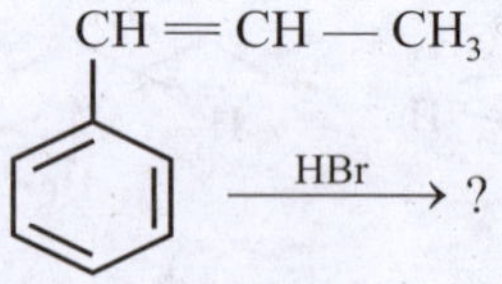

(a) $C_6H_5-CH_2-\underset{\underset{Br}{|}}{CH}-CH_3$
(b) $C_6H_5-\underset{\underset{Br}{|}}{CH}-CH_2-CH_3$
(c) $C_6H_5-CH_2-CH_2-CH_2-Br$
(d) $\underset{\underset{Br}{|}}{C_6H_4}-CH_2-CH_2-CH_3$

49. The number of optical isomers possible for 2-bromo-3-chlorobutane are **[Aug. 19, 2021 (I)]**
(a) 8 (b) 10 (c) 4 (d) 2

50. 1-Chlorobutane on treatment with alcoholic potash forms .... **[Sept. 21, 2020 (I)]**

(a) 2-butanol (b) 1-butene
(c) 1-butanol (d) 2-butene

51. What is the product of the reaction given below? **[Sept. 21, 2020 (I)]**

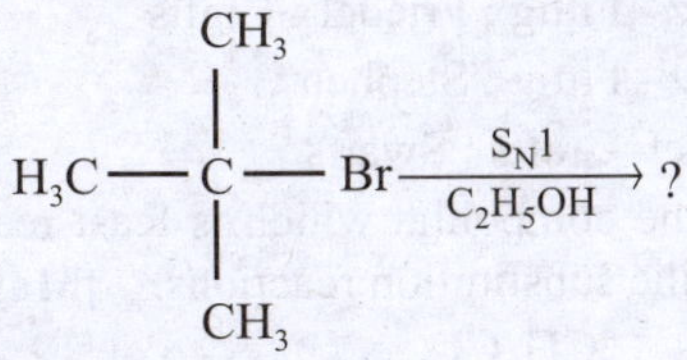

(a) $CH_3—CH_2—CH_2—OC_2H_5$

(b) 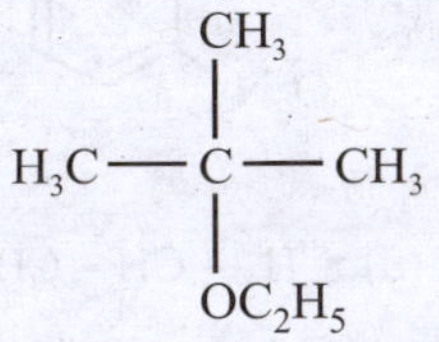

(c) 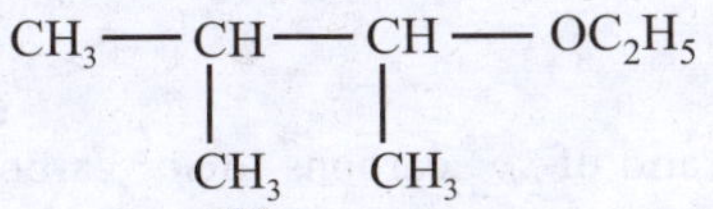

(d) 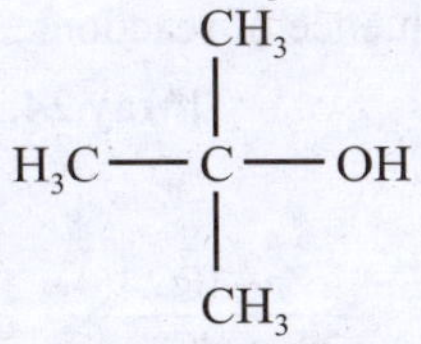

52. The products in the reaction given below are .... '•' denotes a free radical. **[Sept. 17, 2020 (I)]**

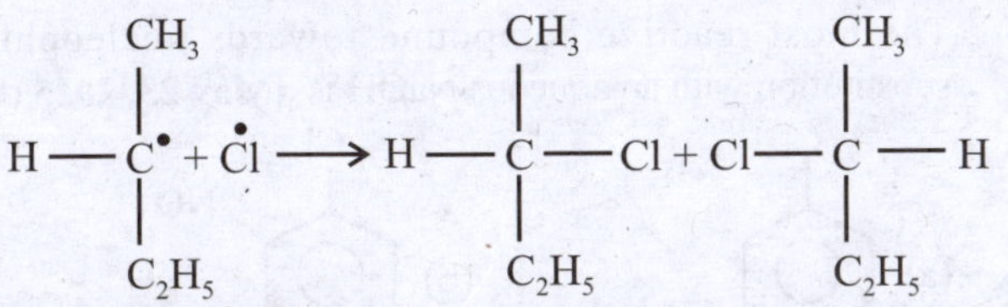

(a) Meso forms (b) Racemic mixture
(c) *d*- and *l*-forms (d) *Cis-trans* isomers

53. Which among the following is most common in alkyl halides? **[Sept. 17, 2020 (I)]**

(a) Nucleophilic substitution
(b) Electrophilic substitution
(c) Electrophilic addition
(d) Nucleophilic addition

54. **Assertion (A) :** S_N1 hydrolysis of optically active 2-bromooctane results in the formation of (±) - octane -2-ol.
Reason (R) : The reaction proceeds through a planar carbocation which can be attacked by the nucleophile from either side.
The correct answer is **[Apr. 22, 2019 (I)]**

(a) (A) and (R) are correct, (R) is the correct explanation of (A)
(b) (A) and (R) are correct but (R) is not the correct explanation of (A)
(c) (A) is correct but (R) is not correct
(d) (A) is not correct but (R) is correct

55. What are X and Y in the following reaction sequence?

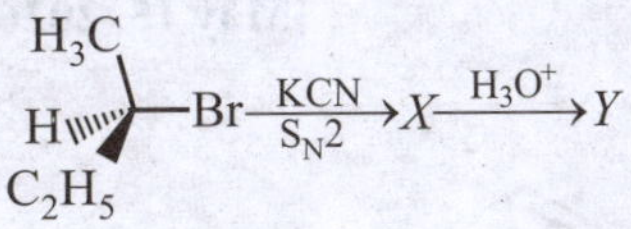

[Apr. 21, 2019 (I)]

	X	*Y*
(a)	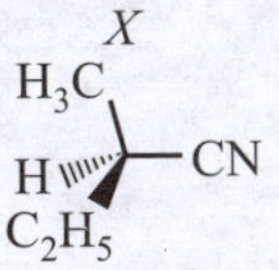	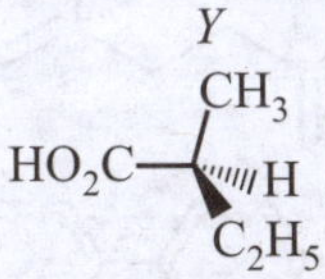
(b)	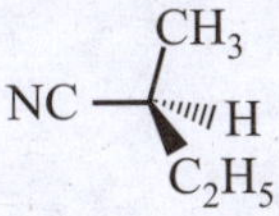	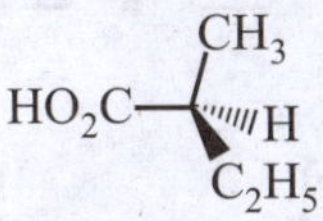
(c)	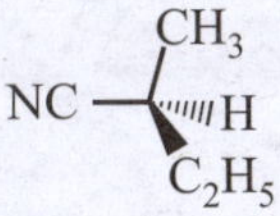	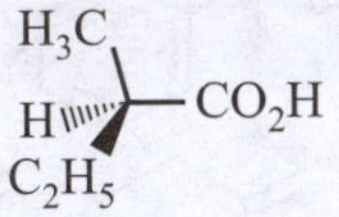
(d)	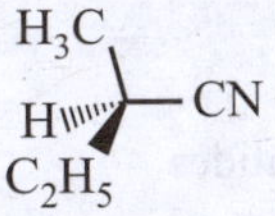	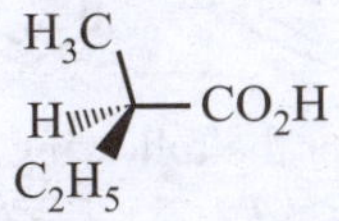

56. Identify the statement which is not correct? **[2017]**

(a) Dehydrobromination of 2-bromopentane gives pent-1-ene as the major product.
(b) Freon 12 is manufactured by Swarts reaction.
(c) $CHCl_3$ is stored in closed, dark coloured bottles.
(d) Chronic exposure to $CHCl_3$ causes liver damage.

57. What is *Z* in the following sequence of reaction?

2-Methyl-2-bromopropane $\xrightarrow[\text{Dry ether}]{\text{Mg}} X \xrightarrow{H_2O} Z$

[2016]

(a) Propane (b) 2-methyl propene
(c) 2-methyl propane (d) 2-methyl butane

Topic 2 Preparation and Properties of Haloarenes

58. Among the following, identify the compound which will form resonance stabilized carbocations after the leaving group is lost **[May 18, 2026 (I)]**

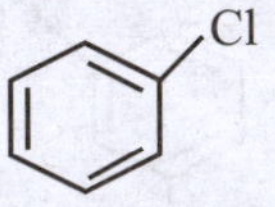
I

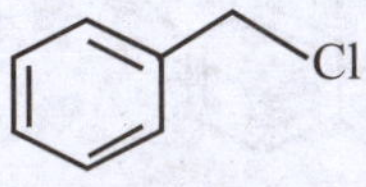
II

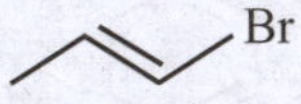
III

IV

The correct answer is

(a) I & II only (b) I & III only
(c) II & III only (d) II & IV only

59. What is Y in the following reaction sequence? (X = major product) **[May 15, 2026 (II)]**

$$C_7H_8 \xrightarrow[\text{dark}]{Br_2/Fe} X \xrightarrow[\text{dry ether}]{2Na} Y$$

(a) 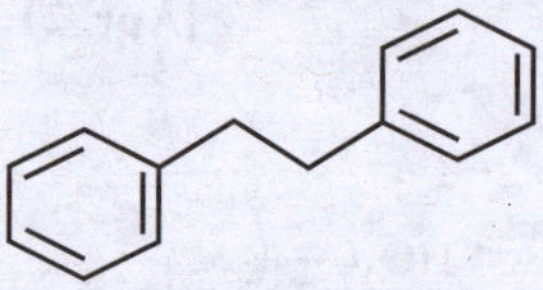

(b) 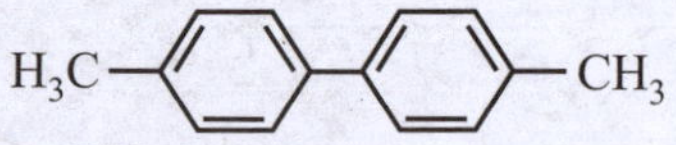

(c) 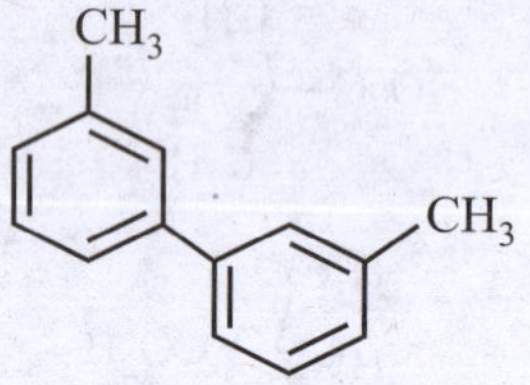

(d) 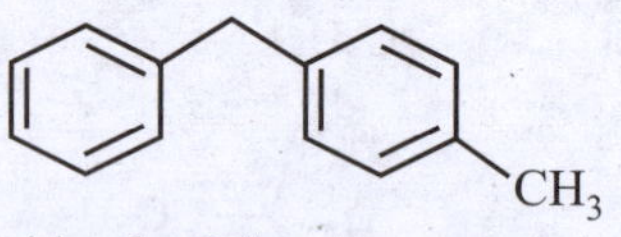

60. Consider the following organic halides

(I) 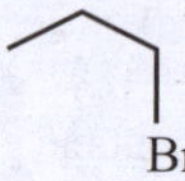 (II) 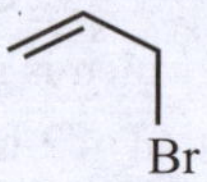 (III) 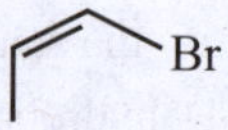

The correct order of reactivity towards S_N2 reaction is **[May 15, 2026 (I)]**

(a) I > II > III (b) III > II > I
(c) II > I > III (d) III > I > II

61. Chlorobenzene (A) on nitration gave B as major product. Reaction of B with NaOH at 443 K followed by acidification formed C. In another reaction of A with CH_3COCl/anhy. $AlCl_3$ gave D (major product). What are C and D respectively? **[May 12, 2026 (II)]**

(a) 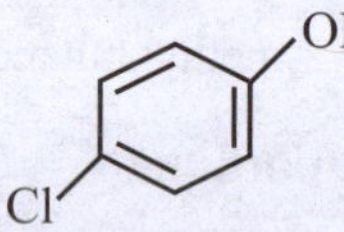 ; 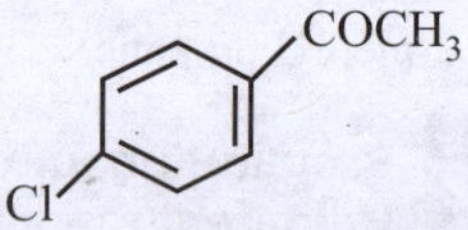

(b) 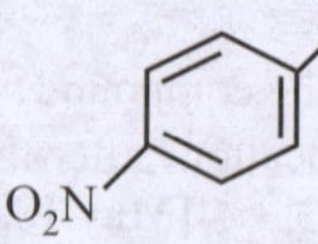 ; 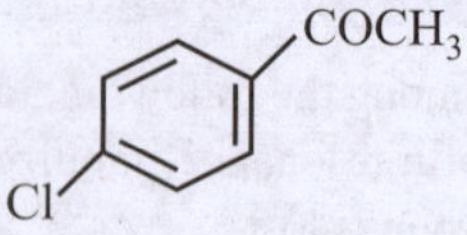

(c) 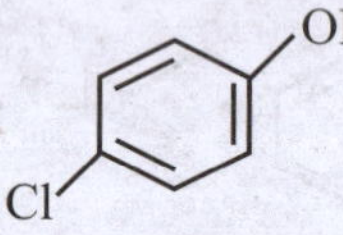 ; 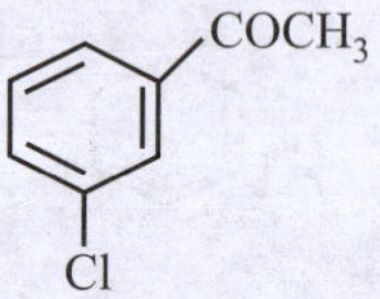

(d) 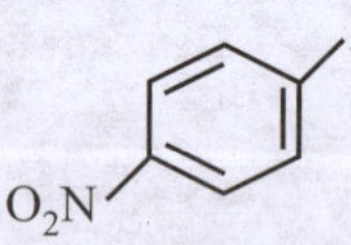 ; 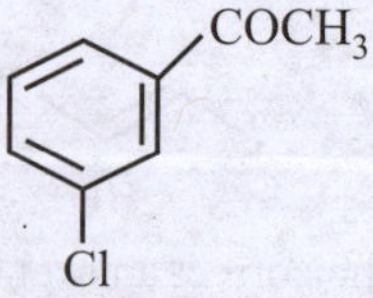

62. Identify the two reactions A(I→II) and B (I→III) respectively in the following set of reactions. **[May 27, 2025 (I)]**

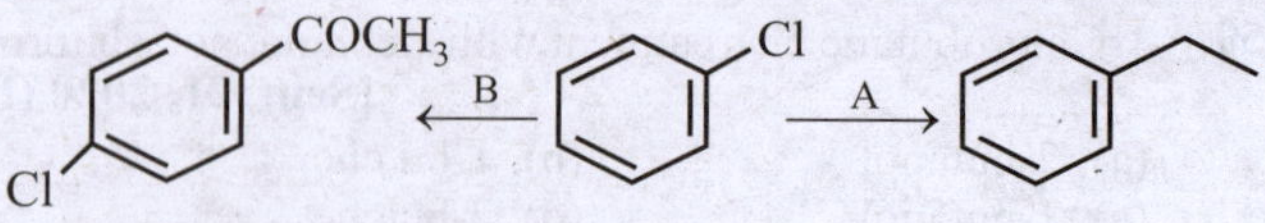

III I II

(a) Fittig ; Friedel - Crafts
(b) Wurtz - Fittig ; Friedel - Crafts
(c) Wurtz - Fittig ; Stephen
(d) Friedel- Crafts ; Swarts

63. Identify the compound which is least reactive towards nucleophilic substitution reactions. **[May 26, 2025 (I)]**

(a) 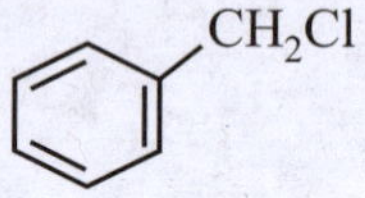 (b) 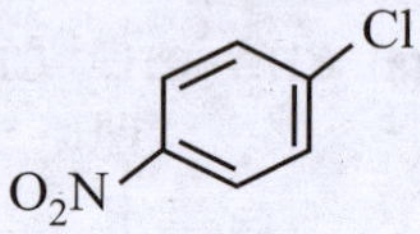

(c) 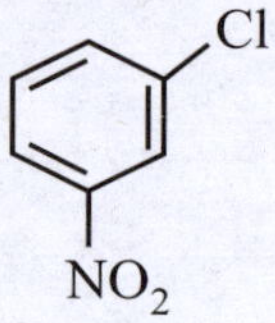 (d) $CH_2 = CH - CH_2Cl$

64. What is the ratio of sp^3 carbons to sp^2 carbons in the product 'P' of the given sequence of reactions ? **[May 24, 2025 (I)]**

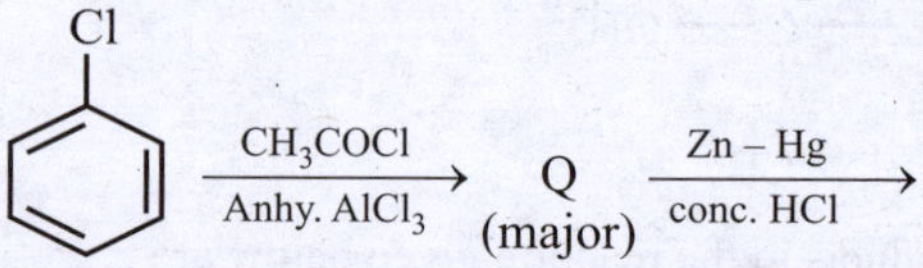

(a) 3 : 1 (b) 2 : 1 (c) 1 : 2 (d) 1 : 3

65. The most reactive compound towards nucleophilic substitution with an aqueous NaOH is **[May 23, 2025 (II)]**

(a) 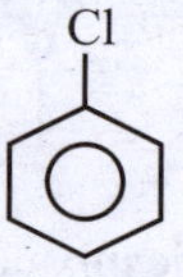 (b) 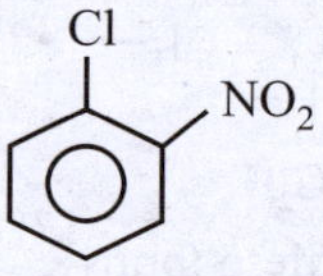

(c) 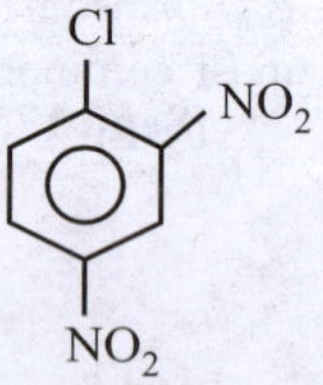 (d) 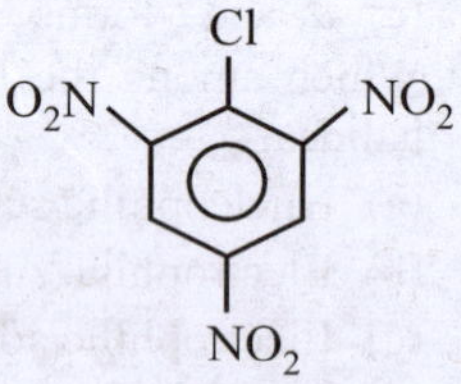

66. Which of the following is the product of Fittig reaction? **[May 22, 2025 (I)]**

(a) 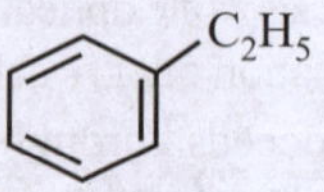

(b) 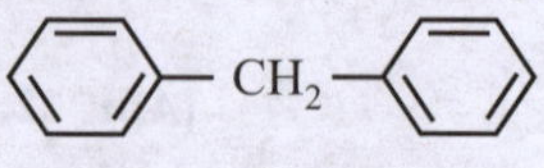

(c) 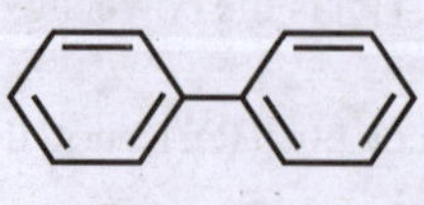

(d) 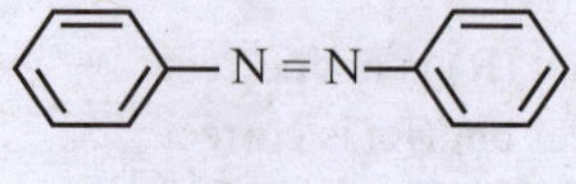

67. What are X and Y respectively, in the following set of reactions? **[May 21, 2025 (II)]**

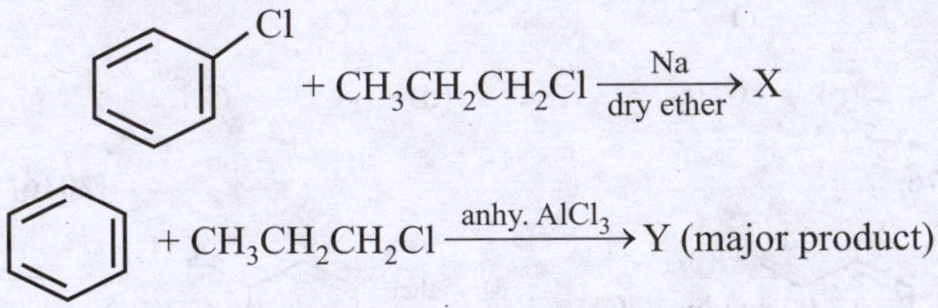

(a) 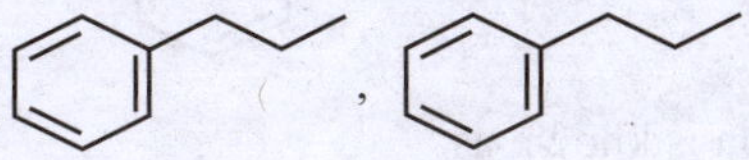

(b) 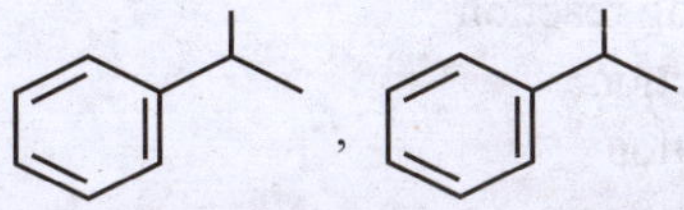

(c) 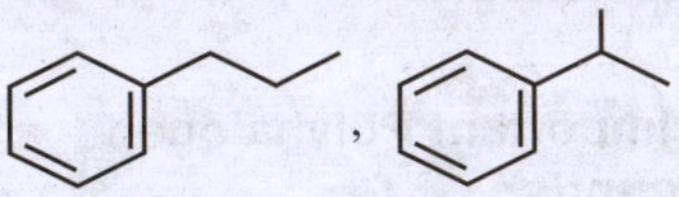

(d) 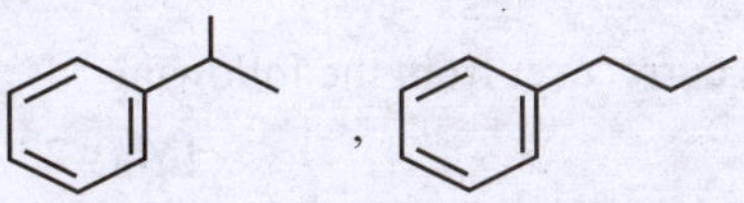

68. Observe the following reactions. **[May 21, 2025 (I)]**

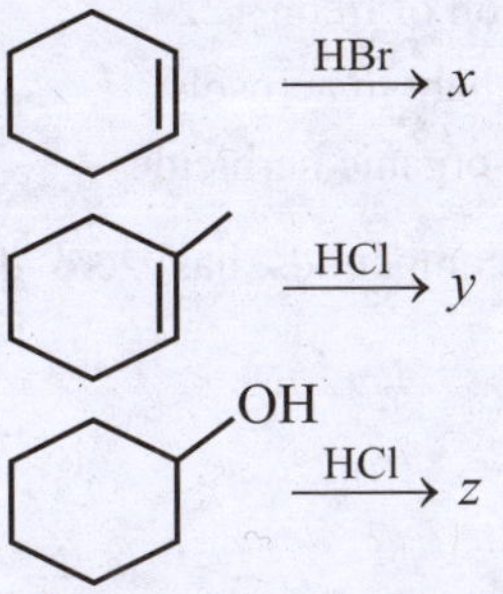

The order of reactivity of *x, y, z* towards S_N1 reaction is

(a) $x > z > y$ (b) $x > y > z$

(c) $y > x > z$ (d) $y > z > x$

69. What are X and Y respectively in the following reactions?

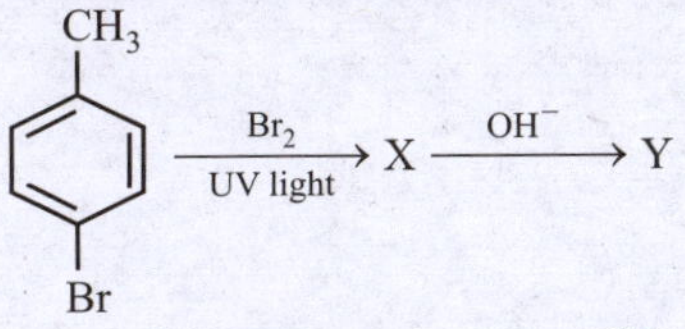

[May 23, 2024 (I)]

(a) 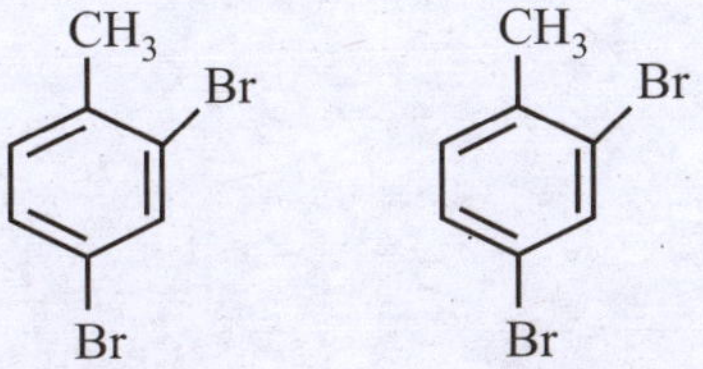

(b) 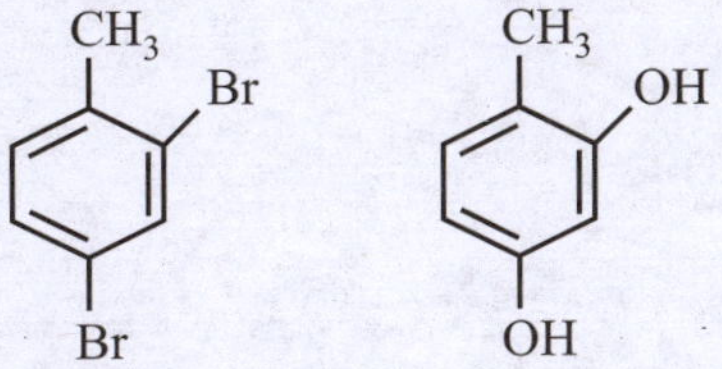

(c) 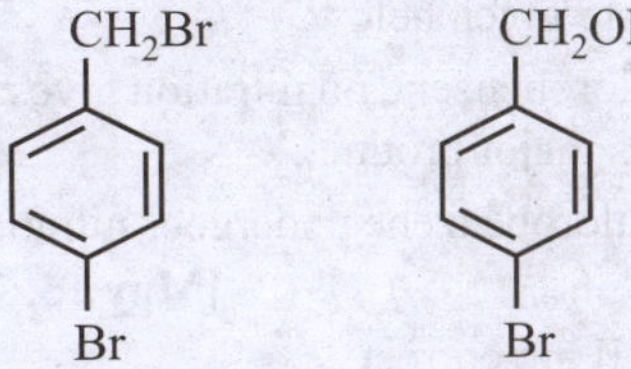

(d) 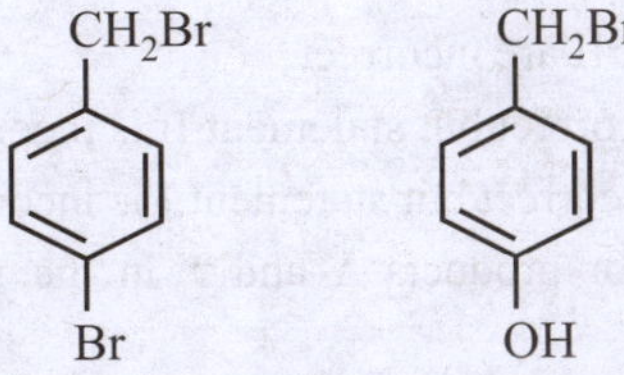

70. 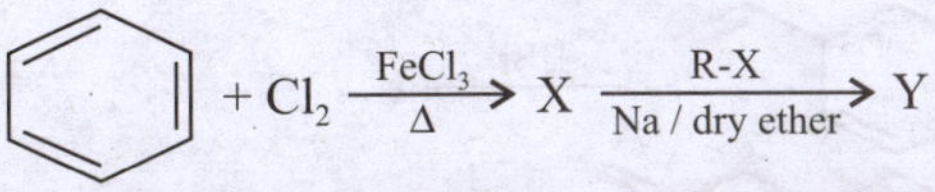

Conversion of X to Y is an example of **[May 22, 2024 (II)]**

(a) Wurtz reaction (b) Fittig reaction

(c) Wurtz-Fittig reaction (d) Friedel-Crafts reaction

71. The product (C) in the following reaction sequence is **[May 22, 2024 (I)]**

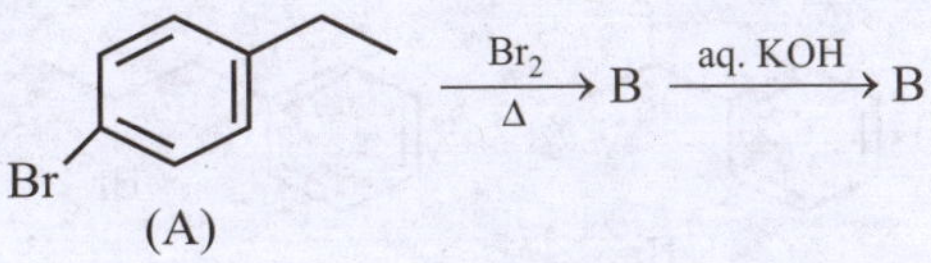

(a) 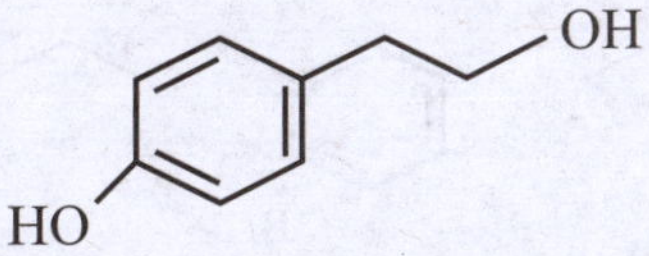

(b) 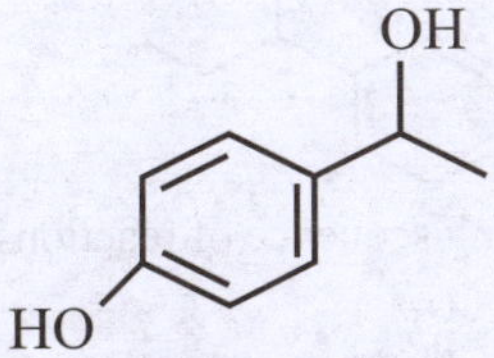

(c) 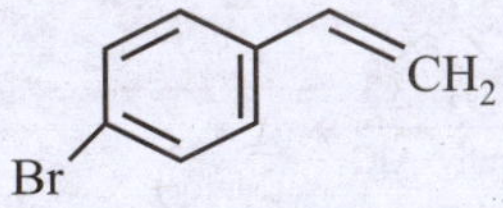

(d) 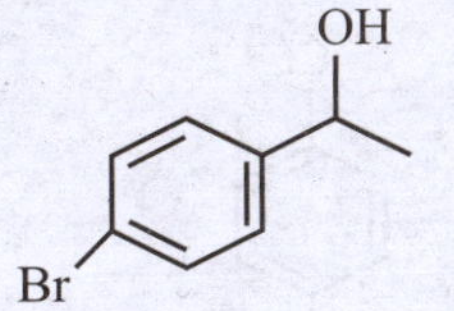

72. Fittig reaction is **[May 18, 2023 (II)]**

(a) Reaction between two aryl halides in the presence of Na/dry ether

(b) Reaction between two alkyl halides in the presence of Na/dry ether

(c) Reaction between aryl halide and alkyl halide in the presence of Na/dry ether

(d) Reaction between two aryl halides in the presence of Fe/dry ether

73. Two statements are given below.

Statement I: Chlorobenzene on nitration gives 1-chloro-4-nitrobenzene as major product.

Statement II: Chlorobenzene undergoes nitration slowly than benzene. **[May 15, 2023 (II)]**

(a) Statement I, II are correct
(b) Statements I, II are incorrect
(c) Statement I correct but statement II is incorrect
(d) Statement II correct but statement I is incorrect

74. Identify the major products *X* and *Y* in the following reactions **[2018]**

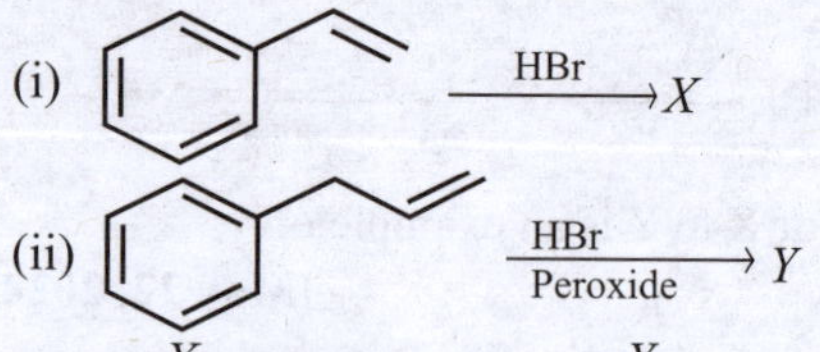

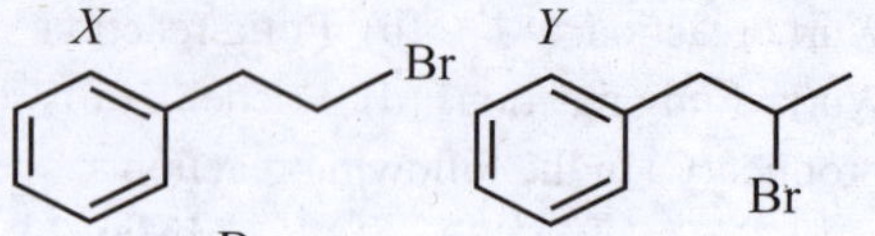

(a)

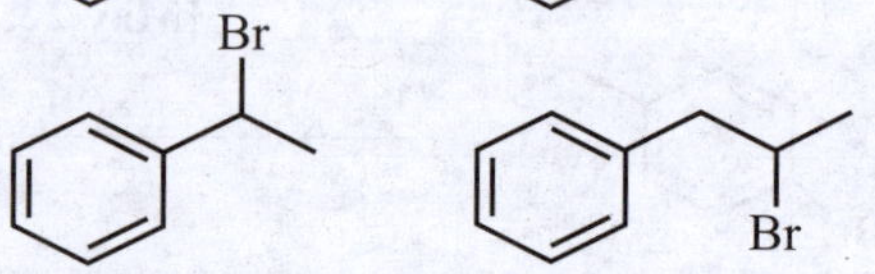

(b)

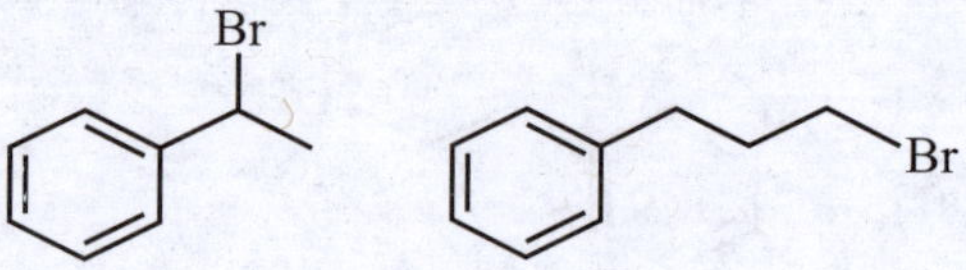

(c)

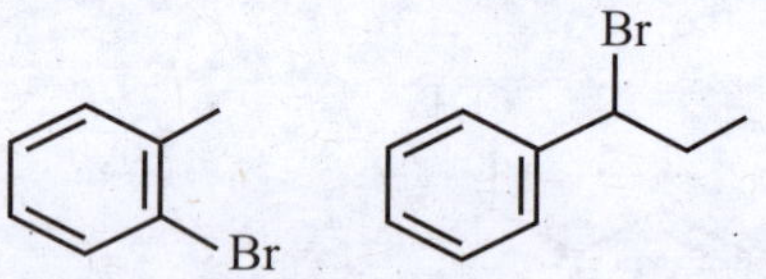

(d)

75. What is $\underline{Z}$ in the following sequence of reactions? **[2017]**

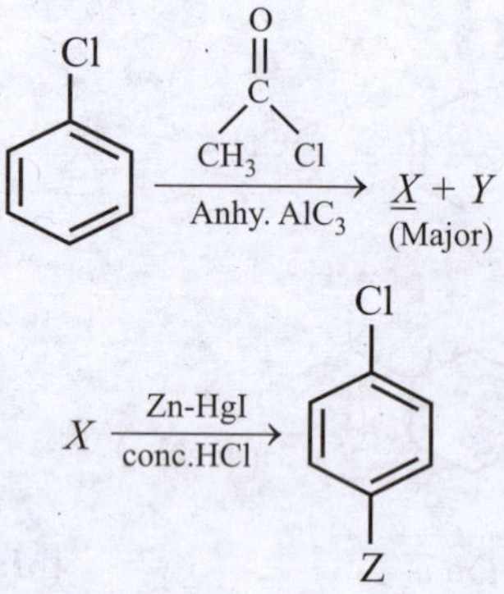

(a) $-\underset{\substack{\parallel \\ O}}{C}-CH_3$ (b) $-\underset{\substack{\parallel \\ O}}{C}-Cl$

(c) $-CH_3$ (d) $-CH_2-CH_3$

76. **[2016]**

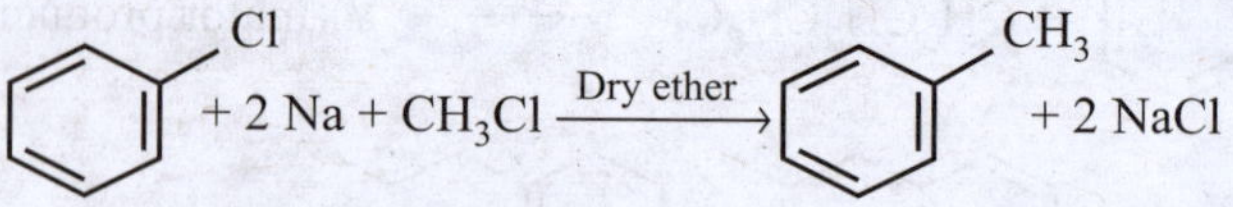

This reaction is known as

(a) Wurtz-Fittig reaction
(b) Wurtz reaction
(c) Fittig reaction
(d) Friedel-Crafts reaction

Topic 3 Some Important Polyhalogen Compounds

77. Identify the correct set from the following **[May 23, 2025 (I)]**

(a) $CHCl_3$ - used in production of freon - 12
(b) CCl_4 - used in production of freon - 22
(c) CH_2Cl_2 - used as propellant in aerosols
(d) DDT - first chlorinated organic herbicide

78. Which of the following compounds has zero dipole moment? **[2015]**

(a) 1, 4-dichlorobenzene
(b) 1, 2-dichlorobenzene
(c) 1, 3-dichlorobenzene
(d) 1-chloro-2-methyl benzene

7 Alcohols, Phenols and Ethers

CHAPTER SYNOPSIS

- Alcohols may be prepared:-

  (1) by hydration of alkenes (i) in presence of an acid, (ii) by hydroboration-oxidation reaction of alkenes and (iii) by oxymercuration-demercuration of alkenes.

  (2) from carbonyl compounds by (i) catalytic reduction and (ii) the action of Grignard reagents.

- Phenols may be prepared by (1) substitution of (i) halogen atom in haloarenes and (ii) sulphonic acid group in aryl sulphonic acids, by –OH group (2) by hydrolysis of diazonium salts and (3) industrially from cumene.

- Alcohols are higher boiling liquids than other classes of compounds, namely hydrocarbons, ethers and haloalkanes of comparable molecular masses. The ability of alcohols and phenols to form intermolecular hydrogen bonding with water makes them soluble in it.

- Alcohols and phenols are acidic in nature. Electron withdrawing groups in phenol increase its acidic strength and electron releasing groups decrease it.

- Alcohols undergo nucleophilic substitution with hydrogen halides to yield alkyl halides. Dehydration of alcohols gives alkenes. On oxidation, primary alcohols yield aldehydes with mild oxidising agents and carboxylic acids with strong oxidising agents, while secondary alcohols yield ketones. Tertiary alcohols are resistant to oxidation.

- The presence of –OH group in phenols activates the aromatic ring towards electrophilic substitution and directs the incoming group to ortho and para positions due to resonance effect.

- Reimer-Tiemann reaction of phenol yields salicylaldehyde with $CHCl_3$ / OH^- and salicylic acid with CCl_4 / OH^-.

- In presence of sodium hydroxide, phenol generates phenoxide ion which is even more reactive than phenol. Thus, in alkaline medium, phenol undergoes Kolbe's reaction.

- Ethers may be prepared by (i) dehydration of alcohols and (ii) Williamson synthesis.

- The boiling points of ethers resemble those of alkanes while their solubility is comparable to those of alcohols having same molecular mass.

- The C–O bond in ethers can be cleaved by hydrogen halides.

- In electrophilic substitution, the alkoxy group activates the aromatic ring and directs the incoming group to ortho and para positions.

Topic 1 Preparation and Properties of Alcohols

1. When vapours of an alcohol X are passed over heated copper at 573 K, gives an alkene. What is X? **[May 18, 2026 (I)]**

(a) $CH_3CH_2CH_2CH_2OH$ (b) $(CH_3)_2CH-CH_2OH$
(c) $(CH_3)_3C-OH$ (d) $CH_3CH(OH)CH_2CH_3$

2. Match the following **[May 15, 2026 (II)]**

List I (Compound)	List II (Common name)
A. C_6H_5OH	I. Quinol
B. 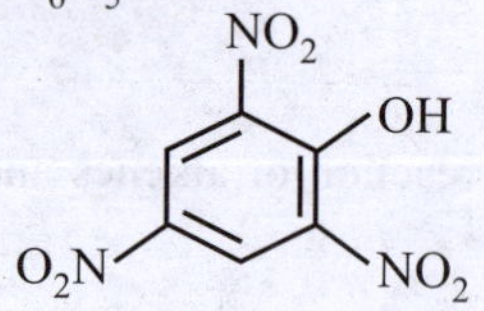	II. Carbolic acid
C. 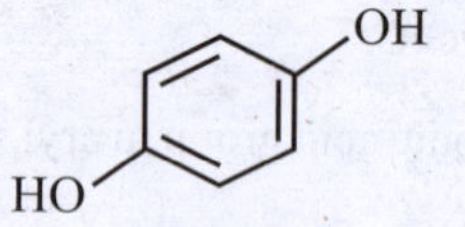	III. p-Cresol
D. 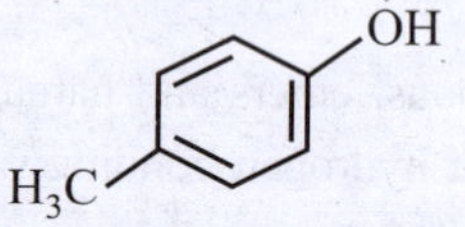	IV. Picric acid

Correct answer is

(a) A-IV, B-II, C-I, D-III (b) A-II, B-IV, C-I, D-III
(c) A-II, B-IV, C-III, D-I (d) A-IV, B-I, C-III, D-II

3. The ratio between number of σ-electrons and number of π-electrons in the final product Z is **[May 14, 2026 (I)]**

$$\underset{CH_2OH}{\overset{CHO}{(CHOH)_4}} \xrightarrow[\Delta]{HI} X \xrightarrow[\substack{773K\\10-20\ atm}]{V_2O_5} Y \xrightarrow[\substack{Anhy\ AlCl_3\\(ii)\ KMnO_4/OH^-\\(iii)\ H_3O^+}]{(i)\ CH_3COCl} Z$$

(Anhy –)

(a) 15 :4 (b) 13 : 5
(c) 12 : 5 (d) 11 : 4

4. Observe the following reactions **[May 12, 2026 (II)]**

I. 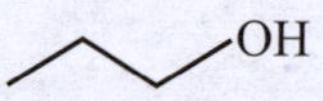 $\xrightarrow[95\%\ H_3PO_4]{KI}$

II. 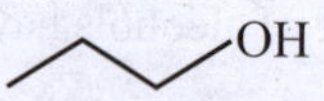 $\xrightarrow[273\ K]{HCl}$

III.  $\xrightarrow[dry\ CH_3COCH_3]{NaI}$

Feasible reactions are

(a) I, II only (b) I only
(c) I, III only (d) I, II, III

5. Isobutyl alcohol can be prepared from which of the following reactions? **[May 12, 2026 (I)]**

I. 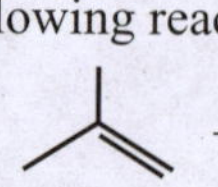 $\xrightarrow[(ii)\ OH^-]{(i)\ HBr/(C_6H_5CO)_2O_2}$

II. 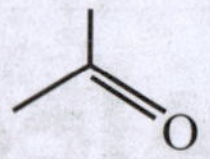 $\xrightarrow[(ii)\ H_2O]{(i)\ MeMgBr}$

III. 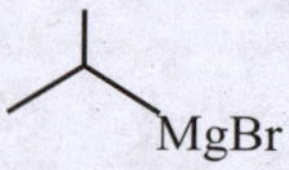 $\xrightarrow[(ii)\ H_2O]{(i)\ HCHO}$

Correct answer is

(a) I, II only (b) II, III only
(c) I, III only (d) I, II, III

6. An alcohol, X ($C_5H_{12}O$) in the presence of Cu/573K gives Y (C_5H_{10}). The reactants required for the preparation of X are **[May 27, 2025 (I)]**

(a) 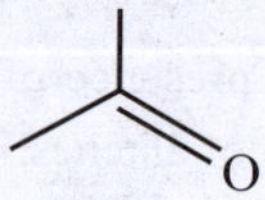 , C_2H_5MgBr

(b) HCHO, $(CH_3)_3$ CMgBr

(c) 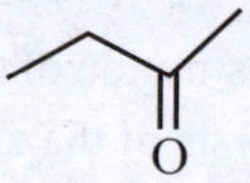 , C_2H_5MgBr

(d) 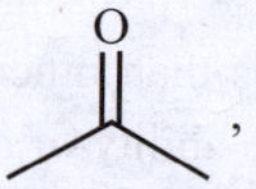 , $(CH_3)_2CHMgBr$

7. Which of the following will undergo methylation with CH_3Cl / anhy. $AlCl_3$? **[May 26, 2025 (II)]**

(a) Aniline (b) Chlorobenzene
(c) Benzoic acid (d) Anisole

8. An alcohol $X(C_5H_{12}O)$ on dehydration gives Y (major product). Reaction of Y with HBr gave $Z(C_5H_{11}Br)$, major product). Z undergoes nucleophilic substitution in two steps. What are X and Y ? **[May 26, 2025 (I)]**

(a) 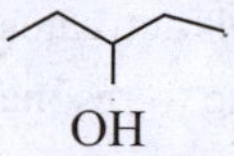 , 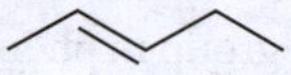

(b)  , 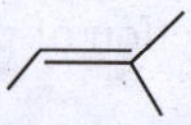

(c) 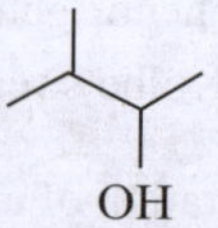 , 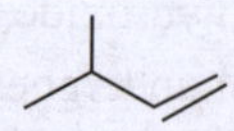

(d) 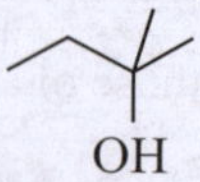 , 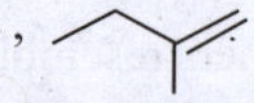

9. The preferred reagent for the preparation of pure alkyl chloride from alcohol is **[May 22, 2025 (II)]**

(a) $HCl + ZnCl_2$ (b) PCl_5
(c) $SOCl_2$ (d) PCl_3

10. Compound 'X' is prepared commercially by the electrolysis of brine solution. Which of the following is not the use of 'X'? **[May 22, 2025 (II)]**

(a) Manufacture of paper (b) Petroleum refining
(c) Antichlor (d) Mercirising cotton fabrics

11. A Grignard reagent (X) on reaction with carbonyl compound (Y) followed by hydrolysis gave Z. Z reacts with conc. HC1 at room temperature. X and Y respectively are **[May 23, 2024 (I)]**

(a) CH_3MgBr, CH_3CH_2CHO
(b) CH_3MgBr, CH_3COCH_3
(c) $CH_3CH_2CH_2MgBr$, HCHO
(d) CH_3CH_2MgBr, CH_3CHO

12. An alcohol X ($C_4H_{10}O$) does not give turbidity with conc. HCl and $ZnCl_2$ at room temperature. X on reaction with reagent Y gives Z. What are X, Y and Z respectively? **[May 21, 2024 (II)]**

(a) 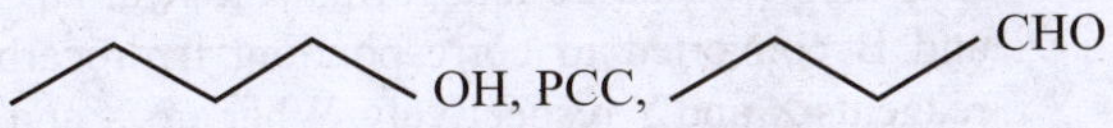

(b) 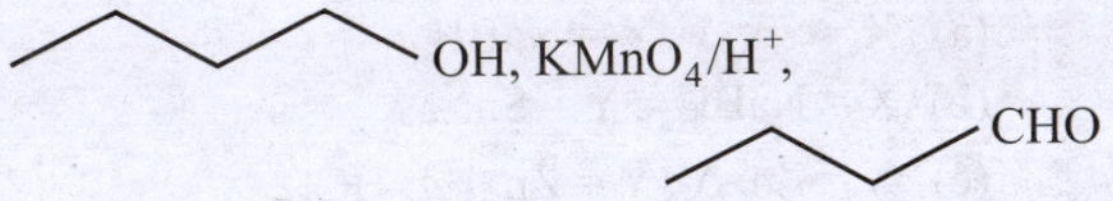

(c) 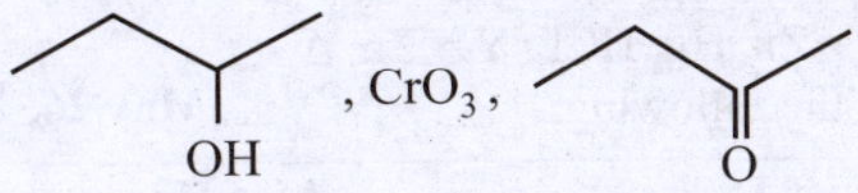

(d) 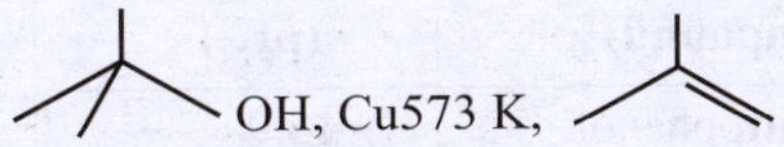

13. The product of which of the following reactions undergo hydrolysis by S_N1 mechanism? **[May 20, 2024 (II)]**

A. 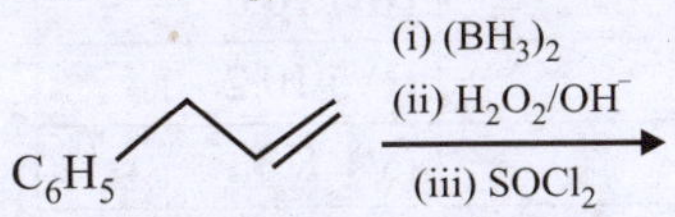

B. 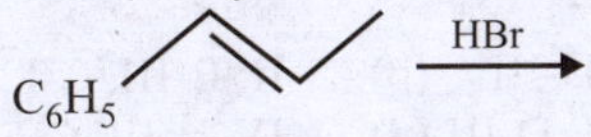

C. 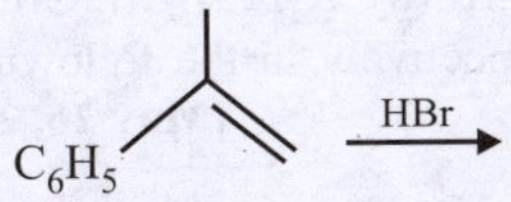

D. 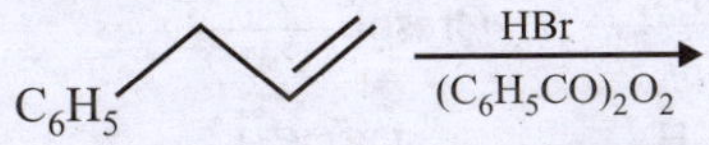

(a) C, D only (b) A, B, C only
(c) B, C only (d) A, D only

14. Which of the following sequence of reagents convert propene to 1-chloropropane? **[May 20, 2024 (II)]**

(a) (i) $(BH_3)_2$ (ii) H_2O_2 / OH^-; HCl, $ZnCl_2$
(b) (i) $(BH_3)_2$ (ii) H_2O_2 / OH^-; NaCl
(c) dil. H_2SO_4; HCl, $ZnCl_2$
(d) dil. H_2SO_4 ; Conc. HCl

15. An alcohol X ($C_4H_{10}O$) reacts with conc. HCl at room temperature to give Y (C_4H_9C1). Reaction of X with copper at 573 K gave Z. What is Z? **[May 19, 2024 (II)]**

(a) 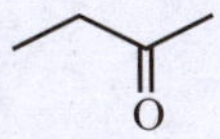

(b) 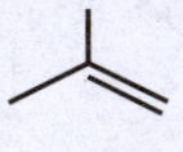
(c) 

(d) 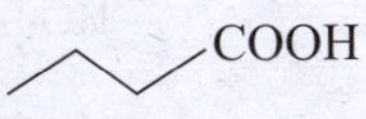

16. Which of the following belongs to benzylic alcohol type? **[May 18, 2023 (I)]**

(a) 1 – Phenyl – 2 – propanol
(b) 1 – Pheny – 1 – propanol
(c) 4 – Phenyl – but – 3 – ene – 2 – ol
(d) 2 – Methyl – but – 3 – ene – 2 – ol

17. Among the following the appropriate reactants for the preparation of 1 – ethyl cyclohexanol are **[May 18, 2023 (I)]**

(a) 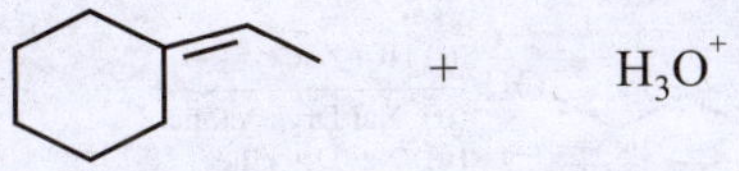

(b) 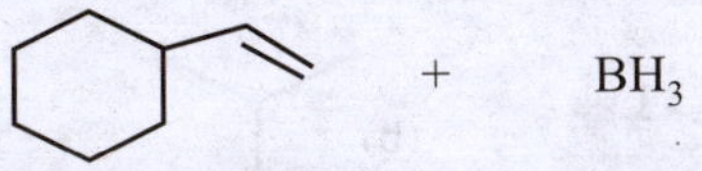

(c) 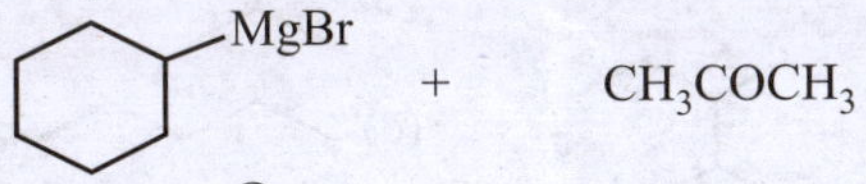

(d) 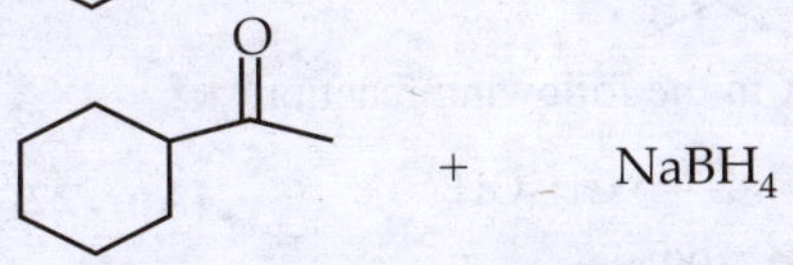

18. Which of the following reactions takes place when tertiary butanol is passed over heated copper at 573 K? **[July 7, 2022 (II)]**

(a) Dehydrogenation reaction
(b) Dehydration reaction
(c) Oxidation reaction
(d) Addition reaction

19. Identify the major product from the following reaction sequence **[July 5, 2022 (II)]**

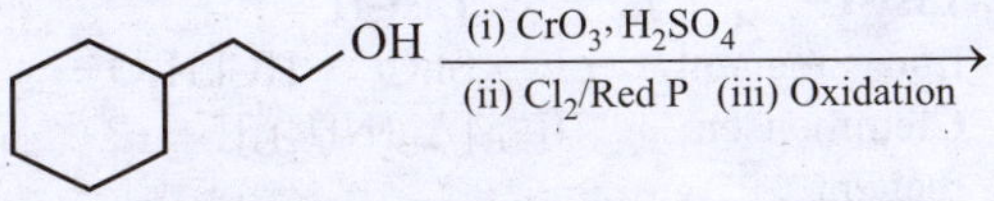

(a) 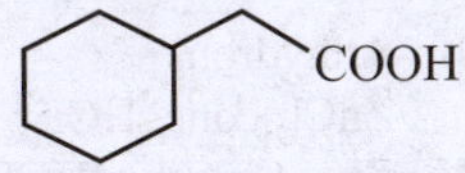

(b) 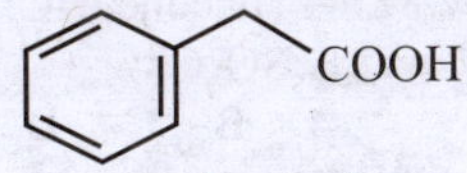

(c) 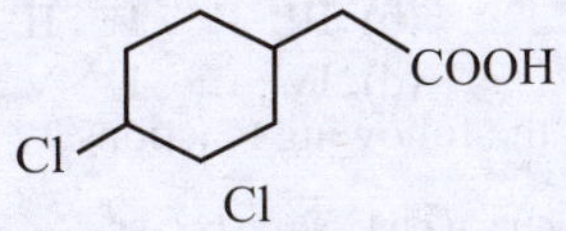

(d) 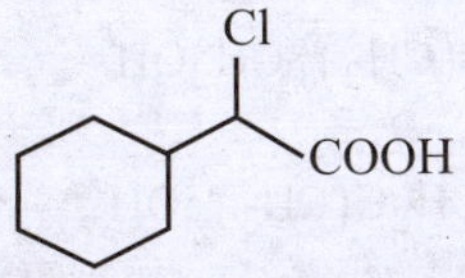

20. Identify the major product (Y) from the following reaction **[July 4, 2022 (II)]**

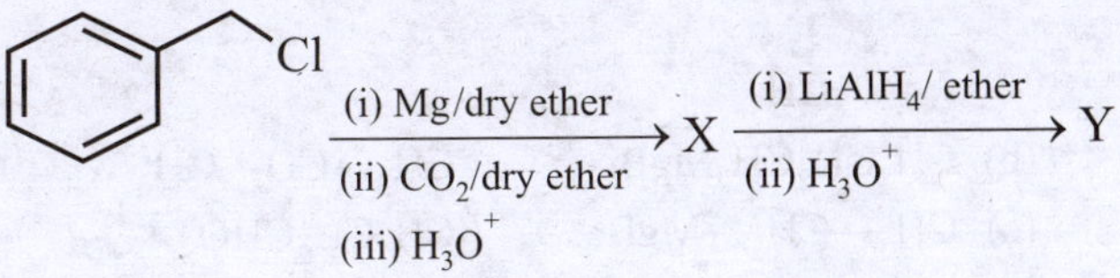

(a) 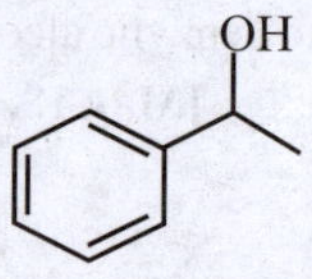

(b) 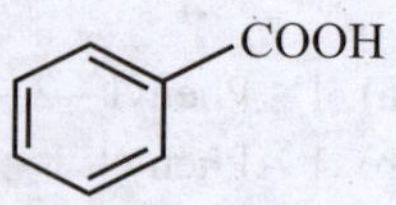

(c) 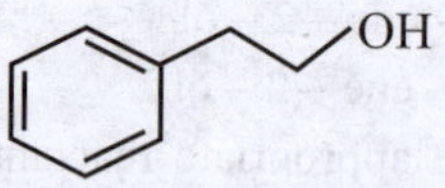

(d) 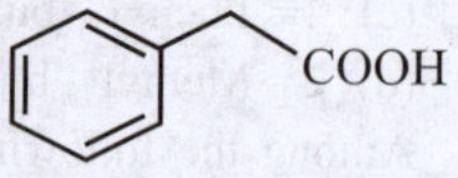

21. Identify the major product formed from the following **[July 4, 2022 (I)]**

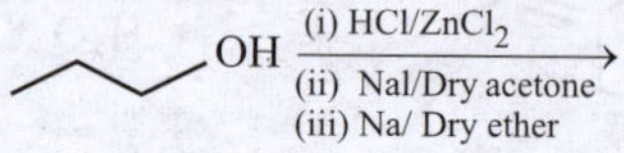

(a) 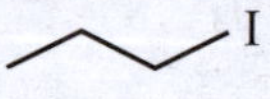

(b) 

(c) 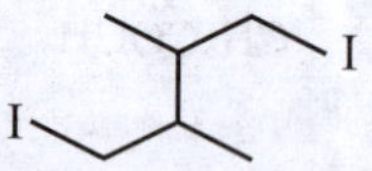

(d) 

22. What is *X* in the following reaction?

$CO + 2H_2 \xrightarrow{x} CH_3OH$ **[Apr. 22, 2019 (I)]**

(a) 623 K /300 atm
(b) $KMnO_4 / H^{\oplus}$
(c) Zn/Δ
(d) $ZnO–Cr_2O_3$, 200-300 atm, 573-673 K

23. The bond angle between C—O and O—H bonds in alcohols is close to **[Apr. 20, 2019 (I)]**

(a) 109° (b) 120° (c) 180° (d) 90°

24. Match the following **[2018]**

	List-I		List-II
A.	Lucas reagent	I.	$SnCl_2 + HCl.H_3O^+$
B.	Clemmensen reagent	II.	$[Ag(NH_3)_2]^+$
C.	Tollens' reagent	III.	Anhydrous $ZnCl_2$|conc. HCl
D.	Stephen reaction	IV.	Zn—Hg|conc. HCl
		V.	$C_6H_5SO_2Cl$

	A	B	C	D		A	B	C	D
(a)	III	IV	II	I	(b)	III	IV	I	II
(c)	IV	II	III	V	(d)	IV	III	I	V

25. What are *X* and *Y* in the following reactions? **[2017]**

$CH_2O \xrightarrow[(ii)\ H_3O^+]{(i)\ X} CH_3(CH_2)_2CH_2OH$

$Y \xrightarrow[(ii)\ H_3O^+]{(i)\ C_2H_5MgBr} CH_3CH_2C(CH_3)_2OH$

	X	*Y*
(a)	$CH_3—CH(CH_3)—MgBr$	$C_2H_5COCH_3$
(b)	$CH_3CH_2CH_2MgBr$	$CH_3—CO—CH_3$
(c)	$CH_3—CH_2—MgBr$	CH_3CH_2CHO
(d)	$(CH_3)_3CMgBr$	$CH_3—CO—CH_3$

26. $C_2H_5OH + 4I_2 + 3Na_2CO_3 \longrightarrow X + HCOONa + 5NaI + 3CO_2 + 2H_2O$

In the above reaction, '*X*' is **[2015]**

(a) diiodomethane (b) triiodomethane
(c) iodomethane (d) tetraiodomethane

Topic 2 Preparation and Properties of Phenols

27. Consider the following reaction **[May 13, 2026 (I)]**

$\text{Cumene} \xrightarrow[(ii)\ H_3O^+]{(i)\ O_2} A + B$

A is acidic in nature and forms salt with aq. NaOH. A and B converted to corresponding hydrocarbons with reagents X and Y respectively. What are X and Y?

(a) X = Sn, Δ ; Y = $NaBH_4$
(b) X = $NaBH_4$; Y = Sn, Δ
(c) X = Zn, Δ ; Y = Zn |Hg, HCl
(d) X = Zn |Hg, HCl ; Y = Zn, Δ

28. Match the following: **[May 26, 2025 (II)]**

List-I (Compound)	List-II (pK_a)
(A) *p*-Nitrophenol	(I) 15.9
(B) Phenol	(II) 7.1
(C) Ethanol	(III) 10.0
(D) *p*-Cresol	(IV) 10.2
	(V) 8.3

The correct answer is

(a) A-II, B-V, C-I D-III (b) A-II, B-III, C-I, D-IV
(c) A-V, B-IV, C-II, D-III (d) A-IV, B-III, C-I, D-V

29. What are X and Y respectively in the following set of reactions? **[May 26, 2025 (II)]**

$Y \xleftarrow[(ii)\ H^+]{(i)(CH_3CO)_2O} p-\text{Cresol} \xrightarrow[\Delta]{Zn} X$

(a) 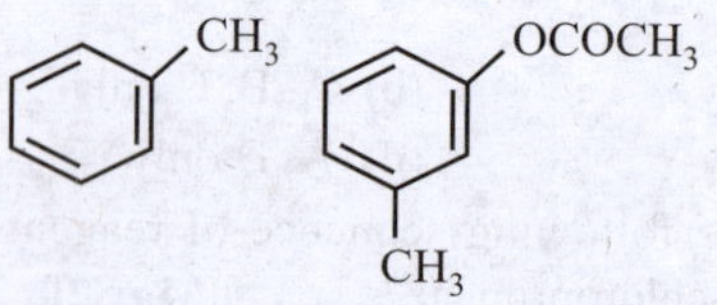

(b) 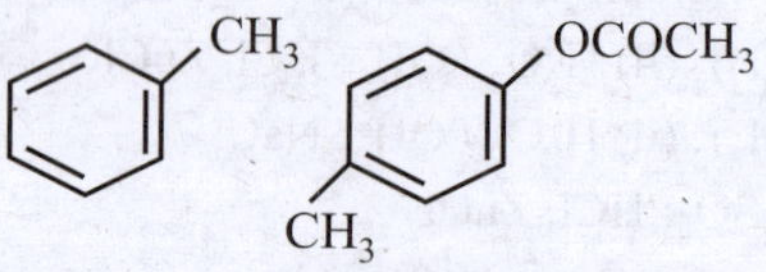

(c) 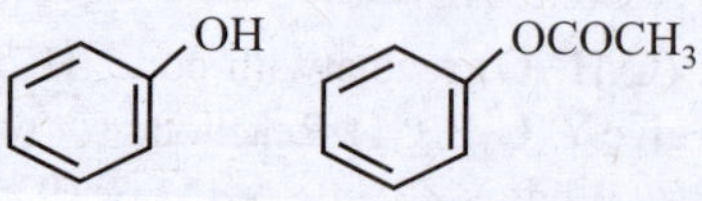

(d) 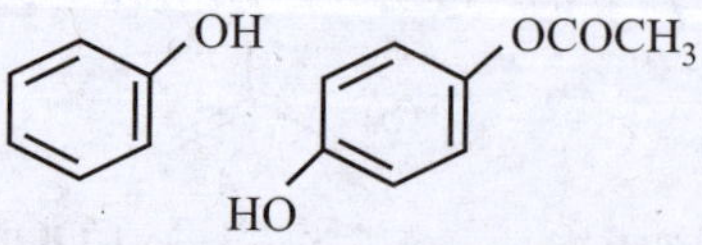

30. Among the following compounds, which one is not responsible for the depletion of ozone layer? **[May 22, 2025 (II)]**

(a) CH_4 (b) $CFCl_3$ (c) NO (d) Cl_2

31. Novolac is formed by the polymerisation of monomer '*x*' in the presence of OH^- ions. What is '*x*'? **[May 22, 2025 (I)]**

(a) 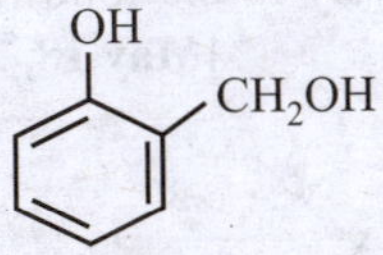

(b) 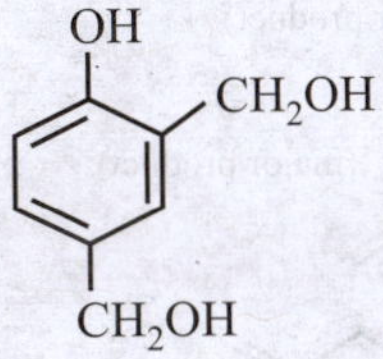

(c) 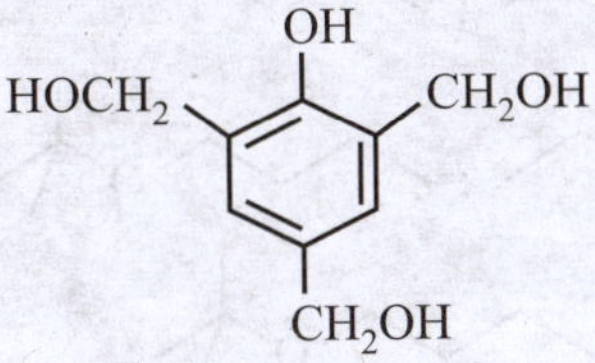

(d) 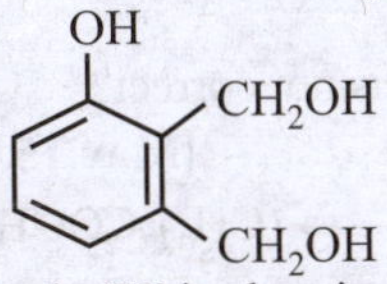

32. What is 'Y' in the given reaction sequence? **[May 22, 2024 (I)]**

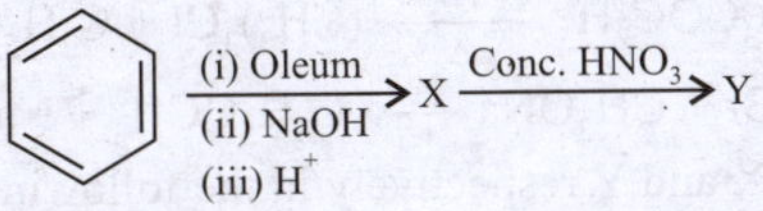

(a) 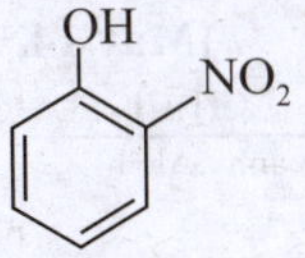
(b) 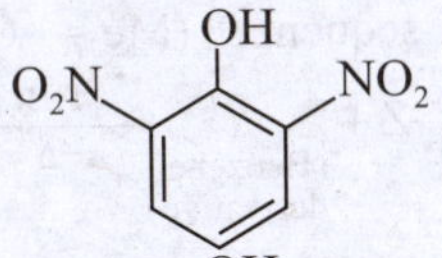

(c) 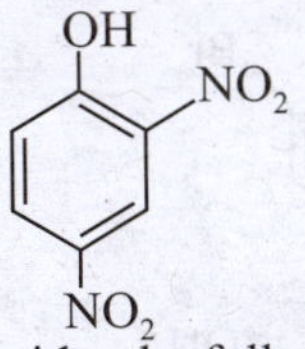
(d) 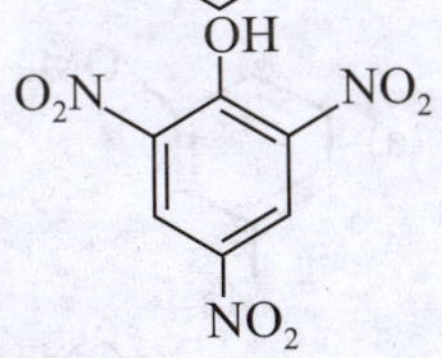

33. Consider the following reactions

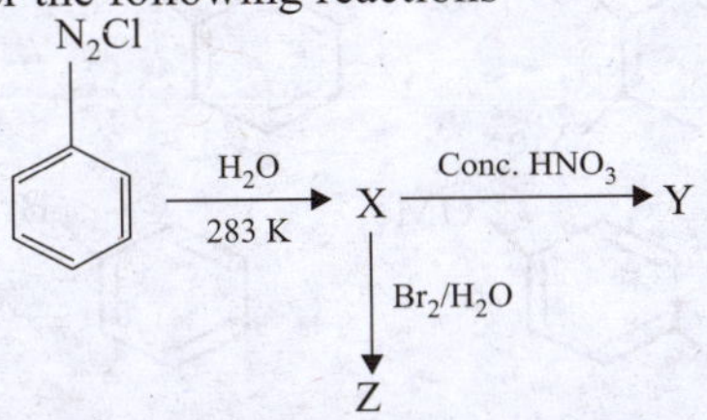

Y and Z respectively are **[May 20, 2024 (I)]**

(a) Picric acid (2,4,6 – Trinitrophenol), 2,4,6 –Tribromophenol
(b) o –nitrophenol, p – bromophenol
(c) p –Nitrophenol, o –bromophenol
(d) 2,4 –dinitrophenol, 2,4 – dibromophenol

34. Chlorobenzene (X) when reacted with reagent 'A' gets converted to phenol (Y). The major product obtained from nitration of X gets converted to p-nitrophenol (Z) by reaction with reagent B. What are A and B respectively? **[May 18, 2024 (I)]**

(a) A = (i) NaOH, 623 K, 300 atm (ii) H^+; B = (i) NaOH, 443K (ii) H^+
(b) A = (i) NaOH, 443 K (ii) H^+; B = H_2O, Δ
(c) A = (i) NaOH, 323 K (ii) H^+: B = (i) NaOH, 443 K (ii) H^+
(d) A = (i) NaOH, 623 K, 300 atm (ii) H^+; B = H_2O, Δ

35. Reaction of phenol with which of the following reagents form picric acid? **[May 19, 2023 (I)]**

(a) Conc. H_2SO_4 (b) dil. H_2SO_4
(c) Conc. HNO_3 (d) dil. HNO_3

36. 1 – Chloro – 4 – nitrobenzene, 1 – chloro – 2, 4 – dinitrobenzene and 1 – chloro – 2, 4, 6 – trinitrobenzene are transformed to corresponding phenols with the reagents X, Y, Z respectively. What are X, Y, Z? **[May 17, 2023 (I)]**

(a) X = H_2O; Y = NaOH, 365K; Z = NaOH, 445K
(b) X = (i) NaOH, 443K, (ii) H^+; Y = (i) NaOH, 368K, (ii) H^+; Z = Warm H_2O
(c) X = (i) NaOH, 625K, (ii) H^+; Y = (i) NaOH, 440K, (ii) H^+; Z = H_2O/H^+
(d) X = NaOH, 625K; Y = H_2O; Z = NaOH, 440K

37. Which of the following is the major product, when p – cresol is treated with zinc dust? **[May 16, 2023 (II)]**

(a) Toluene (b) Heptane
(c) Methyl cyclohexanol (d) Methyl cyclohexane

38. Catechol and m-cresol respectively are **[May 16, 2023 (I)]**

(a) Benzene - 1, 4 - diol; 3 - Methoxy phenol
(b) Benzene - 1, 2 - diol; 3 - Methoxy phenol
(c) Benzene - 1, 3 - diol; 3 - Methyl phenol
(d) Benzene - 1, 2 - diol; 3 - Methyl phenol

39. Which of the following has more pK_a value? **[May 15, 2023 (II)]**

(a) 2-Nitrophenol (b) 3-Nitrophenol
(c) 4-Nitrophenol (d) 2, 4-Dinitrophenol

40. The major product formed in the following reaction sequence is **[July 8, 2022 (I)]**

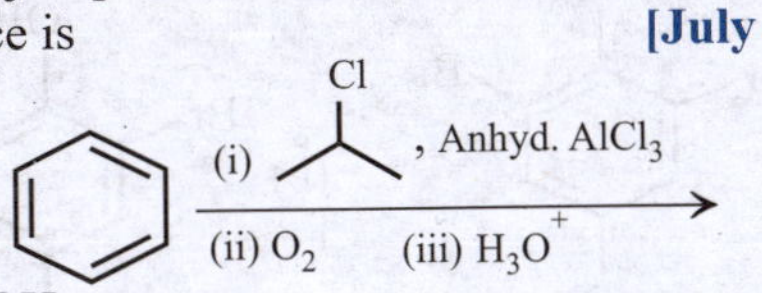

(a) 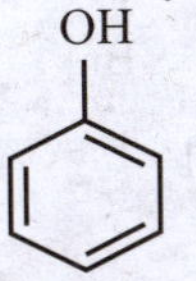
(b) 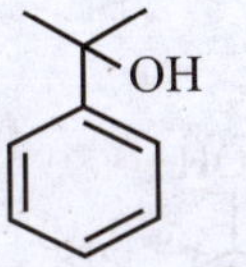

(c) 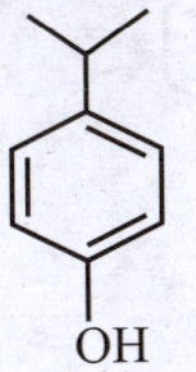
(d) 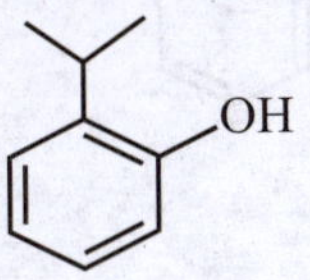

41. The product formed in the given reaction is **[July 7, 2022 (II)]**

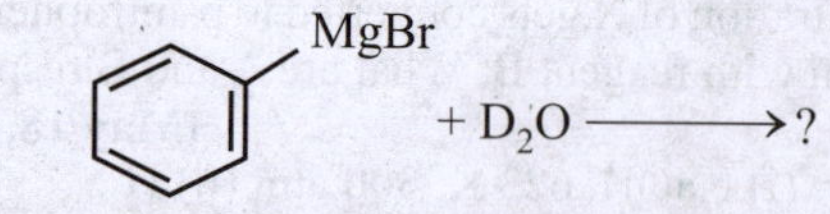

(a) 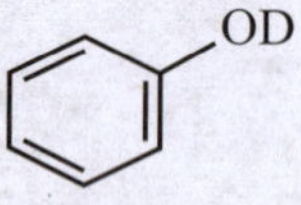 (b) 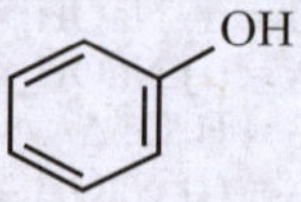

(c) 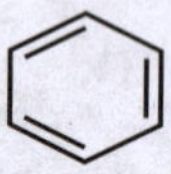 (d) 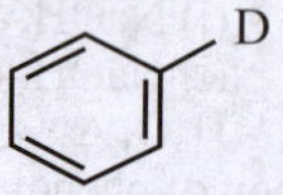

42. Identify the major product formed from the following reaction sequence **[July 6, 2022 (I)]**

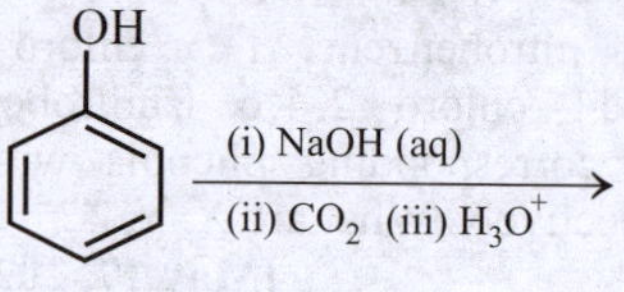

(a) 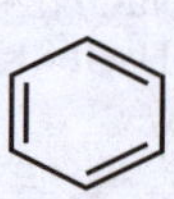 (b) 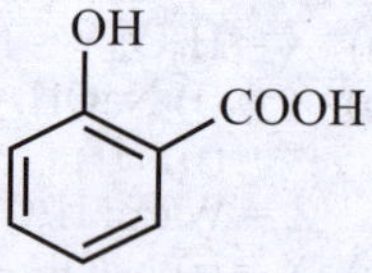

(c) 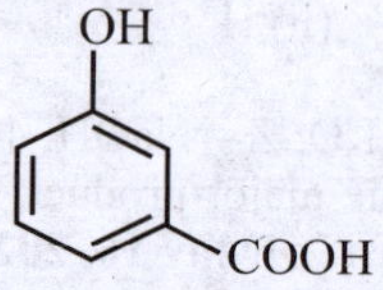 (d) 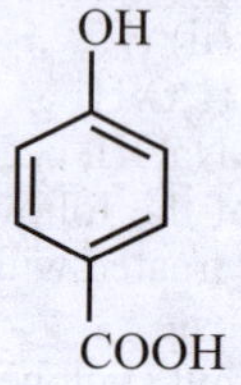

43. The major aromatic product of the following reaction sequence is

[Sept. 21, 2020 (II) Similar to April 22, 2019 (I)]

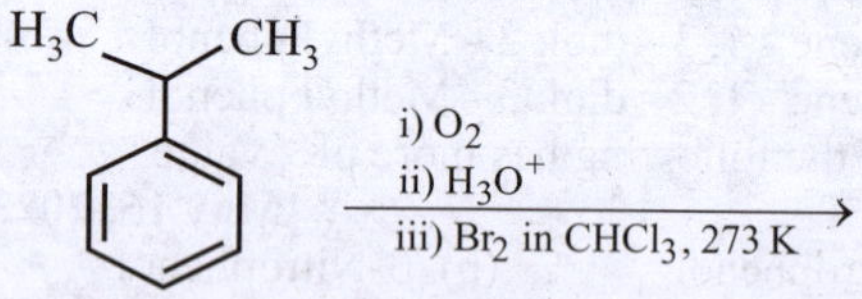

(a) 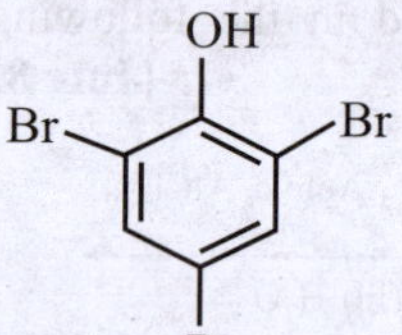 (b) 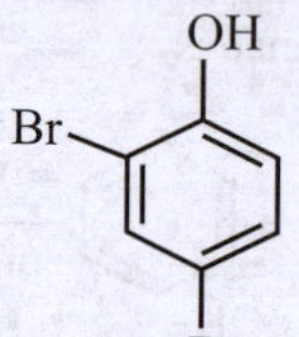

(c) 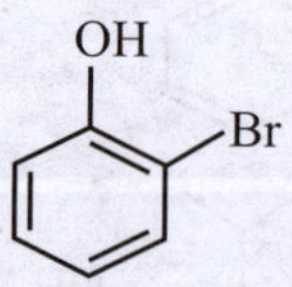 (d) 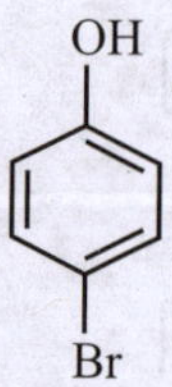

44. Phenol on oxidation in air gives **[2015]**

(a) quinone (b) catechol

(c) resorcinol (d) *o*-cresol

Topic 3 Preparation and Properties of Ethers

45. What are X and Y respectively in the following set of reactions? **[May 18, 2026 (II)]**

(major product =)

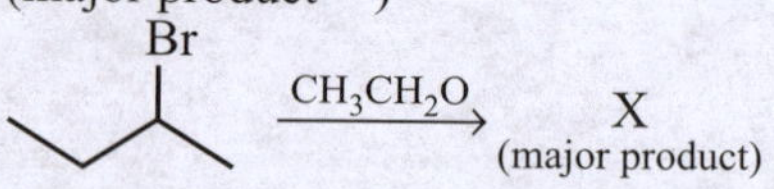

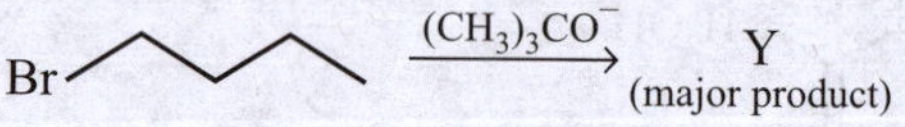

(a) 

(b) 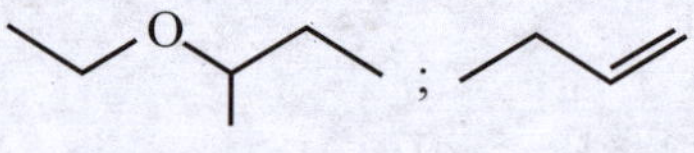

(c) 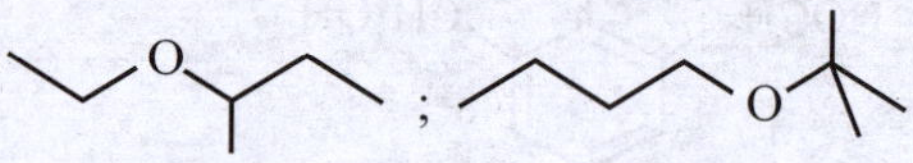

(d) 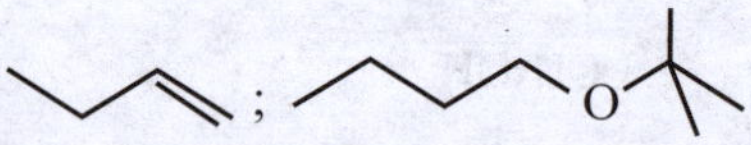

46. Which one of the following is not correct? **[May 15, 2026 (I)]**

(a) $(CH_3)_3CONa + CH_3Br \longrightarrow (CH_3)_3COCH_3$

(b) $(C_2H_5)_2O \xrightarrow[\Delta]{\text{excess HI}} 2\,C_2H_5I + H_2O$

(c) $(CH_3)_3COC_2H_5 \xrightarrow[\Delta]{HI} (CH_3)_3CI + C_2H_5OH$

(d) $C_6H_5Br + CH_3ONa \longrightarrow C_6H_5OCH_3 + NaBr$

47. What are X and Y respectively in the following reaction sequence? (Me = $-CH_3$) **[May 14, 2026 (II)]**

$$Z + \underset{\text{(Benzene derivative)}}{Y} \xleftarrow[\Delta]{HBr} \text{Anisole} \xrightarrow[\text{anhy.}AlCl_3]{CH_3Cl} \underset{\text{(major product)}}{X}$$

(a) 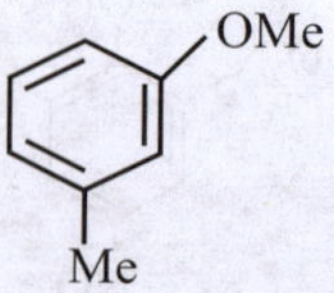 ; 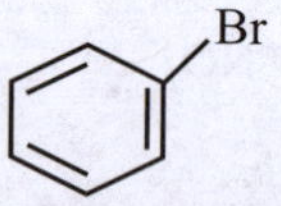

(b) 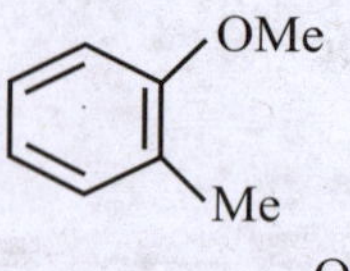 ; 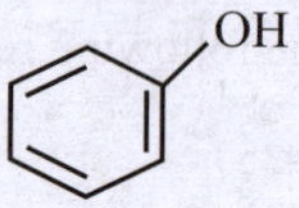

(c) 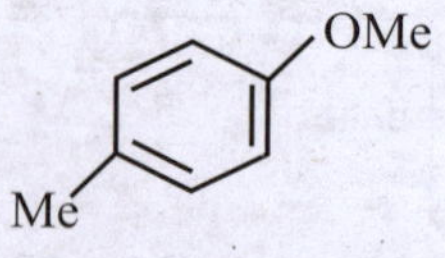 ; 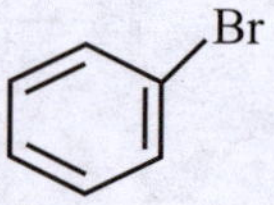

(d) 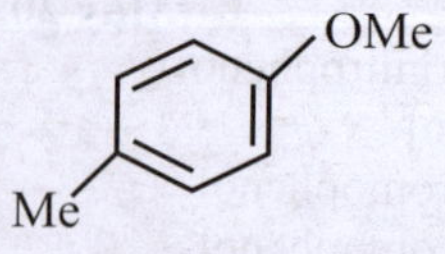 ; 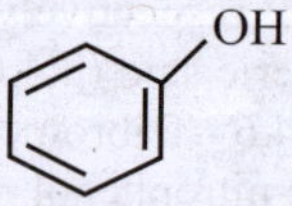

48. What are X and Y respectively in the following set of reactions? **[May 12, 2026 (II)]**

Anisole $\xrightarrow[CH_3CO_2H]{Br_2}$ X (major product)

Toluene $\xrightarrow[\text{(ii) } OH^-]{\text{(i) } Br_2|\text{UV Light}}$ Y (major product)

(a) 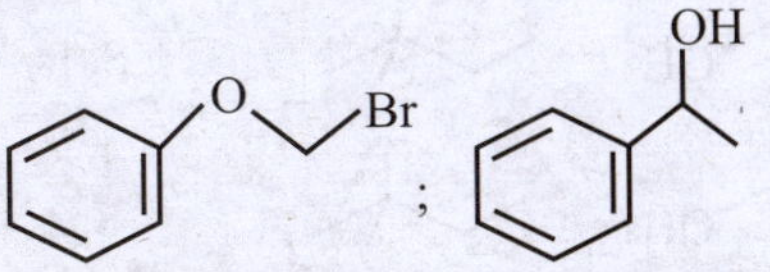

(b) 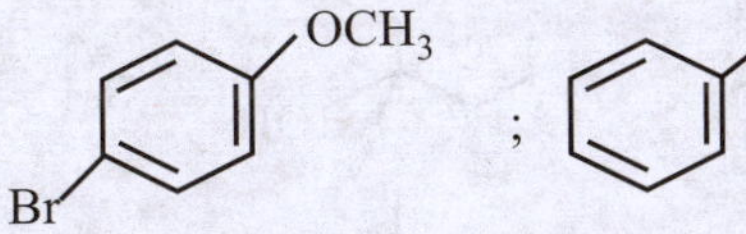

(c) 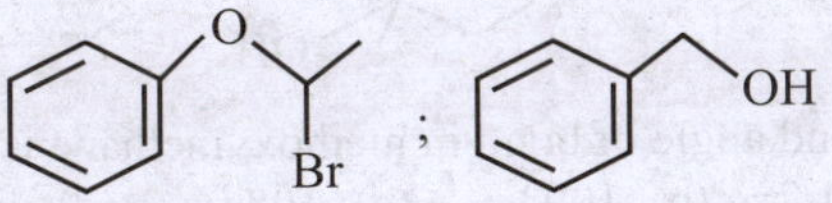

(d) 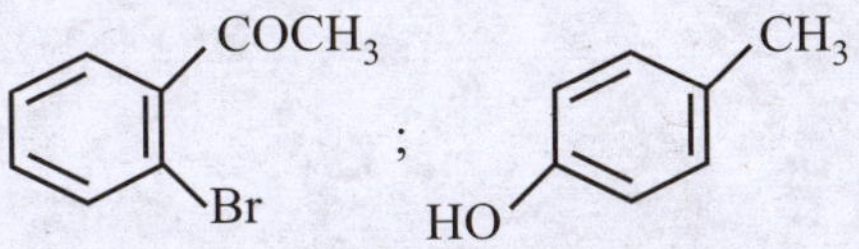

49. The correct statement regarding X and Y formed in the following reaction is **[May 23, 2025 (II)]**

$(CH_3)_3COC_2H_5 \xrightarrow[\Delta]{HI}$ halide (X) + alcohol (Y)

(a) X undergoes substitution by S_N2 mechanism
(b) X undergoes substitution with water in two steps
(c) Y gets converted to corresponding chloride with conc. HCl at room temperature
(d) Reaction of Y with Cu/573 K gives ketone

50. The correct order of boiling points of the compounds given below is **[May 22, 2025 (I)]**

(A) Methoxyethane (B) Propan-l-ol
(C) Propanal (D) Propanone

(a) C > B > A > D (b) B > D > C > A
(c) B > C > D > A (d) C > A > B > D

51. What are X and Y respectively iii the following reactions? **[May 21, 2024 (II)]**

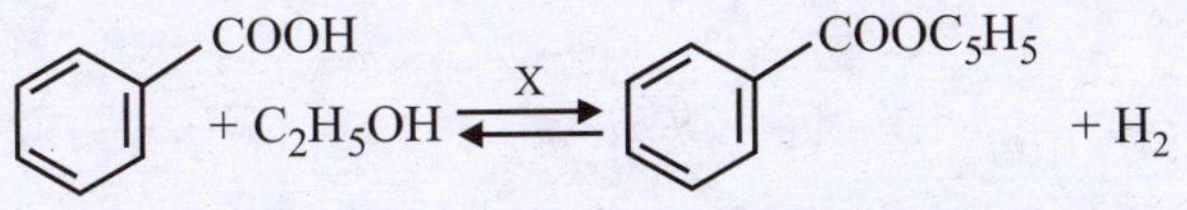

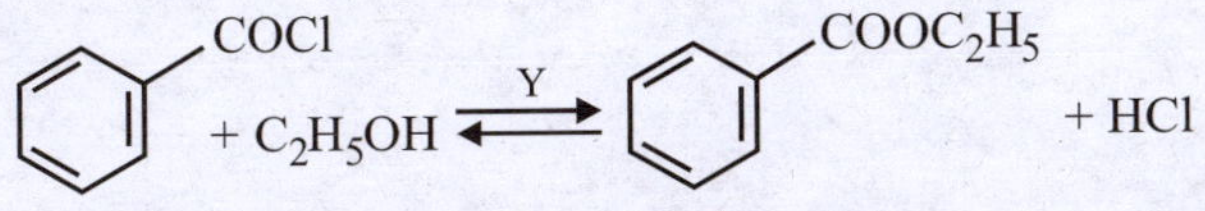

(a) H^+, H^+ (b) H^+, Pyridine
(c) Pyridine, H^+ (d) Pyridine, Pyridine

52. What are the major products X and Y respectively in the following reactions? **[May 21, 2024 (I)]**

$(CH_3)_3\,CONa + CH_3CH_2Br \rightarrow X$

$(CH_3)_3\,CBr + CH_3CH_2ONa \rightarrow Y$

(Elimination due SH)

(a) $CH_2 = CH_2$, $(CH_3)_3\,COCH_2CH_3$
(b) $(CH_3)_3\,COCH_2CH_3$, $(CH_3)_3COCH_2CH_3$
(c) $CH_2 = CH_2$, $(CH_3)_2C = CH_2$
(d) $(CH_3)_3COCH_2CH_3$, $(CH_3)_2C = CH_2$

53. What are X and Y in the following set of reactions? **[May 18, 2024 (I)]**

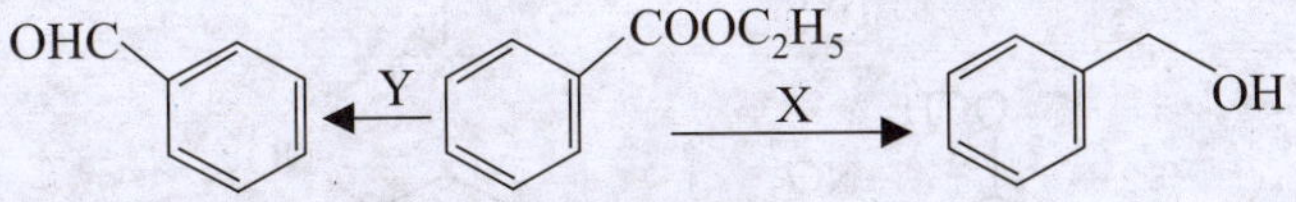

(a) X = (i) DiBAL - H (ii) H_2O
Y = (i) DiBAL - H (ii) H_2O
(b) X = H_2/Catalyst Y = H_2/ Catalyst
(c) X = H_2/ Catalyst Y = (i) DiBAL-H (ii) H_2O
(d) X= (i) DiBAL - H (ii) H_2O Y = H_2/Catalyst

54. What are 'X' and 'Y' respectively in the following reactions?

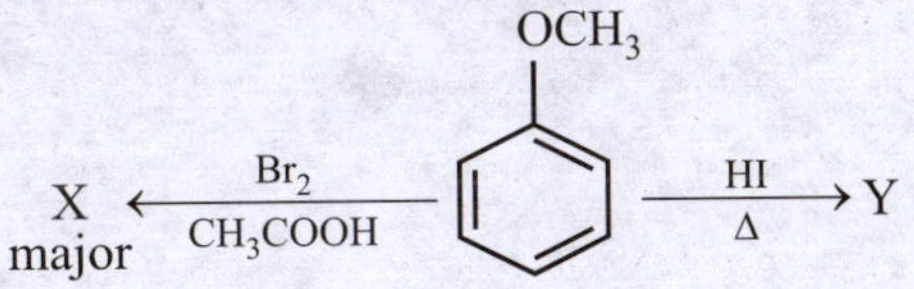

[May 18, 2023 (I)]

(a) 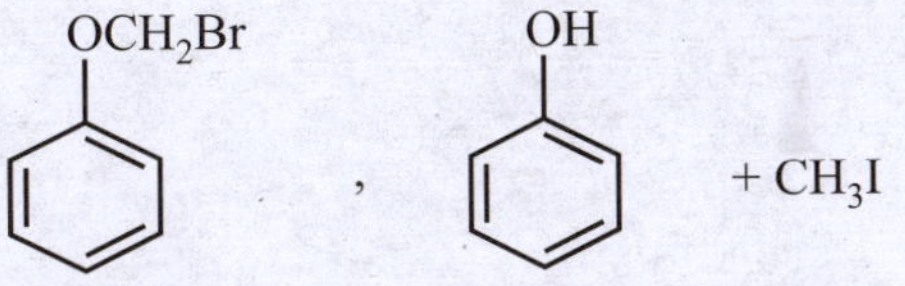

(b) 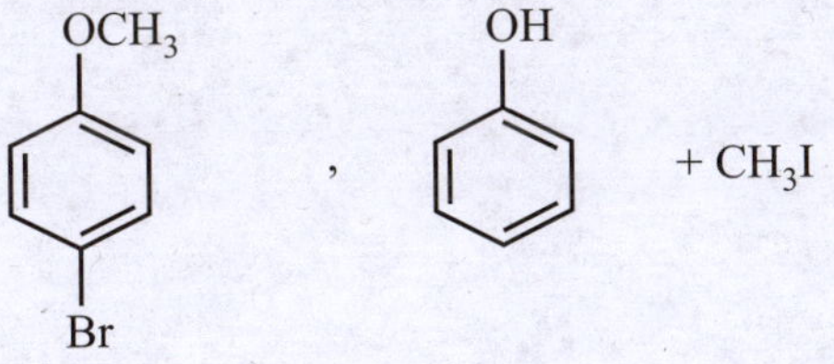

(c) 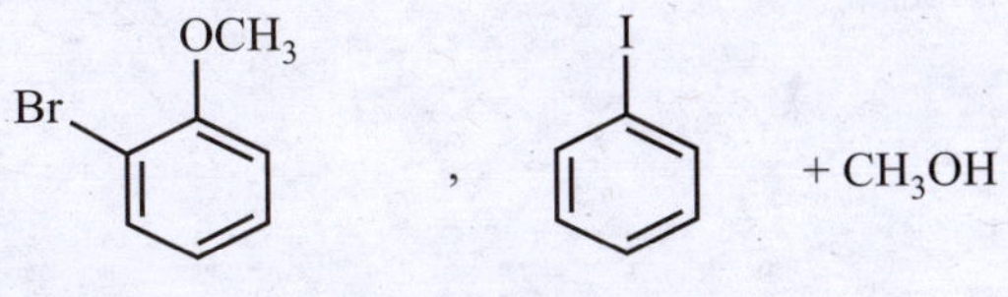

(d) 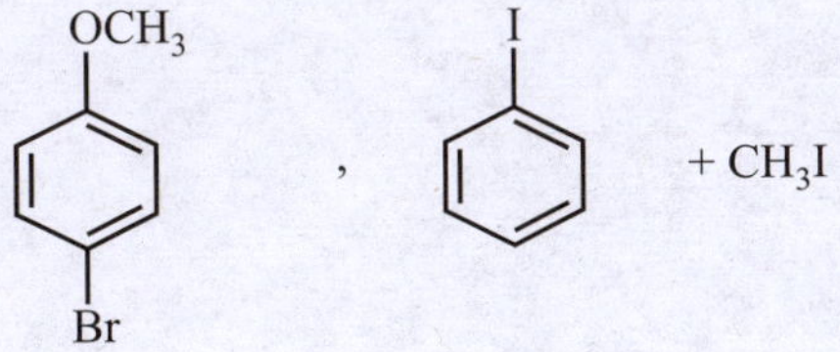

55. Identify the major product of the following reaction.

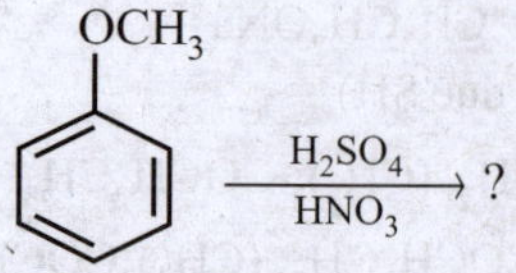

[Aug. 20, 2021 (I)]

(a) 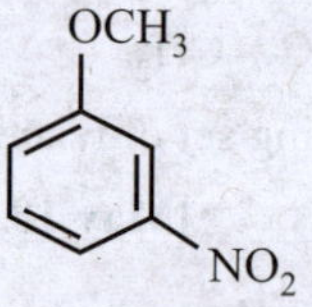

(b) 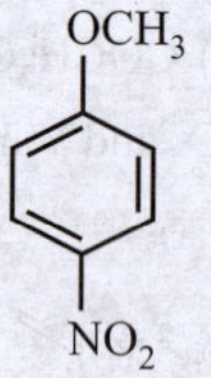

(c) 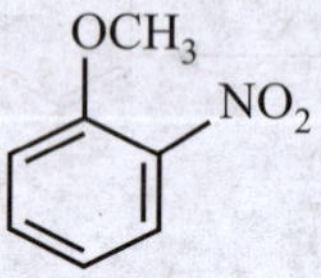

(d) 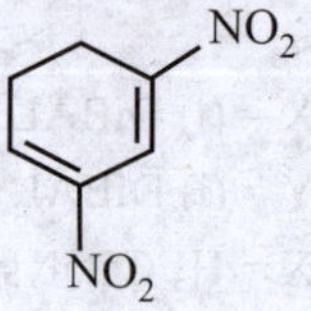

56. Identify the products (*X*, *Y*) and reaction mechanism (*Z*) of the following reaction? **[Apr. 21, 2019 (I)]**

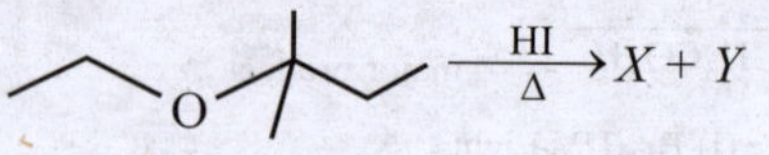

	X	***Y***	***Z***
(a)	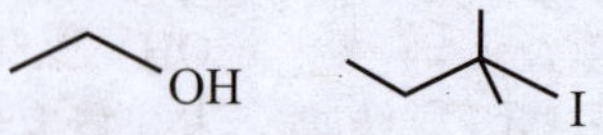		S_N1
(b)	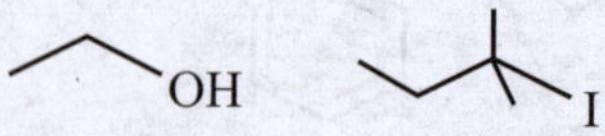		S_N2
(c)	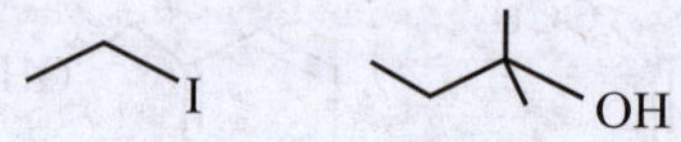		S_N1
(d)			S_N2

57. The bond angle of bond in methoxymethane is **[2015]**

(a) 111.7° (b) 109° (c) 108.9° (d) 180°

8 Aldehydes, Ketones and Carboxylic Acids

CHAPTER SYNOPSIS

- **Beckmann rearrangement :**

Oximes on treatment with catalysts such as conc. H_2SO_4, $SOCl_2$, PCl_5, etc. undergo rearrangement to form substituted amides. This reaction is called **Beckmann rearrangement**.

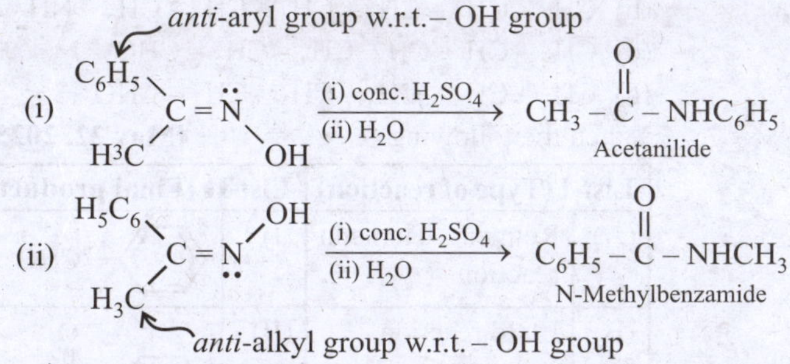

Remember that *anti*-alkyl (aryl) group migrates.

- **Claisen condensation :**

Esters containing α-H-atoms undergo self-condensation in presence of a strong base such as sodium ethoxide to form β-keto esters. For ex :

$$CH_3-\overset{O}{\overset{\|}{C}}\boxed{-OC_2H_5+H-}\overset{\alpha}{C}H_2COOC_2H_5 \xrightarrow{C_2H_5ONa} CH_3-\overset{O}{\overset{\|}{C}}-CH_2COOC_2H_5+C_2H_5OH$$

Ethyl acetate (2 molecules) → Ethylacetoacetate (β-keto ester)

- **Comparative reactivity of acid derivatives :**

The relative reactivities of different acid derivatives towards nucleophilic acyl substitution reactions follow the order :

$$\underset{\text{Acid chloride}}{R-\overset{O}{\overset{\|}{C}}-Cl} > \underset{\text{Anhydride}}{R-\overset{O}{\overset{\|}{C}}-O-\overset{O}{\overset{\|}{C}}-R'} > \underset{\text{Ester}}{R-\overset{O}{\overset{\|}{C}}-OR'} > \underset{\text{Amide}}{R-\overset{O}{\overset{\|}{C}}-NH_2}$$

Since stronger base is a poor leaving group.

$NH_2^- > R'O^- > R'COO^- > Cl^-$. (Basic strength)

Topic 1 Methods of Preparation of Carbonyl Compounds

1. Reaction of benzonitrile (A) with the reagent X gave B. In another reaction of A with the reagent Y gave C. Reaction of B and C in the presence of dil. NaOH at 293 K gave an α, β-unsaturated carbonyl compound. What are X + Y respectively? **[May 18, 2026 (II)]**
   (a) DIBAL-H, H_2O; $(CH_3)_2Cd$
   (b) $SnCl_2 + HCl$, H_3O^+; CH_3MgBr, H_2O
   (c) DIBAL-H, H_2O; $H_2|$ Ni
   (d) $SnCl_2 + HCl$, H_2O; $(CH_3)_2Cd$

2. What is Y in the given sequence of reactions **[May 18, 2026 (I)]**

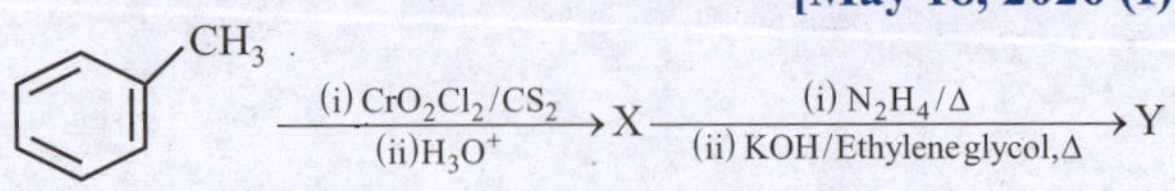

(a) 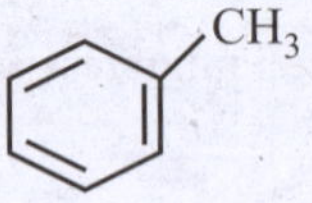

(b) 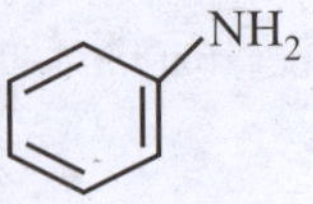

(c) 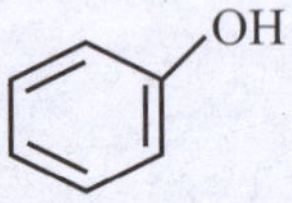

(d) 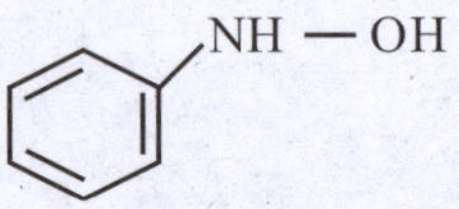

3. Consider the following set of reactions (A = major product) **[May 15, 2026 (II)]**
   (I) $C_3H_6 \xrightarrow[H^+]{H_2O} A \xrightarrow{X} B$
   (II) $C_6H_6 \xrightarrow[\text{anhy. AlCl}_3]{Y} C$
   The product 'B' from reaction (I) gives positive iodoform test whereas product 'C' from reaction (II) does not. What are X and Y respectively?
   (a) H_2CrO_4; CO, HCl (b) $KMnO_4/H^+$; CH_3COCl
   (c) Ag, 573 K ; CO, HCl (d) PCC; $(CH_3CO)_2O$

4. The incorrect statement about Z formed in the sequence of reactions given below is **[May 13, 2026 (II)]**

$$C_6H_{14} \xrightarrow[\substack{773\text{ K}\\ 10-20\text{ atm}}]{V_2O_5} X \xrightarrow[\text{Anhy. AlCl}_3]{CH_3Cl}$$

$$Y \xrightarrow[\text{ii) } H_3O^+]{\text{i) } CrO_2Cl_2,\, CS_2} Z$$

   (a) It does not give test with Fehling's solution
   (b) It can also be obtained by Gatterman-Koch reaction
   (c) It undergoes Cannizaro reaction in the presence of Conc. NaOH solution
   (d) It gives p-nitro derivative as major product in nitration reaction

5. Match the following **[May 13, 2026 (II)]**

List-I (Transformation)	List-II (Reagent)
A. Hexan-1-ol→ Hexanal	I. (i) CrO_2Cl_2/CS_2 (ii) H_2O
B. p-Fluorotoluene → p-Fluorobenzaldehyde	II. DiBAL-H
C. Cyclohexanone→ Cyclohexanaol	III. PCC
D. Ethanenitrile → Ethanal	IV. $NaBH_4$
	V. Pd - $BaSO_4$

   The correct answer is
   (a) A-III, B-IV, C-I, D-II (b) A-III, B-I, C-IV, D-II
   (c) A-IV, B-III, C-II, D-I (d) A-IV, B-I, C-II, D-III

6. What is A in the following reaction? **[May 23, 2025 (II)]**

$$CH_3-CH=CH-CH_2-CH_2-CN \xrightarrow[(2)\ H_2O]{(1)\ AlH(i\text{-}Bu)_2} (A)$$

   (a) $CH_3-CH=CH-CH_2-CH_2-CH_2-NH_2$
   (b) $CH_3-CH_2-CH_2-CH_2-CH_2-CH_2-NH_2$
   (c) $CH_3-CH=CH-CH_2-CH_2-CHO$
   (d) $CH_3-CH_2-CH_2-CH_2-CH_2-CHO$

7. Match the following. **[May 22, 2025 (II)]**

List-I (Type of reaction)		List-II (Final product)	
(A)	Reimer - Tiemann reaction	(I)	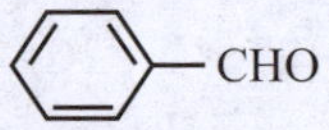
(B)	Etard reaction	(II)	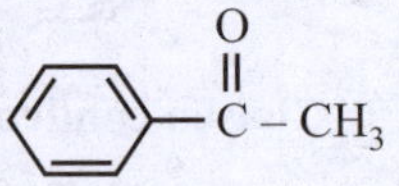
(C)	Sandmeyer reaction	(III)	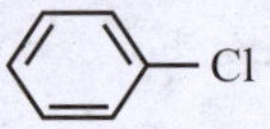
(D)	Friedel-Crafts reaction	(IV)	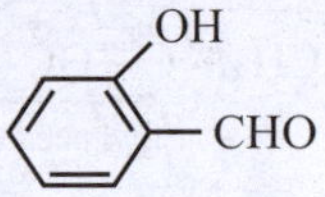

   The correct answer is
   (a) A-IV, B-III, C-II, D-I (b) A-II, B-III, C-I, D-IV
   (c) A-IV, B-I, C-III, D-II (d) A-III, B-IV, C-I, D-II

8. Which of the following represents Etard reaction? **[May 22, 2025 (I)]**
   (a) $RCN \xrightarrow[HCl]{SnCl_2} X \xrightarrow{H_3O^+} RCHO$
   (b) 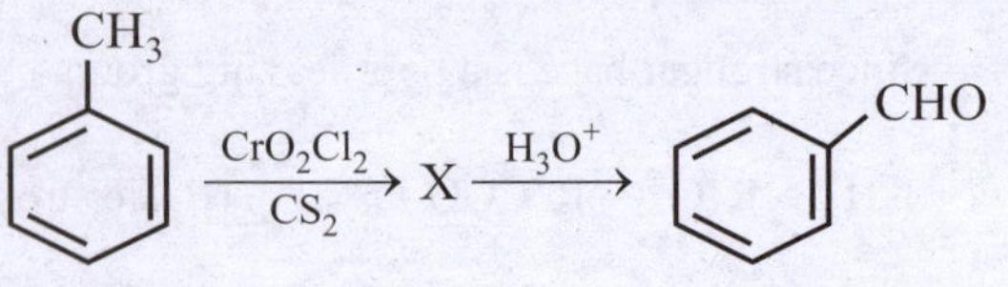

   (c) 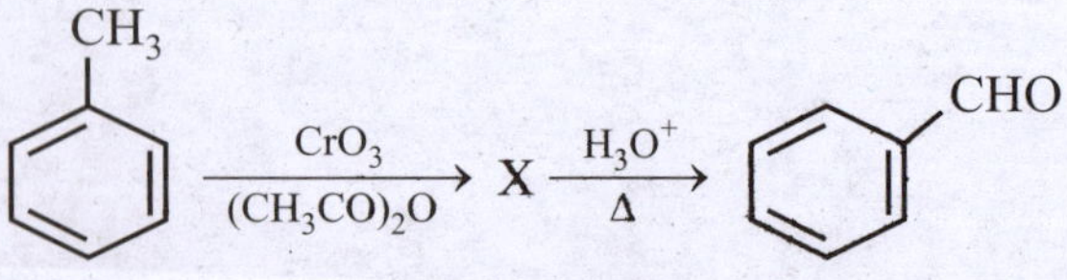

   (d) 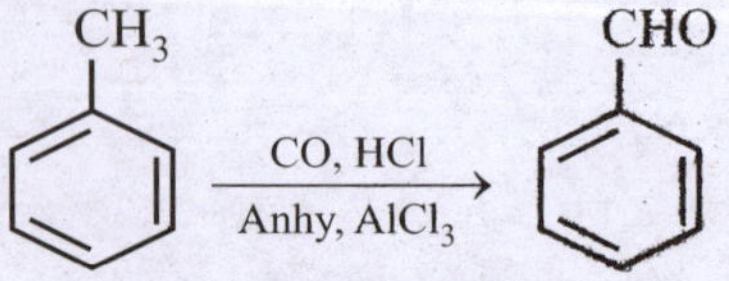

9. In the following sequence of reactions, what is the end product (D)? **[May 21, 2025 (II)]**

$$C_2H_5Br \xrightarrow{KCN} A \xrightarrow{H_3O^+} B \xrightarrow{LiAlH_4} C \xrightarrow[573\ K]{Cu} D$$

(a) Acetaldehyde (b) Acetone
(c) Propionaldehyde (d) Propanol-1

10. The sequence of reagents required to convert ethyl bromide to propanal is **[May 23, 2024 (I)]**
(a) CH_3COOAg, DiBAL-H, H_2O
(b) CH_3COOAg, $LiAlH_4$, H_2O
(c) Mg/ether, HCHO, H_2O
(d) CH_3COOH, $LiAlH_4$, H_2O

11. Toluene on reaction with the reagent X gave Y, which dissolves in $NaHCO_3$ and when reacted with Br_2 / Fe gave Z. What are X and Z? **[May 23, 2024 (I)]**

(a) (i) $KMnO_4$/ OH, Δ (ii) H_3O^+; 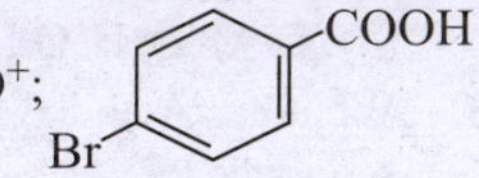

(b) (i) CrO_2Cl_2 (ii) H_3O^+; 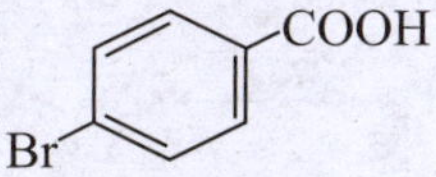

(c) (i) CrO_2Cl_2 (ii) H_3O^+; 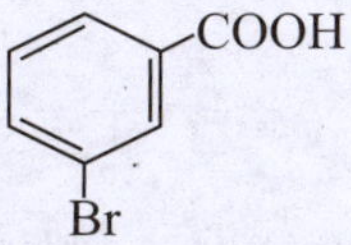

(d) (i) $KMnO_4$/ OH^-, Δ (ii) H_3O^+; 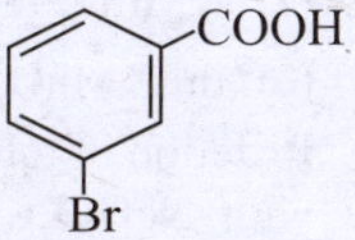

12. Consider the following reactions

$$C_2H_2 + H_2O \xrightarrow[333K]{Hg^{2+}/H^+} [X] \xrightleftharpoons{\text{Isomerisation}} Y$$

Y cannot be obtained from which of the following reactions? **[May 22, 2024 (II)]**

(a) $CH_3COCl + H_2 \xrightarrow{Pd/BaSO_4}$

(b) $CH_3CH_2OH \xrightarrow{Cu/573K}$

(c) $CH_3CN + SnCl_2 + HCl \longrightarrow X \xrightarrow{H_3O^+}$

(d) $CH_3COOH \xrightarrow[(ii)\ H_2O]{(i)\ LiAlH_4/ether}$

13. Identify B in the given reaction sequence **[May 22, 2024 (I)]**

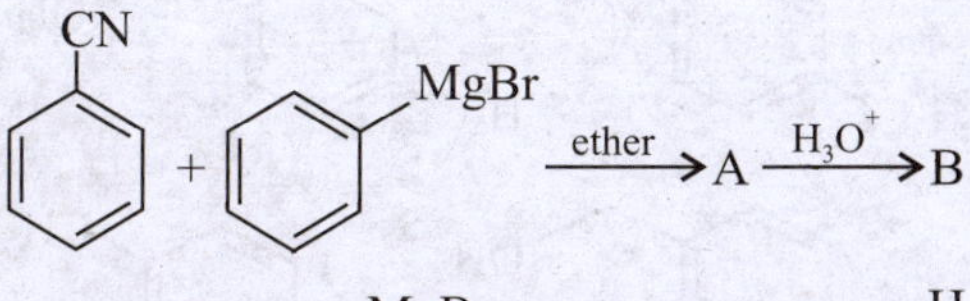

(a) 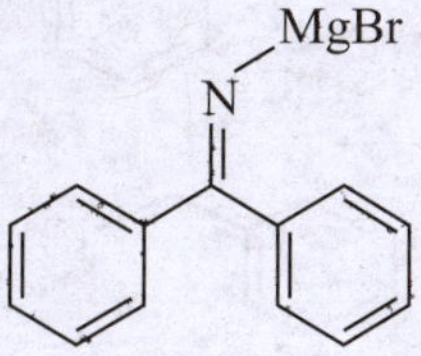

(b) 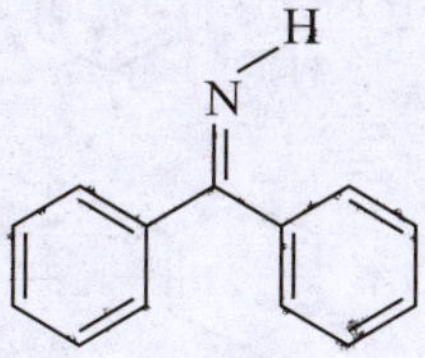

(c) 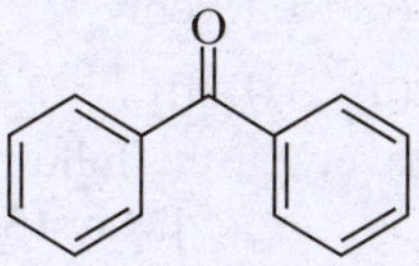

(d) 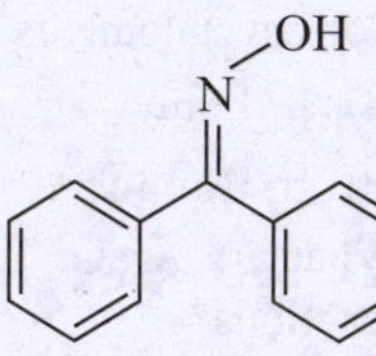

14. The main reactants involved in Etard reaction are **[2016]**
(a) Toluene + CrO_2Cl_2
(b) Toluene + CrO_3 + $(CH_3CO)_2O$
(c) Toluene + Cl_2/hv
(d) Benzene + CO + HCl/Anhy.$AlCl_3$

15. In the presence of peroxide, styrene reacts with HBr to give X. When X reacted with magnesium in dry ether followed by CO_2 and hydrolysis gave Y. Treatment of Y with PCl_5 and then next with H_2, Pd-$BaSO_4$ gave Z. What is Z? **[July 4, 2022 (I)]**

(a) 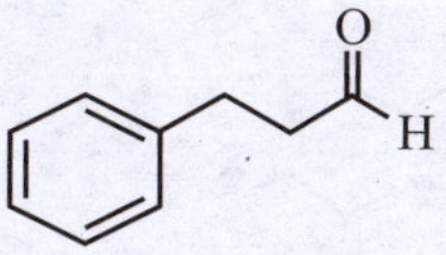

(b) 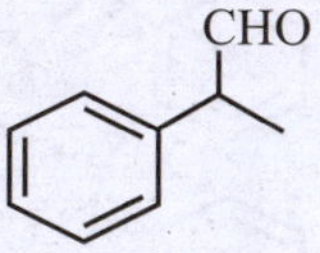

(c) 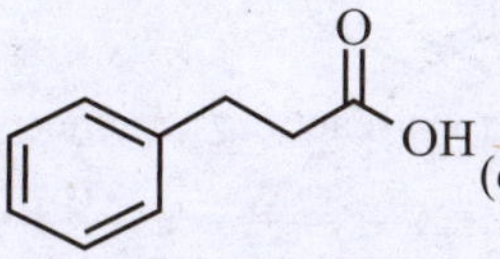

(d) 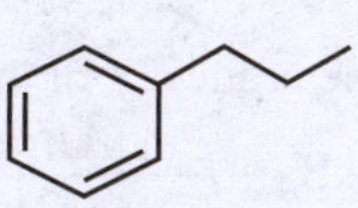

16. The major product in the following reaction is

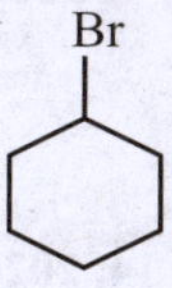

(i) Mg
(ii) CO_2
(iii) H_3O^+
(iv) $SOCl_2$
(v) $(CH_3)_2Cd$

[Aug. 19, 2021 (II)]

(a) 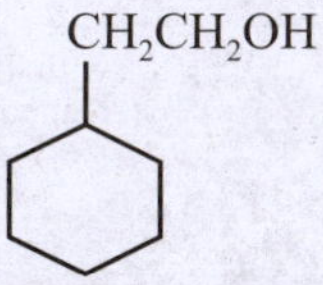

(b) 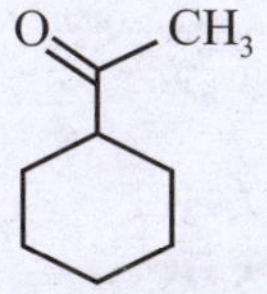

(c) 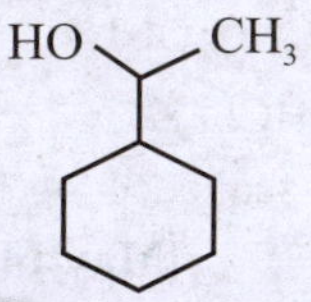

(d) 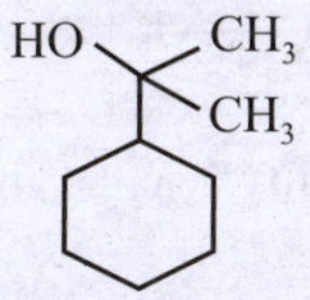

Topic 2 Properties of Carbonyl Compounds

17. Observe the following set of reactions

$$\text{Ethanal} \xrightarrow[(ii)\ H_2O]{(i)\ (CH_3)_2CHMgBr} X$$

$$\text{Propanone} \xrightarrow[(ii)\ H_2O]{(i)\ C_2H_5MgBr} Y$$

Consider the statements regarding X and Y
I. Ease of dehydration is Y > X
II. Acidic character is X > Y
III. Reactivity towards Lucas reagent is X > Y

Correct statements are **[May 18, 2026 (II)]**

(a) I, II only (b) I, III only
(c) II, III only (d) I, II, III

18. What are X and Y respectively in the following set of reactions? **[May 15, 2026 (I)]**

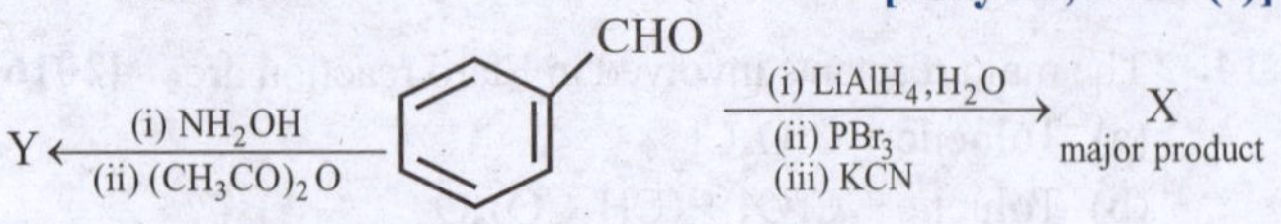

(a) 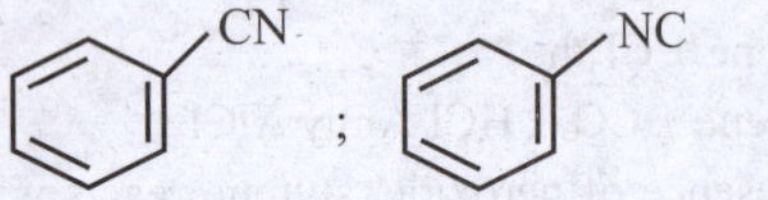

(b) 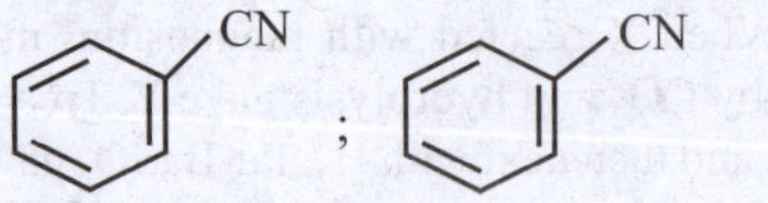

(c) 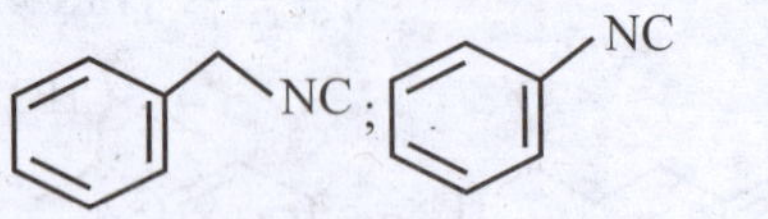

(d) 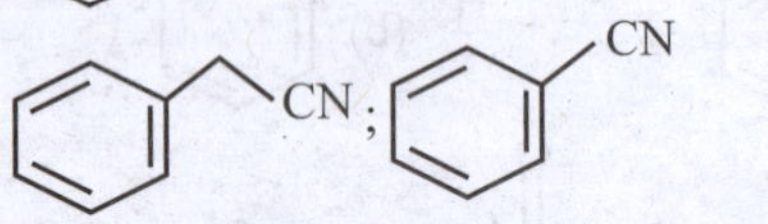

19. The product Z of the given reaction sequence is

$$C_2H_4 \xrightarrow[\text{(ii) } H^+/KMnO_4]{\text{(i) } H^+/H_2O} X \xrightarrow{SOCl_2} Y \xrightarrow{(C_2H_5)_2Cd} Z$$

[May 15, 2026 (I)]

(a) An acid chloride (b) A ketone
(c) An aldehyde (d) An ester

20. What are A and B in the following set of reactions respectively? **[May 14, 2026 (II)]**

$$\underset{\text{does not give iodoform test}}{Y} \xleftarrow[\text{anhy } AlCl_3]{B} \text{Benzene} \xrightarrow[\text{anhy } AlCl_3]{A} \underset{\text{gets oxidised with Tollens' reagent}}{X}$$

(a) CO, HCl ; CH_3CH_2COCl
(b) CO, HCl ; CH_3COCl
(c) CH_3COCl ; CH_3CH_2COCl
(d) CH_3COCl ; CO, HCl

21. Identify C in the given reaction sequence **[May 14, 2026 (I)]**

$$C_6H_5CHO \xrightarrow{\text{Conc. KOH}} A + B \xrightarrow[\Delta]{H^{\oplus}} C$$

(a) $H-CO_2C_6H_5$ (b) $C_6H_5CO_2CH_3$
(c) $C_6H_5CO_2CH_2C_6H_5$ (d) $C_6H_5CO_2C_6H_5$

22. Which of the following gives both iodoform test and Fehling's test? **[May 13, 2026 (II)]**

(a) Acetone (b) Acetaldehyde
(c) Propanal (d) Benzaldehyde

23. The number of secondary alcoholic groups present in the end product 'Y' of the given reaction sequence is **[May 13, 2026 (II)]**

$$C_6H_{12}O_6 \xrightarrow{HCN} X \xrightarrow{H_2O\backslash H^+} Y$$

(a) 4 (b) 3
(c) 5 (d) 6

24. What are X and Y respectively in the following set of reactions? **[May 13, 2026 (I)]**

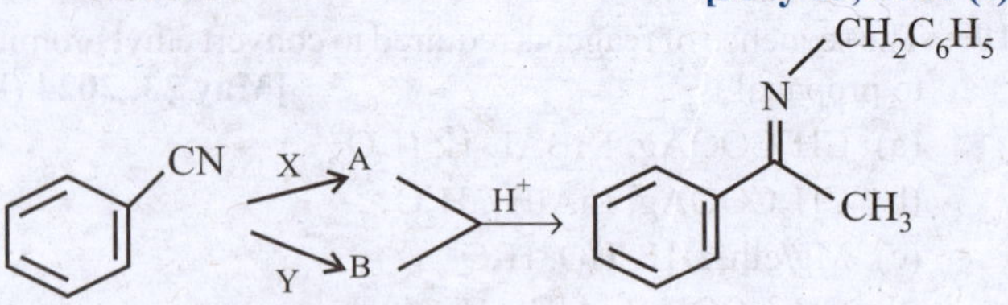

(a) H_2/cat ; $(CH_3)_2Cd$
(b) Na/C_2H_5OH ; CH_3MgBr, H_2O
(c) DIBAL-H, H_2O ; CH_3MgBr. H_2O
(d) $LiAlH_4$, H_2O ; $(CH_3)_2Cd$

25. What are A and B respectively in the following reaction sequence? **[May 12, 2026 (II)]**

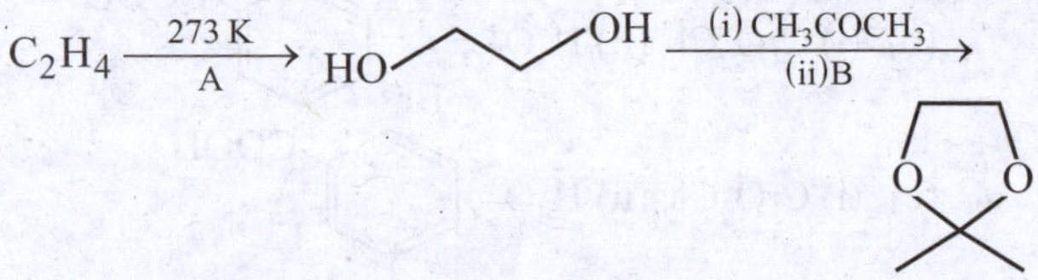

(a) $KMnO_4/H^+$; dil HCl (b) $KMnO_4/H^+$; dry HCl
(c) dil $KMnO_4$; dil HCl (d) dil $KMnO_4$; dry HCl

26. Reaction of toluene with reagent 'A' gave X which reacts with $NaHCO_3$ and liberates CO_2. In another reaction with reagent 'B' toluene gave Y which gives 2, 4-DNP test. What are A and B respectively? **[May 12, 2026 (I)]**

(a) $KMnO_4/OH^-$, H_3O^+ ; $CrO_3/(CH_3CO)_2O$, H_3O^+
(b) Cl_2/hv, H_2O; CrO_3/H^+
(c) CrO_2Cl_2, H_3O^+ ; $KMnO_4/OH^-$, H_3O^+
(d) $KMnO_4/OH^-$, H_3O^+ ; PCC

27. A carbonyl compound X (C_8H_8O) undergoes disproportionation with conc. KOH on heating. Product of X with Zn-Hg/HCl is Y and product of X with $NaBH_4$ is Z. What are Y and Z respectively? **[May 27, 2025 (I)]**

(a) 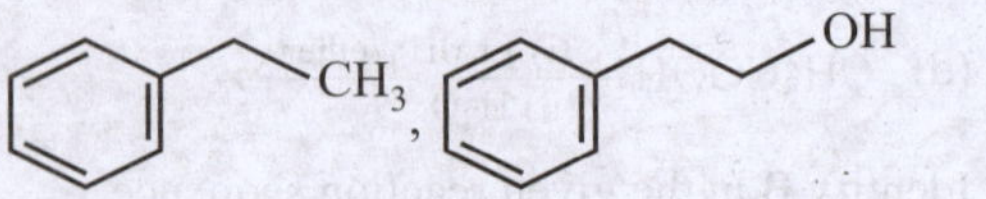

(b) 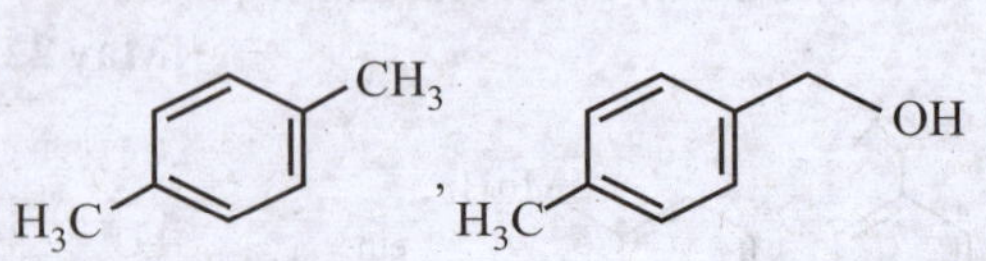

(c) 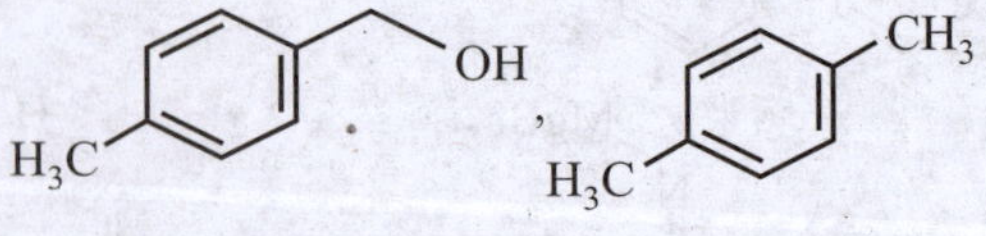

(d) 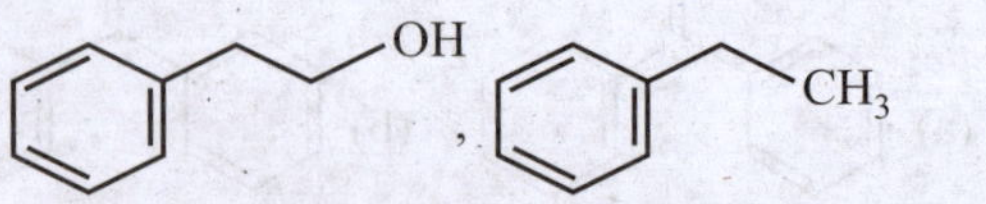

28. What are X and Y respectively in the following reaction sequence ? **[May 26, 2025 (I)]**

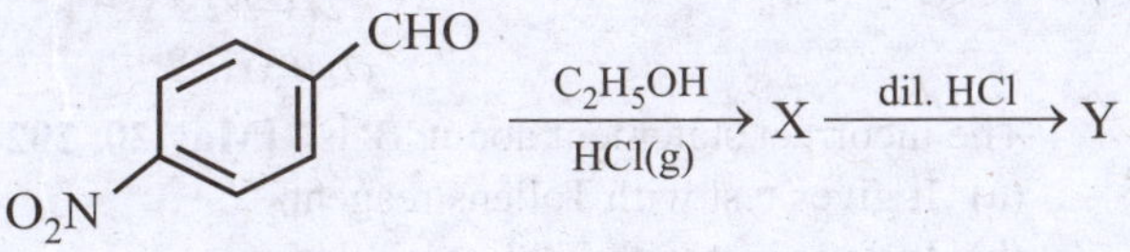

(a) 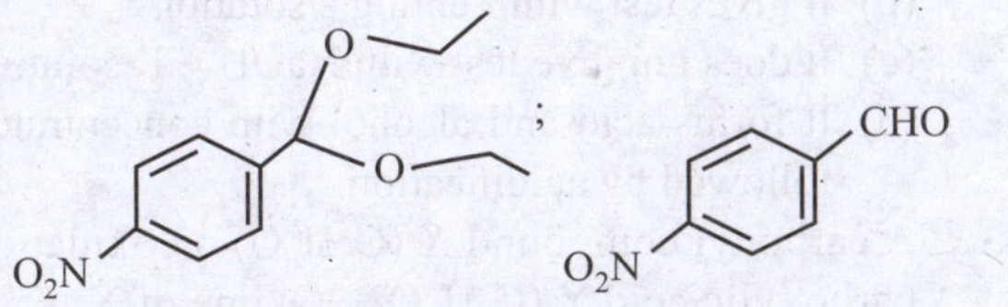

(b) 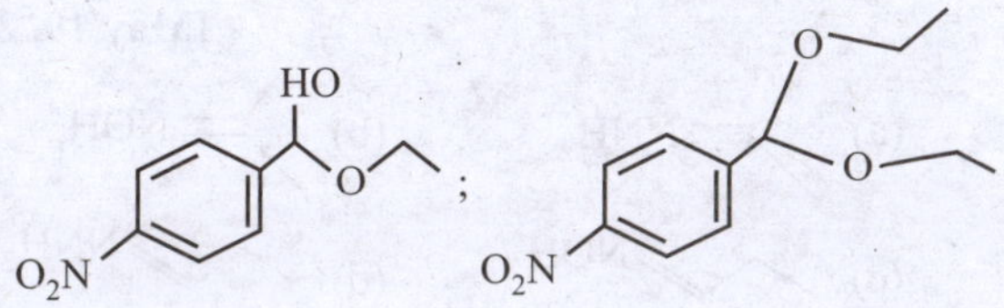

(c) 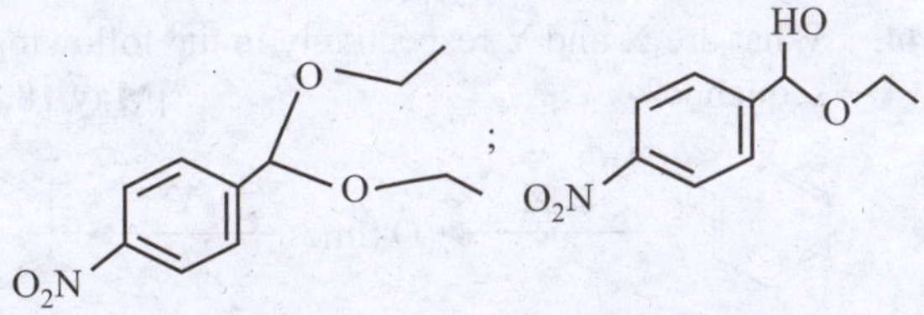

(d) 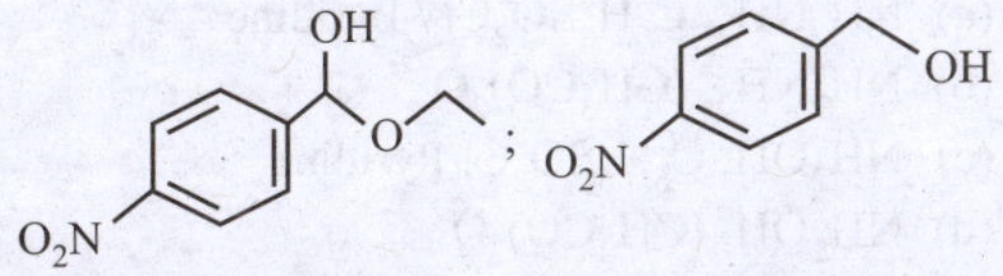

29. Arrange the following in decreasing order of electrophilicity of carbonyl carbon. **[May 24, 2025 (I)]**

(I) 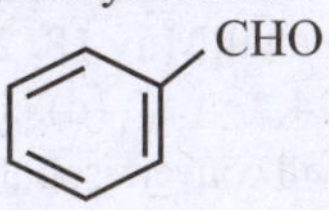 (II) 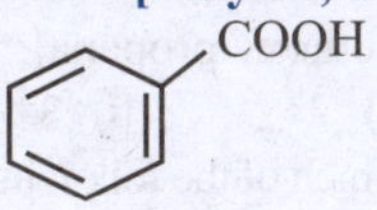

(III) 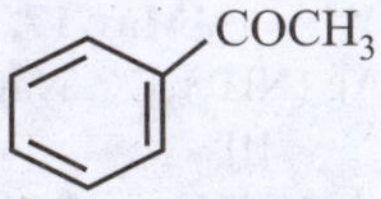 (IV) CH_3CH_2CHO

(a) IV > I > III > II (b) IV > I > II > III
(c) I > IV > III > II (d) I > II > IV > III

30. Consider the following sequence of reactions.

$$C_6H_5COONa \xrightarrow[\Delta]{NaOH/CaO} X \xrightarrow[\text{Anhy. }AlCl_3]{CO + HCl} Y \xrightarrow[NaOH]{conc.} A + B.$$

If A is the reduction product of Y, what is B ? **[May 23, 2025 (II)]**

(a) Sodium formate
(b) Sodium phenoxide
(c) Sodium salt of benzoic acid
(d) Sodium salt of salicylic acid

31. In the given reaction sequence, conversion of X to Y is an example of **[May 23, 2025 (I)]**

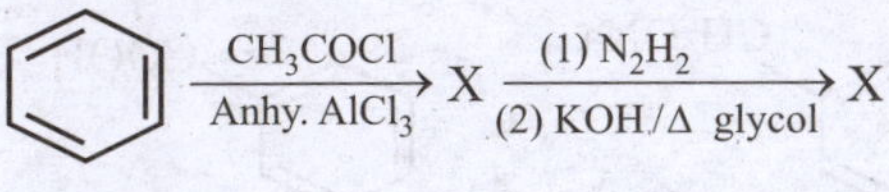

(a) Clemmensen reduction
(b) Stephen reduction
(c) Wolff-Kishner reduction
(d) Rosenmund reduction

32. Consider the reaction sequence **[May 22, 2025 (II)]**

$$\text{Dimethyl ketone} \xrightarrow[\text{(ii) } H_2O]{\text{(i) } CH_3MgCl} X \xrightarrow[\text{(ii) } CH_3Br]{\text{(i) Na}} Y$$

How many sp^3 carbons are present in Y?

(a) 5 (b) 4 (c) 3 (d) 6

33. The correct statement about the product of the following reaction is **[May 22, 2025 (I)]**

$$CH_3CHO \xrightarrow[\text{(ii) } H_2O]{\text{(i) } C_2H_5MgBr} \text{Product}$$

(a) It undergoes dehydration with 20% H_3PO_4 at 358 K.
(b) It gives ketone on oxidation with CrO_3.
(c) It does not give positive iodoform test.
(d) It is a vinylic alcohol.

34. A carbonyl compound $X(C_8H_8O)$ gives yellow precipitate with NaOI. Hemiacetal of X with methanol/dry HCl is **[May 21, 2025 (II)]**

(a) 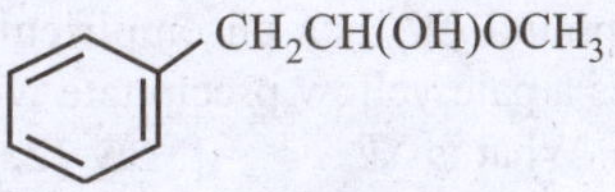

(b) 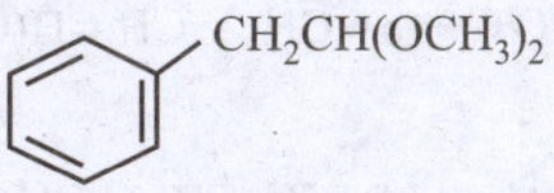

(c) 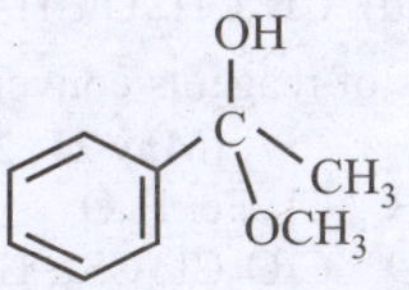

(d) 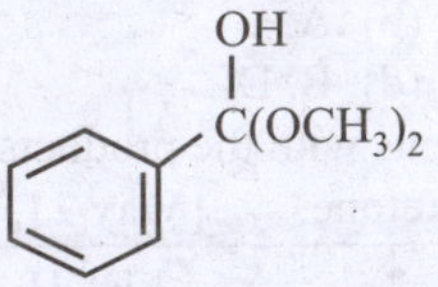

35. What are *x* and *y* in the following reaction sequence? **[May 21, 2025 (I)]**

$$C_2H_2 \xrightarrow[333\text{ K}]{x} CH_3CHO \xrightarrow[\text{(ii) }\Delta]{\text{(i) dil NaOH}} CH_3-CH=CH-CHO$$

$$\uparrow y$$

$$CH_3-CH=CH-CH_2OH$$

(a) H_2O / H_2SO_4; $KMnO_4 / H^+$
(b) H_2O / H_2SO_4; PCC
(c) $H_2O / H_2SO_4, Hg^{2+}$; $KMnO_4 / H^+$
(d) $H_2O / H_2SO_4, Hg^{2+}$; PCC

36. What are X. Y Z in the following reaction sequence respectively? **[May 23, 2024 (I)]**

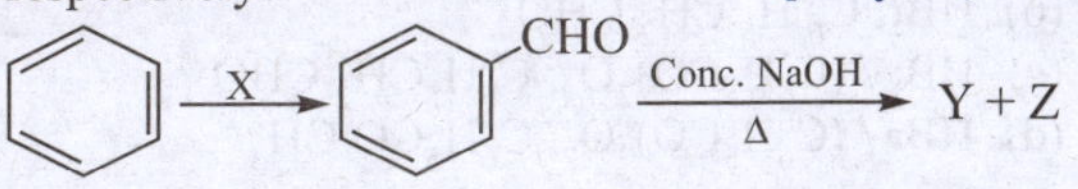

(a) CO, HCl, $AlCl_3$; 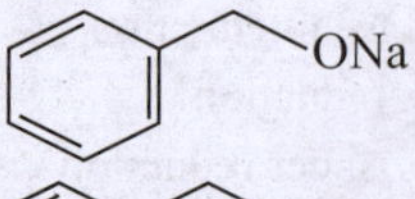

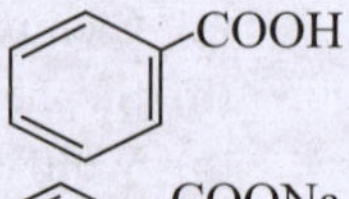

(b) CO, HCl, CuCl: 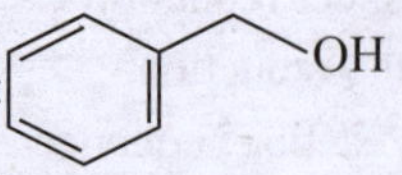

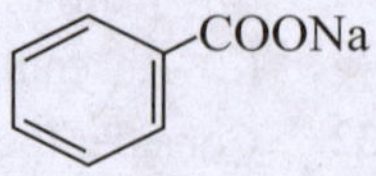

(c) HCHO, HCl, anhy, $AlCl_3$:
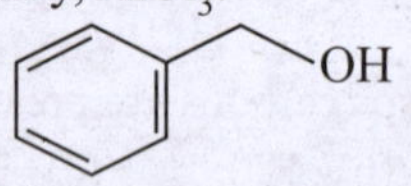

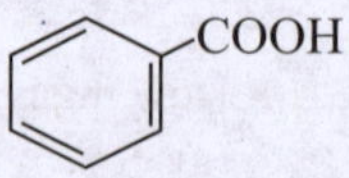

(d) CO, HCl : 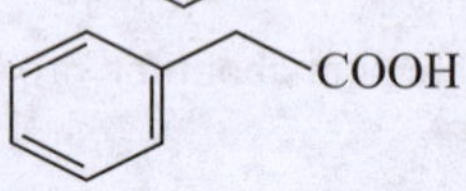

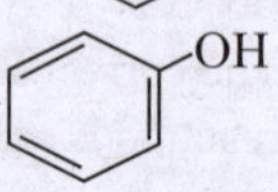

37. What is the major product 'Z' in the following reaction sequence? **[May 22, 2024 (II)]**

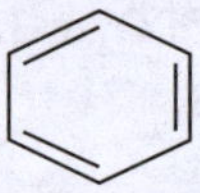 $\xrightarrow{\text{Oleum}}$ X $\xrightarrow[(2)\ H^+]{(1)\ NaOH}$ Y $\xrightarrow[(2)\ H^+]{(1)\ CHCl_3/NaOH}$ Z

(a) o-Hydroxy benzaldehyde
(b) p-Hydroxy benzaldehyde
(c) o-Hydroxy benzoic acid
(d) p-Hydroxy benzoic acid

38. An organic compound (X) has an empirical formula C_4H_8O. This gives a pale yellow precipitate with iodine in NaOH solution. What is X? **[May 22, 2024 (I)]**

(a) $CH_3CH_2CH_2CHO$ (b) $CH_2 = CH\,CH(OH)\,CH_3$

(c) $CH_3 - \underset{}{\overset{CH_2}{\overset{\|}{C}}} - O - CH_3$ (d) $CH_3CH_2\,O\,CH = CH_2$

39. Which of the following sets of reagents convert toluene to benzaldehyde? **[May 21, 2024 (II)]**

A. Cl_2/ hv; H_2O,Δ B. Cl_2/Fe; H_2O
C. $KMnO_4/OH^-$; H^+ D. CrO_2Cl_2/CS_2; H_3O^+
(a) B, C, D (b) A, C
(c) A, D (d) B, D

40. Match the following reagents with the products obtained when they reacted with a ketone. **[May 21, 2024 (I)]**

	List-I		List-II
A.	$C_6H_5NHNH_2$	I.	Schiff base
B.	NH_2OH	II.	Hydrazone
C.	$C_6H_5NH_2$	III.	Oxime
		IV.	Phenyl hydrazone

Correct answer is
(a) A-IV, B-III, C-I (b) A-IV, B-II, C-I
(c) A-II, B-III, C-IV (d) A-II, B-IV, C-III

41. Styrene on reaction with reagent X gave Y which on hydrolysis followed by oxidation gave Z. Z gives positive 2, 4 – DNP test but does not give iodoform test. What are X and Z respectively? **[May 20, 2024 (II)]**

(a) HBr; $C_6H_5COCH_3$
(b) HBr; $C_6H_5CH_2CHO$
(c) HBr / $(C_6H_5CO)_2O_2$; $C_6H_5CH_2CHO$
(d) HBr / $(C_6H_5CO)_2O_2$; $C_6H_5COCH_3$

42. 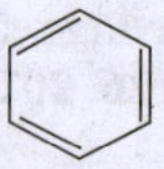 $+CH_3Cl \xrightarrow[AlCl_3]{\text{Anhy.}} A \xrightarrow[273-283K]{(1)\ CrO_3/(CH_3CO)_2O,} \xrightarrow{(2)\ H_3O^+,\ \Delta} B$

The incorrect statement about 'B' is **[May 20, 2024 (I)]**
(a) It gives test with Tollens reagent
(b) It gives test with Fehling's solution
(c) It does not give test with NaOH + I_2 solution
(d) It forms acid and alcohol with concentrated NaOH followed by acidification

43. A carbonyl compound X (C_3H_6O) on oxidation gave a carboxylic acid Y ($C_3H_6O_2$). Oxime of X is **[May 19, 2024 (II)]**

(a) 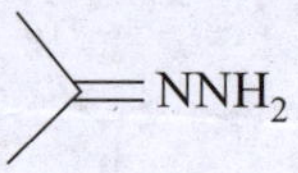

(b) 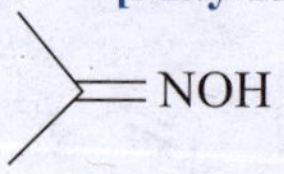

(c) 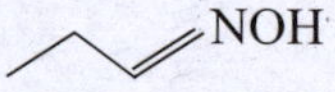

(d) 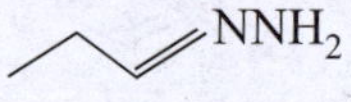

44. What are X and Y respectively in the following reaction sequence? **[May 18, 2024 (I)]**

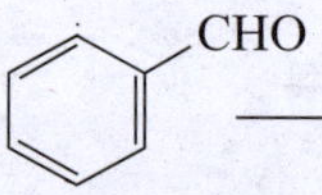

$\xrightarrow{X}$ Oxime $\xrightarrow{Y}$ 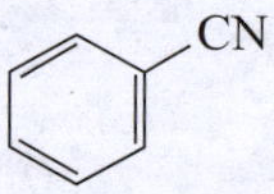

(a) NH_2NH_2, $C_6H_5SO_2Cl$ / Pyridine
(b) NH_2NH_2, $(CH_3CO)_2O$
(c) NH_2OH, $C_6H_5SO_2Cl$/Pyridine
(d) NH_2OH, $(CH_3CO)_2O$

45. The number of aldehydes that undergo Cannizaro reaction from the following are Phenyl ethanal, Methanal, 2 - Methoxy propanal, Trichoroethanal **[May 18, 2023 (II)]**
(a) 2 (b) 3 (c) 4 (d) 1

46. Which of the following reagents will convert isobutyraldehyde to the corresponding acid? **[May 17, 2023 (II)]**

HNO_3	NH_2NH_2/OH^-	$2[Ag(NH_3)_2]^+$	NaOH
I	II	III	IV

(a) I, III (b) I, II (c) II, IV (d) III, IV

47. What are 'X' and 'Y' in the following reaction?

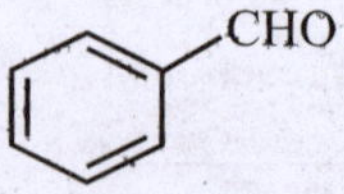

$\xrightarrow[\Delta]{\text{Conc, NaOH}}$ X + Y

[May 17, 2023 (II)]

(a) 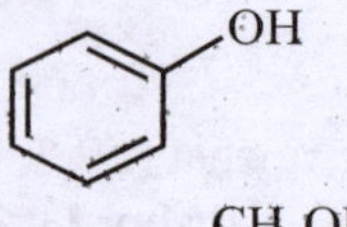

\+ 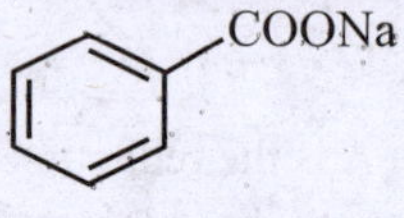

(b) 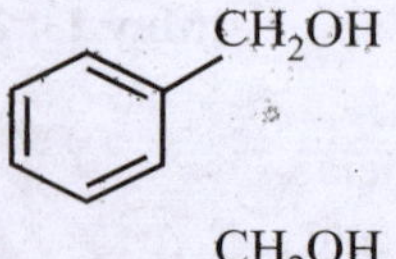

\+ 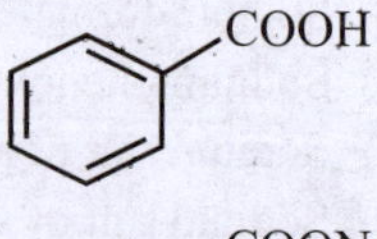

(c) 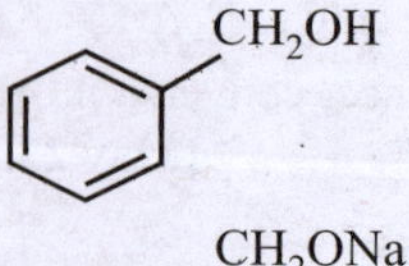

\+ 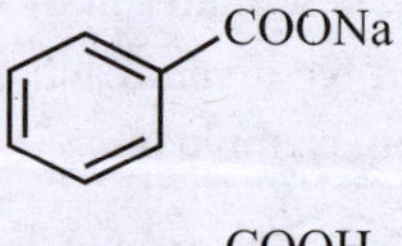

(d) 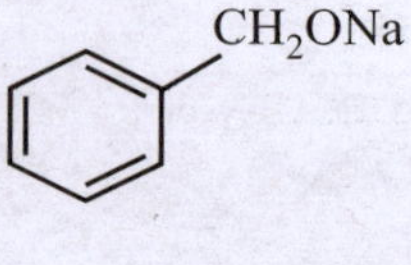

\+ 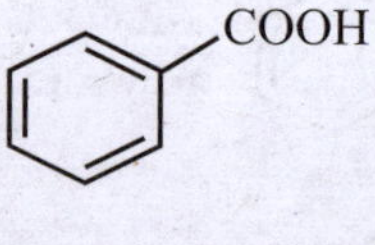

48. Which of the following is a hemiacetal? **[May 17, 2023 (I)]**

(a) 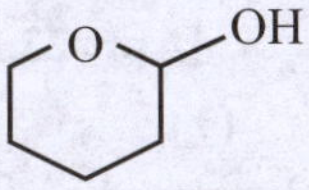

(b) 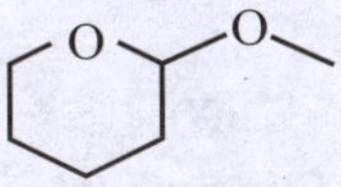

(c) 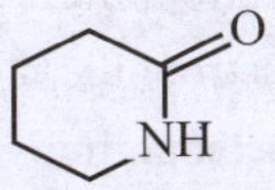

(d) 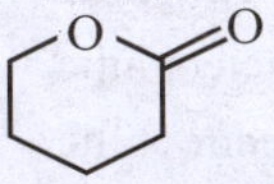

49. What are X and Y respectively in the following reaction?

$CH_3CH_2CHO + 2Cu^{2+} + OH^- \rightarrow X + Y + 3H_2O$

(a) CH_3CH_2COOH, $Cu(OH)_2$ **[May 16, 2023 (I)]**
(b) $CH_3CH_2COO^-$, Cu
(c) CH_3CH_2COOH, Cu_2O
(d) $CH_3CH_2COO^-$, Cu_2O

50. The number of products obtained in the following reaction is **[May 15, 2023 (I)]**

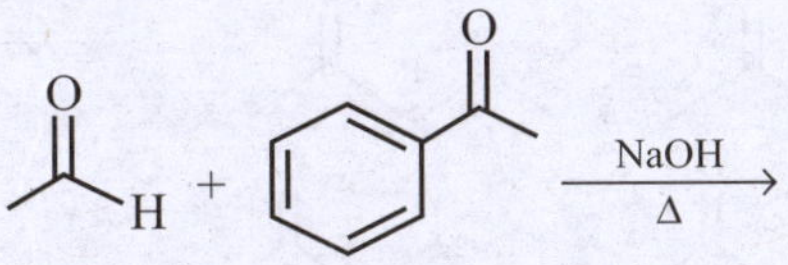

(a) 1 (b) 3 (c) 2 (d) 4

51. What are 'X' and 'Y' respectively in the following reactions? **[May 15, 2023 (I)]**

$$C_6H_5CHO + C_6H_5COCH_3 \xrightarrow[293K]{OH^-} \underset{\text{major}}{X} \xrightarrow{NaBH_4} Y$$

(a) $C_6H_5COCH = C(CH_3)\ C_6H_5$, $C_6H_5CH_2CH_2COC_6H_5$
(b) $C_6H_5COCH = C(CH_3)\ C_6H_5$, $C_6H_5 = CHCH\ (OH)\ C_6H_5$
(c) $C_6H_5CH = CHCOC_6H_5$, $C_6H_5CH = CHCH\ (OH)\ C_6H_5$
(d) $C_6H_5CH = CHCOC_6H_5$, $C_6H_5CH_2CH_2COC_6H_5$

52. With reference to the carbonyl group which statement(s) is/are correct? **[July 7, 2022 (II)]**

A. Carbonyl carbon is electrophilic
B. Carbonyl carbon is nucleophilic
C. Carbonyl oxygen is electrophilic
D. Carbonyl oxygen is nucleophilic

(a) A, D (b) B, C (d) B only (d) C only

53. Identify the major product from the following reaction sequence **[July 6, 2022 (I)]**

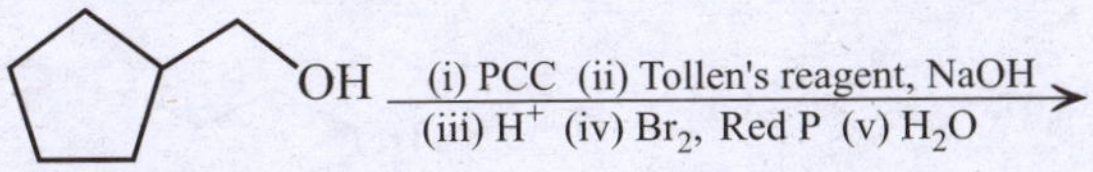

(a) 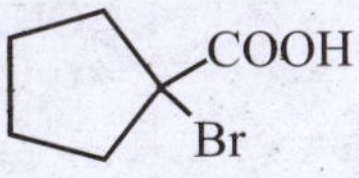

(b) 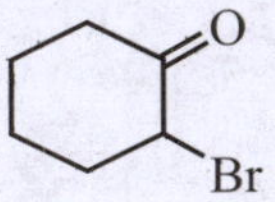

(c) 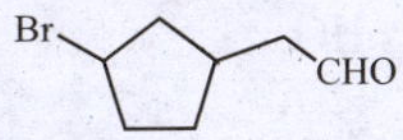

(d) 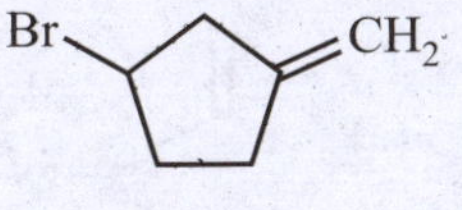

54. Identify the major product formed from the following

$$CH_3-CH{=}CH_2 \xrightarrow[\text{(iii) Cu/573 K} \quad \text{(iv) Ba(OH)}_2,\Delta]{\text{(i) HBr} \quad \text{(ii) NaOH}}$$ **[July 5, 2022 (II)]**

(a) 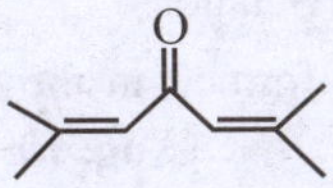

(b) 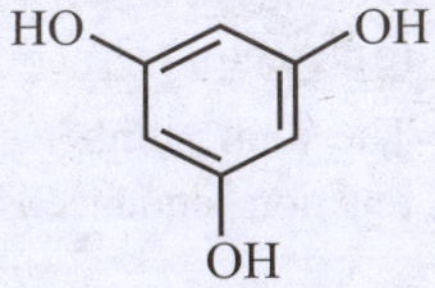

(c) 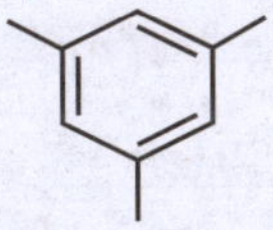
(d) 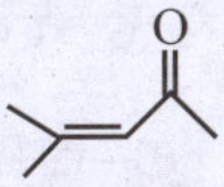

55. Identify the major product of the following reaction **[July 4, 2022 (II)]**

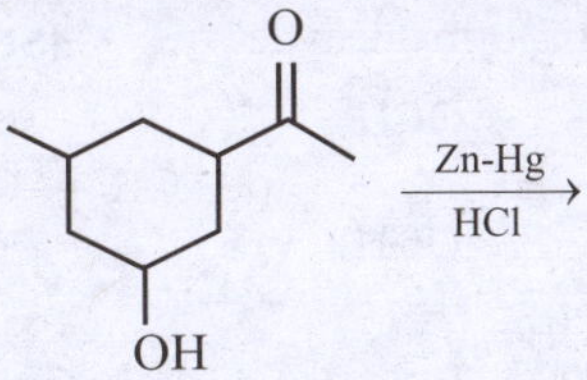

(a) 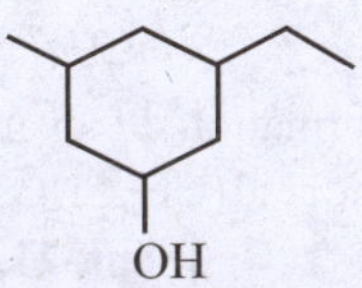

(b) 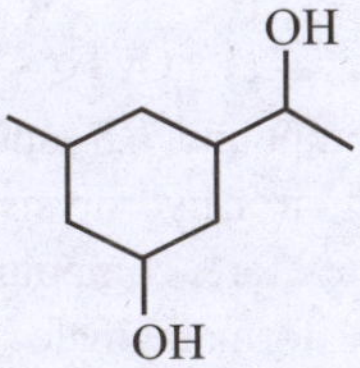

(c) 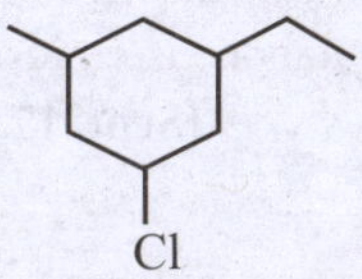

(d) 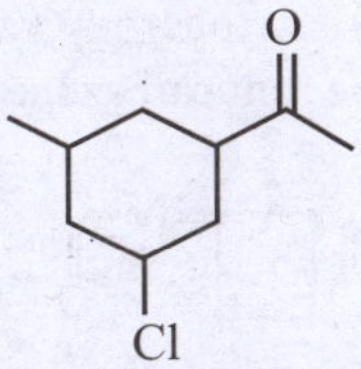

56. Arrange the following in increasing order of their reactivity for nucleophilic addition reaction **[July 4, 2022 (I)]**

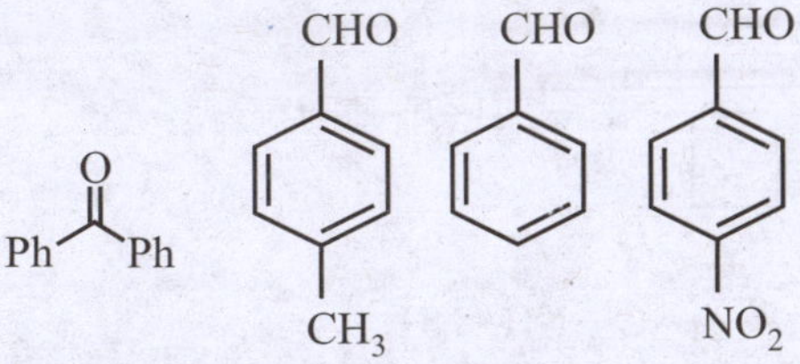

(i) (ii) (iii) (iv)

(a) (i) < (ii) < (iii) < (iv) (b) (i) < (iv) < (iii) < (ii)
(c) (iii) < (ii) < (i) < (iv) (d) (iii) < (i) < (ii) < (iv)

57. What is (*P*) in the reaction given below?

$$(P) \xrightarrow[\text{(ii) } H_3O^+]{\text{(i) } CH_3MgBr} (R) \xrightarrow[\text{(ii) } \Delta]{\text{(i) dil. NaOH}}$$

4-Methyl-pent-3-en-2-one

[Aug. 23, 2021 (I)]

(a) Propanone (b) Ethanamine
(c) Ethane nitrile (d) Ethane

58. Identify (*Z*) in the following reaction.

$$CH_3COOH \xrightarrow{LiAlH_4} (X) \xrightarrow[573\,K]{Cu} (Y) \xrightarrow{dil.\,NaOH} (Z)$$

[Aug. 20, 2021 (II)]

(a) Aldol (b) Ketol
(c) Acetol (d) Butanol

59. The total number of products formed in the following reaction sequence is **[Aug. 19, 2021 (I)]**

$$CH_3COCl \xrightarrow{(i)\,(CH_3)_2Cd} (P)$$

$$(P) + CH_3CHO \xrightarrow{(ii)\,NaOH\,(aq),\,\Delta} ?$$

(a) 2 (b) 4 (c) 1 (d) 3

60. Which of the following represent the structure of methyl hemiacetal of formaldehyde? **[Sept. 21, 2020 (I)]**

(a) $CH_3-CH(OCH_3)(OCH_3)$ (b) $CH_3-CH(OH)(OCH_3)$
(c) $H_2C(OH)(OCH_3)$ (d) $H_2C(OCH_3)(OCH_3)$

61. Compound '*A*' undergoes formation of cyanohydrins, which on hydrolysis gives lactic acid ($CH_3CHOHCOOH$). Therefore, compound '*A*' is **[Sept. 21, 2020 (I)]**

(a) formaldehyde (b) acetaldehyde
(c) acetone (d) benzaldehyde

62. The semicarbazone of cyclobutanone is represented as **[Sept. 17, 2020 (I)]**

(a) 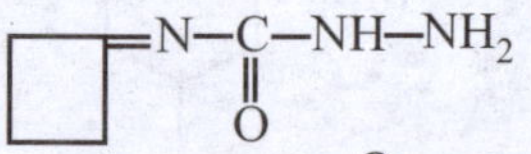

(b) 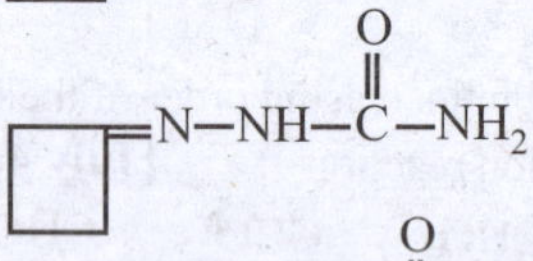

(c) 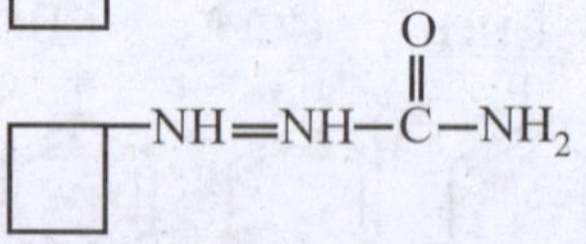

(d) 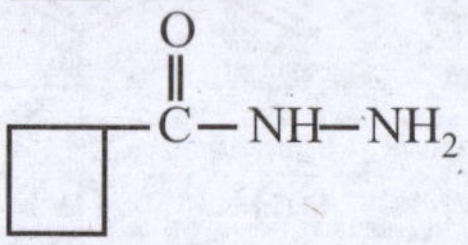

63. Choose the incorrect statement among the following. **[Sept. 17, 2020 (II)]**

A. The reactivity of aromatic aldehydes and ketones is less than that of aliphatic carbonyl compounds toward nucleophilic addition reactions.
B. Benzaldehyde does not give Fehling's test.
C. The H-atoms in ethanal are acidic in nature.
D. *p*-Nitro benzaldehyde is less reactive than benzaldehyde towards nucleophilic addition reactions.

(a) A (b) B (c) C (d) D

64. Alkenes (*X*) and carbonyl compounds (*Y*) participate in which of the following addition reactions? **[Apr. 22, 2019 (I)]**

	(*X*)	(*Y*)
(a)	Electrophilic	Electrophilic
(b)	Nucleophilic	Electrophilic
(c)	Electrophilic	Nucleophilic
(d)	Nucleophilic	Nucleophilic

65. Which one of the following is used for purification of aldehydes? **[Apr. 22, 2019 (I)]**

(a) NaOCl (b) $NaHSO_3$
(c) $C_6H_5SO_2Cl$ (d) Na_2SO_4

66. Mixed aldol products obtained from aldol condensation of ethanal and propanone are **[Apr. 22, 2019 (II)]**

(a) 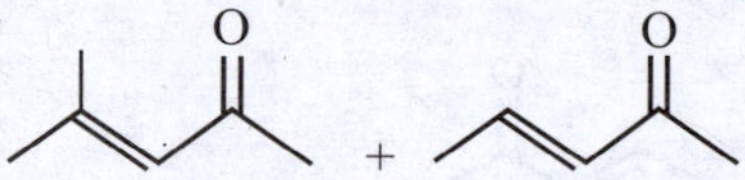

(b) 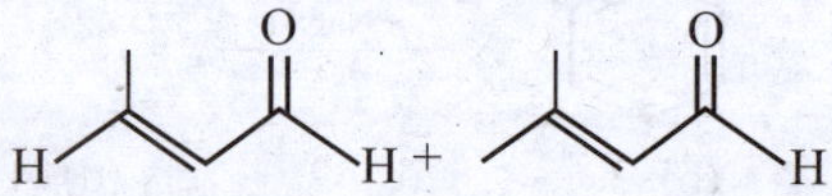

(c) 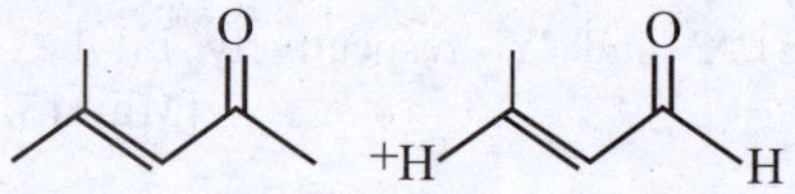

(d) 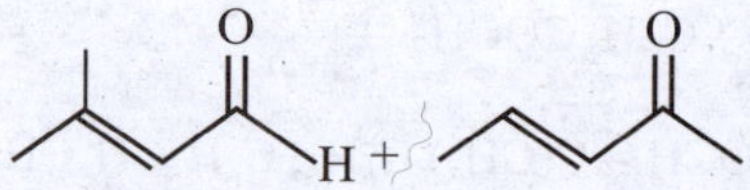

67. What are the products formed when an aldehyde (*R*CHO) is reacted with Tollen's reagent? **[Apr. 21, 2019 (I)]**

(a) Ag, H_2O, RCH_2OH, NH_3
(b) Ag, H_2O, $RCOO^-$, H_2
(c) Ag, H_2O, $RCOO^-$, NH_3
(d) Ag_2, H_2O, $RCOO^-$, NH_3

68. Identify *X, Y, Z* in the following reaction sequence **[Apr. 20, 2019 (II)]**

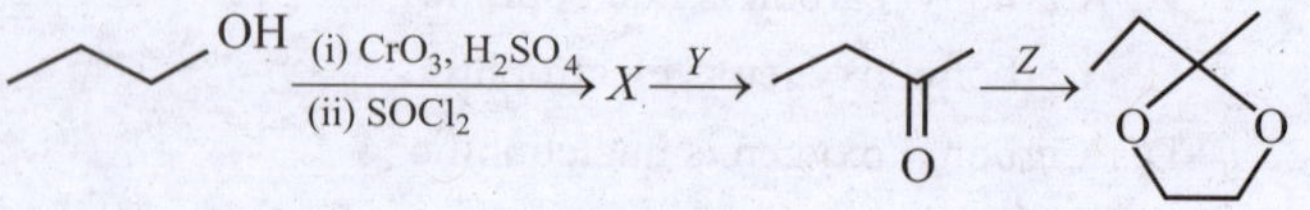

X *Y* *Z*

(a) 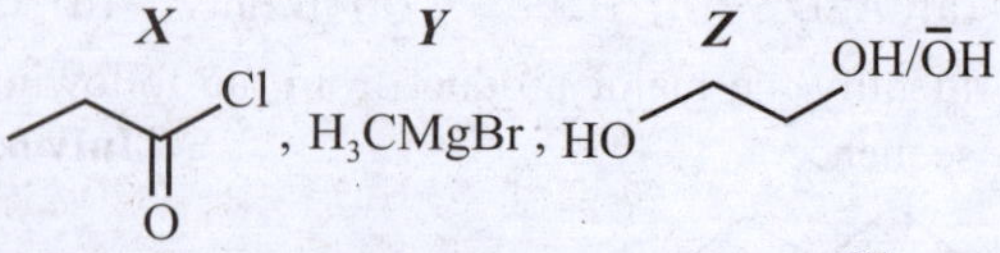

(b) 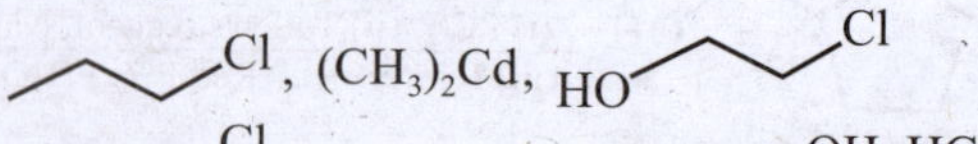

(c) 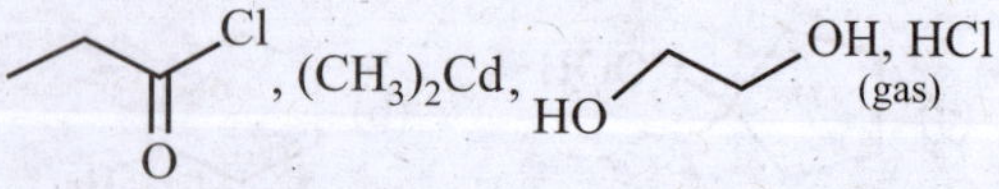

(d) 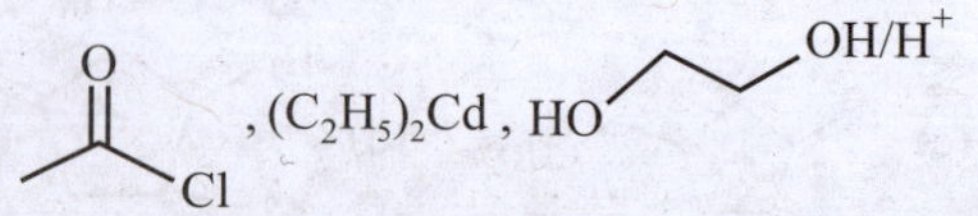

69. Identify *A, B* and *C* in the following reactions. **[2018]**

Isopropyl chloride $\xrightarrow{\text{NaOH}} A \xrightarrow{\text{Cu/573K}} B \xrightarrow{\text{NaOI}} C + \text{Iodoform}$

	A	B	C
(a)	$CH_3CH_2CH_2OH$	$CH_3CH_2CH_2CHO$	CH_3CH_2COONa
(b)	CH_3CH_2OH	CH_3CHO	HCOONa
(c)	$CH_3-CH(OH)-CH_3$	CH_3COCH_3	CH_3COONa
(d)	$CH_3-CH(OH)-CH(OH)-CH_3$	$H_3C-C(=O)-C(=O)-CH_3$	CH_3COONa

70. In which of the following reactions, the product is not correct? **[2016]**

(a) $CH_3CHO \xrightarrow{LiAlH_4} CH_3CH_2OH$

(b) $CH_3COCH_3 \xrightarrow[\text{HCl}]{\text{Zn-Hg}} CH_3-CH(OH)-CH_3$

(c) $CH_3CH_2CHO \xrightarrow[\text{(ii) KOH, Ethylene glycol}/\Delta]{\text{(i) } H_2N-NH_2} CH_3CH_2CH_3$

(d) $CH_3CH_2CHO \xrightarrow{KMnO_4} CH_3CH_2COOH$

Topic 3 Preparation and Properties of Carboxylic Acids and their Derivatives

71. An alkyl halide A (C_4H_9Br) reacts with aqueous NaOH and gives corresponding alcohol B. Reaction of B with reagent C gives a carboxylic acid D. What are C and D? **[May 18, 2026 (II)]**

(a) $[Ag(NH_3)_2]^+$; 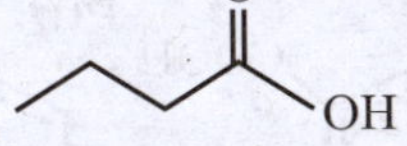

(b) PCC; 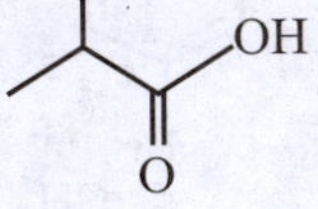

(c) dil. $KMnO_4$, 273K; 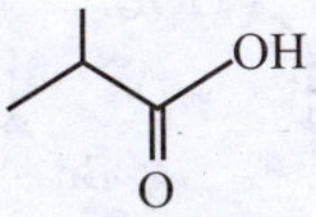

(d) CrO_3-H_2SO_4; 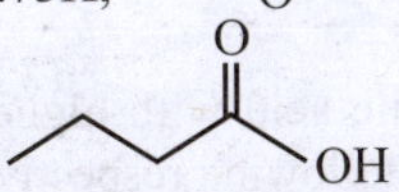

72. Observe the following set of reactions

I. $\underset{X}{C_6H_5COOH} \xrightarrow[\text{Conc. } H_2SO_4]{\text{Conc. } HNO_3} Y$

II. $\underset{A}{C_6H_5CH_2COOH} \xrightarrow[\text{(ii) } H_2O]{\text{(i) } Br_2\text{/Red Phosphorus}} B$

Correct answer regarding the pKa of X, Y and A, B is (Conc. = , Red phosphorus =) **[May 15, 2026 (II)]**

(a) Y < X ; B < A (b) Y > X ; B > A

(c) Y > X ; B < A (d) Y < X ; B > A

73. Which of the following does not form benzoic acid on oxidation with alkaline $KMnO_4$ followed by acidification? **[May 15, 2026 (I)]**

(a) 1-phenylpropane

(b) 2-phenylpropane

(c) Acetophenone

(d) 2-methyl-2-phenylpropane

74. In which of the following sets, reactant and reagent are correctly matched to get corresponding carboxylic acid

I. 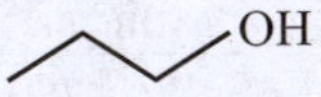 ------ $CrO_3 + H_2SO_4$

II. 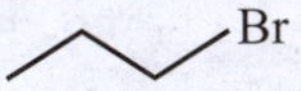 ------ CO_2, H_3O^+

III. 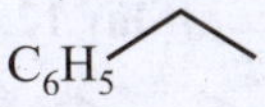 ------ $KMnO_4|OH^-$, H_3O^+

Correct answer is **[May 14, 2026 (II)]**

(a) I only (b) I, II only

(c) I, III only (d) II only

75. What are X and Y in the following set of reaction? **[May 13, 2026 (I)]**

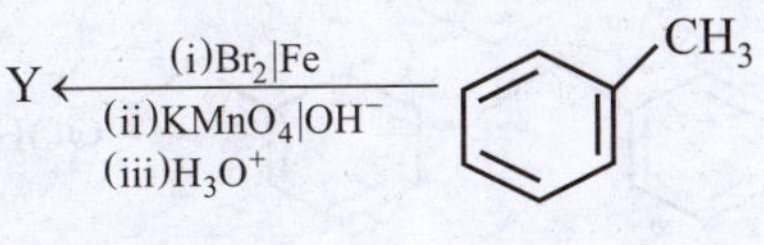

$\xrightarrow[\text{(iii)} Br_2|Fe]{\text{(i)} KMnO_4|OH^- \text{ (ii) } H_3O^+} X$

(a) 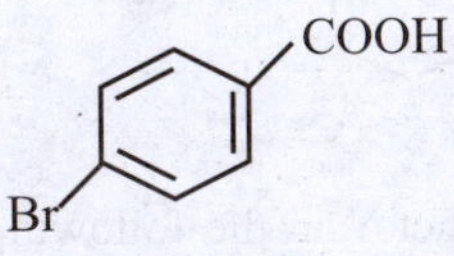 ; 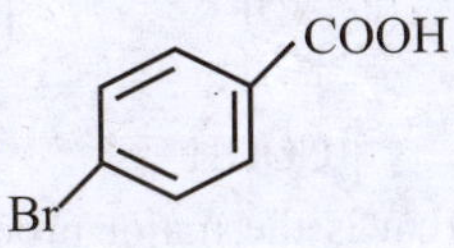

(b) 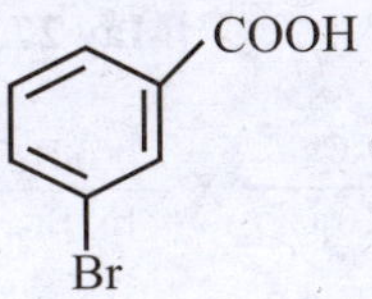 ; 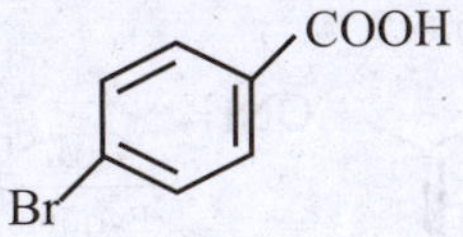

(c) 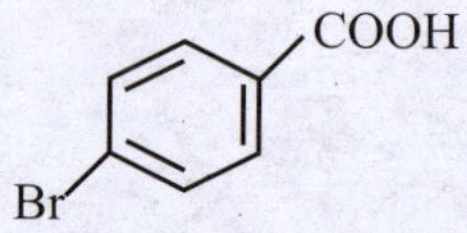 ; 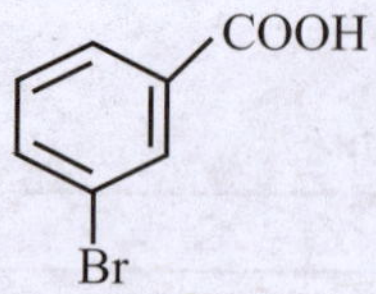

(d) 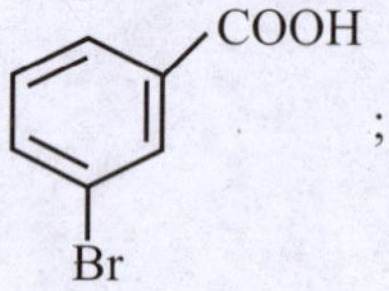 ; 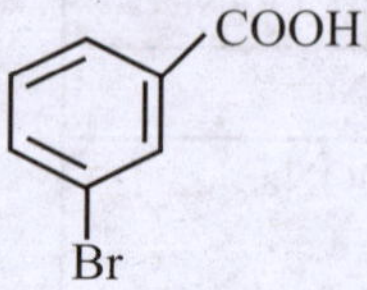

76. Match the following **[May 12, 2026 (II)]**

List-I (compound)		**List-II (pK_a)**
A. C_6H_5COOH	I.	3.41
B. $p-CH_3O-C_6H_4COOH$	II.	4.19
C. $p-O_2N-C_6H_4COOH$	III.	4.46

Correct answer is

(a) A - II, B - I, C - III (b) A - II, B - III, C - I

(c) A - I, B - II, C - III (d) A - III, B - II, C - I

77. What are X and Y in the following set of reactions?

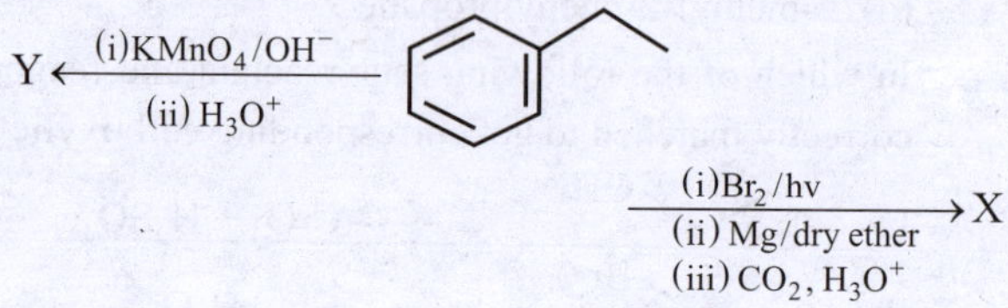

options: **[May 12, 2026 (I)]**

(a) 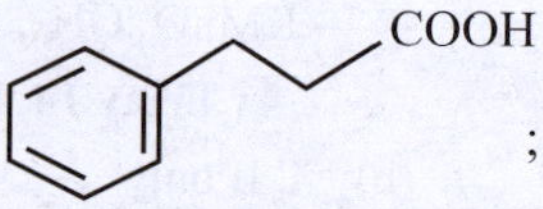 ; 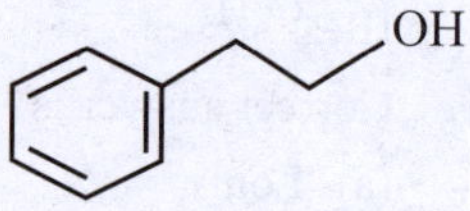

(b) 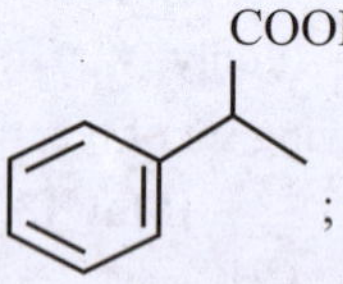 ; 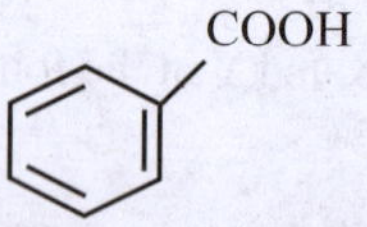

(c) 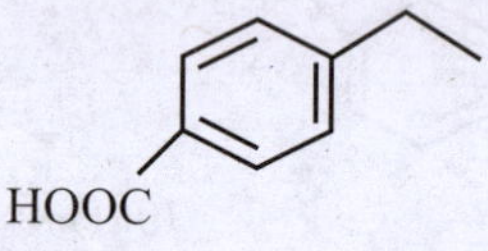 ; 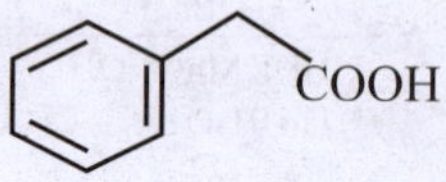

(d) 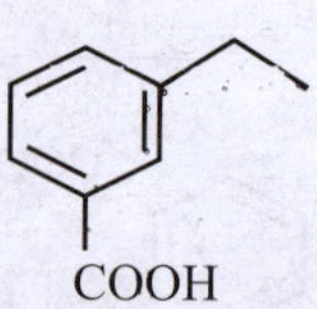 ; 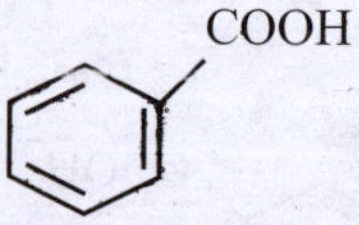

78. What is the major product Y in the following reaction sequence? **[May 27, 2025 (I)]**

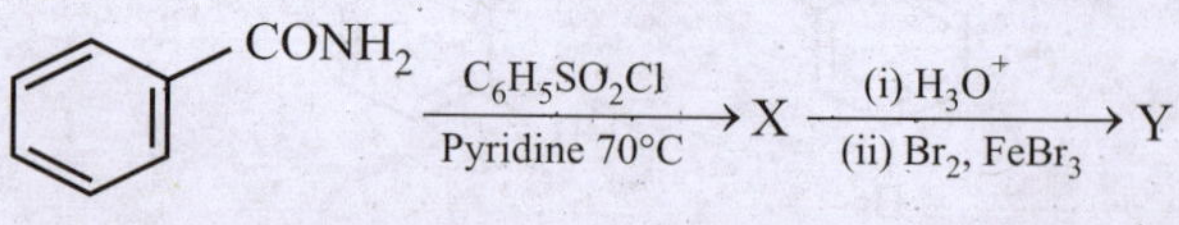

(a) 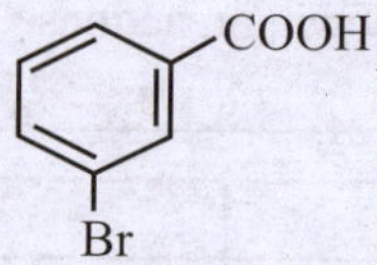 (b) 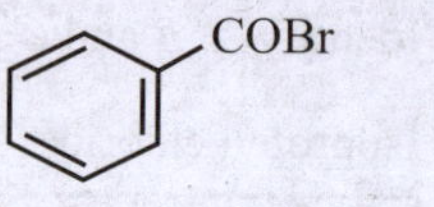

(c) 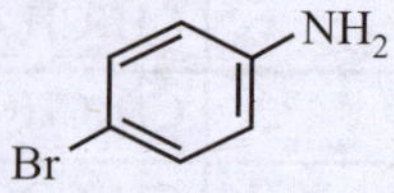 (d) 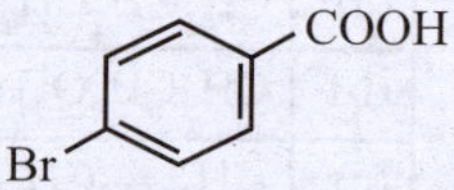

79. The structures of succinic acid (x) and malonic acid (y), respectively, are **[May 26, 2025 (II)]**

(a) 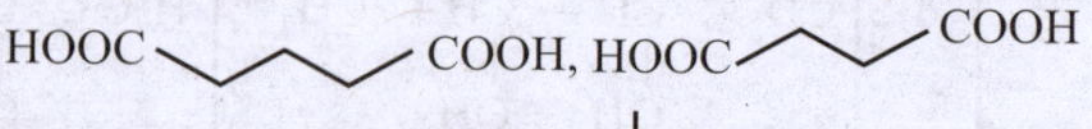

(b) 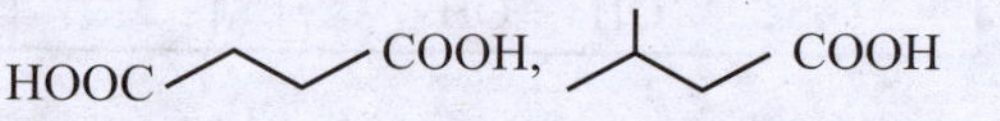

(c) 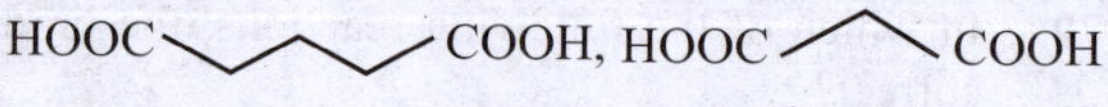

(d) 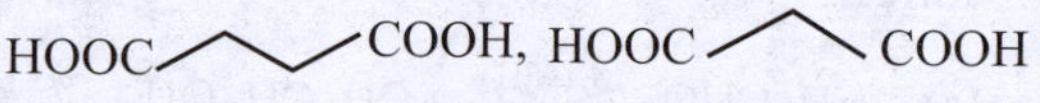

80. What are the major products X and Y respectively in the following set of reactions? **[May 26, 2025 (II)]**

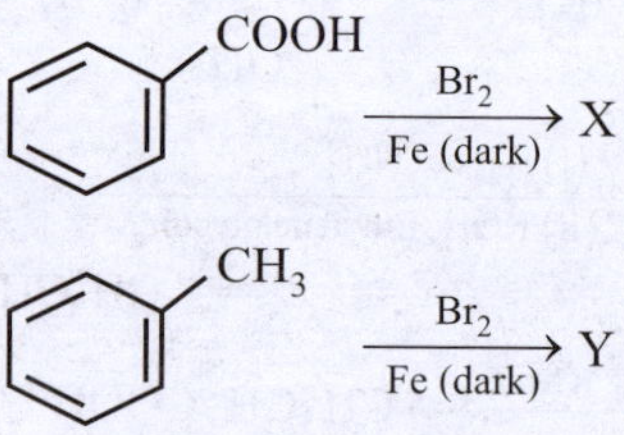

(a) 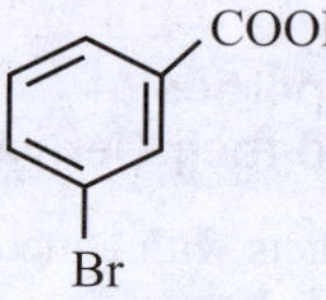 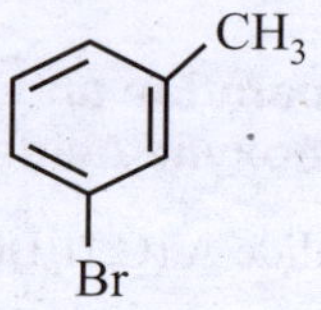

(b) 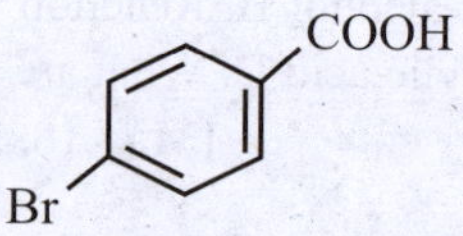 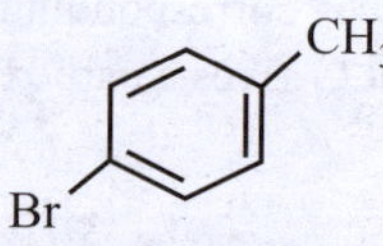

(c) 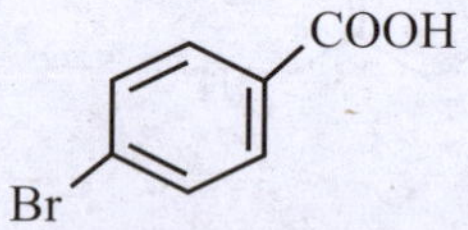 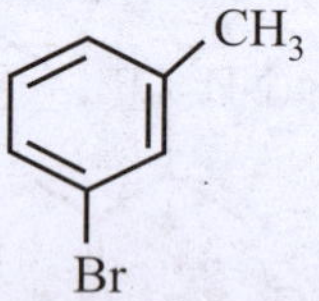

(d) 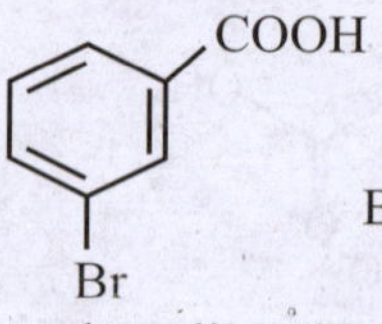 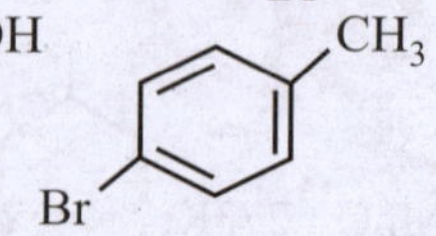

81. The carboxylic acid with highest pK_a and lowest pK_a values of the following respectively are **[May 26, 2025 (I)]**

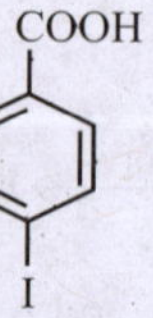 (I) 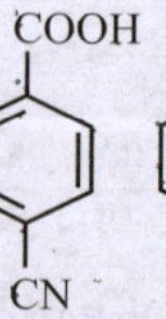 (II) 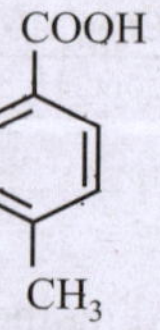 (III) 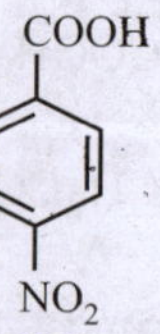 (IV)

(a) I, II (b) I, IV (c) III, II (d) III, IV

82. The final product (C) in the given reaction sequence is

$C_6H_5COOH \xrightarrow{SOCl_2} (A) \xrightarrow[\text{anhy. } AlCl_3]{C_6H_6}$

$(B) \xrightarrow[(ii)\ KOH/(CH_2OH)_2]{(i)\ NH_2-NH_2} (C)$ **[May 24, 2025 (I)]**

(a) Benzophenone (b) Diphenylmethane
(c) Diphenyl methanol (d) Benzoic acid

83. Which one of the following compounds does not give benzoic acid when treated with alkaline $KMnO_4$? **[May 23, 2025 (I)]**

(a) Acetophenone (b) n-Propyl benzene
(c) Styrene (d) t-Butyl benzene

84. What are X and Y respectively in the following set of reactions? **[May 22, 2025 (II)]**

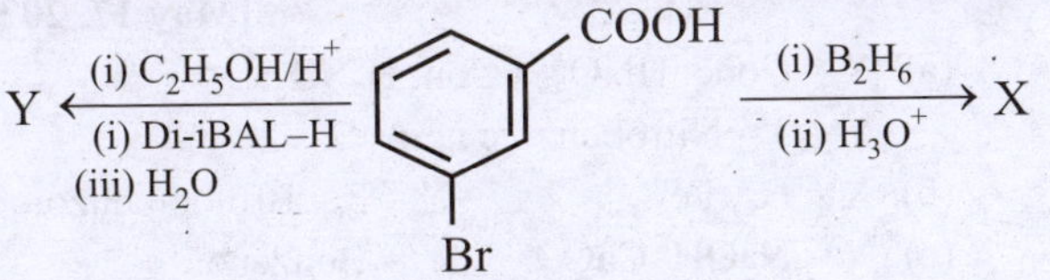

(a) 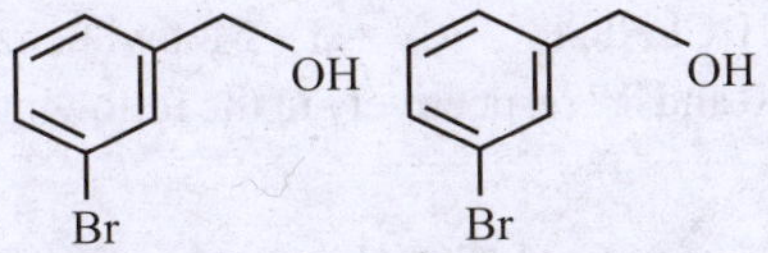

(b) 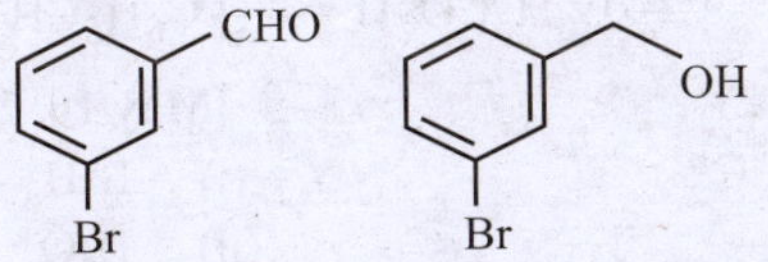

(c) 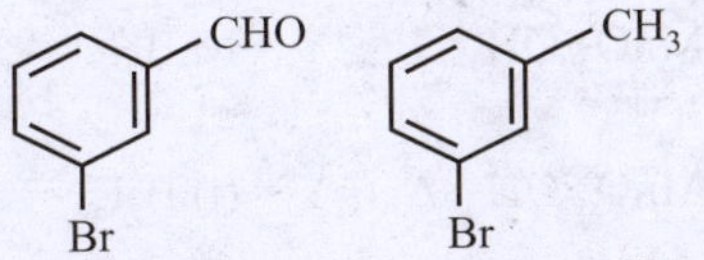

(d) 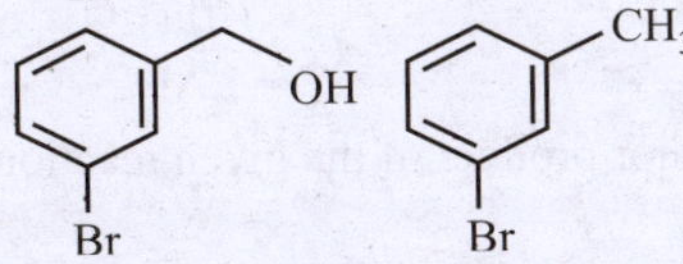

85. The most acidic carboxylic acid is **[May 21, 2025 (II)]**

(a) 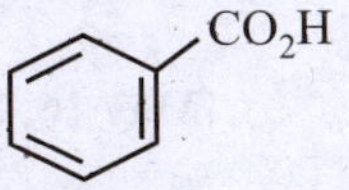

(b) 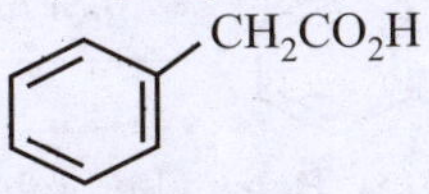

(c) HCOOH (d) CH_3COOH

86. Arrange the products I, II, III from the following reactions in decreasing order of their acid strength. **[May 21, 2025 (I)]**

(A) 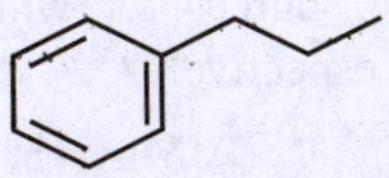 $\xrightarrow[(ii)\ H_3O^+]{(i)\ KMnO_4/OH^-}$ I

(B) $CH_3COOH \xrightarrow[(ii)\ H_2O]{(i)\ Br_2/\text{red P}}$ II

(C) 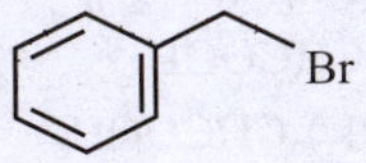

$\xrightarrow[(ii)\ CO_2/\text{dry ether}]{(i)\ Mg/\text{dry ether}}$ (iii) H_3O^+ III

(a) III > II > I (b) III > I > II
(c) II > I > III (d) I > II > III

87. What are X and Y respectively in the following reactions? **[May 21, 2024 (I)]**

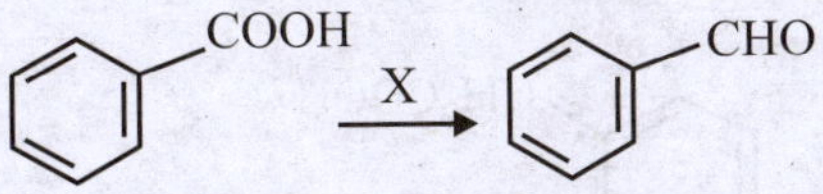

$\xrightarrow[OH^-,\ 293\ K]{C_6H_5COCH_3}$ Y (Major product)

(a) (i) $SOCl_2$, (ii) $H_2|Ni$;

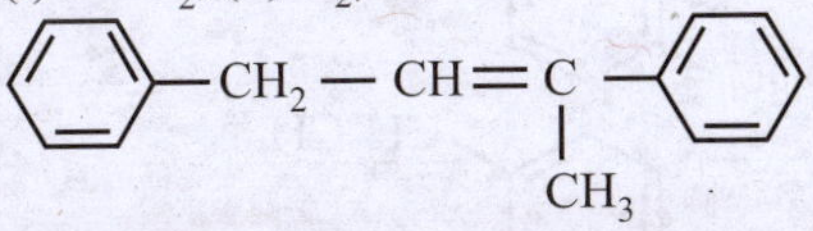

(b) (i) $SOCl_2$, (ii) $H_2|Ni$;

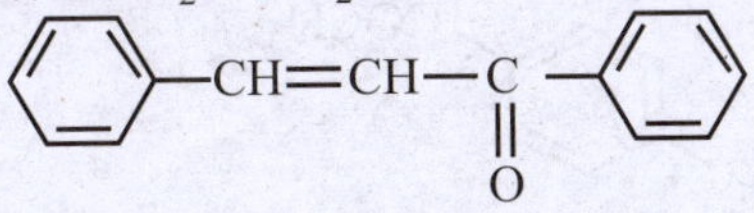

(c) (i) $C_2H_5OH|H^+$, (ii) DiBAL-H (iii) H_2O;

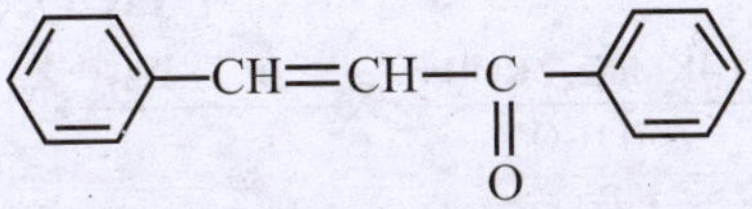

(d) (i) $C_2H_5OH|H^+$, (ii) DiBAL-H (iii) H_2O;

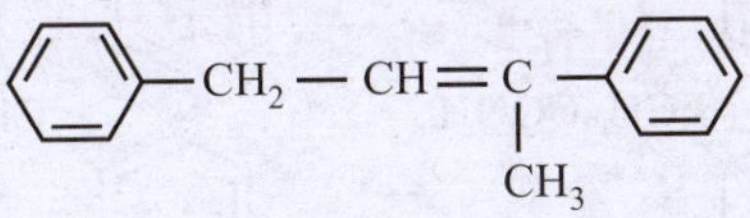

88. What is Y in the following reaction sequence? **[May 19, 2024 (II)]**

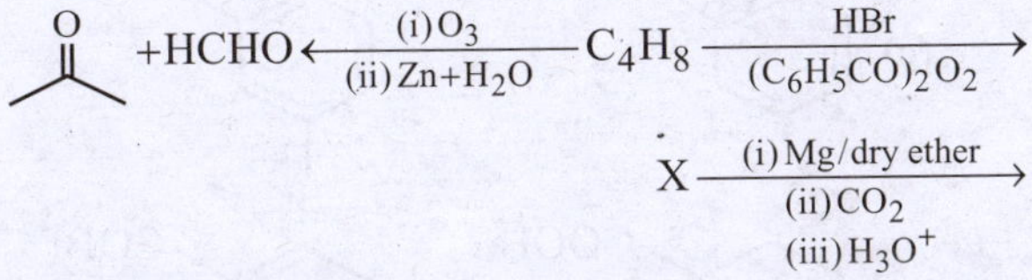

(a) 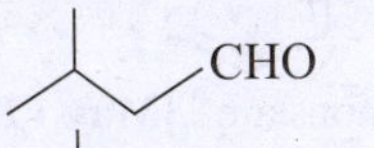

(b) 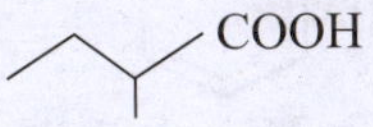

(c) 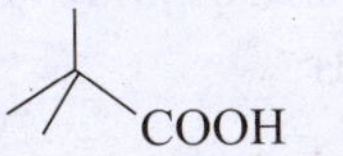

(d) 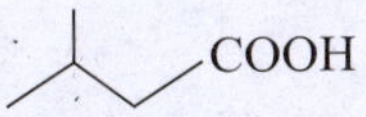

89. The 'X' in the following conversion is

$H_3CCH_2COOH \xrightarrow{x} CH_3CHBrCOOH$ **[May 19, 2023 (I)]**

(a) (i) Br_2/P red, (ii) H_2O
(b) (i) Br_2/CCl_4, (ii) H_2O
(c) Br_2/OH^-
(d) PBr_3

90. The preferred reagent for the following conversion is

$CH_3CH_2COOH \rightarrow CH_3CH_2COCl$ **[May 19, 2023 (I)]**

(a) HCl (b) HOCl
(c) $SOCl_2$ (d) NaOCl

91. What is 'X' in the following reaction? **[May 18, 2023 (II)]**

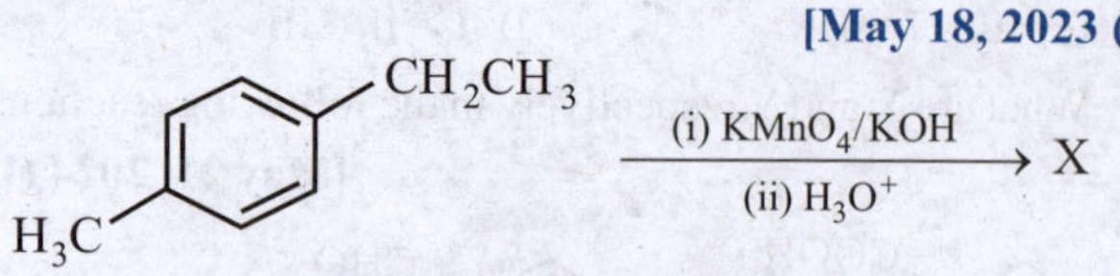

(a) 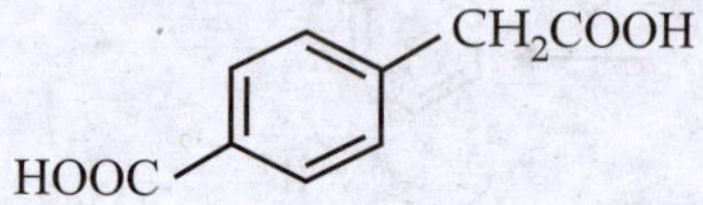

(b) 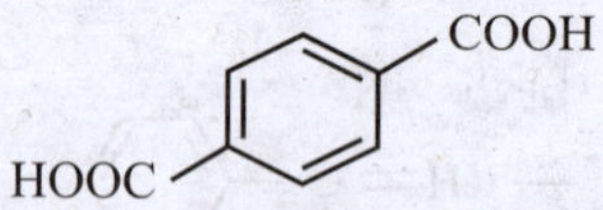

(c) 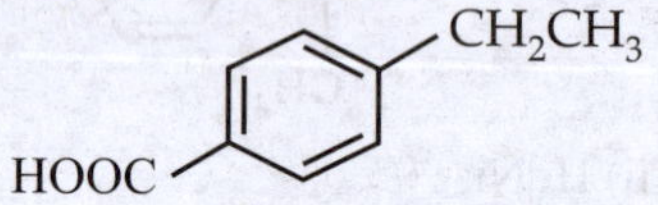

(d) 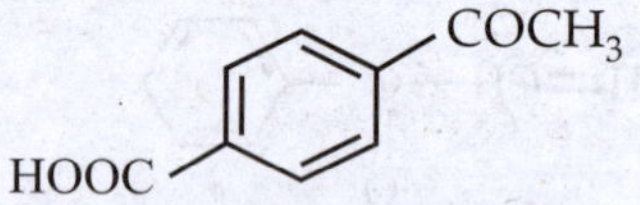

92. What are 'X' and 'Y' respectively in the following reaction sequence? **[May 17, 2023 (II)]**

$$\text{Styrene} \xrightarrow[\text{(ii) } H_3O^+]{\text{(i)} KMnO_4 / KOH} X \xrightarrow{Br_2 / FeBr_3} Y$$

(a) 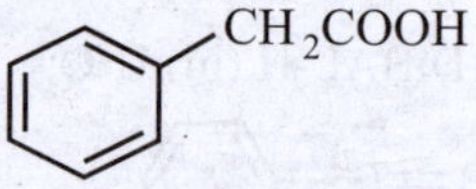 , 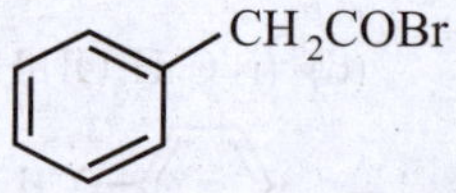

(b) 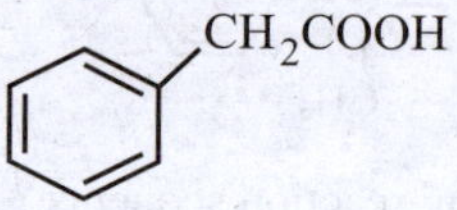 , 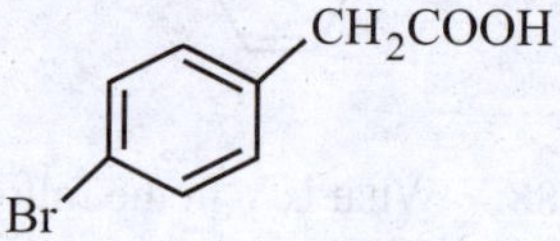

(c) 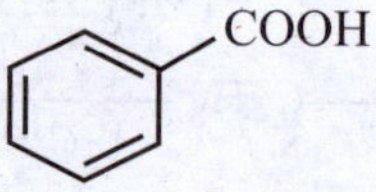 , 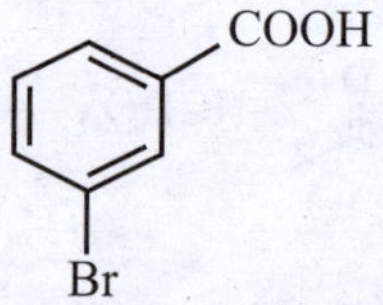

(d) 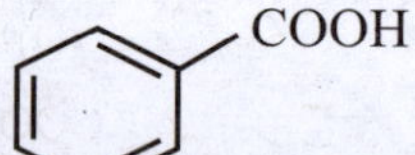 , 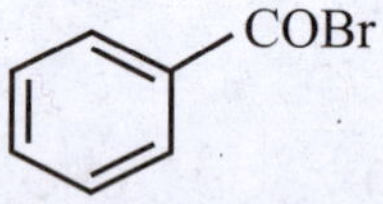

93. X and Y in the following reactions are **[May 17, 2023 (I)]**

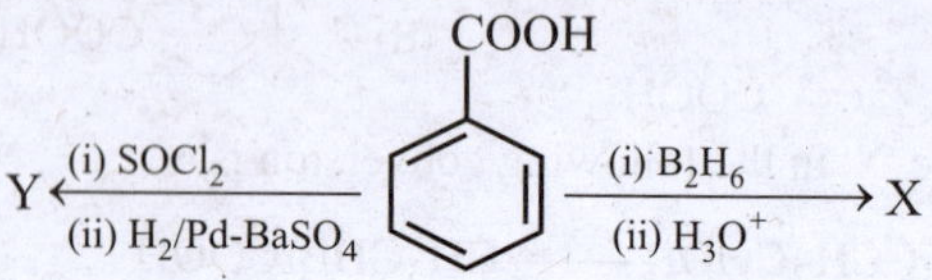

(a) 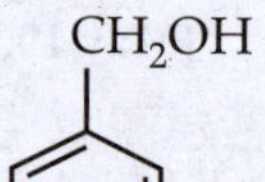 , 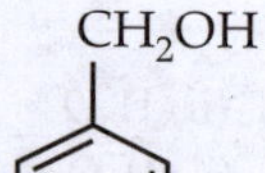

(b) 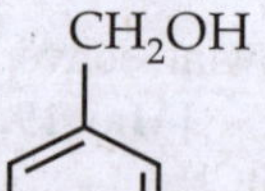 , 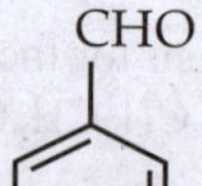

(c) 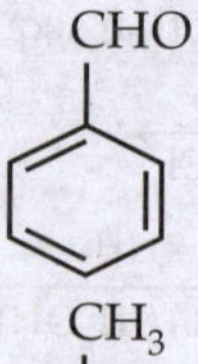 , 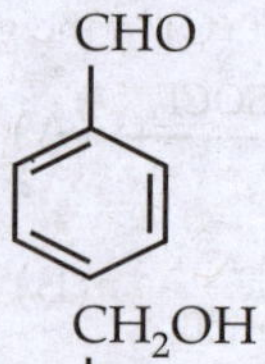

(d) 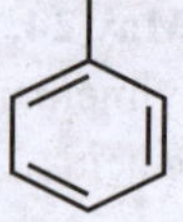 , 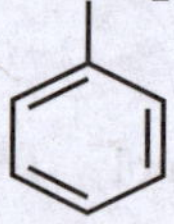

94. In the reaction, if X is the reagent and Y is the product, which of the following is not feasible?

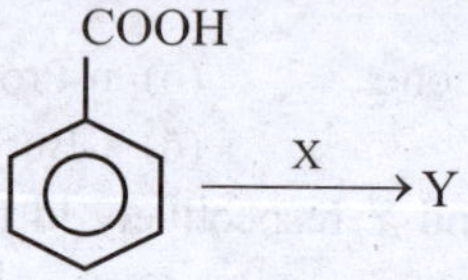

[May 17, 2023 (I)]

(a) X = Conc. HNO_3 + Con. H_2SO_4; Y = 3 – Nitrobenzoic acid

(b) X = Br_2/Fe   Y = 3 – Bromo benzoic acid

(c) X = NaOH, CaO   Y = Benzene

(d) X = $CH_3Cl/AlCl_3$ Y = 3 – Methyl benzoic acid

95. What are 'X' and 'Y' respectively in the following reaction sequence?

$$C_6H_5CH_3 \xrightarrow{X} C_6H_5CO_2H \xrightarrow{Y} C_6H_5CH_2OH$$

[May 16, 2023 (II)]

(a) X = PCC ;   Y = (i) B_2H_6 (ii) H_3O^+

(b) X = (i) $KMnO_4/OH^-$; (ii)H_3O^+ Y = $NaBH_4$

(c) X = (i) $KMnO_4/OH^-$, Δ; (ii) H_3O^+ Y = (i) B_2H_6 (ii) H_3O^+

(d) X = PCC;   Y = LAH

96. Identify the major product of the given reaction

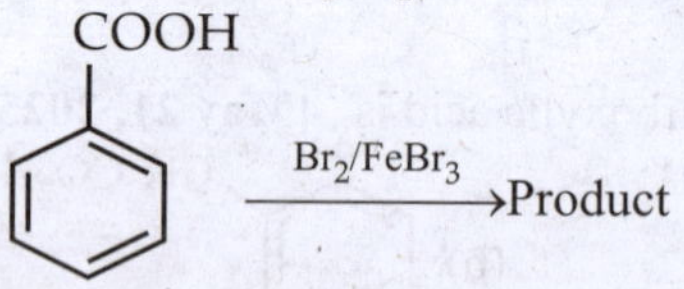

[May 16, 2023 (II)]

(a) Benzoyl bromide
(b) Bromobenzene
(c) 4–bromo benzoic acid
(d) 3–bromo benzoic acid

97. Vinegar and butter are the sources for which of the following carboxylic acids respectively? **[May 15, 2023 (II)]**

(a) $CH_3COOH, CH_3CH_2CH_2CH_2COOH$
(b) $CH_3COOH, CH_3CH_2CH_2COOH$
(c) $CH_3CH_2COOH, (CH_3)_2CHCOOH$
(d) $CH_3CH_2CH_2COOH, (CH_3)_2CHCOOH$

98. Identify X, Y and Z in the following reactions sequence

$$C_6H_5CH_2CH_2OH \xrightarrow{X} C_6H_5CH_2COOH \xrightarrow{Y} Z$$

[May 15, 2023 (II)]

(a) X = PCC Y = NaOH, CaO Z = $C_6H_5CH_3$

(b) X =PCC Y = LAH Z = $C_6H_5CH_2CH_3$

(c) X = Jones reagent Y = NaOH, CaO
Z = $C_6H_5CH_2CH_3$

(d) X = Jones reagent; Y = NaOH, CaO, Δ;
Z = $C_6H_5CH_3$

99. Which of the following is used in perfumery?
[May 15, 2023 (I)]

(a) Esters of benzoic acid

(b) Ethanoic acid

(c) Methanoic acid

(d) Sodium benzoate

100. Arrange the following in increasing order of their acidic strength **[July 8, 2022 (I)]**

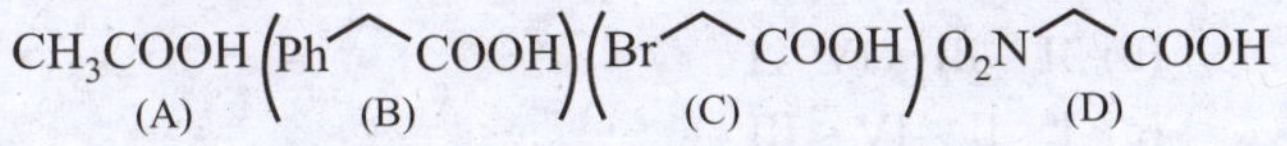

(a) A < C < D < B (b) A < C < B < D

(c) D < C < A < B (d) A < B < C < D

101. Match the name of acid from list-I with source from which is derived. **[July 8, 2022 (I)]**

List-I	List-II
(A) Formic acid	(i) Vinegar
(B) Acetic acid	(ii) Butter
(C) Butyric acid	(iii) Ant

(a) A - (i) B - (ii) C - (iii)

(b) A - (ii) B - (i) C - (iii)

(c) A - (iii) B - (ii) C - (i)

(d) A - (iii) B - (i) C - (ii)

102. Identify the major product from the following reaction sequence. **[July 7, 2022 (II)]**

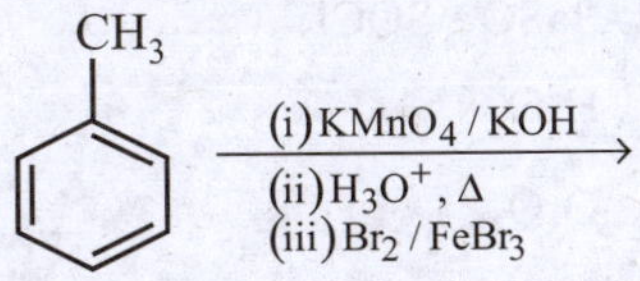

(a) 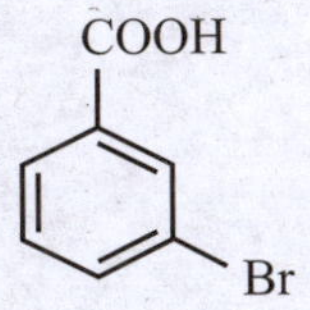

(b) 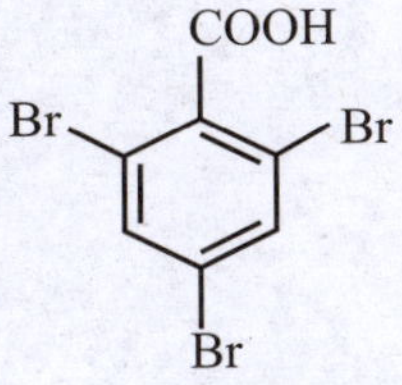

(c) 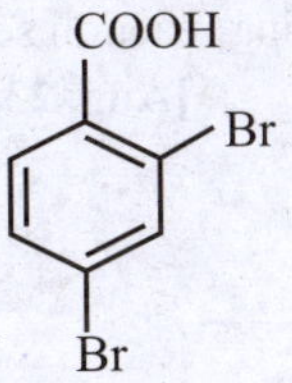

(d) 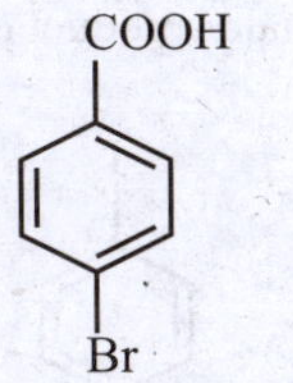

103. Arrange the following in increasing order of pK_a values **[July 6, 2022 (I)]**

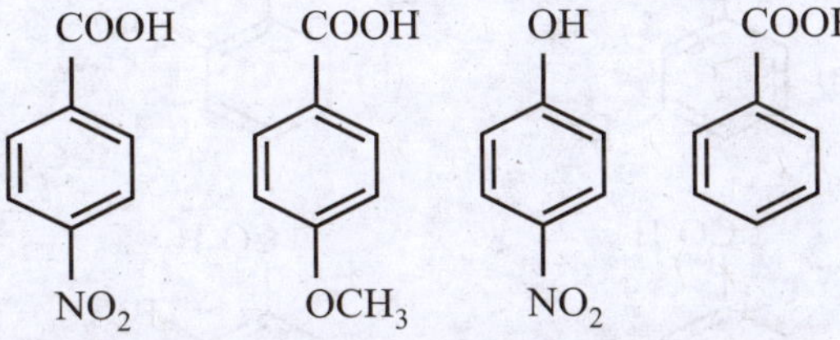

(A) (B) (C) (D)

(a) C < B < A < D (b) B < D < C < A

(c) A < D < B < C (d) A < B < C < D

104. On electrolysis of aqueous solution of sodium butanoate gives a hydrocarbon. The number of carbon atoms present in hydrocarbon are **[July 5, 2022 (II)]**

(a) 6 (b) 4 (c) 8 (d) 3

105. An aryl carboxylic acid on treatment with sodium hydrogen carbonate liberates a gaseous molecule. Identify the gas molecule liberated **[July 4, 2022 (II)]**

(a) H_2 (b) CO_2 (c) CO (d) O_2

106. Identify the major product formed in the following reaction sequence **[July 4, 2022 (I)]**

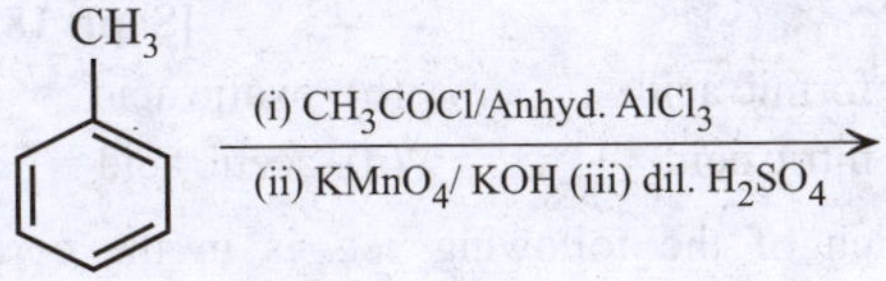

(a) 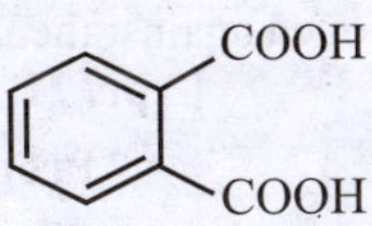

(b) 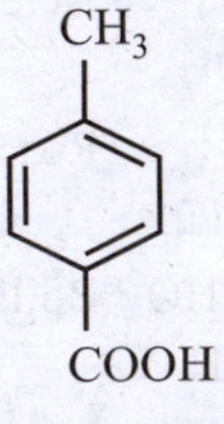

(c) 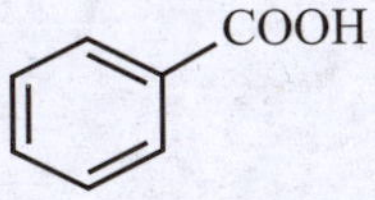

(d) 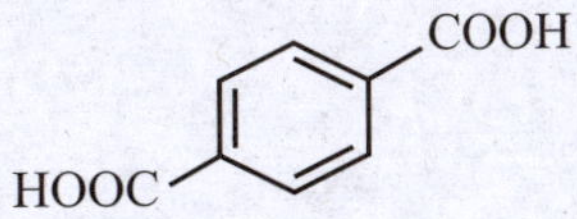

107. The major product of the following reaction sequence is **[Aug. 23, 2021 (I)]**

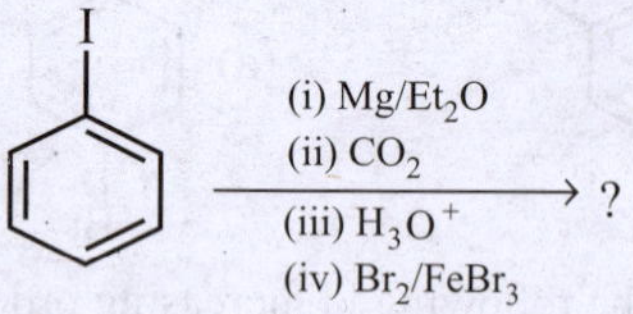

(a) 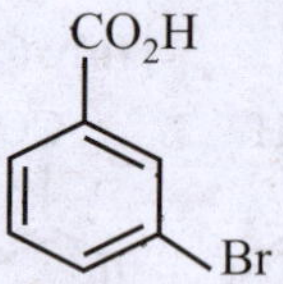

(b) 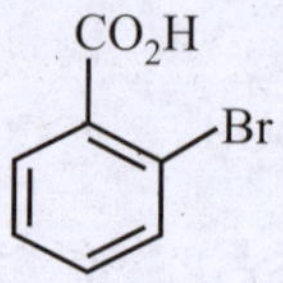

(c) 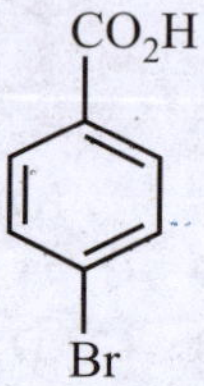

(d) 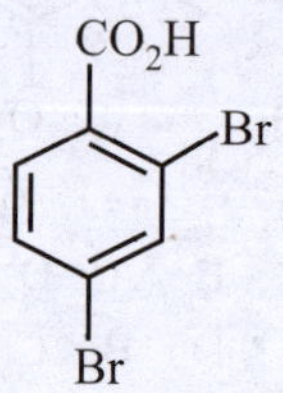

108. The correct order of acidic strength among the followings is **[Aug. 20, 2021 (I)]**

(a) $FCH_2CO_2H > C_6H_5CO_2H > CH_3CH_2CHClCO_2H > CH_3CO_2H$

(b) $C_6H_5CO_2H > CH_3CO_2H > CH_3CH_2CHClCO_2H > FCH_2CO_2H$

(c) $CH_3CH_2CHClCO_2H > FCH_2CO_2H > CH_3CO_2H > C_6H_5CO_2H$

(d) $FCH_2CO_2H > CH_3CH_2CHClCO_2H > C_6H_5CO_2H > CH_3CO_2H$

109. The main constituent of vinegar is .... **[Sept. 18, 2020 (I)]**

(a) formic acid (b) oxalic acid
(c) nitric acid (d) acetic acid

110. Which of the following sets is in the correct order regarding the property mentioned against them? **[Apr. 21, 2019 (II)]**

	Sets	Property
I.	$NCCH_2COOH > FCH_2COOH > H_3CCH_2COOH$	Acidity
II.	$CH_3CH_2CHO > PhCOCH_3 > PhCHO$	Reactivity
III.	$H_3CCOCH_2CH_3 < H_3CCH_2CHO < H_3CCH_2CH_2OH$	Boiling points

(a) I, II only (b) I, III only
(c) II, III only (d) I, II. III

111. The following species are involved in the formation of an ester from a carboxylic acid in the presence of acid. the correct sequence of formation of these species is **[Apr. 21, 2019 (I)]**

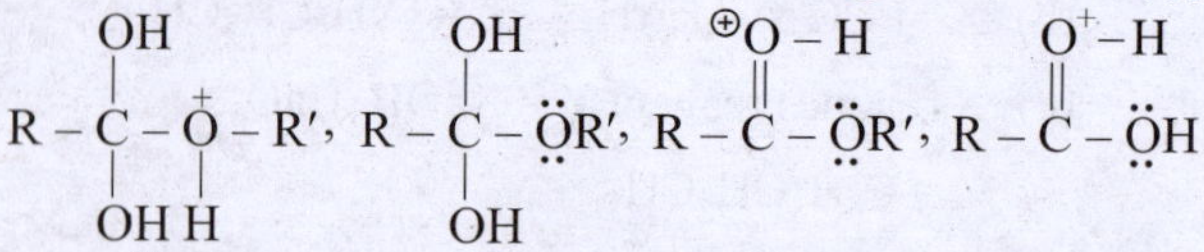

(1) (2) (3) (4)

(a) 2 1 4 3 (b) 4 1 2 3
(c) 1 4 3 2 (d) 2 3 1 4

112. The increasing order of acidity of the following carboxylic acids is **[2017]**

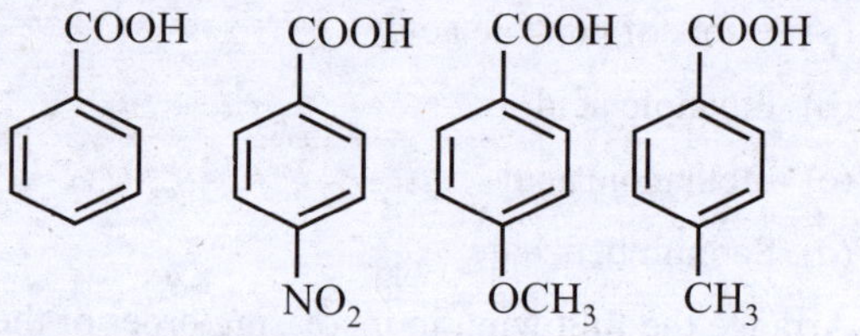

I II III IV

(a) III < IV < II < I
(b) II < III < IV < I
(c) I < II < IV < III
(d) III < IV < I < II

113. What is *C* in the following sequence of reaction? **[2016]**

$$CH_3OH \xrightarrow{PCl_3} A \xrightarrow{KCN} B \xrightarrow{\text{Hydrolysis}} C$$

(a) CH_3CH_2OH
(b) CH_3CHO
(c) CH_3COOH
(d) $HOCH_2—CH_2OH$

114. Identify the reagents *A* and *B* respectively in the following reactions. **[2015]**

$$CH_3COOH \xrightarrow{A} CH_3COCl \xrightarrow{B} CH_3CHO$$

(a) $SOCl_2$, H_2/Pd-$BaSO_4$
(b) H_2/Pd -$BaSO_4$, $SOCl_2$
(c) $SOCl_2$, H_2O_2
(d) $SOCl_2$, O_5O_4

9 Amines

CHAPTER SYNOPSIS

- Methylaniline can be $C_6H_5NHCH_3$, *o*-, *m*- and *p*-$CH_3C_6H_4NH_2$.
- In Hofmann's method, the starting material is amide and final product is an amine having one carbon atom less than the amide. Reaction of alkyl halide with ammonia may lead to the formation of a mixture of amines (1°, 2° and 3°).
- *tert*-Amine molecules cannot associate because of absence of H-bonding.
- Intramolecular H-bonding decreases nucleophilicity and hence reactivity of the —NH_2 group.
- The correct order of basic strength is
  Dimethylamine > Methyl amine > Trimethyl amine > Ammonia (In aqueous solution)
  Trimethyl amine > Dimethylamine > Methylamine > Ammonia (In gas phase)
- The alkyl groups are electron releasing group (+ I), thus increases the electron density around the nitrogen thereby increasing the availability of the lone pair of electrons to proton or Lewis acid and making the amine more basic. Hence more the number of alkyl groups more basic is the amine. Therefore the correct order is
  $$NH_3 < CH_3NH_2 < (CH_3)_2NH$$
- The basic character of an amine in water is determined by (i) electron availability on the N atom and (ii) the extent of stabilization of the cation (protonated amine) due to solvation by hydrogen bonding
- **Hinsberg's reagent** is benzene sulphonyl chloride. A **tertiary amine** does not react with **Hinsberg's** reagent and remains insoluble in aqueous KOH when it is treated with Hinsberg's reagent in presence of excess of KOH.
- Hinsberg test is applicable to liquid amines which are insoluble in water because water solubility of the amine decreases nucleophilicity of nitrogen.
- Hofmann rearrangement involves nitrene ($R-\overset{\overset{O}{\|}}{C}-\ddot{N}:$) intermediate in which nitrogen is electron deficient.
- Carbylamine reaction involves the formation of dichlorocarbene ($:CCl_2$) as intermediate which is electron deficient.
- Aliphatic amines are more basic than aromatic amines. Electron-releasing groups raise basicity, while electron-withdrawing groups lower basicity.
- Arene diazonium cation is a weak electrophile, hence it can couple only with those compounds which bear powerful electron-releasing group like —OH, —NH_2, —NHR, or —NR_2.
- Electron-withdrawing groups (like —NO_2) make arene diazonium cation more electron-deficient, *i.e.*, strong electrophile, while electron-releasing group makes diazonium cation a weak electrophile.
- Presence of electron-withdrawing gp. (—NO_2) in *o*, *p*-position decreases basicity while that of electron-releasing gp. (—CH_3) increases basic character of the aromatic amine.
- Only primary aromatic amines undergo diazotisation followed by coupling.

Topic 1 Aliphatic and Aromatic Amines

1. Consider the following set of reactions and statements given about X and Y

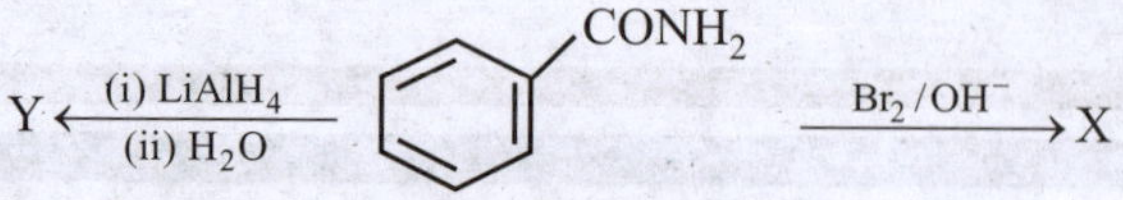

I. pK_b of X is greater than Y

II. Both on reaction with $NaNO_2$ and HCl at 273-298K form stable diazonium salts

III. Both can be prepared by ammonolysis of corresponding chlorides

The incorrect statements are **[May 18, 2026 (II)]**

(a) I, II only (b) II, III only

(c) I, only (d) I, III only

2. The number σ, π – bonds and lone pairs of electrons present in the product C respectively are

$$C_2H_5NO_2 \xrightarrow{Sn+HCl} A \xrightarrow[Heat]{CHCl_3+KOH} B \xrightarrow{HgO} C$$

[May 18, 2026 (I)]

(a) 10, 1, 3 (b) 8, 3, 2

(c) 9, 2, 3 (d) 9, 1, 3

3. Consider the following **[May 15, 2026 (II)]**

$C_6H_5NH_2$	$C_2H_5NH_2$	NH_3	$(C_2H_5)_2NH$
I	II	III	IV

The correct pair with lowest pK_b and highest pK_b values respectively is

(a) IV, I (b) III, II (c) II, IV (d) I, IV

4. Choose the correct statement(s) given below, with regard to N – Ethyl benzene sulphonamide **[May 14, 2026 (I)]**

I. It is soluble in alkali

II. It is formed by reaction between 1° amine and Hinsberg reagent

III. It is formed by reaction between 2° amine and Hinsberg reagent

The correct answer is

(a) II only (b) I & II only

(c) I & III only (d) III only

5. Match the following **[May 13, 2026 (II)]**

List-I (Compound)		**List-II** (b. p/K)	
A.	$n-C_4H_9OH$	I.	310.5
B.	$(C_2H_5)_2NH$	II.	350.8
C.	$n-C_4H_9NH_2$	III.	390.3
D.	$C_2H_5N(CH_3)_2$	IV.	329.3

The correct answer is

(a) A-IV, B-II, C-I, D-III

(b) A-III, B-IV, C-I, D-II

(c) A-III, B-IV, C-II, D-I

(d) A-II, B-III, C-IV, D-I

6. In which of the following set's reactant and reagent are correctly matched to get n-propylamine as major product?

I.  ----- $AgNO_2$, Fe|HCl

II.  ----- NaCH, H_2|Ni

III. 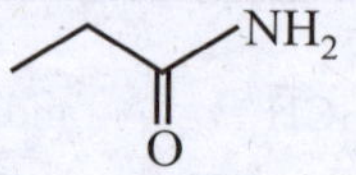 ----- Br_2|OH^-

Correct answer is **[May 12, 2026 (I)]**

(a) II only (b) I, II

(c) II, III (d) I, III

7. Benzyl amine can be prepared from which of the following reactions ? **[May 26, 2025 (II)]**

(a) $C_6H_5Cl \xrightarrow{CH_3NH_2}$

(b) $C_6H_5CH_2Cl \xrightarrow[(ii)\,H_2/Ni]{(i)\,AgCN}$

(c) $C_6H_5CONH_2 \xrightarrow{NaOH/Br_2}$

(d) $C_6H_5CONH_2 \xrightarrow[(ii)\,H_2O]{(i)\,LiAlH_4}$

8. Consider the following:

Statement-I: In the nitration of aniline, more amount of *m*-nitroaniline is formed than expected.

Statement-II: In the presence of a strongly acidic medium, aniline is protonated to form anilinium ion, which is meta directing.

The correct answer is **[May 23, 2025 (II)]**

(a) Both statement-I and statement-II are correct.

(b) Both statement-I and statement-II are not correct.

(c) Statement-I is correct, but statement-II is not correct.

(d) Statement-I is not correct, but statement-II is correct.

9. How many amines with molecular formula C_3H_9N can react with benzene sulphonyl chloride? **[May 22, 2025 (I)]**

(a) 2 (b) 3 (c) 4 (d) 1

10. Consider the following : **[May 21, 2025 (II)]**

Statement-I: CH_3NH_2 is more basic than NH_3 but $C_6H_5NH_2$ is less basic than NH_3.

Statement-II: The order of basic strength of amines in aqueous phase follows the order $(C_2H_5)_3N > (C_2H_5)_2NH > C_2H_5NH_2$

The correct answer is

(a) Both statement-I and statement-II are correct.

(b) Both statement-I and statement-II are not correct.

(c) Statement-I is correct, but statement-II is not correct.

(d) Statement-I is not correct, but statement-II is correct.

11. Which of the following does not involve in Friedel-Craft reaction? **[May 21, 2025 (II)]**

(a) 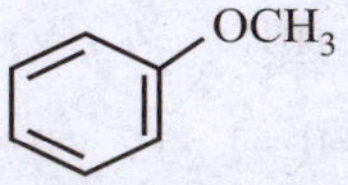

(b) 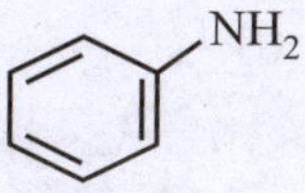

(c) 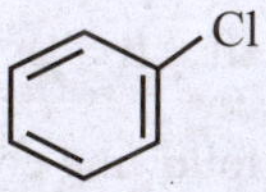

(d) 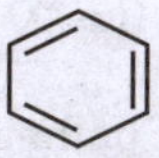

12. What are x and y in the following set of reactions?

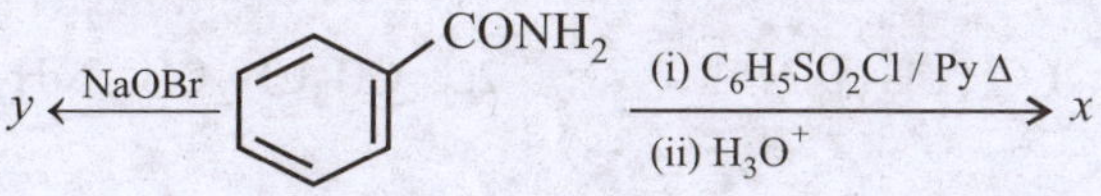

[May 21, 2025 (I)]

(a) 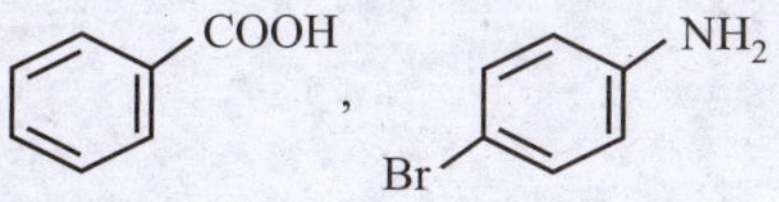

(b) 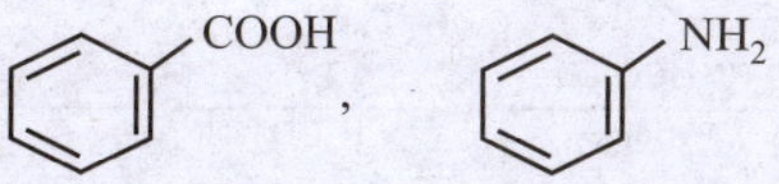

(c) 

(d) 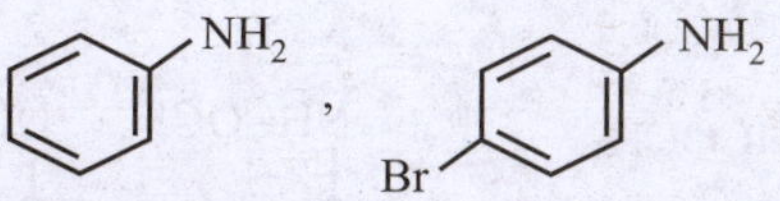

13. When ethyl bromide and n-propyl bromide are allowed to react with Na metal in dry ether, the number of different alkanes formed is **[May 21, 2025 (I)]**

(a) 1 (b) 2 (c) 3 (d) 4

14. In the reaction sequence Y is **[May 22, 2024 (II)]**

$$CH_3CO_2H \xrightarrow[(2)\ \Delta]{(1)\ NH_3} P \xrightarrow{Br_2/NaOH} Y$$

(a) a primary amine with same number of carbons as in P

(b) a primary amine with one carbon less than in P

(c) a secondary amine with same number of carbons as in P

(d) a secondary amine with one carbon less than in P

15. What are X and Y respectively in the following reactions?

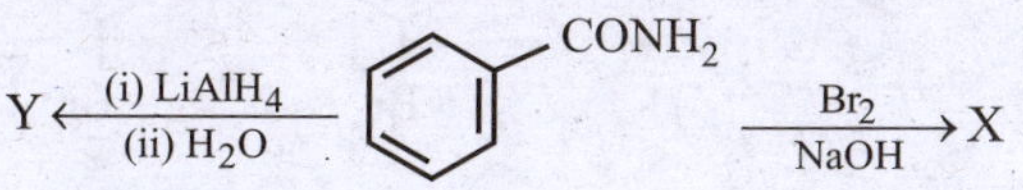

[May 20, 2024 (II)]

(a) 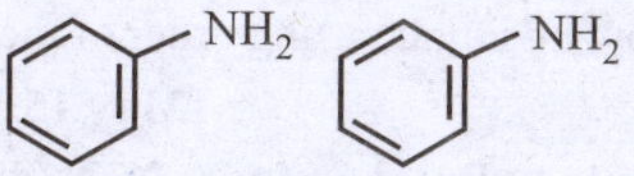

(b) 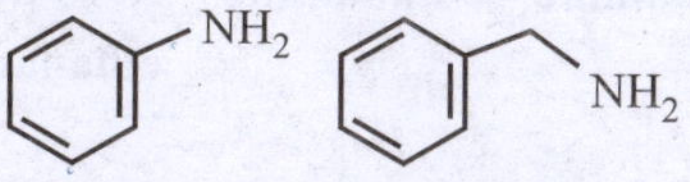

(c) 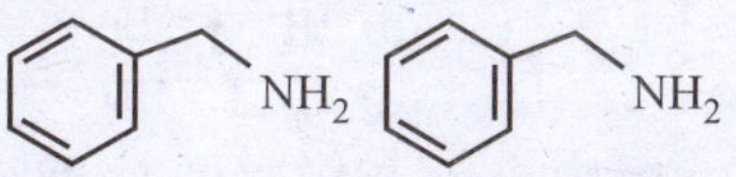

(d) 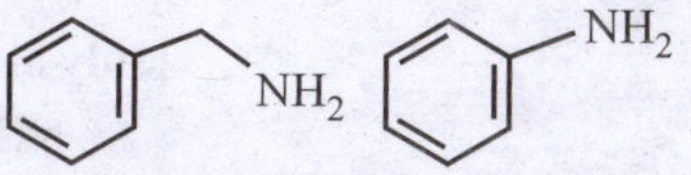

16. Which of the following amine cannot be prepared by the Gabriel phthalimide synthesis method?
[May 19, 2023 (I); Similar to July 5, 2022 (II)]

(a) Ethylamine (b) Benzylamine

(c) Phenylamine (d) Propylamine

17. The product of an amine 'X' with benzene sulphonyl chloride produces the product which is insoluble in alkali. The product of 'X' with ethanoyl chloride is **[May 18, 2023 (II)]**

(a) $C_6H_5NHCOCH_3$ (b) $C_6H_5N(CH_3)COCH_3$

(c) $C_6H_5N(CH_3)CH_2CH_3$ (d) $C_6H_5NHCH_2CH_3$

18. X and Y (major products) in the following reaction sequence are **[May 16, 2023 (I)]**

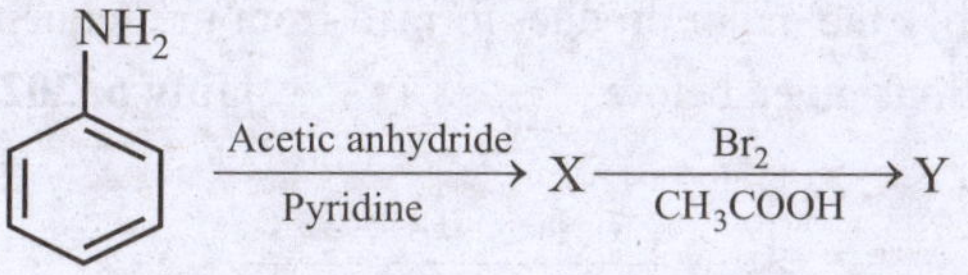

(a) 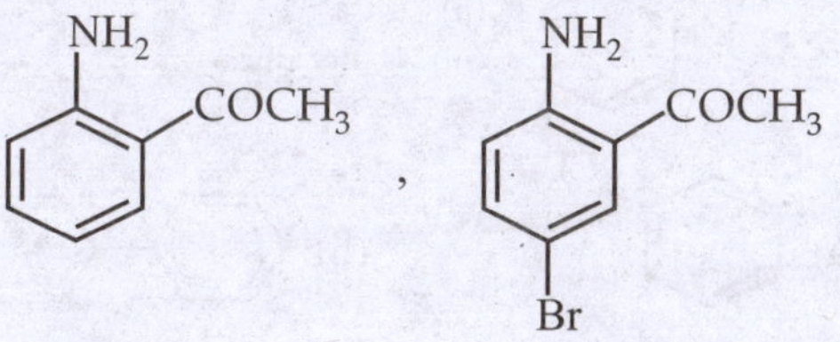

(b) 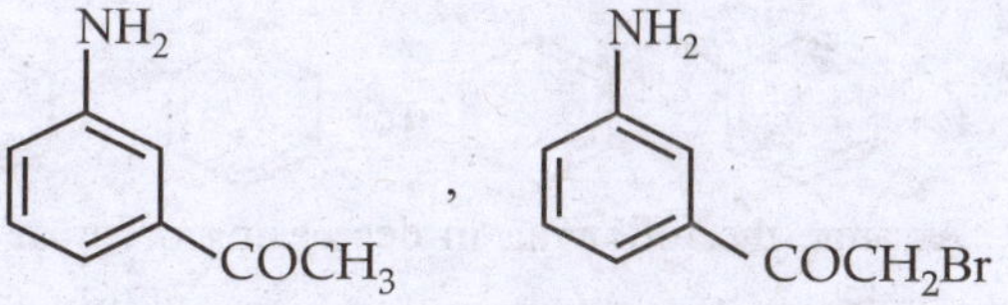

(c) 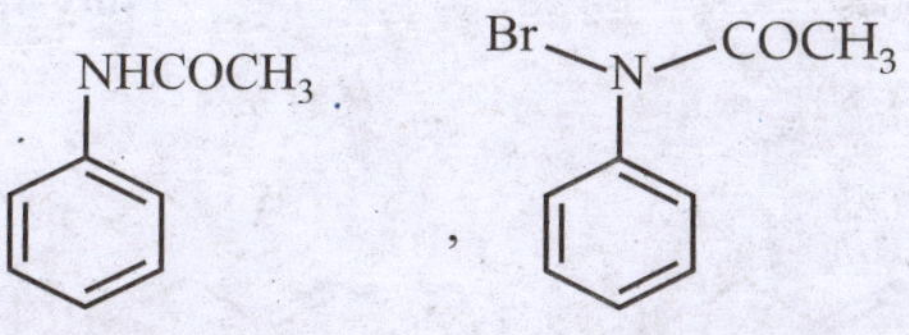

(d) 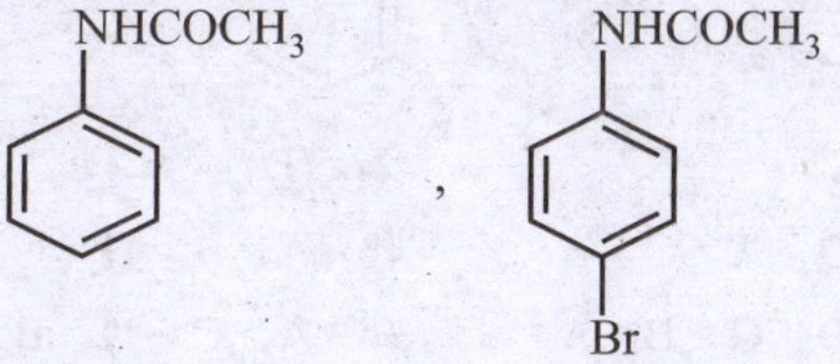

19. Arrange the following in increasing order of their boiling points **[May 15, 2023 (I)]**

N–Ethylethanamine (**I**) **Butanamine** (**II**) **N, N–dimethyl ethanamine** (**III**)

(a) III > II > I (b) III > I > II
(c) II > III > I (d) II > I > III

20. Choose the correct order of basicity of the following **[July 8, 2022 (I)]**

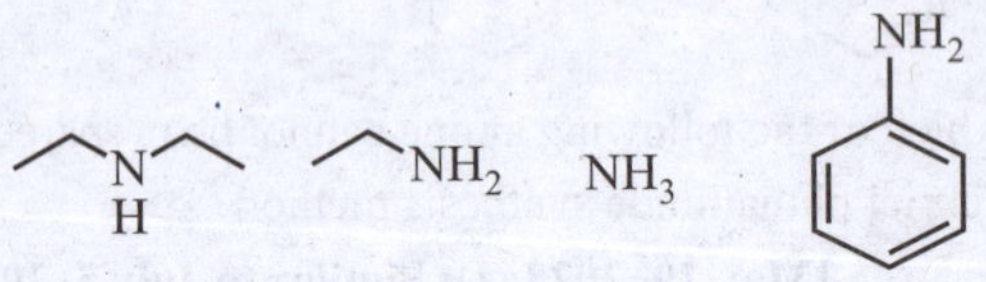

(A) (B) (C) (D)

(a) A > C > D > B (b) A > B > C > D
(c) D > A > C > B (d) D > C > B > A

21. Hydrolysis of the minor product formed from the reaction of 1-bromopropane and ethanolic KCN gives **[July 7, 2022 (II)]**

(a) 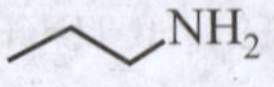 (b) 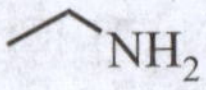
(c)  (d) 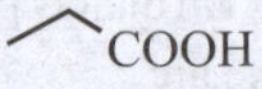

22. Identify the major product formed from the sequence of reactions given below **[July 6, 2022 (I)]**

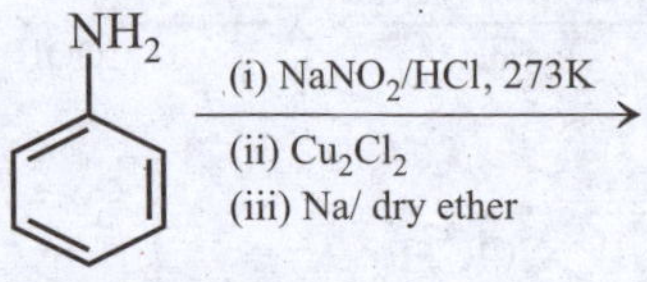

(a) 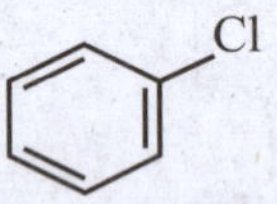 (b) 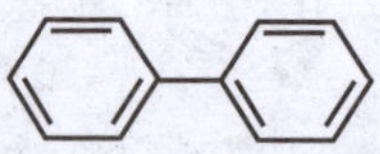
(c) 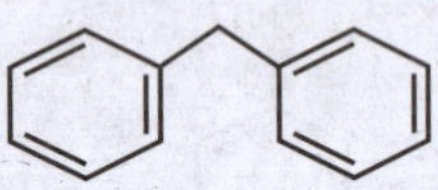 (d) 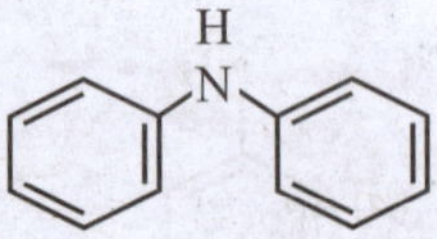

23. Arrange the following in decreasing order of their pK_b values **[July 4, 2022 (I)]**

CH_3NH_2 (A) $(CH_3)_3N$ (B)

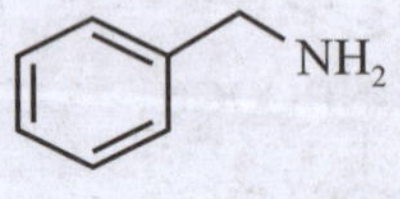 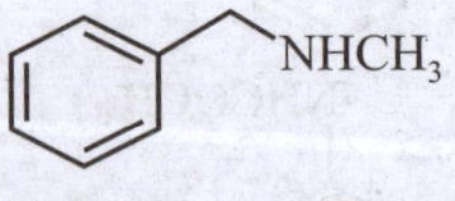

(C) (D)

(a) D > A > C > B (b) A > B > D > C
(c) D > C > B > A (d) A > C > D > B

24. The correct order of basic strength of the following amines is **[2016]**

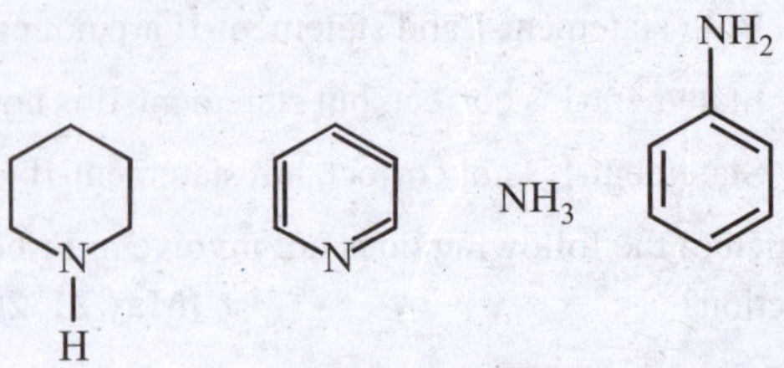

(I) (II) (III) (IV)

(a) I > III > IV > II (b) II > I > IV > III
(c) I > II > III > IV (d) I > III > II > IV

25. The order of boiling points of the following compounds is **[Sept. 18, 2020 (I)]**

1. $(CH_3)_3\ddot{N}$ 2. $CH_3CH_2CH_2\ddot{N}H_2$
3. $CH_3CH_2\ddot{N}HCH_3$

(a) 1 > 3 > 2 (b) 3 > 1 > 2
(c) 2 > 1 > 3 (d) 2 > 3 > 1

26. 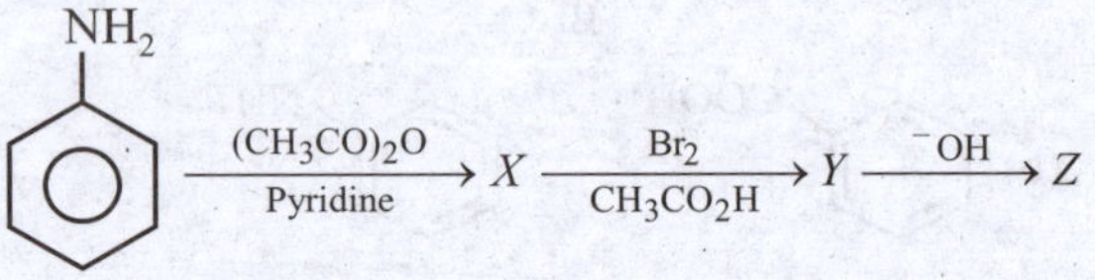

What are structures of *X*, *Y* and *Z* in the above given reaction sequence? **[2017]**

X **Y** **Z**

(a) 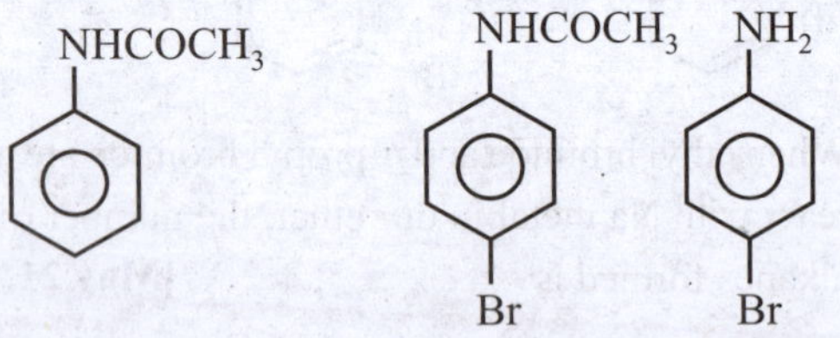

(b) 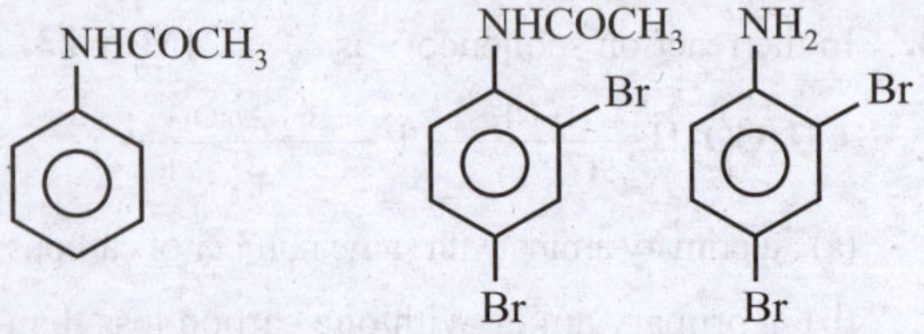

(c) 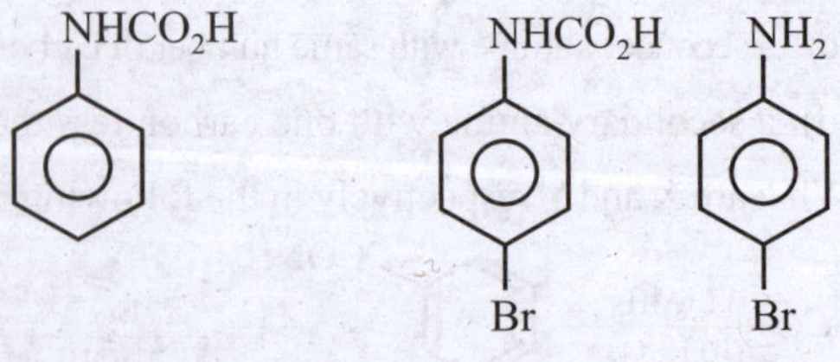

(d) 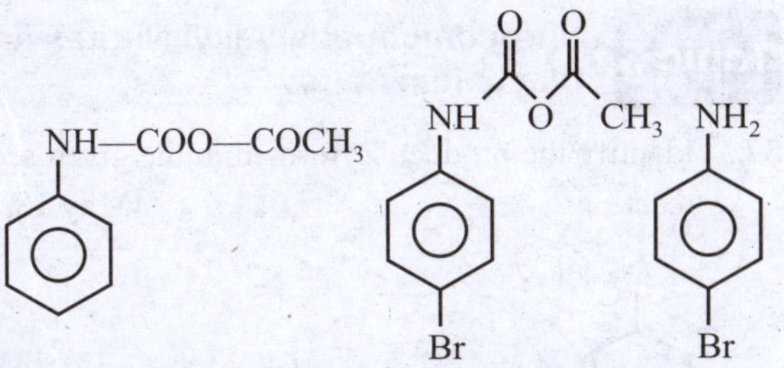

Topic 2 Amides, Cyanides and Isocyanides

27. Identify the product Y in the following reaction sequence

$$C_2H_4 \xrightarrow[\text{(ii) AgCN}]{\text{(i) HBr}} \underset{\text{(major product)}}{X} \xrightarrow{H_2/\text{Catalyst}} Y$$

[May 18, 2026 (I)]

(a) n-propyl amine
(b) Isopropyl amine
(c) Ethyl amine
(d) Ethyl methyl amine

28. Benzamide $\xrightarrow{Br_2/NaOH} X \xrightarrow[\text{alc.KOH}]{CHCl_3} Y$

The conversion of X to Y is **[May 20, 2024 (I)]**

(a) Hoffmann reaction (b) Etard reaction
(c) Stephen reaction (d) Carbylamine reaction

29. The correct sequence of reactions involved in the following conversion is **[May 19, 2024 (II)]**

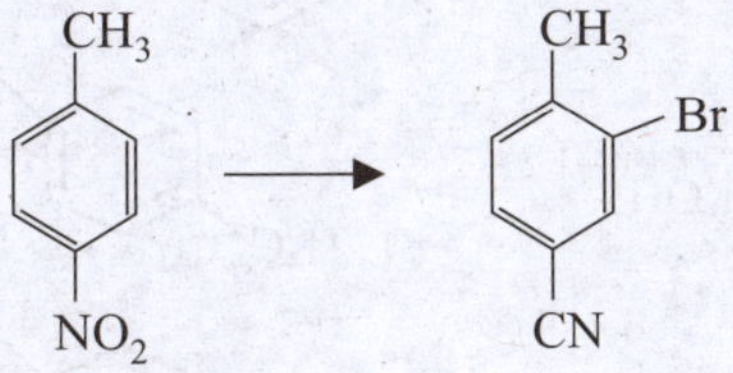

(a) Bromination, reduction, carbylamine reaction
(b) Reduction, bromination, carbylamine reaction
(c) Bromination, reduction, oxidation
(d) Reduction, bromination, oxidation

30. In the given reactions, 'X' and 'Y' respectively are

$$C_6H_5CH_2NH_2 \xleftarrow{X} C_6H_5CONH_2 \xrightarrow{Y} C_6H_5NH_2$$

[May 16, 2023 (II)]

(a) $LiAlH_4$, H_2O; Br_2/OH^-
(b) Br_2/OH^-; $LiAlH_4$, H_2O
(c) Br_2/H^+; $NaBH_4$
(d) $NaBH_4$; Br_2/H^+

31. Identify the product 'Y' in the following sequence of reactions. **[July 4, 2022 (II)]**

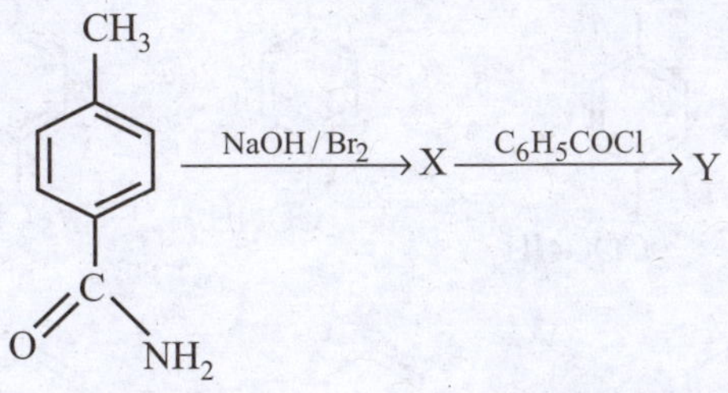

(a) 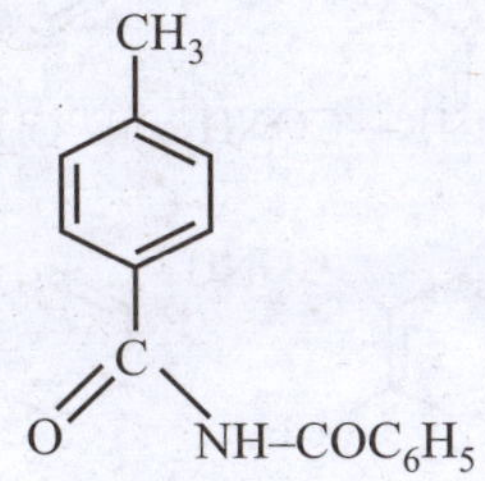
(b) 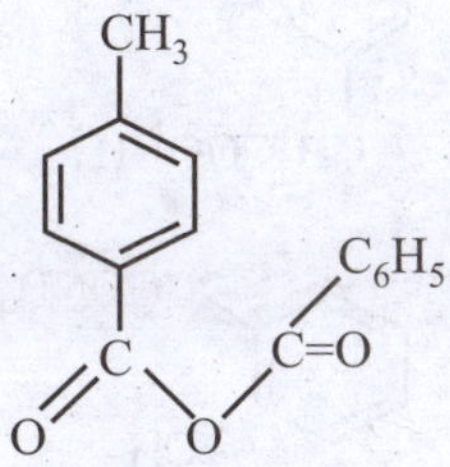
(c) 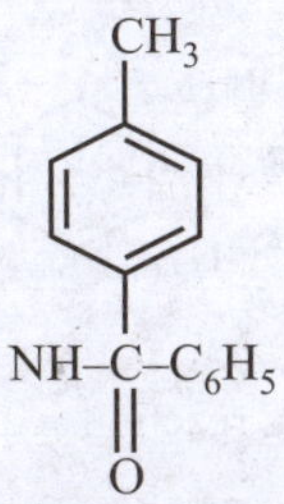
(d) 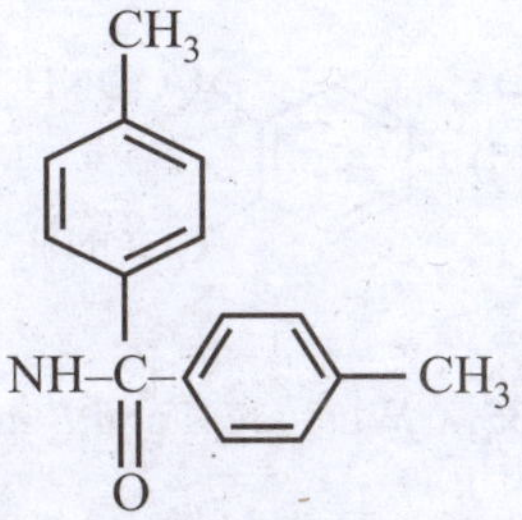

32. The reagent P used for the reaction is **[July 6, 2022 (I)]**

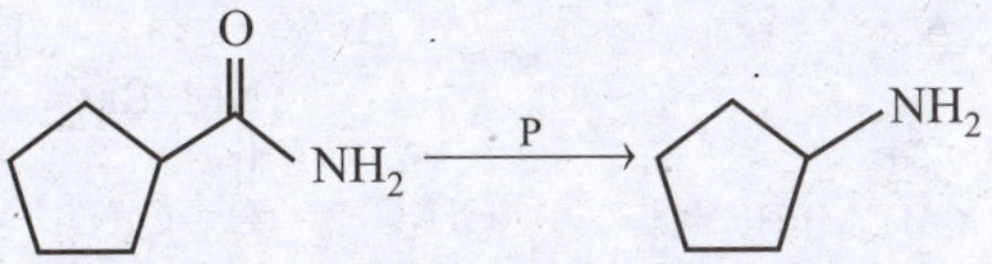

(a) Zn – Hg/HCl (b) $HCl/SnCl_2$
(c) $Br_2/NaOH$ (d) ZnCl/HCl

33. Acetic acid on heating with NH_3 forms *A*. When *A* reacts with $LiAlH_4$ followed by hydrolysis gives *B*. When *B* is heated with chloroform in KOH medium gives *C*. What are *B* and *C* respectively? **[Apr. 20, 2019 (I)]**

(a) CH_3CONH_2, CH_3CH_2NC
(b) $CH_3CH_2NH_2$, CH_3CH_2NC
(c) $CH_3CH_2NH_2$, CH_3COOH
(d) $CH_3CH_2CH_2NH_2$, CH_3CH_2NC

34. What are *A, B* and *C* in the following reactions? **[2018]**

$$\text{Phthalic acid} + NH_3 \longrightarrow A \xrightarrow{\Delta} B \xrightarrow{\text{High temperature}} C$$

	A	B	C

(a) 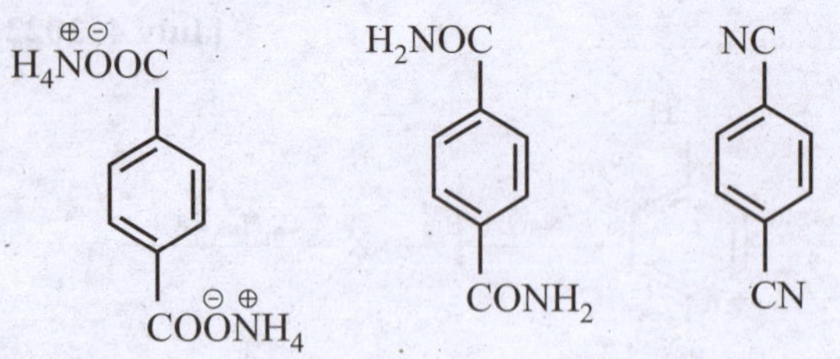

(b) 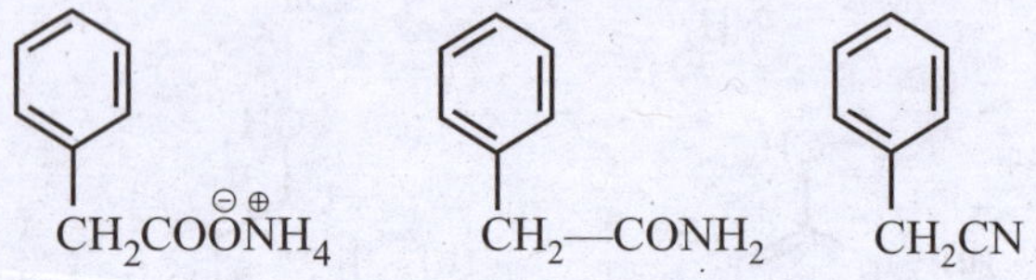

(c) 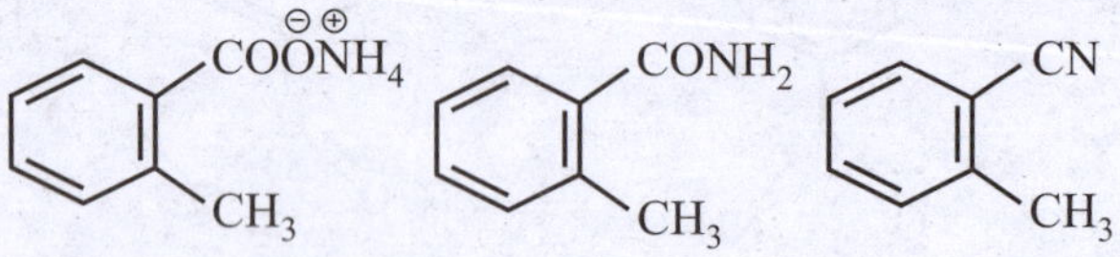

(d) 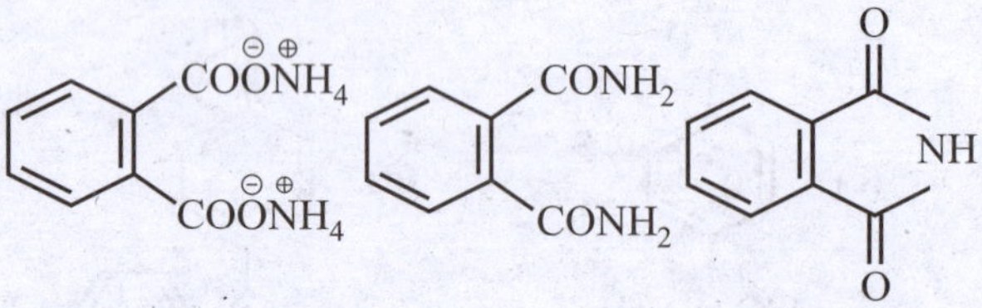

35. What are *A* and *B* in the following reaction sequence?

Propionitrile + $A \longrightarrow B \xrightarrow{H_3\overset{+}{O}}$ Propiophenone

	A	B
(a)	C_2H_5MgBr	$CH_3CH_2—\overset{NMgBr}{\overset{\Vert}{C}}—C_2H_5$
(b)	C_2H_5MgBr	$CH_3CH_2CH_2—\overset{NH}{\overset{\Vert}{C}}—C_2H_5$
(c)	C_6H_5MgBr	$CH_3CH_2—\overset{N.MgBr}{\overset{\Vert}{C}}—C_6H_5$
(d)	$C_6H_5CH_2MgBr$	$CH_3CH_2CH_2—\overset{NH}{\overset{\Vert}{C}}—CH_2C_6H_5$

[2018]

36. $C_2H_5Cl \xrightarrow{KCN} X \xrightarrow{H_2/\text{Catalyst}} Y \xrightarrow[\text{alc.KOH}]{CHCl_3} Z$

What is 'Z' in the above sequence of reactions? **[2018]**

(a) 

(b) 

(c) 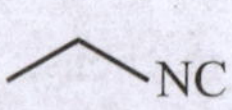

(d) 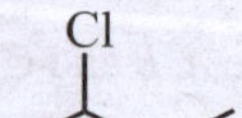

Topic 3 Nitrocompounds, Alkyl Nitrites and Diazonium Salts

37. Identify the product 'Z' formed in the given sequence of reactions **[May 18, 2026 (I)]**

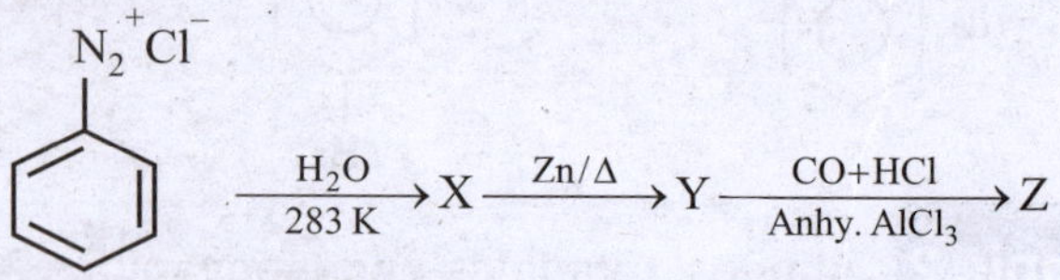

(a) 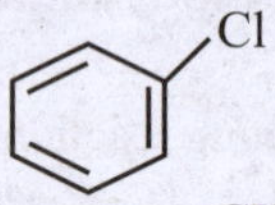

(b) 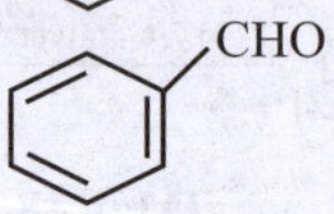

(c) 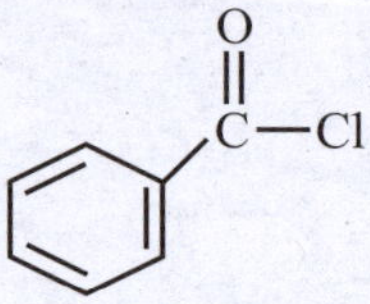

(d) 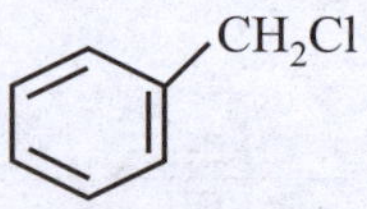

38. Observe the following reaction **[May 14, 2026 (II)]**

$C_7H_7N_2Cl \xrightarrow[283K]{X} Y$

Y reacts with aqueous NaOH solution and forms its sodium salt. What are X and Y?

(a) C_2H_5OH; 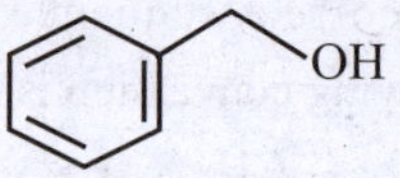

(b) C_2H_5OH; 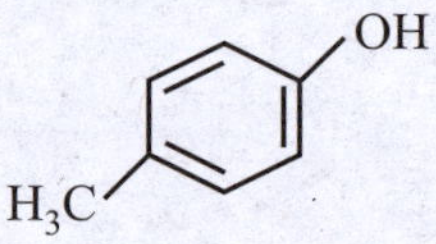

(c) H_2O; 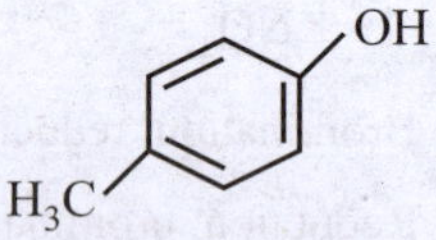

(d) H_2O; 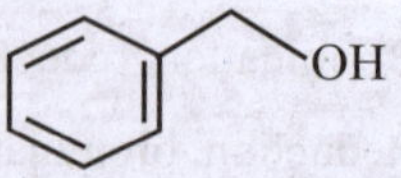

39. Identify the major product 'z' in the given sequence of reactions **[May 14, 2026 (I)]**

(anhy =)

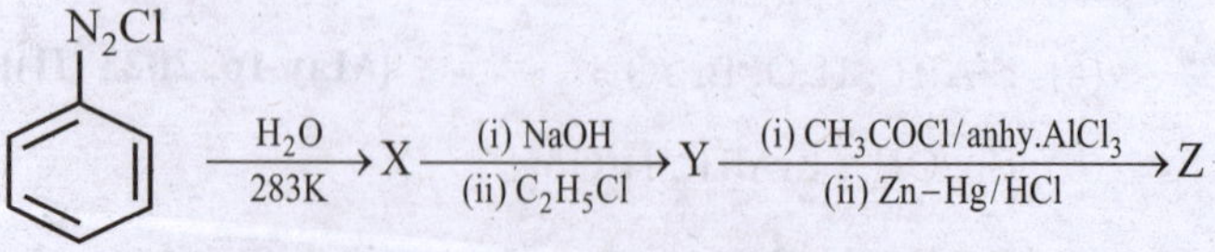

(a) 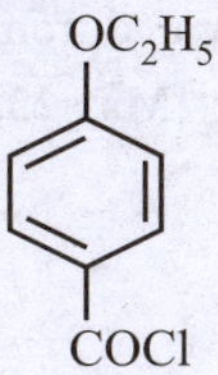 (b) 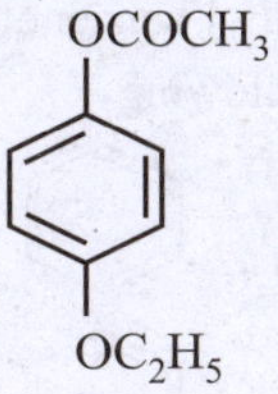

(c) 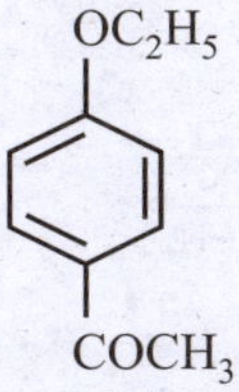 (d) 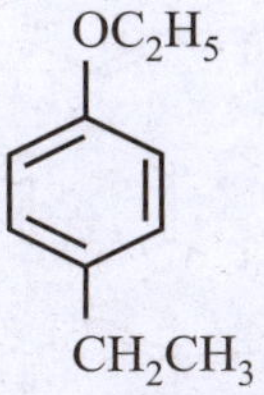

40. What is the end product (Y) in the given sequence of reactions? **[May 13, 2026 (II)]**

$$C_6H_5N_2^+Cl^- \xrightarrow[\text{(ii) } C_2H_5Cl/Na \text{ dry ether}]{\text{(i)}Cu_2Cl_2\backslash HCl} X \xrightarrow[\text{(ii)}H_3O^+]{\text{(i)}KMnO_4/OH^-} Y$$

(a) 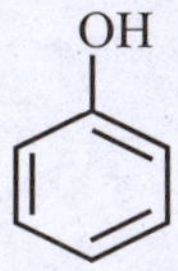 (b) 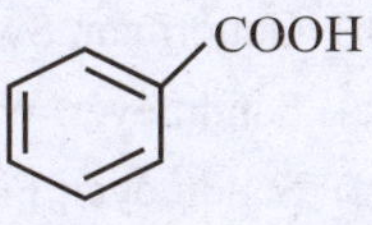

(c) 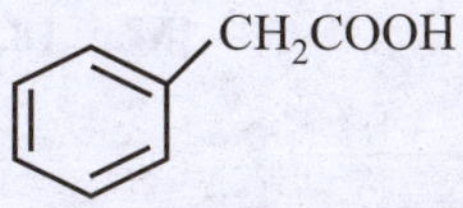 (d) 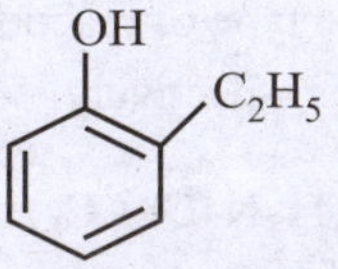

41. Which of the following is not an example of Sandmeyer reaction? **[May 13, 2026 (II)]**

(a) $C_6H_5N_2^+Cl^- \xrightarrow{CuCl\backslash HCl} C_6H_5Cl$

(b) $C_6H_5N_2^+Cl^- \xrightarrow{KI\backslash Warm} C_6H_5I$

(c) $C_6H_5N_2^+Cl^- \xrightarrow{CuBr\backslash HBr} C_6H_5Br$

(d) $C_6H_5N_2^+Cl^- \xrightarrow{CuCN\backslash KCN} C_6H_5CN$

42. In which of the following set/s, reactant and reagent are correctly matched to get ethyl isonitrile as major product? **[May 13, 2026 (I)]**

I.  – AgCN

II. 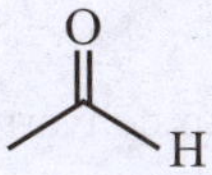 – NH_2OH, $(CH_3CO)_2O$

III. 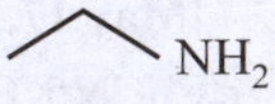 – $CHCl_3/OH^-$, Δ

(a) I, III (b) II, III

(c) I only (d) II only

43. What are X and Y respectively in the following set of reactions? **[May 13, 2026 (I)]**

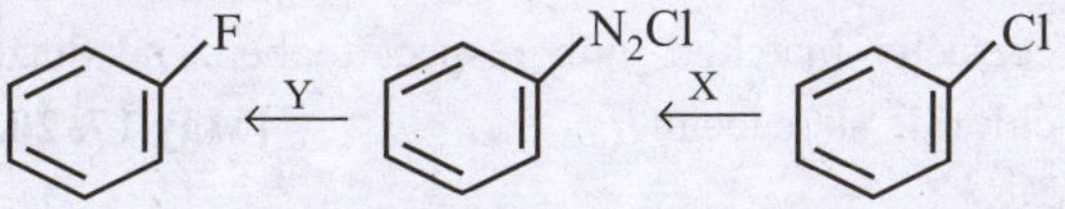

(a) KCl; KF

(b) HCl; KF

(c) HCl; (i) HBF_4 (ii) Δ

(d) Cu|HCl; (i) HBF_4 (ii) Δ

44. What are X and Y respectively in the following set of reactions? **[May 27, 2025 (I)]**

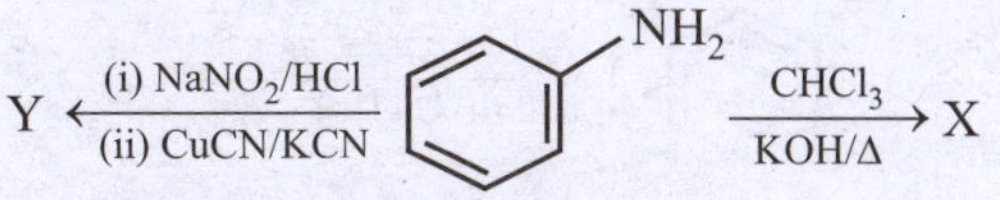

(a) 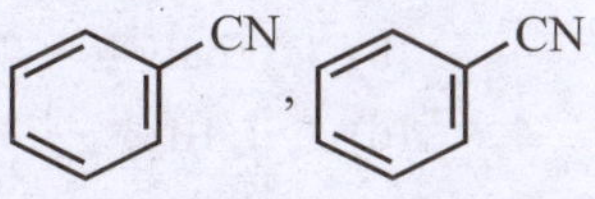

(b) 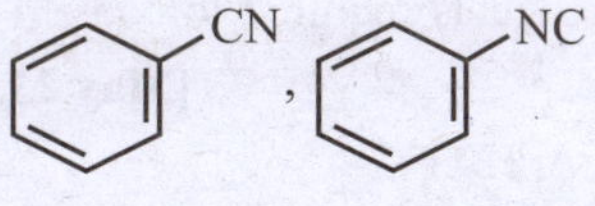

(c) 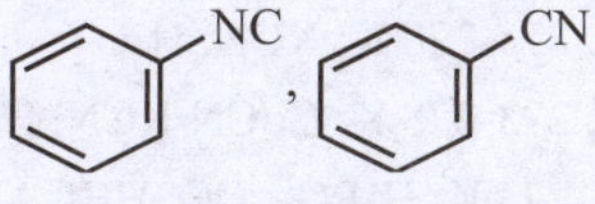

(d) 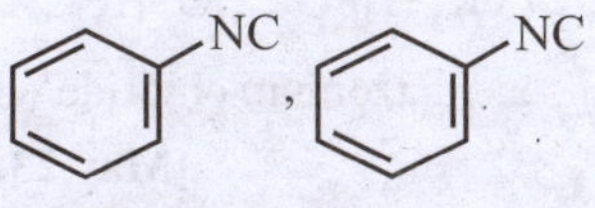

45. The % of carbon in '*z*' is (At.wt. C = 12 u, H = 1 u, N = 14 u, O = 16 u) **[May 26, 2025 (I)]**

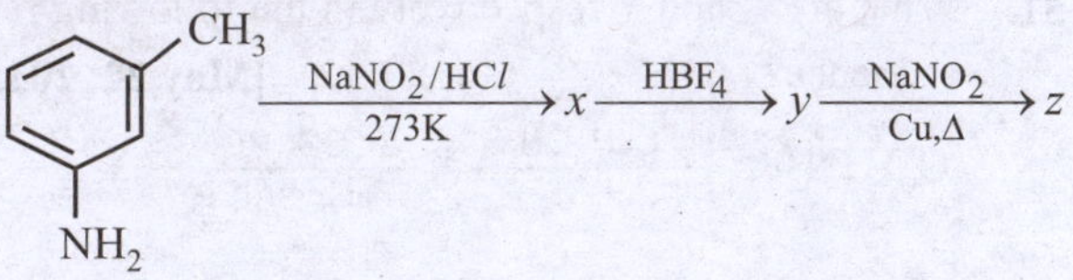

(a) 71.3 (b) 51.3 (c) 61.3 (d) 48.3

46. Which of the following sets of reagents convert aniline to chlorobenzene ? **[May 26, 2025 (I)]**

(a) $NaNO_2$ / HCl, 273 – 278 K; Cu_2Cl_2 / HCl

(b) $NaNO_2$ / HCl, 293 – 298 K; Cu_2Cl_2 / HCl

(c) $NaNO_2$ / HCl, 273 – 278 K; $SOCl_2$

(d) $NaNO_2$ / HCl, 273 – 278 K; Cl_2

47. What are X and Y in the following reaction sequence? **[May 24, 2025 (I)]**

$$C_6H_5N_2^+Cl^- \xrightarrow{X} C_6H_5CN \xrightarrow[\text{(ii) } H_2O]{\text{(i) } CH_3MgBr} Y$$

(a) KCN; $C_6H_5COCH_3$

(b) KCN; $C_6H_5C(OH)(CH_3)_2$

(c) CuCN | KCN; $C_6H_5CH(OH)CH_3$

(d) CuCN | KCN; $C_6H_5COCH_3$

48. *p*-Chlorotoluene is the major product in which of the following reactions? **[May 24, 2025 (I)]**

I. 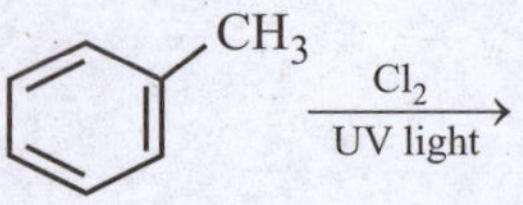

II. 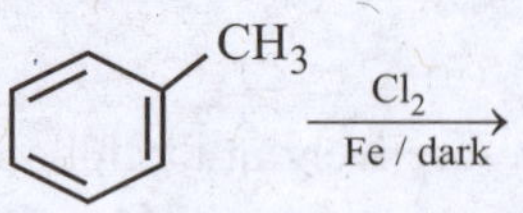

III. 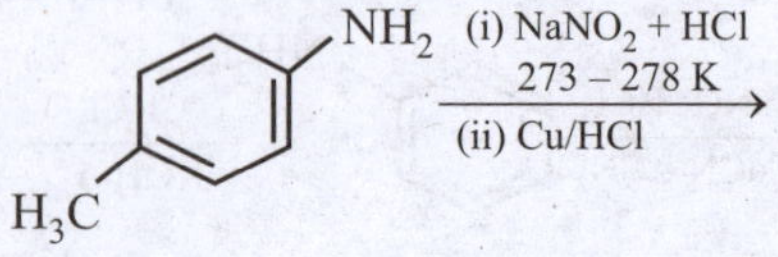

(a) I, III only (b) I, II only
(c) II, III only (d) I, II, III

49. The sequence of reagents required to convert aniline to benzoic acid is **[May 23, 2025 (I)]**
(a) $CHCl_3$ / OH^-, Δ; H_3O^+
(b) $NaNO_2$ / HCl, 273-278 K; KCN, H_3O^+
(c) $NaNO_2$ / HCl, 273-278 K; CuCN/KCN, H_3O^+
(d) $NaNO_2$ / HCl, 273 K; H_3PO_2; CO, HCl, $AlCl_3$

50. The reaction of benzene diazonium chloride with Cu and HCl is known as **[May 23, 2025 (I)]**
(a) Sandmeyer reaction (b) Etard reaction
(c) Finkelstein reaction (d) Gattermann reaction

51. What are X and Y respectively in the following reaction sequence? **[May 22, 2025 (II)]**

$$C_6H_5N_2^+X^- \xrightarrow{C_2H_5OH} X \xrightarrow[\text{anhy. } AlCl_3]{CO,\ HCl} Y$$

(a) 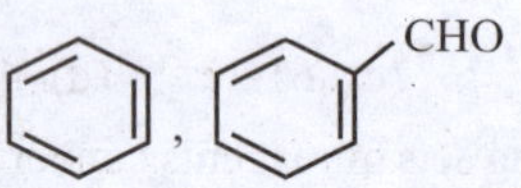

(b) 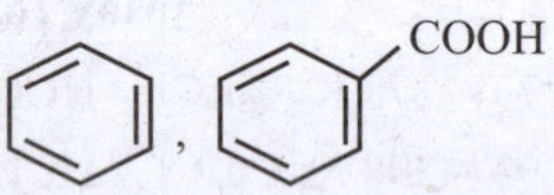

(c) 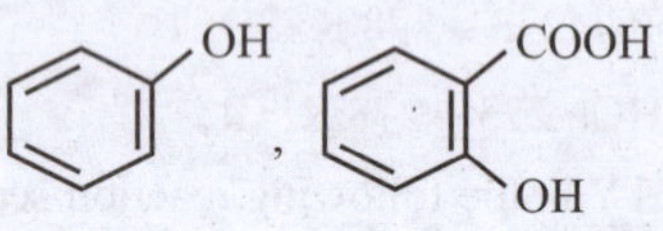

(d) 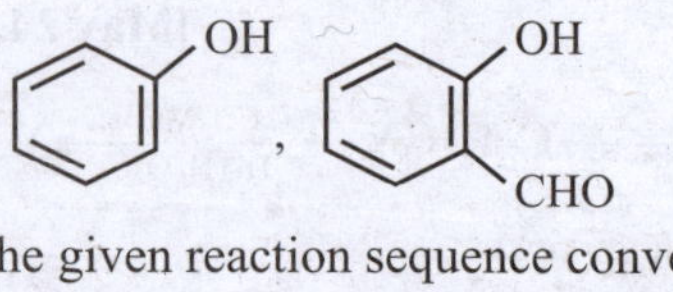

52. In the given reaction sequence conversion of Y to Z is

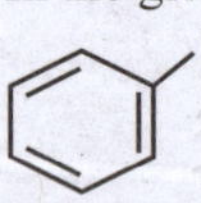 $\xrightarrow[273\text{–}278\ K]{NaNO_2/HCl} X$ **[May 22, 2025 (II)]**

$$\xrightarrow[HBr]{Cu_2Br_2} Y \xrightarrow[\text{dry ether}]{Na} Z$$

(a) Wurtz reaction (b) Wurtz-Fittig reaction
(c) Fittig reaction (d) Swarts reaction

53. *p*-Methyl benzene nitrile can be prepared from which of the following **[May 23, 2024 (I)]**

(a) 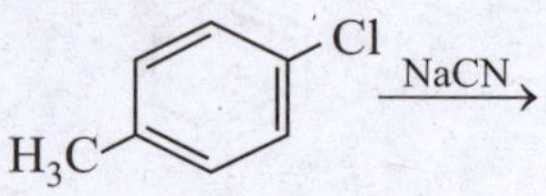

(b) 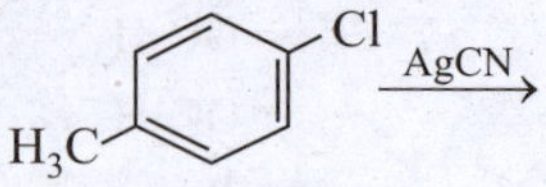

(c) 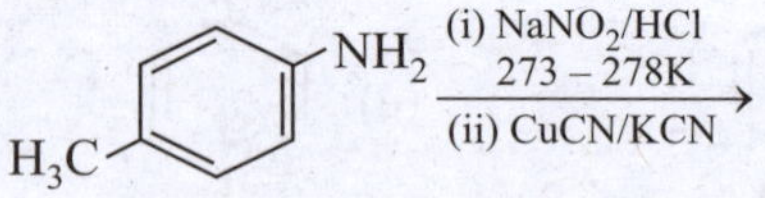

(d) 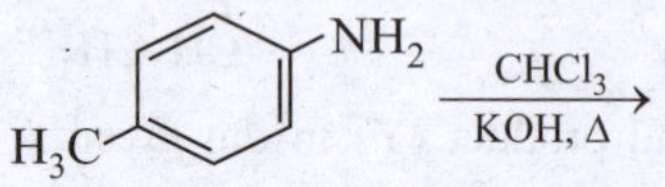

54. The two reactions involved in the conversion of benzene diazonium chloride to diphenyl are respectively **[May 20, 2024 (I)]**
(a) Swarts, Fittig
(b) Gatterman, Swarts
(c) Sandmeyer, Wurtz
(d) Sandmeyer, Fittig

55. The type of reaction 'X' and product 'Y' of the following are respectively **[May 18, 2023 (I)]**

$$C_6H_5N_2Cl + C_6H_5NH_2 \xrightarrow[X]{H^+} Y$$

(a) Electrophilic Substitution,
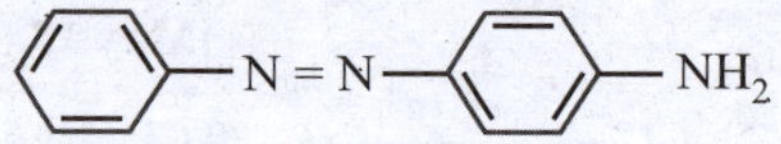

(b) Electrophilic Substitution,
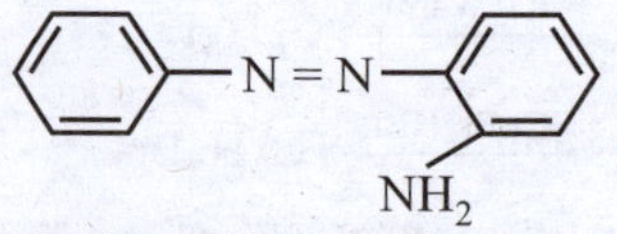

(c) Nucleophilic Substitution,
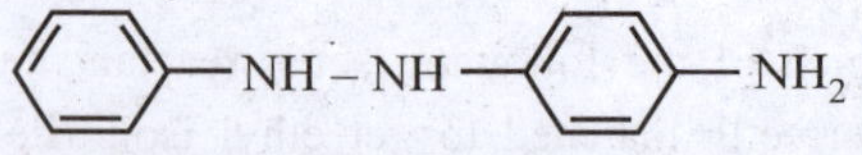

(d) Nucleophilic Substitution,
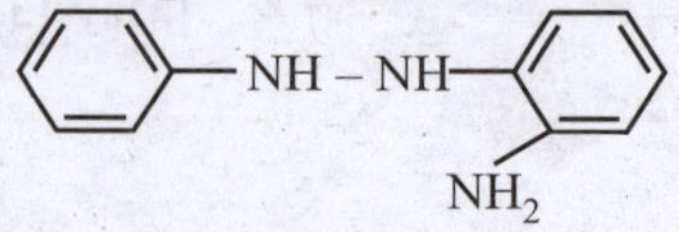

56. The sequence of reagents required to convert aniline to benzene nitrile are **[May 17, 2023 (II)]**
(a) $NaNO_2$ + HCl, 293 – 298 K; CuCN/KCN
(b) $NaNO_2$ + HCl, 273 – 278 K; CuCN/KCN
(c) $NaNO_2$ + HCl, 273 – 298 K; Cu/HCN
(d) Cl_2/ Fe; KCN

57. In which of the following, reagent and product are correctly matched with respect to benzene diazonium chloride as reactant? **[May 17, 2023 (I)]**

(a) Cu_2O ; C_6H_5Br (b) HI ; C_6H_5I

(c) $NaNO_2$; C_6H_5NO (d) CH_3CH_2OH ; C_6H_6

58. Which of the following produces nitrogen gas after the reaction with nitrous acid? **[May 15, 2023 (II)]**

(a) $(CH_3)_3N$ (b) $C_2H_5NHC_2H_5$

(c) $(C_2H_5)_3N$ (d) $C_2H_5NH_2$

59. What are *X* and *Y* in the following reactions? **[Apr. 22, 2019 (II)]**

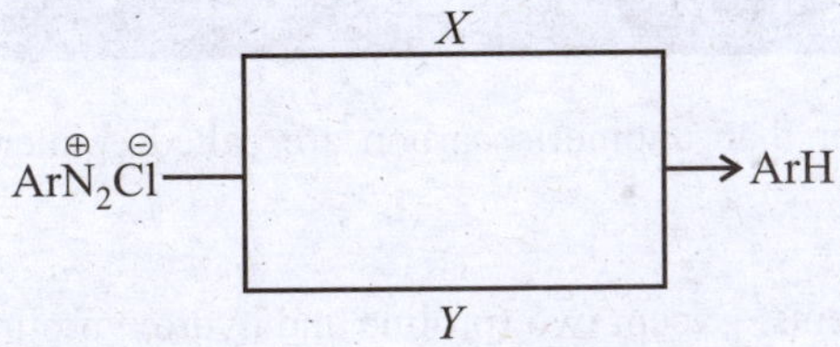

	(*X*)	(*Y*)
(a)	CH_3CH_2OH	H_3PO_2, H_2O
(b)	CH_3MgX	H_3PO_3
(c)	CH_3CHO	H_2O
(d)	$CH_2 = CH_2$	$NaNO_2$/HCl

60. Identify the reagents (*X, Y, Z*) used in the conversion of 3-methylaniline to 3-nitrotoluene. **[Apr. 21, 2019 (II)]**

	X	Y	Z
(a)	$NaNO_2$, HCl 273 K	HBF_4	$NaNO_2$, Cu, Δ
(b)	$NaNO_3$, HCl 273 K	HF	$NaNO_3$, Cu, Δ
(c)	$NaNO_2$, HCl	C_2H_5OH	$NaNO_3$, Δ
(d)	$NaNO_3$, HCl	NaOH	$C_6H_5NO_2$

61. Identify *Z* in the following sequence of reactions. **[Apr. 20, 2019 (II)]**

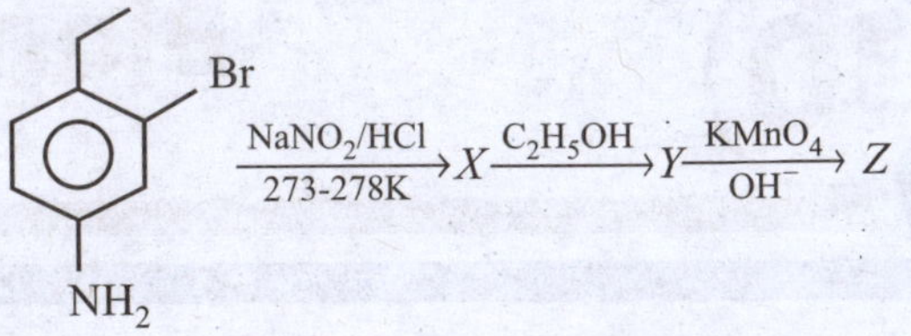

(a)
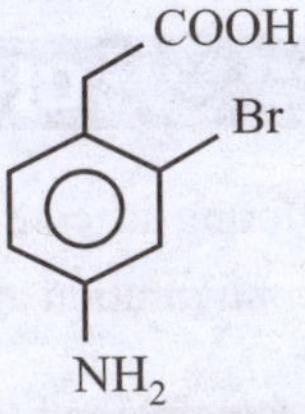

(b)
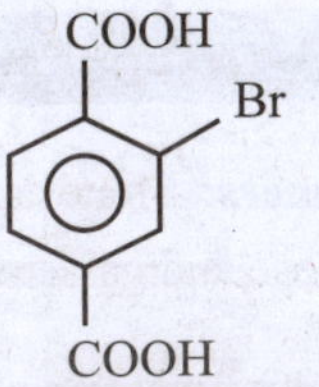

(c)
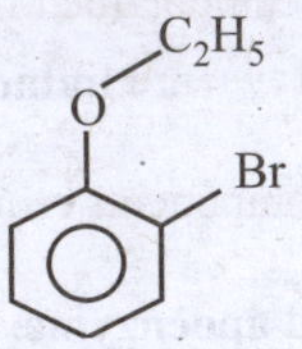

(d)
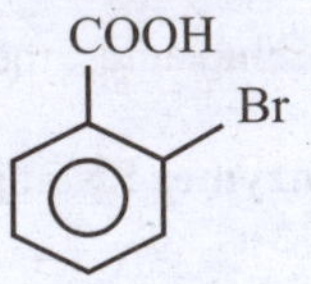

62. Predict respectively '*X*' and 'Y' in the following reactions. **[2015]**

$$Ar-NH_2 \xrightarrow{x} Ar-\overset{+}{N}\equiv NCl^- \xrightarrow{y} Ar-Cl$$

(a) $NaNO_3$ and Cl_2

(b) $NaNO_3$ - HCl and HCl

(c) $NaNO_2$ - HCl and Cu /HCl

(d) $NaNO_2$ - HCl and $NaNH_2$

10 Biomolecules

CHAPTER SYNOPSIS

- **Epimers:** Monosaccharides differing in configuration at a carbon other than anomeric carbon are called epimers e.g. glucose and galactose differ in configuration at C_4 hence called C_4 epimers.

- Twenty five amino acids have been obtained from the hydrolysis of proteins. Except two (proline and hydroxyproline) all are amino acids, the exceptional two are **imino acids**.

- **Coenzymes :** Non proteinous components required for the activity of certain enzymes are known as **coenzymes**.

- Protein part of enzymes is called **apoenzyme.**

- **Types of Hormones**
  - **Steroid hormones :**
    - (a) Estrogens and Progesterones
    - (b) Testosterone
    - (c) Cortisone
  - **Amino acid hormones :**
    - (a) Thyroxine
    - (b) Adrenaline
  - **Peptide hormones :**
    - (a) Insulin
    - (b) Glucagon
    - (c) Oxytocin
    - (d) Vasopressin

- Nucleic acids are polymers of nucleotides.

- Denaturation of proteins causes loss of biological activity without breaking peptide bonds.

- Vitamins are classified as fat-soluble (A, D, E, K) and water soluble (B and C).

Topic 1 Carbohydrates and Lipids

1. Which of the following are the correct statements about D-glucose?

I. It forms oxime with hydroxyl amine

II. It forms addition product with $NaHSO_3$

III. It forms cyanohydrin with HCN

IV. It forms saccharic acid with bromine water

The correct answer is **[May 18, 2026 (II)]**

(a) II & III only (b) I & III only

(c) II & IV only (d) III & IV only

2. Two statements are given below **[May 15, 2026 (II)]**

Statement I: Cane sugar is disaccharide of α – D – glucose and β – D – fructose

Statement II: Milk sugar is disaccharide of β – D – galactose and β – D – glucose

Correct answer is

(a) Statements I and II both are correct

(b) Statements I and II both are not correct

(c) Statement I is correct, but statement II is not correct

(d) Statement I is not correct but statement II is correct

3. Observe the following reactions **[May 15, 2026 (I)]**

I. $\text{D-Glucose} \xrightarrow{NH_2OH}$

II. $\text{D-Glucose} \xrightarrow[\text{(ii) } NH_2OH]{\text{(i) } (CH_3CO)_2O}$

Correct statement regarding the reactions I and II is

(a) Oxime is formed in both the reactions I, II

(b) Oxime is not formed in both the reactions I, II

(c) Oxime is formed in reaction I but oxime is not formed in reaction II

(d) Oxime is not formed in reaction I but oxime is formed in reaction II

4. The incorrect statement is the following is **[May 13, 2026 (I)]**

(a) Amylopection has $C_1 - C_4$ and $C_1 - C_6$ glycosidic linkages

(b) Cellulose is a straight chain polysaccharide of α – D – glucose units through $C_1 - C_4$ glycosidic linkage

(c) Glycogen is found in Yeast and fungi

(d) Glycogen is also known as animal starch

5. Which of the following represents the correct structure of β – D – (–) – fructofuranose? **[May 27, 2025 (I)]**

(a) 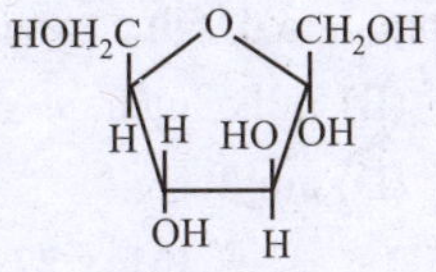

(b) 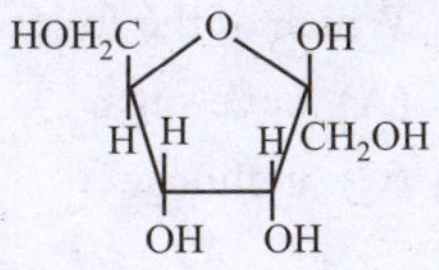

(c) 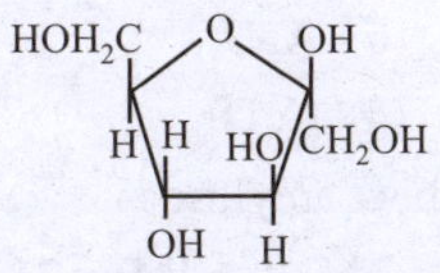

(d) 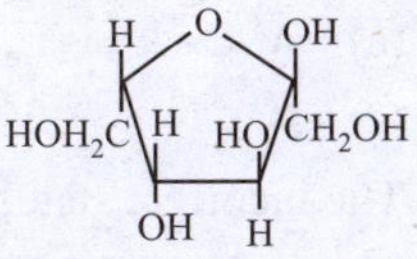

6. Which of the following statement is not correct for glucose? **[May 27, 2025 (I)]**

(a) Glucose does not give Schiffs test.

(b) Glucose exists in two crystalline forms α– and β–.

(c) The pentaacetate of glucose does not react with NH_2OH.

(d) Glucose forms addition product with $NaHSO_3$.

7. Which of the following do not reduce Tollens' reagent ? **[May 26, 2025 (I)]**

A. Fructose B. Sucrose

C. Lactose D. Cellulose

(a) A, B (b) B, D

(c) A, C (d) C, D

8. Match the following. **[May 24, 2025 (I)]**

	List I (Glycosidic linkage)		List II (Polysaccharide)
(A)	α–1,4	(i)	Amylose
(B)	β–1,4	(ii)	Amylopectin
(C)	α–1,4, α–1,6	(iii)	Cellulose

(a) A-II, B-I, C-III (b) A-III, B-I, C-II

(c) A-I, B-II, C-III (d) A-I, B-III, C-II

9. Consider the following

Statement-I: Cane sugar is a disaccharide of α-D-glucose and β-D-fructose

Statement-II: Milk sugar is a diasaccharide of α-D-glucose and β-D-galactose

The correct answer is **[May 23, 2025 (II)]**

(a) Both statement-I and statement-II are correct.

(b) Both statement-I and statement-II are not correct.

(c) Statement-I is correct, but statement-II is not correct.

(d) Statement-I is not correct, but statement-II is correct.

10. Consider the following

Statement-I: Lactose is composed of α-D-glucose and β-D-glucose.

Statement-II: Lactose is a reducing sugar.

The correct answer is **[May 22, 2025 (II)]**

(a) Both statement-I and statement-II are not correct.

(b) Both statement-I and statement-II are correct.

(c) Statement-I is correct, but statement-II is not correct.

(d) Statement-I is not correct, but statement-II is correct.

11. Which of the following contain α-D-glucose units?
(A) cane sugar (B) milk sugar
(C) cellulose (D) amylose
[May 22, 2025 (I)]
(a) A, D (b) A, B
(c) B, C (d) C, D

12. The incorrect statement about amylose is
(a) It is water soluble **[May 21, 2025 (I)]**
(b) In this α-D-(+)-glucose units are held by C-1 to C-4 glycosidic linkages
(c) It is a highly branched polymer of α-D-(+)-glucose units
(d) It is present in starch to an extent of 15-20%

13. The number of –OH groups in open chain and ring structures of D-glucose are respectively
[May 22, 2024 (II)]
(a) 4, 5 (b) 5, 5 (c) 5, 4 (d) 6, 5

14. Which one of the following is NOT a disaccharide?
[May 22, 2024 (I)]
(a) Sucrose (b) Fructose
(c) Maltose (d) Lactose

15. Given below are two statements: **[May 21, 2024 (II)]**
Statement I: Cytosine and guanine are formed in equal quantities in DNA hydrolysis
Statement II: Adenine and uracil are formed in equal quantities in RNA hydrolysis
The correct answer is
(a) Statements I, II both are correct
(b) Statements I, II both are incorrect
(c) Statement I is correct but statement II is incorrect
(d) Statement I is correct but statement II is correct

16. When glucose is oxidized with nitric acid the compound formed is **[May 20, 2024 (I)]**
(a) Gluconic acid (b) n-Hexanoic acid
(c) Saccharic acid (d) Cyanohydrin

17. The carbohydrate which does not react with ammonical $AgNO_3$ solution is **[May 19, 2024 (II)]**
(a) Sucrose (b) Maltose
(c) Lactose (d) Fructose

18. In D – glucose (X) and D – Fructose (Y), which hydroxyl group participates in hemiacetal formation
(a) C – 5 in both X and Y **[May 18, 2023 (I)]**
(b) C – 5 in X and C – 6 in Y
(c) C – 6 in X and C – 5 in Y
(d) C – 4 in both X and Y

19. If sucrose is boiled with dilute. HCl in alcoholic solution the ratio in which glucose and fructose are formed is
[July 8, 2022 (I)]
(a) 1 : 1 (b) 1 : 2 (c) 2 : 1 (d) 4 : 1

20. Which of the following statements are true about carbohydrates? **[Aug. 23, 2021 (I)]**
(i) Monosaccharides can be hydrolysed.
(ii) The two monosaccharide units obtained on hydrolysis of a disaccharide can either be same or different.
(iii) Polysaccharides are not sweet in taste.
(iv) All monosaccharides are not reducing sugars.
(a) (i) and (ii) (b) (ii) and (iii)
(c) (iii) and (iv) (d) (i) and (iv)

21. Identify the product of the following reaction.
[Aug. 19, 2021 (I)]
$$(C_6H_{10}O_5)_n + nH_2O \xrightarrow[393\text{ K},\ 2\text{–}3\text{ atm}]{H^+} ?$$
(a) Fructose (b) Glucose (c) Lactose (d) Maltose

22. Glucose does not react with which of the following.
[Sept. 17, 2020 (I)]
(a) NH_2OH (b) HCN
(c) Br_2/Water (d) $NaHSO_3$

23. Identify the correct set of monosaccharides present in sucrose (*X*), lactose (*Y*) and maltose (*Z*).
[Apr. 20, 2019 (II)]

	X	*Y*	*Z*
(a)	glucose, fructose	galactose, glucose	glucose, fructose
(b)	glucose, fructose	galactose, glucose	glucose, glucose
(c)	glucose, glucose	galactose, glucose	glucose, glucose
(d)	galactose, glucose	glucose, fructose	glucose, glucose

24. Which one of the following is the structure of lactose?
[2018]
(a) 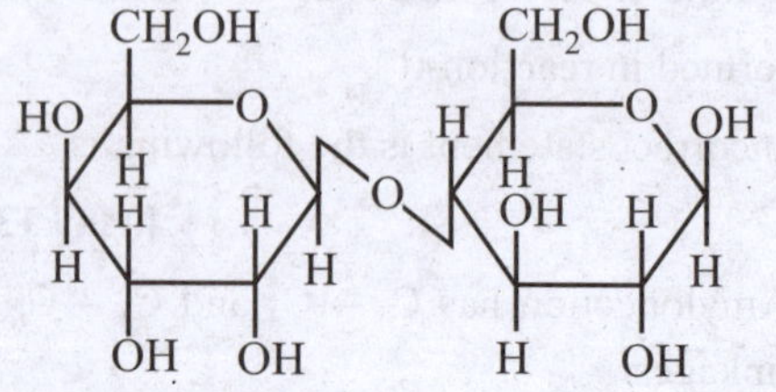
(b) 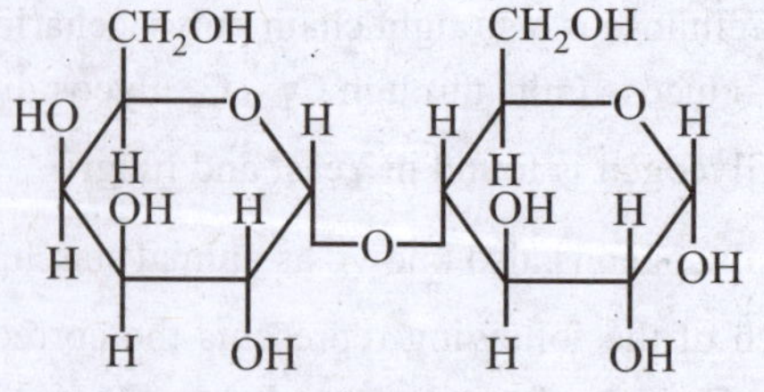

(c) 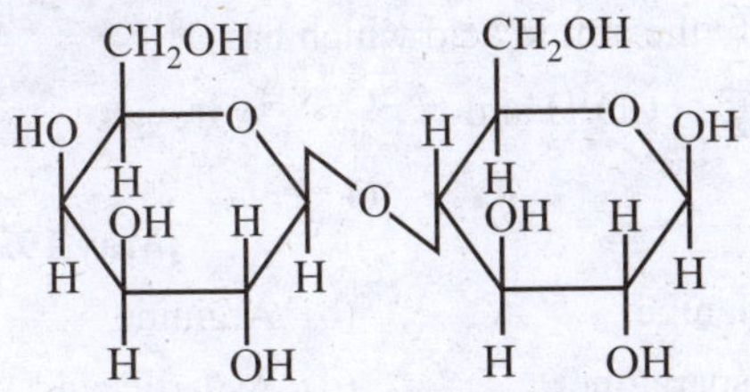

(d) 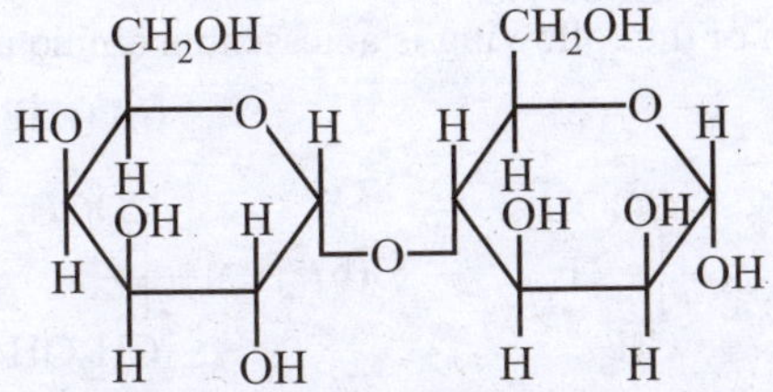

25. Observe the following statements. **[2016]**

I. Sucrose has glycosidic linkage.

II. Cellulose is present in both plants and animals.

III. Lactose contains D-galactose and D-glucose units.

Which of the following statements are correct?

(a) (I), (II) and (III) (b) (I) and (II)

(c) (II) and (III) (d) (I) and (III)

Topic 2 Amino Acids and Proteins

26. In addition to $-NH_2$ and –COOH groups, the functional group present in the amino acid, serine is X̲ and the functional group present in the amino acid cysteine is Y̲, X and Y are respectively. **[May 18, 2026 (I)]**

(a) $-\overset{O}{\overset{\|}{C}}-NH_2$, –SH (b) –OH, –SH

(c) –SH, –OH (d) –OH, $-\underset{O}{\underset{\|}{C}}-NH_2$

27. Match the following **[May 14, 2026 (I)]**

List - I	**List - II**
Name of amino acid	**R̲ part of** $H_2N-\underset{R}{\underset{\mid}{CH}}-COOH$
A Alanine	I $-CH_2-CH(CH_3)_2$
B Leucine	II $-CH_2-OH$
C Serine	III $-CH_3$
D Cysteine	IV $-CH_2SH$

The correct answer is

(a) A-III, B-IV, C-I, D-II (b) A-III, B-I, C-II, D-IV

(c) A-II, B-I, C-IV, D-III (d) A-IV, B-III, C-I, D-II

28. Amino acids containing hetero aromatic ring are

I. Pro II. His

III. Tyr IV. Trp

The correct answer is **[May 12, 2026 (II)]**

(a) I, III only (b) II, IV only

(c) I, III only (d) III, IV only

29. Match the following **[May 12, 2026 (I)]**

List-I	**List-II**
Name of the amino acid	**Description**
A. Tyrosine	I. Basic amino acid
B. Lysine	II. Optically inactive amino acid
C. Glycine	III. Sulphur containing amino acid
D. CYSTEINE	IV. Aromatic amino acid

The correct answer is

(a) A-II, B-I, C-IV, D-III

(b) A-IV, B-III, C-II, D-I

(c) A-IV, B-I, C-II, D-III

(d) A-III, B-IV, C-I, D-II

30. Identify the essential amino acids from the following **[May 26, 2025 (II)]**

(A) Leucine (B) Tyrosine

(C) Cysteine (D) Histidine

(a) A & B only (b) B & C only

(c) B & D only (d) A & D only

31. Consider the following.

Statement-I: Lysine, arginine are essential and basic amino acids.

Statement-II: Leucine, phenylalanine are non essential and neutral amino acids.

Correct answer is **[May 26, 2025 (I)]**

(a) Both statement-I and statement-II are correct.

(b) Both statement-I and statement-II are not correct.

(c) Statement-I is correct, but statement-II is not correct.

(d) Statement-I is not correct, but statement-II is correct.

32. The list given below contains essential amino acids that are basic (X) and also non essential amino acids that are neutral (Y). X and Y, respectively are

(a) Lysine (b) Alanine

(c) Serine (d) Arginine

(e) Tyrosine **[May 24, 2025 (I)]**

(a) X = b, c, e; Y = a, d (b) X = a, d; Y = b, c, e

(c) X = a, c; Y = b, d, e (d) X = a, b, c; Y = d, e

33. Consider the following.

Statement-I: Primary structure of protein represents its constitution.

Statement-II: α-Helix and β-pleated sheet structures of protein represent tertiary structure of it.

Correct answer is **[May 23, 2025 (I)]**

(a) Both statement-I and statement-II are correct.
(b) Both statement-I and statement-II are not correct.
(c) Statement-I is correct, but statement-II is not correct.
(d) Statement-I is not correct, but statement-II is correct.

34. Consider the following sequence of reactions.

Isopropyl benzene 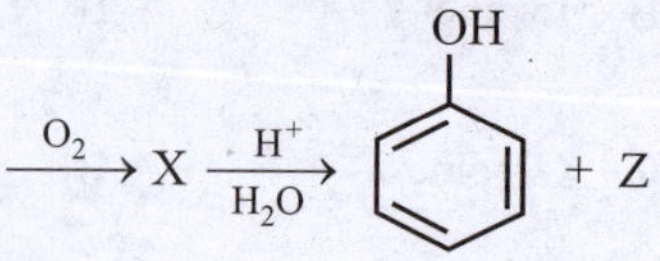

The incorrect statement about Z is **[May 21, 2025 (I)]**

(a) Z gives yellow precipitate of CHI_3 with NaOH + I_2 solution
(b) Z gives isopropyl alcohol on reduction with H_2 in the presence of Pd catalyst
(c) Z on reaction with CH_3MgBr followed by hydrolysis gives 2° alcohol
(d) Z does not give positive test with Fehling's reagent

35. Which of the following is correct statement? **[May 22, 2024 (II)]**

(a) Starch is a polymer of β-D-glucose
(b) Amylose is a component of starch
(c) Proteins are biopolymers of only one type of amino acids
(d) Lactose is a disaccharide of α-D-glucose and β-D-glucose

36. Which of the following is not an essential amino acid? **[May 22, 2024 (I)]**

(a) Lysine (b) Histidine
(c) Glutamine (d) Methionine

37. Which of the following structure of proteins represents its constitution? **[May 21, 2024 (I)]**

(a) Secondary structure (b) Quaternary structure
(c) Primary structure (d) Tertiary structure

38. Which of the following amino acids possess two chiral centres? **[May 20, 2024 (II)]**

(a) Leucine (b) Valine
(c) Serine (d) Threonine

39. The number of essential and non-essential amino acids from the following list respectively is

Val, Gly, Leu, Lys, Pro, Ser **[May 20, 2024 (I)]**

(a) 5, 1 (b) 4, 2 (c) 2, 4 (d) 3, 3

40. Identify the amino acid which has $-NH_2$, $-CO_2H$ and $-\underset{\underset{O}{\|}}{C}-NH_2$ groups **[May 19, 2024 (II)]**

(a) Alanine (b) Arginine
(c) Asparagine (d) Aspartic acid

41. Which of the following is an essential amino acid? **[May 18, 2024 (I)]**

(a) 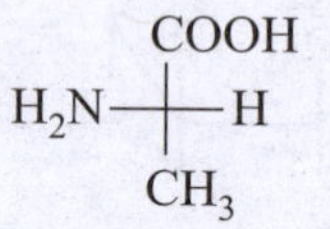
(b) 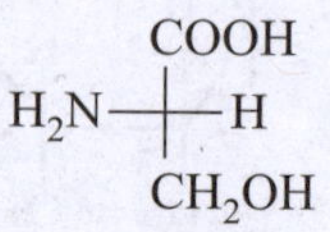
(c) 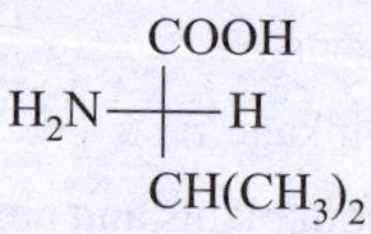
(d) 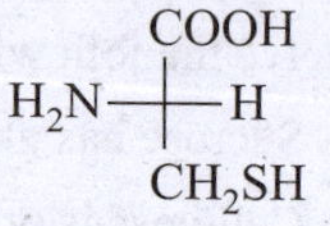

42. Identify the correct statement related to amino acids **[May 19, 2023 (I)]**

(a) Non-essential amino acids cannot be synthesized in the body
(b) These are soluble in ether
(c) These are low melting solid substances
(d) In aqueous solution they exist as zwitter ion

43. In which of the following amino acids - OH group is present? **[May 18, 2023 (II)]**

Lysine	Serine	Tyrosine	Valine
A	B	C	D

(a) A, B (b) A, C (c) B, C (d) B, D

44. Which of the following are fibrous proteins? **[May 17, 2023 (II)]**

Keratin	Insulin	Myosin	Albumin
A	B	C	D

(a) A, B (b) A, C (c) B, D (d) C, D

45. Sulphur containing amino acids of the following are **[May 16, 2023 (I)]**

Serine	Cysteine	Lysine	Methionine
A	B	C	D

(a) A, D (b) A, C (c) B, C (d) B, D

46. The structure of Gly–Ala is **[May 15, 2023 (I)]**

(a) 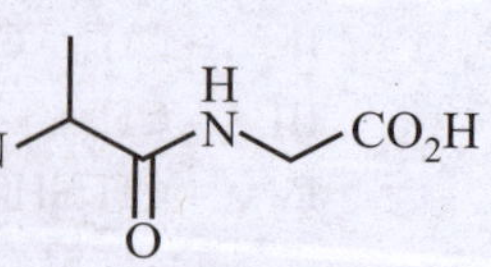

(b) 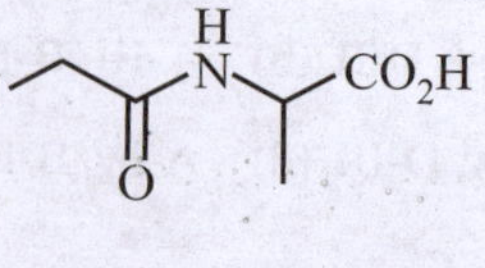

(c) 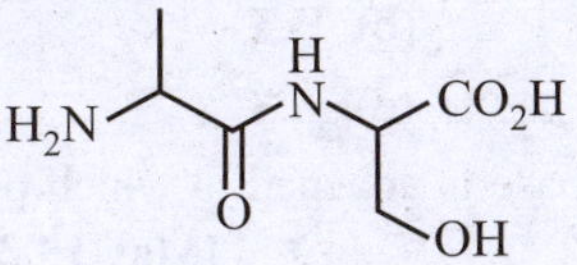

(d) 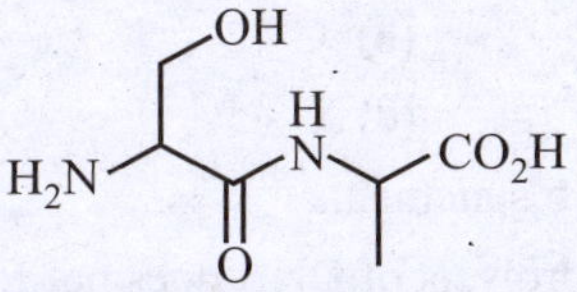

47. In which of the following, keratin, a fibrous protein is absent? **[July 6, 2022 (I)]**
(a) Hair (b) Muscles (c) Silk (d) Wool

48. What is the functional group present in serine, an amino acid in addition to $-NH_2$ and $-COOH$ groups? **[July 5, 2022 (II)]**
(a) $-OH$ (b) $-SH$
(c) $-NH-$ (d) $-\underset{\underset{O}{\|}}{C}-NH_2$

49. Which of the following molecules is eliminated during peptide bond formation? **[July 4, 2022 (I)]**
(a) H_2O (b) NH_3 (c) CH_3OH (d) CO_2

50. The general structural formula of α-amino acid is 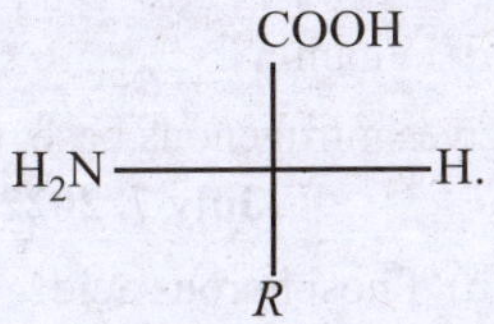. The group *R* in tryptophan (*X*) and histidine (*Y*) are respectively **[Apr. 22, 2019 (II)]**

X Y

(a) 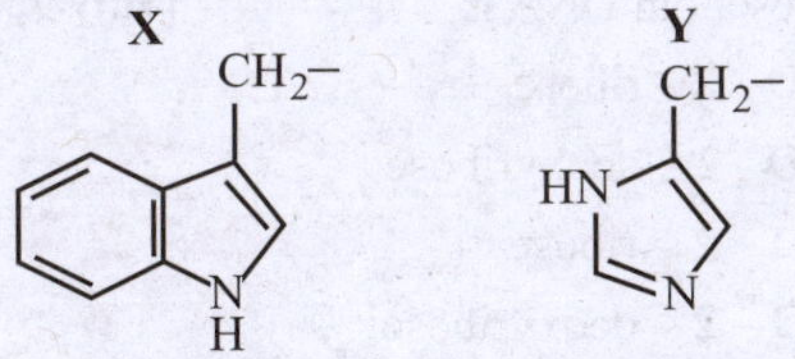

(b) 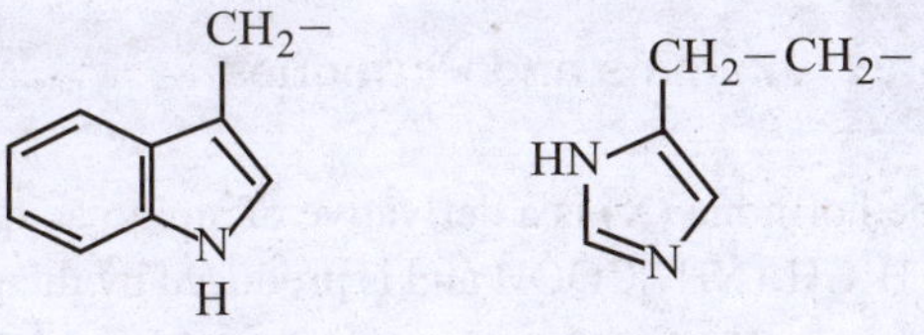

(c) 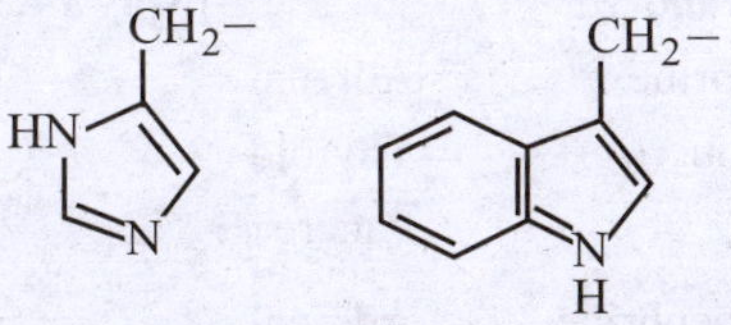

(d) 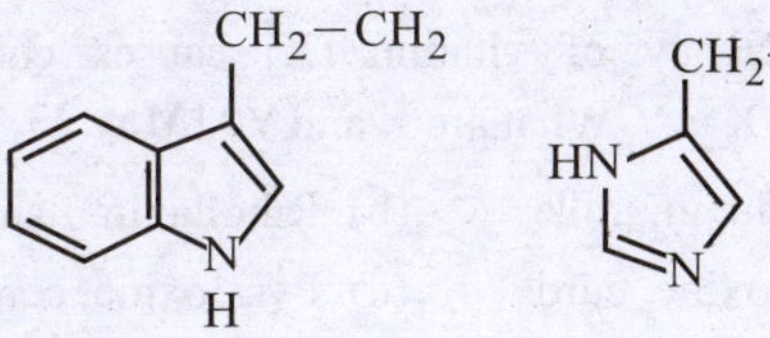

51. The amino acid containing indole part is **[2015]**
(a) tryptophan (b) tyrosine
(c) proline (d) methionine

Topic 3 Nucleic Acid and Enzymes

52. Which of the following represents nucleoside of RNA? **[May 26, 2025 (II)]**

(a) 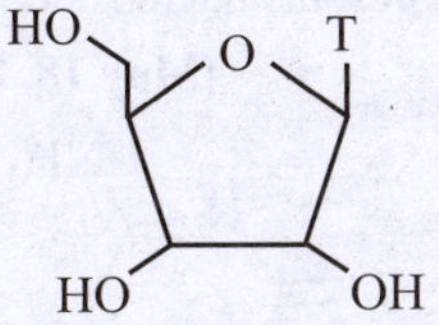

(b) 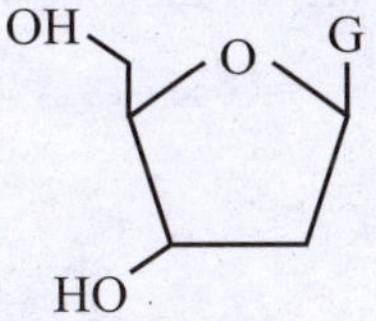

(c) 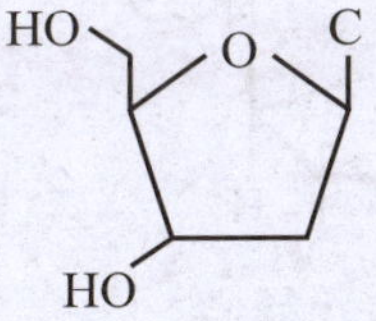

(d) 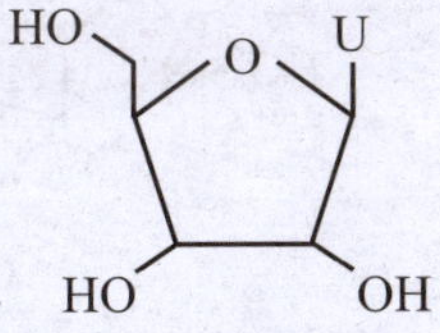

53. Which of the following enzymatic reaction is not correctly matched with enzyme shown against it in brackets **[May 26, 2025 (II)]**
(a) Proteins → Peptides (Pepsin)
(b) Starch → Maltose (Zymase)
(c) Sucrose → Glucose and fructose (Invertase)
(d) Maltose → Glucose (Maltase)

54. Identify the set containing purine and pyrimidine base of DNA respectively. **[May 22, 2025 (I)]**
(a) Adenine, Uracil (b) Cytosine, Guanine
(c) Thymine, Uracil (d) Adenine, Cytosine

55. The structure of the nitrogen containing heterocyclic base given below represents **[May 21, 2025 (II)]**

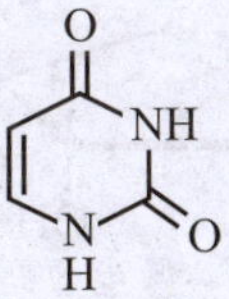

(a) Adenine (b) Thymine
(c) Uracil (d) Cytosine

56. Match List-I with List-II **[May 22, 2024 (I)]**

	List-I (Reaction)		List-II (Enzyme)
A.	Hydrolysis of starch to maltose	I	Diastase
B.	Conversion of proteins to peptides	II	Pepsin
C.	Hydrolysis of sucrose to glucose and fructose	III	Invertase
D.	Glucose to ethanol	IV	Zymase

The correct answer is

(a) A-III, B-II, C-I, D-IV (b) A-I, B-III, C-II, D-IV

(c) A-IV, B-II, C-III, D-I (d) A-I, B-II, C-III, D-IV

57. Which of the following represents simplified version of nucleoside? **[May 20, 2024 (II)]**

(a) Base - sugar - phosphate (b) Sugar - base

(c) Sugar - Phosphate (d) Base - Phosphate

58. Which of the following represents nucleoside? **[May 18, 2023 (II)]**

(a) 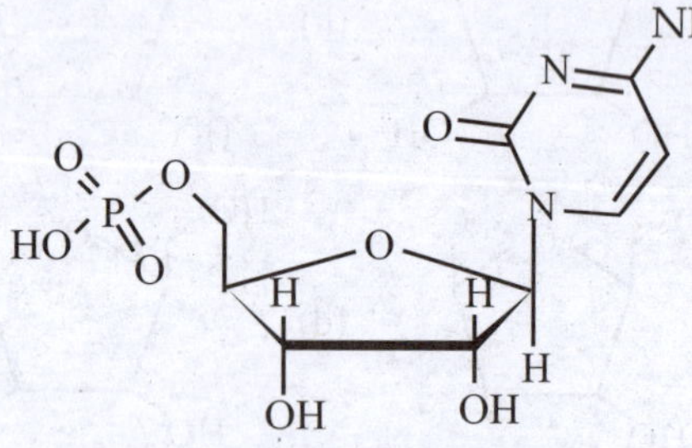

(b) 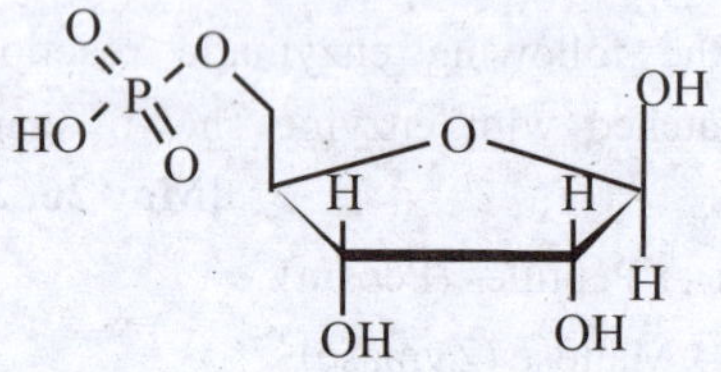

(c) 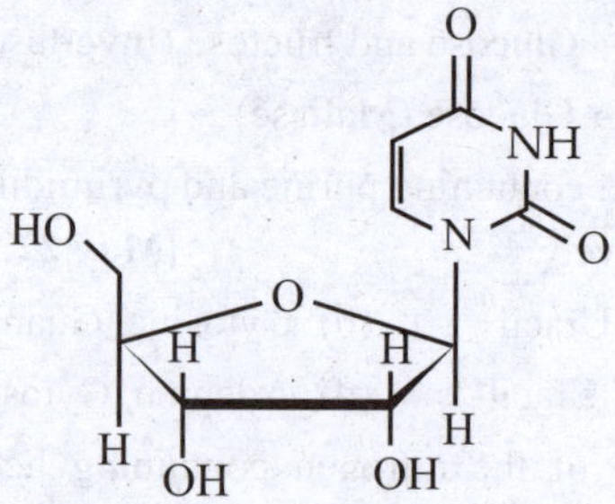

(d) 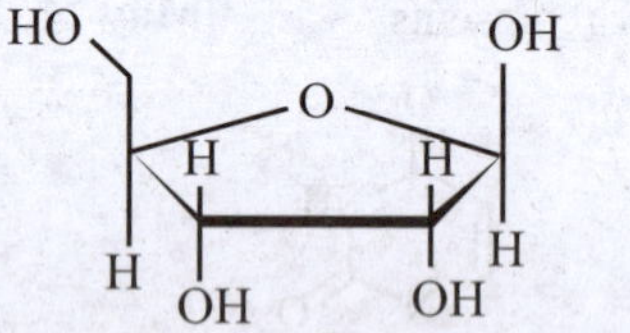

59. Which of the following correctly represents hydrogen bonded pairs in DNA? **[May 18, 2023 (I)]**

(a) G = C; T ≡ A (b) G = C; T = A

(c) G ≡ C; T ≡ A (d) G ≡ C; T = A

60. Which of the following bases are present both in DNA and RNA? **[May 16, 2023 (I)]**

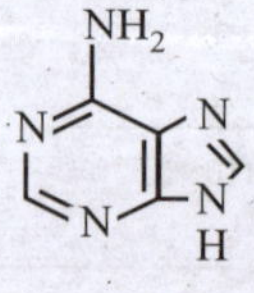
A

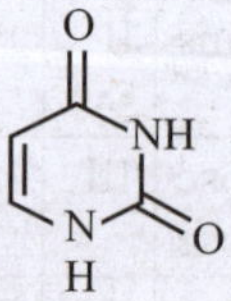
B

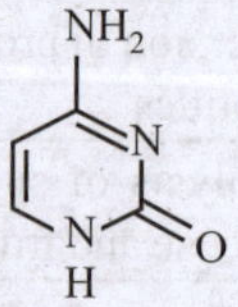
C

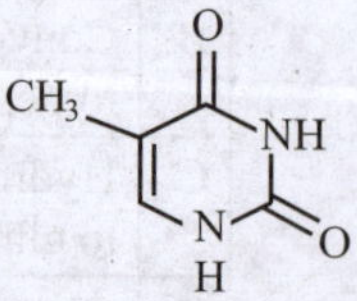
D

(a) C, D (b) B, C

(c) A, B (d) A, C

61. In nucleoside, the base is attached to which position of sugar molecule? **[May 15, 2023 (II)]**

(a) C - 1 (b) C - 2

(c) C - 3 (d) C - 5

62. Given below are two statements

Assertion (A): Hydrolysis of DNA does not form equal number of A and T; G and C

Reason (R): In DNA adenine forms hydrogen bonds with thymine and cytosine forms hydrogen bonds with guanine

The correct answer is **[May 15, 2023 (I)]**

(a) Both A and R are correct and R is the correct explanation of A

(b) Both A and R are correct but R is not the correct explanation of A

(c) A is correct but R is incorrect

(d) A is incorrect but R is correct

63. Thiamine is **[July 8, 2022 (I)]**

(a) Nitrogenous base (b) Amino acid

(c) Hormone (d) Vitamin

64. Hydrolysis of nucleic acid gives nitrogenous base, sugar and ________. **[July 7, 2022 (II)]**

(a) Sulphuric acid (b) Phosphorous acid

(c) Sulphurous acid (d) Phosphoric acid

65. Sugar present in DNA is **[July 7, 2022 (II)]**

(a) β – D - 2 – ribose

(b) β – D - 2 – deoxyribose

(c) α - D – 2 – ribose

(d) α - D – 2 – deoxyribose

Topic 4 Vitamins and Hormones

66. The hormone (X) is a derivative of amino acid p – HO – $C_6H_4CH_2(NH_2)COOH$ and is produced by the gland (Y). What are X and Y? **[May 14, 2026 (II)]**

(a) Epinephrine, Adrenal

(b) Thyroxine, Thyroid

(c) Insulin, Pancreas

(d) Norepinephrine, Adrenal

67. The deficiency of vitamin (X) causes convulsions. Source of X is Y. What are X and Y? **[May 23, 2025 (II)]**

(a) Riboflavin, milk (b) Riboflavin, fish

(c) Pyridoxine, curd (d) Pyridoxine, cereals

68. Match the following. **[May 22, 2025 (II)]**

List-I (Hormones)		List-II (Functions)	
(A)	Glucocorticoids	(I)	In the control of menstrual cycle
(B)	Mineralocorticoids	(II)	Prepares the uterus for implantation of fertilised egg
(C)	Progesterone	(III)	Control the level of excretion of water and salt by the kidneys
(D)	Estradiol	(IV)	Control the carbohydrate metabolsim

(a) A-II, B-III, C-IV, D-I (b) A-IV, B-I, C-II, D-III
(c) A-IV, B-III, C-II, D-I (d) A-IV, B-I, C-III, D-II

69. The improper functioning of 'X' results in Addison's disease. Hormone 'Y' is responsible for the development of secondary female characteristics. 'X' and 'Y' are respectively **[May 21, 2025 (I)]**

(a) Adrenal Cortex, estradiol
(b) Adrenal Cortex, progesterone
(c) Thyroid, progesterone
(d) Thyroid, estradiol

70. Which of the following acts as intracellular messengers? **[May 23, 2024 (I)]**

(a) Enzymes (b) Hormones
(c) Receptors (d) Carrier proteins

71. The deficiency of vitamin (x) causes beri-beri and deficiency of vitamin (y) causes convulsions.
What are *x* and *y* respectively? **[May 23, 2024 (I)]**

(a) B_2, B_{12} (b) B_1, B_{12}
(c) B_2, B_6 (d) B_1 B_6

72. Identify the correctly matched set from the following **[May 21, 2024 (II)]**

(a) Vitamin A - Water soluble - Xerophthamia
(b) Vitamin B_6 - Water soluble - Scurvy
(c) Vitamin D - fat soluble - Rickets
(d) Vitamin C - fat soluble - Convulsions

73. Carrot and curd are sources for the vitamins respectively **[May 21, 2024 (I)]**

(a) A, B_{12} (b) A, B_1
(c) E, Pyridoxine (d) E. Riboflavin

74. Which of the following hormone is responsible for preparing uterus for implantation of fertilised egg? **[May 18, 2024 (I)]**

(a) Estradiol (b) Progesterone
(c) Testosterone (d) Thyroxin

75. From the following, number of fat soluble and water soluble vitamins respectively are
A D C B_1 K B_6. **[May 19, 2023 (I)]**

(a) 2, 4 (b) 4, 2 (c) 3, 3 (d) 6, 0

76. Which of the following hormones modulate inflammatory reactions? **[May 17, 2023 (II)]**

(a) Mineralocorticoids
(b) Glucocorticoids
(c) Epinephrine
(d) Glucagon

77. Match the following

List-I		List-II	
A.	Beri beri	I.	Riboflavin
B.	Scurvy	II.	Thiamine
C.	Cheilosis	III.	Pyridoxine
D.	Rickets	IV.	Ascorbic acid
		V.	Vitamin D

The correct answer is **[May 17, 2023 (I)]**

(a) A – III, B – IV, C – III, D – V
(b) A – II, B – IV, C – I, D – V
(c) A – III, B – V, C – I, D – II
(d) A – III, B – V, C – IV, D – II

78. The source of vitamin, whose deficiency causes scurvy is **[May 17, 2023 (I)]**

(a) Amla (b) Carrot
(c) Egg (d) Fish

79. Deficiency of which vitamin causes convulsions? **[May 16, 2023 (II)]**

(a) Riboflavin (b) Thiamine
(c) Ascorbic acid (d) Pyridoxine

80. Addison's disease is characterized by

A. Hyperglycemia
B. Weakness
C. Increased susceptibility to stress
D. Hypertension **[May 16, 2023 (II)]**

(a) A, C (b) A, D (c) B, C (d) B, D

81. Hypothyroidism is due to

A. High level of iodine in the diet

B. Enlargement of thyroid gland

C. Low levels of iodine in the diet

D. Increased levels of thyroxine

[May 15, 2023 (II)]

(a) A, B (b) B, C (c) A, D (d) C, D

82. The deficiency of which vitamin causes pernicious anaemia? **[July 4, 2022 (II)]**

(a) Vitamin B_2 (b) Vitamin B_6

(c) Vitamin E (d) Vitamin B_{12}

83. The total number of amino acids present in insulin is

[July 6, 2022 (I)]

(a) 55 (b) 1051 (c) 51 (d) 100

84. The product 'Q' of the following reactions is

[July 5, 2022 (II)]

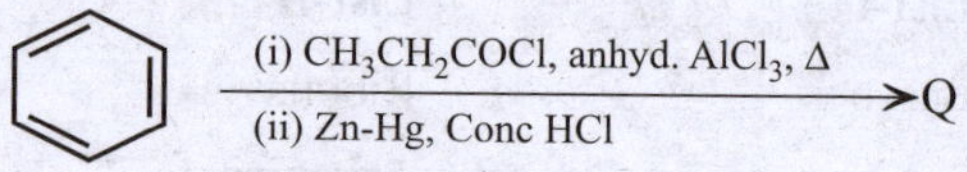

(a) 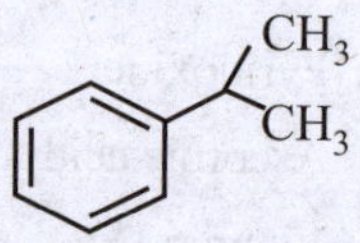

(b) 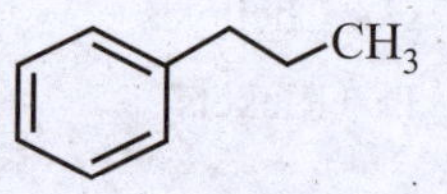

(c) 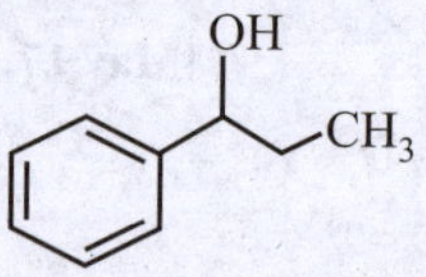

(d) 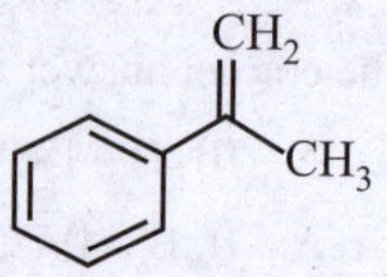

85. Which of the following vitamins cannot be stored in the body? **[July 4, 2022 (II)]**

(a) A (b) C (c) E (d) K

86. Which hormone tends to increase the blood glucose level in human? **[July 4, 2022 (I)]**

(a) Insulin (b) Glucagon

(c) Epinephrine (d) Estrogen

87. Vitamin-B_1 is **[Aug. 20, 2021 (II)]**

(a) riboflavin (b) cobalamine

(c) thiamine (d) pyridoxine

88. Which among the following acts as a vitamin?

[Sept. 21, 2020 (I)]

(a) Aspartic acid (b) Ascorbic acid

(c) Saccharic acid (d) Adipic acid

89. Identify the statement which is not correct from the following. **[2017]**

(i) Carbohydrates are stored as glycogen in animals.

(ii) In glycylalanine, $-\overset{\overset{O}{\|}}{C}-$ of peptide bond belongs to alanine.

(iii) Base - sugar- phosphate unit is known as nucleoside

(iv) Obesity is due to hypothyroidism.

The correct answer is

(a) i, iv (b) ii, iii, iv

(c) i, iii, iv (d) ii, iii

The p-Block Elements (Group 15, 16, 17 & 18)

Appendix

CHAPTER SYNOPSIS

- Hydracid of halogens HF forms two series of salts **($NaHF_2$ and NaF)**.
- Silver halide insoluble in ammonia : AgI
- Metals and non-metals react with HNO_3 under different conditions to give NO or NO_2.
- In laboratory, dioxygen is prepared by heating $KClO_3$ in presence of MnO_2.
- XeF_2 is linear, XeF_4 is square planar and XeF_6 is distorted octahedral.
- XeF_2, XeF_4, and XeF_6 are powerful fluorinating agents.
- Xe form two oxides such as XeO_3 and XeO_4.
- In solid state, PCl_5 exists as an ionic solid, $[PCl_4]^+ [PCl_6]^-$ in which the cation $[PCl_4]^+$ is tetrahedral and the anion $[PCl_6]^-$ is octahedral.
- **SO_3**. is a gas, sp^2 hybridised and planar in nature.

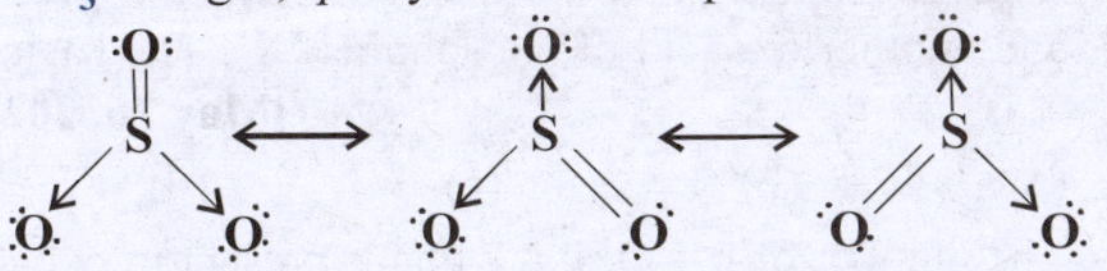

In solid state it exist as a **cyclic trimer $(SO_3)_3$** γ-form or as a **linear** chain cross linked sheets

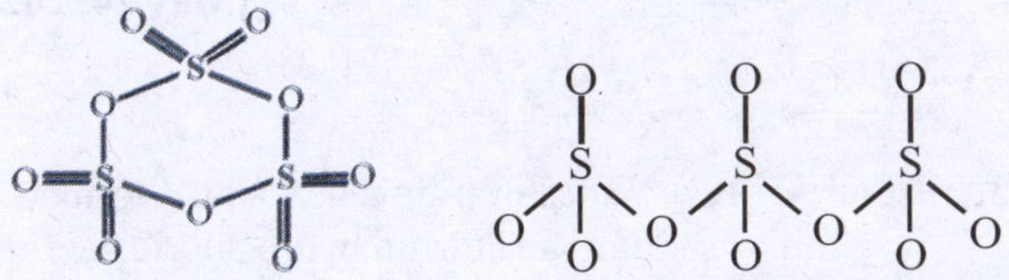

γ-form β- and α-form

- SF_6 is used in high voltage tranformers because of its insulating property.
- Liquid oxygen mixed with finely divided carbon is used in place of dynamite in coal mining.
- Gun powder is a mixture of sulphur, charcoal and KNO_3.
- S_2Cl_2 is used in the vulcanisation of rubber. It is heating of rubber with sulphur and was discovered by, **Charles Goodyear** in 1839.

Topic 1 Nitrogen Family

1. The method by which very pure nitrogen can be obtained is **[May 18, 2026 (II)]**
(a) Thermal decomposition of ammonium dichromate
(b) Thermal decomposition of barium azide
(c) Reaction of aqueous solution of ammonium chloride with sodium nitrite
(d) Thermal decomposition of ammonium nitrate

2. Which anion of the simple salt can be confirmed by Brown ring test? **[May 15, 2026 (I)]**
(a) NO_2^- (b) NO_3^-
(c) Br^- (d) SO_4^{2-}

3. Observe the following reaction **[May 14, 2026 (II)]**
$PH_3(aq) \xrightarrow{\text{Light}} X + H_2$
Which of the following is NOT correct regarding X?
(a) It is non-poisonous, odourless solid
(b) It is insoluble in water and carbon disulphide
(c) It has polymeric structure
(d) It exhibits chemiluminescence in dark

4. Which of the following oxoacids is formed when phosphonic acid is made to react with PCl_3? **[May 14, 2026 (I)]**
(a) $H_4P_2O_6$ (b) $H_4P_2O_7$
(c) $H_4P_2O_5$ (d) $H_3P_3O_9$

5. The reduction products formed when copper and zinc metals are separately oxidised with dilute HNO_3 respectively are **[May 13, 2026 (I)]**
(a) NO, NO_2 (b) N_2O, NO
(c) NO, N_2O (d) NO_2, NO

6. Compound X is formed when dry chlorine is passed over heated white phosphorous. X on hydrolysis gives an acid Y. What are the disproportionation products of Y? **[May 12, 2026 (II)]**
(a) H_3PO_4, H_3PO_2 (b) PH_3, H_3PO_4
(c) H_3PO_3,PH_3 (d) H_3PO_2,PH_3

7. An oxoacid, X is formed by the reaction of P_4O_6 with water. When this acid is heated, it undergoes disproportionation to give a different oxoacid Y and a poisonous gas Z. Identify the correct statement regarding X, Y, Z **[May 12, 2026 (I)]**
(a) X is a tribasic acid
(b) Y has two P-H bonds
(c) X forms another tribasic oxoacid on reacting with PCl_3
(d) Z acts as Lewis base

8. Which oxide of nitrogen can damage the leaves of plants and retard the rate of phatosynthesis, when it is present in higher concentration in air? **[May 12, 2026 (I)]**
(a) NO_2 (b) NO
(c) N_2O (d) N_2O_3

9. The increasing order of N-N bond length of N_2O(A), N_2O_3 (B), N_2O_4(C) is **[May 12, 2026 (I)]**
(a) A, C, B (b) A, B, C
(c) B, C, A (d) C, B, A

10. Observe the following **[May 26, 2025 (II)]**
$P_4 + SOCl_2 \rightarrow$ Products
$P_4 + SO_2Cl_2 \rightarrow$ Products
In both the reactions, a common product '*x*' is obtained. The number of lone pair of electrons on the central atom of *x* is
(a) 1 (b) 2
(c) 3 (d) Zero

11. Orthophosphorus acid on disproportionation gives PH_3 and another oxoacid of phosphorus 'X'. The basicity of X is **[May 26, 2025 (I)]**
(a) 2 (b) 1 (c) 3 (d) 4

12. The number of P = O, P – P bonds present in oxoacid of phosphorus, prepared by treating red P_4 with alkali are respectively **[May 24, 2025 (I)]**
(a) 2, 1 (b) 1, 1
(c) 1, 2 (d) 2, 2

13. Nature of two oxides of nitrogen X and Y formed in the reaction of sodium nitrite with hydrochloric acid **[May 23, 2025 (II)]**
(a) Both X and Y are acidic in nature.
(b) X is acidic and Y is neutral in nature.
(c) Both X and Y are neutral in nature.
(d) X is amphoteric and Y is neutral in nature.

14. White phosphorus on heating with concentrated NaOH solution in an inert atmosphere of CO_2 gives a salt 'X' and gas 'Y'. The oxidation state of central atom in X and Y is respectively **[May 22, 2025 (II)]**
(a) –3, +1 (b) +1, –3 (c) 0, –3 (d) +1, +2

15. The oxides of nitrogen obtained by the reaction of nitric acid with **[May 21, 2025 (II)]**
(i) P_4O_{10}, (ii) P_4 respectively are
(a) NO, N_2O (b) N_2O_3, NO
(c) N_2O_5, NO_2 (d) NO_2, N_2O

16. The shape of colourless neutral gas formed on thermal decomposition of ammonium nitrate is **[May 22, 2024 (II)]**
(a) Angular (b) Linear
(c) Trigonal planar (d) Trigonal pyramidal

17. The basicity of H_3PO_2, H_3PO_3, H_3PO_4 respectively is **[May 22, 2024 (II)]**
(a) 2, 2, 3 (b) 2, 3, 3 (c) 1, 3, 3 (d) 1, 2, 3

18. $P_2O_3 + H_2O \rightarrow X$ **[May 21, 2024 (II)]**
Red P_4 + alkali $\rightarrow$ Y
X, Y are oxoacids of phosphorous. The number of P – OH bonds in X. Y respectively is $P_2O_3 + H_2O \rightarrow X$
(a) 1, 4 (b) 4, 1 (c) 2, 4 (d) 1, 1

19. Which of the following reactions give phosphine?
(i) Reaction of calcium phosphide with water
(ii) Heating white phosphorous with concentrated NaOH solution in inert atmosphere
(iii) Heating red phosphorous with alkali **[May 20, 2024 (I)]**
(a) (i), (ii) only (b) (i), (ii) , (iii)
(c) (ii), (iii) only (d) (i), (iii) only

20. Manganese dioxide on heating with concentrated hydrochloric acid gives a greenish yellow gas, X. With excess of ammonia X gives Y and Z. Y and Z respectively are **[May 18, 2023 (I)]**
(a) NH_4F, N_2 (b) NH_4I, NOCl
(c) NCl_3, HOCl (d) NH_4Cl, N_2

21. Small quantities of NO and HNO_3 are formed as impurities, when N_2 is prepared from NH_4Cl (aq) and $NaNO_2$ (aq), these impurities can be removed by passing the N_2 gas through which of the following? **[July 8, 2022 (I)]**
(a) H_2SO_4 (aq) containing SO_3
(b) H_2SO_4 (aq) containing $K_2Cr_2O_7$
(c) H_2SO_4 (aq) containing $KMnO_4$
(d) HCl (aq) containing $KMnO_4$

22. Arrange the following oxides in correct order of their acidic character. **[July 7, 2022 (II)]**
N_2O_3, P_2O_3, N_2O_5, As_2O_3
I II III IV
(a) I > III > II > IV
(b) III > I > II > IV
(c) IV > II > I > III
(d) III > I > IV > II

23. The moisture present in ammonia can be removed by using which of the following? **[July 6, 2022 (I)]**
(a) P_4O_{10} (b) Conc. H_2SO_4
(c) $CaCl_2$ (anhydrous) (d) CaO

24. In the reaction of phosphorous with conc. HNO_3, the oxidized and reduced products respectively are **[July 4, 2022 (II)]**
(a) H_3PO_4, NO_2 (b) H_3PO_2, NO
(c) H_3PO_3, N_2O (d) HPO_3, NO

25. What are x and y in the following reaction?
$xPb_3O_4 \rightarrow yPbO + O_2$ **[July 4, 2022 (I)]**
(a) x = 3, y = 6 (b) x = 2, y = 4
(c) x = 2, y = 5 (d) x = 2, y = 6

26. The oxoacid of phosphorous which contains 4 P – O – H, 2P = O and one P – O – P bond is **[Sep. 18, 2020 (I)]**
(a) Orthophosphoric acid (b) Metaphosphoric acid
(c) Pyrophosphoric acid (d) Hypophosphoric acid

27. In which of the following reactions there is no liberation of nitrogen gas **[2018]**
(a) $NO_2^-(aq) + NH_4^+(s) \xrightarrow{\Delta}$
(b) $CO(NH_2)_2(s) + HNO_2(l) \longrightarrow$
(c) $NH_3(g) + NaOCl(aq) \xrightarrow{\text{gelatin}}$
(d) $(NH_4)_2Cr_2O_7(s) \xrightarrow{\Delta}$

28. The hybridisation of N-orbitals in NO_3^-, NO_2^- and NH_4^+ respectively are **[Aug. 23, 2021 (II)]**
(a) sp^2, sp^2, sp^3 (b) sp, sp^3, sp^2
(c) sp, sp^2, sp^3 (d) sp^2, sp, sp^3

29. Which among the following is least covalent in nature? **[Aug. 23, 2021 (I)]**
(a) NF_3 (b) BiF_3
(c) PF_3 (d) SbF_3

30. Conc. HNO_3 turns brown on standing due to formation of .... **[Sept. 21, 2020 (II)]**
(a) NO (b) NO_2
(c) N_2O (d) N_2O_4

31. Gas '*X*' is obtained on heating $KClO_3$ with catalyst MnO_2. This gas (in excess) on reaction with white phosphorus forms an acidic oxide '*Y*'. '*Y*' on dissolving in water forms a compound '*Z*'. Identify *X*, *Y* and *Z*. **[Sept. 18, 2020 (I)]**
(a) O_2, P_2O_5, H_3PO_4 (b) O_3, P_2O_5, H_3PO_4
(c) O_2, P_2O_3, H_3PO_3 (d) O_2, P_2O_5, H_3PO_3

32. Which of the compounds among N_2O, NO, N_2O_3, NO_2, N_2O_4, N_2O_5 are diamagnetic? **[Sept. 17, 2020 (II)]**

(a) NO, NO_2, N_2O_3

(b) N_2O, N_2O_3, N_2O_4, N_2O_5

(c) NO, NO_2

(d) N_2O_4, N_2O_5

33. Which one of the following statements is not correct regarding phosphine? **[Apr. 22, 2019 (I)]**

(a) It is a weak base

(b) It reacts with $CuSO_4$ solution to form $CuHPO_4$

(c) It is formed by the reaction of Ca_3P_2 with HCl

(d) It is used in smoke screens

34. White phosphorus is heated with concentrated NaOH in CO_2 atmosphere to form a gas *A* and compound *B*. When *A* is bubbled into aqueous $CuSO_4$ solution copper phosphide and *C* are formed, *B* and *C* are respectively **[Apr. 21, 2019 (II)]**

(a) PH_3, H_2SO_4 (b) NaH_2PO_2, H_2SO_4

(c) $NaHPO_2$, CuS (d) NaH_2PO_2, Cu_2S

35. Noble metals, like gold and platinum are soluble in which of the following mixtures? **[Apr. 20, 2019 (I)]**

(a) 1 : 1 mixture of conc. HNO_3 and conc. H_2SO_4

(b) 1 : 3 mixture of conc. HCl and conc. HNO_3

(c) 1 : 3 mixture of conc. HNO_3 and conc. HCl

(d) 1 : 3 mixture of conc. H_2SO_4 and conc. HCl

36. Which one of the following is correct with respect to basic character? **[2015]**

(a) $P(CH_3)_3 > PH_3$ (b) $PH_3 > P(CH_3)_3$

(c) $PH_3 > NH_3$ (d) $PH_3 = NH_3$

Topic 2 Oxygen Family

37. Consider the following statements about sulphur allotropes and identify the incorrect statement **[May 18, 2026 (I)]**

(a) In both rhombic and monoclinic sulphur, the S_8 ring has crown shape.

(b) In cyclo S_6, the ring adopts the chair form

(c) The bond angle in S_8 ring is more than that of cyclo S_6 ring.

(d) Monoclinic sulphur is stable below 369 K

38. Given below are two statements **[May 15, 2026 (II)]**

Statement I: The formation of $O_2^+[PtF_6]^-$ is the basis for the formation of Xenon flourides

Statement II: O_2 and Xe have almost same first ionisation enthalpy

The correct answer is

(a) Both statements I and II are correct

(b) Statement I is correct, but statement II is not correct

(c) Statement I is not correct, but statement II is correct

(d) Both statements I and II are not correct

39. Which of the following statement is not correct about the structures of ozone and sulphur dioxide?

(a) Both have angular shape **[May 14, 2026 (I)]**

(b) Both have resonance structures

(c) Both have same hybridization

(d) Both have same bond angles

40. How many of the following molecules will give oxygen on thermal decomposition? **[May 13, 2026 (II)]**

$(NH_4)Cr_2O_7$, $KClO_3$, HgO, NH_4NO_3, $KMnO_4$, $CaCO_3$, Pb_3O_4

(a) 4 (b) 2

(c) 5 (d) 3

41. White phosphorous reacts with aqueous NaOH solution to form $PH_3(g)$ and aqueous sodium hypophosphite. 124 g of white phosphorous reacts completely with 1 L of x M NaOH to form three moles of sodium hypophosphite. What is the volume (in L) of x M NaOH that completely reacts with 128 g of rhombic sulphur to form aqueous sulphide, water and aqueous thiosulphate? (P = 31 u; S = 32 u) **[May 13, 2026 (I)]**

(a) 2 (b) 0.5

(c) 1 (d) 4

42. Which of the following is not correct? **[May 23, 2025 (I)]**

(a) Thermal stability : $H_2O > H_2S > H_2Se > H_2Te > H_2Po$

(b) Reducing property : $H_2S > H_2Se > H_2Te > H_2Po$

(c) Boiling point : $H_2S < H_2Se < H_2Te < H_2O$

(d) Melting point : $H_2S < H_2Se < H_2Te < H_2O$

43. In the extraction of copper from copper glance, blister copper is formed by the evolution of gas X. The shape of molecule of X is **[May 19, 2023 (I)]**

(a) Angular (b) Planar trigonal

(c) Tetrahedral (d) Pyramidal

44. The sum of oxygen atoms in the formulae of peroxysulphuric acid and pyrosulphuric acid is **[May 19, 2023 (I)]**

(a) 7 (b) 12 (c) 15 (d) 13

45. In which of the following, the molecules are arranged in the increasing order of their bond angles? **[May 17, 2023 (I)]**

(a) $P_4 < S_6 < O_3 < S_8$ (b) $S_6 < O_3 < S_8 < P_4$

(c) $O_3 < S_8 < P_4 < S_6$ (d) $P_4 < S_6 < S_8 < O_3$

46. The P – P – P bond angle in P_4 and S – S – S bond angle in cyclo S_8 molecule are respectively **[May 16, 2023 (II)]**

(a) 107º, 60º (b) 60º, 40º
(c) 60º, 107º (d) 40º, 60º

47. X + Y → oleum

The sum of oxidation states of central atom in X and Y is **[May 16, 2023 (I)]**

(a) 12 (b) 10 (c) 06 (d) 08

48. For ozone molecule consider the following

(A) It is a linear molecule with bond angle 180°
(B) It is an angular molecule with bond angle 117°
(C) The bond lengths of both O – O bonds are same
(D) With respect to oxygen it is thermodynamically more stable **[May 15, 2023 (I); Similar to 2016]**

The correct options are

(a) (B), (C) only (b) (A), (B) only
(c) (B), (D) only (d) (A), (D) only

49. Among the hydrides of group 16 elements, the hydride X has lowest boiling point and the hydride Y has highest boiling point. X and Y respectively are **[May 17, 2023 (I)]**

(a) H_2Te, H_2Se (b) H_2O, H_2Te
(c) H_2S, H_2Te (d) H_2S, H_2O

50. When KI is reacted with O_3 under aqueous condition the product formed is **[July 8, 2022 (I)]**

(a) I_2O_4 (b) I_2O_5
(c) I_4O_9 (d) I_2

51. Which of the following source materials generate SO_2 that is used in contact process? **[July 6, 2022 (I)]**

(a) S, FeS_2 (b) S, FeS
(c) H_2S, FeS_2 (d) Na_2S, FeS_2

52. The element with highest electronegativity value after fluorine is **[July 5, 2022 (II)]**

(a) Nitrogen (b) Oxygen
(c) Chlorine (d) Bromine

53. Which of the following is formed when SO_3 is absorbed by concentrated H_2SO_4 **[July 4, 2022 (II)]**

(a) $H_2S_2O_8$ (b) $H_2S_2O_3$
(c) $H_2S_2O_7$ (d) $H_2S_2O_5$

54. The correct order of sulphur-oxygen bond in SO_3, $S_2O_3^{2-}$ and SO_4^{2-} is **[Aug. 20, 2021 (I)]**

(a) $SO_4^{2-} < S_2O_3^{2-} < SO_3$
(b) $SO_4^{2-} < SO_3 < S_2O_3^{2-}$
(c) $S_2O_3^{2-} < SO_4^{2-} < SO_3$
(d) $S_2O_3^{2-} < SO_3 < SO_4^{2-}$

55. Potassium cyanide is made alkaline with NaOH and boiled with thiosulphate ions. The solutions is cooled and acidified with HCl and this solution with iron (III) chloride produces **[Aug. 20, 2021 (II)]**

(a) prussian blue colour solution
(b) blood red colour solution
(c) dark brown colour solution
(d) green colour solution

56. Phosphorus reacts with SO_2Cl_2 to form PCl_5 and *X*. At 723 K, HCl gas reacts with O_2 in the presence of $CuCl_2$ to form water and *Y*. *Y* reacts with *X* in water to form two acids *A* and *B*. What are *A* and *B* respectively? **[Apr. 22, 2019 (I)]**

(a) H_2SO_4, HCl (b) H_2SO_4, HNO_3
(c) HCl, HNO_3 (d) H_2SO_4, H_3PO_4

57. Which of the following statements is not correct ? **[Apr. 20, 2019 (II)]**

(a) From SO_2 to TeO_2 reducing power decreases
(b) The order of boiling points of hydrides of 16th group elements is $H_2S < H_2Se < H_2Te < H_2O$
(c) Rhombic sulphur has S_8 molecules while monoclinic sulphur has S_6 molecules.
(d) The bond angle in ozone molecule is 117°

58. Identify the molecules which contains lone pair of electrons on the sulphur atom **[2018]**

(a) H_2SO_5 (b) $H_2S_2O_8$
(c) $H_2S_2O_7$ (d) H_2SO_3

59. S + Conc. $H_2SO_4 \longrightarrow X + Y$

Here *X* is a gas and *Y* is a liquid and both are triatomic molecules. The number of electron lone pairs present on the central atoms of *X* and *Y* are respectively. **[2017]**

(a) 2, 1 (b) 1, 0
(c) 1, 2 (d) 2, 2

60. The Lewis structure for O_3 molecule is given below. The correct formal charges on oxygen atoms labelled 1, 2, 3 are respectively. **[2017]**

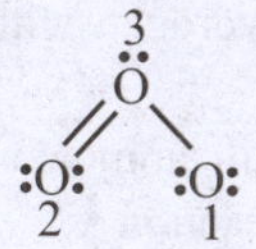

(a) –1, 0, + 1 (b) + 1, 0, – 1
(c) + 1, – 1, 0 (d) 0, + 1, – 1

61. Which of the following statements regarding sulphur is not correct? **[2016]**

(a) At about 1000 K, it mainly consists of S_2 molecules

(b) The oxidation state of sulphur is never less than + 4 in its compounds

(c) S_2 molecule is paramagnetic

(d) Rhombic sulphur is readily soluble in CS_2

62. Sea divers use a mixture of **[2015]**

(a) O_2, N_2 (b) O_2, H_2 (c) O_2, He (d) N_2, H_2

Topic 3 Halogen Family

63. Chlorine gas reacts with cold, dilute NaOH solution to produce NaCl, H_2O and a sodium salt (X). When it reacts with hot, concentrated NaOH solution, it produces NaCl, H_2O and a sodium salt (Y). Identify the correct statements regarding the oxidation states of chlorine in X and Y. **[May 18, 2026 (II)]**

I. The oxidation state of chlorine in Y is same as that of nitrogen in nitric acid

II. The oxidation state of chlorine in X is same as that of phosphorus in phosphinic acid

III. The sum of the oxidation states of chlorine in X and Y is same as that of iodine in iodic acid

The correct answer is

(a) I, II only (b) II, III only

(c) I, III only (d) I, II, III

64. Which of the following reactions is non-spontaneous? **[May 15, 2026 (I)]**

(a) $2F_2 + 2H_2O \rightarrow 4HF + O_2$

(b) $Cl_2 + H_2O \rightarrow HCl + HOCl$

(c) $Br_2 + H_2O \rightarrow HBr + HOBr$

(d) $2I_2 + 2H_2O \rightarrow 4HI + O_2$

65. Chlorine reacts with sodium thiosulphate in the presence of water and forms sodium sulphate, hydrochloric acid and X. Which of the following also produces X when reacted with chlorine? **[May 13, 2026 (II)]**

(a) H_2S (b) H_2SO_4

(c) SO_2 (d) $FeSO_4$

66. Identify the correct statements from the following: **[May 22, 2024 (II)]**

i. Reaction of hydrogen with fluorine occurs even in dark.

ii. Manufacture of ammonia by Haber process is an endothermic reaction

iii. HF is electron rich hydride

(a) i, iii only (b) i, ii, iii

(c) ii, iii only (d) i, ii only

67. 'X' on hydrolysis gives two products. One of them is solid. What is 'X'? **[May 20, 2024 (I)]**

(a) P_4O_{10} (b) F_2 (c) $SiCl_4$ (d) N^{3-}

68. When chlorine reacts with hot and conc. NaOH, the products formed are **[May 18, 2024 (I)]**

(a) NaCl, $NaClO_3$, H_2O (b) NaCl, NaOCl, H_2O

(c) NaCl, H_2O only (d) NaOCl, H_2O

69. Arrange the hydrides NH_3, HF, H_2O, HCl in the increasing order of their boiling points **[May 18, 2023 (II)]**

(a) $HF < NH_3 < HCl < H_2O$

(b) $H_2O < HF < HCl < NH_3$

(c) $NH_3 < HCl < H_2O < HF$

(d) $HCl < NH_3 < HF < H_2O$

70. Which of the following are not in accordance with the property mentioned against them?

I. $F_2 > Cl_2 > Br_2 > I_2$: Oxidising power

II. MI > MBr > MCl > MF : Ionic character of metal halide

III. $F_2 > Cl_2 > Br_2 > I_2$: Bond dissociation enthalpy

IV. HI < HBr < HCl < HF: Hydrogen–halogen bond strength **[May 16, 2023 (II)]**

(a) I & III only (b) II & III only

(c) I & IV only (d) II & IV only

71. Which of the following represents correct order of oxidizing power of halogens with water **[July 7, 2022 (II)]**

(a) $I_2 > Br_2 > Cl_2 > F_2$ (b) $Cl_2 > F_2 > Br_2 > I_2$

(c) $F_2 > Cl_2 > I_2 > Br_2$ (d) $F_2 > Cl_2 > Br_2 > I_2$

72. Assertion (A) : HCl gas is dried by passing through concentrated H_2SO_4.

Reason (R) : HCl gas reacts with NH_3 that gives white fumes **[July 4, 2022 (I)]**

(a) Both (A) and (R) are correct and (R) is the correct explanation of (A)

(b) Both (A) and (R) are correct and (R) is not the correct explanation of (A)

(c) (A) is correct but (R) is incorrect

(d) (A) is incorrect but (R) is correct

73. In the following reaction,

$I_2 + H_2O + Cl_2 \longrightarrow X + Y$, the products X and Y respectively are **[Aug. 23, 2021 (I)]**

(a) $HClO_4$, HI (b) I_2O_7, HCl

(c) HIO_3, HCl (d) ICl_3, HCl

74. Match the following compounds with their corresponding physical properties. **[Aug. 19, 2021 (II)]**

	Column I		Column II
A.	IBr	1.	Orange solid
B.	ClF_3	2.	Yellow-green liquid
C.	BrF_3	3.	Black solid
D.	ICl_3	4.	Colourless gas

	A	B	C	D		A	B	C	D
(a)	2	1	4	3	(b)	1	3	2	4
(c)	3	4	2	1	(d)	4	2	1	3

75. X_2 is used in the refining of Ti metal by van Arkel method. Y_2 does not liberate O_2 from water and does not form HY and HOY with water. X_2 and Y_2 are respectively. **[Apr. 22, 2019 (I)]**

(a) I_2, Cl_2 (b) Cl_2, I_2
(c) I_2, I_2 (d) Cl_2, Cl_2

76. Chlorine oxidises sulphur dioxide in the presence of water to give an oxyacid *A*. Chlorine also oxidises iodine in the presence of water to give an oxyacid *B*. The oxidation states of *S* and I in *A* and *B* are respectively **[Apr. 21, 2019 (II)]**

(a) +4, +5 (b) +6, +3
(c) +6, +5 (d) +4, +7

77. Which of the following reactions does not take place? **[2016]**

(a) $F_2 + 2Cl^- \longrightarrow 2F^- + Cl_2$
(b) $Br_2 + 2I^- \longrightarrow 2Br^- + I_2$
(c) $Cl_2 + 2Br^- \longrightarrow 2Cl^- + Br_2$
(d) $Cl_2 + 2F^- \longrightarrow 2Cl^- + F_2$

Topic 4 Noble Gases

78. Consider the following statements regarding the hydrolysis of XeF_4. **[May 18, 2026 (I)]**

I. It is a disproportionation reaction.
II. Xe and XeO_3 are formed in 2:1 molar ratio
III. O_2 gas is evolved in this reaction.

The correct statements are

(a) I, II only (b) II, III only
(c) I, III only (d) I, II, III

79. In which of the following reactions, chlorine undergoes disproportionation? **[May 14, 2026 (II)]**

I. Reaction with cold, dilute NaOH
II. Reaction with hot, concentrated NaOH
III. Reaction with H_2S

The correct answer is

(a) I, II only (b) I, II, III
(c) II, III only (d) I, III only

80. Consider the following reactions which are not balanced **[May 12, 2026 (I)]**

$XeF_6 + H_2O \rightarrow X + HF$
$XeF_6 + 2H_2O \rightarrow Y + HF$
$XeF_6 + 3H_2O \rightarrow Z + HF$

The correct statement regarding X/Y/Z is

(a) X has square planar geometry
(b) Y has one Xe = O bond
(c) Z has no lone pairs of electrons on its central atom
(d) The oxidation state of Xenon in X, Y and Z is same

81. Complete hydrolysis of Xenon hexafluoride gives HF along with compound X. The hybridisation in X is **[May 27, 2025 (I)]**

(a) sp^3 (b) sp (c) sp^2 (d) sp^3d

82. Hydrolysis of XeF_4 gives HF, O_2, Xe and 'X'. The structure of 'X' is **[May 23, 2024 (I)]**

(a) pyramidal (b) Square pyramidal
(c) octahedral (d) Square planar

83. $Xe(g) + 2F_2(g) \xrightarrow[7\text{bar}]{873K} XeF_4(s)$

The ratio of Xe: F_2 required in the above reaction is **[May 20, 2024 (II)]**

(a) 1 : 2 (b) 1 : 5 (c) 1: 20 (d) 1 : 12

84. Match the following

List-I (molecule/ion)	List-II (Number of lone pairs of electrons on the central atom)
(A) XeF_2	(I) 2
(B) XeO_3	(II) 0
(C) XeF_4	(III) 3
(D) PF_6^-	(IV) 1

The correct answer is **[May 17, 2023 (II)]**

(a) A-III, B-IV, C-I, D-II (b) A-I, B-II, C-IV, D-III
(c) A-II, B-I, C-III, D-IV (d) A-III, B-IV, C-II, D-I

85. Which of the following fluorides of Xenon does not exist? **[May 16, 2023 (I)]**

(a) XeF_3 (b) XeF_2
(c) XeF_6 (d) XeF_4

86. Identify the reaction in which oxygen is not one of the products **[May 15, 2023 (II); Similar to 2016]**

(a) $XeF_2 + H_2O \rightarrow$ (b) $XeF_4 + H_2O \rightarrow$
(c) $XeF_4 + O_2F_2 \rightarrow$ (d) $XeF_6 + H_2O \rightarrow$

87. The shapes of XeF_2, XeF_4, and XeO_3 respectively are **[July 5, 2022 (II); Similar to Aug. 23, 2021 (I)]**

(a) Linear, Tetrahedral, Pyramidal
(b) Angular, Square Planar, Pyramidal
(c) Linear, Tetrahedral, Planar
(d) Linear, Square planar, Pyramidal

88. When SbF_5 reacts with XeF_4 to form an adduct, the shapes of cation and anion in the adduct respectively are **[Sept. 18, 2020 (II)]**

(a) square planar, trigonal bipyramidal

(b) T-shaped, octahedral

(c) square pyramidal, octahedral

(d) plane triangular, trigonal bipyramidal

89. Which of the following reactions are correct with respect to the formation of products? **[Apr. 21, 2019 (I)]**

I. $2NaOH + SO_2 \longrightarrow Na_2SO_4 + H_2$

II. $2XeF_4 + 3O_2F_2 \xrightarrow{143\text{ K}} 2XeO_3 + 7F_2$

III. $PCl_5 + 4H_2O \longrightarrow H_3PO_4 + 5HCl$

IV. $2NaNO_2 + 2HCl \longrightarrow 2NaCl + NO + NO_2 + H_2O$

(a) II, IV (b) III, IV

(c) I, III (d) II, III

90. The reason for the noble gases to have low boiling and low melting point is **[Apr. 21, 2019 (I)]**

(a) atoms of the noble gases have weak covalent interaction

(b) atoms of the noble gases have weak dipole interaction

(c) atoms of the noble gases have weak van der Waal's interaction

(d) atoms of the noble gases have weak dispersion forces

91. XeF_4 is square planar where as CCl_4 is tetrahedral because **[2018]**

(a) in XeF_4, 'Xe' is sp^2 hybridised and in CCl_4 'C' is sp^3 hybridised

(b) in both XeF_4 and CCl_4 the central atom is sp^3 hybridised

(c) in XeF_4, 'Xe' is sp^3d^2 hybridised but due to the presence of 2 lone pairs of electrons shape is square planar whereas in CCl_4 'C' is sp^3 hybridised

(d) Xe is noble gas, whereas C is a non-metal

92. Which statement about noble gases is not correct? **[2018]**

(a) 'Xe' forms XeF_6 under suitable conditions

(b) 'Ar' is used in electric bulbs

(c) The number of lone pair of electrons present on Xe in XeF_2 is 3.

(d) 'He' has the highest boiling point among all the noble gases

93. To prepare XeF_6, Xe and F_2 are mixed at 573 K and 60-70 bar in the ratio of **[2017]**

(a) 20 : 1 (b) 1: 5

(c) 5 : 1 (d) 1: 20

94. **Assertion (A) :** Noble gases have very low boiling points.

Reason (R) : All noble gases have general electronic configuration of $ns^2\ np^6$ (except He). **[2015]**

(a) Both (A) and (R) are true and (R) is the correct explanation of (A)

(b) (A) is false but (R) is true

(c) (A) is true but (R) is false

(d) Both (A) and (R) are true and (R) is the not the correct explanation of (A)

Hints & Solutions

1 Solutions

1. (c) Moles of HCl = 0.5 moles

Since $NaOH + HCl \longrightarrow NaCl + H_2O$

1 : 1

$$X_{NaOH} = \frac{n_{NaOH}}{n_{NaOH} + n_{H_2O}} = 0.02$$

$n_{NaOH} = 0.5$ moles

$$0.02 = \frac{0.5}{0.5 + n\ H_2O} = 24.5 \text{ mol}$$

Mass of NaOH = 20g

Mass of H_2O = 441g

Total mass of solution = 461 g

$$\text{Volume of water} = \frac{441\text{g}}{1\text{g/mL}} = 441 \text{ mL}$$

2. (d) Mole fraction of CH_3OH, x = 0.02

So, mole fraction of water = 1 – x = 1 – 0.02 = 0.98

$$\text{Molality} = \frac{x \times 1000}{1 - x \times M_{H_2O}} = \frac{0.02 \times 1000}{0.98 \times 18}$$

$$= \frac{20}{17.64} = 1.13 \text{ m}$$

3. (b) $\text{Molality (m)} = \frac{\text{number of moles}}{\text{weight of the solvent}}$

Weight of solute = 10g

Weight of solvent = 90g

$$\text{Moles of solute} = \frac{10}{180}$$

$$\text{Molality} = \frac{10 \times 1000}{180 \times 90}$$

$\Rightarrow$ Molality = 0.62 m

4. (c) $x_{H_2O} = 40 \times x_{glucose}$

$x_{H_2O} = 1 - x_{glucose}$

$\Rightarrow \quad 1 - x_{glucose} = 40x_{glucose}$

$$\Rightarrow \quad x_{glucose} = \frac{1}{41}$$

Now, we take 1L of H_2O $\Rightarrow$ Mass of H_2O = 1000 g

$$\Rightarrow \quad n_{H_2O} = \frac{1000 \text{ g}}{18.0 \text{ g mol}^{-1}} = 55.56 \text{ mol}$$

$$\text{Thus, } x_{H_2O} = \frac{n_{H_2O}}{n_{glucose} + n_{H_2O}}$$

$$= \frac{55.56}{n_{glucose} + 55.56} = 40x_{glucose}$$

$$= 40 \times \frac{1}{41} = 0.975$$

Thus, 0.975 $n_{glucsoe}$ + 54.171 = 55.56

$\Rightarrow \quad n_{glucose} = 1.424$ mol

$\Rightarrow \quad$ Mass(glucose) = 1.424 × 180 = 256.32 g

Therefore, mass % of glucose

$$= \frac{256.32 \text{ g}}{(256.32 + 1000) \text{ g}} \times 100$$

= 20.4 % ≈ 20 %

5. (c) Mole fraction of glucose (χ_g) = 0.0244

Mole fraction of water (χ_w) = 0.9756

$$\frac{\chi_g}{\chi_w} = \frac{0.0244}{0.9756} = 0.025 = \frac{25}{1000} = \frac{1}{40}$$

$$\Rightarrow \quad \frac{n_g}{n_w} = \frac{1}{40} \Rightarrow \frac{W_g}{W_w} = \frac{1}{4}$$

$\therefore \quad W_g$ = 1 part of glucose

W_w = 4 part of water

$W_g + W_w$ = 5 part

$$\therefore \quad \frac{W_g}{W_g + W_w} = \frac{1}{5} \times 100 = 20\%$$

6. (c) Mole of ethylene glycol

$$= \frac{248}{12 \times 2 + 6 + 32} = \frac{248}{62} = 4 \text{ mol}$$

$$\text{Molarity} = \frac{4}{200/1000} = \frac{4 \times 1000}{200} = \frac{40 \text{ m}}{2} = 20 \text{ m}$$

Molality of resulting solution = 20 m

7. (c)

Gas	Temperature	K_H/kbar
He	293	144.97
H_2	293	69.16
O_2	293	34.86
N_2	293	76.48

So, He has the highest Henry's law constant.

8. (c) We know that

Normality = Molarity × Z factor

$$N_1 = \frac{1}{10} \times 2 = \frac{1}{5}$$

$$N_2 = \frac{1}{10} \times 1 = \frac{1}{10}$$

$$\therefore \quad \text{no. of mole } (n_1) = \frac{1}{5} \times 100 = 20 \text{ mole}$$

$$\text{no. of mole } (n_2) = \frac{1}{10} \times 200 = 20 \text{ mole}$$

Total mole ($n_1 + n_2$) = 40 mole

$$\text{Concentration/Normality of solution} = \frac{n_1 + n_2}{V_1 + V_2}$$

$$= \frac{40}{300} = 0.13\text{N}$$

9. (b) Amount of urea = 60g

$$\text{Moles of urea} = \frac{60}{60} = 1 \text{ mole}$$

$$\text{Molarity} = \frac{\text{Moles}}{\text{Volume of solution}}$$

$$= \frac{1 \text{ Mole}}{1 \text{ Litre}} = 1.0 \text{ M}$$

10. (d) Given - Density (δ) = 1.5 g/ml

Volume (v) = 1000 ml

Weight percentage = 68

Mass of solution = density × volume

1.5 g/ml × 1000 ml = 1500g

Mass of Nitric Acid = weight percentage × Total mass of solution.

Mass of Nitric acid = 0.68 × 1500g = 1020g

Molar mass of Nitric Acid (HNO_3)

= 1(H) + 14(N) + 3 × 16(0) = 63 g/mol

$$\text{Moles of Nitric acid} = \frac{\text{mass}}{\text{molar mass}}$$

$$\text{Moles of Nitric acid} = \frac{1020\text{g}}{63\text{g/mol}} = 16.19\text{mol}$$

$$\text{Molarity(m)} = \frac{\text{moles of solute}}{\text{Volume of solution in litres}}$$

$$\text{Molarity} = \frac{16.19\text{mol}}{1\text{L}} \approx 16.2$$

11. (d)

$$\text{ppm (parts per million)} = \frac{\text{mg of solute}}{\text{L of solution}}$$

Given, ppm = 1000

volume = 1L

mg of solute = ppm × L of solution

= 10^3 × 1

weight of solute = 10^3 mg

$$\text{Concentration} = \frac{\text{no. of moles}}{\text{volume}}$$

$$\text{no. of moles} = \frac{\text{weight of solute}}{\text{molecular weight of solute}}$$

$$= \frac{10^3 \times 10^{-3} \text{g}}{100 \text{ g mol}^{-1}} \left[1 \text{ mg} = 10^{-3} \text{g}\right]$$

= 10^{-2} mol

$$\text{Concentration (C)} = \frac{10^{-2} \text{ mol}}{1\text{L}} = 10^{-2} \text{mol L}^{-1}$$

12. (d) According to Henry's Law,

$p = K_H \times x$

p = partial pressure

K_H = Henry constant

x = mole fraction

given

p = 1 bar

$K_H = 0.4 \times 10^3$ bar [1k bar = 10^3 bar]

$\therefore p = K_H x$

1 bar = 0.4 × 10^3 bar × x

$$x = \frac{1}{0.4\times10^3}$$

$$\frac{n_{methane}}{n_{methane}+n_{H_2O}} = \frac{1}{0.4\times10^3}$$

$n_{methane} << n_{H_2O}$

$$\therefore \frac{n_{methane}}{n_{H_2O}} = \frac{1}{0.4\times10^3}$$

$$\frac{n_{methane}}{n_{H_2O}} = \frac{1}{0.4\times10^3}$$

$$\left[n_{H_2O} = \frac{1000}{18} = 55.55 \text{ mol}\right]$$

$$= \frac{55.55}{0.4\times10^3} = 138 \times 10^{-3}$$

$$\boxed{n_{methane} = 1.38\times10^{-1}}$$

13. (d) According to Henry's law :-

$P = x\,K_H$

For N_2 :- $P_{N_2} = x_{N_2}\,K_H\,(N_2)$

For O_2:- $P_{O_2} = x_{O_2}\,K_H\,(O_2)$

We have, $P_{N_2} = P_{O_2}$, $K_H\,(N_2) = 76.48$ k bar,

$K_H\,(O_2) = 3486$ k bar

$$\Rightarrow \frac{x_{N_2}}{x_{O_2}} = \frac{\left(\frac{P_{N_2}}{K_H(N_2)}\right)}{\left(\frac{P_{O_2}}{K_H(O_2)}\right)} = \frac{P_{N_2}}{K_H(N_2)} \times \frac{K_H(O_2)}{P_{O_2}}$$

$$= \frac{K_H(O_2)}{K_H(N_2)} = \frac{34.86}{76.48} = 0.45$$

14. (b)

$$\text{Molarity} = \frac{\frac{4.9\text{ g}}{98.0\text{ g mol}^{-1}}}{0.250\text{ L}} = 0.2\text{ mol L}^{-1}$$

15. (b) n_{HCl} = 0.1 M × 0.02 L = 0.002 mol

n_{NaOH} = 0.1 M × 0.03 L = 0.003 mol

Number of moles of NaOH remaining after neutralization.

= 0.003 – 0.002 = 0.001 mol.

Total final volume = 50 mL+ 50 mL = 100 mL = 0.1 L

$$\Rightarrow \text{Molarity} = \frac{0.001}{0.1} = 0.01\text{ M}$$

16. (b) Relation between molality and molarity is

$$\frac{1}{m} = \frac{d}{M} - \frac{M}{1000} \quad [M = \text{molar mass of glucose}]$$

$$\therefore \frac{1}{1} = \frac{d}{M} - \frac{180}{1000}$$

$$\Rightarrow \frac{1180}{1000} = \frac{1.2}{M}$$

$$\therefore M = \frac{1200}{1180}$$

M = 1.01

17. (b) According to Henry's Law,

$P_{O_2} = K_H\chi_{O_2}$; $P_{O_2} = 1$ bar, $(K_H)_{O_2} = 50$ k bar at T(K)

$\therefore 50\times10^3\chi_{O_2} = 1$

$$\text{or } \chi_{O_2} = \frac{10^{-3}}{50}$$

$$\text{or } \frac{n_{O_2}}{n_{O_2}+n_{H_2O}} = \frac{10^{-3}}{50}$$

Approximating $n_{O_2} << n_{H_2O}$, $\frac{n_{O_2}}{n_{H_2O}} = \frac{10^{-3}}{50}$

[1L H_2O = 55.5 mol H_2O]

$$\therefore n_{O_2} = \frac{55.5\times10^{-3}}{50} = 1.11\times10^{-3}\text{ mol}$$

$$= \frac{C = 1.11\times10^{-3}}{1}$$

C = 1.11 × 10^{-3} mol L^{-1}

The amount of O_2 dissolved in 1L of solution is

= 1.11 × 10^{-3} × 32 g/L

= 32 × 1.11 × 10^{-3} × 10^3 mg/L = 35.5 ppm

18. (b) Increase in temperature in an endothermic dissolution process enhance the kinetic energy of the solvent molecules by allowing them to break apart more efficiently. This results into the more solubility of solute molecules.

19. (a) Concentration of the solution at 20°C

$$= \frac{n}{V} = \frac{\frac{2}{40}}{\frac{200}{1000}} = 0.25(M) \quad [\text{Mw of NaOH} = 40]$$

As temperature increases the volume of the solution increases but the no. of moles remains the same.

Hence, concentration of the solution decreases.

20. (d) Higher the value of K_H, lower is the solubility of the gas in the liquid at given pressure.

$$\text{i.e., solubility} \propto \frac{1}{K_H}$$

So, the correct order is Ar < CO_2 < CH_4 < HCHO

21. (a) $CaCl_2 \rightarrow Ca^{2+} + 2Cl^-$

Cl^- in solution = 3.01 × 10^{22} ions

$$\text{No. of } CaCl_2 \text{ present in solution} = \frac{3.01\times10^{22}}{2}$$

= 1.505 × 10^{22} $CaCl_2$

$$\text{Molarity of solution} = \frac{\text{No. of moles of } CaCl_2}{\text{Vol. of solution (in litre)}}$$

$$= \frac{1.51\times10^{22}}{6.022\times10^{23}} \times \frac{1000}{500} = 0.05$$

22. (c) Therefore, normality = *n*-factor × molarity

n-factor for Na_2CO_3 = 2

$\Rightarrow$ Molarity = 0.2/2 = 0.1 M

23. (c) Given, density (*d*) = (1.2 g mL^{-1}),

$$\text{Vol. of sol.} = \frac{\text{mass}}{\text{density}} = I = \frac{100}{1.2}\text{ mL}$$

$$\Rightarrow \text{Molarity} = \frac{\text{moles of solute}}{\text{Vol. of solution (in litre)}}$$

$$M = \frac{\text{Given mass}}{\text{Molarmass}}\ \frac{1000}{V_I\text{(in Litre)}}$$

$$M = \frac{40\times1.2\times1000}{36.5\times100} = 13.1\text{ M.}$$

24. (a) I. Moles of solute NaOH

= molarity × volume of solution (in L)

$$= \frac{0.2\times500}{1000} = 0.1$$

II. Molarity of H_2SO_4 $= \frac{0.1}{2} = 0.05$ M

$$\text{Moles of } H_2SO_4 = \frac{0.05\times200}{1000} = 0.01$$

$$\text{III. Moles of area} = \frac{\text{Mass of urea}}{\text{Molecular mass of urea}}$$

$$= \frac{6}{60} = 0.1$$

25. (b) Given,

Mass of solute (*W*) = 120 g

Molar mass of solute (*M*) = 60

Mass of solvent (*w*) = 1000 g

∴ Total mass of solution = 1000 + 120 = 1120 g

$$\because d = \frac{\text{Mass}}{\text{Volume }(V)}$$

$$\therefore \text{Total volume }(V) = \frac{1120}{1.12} = 1000\text{ mL}$$

$$\because \text{Molarity} = \frac{w}{M} \times \frac{1000}{V}$$

$$\because \text{Molarity} = \frac{120}{60} \times \frac{1000}{1000} = 2.0$$

26. (c) P= $K_H\chi$

$$K_H = \frac{p}{\chi} = \frac{2}{0.02} = 100$$

$$\chi' = \frac{P'}{K_H} = \frac{4}{100} = 0.04$$

χ'_{H_2O} = 1 – 0.04 = 0.96

27. (b) x axis represent mol fraction and *y* axis represent vapour pressure of solution.

28. (a) $P^o_{benzene}$ = 75 mm Hg

$P^o_{toluene}$ = 22 mmHg

$$\text{Mole of benzene} = \frac{23.4}{78} = 0.3\text{ mol}$$

$$\text{Mole of toluene} = \frac{64.4}{92} = 0.7\text{ mol}$$

$$\text{Mole fraction of benzene} = \frac{0.3}{1.0} = 0.3$$

Mole fraction of toluene = 1 – 0.3 = 0.7

Partial pressure of benzene = 0.3 × 75 = 22.5 mmHg

Partial pressure of toluene = 0.7 × 22 = 15.4 mmHg

Total pressure of solution = 22.5 + 15.4
= 37.9 mmHg

Mole fraction toluene = $\frac{15.4}{37.9} = 0.406$

Mole fraction of toluene in vapour phase approximately 0.406.

29. (d) As, $p_{total} = x_1p_1^\circ + x_2p_2^\circ$

$= (1 - x_2)p_1^\circ + x_2p_2^\circ$

$\therefore \quad p_{total} = p_1^\circ + (p_2^\circ - p_1^\circ)x_2$ ...(i)

Now, $p_{total} = 475$ torr

$p_1^\circ = 280.7$ torr (for liquid A)

$p_2^\circ = ?$ (for liquid B)

For mole fraction of liquid B :

$$X_2 = \frac{n_2}{n_1 + n_2} = \frac{5.555}{5.555 + 0.714} = \frac{5.555}{6.269} = 0.8861$$

So, using equation (i) we get –

$475 = 280.7 + (p_2^\circ - 280.7)\ 0.8861$

$475 - 280.7 = 0.8861\ p_2^\circ - 280.7 \times 0.8861$

$$\frac{194.3 + 248.72}{0.8861} = p_2^\circ$$

$$\frac{443}{0.8861} = p_2^\circ = 500$$

30. (b) Vapour pressure of aqueous solution (p) = 34.65 mm Hg

Mole fraction of non volatile solute is = 0.02

Mole fraction of water = 1 – 0.02 = 0.98

Vapour pressure of pure water ($p°$) = $\frac{p}{x}$

$$= \frac{34.65}{0.98} = 35.36$$

31. (a) $p_A^\circ = 70$ mmHg, $x_B = 0.2$

$P_T = 84$ mm Hg, $x_A = 1 - x_B = 0.8$

$P_T = p_A^\circ x_A + p_B^\circ x_B \Rightarrow 84 = 70 \times 0.8 + p_B^\circ \times 0.2$

$\Rightarrow \quad p_B^\circ = \frac{28}{0.2} = 140$ mm Hg.

32. (c) Mass of urea = 7.5 gm

Mole of urea = $\frac{7.5}{60}$

Mole of $x = \frac{15}{M}$

Since mass of water is same thus molality equal to mole.

T_f is same for both solution

$$\frac{T_{f1}}{T_{f2}} = \frac{m_1}{m_2}$$

$$1 = \frac{7.5/60}{15/M}$$

$$M = \frac{15 \times 60}{7.5} = 120\ g$$

33. (a)

Ideal	Non-Ideal
(i) follow Raoult's law	(i) not follow Raoult's law
(ii) $\Delta H = 0$, $\Delta V = 0$	(ii) $\Delta H \neq 0$, $\Delta V \neq 0$
(iii) Interaction between A and B equal to A-A and B-B interaction	(iii) For positive deviation A and B weaker then A-A and B-B but in Negative deviation A and B interaction greater then A-A and B-B interaction.

So both statement are correct.

34. (d) $P_A^o = 500 \quad n_A = 1 \quad x_A = 0.5$

$P_B^o = 400 \quad n_B = 1 \quad x_B = 0.5$

$\therefore \quad P_A = P_A^o x_A$

$P_A = 500 \times 0.5 = 250$

$P_B = 400 \times 0.5 = 200$

$P_T = P_A + P_B = 250 + 200 = 450$

In vapour state

$P_A = P_T \times x_A'$

$$x_A' = \frac{P_A}{P_T} = \frac{250}{450} = 0.555$$

$$x_B' = \frac{P_B}{P_T} = \frac{200}{450} = 0.444$$

35. (a)

A + B + C liq + vap I	A + B + C vapour only II	→ after heating

Boiling point $\propto \frac{1}{\text{vapour pressure}}$

Boiling point : C < A < B

Vapour pressure : B < A < C

I. Vapour pressure of B is lowest so it is in liquid phase.

II. Vapour pressure of C is highest so it is in the gaseous phase.

III. Order of vapour pressure : C > A > B.

36. (c) $P_A^o = 400 \quad P_B^o = 600$

$x_A = 0.7$

$x_B = 0.3 \quad [x_A + x_B = 1]$

$P_A = P_A^o\ x_A$

$P_A = 0.7 \times 400 = 280$

$P_B = P_B^o\ x_B$

$= 0.3 \times 600 = 180$

$P_T = P_A + P_B = 460$

$\therefore$ In vapour phase,

$P_A = P_T X_{1A}$

$P_B = P_T X_{1B}$

$$\therefore X_{1A} = \frac{280}{460} = 0.609$$

$$\therefore X_{1B} = \frac{180}{460} = 0.391$$

37. (c) Boiling point is the temperature at which vapour pressure equal to the atmospheric pressure.

According to given graph, Solution of urea boil at T_3 where boiling point down the line of 1.0 atm.

38. (c) Relative lowering of vapour pressure

$= \frac{\Delta P}{P}$

$\therefore \quad \frac{\Delta P}{P} = \chi_{solute}$

$$\frac{\Delta P}{P} = \frac{n_{solute}}{n_{solute} + n_{solvent}}$$

$$= \frac{0.1}{0.1 + 0.9}$$

$$= \frac{0.1}{1}$$

$\therefore \quad \frac{\Delta P}{P} = 0.1$

39. (d) Ethanol has hydrogen bonding while acetone has dipole-dipole forces. Thus, their mixture would form a non-ideal solution.

40. (a) The vapour pressure will be lowest for least volatile liquid for which the boiling point will be highest. Since toluene has the lowest vapour pressure, its boiling point will be highest.

41. (b) $P_{total} = x_1 P°_1 + x_2 P°_2$

$= P_1 + P_2 = 285.5 + 62.4 = 347.9$ mm Hg.

(as chloroform and dichloromethane form an ideal solution)

42. (d) An ideal solution follows Raoult's law over a wide range of concentration and has zero enthalpy and volume of mixing of the components.

43. (a) $n_X = \frac{3.1}{62} = 0.05$; $n_Y = \frac{19.5}{78} = 0.25$

$$\chi_X = \frac{0.05}{0.05 + 0.25} = \frac{0.05}{0.30}$$

$$\chi_Y = \frac{0.25}{0.30} \quad \therefore \quad \frac{\chi_X}{\chi_Y} = \frac{0.05}{0.25} = 1:5$$

44. (a) In ethyl chloride and ethyl bromide the intermolecular attraction is mostly Van der Waal's force. Therefore, A–B interactions are almost same as A–A and B–B.

$\therefore \quad \Delta H_{mix} = 0$ and $\Delta V_{mix} = 0$

Acetone breaks the H-bonding in ethanol on mixing. So, the acetone-ethanol mixture shows positive deviation.

Phenol-aniline mixture has stronger H-bonding than A–A and B–B. So, negative deviation is observed.

Chloroform-acetone mixture has dipolar interactions among A–B. Hence, negative deviation is observed.

45. (b) In reverse osmosis, the solvent molecules moves from high concentration solution to low concentrated solution through a semipermeable membrane when the external pressure exceeds the osmotic pressure.

46. (d)

$P°_{H_2O} = 25$ torr; $n_u = \frac{12}{60} = 0.2$ moles;

$n_g = \frac{36}{180} = 0.2$ moles; $n_{H_2O} = \frac{100}{18} = 5.55$ moles

$\therefore\ \chi_{H_2O} = \frac{5.55}{5.55+0.2+0.2} = \frac{5.55}{5.95}$

$\therefore\ P_{H_2O} = \chi_{H_2O}\, P^{\circ}_{H_2O} = \frac{5.55}{5.95} \times 25 = 23.32$

47. (d) Benzene and toluene have very similar molecular structure. Thus, they form an ideal solution.

48. (a) According to Raoult's law, relative lowering of vapour pressure is directly proportional to mole fraction of solute. So, mole fraction is used in relating concentration of solution with its vapour pressure.

49. (c) Relative lowering in vapour pressure

$= \frac{(p^{\circ} - p)}{p^{\circ}} = X_A$

[Given $p^{\circ} = 760$ torr. Let, d water = 1 g/mL

$\therefore$ 54 mL = 54 g water]

$\Rightarrow X_A = \frac{n_A}{n_A + n_{H_2O}}$

$\Rightarrow \frac{760 - p}{760} = \frac{\frac{160}{160}}{\frac{160}{160} + \frac{54}{18}} = \frac{1}{4}$

$\Rightarrow p = \frac{3}{4} \times 760 = 570$ torr.

50. (d) Moles of toluene, $n_t = \frac{w_t}{M_t} = \frac{460}{92}$

Moles of benzene, $n_b = \frac{w_b}{M_b} = \frac{390}{78}$

Hence, mole fraction of toluene,

$x_t = \frac{\frac{460}{92}}{\frac{460}{92} + \frac{390}{78}} = \frac{1}{2}$

Mole fraction of benzene $x_b = \frac{\frac{390}{78}}{\frac{460}{92} + \frac{390}{78}} = \frac{1}{2}$

$p_{total} = p^{\circ}_t X_t + p^{\circ}_b X_b$

$p_{total} = 32 \times \frac{1}{2} + 40 \times \frac{1}{2}$

$p_{total} = 36$ mm

By Dalton's law : $p^{\circ}_t x_t = Y_t p_{total} \Rightarrow y_t = \frac{p^{\circ}_t x_t}{p_{total}}$

$\Rightarrow\ y_t = \frac{32 \times \frac{1}{2}}{36} \Rightarrow y_t = \frac{16}{36} = 0.444$

51. (b) Given,

Mass of solute $(w_B) = 10$ g

Molar mass of solute $(M_B) = M_B$

Mass of solvent $(w_A) = 360$g

Molar mass of water $(M_A) = 18$ g mol^{-1}

$\frac{\Delta p}{p^{\circ}} = \chi_B = \frac{n_B}{n_A + n_B} = 5 \times 10^{-3}$

$\frac{\Delta p}{p^{\circ}} = \frac{\frac{w_B}{M_B}}{\frac{w_A}{M_A} + \frac{w_B}{M_B}} \Rightarrow 5 \times 10^{-3} = \frac{\frac{10}{M_B}}{\frac{360}{18} + \frac{10}{M_B}}$

$5 \times 10^{-3} = \frac{10}{20M_B + 10}$

$\Rightarrow (20\ M_B + 10)\ 5 \times 10^{-3} = 10$

$M_B = \frac{1990}{20} = 99.5$ g mol^{-1}

52. (d) For equimolar solution, $\chi_b = \chi_t = 0.5$

$P_b = \chi_t \times P_b^0 = 0.5 \times 160 = 80$ mm

$P_t = \chi_t \times P_t^0 = 0.5 \times 60 = 30$ mm

$P_{total} = 80 + 30 = 110$ mm

Mole fraction of benzene in vapour phase

$= \frac{P_b}{P_{total}} = \frac{80}{110} = 0.727 = 0.73$

53. (b) For anti-freezing effect, ΔT_f must be same for both solution.

$\Delta T_f = i.k_f.m$ since v = same

$\therefore$ For equal T_f

$I_{NaCl} \cdot n_{NaCl} = i_{glycerol} \cdot n_{glycerol}$ ... (i)

For NaCl

$i = 1 + (n - 1)\alpha$

$= 1 + (2 - 1)0.97$

$i = 1.97$

moles $= \frac{20}{58.5}$

$= 0.341$ mol

For glycerol, i = 1 as it is a non electrolyte

Putting all values in (i)

$1.97 \times 0.341 = 1 \times n_{glycerol}$

$n_{glycerol} = 0.673$ mole

Molar mass = 92 g/mol

mass required = moles × molar mass

= 0.673 × 92 = 61.96g

54. (a) Given, moles of $CaCl_2$ = x

i = 2.5

volume = 2.5L

$\pi = 0.75$ atm

Density (d) = 1 g mL^{-1}

$\therefore$ weight of solvent = 2500 g

$\pi = i \times C \times R \times T$

$0.75 = 2.5 \times \frac{n}{v} \times 0.08 \times 300$

$\Rightarrow 0.75 = 2.5 \times \frac{x}{2.5} \times 0.08 \times 300$

$\Rightarrow$ x = 0.03125 moles

$\therefore$ molality (m) $= \frac{0.03125}{2500} \times 1000$

= 0.0125

$\Delta T_b = i \times K_b \times m$

$= 2.5 \times 0.52 \times 0.0125$

$= 0.01625$

55. (b) $\Delta T_b = i \times K_b.m$

$= 1.85 \times 0.52 \times 1.0357 \approx 0.9963°C$

Boiling point of pure water $(T_b^{\circ}) = 100°C$

$T_b = T^{\circ}_b + \Delta T_b = 100°C + 0.9963°C = 100.996°C$

56. (a) Using osmotic pressure equation,

$\pi = iCRT$

i = 1(For glucose and non-electrolyte)

So, $\pi = \frac{n}{v}RT$

Since, $\pi_1 = \pi_2$, $V_1 = V_2$ and $T_1 = T_2$

Comparing n_1 and n_2

So, $n_1 = n_2$

$\frac{x}{180} = \frac{y}{92}$

$\frac{x}{y} = \frac{180}{92} = \frac{45}{23}$

57. (c) At 300K, 0.1 M solution of $K_4[Fe(CN)_6]$ is 50% dissociated.

$K_4[Fe(CN)_6] \rightarrow 4K^+ + [Fe(CN)_6]^{-4}$

No. of ions formed after dissociation = 5

For dissociation: Van't Hoff factor (i)

$i = 1 + \alpha\,(n - 1)$

Where α = degree of dissociation

n = no. of ions

$i = 1 + 0.5\,(5 - 1)$

$= 1 + 2 = 3$

So, Osmotic pressure (π)

$\pi = iCRT$

$= 3 \times 0.1 \times 0.082 \times 300$

= 7.38 atm

58. (c) Given, Mass of solute 1 g.

Mass of water (solvent) = 20.4g = 0.0204 kg

since, solute is non-electrolyte so i = 1

$\Delta T_f = 0 - (-1.05) = 1.05$ k

and, $\Delta T_f = i\,K_f\,m$

$M = \frac{\Delta T_f}{K_f} = \frac{1.05}{1.86} = 0.5645$ mol kg^{-1}

$M = \frac{\text{Moles of solute}}{\text{kg of solvent}}$

Moles = 0.5645 × 0.0204 = 0.01152 mol

Molar Mass $\frac{\text{Mass}}{\text{No. of Moles}} = \frac{1}{0.01152} = 86.8$g mol^{-1}

59. (b) $\Delta T_b = K_b.m$

$m = \frac{\Delta T_b}{K_b}$

$= \frac{0.5}{0.512} \approx 0.976$ m

$\Delta T_f = K_f \cdot m$

$= 1.86 \times 0.976$

$\Delta T_f \approx 1.81536$

$\Delta T_f \approx 1.815°C$

$T_f = T_f^\circ - \Delta T_f$
$= 0 - 1.815$
$\boxed{T_f = -1.815°C}$

60. (c) Let the value of K_b is x
$K_b = x$
So, $K_f = 4x$
Case-I:
Weight of non volatile solute = 2g
Weight of solvent = 200g
$\Delta T_b = YK$
Case-II
Weight of nonvolatile solute = 4g
Weight of solvent = 200g
$\Delta T_f = ZK$
$\Delta T_b = m \times K_b$ ... (1)
$\Delta T_f = m \times K_f$ ... (2)
Putting values in (1) & (2)

$$\frac{Y}{Z} = \frac{\frac{2\times1000}{100\times200}\times x}{\frac{4\times1000}{100\times200}\times 4x}$$

$$\frac{Y}{Z} = \frac{1}{8}$$

61. (d)
w = 124g ethylene glycol (mm-62 g mol^{-1})
x - g water
Solution 10 m

$$\text{Molality} = \frac{\text{no. of mol of solute}}{\text{wt. of solvent in kg}}$$

$$\log\frac{x}{m} = \log k + \frac{1}{n}\log p$$

$$0.052 = \frac{x}{y} \times \frac{0.52\times1000}{60}$$

$$x = \frac{2\times1000}{10}$$

= 200 g water

62. (c) Van't Hoff factor (i)

$$= \frac{\text{observed colligative properties}}{\text{calculated colligative properties}}$$

Obserbed colligative properties = $\Delta T_f(1)$
Caclulated colligative properties,
$\Delta T_f(2) = m \times K_f$
$= 0.5 \times 1.86 = 0.93$

$$\therefore\ i = \frac{\Delta T_f(1)}{\Delta T_f(2)} = \frac{\Delta T_f(1)}{0.93}$$

$\Rightarrow \Delta T_f(1) = 1.075 \times 0.93 \approx 1$

63. (d) Let x is the atomic weight of XY and y is the atomic weight of XY_3.
$\Delta T_f = m \times K_f$

$$\Rightarrow\ m = \frac{\Delta T_f}{k_f} = \frac{5.333}{2}$$

$$\Rightarrow \frac{\text{weight}\times1000}{\text{Molecular weight of XY} \times \text{Weight of solvent}} = 2.6665$$

$$\Rightarrow \frac{10\times1000}{M_{xy}\times50} = 2.665$$

$$\Rightarrow\ M_{xy} = \frac{200}{2.665} = 75$$

Again for XY_3 compound.

$$M_{xy_3} = \frac{10\times1000}{1.1428\times50}$$

$$\left[m = \frac{\Delta T_f}{k_f} = \frac{2.2857}{2} = 1.1428\right]$$

$M_{xy_3} = 175$
$\therefore\ x + y = 75$ ...(i)
$x + 3y = 175$ ...(ii)
By solving equation (i) and (ii) we get
$x = 25$
$y = 50$

64. (d) $p° = x$kPa
Let p is the vapour pressure of non-volatile solute.

$$\frac{p° - p}{p°} = \frac{n_{solute}}{n_{solute} + n_{solvent}}$$

$$\Rightarrow \frac{x-p}{x} = \frac{1}{1+55.55} = \frac{1}{56.55}$$

$\Rightarrow 56.55x - 56.55p = x$

$$\Rightarrow\ p = \frac{55.55x}{56.56} = 0.982$$

65. (b) As per the formula relative lowering of vapour pressure:

$$\frac{p_1^0 - p_1}{p_1^0} = \frac{n_2}{n_1}$$

Where, p_1 is vapour pressure of the solvent = 12.078 kPa
$p_1{}^0$ is the vapour pressure of pure solvent = 12.3 kPa
n_1 is no. of moles of solvent
n_2 is no. of moles of solute

$$\therefore \frac{12.3-12.078}{12.3} = \frac{n_2}{n_1}$$

$$i.e., 0.0180 = \frac{n_2}{n_1}$$

$$\text{as } n_1 = \frac{1000}{18} \text{ (for } H_2O \text{ as solvent)}$$

$\therefore\ n_1 = 555.5$
$\therefore\ 0.0180 \times 55.5 = n_2 = 0.999 \approx 1$

$$\therefore\ \text{Molality } (m) = \frac{n_2}{\text{Mass of solvent (kg)}}$$

$$= \frac{1}{1 \text{ kg of water}} = 1 \text{ mol/kg}$$

66. (d) The depression in freezing point is calculated as :
$\Delta T_f = T_f^\circ - T_f$
Where, T_f° is the freezing point of pure solvent which is 273.16 K
T_f is the freezing point of the solution which is 272.814 K
m is molality
k_f is freezing point depression constant
So, $\Delta T_f = 273.15 \text{ K} - 272.814 \text{ K}$
$\Delta T_f = 0.336 \text{ K}$
As, $\Delta T_f = k_f m$

$$\therefore\ m = \frac{\Delta T_f}{k_f}$$

$$\therefore\ m = \frac{0.336 \text{ K}}{1.86 \text{ K kg mol}^{-1}}$$

$m = 0.18065$ mol/kg

$$\text{As, molality (m)} = \frac{\text{no. of moles of solute}}{\text{Mass of solvent in kg}}$$

and as Mass of solvent = 21.5 g = 0.0215 kg
$\therefore$ no. of moles of solute

$$= 0.18065\frac{\text{mol}}{\text{kg}}\times0.0215 \text{ kg}$$

$\therefore$ no. of moles of solute = 0.00388 mol

$$\text{As, Molar mass of solute} = \frac{\text{mass of solute}}{\text{no. of moles of solute}}$$

$\therefore$ Molar mass of solute

$$= \frac{0.2}{0.00388} = 51.5 \text{ g/mol}$$

67. (a) $\Delta T_F = iK_F m \Rightarrow i = \frac{\Delta T_F}{K_F m}$

$$= \frac{2}{5\times\left(\frac{2.44/122.12}{30/1000}\right)} = 0.6$$

Now, $2C_6H_5COOH$(benzene) $\rightarrow (C_6H_5COOH)_2$(benzene)

Initial	1 mol	0 mol
After association	$1 - x$ mol	$\frac{x}{2}$ mol

Where, x = degree of association
Thus, total moles at equilibrium (after association)

$$= (1-x) + \frac{x}{2} = 1 - \frac{x}{2}$$

$$\text{Thus, } i = \frac{\text{Moles after association}}{\text{Moles before association}}$$

$$= \frac{1-\frac{x}{2}}{1} = 1 - \frac{x}{2}$$

$\Rightarrow$ Degree of association $(x) = 2(1 - i)$
$= 2(1 - 0.6) = 0.8$ or 80 %

68. (c) $T_b = 100.18$ $K_b = 0.52$
$T_f = ?$ $K_f = 1.86$
$\Delta T_b = K_b$ m
$0.18 = 0.52$ m

$$m = \frac{0.18}{0.52} = 0.34$$

$\Delta T_f = 1.86 \times 0.34 = 0.6324 \approx 0.64$

69. (b) As, $\Delta T_f = K_f m$
Where, K_f = depression in freezing point constant
m = molality
ΔT_f = depression in freezing point
$0.64 = 5.12$ m

$$\therefore\ m = \frac{0.64}{5.12}$$

m = 0.125 mol/kg

as molality $= \dfrac{\text{no. of moles of solute}}{\text{Mass of solvent (kg)}}$

$0.125 = \dfrac{\text{no. of moles of solute}}{\dfrac{100}{1000}}$

(as, 100 g of benzene as solvent used here)

$\therefore$ 0.125×0.1 = no. of moles of solute

$\therefore$ no. of moles of solute = 0.0125 mol

As no. of moles of solute $= \dfrac{\text{mass of solute}}{\text{Molas mass of solute}}$

$\therefore$ Molar mass of solute $= \dfrac{1.95}{0.0125} = 156$ g/mol

70. (a) $\alpha = 0.5$

$i = 1 + (n-1)\alpha = 1 + (2-1) \times 0.5 = 1.5$

$\therefore$ $\pi = i \times cRT = 1.5 \times 0.01 \times 0.083 \times 2.98 = 0.37$

71. (c) Osmotic pressure (π) = CRT

Given,

Weight of urea = 6g

Molecular weight of urea $\left(H_2N-\overset{\overset{O}{\|}}{C}-NH_2\right)$

$= 4 \times 1 + 2 \times 14 + 12 + 16 = 60 \text{ g mol}^{-1}$

$\therefore$ Number of mole of urea $= \dfrac{\text{Weight}}{\text{Molecular weight}}$

$\Rightarrow \dfrac{6}{60} = 0.1$ mole

concentration (C) $= \dfrac{\text{mole}}{\text{volume}}$

$= \dfrac{0.1}{0.5}$ [1 L = 10^3 mL]

(C) = 0.2 mole/liter

$\pi = 0.2 \times 0.082 \times 300$

$\pi = 4.92$ atm

72. (a) Given, weight of benzoic acid = x g

Molar mass of benzoic acid = 122 g mol^{-1}

Weight of benzene = 49g

Molar mass of benzene = 78 g mol^{-1}

depression in freezing point (ΔT_f) = 1.12 K

degree of association (α) = 88% = 0.88

K_f for benzene = 4.9 k kg mol^{-1}

For association,

Van't Hoff factor (i) $= 1 + \left(\dfrac{1}{n} - 1\right)\alpha$

$= 1 + \left(\dfrac{1}{2} - 1\right) \times 0.88$

i = 0.56

$\Delta T_f = i \times K_f \times m$

$1.12 = 0.56 \times 4.9 \times \dfrac{x \times 1000}{122 \times 49}$ m =

$\left[m = \dfrac{\text{weight of solute} \times 100}{\text{Molecular} \times \text{Weight} \quad \text{Weight of solute} \quad \text{of solvent}} \right]$

x = 2.44 g

73. (d) In case of negative deviations from Raoult's law, the intermolecular attractive forces between A – A and B – B are weaker than those between A – B and leads to decrease in vapour pressure resulting in negative deviations.

In reverse osmosis the applied pressure must be higher than the osmotic pressure of solution. Hence Statement I is incorrect but II is correct.

74. (d) Given

$\Delta T_b = 0.052$ K

$\Delta T_b = K_b \times m$

$0.052 = 0.52 \times m$

m = 0.1

$\Delta T_f = m\,K_f = 0.1 \times 1.86 = 0.186$

Freezing point of solution = 273 – 0.186 = 272.81 K.

75. (a) I and III only

In this experiment the process of reverse osmosis take place. Reverse osmosis is a process in which a larger pressure is applied to the solution side as to overcome the osmatic pressure. This pushes the pure solvent under pressure. Out of the solution through the semi-permeable membrane. By the table if pressure applied in part I of the vessel than pure water can be obtain by part II of vessel through semi-permeable membrane.

76. Given, $\Delta T_b = 0.01$ K

Molality = 0.01 m

$K_b = 0.52$ K kg mol^{-1}

We know, $\Delta T_b = i\,K_b\,m$

$i = \dfrac{\Delta T_b}{K_b m} = \dfrac{0.01}{0.52 \times 0.01} = 1.92$

77. (c) Given,

$T_b° = 373.15$, $K_b = 0.52$ K kg mol^{-1}

$T_b = 373.202$

$T_f° = 273.15$, $K_f = 1.86$ K kg mol^{-1}

$\therefore$ $(T_b - T_b°) = m \times K_b$

m = 0.1

Again,

$(T_f° - T_f) = m \times K_f$

$(273.15 - T_f) = 0.1 \times 1.86$

$273.15 - 0.186 = T_f$

$\therefore$ $T_f = 272.964$

78. (d) $\Delta T_f = m \times K_f = \dfrac{n_2}{m_1} \times K_f$

We have, $x_2 = \dfrac{n_2}{n_1 + n_2} \approx \dfrac{n_2}{n_1} = 0.01$

Taking 1L of water, mass of water = 1 kg = 1000 g

$\Rightarrow$ $n\,(H_2O) = n_1 = \dfrac{1000 \text{ g}}{18 \text{ g mol}^{-1}} = 55.55$ mol

$\Rightarrow$ $0.01 = \dfrac{n_2}{55.55 + n_2}$

$n_2 = 0.5611$

$\Rightarrow \Delta T_f = \dfrac{n_2}{m_1} \times K_f = \dfrac{0.5611}{1\text{kg}} \times 1.86$

= 1.043 K

79. (b)

$\Delta T_b = K_b \times m \times i = (0.52)(0.1)(2) = 0.104$ K

$\Rightarrow T_b = T_b° + \Delta T_b = 373 + 0.104 = 373.104$ K

80. (a) $\pi = CRT$

$\Rightarrow C = \dfrac{\pi}{RT} = \dfrac{2.46}{0.082 \times (27 + 273)} = 0.1 \text{ mol L}^{-1}$.

81. (d) $\dfrac{\Delta P}{P^0} = 0.006$, $m_1 = 100$ g,

$m_2 = 6$g, $M_1 = 18.0$ g mol^{-1}

$\dfrac{\Delta P}{P^0} = x_2 = \dfrac{n_2}{n_1 + n_2} \cong \dfrac{n_2}{n_1} (n_1 >> n_2)$

$\Rightarrow n_2 = \dfrac{\Delta P}{P^0} \times n_1 = 0.006 \times \dfrac{100.0}{18.0} = 0.0334$

$\Rightarrow M_2 = \dfrac{m_2}{n_2} = \dfrac{6.0}{0.0334} \cong 180 \text{ g mol}^{-1}$

82. (d)

$\Delta T_f = 0.0\,°C - (-0.0186\,°C) = 0.0186\,°C$ (glucose)

$\Delta T_f = i \times m \times k_f$

Both solutions have the same molar concentrations so their molal concentration will also be the same.

Also, i for NaCl = 2

$\Rightarrow$ ΔT_f (NaCl) = $2 \times \Delta T_f$ (glucose)

$= 2 \times 0.0186\,°C = 0.0372\,°C$

Thus, the NaCl solution will freeze at – 0.0372 °C

83. (a) The molal depression constant or cryoscopic constant is a characteristic property of a solvent.

84. (b)

$\pi = CRT = (0.02)(0.082)(300) = 0.492$ atm.

85. (c) $\Delta T_b = 0.104$ K,

$K_b = 0.52$ K kg mol^{-1}, $K_f = 1.86$ K kg mol^{-1}

Thus, $\Delta T_b = m\,K_b$

$\Rightarrow m = \dfrac{\Delta T_b}{K_b} = \dfrac{0.104}{0.52} = 0.2 \text{ mol kg}^{-1}$

$\Rightarrow \Delta T_f = m\,K_f = 0.2 \times 1.86 = 0.372$ K.

86. (c) Ferric sulphate = $Fe_2(SO_4)_3$

$Fe_2(SO_4)_3 \rightarrow 2Fe^{3+} + 3\,SO_4^{2-}$

(complete ionization)

$\Rightarrow$ van't Hoff factor = i = 2 + 3 = 5.

87. (c) Total no. of species will increases for the dissolution of strong electrolytes, KCl and K_2SO_4.

$KCl \rightarrow K^+ + Cl^-$; $K_2SO_4 \rightarrow 2K^+ + SO_4^{2-}$

Therefore, depression in freezing point will be in greater extent than undissociated organic compounds like urea and glucose is they don't dissociate in aqueous solution.

Now, 30g of glucose $= \dfrac{30}{180} = \dfrac{4}{6} = 0.167$ mol

Therefore, no. of moles of solute of glucose is greater than that of urea of 1 kg water. So, depression (ΔT_f) in freezing point is more than that of urea.

$\Delta T_f = im\,K_f$

$\therefore$ The highest freezing point is for 0.1 mol urea in 1 kg water.

88. (b) Two solutions having same osmotic pressure at a given temperature are called isotonic solutions.

Mol. Wt. of area $[CO(NH_2)_2] = 60$

$\pi_{CO(NH_2)_2} = \pi_X$ or, $C_1RT = C_2RT$

∴ The molar mass (X) = 100 g/mol

or, $\frac{6}{60}RT = \frac{10}{X}RT$

X = 100

89. (a) $m_2 = 4\%$ (w/v) = 4g in 100 ml solution.
= 40g in 1000 ml solution.
∴ For isotonic solution,
$\pi_1 = \pi_2$ or, $C_1RT = C_2RT$

or, $\frac{n_1}{v} = \frac{n_2}{v}$ or, $\frac{m_1}{M_1} = \frac{m_2}{M_2}$.

or, $\frac{x}{60} = \frac{4}{120} \Rightarrow x = 2$

90. (b) Molality of the solution

$$= \left(\frac{x}{78}\right) \times \frac{1000}{500} = \frac{x}{39}(m)$$

$\Delta T_f = m(K_f)_{H_2O}$

$\therefore \frac{x}{39} = \frac{1}{1.86}$ ∴ $x = \frac{39}{1.86} = 20.96$

91. (c) The osmotic pressure of the fluid inside the blood cells are same as 0.9% (mass/volume) saline water. This particular percentage of saline water is known as normal saline water. When the concentration of the saline water > 0.9%, then the osmotic pressure becomes more in comparison to that blood cell. Therefore, water starts come out of the cell resulting into the shrinking of cell.
And when it is < 0.9%, water enters into the blood cells and thus it swells resulting into the disease edema.

92. (b) Osmotic pressure π = CRT; C is in moles/L.

$C = \frac{n}{V} = \frac{m}{MV}$

m = mass of solute and M = mol. wt. of solute
V = Volume in L.
At a given T, isotonic solution; $\pi_1 = \pi_2$; $C_1RT = C_2RT$

(A) 18g/L of glucose = (18/180)/L = 0.1 mol/L = 0.1(M) and 6g\L of Urea = (6/60)/L = 0.1 mol/L = 0.1 (M)

(B) 10g/L of glucose

$$= \left(\frac{10}{180}\right)/L = \left(\frac{1}{18}\right)/L = 0.06(M)$$

10g/L of urea $= \left(\frac{10}{60}\right)/L = \left(\frac{1}{6}\right)/L = 0.17(M)$

∴ $C_1 \neq C_2$

(C) 0.01(M) NaOH solution and 0.02(M) glucose solution are isotonic.
$\pi_{NaOH} = 2 \times 0.01 \times RT = 0.02\ RT$
$\pi_{glucose} = 0.02\ RT$
$\therefore \pi_{NaOH} = \pi_{glucose}$ ∴ $C_1 \neq C_2$

(D) 0.01(M) NaCl solution are 0.01(M) glucose solution
$\pi_{NaCl} = 0.02\ RT$
$\pi_{glucose} = 0.01 \times R \times T$
∴ $\pi_{NaCl} \neq \pi_{glucose}$

93. (b) $\Delta T_b = K_b \times m \Rightarrow K_b = \frac{\Delta T_b}{m}$

94. (d) Standard boiling point (b.p. at 1 bar pressure) of a liquid is slightly lower than the normal boiling point (b.p. at 1 atm pressure). It is because 1 bar pressure is sightly lower than 1 atm pressure.

95. (b)
Moles of non-volatile solute X = 9/180
Moles of non-volatile solute Y = 1/50
Mass of solvent water (approx.) = 90 gm
$K_b = 0.52$ Kkg mol^{-1}
$\Delta T_b = K_b \times m$

$$= 0.52\left(\frac{9}{180} + \frac{1}{50}\right)\frac{1000}{90}$$

= 0.52(0.05 + 0.02)10 = 0.40

Thus, boiling point = 100 + 0.40 = 100.4 °C

96. (d) Given,
Mass of $MgSO_4$ (W) = x g
Volume of solution (V) = 2.5 L
vant Hoff factor (i) = 1.8
Osmotic pressure (π) = 2.463 atm
Temperature (T) = 27 + 273 = 300 K
Molar mass of $MgSO_4$ (M) = 120 g mol^{-1}

$$\pi = iCRT = \frac{i \times W \times RT}{M \times V(L)}$$

$$2.463 = \frac{1.8 \times x \times 0.0821 \times 300}{120 \times 2.5}$$

(R = 0.0821 - atm K^{-1} mol^{-1})

x = 16.68g

97. (b) $\Delta T_f = K_f \times m \Rightarrow 0.70 = 5.1 \times m$

$\Rightarrow m = \frac{0.70}{5.1} = \frac{\text{Moles of solute}}{\text{Total mass of solvent (kg)}}$

Lets, assume x g napthalene is present.

$$0.137 = \frac{\left(\frac{x}{m_{C_{10}H_8}} + \frac{6-x}{m_{C_{14}H_{10}}}\right) \times 1000}{300}$$

$\Rightarrow 0.041 = \frac{x}{128} + \frac{6-x}{178} = 3.4$ g

Mass of anthracene = 6 – x = 6 – 3.4 = 2.6 g

98. (b) Given, π = 3.735 × 10^{-3} bar
Mass of K_2SO_4 = 17.4 mg
Molar mass (M) H_2SO_4 = 174 i = 3.0
Volume = 2L
From osmotic pressure of solution.
π = iCRT
i = van't-Hoff factor
i = π/CRT

$$= \frac{\pi \times M \times V}{W \times R \times T} = \frac{3.735 \times 174 \times 2}{17.4 \times 0.083 \times 300} \approx 3.0$$

99. (b) Given,
W_B (mass of ethylene glycol) = 31 g
W_A (mass of water) = 600 g
K_f (for water) = 1.86 K kg mol^{-1}
and M_B (for $C_2H_6O_2$) = 62

$\because \Delta T_f = K_f \cdot \frac{W_B}{M_B} \times \frac{1000}{W_A}$

$\therefore \Delta T_f = \frac{1.86 \times 31 \times 1000}{62 \times 600} = 1.55K$

100. (d) ∵ π = iC RT.

(a) π for 5.0 M urea is
π = 1 × 5 × 0.0821 × 340 K
π = 139.57 atm

(b) π for 1.5 M A_2B_3 type is (i = 4)
π = 4.1 × 1.5 × 0.0821 × 300 K
π = 151.47 atm

(c) π for 3.0 M AB type is (i = 1.6)
π = 1.6 × 3 × 0.0821 × 300 K
π = 1440 R = 118.22 atm

(d) π for 2.5 M AB_2 type is (i = 2.5)
π = 2.5 × 2.5 × 0.0821 × 330 K
π = 169.33 atm

Hence AB_2 shows highest osmotic pressure at 57°C.

101. (d) $\Delta T_f = K_f m$

$0.93 = \frac{1.86 \times 6 \times 1000}{M \times 100} \Rightarrow M \approx 120$

102. (d) From Rault's law for non-volatile solute, we know that

$$\frac{p^\circ - p_s}{p^\circ} = \frac{n_2}{n_1 + n_2}$$

For dilute solution, relative lowering of vapour pressure, $n_1 + n_2 \approxeq n_1$

$n_2 = \frac{18}{180} = 0.1$; $n_1 = \frac{90}{18} = 5$

$$= \frac{p^\circ - p_s}{p^\circ} = \frac{0.1}{5} = 0.02$$

2 Electrochemistry

1. **(b)** The limiting molar conductivity $(\overset{\circ}{\lambda}m)$ for CsCl is higher than NaCl so CsCl plot sits higher on the graph than the NaCl plot.

2. **(c)** Given, Resistance (R) of KCl solution $= 85\Omega$

Conductivity of KCl solution $(K_1) = 0.3\ sm^{-1}$

Using formula $R = \rho\frac{\ell}{A}$ or $R = \frac{1}{K}\frac{\ell}{A}$

Where R = Resistance

ρ = resistivity

$\frac{\ell}{A}$ = Cell constant

K = Conductivity

So, Cell constant $\left(\frac{\ell}{A}\right) = R \times K$

$= 85 \times 0.3 = 25.5\ m^{-1}$

Conductivity (K_2) of K_2SO_4 solution

$K_2 = \frac{1}{R}\times\frac{\ell}{A}$

$K_2 = \frac{25.5 m^{-1}}{300\Omega} = 0.085\ Sm^{-1}$

Molar conductivity of K_2SO_4 solution (λm)

$= \frac{K_2}{1000 \times C}$

$\lambda m = \frac{0.085}{1000 \times 0.0025}$

$\lambda m = 0.034\ S^2\ m^2\ mol^{-1}$

or

$3.4 \times 10^{-2}\ S\ m^2\ mol^{-1}$

3. **(b)** Given k (0.001m acetic acid)

$= 5 \times 10^{-5}\ S\ cm^{-1}$

$\lambda_m^o = 390\ S\ cm^2\ mol^{-1}$

We know that

$\lambda_M^\lambda = \frac{K \times 1000}{C}$

$\lambda_M = \frac{5\times10^{-5}\times1000}{0.001}$

$\lambda_m = 50\ S\ cm^2\ mol^{-1}$

$\alpha = \frac{\lambda_m}{\lambda_m^o} = \frac{50}{390} = 0.128$

4. **(a)**

$\Lambda_m^o (NaCl) = \lambda^o(Na^+) + \lambda^o(Cl^-) = 50 + \lambda^o(Cl^\ominus)$

$\Lambda_m^o (KCl) = \lambda^o(K^+) + \lambda^o(Cl^-) = 73 + \lambda^o(Cl^-)$

$\Lambda_m^o (CsCl) = \lambda^o(Cs^+) + \lambda^o(Cl^-) = 77 + \lambda^o(Cl^-)$

$\Lambda_m^o\ CsCl > \Lambda_m^o\ KCl > \Lambda_m^o\ NaCl.$

5. **(d)**

Conductivity of 0.01M KCl = p $Ohm^{-1}\ cm^{-1}$

Conductance of 0.01M KCl = q Ohm^{-1}

As we know,

Cell constant $\left(\frac{1}{A}\right) = \frac{K\ (Conductivity)}{G\ (Conductance)}$

So for 0.01 M KCl

$\frac{1}{A} = \frac{p}{q}$

Conductivity of H_2SO_4 solution:

$K(H_2SO_4)$ = Cell constant × Conductance

$K(H_2SO_4) = \frac{p}{q} \times r = \frac{pr}{q}$

6. **(b)** Λ_m (molar conductivity) $= S\ Cm^2\ mol^{-1}$

G (conductance) = S

K (specific conductance) $= S\ Cm^{-1}$

G* (cell constant) $= m^{-1}$

7. **(a)** $R_1 = 100\ \Omega$

$C_1 = 0.1$ M

$K = 1.29\ Sm^{-1} = 1.29 \times 10^{-2}\ Scm^{-1}$

$R_2 = 520$ W

$C_2 = 0.2$ M

$\Lambda_m = \gg$ for 0.02 M solution

Where, $R_1 = R_2$ = resistance

$C_1 = C_2$ = concentration

Λ_m = molar conductivity

K = conductivity

Now, $G = K\left(\frac{A}{l}\right)$

$\frac{l}{A} = \frac{K}{G}$

$\frac{l}{A} = \frac{K}{G} = KR = 1.29\times10^{-2}\times1000 = 1.29\ cm^{-1}$

$\Lambda_m = \frac{K\times1000}{C} = \frac{K\times1000}{0.02} = \frac{\frac{1}{520}\times1.29\times1000}{0.02}$

$= 124\ Scm^2\ mol$

8. **(d)** $C = 0.05$

$K = 0.0115\ S\ cm^{-1}$

$\Lambda_m = \frac{K\times1000}{M} = \frac{0.0115\times10^3}{0.05}$

$= 230\ S\ cm^2\ mol^{-1}$

9. **(b)** With the increase in concentration, conductivity of solution increases due to an increase in the number of ions.

Thus, Z > X > Y.

10. **(d)** $\Lambda_m^o(HCOOH) = \lambda_{H^+}^o + \lambda_{HCOO^-}^o$

$= 349.6 + 54.6 = 404.2\ S\ cm^2\ mol^{-1}$.

$\Rightarrow \alpha = \frac{\Lambda_m}{\Lambda_m^o} = \frac{40.42}{404.2} = 0.1$

$\Rightarrow \kappa_a = \frac{C\alpha^2}{1-\alpha} = \frac{0.027(0.1)^2}{1-0.1}$

$= 0.0003 = 3.0 \times 10^{-4}$.

11. **(c)** Conductivity (K) = Number of ions dissolved in unit volume of the solution.

Thus, upon dilution, the number of ions per unit volume decreases because of which conductivity decreases.

Thus, Assertion (A) is correct but Reason (R) is not correct.

12. **(a)** Conductivity (k) $= 6 \times 10^{-3}\ \Omega^{-1}\ cm^{-1}$

V = 200 mL = 0.2 L

mass = 2.08 g

$\Rightarrow C = \frac{n}{V} = \frac{\left(\frac{mass}{molar\ mass}\right)}{V} = \frac{\left(\frac{2.08}{208}\right)}{0.2} = 0.05\ M.$

$\Rightarrow \Lambda_m = \frac{K\times1000}{C} = \frac{(6\times10^{-3})(1000)}{0.05}$

$= 120 = 1.20 \times 10^2$

Thus, x = 1.2

13. **(a)** $CH_3COOH \rightleftharpoons CH_3COO^- + H^+$; $HCl \rightarrow H^+ + Cl^-$

$(CH_3COO)_2Ba \longrightarrow 2CH_3COO^- + Ba^{2+}$;

$BaCl_2 \rightarrow Ba^{2+} + 2Cl^-$

$2(\Lambda^o_m)_{CH_3COOH} = 2(\Lambda^o_m)_{CH_3COO^-} + 2(\Lambda^o_m)_{H^+}$

$= \left[2(\Lambda^o_m)_{CH_3COO^-} + (\Lambda^o_m)_{Ba^{2+}}\right] + \left[2(\Lambda^o_m)_{H^+} + 2(\Lambda^o_m)_{Cl^-}\right] - (\Lambda^o_m)_{Ba^{2+}} - 2(\Lambda^o_m)_{Cl^-}$

$= (\Lambda^o_m)_{(CH_3COO)_2Ba} + 2(\Lambda^o_m)_{HCl} - (\Lambda^o_m)_{BaCl_2}$

$= x_1 + 2x_3 - x_2$

$\therefore\ (\Lambda^o_m)_{CH_3COOH} = \frac{x_1 - x_2}{2} + x_3$

14. **(d)**

$R_1 = 100\Omega;\ R_1 = \rho_1\frac{\ell}{A};\therefore \frac{\ell}{A} = R_1\lambda_1 = 1.29\times100\ cm^{-1}$

$R_2 = 258\Omega;$ Now, $\frac{\ell}{A} = R_2\lambda_2;\ \lambda_2 = \frac{100\times1.29}{258} = \frac{1}{2}Scm^{-1}$

$= 0.5\ Scm^{-1}$

15. **(a)** Given, $\kappa = 0.013\ cm^{-1}$, $R = 300\ \Omega$

Cell constant G* = conductivity(κ) × Resistance(R)

Cell constant $= 0.013 \times 300 = 3.9\ cm^{-1}$

16. **(d)** $\lambda^o_m(NH_4OH) = \lambda^o_m(NH_4^+) + \lambda^o_m(OH^-)$

$= \lambda^o_m(NH_4Cl) + \frac{1}{2}\lambda^o_m(Ba(OH)_2) - \frac{1}{2}\lambda^o_m(BaCl_2)$

$= 2130 + \left(\frac{1}{2}\times457.0\right) - \left(\frac{1}{2}\times240.6\right)$

$= 2238.2\ S\ cm^2\ mol^{-1}$.

17. (c) Electrolysis of NaCl:

at cathode: $2H_2O(l) + 2e^- \longrightarrow H_2(g) + 2OH^-(aq)$

2 moles of e^- required for 1 mole of H_2

$Q = It$

$= 10 \times 10^{-3} A \times 19.3 \times 10^4 S$

$Q = 1930$ C

moles of $e^- = \frac{Q}{F} = \frac{1930}{96500}$

= 0.02 moles

2 moles of e^- give 1 mol of H_2

So, 0.02 moles of e^- will give 0.01 mol of H_2

18. (b) Given:- Time (t) = 10 min = 10 × 60 = 600 sec.

Current (A) = 2.0 Amp.

The reaction at Cathode as:-

$Cu^{+2} + 2e^- \rightarrow Cu$

$2e^-$ are transfer in this reaction

The mass of copper is 63.5 g mol^{-1}

Charge = time × current

Charge = 600 × 2 = 1200 C

Now the mass of copper deposited

$= \frac{\text{molar mass} \times \text{charge}}{\text{electron transferred} \times \text{Faraday constant}}$

$\Rightarrow \frac{63.5 \times 1200}{2 \times 96500} = \frac{762}{1930} = 0.39$ g

19. (a) $M^{2+} + 2e^- \rightarrow M$

8040 coulombs deposited = 2.644g of metal

2 × 96500 coulombs will deposit $= \frac{2.644}{8040} \times 2 \times 96500$

= 63.46g

Hence, atomic mass of metal is 63.46g mol^{-1}.

20. (b) Oxidation : (anode)

$2H_2O\ (l) \rightarrow O_2\ (g) + 4H^+\ (aq.);\ E^\circ_{RP} = +1.23$ V

Reduction : (cathode)

$Cu^{2+}\ (aq.) + 2e^- \rightarrow Cu\ (s)\ ;\ E^\circ_{RP} = +0.34$ V

$E^\circ_{cell} = E^\circ_{cathode} - E^\circ_{anode} = (0.34) - (+1.23) = -0.89$ V.

Thus, a potential of minimum of +0.89 V would be required to carry out the given reaction.

21. (b) i = 2.0 A, t = ?

$3Fe^{3+} + 3e^- \rightarrow 3Fe^{2+}$

Charge of 3 moles of e^- = 3 × 96500 = 289,500 C.

$\Rightarrow t = \frac{Q}{i} = \frac{289,500}{2.0} = 144,750$ seconds

= 40.208 hours.

22. (a) $MgCl_2 \rightarrow Mg^{2+} + 2\ Cl^-$

$Mg^{2+} + 2e^- \rightarrow Mg\ (s)$

2 moles of e^- are required to deposit 1 mole of Mg (s).

$\Rightarrow$ 1 mole of e^- = 1F

$\Rightarrow$ 2 moles of e^- = 2F

$n(MgCl_2) = 0.1\ M \times 1\ L = 0.1$ mol.

$n(Mg^{2+}) = 0.1$ mol.

Therefore, the number of moles of electrons/faradays required to deposit 0.1 mol of Mg will be 2 × 0.1 = 0.2 mol.

23. (a) Charges passing through solution = 5 × 193 = 965C

$Cu^{n+} + ne^- \rightarrow Cu$

965C charge deposit 0.32g

or 96500n C charge deposit

$= \frac{0.32 \times 96500n}{965} = 63.5 \ \therefore\ n = \frac{64}{32} = 2$

24. (b) Equivalent weight $= \frac{W \times F}{I \times t}$

$= \frac{0.96 \times 96500}{1.2 \times 40 \times 60} = 32.1g \simeq 31.75g$

25. (c) Charges passed through solution = 38.6 × 100 = 3860 C

At Cathode : $Cu^{2+} + 2e \rightarrow Cu$

At Anode : $2H_2O \rightarrow O_2\uparrow + 4H^+ + 4e$

2F = 96500 × 2 C charge deposit 1 mole = 63.5g of Cu

3860C charge deposit $= \frac{63.5 \times 3860}{96500 \times 2} = 1.27$g of Cu

4F = 96500 × 4 C charge liberate 1 mole = 22.4 L O_2 at STP

$\therefore$ 3860 C charge liberate

$= \frac{22.4 \times 3860}{4 \times 96500} = 0.224$L of O_2

26. (a) Time, t = 1.608 min or 96.5 s

Formula, $W_{Al} = \frac{z \times i \times t}{96500} \Rightarrow W_{Al} = \frac{27}{3} \times \frac{10 \times 96.5}{96500}$

$\Rightarrow W_{Al} = 0.09$ g

27. (c) $p = V \times i_o$

$200 = 100 \times i$ $\quad$ [i = 2]

$\therefore w = \frac{Eit}{F} = \frac{M \times i \times t}{n \times F}$

$\Rightarrow n = \frac{M \times i \times t}{w \times F} = \frac{118.7 \times 2 \times (5 \times 3600)}{11.1 \times 96500} = 3.989$

SnO and SnO_2 are non-electrolytes (aqueous). Hence, the compound is $SnCl_4$

28. (c) When an aqueous solution of $CuCl_2$ is electrolysed using Pt inert electrodes. The chloride ion is oxidised to chlorine (Cl_2) at anode and Cu^{2+} ion is reduced to Cu at cathode.

At anode: $2Cl^- \xrightarrow{-2e^-} Cl_2(g)$

At cathode: $Cu^{2+} + 2e^- \longrightarrow Cu$

29. (b) When same amount of electricity is passed through $AgNO_3$ and $CuSO_4$ aqueous solution.

Then 1 mole of Ag^+ will deposit and half mole of Cu^{2+} will deposit.

The relation between Ag^+ and Cu^{2+} ion is as follows

1 mol of $Ag^+ = \frac{1}{2}$ mol of Cu^{2+}

Thus for, $\frac{x \text{ mol of } Ag^+}{y \text{ mol of } Cu^{2+}} = \frac{1 \text{ mol}}{1/2 \text{ mole}}$

$\therefore\ x = 2y$

30. (c) When sodium acetate is electrolysed in aqueous medium, it react as follows

$2CH_3COONa + 2H_2O \longrightarrow 2CO_2 + 2C_6H_6 + 2H_2$

At anode (Y): $2C_6H_6 + 2CO_2$

At cathode (X): H_2

31. (b) $K_2SO_4 \rightarrow 2K^+ + SO_4^{2-}$

Due to platinum electrodes, self ionization of water will take place.

$H_2O \rightarrow 2H^+ + OH^-$

At cathode: $2H^+ + 2e^- \rightarrow H_2$

At anode: $4OH^- \rightarrow 2H_2O + O_2 + 4e^-$

Due to lower electrode potentials, H_2 gas will generate at cathode and O_2 gas will generate at anode.

32. (c) $E^\circ_{cell} = E^\circ_C - E^\circ_A = 0.80 - 0.34$

$E^\circ_{cell} = 0.46$V

$E^\circ_{cell} = \frac{2.303RT}{nF} \log K_c$

Given $\frac{2.303RT}{F} = 0.06$

$\therefore E^\circ_{cell} = \frac{0.06}{n} \log K_c$

$\log K_c = \frac{0.46 \times 2}{0.06}$

$= \frac{46}{3} \approx 15.33$

$\log K_c = 15.33$

33. (a) $M(S) \rightarrow M^{2+}(xM)$

$2H^+\ (0.02M) \rightarrow H_2(g)$

$\therefore E^\circ = E^\circ_{oxidation} + E^\circ_{Reduction}$

$= E_{M/M^{2+}} + E_{H^+/H_2}$

$= 0.14 + 0 \Rightarrow E^\circ = 0.14$ V

$\therefore E_{cell} = E^\circ - \frac{0.059}{n} \log \frac{[M^{2+}]}{[H^+]^2}$

$\Rightarrow 0.077 = 0.14 - \frac{0.059}{2} \log \frac{x}{[2 \times 10^{-2}]^2}$

$\Rightarrow$ 2.13 = log x – log 4 × 10^{-4}

$\Rightarrow$ 2.13 = 10gx + 3.398

$\Rightarrow$ logx = –1.268

x = 0.054

34. (a) $Zn|Zn^{+2}(c_1)\ ||\ Cu^{+2}c_2)\ |\ Cu$

Anode- $Zn \longrightarrow Zn^{+2} + 2e^-$;

Cathode - $Cu^{+2} + 2e^- \rightarrow Cu$

Net reaction– $Zn + Cu^{+2} \longrightarrow Zn^{+2} + Cu$, n = 2

$E_{cell} = E^\circ_{cell} - \frac{2.303RT}{nF} \log \frac{[Zn^{+2}]}{[Cu^{+2}]}$

Cell-1 $Zn|Zn^{+2}||\ Cu^{+2}|Cu$

$E_1 = E^\circ_{cell} - \frac{0.0591}{2} \log\left(\frac{1}{0.1}\right) = E^\circ_{cell} - 0.0295$

Cell-2 $Zn|Zn^{+2}|Cu^{+2}\ |Cu$

$E_2 = E^\circ_{cell} - \frac{0.0591}{2} \log\left(\frac{1}{1}\right) = E^\circ_{cell} = 0$

Cell- 3 $Zn|Zn^{+2}||Cu^{+2}\ |Cu$

$E_3 = E^\circ_{cell} - \frac{0.0591}{2} \log\left(\frac{0.1}{1}\right) = E^\circ_{cell} + 0.0295$

$E_3 > E_2 > E_1$

35. (c) For the given cell,
$Fe | Fe^{2+} || Cu^{2+} | Cu$
So, n = 2
Using nernst equation-

$$E = E^\circ_{cell} - \frac{2.303\,RT}{nF}\log\frac{[Fe^{2+}]}{[Cu^{2+}]}$$

$$E = E^\circ_{cell} - \frac{0.06}{n}\log\frac{0.001}{0.1}$$

$$0.82 = E^\circ_{cell} - \frac{0.06}{2}\log(10^{-2})$$

$$0.82 = E^\circ_{cell} - \frac{0.06}{2}(-2)$$

$E^\circ_{cell} = 0.82 - 0.06 = 0.76V$

36. (b) Given, I = 965A
t = 1000s
Charge passed = Q = it
Q = 965 × 1000
= 965000
No. of moles of electron

$$= \frac{Q}{F} = \frac{965000}{96500} = 10 \text{ mol}$$

In molten Al_2O_3: $Al^{3+} + 3e^- \rightarrow Al$
3 moles of electrons deposit 1 mol of Al
So, 10 moles of electron deposit

$$= \frac{10}{3} \text{ moles of Al}$$

= 3.33 moles
Mass of Al = 3.33 × 27 = 90g

37. (a) For the reaction,
$2\,Al(s) + 3\,Cu^{2+}(aq) \rightarrow 2Al^{3+}(aq) + 3\,Cu(s)$
$E^\circ_{cell} = E_{cathode} - E_{anode}$
= 0.34 – (–1.66)
$E^\circ_{cell} = 2V$
No. of electron (n): $2Al \rightarrow 2Al^{3+} + 6e^-$
$3Cu^{2+} + 6e^- \rightarrow 3\,Cu$
So, n = 6
Using, ΔG = –nFE°
= – 6 × 96500 × 2
= –1158000 J mol^{-1}
= –1158 kJ mol^{-1}

38. (c)
$$2M^{+3}(aq) + 2I^{\ominus}(ag) \rightarrow 2M^{2+}(aq) + I_2(s)$$

$$E^\circ_{cell} = \frac{2.303 \times RT}{nF}\log K_c$$

$$E^\circ_{cell} = \frac{0.0591}{2} \times 7.98 \approx 0.2358V$$

39. (c) (I) ΔG° = –RT ln K_c is a standard thermodynamic relation hence it is correct.

(II) $E^\circ_{cell} = \frac{0.059}{n}$ ln K_c is incorrect. The correct relation is $E^\circ_{cell} = \frac{0.059}{n}\log K_c$

Hence, Statement I is correct while Statement II is incorrect.

40. (a) According to nernst equation:
EMF of hydrogen concentration cell

$$E_{cell} = \frac{2.303RT}{nF}\log\frac{[H^+]_{cathode}}{[H^+]_{anode}} \quad (\because \text{As } n = 1)$$

$[H^+]_{cathode} = 0.01$ M, $[H^+]_{anode} = 10^{-8}$M

$$E_{cell} = 0.06\log\frac{[10^{-2}]}{[10^{-8}]}$$

$= 0.06 \log [10^6]$
= 0.06 × 6 = 0.36 V

41. (b) $E = E^\circ - \frac{2.303\,RT}{nF}$

$$E = 0.34 - \frac{0.06}{2}$$

= 0.34 – 0.03
= 0.31 V

42. (a) As $\Delta G = -nFE_{cell}$
Where, n = no. of electrons transferred in a reaction
F = Faraday's = 96500 C/mol
E_{cell} = *emf* of the cell = 0.237 V
ΔG = Gibbs free energy of cell
Now, as per the reactions 2 electrons (*n* = 2) are transferred :
$2Fe^{+3} + 2e^{-1} \longrightarrow 2Fe^{+2}$
$2I^- \longrightarrow I_2 + 2e^{-1}$
∴ ΔG = –2 × 96500 × 0.237
ΔG = – 45741 J/mol
as, $\Delta G = -2.303\,RT\log k_{eq}$
Where, k_{eq} = equilibrium constant = 10^x
R = Universal G as constant
T = Temperature (K)
∴ ΔG = –2.303 × 8.3 × 298 × log 10^x
as ΔG = –45741 J/mol
so, –45741 = – 2.303 × 8.3 × 298 × log 10^x

$$\frac{45741}{2.303 \times 8.3 \times 298} = \log 10^x$$

$$\frac{45741}{5696} = \log 10^x$$

8 = *x* or $\boxed{x = 8}$

43. (a) $E = E^0 - \frac{2.303RT}{nF}\log\frac{[P\,H_2]^{1/2}}{[H^+]}$

$$E = 0 - \frac{2.303RT}{F}\log\frac{1}{10^{-10}}$$

= – 0.06 log10 = – 0.06 × 10 = – 0.6V

44. (b) $E^\circ_{Fe^{2+}/Fe} = -0.441$ V; $E^\circ_{Fe^{3+}/Fe^{2+}} = 0.771$ V
$Fe(s) + 2Fe^{3+}(aq) \longrightarrow 3Fe^{2+}(aq)$
$E^\circ = E_{Fe/Fe^{2+}} + E_{Fe^{3+}/Fe^{2+}}$
E° = 0.441 + 0.771 = 1.212 V

45. (d) $E^\circ_{cell} = E^\circ_{cathode} - E^\circ_{anode}$
= – 0.25 – (–0.76) = +0.51 V

$$E_{cell} = E^\circ_{cell} - \frac{2.303\,RT}{2\,F}\log\frac{0.01}{0.1}$$

$$= 0.51 - \left(\frac{0.06}{2}\right)\log 10^{-1}$$

= 0.51 – 0.03 × –1
= 0.51 + 0.03
= 0.54 V

46. (a) Given, $\Delta_r S^\circ = 100\ JK^{-1}\ mol^{-1}$
$E^\circ_{cell} = 1.0$ v
n = 2
ΔG° = –nFE°
= – 2 × 96500 × 1 J mol^{-1}
= – 193 kJ mol^{-1}
∴ ΔG° = ΔH° – TΔS°
ΔH° = ΔG + TΔS°

$$= -193 + \frac{300 \times 100}{1000} = -193 + 30$$

ΔH° = – 163 kJ mol^{-1}

47. (b) Given,
E° = 1.0V
$\Delta_r H^\circ = -163$ kJ mol^{-1}
n = 2
T = 300 K
∴ ΔG° = – nFE°
= – 2 × 96500 × 1.0
= 193000 CV [1J = 1CV]

$$= \frac{193000}{1000}\text{kJ} \quad [1\text{ kJ} = 10^3\text{J}]$$

ΔG° = 193kJ
∴ ΔG = ΔH – TΔS

$$\text{or, } \Delta S = \frac{\Delta H - \Delta G}{T}$$

$$\Rightarrow \Delta S = \frac{-163 + 193}{300} = \frac{30}{300} = 0.1\text{ kJ K}^{-1}$$

∴ ΔS = 0.1 × 10^3 JK^{-1}
ΔS = 100 JK^{-1}

48. (d)
$$Mg \rightarrow Mg^{2+} + 2e^-$$
$$Cl_2 \rightarrow +2e^- \rightarrow 2Cl^-$$
$$\overline{Mg + Cl_2 \rightarrow Mg^{2+} + 2Cl^-}$$

(a) $E_{cell} = E^\circ - \frac{RT}{nF}\ln[Cl]^{-2} \times [Mg^{2+}]$

$E_{cell} = 3.72 - \frac{RT}{nF}\ln(1)^2 \times 1$

$E_{cell} = 3.72 - \frac{RT}{nF}\ln 1$

(b) $E_{cell} = E^\circ - \frac{RT}{nF}\ln(1)^2 \times 10^{-2}$

$= E^\circ + 2\frac{RT}{nF}\ln 10$

(c) $E_{cell} = E^\circ - \frac{RT}{nF}\ln(10^{-2})^2 \times 1$

$= E^\circ + 4\frac{RT}{nF}\ln 10$

(d) $E_{cell} = E^\circ - \frac{RT}{nF}\ln(10^{-2})^2 \times 10^{-2}$

$= E^\circ + 6\frac{RT}{nF}\ln 10$

∴ So option (d) have highest emf.

49. (d) According to the given standard potential data
$E^o_{T\ell^+/T\ell} < E^o_{A\ell^+/A\ell}$
It mean that Tl^+ is more stable as compare to Al^+. Tl^+ is act as reducing agent whereas Tl^{3+} act as powerful oxidixing agent which make is unstable.

50. (a) $3Ca(s) + 2Au^{3+}(aq\ 1M) \rightarrow 3Ca^{2+}(aq\ 1M) + 2Au(S)$
$E^\circ = E^\circ_L + E^\circ_R$
$= E^\circ_{Ca/Ca^{2+}} + E^\circ_{Au^{3+}/Au}$
= 2.87 + 1.50

$E^o = 4.37V.$
Total no. of electron envolved by balancing the electron.
$n = 6$

$\therefore \quad \Delta G^o = -nFE^o$
$= -6 \times 96500 \times 4.37$ mol . C $mol^{-1}.V$
$= -2530230$ CV $\quad [1 J = 1 CV]$
$= -2530.23$ kJ $[1 kJ = 10^3 J]$
$\Delta G^o = -2.53 \times 10^3$ kJ

51. (c) According to Nernst equation,

$$E = E^\circ - \frac{2.303\ RT}{nF}\log\frac{[\text{product}]}{[\text{reactant}]}$$

$$M \longrightarrow M^2 + 2e^{-1}$$
$$2e^{-1} + Cu^{2+} \longrightarrow Cu$$
$$M + Cu^{2+} \longrightarrow M^{2+} + Cu$$

$$E = E^\circ - \frac{2.303\ RT}{nF}\log\frac{[M^{2+}]}{[Cu^{2+}]}$$

Given, $E^\circ = 0.3V$

$\frac{2.303RT}{F} = 0.06$

$n = 2$

$M^{2+} = 0.1M$

We have to take $E_{cell} = 0$. According to question.

$$0 = 0.3V - \frac{0.06}{3}\log_{10}\frac{10^{-1}}{[Cu^{2+}]}$$

$$-0.3 = -0.03\log_{10}\frac{[10^{-1}]}{[Cu^{2+}]}$$

$$10 = \log_{10}\frac{[10^{-1}]}{[Cu^{2+}]} \Rightarrow \therefore \frac{[10^{-1}]}{[Cu^{2+}]} = 10^{10}$$

$$\text{or, } [Cu^{2+}] = \frac{10^{-1}}{10^{10}} = 10^{-1-10} = 10^{-11}$$

$$\boxed{Cu^{2+} = 10^{-11}}$$

52. (a) $(M \rightarrow M^{3+} + 3e) \times 2; (N^{2+} + 2e \rightarrow N) \times 3$

Overall reaction : $2M(s) + 3N^{2+}(aq) \rightarrow 2M^{3+}(aq) + 3N(s)$

$$\therefore E_{cell} = E^\circ_{cell} - \frac{0.059}{6}\log\frac{[M^{3+}]^2}{[N^{2+}]^3}$$

$$= -0.6 + 0.1 - \frac{0.059}{6}\log\frac{(10^{-2})^2}{(10^{-1})^3}$$

$$= -0.5 - \frac{0.059}{6}\log 10^{-1} = 0.51\ V$$

53. (c) $A + B^{2+} \rightleftharpoons A^{2+} + B$

$G^\circ = -RT \ln K_c$

$= -8.314 \times 298 \times 2.303 \times \log 10^{12} = 68.47$ kJ/mol

54. (c) Reduction process: $2H^+ + 2e \rightarrow H_2$

$$E = E^\circ - \frac{0.059}{2}\log\frac{p_{H_2}}{[H^+]^2} \quad \left[\begin{array}{l}\text{neutral pH at 25°C,}\\ \log[H^+] = 7\\ \therefore [H^+] = 10^{-7}\end{array}\right]$$

$$= 0.00 - \frac{0.059}{2}\log\frac{1}{(10^{-7})^2} = -\frac{0.059}{2} \times 14 = -0.413V$$

55. (a) pH of solution 1 = 3

$\therefore \quad [H^+]_1 = 10^{-3}$ M

pH of solution 2 = 6

$\therefore \quad [H^+]_2 = 10^{-6}$ M

$$\text{Now, } E_{cell} = E^\circ_{cell} - \frac{0.059}{1}\log\frac{10^{-6}}{10^{-3}} = 0 + 0.059 \times 3$$

$E_{cell} = 0.177$ V

56. (a) On applying an external voltage greater than E_{cell} V in a Daniell cell the current flows in the reverse direction i.e., from Zn to Cu (cathode to anode) and electrons flow from Cu to Zn.

57. (b) The correct cell representation is
Cd/Cd^{2+} (0.01 M) || Cu^{2+}(0.01 M) | Cu

Given $\quad E_{Cu^{2+}/Cu} = 0.35$ V

$E_{Cd^{2+}/Cd} = -0.4$ V

$E^\circ_{Cell} = E_{Cu^{2+}/Cu} - E_{Cd^{2+}/Cd} = 0.35 - (-0.4) = 0.75$ V

$$E_{Cell} = E^\circ_{Cell} - \frac{0.059}{2}\log\frac{[Cd^{2+}]}{[Cu^{2+}]}$$

$$E_{Cell} = 0.75 - \frac{0.059}{2} - \log\frac{[0.01]}{[0.01]} \quad (\because \log 1 = 0)$$

$E_{Cell} = 0.75.$

$$\Rightarrow E_{cell\ observed} = E_{internal} - E_{external}\left[\begin{array}{l}E = V\\ V = IR\end{array}\right]$$

$= 0.75 - (\text{resistance} \times \text{current})$

$= 0.75 - (4 \times 0.15) = (0.75 - 0.60)$ V $= 0.15$ V

58. (d) For the reaction,

$$A + 2B^{2+}(aq) \rightleftharpoons A^{2+}(aq) + 2B(s)$$

$$E^\circ_{cell} = \frac{0.059}{n}\log K_c$$

$$\log K_c = \frac{nE^\circ_{cell}}{0.059} = \frac{2 \times 0.59}{0.059} = 20 \Rightarrow K_c = 1 \times 10^{20}$$

59. (c) Given,

Free energy, $[\Delta G = -nFE^\circ]$

where n = number of electron involved

E° = standard electrode potential

F = Faraday's constant $\Delta G^\circ_3 = n_3 = f E^\circ_3$

$$\text{(iii)} \quad M^{2+}_{(aq)} + 2e^- \longrightarrow M_{(s)} \Delta G^\circ_3 = n_3 FE^\circ_3$$

For reaction (iii) $\Delta G^\circ_3 = \Delta G^\circ_1 + \Delta G^\circ_2$

$$-n_3 FE^\circ_3 = -(n_1 FE^\circ_2 + n_2 FE^\circ_2)$$

$$-2E^\circ_3 = -(n E^\circ_1 + nE^\circ_2) \Rightarrow 2E^\circ_3 = E^\circ_1 + E^\circ_2$$

$$2E^\circ_3 = 0.15 + 0.5 \quad \therefore E^\circ_3 = \frac{0.65}{2} = 0.325\ V$$

60. (a)

$E^\circ_{cell} = E^\circ_C - E^\circ_A = 0.34 - (-0.76)V = 1.1V$

$$E_{cell} = E^\circ_{Cell} - \frac{2.303RT}{nF}\log\left(\frac{Zn^{2+}}{Cu^{2+}}\right)$$

$$\Rightarrow E_{cell} = 1.1 - \frac{0.059}{n}\log\frac{C_2}{C_1} \quad \left(\begin{array}{l}Zn^{2+} = C_2\\ Cu^{2+} = C_1\end{array}\right)$$

E_{Cell} value wil be maximum when, $\log\frac{C_2}{C_1}$ will be minimum.

From the given option $\log\frac{0.01}{0.1} = \log 10^{-1}$ will give the maximum value of E_{Cell}.

61. (b)

$$E^\circ_{cell} = E^\circ_C - E^\circ_A = 0.80 - (-0.76) = 1.56V$$

From the equation $\Delta G^\circ = -nFE^\circ$

$= -2 \times 96500 \times 1.56 \quad (n = 2)$

$= -301080$ J/mol

$= -301$ kJ/mol

62. (a) (I) Dry cell- it is also known as Leclanche cell

(II) Anode Zn container, Cathode - Graphite rod surrounded by MnO_2 + C powder. Electrolyte:- Moist paste of NH_4Cl and $ZnCl_2$ is filled between them. That's why it is called dry cell.

(III) $MnO_2 + NH_4^+ + e^- \longrightarrow MnO(OH) + NH_3$

$MnO_2 + NH_4^+ + e^- \longrightarrow MnO(OH) + NH_3$

at cathode- MnO_2 gets reduces by NH_4^+ion,

at Anode- $Zn \rightarrow Zn^{+2} + 2e^-$

63. (b) Statement II: In lead storage battery, spongy Pb is anode and the PbO_2 packed lead grid is cathode, so statement II is false.

Statement III: The electrolyte used in lead storage battery is 38% H_2SO_4 not 98% H_2SO_4

Hence only statement I, IV is correct.

64. (c) Overall reaction in $H_2 - O_2$ fuel cell is

$2H_2(g) + O_2(g) \longrightarrow 2H_2O$ (l)

65. (c) In dry cell Zinc vessel acts as anode.

66. (c) For Lead Storage Battery :

At anode: $Pb(s) + SO_4^{2-}(aq) \rightarrow PbSO_4(s) + 2e^-$

At cathode: $PbO_2(s) + SO_4^{2-}(aq) + 4H^+(aq) + 2e^- \rightarrow PbSO_4(s) + 2H_2O(l)$

67. (a) Leclanche' cell:-

Anode : Zn Container

$Zn(s) \rightarrow Zn^{2+}(aq.) + 2e^-$

Cathode : Carbon (graphite) + MnO_2 + Carbon powder.

$MnO_2 + NH_4^+ + e^- \rightarrow MnO(OH) + NH_3$

Electrolyte = $NH_4Cl + ZnCl_2$ paste

Thus, I and II are correct.

68. (c) Mercury cell uses a paste of KOH and ZnO.

Anode = Zn – Hg amalgam

Cathode = HgO + C paste.

3 Chemical Kinetics

1. **(c)**

$$N_2O_5 \longrightarrow N_2O_4 + \frac{1}{2}O_2$$

Initial: 1, 0, 0

at t = t: $1 - x$, x, $\frac{x}{2}$

x = moles of N_2O_5 decomposed.

Initial moles of N_2O_5

$n = M \times V$

$= 2 \times \frac{50}{1000} = 0.1$ mol

Moles of O_2 at STP

$n = \frac{\text{vol. of } O_2}{\text{Molar vol. at STP}}$

$= \frac{0.28}{22.4} = 0.0125$ mol

1 mole of N_2O_5 gives $\frac{1}{2}$ mol of O_2

So moles of N_2O_5 decomposed = 2 × moles of O_2

= 2 × 0.125

= 0.025 moles

Remaining N_2O_5 = 1 – 0.025 = 0.075 moles

$\text{Conc.} = \frac{\text{Remaining moles}}{\text{vol. of sol}^n (L)} = \frac{0.075}{0.05} = 1.5M$

$\text{Average Rate (Y)} = \frac{-\Delta[N_2O_5]}{\Delta t} = \frac{C_i - C_f}{t}$

$= \frac{2 - 1.5}{30} = 0.166$

$Y = 1.66 \times 10^{-2}$ mol L^{-1} min^{-1}

2. **(b)** Average velocity =

$-\left[\frac{\text{Change in concentration}}{\text{Change in time}}\right]$

$= -\left[\frac{C_2 - C_1}{t_2 - t_1}\right]$

$= -\frac{[0.03 - 0.04]}{[2400 - 0]}$

$= \frac{0.01}{2400} = 4.167 \times 10^{-6}$

3. **(a)** Rate of reaction =

$\frac{\text{Change in concentration}}{\text{Change in time}} = \frac{|x - y|}{100}$

4. **(a)** $A + 2B \rightarrow 3C + 2D$

$-\frac{dA}{dt} = -\frac{1}{2}\frac{dB}{dt} = \frac{1}{3}\frac{dC}{dt} = \frac{1}{2}\frac{dD}{dt}$

Rate of disappearance of $B = -\frac{dB}{dt} = x \times 10^{-2}$

Rate of reaction $= \left(-\frac{1}{2}\frac{dB}{dt}\right) = -\frac{1}{2}x \times 10^{-2}$

Rate of appearance of $C = \frac{dC}{dt} = -\frac{3}{2}\frac{dB}{dt}$

$= -\frac{3}{2} \times x \times 10^{-2}$

∴ Ratio of reaction : Rate of appearance

$-\frac{x}{2} \times 10^{-2} : -\frac{3}{2} \times x \times 10^{-2}$

1 : 3

5. **(b)** $R_{inst} = \frac{-d[R]}{dt} = \frac{d[P]}{dt}$

So, the instantaneous rate of reaction at point C is slope i.e m.

6. **(a)** $K = 3.3 \times 10^{-4}$ s^{-1}

$K = \frac{2.303}{t}\log\frac{a}{a - x}$

A	⟶	B
100		0
10		90

$\therefore K = \frac{2.303}{t}\log\frac{100}{10}$

$t = \frac{2.303}{3.3 \times 10^{-4}} \times 1 \quad [\log 10 = 1]$

$t = \frac{2.303}{3.3} \times 10^4$

$t = 0.70 \times 10^4$ second

t = 7000 s

$t = \frac{7000}{60} = 116.6$ min

7. **(a)** Given,

$K = 10^{-3}$ mol L^{-1} s^{-1}

$[A_o] = 0.1$ mol L^{-1}

t = 10s

for zero order,

$[A_+] = [A_0] - kt$

$[A_+] = 0.1 - 10^{-3} \times 10$

$= 0.1 - 10^{-2}$

$= 0.09$ mol L^{-1}

8. **(c)** Given reaction,

$5Br^-(aq) + BrO_3^-(aq) + 6H^+(aq) \rightarrow 3Br_2(aq) + 3H_2O(l)$

$-\frac{\Delta[Br^-]}{\Delta t} = x$ mol L^{-1} min^{-1}

Rate of Reaction $= -\frac{1}{5}\frac{d[Br^-]}{dt}$

$= \frac{1}{5}x$

9. **(a)** Given :- Time = 25 × 60 sec.

Concentration of Reactant = 0.03 mol L^{-1}

Concentration of Product = 0.02 mol L^{-1}

$\text{Rate} = \frac{\Delta[R]}{\Delta t} \frac{[-(0.02 - 0.03)]}{25 \times 60}$

⇒ 6.67×10^{-6} mol L^{-1} s^{-1}

10. **(d)** From first order reaction,

$\ln\frac{a}{a - x} = Kt$

ln a – ln (a – x) = Kt

ln (a – x) = ln a – Kt

y = c – mx

C(intercept) = ln a

m (slope) = –K

∴ given,

C = ln a

or, ln a = –2.303

2.303 log a = –2.303

log a = –1

$\therefore \boxed{a = 10^{-1}}$

again,

$-K = -(10)^{-2}$

$\boxed{K = 10^{-2}}$

11. **(b)** $-\frac{1}{3}\frac{d[X]}{dt} = \frac{1}{2}\frac{d[Y]}{dt} = \frac{d[Z]}{dt}$

$\Rightarrow \frac{d[Y]}{dt} = \frac{2}{3}\frac{d[X]}{dt} = \frac{2}{3} \times 7.2 \times 10^{-3}$

$= 4.8 \times 10^{-3}$ mol L^{-1} S^{-1}

12. **(d)**

$\frac{1}{2}\frac{d[A]}{dt} = \frac{1}{4}\frac{d[B]}{dt} \Rightarrow \frac{d[A]}{dt} = \frac{1}{2} \times \frac{d[B]}{dt}$

$= \frac{1}{2} \times \frac{\Delta B}{\Delta t}$

$\Rightarrow \frac{1}{2} \times \frac{5 \times 10^{-3}}{10} = 2.5 \times 10^{-4}$ Ms^{-1}.

13. **(c)** According to the rate law:-

When $[A]_2 = 4[A]_1$ and $[B]_2 = 2[B]_1$

rate=r=z=$k[4A][2B]^2 = k \times 4 \times 4 \times [A]_1[B]_1 = 16R$.

And when [B] is kept constant, and $[A]_2 = x$

⇒ rate = r_2 = 2 R = 2k (0.05) $(0.05)^2$

= k (0.10) $(0.05)^2$ = k (x) $(0.05)^2$

Thus, x = 0.10.

14. **(c)** Order = 1, k = 1.15 × 10^{-3} S^{-1}, $C_1 = 10$, $C_2 = 6$

$\Rightarrow t = \frac{2.303}{k}\log\frac{C_1}{C_2} = \frac{2.303}{1.15 \times 10^{-3}}\log\frac{10}{6}$

$= 444.27 \cong 4.4 \times 10^2$

Thus, x = 4.4

15. **(c)** $r = K[NH_3]^\circ = K = y \times 10^{-4}$ mol L^{-1} s^{-1}

Now, $\frac{1}{3}\frac{d[H_2]}{dt} = r$

$\Rightarrow \frac{d[H_2]}{dt} = 3r = 3y \times 10^{-4}$ mol L^{-1} s^{-1}

16. **(c)** $-\frac{d[A]}{dt} = \frac{1}{3}\frac{d[B]}{dt} = k$ (zero order reaction)

From the table, it is found that $t_{1/2} = 15s$

$$\therefore \ K = \frac{[A]_0}{2t_{1/2}} = \frac{0.1}{2 \times 15} = \frac{1}{300}$$

$$\begin{array}{lll} & A \longrightarrow & 3B \\ t = 205 & 0.1 - x & 3x \end{array}$$

$A_0 = A + Kt$

$$0.1 - (0.1 - x) = \frac{1}{300} \times 20 \quad x = 6.6 \times 10^{-2}$$

$3x = 1.98 \times 10^{-1}$

17. (c) The rate equation for zero order reaction,

$[A]_t = [A]_0 - kt$ or, $0.075 = 0.1 - 0.003\ t$

or $t = (0.1 - 0.075)/0.003 = \frac{0.025}{0.003} = \frac{25}{3} = 8.33\ s$

18. (d) k depends on order of reaction and unit of k for 1st order reaction is s^{-1}.

19. (c) $C_2H_2I\,(g) \longrightarrow C_2H_4\,(g) + HI\,(g)$

$$\begin{array}{llll} \text{At } t = 0 & 2 \text{ bar} & 0 & 0 \\ t = 1000 \text{ min.} & 0.1 & (2-0.1) & (2-0.1) \\ & & = 1.9 & = 1.9 \end{array}$$

Since, the reaction is first order,

$$k = \frac{2.303}{t} \log \frac{p_0}{p_0 - x}$$

$$\Rightarrow \quad k = \frac{2.303}{1000} \log \frac{2}{0.1}$$

$$\Rightarrow \quad k = \frac{2.303}{1000} \log 20 = \frac{2.996}{1000}$$

$$\Rightarrow \quad k = 3 \times 10^{-3}\ \text{min}^{-1}.$$

20. (b) Rate of reaction at t = 10 min is x mol L^{-1} min^{-1}.

rate of reaction = $K[C]^0 = K$

$\therefore$ for zero order reaction rate of reaction does not depend on the concentration so after 20 mint rate is also x mol L^{-1} min^{-1}.

21. (a) For first order reaction,

$$t = \frac{2.303}{K} \log \frac{[A_o]}{[A]}$$

For $t^{1/8}$:

$$t^{1/8} = \frac{2.303}{k} \log \frac{[A_o]}{\frac{[A_o]}{8}}$$

$$t^{1/8} = \frac{2.303}{k} \log(8)$$

$$t^{1/8} = \frac{2.303}{k} \times 0.90 \qquad \text{... (1)}$$

For $t^{1/10}$:

$$t^{1/10} = \frac{2.303}{k} \log \frac{[A_o]}{\frac{[A_o]}{10}}$$

$$t^{1/10} = \frac{2.303}{k} \log(10)$$

$$t^{1/10} = \frac{2.303}{k} \times 1 \qquad \text{... (2)}$$

Dividing (1) ÷ (2)

$$\frac{t^{1/8}}{t^{1/10}} = \frac{0.9}{1} \text{ or } \frac{9}{10}$$

So, ratio $t^{1/8} : t^{1/10} = 9:10$

22. (a) For first order reaction:

$$t^{1/2} = \frac{0.693}{K} \qquad (\therefore \text{ Given } t^{1/2} = 10 \text{ min}$$

$$k = \frac{0.693}{10}$$

$k = 0.0693\ min^{-1}$

For t = 20 min, no. of half life passed in 20 min.

$$n = \frac{\text{Total Time}}{\text{Half life}} = \frac{20}{10} = 2 \text{ half life}$$

Remaining concentration after 2 half life.

$$[A] = \frac{[A_o]}{2^n} \Rightarrow [A] = \frac{10}{2^2} \qquad (\therefore \ [A_o] = 10m)$$

$$[A] = \frac{10}{4} = 2.5\ M$$

For first order reaction:

Rate = k[A]

$= 0.0693\ min^{-1} \times 2.5\ M$

$= 0.17325\ M\ min^{-1}$

$= 1.73 \times 10^{-1}\ M\ min^{-1}$

23. (a) For first order reaction:

$$K = \frac{1}{t} \ln \frac{[A_o]}{[A_t]} \text{ or } K = \frac{1}{t} \ln \frac{P_A^{\circ}}{P_A}$$

$$\begin{array}{llll} & A(g) \longrightarrow & B(g) + & C(g) \\ \text{At } t = 0 & P_A^{\circ} & 0 & 0 \\ \text{At } t = 10 & P_A^{\circ} - x & x & x \end{array}$$

P_t after 10 min = $(P_A{}^{\circ} - x) + x + x$

$P_t = P_A{}^{\circ} + x$

$x = P_t - P_A{}^{\circ}$

Pressure of A after 10 min.

$P_A = P_A{}^{\circ} - x$

$= P_A{}^{\circ} - (P_t - P_A{}^{\circ})$

$= 2P_A{}^{\circ} - P_t$

$$\text{So, } K = \frac{1}{t} \ln \left(\frac{P_A^{\circ}}{2P_A^{\circ} - P_t} \right)$$

24. (b) Rate constant (K) = 0.02 mol L^{-1} min^{-1}

Unit of rate constant is mol L^{-1} which signifies it is zero order reaction.

So, $[A_o] = 1.0$ mol/L

t = 20 min.

For zero order reaction,

$$K = \frac{[A_o] - [A_t]}{t}$$

$[A_t] = [A_o] - kt = 1.0 - (0.02 \times 20)$

$= 1.0 - 0.4 = 0.6$ mol/L

25. (c) For first order kinetics,

$$k = \frac{2.303}{t} \log \frac{a_o}{a_t}$$

$a_o = 8 \times 10^{-3}$ mol L^{-1}

For 80% decomposition, remaining 20%

$$a_t = \frac{20}{100} \times a_o$$

$$a_t = \frac{20}{100} \times 8 \times 10^{-3} \Rightarrow 1.6 \times 10^{-3} \text{ mol } L^{-1}$$

$$K = \frac{2.303}{80} \times \log \left(\frac{8 \times 10^{-3}}{1.6 \times 10^{-3}} \right)$$

$$K = \frac{2.303}{80} \times \log 5$$

$$K = \frac{2.303}{80} \times 0.70$$

$K = 0.02\ min^{-1}$

26. (a) For a first order reaction, the time taken is given by:–

$$t = \frac{2.303}{k} \log \left(\frac{A_0}{A} \right)$$

Where, t = time taken

k = rate constant

A_0 = initial concentration of reactant

A = concentration of reactant at time t

$t_{1/2}$ = half time

$$\text{for } t_{1/2} = \frac{2.303}{k} \log \left(\frac{A_0}{\frac{A_0}{2}} \right)$$

$$t_{1/2} = \frac{2.303}{k} \log 2 \qquad \text{...(i)}$$

$$\text{for } t_{3/4} = \frac{2.303}{k} \log \left(\frac{A_0}{\frac{A_0}{4}} \right)$$

$$t_{3/4} = \frac{2.303}{k} \log 4 \qquad \text{...(ii)}$$

Dividing equation (ii) by equation (i)

$$\frac{t_{3/4}}{t_{1/2}} = \frac{\frac{2.303}{k} \log (2)^2}{\frac{2.303}{k} \log 2} = \frac{\frac{2.303}{k} 2 \log (2)}{\frac{2.303}{k} \log 2} = 2$$

27. (c) For a 1st order reaction :

$$kt = 2.303 \log \frac{[A]_0}{[A]}$$

Where, k = rate constant

t = time taken

$[A]_0$ = initial concentration of reactant

$[A]$ = concentration of reactant at time 't'

Now, for t = 75 min

$$[A] = \frac{[A]_0}{8}$$

$$\therefore \ k = \frac{2.303}{15} \log \left(\frac{[A]_0}{\frac{[A]_0}{8}} \right)$$

$$\therefore \ k = \frac{2.303}{75} \log (8)$$

$$\therefore \ k = \frac{2.303}{75} \times 3 \log 2$$

$$\text{hence, } k = \frac{2.303}{75} \times 3 \times 0.30$$

$$\text{Now, for } t = t^{1/2} = \text{half life } [A] = \frac{[A]_0}{2}$$

$\therefore\ t^{1/2} = \dfrac{2.303 \log 2}{\dfrac{2.303}{75} \times 3 \times 0.30}$

so, $t^{1/2} = \dfrac{2.303 \times 0.30}{\dfrac{2.303}{75} \times 3 \times 0.30} = \dfrac{75}{3} = 25$

28. **(d)** $A \rightarrow$ Product

rate = $K[A]$ (1st order reaction)

$0.2 = K \times 0.02$

$K = 10$

For x

$0.4 = 10[x]$

$x = \dfrac{0.4}{10} = 0.04$

For y $1.0 = 10[y]$

$y = \dfrac{1}{10} = 0.1$

Ratio x : y

$\dfrac{x}{y} = \dfrac{0.04}{0.1} = \dfrac{4}{10} = \dfrac{2}{5}$

29. **(c)** $A(g) \rightarrow B(g) + 2C(g)$

t = 0	100	0	0
t = 24	100–x	x	2x

$\dfrac{\text{Amount of product}}{\text{Amount of reactant}} = \dfrac{1}{3} = \dfrac{x + 2x}{100 - x}$

$\Rightarrow$ x = 10,

Hence at t = 24 min, amount of A left is 90

$K = \dfrac{2.303}{24} \log \dfrac{100}{90}$

$\Rightarrow$ K = 0.00441

$t_{1/2} = \dfrac{0.693}{K} = \dfrac{0.693}{0.00441} = 157.14$ min

30. **(b)** For a zero order reaction :

Rate = $K[A]^0 = K$

Thus, the rate does not change with concentration. Therefore, I is of zero order reaction.

For the integrated rate law of zero order :

$C = -kt + C_0$

Thus, the graph II is for a zero order reaction.

For a first order reaction:-

$t = \dfrac{2.303}{K} \log \dfrac{[R]_0}{[R]}$ or $\log \dfrac{[R]_0}{[R]} = \dfrac{K}{2.303} t$

Thus, III is a graph for a first order reaction.

31. **(a)** When initial concentration of A is kept constant and that of B is changed (tripled), the rate of the reaction increases by 9 times.

Thus, the order of the reaction will be α with respect to B.

When the concentration of B is kept constant and that of A is increased by 3 times, the rate of the reaction increases by 3 times too.

Thus, the order of the reaction is 1 with respect to A.

32. **(d)** $r_1 = k[A]^n$ and $r_2 = k[2A]^n$

$\because\ r_1 = r_2 \quad \therefore k[A]^n = k(2[A])^n$

or, $2^n = 1$

or, $2^n = 2^\circ \Rightarrow n = 0$

It is a zero order reaction.

33. **(d)** $A \longrightarrow$ products; Ist order reaction

$k = \dfrac{0.693}{t_{1/2}} = \dfrac{0.693}{60 \times 60} = 1.92 \times 10^{-4}\ s^{-1}$

34. **(c)** $A \rightarrow$ Products

$t = 0, A_0 = 1$

$t = t, A_t = 1 - 0.9375 = 0.0625$

$\therefore\ A_t = A_0 e^{-kt}$

or, $\ln\left(\dfrac{A_t}{A_0}\right) = -kt$

$\Rightarrow\ kt = \ln\left(\dfrac{A_0}{A_t}\right)$

or, $k = \dfrac{1}{x} \ln\left(\dfrac{1}{0.0625}\right) = \dfrac{2.77}{x}$

$\therefore\ t_{1/2} = \dfrac{0.693}{k} = 0.25x = \dfrac{x}{4}$

35. **(c)** $\because$ Given that k is $2.4 \times 10^{-4}\ S^{-1}$

$\because$ It is first order reaction

$t_{99.9\%} = \dfrac{2.303}{k} \log \dfrac{100}{01}$

$= \dfrac{2.303}{k} \log 1000 = \dfrac{2.303}{k} \log 10^3$

$= \dfrac{2.303}{k} \times 3 \log 10 = \dfrac{2.303}{k} \times 3\ [\because \log 10 = 1]$

$t_{50\%} = \dfrac{0.693}{k}$

Ratio of $t_{99.9\%}$ and $t_{50\%}$ is

$\dfrac{t_{99.9\%}}{t_{50\%}} = \dfrac{3 \times 2.303 / k}{0.693 / k} = 10$

36. **(d)** For zero order reaction,

$[A] = [A_0] - kt$ ...(i)

When $t = t_{1/2}$, $[A] = \dfrac{[A_0]}{2}$ ...(ii)

From eqs. (i) and (ii)

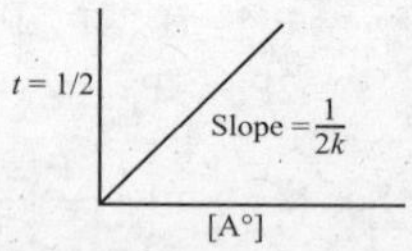

$\dfrac{[A_0]}{2} = [A_0] - kt_{1/2}$

$\Rightarrow t_{1/2} = \dfrac{[A_0]}{2k}$

Plot of $t_{1/2}$ *versus* $[A_0]$ will be straight line.

37. **(c)** For first order reaction;

$t = \dfrac{2.303}{k} \log\left(\dfrac{a}{a-x}\right)$

$t = \dfrac{2.303}{2.303 \times 10^{-3}} \log\left(\dfrac{4}{0.2}\right)$

$\Rightarrow\ t = 10^3 \times \log 20 \Rightarrow\ t = 1301\ s = 0.36$ hr

38. **(c)** We know, $r_1 = k[A]^n$ ...(i)

If conc. of A is increased four times rate of reaction on doubles.

$2r_1 = k[4A]^n$ ...(ii)

Divide Eq. (ii) by (i).

$\dfrac{2r_1}{r_1} = \dfrac{k(4A)^n}{k(A)^n} \Rightarrow 2 = (4)^n \Rightarrow 2n = (2)^{2n}$

$\Rightarrow n = 0.5$

39. **(b)** Final quantity $(a - x) = (100 - 90) = 10$

Initial quantity $(a) = 100\%$

$k = 4.606 \times 10^{-3} s^{-1}$

First order reaction

$k = \dfrac{2.303}{t} \log \dfrac{a}{(a-x)}$

$k = 4.606 \times 10^{-3}\ s^{-1}$

$t = \dfrac{2.303}{4.606 \times 10^{-3}} \log \dfrac{100}{10}$

$t = 500s$

40. **(b)** For $t = 90$ min (from 10 a.m. to 11:30 a.m.)

As 20% was already completed $\therefore\ a = 80$

$(a - x) = (100 - 80) = 20$

$\because\ k = \dfrac{2.303}{t} \log \dfrac{a}{a-x} \Rightarrow k = \dfrac{2.303}{90} \log \dfrac{80}{20}$

$\Rightarrow\ k = \dfrac{2.303}{90} \log 4 = \dfrac{2.303 \times 0.6020}{90}$

$k = 0.015$ min

$\because\ t_{1/2} = \dfrac{0.693}{k} \Rightarrow t_{1/2} = \dfrac{0.693}{0.015} \approx 45$

41. **(b)**

$\log\left(\dfrac{K_2}{K_1}\right) = \dfrac{E_a}{2.303R}\left(\dfrac{T_2 - T_1}{T_1 T_2}\right), \dfrac{K_2}{K_1} = \dfrac{10 \times 10^3}{5 \times 10^3} = 2$

$\log 2 = 0.3$

$0.3 = \dfrac{50000}{2.303 \times 8.3}\left(\dfrac{T - 300}{300 \times T}\right)$

$T = 310.7K$

42. **(d)** Given, $T_1 = 300°C = 573K$

$K_1 = 2.5 \times 10^{-4}\ s^{-1}$

$E_a = 42$ Kcal mol^{-1}

$R = 2$ Cal $K^{-1}\ mol^{-1}$

$t_{1/2}$ at $T_2 = 138.6$

For first order reaction

$t_{1/2} = \dfrac{0.693}{K}$

so, $K_2 = \dfrac{0.693}{t_{1/2}} \Rightarrow \dfrac{0.693}{138.6} \Rightarrow 5 \times 10^{-3} s^{-1}$

Using Arrhenius equation:

$\log \dfrac{K_2}{K_1} = \dfrac{E_a}{2.303R}\left(\dfrac{1}{T_1} \dfrac{-1}{T_2}\right)$

$\log \dfrac{5 \times 10^{-3}}{2.5 \times 10^{-4}} = \dfrac{42000}{2.303 \times 2}\left(\dfrac{1}{573} - \dfrac{1}{T_2}\right)$

$\log 20 = 9118.54\left(\dfrac{1}{573} - \dfrac{1}{T_2}\right)$

$1.30 = 9118.54\left(\dfrac{1}{573} - \dfrac{1}{T_2}\right)$

$\dfrac{1}{573} - \dfrac{1}{T_2} = \dfrac{1.30}{9118.54}$

$T_2 = 624.21\ K \simeq 625\ K$

43. **(b)** $\log\left(\dfrac{K_2}{K_1}\right) = \dfrac{Ea}{2.303R}\left[\dfrac{T_2 - T_1}{T_1 \times T_2}\right]$

$\log_{10}\left(\dfrac{K_2}{K_1}\right) = \dfrac{198870}{2.303 \times 8.3}\left[\dfrac{700 - 600}{600 \times 700}\right]$

$\log_{10}\left(\frac{K_2}{K_1}\right) = 2.4771$

$\left(\frac{K_2}{K_1}\right) = 300,$

$K_2 = 300 \times K_1 = 300\ (1.6 \times 10^{-5}\ s^{-1})$

$K_2 = 4.8 \times 10^{-3}$

44. (b) Arrhenius equation

$k = A_e^{-E_a/RT}$

Where

k = Rate instant of reaction

A = Pre-exponential factor

$e^{-E_a/RT}$ = Boltzmann factor or fraction of molecules that have KE, equal to or greater than E_a.

45. (c) The Arrhenius equation expressed as

$K = A\exp\left(-\frac{E_a}{RT}\right)$

Taking log both side

$\ln K = \ln A - \frac{E_a}{R}.\frac{1}{T}$

$y\text{-axis} = m \times x\text{-axis}$

$\text{Slope} = m = -\frac{E_a}{R}$

$E_a = 2 \times 10^4 K \times R$

$E_a = 2 \times 10^4\ K \times 8.3\ JK^{-1}\ mol^{-1}$

$E_a = 16.6 \times 10^4\ J\ mol^{-1}$

$E_a = 16.6 \times 10^4 \times \frac{1}{1000}$

$= 166\ kJ\ mol^{-1}$

46. (b) $E_a = 25 - 10 = 15\ kJ\ mol^{-1}$

$|\Delta H| = |5 - 10| = 5\ kJ\ mol^{-1}$

47. (a) According to Arrhenius equation :

$\ln K = -\frac{E_a}{RT} + \ln A$

$= \ln A - \frac{E_a}{RT}$

$\Rightarrow \log K = \log A - \frac{E_a}{2.303\ RT}$

$\Rightarrow \frac{E_a}{2.303\ RT} = \log A - \log K$

$= \log\frac{A}{K}$

$\Rightarrow -\frac{E_a}{2.303\ RT} = \log\frac{K}{A} = 0.00174$ (Given)

$\Rightarrow -E_a = (2.303 \times 8.314 \times 300 \times 0.00174)$

$= 10.0\ J\ mol^{-1}$

48. (a) Arhenius equation is

$K = A \times e^{-E_a/RT}$

$\therefore \quad \log K = \log A - \frac{E_a}{2.303RT}$ ...(i)

Given equation is

$\log K/A = -\frac{x}{T}$

$\log A = \log A - \frac{x}{T}$ ...(ii)

Comparing equation (i) and (ii) we get,

$\frac{x}{T} = \frac{E_a}{2.303RT}$

$2.303\ Rx = E_a$

Activation energy $(E_a) = 2.303\ Rx$

49. (a) Activation energy for acid hydrolysis of sucrose is 6.22 kJ mol^{-1}, while the activation energy is only 2.15 kJ mol^{-1} when hydrolysed by the enzyme.

50. (d) According to Arrhenius theory.

$K = A \times e^{-E_a/RT}$

$\log\frac{K_2}{K_1} = \frac{E_a}{2.303R}\left[\frac{1}{T_1} - \frac{1}{T_2}\right]$

Given,

$K_1 = x, \quad T_1 = 300$

$K_2 = 2x \quad T_2 = 310$

$\log\frac{2x}{x} = \frac{E_a}{2.303 \times 8.3}\left[\frac{1}{300} - \frac{1}{310}\right]$

$E_a = \frac{\log 2 \times 2.303 \times 8.3 \times 300 \times 310}{10}$

$E_a = 53.49\ kJ\ mol^{-1}$.

51. (b) $K_1 = 3.46 \times 10^{-2}$

$T_1 = 298k$

$K_2 = ?$

$T_2 = 350$

$E_a = 50.1\ kJ\ mol^{-1}$

$R = 8.314\ JK^{-1}\ mol^{-1}$

According to Arrhenius theory,

$\log\frac{K_2}{K_1} = \frac{E_a}{2.303R}\left[\frac{1}{T_1} - \frac{1}{T_2}\right]$

$\log\frac{K_2}{3.46 \times 10^{-2}} = \frac{50.1 \times 10^3}{2.303 \times 8.314}\left[\frac{1}{298} - \frac{1}{350}\right]$

$\log\frac{K_2}{3.46 \times 10^{-2}} = 1.30$

$\frac{K_2}{3.46 \times 10^{-2}} = 10^{1.30} = 20$

$K_2 = 3.46 \times 10^{-2} \times 20$

$K_2 = 69.03 \times 10^{-2}$

$\therefore \quad K_2 = 0.69\ s^{-1}$

52. (a) $\log\frac{k_2}{k_1} = \frac{E_a}{2.303R}\left(\frac{T_2 - T_1}{T_1 T_2}\right)$

$\log\left(\frac{4x}{x}\right) = \frac{E_a}{2.303(8.314)}\left(\frac{700 - 600}{700 \times 600}\right)$

$0.602 = \frac{E_a}{19.147}\left(2.38 \times 10^{-4}\right)$

$\Rightarrow E_a = 48548.3\ J = 48.54\ kJ \approx 48.16\ kJ.$

53. (a) From Arrhenius equation,

$\log\frac{k_{310}}{k_{300}} = \frac{E_a}{2.303R}\left(\frac{1}{300} - \frac{1}{310}\right)$

$\Rightarrow \log 2 = \frac{E_a}{2.303 \times 8.314 \times 10^{-3}}\left(\frac{10}{300 \times 310}\right)$

$E_a = 53.6\ kJ\ mol^{-1}$

54. (d) The temperature dependence of the rate of a chemical reaction can be explained by Arrhenius equation,

$k = A.e^{E_a/RT}$

Taking ln on both side

$\Rightarrow \ln k = \ln A - \frac{E_a}{RT}$

$\Rightarrow \frac{E_a}{RT} = \ln A - \ln k.$

55. (a)

56. (c) Rate constant $k = \frac{0.693}{t_{1/2}}$

$\therefore \quad k_1\ (\text{at } 300\ K) = \frac{0.693}{50} = 0.014 s^{-1}$

and $k_2(\text{at } 400K)\frac{0.693}{10} = 0.07 s^{-1}$

According to Arrhenius theory

$\log\frac{k_2}{k_1} = \frac{E_a}{2.303R}\left[\frac{T_2 - T_1}{T_1.T_2}\right]$

Thus,

$\log\frac{0.07}{0.014} = \frac{E_a}{2.303 \times 8.314}\left[\frac{400 - 300}{400 \times 300}\right]$

$\log 5 = \frac{E_a}{2.303 \times 8.314}\left[\frac{100}{400 \times 300}\right]$

or, $0.70 = \frac{E_a}{19.15 \times 1200}$

or, $E_a = 16086\ J = 16.08\ kJ\ mol^{-1}$

$E_a = 16.10\ kJ\ mol^{-1}$

57. (c) Arrhenius equation,

$k = Ae^{-Ea/RT}$

On taking log on both sides, we get

$\ln k = \ln A - \frac{E_a}{RT}$

A graph between in k and 1/T is a straight line with $-\frac{E_a}{R}$ slope.

4 The *d*-and *f*-Block Elements

1. **(d)** The components of German silver are copper (50 – 60%), zinc (20%) and Nickel (20%).

2. **(a)** $\mu = \sqrt{n(n+2)}$ B.M $\quad \mu = \sqrt{15}$ B.M

$n(n+2) = 15$

$n^2 + 2n - 15 = 0 \Rightarrow (n+5)(n-3) = 0$

Chromium Z = 24

3. **(b)** Among Ti, V, Cr, Mn and Fe Mn has the highest third ionization enthalpy among them because removal of an electron from stable half filled d^5 configuration of Mn^{2+} is difficult.

So, electronic configuration of $Mn^{3+} = d^4$.

Mn^{3+} = [Ar]

↑	↑	↑	↑			

$3d^4$ (five boxes), $4s^0$ (one box, empty)

It has 4 unpaired electrons.

Magnetic Moment $= \mu = \sqrt{n(n+2)}$

$= \sqrt{4(4+2)} = \sqrt{24} = 4.90$ B.M.

4. **(d)** Ni : $3d^8 \rightarrow$

↑↓	↑↓	↑↓	↑	↑

no. of unpaired e^- = 2

Co : $3d^7 \rightarrow$

↑↓	↑↓	↑	↑	↑

unpaired e^- = 3

Fe : $3d^6 \rightarrow$

↑↓	↑	↑	↑	↑

unpaired e^- = 4

Mn: $3d^5 \rightarrow$

↑	↑	↑	↑	↑

unpaired e^- = 5

5. **(b)** Out of Ti, V, Cr, Mn, Fe. Mn has anomalously law melting point due to its complex crystal structure and weak metallic bonding so it has lowest melting point among them.

$[Mn] = [Ar]\ 3d^5\ 4s^2$

$Mn^{3+} = [Ar]\ 3d^4$

↑	↑	↑	↑	

It has 4 unpaired electrons.

$\mu = \sqrt{n(n+2)} = \sqrt{4(4+2)}$

$= \sqrt{4 \times 6} = \sqrt{24}$ B.M

6. **(a)**

Metal	Valence shell Electronic configuration	Unpaired electron	Magnetic moment ($\mu = \sqrt{n(n+2)}$)
Cr^{3+}	$3d^3 4s^0$	3	$\mu = \sqrt{15} = 3.87$
Cu^{3+}	$3d^9 4s^0$	1	$\mu = \sqrt{3} = 1.73$
CO^{3+}	$3d^6 4s^0$	4	$\mu = \sqrt{24} = 4.90$
Fe^{2+}	$3d^6 4s^0$	4	$\mu = \sqrt{24} = 4.90$

7. **(b)** Interstitial compounds retain metallic conductivity.

8. **(c)** Standard Electrode potential ($E^\circ_{M^{2+}/M}$) :
$Mn^{2+} < Cr^{2+} < Fe^{2+} < Ni^{2+}$

This order shows that the tendency to get reduced from M^{2+} to M increases from Mn to Ni.

It is minimum for Mn^{2+} due to very high sum of ionization energies ($\Delta_i H_1 + \Delta_i H_2$) and low sublimation enthalpy due to weaker metallic bonding.

It is maximum for Ni^{2+} due to high enthalpy of hydration and lower sublimation enthalpy.

9. **(d)** The Cr^{+3}/Cr^{+2} reduction potential is negative because Cr^{+3} is more stable than Cr^{+2} due to its half filled t_2g orbitals in an octahedral crystal field. This means Cr^{+2} readily oxidized to Cr^{+3} making Cr^{+2} a strong reducing agent.

10. **(d)**

Aquated ion	Colour
Ni^{2+}	green
Fe^{3+}	yellow
Mn^{3+}	violet
V^{4+}	blue

11. **(d)** W has highest melting point. More the unpaired in d-orbital strong the intermolecular interaction which leads to high melting points.

12. **(c)** The splitting energy order is (due to strong-field ligand 'en') :-

$[Ni(H_2O)_6]^{2+} < [Ni(H_2O)_4(en)]^{2+} <$
$[Ni(H_2O)_2(en)_2]^{2+} < [Ni(en)_3]^{2+}$

Thus, the colour shifts from large wave length to short or small frequency to high frequency which is from **green** to pale blue to blue to violet.

13. **(c)** V^{2+} is a strong reducing agent and liberates hydrogen from a dilute acid. Thus, (i) is correct.

In chemical behaviour, the earlier members of the lanthanide series behave more like calcium. Thus, (ii) is incorrect.

Silver UK coins = Cu + Ni alloy.

Thus, (iii) is correct.

Neptunium (Np) belongs to the actinides series and has the configuration $5f^4\ 6d^1\ 7s^2$ because of which it can show a maximum of +7 oxidation state.

Thus, (iv) is correct.

14. **(a)** Cr in higher oxidation state will be more acidic.

Thus, the order of acidic strength will be :-

$\overset{+6}{CrO_3} > \overset{+3}{CrO_3} > \overset{+2}{CrO}$

15. **(c)** Due to absence of unpaired electrons, Zn has the lowest enthalpy of atomization.

16. **(c)**

(i) $[Fe(CN)_6]^{3-}$:-

Fe is in +3 state and CN^- is a strong-field ligand. Thus, $Fe^{3+} = [Ar]\ 3d^5$ or

↑↓	↑↓	↑		

3d

Thus, there is only one unpaired electron.

(ii) $[MnCl_6]^{3-}$:-

Mn is in +3 state and Cl^- is a weak-field ligand. Thus, $Mn^{3+} = [Ar]\ 3d^4$ or

↑	↑	↑	↑	

3d

Thus, there are four unpaired electrons.

(iii) $[FeF_6]^{3-}$:-

Fe is in +3 state and F^- is a weak-field ligand. Thus, Fe will be [Ar] $3d^5$ with five unpaired electron.

Fe^{3+} =

↑	↑	↑	↑	↑

3d

(iv) $[Co(NH_3)_6]^{3+}$:-

Co is in +3 state here and NH_3 is a strong-field ligand. Thus, Co will be [Ar] $3d^6$ with zero unpaired electrons.

Co^{3+} =

↑↓	↑↓	↑↓		

3d

Thus, the increasing order of the number of unpaired electrons will be :-

(iv) < (i) < (ii) < (iii)

17. **(a)**

$E^\circ_{Cu^{2+}/Cu} = +0.34$ V, $E^\circ_{I_2/I^-} = 0.54$

$2Cu^{2+} + 4I^- \rightarrow 2CuI + I_2$

Despite the above values of the standard reduction potentials, Cu^{2+} is able to oxidize iodide to I_2 due to all the species like Cu^{2+}, Cu^+, and CuI being present together in the solution.

The cumulative effect of this results in the $Cu^{2+} \rightarrow CuI$ reduction potential being + 0.88 V that makes the reaction feasible.

Therefore, CuI or Cu_2I_2 exists instead of CuI_2 as Cu^{2+} oxidises I^- to I_2 and so (A) and (R) are true with (R) explaining (A).

18. **(a)** More the no. of valence electrons more is the overlapping. This phenomenon also leads to the high melting and boiling point.

19. (a) General electronic configuration of valence shell of Gr 12 elements: $(n-1)\,d^{10}ns^2$

20. (a) Many of transition metals are sufficiently electro-positive to react with dilute acid in order to produce hydrogen gas. But those having lower standard reduction potential are not able to liberate H_2 from dilute acid

21. (b) Catalysts lower the activation energy of the reaction by altering reaction mechanism.

22. (d) The catalyst used in manufacturing polyethylene is known Ziegler-Natta catalyst. It is a mixture of $TiCl_4$, $Al(C_2H_5)_3$ or $Al(CH_3)_3$ works at 333 – 343K at pressure 6 - 7 atm pressure in a hydrocarbon solvent.

23. (c) n = number of unpaired electron

Configuration	No. of unpaired	Magnetic moment
d^5	5	5.90
d^3	3	3.82
d^1	1	1.92
d^4	4	4.90

So, the correct order of magnetic moment is $d^5 > d^4 > d^3 > d^1$

24. (c) In all other compounds

$CuCl_2 \rightarrow [Cu^{2+}] \Rightarrow [Ar]\,3d^9$

$CuCl \rightarrow [Cu^{+}] \Rightarrow 3d^{10}\,4s^0$

$ScCl_3 \rightarrow [Sc^{3+}] \Rightarrow 3d^0\,4s^0$

$TiCl_4 \rightarrow [Ti^{4+}] \Rightarrow 3d^0\,4s^0$

$CuCl_2$ contains one unpaired electron.

Hence, it is coloured compound.

25. (c) Transition metals commonly exhibit +2 oxidation state because two electrons present in valance s-orbitals and removing the electrons from the sub shell below s-orbitals requires immense amount of energy.

26. (c)

27. (a) $Cr^{2+} \Rightarrow [Ar]\,3d^4,\ E^0_{Cr^{3+}/Cr^{2+}} = -0.41\ V$

$Mn^{3+} \Rightarrow [Ar]3d^4,\ E^0_{Mn^{3+}/Mn^{2+}} = +1.51\ V$

So, reducing power $Cr^{2+} > Mn^{2+}$.

28. (d) Catalytic activity of transition elements is due to their variable oxidation states and to form complexes.

29. (d)

$$(NH_4)_2Cr_2O_7 \xrightarrow{\Delta} Cr_2O_3 + N_2 + 4H_2O$$

Cr_2O_3 is amphoteric in nature.

Transition metal oxides in lower oxidation state are basic, higher oxidation state are acidic.

Here Cr is in +3 Oxidation state

30. (a) In acidic medium balanced equation is

$$5Fe^{2+} + MnO_4^- + 8H^+ \rightarrow Mn^{2+} + 8H_2O + 5Fe^{3+}$$

$$\text{Moles of } FeSO_4 = \frac{1.52}{152} = 10^{-2}$$

$$\text{moles of } KMnO_4 = \frac{\text{moles of } FeSO_4}{5} = \frac{10^{-2}}{5}$$

$$\therefore \quad \text{Molarity} = \frac{\text{moles}}{\text{volume(L)}}$$

$$\text{Volume(L)} = \frac{10^{-2}}{5} \times \frac{1}{0.05} = 0.04\ L$$

Volume (mL) = 0.04 × 1000 = 40 mL

31. (b) Chromite ore is fused with sodium carbonate in the presence of air as:

$$\underset{(A)}{4\,Fe\,Cr_2O_4} + 8Na_2CO_3 + 7O_2 \rightarrow 8Na_2\,CrO_4 + \underset{(B)}{2Fe_2O_3} + 8CO_2$$

I: Compound A is CrO_4^{2-} which has tetrahedral geometry so, statement I is false it doesn't have Cr–O–Cr linkage.

II: B is Fe_2O_3.

III: Oxidation state of Cr in Na_2CrO_4 is + 6

Only statement II and III are correct.

32. (b) During the preparation of $K_2Cr_2O_7$ from chromite are yellow Na_2CrO_4 converts into orange $Na_2Cr_2O_7$.

Chromate and dichromate ions exists in equilibrium as:

$$\underset{\text{(yellow)}}{2CrO_4^{2-}} + 2H^+ \rightleftharpoons \underset{\text{(orange)}}{Cr_2O_7^{2-}} + H_2O$$

Adding acid (decreasing pH) or increasing H^+ concentration shifts the equilibrium to the right according to Le-Chatelier principle, converting chromate ions into dichromate.

33. (a) $K_2Cr_2O_7$ is orange red crystalline solid. A powerful oxidising agent and it is used as a primary standard in volumetric analysis. While Cr–O–Cr bond angle in $Cr_2O_7^{2-}$ is around 126° not 118°.

34. (b) From the given reaction.

$$2MnO_4^- + 6H^+ + 5H_2O_2 \rightarrow 2Mn^{2+} + 8H_2O + 5O_2$$

No. of millimoles of 0.02M $KMnO_4$ in 100 ml of solution.

No. of Moles = Molarity × Volume

= 0.02 × 100 ml

= 2 m mol.

From the Balanced chemical reaction, ratio of $KMnO_4 : H_2O_2$ is 2:5.

So no. of m mol of H_2O_2 required in the reaction:

$$n(H_2O_2) = \frac{5}{2} \times n(KMnO_4)$$

$$n(H_2O_2) = \frac{5}{2} \times 2\ \text{mmol}$$

$n(H_2O_2) = 5$ mmol

Molarity of H_2O_2 solution:

$$M(H_2O_2) = \frac{n}{v} = \frac{5\ \text{mmol}}{10\text{ml}} = 0.5\ \text{mol/L}$$

Note- Volume strength of H_2O_2 is defined as the volume of O_2 gas liberated by the complete decomposition of 1L of H_2O_2 solution.

$$2H_2O_2 \longrightarrow 2H_2O + O_2$$

2 Mol of H_2O_2 give 1 mol of O_2 = 22.4 L of O_2 at STP

So, 1 mol of H_2O_2 gives = 11.2 L of O_2 at STP

Volume strength = Molarity × Volume

X = 0.5 × 11.2 = 5.6

35. (c) Balanced equation is

$$2KMnO_4 + 3H_2SO_4 + 5H_2S \rightarrow K_2SO_4 + 2MnSO_4 + 8H_2O + 5S$$

5 mole H_2S required 2 mol of $KMnO_4$

1 mol H_2S required $\frac{2}{5} = 0.4$ mol of $KMnO_4$

36. (d) While both lanthanides and aluminium are metals their reactivity varies. The early lanthanides are more reactive due to the factors like their electronic configuration and ability to readily form ions.

37. (c) V_2O_5 is amphoteric

$V_2O_5 + NaOH \rightarrow VO_4^{3-}$

$V_2O_5 + H_2SO_4 \rightarrow VO_2^+$

Thus, oxidation state of V in products is +5, +5

38. (a) $2KMnO_4 \xrightarrow{\Delta} K_2MnO_4 + MnO_2 + O_2$

So statement I is incorrect because it is oxygen also.

39. (b) $2Na_2CrO_4 + 2H^+ \longrightarrow Na_2Cr_2O_7 + 2Na^+ + H_2O$

$Na_2Cr_2O_7$

$+2 + 2x - 14 = 0$

$2x - 12 = 0$

$x = +6$

40. (b) In acidic medium hydrogen sulphide is oxidised, sulphur being precipitated

$H_2S \longrightarrow 2H^+ + S^{2-}$

$$5S^{2-} + 2\,MnO_4^- + 16H^+ \longrightarrow 2Mn^{2+} + 8H_2O + 5S$$

41. (a) In VO_2^+, V is in +3 oxidasion state.

$Cr_2O_7^{2-}$ Cr is in +6 oxidasion state.

MnO_4^- Mn is in +7 oxidation state.

Oxidising power means substance have more tendency to accept electron. Mn is in highest oxidation state so it have more oxidising power.

$MnO_4^- > Cr_2O_7^{2-} > VO_2^+$

42. (d) In Neutral or fainty alkaline solutions Oxidation of iodide to iodate

$$2MnO_4^- + H_2O + I^- \rightarrow 2MnO_2 + 2OH^- + IO_3^-$$

43. (d) Sc electronic configuration = $1s^2\,2s^2\,2p^6\,3s^2\,3p^6\,4s^2\,3d^1$ to form the oxide Sc have to remove 20th electrons from its d and s-orbital. It form a very unstable configuration. Sc will show +3 oxidation state and make inert gas configuration does not form oxide.

44. (b) In neutral or faintly alkaline medium, iodide ion oxidised to iodate as:

$$2MnO_4^- + H_2O + I^- \rightarrow 2MnO_2 + 2OH^- + \underset{\text{Iodate ion}}{IO_3^-}$$

45. The oxides of transition metal that contain metals in lower oxidation state are considered to be basic and basic character of metal oxide decreases along the period.

Cr_2O_3	CrO_3	V_2O_5	V_2O_3
$2x-6=0$	$x-6=0$	$2x-10=0$	$2x-6=0$
$x=+3$	$x=6$	$x=\pm5$	$x=\pm3$
Cr^{+3}	Cr^{+6}	V^{+5}	V^{3+}

V_2O_3 present in its lowest oxidation state.

The vanadium tends to donate the pair of electrons

Hence it is basic oxide.

46. (c) Ti O is a white pigment used in coating industries. MnO_2 is used in dry battery cells as it possesses good energy.

The traditional UK copper coins are mainly made of Cu, Zn and Sn.

Thus, Statement (iii) is incorrect.

47. (c) $\underset{(B)}{Zn(OH)_2} \xrightarrow{\Delta} \underset{(A)}{ZnO} + H_2O$

$$\underset{(B)}{Zn(OH)_2} + 2NaOH \longrightarrow Na_2[Zn(OH)_4]$$

$$\xrightarrow[H_2O]{} \underset{(C)}{Na_2ZnO_2}$$

$$\underset{\text{Zinc oxide}}{ZnO} + C \longrightarrow \underset{(D)}{Zn} + \underset{\substack{(E)\\ \text{Carbon monoxide}}}{CO}$$

48. (b) Cr is present in +6 oxidation state. In both of chromate (CrO_4^{2-}) and dichromate ($Cr_2O_7^{2-}$) ions i.e. d^0-configuration. So, d-d transition is absent in them.

The yellow colour of CrO_4^{2-} and orange colour of $Cr_2O_7^{2-}$ is due to charge transfer of oxygen ligand get transfered into vacant *d*-orbital of metal Cr (VI).

49. (c)

$$SO_3^{2-} + H_2SO_4 \longrightarrow SO_4^{2-} + SO_2 + H_2O$$

$$5SO_2 + 2KMnO_4 + 2H_2O \longrightarrow K_2SO_4 + 2MnSO_4 + 2H_2SO_4$$

∴ Oxidation state of Mn in $MnSO_4$ is + 2.

50. (d) In neutral or faintly alkaline solution,

$$8MnO_4^- + 3S_2O_3^{-2} + H_2O \longrightarrow 8MnO_2 + 6SO_4^{-2} + 2OH^-$$

In acidic medium,

$$2MnO_4^- + 5NO_2^- + 6H^+ \longrightarrow 2Mn^{+2} + 5NO_3^- + 3H_2O$$

51. (b)

(a) $2MnO_4^- + 10I^- + 16H^+ \longrightarrow 2Mn^{2+} + 5I_2 + 8H_2O$

(b) $2MnO_4^- + I^- + H_2O \longrightarrow 2MnO_2 + \underset{Y}{IO_3^-} + \underset{X}{2OH^-}$

Hence, (X) and (Y) are respectively I_2 and IO_3^-

52. (d) Eu^{2+} and Yb^{2+} have more tendency to accept electrons so they are act as good reducing agents.

53. (a) Ce, Nd, Pr, Tb and Dy exhibit in +4 oxidation state.

54. (c

Atomic number	Symbol with oxidation state	Electronic configuration
59	Pr^{3+}	$4f^2$
71	Lu^{3+}	$4f^{14}$
63	Eu^{2+}	$4f^7$
58	Ce^{4+}	$4f^0$

55. (c) Ce, Gd and Lu have [Xe] $4f^x\ 5d^1\ 6s^2$ configuration.

Ce = [Xe] $4f^1\ 5d^1\ 6s^2$

Gd = [Xe] $4f^7\ 5d^1\ 6s^2$

Lu = [Xe] $4f^{14}\ 5d^1\ 6s^2$

56. (c) Yb^{2+} = [Xe] $4f^{14}$

Thus, it prefers to lose one electron as shielding is strong and it can form Yb^{3+} so it acts as a reductant.

Lu^{3+} = [Xe] $4f^{14}$ so it is diamagnetic.

CrO is basic in its low oxidation state of +2 and prefers to attain a state of +6.

Brass = Cu + Zn and Bronze = Cu + Sn

57. (b) The correct order of ionic radii :-

$_{70}Yb^{3+} < {_{66}Dy^{3+}} < {_{62}Sm^{3+}} < {_{59}Pr^{3+}}$

(86 Pm) (91) (96) (101)

This order can be explained on the basis of lanthanide contraction due to which the atomic and ionic radii decrease steadily.

58. (c) The atomic numbers of the given lanthanides are:-

Ce = 58, Eu = 63, Lu = 71

Since the metallic character decreases from left to right in a period, the order of metallic character for the given metal will be Lu < Eu < Ce.

Thus, the basic strength of their hydroxides will be:- Lu $(OH)_3$ < Eu $(OH)_3$ < Ce $(OH)_3$.

59. (b) Pr, Nd, Tb and Dy exhibit +4 state in their oxides as they acquire configurations closer to stable $4f^\circ$ and $4f^7$ configurations.

Pr^{4+} = [Xe]$4f^1$, Nd^{4+} = [Xe] $4f^2$, Pm^{4+}= [Xe] $4f^3$,

Sm^{4+} = [Xe] $4f^4$, Eu^{4+} = [Xe] $4f^5$, Gd^{4+}= [Xe] $4f^6$,

Tb^{4+} = [Xe]$4f^7$, Dy^{4+} = [Xe]$4f^8$.

60. (a) Due to more e^- in inner shells, shielding effect is more effective.

61. (d)

(i) The ionic radius of lanthanoids decreases as, we move along the period.

Hence, order of ionic radius,

$_{59}Pr^{3+} > {_{62}Sm^{3+}} > {_{66}Dy^{3+}}$

(ii) Element Eu (z = 63) can exits in (+) 2 and (+) 3 oxidation state.

+3 oxidation state is the most common oxidation state for lanthanoids.

Thus, E_u^{2+} can easily oxidise to Eu^{3+} and act as strong reducing agent.

(iii) The electronic configuation for

$_{94}P_u = [R_n]5f^6 6d^0 7s^2$

Thus, it can show +7 oxidation state.

62. (c) Electronic configurations of

(i) Lanthanum : (Z = 57) $[Xe]_{54}\ 5d^1\ 6s^2$

(ii) Uranium : (Z = 92) $[Rn]_{86}\ 5f^3\ 6d^1\ 7s^2$

(iii) Lawrencium : (Z = 103) $[Rn]_{86}\ 5f^{14}\ 6d^1\ 7s^2$

(iv) Thorium : (Z = 90) $[Rn]_{54}\ 6d^2\ 7s^2$

(v) Actinium : (Z = 89) $[Rn]_{86}\ 6d^1\ 7s^2$

(vi) Cerium: (Z = 58) $[Xe]_{54}\ 4f^1\ 5d^1\ 6s^2$

Hence, elements La, Ac, and Th do not possess f-electrons.

63. (b) Cerium exihibit + 4 oxidation state.

E.C. of Ce (58) = [Xe] $4f^1\ 5d^1\ 6s^2$

Ce^{+4} = [Xe] $4f^0\ 5d^0\ 6s^0$ (stable configuration)

64. (d)

5 Co-ordination Compounds

1. **(c)** $[Co(NH_3)_3(NO_3)_3]$ is MA_3B_3 type complex it shows fac-mer geometrical isomerism only.

Since, both fac and mer isomer have plane of symmetry. So it does not show optical isomerism.

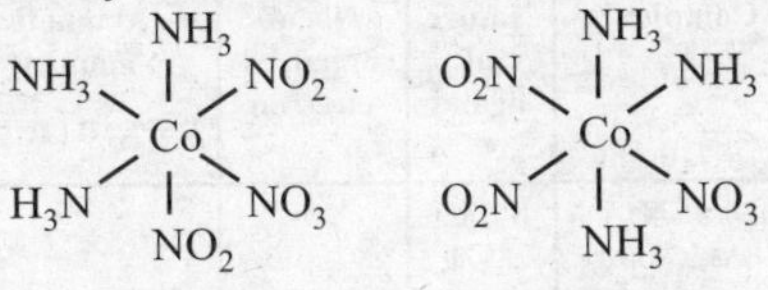

fac-isomer mer-isomer

2. **(b)** I : $K[Cr(H_2O)_2(C_2O_4)_2]$ in $[M(AA)_2B_2]$ type octahedral complex it does show cis/trans geometrical isomerism as:

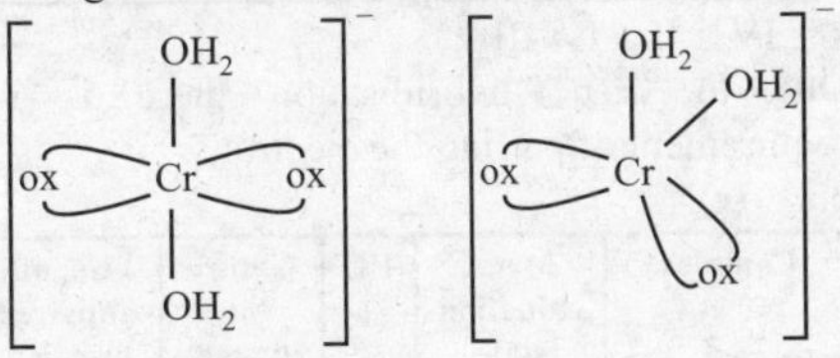

Trans Cis

II: $[Co(en)_3]Cl_3$ is $[M(AA)_3]$ type octahedral complex, hence only one geometrical arrangement possible, it doesn't shows geometrical isomerisms.

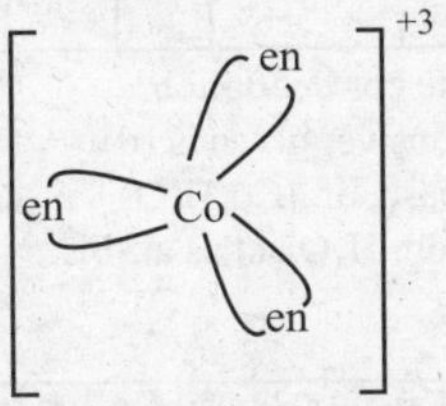

III: $[CO(NH_3)_5(NO_2)](NO_3)_2$ is $[MA_5B]$ type octahedral complex, hence only one spatial arrangement is possible, so no geometrical isomerism exists.

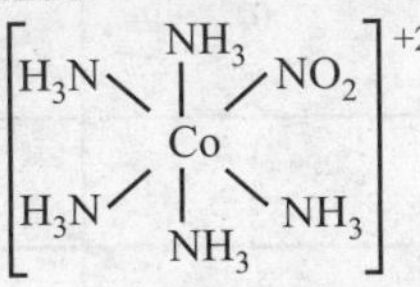

So, complex II and III doesn't show geometrical isomerism.

3. **(a)** Ambidentate ligands are the ligands which can bind through either of two donor atoms.

NO_2^-, CN^-, SCN^- are all ambidentate ligands.

4. **(d)** $[Co(en)_3]_4[Fe(CN)_6]_3$

5. **(a)**

(I) $PtCl_4.2HCl$ exists as $H_2[PtCl_6]$ hence, all Cl^- are inside coordination sphere, no free Cl^- present.

(II) $PtCl_4.2NH_3$ exists as $[Pt(NH_3)_2Cl_4]$, all Cl^- are inside coordination sphere, no free Cl^- present.

(III) $CoCl_3.4NH_3$ exists as $[Co(NH_3)_4Cl_2]Cl$, hence one Cl^- present as free, it gives AgCl as precipitate.

(IV) $PdCl_4{\cdot}4NH_3$ exists as $[Pd(NH_3)_4]Cl_4$, hence four Cl^- present as free, it gives AgCl as precipitate.

Compound I & II have all Cl^- inside coordination sphere- they do not precipitate AgCl.

6. **(b)** $C_2O_4^-$ – didentate

H_2O – Monodentate

SO_4^{2-} – monodentate, or didentate as per oxidation number of complex

7. **(d)** $K_3[Co(ox)_3]$

Oxidation state of Co is $3 \times (+1) + x + (-2) \times 3 = 0$

$x = +3$

IUPAC name : Potassium trioxaltocobaltate (III)

8. **(a)** Ionisation isomerism

$[Ti(H_2O)_5Cl](NO_3)_2$ and $[Ti(H_2O)_5NO_3]ClNO_3$

$[Pt(en)(NH_3)Cl]NO_3$ and $[Pt(en)(NH_3)NO_3]Cl$

9. **(c)** The coordination number is the number of ligand donor atoms to which the metal is directly bonded.

As H_2O = unidentate ligand

and $C_2O_4^{2-}$ = oxidate ion = bidentate ligand

hence coordination number of chromium is 6.

10. **(b)** Prussian blue ppt formula is :

$Fe_4[Fe(CN)_6]_3$

Where X = 4

Y = 1

11. **(c)**

$$COCl_3 \xrightarrow{NH_3} \underset{\text{(Grean colour)}}{COCl_3.4NH_3} \xrightarrow{\text{excess } Ag^+} AgCl$$

Volume given = 100 ml = 10^{-1} L

Concentration = 1 M

$$\text{Concentration} = \frac{\text{number of mole}}{\text{Volume}}$$

$\therefore$ Number of mole = $1 \times 10^{-1} = 0.1$ mole

12. **(d)** $4M(S) + 8CN^-(aq) + 2H_2O(aq) + O_2(g)$

$\downarrow$

$4[M(CN)_2]^-(aq) + 4\bar{O}H$ [M = Ag or Au]

$2[M(CN)_2]^-(aq) + Zn(s) \rightarrow [Zn(CN)_4]^{2-}(aq) + 2M(s)$

$\therefore$ CN no. of Ag = 2 CN no. of Zn = 4

13. **(c)** The ligands are classified as weak and strong ligand.

According to spectrochemical series.

$I^- < Br^- < S^{2-} < SCN^- < Cl^- < N_3^- < F^- <$ urea $< OH^- < C_2H_5OH < C_2O_4^{2-} < O^{2-} < H_2O < NCS^- <$ gly $< NH_3 <$ en $< NH_2OH <$ bPy $< NO_2^- < CH_3^- < C_6H_5^- < CN^- < CO$

$\therefore$ 4 ligands are strong than H_2O

14. **(c)** To be optically active a molecule must not posses any one of the following symmetry elements.

1. Centre of symmetry
2. Plane of symmetry

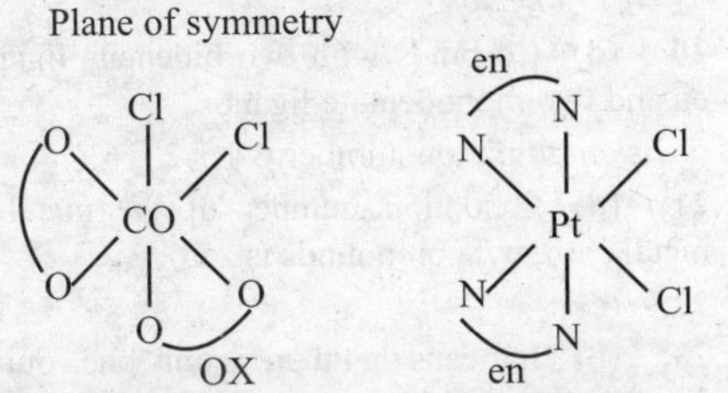

[POS absent] Optically Active [POS absent] Optically Active

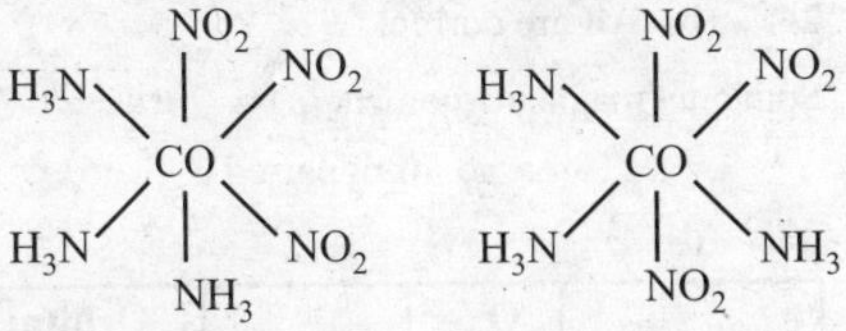

POS present Fac-optically inactive POS present mer-optically inactive

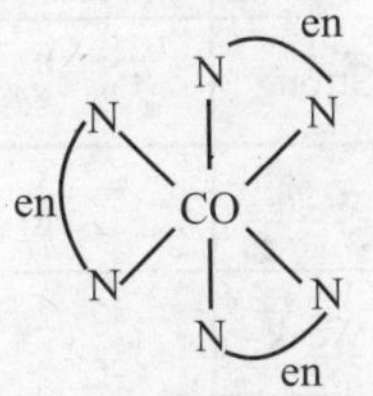

POS absent Optically Active

15. **(a)** No optical isomerism is exhibited by the given complex as there is a plane of symmetry.

Linkage isomers :-

$[Co(NH_3)_5(NO_2)]^{2+}$ and $[Co(NH_3)_5(ONO)]^{2+}$

Ionization isomers:-

$[Co(NH_3)_5(NO_2)]^{2+}$ and $[Co(NH_3)_5(NO_3)]^+$

For coordination isomerism, both, cationic and anionic entities are required.

16. **(c)** The complex is a cationic complex with two ammine (NH_3), one chloro (Cl) and one methanamine ligand.

Thus, the name will be :-

Diamminechloro (methanamine) platinum (II) chloride.

17. **(c)** Highest molar conductivity (for equimolar solutions) will be exhibited by the complex that will dissociate into a greater number of ions in the solution.

$[Pt(NH_3)_2Cl_2] = 0$

$[Co(NH_3)_4Cl_2]Cl = 2$

$K_4[Fe(CN)_6] = 5$

$[Cr(H_2O)_6]Cl_3 = 4$

Thus, potassium hexacyano ferrate (II) will have the highest molar conductivity.

18. (d)

Ethane- 1,2 - diamine = $\begin{array}{cc} NH_2 & NH_2 \\ | & | \\ CH_2 & - CH_2 \end{array}$ (neutral ligand)

$\Rightarrow$ formula = $[Co\ (NH_2CH_2CH_2NH_2)_3]_2\ (SO_4)_3$

19. (b) The ligands containing two donor sites but use only one at a time are known as ambidentate ligand

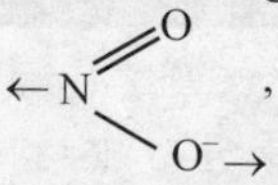 , $\leftarrow \overset{\ominus}{C} \equiv N\rightarrow$, $\leftarrow \overset{\ominus}{S} - C \equiv N \rightarrow$

20. (d) Co binds with two bidentate ligands en and two monodentate ligands.

$\therefore$ Its coordination number = 4 + 2 = 6

21. (d) Oxidation number of the metal in metal carbonyl compounds is zero.

22. (c)

23. (b) It means that there is only one counter ion, i.e., the possible complex is $[Co(NH_3)_4Cl_2]$ Cl. Hence, *X* is 4.

24. (b) All are correct.

Spin only magnetic moment (μ) = $\sqrt{n(n+2)}$ BM

n = no. of unpaired e^-

25. (d)

Complex	Oxidation state	Nature of ligand	Orbital electronic configuration
$[Fe(CN)_6]^{3-}$	Fe^{3+}	Strong	$t_{2g}^5\ e_g^0$
$[Fe(Cl)_6]^{3-}$	Fe^{3+}	Weak	$t_{2g}^3\ e_g^2$
$[Co(Cl)_6]^{3-}$	Co^{3+}	Weak	$t_{2g}^4\ e_g^2$
$[Co(NH_3)_6]^{3-}$	Co^{3+}	Strong	$t_{2g}^6\ e_g^0$

So $[Co(NH_3)_6]^{3+}$ has maximum number of electrons in t_{2g} orbital.

26. (a) $[Cr\ (H_2O)_6]^{2+}$ $Cr^{+2} = 3d^4$

$[Fe(H_2O)_6]^{+2}$ $Fe^{+2} = d^6$

$[CoF_6]^{-3}$ $Co^{+3} = d^6$

27. (a). $[FeF_6]^{3-}$: Fe present as Fe^{3+}

$Fe^{3+} \Rightarrow [Ar]\ 3d^5$

As F^- is weak field ligand, So no pairing occurs.

Filling of e^- in d - orbitals as:

[↑][↑] e_g

[↑][↑][↑] t_{2g}

$t_{2g}^3 : e_g^2$

- $[CoF_6]^{3-} \Rightarrow$ Co as Co^{+3}

Co^{+3} : [Ar] $3d^6$ [↑][↑] e_g^2

$F^- \Rightarrow$ weak field ligand [↑↓][↑][↑] t_{2g}^4

- $[Fe(CN)_6]^{3-} \Rightarrow$ Fe as Fe^{+3}

Fe^{+3} : [Ar] $3d^5$ [ ][ ] e_g^0

$CN^- \Rightarrow$ Strong field ligand. [↑↓][↑↓][↑] t_{2g}^5

- $[Co\ (NH_3)_6]^{+3} \Rightarrow$ Co as Co^{+3}

Co^{+3} $[Ar]3d^6$ [ ][ ] e_g^0

$NH_3 \Rightarrow$ Strong field ligand [↑↓][↑↓][↑↓] t_{2g}^6

28. (d) $[MnCl_6]^{3-} \Rightarrow Mn^{3+} = [Ar]3d^4$

or [↑][↑][↑][↑][ ]
3d

Thus, μ_s =

$\sqrt{n(n+2)} = \sqrt{4(4+2)} = \sqrt{24} = 4.90$ B.M.

29. (a) $[(Mn\ (H_2O)_6]^{2+}$ have Mn^{2+}

$Mn^{2+}\ 1s^2\ 2s^2\ 2p^6\ 3s^2\ 3p^6\ 4s^0\ 3d^5$

is octahedral splitting t_{2g}^3 and e_g^2

30. (d) Stronger the ligand more will be the magnitude of crystal field splitting.

NH_3 is stronger ligand as compare to H_2O so the magnitude of crystal field splitting $[Fe(NH_3)_6]^{2+}$ is more than $[Fe(H_2O)_6]^{2+}$

31. (c) In $[CO(en)_3]Cl_3$ all secondary valency joint with same type of linkage thus Geometrical isomer not formed.

32. (d)

Complex	Nature of ligand	No. of unpaired electron	Magnetic moment $x = \sqrt{n(n+2)}$
I $[Mn(CN)_6]^{3-}$	Strong	2	$\sqrt{8} = 2.82$
II $[MnCl_6]^{3-}$	Weak	4	$\sqrt{24} = 4.89$
III $[Fe(CN)_6]^{3-}$	Strong	1	$\sqrt{3} = 1.72$
IV $[FeF_6]^{3-}$	Weak	5	$\sqrt{35} = 5.92$

x = IV > II > I > III

Due to d^2sp^3 hybridisation there is no requirement of pairing the electrons.

33. (c)

Complex	Metal oxidation state	EC	Nature of ligand	No. of unpaired electron
$[Co(NH_3)_6]^{2+}$	Co^{2+}	$3d^7$	Strong	1
$[Co(NH_3)_6]^{3+}$	Co^{3+}	$3d^6$	Strong	0
$[Co(H_2O)_6]^{2+}$	Co^{2+}	$3d^7$	Weak	3
$[CO(H_2O)_6]^{3+}$	Co^{3+}	$3d^6$	Strong	0

So, (c) is the correct option.

but offical answer given is (d).

Note: In case of $[Co(H_2O)_6]^{+3}$ due to CFSE consideration, H_2O act as a SFL.

34. (c)

Complex	Oxidation state of metal	Valence shell electron of metal ion	Nature of ligand	Valence bond electrons description	No. of unpaired electron	Hybridisation
$Ni(CO)_4$	0	$3d^84s^2$	strong	[↑↓][↑↓][↑↓][↑↓][↑↓] [↑↓] [↑↓][↑↓][↑↓]	0	sp^3
$[Ni(CN)_4]^{2-}$	+2	$3d^8$	strong	[↑↓][↑↓][↑↓][↑↓][↑↓] [↑↓] [↑↓][↑↓]	0	dsp^2
$[CoF_6]^{3-}$	+3	$3d^6$	weak	[↑↓][↑][↑][↑][↑] [↑↓] [↑↓][↑↓][↑↓] [↑↓][↑↓][ ][ ]	4	sp^3d^2
$[Co(NH_3)_6]^{3+}$	+3	$3d^6$	strong	[↑↓][↑↓][↑↓][↑↓][↑↓] [↑↓] [↑↓][↑↓][↑↓] [ ][ ][ ][ ][ ]	0	d^2sp^3

35. (c)

Complex	Oxidation state of metal	Electronic configuration	Nature of ligand	No. of unpaired electron
I. $[MnCl_6]^{3-}$	Mn^{3+}	$3d^4$	Weak	4
II. $[Fe F_6]^{3-}$.	Fe^{3+}	$3d^5$	Weak	5
III. $[Mn(CN)_6]^{3-}$	Mn^{3+}	$3d^4$	Strong	2`
IV. $[Fe (CN)_6]^{3-}$	Fe^{3+}	$3d^5$	Strong	1

So order will be IV < III < I < II.

36. (d) $[Ni(NH_3)_6]^{+2}$

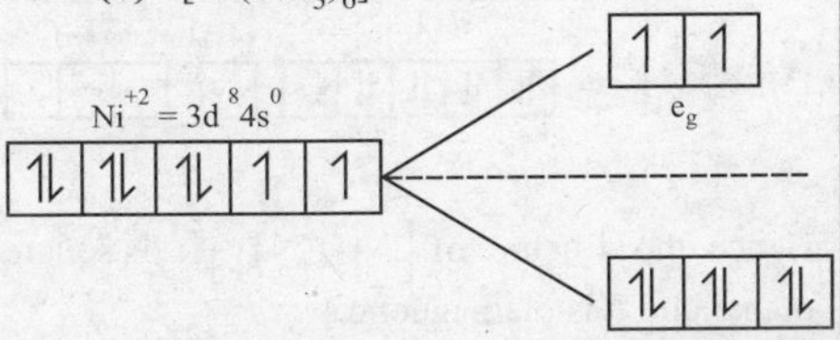

In t_{2g} all electrons are paired.

37. (a) In $[Mn(CN)_6]^{3-}$, oxidation state of Mn is +3 Mn^{3+}: $3d^4$

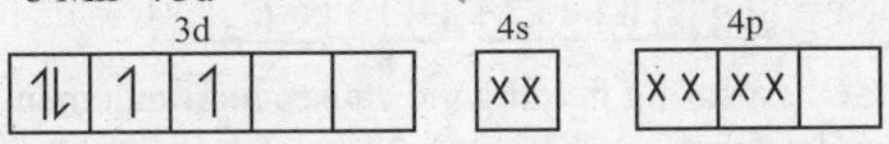

Unpaired electron = 2

$\mu_{\text{spin only}} = \sqrt{n(n+2)}\text{BM}$

$= \sqrt{2(2+2)}\text{BM}$

= 2.84 BM

In $[Co(C_2O_4)_3]^{3-}$, oxidation state of Co is + 3.

CO^{3+} : $3d^6$

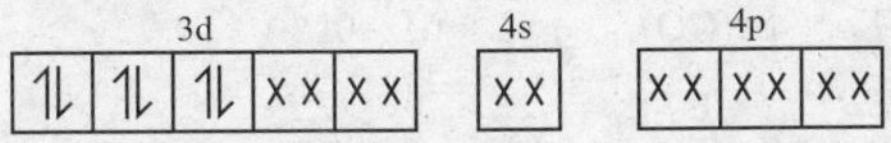

n = 0

$M_{\text{spin only}} = 0$ BM

38. (d) The configuration $t_{2g}^3\, e_g^1$ represents a total of 3 + 1 = 4 electrons in the d-subshell with all electrons unpaired as there is a weak-field ligand.

Thus, Mn is in +3 state and the complex 'A' will be $[Mn(H_2O)_6]^{3+}$.

The configuration $t_{2g}^4\, e_g^0$ represents the same oxidation state of Mn but with a strong-field ligand.

Thus, the complex 'B' will be $[Mn (CN)_6]^{3-}$.

39. (d) $\mu_s = \sqrt{n(n+2)} = 5.9$ B. M.

$\Rightarrow \quad \mu^2 = n(n+2) = 34.81 \Rightarrow n = 5$

Thus, Mn will have five unpaired electrons so Mn will be in +2 state with Br^- being weak- field ligands.

Thus, x = 2 for $[MnBr_4]^{2-}$

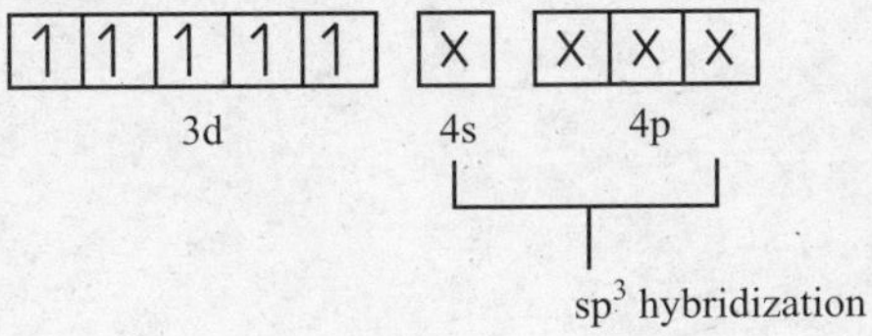

40. (a) $[Mn (CN)_6]^{3-}$:-

$Mn^{3+} \Rightarrow [Ar]3d^4$

CN^- is a strong-field ligand so it pairs the electrons.

Thus,

$[Mn (CN)_6]^{3-}$

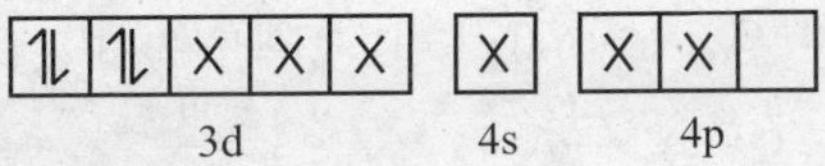

Thus, it is an inner-orbital but a diamagnetic complex.

$[Fe (CN)_6]^{3-}$:-

$Fe^{3+} \Rightarrow [Ar]\ 3d^5$

CN^- will pair - up the electrons so :-

$[Fe (CN)_6]^{3-}$

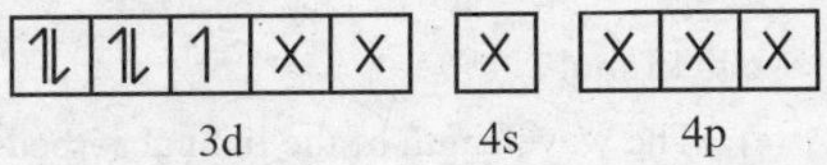

Thus, it is an inner-orbital and a paramagnetic complex.

$[Co (C_2O_4)_3]^{3-}$:-

$Co^{3+} \Rightarrow [Ar]\ 3d^6$

$C_2O_4^{2-}$ is a weak-field ligand so :-

$[Co(C_2O_4)_3]^{3-}$

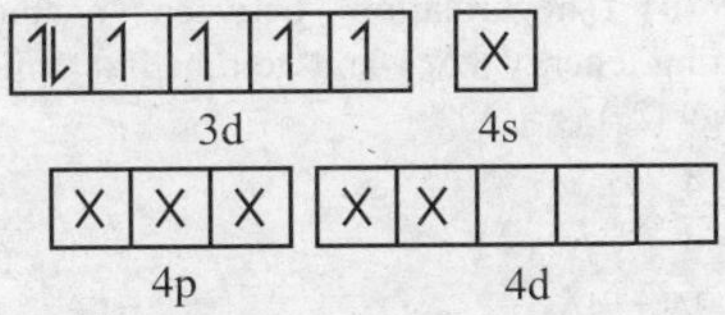

Thus, it is an outer-orbital and paramagnetic complex

$[MnCl_6]^{3-}$:-

$Mn^{3+} \Rightarrow [Ar]\ 3d^4$

Cl^- is a weak-field ligand so :-

$[Mn\ Cl_6]^{3-}$

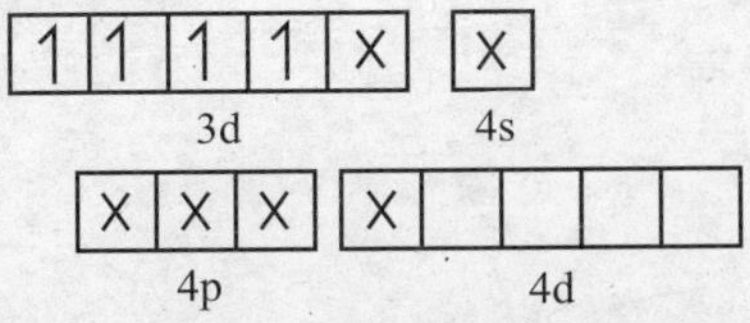

Thus, it is an inner-orbital and paramagnetic complex

$[Fe(CN)_6]^{4-}$:-

$Fe^{2+} \Rightarrow [Ar]\ 3d^6$ and CN^- is a strong-field ligand.

Thus,

$[Fe(CN)_6]^{4-}$

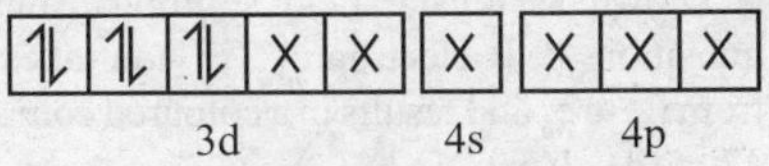

Thus, it is an inner-orbital and diamagnetic complex.

$[CoF_6]^{3-}$:-

$Co^{3+} \Rightarrow [Ar]\ 3d^6$ and F^- is a weak-field ligand.

Thus,

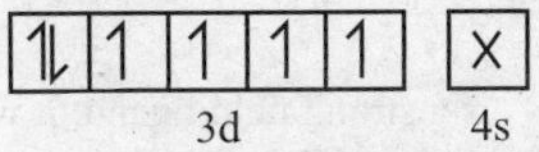

$[CoF_6]^{3-}$

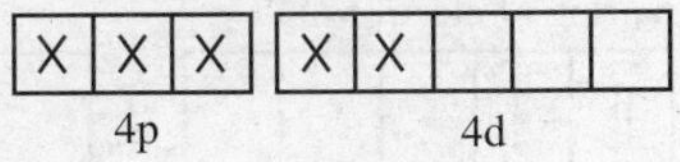

Thus, it is an outer-orbital and paramagnetic complex.

Therefore, there are two inner-orbital and paramagnetic complexes.

41. (b) $[NiCl_4]^{2-}$ has Ni^{2+} that has the configuration $[Ar]3d^8$. Since Cl^- is a weak-field ligand, the configuration of the complex will be:-

$[NiCl_4]^{2-}$

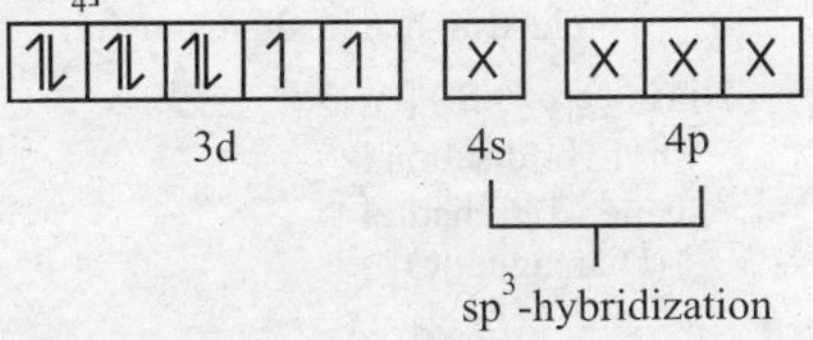

Thus, it is a tetrahedral complex.

It is paramagnetic due to unpaired electrons.

$[Ni (CO)_4]$ has neutral and strong-field ligand CO.

Thus,

$[Ni(CO)_4]$

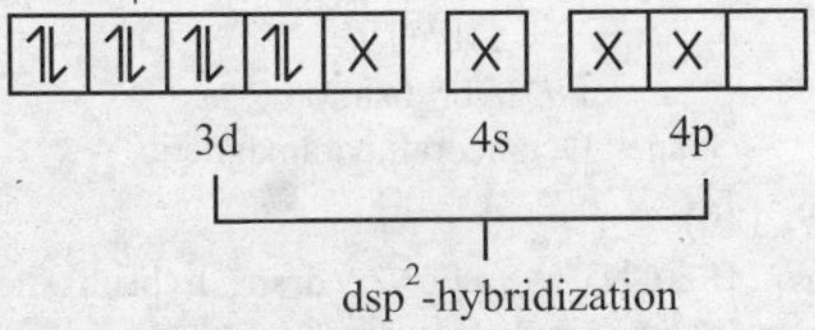

Thus, $[Ni (CO)_4]$ is a square-planar and diamagnetic complex.

Therefore, (ii) is incorrect and only (i) and (iii) are correct.

42. (b) (n – 1)d; ns, np

43. (d) CN^- being a strong field ligand facilitates the participation of inner orbital in hybridization $[Mn(CN)_6]^{3-} \rightarrow d^2sp^3$ hybridization.

F^- is a weak field ligand $\rightarrow sp^3d^2$ hybridization.

Both the complexes are of octahedral geometry.

44. (b) $Fe^{2+}(d^6)$: Unpaired electrons (n) = 4

$\therefore \quad \mu_s = \sqrt{4(4+2)} = 2\sqrt{6} = 4.89 \simeq 4.90$ BM

45. (b) One of the assumptions in CFT is ligands are considered as point charges.

46. (b) $TiCl_3 \rightarrow Ti^{3+}$ (d^1 system). Due to presence of unpaired e^- in d-orbital $TiCl_3$ will show purple colour solution.

$[Ti(H_2O)_6]\,Cl_3 \rightarrow$ Hexacoordinated Ti^{3+} leads to the splitting of degenerated d-orbitals, which is known as crystal field splitting. Thus, d-d transition of d^1 electron of Ti^{3+} ion takes place from t_{2g} to e_g and results in a coloured compound.

47. (d) $[Cr(CN)_6]^{3-}$

Oxidation state of Cr is + 3

$Cr^{3+} = [Ar]\ 3d^3$

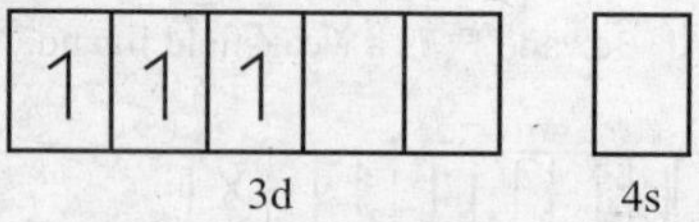

Since, CN^- is a strong field ligand, it will cause pairing of electrons in Cr^{3+}

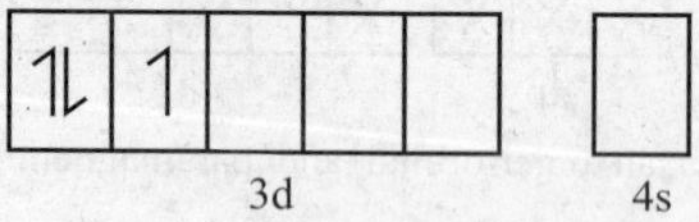

So, there is one unpaired electron in 3d-orbital of Cr^{3+} which makes the compound $[Cr(CN)_6]^{3-}$ paramagnetic.

48. (c) (a) $Ni^{2+} : [Ar]3d^8$

dsp^2 hybridisation

Shape : Square planar

(CN^- causes pairing of electron hence, diamagnetic)

(b) Ni (in zero O.S.) $[Ar]3d^8$

sp^3 hybridisation

Shape : Tetrahedral

(Diamagnetic)

(c) $Ni^{2+} : [Ar]3d^8$

sp^3 hybridisation

Shape : Tetrahedral

(Cl^- weak field ligand cause no pairing of electron hence, paramagnetic)

(d) $Ni^{2+} : [Ar]3d^8$

sp^3d^2 hybridisation

Shape : Octahedral, paramagnetic

49. (d)

(a) $[Fe(CN)_6]^{3-}$: Fe^{3+} : d^2sp^3 hybridisation with one unpaired electron

$\mu = \sqrt{n(n+2)} = \sqrt{1(1+1)} = 1.732$ B.M.

(b) $[Fe(CN)_6]^{4-}$: Fe^{2+} :

d^2sp^3 hybridisation with no unpaired electron $\mu = 0$.

(c) $[Ni(CN)_4]^{2-}$: Fe^{+2}

no unpaired electron $\therefore\ \mu = 0$.

(d) $[Ni(CN)_4]^{2-}$: Ni^{2+}

sp^3 hybridisation, Cl^- is a weak ligand so, there is no pairing of electrons.

Number of unpaired electron = 2.

$\therefore\ \mu = \sqrt{2(2+2)} = 2.82$

50. (b) The field strength order of the ligands is

$H_2O < NH_3 < NO_2^-$

So, the order of CFSE values:

$[Ni(H_2O)_6]^{2+} < [Ni(NH_3)_6]^{2+} < [Ni(NO_2)_6]^{4-}$

We know, $E = \dfrac{hc}{\lambda}$ or $E \propto \dfrac{1}{\lambda}$

Hence, the order of wavelength of absorption in visible region will be,

$[Ni(H_2O)_6]^{2+} > [Ni(NH_3)_6]^{2+} > [Ni(NO_2)_6]^{4-}$

51. (a) $\Delta_t = \dfrac{4}{9}\Delta_o \Rightarrow \Delta_o = \dfrac{9}{4}\Delta_t = \dfrac{9x}{4}$

52. (b) Given, Δ_0 for $(3d^2) = 1000$ kJ mol^{-1}

Energy of (t_{2g}) $E(t_{2g}) = -400$ kJ mol^{-1}

Q Δ_0 = Energy of e_g – Energy of t_{2g}

$1000\ E_{(2g)} - (-400)$

$E_{(eg)} = 1000 - 400$

$E_{(eg)} = 600$ kJ/mol

53. (c) The wavelength of the light absorbed by the complexes $\propto \dfrac{1}{\text{strength of ligands}}$.

Strength of ligand : en > H_2O.

Hence, order of wavelength :

$\underset{(\lambda_1)}{[Ni(H_2O)_6]^{2+}} > \underset{(\lambda_3)}{[(Ni(H_2O)_4en)]^{2+}} > \underset{(\lambda_2)}{[Ni(en)_3]^{2+}}$

54. (b) The relation between octahedral splitting energy (Δ_0) and tetrahedral splitting energy (Δ_t) is

$\Delta_t = \dfrac{4}{9}\Delta_0$

$\therefore\ 9\Delta_t = 4\Delta_0$

55. (d)

(a) Ni in $[Ni(Cl)_4]^{2-}$ exist as Ni^{2+} ion.

Cl^- is a weak field ligand (high spin). It will not cause pairing of electrons.

Hence, configuration of $[Ni(Cl)_4]^{2-}$ is

$[Ni(Cl)_4]^{2-}$ = 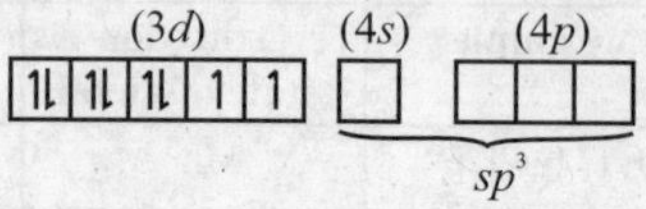

Tetrahedral with two unpaired electrons (i.e., paramagnetic) and has sp^3 hybridisation.

(b) In $\left[Co(C_2O_4)_3\right]^{3-}$, $(C_2O_4)^{2-}$ is a bidentate ligand thus, give octahedral structure.

(c) In $\left[Ni(CN)_4\right]^{2-}$, Ni exist as Ni^{2+} ion.

CN^- is a strong field ligand (low spin). Causes pairing of electrons of 3*d* orbital.

$[Ni(CN)_4]^{2-}$ = 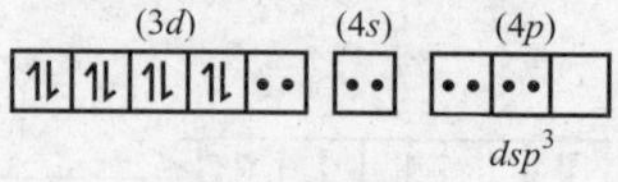

Hence, the structure of $\left[Ni(CN)_4\right]^{2-}$ is square planar and it is diamagnetic.

(d) In $[Ni(CO)_4]$, Ni has zero oxidation state. i.e.,

Ni = 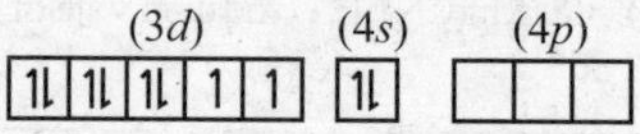

CO is a strong field ligand causes rearrangement and pairing of electrons of 3*d* and 4*s* orbital.

$[Ni(CO)_4]$ = 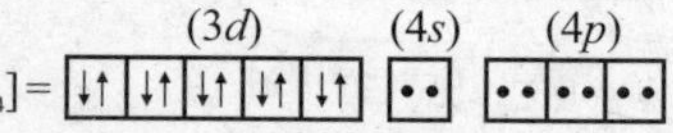

Structure of $Ni(CO_4)$ is tetrahedral with sp^3 hybridisation and it is diamagnetic.

Hence, (d) is the correct answer.

56. (c) Let oxidation state of Fe = *x*

For $Fe(CO)_5$, $x + (5 \times 0) = 0$

$\Rightarrow\ x = 0$

57. (b) Wilkinson's Catalyst : $RhCl(PPh_3)_3$

58. (b) Ruby is Al_2O_3 in which red colour is obtained when Cr^{3+} replaces Al^{3+} ions in octahedral sites. Emerald is $Be_3Al_2(SiO_3)_6$ in which green colour is obtained when Cr^{3+} replaces Al^{3+}.

59. (d) The atomic number of gadolinium is 64. Electronic configuration of Gd $[Xe]\ 4f^7 5d^1 6s^2$

6 Haloalkanes and Haloarenes

1. (a) Order of reactivity towards S_N2 reaction : 1° > 2° > 3° also more the steric hindrance, slower will be the rate.

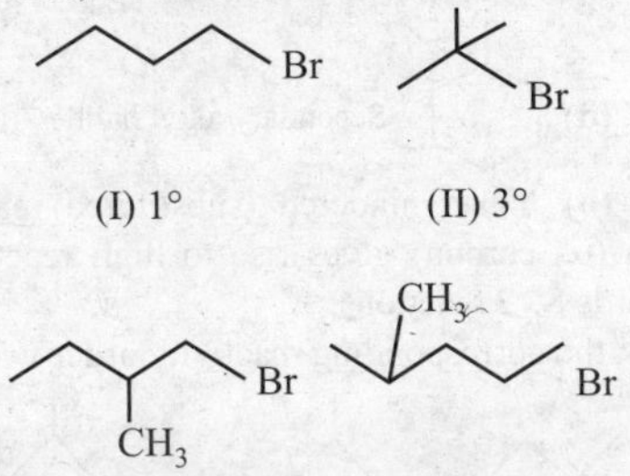

2. (c) $H-\underset{Cl}{\overset{CH_3}{C}}-CH_2-CH_2-CH_3$

(R)-2-chloropentane

2° alkyl halide but with less steric hindrance. S_N2 reaction is single step reaction. Inversion of configuration.

$CH_3-CH_2-\underset{Cl}{CH}-CH_2-CH_2-CH_3$

(R)-3-chloroheptane

3°/2° alkyl halide with more substitution S_N1 reaction.

3. (d) According to Zaitsev rule elimination occurs to form the most substituted and highly conjugated stable alkene.

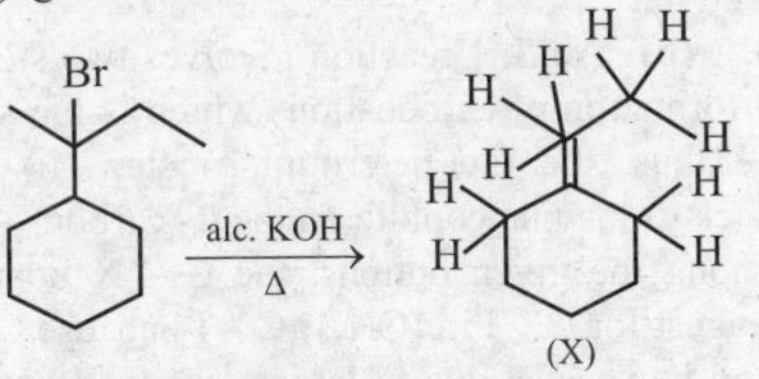

No. of α-hydrogen = 9

4. (a) I is 1-Bromo-1-phenyl propane

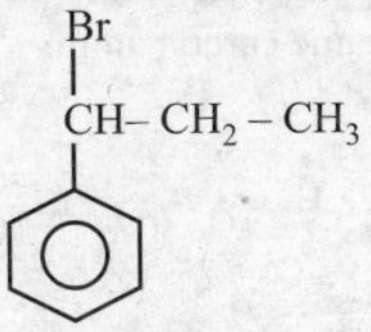

The bromine is attached to the carbon which is directly attached to benzene ring i.e., at benzylic positive. So I is benzylic halide.

II is 1-Bromo-3-nButyl-2-methyl benzene

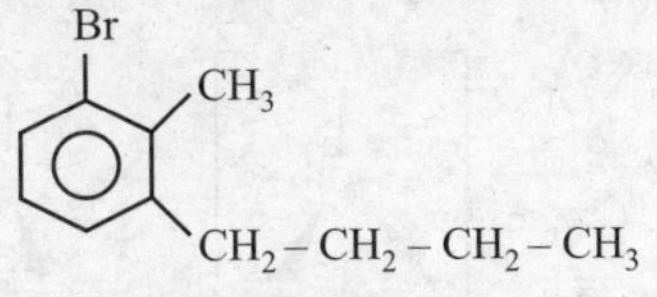

Bromine is directly attached to the benzene ring hence it is aryl halide.

5. (a) Isomer of C_4H_8 exhibiting cis-trans isomerism.

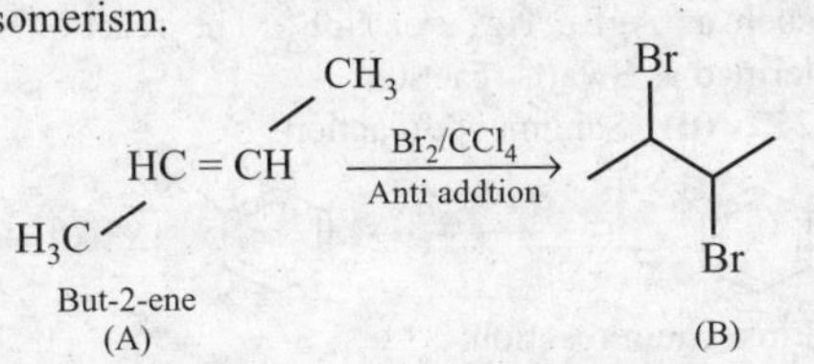

Isomer of C_4H_6 that forms sod. derivative with $NaNH_2$ that means it is a terminal alkyne.

$CH_3-CH_2-C\equiv CH \xrightarrow{NaNH_2}$ (But–1–yne) (C)

$CH_3-CH_2-C\equiv C^-Na^+$

$CH_3-CH_2-CH\equiv CH \xrightarrow[\text{Markovanikov addition}]{HBr}$

$CH_3-CH_2-\underset{Br}{\overset{Br}{C}}-CH_3$ or 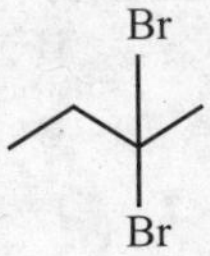

6. (c)

$\underset{(A)}{CH_3-CH_2-CH_2-CH_2-Br} \xrightarrow{Na/Dry\ ether} CH_3-CH_2-$

$CH_2-CH_2-CH_2-CH_2-CH_2-CH_3 \xrightarrow{\text{Photochemical chlorination}}$

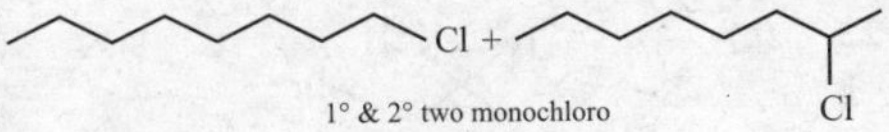

1° & 2° two monochloro product

7. (d)

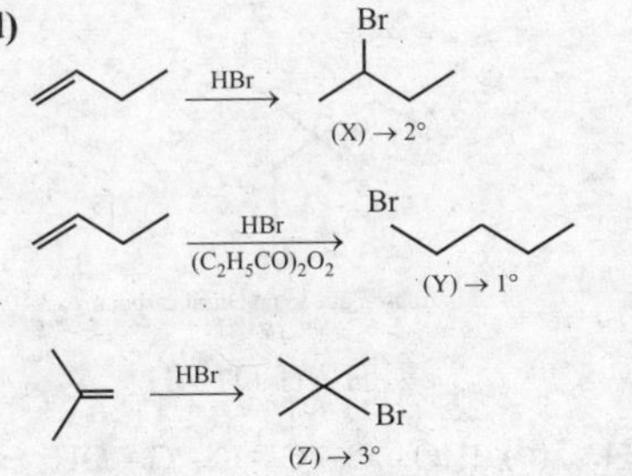

Reactivity towards S_N1: 3° > 2° > 1°

8. (a)

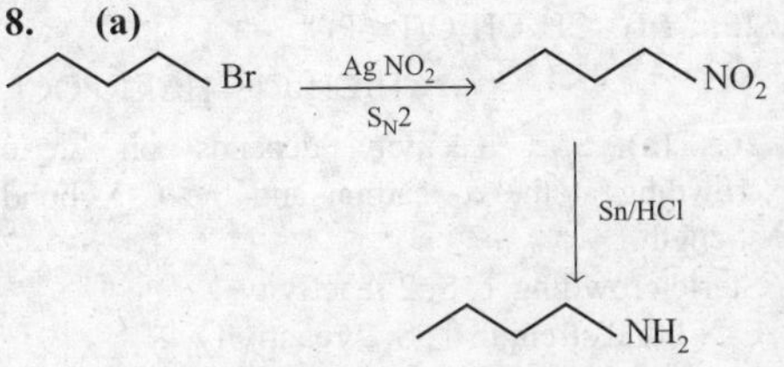

A : $AgNO_2$, B: 

9. (c)

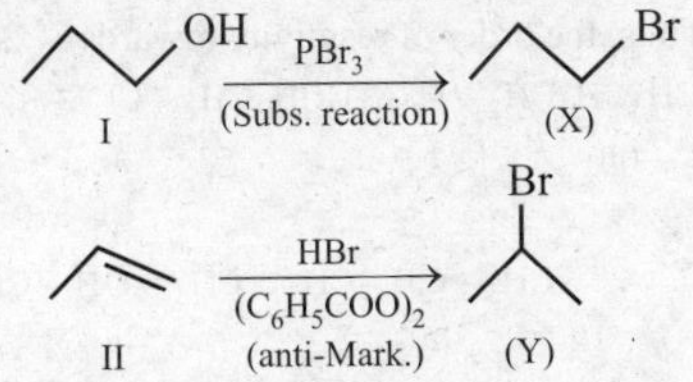

10. (d) S_N1 mechanism is based on stability of carbocation formed during the reaction. Hence, for ethyl chloride $CH_3CH_2^+$ carbocation *i.e.* primary carbocation is generated which is least reactive towards hydrolysis by S_N1 mechanism.

11. (d) $C_5H_{11}Br$ undergoes hydrolysis in two steps (S_N1 reactions) so it must be a 2° or 3° bromide.

X reacts with Mg to form Grignard reagent which then reacts with CO_2 in dry ether and further acidification gives a carboxylic acid.

$$R-Br \xrightarrow[ether]{Mg} R-MgX \xrightarrow{CO_2,\ H_3O^+} R-COOH$$

According to the given options, the *R*-part cannot be a secondary carbocation so it is a tertiary carbocation

Thus, $R = CH_3CH_2-\underset{CH_3}{\overset{\oplus}{C}}-CH_3$

thus, $X = CH_3-CH_2-\underset{CH_3}{\overset{Br}{C}}-CH_3$

Therefore :

$$CH_3CH_2-\underset{CH_3}{\overset{Br}{C}}-CH_3 \xrightarrow[ether]{Mg} \left(CH_3CH_2-\underset{CH_3}{\overset{MgBr}{C}}-CH_3\right) \xrightarrow{(i)\ CO_2,\ (ii)\ H_3O^+} \underset{(Y)}{CH_3CH_2-\underset{CH_3}{\overset{COOH}{C}}-CH_3}$$

12. (b)

Halide	Example
Vinyl (A)	1-Bromo-3-methylcyclohexene 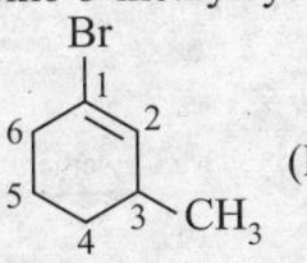 (III)
Allyl (B)	3-Bromo-4-methylcyclohexene 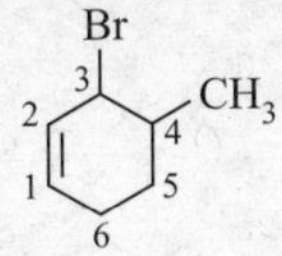 (IV)

Benzyl (C)	1-Bromo-1-phenylethane 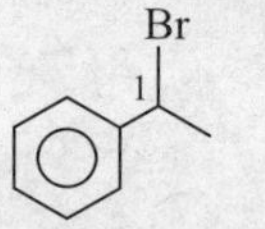 (I)
Aryl (D)	3-Bromotoluene 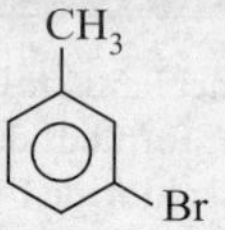 (II)

13. (a) The halogen group is attached to a sp^3 hybridised carbon atom, which in turn is attached to sp^2 hybridised carbon atom is said to be allylic halogen.

For example, $\overset{sp^3}{}CH_3 - CH = CH - \underset{sp^3}{CH_2} - Cl$

Allylic halide

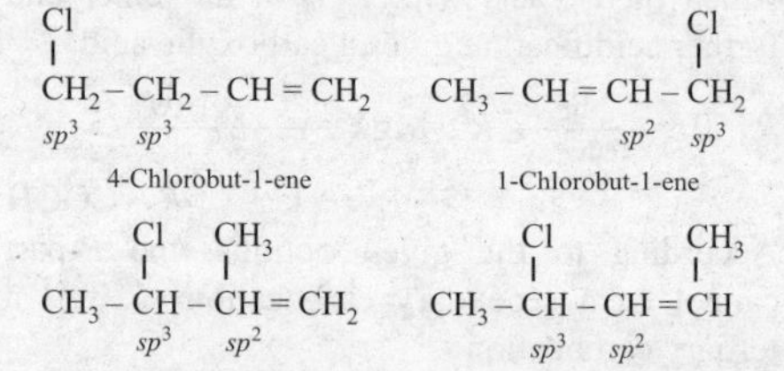

4-Chlorobut-1-ene; 1-Chlorobut-1-ene; 3-Chloro-2-methylbut-1-ene; 4-Chloropent-2-ene

14. (b) The Wurtz-Fittig reaction is the chemical reaction of an aryl halide, alkyl halide and sodium metal (in presence of dry ether) to give substituted aromatic compounds.

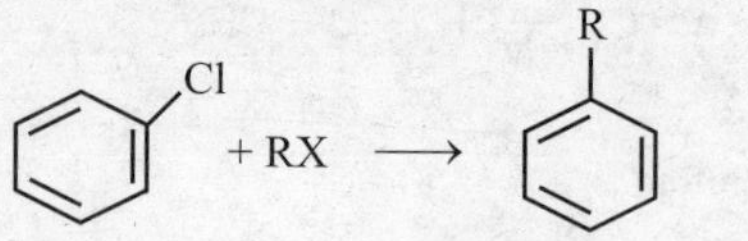

(Substituted benzene)

15. (b)

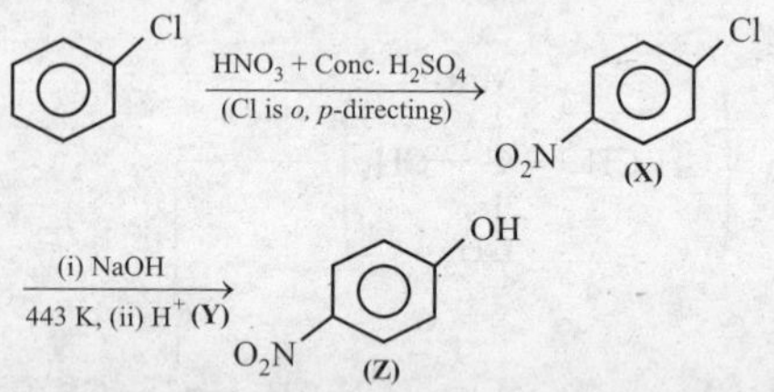

16. (d) First order kinetics of hydrolysis of $C_5H_{12}Br$ indicates the formation of a stable carbocation intermediate, i.e. $3°C_5H_{12}^+$, so X should be corresponding *ter*-bromide.

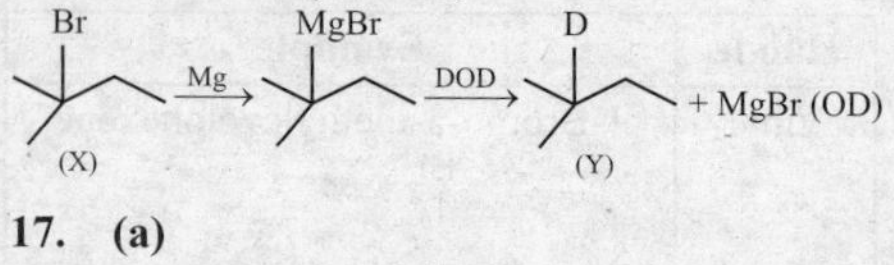

17. (a)

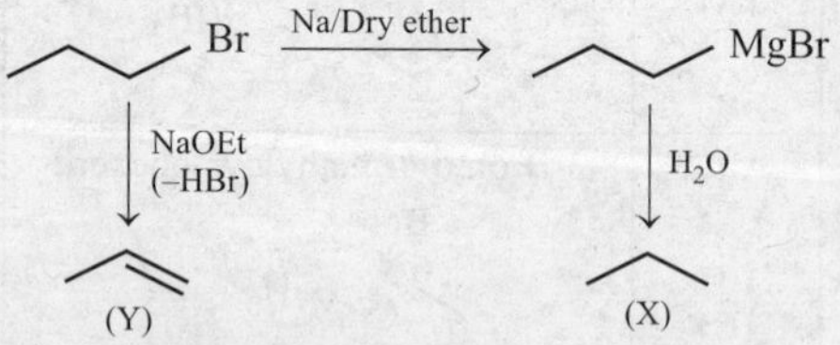

18. (d)

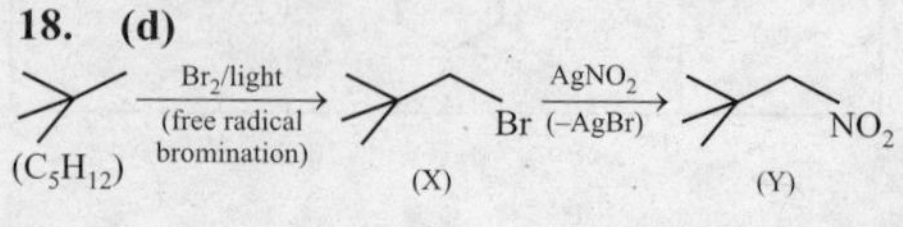

19. (b) anti-Markovnikov addition.

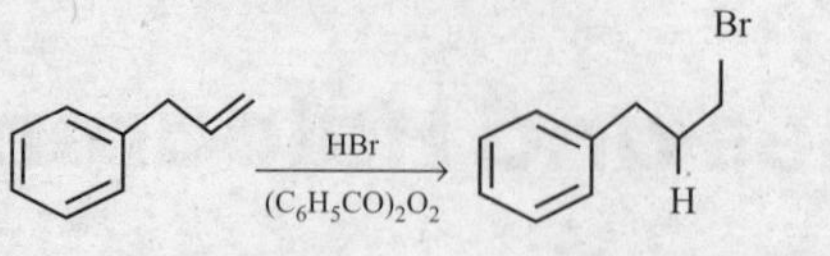

Primary alkyl halide

20. (d) The synthesis of alkyl flurorides is best accomplished by heating an alkyl chloride/ bromide in the presence of a metallic fluoride such as AgF_2, HgF_2 or SbF_3. The reaction is termed as Swarts reaction.

21. (d) Sandmeyer reaction

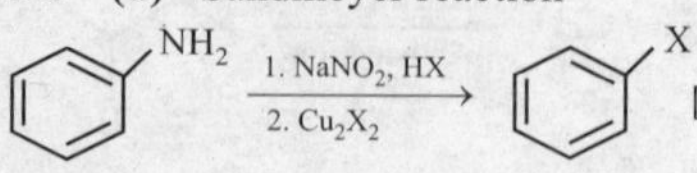

[X = Cl, Br]

Finkelstein reaction:

$R - X + NaI \longrightarrow R - I + NaX$

(X = Cl, Br)

Swarts reaction

$R - Br + AgF \longrightarrow RF + AgBr$

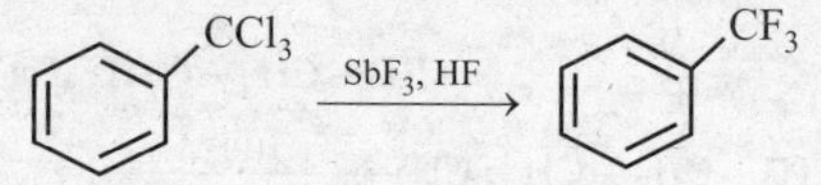

22. (b)

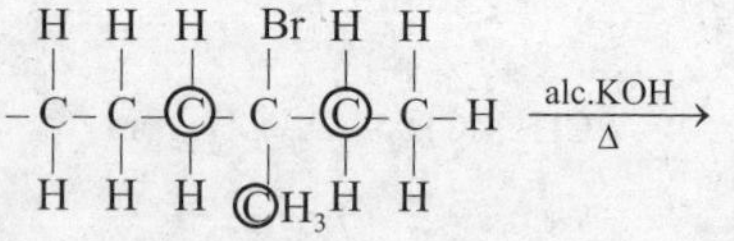

3 different alkenes obtained

3-Bromo-3- methylhexane

As there are three distinct β-hydrogens (on β-carbons), we can get three different alkenes.

23. (c)

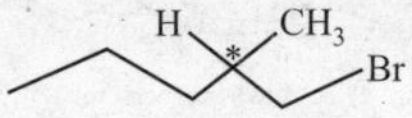

Chiral molecule (X)

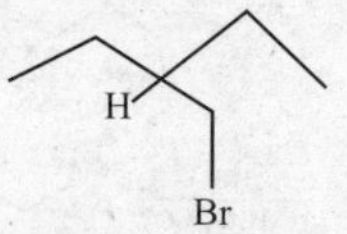

Achiral due to no chiral carbons (Y)

24. (d) $HO - \underset{H}{\overset{H}{C}} - \underset{Br}{\overset{H}{C^*}} - \underset{Br}{\overset{H}{C^*}} - \underset{H}{\overset{H}{C}} - OH$

25. (d) $CH_3CH_2OH + PCl_5 \rightarrow CH_3CH_2Cl + HCl + POCl_3$

26. (a) S_N2 reactivity depends on steric crowding at the α- carbon and the C-X bond strength.

Steric crowding ↑, S_N2 reactivity ↓

C-X bond strength ↑, S_N2 reactivity ↓

Remember the following order of bond length

H – I > H – Br > H – Cl

Thus, the order of reactivity towards S_N2 will be :-

$\underset{(III)}{CH_3CH_2CH_2 - I} > \underset{(I)}{CH_3CH_2CH_2 - Cl}$

$> \underset{(IV)}{CH_3 - \overset{I}{CH} - CH_3} > \underset{(II)}{CH_3 - \overset{Cl}{CH} - CH_3}$

27. (d)

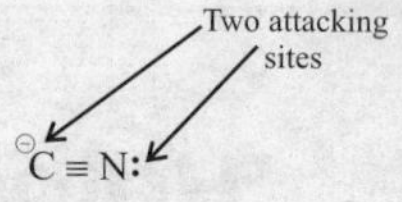

Cyanide ion

28. (a) $CH_2 = CH_2 \xrightarrow[\text{(electrophilic addition)}]{\text{(i) HBr(x)}} \overset{H}{CH_2} - \overset{Br}{CH_2}$

$\xrightarrow[\text{(Finkelstein reaction)}]{\text{(i) NaI/dry acetone (Y)}} CH_3 - \overset{I}{CH_2}$

29. (d) 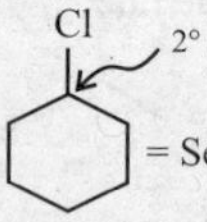 = Secondary alkyl halide

30. (b) Least hindered (substituted) carbon atom (α- carbon) gives rise to high reactivity towards S_N2 reactions.

Thus, the corresponding reactivity order will be:

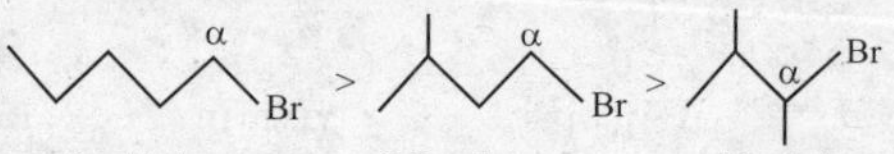

Least bulky (iii) > Bulky alkyl group (i) > Most bulky (ii)

31. (a) The elimination reaction (dehydrohalogenation) is favoured by those substrates that form a more stable carbocation intermediate.

Thus, the order of reactivity will be :-

$\underset{\substack{1° \text{ ethyl} \\ (A)}}{CH_3CH_2Br} < \underset{\substack{1° \text{ propyl} \\ (B)}}{CH_3CH_2CH_2Br} < \underset{\substack{2° \text{ halide} \\ (C)}}{CH_3\overset{Br}{C}H CH_3} < \underset{\substack{3° \text{halide} \\ (D)}}{(CH_3)_3C\,Br}$

32. (c) An S_N2 reaction involves a single-step concerted mechanism and the alkyl halide that is most hindered or substituted at the α-position will be least reactive.

Thus, 2-chloro-2-methyl propane will be least reactive.

33. (b) An S_N1 reaction involves two steps : (i) formation of carbocation (which is the slow and thus, the rate-determining) step (ii) and attack of the nucleophile on the α- carbon.

Among the given options, the C – X bond is weakest for C – I in $(CH_3)_3$ C – I because C – I bond is weakest due to largest size of I among C – X bonds.

34. (a) A geminal dihalide has two halogen atoms at the same carbon atom.

$H - \underset{Cl}{\overset{Cl}{C}} - \underset{H}{\overset{H}{C}} - \underset{H}{\overset{H}{C}} - H$

1, 1- Dichloropropane

35. (d) Grignard reagent = $R - \overset{\delta+\delta-}{Mg\,X}$

Thus, it is an organomagnesium compound.

36. (b)

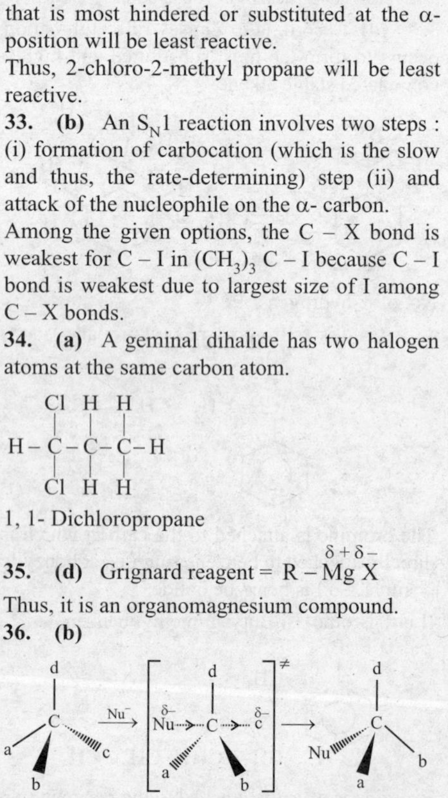

Penta-coordinated transition state

37. **(b)** $Br - CH_2 - CH_2 - CHO$
3- Bromopropanal is optically- inactive as there is no chiral centres.

38. **(a)** $2\,CH_3CH_2Br \xrightarrow{2Na/\text{dry ether}} CH_3CH_2CH_2\,CH_3 + 2NaBr$

This reaction is known as **Wurtz reaction**.

39. **(b)** Br attached to secondary carbon has less steric hindrance in order to occur S_N2 reaction.

40. **(d)**

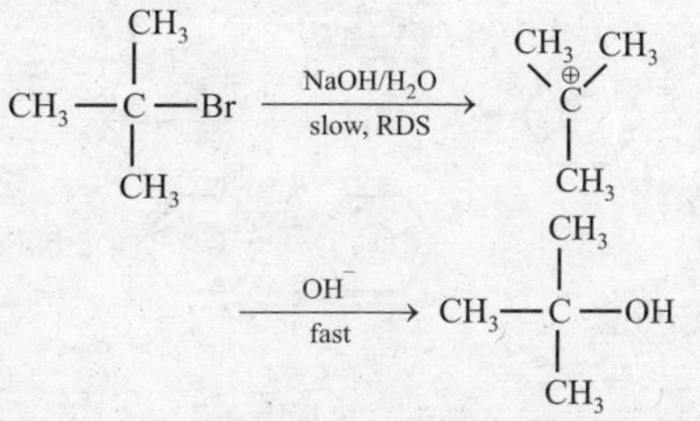

Note that rate determining step (RDS) involves only *t*-butyl bromide as reactant.

41. **(c)**

$CH_3 \left(CH_2\right)_5 Br \xrightarrow[S_N2]{\text{aq. NaOH}} CH_3 \left(CH_2\right)_5 OH$

42. **(a)**

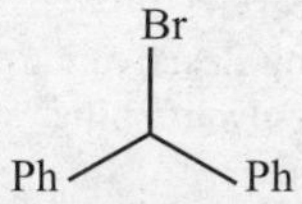

Forms the carbocation in S_N1 mechanism, which gets the stability by delocalization of positive charge through two benzene rings.

43. **(c)** AgCN is covalent in nature. Thats why haloalkane produces isocyanide compound with AgCN and cyanide compound with KCN.

44. **(b)** $I^{\ominus}$ is a good nucleophile than other halides.

45. **(b)** Higher the molecular or atomic size, stronger is the van der waal's interaction. Therefore, mass per unit volume increases.

46. **(d)** This reaction is an evidence of solvent effect on the mechanism of a reaction.

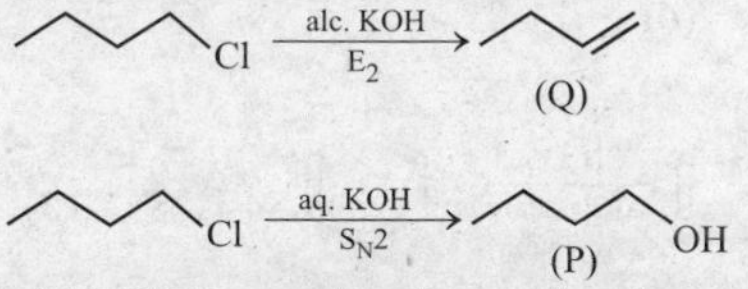

47. **(a)** C_5H_{12}, pentane has moleculars mass 48 g i.e. the isomer of pentane which yields single monochloro- derivative and two dichloro derivative is 2, 2-dimethyl, propane as it has all equivalent hydrogens.

The compound A is 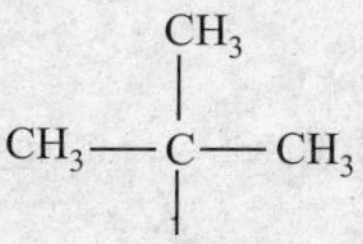

One mono chloro derivative is 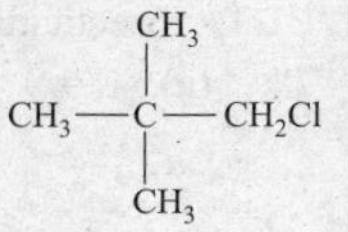

Two dichloro derivatives are

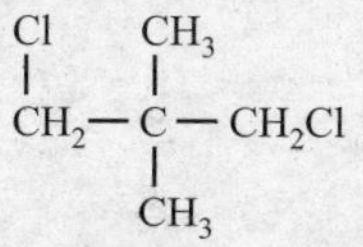 and 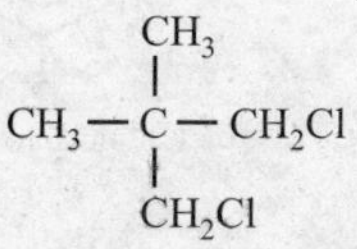

48. **(b)**

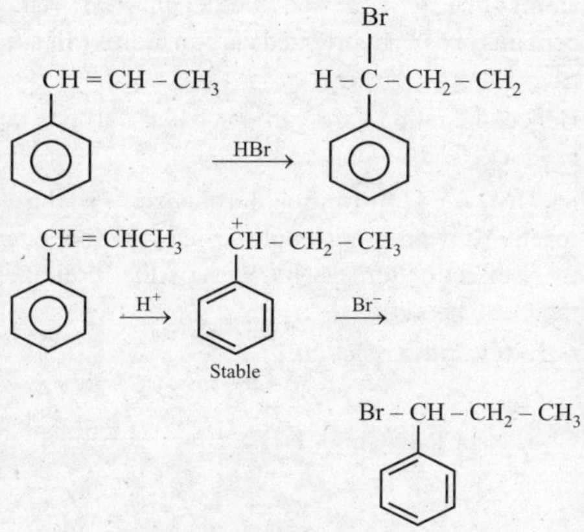

49. **(c)** 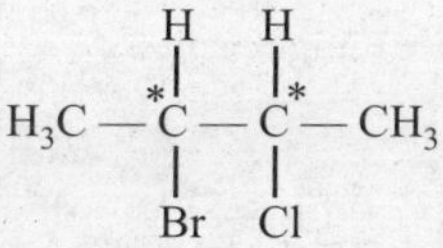

Number of optical isomers = $2^n = 2^2 = 4$

50. **(b)**

$$\underset{\text{1-chlorobutane}}{CH_3CH_2CH_2CH_2Cl} \xrightarrow[\text{(dehydrohalogenation)}]{\text{Alc. KOH}} \underset{\text{1-butene}}{CH_3CH_2CH = CH_2}$$

51. **(d)** Unimolecular nucleophilic substitution reaction (S_N1) proceeds throuth two steps. First step is formation of carbocation and the second step is the attack of the nucleophile OH^- to the carbocation.

Step 1: 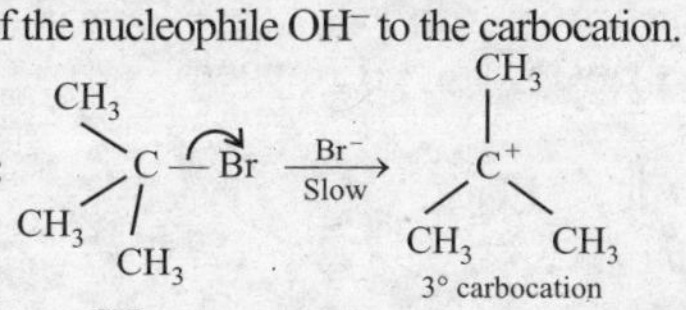

Step 2: 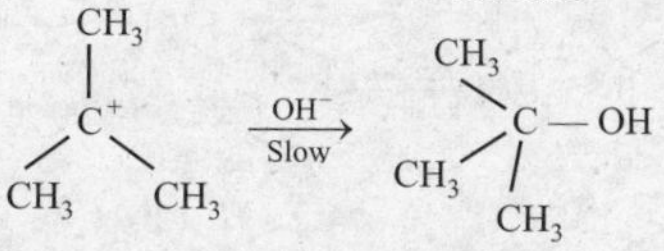

52. **(b)** Carbon free radical is sp^2 hybridised and is triangular planar. The given reaction is the chain termination step of a free radical reaction. Here, the trigonal planar free radical ($C_2H_5-\dot{C}H-CH_3$) gets attracked by Cl^- with equal ease of retention and inversion in configuration. So, the final product is the equimolar mixture of *d*- and *l*-forms (racemic mixture), which is optically inactive.

53. **(a)** Alkyl halides readily undergo nucleophilic substitution, viz. S_N2 and S_N1.

Here a stronger nucleophile, $\overset{\ominus}{Nu}$ substitutes a weaker nucleophile (leaving group: X^-) from an alkyl halide.

54. **(a)**

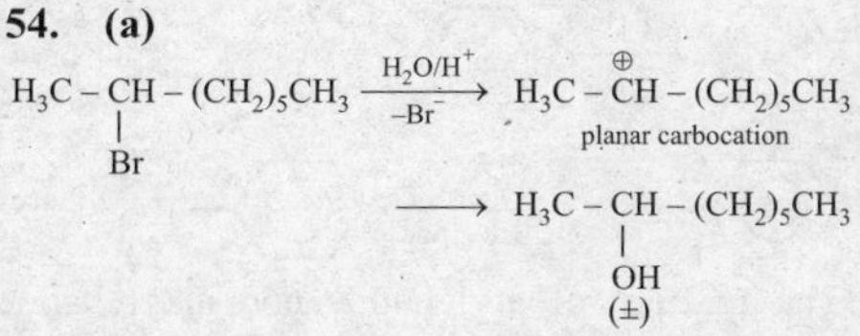

55. **(b)** 2-Bromobutane (2° haloalkane) reacts with KCN via S_N2 mechanism due to less steric hinderance and we get 2-methyl butane nitrile (X) with inversion in structure which on hydrolysis gives methylbutanoic acid (Y) having inverted structure to that of haloalkane.

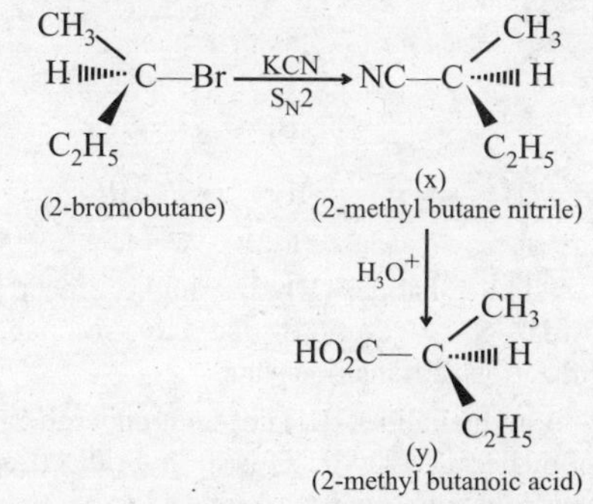

56. **(a)** Elimination of 2-bromopentane follow Saytzeff's rule and give pent-2-ene as major product. Some pent-1-ene also form according to Hofmann rule:

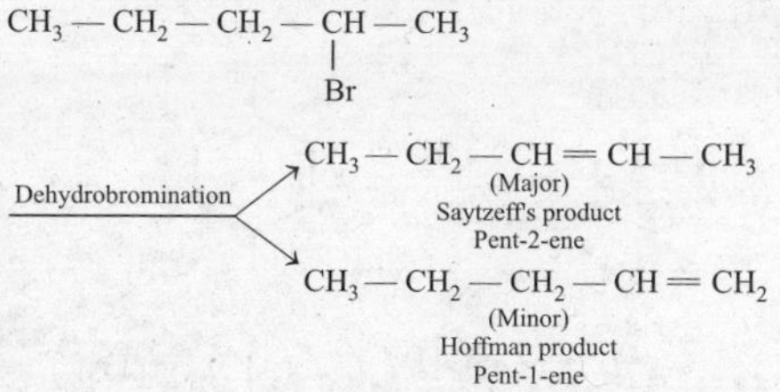

57. **(c)**

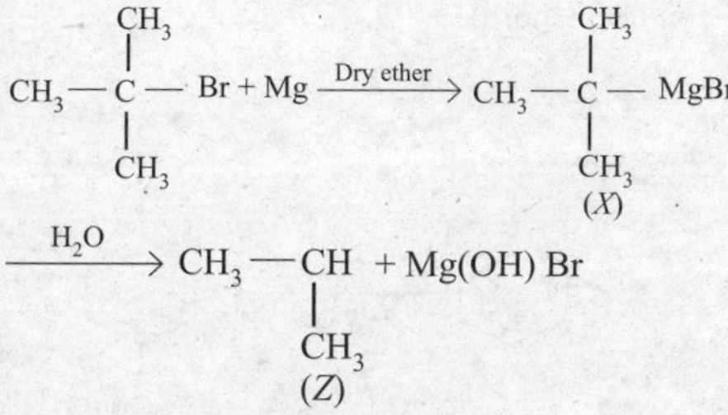

Z-Methylpropane

58. **(d)**

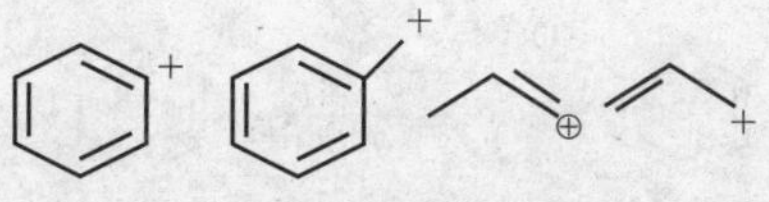

I II III IV

Compound II and IV are stabilized by resonance while I and III are not stable carbocation because they are on the sp^2 Hybridization.

II. 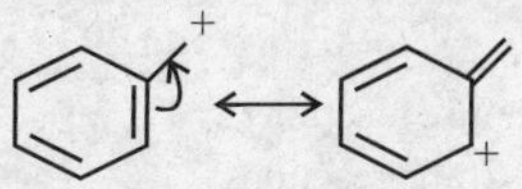

III. 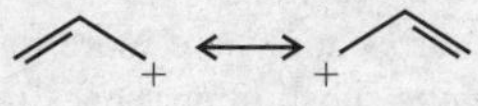

59. **(b)**

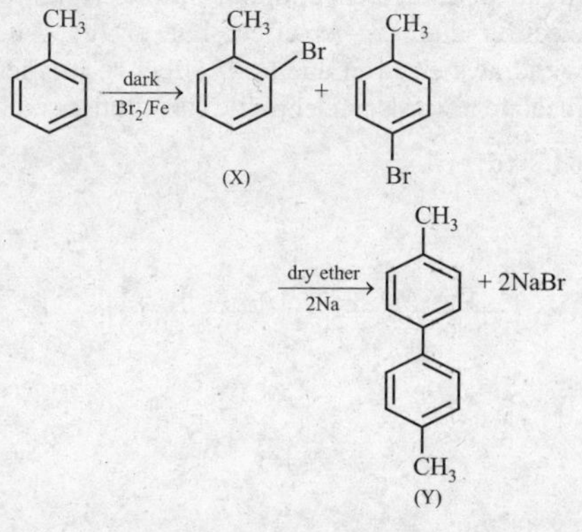

60. (c)

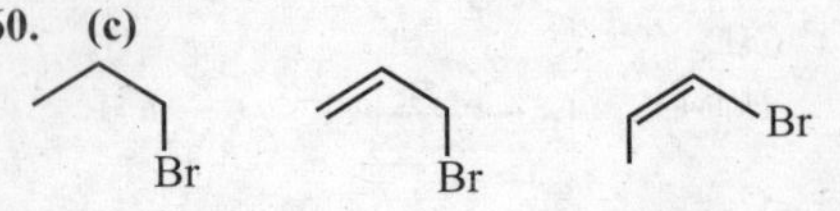

(I) (II) (III)

1° halide allylic halide Vimyl halide

- Allylic halide (II) are highly reactive towards S_N2 reaction due to resonance stabilization of transition state.
- Vinylic halides (III) does not undergo S_N2 reaction because vinylic 'C' is sp^2 hybridised and attack from backside is also hindered.

Reactivity order ⇒ Allylic > 1° halide > Vinyl-halide

⇒ II > I > III

61. (b)

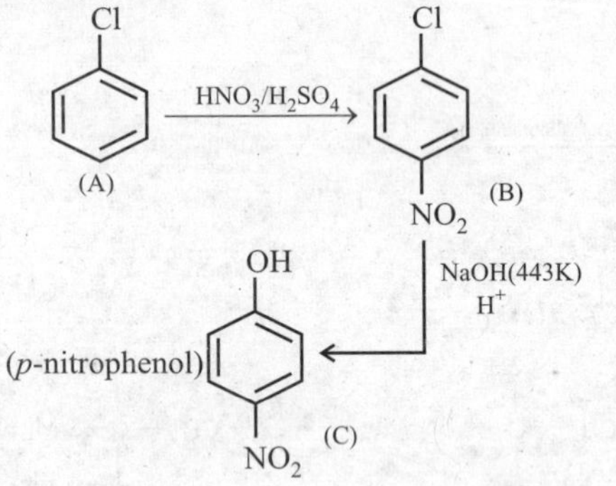

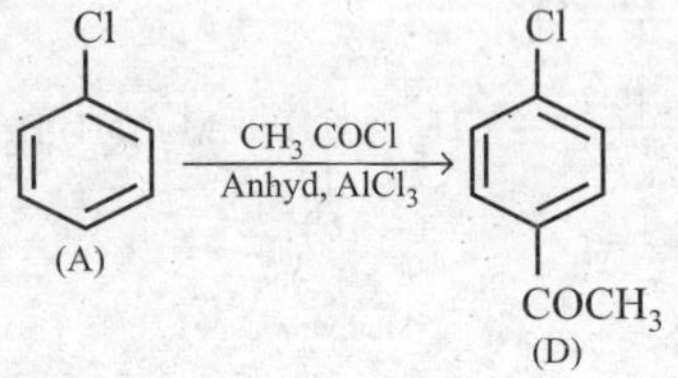

62. (b)

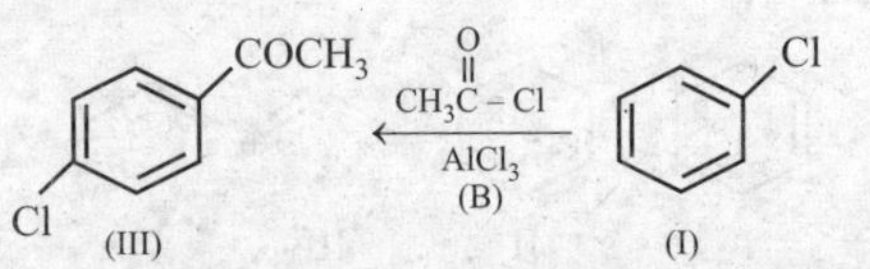

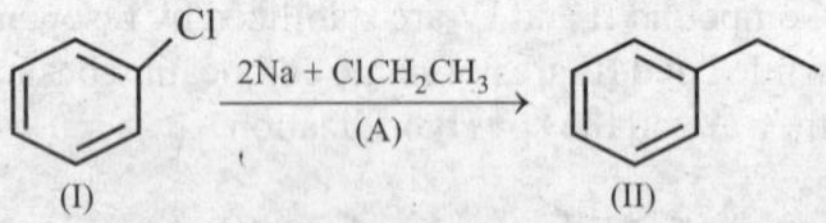

A ⇒ Wurtz – Fittig reaction

B ⇒ Friedel - Crafts reactions

63. (c) Stable carbocations are more reactive towards nucleophilic substitution, hence (a) and (d) are discarded. In option (b) $-NO_2$ withdraws electron due to $-M$ effect but in (c) $-NO_2$ withdraws electron due to $-I$ effect so it is less reactive towards nucleophilic substitution.

64. (d)

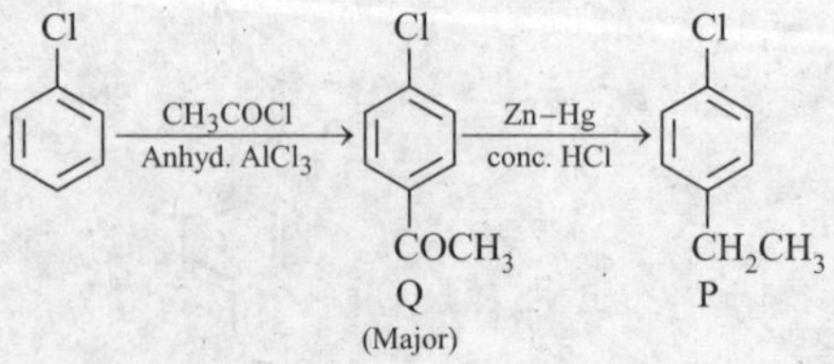

The product P contains $2sp^3$ hybridized carbon atoms (one in $-CH_2$ and another in $-CH_3$) and contains six sp^2 hybridized carbon atoms (all six ring carbons).

Hence, the ratio of sp^3 carbons to sp^2 carbons in product P is 2 : 6 or 1 : 3

65. (d) 2, 4, 6-trinitrochlorobenzene is most reactive towards nucleophilic substitution due to $-I$ effect of three $-NO_2$ groups that polarize the C – Cl bond.

66. (c) Fittig reaction

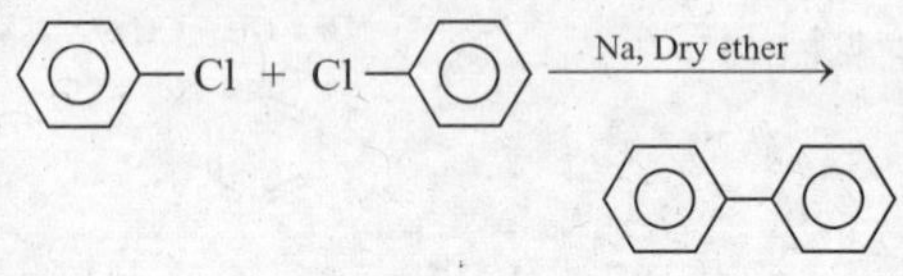

67. (c) Wurtz Fittig reaction

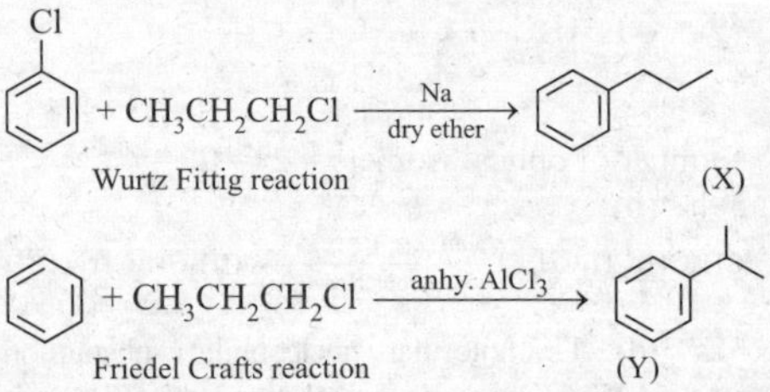

68. (c) Greater the stability of carbocation formed from *x, y* and *z*, greater will be their reactivity toward S_N1 reaction

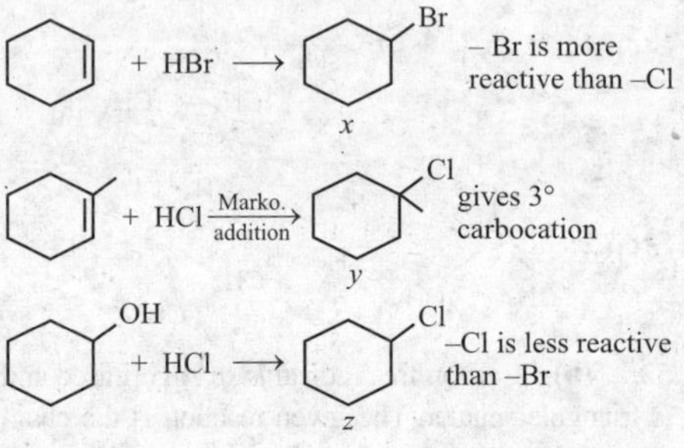

Hence the correct order of S_N1 reaction of *x, y* and *z* is *y* > *x* > *z*

69. (c)

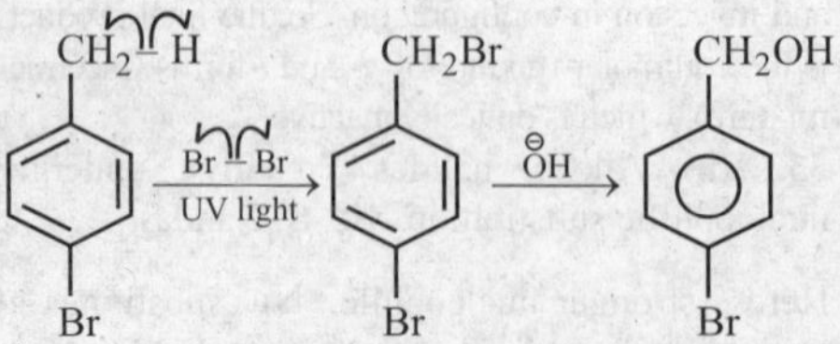

70. (c) $FeCl_3 + Cl_2 \longrightarrow FeCl_4^- + Cl^+$

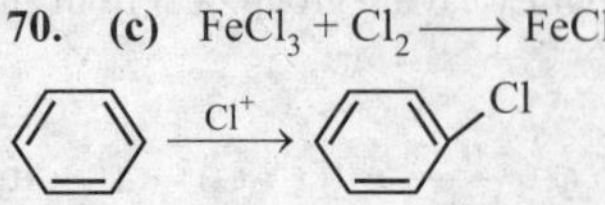

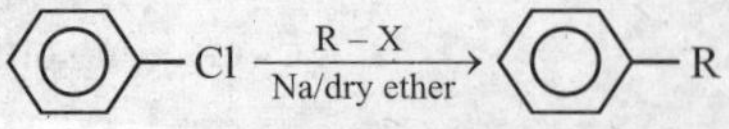

The reaction of aryl halide and alkyl halide in presence of sodium metal and dry ether is Wurtz-Fittig reaction.

71. (d) In the presence of heat, side chain halogenation occurs at the benzylic hydrogen.

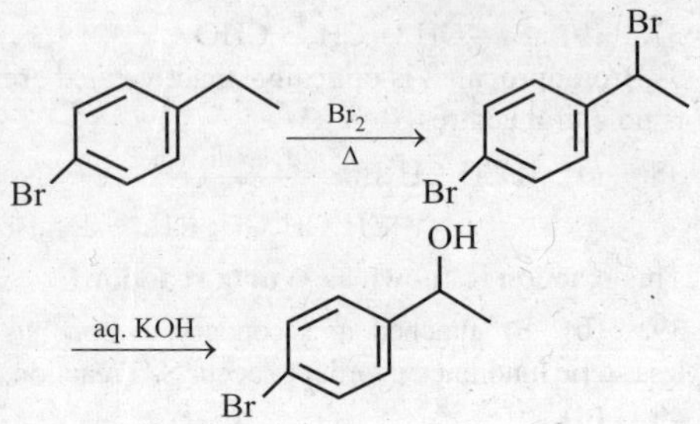

72. (a) Fittig reaction:-

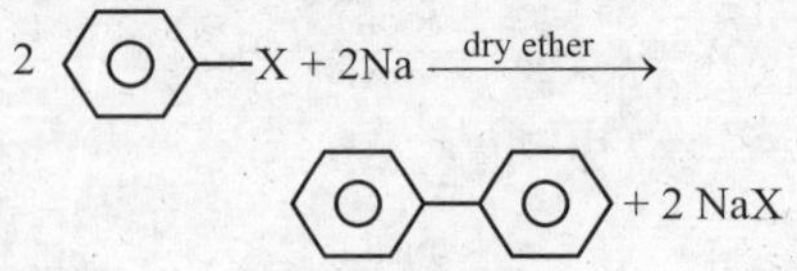

73. (a)

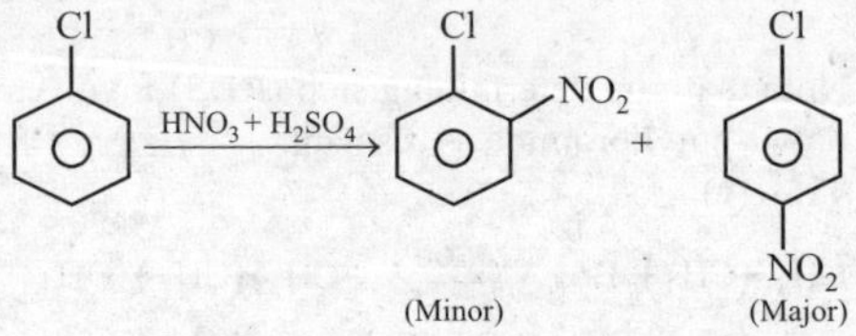

Thus, Statement I is correct.

Since – Cl is a ring-deactivating group, so it slows down the electrophilic substitution reactions like nitration.

Thus, Statement II is also correct.

74. (c)

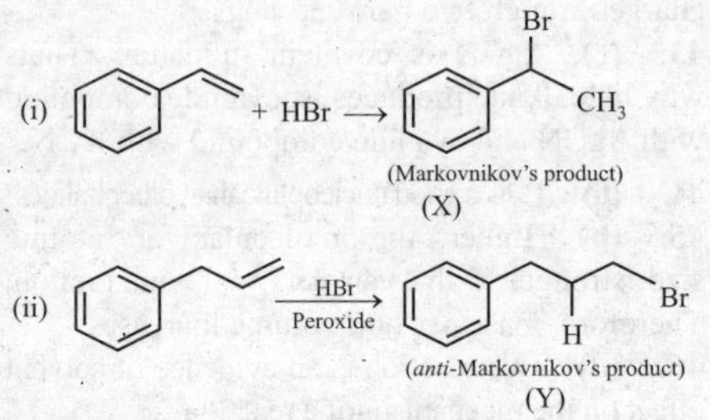

75. (d)

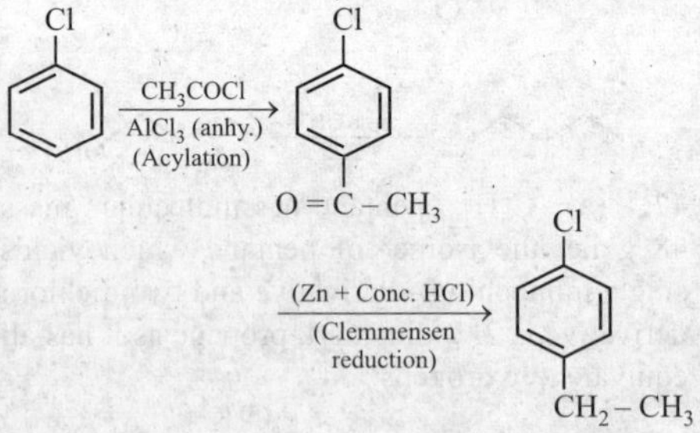

76. (a)

77. (c) $CHCl_3$ – used for production of freon-22

CCl_4- used for production of freon-12

DDT - Insecticide

78. (a) $\mu = 0$

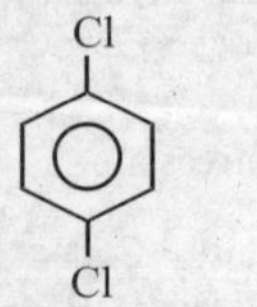

1,4-Dichlorobenzene

7 Alcohols, Phenols and Ethers

1. **(c)**

$CH_3-CH_2-CH_2-CH_2-OH \xrightarrow{Cu,\ 573K} CH_3-CH_2-CH_2-CHO$

$(CH_3)_2CH-CH_2OH \xrightarrow{Cu,\ 573K} (CH_3)_2CH-CHO$

$(CH_3)_3C-OH \xrightarrow[\text{elimination}]{Cu,\ 573K} (CH_3)_2-C{=}CH_2$ alkene (X)

$CH_3CH(OH)CH_2CH_3 \xrightarrow{Cu,\ 573K} CH_3-\overset{O}{\overset{||}{C}}-CH_2-CH_3$

2. **(b)** A-phenol is commonly known as carbolic acid

B-

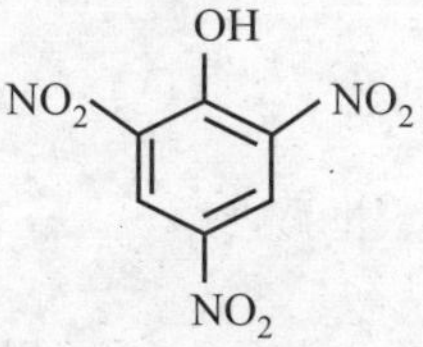

Picric acid

C-

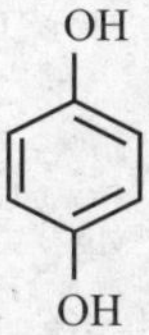

quinol

D-

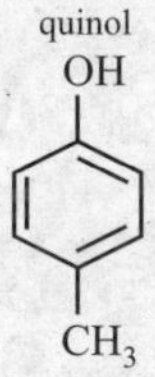

p-Cresol

3. **(a)**

$CHO-(CHOH)-CH_2OH \xrightarrow[\Delta]{HI} CH_3CH_2CH_2CH_2CH_2CH_3$ (n-hexane) (X) $\xrightarrow{V_2O_5,\ 773K,\ 10\text{-}20\ atm}$

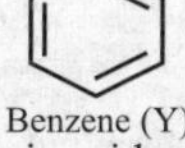

Benzene (Y)

No. of σ bonds in benzoic acid = 15

No. of π bonds in benzoic acid = 4

Ratio = 15 : 4

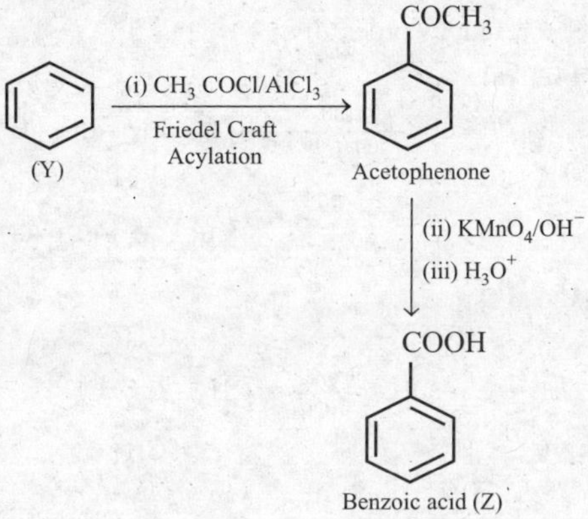

4. **(c)**

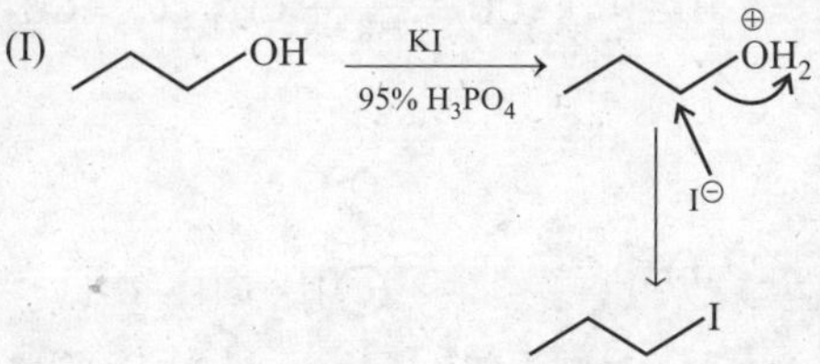

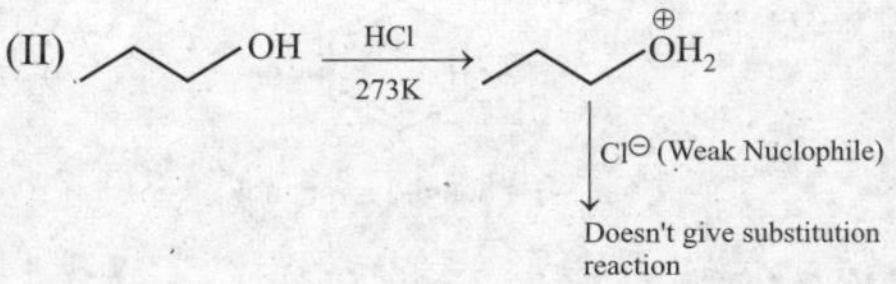

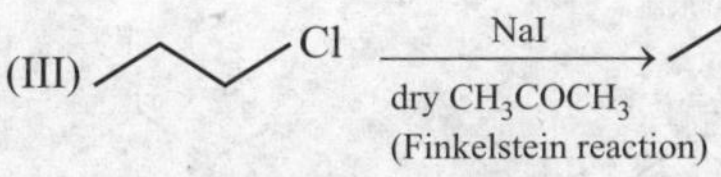

Hence, only I, III are feasible.

5. **(c)** Isobutyl alcohol : $(CH_3)_2CH-CH_2-OH$

(I)

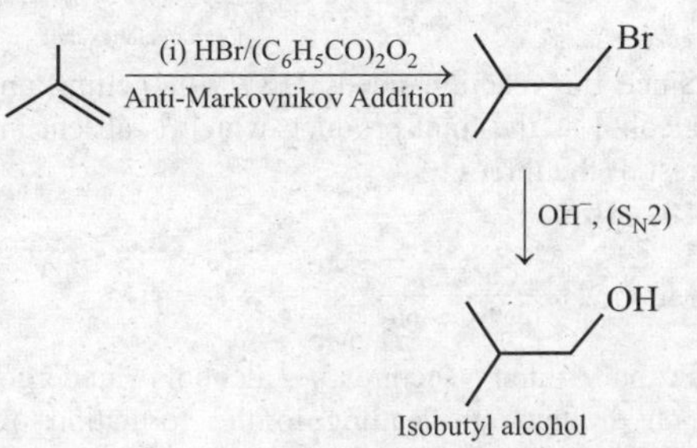

(II)

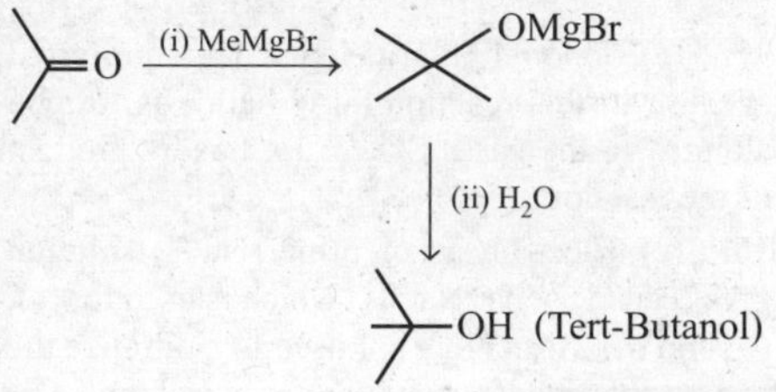

(III)

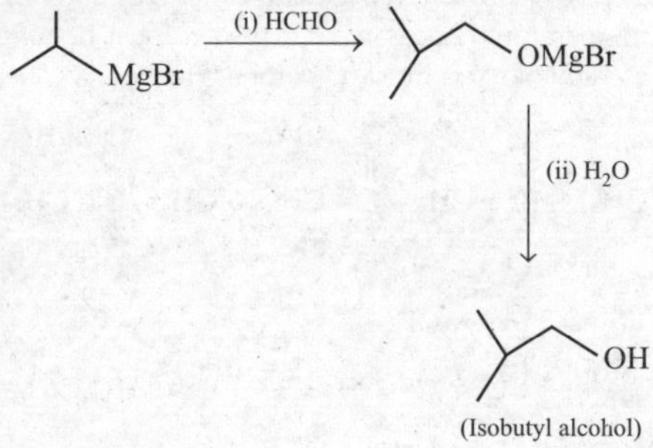

6. **(a)**

$CH_3-CH_2-\underset{CH_3}{\overset{OH}{C}}-CH_3 \xrightarrow{Cu/573K} CH_3CH=\underset{CH_3}{C}-CH_3$

(X) $C_5H_{12}O$ Alcohol; (Y) C_5H_{10} (Stable)

Preparation of X:

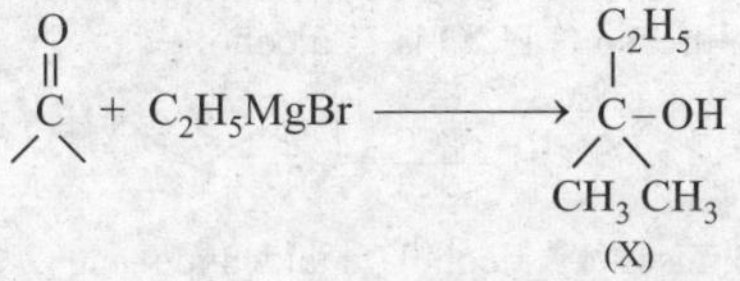

7. **(c)**

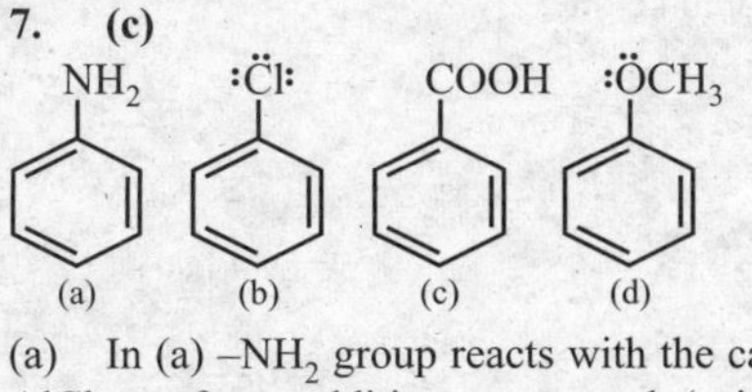

(a) In (a) $-NH_2$ group reacts with the catalyst $AlCl_3$ to form addition compound (acid-base reaction) and thus consumes all $AlCl_3$, hence Friedel-Craft reaction does not occur.

(b) – Cl is although *o*, *p*-directing due to lone pair of electrons on Cl (+ R effect) but deactivated due to – I effect of – Cl, hence methylation does not occur effectively.

(c) – COOH group deactivates the benzene ring due to – R effect.

(d) – OCH_3 group activates the benzene ring due to + R effect (lone pair of electrons on O), hence methylation takes place easily.

8. (b)

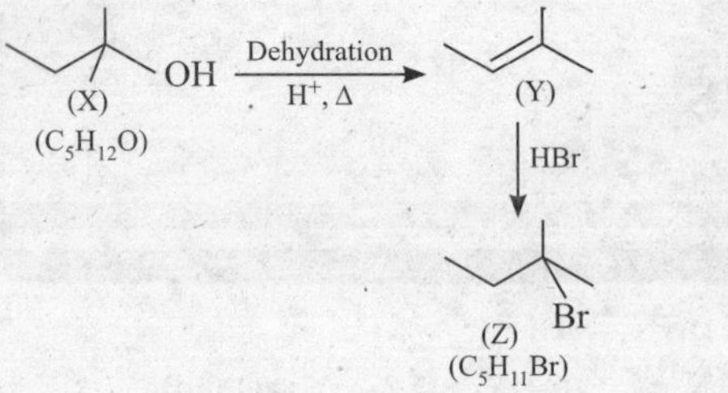

9. (c) Thionyl chloride ($SOCl_2$) is preferred because in this reaction alkyl halide is formed along with the gases SO_2 & HCl as by-product of the reaction.

10. (c) Electrolysis of brine (NaCl) solution gives caustic soda (NaOH) which is used for (a), (b) and (d). Antichlors are used to neutralize the excess chlorine left behind after bleaching.

11. (b) Since Z reacts with conc. HCl at room temperature (Lucas reagent), so it must be *ter*-alcohol, so Y is must be ketone. Hence

$$\overset{\delta^-}{CH_3}\overset{\delta^+}{MgBr} + CH_3-\overset{O^-}{\overset{\|}{\underset{\delta^+}{C}}}-CH_3 \rightarrow CH_3-\overset{OMgBr}{\overset{|}{\underset{CH_3}{\underset{|}{C}}}}-CH_3$$
(X) (Y)

$$\xrightarrow{H_3O^+} CH_3-\overset{OH}{\overset{|}{\underset{CH_3}{\underset{|}{C}}}}-CH_3 \xrightarrow{\text{Conc. HCl}} \underset{\text{Turbidity}}{(CH_3)_3CCl\downarrow}$$
(Z)

12. (a) Lucas test generally used to distinguish 1°, 2° and 3° alcohols.

$$\underset{(1°, 2° \text{and} 3°)}{R-OH} \xrightarrow[ZnCl_2]{\text{Conc. HCl}} \underset{(\text{turbidity})}{R-Cl}$$

1° alcohol does not give any turbidity at room temperature, so $C_4H_{10}O$ is 1° alcohol.

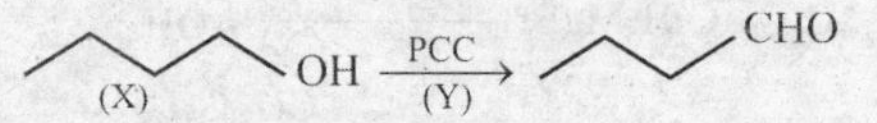

PCC oxidises 1° alcohol to aldehyde and 2° alcohol to ketone.

13. (c)

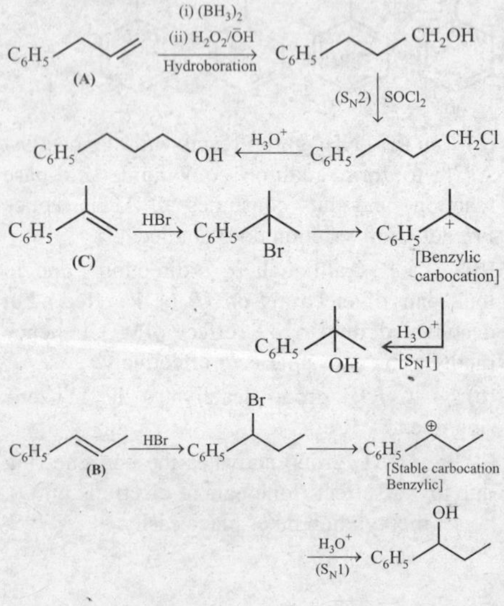

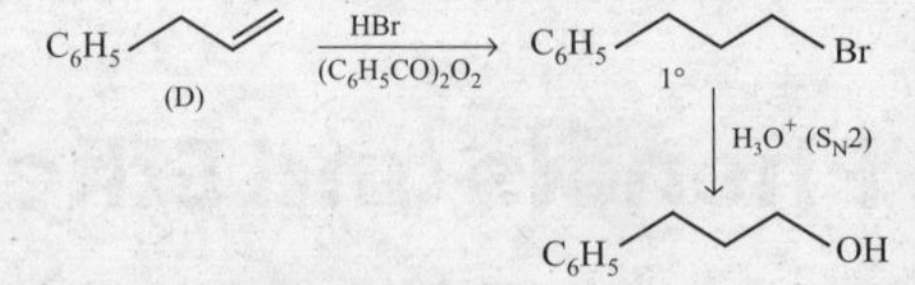

So only B and C formed stable benzylic carbocation, so it will undergo hydrolysis by S_N1 mechanism.

S_N1 reactivity order : benzylic > 3° > 2° > 1° > 0°

S_N2 reactivity order : 0° > 1° > 2° > 3°

14. (a)

$$CH_3-CH=CH_2 \xrightarrow[(ii)\ H_2O_2/\ OH]{(i)\ (BH_3)_2} CH_3-CH_2-CH_2-OH \xrightarrow{HCl,\ ZnCl_2} \underset{\text{1-Chloropropane}}{CH_3-CH_2-CH_2-Cl}$$

15. (b)

$$\underset{(X)}{CH_3-\overset{CH_3}{\overset{|}{\underset{CH_3}{\underset{|}{C}}}}-OH} \xrightarrow[HCl]{\text{Conc.}} \underset{(Y)}{CH_3-\overset{CH_3}{\overset{|}{\underset{CH_3}{\underset{|}{C}}}}-Cl}$$

$$\underset{(X)}{CH_3-\overset{CH_3}{\overset{|}{\underset{CH_3}{\underset{|}{C}}}}-OH} \xrightarrow[573K]{Cu} \underset{(Z)}{CH_3-\overset{CH_3}{\overset{|}{C}}=CH_2}$$

16. (b)

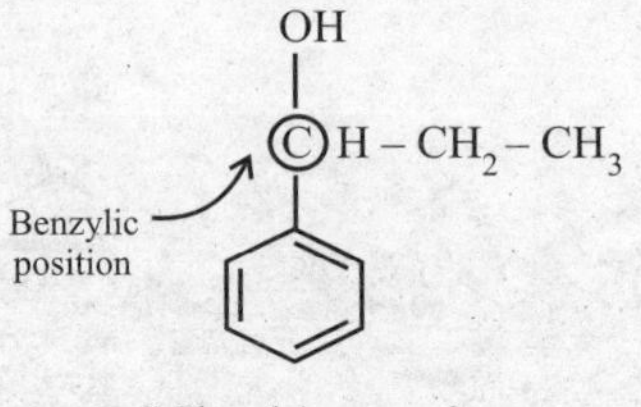

1-Phenyl-1-propanol

17. (a)

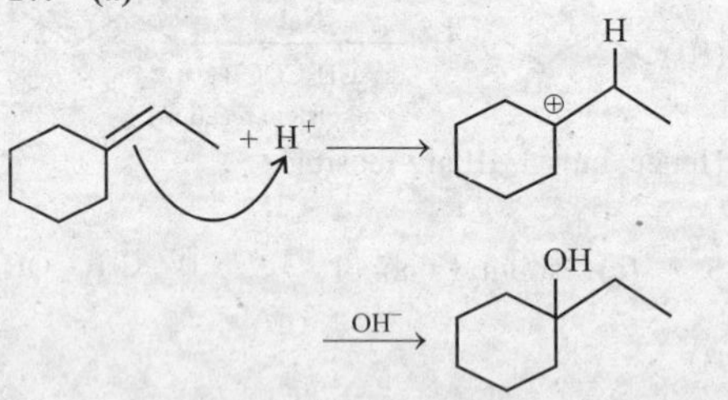

1-Ethyl cyclohexanol

Since the reaction needs H_3O^+ for getting an alcohol as the final product, which is absent in rest of the three.

18. (b)

$$Me_3COH \xrightarrow[(\text{dehydration})]{Cu,\ 573K} \overset{Me}{\underset{Me}{>}}C=CH_2$$

Primary and secondary alcohols undergo dehydrogenation leading to the formation of aldehyde and ketone, respectively.

19. (d)

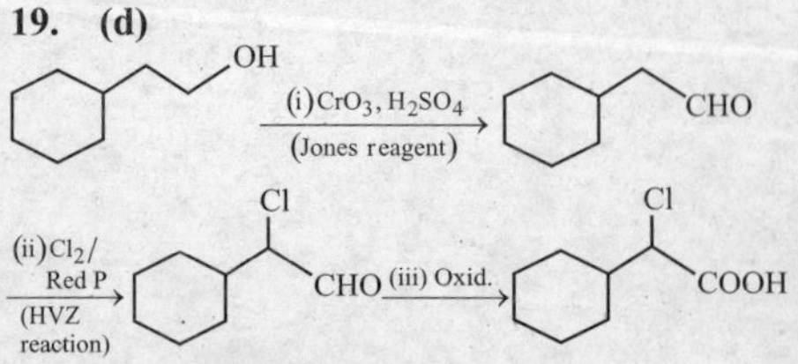

20. (c)

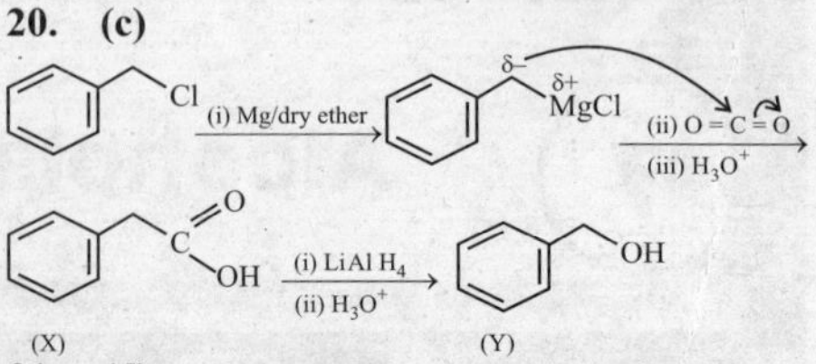

21. (d)

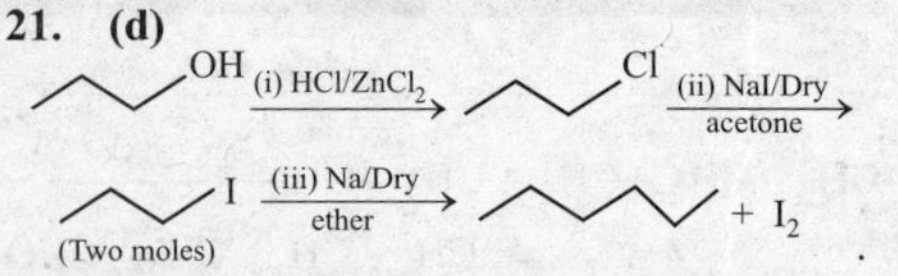

22. (d)

23. (a) The bond angle between C – O and O – H bonds in alcohols is close to 109°. (i.e. 109°28')

24. (a) A–(III), B–(IV), C–(II), D–(I)

(A) Anhydrous $ZnCl_2$ + conc HCl is known as Lucas reagent and used to distinguish between primary, secondary, tertiary alcohols.

(B) Zn–Hg/HCl is called Clemmensen reagent. This reagent is used in conversion of carbonyl into alkane i.e., Clemmensen reaction.

(C) Tollen's reagent $[Ag(NH_3)_2]^+$ used as oxidising reagent to distinguish between aldehyde and ketones.

(D) Stephen reagent ($SnCl_2$ + HCl) is used in reduction of nitrogen compounds.

25. (b)

(*i*)

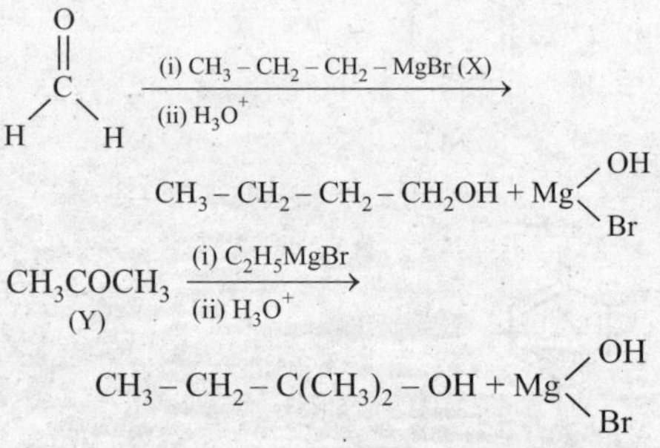

26. (b) $C_2H_6OH + 4\,I_2 + 3\,Na_2CO_3 \longrightarrow \underset{\text{Triiodomethane}}{CHI_3} + \underset{\text{Sodium formate}}{HCOONa} + 5\,NaI + 3\,CO_2 + 2\,H_2O$

27. (c) Cumene

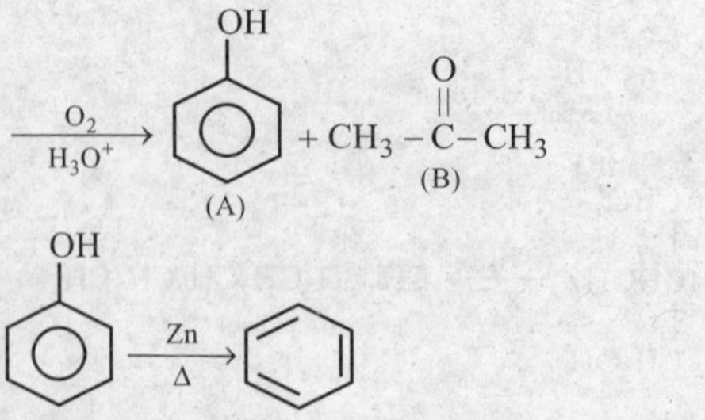

$$CH_3\overset{O}{\overset{\|}{C}}-CH_3 \xrightarrow[HCl]{Zn\ /\ Hg} CH_3CH_2CH_3$$

28. (b) Acidity $\propto \dfrac{1}{pK_a}$

Electron withdrawing group increases the acidity of the compound so *p* nitrophenol is more acidic than phenol and electron donating group decreases the acidity of the compound. So *p*-cresol is less acidic than phenol.

pK_a
(A) *p*-Nitrophenol = 7.1 (II)
(B) Phenol = 8.3 (V)
(C) Ethanol = 15.9 (I)
(D) *p*-Cresol = 10.0 (III)

29. (b)

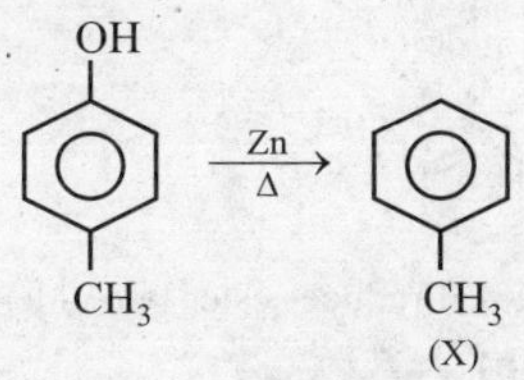

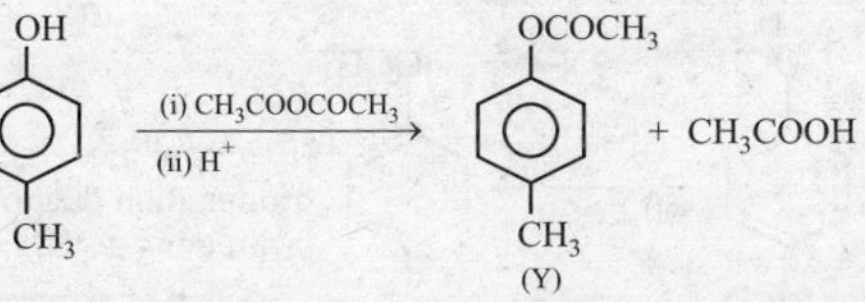

30. (a) Methane is not responsible for O_3 layer depletion because the main substances responsible for O_3 layer depletion are CFCs (chlorofluorocarbons) and other halogenated substances.

31. (a) Novolac is formed by the monomer of o-hydroxy- methyl-phenol *i.e.*,

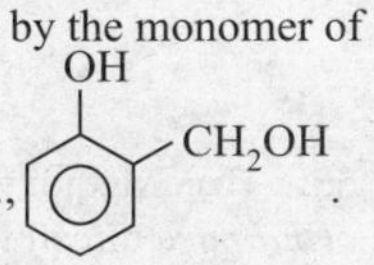

32. (d)

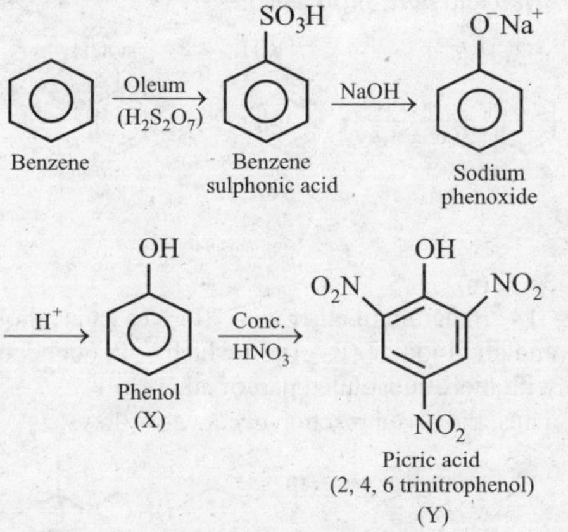

33. (a)

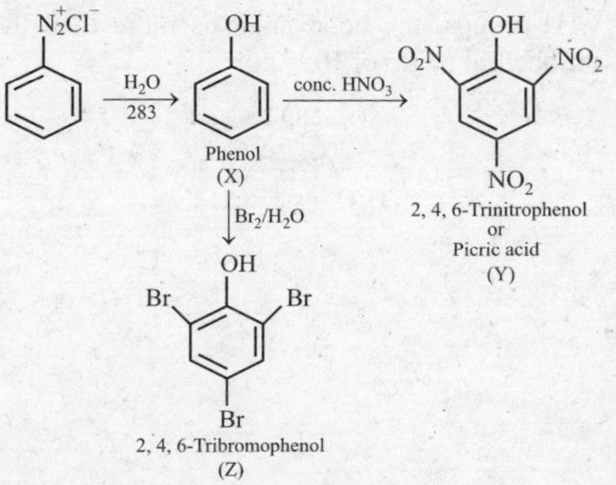

34. (a)

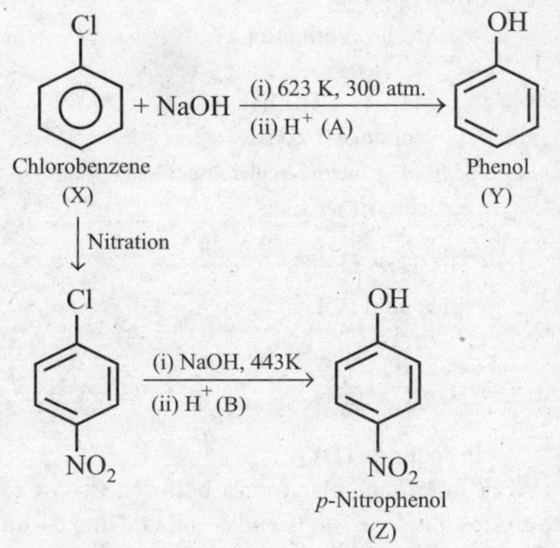

35. (c)

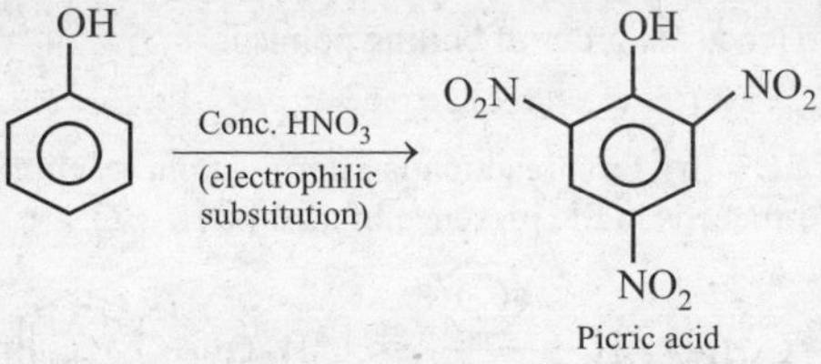

36. (b)

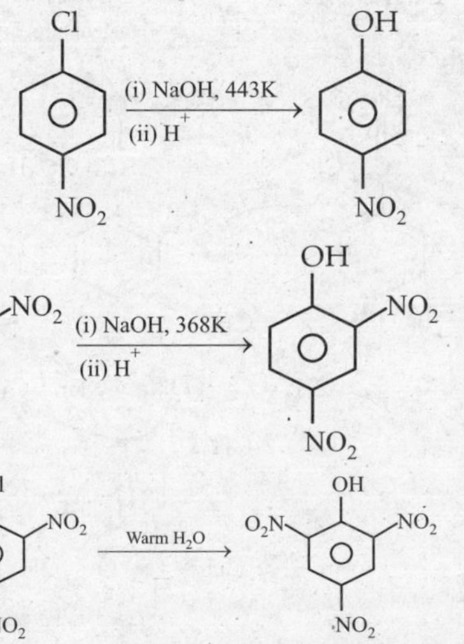

The reactivity of chlorobenzene increases with more $-NO_2$ groups and thus, nucleophilic substitution requires milder conditions.

37. (a)

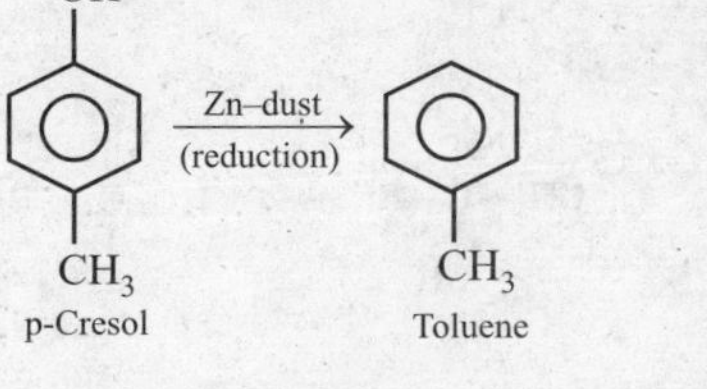

38. (d)

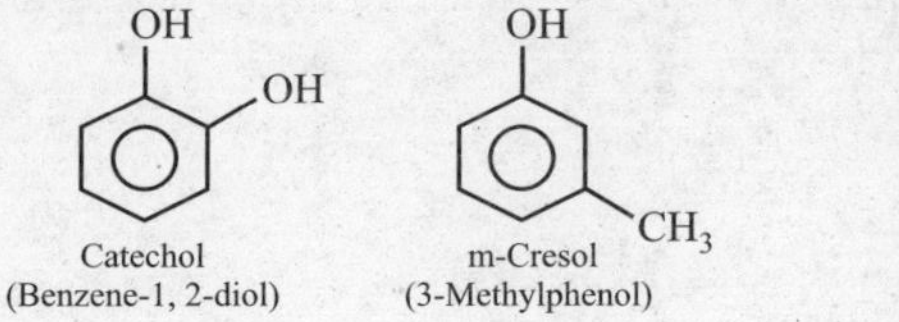

39. (b) Greater pK_a value means smaller K_a or weaker acid. Due to the presence of an electron-withdrawing $-NO_2$ group at the meta position, 3- nitrophenol is the weakest acid among the given options.
The effect of $-NO_2$ is nullified at the meta position.

40. (a)

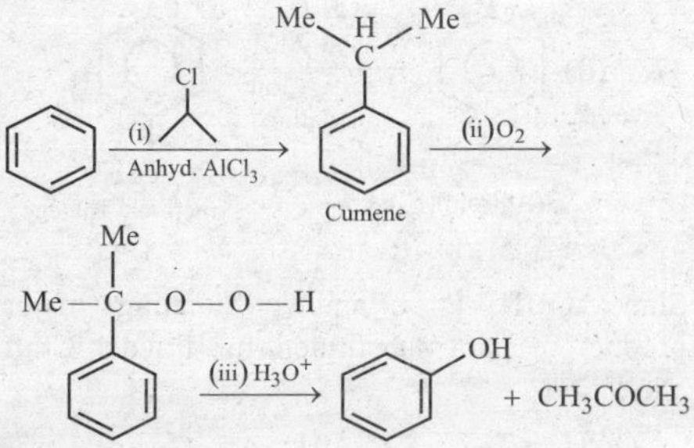

41. (d)

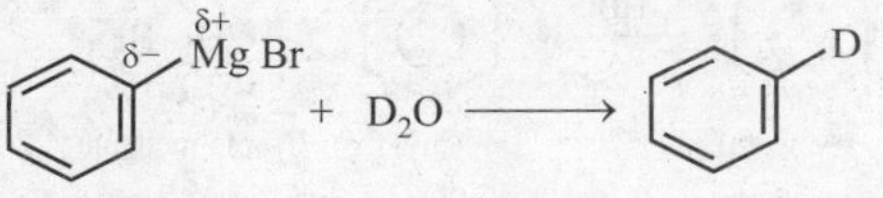

42. (b)

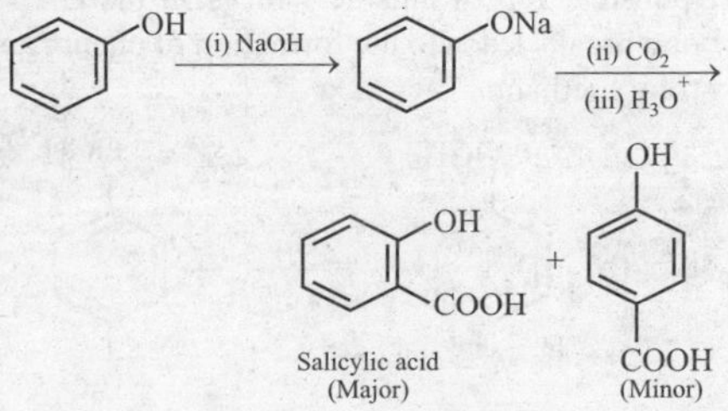

43. (d)

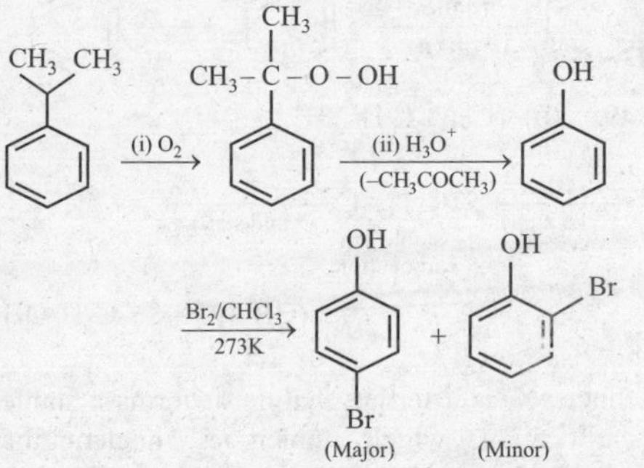

44. (a)

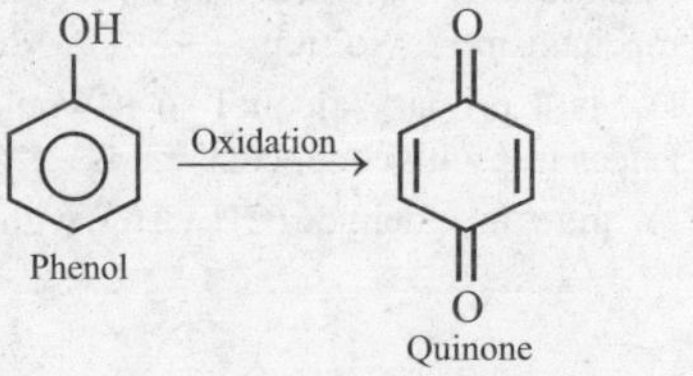

45. (b)

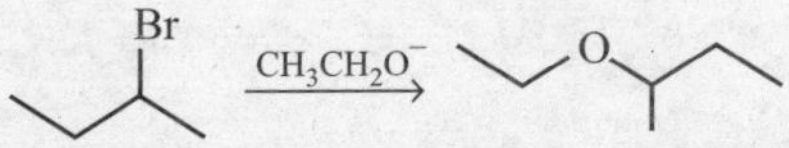

$CH_3CH_2O^-$ is small base but less stable than $(CH_3)_3CO^-$. So it performs nucleophilic substitution reaction instead of elimination reaction.

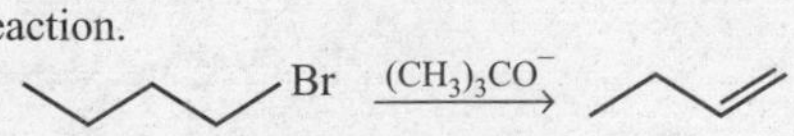

46. (d) $C_6H_5Br + CH_3ONa \xrightarrow{\times} C_6H_5OCH_3 + NaBH$

Aryl halides do not undergo nucleophilic substitution reaction because of partial double bond character between C-Br Bond.

47. (d) 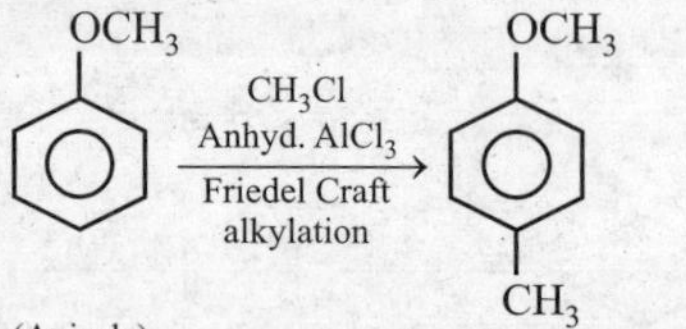

(Anisole) P-methoxy Toluene (X)

Since $-OCH_3$ is -o and -p directing, major product in para substituted for Friedel Craft alkylation.

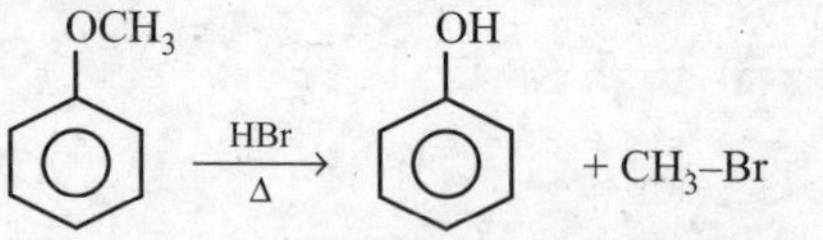

(Anisole) Phenyl (Y) Bromo methane (Z)

Upon reaction of anisole with HBr, the O-CH_3 bond breaks leads to the formation of phenol and bromomethane.

48. (b) 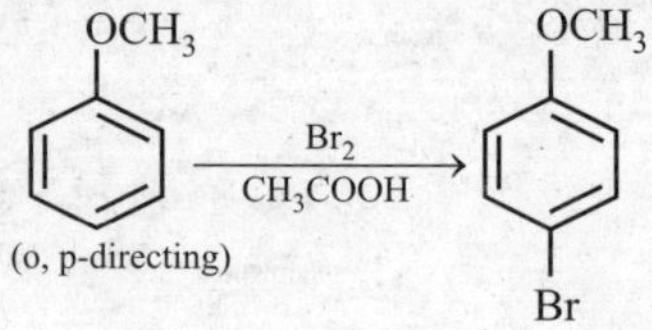

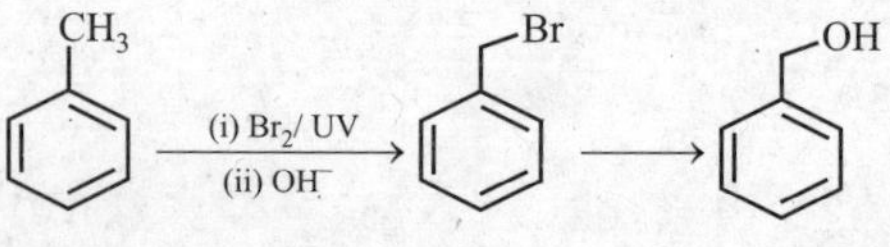

49. (b) $(CH_3)_3C{\cdot}OC_2H_5$

$\xrightarrow[\text{(1st step)}]{HI/} (CH_3)_3C^{+}$ (stable 3° carbocation) $\xrightarrow[\text{(2nd step)}]{I^-}$

$(CH_3)_3C-I + C_2H_5OH$
(X) (Y)

Since 'X' is a tertiary halide, it forms a stable carbocation which undergoes nucleophilic substitution (hydrolysis) through S_N1 mechanism in two steps.

'Y' is a primary alcohol so it would not give Lucas test with conc. HCl

'Y' gives an aldehyde (CH_3CHO) with Cu/573 K.

50. (a) $CH_3CH_2-O-CH_3$
Methoxyethane **(A)**
(No intermolecular forces operate)
$CH_3CH_2CH_2OH$
Propanol-1 **(B)**
(Strong intermolecular association operates)

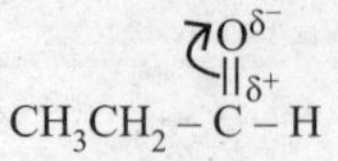

Propanal **(C)**

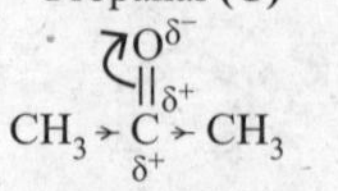

Propanone **(D)**

(Weak intermolecular forces between two –CO –groups due to δ^+ on C and δ^- on O. Note δ^+ on C of ketone is lower than that of aldehyde due to decreases δ^+ on C).

Hence the order of boiling points is

$B > C > D > A$

51. (b) First reaction is esterification, reaction proceeds in the presence of acid i.e H^+ (X).

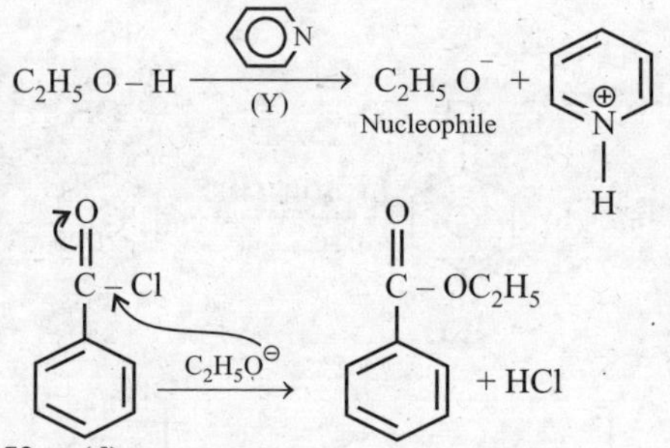

52. (d)

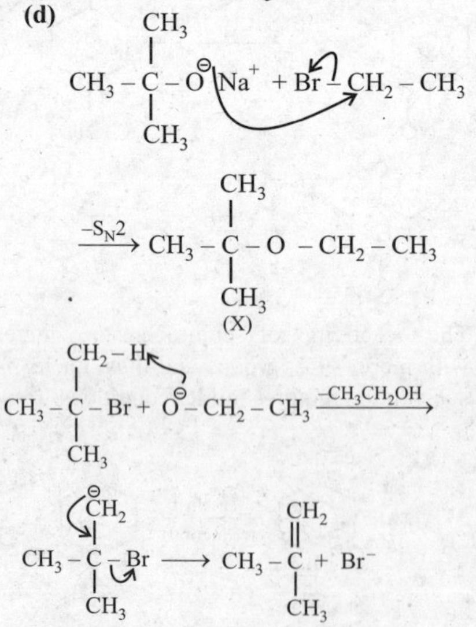

53. (c)

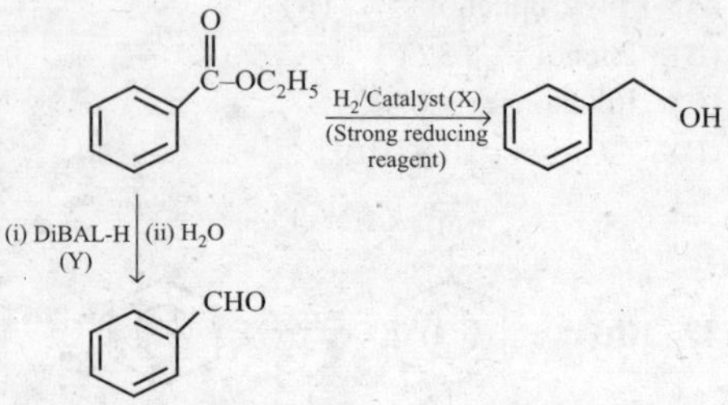

DiBAl – H reduces ester into aldehyde

54. (b)

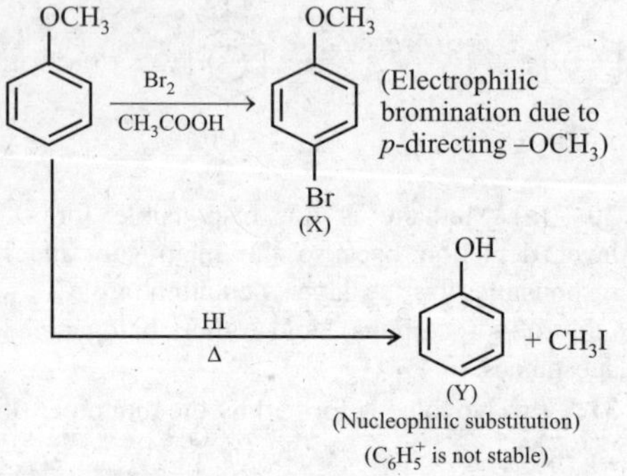

55. (b) Methoxy group is activating and *ortho-para* directing group. Hence with mixture of conc. HNO_3 and conc. H_2SO_4, anisole gives *ortho* and *para*-nitro anisoles.

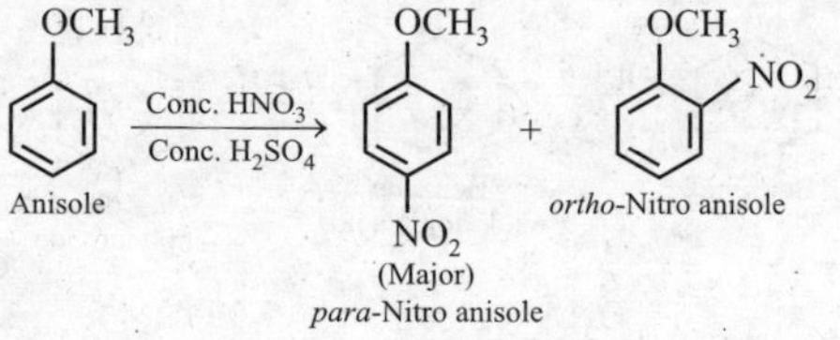

56. (a)

(i) Reaction of ether with HI gives an alcohol and alkyl iodide (R—I), in which —I is bonded with more substituted part of ether.

Thus, the given reaction occurs as follows:

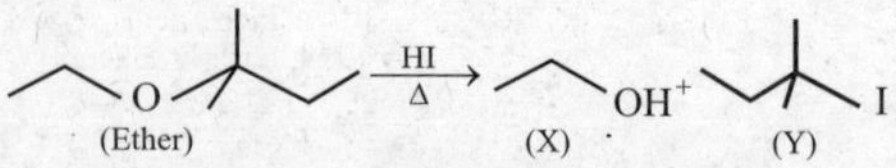

57. (a) Due to repulsion between two –CH_3 groups, the bond angle is more than the tetrahedral angle of 109°28′.

8 Aldehydes, Ketones and Carboxylic Acids

1. (b)

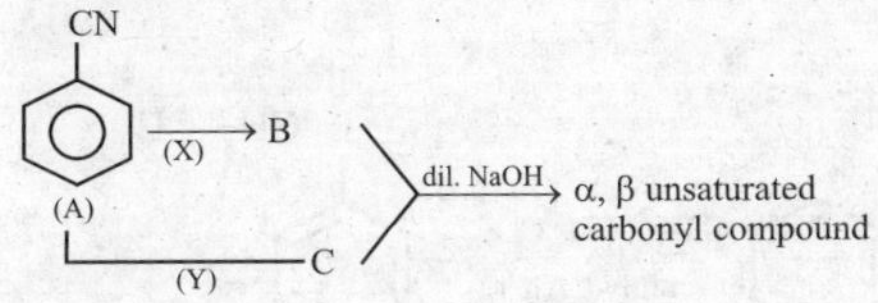

B and C must be aldehyde and ketone, so (X) can be ($SnCl_2$ + HCl)

A on reaction with X gives benzal aldehyde

B = 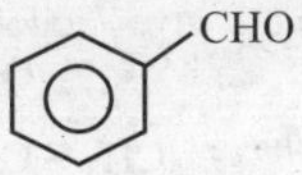

Y can be CH_3MgBr which reacting with (A) gives acetophenone

C = 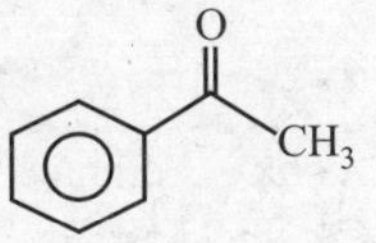

2. (a)

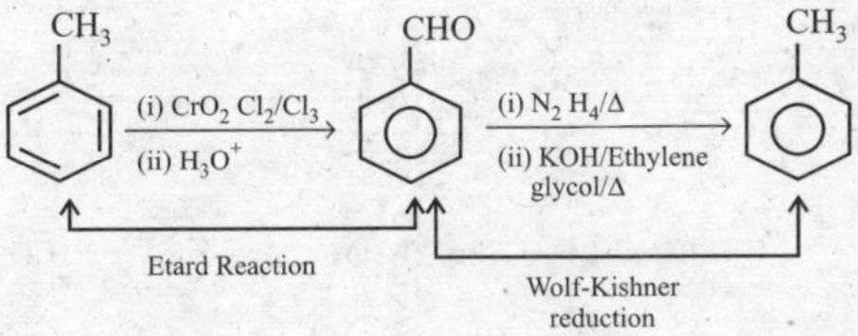

3. (c)

$$CH_3-CH=CH_2 \xrightarrow{H_2O|H^{\oplus}} \underset{\text{Propan-2-ol}}{CH_3-\overset{OH}{\overset{|}{C}H}-CH_3} \xrightarrow[573K]{Ag}$$

$$CH_3-\overset{O}{\overset{||}{C}}-CH_3$$

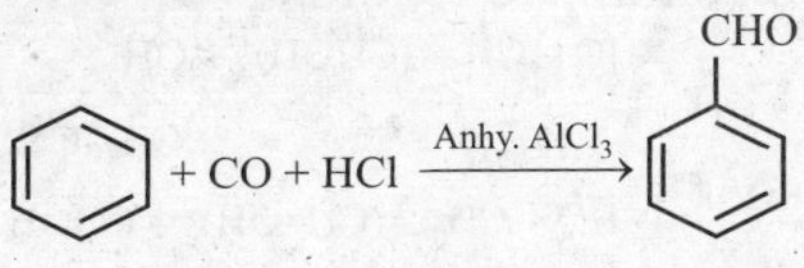

4. (d) $C_6H_{14} \xrightarrow{V_2O_5,\ \Delta}$

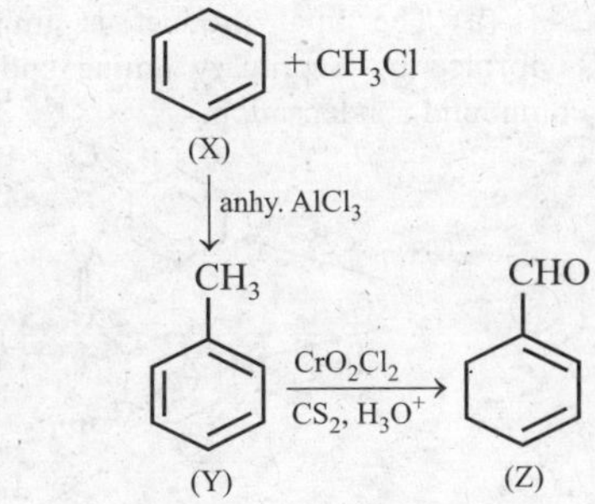

5. (b) (A) 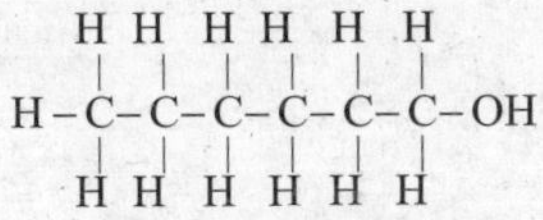

Hexan – 1 – ol

$$\xrightarrow{PCC} \underset{\text{Hexanal}}{CH_3-(CH_2)_4-CHO}$$

(B) 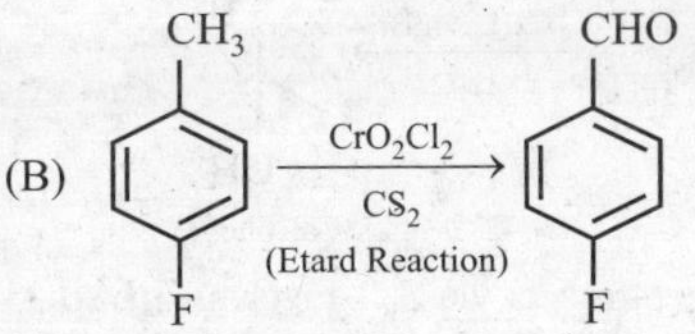

(C) 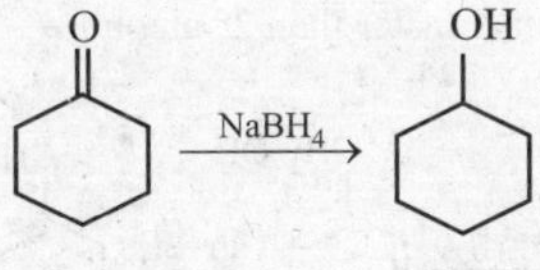

(D) $CH_3-CH_2-C\equiv N \xrightarrow{DIBAL-H} CH_3CHO$

6. (c)

$$CH_3CH{=}CH{-}CH_2CH_2{-}CN \xrightarrow[(2)\ H_2O]{(1)\ AlH\ (i-Bu)_2}$$

$$\underset{(A)}{CH_3CH=CH-CH_2CH_2-CH_2NH_2}$$

Di-iBAL – H (AlH (i – Bu)$_2$) selectively reduces nitrile group to $-CH_2NH_2$ group.

7. (c) Reimer-Tiemann reaction

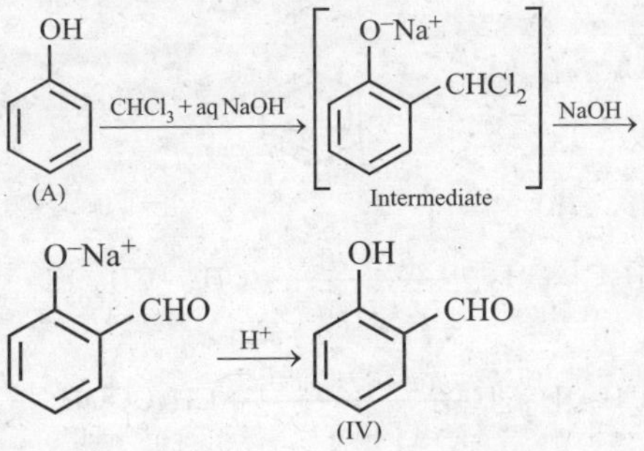

Etard reaction

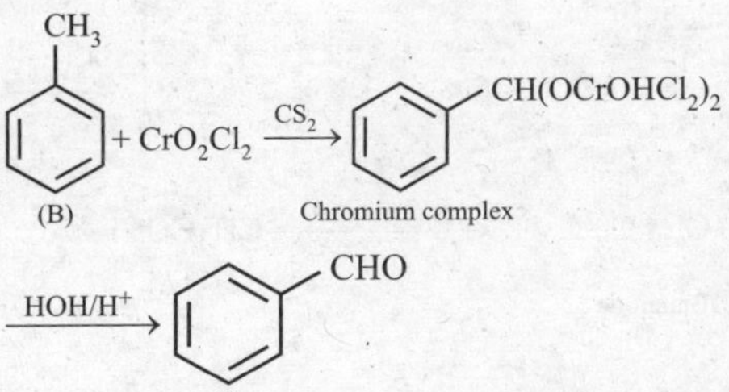

Sandmeyer reaction

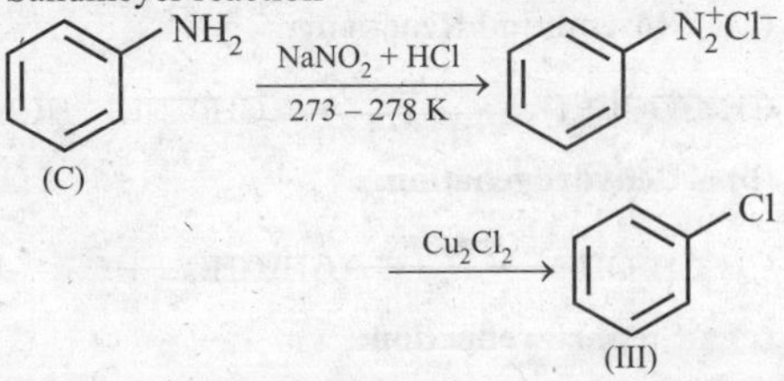

Friedel-Crafts reaction

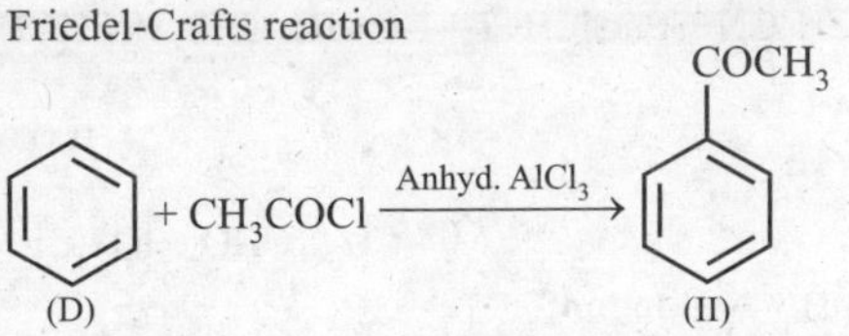

8. (b) Etard reaction :

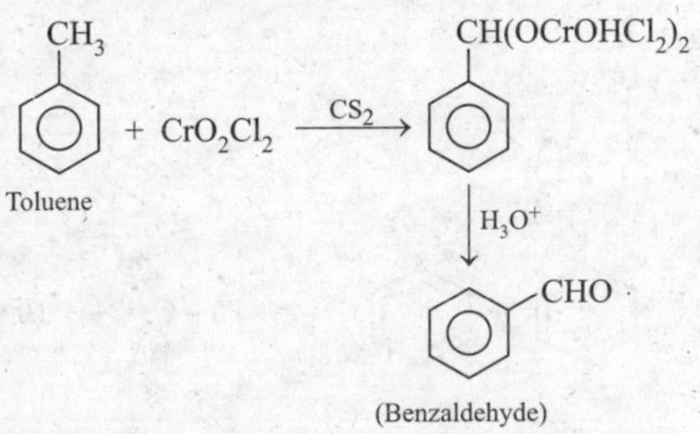

9. (c)

$$C_2H_5Br \xrightarrow{KCN} \underset{(A)}{C_2H_5CN} \xrightarrow{H_3O^+} \underset{(B)}{C_2H_5COOH} \xrightarrow{LiAlH_4} C_2H_5CH_2OH \xrightarrow[573\,K]{Cu} \underset{\text{(Propinaldehyde)}}{CH_3-CH_2-CHO}$$

10. (a)

$$\underset{\text{Silver acetate}}{CH_3COOAg} + BrCH_2CH_3 \longrightarrow \underset{\text{Ethyl ethanoate}}{CH_3-\overset{O}{\overset{||}{C}}-O-C_2H_5} + AgBr\downarrow$$

$$\xrightarrow{DIBAL-H/H_2O} CH_3-CH_2-\overset{O}{\overset{||}{C}}-H$$

11. (d)

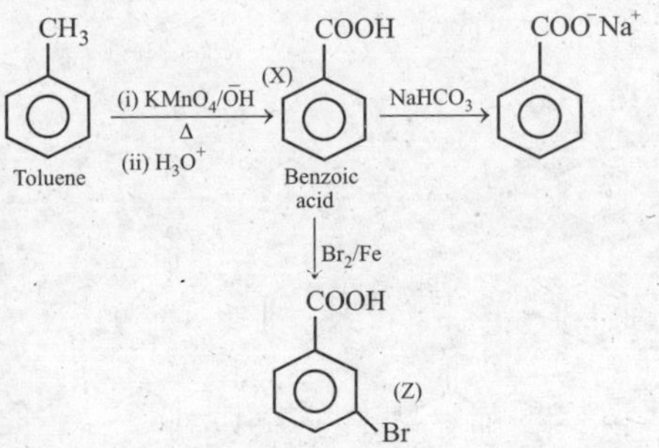

Carboxylic acid is meta directing group.

12. (d)

$$HC \equiv CH + H - OH \xrightarrow[333k]{Hg^{2+}/H^{+}} CH_2 = \underset{OH}{\underset{|}{C}} - H$$

Ethyne

$$\xrightleftharpoons{\text{isomerisation}} CH_3 - \underset{O}{\underset{||}{C}} - H$$

Ethanal

(a) Rosenmund Reaction:

$$CH_3COCl + H_2 \xrightarrow{Pd/BaSO_4} CH_3CHO + HCl$$

(b) Dehydrogenation:

$$CH_3CH_2OH \xrightarrow{Cu/573\,K} CH_3CHO + H_2$$

(c) Stephen reduction:

$$CH_3CN + SnCl_2\ HCl \longrightarrow CH_3{-}CH = NH.HCl$$

$$\downarrow H_3O^+$$

$$CH_3{-}CHO + NH_4Cl$$

(d) Reduction:

$$CH_3COOH \xrightarrow[(ii)\ H_2O]{(i)\ LiAlH_4/ether} CH_3CH_2OH$$

13. (c)

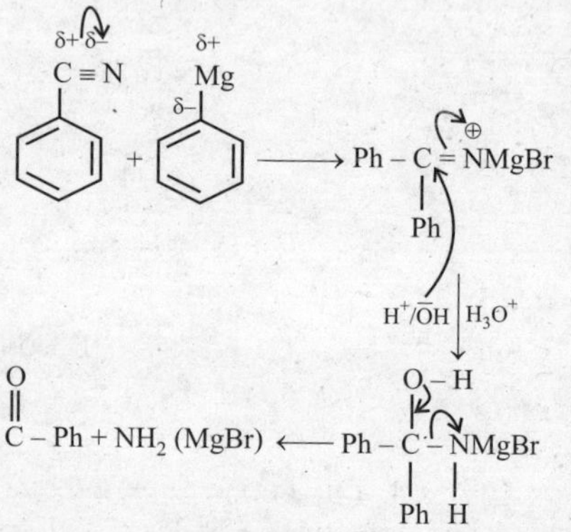

14. (a) In Etard reaction, chromyl chloride oxidises methyl group to a chromium complex, which on hydrolysis gives corresponding benzaldehyde.

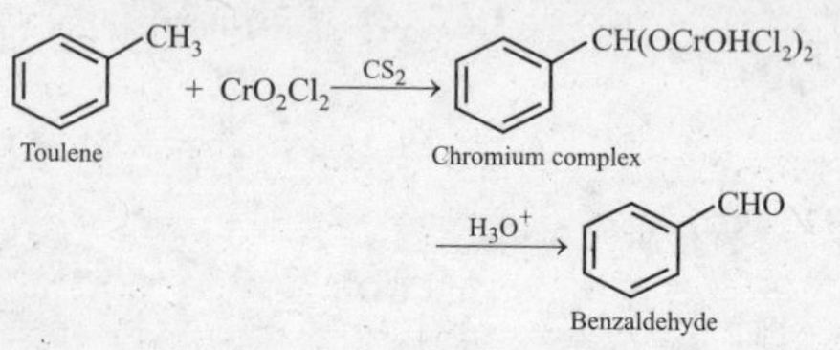

15. (a)

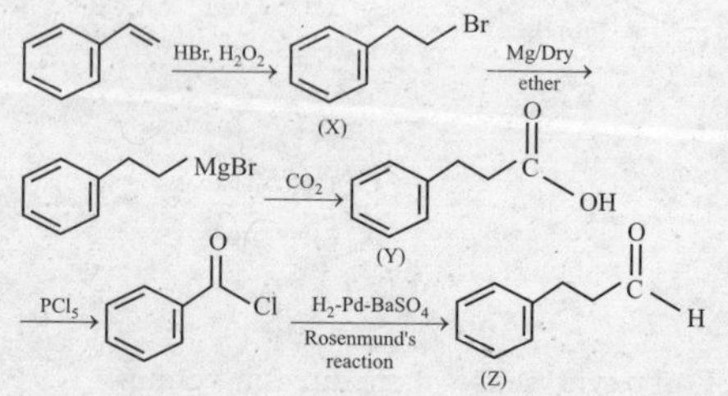

16. (b)

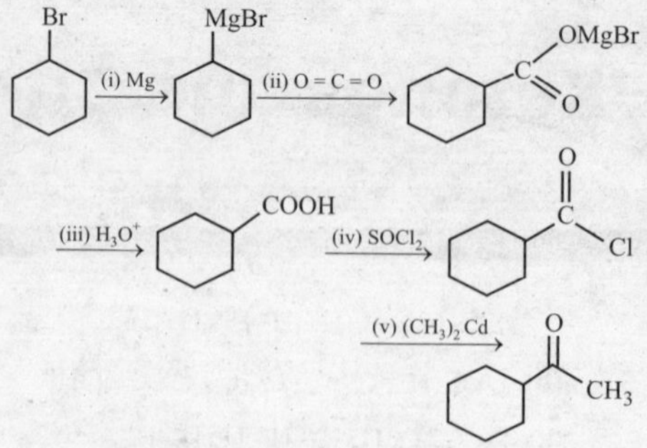

17. (a)

$$CH_3CHO \xrightarrow[(H_2O)]{(CH_3)_2CHMgBr} CH_3 - \overset{OH}{\overset{|}{CH}} - CH - (CH_3)_2$$

2° (alcohol) (X)

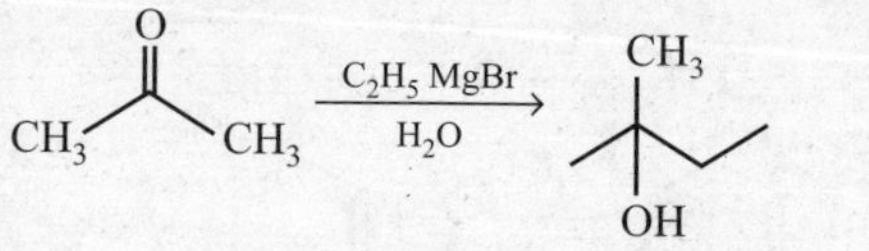

3° alcohol (Y)

Lucas reagent reacts via S_N1 mechanism, so 3° alcohol will react faster than 2° alcohol.

18. (d)

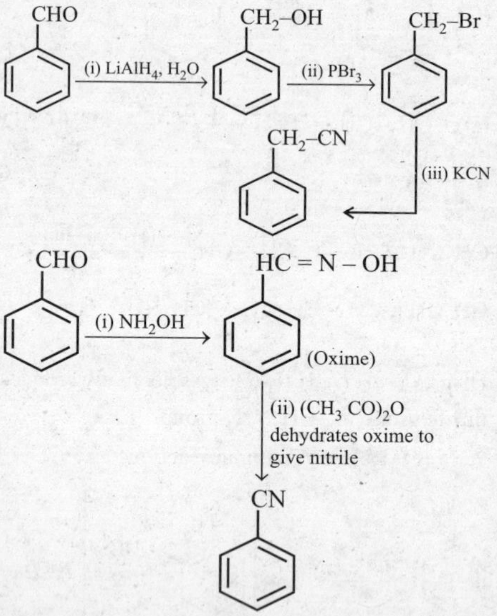

19. (b)

$$\underset{(C_2H_4)}{H_2C = CH_2} \xrightarrow{(i)\ H^+/H_2O} \underset{\text{ethanol}}{CH_3 - CH_2OH}$$

$$CH_3CH_2OH \xrightarrow{(ii)\ H^+/KMnO_4} \underset{\text{acetic acid (X)}}{CH_3COOH}$$

$$\downarrow SOCl_2$$

$$\underset{\text{Butanone (Z)}}{CH_3\overset{O}{\overset{||}{C}}{-}C_2H_5} \xleftarrow{(C_2H_5)_2\,Cd.} \underset{(Y)}{CH_3COCl}$$

20. (a)

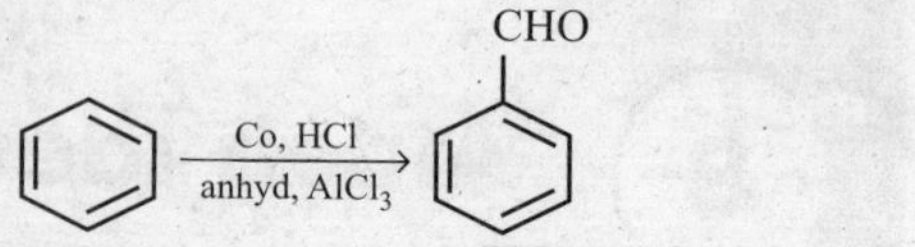

(X) Benzaldehyde

Benzaldehyde is obtained from benzene via Gaterman-Koch reaction and Benzaldehyde (X) gets oxidised with Tollen's reagent and gives a positive silver mirror (Tollen's) Test.

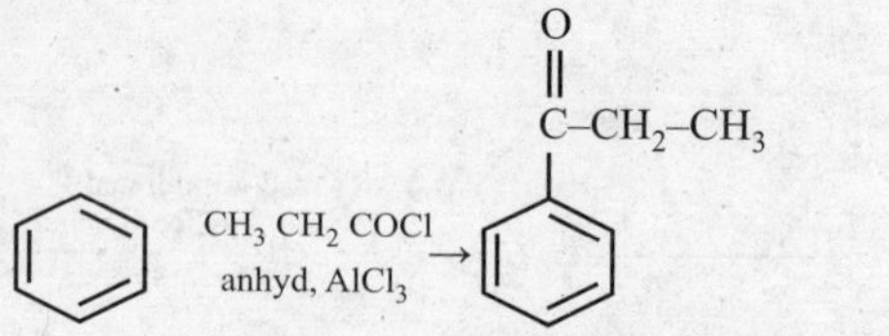

(Y) Propiophenone

Propiophenone is obtained upon reaction with CH_3CH_2COCl via friedel craft acylation reaction and it does not give iodoform test because it doesn't have $CH_3 - \overset{O}{\overset{||}{C}}$ or $CH_3 - \overset{OH}{\overset{|}{CH}}$ group, therefore it does not give positive iodoform test.

21. (c)

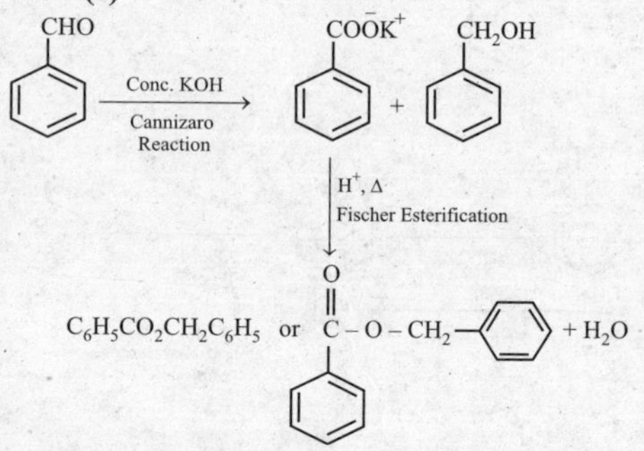

22. (b) Iodoform Test: The compound must contain a methyl carbonyl group.

Fehling Test: The compound must contain an aliphatic aldehyde.

23. (c)

$$\underset{\underset{OH}{|}}{CH_2} - (CHOH)_4 - CHO + HCN \longrightarrow HO - CH_2 - (CHOH)_4 - \underset{\underset{CH-CN}{|}}{OH}$$

(X)

$$\xrightarrow{H_2O/H^{\oplus}} HO - CH_2 - (CH{-}OH)_4 - COOH$$

(Y)

Secondary alcoholic groups = 1 + 4 = 5

24. (b) The final product is imine which is formed by a primary amine and carbonyl compound condensation.

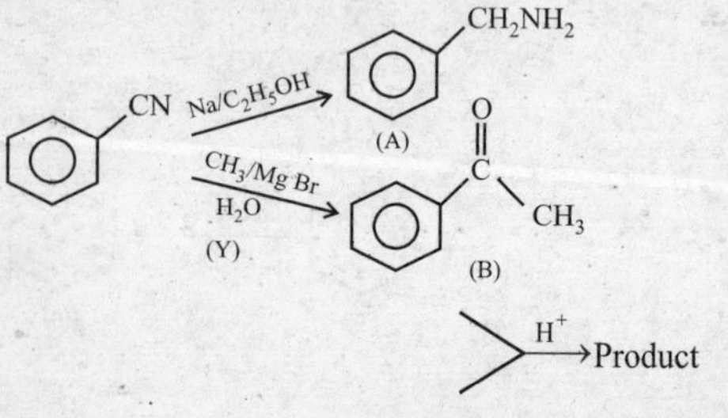

25. (d)

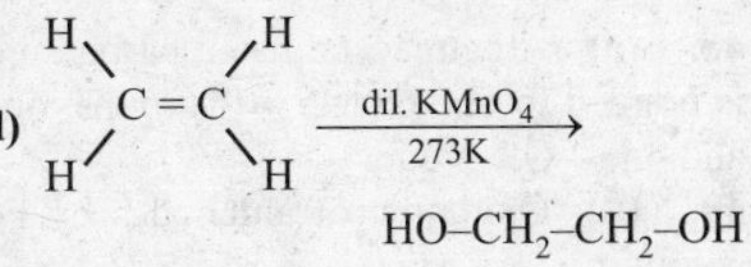

Cold, dil. $KMnO_4$ gives syn-dihydroxylation of alkenes.

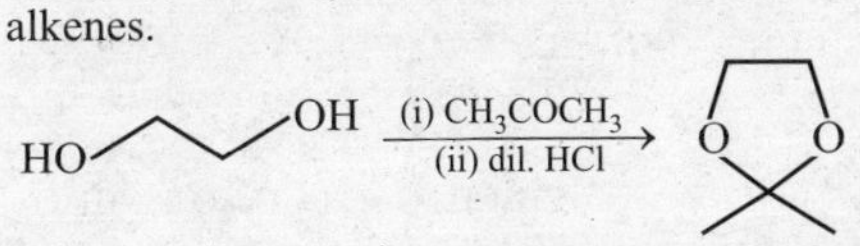

Ethylene glycol reactes with acetone to form a cylic ketal. This reaction requires an acid catalyst like dil. HCl.

26. (a)

- Toluene + A → X, which reacts with $NaHCO_3$ to give CO_2 ⇒ So, X is a carboxylic acid, so complete oxidation of toluene needs a strong oxidant.

So A = $KMnO_4/OH^-$ then H_3O^+ gives benzoic acid (X)

- Toluene + B → Y, which gives positive 2, 4 DNP Test ⇒ So, Y is an aldehyde. This is an controlled oxidation reaction, it gives Benzaldehyde as the product. (Y)

So A = $KMnO_4/OH^-$, H_3O^+

B = $CrO_3/(CH_3CO)_2O$, H_3O^+

27. (b) Less number of H atoms in relation to C in X (C_8H_8O) indicates the presence of benzene ring. Further X undergoes disproportionation (Cannizaro reaction) indicating it to be an –CHO group having no α-hydrogen. Thus X should be

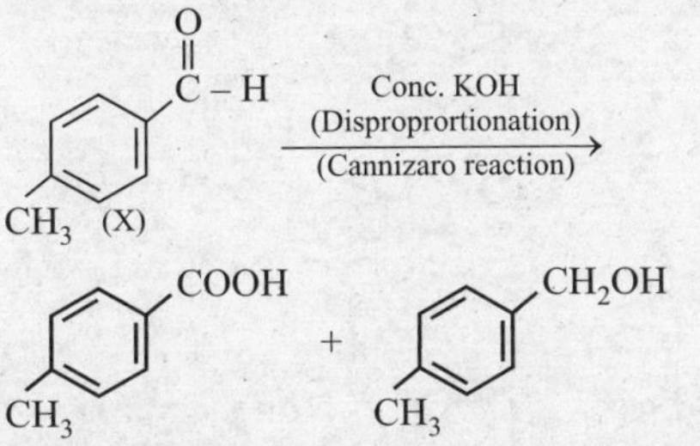

Above structure of X also explains its other given reactions.

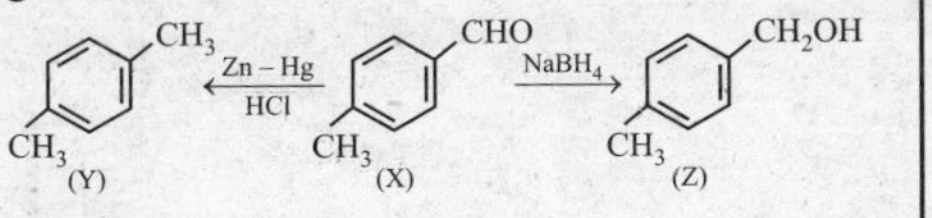

28. (a)

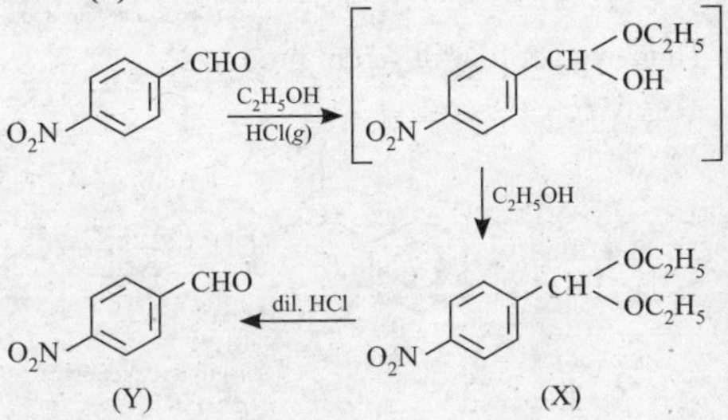

29. (a)

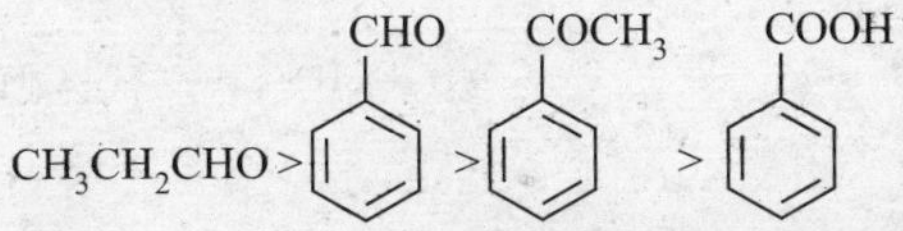

Aldehydes are generally more electrophilic than ketones because in ketones the presence of 2 (+I) alkyl groups reduce the electrophilicity of carbonyl carbon in comparison to aldehydes.

In case of –COOH group due to resonance

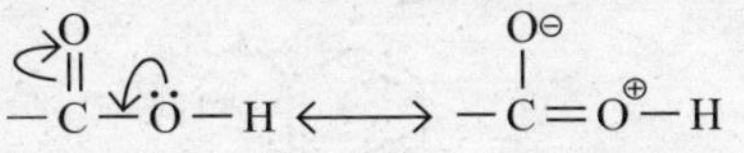

the electrophilicity of carbonyl carbon is further reduced.

30. (c) C_6H_5COONa

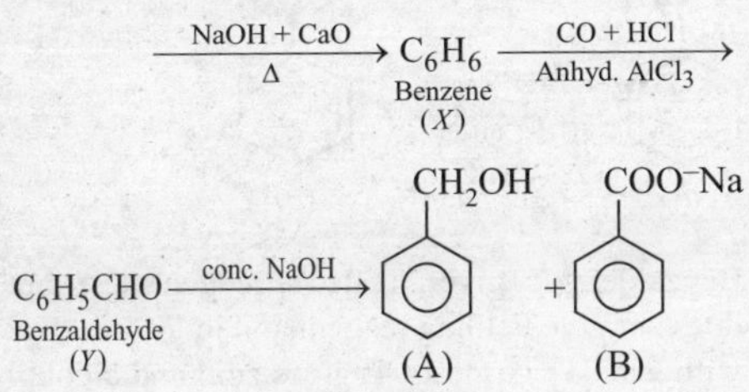

31. (c) Wolf-Kishner reduction.

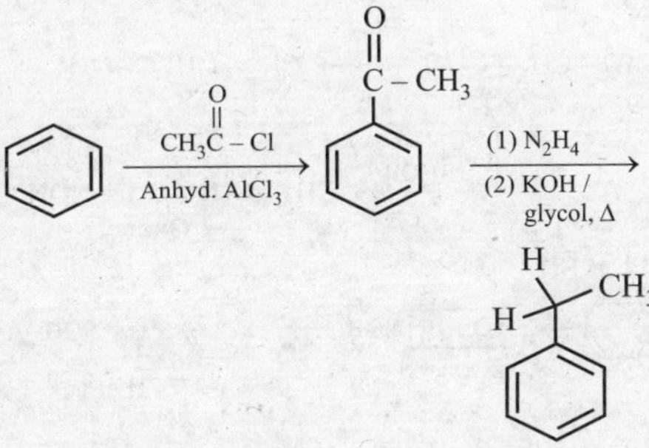

32. (a)

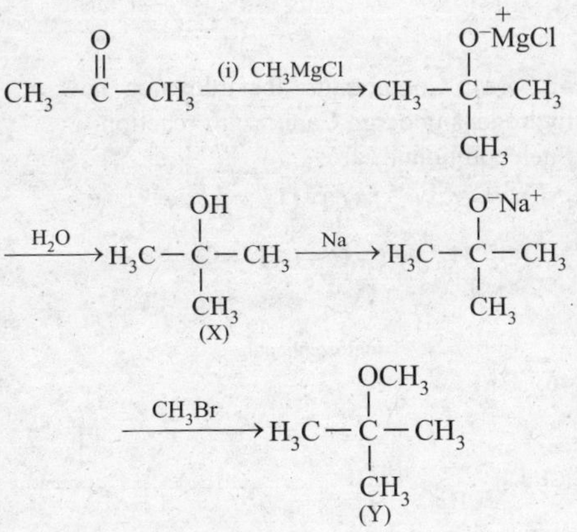

(Y) = Five sp^3 carbons.

33. (b)

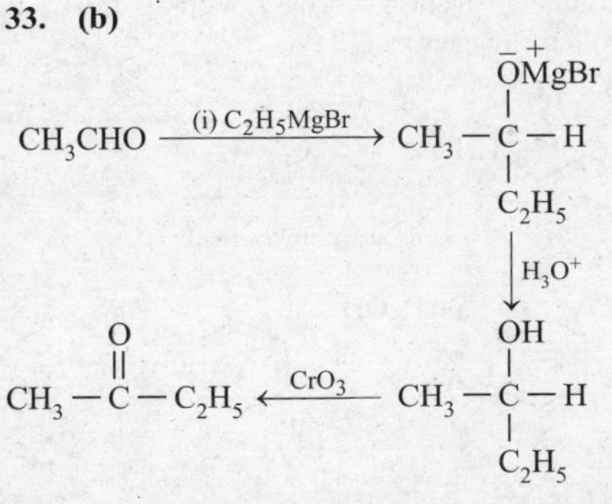

34. (c)

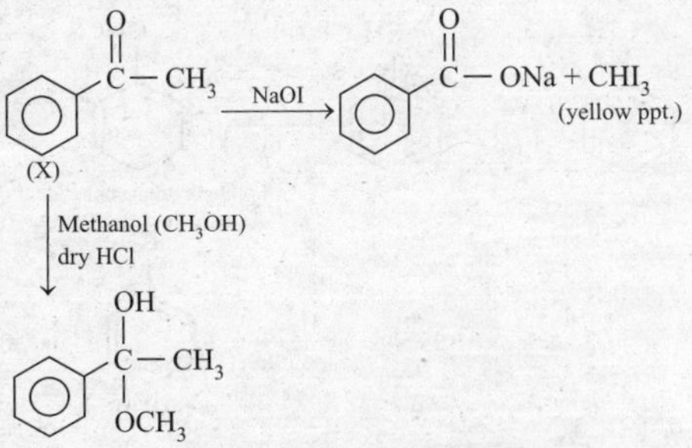

35. (d)

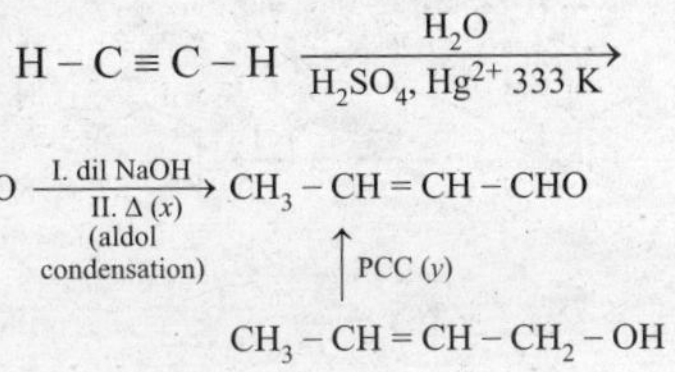

Thus $x = H_2O/H_2SO_4, Hg^{2+}$

y = PCC (Pyridinium chlorochromate)

36. (b) Gattermann-Koch reaction

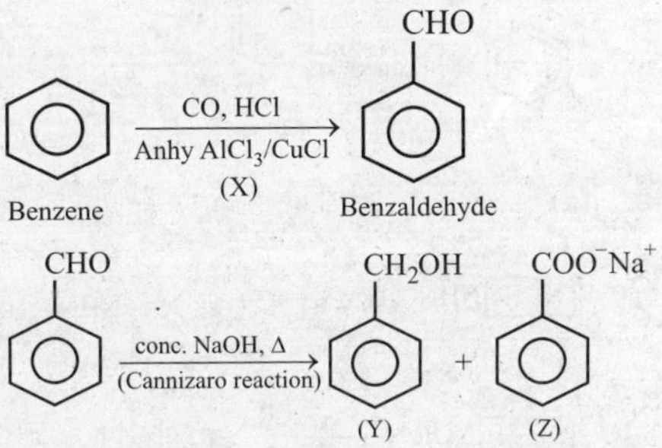

37. (a)

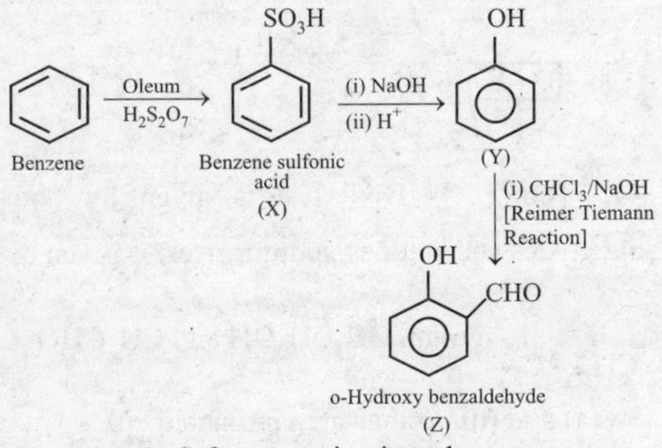

38. (b) Iodoform test is given by 2° alc. having at least one $-CH_3$ group, i.e., $RCHOH.CH_3$–

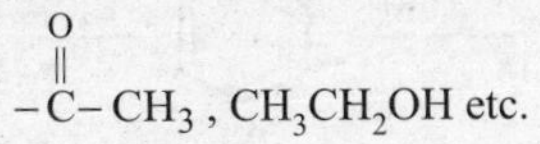

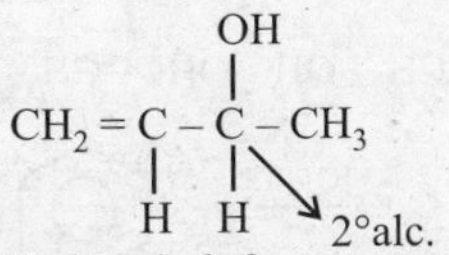

It gives iodoform test.

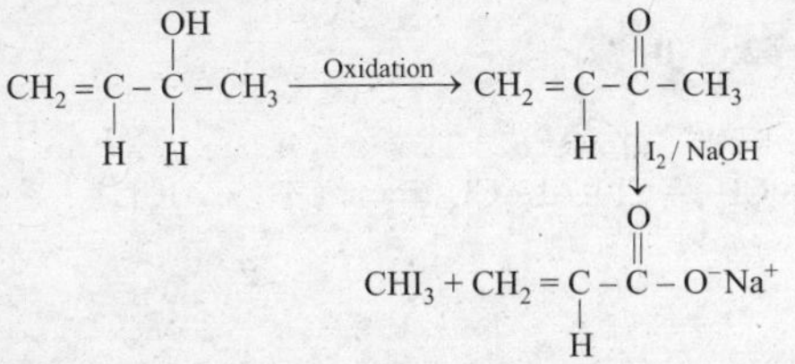

39. (c)

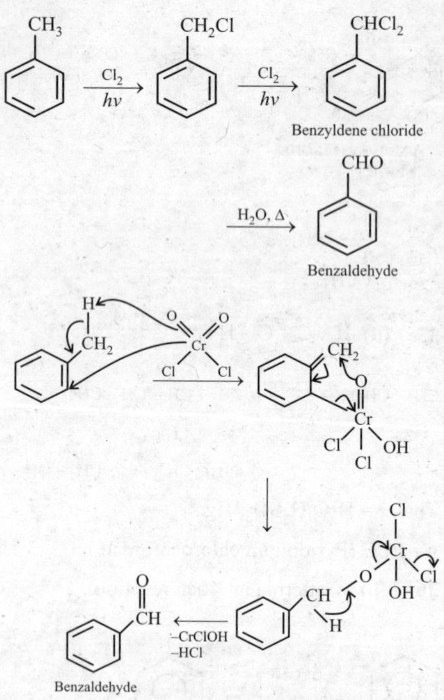

40. (a)

$$\begin{matrix}R\\R\end{matrix}\!\!>C=\boxed{O+H_2}NHNC_6H_5 \longrightarrow \begin{matrix}R\\R\end{matrix}\!\!>C=NHNC_6H_5$$
Phenyl hydrazone

$$\begin{matrix}R\\R\end{matrix}\!\!>C=\boxed{O+H_2}NOH \longrightarrow \begin{matrix}R\\R\end{matrix}\!\!>C=NOH$$
Oxime

$$\begin{matrix}R\\R\end{matrix}\!\!>C=\boxed{O+H_2}NC_6H_5 \longrightarrow \begin{matrix}R\\R\end{matrix}\!\!>C=NC_6H_5$$
Schiff base

41. (c) 2, 4- DNP test is given by both aldehydes and ketones, iodoform test is given by $CH_3-\overset{O}{\overset{||}{C}}-$ group, CH_3CH_2OH and CH_3CHO

So (a) and (d) options are eliminated.

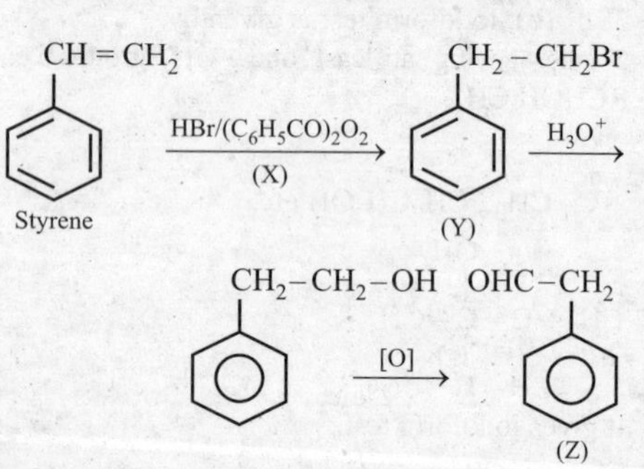

42. (b)

$$CH_3-Cl+Al-Cl_3 \rightleftharpoons \overset{+}{C}H_3+AlCl_4^-$$

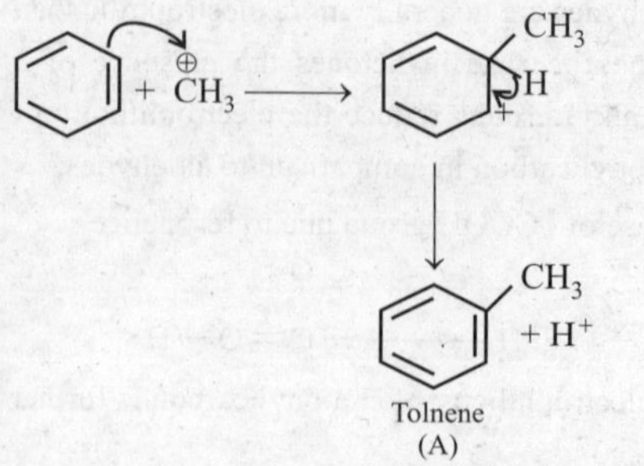

$$H^+ + AlCl_4^- \longrightarrow HCl + AlCl_3$$

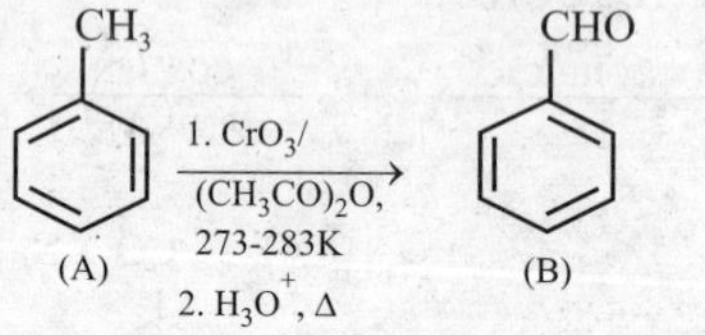

Benzaldehyde gives Tollen's reagent test but does not give Fehling reagent and iodoform (test with NaOH + I_2) tests. It gives acid and alcohol with conc. NaOH (Cannizaro reaction)

43. (c)

$$\underset{(X)}{CH_3-CH_2-CHO} \xrightarrow{(O)} \underset{(Y)}{CH_3-CH_2\,COOH}$$

$$\xrightarrow{NH_2OH} \underset{\text{Oxime}}{CH_3-CH_2-CH=NOH}$$

44. (d)

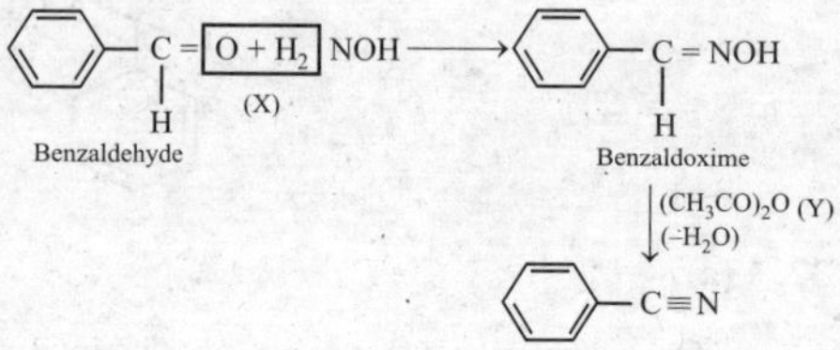

45. (a) Compounds that do not have α-hydrogens undergo Cannizzaro reaction. Such compounds are:-

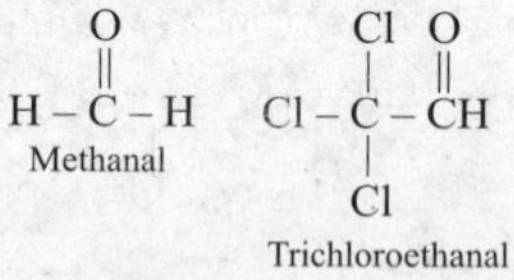

46. (a)

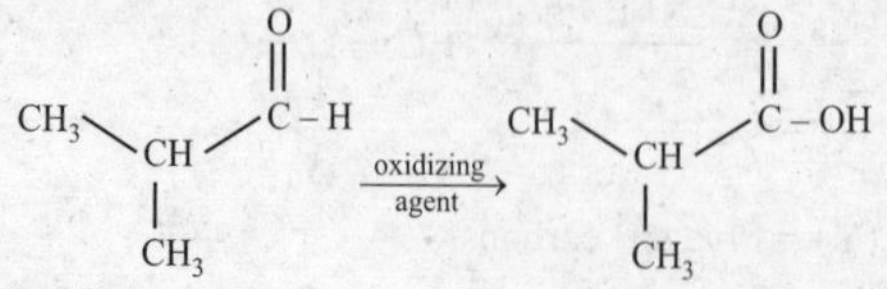

Oxidizing agents = HNO_3, $2[Ag\ (NH_3)_2]^+$ (Tollen's reagent).

47. (c)

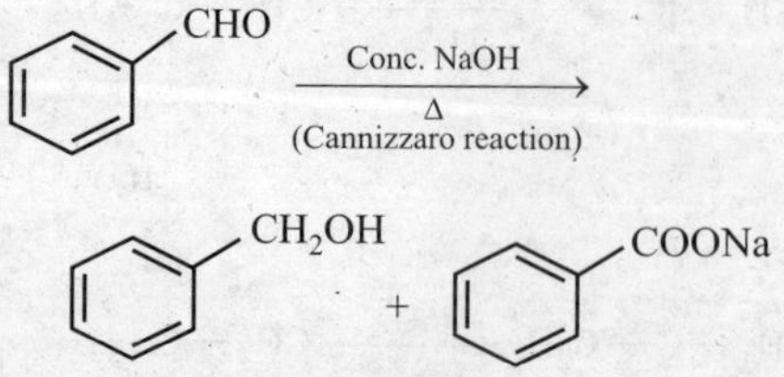

48. (a) A hemiacetal has a carbon atom that is bonded to one or two – R groups, one – OH and one – OR group.

49. (d) Oxidation of aldehydes by Fehling's solution:-

$$CH_3CH_2-\overset{O}{\overset{||}{C}}-H+\underset{\text{Fehling solution}}{2Cu^{2+}+OH^-} \longrightarrow$$

$$\underset{(X)}{CH_3CH_2\overset{O}{\overset{||}{C}}-O^-}+\underset{\substack{(Y)\\ \text{(red ppt.)}}}{Cu_2O\downarrow}+3H_2O$$

50. (d) Cross-aldol condensation : Both reactants have α-H atom.

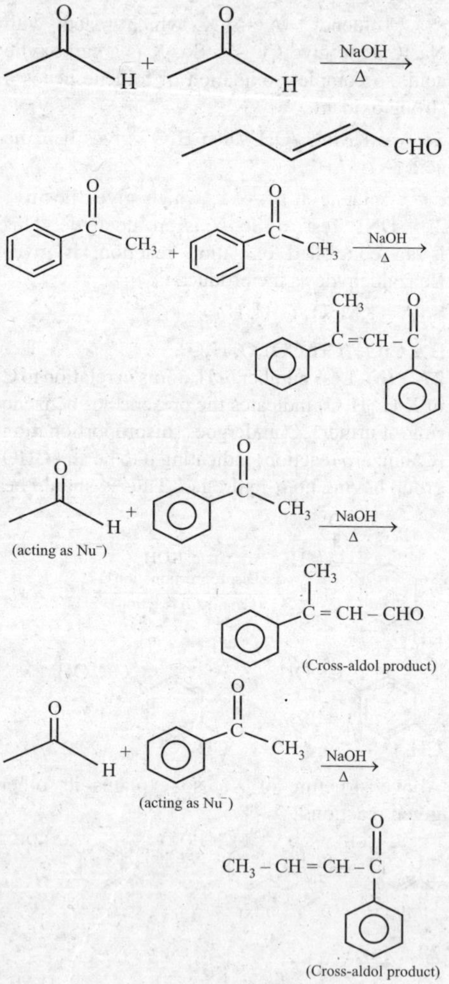

Thus, we get four different products.

51. (c)

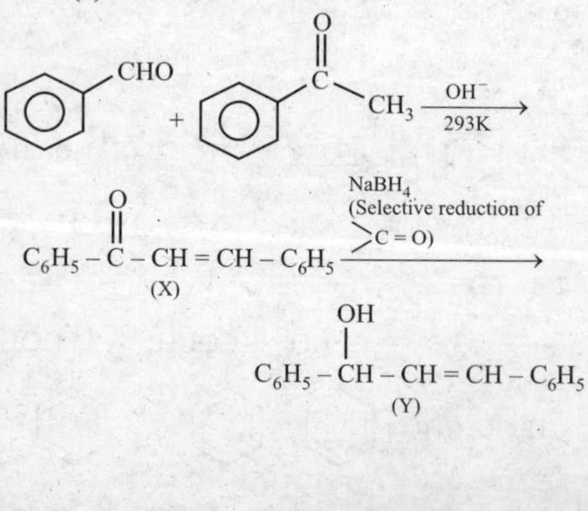

52. (a)

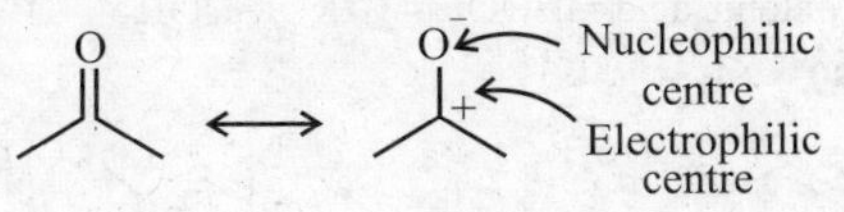

53. (a)

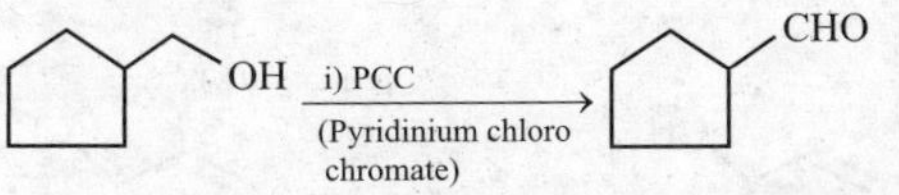

Best method for preparing aldehyde from primary alcohol.

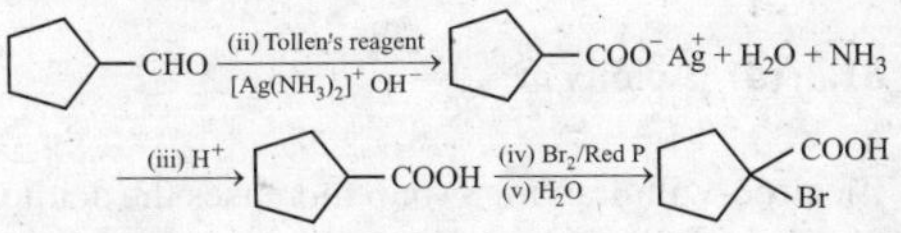

54. (d)

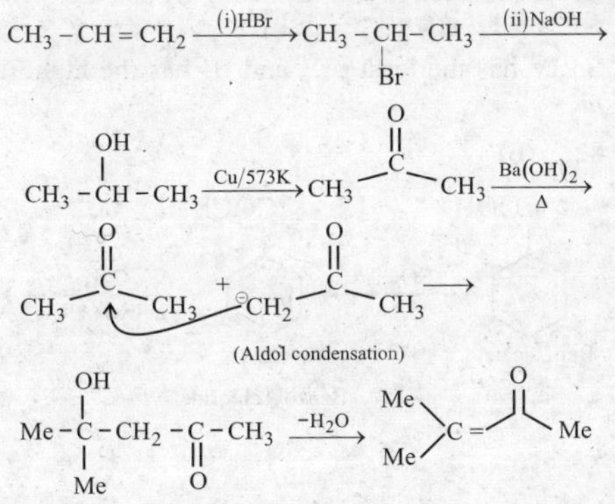

55. (c)

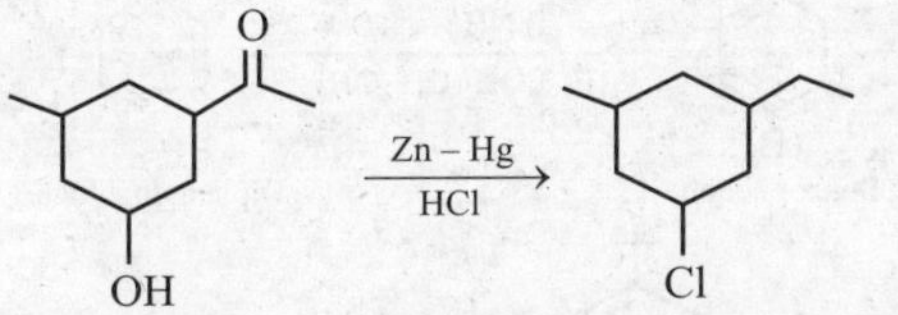

Carbonyl ($>C=O$) group is reduced to ($>CH_2$) by Zn-Hg, HCl, known as Clemmensen reduction. Since, –OH is present, in acidic medium it will be replaced by Cl^-.

56. (a) Ketones are more stable than aldehydes. Phenyl ring has (–I) effect nd (+R) effect due to the delocalized π-electrons over the ring.

+I effect of substituents $-CH_3 > H > -NO_2$

Therefore, the stability of transition states of nucelophilic addition to $\underset{H}{>}C=O$ group decreases and as a result reactivity increases.

$\therefore$ correct order : (i) < (ii) < (iii) < (iv)

57. (c)

$$\underset{\text{Ethane nitrile}}{\underset{(P)}{CH_3C\equiv N}} \xrightarrow[(ii) H_3O^+]{(i) CH_3MgBr} \underset{\text{Propanone}}{\underset{(R)}{CH_3-CO-CH_3}} + NH_3$$

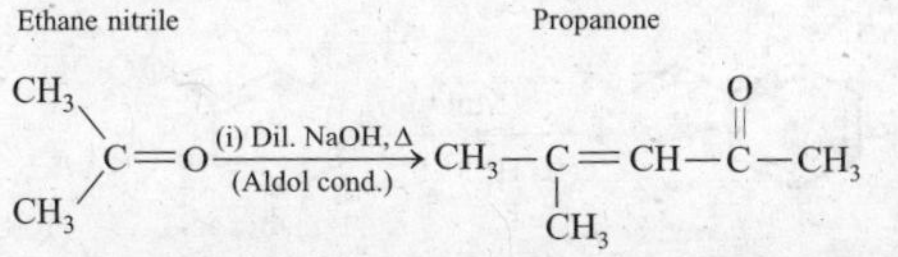

58. (a)

$$\underset{\text{Acetic acid}}{CH_3COOH} \xrightarrow[\text{(reduction)}]{LiAlH_4} \underset{\text{Ethyl alcohol}}{CH_3CH_2OH} \xrightarrow[\text{(oxidation)}]{Cu,\ 573K} \underset{\text{Acetaldehyde}}{CH_3CHO}$$

$$\xrightarrow[\text{(Aldol condensation)}]{\text{Dil. NaOH}} \underset{\text{3 Hydroxy butanal}}{\underset{\text{(Aldol)}}{CH_3-\underset{OH}{\underset{|}{CH}}-CH_2CHO}}$$

59. (b) When CH_3COCl react with $(CH_3)_2$ Cd, it will form acetone as a product (P). On further step, acetone (P) react with acetaldehyde to give aldol condensation reaction and formed α, β–unsaturated alkene product.

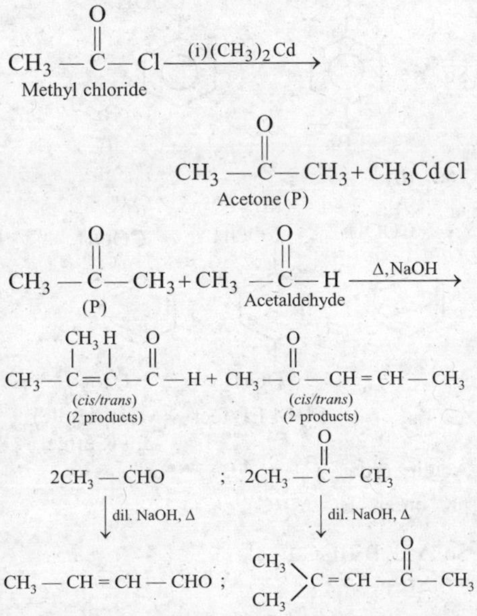

Hence, total number of products = 4 (without considering isomers).

60. (c)

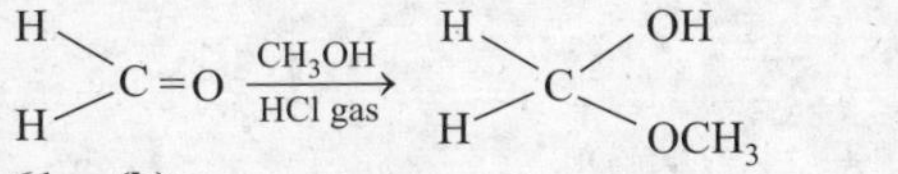

61. (b)

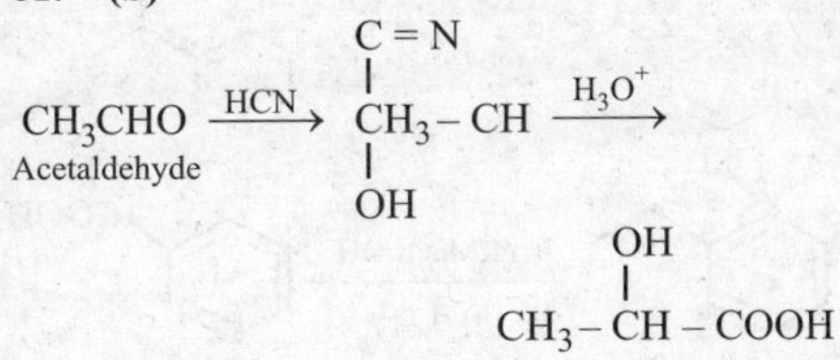

Therefore compound *A* is acetaldehyde.

62. (b)

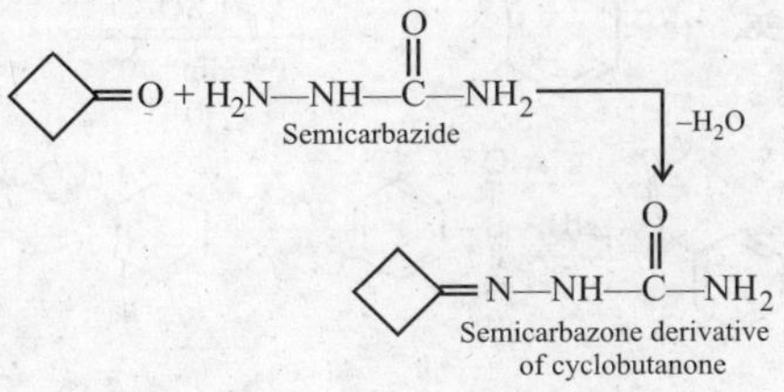

63. (d)

(A) Reactivity of aromatic aldehyde and ketones is less than aliphatic carbonyl compound due to steric hindrance caused due to bulkier aryl group.

(B) Fehling's solution is being a very mild oxidising agent, benzaldehyde does not respond to it.

(C) Ethanal on tautomerisation produces its enol form.

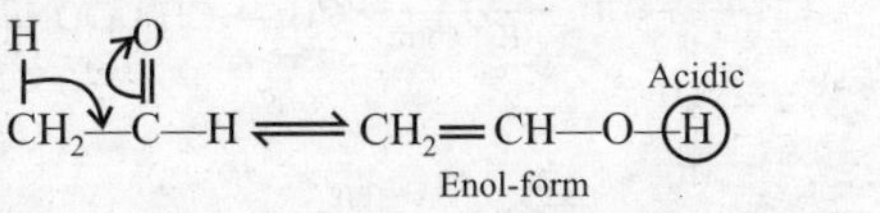

(D) Because of the presence of $-NO_2$ group at *para* position (– *R* effect), the carbon atom. of $>C=O$ group becomes electron deficient and hence more susceptible for nucleophilic attack.

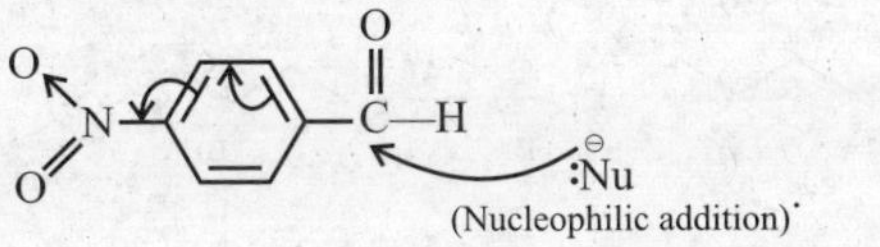

(Nucleophilic addition)

64. (c) Here, *X* = electrophile and *Y*- nucleophile. Alkenes (*X*) undergo electrophilic reactions due to reactive π-electrons.

Carbonyl compounds undergo nucleophilic reaction due to polar nature of C = O group.

65. (b)

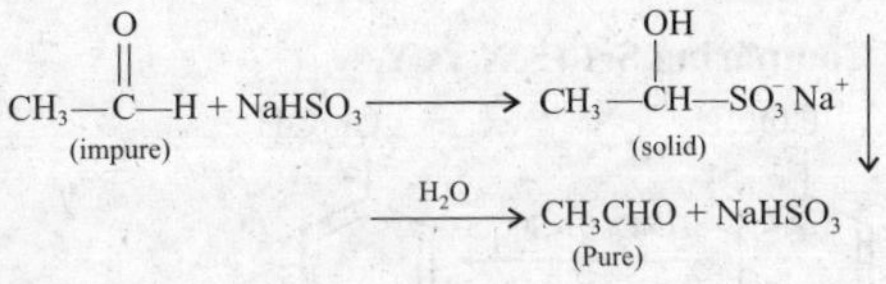

66. (d) (i)

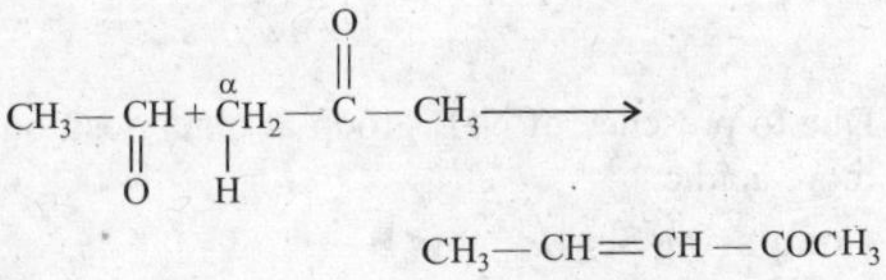

(ii)

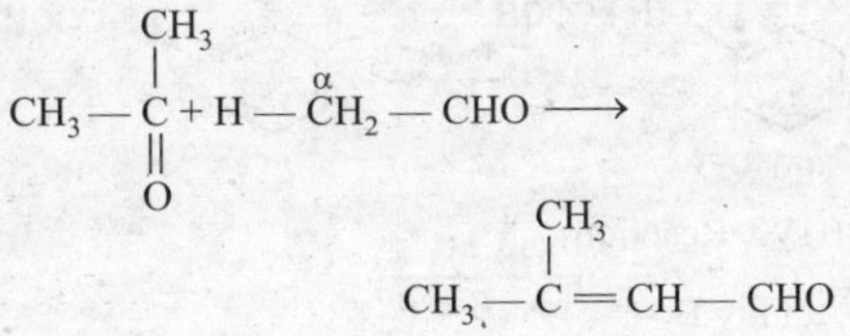

67. (c)

$$R-CHO + \underset{\text{(Tollen's reagent)}}{2[Ag(NH_3)_2]^+} + 3OH^- \longrightarrow RCOO^- + 2Ag + 4NH_3 + 2H_2O$$

68. (c)

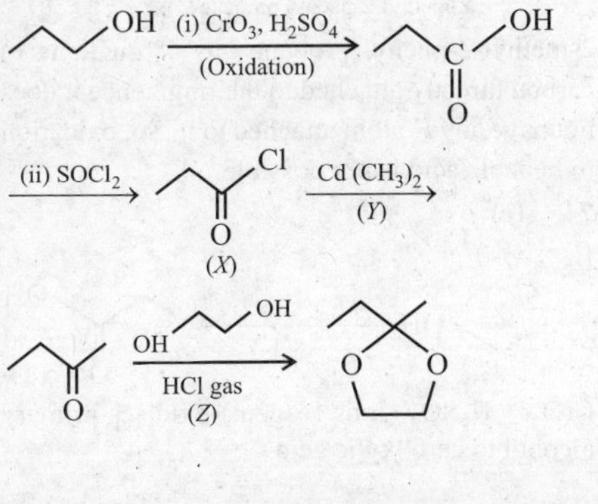

69. (c)

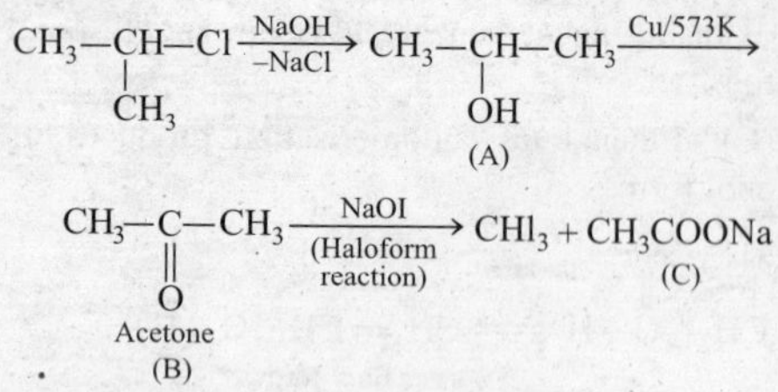

70. (b) Clemmensen reduction:

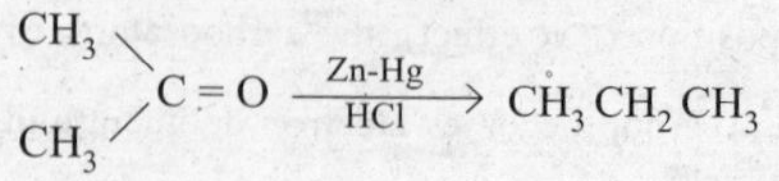

71. (d)

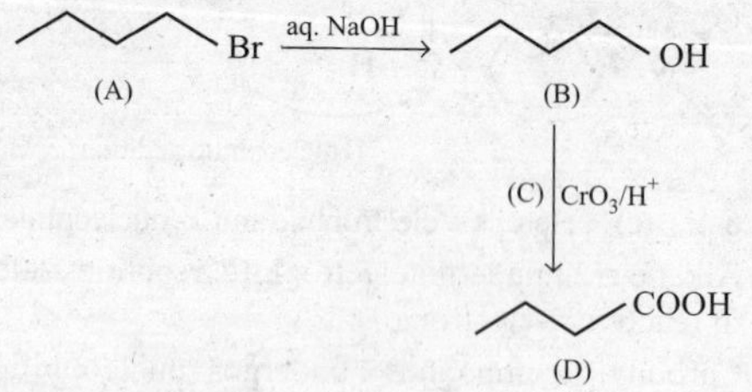

72. (a) Acidity μ K_a α $\frac{1}{pK_a}$

Comparing Set I:- X vs Y

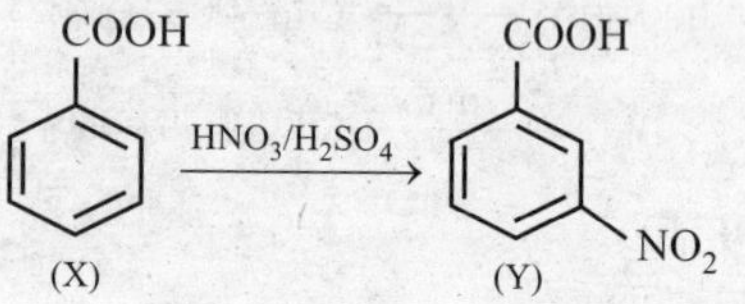

Due to presence of NO_2 group at meta position more acidic.

Comparing Set II:- A vs B

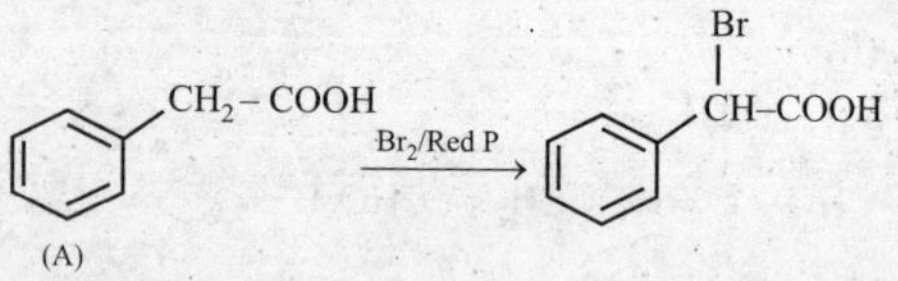

(HVZ Reaction)

Acidity B > A pK_a B < A

73. (d)

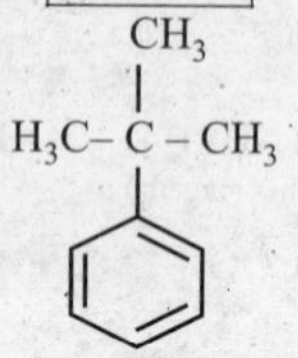

2-methyl-2-phenyl propane

2-methyl-2-phenyl propane has 4°(quaternary) carbon directly attached to the ring hence it does not have any H atom attached to it. So, oxidation to benzoic acid is not possible.

74. (c)

I:

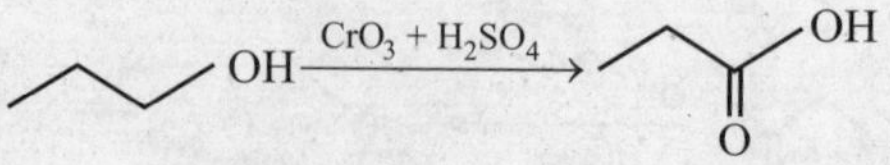

$CrO_3 + H_2SO_4$ (Jons reagent) oxidises primary alcohol to carboxylic acid.

III:

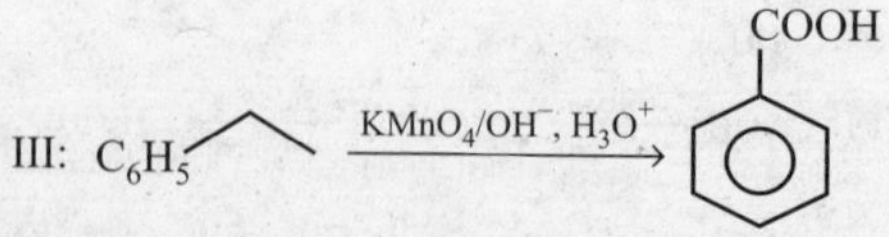

Strong oxidising agents like $KMnO_4$ oxidises any alkyl side chain attached to benzene ring to –COOH.

Hence, I and III gives corresponding carboxylic acid.

75. (b) $-CH_3$ group is o-and p-directing while –COOH is m-directing group.

So Y = X =

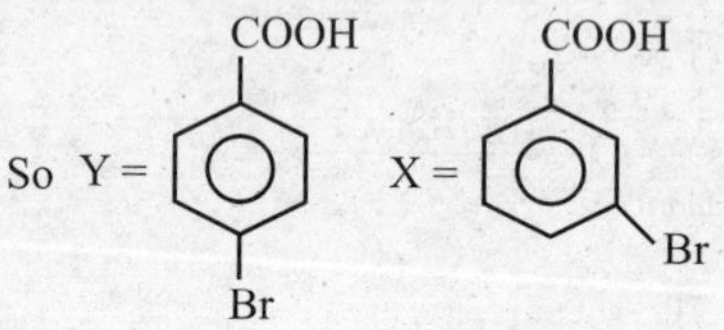

76. (b)

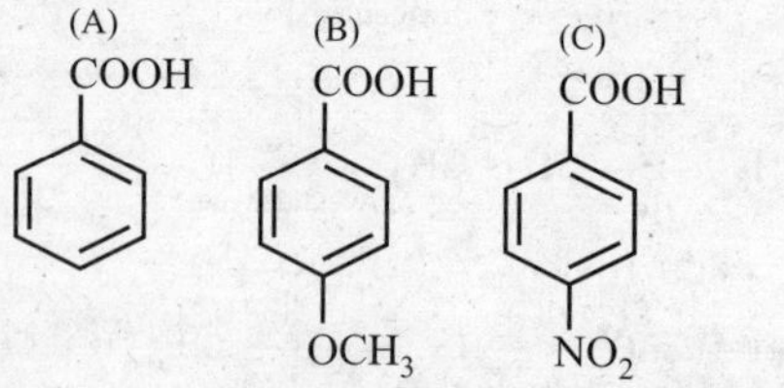

–I, +M Ef fect (Most Acidic) –I, –R effect

Acidity order - C > A > B

pK_a order - B > A > C

So, A-II, B-III, C-I

77. (b)

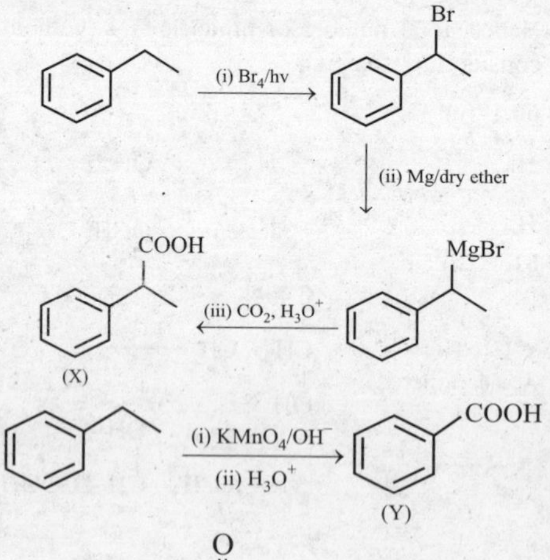

78. (a)

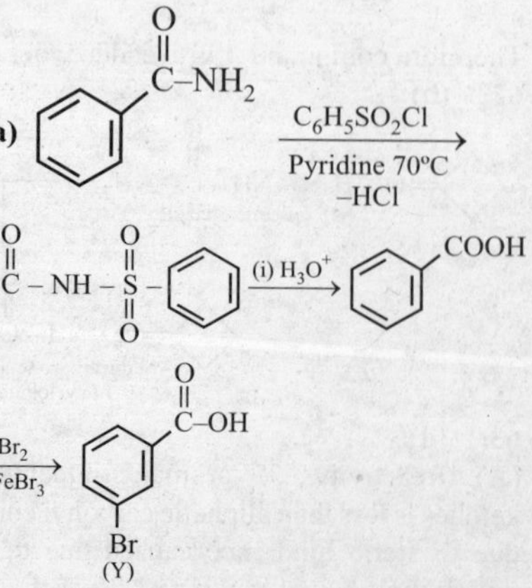

79. (d) Succinic acid $= HOOC-(CH_2)_2-COOH$

Malonic acid $= HOOC-CH_2-COOH$

80. (d)

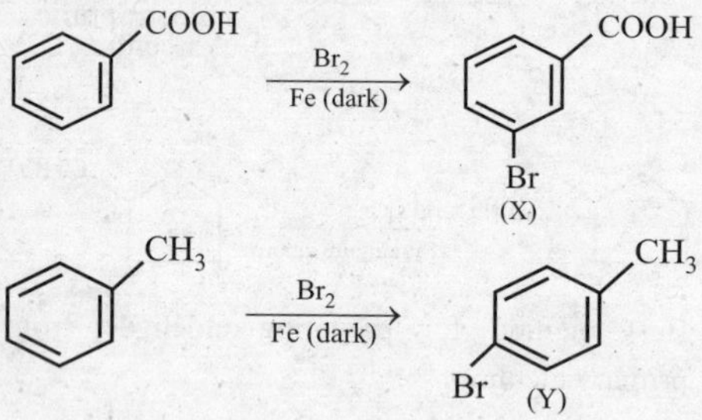

81. (d) Acidity $\propto \frac{1}{pK_a}$

Electron-withdrawing group increases the acidic strength of the carboxylic acid.

Order of Electron-withdrawing groups are $NO_2 > CN > I > CH_3$

So IV has the least pK_a and III has the highest pK_a.

82. (b)

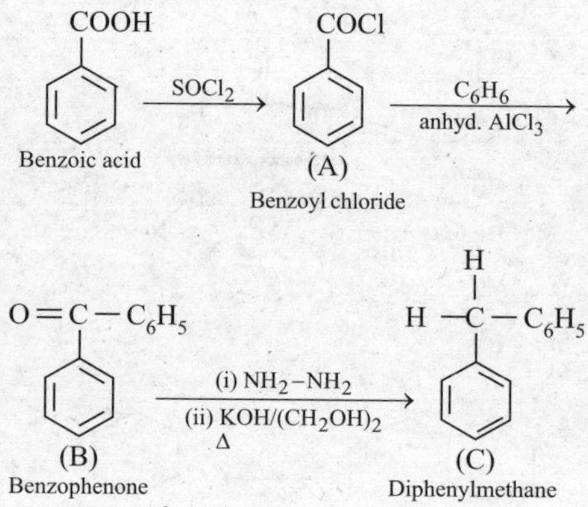

83. (d)

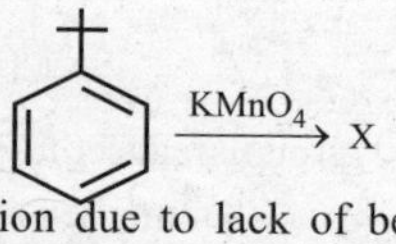

No reaction due to lack of benzylic hydrogen atom.

84. (b)

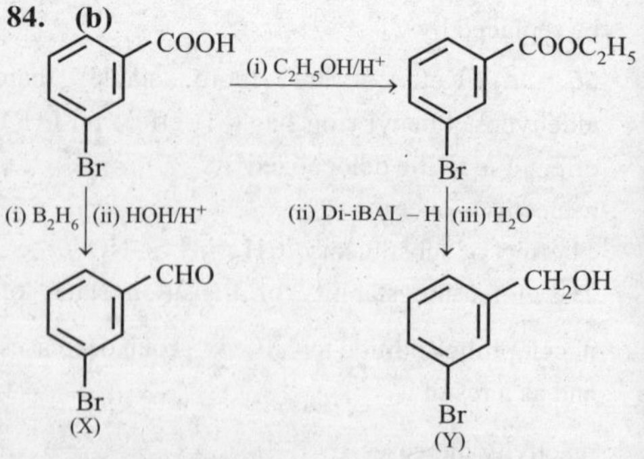

85. (c) Formic acid is more acidic because it is the first member of the carboxylic acid homologous series and therefore no electron-donating alkyl group (that destablises the carboxylate ion) is present.

86. (c)

A.

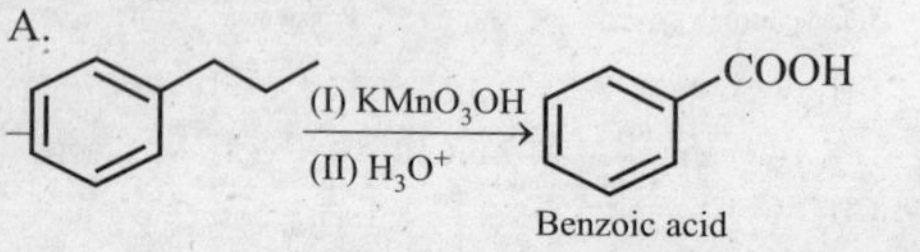

B. –

$$CH_3-COOH \xrightarrow[\text{(II) } H_2O]{\text{(I) } Br_2/\text{Red P}} Br-CH_2-COOH$$

2. Bromoacetic acid

C. –

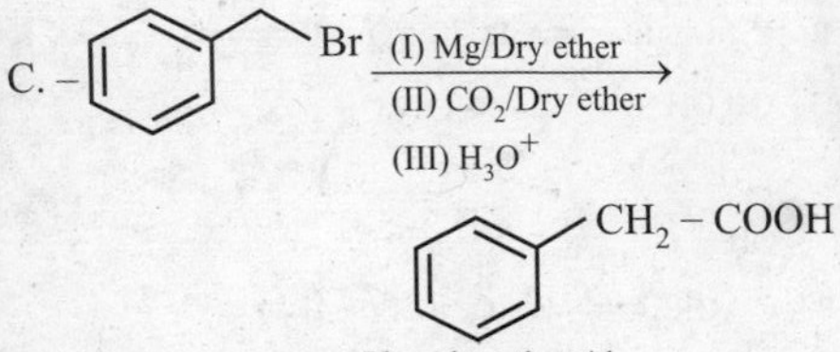

Phenyl acetic acid

Order of Acidity

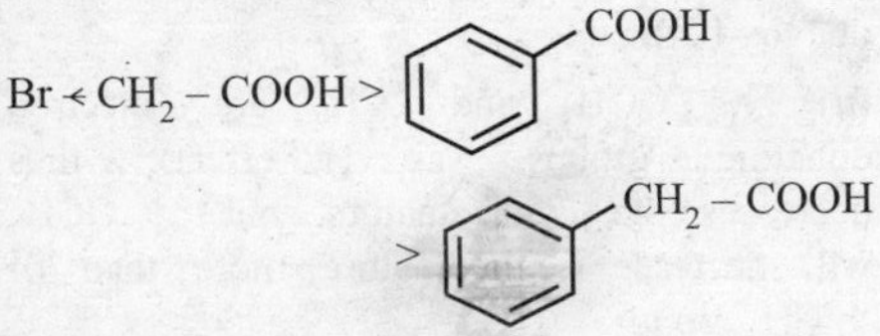

87. (c)

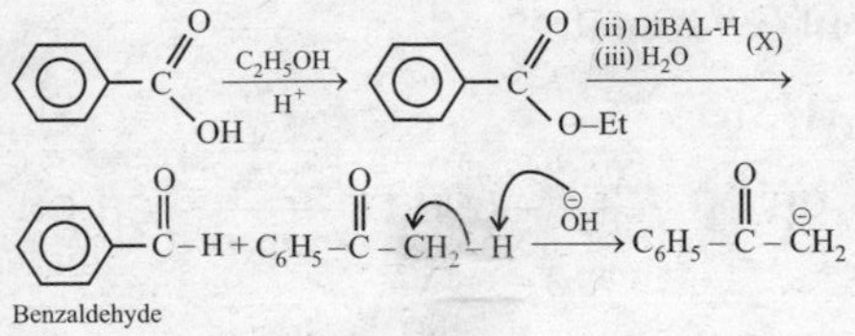

Benzaldehyde undergoes cross aldol condensation with $C_6H_5COCH_3$ in presence of OH^-. Different steps are

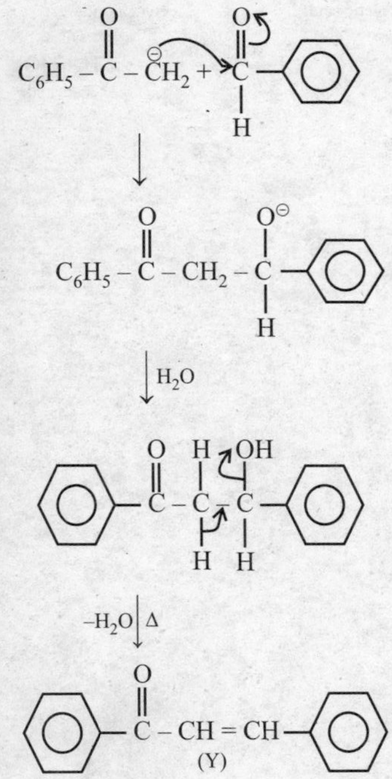

88. (d)

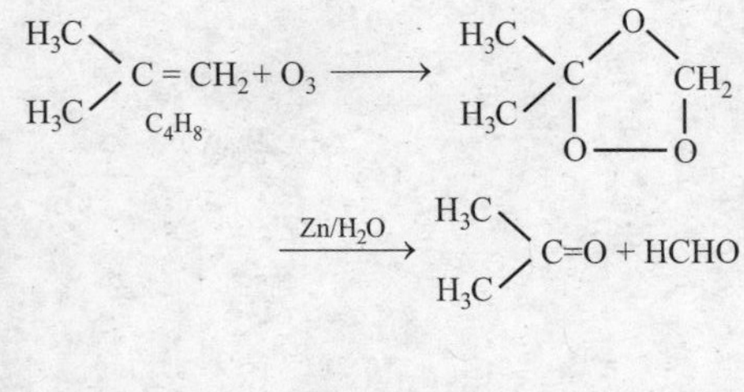

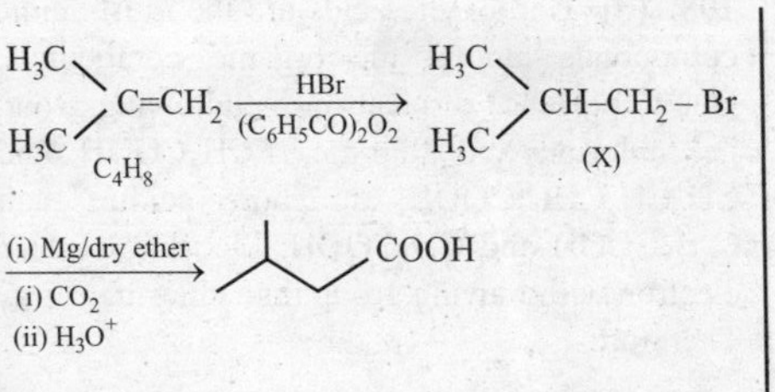

89. (a)

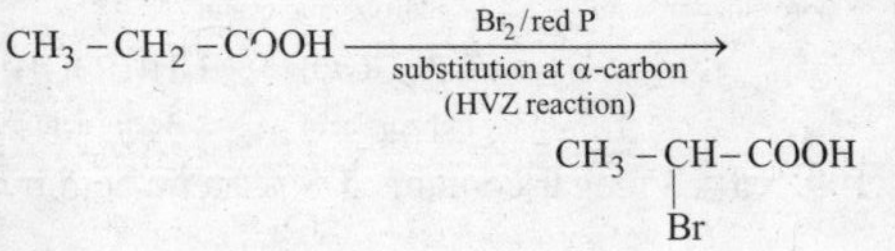

90. (c) A carboxylic acid can be converted into its acyl halide by use of thionyl chloride, $SOCl_2$.

$$CH_3CH_2-\overset{O}{\overset{\|}{C}}-OH \xrightarrow{SOCl_2(Nu^-)} CH_3CH_2-\overset{O}{\overset{\|}{C}}-Cl$$

This reaction is a nucleophilic acyl substitution with $SOCl_2$ acting as a good nucleophilic reagent.

91. (b)

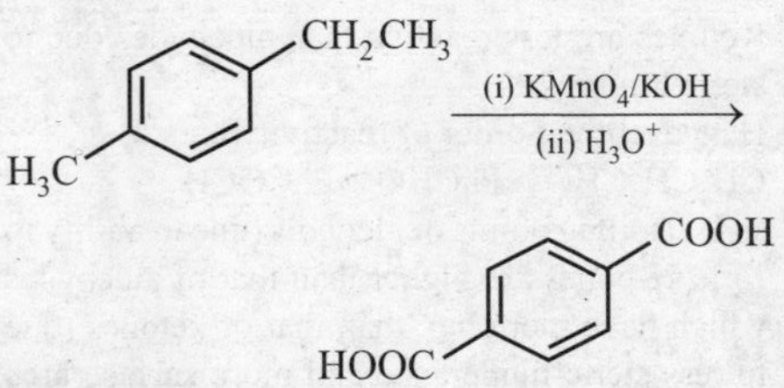

92. (c)

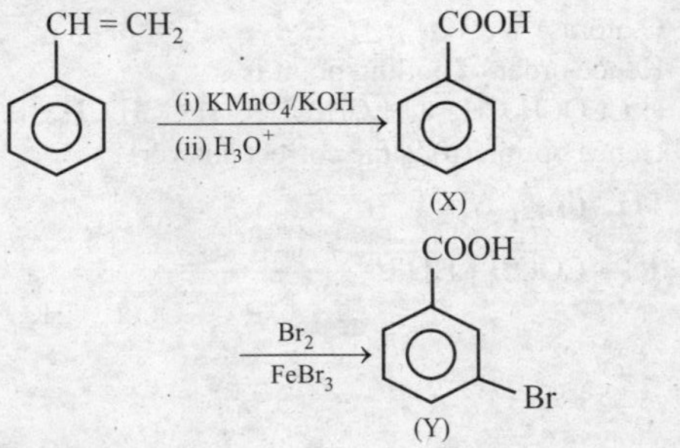

93. (b)

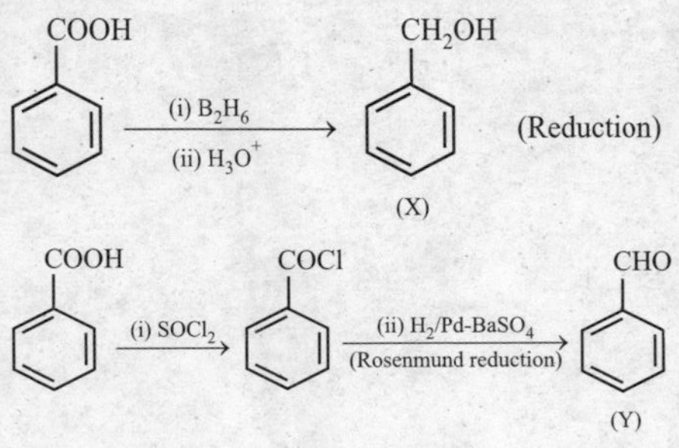

94. (d)

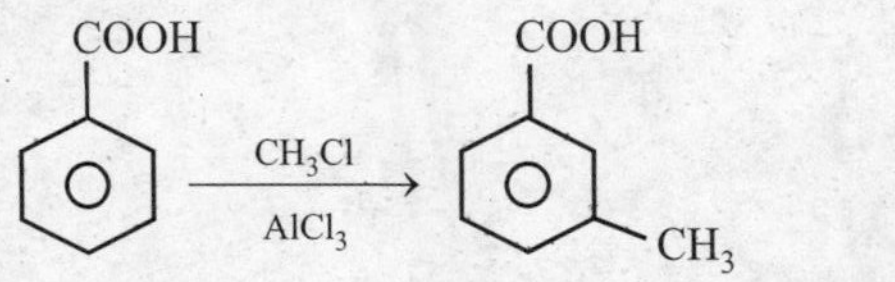

This reaction is not feasible because the –COOH group interacts with the Lewis acid $AlCl_3$ and forms acylium ion instead of the usual electrophilic substitution at the ring.

95. (c)

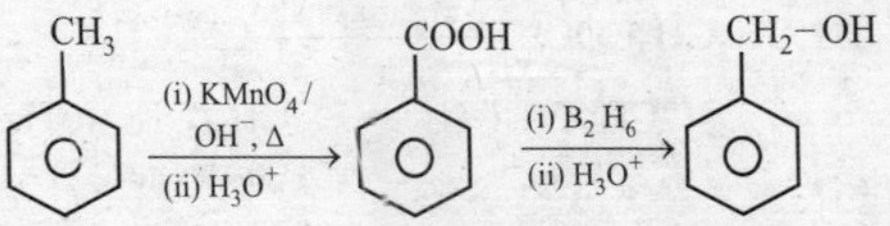

X = (i) $KMnO_4/OH^-$, Δ, (ii) H_3O^+ (strong oxidising agent side-chain oxidation)

Y = (i) B_2H_6, (ii) H_3O^+ (reduction to alcohols)

96. (d)

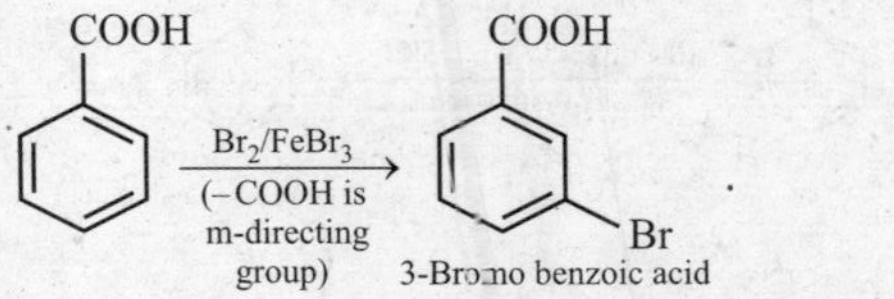

97. (b) Vinegar = acetic acid (CH_3COOH)

Butter = Butyric acid ($CH_3CH_2CH_2COOH$)

98. (d)

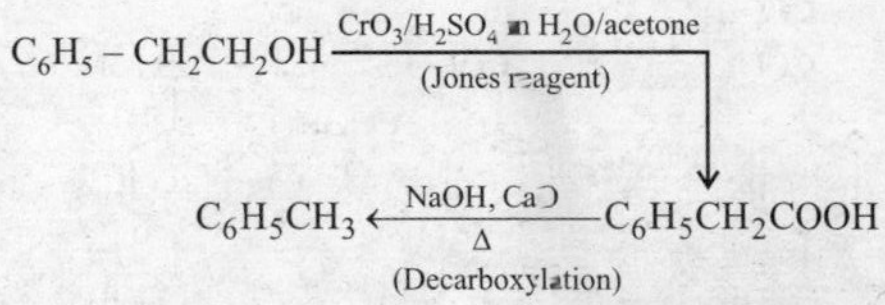

Thus, X = Jones reagent ; Y = NaOH, CaO, Δ; Z = $C_6H_5CH_3$

99. (a) Esters $\left(R-\overset{O}{\overset{\|}{C}}-OR'\right)$ are derivatives of carboxylic acids and are characterized by fruity smell so they are used in perfumery.

100. (d) More the stability of conjugate bases, more is the acidity of the parent acid. Ph, Br, NO_2 exert the –I effect to the C_2 which, further, stabilizes the carboxylate ion.

Order of (–I) effect of the substituents :

$H < Ph < Br < NO_2$

101. (d) Formic acid – HCOOH; Acetic acid – CH_3COOH

Butyric acid – $CH_3CH_2CH_2COOH$

102. (a)

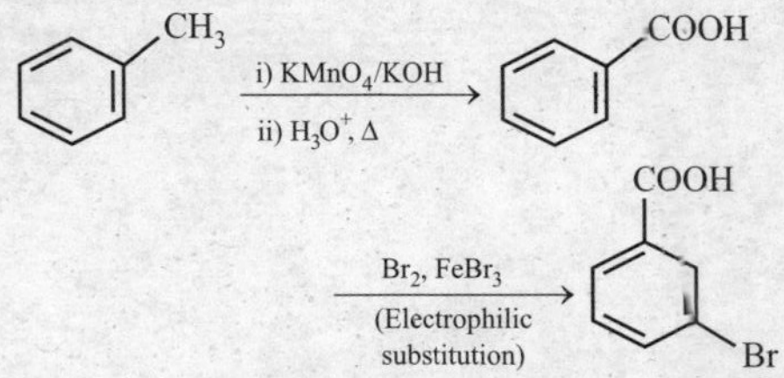

103. (c) (i) Carboxylic acids are stronger acids than phenols because the corresponding carboxylate ions (or conjugate base) are more stabilised by resonance than the corresponding phenoxide ions due to equivalent structures of their canonical forms.

(ii) Groups having –I effect (e.g. $-NO_2$, –X) increase acidity while those having +I effect (e.g. $-OCH_3$, –R) decrease acidity.

Thus acidic (K_a value) order of the four acids is

A > D > B > C

Hence order of pK_a of the four acids is

A < D < B < C

9 Amines

1. (b)

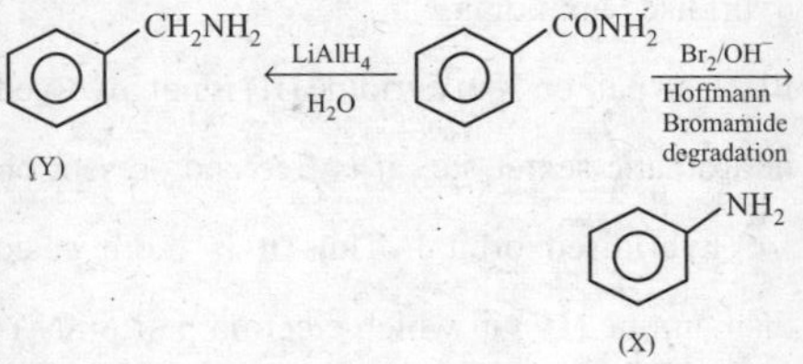

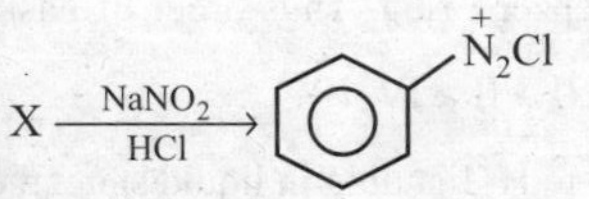

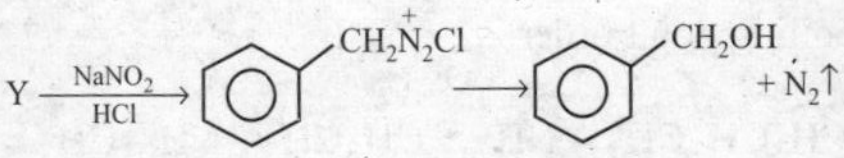

So (Y) does not form stable diazonium salt because its aliphatic amine.

Y can be prepared by ammonolysis of

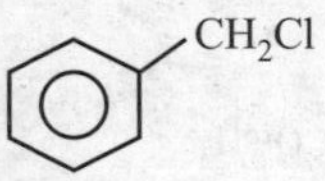

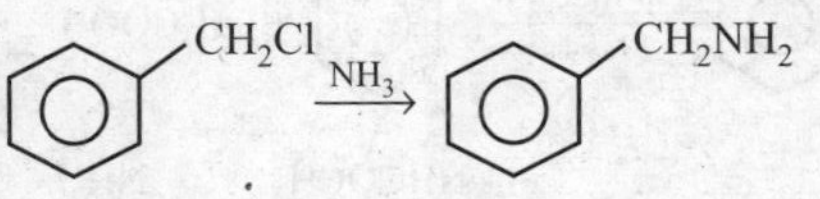

But X does not show this reaction because of partial double bond character of chloro benzene.

2. (c)

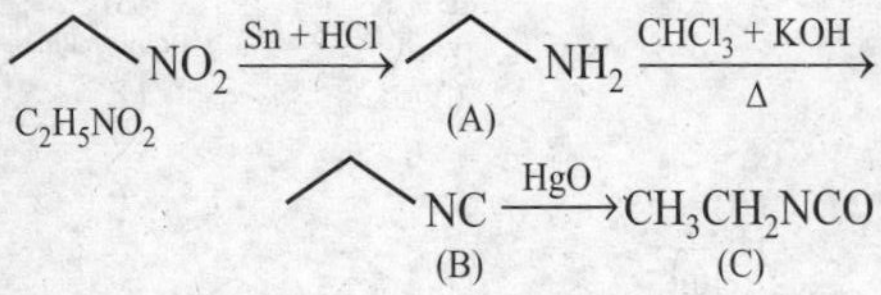

∴ 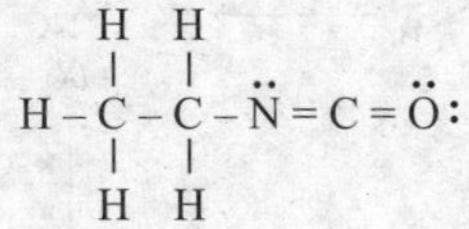

σ bond = 9, π bond = 2, lone pair = 3

3. (a) Basicity $\propto K_b \; \alpha \; \frac{1}{pK_b}$

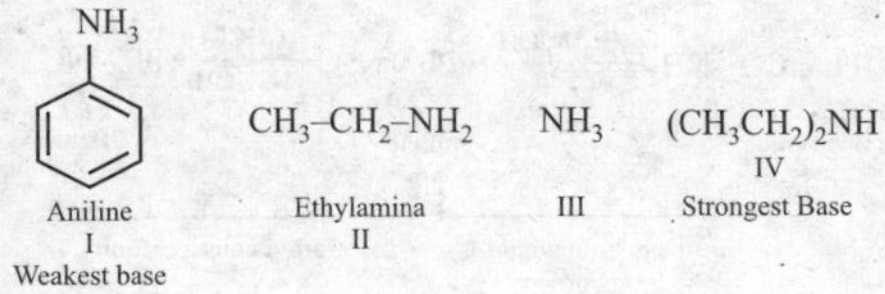

4. (b)

I. The H-atom attached to nitrogen atom in highly acidic, because of this acidic H, it is readily soluble in alkali.

II. It is formed by reaction of Hinsberg reagent

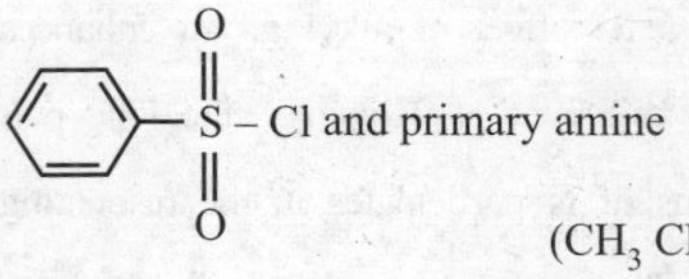

$(CH_3\ CH_2 - NH_2)$

not secondary amine.

5. (b)

(A) n-C_4H_9OH (1°alcohol $\longrightarrow$ 390.3K

(B) $(C_2H_5)_2NH$ (2° amine) $\longrightarrow$ 239.3K

(C) n-$C_4H_9NH_2$ (1° Amine) $\longrightarrow$ 350.8K

(D) $C_2H_5N\ (CH_3)_2$ (3° amine) $\longrightarrow$ 310.5K

6. (b)

(I)

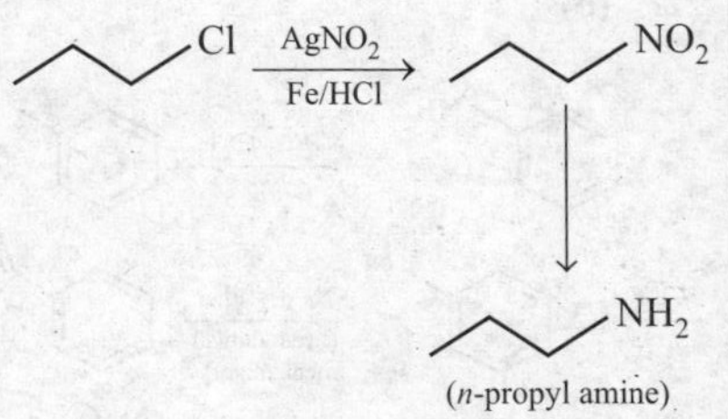

(II)

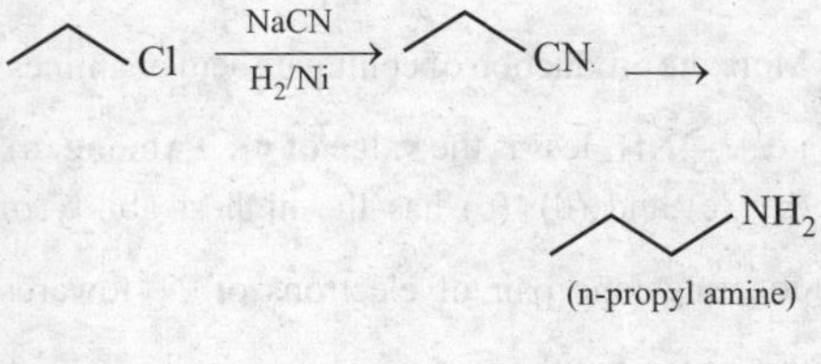

(III)

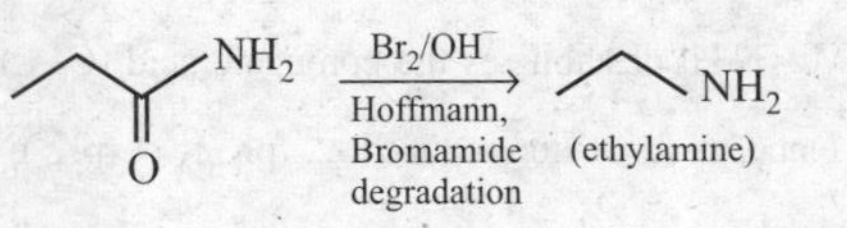

7. (d) $C_6H_5Cl \xrightarrow{CH_3NH_2} C_6H_5NH - CH_3$

$C_6H_5CH_2Cl \xrightarrow{\text{(i) AgCN}} C_6H_5CH_2NC$

$\xrightarrow{\text{(ii)}H_2/Ni} C_6H_5CH_2NH - CH_3$

$C_6H_5CONH_2 \xrightarrow{NaOH/Br_2} C_6H_5NH_2$ (Aniline)

$C_6H_5CONH_2 \xrightarrow[\text{(ii)}H_2O]{\text{(i)}LiAlH_4} C_6H_5CH_2NH_2$ (Benzyl amine)

8. (a) *m*-Nitroaniline is formed in significant amount (47%) due to formation of anilinium ion ($-NH_3^+$) which is a meta-directing group. Thus, statement-I is correct. Statement-II is also correct for the given reason.

9. (b) Benzene sulphonyl chloride ($C_6H_5SO_2Cl$), which is also known as Hinsberg's reagent reacts with primary and secondary amines.

For C_3H_9N

$CH_3 - CH_2 - CH_2 - NH_2$ (1° amine)

$CH_3 - \underset{NH_2}{\overset{H}{\underset{|}{\overset{|}{C}}}} - CH_3$ (1° amine)

$H_3C - \underset{H}{\underset{|}{N}} - CH_2 - CH_3$ (2° amine)

So 'three' amines react with benzene sulphonyl chloride.

10. (c) In the aquecus phase a secondary amine salt $(C_2H_5)_2NH_2^+$ is a balanced interaction of hydrogen bonding and (solvation effect) and inductive effect therefore it is the most basic in water. So the order of basic strength is

$(C_2H_5)_2NH > (C_2H_5)_3N > C_2H_5NH_2$

11. (b) Aniline ($C_6H_5NH_2$) is a Lewis base that reacts with $AlCl_3$ catalyst which is a Lewis acid and therefore Friedel Crafts reaction is not given by aniline due to the formation of salt.

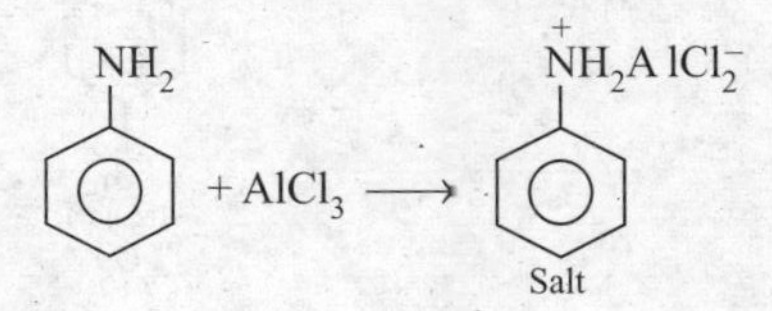

12. (b)

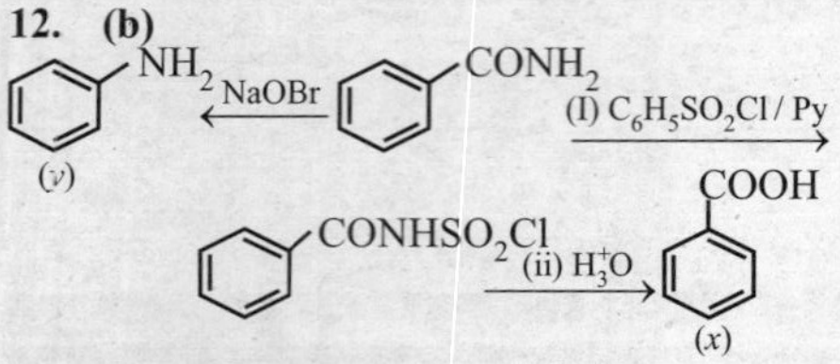

13. (c)

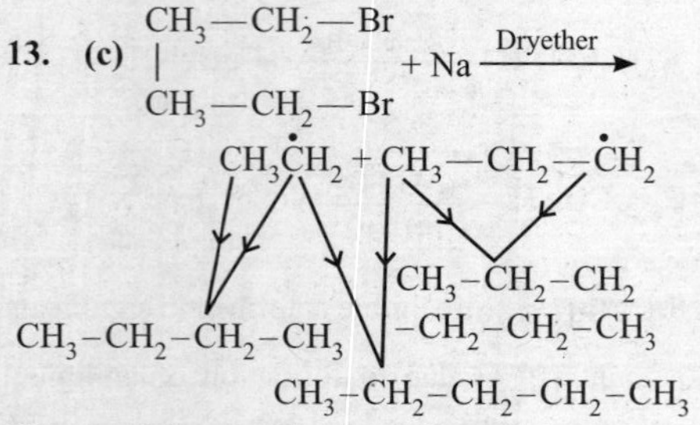

Thus total three products are formed.

14. (b)

$$CH_3-\overset{O}{\overset{||}{C}}-OH \xrightarrow[(2)\ \Delta]{(1)\ NH_3} CH_3CONH_2$$

$$\xrightarrow[\text{(Reaction Hoffmann bromamide)}]{Br_2/NaOH} CH_3-NH_2$$

15. (b)

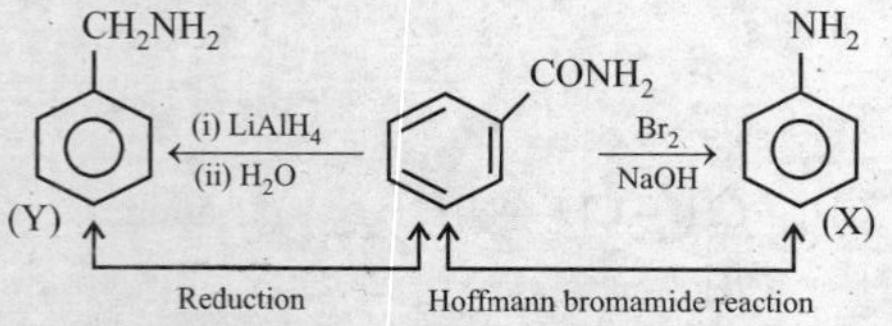

16. (c) Gabriel phthalimide synthesis cannot be used for the preparation of aromatic primary amines because the C – X bond in an aromatic halide (aryl halide) is stronger and thus difficult to break.

17. (b) A secondary amine gives an insoluble compound upon reaction with Hinsberg reagent.

$$\underset{2^\circ \text{ amine}}{R_1-\overset{H}{\overset{|}{N}}-R_2} - \underset{\text{ethanoyl chloride}}{CH_3-\overset{O}{\overset{||}{C}}-Cl} \rightarrow \underset{\text{Amide}}{R_1-\overset{\overset{O}{||}}{\overset{C-CH_3}{|}}{N}-R_2}$$

Thus, 'X' will be $C_6H_5-N(CH_3)-\overset{O}{\overset{||}{C}}-CH_3$

18. (d)

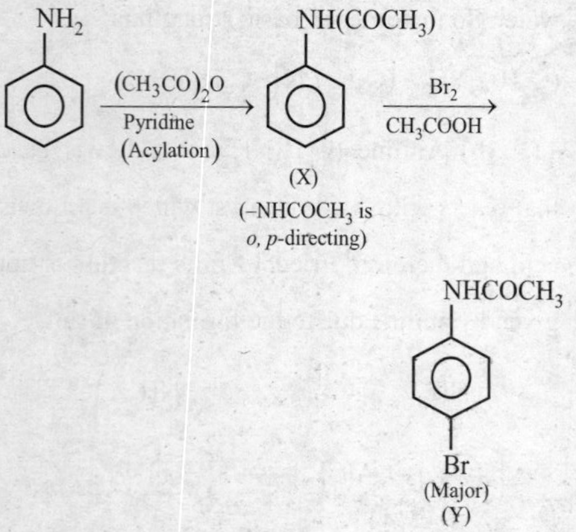

19. (d) The boiling point of amines increases with increasing molecular mass and with decreasing number of alkyl groups to the amino N-atom because of H-bonding.

$$\underset{\substack{1^\circ \text{Amine} \\ \text{(Max. H-bonding} \\ \because \text{ 2 H atoms on N)}}}{CH_3CH_2CH_2CH_2NH_2} > \underset{2^\circ \text{Amine}}{CH_3CH_2NH_2CH_5} > \underset{\substack{3^\circ \text{Amine} \\ \text{(Min. H-bonding} \\ \because \text{ no H atom on N)}}}{CH_3CH_2N(CH_3)CH_3}$$

20. (b) (+R) effect of alkyl group enhances the donor ability of N. However, the lone pair of electrons of N participates in the resonating structures. Thus, it shows very low basic property.

21. (a)

$$CH_3CH_2\ CH_2Br \xrightarrow[C_2H_5OH]{KCN} \underset{\text{Major}}{CH_3CH_2CH_2CN} + \underset{\text{Minor}}{CH_3CH_2CH_2NC}$$

$$CH_3CH_2CH_2CN \xrightarrow{H_3O^+} CH_3CH_2CH_2NH_2 + HCOOH$$

22. (b)

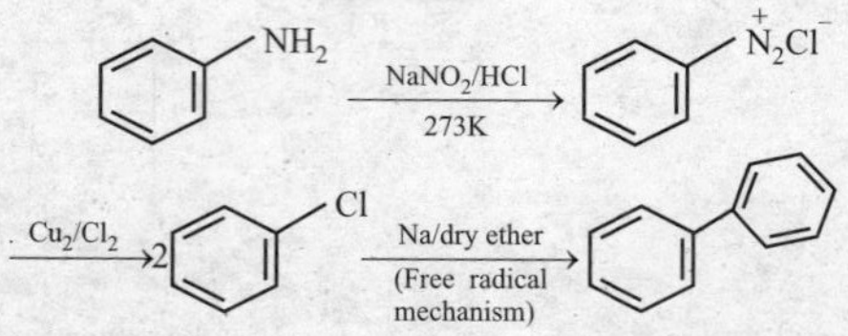

23. (c) $pK_b = -\log\frac{[\text{conjugate acid}]}{[\text{Base}]}$

More the production of conjugate acid of amines, i.e., $\geq\overset{\oplus}{N}H$, less is the value of pK_b. Among (a), (b), (c) and (d), (b) has the highest ability of donating lone pair of electrons of 'N' towards the proton but the steric factor of conjugate acid, $Me_3\overset{\oplus}{N}H$ destabilizes the conjugate acid (C.A.). Hence, its formation reduced. $\therefore$ $(pK_b)_A < (pK_b)_B$. As the phenyl group exerts (–I) effect, the donating capability of lone pairs of 'N' decreases than alkyl amines. However, the steric reason is also valid for the formation of CA. of (c) and (d) and $[C.A.]_{(C)} > [C.A.]_{(D)}$.

Therefore, $(pK_b)_C < (pK_b)_D$.

Hence, the correct order of pK_b

$\Rightarrow$ (D) > (C) > (B) > (A)

24. (d) Piperidine (A) is the most basic. The N lone pair is on sp^3 hybrid orbital and there is no resonance and due to + I effect of alkyl group attached, it becomes more basic than sp^2 hybridised ammonia.

Electron pair on N in pyridine (II) is not involved in aromatic sextet, i.e., it is free and present on sp^2 hybridised orbital. Thus it is more basic than aniline (IV) in which electron pair on N is dispersed to benzene ring. Thus order of basic strength is I > III > II > IV

25. (d) Due to H- bonding in liquid state, the boiling point order is :

$$\underset{(2)\ 1^\circ \text{ Amine}}{CH_3CH_2CH_2-NH_2} > \underset{(3)\ 2^\circ \text{ Amine}}{CH_3CH_2-NH-CH_3} > \underset{(1)\ 3^\circ \text{ Amine}}{CH_3-\underset{\underset{CH_3}{|}}{N}-CH_3}$$

26. (a)

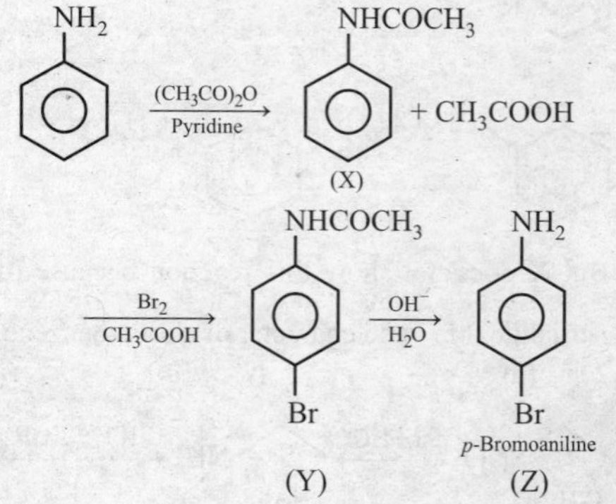

27. (d)

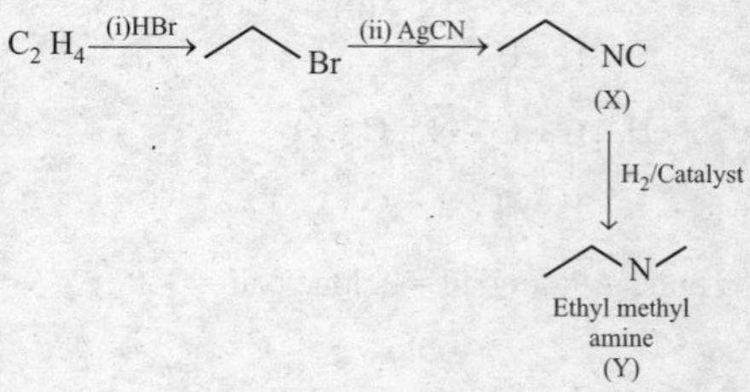

28. (d)

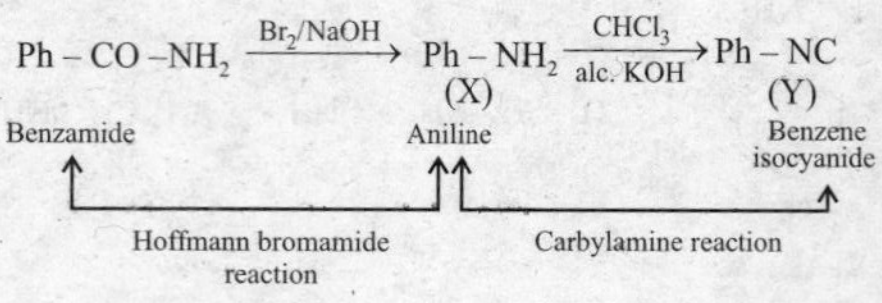

29. (a)

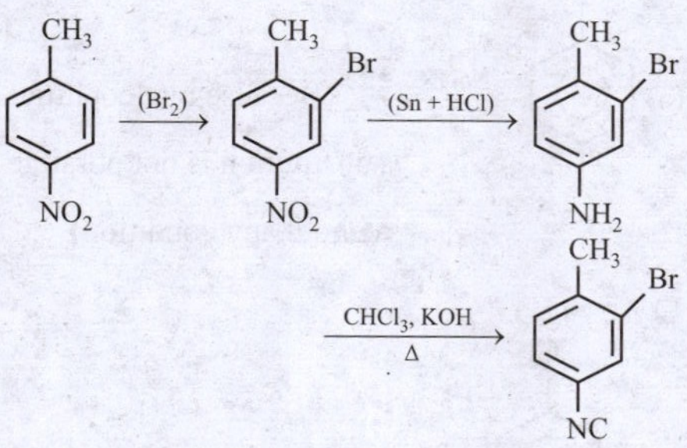

30. (a)

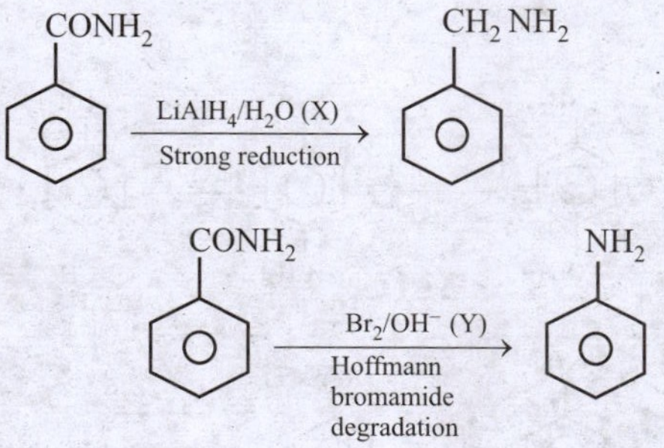

31. (c)

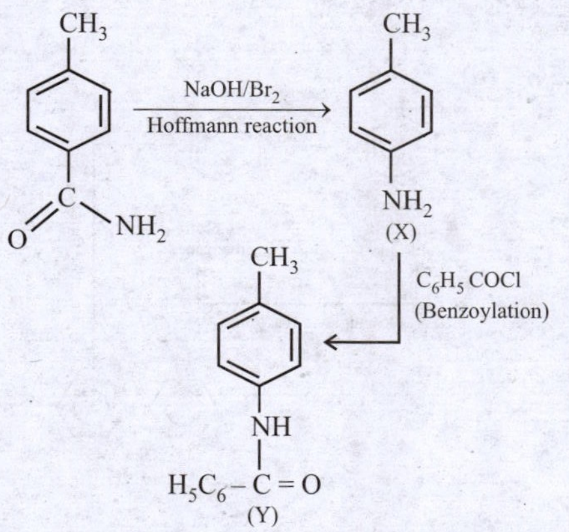

32. (c) Hoffmann bromamide reaction.

33. (b)

$$\underset{\text{(Acetic acid)}}{CH_3COOH} \xrightarrow{NH_3} CH_3CO\overset{-}{O}\overset{+}{N}H_4$$

$$\xrightarrow[-H_2O]{\Delta} \underset{(A)}{CH_3CONH_2}$$

$$\xrightarrow{LiAlH_4} \underset{(B)}{CH_3-CH_2-NH_2}$$

$$\xrightarrow{CHCl_3,\ KOH} \underset{(C)}{CH_3-CH_2-N\equiv C}$$

34. (d)

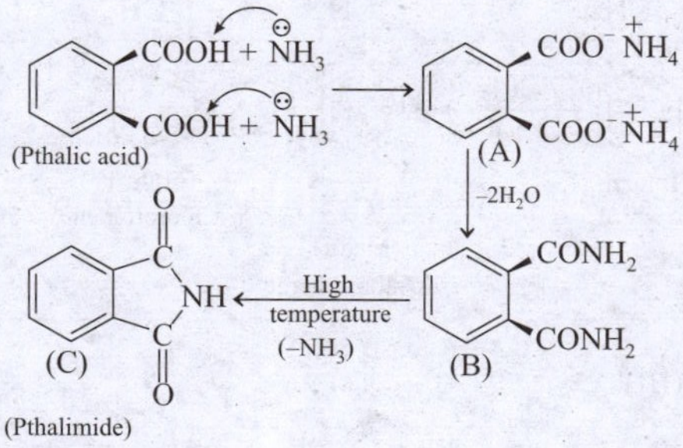

35. (c)

$$\underset{(A)}{C_6H_5MgBr} + \underset{\text{Propionitrile}}{CH_3CH_2C\equiv N} \longrightarrow \underset{(B)}{CH_3CH_2\overset{NMgBr}{\overset{\|}{C}}-C_6H_5}$$

$$\downarrow H_3O^+$$

$$Mg(Br)(NH_2) + \underset{\text{Propiophenone}}{CH_3-CH_2-\overset{O}{\overset{\|}{C}}-C_6H_5}$$

36. (a)

$$C_2H_5-Cl \xrightarrow{KCN} \underset{(X)}{C_2H_5-CN} \xrightarrow{H_2/\text{Catalyst}}$$

$$\underset{(Y)}{CH_3-CH_2-CH_2-NH_2} \xrightarrow[\substack{\text{ak.KOH} \\ \text{(Carbylamine test)}}]{CHCl_3} \underset{(Z)}{CH_3-CH_2-CH_2-NC}$$

37. (b)

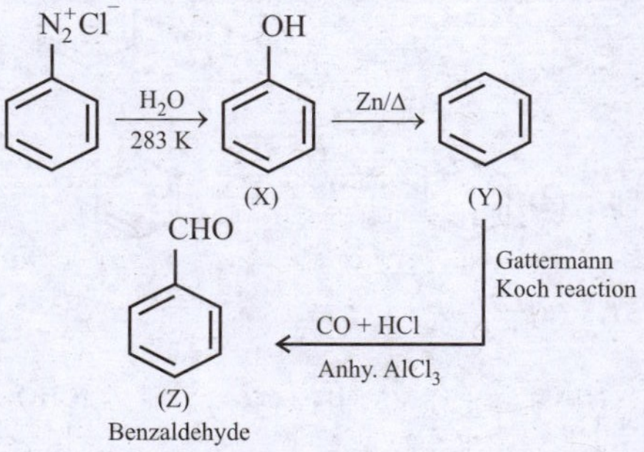

38. (c)

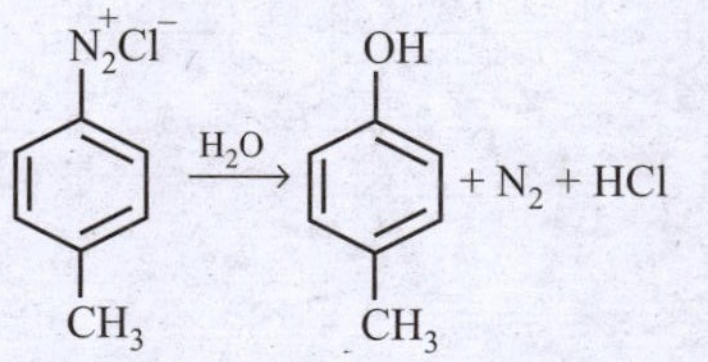

A diazonium salt undergoes hydrolysis upon reaction with H_2O to give corresponding phenol.

So X is H_2O and Y is 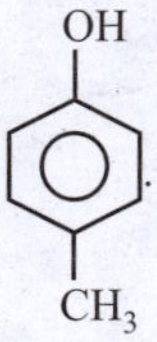.

39. (d)

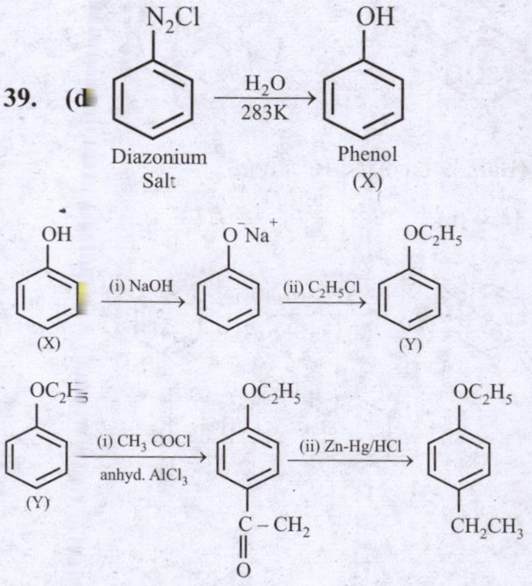

40. (b)

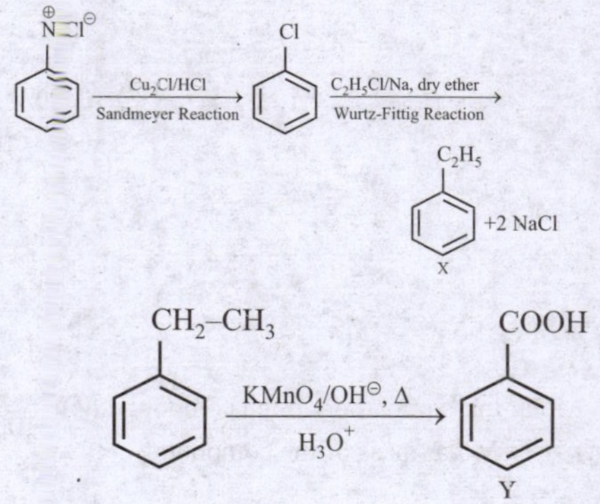

41. (b) Sandmeyer reaction:

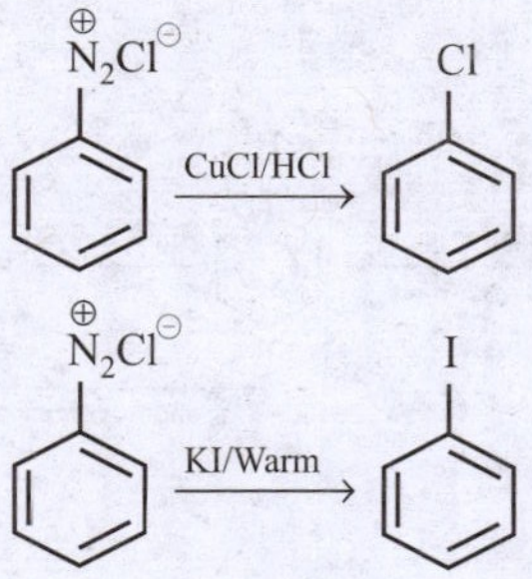

⇒ Synthesis of iodobenzene does not require a copper catalyst because the iodide ion is a powerful enough reducing agent.

42. (a) AgCN is covalent compound so nitrogen attacks the alkyl halide forming isonitrile.

II → Carbylamine reaction where 1° amines react with chloroform to give isonitrile as product.

43. (d) 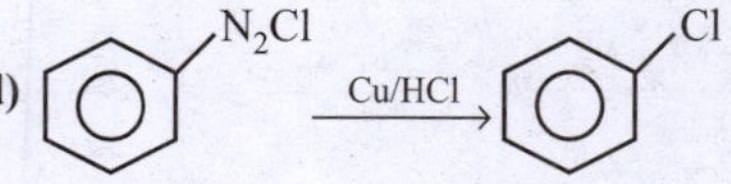

(Sandmayer's Reaction)

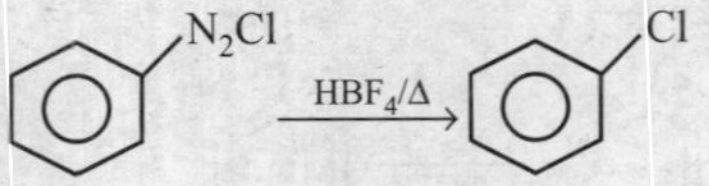

(Balz-Schiemann Reaction)

44. (c)

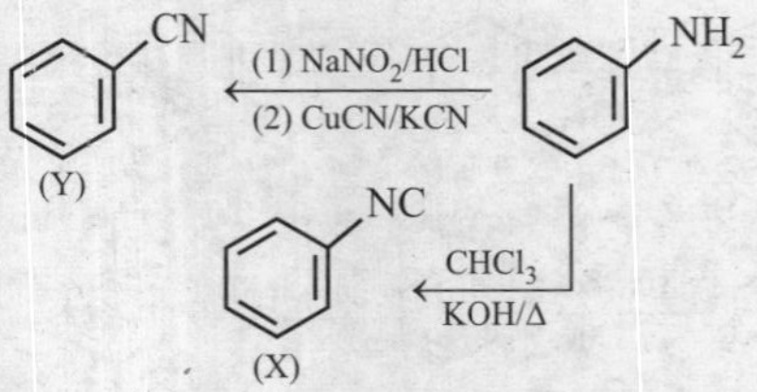

45. (c)

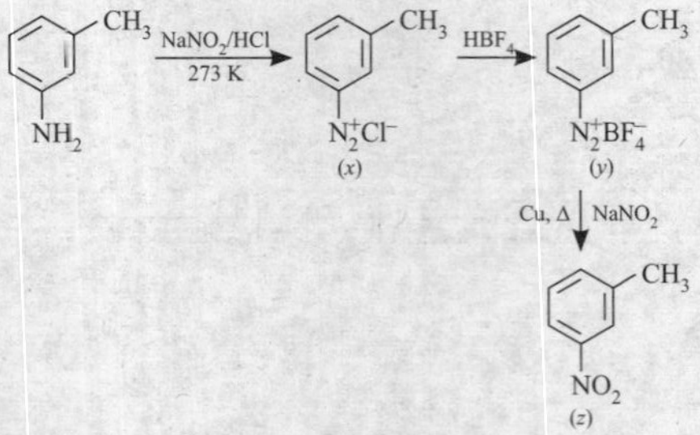

% of carbon =

$$\frac{\text{Molar mass of carbon in the compound (Z)}}{\text{Molar mass of the compound}}\times 100$$

$$= \frac{84}{137}\times 100 = 61.3\%$$

46. (a)

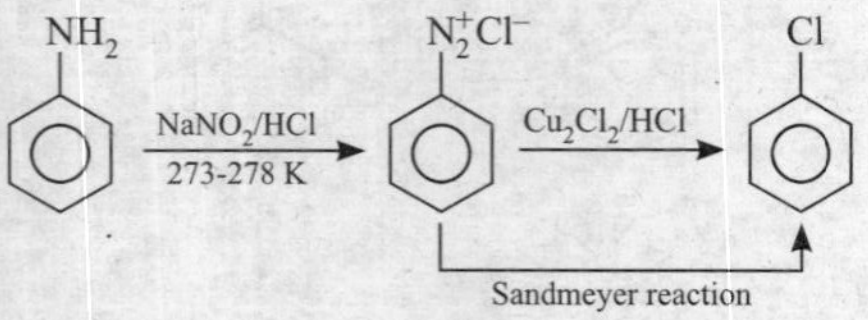

47. (d)

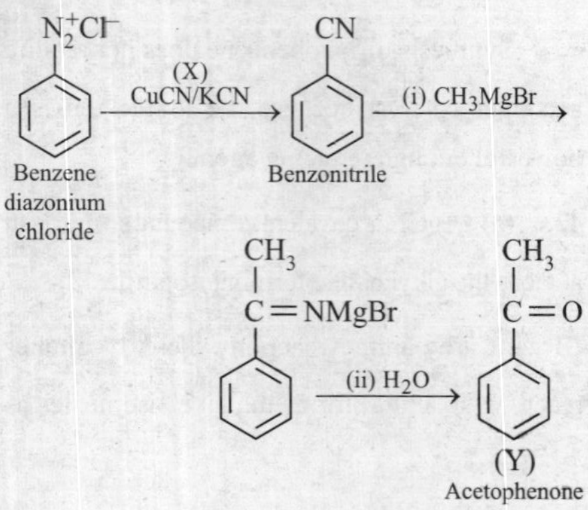

48. (c) (II)

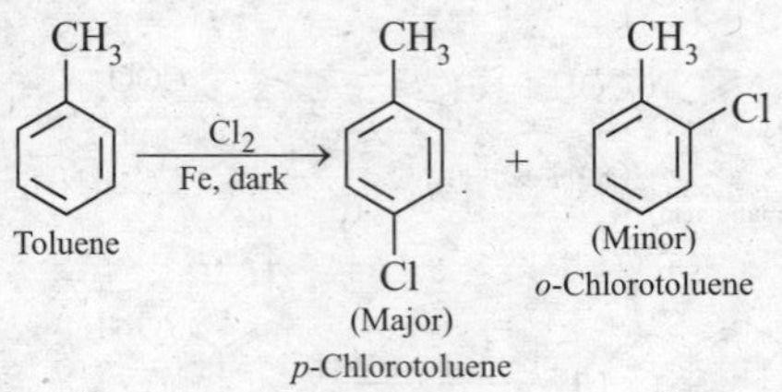

(III)

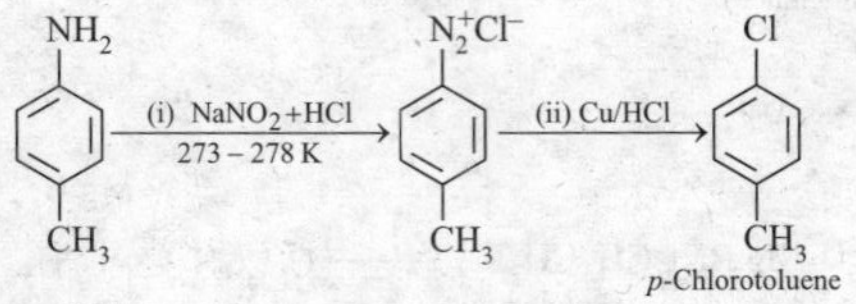

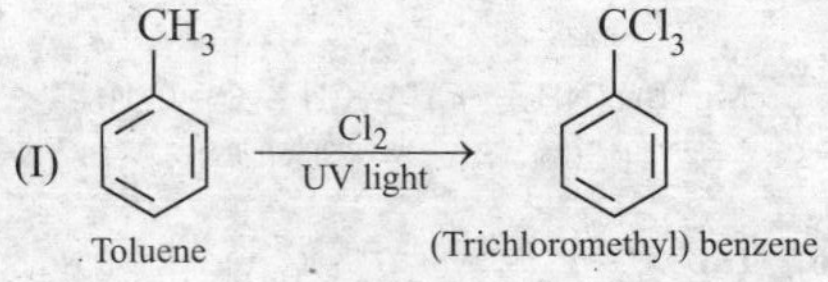

49. (c)

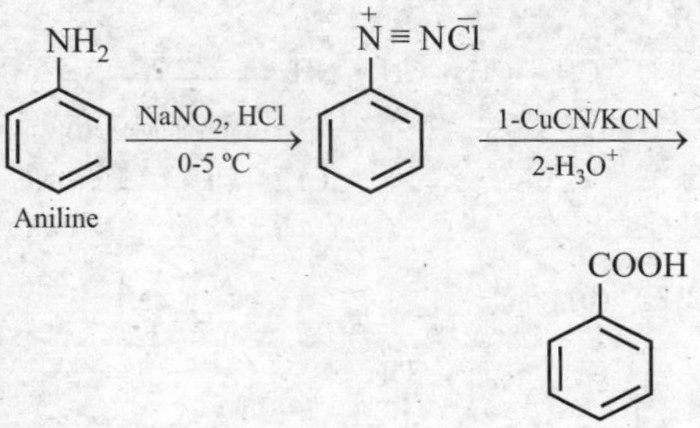

50. (d)

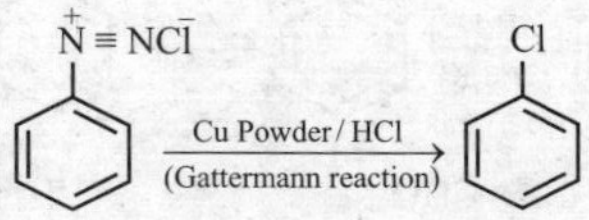

51. (a)

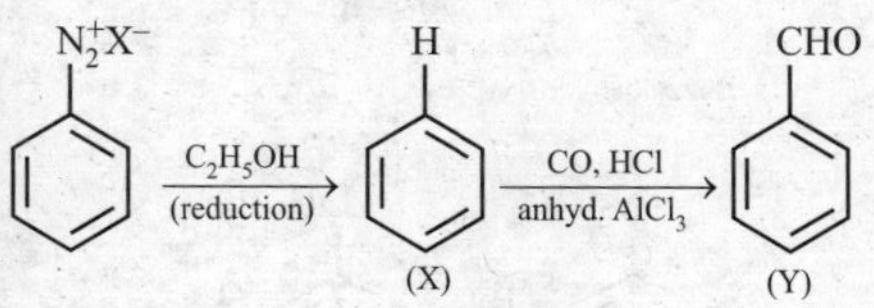

52. (c)

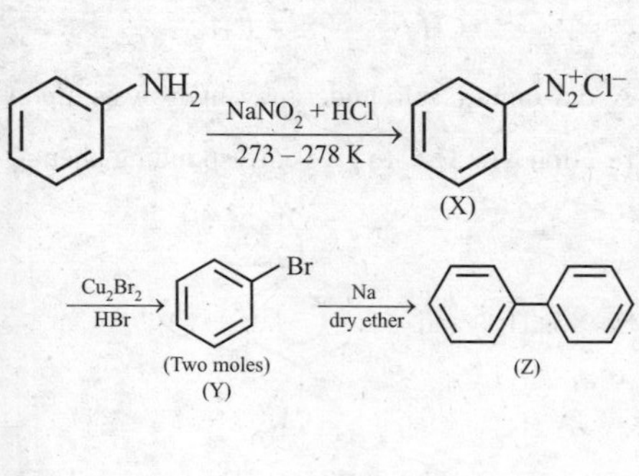

53. (c)

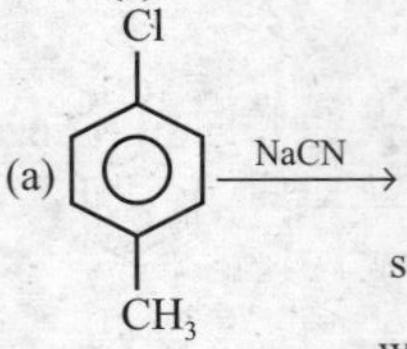

X (Because nucleophilic substitution is not possible without any condition)

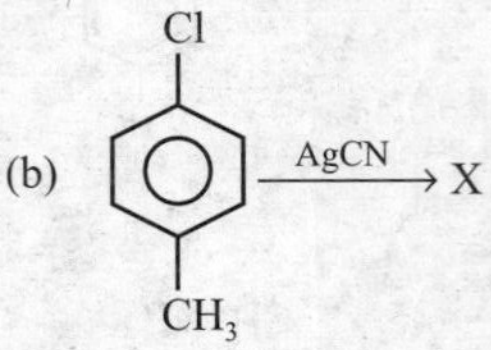

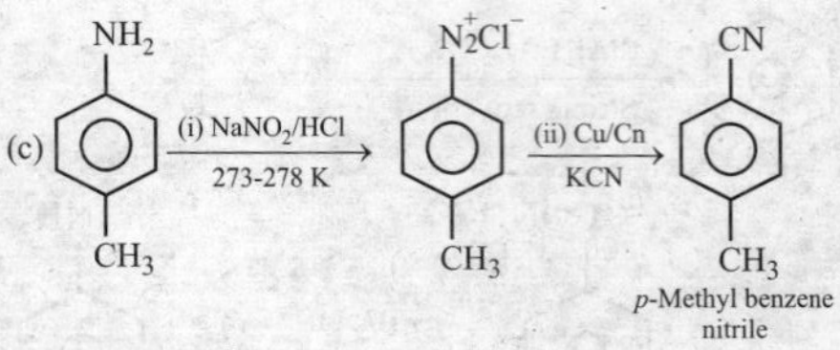

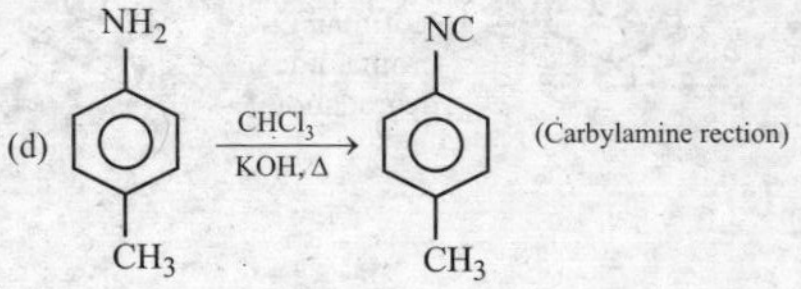

54. (d)

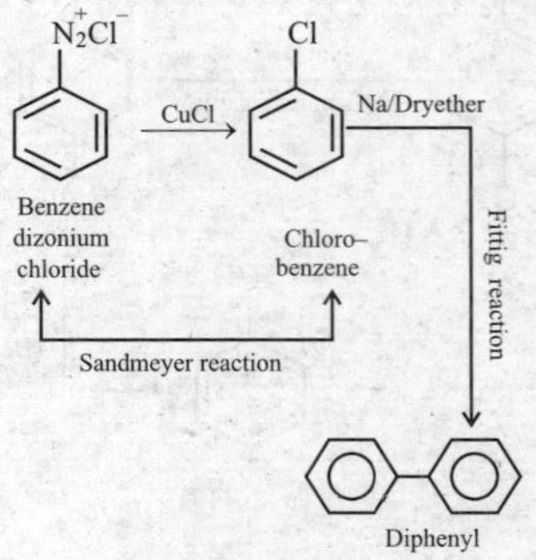

55. (a)

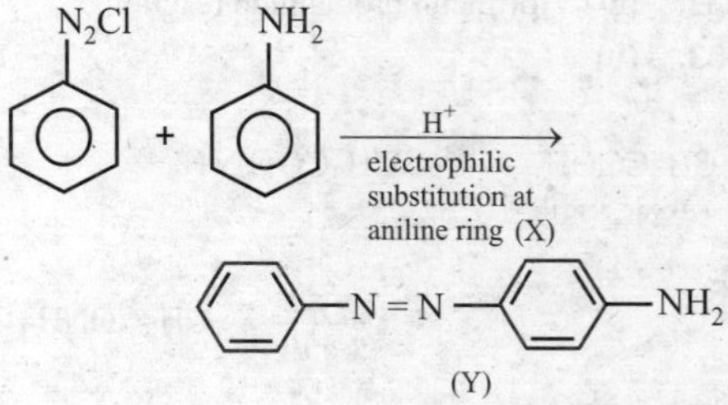

56. (b)

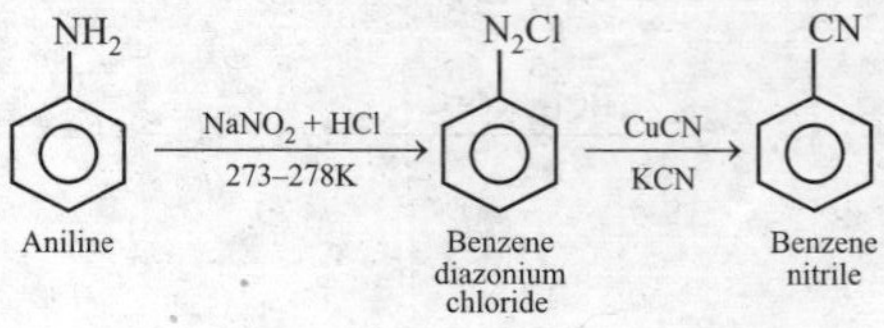

57. (d)

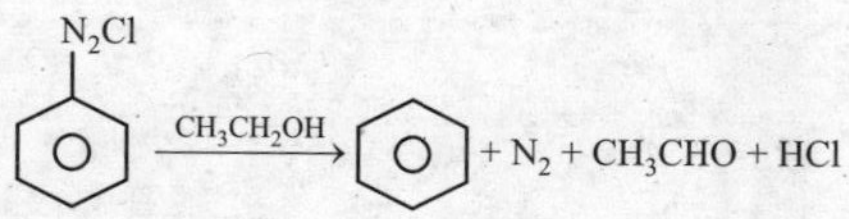

58. (d)

$$C_2H_5NH_2 + HNO_2 \xrightarrow[NaNO_2 + HCl]{0–5°C} C_2H_5N_2Cl$$

1° amine (aliphatic) (unstable)

$$\xrightarrow{H_2O} C_2H_5OH + HCl + N_2\uparrow$$

59. (a)

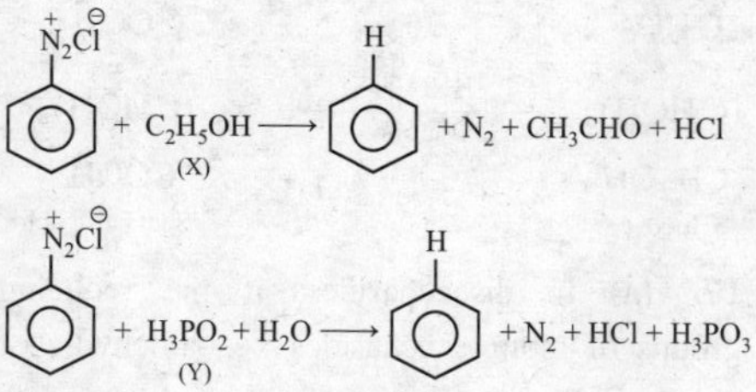

60. (a)

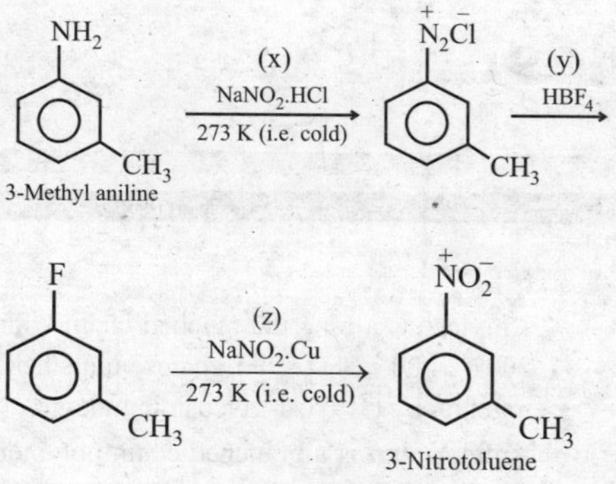

61. (d)

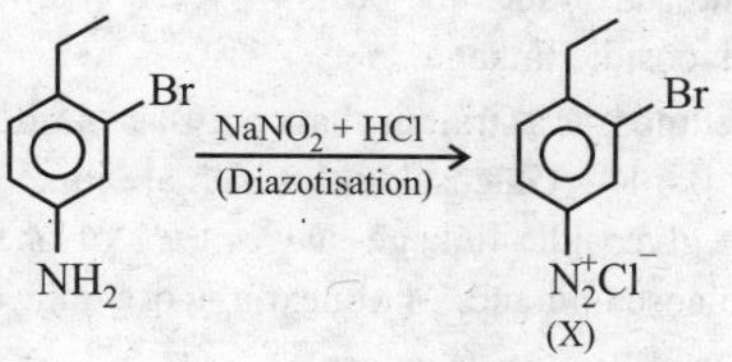

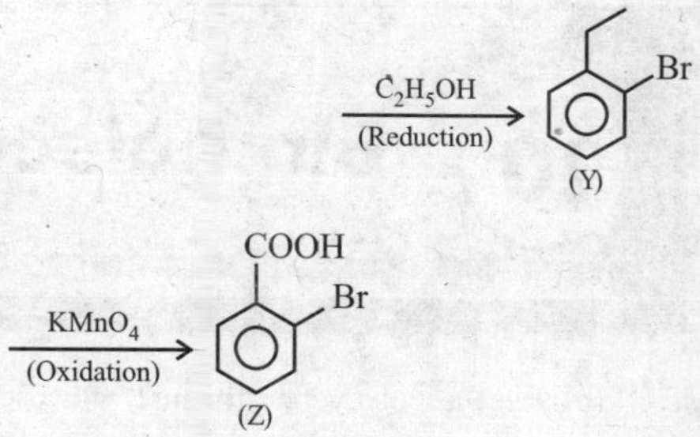

62. (c) The sequence of reaction is

$$Ar_2 - NH_2 \xrightarrow[(X)]{NaNO_2 + HCl} Ar - \overset{+}{N} \equiv NCl^-$$

$$\xrightarrow[(Y)]{Cu/HCl} Ar - Cl + N_2$$

10 Biomolecules

1. **(b)** Because of cyclic structure, glucose does not react with $NaHSO_3$.
(Br_2/H_2O) is mild oxidising agent so it only oxidises aldehydic group to produce gluconic acid.

2. **(a) Statement-I:** Cane sugar is sucrose, it is a disaccharide composed of an α-D glucose unit and β-D fructose unit. These 2 units are held by a glycosidic linkage.
Statement-II : Milk sugar is lactose it is diasaccharide compose d of β-D galactose unit and β-D glycose unit.

3. I:

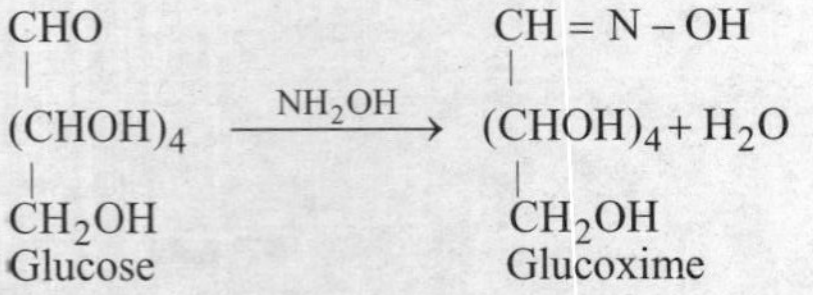

Glucose has free –CHO group that react with NH_2OH to form an oxime.

II:

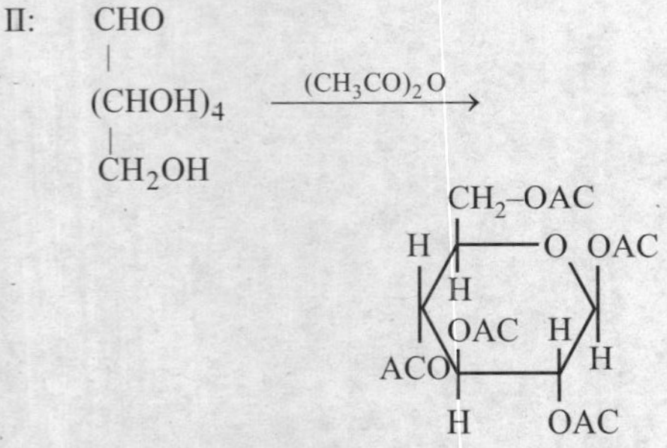

Acetic anhydride acetylates all –OH groups, forming penta acetate and converting glucose in its cyclic form so, there is no free aldehyde group present. Since, there is no free-CHO available NH_2OH connot form an oxime. So, oxime is formed in reaction I but not in reaction II.

4. **(b)** Cellulose is straight chain polysaccharide of β-D-glucose units through C_1–C_4 glucosidic linkage.

5. **(c)**

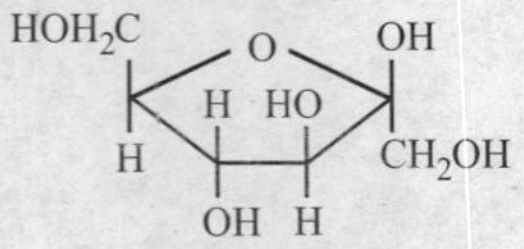

β-D- (–) – Fructofuranose

6. **(d)** Glucose predominanty present in cyclic hemiacetal form in which –CHO group is not free, so it does not react with sodium bisulphite under normal condition.

7. **(b)** Sucrose and cellulose does not give Tollen's reagent.

8. **(d)**

→ Amylose is a long unbranched chain with 200 – 1000 α – D – (+)-glucose units held together by C1 – C4-glycosidic linkage.

→ Amylopectin is a branched chain polymer of α – D-Glucose units in which chain is formed by C1 – C4-Glycosidic linkage whereas branching occurs by C1 – C6-Glycosidic linkage.

→ Cellulose is a straight chain polysaccharide of β – D – Glucose units which are joined by glycosidic linkage between C1 of one glucose unit and C4 of next glucose unit.

9. **(c)** Milk sugar (Lactose)
= β – D – glucose + β – D – galactose
Thus, statement I is correct but II is incorrect.

10. **(d)** Lactose is more commonly known as milk sugar. It is composed of β-D-galactose and β-D-glucose. Free aldehyde group may be produced at C–1 of glucose unit hence it is a reducing sugar.

11. **(a)** Cane sugar and amylose contain α-D-glucose unit.

12. **(c)** Amylose is an unbranched polymer of α-D-(+)-glucose.

13. **(b)**

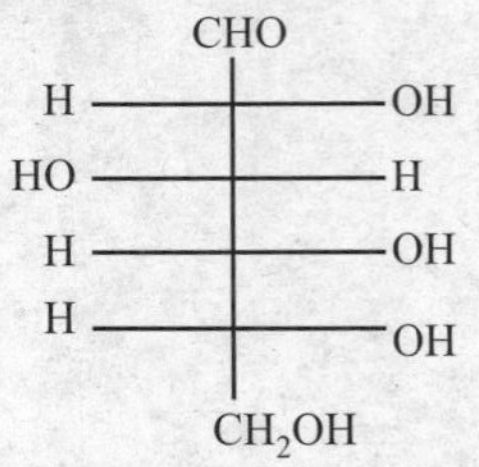

Glucose

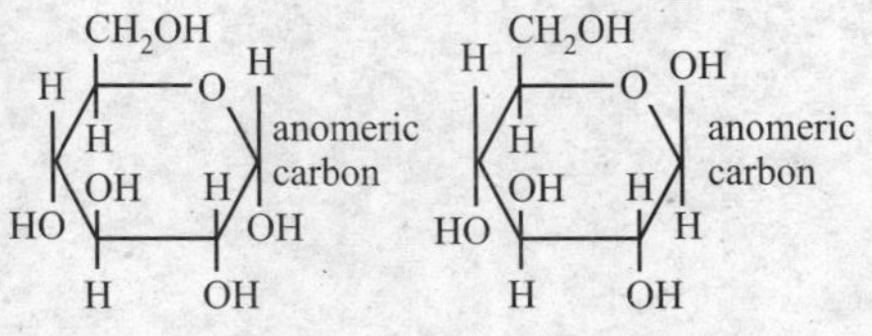

α-D-(+) Glucopyranose β-D-(+)-Glucopyranose

No. of –OH groups are 5 in open chain and ring structure.

14. **(b) Monosaccharides:** A carbohydrate that cannot be hydrolysed further to give simpler unit of polyhydroxy aldehyde or ketone is called a monosaccharide.

Example: Glucose, Fructose, Ribose

Disaccharides: The sugar formed when two monosaccharides are joined by glycosidic linkage.

Example: Sucrose, Lactose, Maltose.

15. **(c)** Chargaff's rule states that in DNA, amount of guanine should be equal to the amount of cytosine and the amount of adenine should be equal to the amount of thymine.
So statement (I) is correct but (II) is incorrect.

16. **(c)**

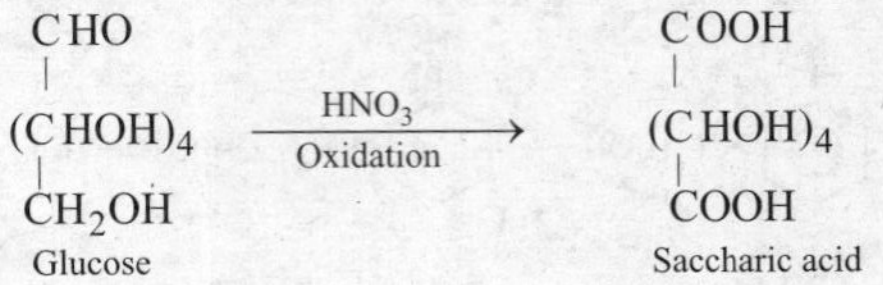

17. **(a)** In disaccharides, if the reducing groups of mono-saccharides i.e., aldehydic of aldose or ketonic groups of ketose are bonded, these are non-reducing sugar e.g., sucrose. On the other hand, sugars in which these functional groups are face, are called reducing sugars for example, maltose and lactose.

18. **(a)** In both, glucose and fructose, C-5 atom participates in hemiacetal formation.

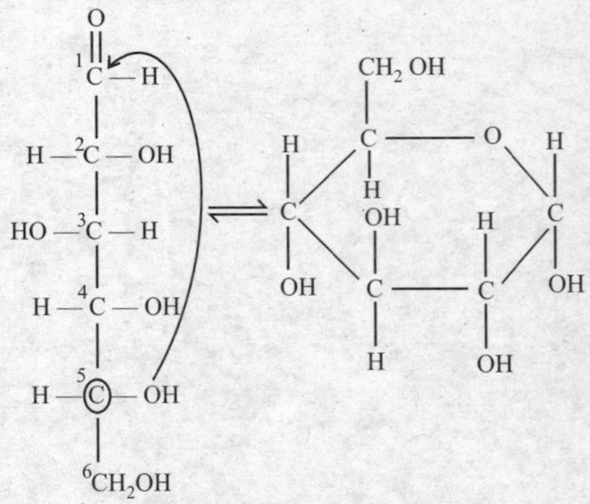

D-glucose

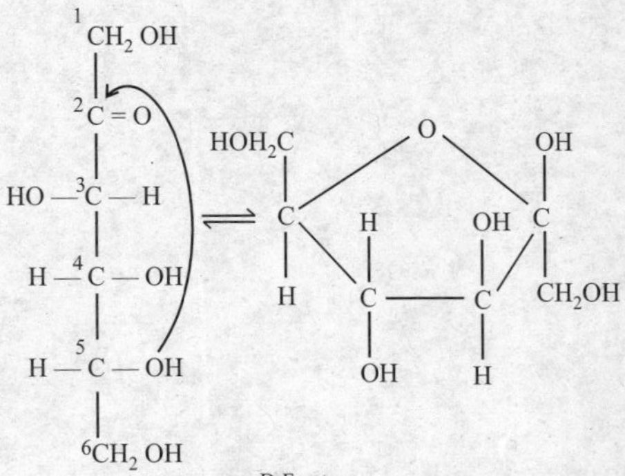

D-Fructose

19. **(a)** It is an equimolar mixture.

20. **(b)**

(i) Monosaccharides are smallest carbohydrates that cannot be hydrolysed. Hence statement (i) is not correct.

(ii) Disaccharides are made up of two units of monosaccharides, so their hydrolysis will also give two monosaccharide units that can be same or different.

e.g., Sucrose → Glucose + Fructose

Maltose → Glucose + Glucose

Hence, statement (ii) is correct

(iii) Polysaccharides are polymers of many monosaccharides and have no sweet taste.

Hence, statement (iii) is correct

(iv) Monosaccharides are categorised as reducing sugars.

Hence, statement (iv) is not true.

21. (b)

$$\underset{\text{Starch}}{(C_6H_{10}O_5)_n} + nH_2O \xrightarrow{343\text{K},2\ 3\text{atom}} \underset{\text{Glucose}}{nC_6H_{12}O_6}$$

22. (d) Glucose does not react with $NaHSO_3$, to form hydrogen sulphide addition product. Glucose reacts with NH_2OH, HCN and Br_2/H_2O and give oxime, cyanohydrin, gluconic acid respectively.

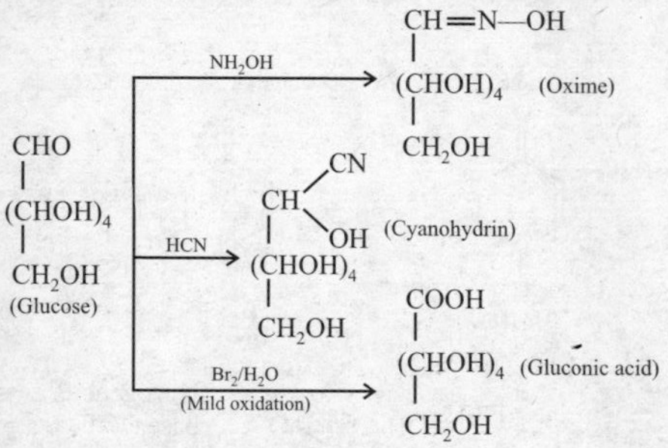

23. (b)

24. (c) Lactose is composed of β-D-galactose (C-1) linked to β-D glucose at (C-4).

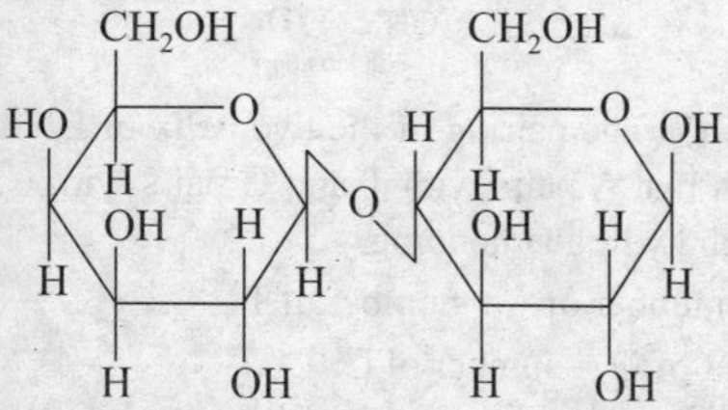

25. (d)

26. (b) Amino acid **Structure**

Serine

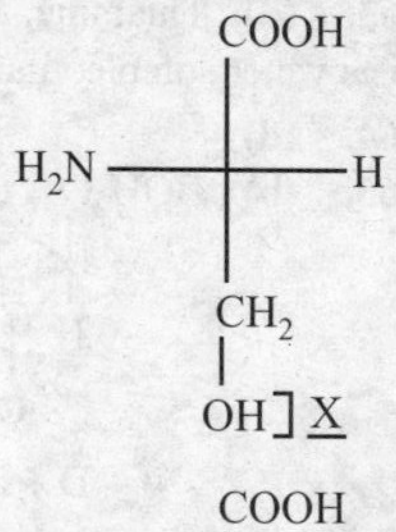

Cysteine

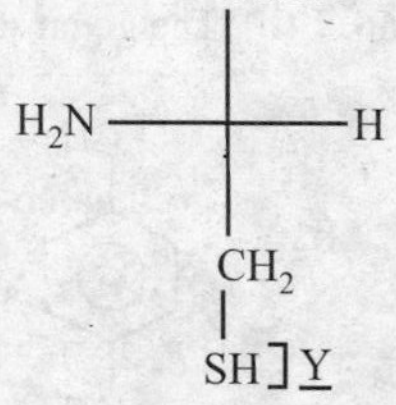

So X = –OH, Y = –SH

27. (b) Alanine: $H_2N-CH(CH_3)-COOH$

Leucine: $H_2N-CH(CH_2-CH(CH_3)_2)-COOH$

Serine : $H_2N-CH(CH_2-OH)-COOH$

Cysteine: $H_2N-CH(CH_2-SH)-COOH$

So, A-III, B-I, C-II, D-IV.

28. (b) Histidine (His) and Tryptophan (Trp) contains heterocyclic aromatic ring.

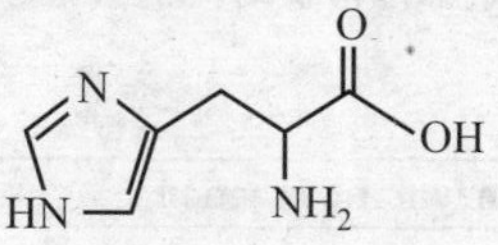

Histidine

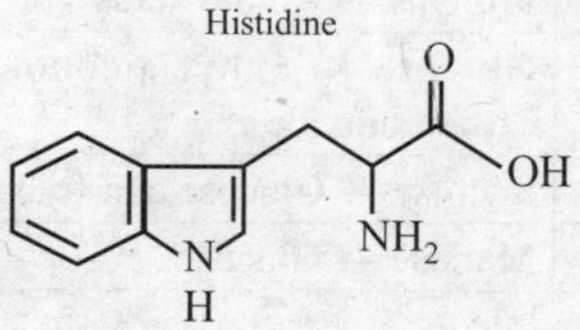

Tryptophan

29. (c)

(A) Tyrosine ⇒

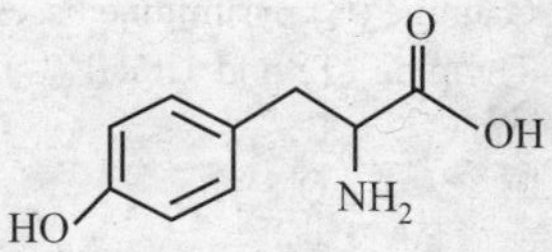

(Aromatic amino acid)

(B) Lysine ⇒

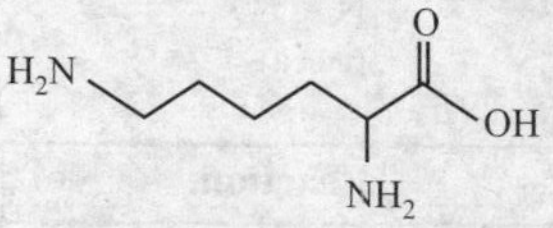

Extra amino group ⇒ (Basic amino acid)

(C) Glycine ⇒

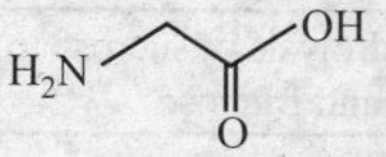

No chiral centre ⇒ (Optically inactive amino acid)

(D) Cysteine ⇒

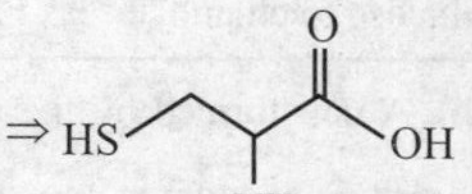

(Sulphur) containing amino acid)

A-IV, B-I, C-II, D-III

30. (d) Essential amino acids are leucine and histidine.

31. (b) Leucine and phenylalnine are essential and neutral amino acids.

32. (b) Amino acids are classified as acidic, basic or neutral depending upon the relative number of amino acid and carboxyl group in their molecule. Equal number of amino and carboxyl group makes it neutral, more number of amino than carboxyl group makes it basic.

Lysine and arginine are basic amino acids because their structures contain more amino groups ($-NH_2$) than carboxyl groups (–COOH).

Alanine, Tyrosine and Serine are neutral amino acids because they have an equal number of amino ($-NH_2$) and carboxyl (–COOH) groups.

33. (c) Primary structure of protein represent its constituent but α-helix and β-pleated sheet structures are formed by H-bonding regular folding. They represent secondary structure of proteins.

34. (c)

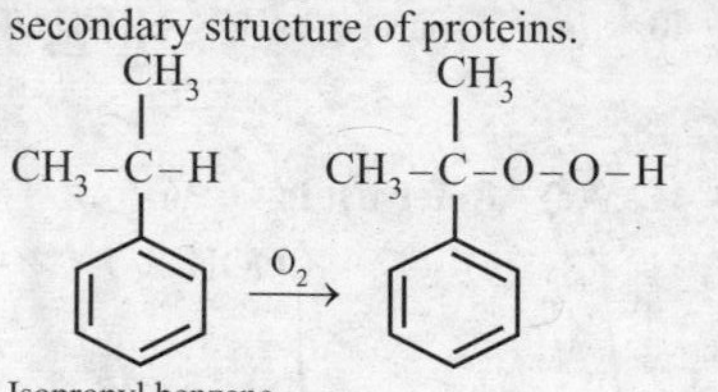

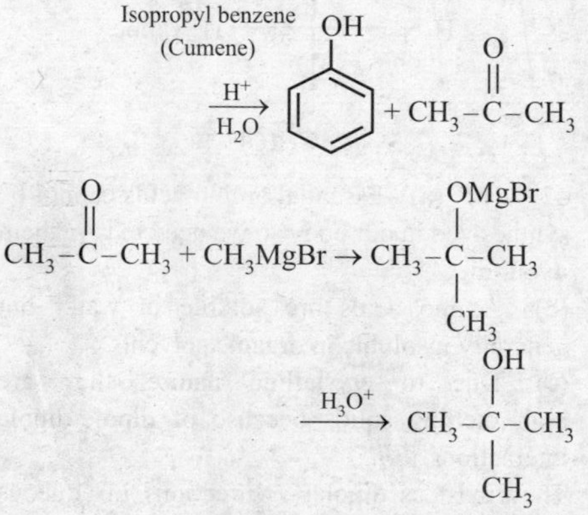

35. (b) Starch is a polymer of α-glucose. Amylose and Amylopectin are components of starch. Lactose is composed of β-D- galactose and β-D-glucose. Proteins are composed of many type of amino acid.

36. (c)

Essential amino acids	Non-essential amino acids
Arginine (Arg)	Alanine (Ala)
Histidine (His)	Asparagine (ASN)
	Isoleucine (Ile)
	Aspartate (ASP)
Leucine (Leu)	Glutamic acid (Glu)
Lysine (Lys)	Glycine (Gly)
Methionine (Met)	Serine (Ser)
Phenyl alanine (Phe)`	Proline (Pro)
	Threonine (Thr)
	Tryptophan (Trp)
	Valine (Val)

37. (c) Primary protein structure represents sequence of amino acids present in a chain.

Secondary protein structure involves hydrogen bonding of the peptide backbone.

Tertiary protein structure represents three dimensional folding pattern of a protein due to side chain interaction.

Quaternary protein structure indicates number of chains of amino acids in protein.

104. (a)

$$CH_3CH_2CH_2COONa \xrightarrow{\text{electrolysis}} CH_3CH_2\dot{C}H_2$$

$$2CH_3CH_2\dot{C}H_2 \longrightarrow \underset{n\text{-Hexane }(C_6)}{CH_3(CH_2)_4CH_3}$$

105. (b) $Ar-COOH \xrightarrow{NaHCO_3} Ar-COONa + CO_2\uparrow + H_2O$

106. (d)

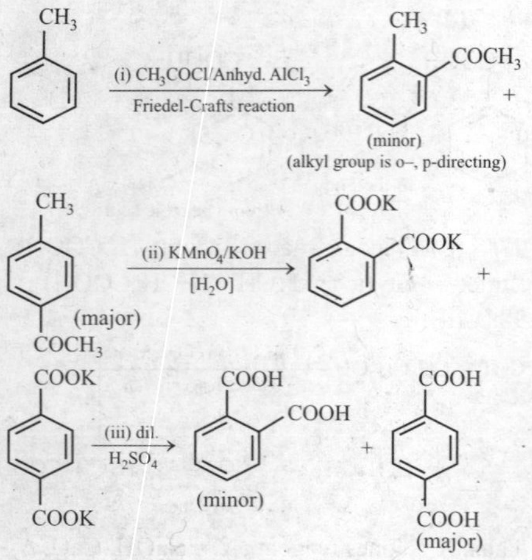

107. (a)

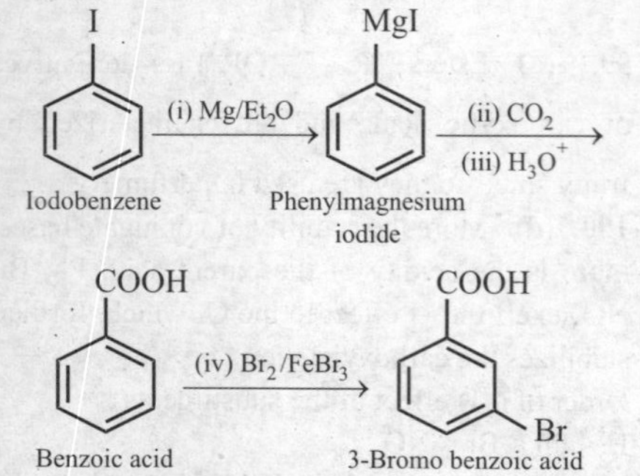

108. (d) Carboxylic acids are the most acidic compounds among the organic compounds. Due to presence of electron withdrawing group i.e. chlorine and fluorine, FCH_2COOH and $CH_3CH_2CHClCOOH$ are more acidic, than C_6H_5COOH and CH_3COOH. Fluorine is more electron withdrawing group than chlorine. Therefore,

$$\underset{\text{Fluoro ethanoic acid}}{FCH_2COOH} > \underset{\text{2-Chlorobutanoic acid}}{CH_3CH_2CHClCOOH} > \underset{\text{Benzoic acid}}{C_6H_5COOH} > \underset{\text{Acetic acid}}{CH_3COOH}$$

109. (d) Vinegar contains 5-8% acetic acid by volume.

110. (b) (–) I group, if present along with – COOH group in an acid, it increases the acidic property while (+) I groups (e.g. CH_3) will decrease the acidic property.

∴ $NCCH_2COOH > FCH_2COOH > H_3C\,CH_2COOH$

(II) Structures which show more resonance structures or hyperconjugation among aldehydes are less reactive.

Ketones are less reactive than aldehydes due to steric hindrance.

Hence, correct order of reactivity is:

$CH_3CH_2CHO > PhCHO > PhCOCH_3$

(III) Boiling points of alcohols (due to ability to form H-bond) are higher than that of aldehydes which have more b.p. than that of ketones (due to less steric-hinderance and more surface area in aldehyde group, having same number of C-atoms)

Hence order of boiling point is

$H_3CCOCH_2CH_3 < CH_3CH_2CHO < H_3CCH_2CH_2OH$

Hence option (b) is the correct answer.

111. (b)

$$R-COOH + HOR' \xrightarrow{\text{Conc. } H_2SO_4} R-COOR' + H_2O$$

Mechanism of esterification

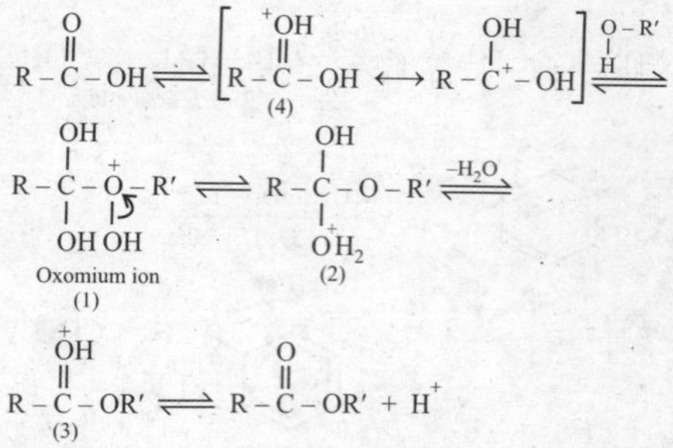

112. (d)

(*i*) ∵ NO_2 group increases the acidic nature due to –I effect.

(*ii*) ∵ OCH_3 and CH_3 are electron donating groups (i.e.,+I effect), thus decreases the acidic nature, but ∵ OCH_3 will decrease acidic nature more than of ∵ CH_3 group

Hence, correct order is

III < IV < I < II

113. (c)

$$CH_3OH \xrightarrow{PCl_3} \underset{(A)}{CH_3Cl} \xrightarrow{KCN} \underset{(B)}{CH_3CN} \xrightarrow{H_3O^+} \underset{(C)}{CH_3COOH}$$

Hence, C is CH_3COOH.

114. (a) $\underset{\text{Acetic acid}}{CH_3COOH} \xrightarrow{SOCl_2} \underset{\text{Acetyl chloride}}{CH_3COCl} \xrightarrow{H_2/Pd-BaSO_4} \underset{\text{Acetaldehyde}}{CH_3CHO}$

38. (d) 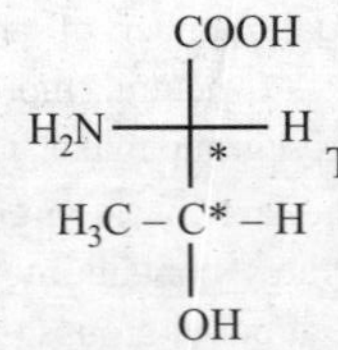 Threonine

Threonine has 2 chiral centres.

39. (d) Val, Leu and Lys are essential and Gly, Pro and Ser are non essential amino acids (3 and 3). **Refer Q. 36**

40. (c) Asparagine 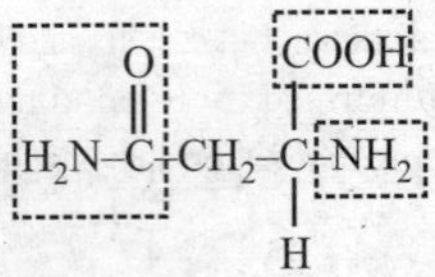

41. (c) **Refer list in Q. 36**

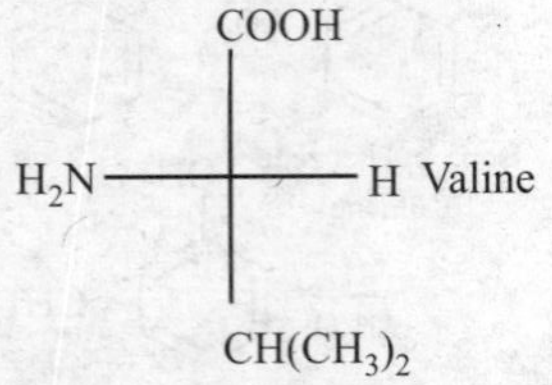

42 (d) (a) Essential amino acids cannot be synthesized in our body so we need to take them in our diet.

(b) Amino acids are soluble in water but generally insoluble in organic solvents.

(c) Due to crystalline nature, they are high melting solids because of dipole-dipole interactions.

They exist as dipolar zwitter ions in aqueous solutions.

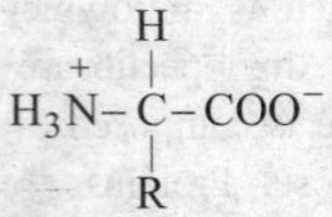

43. (c)

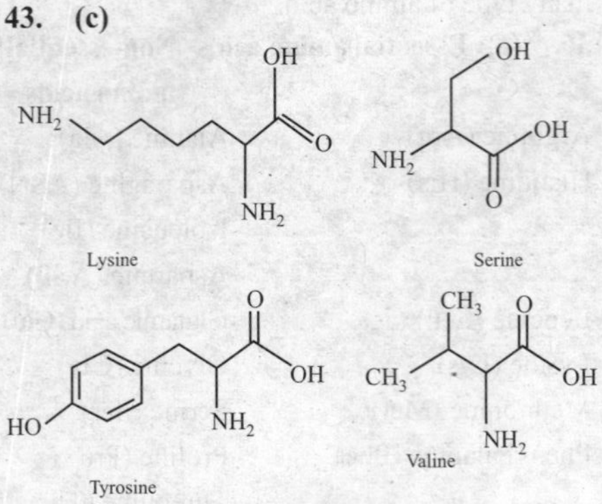

44. (b) Fibrous proteins = Keratin, Myosin

Globular proteins = Insulin, Albumin

45. (d) S-Containing amino acids = Cysteine, methionine.

OH- Containing amino acid = Serine

NH_2- Containing amino acid = Lysine.

46. (b)

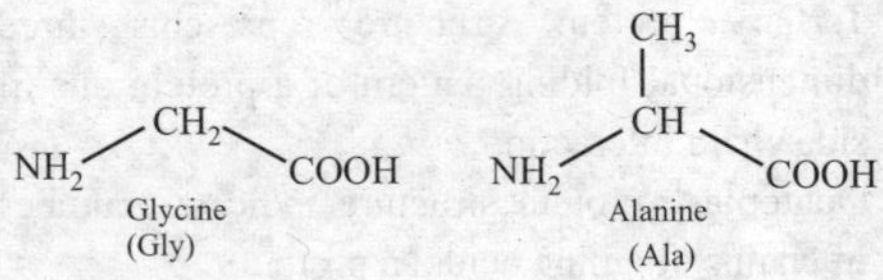

47. (b) Keratin is a natural structural protein that is found in many outer body parts, e.g., hair, skin, nail etc. It is not present in muscles.

48. (a) Serine

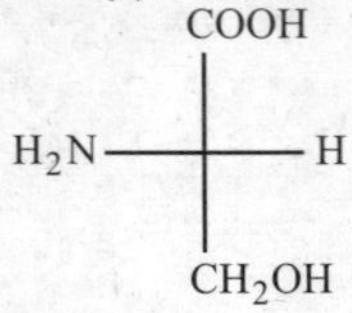

49. (a)

50. (a)

51. (a) 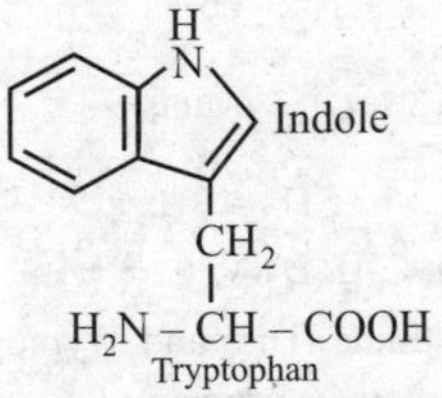

Indole

Tryptophan

52. (d) Nucleoside of RNA has ribose sugar and uracil (U).

53. (b)

Enzyme	Enzymatic reaction
Pepsin	Proteins → Amino acids
Zymase	Glucose → Ethyl alcohol and carbon dioxide
Invertase	Sucrose → Glucose and fructose
Maltase	Maltose → Glucose

So 'b' is incorrect.

54. (d) Purine bases one Adenine (A) and Gaunine (G) pyrimidine bases are Cytosine (C), Thymine (T) and Uracil (U). DNA contains A and C.

55. (c) 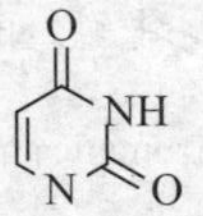

(uracil)

56. (d)

Reaction	Enzyme
(A) Hydrolysis of starch to maltose	Diastase (I)
(C) Hydrolysis of sucrose to glucose and fructose	Invertase(III)
(B) Conversion of proteins to peptides	Pepsin (II)
(D) Glucose to ethanol	Zymase (IV)

57. (b) A unit formed by the attachment of a base to 1 psition of sugar is known as nucleoside. In nucloside, the sugar carbons are numbered as 1', 2', 3' etc.

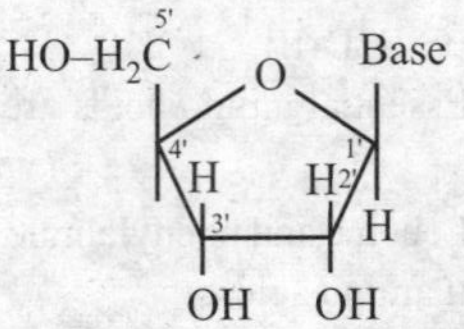

58. (c) Nucleoside = Pentose Sugar + Nitrogenous base.

Nucleotide = Nucleoside + Phosphate

59. (d)

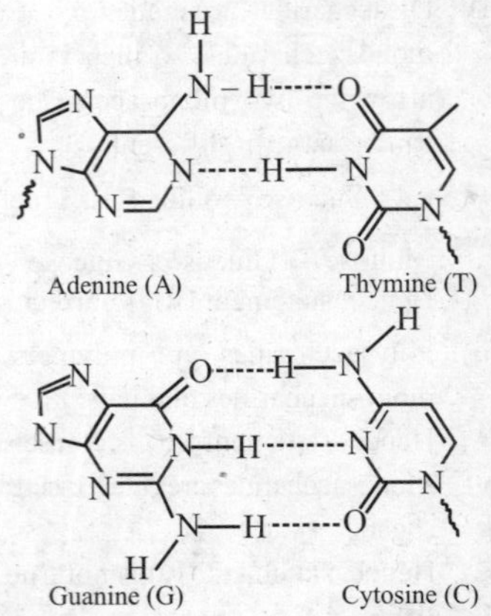

60. (d) Adenine (A), Guanine (G) and cytosine (C) are present in both, DNA and RNA. Thymine (T) is present in DNA and Uracil (U) is present in RNA.

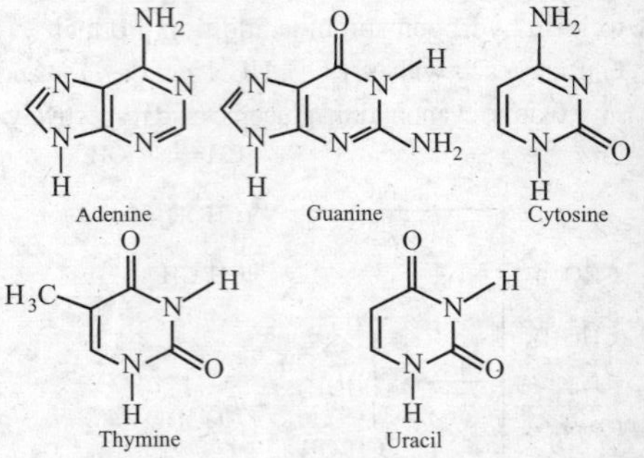

61. (a)

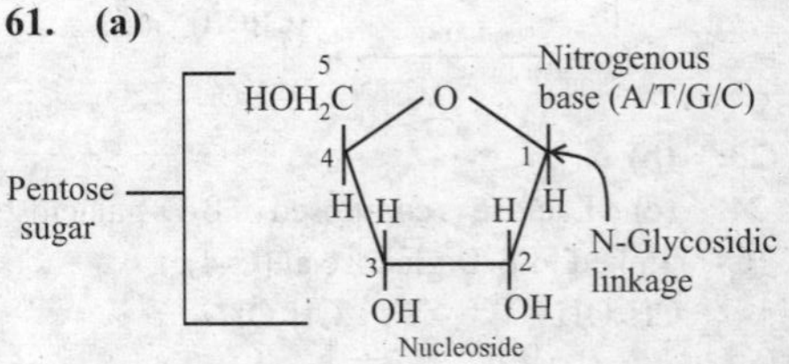

62. (d) The pairing of the two helix of DNA is such that A pairs with T and G pairs with C, through hydrogen bonding.

Thus, number of A = number of T

number of G = number of C

Therefore, statement in Assertion (A) is wrong and Reason (R) is correct.

63. (d) Thiamine, also known as Vitamin B_1, is a water soluble vitamin.

64. (d)

65. (b) 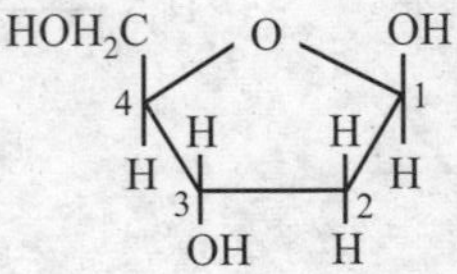

β – D – 2 – Deoxyribose

66. (b) The given structure of amino acid.

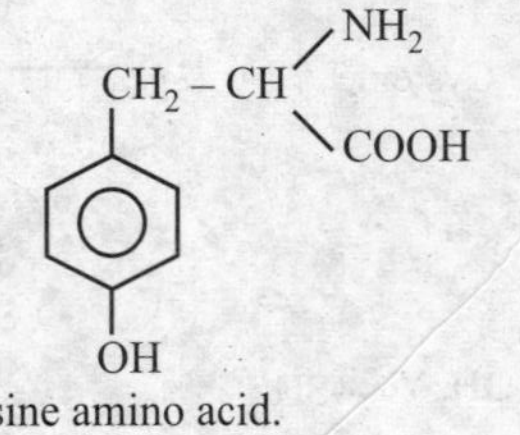

is of tyrosine amino acid.

Among tyrosine derived hormones, thyroxine is synthesized by thyroid gland. So (X) is thyroxine and (Y) is thyroid gland.

67. (d) Deficiency of Vitamin B_6 (pyridoxine) causes convulsions.

Thus, X = Pyridoxine.

Good source of Vitamin B_6 = Cereals (Y).

68. (c) Glucocorticoids control the carbohydrate metabolism, modulate inflammatory reactions and are involved in reactions to stress.

The mineralocorticoids control the level of excretion of water and salt by the kidney.

The progestrone is responsible for preparing the uterus for implantation of fertilised egg.

The estradiol is main female sex hormone and is responsible for development of secondary female characteristics & participates in the control of menstrual cycle.

69. (a) Addison's disease a rare disorder when adrenal gland can't produce enough hormone.

Estradiol drives the development of secondary sexual characteristics in females.

70. (b) Intra cellular messengers are hormones.

71. (d) The deficiency of vitamin B_1 or thiamine in the diet will lead to beri-beri.

The deficiency of vitamin B_6 leads to convulsion.

72. (c)

Vitamin	Solubility	Deficiency
A	Fat soluble	Night blindness
Vitamin B_6	Soluble in water	Anemia
Vitamin D	Fat soluble	Rickets
Vitamin C	Water soluble	Scurvy

73. (a)

Vitamin	Source
Vitamin A	Carrots, guavas, eggs, Papayas, Mangoes, Peas
Vitamin B_1(Thiamine)	Oats, groundnuts, cashew, milk, meat
Vitamin B_{12}	Chicken, beef, curd, milk, fish, cheese
Riboflarin, (B_2)	Egg, organ meats, milk Guava, Mangoes, Potatoes, egg, almonds
Pyridoxine (B_6)	Bananas, dates, Strawberries, beetroot, peas, egg

∴ Vitamin A, source is carrots and B_{12} source is curd.

74. (b) Progesterone (P4) is an endogenous steroid. It is a sex hormone involved in the menstrual cycle, pregnancy and embryo genesis of humans and other species.

75. (c) Fat soluble vitamins = A, D, K

Water soluble vitamins = All B, C

76. (b) Glucocorticoids are steroidal hormones that control the carbohydrate metabolism, modulate inflammatory reactions and react to stress.

77. (b) Beri-beri caused by deficiency of vitamin B_1 (thiamine)

Scurvy caused by deficiency of vitamin C (ascorbic acid)

Cheilosis caused by deficiency of vitamin B_2 (riboflavin)

Rickets caused by deficiency of vitamin D (calciferol)

78. (a) Scurvy is caused by deficiency of vitamin C which is present in citrus fruits, amla.

79. (d) Deficiency of vitamin B_6 (pyridoxine) causes nerve-related issues like convulsions.

80. (c) Addison's disease is characterized by:-

Muscle weakness, stress, nausea, low-blood pressure, etc.

81. (b) Hypo-thyroidism is a condition in which the deficiency of required iodine content in the diet results in the enlargement of thyroid gland.

Thus, B, and C are correct.

82. (d) The deficiency of vitamin B_{12} causes pernicious anemia.

83. (c) Human insulin has 51 amino acids.

84. (b)

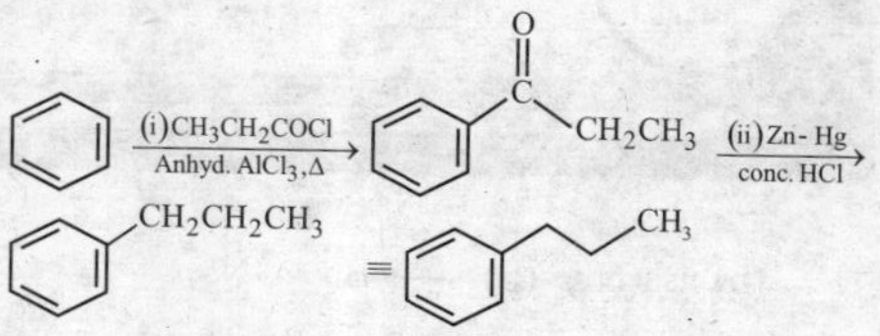

85. (b) Water soluble vitamins (like vitamin C) are readily excreted from the body.

86. (b) Glucagon increases the glucose and fatty acid in the blood stream. It is a peptide hormone, produced in pancreas.

87. (c) Thiamine – Vitamin B_1

Riboflavin – Vitamin B_2

Cobalamine – Vitamin B_{12}

Pyridoxine – Vitamin B_6

88. (b)

89. (d)

(i)

$$\underset{\text{Glycine}}{H_2N-CH_2-\overset{\overset{O}{||}}{C}-OH} + \underset{\text{Alanine}}{H-\underset{H}{N}-\underset{H}{\overset{CH_2}{C}}-\overset{O}{\overset{||}{C}}-OH}$$

$$\longrightarrow H_2N-CH_2-\underbrace{\overset{\overset{O}{||}}{C}-\underset{H}{N}}_{\text{Peptide bond}}-\underset{H}{\overset{CH_3}{C}}-\overset{\overset{O}{||}}{C}-OH$$

Hence, $-\overset{\overset{O}{||}}{C}-$ of peptide bond belongs to glycine

(ii) glycylalanine is:

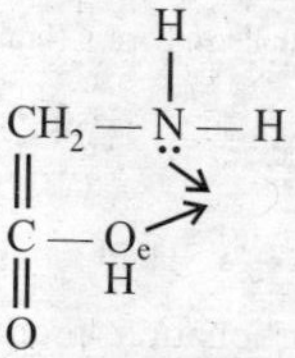

(iii) Phosphate group – pentose sugar – nitrogenous base units joined as shown above is known as nucleotide.

Appendix

The p-Block Elements (Group 15, 16, 17 & 18)

1. **(b)** $Ba(N_3)_2\,(S) \longrightarrow Ba + 3N_2\uparrow$
(Pure nitrogen)

2. **(b)** The brown ring tests specifically detects nitrate ion (NO_3^-). A brown ring forms at the junction due to formation of brown ring complex ($[Fe(H_2O)_5NO]SO_4$).

3. **(d)** $PH_3(aq.) \xrightarrow{\text{light}} P + H_2$
(red P)

Photolysis of phosphine (PH_3) given red phosphorus. Red P is non-poisnous, odourless insoluble in water and CS_2 and polymeric in structure. While chemiluminescence shown in dark is property of white phosphorus not red phosphorus.

4. **(c)** Phosphoric acid (H_3PO_3) when treated with PCl_3, PCl_3 acts as dehydrating agent and forms pyro phosphorous acid.

$2H_3PO_3 + PCl_3 \rightarrow H_4P_2O_5 + HCl$

5. **(c)** $3Cu + 8HNO_3\,(dil.) \rightarrow 3Cu(NO_3)_2 + 2NO + 4H_2O$

$4Zn + 10HNO_3(dil.) \rightarrow 4Zn\,(NO_3)_2 + N_2O + 5H_2O$

6. **(b)** P_4 (White Phosphorus) + Cl_2 (limited) $\longrightarrow PCl_3$ (X)

$PCl_3 + H_2O \longrightarrow \overset{+3}{H_3PO_3}$ (Y)

$4H_3PO_3 \longrightarrow 3H_3PO_4 + PH_3$

Disproportionation product of H_3PO_3 (Y) is H_3PO_4 and PH_3.

7. **(d)** $P_4O_6 + 6H_2O \longrightarrow 4H_3PO_3$
(X)
Phosphorous acid

$H_3PO_3 \Rightarrow$ 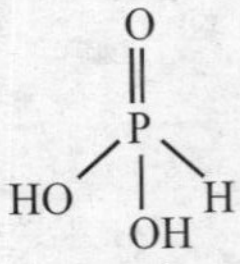 (Dibasic acid)

$4H_3PO_3 \longrightarrow 3H_3PO_4 + PH_3$ (Phosphine)
(Y) (Z)

$H_3PO_4 \Rightarrow$ 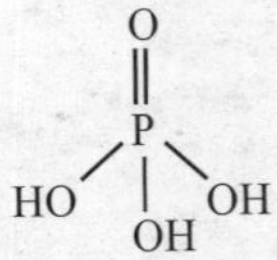 $PH_3 =$ 

- Z(PH_3) has a lone pair on phosphorous and it can act as a Lewis base.

8. **(a)** NO_2, when present in higher concentration in air, damages leaves and retards the rate of photosynthesis by dissolving into the water on leaf surfaces to form corrosive nitric acid.

9. **(a)** $A : N_2O$

$:N \equiv N - \ddot{\underset{..}{O}}:$

N-N has triple bond present between them, so Bond length is shortest.

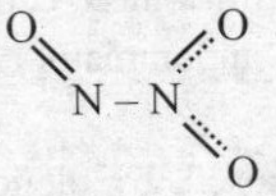

$B : N_2O_3$

N-N single bond present between NO and NO_2 units, this bond is unusually weak and long because of poor orbital overlap.

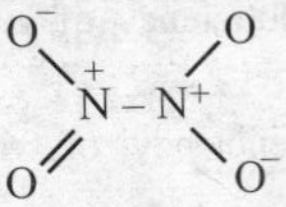

$C : N_2O_4$

In N_2O_4, two NO_2 units are joined by N-N single bond. So, order of bond length is:
A < C < B.

10. **(a)** $P_4 + 8SOCl_2 \rightarrow PCl_3 + 4SO_2 + 2S_2Cl_2$
(x)

$P_4 + 10SO_2Cl_2 \rightarrow PCl_5 + 10SO_2$
(x)

SO_2 is common product and it has only one lone pair of electron in central atom.

11. **(c)**

$4H_3PO_3$ (ortho phosphorous acid) $\rightarrow$ $4H_3PO_3$ (ortho phosphoric acid) (X) $+ PH_3$

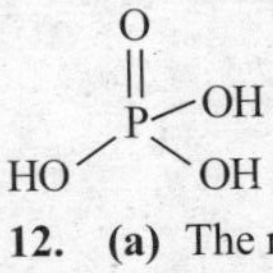 Basicity = 3

12. **(a)** The reactions are:

$P_4 + 3NaOH + 3H_2O \rightarrow Na_4P_2O_6 + PH_3 + 3H_2$

$Na_4P_2O_6 + 4H_2O \rightarrow H_4P_2O_6 + 4NaOH$

Structure of $H_4P_2O_6$

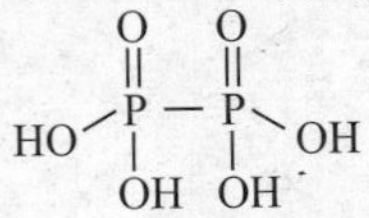

Number of P = 0 bonds = 2

Number of P – P bond = 1

13. **(b)** $NaNO_2 + HCl \rightarrow NaCl + HNO_2$

$2HNO_2 \rightarrow NO_2 + NO + H_2O$
(X) (Y)

NO_2 = acidic, NO = neutral

14. **(b)**

P_4 (white phosphorous) $+ 3NaOH + 3H_2O \rightarrow PH_3$ (Y) $+ 3NaH_2PO_2$ (X)

Where $(X) = H_2PO_2^- \Rightarrow 2 + x - 4 = 1$

So, $x = -1 + 4 - 2 = 1$

& $(Y) = PH_3 \Rightarrow x + 3 = 0$ so, $x = -3$

15. **(c)** $4HNO_3 + P_4O_{10} \rightarrow 4HPO_3 + 2N_2O_5$

$P_4 + 20HNO_3 \rightarrow 4H_3PO_4 + 20NO_2 + 4H_2O$

16. **(b)** Ammonium nitrate (NH_4NO_3) on thermal decomposition produces N_2O and H_2O

$NH_4NO_3 \rightarrow N_2O$ (colourless gas) $+ H_2O$

N_2O

$:N \equiv N - \ddot{O}:$

Linear

N_2O is also known as laughing gas.

17. **(d)**

H_3PO_2 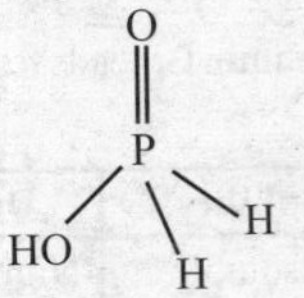 Basicity = 1

H_3PO_3 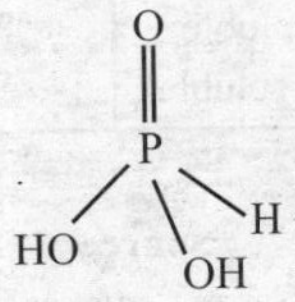 Basicity = 2

H_3PO_4 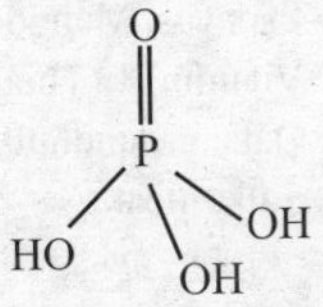 Basicity = 3

18. **(c)** $P_2O_3 + 3H_2O \longrightarrow 2H_3PO_3$
Ortho phosphorous acid

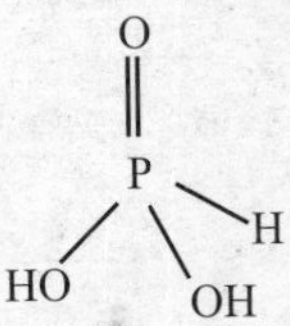

2 P-OH bond

Red P_4 + alkali $\longrightarrow H_4P_2O_6$

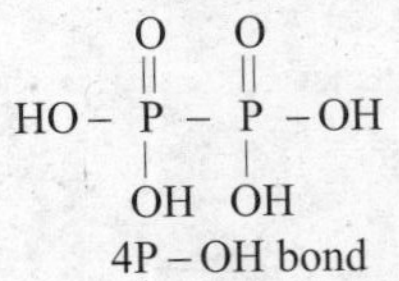

4P – OH bond

19. (a) (i) The reaction of calcium phosphide with water

$Ca_3P_2 + 3H_2O \longrightarrow \underset{\text{Phosphine}}{2PH_3} + 3CaO$

(ii) Heating white phosphorous with concentrated NaOH solution

$P_4 + 3NaOH + H_2O \longrightarrow \underset{\text{Phosphine}}{PH_3} + \underset{\text{sodium hypophosphite}}{3NaH_2PO_2}$

(iii) Red phosphorous does not react with Alkali.

20. (d) $MnO_2 + 4HCl\ (conc.) \rightarrow MnCl_2 + \underset{(X)}{Cl_2} + 2H_2O$

$3Cl_2 + 8NH_3\ (excess) \rightarrow \underset{(Y)}{6NH_4Cl} + \underset{(Z)}{N_2}$

21. (b) $NH_4Cl(aq) + NaNO_2(aq) \rightarrow N_2\uparrow + 2H_2O + NaCl$

The impurities of NO and HNO_3 in the N_2 gas can be removed by passing the gas through an aqueous H_2SO_4 solution containing $K_2Cr_2O_7$.

22. (b) $N_2O_5 > N_2O_3 > P_2O_3 > As_2O_3$

III > I > II > IV

Higher the oxidation state (O.S.) higher is the acidic character. However, elements of same O.S. with larger size enhance the basic character.

23. (d) NH_3 is basic in nature. Therefore, the drying agent has to be basic in nature so that it doesnot react with drying agent.

24. (a)

$\overset{0}{P_4} + 20\ H\overset{+5}{N}O_3 \rightarrow 4H_3\overset{+5}{P}O_4 + 20\ \overset{+4}{N}O_2 + 4H_2O$

Ox (P: 0 → +5); Red (N: +5 → +4)

25. (d) $2Pb_3O_4 \longrightarrow 6PbO + O_2$

x = 2, y = 6.

26. (c) The structure of pyrophosphoric acid is

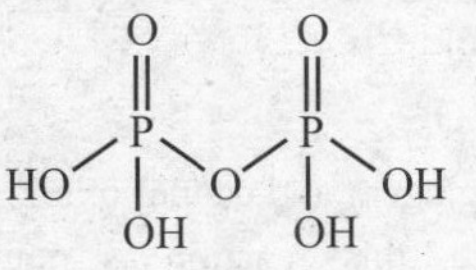

No. of P – O – H bond = 4

No. of P = O bond = 2

No. of P – O – P bond = 1

27. (c) (a) $NH_4^+ + NO_2^- \xrightarrow{\Delta} N_2 + 2H_2O$

(b) $CO(NH_2)_2(s) + 2HNO_2(l) \rightarrow 2N_2 + CO_2 + 3H_2O$

(c) This is Raschig process used for manufacturing hydrazine

$NH_3 + NaOCl(aq) \xrightarrow{\text{gelatin}} NH_2Cl + NaOH(\text{fast})$

$2NH_3 + NH_2Cl \longrightarrow NH_2NH_2 + NH_4Cl(\text{slow})$

Gelatin is used to mask the heavy metal ions which may present in water used for the reaction. The metal ions catalyse other side reactions.

(d) $(NH_4)_2Cr_2O_7(s) \xrightarrow{\Delta} N_2\uparrow + Cr_2O_3 + 4H_2O$

28. (a) As we know,

$\text{Hybridisation} = \frac{1}{2}[V + M - C + A]$

$I_nNO_3^- = \frac{1}{2}[5 + 0 - 0 + 1] = 3(sp^2)$

$I_nNO_2^- = \frac{1}{2}[5 + 0 - 0 + 1] = 3(sp^2)$

$I_nNH_4^+ = \frac{1}{2}[5 + 4 - 1 + 0] = 4(sp^3)$

The hybridisation of N in NO_3^-, NO_2^- and NH_4^- are sp^2, sp^2 and sp^3 respectively.

29. (b) According to the Fajan's rule, smaller the cation, stronger is the covalent bond it forms, more is the covalent nature.

Size of cation of Bi is largest in the group more over it is metally in nature and bond between metal and nonmetal is ionic hence, it is least covalent in nature.

30. (b) On standing conc. HNO_3 under goes decomposition.

$4HNO_3 \rightarrow 2H_2O + 4NO_2 + O_2$

Due to the formation of nitrogen dioxide, it turns yellow brown.

31. (a)

$KClO_3 \xrightarrow[-KCl]{MnO_2/\Delta} \underset{(X)}{O_2} \xrightarrow{P_4(\text{white})} \underset{(Y)}{P_2O_5} \xrightarrow{H_2O} \underset{(Z)}{H_3PO_4}$

32. (b)

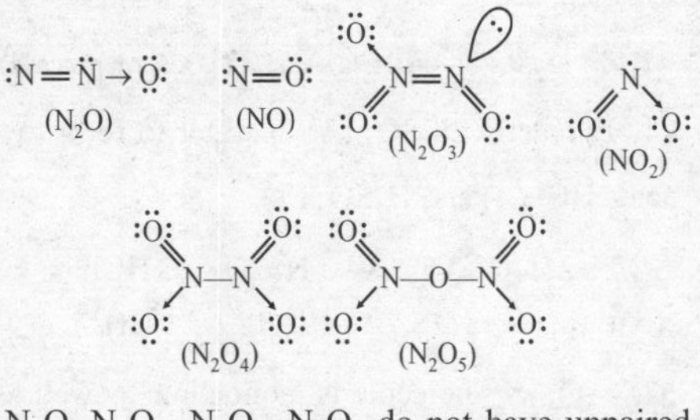

N_2O, N_2O_3, N_2O_4, N_2O_5 do not have unpaired electrons. So, they are diamagnetic

33. (b) Phosphine gives a black precipitate of cupric phosphide on reacting with $CuSO_4$ solution.

$3CuSO_4 + 2PH_3 \rightarrow Cu_3P_2 + 3H_2SO_4$

34. (b)

(i) $\underset{\text{White phosphorus}}{P_4} + 3NaOH + 3H_2O \xrightarrow[\Delta]{CO_2} \underset{(A)}{PH_3(g)} + \underset{\text{(Sodiumhypophosphite) (B)}}{3NaH_2PO_2}$

(ii) When (A), i.e. $PH_3(g)$ is bubbled in aqueous $CuSO_4$ solution, copper phosphide (Cu_3P_2) and H_2SO_4 (C) is formed. The reaction occurs as follows :

$2PH_3 + 3CuSO_4 \longrightarrow \underset{\text{(Copper phosphide)}}{Cu_3P_2} + \underset{(C)}{3H_2SO_4}$

35. (c) Nobel metal like gold and platinum are soluble in aqua-regia which is a mixture of nitric acid and hydrochloric acid in molar ratio of 1 : 3.

36. (a) Due to +I effect of 3 methyl groups, the correct basic order is: $P(CH_3)_3 > PH_3$

37. (d) Monoclinic sulphur is stable above 369 K

38. (a) Statement-I : In 1962 Neil Bartlett prepared $O_2^+[P+F_6]^\ominus$ by reacting O_2 with $P+F_6$. This led to the 1st noble gas compound $Xe^+[P+F_6]^-$, and later XeF_2, XeF_4, XeF_6

Statement-II : O_2 and Xe have almost same 1st ionisation enthalpy

1st I. E. of O_2 = 1175 kJ/mol.

1st I. E. of Xe = 1170 kJ/mol

39. (d)

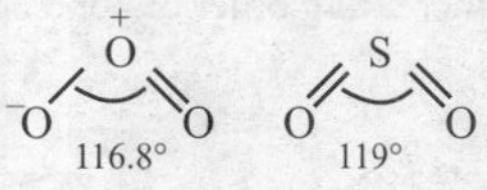

O_3 SO_2

O_3 and SO_2 both are bent/angular, both having resonating structures and both sp^2 hybridized but bond angles are different, O_3 have bond angle approx 116.8° and SO_2 have bond angle 119°.

40. (a) (1) $(NH_4)_2Cr_2O_7 \xrightarrow{\Delta} N_2\uparrow Cr_2O_3 + 4H_2O$

(2) $2KClO_3 \xrightarrow{\Delta} 2KCl + 3O_2\uparrow$

(3) $2HgO \xrightarrow{\Delta} 2Hg + O_2\uparrow$

(4) $NH_4NO_3 \xrightarrow{\Delta} N_2O\uparrow + 2H_2O$

(5) $2KMnO_4 \xrightarrow{\Delta} K_2MnO_4 + MnO_2 + O_2$

(6) $CaCO_3 \xrightarrow{\Delta} CaO + CO_2\uparrow$

(7) $2Pb_3O_4 \xrightarrow{\Delta} 6PbO + O_2\uparrow$

41. (a) $P_4 + 3NaOH + 3H_2O \longrightarrow PH_3 + 3NaH_2PO_2$ ... (i)

$\text{no. of moles of } P_4 = \frac{124g}{124\,g/mol} = 1\text{ mol}$

1 mol P_4 requires 3 moles of NaOH

∴ NaOH used in 1L of xM solution = 3 mol

$\text{Hence, } x = \frac{3\,mol}{1L} = 3M$

Reaction of rhombic sulphur with NaOH

$4S + 6NaOH \longrightarrow 2Na_2S + Na_2S_2O_3 + 3H_2O$ ... (ii)

Moles of sulphur $= \frac{128g}{32\,g/mol} = 4$ mol

From eq^n (2)

4 mole of S requires 6 mol of NaOH

Volume of NaOH (3M) required:

n = MV

$V = \frac{n}{M} = \frac{6}{3} = 2L$

42. (b) Reducing power decrease down the group

Thus $H_2S > H_2Se > H_2Te > H_2Po$ is not correct.

43. (a) $2Cu_2S + 3O_2 \rightarrow 2Cu_2O + 2SO_2$

$2Cu_2O + Cu_2S \rightarrow 6\,Cu + \underset{(X)}{SO_2}$

Shape of SO_2 = Angular/bent

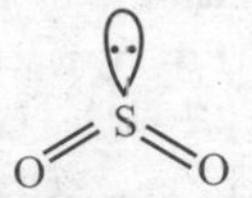

44. (c) Peroxysulphuric acid

(Peroxydisulphuric acid) = $H_2S_2O_8$.

Pyrosulphuric acid = $H_2S_2O_7$

⇒ Sum of O-atoms = 8 + 7 = 15

45. (d) Increasing order of bond angles :-

$P_4 < S_6 < S_8 < O_3$.

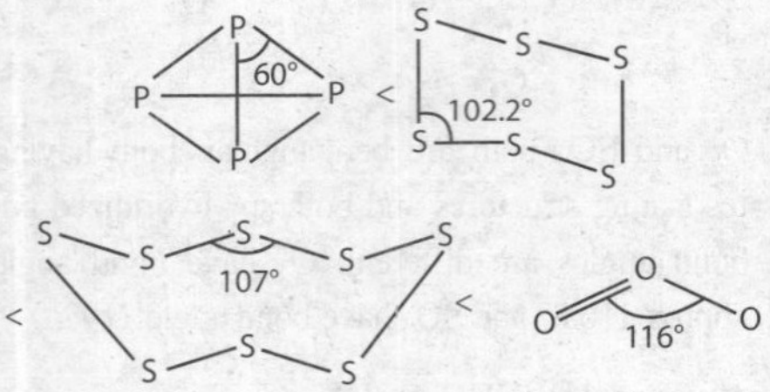

46. (c)

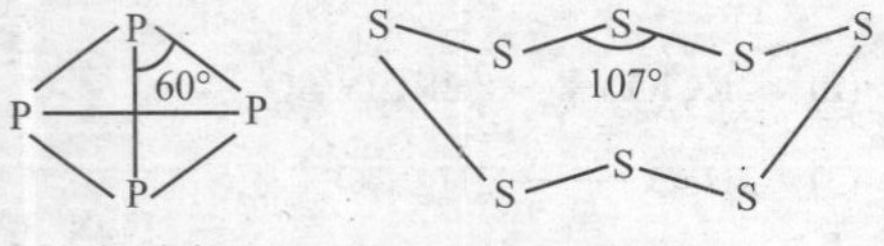

Strained ring Crown Structure

47. (a) $\overset{+6}{H_2SO_4} + \overset{+6}{SO_3} \rightarrow H_2S_2O_7$ (oleum)

⇒ Sum of oxidation states

= 6 + 6 = 12

48. (a) Ozone (O_3) is a bent molecule with a bond angle of about 117°.

Thus, (A) is incorrect.

The bond lengths of both O-O bonds are the same due to resonance.

It is less stable than oxygen and is electrophilic in nature. Thus, (D) is incorrect.

Therefore, only (B) and (C) are correct statement.

49. (d) On moving down the group from S to Te, the boiling point of hydrides increases due to increase in van der waal force of attraction. But H_2O has highest boiling point due to presence of hydrogen bonding.

Hence, the increasing order of boiling point of group 16 hydrides is given as : $H_2S < H_2\,Se < H_2\,Te < H_2O$

Thus, H_2S has lowest boiling point while H_2O has highest boiling point.

50. (d) $O_3(g) + 2I^-(aq) + H_2O(l) \rightarrow 2OH^-(aq) + I_2(s) + O_2(g)$

51. (a) Preparation of H_2SO_4 from iron pyrite (FeS_2): $FeS_2 + O_2 \rightarrow Fe_2O_3 + SO_2$

and from S: $S + O_2 \rightarrow SO_2$

52. (b) Oxygen is the second most electronegative element.

53. (c) $H_2SO_4 + SO_3 \rightarrow H_2S_2O_7$

54. (c) (i) SO_4^{2-} :

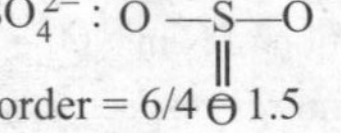

Average bond order = 6/4 ⊖ 1.5

(ii) SO_3 :

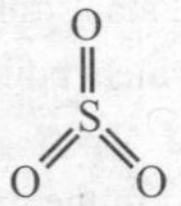

Average bond order = 6/3 = 2

(iii) $S_2O_3^{2-}$:

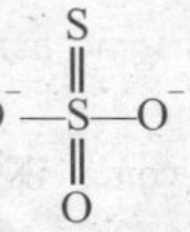

Average bond order = 4/3 = 1.33

Correct sequence of bond order is

$SO_3 > SO_4^{2-} > S_2O_3^{2-}$

55. (b) $KCN \xrightarrow[S_2O_3^{2-}]{NaOH} \underset{\text{Potassium thiocyanate}}{KSCN}$

$FeCl_3 + 3KSCN \longrightarrow \underset{\text{Blood red colour}}{Fe(SCN)_3} + 3KCl$

Reaction of $FeCl_3$ with KSCN gives a blood red solution.

56. (a) $P_4 + 10\,SO_2Cl_2 \rightarrow 4\,PCl_5 + 10\,SO_2$

$4HCl + O_2 \xrightarrow[CuCl_2]{723} 2Cl_2 + 2H_2O$ (Deacon process)

$Cl_2(Y)$ react with SO_2 (X) in water to form two acids HCl (A) and H_2SO_4 (B).

$\underset{(X)}{SO_2} + 2H_2O + \underset{(Y)}{Cl_2} \longrightarrow \underset{(B)}{H_2SO_4} + \underset{(A)}{2HCl}$

57. (c) S_8 molecule is monoclinic as well as rhombic.

58. (d) Sulphur atom contains lone pair in only in sulphurous acid among the given acids.

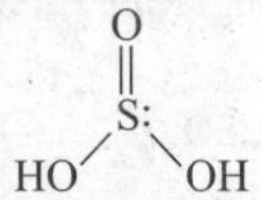

Sulphurous acid

59. (c)

$S + 2H_2SO_4(conc.) \longrightarrow \underset{(X)}{3SO_2} + \underset{(Y)}{2H_2O}$

As SO_2 has one lone pair of electrons on central atom i.e., sulphur.

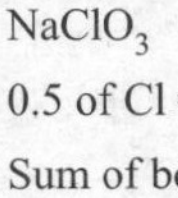

(X)

And H_2O has two lone pair of electrons on the central atom i.e., oxygen.

60. (a) ∵ Formal charge = No. of valency electron in central atom – [No. of lone pair + $\frac{1}{2}$ No. of bond pair of electron]

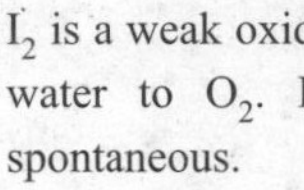

F.C for O labelled as 1 = 6 – [6 + 1] = –1

F.C for O labelled as 2 = 6 – [4 + 2] = 0

F.C for O labelled as 3 = 6 – [2 + 3] = +1

61. (a) At high temperature about 1000K, sulphur consists of mixture of forms S_2, S_4, S_6, S_8, etc.

62. (c) In place of nitrogen, helium is mixed with oxygen because helium is not soluble in blood even under high pressure.

63. (a)

$\underset{\text{(Cold)}}{Cl_2 + 2\,dil.NaOH} \longrightarrow NaCl + \underset{(X)}{NaClO} + H_2O$

$\underset{\text{(Hot, conc)}}{3Cl_2 + 6NaOH} \longrightarrow 5NaCl + \underset{(Y)}{NaClO_3} + 3H_2O\,NaClO$

0.5 of Cl = + 1

$NaClO_3$

0.5 of Cl = + 5

Sum of both = + 6

O.S of I in iodic acid (HIO_3) = + 5

∴ Statement III is wrong.

64. (d) Reactivity of halogens with water decrease down the group. (F_2 is most reactive and I_2 is least reactive).

$2I_2 + 2H_2O \rightarrow 4HI + O_2$

I_2 is a weak oxidizing agent and cannot oxidize water to O_2. Hence, this reaction is non-spontaneous.

65. (a) $Na_2S_2O_3 + 4Cl_2 + 5H_2O \longrightarrow Na_2S_4 + 8HCl + S\downarrow$ $H_2S + Cl_2 \longrightarrow 2HCl + S\downarrow$

66. (a) $H_2(g) + F_2(g) \longrightarrow 2\,HF\,(g)$

F_2 is highly reactive so it reacts with hydrogen even in dark.

$N_2 + 3H_2 \xrightarrow[200\text{ atm}]{Fe(Catalyst)\;400-450°C} 2NH_3 + Heat$

The reaction is an exothermic reaction, these is a release of energy.

HF is electron rich hydride because its fluorine atom having extra electrons present as lone pair. So any (i) and (iii) are correct.

67. (c) $SiCl_4$

1. Hydrolysis of $P_4O_{10} \rightarrow$

$P_4O_{10} + 6H_2O \longrightarrow 4H_3PO_4$

H_3PO_4 and P_4O_{10} are not solid under standard conditions.

2. Hydrolysis of $F_2 \rightarrow$

$2F_2 + 2H_2O \longrightarrow 4HF + O_2$

HF is a liquid or gas and O_2 is a gas

3. Hydrolysis of $SiCl_4 \rightarrow$

$SiCl_4 + 2H_2O \longrightarrow SiO_2 + 4HCl$

SiO_2 is a solid and HCl is a gas

Hydrolysis of Azide ion

Azide ion does not hydrolyse under normal conditions.

68. (a) $3Cl_2 + 6NaOH \longrightarrow 5NaCl + NaClO_3 + 3H_2O$

69. (d) H_2O, HF and NH_3 have hydrogen bonding as the intermolecular forces while HCl has weaker dipole-dipole interaction.

Thus, HCl has the lowest boiling point.

Among H_2O, HF, and NH_3 H_2O has the highest boiling point due to extensive network of hydrogen bonds.

Among NH_3 and HF, HF forms stronger hydrogen bonds due to very high electronegativity of fluorine.

Thus, the order of boiling point will be :-

$HCl < NH_3 < HF < H_2O$

70. (b) Ionic character of metal halide :-

$M - F > M - Cl > M - Br > M - I$

This is due to low polarizability of fluorine due to very small size which gives more ionic character.

Thus, II is incorrect.

Order of bond dissociation enthalpy :- $Cl_2 > Br_2 > F_2 > I_2$

This is due to very small size and F – F bond length that causes repulsion between the atoms and possible multiple bonds between Cl_2, Br_2 and I_2 due to availability of d- orbitals.

Thus, III is incorrect.

71. (d) The oxidizing power decreases down the group.

72. (b) HCl and H_2SO_4 both are acidic, Therefore, concentrated H_2SO_4 is used for drying HCl gas.

$NH_3(g) + HCl(g) \longrightarrow NH_4Cl(s)$

73. (c) The products X and Y are HIO_3 and HCl respectively,

$I_2 + 5Cl_2 + 6H_2O \rightarrow 2HIO_3 + 10HCl$

74. (c)

75. (c)

$Ti + 2I_2 \rightarrow TiI_4 \xrightarrow{\Delta} Ti + 2I_2$ (van Arkel)

$I_2 + H_2O \rightarrow IO^- + 2H^+ + I^-$

76. (c)

(i) When chlorine oxidises sulphur dioxide in presence of water, it gives H_2SO_4 as oxyacid(A). The reaction occurs as follows :

$Cl_2 + SO_2 + 2H_2O \longrightarrow H_2SO_4 + 2HCl$

The oxidation number of sulphur in H_2SO_4

$= 2 + x + (4 \times -2) = 0$

$\Rightarrow x = +6$

(ii) When chlorine (Cl_2) oxidises iodine (I_2) in presence of water, it gives HIO_3 as oxyacid (B), the reaction occurs as follows :

$5Cl_2 + I_2 + 6H_2O \longrightarrow 2HIO_3 + 10HCl$

The oxidation state of (1) in HIO_3 is

$= 1 + y + 3 \times (-2) = 0$

$\Rightarrow y = +5$

77. (d)

78. (d) Hydrolysis of XeF_4:

$6XeF_4 + 12H_2O \rightarrow 4Xe + 2XeO_3 + 24HF + 3O_2$

So all statements are correct.

79. (a)

I: $\overset{(0)}{Cl_2}$ + cold dil. NaOH $\rightarrow$ $\overset{(-1)}{NaCl} + \overset{(+1)}{NaOCl} + H_2O$

Cl_2 upon reaction with cold dilute NaOH shown disproportionation.

II: $\overset{(0)}{Cl_2}$ + hot conc. NaOH $\rightarrow$ $\overset{(-1)}{NaCl} + \overset{(+5)}{NaClO_3} + 3H_2O$

Cl_2 upon reaction with hot conc. NaOH shows disproportionation.

III : $\overset{(0)}{Cl_2} + H_2S \rightarrow \overset{(-1)}{2HCl} + S$

Cl_2 upon reaction with H_2S doesn't shows disproportionation.

80. (d) $XeF_6 + H_2O \longrightarrow XeOF_4\ (X) + 2HF$

$XeF_6 + 2H_2O \longrightarrow XeO_2F_2\ (Y) + 4HF$

$XeF_6 + 3H_2O \longrightarrow XeO_3\ (Z) + 6HF$

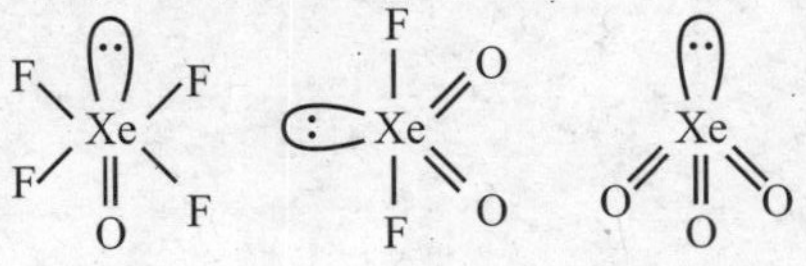

$XeOF_4$ (X) XeO_2F_2 (Y) XeO_3 (Z)

Oxidation date of Xe

- $XeOF_4$: $x + (-2) + (-4) \Rightarrow x = 6$
- XeO_2F_2 : $x + 2(-2) + (-2) \Rightarrow x = 6$
- XeO_3 : $x + 3(-2) \Rightarrow x = 6$

Oxidation state of Xe in X, Y, Z is same (+6)

81. (a) $XeF_6 + H_2O \rightarrow XeO_3 + 6HF$

$H = \frac{1}{2}(V + M - C + A)$

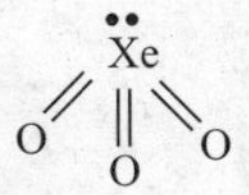

$= \frac{1}{2} \times 8 = 4 \Rightarrow sp^3$ hybridisation

82. (a) $6XeF_4 + 12H_2O \longrightarrow 4Xe + 2XeO_3 + 24HF + 3O_2$

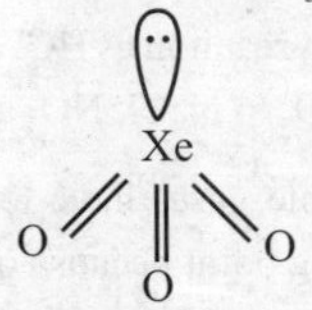

pyramidal

83. (b) Xenon forms three binary fluorides XeF_2, XeF_4 and XeF_6 by direct reaction of elements under appropriate conditions.

$Xe(g) + 2F_2(g) \xrightarrow{873\text{ K, 7bar}} XeF_4(s)$

(1 : 5 ratio)

84. (a)

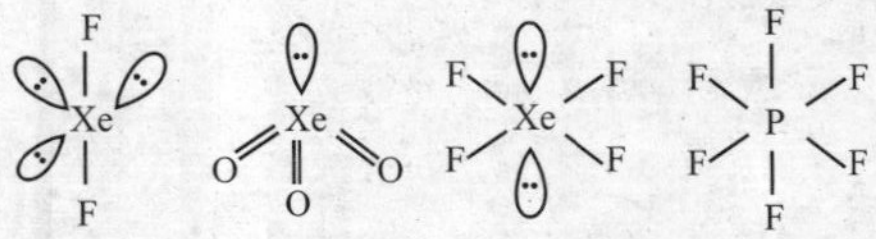

85. (a) Xe forms fluorides of even number of fluorine atoms. This is so because the promotion of one, two or three electrons from the 5p-orbital will result in two, four or six half-filled orbitals and this will give XeF_2, XeF_4 or XeF_6 respectively.

86. (d) $XeF_6 + 3H_2O \rightarrow XeO_3 + 6HF$

87. (d)

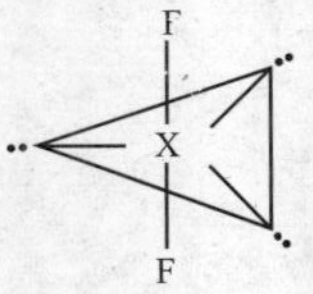

XeF_2 (sp^3d)

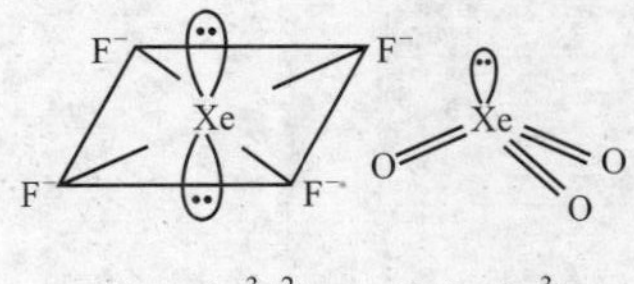

XeF_4 (sp^3d^2) XeO_3 (sp^3)

88. (b)

$XeF_4 + SbF_5 \longrightarrow [:\ddot{X}eF_3]^{\oplus}[SbF_6]^-$

Cation Anion

Hybridisation	sp^3d (Xe)	sp^3d^2 (Sb)
Geometry:	Trigonal bipyramidal	octahedral
Shape:	T-shaped	octahedral

89. (b) For the given reactions :

(I) $2NaOH + SO_2 \rightarrow Na_2SO_3 + H_2O$

(II) $XeF_4 + O_2F_2 \xrightarrow{143\text{ K}} XeF_6 + O_2$

(III) $PCl_5 + H_2O \rightarrow POCl_3 + 2HCl$

$POCl_3 + 3H_2O \rightarrow H_3PO_4 + 3\ HCl$

Overall reaction,

$PCl_5 + 4H_2O \longrightarrow H_3PO_4 + 5HCl$

(IV) $2NaNO_2 + 2HCl$

$\longrightarrow 2NaCl + NO_2 + H_2O$

Also the correct reaction as HCl can decomposes salts like $NaNO_2$ to NaCl, NO_2 and H_2O.

90. **(c,d)** Noble gases have low boiling point and low melting point because of

(i) weak van der Waal's interactions and,

(ii) weak dispersion forces.

Hence, option (c) and (d) both are the correct answer.

91. **(c)** XeF_4 is sp^3d^2 hybridised and due to presence of 2 lone pair of electrons its shape is square planar.

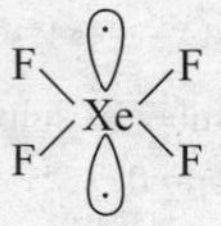

sp^3d^2

CCl_4 is sp^3 hybridised due to 4 bonds. Its geometry is sigma.

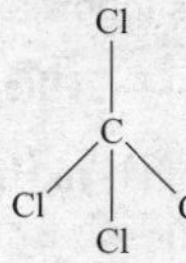

$(sp)^3$

92. **(d)** (d) Helium has lowest boiling point among all the noble gases. Due to minimum van der Waal's force of attraction.

(a) $Xe(g) + 3F_2(g) \xrightarrow[60-70\,bar]{573\,k} XeF_6(s)$

(b) Ar used in electric bulbs.

(c) 3 lone pairs are present in XeF_2.

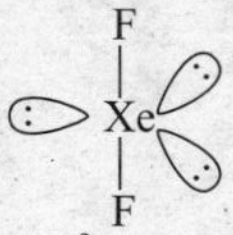

(sp^3d) Linear

93. **(d)** $Xe + F_2 \xrightarrow[60-70\,bar]{573\,K} XeF_6$ (1:20)

94. **(d)** Boiling points of noble gases are low due to only acting weak van der Waal's forces of attraction between the atoms.